Conservative
Management of

CERVICAL SPINE
Syndromes

Conservative Management of

CERVICAL SPINE

Syndromes

Edited by
Donald R. Murphy, DC, DACAN

Clinical Director
Rhode Island Spine Center
Providence, Rhode Island
Clinical Teaching Associate
Department of Community Health
Brown University School of Medicine
Providence, Rhode Island
Postgraduate Faculty:
University of Bridgeport College of Chiropractic
Bridgeport, Connecticut
New York Chiropractic College
Seneca Falls, New York
Los Angeles College of Chiropractic
Whittier, California

McGraw-Hill
Health Professions Division

New York   St. Louis   San Francisco   Aukland   Bogotá   Caracas   Lisbon   London
Madrid   Mexico City   Milan   Montreal   New Delhi   San Juan
Singapore   Sydney   Tokyo   Toronto

McGraw-Hill
A Division of The McGraw-Hill Companies

Conservative Management of Cervical Spine Syndromes

123456789   CCWCCW   99

ISBN 0-8385-6386-4

This book was set in Goudy by Clarinda Prepress, Inc.
The editor was Robin Lazrus.
The production supervisor was Shirley Dahlgren.
The production service was Andover Publishing Services.
The designer was Janice Barsevich Bielawa.
The art manager was Eve Siegel.
The illustrators were Anne Greene and ElectraGraphics, Inc.
The index was prepared by Louise Martin.

Courier Printing was printer and binder.

This book is printed on acid-free paper.

Library of Congress Cataloging-in-Publication Data
Murphy, Donald R.
    Conservative management of cervical spine syndromes / Donald R.
Murphy.
        p.   cm
    Includes index.
    ISBN 0-8385-6386-4 (case : alk. paper)
    1. Cervical vertebrae—Wounds and injuries—Treatment.   I. Title.
    [DNLM: 1. Cervical Vertebrae—injuries.   2. Spinal Diseases—
therapy.   WE 725 M978c 2000]
    RD533.M87   2000
    617.5′6—dc21
    DNLM/DLC   99-35198
    for Library of Congress   CIP

This book is dedicated to the loves of my life. My wonderful wife, Laura, whose support and encouragement served as the "wind beneath my wings" throughout the writing of this book, and my beautiful daughters, Jessica and Alison, who are a constant inspiration to me and a reminder that innocence is the key to knowing God.

Contents

Contributors

Michael Barnum, MD
Spine Fellow
Department of Orthopedics
Brown University School of Medicine
Providence, Rhode Island

Darryl Curl, DDS, DC
Head, Neck, and Spine Center of San Diego
La Jolla, California
Attending Clinician and Lecturer
Orofacial Pain Clinic at UCLA
Los Angeles, California

George G. DeFranca, DC
Private Practice
West Boylston, Massachusetts

Giuseppe Di Stefano, PhD
Psychiatrische Universitätspoliklinik
Berne, Switzerland

David Eliot, PhD
Associate Professor of Basic Sciences
University of Bridgeport College of Chiropractic
Bridgeport, Connecticut

Don Fitz-Ritson, HonsBA, DC, RCCRS-C
Private Practice
Toronto, Ontario, Canada

Joanne Fowler, PhD
Institute for Behavioral Medicine
Cranston, Rhode Island

Kim Garges, DC
Spine Institute of Alabama and Pain Management Center
Alabama Bone and Joint Center
Cullman, Alabama

Martin I. Gruder, DC, DACAN, DABCO
Private Practice
Plainville, Massachusetts

Beverly L. Harger, DC, DACBR
Associate Professor of Radiology
Director of Radiology
Western States Chiropractic College
Portland, Oregon

Steven Heffner, DC, Dip MDT
Laurel Wellness Center
Blossburg, Pennsylvania

Lisa E. Hoffman, BS, DC, DACBR
Associate Professor of Radiology
Western States Chiropractic College
Portland, Oregon

Kim Humphreys, BSc, DC, PhD
Head of Academic Affairs
Anglo-European College of Chiropractic
Bournemouth, England

Eric L. Hurwitz, DC, MS, PhD
Assistant Professor
Department of Epidemiology
UCLA School of Public Health
Los Angeles, California
Department of Research
Los Angeles College of Chiropractic
Whittier, California

Gary F. Ierna, DC
Postgraduate Faculty
Canadian Memorial Chiropractic College
Private Practice
Riverhead, New York

Mary Koestler, RN
Spine Care Medical Group and
    San Francisco Spine Institute
Daly City, California

Pavel Kolár, PT, PhD
Rehabilitation Clinic
Prague, Czech Republic

P. Michael Leahy, CCSP, DC
Private Practice
Colorado Springs, Colorado

Karel Lewit, MUDr, DrSc.
Professor
Charles University
Rehabilitation Clinic
Prague, Czech Republic

Donald R. Murphy, DC, DACAN
Clinical Director
Rhode Island Spine Center
Providence, Rhode Island
Clinical Teaching Associate
Department of Community Health
Brown University School of Medicine
Providence, Rhode Island
Postgraduate Faculty:
University of Bridgeport College of Chiropractic
Bridgeport, Connecticut
New York Chiropractic College
Seneca Falls, New York
Los Angeles College of Chiropractic
Whittier, California

Laura B. Murphy, DC
Rhode Island Spine Center
Providence, Rhode Island

Craig Nelson, DC
Associate Professor
Northwestern College of Chiropractic
Bloomington, Minnesota

Lawrence S. Nordhoff, Jr., BS, DC, QME
Postgraduate Faculty
Life Chiropractic College West
Traffic Accident Reconstructionist
Pleasanton, California

Mark Palumbo, MD
Assistant Professor
Department of Orthopedics
Brown University School of Medicine
Providence, Rhode Island

Bogdan P. Radanov, MD
Associate Professor of Psychiatry
Faculty of Medicine and Psychology
University of Berne
Berne, Switzerland

John M. Schneider, DC
Private Practice
Colorado Springs, Colorado

Allan P. Shapiro, PhD
Adjunct Assistant Professor for Physical Medicine and
    Rehabilitation
Faculty of Medicine and Dentistry
University of Western Ontario
London Health Sciences Centre
London, Ontario, Canada

Clayton D. Skaggs, DC, CCRD
Director, Clayton Physical Medicine
St. Louis, Missouri
Faculty Instructor, Logan College of Chiropractic
Chesterfield, Missouri
Postgraduate Faculty
Los Angeles College of Chiropractic
Whittier, California

Rowena Tabamo, MD
Chief Resident in Neurology
Rhode Island Hospital
Assistant Instructor in Neurology
Brown University School of Medicine
Providence, Rhode Island

Robert W. Teasell, BSc, MD, FRCC
Associate Professor and Acting Chair
Department of Physical Medicine and Rehabilitation
University of Western Ontario
London Health Sciences Centre
London, Ontario, Canada

**Allan G. J. Terrett, DipAppSc, BAppSc, MAppSc,
DAc, GradDipTertEd., MACE, FACCS, FICC**
Associate Professor
Faculty of Biomedical and Health Sciences
RMIT University
Bundoora, Australia

Ronald J. Tyszkowski, DC
Rhode Island Spine Center
Providence, Rhode Island

Arthur H. White, MD
Medical Director
Spine Care Medical Group and San Francisco
    Spine Institute
Daly City, California

Janet Wilterdink, MD
Brown University School of Medicine
Rhode Island Hospital
Providence, Rhode Island

Steven G. Yeomans, DC, DABCO
Director, Yeomans Chiropractic Center
Ripon, Wisconsin
Postgraduate Faculty
Northwestern College of Chiropractic
Bloomington, Minnesota

Foreword

The entire locomotor system depends on a proper functioning cervico-cranial region. Preventing activity intolerances due to head and neck pain is a challenge which chiropractors, physical therapist, orthopedists, neurologists, and physiatrists all face. Headache pain is the most common reason patients take pain medicine and it is one of the most frequent causes of absence from work. Biomechanical, neurophysiological, and psycho-social components are all relevant to managing problems related to the head/neck region. The biomedical model is being replaced by a new biopsychosocial paradigm which this book presents in a broad yet practical fashion.

Emphasis on pathoanatomy—x-rays, CT scans, MRIs, electrodiagnosis, and so forth—has not resulted in significant relief of suffering for the majority of pain suffers. This book presents an alternative approach for the base majority of patients whose problem is loss of function due to pain. Tests of the function of the cervical region relating to mobility, posture, balance, vision, coordination, and endurance are all presented as a substrate for a "best practice" scenario in the conservative management of pain arising from the head/neck region. This book provides a roadmap for providing pain relief treatments and restoring functional integrity. The approach presented can be followed by anyone who chooses to study the importance of this vital region to the functioning of the entire locomotor system.

The head and neck region has a place of special importance in disorders of the locomotor system. Rudolph Magnus of Utrecht first suggested that the base of the skull is the postural center of the body. For this reason the deadly "rabbit punch" in boxing is outlawed. This is the basis of the work of F. Mathias Alexander, who demonstrated that improved postural control of the head/neck region could have far-reaching effects on conditions such as Morton's neuroma, sacro-iliac dysfunction, and even dysphasia. Dr. Murphy has focused our attention on the importance of rehabilitation of functional disturbances of the head/neck region, and in particular, on faulty motor control of the cervico-cranial junction.

The subcortical nature of the cervico-cranial area's control over human posture is not to be underestimated. B Kinnear Wilson in his *Modern Problems in Neurology* says ". . . . with each displacement of the head a given attitude of the whole body is determined." In 1924, R. A. Dart after studying the fossils of *Australopithicus africanus* noted that this creature had assumed a nearly erect posture. He explained the key role of the upright head. "The improved poise of the head, and the better posture of the whole body framework which accompanied this alteration in the angle at which its dominant member was supported, is of great significance." It is the pivotal changes in head/neck orientation with respect to our center of gravity that allowed for development of an upright posture and with it better tool-making ability.

Although the phylogenetic development of upright posture may have taken many millions of years, modern society has wreaked havoc with this evolution in less than 100 years. Early in the 20th century Lord Sherrington suggested that urbanized culture inspired poor posture through our altered motor behavior. Vladimir Janda drew attention to the negative effects of sedentarism by pointing out the pathogenesis of reduced endurance capability of our postural control system. His influence has shown how postural stress results in muscle imbalances, faulty movement patterns, and joint dysfunction, which are all part of a predictable cascade of events. The fundamental underpinnings of this book are its clear focus on functional restoration. This provides a clear guide to clinicians who desperately need to do a better job caring for the multitudes of patients who are suffering from activity-limiting pain arising in this region and to the scientists who have for too long focused exclusively on the pathoanatomical rather than the functional aspects of the cervical spine.

Craig Liebenson, DC
Los Angeles, California

Foreword

Preface

The cervical spine has always been for me the most fascinating area of the body. The functional complexity of this area and the impact that it has on the rest of the locomotor system—both in normal function and in dysfunction—are astounding. Every time I feel I have seen everything that can result from problems in the cervical spine, a patient comes along to remind me that the potential clinical manifestations of cervical spine dysfunction are nearly limitless. With *Conservative Management of Cervical Spine Syndromes*, I hope to capture the complexities of the cervical spine and present a systematic way of approaching problems in this area so that other clinicians can both experience the awe and inspiration that I experience when studying the cervical spine and feel more confident in their ability to manage patients with cervical spine syndromes.

I also want to present to the nonsurgical clinician, and the student training to become a nonsurgical clinician, information about the cervical spine that is most relevant to the types of cervical spine syndromes seen on a regular basis. Nonsurgical clinicians, particularly neuromusculoskeletal specialists, are daily faced with patients complaining of neck or arm pain, headache, disequilibrium, vertigo, and whiplash with its multitude of resultant symptoms. I would like this book to be a resource to which they can turn for basic scientific, diagnostic, treatment, rehabilitative, and referral information to help them manage these patients with maximum effectiveness. The major focus is thus on the types of problems that are seen regularly; less common problems, such as spinal cord injuries, tumors, and infections, although presented in the context of differential diagnosis, are left to the many books on the cervical spine that cover these disorders almost exclusively.

Because of the near ubiquitousness of low back pain and its tremendous cost to society, much of the attention (and research dollars) regarding spinal pain has been given to the lumbar spine. The cervical spine has been relatively neglected. But cervical syndromes cause a tremendous amount of pain and suffering to millions of people, and the societal cost of these syndromes is substantial. If one considers neck and upper extremity pain and headache, both the prevalence (50 to 70 percent and 88 percent, respectively) and cost ($57 billion annually for headache alone) probably equal or surpass those of low back pain. Also, one third or more of people who develop cervical pain are likely to have continued pain for years afterward. The ongoing pain and disability of many people with cervical spine syndromes should serve as continued inspiration to those of us who are in a position to effectively treat chronic cervical-related pain, and to prevent chronicity in patients with acute cervical syndromes.

It is often assumed that the information that is obtained from studies related to the lumbar spine can be applied to the cervical spine. However, there are significant anatomical, functional, and clinical differences between these two portions of the spine, and the disorders that affect one are distinct from those that affect the other. Because of this, the cervical spine must be seen as a distinct and unique area of the body, with its own set of mechanical, neurophysiological, and pathological processes. Patients with cervical spine syndromes must be approached with this in mind. In most cases, the information presented in this book is taken from studies on the cervical spine, with a minimum of extrapolation from lumbar studies.

This book is not designed to be "everything possible there is to know about the cervical spine," but rather to present the information that is most important for the clinician in dealing effectively with patients with cervical syndromes. My approach to the book is reflective of my approach to the cervical spine patient: one of looking at the cervical spine in the context of the entire individual—mind, body and spirit—and in so doing looking at the ways in which the function of the person as a whole can become disrupted to the extent that specific clinical syndromes related to the cervical spine can result. In order to understand this approach, one must first have a keen understanding of the normal anatomy and function of the cervical spine as well as the types of dysfunction that can occur, with reference to the rest of the locomotor (neuromusculoskeletal) system. This must be combined with a global perspective on the incidence, prevalence, and risk and prognostic factors of cervical spine syndromes in western society. This information is covered in Section I of the book.

Next, the clinician must develop an understanding of the specific clinical syndromes that can result from dysfunction in the cervical spine and the rest of the locomotor system. This is especially important as each type of disorder has its own unique characteristics. This content is covered in Section II.

The clinician then must become familiar with the ways in which one can assess the cervical spine in order to establish a diagnosis of the specific functional or pathoanatomical disorder that is present, differentiate between the various disorders that can potentially cause the symptoms with which the patient is presenting, and be able to tie this in with the clinical syndrome that the patient is experiencing. Section III covers this information.

Treatment and rehabilitation of the cervical spine are covered in Sections IV and V, and these sections naturally flow out of the evaluation section, as the specific treatment that is provided must be directed at specific identified dysfunctions that have been noted during assessment. The chapters in this section continually refer to the preceding section on evaluation.

Finally, all these concepts must be tied into an overall management approach for the cervical spine patient, with specific principles for effective management. This information is covered in Section VI.

The various "clinical pearls" that appear throughout the book's chapters are designed to continually bring the material to a clinical level. These are personal messages in which each chapter author shares bits of his or her clinical experience with the reader. They help make the reader feel as if he or she is being instructed directly by the author.

In the treatment, rehabilitation, and management sections of the book, every attempt is made to present the available research literature that has investigated the efficacy of the methods presented. However, it will be seen that in many cases, little or no data are available. There are several reasons for this. One reason is that there is very little data available for any treatment for cervical spine syndromes. Another is that the methods presented in the book have been recently developed or have been previously utilized in environments that were not research oriented, and thus data were never generated. Finally, and most importantly, it is quite difficult to study the work presented in the book, because the approach to patients with cervical spine syndromes that is presented does not simply involve a group of isolated treatment methods, but, rather, is a *model* for the management of these patients. This model represents a way of approaching patients that is based on a particular perspective regarding the cervical spine and its integration with the rest of the locomotor system, and the individual as a whole. It is far easier to conduct a randomized, controlled trial on, say, a certain medication or a certain type of manipulation for neck pain. But this is not how neck pain is (or should be) treated in clinical practice. The model presented here involves an integrated approach that is designed to help the clinician identify those specific factors in the patient that are most significant in producing the clinical syndrome from which the patient suffers, and to apply a certain treatment strategy that is designed to address those factors. This approach is very difficult to study because the model, by its very nature, necessitates individualizing the approach to each patient. Thus, the methods cannot be generalized to a patient population.

The field of quality clinical research is in its infancy and, as a result, the current scientific literature cannot possibly be depended on to provide us with the answers to the plethora of questions with which we are faced on a daily basis. For this reason, the clinician must apply an empirical approach in which he or she is *guided* by the literature, but is able to feel comfortable with the fact that the efficacy of much of what he or she is doing with patients every day has not yet been proven. Nonetheless, one of the purposes of this book is to allow analysis of this model of patient management so that interest will be stimulated, leading to further clinical research.

Donald R. Murphy

Acknowledgments

The number of people who have influenced the creation of this book is staggering, and merely mentioning their names cannot provide thanks enough. However, I would like to acknowledge each of those whose input was particularly valuable.

First, I would like to thank my editorial team at Appleton & Lange, Lin Marshall, Philip Gardiner, and John Butler, for their dedication and patience.

For information gathering, I would like to thank Mary Ellen Bowen of the University of Bridgeport College of Chiropractic library; Daniel Canale and Mary Ott of the New York Chiropractic College library; Philip Bolton, DC, PhD; David Winter, PhD; Michael Schneider, DC; and Craig Liebenson, DC.

I would like to thank my father, Charles A. Murphy, for editorial assistance in this and many other of my writing projects over the years and for the ongoing influence that he has had on my writing.

I would also like to thank Céleste Ryfa, LMT, and William Brady, DC, for posing for photographs, and Céleste Ryfa, LMT, for the many hours of assistance in manuscript preparation, coordination of contributors' manuscripts and figures, and for generally being my "go to" person for just about everything.

I would like to give special thanks to all those individuals who have served as mentors to me in my career and who have influenced me in ways that I am sure none of them realize. These are Vladimir Janda, MD, Karel Lewit, MD, Janet Travell, MD, George DeFranca, DC, Gwendolen Jull, Grad DipManip Ther, FACP, Dennis Morgan, PT, DC, John Mennel, MD, Joseph Ferezy, DC, Philip Bolton, DC, PhD, Anthony Onorato, DC, Warren Hammer, DC, Lillian Ford, DC, Hunter Mollin, DC, Don Fitz-Ritson, DC, Adrian Grice, DC, Greg Bruno, DC, Joseph Friedman, MD, James Gilchrist, MD and Leonard J. Faye, DC.

I would also like to thank Craig Liebenson, DC, Gary Ierna, DC, and Charles Rybeck, DC, each for countless hours discussing the cervical spine and the principles of optimizing clinical care for patients with cervical spine syndromes.

Special thanks goes to my fine staff at the Rhode Island Spine Center—Laura, Ron, Kaycie, Céleste, Sharon, Jo-Ann, and Melissa—and my loving family—Laura, Jessica, and Alison—for supporting (and putting up with) me throughout the course of this project.

Finally, I would like to thank God for Being.

Conservative Management of

CERVICAL SPINE

Syndromes

PART

1

Basic Science

CHAPTER 1

Functional Anatomy of the Cervical Spine

DAVID ELIOT

"Anatomy is to physiology as geography is to history."

—Fernel

INTRODUCTION

Readers of this volume probably do not need to be reminded of how hard it is to learn gross anatomy. However, it may be useful to recognize that the subject also provides anatomy instructors with some challenges. Our job is to show students how to cut a body into pieces, but from that we want the students to learn how a living person is put together. We assume that a synergistic learning experience occurs when rote memorization is combined with practical correlations, hands-on experience, communication exercises, and thinking exercises. But how do we encourage students to think about anatomy, when so much of the material must be learned by memorization rather than by cogitation? What is there to think about?

For thinking we want integrative issues, issues that will encourage students to combine facts not only accurately and memorably, but also in ways that generate understanding. The four major integrative issues in anatomy are development, evolution, clinical application, and function. Thus, an anatomist can choose to describe how structures came to be as they are (development and evolution), what to do with them (clinical application), or why they are as they are (function). To complement the themes that run through the subsequent chapters of this book, function is emphasized here. Even when developmental, evolutionary, and clinical issues are given minimal attention, there is more anatomy in the neck than this one chapter can contain. Several chapters could be devoted to items that are covered briefly here, without straying from the structure and function approach. Most nonmusculoskeletal issues are avoided, so readers will have to refer to a comprehensive anatomy text for details of the vasculature, cervical viscera, and nervous system. Very little anatomy of the head or thorax is included, although considerable knowledge of those regions is essential to an understanding of the neck that connects them. And one hopes that the reader will be able to wait patiently for more clinical applications in the rest of the book.

BONES, JOINTS, AND JOINT COMPLEXES

SOME GENERAL TERMINOLOGY

The terms *segmental joint complex* and *motion segment* are herein used to refer to two contiguous vertebrae and all of the articulations between them. Such terms are necessary because all vertebrae meet their neighbors in the spinal column at more than one joint. For example, typical cervical vertebrae meet both their superior and inferior neighbors at two facet joints, two uncovertebral joints, and a symphysis (the intervertebral disc). When discussing postural relationships or movements, one is often concerned with the vertebrae as whole units and not with each joint individually. Joint complex and motion segment are very helpful terms in such instances.

The cervical vertebrae are defined by their location between the skull and rib cage, by the absence of ribs, and by several unique osteological features, not the least of which is relatively small size. All but a few mammalian species have a count of seven cervical vertebrae. The first two (atlas and axis) show such a high degree of anatomical and functional specialization that they can be referred to as the upper cervicals while the remaining five are the lower cervicals. Among the lower cervical vertebrae, the third through sixth have few distinguishing characteristics, and so they are the four typical cervicals. The seventh has several specializations that are related to its contribution to the cervicothoracic transition.

TYPICAL CERVICAL VERTEBRAE

A vertebral body makes up the anteromedial portion of each cervical vertebra below the atlas (Fig. 1–1). The curved superior surface of each lower cervical vertebral body is marked by a pair of uncinate processes, which are situated laterally to give the body a saddle appearance. The uncinate processes develop from the neural arch rather than from the centrum (embryonic vertebral body); growth plates separating them from the centrum are evident in the cervical vertebrae of children.[1, 2] The uncinate process contributes to the anteromedial wall of the intervertebral foramen (IVF) (Fig. 1–2), and osteophytes that develop on the process can encroach upon the IVF and its contents. According to Penning and Wilmink,[3] the angled orientation of the uncovertebral joints and surfaces of the vertebral bodies contribute to the production of coupled movement in the cervical spine.

When viewed from above or below, the posterior portion of all cervical vertebrae (including the atlas and axis) takes the form of an arch, which is called the neural arch (see Fig. 1–2). The neural arch features a single midline spinous process and six paired structures: the lamina, the superior and inferior articular processes which are connected by the pars interarticularis, the transverse process,

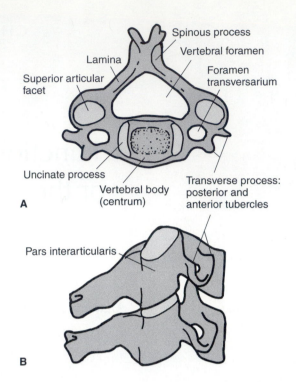

Figure 1–1. **A.** Superior view of an isolated fourth cervical vertebra. **B.** Lateral view of fourth and fifth cervical vertebrae. The third, fourth, and fifth cervical vertebrae are the typical cervicals, and they are not easily distinguished from each other.

and the pedicle. Each pedicle forms the floor of the IVF superior to it, and the roof of the IVF inferior to it. In the adult, pedicles lie at the junction of the neural arch with the vertebral body. Thus, each vertebra forms a ring of bone around a large vertebral foramen. When two or more vertebrae are articulated, their aligned vertebral foramina form the vertebral canal, which surrounds and protects the spinal cord and meninges.

The transverse processes of typical cervical vertebrae are oriented anterolaterally, and they slope inferiorly. A groove or gutter on the superior surface of the transverse process supports the ventral ramus of the spinal nerve as it courses anterolaterally from the IVF. The groove is formed by a collection of features that are unique to the cervical spine: the anterior tubercle, the posterior tubercle, and the costal lamella. The costal lamella connects the two tubercles, and it serves as the floor of the groove. It is pierced by the transverse foramen. Developmentally, all parts of the transverse process that are distal to the transverse foramen are derived from costal elements. Muscles that attach there are hypaxially derived; they are therefore innervated by branches of the ventral rami of spinal nerves. Owing to its muscle attachments, the anterior tubercle of C6 is often particularly well developed; it is called the carotid tubercle because one can digitally compress the common carotid artery against its prominence. The transverse foramina of vertebrae from C1 to C6 transmit the vertebral artery. The

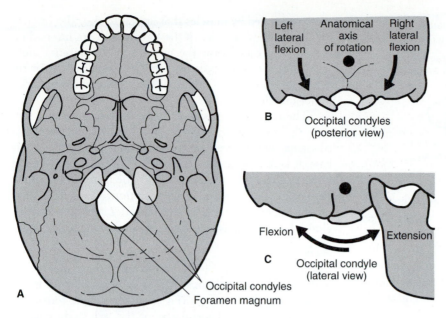

Figure 1–2. A. An inferior view of the skull shows the position of the occipital condyles adjacent to the anterior part of the foramen magnum. **B.** The orientation of the occipital condyles and the distance between them determine or strongly influence the axis of rotation for lateral flexion of the head on the atlas. **C.** Similarly, the sagittal curvature of the occipital condyles may determine the axis of rotation for flexion and extension of the head on the atlas. The shape of the condyles prevents rotation of the head on the atlas unless distraction also occurs. Because the alar ligaments severely limit distraction, rotation is limited to a few degrees.

transverse foramen of C7 is typically rather large, and yet the vertebral artery does not pass through it. Variation in its size may be associated with the presence or size of the vein(s) it conveys.

Situated posterolaterally on the superior aspect of the neural arch of each vertebra below C2, one finds a pair of superior articular facets, which are directed posterosuperiorly. The inferior aspect of each vertebra after C1 has inferior articular facets, which are directed anteroinferiorly to meet the superior facets of the vertebra below. The resulting facet joints (zygapophyseal joints) are rotated approximately 125 degrees from the plane of the superior end plate of the vertebral body.[4] This orientation guides lateral flexion and rotation movements such that rotation and lateral flexion to the same side tend to occur together in the primary coupled movement pattern of the cervical spine. Obviously, normal symmetrical motion requires that the right and left facet joints be symmetrically arranged. At the C3–C4 level and below, the right and left facet joints are nearly coplanar.[4] The medial edges of the facets at the C2–C3 joints are anterior to the lateral edges; such angulation limits rotation at the C2–C3 joint complex.

The facet joints are true synovial joints: thin ligamentous capsules seal them, and hyaline cartilage covers their articular surfaces. Osteophytes formed on the superior articular process can encroach upon the IVF. The facet joint capsules are innervated by the medial branch of dorsal ramus of the spinal nerve at that segment, and also by the medial branches of adjacent dorsal rami. (For example, the facet joints of the C3–C4 segmental joint complex are innervated not only by the dorsal ramus of C4, but also by dorsal rami of C3 and C5.) Detaching the neighboring muscles from the joint capsules is a delicate procedure in anatomical dissection.

The spinous processes of the second to sixth cervicals are usually bifid; that is, they are marked by a midline cleft dividing the tip into right and left processes. One or the other of these small processes may be absent, and they are often asymmetrical in length and shape, so the positional information obtained from palpation of cervical spinous processes is limited. The spinous process of C2 is stout and easily palpated; that of C6 is moderately elongated, and its tip is often bulbous rather than bifid.

THE OCCIPITO-ATLANTO-AXIAL COMPLEX

The many specializations of the osseous anatomy of the occiput, atlas, and axis are related to the geometric requirements of the transition between the skull and spine and to the functional requirements of a high degree of mobility in the motion segments near the head.

Occiput

The intracranial and extracranial surfaces of the occipital bone have many features of biomechanical and clinical significance; only the foramen magnum and occipital condyles will be considered here. The foramen magnum of the occipital bone connects the posterior cranial fossa to the vertebral canal (Fig. 1–2); through it pass the vertebral arteries, meninges, membrana tectoria, and the caudal end of the medulla oblongata. Its cross-sectional area is, therefore, larger than that of the spinal cord. The foramen is narrower anteriorly than posteriorly. The dens of the axis stands immediately inferior to basion, the anteriormost midline point on the foramen magnum.

The convex, somewhat kidney-shaped occipital condyles are found at the anterolateral edges of the foramen magnum. Each condyle is obliquely oriented, with its anterior end closer to the midline than its posterior end,

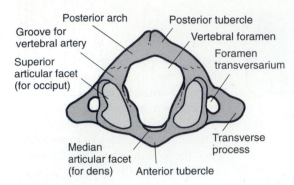

Figure 1–3. In a superior view of an isolated atlas (first cervical vertebra), one sees that the vertebral foramen is large enough to house not only the spinal cord and meninges but also the dens of the axis. Notice that the posterior tubercle is considerably smaller than the typical cervical spinous process; only the rectus capitis posterior minor muscles and a small part of the nuchal ligament attach there.

and the medial edge inferior to the lateral edge. Two aspects of the geometry of the condyles contribute much to upper cervical kinematics. First, the prominent anteroposterior convexity determines the axis of rotation for sagittal movements of the head on the neck, and helps to prevent rotational movement. Second, the distance between the right and left condyles matches their tilted orientation to define the axis of rotation for lateral flexion movements.

Atlas

The atlas lacks a vertebral body, so it takes the shape of a ring: anterior and posterior arches connect the right and left lateral masses to form a uniquely shaped vertebral foramen (Fig. 1–3). The anteroposterior length of the vertebral foramen is greater than that of the other cervicals, allowing room for the dens of the axis and its associated ligaments. These occupy the narrow anterior one third of the foramen, between the lateral masses, while the spinal cord and meninges pass through the wider posterior two thirds. The placement of the atlanto-occipital joints lateral to the foramen magnum and vertebral foramen (rather than anterior to them) minimizes distension of the spinal cord and medulla oblongata during flexion of the head.

The weight of the head and other sagittal forces are borne by the lateral masses of the atlas rather than being distributed between a vertebral body and articular pillars, as is the case for the other cervicals. The superior aspect of each lateral mass is marked by a concave articular facet that meets the convex surface of the occipital condyle. The inferior surface of each lateral mass features a large, sloping articular facet that allows rotation of the atlas on the axis.

The anterior and posterior arches of the atlas do not bear the weight of the head, but craniocaudal compression of the upper cervical spine subjects them to tension and bending forces as the trapezoid-shaped lateral masses are forced laterally. The arches must also withstand the forces

that are applied by muscles that attach to the atlas or cross it. The superior fascicles of the longus colli are inserted on the anterior tubercle at the midline of the anterior arch. Instead of a spinous process, there is a small posterior tubercle which serves as origin for the rectus capitis posterior minor muscle.

The transverse process of the atlas is large with a bulbous tip. Viewing the vertebra from above, the process is triangular and pierced by the transverse foramen near its base. It lacks the trough one finds on the superior surface of lower cervical transverse processes. The first cervical spinal nerve exits the vertebral canal posterior to the lateral mass on the superior surface of the posterior arch rather than along the superior aspect of the transverse process.

Axis

The unique features of the axis are found on its superior portion. Of these features, the most characteristic is the dens, or odontoid process (Fig. 1–4). In simple terms, the dens and a small adjacent part of the axis body develop from an ossification center that could have become the centrum of the atlas. (Jenkins[5] offers details of comparative and developmental anatomy.) Anteriorly, the dens has a hyaline cartilage-covered midline facet for articulation with the anterior tubercle of the atlas (the median atlanto-axial joint). Posteriorly, the neck of the dens is usually marked by a groove where the transverse ligament of the atlas passes. A synovial bursa may be found between the ligament and the cortical bone of the dens. Surgical aspects of the external and internal dimensions of the dens have been quantified by various authors.[6–8]

The relatively large superior articular facets of the axis lie lateral to the dens, directly on the surface of the vertebral body (i.e., not on an articular process). They slope considerably downward from medial to lateral to match the orientation of the atlas inferior facets. This angulation of the lateral atlanto-axial joint is readily recognized on AP radiographs. Because articular processes and an intervertebral disc are lacking, rotation at the atlanto-axial motion segment is free. The lateral atlanto-axial joints must convey

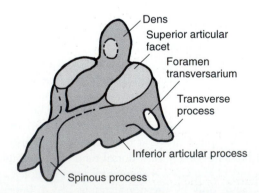

Figure 1–4. The prominent and unique features of the axis (second cervical) are found on its superior aspect. These features are the dens and the large, superolaterally oriented superior articular facets.

the entire weight of the atlas and head to lower structures. They are therefore situated anteroposteriorly in an intermediate position that is not as far anterior as an intervertebral disc and not as far posterior as a typical facet joint (see Fig. 1–4). The unique shapes of the atlas and axis eliminate the IVF, and the C2 spinal nerve passes through the slit between the posterior arch of atlas and the lamina of axis. There is an intervertebral disc below the axis, and the inferior articular processes and facets resemble those of lower cervicals in size, shape, position, and angulation. The stout, moderately long, bifid spinous process affords the superiormost opportunity for muscle attachment to a bone with movements that are essentially lower cervical in nature.

The axis transverse processes are slightly shorter than those of the lower cervicals, and so the axis is much narrower transversely than the atlas. As the vertebral artery ascends through the base of the axis transverse process, it begins to pass laterally on its way to the atlas transverse foramen. This curve and three others in the upper cervical and cranial course of the vertebral artery are described next.

SEVENTH CERVICAL VERTEBRA

The specializations of C7 (Fig. 1–5), the atypical lower cervical vertebra, are less obvious than those of the upper cervicals. Its long and horizontally oriented spinous process has a readily palpable, bulbous tip; C7 thereby earns the name *vertebra prominens*. Occasionally the spinous process is not so prominent as that of T1. The uncinate processes of T1 are small or absent, so the inferior surface of C7 usually lacks the indented facets for them. The orientations of the IVFs at the C6–C7 and C7–T1 levels (the passages for the C7 and C8 spinal nerves) are more coronal than those of the other cervical IVFs; they approach the angle of the thoracic IVFs. This angulation has obvious consequences for patient positioning in radiographic examination of the IVF.

The anterior tubercle of C7's transverse process is small or absent. And yet, the transverse process is longer than those of other lower cervicals. Its length is achieved by the costal element of the posterior tubercle. Unusually long transverse processes and cervical ribs are more common at C7 than at higher levels. A cervical rib is present when there is an articulation between the distal part of the transverse process and the rest of the vertebra. When this anomalous rib is present, it usually attaches to the superior surface of the first rib distally, but it may reach the sternum. The subclavian artery and lower trunk of the brachial plexus do not pass between the cervical rib and first rib. Rather, they pass superior to the cervical rib or anteromedial to its tip.[9] The presence of a cervical rib reduces the dimensions of the scalene triangle; compression of the subclavian artery or the lower trunk of the brachial plexus may result. Radiographic assessment of transverse process length and the presence of cervical ribs can therefore be part of an examination for thoracic outlet syndrome. A ligamentous band that connects the C7 transverse process or a short

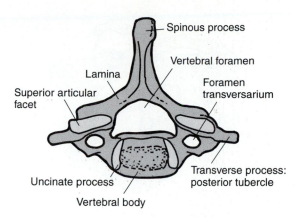

Figure 1–5. The transverse processes and spinous process of the seventh cervical are elongated; these unique proportions are related to the bone and its role in the cervicothoracic transition.

cervical rib to the first rib will not be visualized in a standard radiograph, but it may produce thoracic outlet signs and symptoms as if it were a full-sized, osseous cervical rib. As it has traditionally been defined, thoracic outlet syndrome covers a variety of neurological or vascular conditions in or near the root of the neck. Recently, Ranney[10] proposed the general term *cervicoaxillary syndrome* for such ailments. Within the cervicoaxillary syndrome, one would distinguish compression syndromes of the scalene triangle (thoracic outlet), costoclavicular space, and the space between the pectoralis minor and coracoid process.

A FEW POINTS ABOUT THE THORACIC SKELETON AND SHOULDER GIRDLE

One should not be led to think that the few points of the osseous anatomy of the thorax and shoulder that are presented here are more important than other features. Rather, some issues have been chosen that can easily be forgotten, but should not be. How does an upper thoracic vertebra differ from a lower cervical vertebra? Of course, the ribs articulate with thoracic vertebrae, and the thoracic transverse process lacks the details of a cervical transverse process, since those details are derived embryonically from costal elements. Uncinate processes are sometimes present at T1, but they are lacking on all subsequent vertebrae. Relative to the height of the vertebral body, the discs between upper thoracic vertebrae are thin. The IVFs are oriented more transversely in the thoracic spine. The facets are oriented more vertically, but they acquire a slight rotation, such that the inferior facets are directed anteromedially and the superior facets are directed posterolaterally to meet them.[11] This orientation would seem to favor rotation over lateral flexion, and to uncouple the two movements.

The s-curve shape of the clavicle is essential to its mechanical function during upper limb elevation. The medial third runs slightly posteriorly, and the lateral third runs nearly in the coronal plane. However, the medial third is

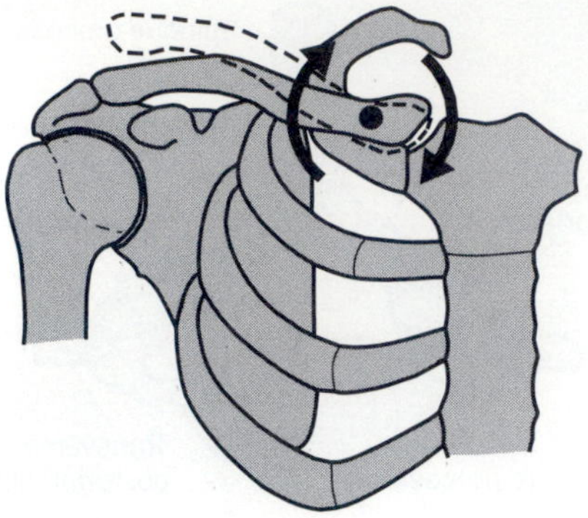

Figure 1–6. During elevation of the shoulder or upper limb, the distal end of the clavicle elevates. The antero-posterior axis of rotation is lateral to the sternoclavicular joint, so there is a slight depression of the proximal end of the clavicle. Rotation about the transverse axis (along the length of the bone) also contributes to elevation of the distal end of the clavicle; the superior surface of the bone comes to face forward. For clarity, the humerus and scapula are not shown in the elevated position.

well anterior to the lateral third. It should then be obvious that the middle third of the clavicle connects the bone's ends by running from anteromedial to posterolateral. During shoulder or upper limb elevation, the anteroposterior axis of rotation for angulation of the clavicle is a few centimeters lateral to the proximal end of the bone, near the attachment of the costoclavicular ligament (Fig. 1–6). The resulting depression of the proximal end of the clavicle (inferior glide at the sternoclavicular joint) is easily palpated. Elevation of the shoulder and upper limb also involves rotation of the clavicle about an axis that runs through the length of the proximal third of the bone (spin of the clavicle at the sternoclavicular joint). In order to elevate the distal end of the clavicle, the bone must spin such that its superior surface rotates anteriorly. Other elements of shoulder girdle movement are discussed in Chapter 2.

A disc of fibrocartilage divides the sternoclavicular joint into two completely separate compartments. An incomplete disc can often be found at the distal end of the clavicle; the space it fills should be kept in mind when assessing the gap between the clavicle and acromion in a radiographic evaluation of separated shoulder. At the acromioclavicular joint, the superior aspect of the clavicle is often more prominent than the acromion.

LIGAMENTS OF THE TYPICAL CERVICAL SEGMENTAL JOINT COMPLEX

Other than the ligaments that are associated with the spinal cord, the ligaments in the cervical region attach to bone, and they guide or prevent the movements of bones. The movements that any particular ligament is capable of guiding or preventing depend on its location and attach-

ments, but the character of the limitation to movement depends also on the ligament's mechanical properties. The more elastic ligaments in the cervical region—the ligamentum nuchae and ligamentum flavum—can store energy when they are stretched during flexion of the head and neck; they will return that energy as work during the extension movement that restores the ligaments to their pre-stretched positions. The important ligamentous structures in the cervical spine are the intervertebral discs, anterior and posterior longitudinal ligaments, ligamenta flava, the special ligaments of the occipito-atlanto-axial complex, and the nuchal ligament. Although the meninges surrounding the spinal cord serve certain ligamentous functions, they are beyond the scope of this chapter.

The principal connecting structure at each typical cervical joint complex is the intervertebral disc. In the cervical spine, the intervertebral discs are approximately three fifths of the thickness of a vertebral body (Fig. 1–7). The disc is composed of the anulus fibrosus surrounding the more gelatinous material of the nucleus pulposus. The outer concentric rings of the anulus are collagenous, and there is progressively less fibrous material in the inner fibrocartilaginous rings. Tearing injury to the outer layer of anulus fibrosus appears to be capable of causing pain, as nerve endings that have the anatomical characteristics of nociceptors are embedded in the anular tissue. Blood vessels and sensory nerve endings are not found in the nucleus pulposus. Relative to the size of the entire disc, the nucleus is smaller in the cervical disc than the lumbar disc. The center of the nucleus is posterior to the middle of the disc. Beginning in a child's teenage years, the mucoid tissue of the nucleus pulposus is replaced with fibrocartilage that arises from the hyaline cartilage of the end plates of the vertebral bodies.

Knowing something of the anatomy of the vertebral body and intervertebral disc, one can consider the uncovertebral joint and developmental changes in the cervical intervertebral disc. The uncovertebral joint is an articulation between the uncinate process (uncus) and a small indentation on the inferior surface of the vertebral body (Fig. 1–8). It is often referred to as Luschka's joint (Dvorak and Sandler[8] provide biographical information on Hubert von Luschka). In the fetal and preadolescent spine, there is loose fibrous connective tissue in the space between the uncus and the neural arch of the vertebra above.[2] Denser, more organized tissue of the nascent or young anulus fibrosus is found medially. The uncovertebral joint forms in the teen years when a space opens within the loose connective tissue. The joint, therefore, does not develop initially as a cleft in the anulus. However, formation of clefts within the disc generally accompanies the progressive disc dehydration that occurs in adulthood.

Several investigators have interpreted the process of discal cleft formation to be a combination of normal development and pathological degeneration.[2, 13, 14] Discal clefts probably can initiate centrally (as suggested in Fig. 1–7) or as expansions of Luschka's joints; in the former case, the

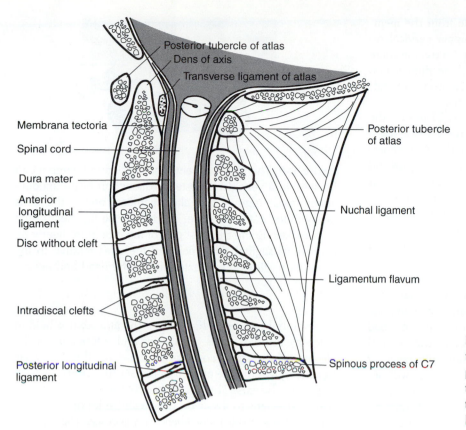

Membrana tectoria

Spinal cord

Dura mater

Anterior
longitudinal
ligament

Disc without cleft

Intradiscal clefts

Posterior longitudinal
ligament

Posterior tubercle of atlas
Dens of axis
Transverse ligament of atlas

Posterior tubercle
of atlas

Nuchal ligament

Ligamentum flavum

Spinous process of C7

Figure 1–7. A sagittal section through the neck shows the intervertbral discs, posterior longitudinal ligament, and anterior longitudinal ligament. Several intradiscal clefts are also evident in this illustration.

Figure 1–8. In an anterolateral oblique view of articulated cervical vertebrae one can see that the uncinate processes contribute to the anteromedial wall of the intervertebral foramen.

(Photo Courtesy of Aparna Annam.)

cleft and joint can eventually come to be united. If cleft formation follows disc dehydration, it will serve to maintain the mobility of the motion segment despite loss of the youthful resilience that the nucleus provides. However, the concomitant loss of disc height may lead to decreased height of the IVF or protrusion of anular material into the vertebral foramen, or both. Furthermore, the hyaline cartilage of the cervical vertebral end plate is replaced with bone in middle age.[13] This resembles the degenerative process that occurs at damaged joints. (Whether hyaline cartilage is retained into old age in segments that do not show osteophyte formation or other signs of degenerative disc disease is unknown.) It seems likely that herniation or shifting of the nucleus will occur if the nucleus is not sufficiently desiccated at the time of cleft formation (Fig. 1–7).

On the anterior side of the vertebral canal, between the dura mater and the vertebral bodies and discs, one finds a ligamentous surface. This is the posterior longitudinal ligament (PLL), which is named according to its relationship to the vertebral body and disc. The PLL is broader and much thicker in the cervical region than it is in the thoracic and lumbar regions. Its ability to prevent disc protrusion may be as important as its routine function in preventing flexion of the cervical spine. The cranialmost attachment of the PLL is to the inferior part of the body of C2; the ligament that continues superiorly from there to reach the occiput is called the membrana tectoria. Dura mater is tightly adherent to the PLL at C3 and at the caudal end of the axis; it is usually separable from the membrana tectoria in the remainder of the upper cervical region. Between C3 and the lower thoracic vertebrae there are generally few attachments of the PLL to dura mater. Like the outer anulus fibrosus, the PLL contains nerve endings with anatomical features of nociceptors.

The anterior longitudinal ligament (ALL) lies on the anterior surface of vertebral bodies and intervertebral discs. Cramer and associates[15] have shown that the ALL generally has strong attachments to the superior and inferior end plates of cervical vertebrae, but not to cervical discs. It is narrow at the atlas, and wider in the lower cervical region than it is in the thoracic region. It prevents extension of the neck and is vulnerable to extension injury.

The laminae of successive vertebrae at segments from C1–C2 to L5–sacrum are connected by ligamenta flava. The yellow color that gives these ligaments their name is due to the presence of elastic fibers. At each segment, the ligamentum flavum can form a single sheet crossing the midline; however, small midline gaps for passage of blood vessels are common. The ligamenta flava of the cervical spine are relatively long, allowing considerable range of motion in flexion. Since the ligament is elastic, it will not be slack when the head and neck are in the neutral position. When the normal, healthy elasticity of the ligament is lost due to scarring or fatty infiltration, the contents of the vertebral canal may be compressed by lax ligamentous tissue during extension of the head and neck. Elasticity also allows the ligaments to contribute extensor force to the neck, as when returning the head to neutral from a flexed position. The highly mobile space between the posterior arch of the atlas and laminae of the axis is often bridged by a thin, loose, relatively inelastic membrane rather than a ligamentum flavum.

LIGAMENTS OF THE UPPER CERVICAL SPINE

Conceptually, the ligamentous structures of the occipito-atlanto-axial complex can be divided into three groups: a collection of flexible membranous rings, the membrana tectoria and ligaments associated with the dens, and the meninges. Included in the rings of flexible membranes are the anterior atlanto-occipital membrane, posterior atlanto-occipital membrane, the anterior atlanto-axial membrane and the tissues between the posterior arch of the atlas and lamina of the axis.

The PLL breaks its connection to the vertebral bodies on the posterior surface of the vertebral body of C2. Without attaching to the superior part of the body of the axis or the dens, the ligament continues superiorly to make an attachment on the intracranial surface of the occiput, just inside the anterior edge of the foramen magnum. This bridging ligament is called the membrana tectoria; it is an important limiter of upper cervical flexion. Anterior to the membrana tectoria are the cruciform ligament and the paired alar ligaments (Fig. 1–9). The former is composed of

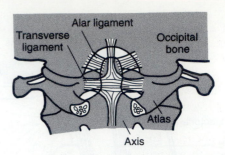

Figure 1–9. The alar ligaments and cruciform ligament can be seen in a very deep posterior dissection of the median atlanto-axial region. The alar ligaments attach the dens firmly to the occipital bone. The transverse ligament of the atlas makes up the sturdiest part of the cruciform ligament. It prevents sagittal movements of the atlas relative to the dens during flexion and extension of the head and neck.

a substantial transverse ligament of the atlas that is held in place by thinner bands of superior and inferior fibers. By closing off the space posterior to the dens, the transverse ligament prevents the atlas from translating anteriorly with respect to the axis. The alar ligaments connect the superior part of the dens to fossae on the medial sides of the occipital condyles. Additional fibers that connect the dens to the atlas lateral mass are common.[16] These stout ligaments keep the skull firmly on the neck, and they are the primary structures responsible for limiting rotation of the skull and atlas on the axis. Different parts of the alar ligament are drawn tight at the end-ranges of ipsilateral and contralateral atlanto-axial rotation. Finally, the apical dental ligament connects the anterior edge of the foramen magnum to the tip of the dens. It is revealed in anatomical dissection by reflecting the membrana tectoria and carefully removing the superior fibers of the cruciform ligament. One expects to find the anterior atlanto-axial membrane immediately anterior to it. The apical dental ligament is too small to have major mechanical significance.

NUCHAL LIGAMENT

The last nonmuscular supporting structure to be discussed is the nuchal ligament. It is comprised of a superficial, cord-like funicular part and a thin deeper sheet, the lamellar part.[17] The funicular part is an extension of the supraspinous ligament. It runs from lower cervical and upper thoracic spinous processes to the external occipital protuberance, and it serves as part of the origin of the upper trapezius, rhomboideus minor, serratus posterior superior, and splenius capitis muscles. The deeper fibrous sheet of the lamellar nuchal ligament attaches to the skull at the external occipital crest, which lies on the midline deep to the external occipital protuberance. Recently, Mitchell and colleagues[18] described two details of the deep upper cervical anatomy of the nuchal ligament. A small midline slip attaches to the dura mater at the interspace between atlas and axis, and portions of the ligament fan deep to the semispinalis capitis muscle to form lateral attachments on the superior nuchal lines. The dural attachment may assist in preventing inward buckling of the dura mater during head and neck extension. Mitchell and colleagues[18] suggest that the lateral fibers may guide or limit rotation of the head.

In many large obligate quadruped mammals, the nuchal ligament is large and strong, and it is yellow in color owing to a wealth of elastic fibers.[17] Since a large, elastic ligament provides torque to extend the head and neck, animals with well-developed nuchal ligaments are able to utilize cervical postures that minimize muscular effort by balancing ligament tension against gravity. One might infer from this that the relatively small human nuchal ligament makes a nearly balanced head position optimal for humans. However, the nuchal ligament is small or absent in all primates, including those with forward head postures, so such a conclusion would not be wise.

ADDITIONAL ISSUES IN NONMUSCULAR ANATOMY OF THE CERVICAL SPINE

NORMAL LORDOTIC CURVATURE

Anatomically, the curvatures of both the normal and ailing cervical spine are determined by the geometries of the intervertebral disc, vertebral bodies, partes interarticulares and, to a lesser extent, the pedicles. The cervical intervertebral discs are taller anteriorly than posteriorly, contributing much to the normal curve. The partes interarticulares of some individuals are unusually high relative to the heights of the vertebral bodies.[19] In such cases, a curve that is straighter than the healthy curve of a typical individual may be healthy and normal. Curvature will decrease if the anterior muscles shorten, whether by contracture, spasm, or volitional contraction; only the latter two causes of altered curvature can occur in the short term. It seems that shortening of the small posterior and anterior muscles in appropriate combinations could result in a temporary and modifiable loss of lordotic curvature at a single segmental joint complex. The precise nature of the short-term and long-term detrimental effects of moderately straightened and hyperlordotic curves is poorly understood. Radiographically, several different geometric and positional techniques have arisen to evaluate the lordotic curve or loss of it at one or more segments (see Chaps. 2 and 16).

PROMINENT BONY LANDMARKS FOR PALPATION OF THE CERVICAL SPINE

The spinous processes of C2 and C7 are readily palpable. Although the spinous processes from C3 through C6 are less prominent and their shapes are more variable, they are valuable for motion palpation (e.g., one may examine sagittal movements of C6 on C7 by palpation of spinous processes). The posterior aspects of the partes interarticulares of cervical vertebrae from C2 to C7 can be palpated through several layers of muscle; they are less anatomically variable than the cervical spinous processes and less tender than the transverse processes. When palpating the neck anteriorly, the carotid tubercle on C6 is often more prominent than the anterior tubercles of the other cervical vertebrae.

The skilled palpator will acquire some information about the position or movements of the posterior tubercle of C1 by palpation of the interspace between the spinous process of C2 and the occiput. The transverse process of C1 is felt in a moderately deep palpation anterior to the mastoid process of the temporal bone. If the mastoid process is short, the atlas transverse process will be anteroinferior to it. In most individuals, the styloid process of the temporal bone is no deeper than the tip of the atlas transverse process and less than a centimeter anterior to it.

Prominent bony landmarks of the shoulder girdle include the episternal notch and proximal end of the clavicle, the curvatures of the clavicle, the distal end of the clavicle, and the acromioclavicular joint; on the scapula, the acromion, spine, coracoid process (moderately deep), medial or vertebral border, superior angle (located somewhat anteriorly), and inferior angle.

MUSCLES IN THE NECK

The conversion of neural information to contractile force can be thought of as the primary function of muscles. However, the relationship between skeletal muscles and the nervous system is bidirectional: muscles receive information from the nervous system, and they deliver information to it. With their mechanoreceptors, the joints and muscles begin the chain of neurophysiological events that produces proprioception—the sense of where one's anatomical parts are in relation to other parts—and kinesthesia—the sense that one's anatomical parts are moving. Of course, muscles are of great interest as sources of pain and targets of therapy to relieve pain, restore motion, and improve performance.

ACTION, ACTIVITY, AND FUNCTION

After the anatomical description of each muscle in most anatomy texts, one usually finds a brief account of the muscle's mechanical attributes and its roles in various behaviors. This synopsis, which commonly has the title "Actions," is useful; students learning the muscles for the first time must know something of what individual muscles and groups of muscles do, but they should not be burdened with excessive factual and conceptual information. However, the more advanced student may find the same synopsis inadequate, and sometimes a little frustrating. The reader is left wondering what is known and what has been assumed by the author to be true. This confusion can be clarified by using a cohesive set of carefully delineated terms to describe multiple aspects of knowledge about muscles. The terms must distinguish anatomical facts from physiological ones, and distinguish fact from understanding. Action, activity, and function will be used hereinafter to describe anatomical, physiological, and conceptual knowledge of muscles.

Action is a description of the anatomical effect of the torques and forces a muscle exerts. In the anatomy lab one will ask, "What movements occur when this muscle contracts?" Action is, therefore, a matter of mechanical fact that is inferred from the geometry of body parts: hence the term *anatomical action*. Consider the following useful statements concerning the actions of neck muscles.

1. All neck muscles have the action of lateral flexion toward their side of the body.
2. Muscles that cross the atlanto-axial joint have more prominent head rotating actions than muscles that are confined to the lower cervical spine.
3. Some muscles in the neck act on the axial skeleton only (we can call them the intrinsic neck muscles), and others act on the shoulder girdle (the axioscapular muscles).
4. Certain axioscapular muscles exert anatomical actions on the head and neck, even when they are recruited during efforts of the shoulder or upper limb.

Clearly, even though the four statements may be difficult to demonstrate or quantify precisely, all are matters of fact, not of understanding.

Muscle activity is another matter of fact. It answers the question, "During which behaviors is the muscle recruited by the nervous system?" One observes such physiological facts by palpation, electromyography, or other in vivo means. Palpation and inspection remain the most common and important means of assessing muscle activity. For example, an electromyographer may palpate actively contracting muscles to identify targets for electrode placement, and specific procedures for visual inspection of superficial muscles are described in Chapter 14. Recruitment can be used synonymously with activity of a muscle. The term *muscle contraction* can be reserved for instances when the force that the muscle exerts when it is active is of interest (e.g., during a manual muscle test).

A muscle's function is the role that it plays in a specific behavior. Here one asks the question, "Why is a muscle recruited when it is?" Function is a matter of understanding, not of fact. (This is not to say that there cannot be correct or incorrect functional interpretations.) To answer a functional question, one will want to know the action and activity patterns of the muscle and one may have to study other muscles, too. In a clinical context, the word *function* sometimes refers to the ability to perform a role, not to the role itself. This is the difference between "What is a structure's function?" and "How well is a structure functioning?" Function in the sense of "role" cannot be improved or impaired. On the other hand, function in the sense of "ability to do things" can be impaired or improved. Obviously, function is not limited to muscles in the way that action and activity are; any anatomical structure or physiological phenomenon can have a function.

TRAPEZIUS

The trapezius is the most superficial back muscle, and it is the largest of the axioscapular muscles (Fig. 1–10). Its origin, which typically runs from the occiput to the spinous process of T12, is the longest muscle attachment in body. The insertion of trapezius can be traced from the lateral third of the clavicle, across the acromioclavicular joint, onto the superficial surface of the acromion process, along the superior lip of the spine of the scapula, through a 180-degree turn, and finally onto the medial part of the inferior lip of the spine of the scapula. The trapezius is traditionally divided into upper, middle, and lower parts. Upper trapezius has the greatest mechanical, neurophysiological, and clinical importance to the cervical spine. The highest fascicles of upper trapezius arise either from the superior nuchal line of the occiput or from the midline of the occiput at or near inion. They are inserted on the distal third of the clavicle. The part of upper trapezius that arises from the nuchal ligament is inserted on or near the acromioclavicular joint. With the origin from C7, one may refer to middle trapezius; from C7, fascicles can be traced to the acromion. A triangular sheet of tendon several centimeters long attaches the muscle to its origin from C7 and upper thoracic transverse processes. In some instances muscle fascicles arise from the deep surface of the tendon and, in general, the trapezius is thickest just lateral to the tendon. Fascicles of lower trapezius ascend from their origin on thoracic spinous processes to the root of the spine of the scapula; they are inserted on the inferior lip of the spine. A small tubercle on that lip—the tubercle of the spine of the scapula—usually marks the lateral extent of the lower trapezius insertion.

The motor innervation of the trapezius is by the accessory nerve (cranial nerve [CN] XI). The branch of the accessory nerve that supplies the trapezius is joined by branches of the ventral rami of the third and fourth cervical spinal nerves; this cervical component usually conveys all or most of the sensory information from the muscle. Variations from this typical plan are of particular interest to surgeons, because the accessory nerve and the branches that connect to it are commonly excised in radical neck dissections, as when removing cancerous lymph nodes.[20,21] The greater occipital nerve occasionally passes through the trapezius near its superior border to reach the scalp.[22] Branches of the subclavian artery in the neck deliver blood to most of the muscle.

Obviously, the different parts of the trapezius have different actions on the shoulder girdle. All three parts retract

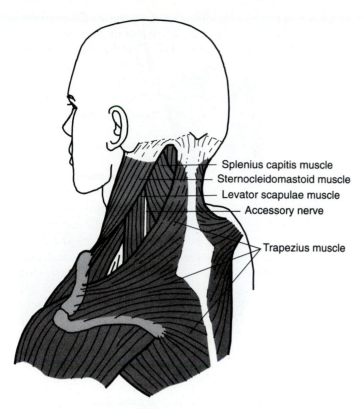

Splenius capitis muscle
Sternocleidomastoid muscle
Levator scapulae muscle
Accessory nerve

Trapezius muscle

Figure 1–10. The trapezius muscle is broad and flat; its origin from the occipital bone, nuchal ligament, and spinous processess is the longest muscular attachment in the body. The upper trapezius is thin; this is especially true of its highest parts, which pass from the occipital bone to the clavicle. Middle trapezius can be defined as the part that is inserted to the spine of the scapula; it is the thickest part of the muscle. The muscle thins again in its lower portion.

the scapula. Upper trapezius also elevates the shoulder girdle; lower trapezius depresses it. When the actions of the three parts of trapezius and serratus anterior are combined, the result is lateral rotation of the scapula and elevation of the shoulder girdle. Lower trapezius and serratus anterior act to draw the medial border and inferior angle of the scapula inferiorly and laterally whereas upper trapezius draws the acromion superiorly. Therefore, the axis about which "glenoid up" rotation occurs is within the scapula. In addition to its actions on the shoulder girdle, upper trapezius exerts contralateral rotation, lateral flexion, and extension torques on the head and neck. These actions must be counteracted to maintain head position when upper trapezius is recruited during upper limb and shoulder efforts.[23,24]

The trapezius is recruited during shoulder elevation and retraction, and during upper limb elevation.[25] All three parts show more activity during abduction of the upper limb than during flexion. This effect is most prominent for lower trapezius. Trapezius activity can be very low during far forward reaches. (Serratus anterior is more active then.) Upper trapezius is not recruited to perform contralateral head rotation or other head movements in the absence of upper limb effort. However, during upper limb efforts there is greater upper trapezius activity when the head is rotated contralaterally (i.e., right upper trapezius is more active during right-sided upper limb elevation efforts with left head rotation). Functional explanations for this observed recruitment pattern are a topic of ongoing electromyographic research.

LEVATOR SCAPULAE

The levator scapulae is the smaller of the two major axioscapular muscles in the neck. Typically it originates from the transverse process of C1 and from the posterior tubercles of transverse processes from C2, C3, and C4; it is inserted on the vertebral border of the scapula between the superior angle and the point where the spine of the scapula meets the vertebral border (Fig. 1–11). Often one can trace individual fascicles from transverse processes to the scapula. The fascicles do not cross each other; the atlantal attachment is, therefore, continuous with the insertion nearest the spine of the scapula and the lower cervical fascicles attach nearer the superior angle of the scapula. The superior portion of the levator scapulae lies next to the splenius capitis and it is superficial to the splenius cervicis. Contraction of levator scapulae is readily palpated over the superior portion, and its superficially exposed surface is amenable to electromyographic (EMG) monitoring. The deeper inferior portion with its scapular attachment lies deep to the upper trapezius. Here the deviation of the levator scapulae's fibers away from those of the splenii is very obvious, since the latter muscles curve toward the spinous processes while the levator scapulae continues straight to the scapula.

The levator scapulae acts to elevate the shoulder girdle with some protraction, and at the same time it internally rotates the scapula. (This rotation is sometimes referred to as glenoid down rotation.) A concentric contraction of levator scapulae occurs reliably during shoulder elevation

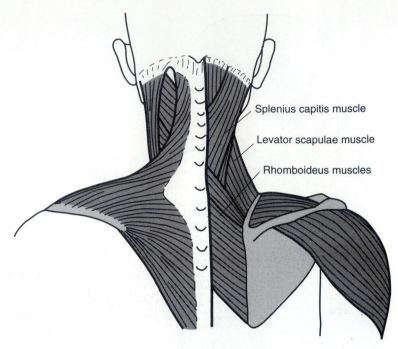

Splenius capitis muscle

Levator scapulae muscle

Rhomboideus muscles

Figure 1–11. Reflection or removal of the sterno-cleidomastoideus and trapezius reveals the splenius capitis, levator scapulae, and rhomboideus muscles. Despite their very different attachments, the splenius and levator scapulae have nearly parallel fibers. Both muscles exert extension, lateral flexion, and ipsilateral rotation actions on the neck. However, the levator scapulae is not recruited to perform such efforts unless much force is required.

with the upper limb at rest; the addition of shoulder protraction elicits greater activity. The muscle's scapula-elevating action suggests that it might be recruited during upper limb elevation, but its rotating action suggests that it might not, since glenoid up rotation is required. In fact, recruitment during upper limb efforts is controversial. Indwelling fine-wire EMG electrodes that I placed in the superior, superficial part of the muscle showed no activity during upper limb abduction, flexion, and scapular plane elevation, and reliable low to moderate level activity accompanying scapular elevation during extension of the upper limb.[24] However, needle electrodes placed with appropriate regard to proper position in the inferior part of the muscle by Behrsin and Maguire[26] indicated considerable activity during upper limb abduction and flexion, and no activity during upper limb extension.

Its attachments to cervical transverse processes give the levator scapulae direct anatomical actions on the neck and indirect actions on the head: it is an ipsilateral rotator, lateral flexor, and weak extensor of the neck. As was true of the trapezius, levator scapulae is not recruited to produce isolated head movements, but the actions it exerts on the neck are relevant because neck muscles have to be recruited to stabilize the head and neck during shoulder and upper limb efforts that involve levator scapulae contraction.[24]

RHOMBOID MINOR AND MAJOR

The rhomboid minor is the smallest and caudalmost axioscapular muscle in the neck (see Fig. 1–11). Its origin from the lowest part of the nuchal ligament and the spinous processes of C7 and T1 indicates that it has small mechanical effects on the head and neck. The rhomboid mus-

cles cannot be studied with surface EMG electrodes because they are covered by the trapezius. Therefore, little is known with certainty about their activity patterns and functions. Their actions suggest that they will be recruited for concentric contraction during rowing exercises or other instances of scapular retraction. Moseley and associates[27] detected such activity using indwelling EMG electrodes. Scapular retraction will not serve as a test of isolated rhomboideus activity because the middle trapezius will also be particularly active. Rhomboideus major is inactive during isolated head and neck movements.[28] Perhaps the strongest association of the rhomboids with the cervical spine is that their innervation is by the dorsal scapular nerve (ventral ramus of C5 with some contribution from C4).

SPLENIUS CAPITIS AND CERVICIS

The splenius capitis and splenius cervicis muscles are two important head and neck rotators that lie immediately adjacent to each other in the nuchal region and posterior triangle of the neck (Fig. 1–12). From their origins on the nuchal ligament and the spinous processes of C7 and upper thoracic vertebrae, they course obliquely into the neck. The splenius capitis is inserted on the lateral part of the superior nuchal line and on the mastoid process deep to the sternocleidomastoid muscle. Splenius cervicis is inserted on the posterior tubercles of cervical transverse processes, medial to levator scapulae. By their attachments it is clear that both splenii are capable of ipsilateral rotation, lateral flexion, and extension at the spinal joints they cross. The lever arms and available ranges of motion for each of these movements are less for most of the splenius cervicis than for the splenius capitis. However, the highest fascicles of

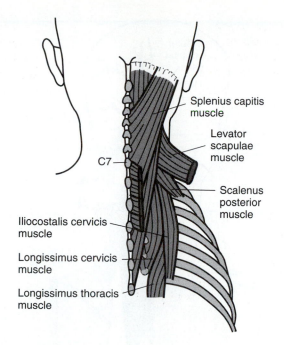

Figure 1–12. Removing the axioscapular muscles and the thin sheet of the serratus posterior superior muscle reveals the extent of the long, narrow splenius origin from upper thoracic spinous processes. The insertions of longissimus thoracis and cervicis are on the deep surface of the muscles themselves, and so they are not seen. However, the iliocostalis cervicis does not extend so far superiorly, and its final tendinous insertions on the posterior tubercles of lower cervical transverse processes can be seen without lifting or displacing the muscle. The thorough dissector may also find the scalenus posterior immediately lateral to iliocostalis cervicis.

splenius cervicis, those that are inserted on the transverse process of the atlas, have nearly as much rotating action as the splenius capitis. The epaxial developmental derivation of the splenii is revealed by their insertion medial to the origin of levator scapulae and by the innervation they receive from dorsal rami of cervical spinal nerves.

Splenius capitis is recruited ipsilaterally in almost all typical head rotations; it is not recruited to produce lateral flexion.[29] In the course of EMG experiments I have observed elevated splenius capitis activity during the common behavior of looking to the side and slightly downward with the trunk in a forward flexed position (e.g, when tying a shoe). The splenius can then provide rotatory torque, and it counteracts the flexion torque that gravity exerts on the head.

CERVICAL ERECTOR SPINAE

The cervical representatives of the iliocostalis, longissimus, and spinalis muscles are much smaller than the like-named muscles in the back. The iliocostalis cervicis is a deep muscle that arises from the angles of ribs 3 through 6 and passes to its insertions on posterior tubercles of transverse

processes from C4 to C6. The superior portion of the muscle is covered by the splenius cervicis. One assumes that it functions as a stabilizer of the cervicothoracic junction and lower cervical spine. Slightly medial to this muscle are the longissimus cervicis and capitis; they are thin continuations of the longissimus thoracis. In dissection, one can follow the bladelike posterior edge of longissimus capitis to the mastoid process. It is the deepest neck muscle attached there, and it is the only erector spinae muscle to reach the head. The shorter, more anterior longissimus cervicis fibers are inserted on posterior tubercles of cervical transverse processes. The least of the cervical erector spinae muscles is the spinalis cervicis, a worm-shaped, variably present muscle that connects the spinous process of C6 or C7 to the spinous process of the axis. Right and left spinalis cervicis muscles are found on either side of the lamellar nuchal ligament.

SEMISPINALIS CAPITIS AND THE TRANSVERSOSPINALIS CERVICIS

Semispinalis capitis is among the largest nuchal muscles; it approaches the size of the two splenii taken together (Figs. 1–13 and 1–14). It lies deep to the splenii, and it is readily distinguished from them by its longitudinally oriented

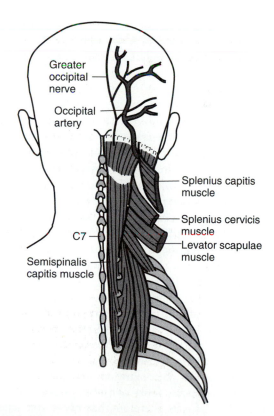

Figure 1–13. In a posterior dissection of the neck, removal or reflection of the axioscapular muscles and the splenii reveals the full extent of the semispinalis capitis muscle. The semispinalis capitis is moderately thick; it is the most powerful extensor of the head and neck.

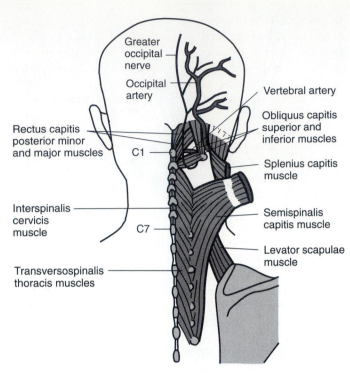

Figure 1–14. Reflection of the splenius muscles and the semispinalis capitis reveals the transversospinalis cervicis, the suboccipital muscles, and the interspinalis muscles. The most superficial fascicles of all three parts of transversospinalis (semispinalis, multifidus, and rotatores) are inserted on the spinous process of C2. The suboccipital triangle is formed of the rectus capitis posterior major and the two obliquus muscles. Notice that the third part of the vertebral artery is found in the triangle, and that only one angle of the triangle approaches the midline of the body. The interspinalis cervicis muscles are among the smallest muscles that serve locomotor or postural functions.

fibers. Reflection of the upper trapezius reveals a triangular surface of semispinalis capitis inferior to the occiput and between the superior borders of the right and left splenius capitis. Depending on the lengths of the attachments of upper trapezius and the sternocleidomastoid muscle on the superior nuchal line, a few square centimeters of semispinalis capitis in the lateral portion of this triangle are not covered by any muscle at all. Semispinalis capitis is considered to be a member of the transversospinalis group, but its attachments do not match that classification perfectly. It does originate from transverse processes of C7–T6 and from the posterior surfaces of the pars interarticularis of C4–C6; but often a few fascicles arise from upper thoracic spinous processes, too. Its insertion deep to the superior nuchal line fills the surface of the occipital bone between the superior and inferior nuchal lines. The right and left semispinalis capitis muscles are separated by the lamellar portion of the nuchal ligament.

The remaining muscles of the cervical transversospinalis group really do run from transverse processes to spinous processes (see Fig. 1–14). The chief insertion of the semispinalis cervicis, multifidus cervicis, and rotatores cervicis is the spinous process of axis, and the three differ primarily in their origins. By definition, fascicles of the semispinalis cervicis cross four or more segmental joint complexes. The muscle, therefore, has no origins superior to the transverse process of C7. Most of the muscle arises from upper thoracic vertebrae, and it is the largest muscle that acts to extend the lower cervical spine exclusively. Fascicles arising from C6 or C5 will cross three or four segmental joint complexes on their way to the axis, and so

they are defined as multifidus cervicis. The rotatores muscles act across only one or two joint complexes; upon reflection of the semispinalis capitis they can be seen running from C4 and C3 to the axis. Small fascicles of multifidus and rotatores with insertions on the bases of lower cervical spinous processes can be found deep to semispinalis cervicis in a thorough dissection of the nuchal region.

ACTIONS AND ACTIVITY PATTERNS OF THE NUCHAL MUSCLES

Extension of the head and neck or of the neck alone is the primary anatomical action of the cervical erector spinae, semispinalis capitis, and transversospinalis muscles. The more lateral parts of the erector spinae and semispinalis capitis are also able to exert considerable lateral flexion torque. The transversospinalis muscles are contralateral rotators of the lower cervical spine, with the deeper, shorter muscles being most capable of this action. Geometry requires that the deep muscles of the lower cervical spine are shorter than the more superficial muscles. They therefore act over just one or a few segments, which suggests that they are involved in segmental dysfunction. However, the activities of the deep nuchal muscles have not been studied thoroughly in a biomechanical context.

When the head is in the neutral position, low-level, intermittent semispinalis capitis activity functions to prevent head flexion. One would expect flexion-preventing postural activity to increase when one assumes a slightly flexed head posture, but this is not always detected electromyographically. A second postural function of the nuchal muscles is to prevent flexion of the head and neck when the scalenes or sternocleidomastoid contract to elevate the rib cage, or when the suprahyoid and infrahyoid muscles are recruited for their actions on the cervical viscera. Ongoing activity of semispinalis capitis and other nuchal muscles can become variable and show momentary increases in activity during mastication and speech. This appears to serve several functions. The head is being stabilized against anterior neck muscle torques and also against reaction forces associated with mandibular acceleration (especially during mastication), and small, expressive head movements (including head extension) are all but unavoidable during speech.

Semispinalis capitis activity increases phasically during head extension movements, and the muscle is tonically active during isometric head extension exercises. Differences between activity during isometric extension and retraction efforts could be studied with exercise equipment that allowed quantification of torques applied to the head. Although it exerts a lateral flexion torque on the head, semispinalis capitis activity has been found not to increase during unresisted lateral flexion movements[29] nor during gently resisted lateral flexion efforts unless extension activity is also appropriate. (That is to say, the muscle will be active to prevent flexion if the manual muscle tester's hand contacts the subject's head posterolaterally.) An explicit attempt to sample the lateral fibers of the muscle would be interesting in this regard.

SUBOCCIPITAL MUSCLES AND SUBOCCIPITAL TRIANGLE

The four suboccipital muscles are the rectus capitis posterior major, rectus capitis posterior minor, obliquus capitis inferior, and obliquus capitis superior. All four are found deep to the semispinalis capitis (see Fig. 1–14), and they are innervated by the suboccipital nerve, a branch of the dorsal ramus of C1.

The rectus capitis posterior major muscle arises from the superior surface of the spinous process of axis, and it is inserted on the occiput deep to the inferior nuchal line. It is, therefore, an ipsilateral rotator, lateral flexor, and extensor of the head and atlas. Contraction of the muscle when the head is stabilized will rotate the axis under the atlas and flex the axis on C3; the resulting displacement of the axis spinous process upward and toward the side of the active muscle should be recognizable on radiographs.[30, 31]

Pain and vagaries of electrode placement have limited my success with EMG of the rectus capitis posterior major. In three subjects it was active during all ipsilateral head rotations and most returns to a nonrotated head position from contralateral rotation. It showed intermittent, prolonged phases of activity when little or no head rotation was evident, so it seems to be recruited for its head extending action, as well. The curious finding that it is active contralateral to resisted or unresisted lateral flexion is in keeping with Jirout's predictions based on upper cervical

radiography.[30] The muscle has been a target of some interesting anatomical research with a neurophysiological focus: fatty infiltration into the muscle, as recognized on magnetic resonance imaging (MRI), is associated with chronic neck pain, soft tissue palpatory findings, and poor balance.[32, 33]

The rectus capitis posterior minor is deeper than the rectus capitis posterior major. It connects the posterior tubercle of atlas to a portion of the occipital bone that is medial to the insertion of its slightly larger lateral neighbor. An attachment to dura mater has been described near the muscle's origin.[34] Head extension is the primary action of the rectus capitis posterior minor; it also has some ability to rotate over a very small range of motion. It may be worth noting that it is capable of flexing the atlas relative to the axis when the head is stabilized. When the head is in an extended position, the rectus capitis posterior minor has a markedly anteroposterior course. Fibers that have a connection to the dura may, therefore, function to draw the dura posteriorly, preventing folding into the vertebral canal. The muscle's activity patterns are unknown.

The obliquus capitis inferior runs from the side of the spinous process of C2 to the posterior aspect of the transverse process of C1. The greater occipital nerve—the major branch of the dorsal ramus of C2—curves around the inferior border of the muscle before it pierces the semispinalis capitis muscle on its way to the scalp. The obliquus capitis inferior is round in cross-section and sometimes surprisingly thick. Since its only action is ipsilateral rotation at the atlanto-axial joint, it is likely to play a role in compensating for postural alterations of the lower cervical spine. I have not succeeded in collecting EMG data from obliquus capitis inferior.

The relationships and actions of obliquus capitis superior are very different from those of obliquus capitis inferior. The former muscle leaves the transverse process of C1 and passes posterosuperiorly to its insertion on the inferior nuchal line of the occiput. Much of the broad, thin distal portion of the muscle is immediately superficial to the rectus capitis posterior major. Obliquus capitis superior is primarily an extensor of the head. The force it applies for lateral flexion is weak because the muscle approaches the skull tangentially.[35] However, that force is applied over a rather long lever arm. The muscle's tangential alignment makes it a contralateral rotator at the atlanto-occipital motion segment, but there is very little range of motion for that movement. Several electrodes that I intended to place in the rectus capitis posterior major reported activity during lateral flexion, extension, and contralateral rotation head movements. These electrodes seem to have sampled either obliquus capitis superior or high, lateral fibers of semispinalis capitis.

The rectus capitis posterior major and the two obliquus muscles make up the borders of the suboccipital triangle. When seeking either the third part of the vertebral artery within the triangle or the rectus capitis posterior minor medial to it, an anatomist must remove a considerable amount of fibrofatty tissue investing the suboccipital plexus of veins. In living subjects, palpable changes in the consistency of this tissue may provide diagnostic information; on the other hand, such changes may obfuscate palpatory findings for the suboccipital muscles themselves.

INTERSPINALIS CERVICIS

The last of the nuchal muscles are the six pairs of interspinales cervicis muscles that connect the tips of spinous processes from C2 to C7 (see Fig. 1–14). The muscles of this elegant chain are likely to function as sensory organs for reflexes and the proprioceptive pathway, and as regulators of the low amplitude sagittal movements that the maintenance of posture requires.

STERNOCLEIDOMASTOID

The sternocleidomastoid (SCM) is the smaller of the two muscles innervated by the accessory nerve (Fig. 1–15). Like the trapezius, it is a relatively superficial muscle. SCM originates from the proximal part of the clavicle and the superior aspect of the manubrium. Most of its fascicles are inserted on the mastoid process of the temporal bone, but a thin sheet of muscle and tendon extends posteriorly from the mastoid process along the superior nuchal line. The presence of two origins and two insertions suggests the possibility of four parts of the muscle, which can be called sternomastoideus, cleidomastoideus, sterno-occipitalis, and cleido-occipitalis. In fact, the cleido-occipitalis is typically small when it is present at all; most or all of the clavicular fascicles attach to the mastoid process and are separated from the overlying sterno-occipital and sternomastoid fibers by a variably distinct fascial layer. It is not always possible to trace this fascial layer as far superiorly as the mastoid process.

In broad terms, the anatomical actions of SCM are flexion, lateral flexion, and contralateral rotation of the head and neck. The clavicular and sternal parts have different actions on the shoulder girdle: the former elevates the clavicle directly, while the latter elevates the entire rib cage and thereby elevates both the right and left shoulder girdles without directly influencing the angle of the clavicle. In far contralateral head rotations, the mastoid process passes medial to the clavicular attachment of cleidomastoideus and the muscle loses its rotating action. The orientations of the zygapophyseal and uncovertebral joints in the human cervical spine produce coupling of lateral flexion and rotation;[35–37] the lateral flexion action of all parts of SCM opposes the coupled movement pattern. Right SCM is a left rotator and right lateral flexor, but typical left head rotations are accompanied by lower cervical left lateral flexion. Since cleidomastoideus has a slightly greater lever arm for lateral flexion of the head than the sternal parts of SCM, its action will be affected more strongly by the coupling of lateral flexion and rotation, and the action

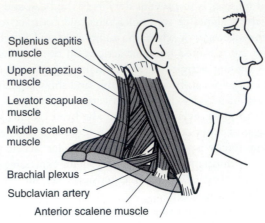

Splenius capitis muscle
Upper trapezius muscle
Levator scapulae muscle
Middle scalene muscle
Brachial plexus
Subclavian artery
Anterior scalene muscle
Sternocleidomastoid muscle

Figure 1–15. The lateral aspect of the neck is dominated by muscular and neural structures: between the sternocleidomastoid and trapezius muscles are the superficial surfaces of the splenius capitis, levator scapulae, scalenus medius, scalenus anterior, and inferior belly of omohyoid. The brachial plexus, cervical plexus, and subclavian vessels also pass through this region. It is worth remembering that the subclavian artery can extend one or two fingerbreadths superior to the clavicle.

of the cleidomastoideus may be slightly less suited to rotation of the head than the action of sternomastoideus. The attachments of the SCM to the mastoid process and occiput also result in regional differences in anatomical action: the occipital fibers (primarily sterno-occipitalis) exert a slight head extending torque while the fascicles that are inserted on the mastoid process exert a slight flexion torque.

Electromyographically, the SCM is the most thoroughly studied intrinsic neck muscle. The elaborate anatomy of the SCM causes problems for the electromyographer. Precise verification of electrode position is difficult. Two sites provide relative certainty of electrode placement: an electrode placed within the medial two thirds of the clavicular head of SCM will sample the cleidomastoideus even if cleido-occipitalis is present, and the anterior edge of the sternal head of SCM is almost certain to be sternomastoideus. In general, SCM is unilaterally active to produce lateral flexion and contralateral rotation of the head. The clavicular head of SCM is slightly less active than the sternal head during head rotations.[38] I have observed low-level contralateral SCM activity (and ipsilateral splenius capitis activity) when the head is held still in a rotated position. Unlike the splenius, SCM is less active during head rotation with a flexed head posture. The muscle is recruited bilaterally during end range or resisted head flexion efforts, including rising from a supine position. Bilateral activity functions to elevate the rib cage during deep inspirations or other instances of costal respiration.

No published studies have attempted to distinguish activity in the mastoid and occipital parts of SCM. However, variation in activity to produce or control head extension is found both within and across studies of the muscle as a whole. Machado de Sousa and colleagues[38] and Vitti and associates[39] found few subjects who recruited the SCM for unresisted head extension. On the other hand, Costa and colleagues[40] recorded low-level, moderate, or strong recruitment during unresisted head extension in approximately half of their subjects. Whether the subjects who recruited the muscle in the various studies did so to produce the head extension movement or to prevent excessive extension is unclear. It is possible that the sterno-occipitalis was inadvertently sampled in some but not all subjects.

ANTERIOR, MIDDLE, AND POSTERIOR SCALENE MUSCLES

The three scalene muscles—the anterior, middle, and posterior scaleni—are cervical homologues of the innermost, internal and external intercostal muscles. This is recognized by their attachments to ribs and cervical anterior tubercles, their innervation by cervical ventral rami, and by the passage of the brachial plexus between the anterior and middle scaleni (Figs. 1–15 and 1–16).

The anterior and middle scaleni attach to the first rib. The former is inserted on anterior tubercles of cervical transverse processes from C3 to C6, while the cervical attachment of the latter is from C2 to C6, occasionally reaching the atlas. The two muscles flex and laterally flex the neck and weakly rotate it contralaterally; at the end range of contralateral rotation the scalenus medius especially will have little or no rotary action. The features of osseous anatomy that couple lateral flexion and contralateral rotation movements in the human lower cervical spine[35–37] cause the scaleni to be more effective flexors than lateral flexors or contralateral rotators. Briefly put, the muscles exert a force that is nearly perpendicular to the zygapophyseal joint plane, which limits their ability to produce lateral flexion or rotation. Mathematical modeling and in vitro experiments in which displacements are measured when forces that mimic contraction of the scaleni are applied to isolated cadaveric spines could be used to test this analysis.

In a typical scalenus group, the only fascicles that attach to the second rib are found posterior to the middle scalene; these are defined as the posterior scalene muscle. Its coronal orientation suggests that the posterior scalene's actions are limited to lateral flexion of the neck and elevation of the rib cage, but coupling of lower cervical lateral flexion and rotation will grant it some rotating action, too.

A short, variably present muscle called scalenus minimis connects the transverse process of C7 to the medial

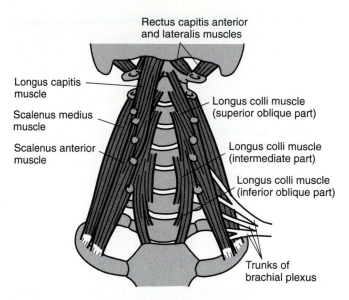

Figure 1–16. The scalenus anterior and scalenus medius muscles, the brachial plexus, and the longus muscles are readily visible when the vasculature and visceral structures are removed from the anterior aspect of the neck. The scalenus posterior, however, is often obscured by the scalenus medius in a directly anterior view of the neck. As they cross the middle scalene muscle, the roots of the brachial plexus (the ventral rami of spinal nerves from C5 to T1) unite to form the upper, middle, and lower trunks. Prior to dissection, these trunks are bundled together in a tight investing fascia.

border of the first rib and to the suprapleural membrane. It passes inferior to the subclavian vessels. Whether individuals who possess this muscle are particularly vulnerable to compression syndromes involving the ventral ramus of T1 is unclear.

One expects the scaleni to function as postural stabilizers that prevent posterolateral displacement of the head, as when an external force is applied to the temple. Electromyographically, I have detected only slight activity during typical unresisted lateral flexion and flexion movements; presumably gravity provides sufficient force to move the head after it deviates from neutral. However, considerable activity can be elicited when one rises from a supine position[41] and during resisted flexion or lateral flexion efforts. One could study the transient bursts of scalenus activity that occur during locomotion and other impromptu behaviors as a means to explore interactions between posture and movement. By comparing MRI images obtained before and immediately after resisted head movement exercises, Conley and associates[42] inferred activity in the middle scalene during ipsilateral head rotation and lateral flexion, but not during contralateral rotation; my EMG observations concur.

When the head and neck are stabilized, the scalene muscles will have the action of elevating the first rib (or, in the case of the posterior scalene, the second rib), and thereby elevating the entire rib cage. The anterior and middle scalene muscles have been demonstrated to be active during the inspiratory phase of respiration, with inconsistent, very low level rhythmic activity during quiet breathing, low-level activity during moderately forceful costal inspiration, and greater activity during deep inspiration.[41] In general, the scaleni are more active during respiration than the SCM.

LONGUS COLLI AND LONGUS CAPITIS

The longus colli and longus capitis are found deep in the anterior neck, on the anterior surfaces of the vertebrae (see Fig. 1–16). In dissection of the neck, they are exposed upon retraction of the pharynx and carotid axis. The longus colli is medial to the longus capitis in the regions where they overlap. Longus colli has lower and upper oblique portions between a vertical portion. The lower oblique fibers originate from upper thoracic vertebral bodies and are inserted slightly lateral, on the bases or anterior tubercles of lower cervical transverse processes. The upper oblique portion ascends from origins on lower cervical transverse processes to somewhat more medial insertions on vertebral bodies and the anterior tubercle of the atlas. The transition between the upper and lower parts occurs at C6; the vertically oriented fascicles are found bridging across the ventral surface of C6.

The longus capitis arises from anterior tubercles of cervical transverse processes. The fibers that are readily visible in dissection pass all vertebrae to reach an insertion immediately lateral to the pharyngeal tubercle on the occiput. A few of the longus capitis fascicles that lie closest to the vertebrae and arise from the lower cervical spine may fail to reach the head. They are instead inserted on cervical transverse processes and are, therefore, anatomically equivalent to fascicles of anterior intertransversarius that cross more than one segmental joint complex. Longus colli and longus capitis receive their innervation by short twigs from the ventral rami of spinal nerves.

By action, the lower parts of longus colli are specific flexors and lateral flexors of the lower cervical spine and cervicothoracic junction. The longus capitis and the more superior parts of longus colli are able to flex and laterally flex the upper cervical spine selectively. The fascicles of longus colli that pass superomedially to their insertion on the atlas are angled for ipsilateral rotation, but their lever arm is small since the anterior tubercle is close to the axis of rotation within the dens. Although longus capitis also crosses the atlanto-axial joint, its orientation limits its actions to flexion and lateral flexion.

Despite its depth and proximity to important neural and vascular elements, the longus colli has been monitored with indwelling EMG electrodes. Vitti and associates[39] found the longus colli to be active during flexion of the head, and it was also active ipsilateral to the side of head rotation.

CERVICAL INTERTRANSVERSARII, RECTUS CAPITIS ANTERIOR, AND RECTUS CAPITIS LATERALIS

The anterior and posterior intertransversarii are small muscles with interesting anatomical and developmental characteristics. They constitute seven pairs of muscles connecting transverse processes from atlas to T1 (Fig. 1–17). The anterior intertransversarii connect anterior tubercles, and the posterior intertransversarii connect posterior tubercles. The two muscles of each pair surround the proximal portion of the ventral ramus. The intertransversarii between atlas and axis are sometimes absent; when present they must be capable of considerable distension to allow rotatory movements.

Recall that the anterior tubercle and part of the posterior tubercle are derived from embryonic rib elements. One might therefore expect that the anterior and posterior intertransversarii are serially homologous to innermost and internal intercostal muscles, respectively. However, the medial part of the posterior intertransversarius is innervated by the dorsal ramus, and so it is not serially homologous to any intercostal muscle. Anatomically, the anterior intertransversarii are closely related to longus capitis; one may think of the anterior intertransversarius muscles as longus capitis fascicles that cannot reach the skull because the next vertebra superiorly intervenes. The primary anatomical action of the anterior and posterior intertransversarius muscles is lateral flexion.

Immediately deep (posterior) to the highest part of longus capitis is a separate sheet of obliquely oriented muscle connecting the anterior arch of atlas to the occiput. This short muscle, which is called the rectus capitis ante-

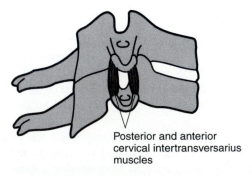

Posterior and anterior cervical intertransversarius muscles

Figure 1–17. The anterior and posterior cervical intertransversarius muscles are immediately distal to the intervertebral foramen. Therefore, they have a close relationship to the dorsal and ventral rami of spinal nerves. The ventral ramus passes between the two muscles and the dorsal ramus passes through the posterior intertransversarius or between the muscle and the superior articular process.

rior, is considered to be homologous to the anterior intertransversarius of lower cervical segments. It acts primarily to flex the head on the atlas, but its fiber direction also causes it to exert an ipsilateral rotation torque on the head. Another short muscle, the rectus capitis lateralis, connects the transverse process of the atlas to the occiput. The ventral ramus of the C1 spinal nerve passes medial to rectus capitis lateralis, so it is homologous to the posterior intertransversarius. Similar to lower intertransversarii, rectus capitis lateralis has a lateral flexion action. Twigs from the ventral rami of C1 and C2 innervate the rectus capitis anterior and lateralis.

It should come as no surprise that experimental evidence of the activity patterns of these small deep muscles is lacking. They may play important roles in segmental mechanics, and they may be partially responsible for segmental dysfunction. It is conceivable that fine upper cervical movements can be initiated and controlled by the use of gravity and long muscles such as the semispinalis and SCM alone. However, it is very likely that an ability to control the activity of rectus capitis anterior, rectus capitis lateralis, and the suboccipital muscles is necessary to stabilize this region.

SUPRAHYOID AND INFRAHYOID CHAINS

The suprahyoid and infrahyoid muscles are recruited primarily for their actions on the oral cavity, tongue, mandible, larynx, and pharynx during mastication, swallowing, and phonation. These muscles are not recruited during typical unresisted head flexions.[43] However, suprahyoid muscle contraction can be palpated during forceful head flexion efforts. Regardless of when they are recruited, the simultaneous contraction of suprahyoid and infrahyoid muscles exerts a flexing action on the head and neck. So the most important aspect of these muscles in head and neck mechanics may be the need to counteract head flexion torque when they are recruited for their effects on the oral structures and the cervical viscera. In fact, the head extensor muscles show moderate levels of activity during mastication and both recitative and spontaneous speech.

SPINAL CORD AND SPINAL NERVES

Details of the anatomy of the spinal cord, meninges, and peripheral nervous system are outside the scope of this chapter. However, several functionally relevant anatomical relationships between the cervical vertebrae and neural structures are considered here.

At the foramen magnum, the anterior portions of the end of the medulla oblongata and the beginning of the spinal cord pass medial to the posterior portions of the occipital condyles. The position of the condyles determines the anteroposterior location of the transverse axis for sagittal movement of the head; the result is that little distension of the spinal cord occurs when the head flexes on the neck. The vertebral canal has a greater cross-sectional area in the cervical region than in the thoracic region. The larger canal allows room for the cervical enlargement of the spinal cord, and also allows the bones to move more than the spinal cord during typical movements. But a comparison within cervical vertebrae shows that the narrowing of the vertebral canal begins as high as C4. The cervical enlargement of the spinal cord, which corresponds roughly to the roots of the brachial plexus, runs from C4 to T1. The lower cervical spine is, therefore, a region where it is relatively easy for the spinal cord or nerve roots to be compromised by stenosis of the vertebral canal.

NEURAL STRUCTURES WITHIN AND NEAR THE INTERVERTEBRAL FORAMEN

To review, the borders of the IVF are the posterolateral disc, the inferior surface of the pedicle of the vertebra above, and three surfaces on the vertebra below. These three are the superior surface of the pedicle, the posterolateral surface of the uncinate process, and the anterior surface of the superior articular process.

Neural structures occupy nearly half of the space in a cervical IVF. (Neural structures occupy relatively less space in thoracic and lumbar IVFs.) The neural contents of the IVF include the ends of the ventral and dorsal spinal nerve roots, the dorsal root ganglion, the spinal nerve itself, the meninges that surround these four structures, and the recurrent meningeal nerve (Fig. 1–18). The union of ventral and dorsal roots forms the spinal nerve, which contains both motor and sensory fibers. Exceptions to the rule that the dorsal and ventral roots are encased in a single dural sheath appear to be more common in the cervical IVFs than in the thoracic or lumbar spine. The spinal nerve is

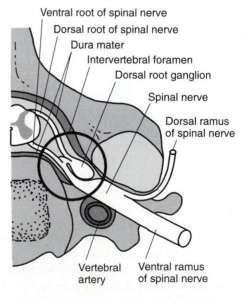

Ventral root of spinal nerve
Dorsal root of spinal nerve
Dura mater
Intervertebral foramen
Dorsal root ganglion
Spinal nerve
Dorsal ramus of spinal nerve
Vertebral artery
Ventral ramus of spinal nerve

Figure 1–18. Neuroanatomical features of the typical cervical intervertebral foramen. (See text for description.)

only a few millimeters long. At the point where the IVF becomes the groove on the transverse process, the spinal nerve splits into its dorsal and ventral rami and the sympathetic gray ramus communicans is given off. The meninges fuse to the epineureum at approximately this point. The ventral ramus continues anterolaterally in the groove on the transverse process. Here the epineureum is tightly bound to the periosteum of the transverse process. Cervical ventral rami below C4 are particularly large because they contribute to the brachial plexus. Below the C2 level, the dorsal ramus is smaller than the ventral ramus; its course is posterolateral, between the superior articular process and posterior intertransversarius muscle.

Small veins and spinal branches from the deep cervical artery, ascending cervical artery, or vertebral artery are also present at each cervical IVF; these branches are of variable size.

THE VERTEBRAL ARTERY

The anatomy of the many blood vessels in the neck is complicated by a great many twists, forks, and turns. Details of the course of the vertebral artery are presented here be-

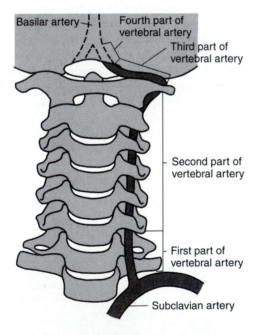

Figure 1–19. The vertebral artery is divided into four parts in its course from the subclavian artery to the posterior cranial fossa. The first part arises from the subclavian artery. The intravertebral second part begins as the artery enters the sixth cervical transverse foramen. The third part, which is superior to the atlas transverse process, curves abruptly posteromedially to pass between the atlas and occipital bone. The intradural fourth part ends where the right and left vertebral arteries meet to form the basilar artery. (See text for further details.)

cause they are great importance to clinical issues, both diagnostic and therapeutic, in the neck. The literature on the anatomy of the vertebral artery has been reviewed thoroughly by Thiel.[44] In its course from the root of the neck to the posterior cranial fossa, the vertebral artery is divided into four parts (Fig. 1–19). The first part branches from the first part of the subclavian artery, and it travels superiorly along the anterior aspects of the first rib and C7. The second part begins when the artery passes between the anterior tubercles of C6 and C7 to enter the transverse foramen of C6. The third part is superior to the atlas transverse process, and the fourth is within the neural canal and posterior cranial fossa.

Within transverse processes from C6 to C2, the second part of the artery crosses immediately anterior to spinal nerves. It is accompanied by vertebral veins; one, two, or none of the veins may be large enough to be demonstrated easily in anatomical dissection. The nerve plexus (formed by one or more branches of the stellate sympathetic ganglion) is large. In the upper cervical spine and within the skull, the vertebral artery has four curves. First, between C2 and C1 the artery bends laterally and slightly anteriorly. The length of this segment necessarily varies with head position: it is elongated on the side contralateral to head rotation. The artery completes its second part by curving superiorly within the transverse foramen of C1. The third part arcs around the lateral and posterior sides of the lateral mass of C1, making a pronounced groove on the superior surface of the posterior arch. In its fourth part, the artery enters the dural sac by passing between the occipital bone and the posterior arch and piercing the posterior atlanto-occipital membrane and dura mater. After entering the skull via the foramen magnum, the right and left vertebral arteries curve superiorly (the fourth curve) to meet on or near the midline of the clivus, forming the unpaired basilar artery. The internal carotid artery has a convoluted intracranial course that bears a superficial resemblance to the third and fourth parts of the vertebral artery. One should examine the branching patterns to distinguish the two arteries on anteroposterior angiograms.

Deep cervical tissues, including the cervical spinal cord, receive blood from small branches of the first three parts of the vertebral artery. The fourth part supplies the upper cervical cord and medial medulla oblongata by way of the anterior spinal arteries, while the lateral medulla, the cerebellum, and dorsal parts of the spinal cord are served by the posterior inferior cerebellar arteries. The basilar artery serves much of the medulla, pons, and cerebellum, and it contributes to the arterial circle of Willis by way of its terminal branches, the right and left posterior cerebral arteries. Visual centers in both the right and left occipital lobes of the cerebrum are vulnerable when a vertebral artery occlusion occurs in an individual lacking one or both posterior communicating arteries. For additional clinical aspects of the course and circulation of the vertebral artery see Chapter 22.

REFERENCES

1. Hall MC. *Luschka's Joint.* Springfield Ill: Charles C. Thomas; 1965.
2. Hayashi K, Yabuki T. Origin of the uncus and of Luschka's joint in the cervical spine. *J Bone Joint Surg* 1985;67A:788–791.
3. Penning L, Wilmink JT. Rotation of the cervical spine: A CT study in normal subjects. *Spine* 1987;12: 732–738.
4. Milne N. The role of zygapophyseal joint orientation and uncinate processes in controlling motion in the cervical spine. *J Anat* 1991;178:189–201.
5. Jenkins FA. The evolution and development of the dens of the mammalian axis. *Anat Rec* 1969;164: 173–184.
6. Schaffler MB, Alson MD, Heller JG, Garfin SR. Morphology of the dens. A quantitative study. *Spine* 1992;17:738–743.
7. Heller JG, Alson MD, Schaffler MB, Garfin SR. Quantitative internal dens morphology. *Spine* 1992; 17:861–866.
8. Doherty BJ, Heggeness MH. Quantitative anatomy of the second cervical vertebra. *Spine* 1995;20: 513–517.
9. Short DW. The subclavian artery in 16 patients with complete cervical ribs. *J Cardiovasc Surg (Torino)* 1975;16:135–141.
10. Ranney D. Thoracic outlet: An anatomical redefinition that makes clinical sense. *Clin Anat* 1996;9:50–52.
11. Davis PR. The medial inclination of the human thoracic intervertebral articular facets. *J Anat* 1959;93: 68–74.
12. Dvorak J, Sandler A. Historical perspective: Hubert von Luschka. *Spine* 1994;19:2478–2482.
13. Oda J, Tanaka H, Tsuzuki N. Intervertebral disc changes with aging of human cervical vertebra. From the neonate to the eighties. *Spine* 1988;13:1205–1211.
14. Bland JH, Boushey DR. Anatomy and physiology of the cervical spine. *Sem Arthritis Rheumatism* 1990; 20:1–20.
15. Cramer G, Roberts V, Tuck N, Skogsberg D, Yu S. Identification of the anterior longitudinal ligament on cadaveric spines and comparison with appearance on MRI. Internatational Conference on Spinal Manipulation, Bournemouth, England, 1996. Foundation for Chiropractic Education and Research, pp. 151–152.
16. Dvorak J, Panjabi MM. Functional anatomy of the alar ligaments. *Spine* 1987; 12:183–189.
17. Fielding JW, Burstein AA, Frankel VH. The nuchal ligament. *Spine* 1976;1:3–14.
18. Mitchell BS, Humphreys BK, O'Sullivan E. Attachments of the ligamentum nuchae to cervical posterior spinal dura and the lateral part of the occipital bone. *J Manipulative Physiol Ther* 1998;21:145–148.
19. Peterson CK, Kirk RJ, Isdahl M, Humphreys BK. Prevalence of hyplastic articular pillars in the cervical spine and relationship with cervical lordosis. International Conference on Spinal Manipulation, Bournemouth, England, 1998. Foundation for Chiropractic Education and Research, pp. 124–125.
20. Krause HR, Bremerich A, Herrmann M. The innervation of the trapezius muscle in connection with radical neck dissection. An anatomical study. *J Craniomaxillofacial Surg* 1991;19:87–89.
21. Stacey RJ, O'Leary ST, Hamlyn PJ. An anomaly in the nerve supply of the trapezius muscle. *Clin Anat* 1996;9:414–416.
22. Bovim G, Bonamico L, Fredriksen TA, Lindboe CF, Stolt-Nielsen A, Sjaastad O. Topographical variations in the peripheral course of the greater occipital nerve. Autopsy study with clinical correlations. *Spine* 1991;16:475–478.
23. Duchenne GB. *Physiology of Motion.* Philadelphia: J.B. Lippincott; 1866.
24. Eliot DJ. Electromyography of levator scapulae: New findings allow tests of a head stabilization model. *J Manipulative Physiol Ther* 1996;19:19–25.
25. Mathiassen SE, Winkel J. EMG activity in the shoulder-neck region according to arm position and glenohumeral torque. *Eur J Appl Physiol* 1990;61:370–379.
26. Behrsin JF, Maguire K. Levator scapulae action during shoulder movement: A possible mechanism for shoulder pain of cervical origin. *Austr J Physiother* 1986;32:101–106.
27. Moseley JB, Jobe FW, Pink M, Perry J, Tibone J. EMG analysis of the scapular muscles during a shoulder rehabilitation program. *Am J Sports Med* 1992;20:128–134.
28. de Freitas V, Vitti M. Electromyographic study of the trapezius (pars media) and rhomboideus major muscles in free movements of the head. *Electromyogr Clin Neurophysiol* 1980;20:351–357.

29. Takebe K, Vitti M, Basmajian JV. The functions of semispinalis capitis and splenius capitis muscles: An EMG study. *Anat Rec* 1974;179:477–480.

30. Jirout J. Changes in the atlas-axis relations on lateral flexion of the head and neck. *Neuroradiol* 1973; 6:215–218.

31. Jirout J. Rotational synkinesis of occiput and atlas on lateral inclination. *Neuroradiol* 1981;21:1–4.

32. Hallgren RC, Greenman PE, Rechtien JJ. Atrophy of suboccipital muscles in patients with chronic pain: A pilot study. *J Am Osteopathic Assoc* 1994;94:1032–1038.

33. McPartland JM, Brodeur RR, Hallgren RC. Chronic neck pain, standing balance, and suboccipital muscle atrophy—a pilot study. *J Manipulative Physiol Ther* 1997;20:24–29.

34. Hack GD, Koritzer RT, Robinson WL, Hallgren RC, Greenman PE. Anatomic relation between the rectus capitis posterior minor muscle and dura mater. *Spine* 1995;20:2484–2486.

35. Penning L. Normal movements of the cervical spine. *Am J Roentgenol* 1978;130:317–326.

36. Lysell E. Motion in the cervical spine: An experimental study on autopsy specimens. *Acta Orthop Scand Suppl* 1969;123:5–61.

37. Penning L. Differences in anatomy, motion, development and aging of the upper and lower cervical disk segments. *Clin Biomech* 1988;3:37–47.

38. Machado de Sousa O, Furlani J, Vitti M. Etude electromyographique du m. sternocleidomastoideus. *Electromyogr Clin Neurophysiol* 1973;13:93–106.

39. Vitti M, Fujiwara M, Basmajian JV, Iida M. The integrated roles of longus colli and sternocleidomastoid muscles: An EMG study. *Anat Rec* 1973;177:471–484.

40. Costa D, Vitti M, Oliviera-Tosello DD. Electromyographic study of the sternocleidomastoid muscle in head movements. *Electromyogr Clin Neurophysiol* 1990;30:429–434.

41. Campbell EJM. The role of the scalene and sternomastoid muscles in breathing in normal subjects. An electromyographic study. *J Anat* 1955;89:378–386.

42. Conley MS, Meyer RA, Bloomberg JJ, Feeback DL, Dudley GA. Noninvasive analysis of human neck muscle function. *Spine* 1955;23:2505–2512.

43. Berzin F. Electromyographic analysis of the sternohyoid muscle and anterior belly of the digastric muscle in head and tongue movements. *J Oral Rehabil* 1995;22:825–829.

44. Thiel HW. Gross morphology and pathoanatomy of the vertebral arteries. *J Manipulative Physiol Ther* 1991;14:133–141.

CHAPTER 2

Normal Function of the Cervical Spine I

Biomechanics and Posture

DONALD R. MURPHY

"To take a step is an affair, not of this or that limb solely, but of the total neuromuscular activity of the moment—not least of the head and neck."

—Sir Charles Sherrington, *The Endeavour of Jean Fernel*

INTRODUCTION

The opening quote to this chapter sums up the essential theme of this and the next chapter—that the cervical spine is involved in virtually all activities of the locomotor system. The cervical spine is an area of great mobility compared to the thoracic spine, lumbar spine, and pelvis. Exceptional demands are placed on the central nervous system in providing postural stability and motor control in the presence of this great mobility.[1] Also, because the cervical spine has the responsibility of maintaining position of the sense organs for sight, sound, balance, and olfaction, proper function of the cervical spine is essential for effective interaction with the environment. Finally, activity of muscles throughout the trunk and extremities is affected by events that occur in the cervical spine.

An understanding of the most common painful conditions of the cervical spine requires an understanding of *dysfunction*. The majority of patients with cervical related complaints have some type of dysfunction as an important component of their clinical picture. Therefore, understanding and being able to identify dysfunction, and relate it the specific clinical syndrome with which the patient is presenting, is at the heart of effectively managing this patient population. To understand dysfunction in the cervical spine and related aspects of the locomotor system, one must also have a fundamental knowledge of normal function. And, as illustrated by the opening quote to this chapter, one must have an appreciation for the ways in which the cervical spine interacts with the rest of the locomotor system.

In this discussion of normal function, for purposes of ease of understanding, the cervical spine is broken down into its component parts; that is, biomechanics, muscle function, posture, neurophysiology, and stability. It is important to recognize that in life, there is a highly complex interaction among these components; this interaction will be emphasized throughout the remainder of the book. This chapter on biomechanics and Chapter 3, focusing on neurophysiology, are not meant to provide intricate details of these topics, but rather are designed to provide the clinician with an understanding of the most important concepts required for application of the clinical sections of the book.

BIOMECHANICS

Much has been published in the area of cervical biomechanics. This discussion will attempt to synopsize the information that is available in the literature with the goal of providing a basic understanding of its clinical relevance.

The cervical spine is generally separated into two distinct functional parts: the upper cervical spine (C0–C2) and the lower cervical spine (C3–C7). The directions of rotation that spinal joints undergo are, in common language, expressed as flexion, extension, lateral flexion, and rotation. Translations are expressed as anterior, posterior, and left and right lateral translation. A more precise system is described by White and Panjabi[2] and is known as the right-handed orthogonal coordinate system. This system allows for more accurate communication of biomechanical concepts, but it is not necessary for common usage.

The right-handed orthogonal coordinate system (Fig. 2–1) utilizes three lettered axes about which rotations take place and along which translations take place. The y axis is that which lies along an imaginary plumb line hung in the center of the body. The x axis lies in a left to right configuration at a 90-degree angle to the y axis, and the z axis lies in a front to back configuration at a 90-degree angle to the y axis. Each axis originates from a point in the center of the body. For descriptive purposes, each direction to which an axis points is labeled either positive or negative. For the y axis, upward is positive and downward is negative. For the x axis rightward is positive and leftward is negative. For the z axis, anteriorward is positive and posteriorward is negative. Therefore, translations are described in terms of the axis along which they are occurring and the direction in

which they are occurring. The various translations are listed in Table 2–1.

Rotations are described in terms of the axis about which they take place and the direction in which they occur. As with translations, opposite directions are distinguished by labeling them as either positive or negative. The various rotations are illustrated in Figure 2–2 and listed in Table 2–2.

Table 2–1: Identification of Translations According to the Right-handed Orthogonal Coordinate System

Forward translation	+z
Rearward translation	−z
Superiorward translation	+y
Inferiorward translation	−y
Leftward translation	+x
Rightward translation	−x

> ! **CLINICAL PEARL**
>
> As stated earlier, for common usage, the traditional language of flexion, extension, left and right lateral flexion, and so forth, is used in this book except in those specific areas in which greater precision is required for clarity.

Before discussing the specifics with regard to the kinematics of the cervical spine, the ranges of motion, neutral zone, instantaneous axis of rotation, and coupled motions of each segment will be presented. Definitions of each of

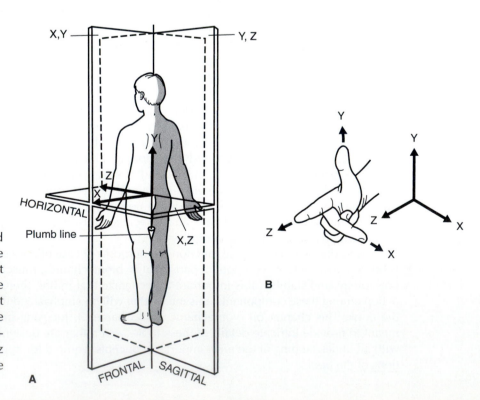

Figure 2–1. A and **B.** The right-handed orthogonal coordinate system. Three axes are illustrated. The directions that constitute positive translations can be understood by holding one's right hand in the manner shown in **B.** The thumb points in the positive y direction, the index finger in the positive z position, and the middle finger in the positive x position.

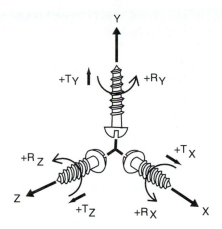

Figure 2–2. The direction that each screw turns when driving it inward represents the positive direction of rotations about that axis.

(Adapted from Figure 6.9B in Curl DD, ed. Chiropractic Approach to Head Pain. *Baltimore, Md: Williams and Wilkins, 1994:101.)*

these properties are necessary for a complete understanding of these kinematics. The following definitions are adapted from White and Panjabi[2] unless otherwise indicated.

> **Range of motion:** displacement from one extreme to the other extreme of the physiological range of translation or rotation of a joint, for each of its six degrees of freedom.
> **Neutral zone:** that part of the range of motion starting from the neutral position up to the beginning of some resistance offered by the joint (Fig. 2–3). It is a measure of the laxity of the joint; thus, it is a better indicator of the stability of the joint than is range of motion.[3]
> **Instantaneous axis of rotation:** the imaginary line in a vertebra that does not move and about which rotation takes place at any given moment.
> **Coupled motions:** a phenomenon of consistent association of one motion (translation or rotation) about an axis with another motion about a second axis.

Also essential to an understanding of the function and dysfunction of the cervical joints is the concept of joint play. Joint play is the subtle, accessory movement that all joints possess, and its purpose is to allow a joint to move through a wide range of motion without excessive strain.[3] This is

Table 2–2: Identification of Rotations According to the Right-handed Orthogonal Coordinate System

Right lateral flexion	$+ \theta z$
Left lateral flexion	$- \theta z$
Left rotation	$+ \theta y$
Right rotation	$- \theta y$
Flexion	$+ \theta x$
Extension	$- \theta x$

The designation θ is used to distinguish rotations from translations.

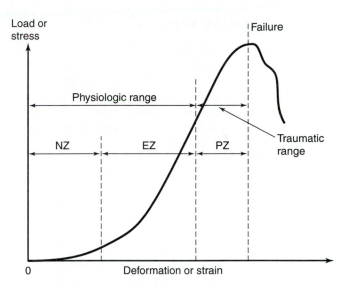

Figure 2–3. Load-displacement curve demonstrating the neutral zone (NZ), elastic zone (EZ), and plastic zone (PZ).

(Adapted from Figure 1-14 in White AA, Panjabi MM. Clinical Biomechanics of the Spine. *2nd ed. Philadelphia, Pa: Lippincott, 1990:21.)*

much like the play that is built into the parts of a machine, allowing the parts to move against one another smoothly and easily. This play is not under voluntary control and thus cannot be produced by the individual; it can only be produced by an outside force. Joint play and its clinical significance will be discussed in more detail in Chapters 13 and 18.

! CLINICAL PEARL

One can experience joint play simply by taking one's proximal phalanx of the first digit and gently pulling it out along its long axis while observing what occurs at the metacarpophalangeal joint (Fig. 2–4). Then glide the proximal phalanx left and right, anterior and posterior. The small movements that are produced represent joint play.

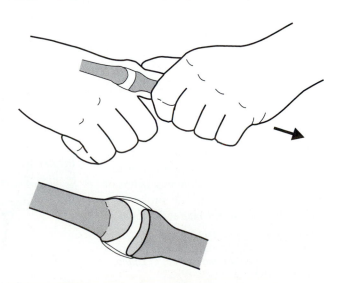

Figure 2–4. Joint play at the metacarpophalangeal joint.

UPPER CERVICAL SPINE

The upper cervical spine is comprised of the motion segments of C0–C1 and C1–C2. As will be discussed later, this is the most dynamic area of the spine (and perhaps the entire body) from a neurophysiological standpoint, and knowledge of the mechanics of these segments is essential if one is to understand the effect of dysfunction in this area on the entire locomotor system.

Ranges of Motion

Because of the differences in the configurations in the joint surfaces, the presence of the dens, and other factors, the ranges of motion (ROMs) of the C0–C1 and C1–C2 joints, and the role they play in overall cervical biomechanics, differ. According to Panjabi et al,[4] the C0–C1 joint acts as a pivot upon which flexion and extension can occur, and it is this pivot upon which occipital nodding occurs. The ROM for flexion and extension is approximately 25 degrees. The C1–C2 segment contributes almost equally to cervical flexion and extension, with approximately 20 degrees of range.

❗ CLINICAL PEARL

As Grice,[5] Taylor and Skippings,[6] and Henderson and Dormon[7] have pointed out, a paradoxical motion of extension of the occiput occurs in over 80 percent of normal individuals upon flexion of the cervical spine as a whole. This motion is most likely caused by the normal tension in the nuchal ligament. Even when the individual retracts the chin prior to flexing the cervical spine, this paradoxical motion may take place. It is thus important, when interpreting flexion radiographs of the cervical spine, to avoid mistaking this paradoxical motion as an indication of hypomobility.

Axial rotation in the upper cervical spine occurs primarily at C1–C2. In fact, approximately 50 to 60 percent of the rotation ROM of the entire cervical spine takes place at this level.[2, 4] Because of the biconvex configuration of its articular surfaces, the presence of the dens, the absence of an intervertebral disc, and the freedom allowed by the transverse, apical, and alar ligaments, a large amount of axial rotation can occur.[8] The range is approximately 23 to 39 degrees to each side.[9]

Table 2–3: Neutral Zones in the Upper, Middle, and Lower Cervical Spine

LEVEL	FLEXION/ EXTENSION	LATERAL FLEXION	ROTATION
C0–C1	1.1	1.6	1.5
C1–C2	3.2	1.2	29.6
C3–C6	4.9	4.0	3.8
C7–T1	1.5	1.6	0.7

Figures are given in degrees and to one side of the neutral position. (From White and Panjabi.[2])

The C0–C1 segment, because of the cuplike design of its articular surfaces, contributes little to axial rotation. In fact, it used to be thought that no rotation at all took place here. More recently, however, it has been discovered that up to 5 degrees of rotation may occur here.[4] Lateral flexion in the upper cervical spine is limited to approximately 5 degrees at each of the C0–C1 and C1–C2 segments.[4]

Translation movements in the upper cervical spine are minimal. Worth mentioning, however, is the small amount of translation that occurs along the ±z axis. Normal translation in this direction is measured as 2 to 3 mm during upper cervical flexion on radiographic examination and is limited by the intact transverse ligament. Excessive translation at this level suggests the presence of gross instability due to inadequacy of the transverse ligament.[10]

Neutral Zone

The neutral zones (NZs) for each segment and each direction of movement are provided in Table 2–3.[2]

Instantaneous Axis of Rotation

The instantaneous axis of rotation (IAR) of a spinal segment is that point about which a vertebra rotates in a certain direction. In the cervical spine, the IAR is different for the various levels and directions of rotation. At the C0–C1 level, the IAR for flexion and extension and lateral flexion has been estimated to be just above the tip of the dens (Fig. 2–5). At the C1–C2 level, the IAR for flexion and extension has been estimated to be approximately at the level of the middle third of the dens (Fig. 2–6). For

Figure 2–5. A. The IAR for lateral flexion at the C0–C1 segment. The broken line represents that IAR for flexion and extension. **B.** The IAR for flexion and extension at the C1–C2 segment. The broken line represents that IAR for lateral flexion.

(Adapted from Figure 2-11A and B in White AA, Panjabi MM. Clinical Biomechanics of the Spine. 2nd ed. Philadelphia, Pa: Lippincott, 1990:96.)

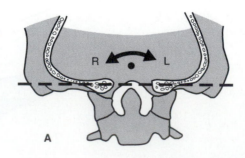

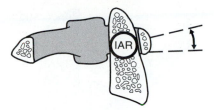

Figure 2–6. The IAR for flexion and extension at the C1–C2 segment.

(Adapted from Figure 2-7A in White AA, Panjabi MM. Clinical Biomechanics of the Spine. 2nd ed. Philadelphia, Pa: Lippincott, 1990:93.)

axial rotation, it has been estimated to be at the dens (Fig. 2–7). The IAR for lateral flexion at C1–C2 has not been identified.

Coupled Motions

In the locomotor system, no movement occurs in isolation. Even at the spinal intersegmental level, when a joint moves through rotation about a certain axis, it will inevitably rotate or translate about or along another axis. In the upper cervical spine, rotation to one side is coupled with lateral flexion to the opposite side; that is, when the C1–C2 segment goes through $+\theta$ y rotation there occurs a coupled $+\theta$ z rotation.[4] As will be seen, the opposite coupling pattern occurs in the lower cervical spine, and these opposing coupled patterns allow the head to remain neutral during cervical spine movements. There also occurs a $\pm$ y translation during axial rotation of the C1–C2 segment. In addition, as Penning and Wilmink[11] have shown, the atlas translates laterally (along the x axis) during rotation of the upper cervical spine. This translation occurs in the opposite direction as rotation; that is, with right rotation of the upper cervical spine the atlas translates to the left.

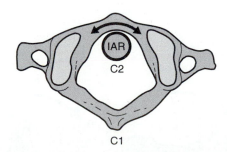

Figure 2–7. The IAR for axial rotation at the C1–C2 segment.

(Adapted from Figure 2-12 in White AA, Panjabi MM. Clinical Biomechanics of the Spine. 2nd ed. Philadelphia, Pa: Lippincott, 1990:96.)

LOWER CERVICAL SPINE

The lower cervical spine consists of the segments C2–C3 through C7–T1. C2 is the transition vertebra between the two sections of the cervical spine. As will be seen, the mechanics of this section are different in some ways from those of the upper cervical spine and these differences compliment each other for more efficient function of the cervical spine as a whole.

Range of Motion

The data that follow are taken from the work of White and Panjabi.[2,4] For flexion and extension, the segments of the lower cervical spine have an ROM of between 10 and 20 degrees, with the greatest ROM occurring at the levels C4–C5 and C5–C6. Axial rotation of the cervical spine, as stated earlier, takes place primarily at C1–C2. There being very little axial rotation taking place at C0–C1, the remaining total axial rotation in the cervical spine is somewhat evenly distributed among the lower cervical spine segments. This adds up to approximately 3 to 7 degrees at each segment from C2–C3 to C7–T1. It should be noted that there is a wide individual variability of ROM in rotation in the lower cervical spine.[11] For lateral flexion, approximately 5 to 10 degrees occurs at each segment, with the greatest amount occurring at the C3–C4 and C4–C5 segments. Figure 2–8 provides graphic representation of the representative ROMs at each level of the cervical spine.

Neutral Zone

The neutral zones for each segment and each direction of movement are provided in Table 2–3.[2]

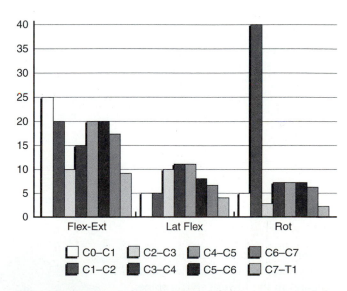

Figure 2–8. Representative ROM at each segment of the cervical spine.

(Adapted from White AA, Panjabi MM. Clinical Biomechanics of the Spine. 2nd ed. Philadelphia, Pa: Lippincott, 1990.)

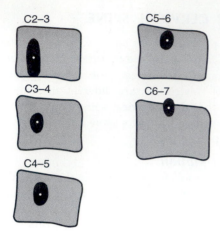

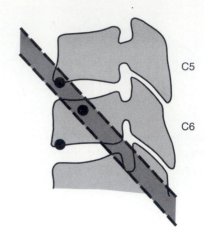

Figure 2–9. Location of the IAR for flexion in the lower cervical spine.

(Adapted from Amevo B, Worth D, Bogduk N. Instantaneous axes of rotation of the typical cervical motion segments: A study in normal volunteers. Clin Biomech 1991;6:111–117.)

Figure 2–10. Location of the IAR for rotation in the lower cervical spine.

(Adapted from Penning L, Wilmink JT. Rotation of the cervical spine: A CT study in normal subjects. Spine 1986;12:732–738.)

Instantaneous Axis of Rotation

Amevo et al[12] have studied the area of IAR for flexion and extension in the lower cervical spine. They showed the IAR to be located at various points within the vertebral bodies of the vertebra below the one that was moving (Fig. 2–9). For axial rotation, the IAR has been estimated to be located close to the spinal cord to allow for large ROM with impingement of the cord.[4] Penning and Wilmink[11] have demonstrated that the IAR for rotation is perpendicular to the plane of the zygapophyseal joints (Fig. 2–10). Less is known about the IAR for lateral flexion in the lower cervical spine, but it is speculated that it lies in the body of the lower vertebra (Fig. 2–11).

Coupled Motions

Lysell[13] showed that during flexion and extension, the motion of each vertebra is a combination of rotation and translation, with flexion being coupled with +z axis translation and extension being coupled with −z axis translation. For lateral flexion, axial rotation occurs as a coupled motion such that the spinous processes move toward the convexity of the curve (Fig. 2–12). Likewise, axial rotation is coupled with lateral flexion to the same side. Moroney et al[14] showed that along with this coupling of rotation and lateral flexion, there is additional translation movement that occurs in the same direction as the lateral bending movement; that is, with −y rotation (right rotation) as the primary movement, an associated +z rotation (right lateral flexion) and −x translation occurs. With −z rotation (left lateral flexion) as the primary movement, an associated +y rotation (left rotation) and +x translation occur.

According to Onan et al[15] the magnitude of the rotation–lateral bending coupling decreases in the more caudal segments of the lower cervical spine. They felt that this coupling is primarily produced by the orientation of the zygapophyseal joints, as cutting of the anterior and posterior longitudinal ligaments, intervertebral discs, and interspinous ligaments did not change the coupling ratios in the lower cervical spine.

Figure 2–11. Location of the IAR for flexion/extension, lateral flexion, and rotation in the lower cervical spine.

(Adapted from Figure 2–17 in White AA, Panjabi MM. Clinical Biomechanics of the Spine. 2nd ed. Philadelphia, Pa: Lippincott, 1990:102.)

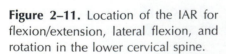

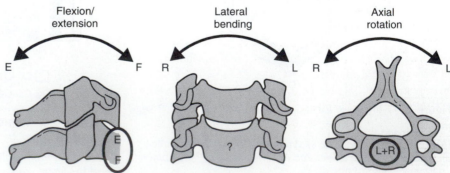

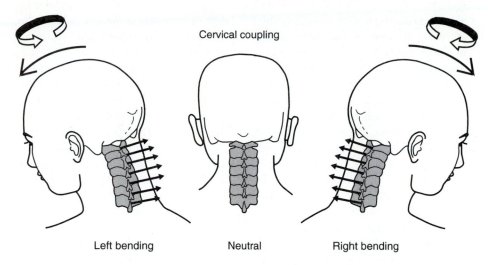

Figure 2–12. Coupled motion of lateral flexion with rotation to the same side, such that the spinous processes move toward the convexity of the curve.

(Adapted from White AA, Panjabi MM. Clinical Biomechanics of the Spine. 2nd ed. Philadelphia, Pa: Lippincott, 1990:100)

<table>
<tr><td>Left bending</td><td>Neutral</td><td>Right bending</td></tr>
</table>

> ### ❗ CLINICAL PEARL
>
> As Krausova and Lewit[16] and Lewit[17] have noted, when there is joint dysfunction at C2–C3, the normal coupled rotation of C2 with lateral flexion does not occur. Thus, in a patient with acute antalgia in lateral flexion, it can often be noted on radiograph that there is no coupled deviation of the spinous process with the lateral flexion of C2. This may indicate that C2–C3 is the significant dysfunction, or key link.

DISC MECHANICS

Most of the research investigating the biomechanical properties of the intervertebral disc has focused on the lumbar spine. However, because of the larger loads and smaller ROM of this area, the information derived from these studies may not translate well to the cervical spine. Studies that have looked specifically at the cervical disc have demonstrated that it is markedly different in many respects from its lumbar counterpart.[18] Consequently, information regarding the mechanics of the cervical discs cannot be inferred from studies of lumbar discs without an appreciation of these differences.

In the lumbar spine, the primary function of the nucleus pulposus is to distribute stress produced by axial loading evenly throughout the disc.[2] However, this role is likely to be greatly reduced in the cervical spine as, while the nucleus of the cervical spine is primarily gelatinous in nature at birth and during childhood, by the mid-teens the gelatinous material starts being replaced by fibrocartilage and fibrous components.[19,20] During adulthood, dehydration occurs rapidly so that by age 40 the nucleus is dry and ligamentouslike, composed of fibrocartilage, islands of hyaline cartilage, and tendonlike material, with little or no proteoglycans.[20] Even during childhood and very young adulthood, the cervical nucleus pulposus only comprises 25 percent of the entire disc, dramatically different from the 50 percent seen in the lumbar spine.[18]

The smaller size of the nucleus and its early dehydration suggests a lesser need to resist compressive forces than would be seen in the lumbar spine. Scott et al[21] suggest that the greater collagen content of the cervical nucleus reflects the greater need in the cervical spine to resist torsion and shear forces. So the role of the cervical discs is most likely more related to resistance of forces during rotation and translation and less related to resistance of axial load forces.

CERVICAL LORDOSIS

Much controversy exists regarding whether what is considered the "normal" cervical lordosis is necessary for a healthy cervical spine or whether loss of or reversal of the cervical curve can be considered a normal variant. Harrison et al[22] have suggested a mathematical model for the ideal cervical curve that is based on the height-to-length ratio. They have compared it to a sample of 400 patients from a clinic. These were patients with clinical problems, but a subset of 252 patients was included who did not have cervical complaints. The authors included only those radiographs that exhibited a lordotic shape of any radius of curvature. They found that the average lordosis was 34 degrees, with a range of 16.5 to 66 degrees. They also found that their model was predictive of degree of lordosis in the subjects with an average error of less than 10%. They argue that lordosis is the normal configuration of the cervical spine and that deviation from the ideal should be considered abnormal and should be corrected.[23]

This model and its accompanying notion regarding the necessity of an intact cervical lordosis has been criticized,[24–26] primarily on the grounds that, as Gay concluded in a review of the literature on the topic,[27] several studies of asymptomatic subjects have shown a number of instances of loss or reversal of the cervical lordosis. The suggestion, therefore, is that loss or reversal of the cervical curve can be seen as a normal variant. For example, Helliwell et al[28] examined lateral cervical radiographs in 33 patients with acute neck pain due to trauma, 83 patients with chronic neck pain, and 80 controls. They found the prevalence of a "straight" cervical spine in 19 percent of the acute cases, 26 percent of the chronic cases, and 42 percent of the controls. Gore et al[29] found that among 200 asymptomatic subjects, 9 percent had actual kyphotic deformities in the cervical spine. They do not provide the percentage of subjects that demonstrate simple loss of curve, but they suggest that loss or reversal of the cervical lordosis are "probably normal variations." Mayoux-Benhamou et al,[30] in studying the effect of muscle function on the cervical lordosis, noted a wide variation in the natural curvature in 36 healthy young women. Harrison et al[31] argue that absence of symptoms should not be the criteria for "normal" as there are a number of disorders, heart disease and hypertension among them, that develop in early stages without the presence of symptoms. They suggest that abnormal cervical curve falls into this category and present some evidence that the biomechanical stresses that are produced create sufficient strain to the locomotor system to create significant problems.

It has been demonstrated that abnormalities in the cervical curve can be a significant factor in relation to the severity and duration of cervical trauma. Hohl,[32] in a review of 146 patients who experienced cervical trauma and in whom no degenerative changes were found immediately after the accident, found that sharp reversal of the cervical curve was associated with the development of degenerative changes 5 years or more after the accident. However, there was no difference in the cervical curve in those patients whose pain lasted greater than 18 months as compared to those whose pain lasted less than 6 months. Norris and Watt[33] retrospectively evaluated 61 consecutive patients up to 2 years after cervical trauma. They found that abnormality in the cervical curve was associated with both greater severity of injury immediately following trauma and poorer prognosis. More recently, Robinson and Cassar-Pullicino[34] found that among 21 patients followed 10 to 19 years after cervical trauma, those with a fixed localized kyphosis had the worst clinical outcome.

It must be realized, of course, that these studies were retrospective and there is no way of telling whether the loss or reversal of lordosis was preexisting, and thus increased the severity of the injury as a result of its presence, or occurred as a result of muscle spasm that was severe enough to alter the curve, thus perhaps reflecting a greater degree of spasm and a more severe injury. However, Ono et al[35] showed that when the cervical spine was placed in a position of kyphosis, a greater degree of compression force resulted from low-speed rear-impact collision than when there was a neutral cervical spine or lordosis. Compression force was lowest when lordosis was present. In this experiment, the lordotic, neutral, or kyphotic cervical curve was induced by specific positioning of the subjects and was not necessarily their natural curve, so it is not clear whether this finding truly reflects clinical reality.

Marshall and Tuchin[36] analyzed 500 cervical radiographs retrospectively and found that the incidence of abnormal lordosis was significantly higher in patients who had been involved in a motor vehicle accident as compared to those who had not. The abnormal lordosis may have been in the form of an increased or decreased curve, but decreased curve was more common. Interestingly, there was no significant correlation between lordosis and complaint of neck pain. And there was a significant correlation between a lower likelihood of abnormality with the duration of time between the accident and the time of the radiograph.

More work needs to be done to clarify exactly what impact an abnormal cervical curve has on the mechanics of the cervical spine and the health of the individual. The cervical curve, as with all spinal statics, should be looked at in terms of the effect, if any, it has on function. As Lewit says, "We are not doctors of cosmetics."[37] The significance of any alteration of spinal statics should be evaluated on an individual basis and should be considerate of the effect that it has on the function of the locomotor system as a whole and the cervical spine in particular. Based on the work of Gore et al[29] and Harrison et al,[22] the normal cervical lordosis can be considered to be in the range of 23 to 44 degrees.

The decision to treat any abnormality that is thought to be clinically significant should be based on the needs of the patient as well as appropriate justification for the cost and time commitment of the patient. For example, a few studies have demonstrated that certain treatment approaches can be effective in restoring to normal an abnormal cervical curve.[38–40] Perhaps the most impressive of these was a controlled trial by Harrison et al[38] in which manipulation combined with extension-compression traction was compared to manipulation alone and a control group. The authors showed that the manipulation plus traction group demonstrated significant improvement in absolute rotation angle as well as relative rotation angle (with the exception of C6–C7). The other two groups showed no significant change. In the manipulation plus traction group, 24 patients had demonstrated no lordosis on pretreatment films. Of these, 18 had lordosis measured on post-treatment film. Although this was an impressive result, the treatment group required 60 visits to produce the changes. If one is going to suggest a treatment plan that requires 60 visits to achieve the desired outcome, it would be imperative that the outcome truly be a desired one, and that the treatment approach be worth the time, money, and effort.

Another factor that must be considered in evaluating the cervical curve is radiographic positioning. It has been shown that minor changes in the position of the patient, particularly even a slight chin tuck, can cause what would normally be a normal cervical curve to appear as a "straight" spine.[41] Certainly, correct positioning can be established reliably[38, 39] but one must be meticulous to be sure that positioning does not affect the radiographic findings.

Loss or reversal of lordosis is often attributed to acute muscle spasm, particularly of the longus capitis, longus colli, and scalenes.[42] On the surface, this seems unlikely as the bulk of the muscles in the cervical spine are located posterior to the axis of rotation for extension, so that, if muscle spasm were to alter the curve, one would expect this alteration to be one of increased lordosis. However, antalgic postures related to reflex muscle spasm are most typically flexion, as with the flexed posture of the acute "locked back," or of acute appendicitis. This is no different in the cervical spine. Thus, loss or reversal of lordosis in the presence of acute cervical pain is a reflection of this flexion tendency.

MUSCLE FUNCTION

To understand the normal function of the cervical spine, it is essential to have a good grasp of how the muscular system in this vital part of the body works and the influence it has on the rest of the locomotor system. As will be seen in Chapter 3, focusing on neurophysiology, the cervical musculature has body-wide effects, and delicate alterations in the function of the cervical muscles can significantly alter locomotor processes elsewhere in the body.

The head–neck system consists of approximately 30 to 32 muscles.[1, 43] The way in which this chapter will examine these muscles will be to look at the movements the cervical spine is capable of and explore the muscles that are involved in those movements. We will look at the specific role each muscle plays, and the extent to which they influence particular movements. This coordinated function approach will be stressed throughout the remainder of this book. This is preferable to the standard approach of isolating the individual muscles and discussing their functions separate from the complex system in which they operate. It is important to remember that the cervical spine, like the rest of the locomotor system (and the other systems in the body, for that matter), functions in such a way that individual parts normally operate in harmony with the other parts. It, therefore, makes no sense to separate the individual components from the overall function for study purposes.

In studying muscle function, it is also important to realize that muscles contract in a variety of ways and that, for any given movement of the cervical spine, different muscles may be contracting concentrically, eccentrically, or statically, depending on the particular situation in which the movement is occurring. For example, flexion of the cervical spine performed in the supine position involves an entirely different pattern of muscle contraction than that performed in the upright position. This is due to the position of the body with respect to gravity. Thus, simply looking at muscle "contraction" without consideration of the functional circumstances and the environment in which the action is occurring will provide an inaccurate picture.[44] This is especially true in the cervical spine, for most movements in this region involve a combination of concentric contraction of the muscles that are moving the head and neck against resistance and eccentric contraction of the "antagonists" for the purpose of controlling the movement and ensuring that the movement occurs smoothly.[45] As a result, the cervical spine is one of the few areas of the locomotor system in which reciprocal inhibition does not occur.[46]

! CLINICAL PEARL

In Chapter 19, which discusses evaluation and treatment of muscle dysfunction, the importance of understanding those circumstances in which a given muscle contracts against gravity will become clear. As described there, treating a muscle with postisometric relaxation (PIR) requires that the muscle be placed in a position in which it is completely relaxed, and thus not contracting against gravity.

Furthermore, we must remember that the primary action of the muscles of the cervical spine, as with muscles throughout the spinal column, is the maintenance of upright posture. They do this through a series of co-contractions that occur continuously as we move about in the upright position. The specific muscles that are acting and the degree to which each is involved varies with the alterations, or potential alterations, of the position of the head and neck with respect to gravity. There are also individual variations.[47] Nonetheless, in order to understand the cervical muscles from a functional and clinical standpoint, we must be familiar with the specific actions they create when contracting concentrically.

For simplicity, we will look at the six cardinal planes of movement of the cervical spine and the muscles that contract concentrically when this movement is being carried out against resistance. It is critically important to remember, once again, that when the movement is occurring in an environment in which the force of gravity is exerted in a direction such that eccentric contraction is the primary contraction occurring, a completely different contraction pattern may be occurring.

FLEXION

Flexion of the cervical spine can be carried out in one of two ways—with the upper cervical spine in flexion, and with the upper cervical spine in extension. Flexion of the cervical spine as a whole with the upper cervical spine flexed is generally considered more efficient, more stable, and produces less strain on the upper cervical joints.[48, 49] In order to carry out flexion with the upper cervical spine flexed, several muscles must contract concentrically in coordination with one another.

Conley et al[50] studied muscle activity in the cervical spine through the novel use of shifts in signal relaxation times of T2-weighted magnetic resonance images (MRIs). MRI examinations were done following performance of movement against resistance in flexion, extension, lateral flexion to each side, and rotation. During the flexion movement, they did not take into consideration the position of the upper cervical spine relative to the lower cervical spine. They showed that the greatest contribution to cervical flexion was provided by the sternocleidomastoid muscle (SCM) and the deep neck flexors (longus capitis and colli), as measured by the cross-sectional area of these muscle following the movement.

Fountain et al,[42] using copper wire electromyogram (EMG), showed activity in the longus colli during flexion against resistance that increased in intensity with increased resistance. Interestingly, they showed that the longissimus cervicis, typically thought of as a "cervical extensor," was active during cervical flexion against resistance and its activity increased markedly as resistance increased. These findings demonstrate the absence of reciprocal inhibition in the cervical spine and show the complex interaction between cervical muscles for the purpose of maintaining stability and smooth movement. The contraction of the SCM and the deep neck flexors is synchronous and coordinated[51] and proper balance of this synchronization is essential to proper function of the flexion movement pattern. Moroney et al,[52] using biomechanical analyses and surface EMG, showed that the infrahyoids and scalenes are also important components to the cervical flexion movement pattern. The muscles involved in cervical flexion, in order of intensity of action, are listed in Table 2–4.

Fountain et al[42] further showed that with flexion in the upright position, such that the force of gravity is causing eccentric contraction of the posterior cervical muscles,

the longissimus cervicis maintains its activity throughout the entire movement, as well as in the fully flexed position. Harms-Ringdahl et al,[53] Carlsoo,[54] and Steen[55] have also shown that, unlike the lumbar spine, the cervical spine displays no flexion relaxation phenomenon.

It must be remembered that, for functional purposes, movement of the upper cervical spine occurs in coordination with that of the lower cervical spine, and the quality of the movement is in part dependent on the relationship between the movement of these two areas. The muscles that are primarily involved in creating movement in each of these areas of the cervical spine will be different. Flexion of the upper cervical spine is created by the longus capitis, the rectus capitis anterior, and the supra- and infrahyoids. Flexion of the lower cervical spine is carried out by the SCM and scalenes. The longus colli assists in flexion of the cervical spine as a whole. The SCM, if the flexors of the upper cervical spine are not active, creates flexion of the lower cervical spine along with extension of the upper cervical spine (Fig. 2–13). The scalenes are capable of flattening the lordosis[42] (this is not to be confused with their alleged role in causing loss or reversal of lordosis after trauma), but when the lordosis is exentuated, they act merely to flex the cervical spine on the thoracic spine while maintaining cervical lordosis. This action makes the scalenes the cervical analogue to the iliopsoas.[56] So it can be seen that the movement of flexion of the cervical spine is complex and cannot be reduced to simplified terms.

EXTENSION

As previously mentioned, when considering extension of the cervical spine, it is important to recognize that the upper cervical and lower cervical spine are functionally

Table 2–4: Muscles Involved in Flexion of the Cervical Spine Against Resistance

Sternocleidomastoid

Longus colli

Longus capitis

Infrahyoids

Suprahyoids

Rectus capitis anterior

Scalenes

All muscles contract bilaterally.

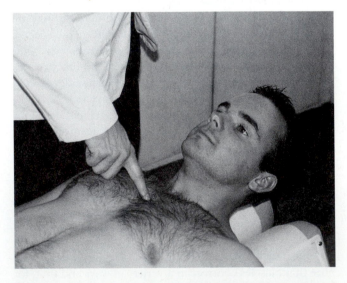

Figure 2–13. Flexion of the lower cervical spine combined with extension of the upper cervical spine, carried out primarily by the SCM.

separated and are capable of moving independent of one another. Extension of the upper cervical spine is primarily carried out by the semispinalis capitis, splenius capitis, suboccipital group (except the obliquus capitis posterior), and SCM. The SCM is generally considered a flexor of the cervical spine, but it must not be overlooked that when it contracts concentrically, in addition to causing the lower cervical spine to flex, it causes the upper cervical spine to extend. This action is probably not prominent when a heavy load is being moved, but it does become important during common movements of the head in the upright position. In addition to these muscles, the upper trapezius contributes to extension of the upper cervical spine.[50]

The most important extensors of the lower cervical spine are the semispinalis cervicis, multifidis, and longissimus cervicis.[50, 52, 53] The extensors of the cervical spine, in general, are more bulky and powerful than the flexors. The semispinalis muscles, in particular, are powerful extensors[57] and, along with the multifidis, are important stabilizers of the lower cervical spine and, in the case of the semispinalis cervicis, the upper thoracic spine. In the lower cervical and upper thoracic spine, the semispinalis cervicis is assisted by the spinalis cervicis, longissimus cervicis, and iliocostalis cervicis, all part of the erector spinae group.[57] As Nolan and Sherk[58] have shown, when surgical procedures, such as multilevel laminectomies, are performed that damage these muscles, swan-neck deformities commonly develop. Even in the absence of destruction such as that from surgery, normal activity of these muscles, particularly in the lower cervical and upper thoracic spine, is essential to the maintenance of normal head posture and prevention of forward head carriage.

ROTATION

Rotation of the cervical spine involves activity by a wide variety of muscles.[48] This is because of the importance of fine motor control of this movement during functional movements involving rotation, such as smooth pursuit movements of gaze and normal rotational head movements while talking, especially to a group. Rough, uncontrolled movement of the cervical spine in these situations would be functionally inefficient and disturbing to the normal carrying out of these everyday activities. The movement of the head and neck into rotation is primarily carried out by the ipsilateral splenius capitis, contralateral SCM, and ipsilateral semispinalis capitis.[50] In the upper cervical spine, the obliquus capitis inferior and rectus capitis posterior major also play an important role.[57] In the lower cervical spine, the splenius cervicis contributes.[57] In addition to these muscles, the contralateral upper trapezius, ipsilateral levator scapulae, and ipsilateral longissimus capitis and cervicis are important rotators[50] (although the upper trapezius and levator scapulae only perform this function in the presence of upper limb activity). On an intersegmental level, the multifidis and rotatores are the prime movers.

The SCMs are of particular importance in maintaining the smooth, even cervical movement during rotation. As Mazzini and Schieppati have shown,[59] when head rotation is performed in response to a stimulus, both SCMs contract, with the muscle on the side opposite the direction of rotation contracting earlier and concentrically to create the movement and that on the same side as the movement displaying a slightly delayed onset of eccentric contraction for control. This action is also seen in the semispinalis and splenius capitis muscles. In the case of these muscles, concentric contraction on the side to which rotation occurs is seen while eccentric contraction on the side opposite takes place simultaneously.

Other muscles are active as well in controlling cervical movement, most likely to prevent unnecessary flexion, extension, and lateral flexion movements during rotation. These include the anterior and middle scalenes, semispinalis cervicis, and the longus capitis and colli.

LATERAL FLEXION

Lateral flexion is a less important and less well-studied movement in the cervical spine. Conley et al[50] found that the SCM shows the greatest activity with this movement, with substantial contribution from the levator scapulae, longissimus capitis and cervicis, and scalenes. The iliocostalis cervicis and upper trapezius also make substantial contributions.[57] On an intersegmental level, the obliquus capitis superior and inferior in the upper cervical spine and the intertransversarii and multifidis in the lower cervical spine are the prime movers. As most of the muscles involved in lateral flexion of the cervical spine are also extensors, the longus capitis and colli are active in preventing flexion during this movement.[50, 57]

Figures 2–14 through 2–18 illustrate the directions of pull for the cervical muscles.

INVOLVEMENT OF CERVICAL MUSCLES IN UPPER EXTREMITY MOVEMENTS

When the upper extremity is used in common movements, the muscles that attach to the cervical spine and scapula play an important role in controlling and stabilizing the shoulder and neck. This is particularly important as the activity of prehension (grasping) of an object and bringing it to the mouth is a basic survival function that

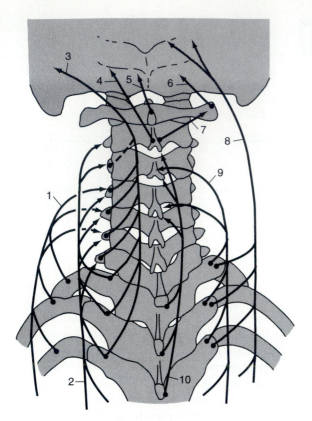

Figure 2–14. Directions of pull for the deeper muscles of the cervical spine: (1) iliocostalis cervicis, (2) longissimus cervicis, (3) longissimus capitis, (4) rectus capitis posterior major, (5) rectus capitis posterior minor, (6) obliquus capitis posterior superior, (7) obliquus capitis posterior inferior, (8) semispinalis capitis, (9) semispinalis cervicis, (10) spinalis cervicis.

(Adapted from Parke WW, Sherk HH. Normal adult anatomy. In: The Cervical Spine Research Editorial Committee, eds. The Cervical Spine. 2nd ed. Philadelphia, Pa: Lippincott, 1989:17.)

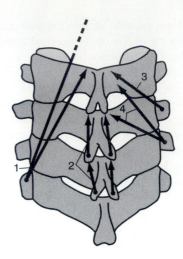

Figure 2–15. Directions of pull for the short muscles of the cervical spine: (1) mutifidis, (2) interspinalis, (3) short rotator, (4) long rotator.

(Adapted from Parke WW, Sherk HH. Normal adult anatomy. In: The Cervical Spine Research Editorial Committee, eds. The Cervical Spine. 2nd ed. Philadelphia, Pa: Lippincott, 1989:17.)

the glenohumeral joint capsule and the rotator cuff.[62, 63] Scapular rotation is also important in order that the muscles that attach to the scapula may assist in abduction of the humerus through the point in the movement at which the greatest resistance occurs.[61] During the first 30 to 60 degrees of shoulder abduction or flexion, there is normally no scapular or spinal motion and the movement is purely glenohumeral. After 30 to 60 degrees, the scapula starts to rotate and thereafter, the ratio of glenohumeral movement to scapular movement is thought to be roughly 2:1,[63] though one study found it to be smaller, at 5:4.[64] This

is a phylogenetically old and neurologically well-established movement pattern.

Clinically, the most important movements to consider are flexion and abduction. To produce these movements, motion at the glenohumeral, acromioclavicular, sternoclavicular, scapulothoracic, and lower cervical and upper thoracic joints is required. This involves a complex pattern of contraction of a variety of muscles, some of which are designed to move, others for stabilization, and others for midcourse correction.[60] Some muscles provide a combination of these functions during various points in the ROM.[61]

Approximately 180 degrees of shoulder flexion and abduction are possible,[60] with 90 to 100 degrees occurring at the glenohumeral joint, while approximately 60 degrees occurs as a result of rotation of the scapula. The remaining 20 to 30 degrees occur in the lower cervical and upper thoracic spine. The purpose of scapular rotation is to maintain a consistent position of the glenohumeral joint to allow further flexion or abduction with a minimum of stress to

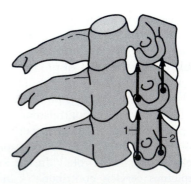

Figure 2–16. Directions of pull for additional short muscles of the cervical spine: (1) posterior intertransversarii, (2) anterior intertransversarii.

(Adapted from Parke WW, Sherk HH. Normal adult anatomy. In: The Cervical Spine Research Editorial Committee, eds. The Cervical Spine. 2nd ed. Philadelphia, Pa: Lippincott, 1989:17.)

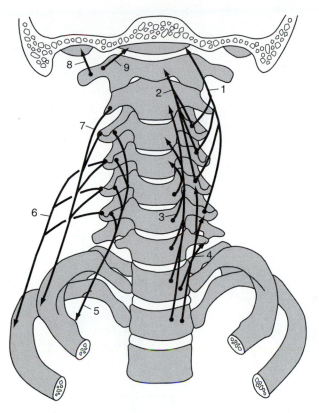

Figure 2–17. Directions of pull for the anterior muscles of the cervical spine: (1) longus capitis, (2) longus colli (superior oblique part), (3) longus colli (vertical part), (4) longus colli (inferior oblique part), (5) anterior scalene, (6) posterior scalene, (7) middle scalene, (8) rectus capitis lateralis, (9) rectus capitis medialis.

(Adapted from Parke WW, Sherk HH. Normal adult anatomy. In: The Cervical Spine Research Editorial Committee, eds. The Cervical Spine. 2nd ed. Philadelphia, Pa: Lippincott, 1989:16.)

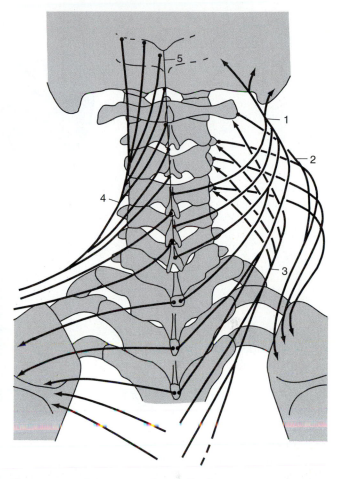

Figure 2–18. Directions of pull for the superficial muscles of the posterior cervical region: (1) splenius capitis, (2) levator scapulae, (3) splenius cervicis, (4) trapezius (cervical part).

(Adapted from Parke WW, Sherk HH. Normal adult anatomy. In: The Cervical Spine Research Editorial Committee, eds. The Cervical Spine. 2nd ed. Philadelphia, Pa: Lippincott, 1989:16.)

movement is very delicately coordinated and is known as scapulohumeral rhythm.[59, 63] The rhythm requires a precise pattern of muscle contractions to allow for uniform, synchronous movement that requires as little effort as necessary.

During abduction of the shoulder to less than 30 degrees, the supraspinatus and deltoid contract concentrically as prime movers, while the upper, middle, and lower trapezius; levator scapulae; rhomboid; and serratus anterior all contract statically to stabilize the scapula.[60, 65] At the same time, the infraspinatus, teres minor, and subscapularis contract concentrically to depress the humeral head within the glenoid fossa and prevent impingement at the acromion process. This stabilization of the humeral head continues throughout the ROM. After 30 degrees, the scapula starts to elevate and rotate through the finely coordinated concentric contraction of the upper, middle, and lower trapezius and serratus anterior.[62] Here, the acromion moves superiorward, the superior angle inferiorward, and the inferior angle laterally (Fig. 2–19). Behrsin and MaGuire[66] showed

that the levator scapulae, after initially contracting concentrically, shortens slightly during the first 90 degrees of abduction, then contracts concentrically after 90 degrees to help ensure smooth rotation of the scapula. However, Eliot[67] found no activity in the levator scapulae in normal individuals.

The instantaneous axis of rotation (IAR) for scapular rotation changes as shoulder abduction occurs.[68] In the beginning, it is located either at the root of the spine of the scapula or just lateral to this and, as scapular rotation proceeds, the IAR migrates toward the acromion process. Finally, the scapula and clavicle rotate together at the end of the ROM about an axis that passes through the clavicle.[66] Thus, the mechanical advantage of the various muscles involved in rotation of the scapula changes as the movement proceeds.

Activity in the upper trapezius can be seen from the very beginning of shoulder abduction for the purpose of

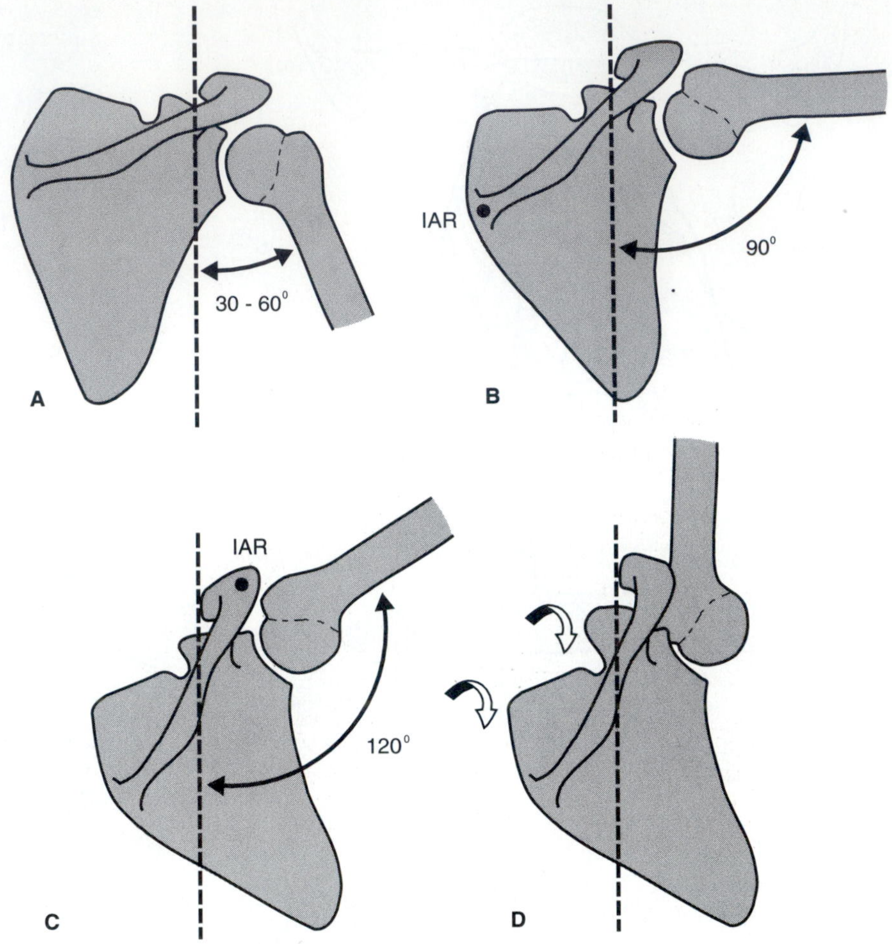

Figure 2–19. Movement of the scapula during shoulder abduction. There is no rotation during the first 30 degrees, after which the scapula starts to rotate about an axis located at the root of the spine or just lateral to this to about 90 degrees, followed by rotation about an axis at the acromion and, at the end, about the long axis of the clavicle to 180 degrees.

stabilizing the scapula while rotation is occurring in the glenohumeral joint.[61] It is important that this activity not be great enough to move the scapula, particularly in the absence of a similar level of activity in the lower trapezius and lower fibers of the serratus anterior, as this would create excessive scapular elevation. The activity in the upper trapezius increases steadily until the shoulder has been abducted to approximately 15 to 45 degrees, after which the increase in activity plateaus somewhat until 90 to 120 degrees of abduction. The onset of this plateau corresponds to the point at which the upper trapezius is assisted by the middle and lower trapezius and the serratus anterior in rotating the scapula.

The middle trapezius, while not playing an essential role in rotating the scapula, provides an important stabilization function during this movement.[61] It is active from the very beginning of the movement and, though its activity plateaus somewhat between 15 and 105 degrees of abduction, it remains active throughout the ROM to maintain constant stability of the scapula while it rotates.

The lower trapezius shows a small degree of activity until approximately 90 degrees of abduction, after which its activity rapidly increases.[61] The purpose of this increased activity is to play an important role in rotating the scapula as the IAR moves toward the acromion process.

Activity in the serratus anterior gradually increases throughout shoulder abduction, with a brief plateau as the humerus passes through the 90-degree position. It rotates the scapula by, primarily through the action of its lower fibers, moving the inferior angle anterolaterally. Refer to Figure 2–20. The pattern of motion of shoulder flexion is

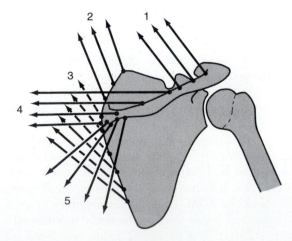

Figure 2–20. Directions of pull for the muscles involved in shoulder abduction. (1) upper trapezius, (2) levator scapulae, (3) rhomboid, (4) middle trapezius, (5) lower trapezius.

similar and the pattern of muscle contraction is virtually the same as with abduction,[60] with the exception that there is less activity in the trapezius, particularly the middle part, to allow for protraction of the scapula during this movement.[69]

INVOLVEMENT OF CERVICAL MUSCLES IN OTHER ACTIVITIES

The cervical spine is involved in processes that occur in virtually the entire locomotor system. Much of this involvement is reflex based. This aspect will be addressed in Chapter 3 in the discussion of neurophysiology there. However, the cervical spine musculature also displays activity in a variety of processes related to mastication and breathing.

During normal breathing, there is little or no activity in the muscles of the cervical spine. With deep breathing, however, the accessory muscles of respiration contract. These include the SCM, scalenes, upper trapezius, and pectorales minor.[51] During coughing, there is slight activity in the deep neck flexors to stabilize the head and neck.[51] This is also seen in forceful blowing, along with activity in the SCM. The deep neck flexors are also active during talking and swallowing,[42] for the purpose of preventing excessive anterior movement of the head and neck during these activities. The SCM normally shows no activity during swallowing. See Chapter 1 for additional information regarding involvement of cervical muscles in orofacial activities.

POSTURE

While it is important to understand the role that each of the cervical muscles plays in the various ranges of motion of the neck, from a functional standpoint it must be appreciated that the most important role of the spinal muscles is co-contraction to maintain stability of the spine during static and dynamic activity.[69] With this co-contraction, there is variable activity in the muscles involved because in the "real world," we generally do not (with certain notable exceptions) maintain one static position for any length of time. Rather, we are constantly changing the positional relationships of the different parts of the body with respect to each other as well as to gravity. If one watches an individual standing in a line at a store, for example, one sees that he or she rarely maintains one static position for any longer than a few seconds. Weight is shifted from one side to another; the head moves as the person gazes around the room; swallowing, speaking, coughing, and breathing activities alter muscle activity and positional relationships; and, perhaps most important, movement eventually takes place, such as moving up in line or gesturing while speaking. It is for this reason that, in looking at static posture, we must consider not only the muscle activity (or lack thereof) and positional relationships as they apply to maintaining a given posture, but also the role that that activity and those

relationships play in preparing the locomotor system to move comfortably and with stability within and from that posture.

All static postures should be viewed not only in terms of the position of the body and the activity of muscles at any given moment in time, but as a "postural set" from which is derived any movement in which the person engages following the maintenance of that posture. As Jones demonstrated,[70] the quality of the postural set in which a person engages has an impact on the quality of the movement that is derived from that set. An example of this is standing from a sitting position. The manner in which the sit-to-stand movement is carried out is in part determined by the precise posture that was taken during the sitting activity from which the sit-to-stand movement pattern was derived. The more upright the head is, with correct alignment as described in the following paragraph, and the closer the feet are to the sitting surface, the less lumbar flexion and upper cervical extension take place. This has particular relevance in the cervical spine patient when head position is considered as part of the postural set in which the individual engages prior to the sit-to-stand pattern. This aspect will be explored in Chapter 3.

From the clinical standpoint, it is helpful to examine the "ideal" posture in order to have a standard to which to compare an individual's posture. In standing, no muscular activity should be required to maintain postural equilibrium, provided the center of mass of each body segment is positioned exactly over its base of support.[71] Muscular activity is only required to bring about postural adjustments to return the body to equilibrium following disturbance of that equilibrium due to perturbation.

Kendall and McCreary[72] present what they feel is the ideal standing posture (Fig. 2–21). Viewed from the side, a plumb line will pass through the earlobe, midway through the shoulder joint, midway through the trunk, through the greater trochanter, slightly anterior to the midpoint of the knee, and slightly anterior to the lateral malleolus. Lewit[48] suggests that the external auditory meatus should be aligned vertically over the clavicle and slightly anterior to the lateral malleolus. In addition, the SCM should form an angle of approximately 45 to 60 degrees. The hyoid bone should be located just anterior and superior to the C3 vertebral body.[73] From the rear view, the plumb line should simply fall exactly through the midline of the body, and there should be alignment of the symmetrical body parts on each side: the head should be neutral, the shoulders aligned, the hips aligned, and the feet rotated outward slightly (Fig. 2–22).

In sitting, the relationships of the structures of the upper body should be the same; that is, alignment of the head, shoulders and torso should be identical to those in the ideal standing posture. The posture of the cervical spine in sitting, however, is effected by the position of the pelvis and lumbar spine,[74] and must be taken into consideration. This effect will be discussed in detail in subsequent chapters.

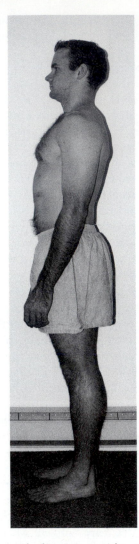

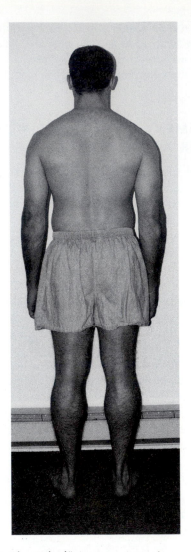

Figure 2–21. The "ideal" posture, side view.

Figure 2–22. The "ideal" posture, rear view.

The tongue is normally held against the hard palate by negative pressure.[75] It should be in contact with the upper incisors but should not push against them. This position occurs because the tongue is suspended from the styloid processes of the temporal bones to the anterior region of the mandible. This normal position is essential for swallowing to take place in a smooth, nonstraining manner. It also has an impact on the stabilizing mechanisms of the cervical spine. The clinical importance of alteration in the ideal resting position of the tongue and faulty swallowing will be discussed in subsequent chapters.

As was stated earlier, the significance of suspected abnormalities of posture must be considered in terms of the effect they have on function. Most important is the degree to which the postural alignment in question serves as the postural set from which movements are derived and the way in which the posture helps to determine the quality of those movements. The most prominent notable exception is the person who sits or stands in one position for prolonged periods of time, as in the case of a secretary who sits in front of a computer for a good part of the work day. In this case, the static posture in and of itself may have a great impact on the production of pain and dysfunction in the cervical spine. But the entire clinical picture must always be taken into consideration.

CONCLUSION

The purpose of this chapter was to present the basic biomechanics, muscle functions, and postural relationships that are important for the development of an understanding of normal cervical function. This information provides the clinician and student with a foundation for understanding dysfunction in the cervical spine that can be applied to the diagnosis and treatment of clinical syndromes involving the cervical spine. In the next chapter, we will explore important concepts regarding the neurophysiology and stability of the cervical spine.

REFERENCES

1. Dutia MB. The muscles and joints of the neck: Their specialisation and role in head movement. *Prog Neurobiol* 1991;37:165–178.
2. White AA, Panjabi MM. *Clinical Biomechanics of the Spine*. 2nd ed. Philadelphia, Pa: Lippincott; 1990.
3. Mennel JM. *Joint Pain*. Boston, Mass: Little, Brown; 1964.
4. Panjabi MM, Vasavada A, White AA. Cervical spine biomechanics. *Sem Spine Surg* 1993;5:10–16.
5. Grice AS. Preliminary evaluation of 50 sagittal cervical motion radiographic examinations. *J Can Chiro Assoc* 1977;21:33–34.
6. Taylor M, Skippings R. Paradoxical motion of the atlas in flexion: A fluoroscopic study of chiropractic patients. *Eur J Chiropr* 1987;35:116–134.
7. Henderson DJ, Dormon TM. Functional roentgenometric evaluation of the cervical spine in the sagittal plane. *J Manipulative Physiol Ther* 1985;8:219–227.
8. Crisco JJ, Panjabi M, Dvorak J. A model of the alar ligaments of the upper cervical spine in axial rotation. *J Biomech* 1991;24(7):607–614.
9. Goel VK, Clark CR, Gallaes K, et al. Moment-rotation relationships of the ligamentous occipito-atlanto-axial complex. *J Biomech* 1988;21:673–680.
10. Yochum TR, Rowe LJ. *Essentials of Skeletal Radiology*. Vol 1. Baltimore, Md: Williams and Wilkins; 1987.
11. Penning L, Wilmink JT. Rotation of the cervical spine: A CT study in normal subjects. *Spine* 1986;12:732–738.
12. Amevo B, Worth D, Bogduk N. Instantaneous axes of rotation of the typical cervical motion segments: A study in normal volunteers. *Clin Biomech* 1991;6:111–117.
13. Lysell E. Motion of the cervical spine. *Acta Orthop Scand* 1969;123(suppl).
14. Moroney SP, Schultz AB, Miller JAA, Andersson GBJ. Load-displacement properties of the lower cervical spine motion segments. *J Biomech* 1988;21:769–779.
15. Onan OA, Heggeness MH, Hipp JA. A motion analysis of the cervical facet joint. *Spine* 1998;23(1):430–439.
16. Krausova L, Lewit K. The mechanism and the measuring of the motility in the craniocervical joints during lateral inclinations. *Acta Universitatis Carolinae Medica Suppl* 1965;21:123–126.
17. Lewit K. Functional anatomy and radiography of the spinal column. In: Lewit K, ed. *Manipulative Therapy in the Rehabilitation of the Locomotor System*. 2nd ed. Oxford: Butterworth-Heinemann; 1991:33–54.
18. Mercer SR, Jull GA. Morphology of the cervical intervertebral disc: Implications for McKenzie's model of the disc derangement syndrome. *Man Ther* 1996;2:76–81.
19. Oda J, Tanaka H, Tsuzuki N. Intervertebral disc changes associated with aging of human cervical vertebra: From the neonate to the eighties. *Spine* 1988;13:1205–1211.
20. Bland JH, Boushey DR. Anatomy and physiology of the cervical spine. *Sem Arthritis Rheum* 1990;20:1–20.
21. Scott JE, Bosworth TR, Cribb AM, Taylor JR. The chemical morphology of age-related changes in human intervertebral disc glycosaminoglycans from cervical, thoracic and lumbar nucleus pulposis and annulus fibrosus. *J Anat* 1994;184:73–82.
22. Harrison DD, Janik TJ, Troyanovich SJ, Holland B. Comparisons of lordotic cervical spine curvatures to a theoretical model of the static sagittal cervical spine. *Spine* 1996;21(6):667–675.
23. Harrison DD, Troyanovich SJ, Harrison DE, et al. A normal sagittal spinal configuration: A desirable clinical outcome. *J Manipulative Physiol Ther* 1996;19(6):398–405.
24. Morgan L. A normal sagittal spinal configuration: A desirable clinical outcome. Letter to the editor. *J Manipulative Physiol Ther* 1997;20(2):130–131.
25. Owens EF. A normal sagittal spinal configuration: A desirable clinical outcome. Letter to the editor. *J Manipulative Physiol Ther* 1997;20(2):133–134.
26. Cooperstein R. A normal sagittal spinal configuration: A desirable clinical outcome. Letter to the editor. *J Manipulative Physiol Ther* 1997;20(2):135–137.
27. Gay RE. The curve of the cervical spine: Variations and significance. *J Manipulative Physiol Ther* 1993;16(9):591–594.
28. Helliwell PS, Evans PF, Wright V. The straight cervical spine: Does it indicate muscle spasm? *J Bone Joint Surg* 1994;76-B:103–106.
29. Gore DR, Sepic SB, Gardner GM. Roentgenographic findings of the cervical spine in asymptomatic people. *Spine* 1986;11:521–524.

30. Mayoux-Benhamou MA, Revel M, Valee C, et al. Longus colli has a postural function on cervical curvature. *Surg Radiol Anat* 1994;16:367–371.

31. Harrison DD, Janik TJ, Troyanovich SJ, et al. Evaluation of the assumptions used to derive an ideal normal cervical spine model. *J Manipulative Physiol Ther* 1997;20(4):246–256.

32. Hohl M. Soft tissue injuries of the neck in automobile accidents. *J Bone Joint Surg* 1974;56A:1675–1682.

33. Norris SH, Watt I. The prognosis of neck injuries resulting from rear-end vehicle collisions. *J Bone Joint Surg* 1983;65-B:608–611.

34. Robinson DD, Cassar-Pullicino VN. Acute neck sprain after road traffic accident: A long-term clinical and radiological review. *Injury* 1993;24:79–82.

35. Ono K, Naneoka K, Wittek A, Kajzer J. Cervical injury mechanism based on the analysis of human cervical vertebral motion and head-neck-torso kinematics during low speed rear impacts. *SAE Technical Paper Series* 973340, 1997:339–356.

36. Marshall DL, Tuchin PJ. Correlation of cervical lordosis with incidence of motor vehicle accidents. *ACO* 1996;5:79–85.

37. Lewit K. *Advanced Manual Medicine Course*. Prague, Czech Republic; 1997.

38. Harrison DD, Jackson BL, Troyanovich S, Robertson G, Dwight G, Barker WF. The efficacy of cervical extension-compression traction combined with diversified manipulation and drop table adjustments in the rehabilitation of cervical lordosis: A pilot study. *J Manipulative Physiol Ther* 1994;17(7):454–464.

39. Wallace HL, Jahner S, Buckle K, Desai N. The relationship of changes in cervical curvature to visual analogue scale, Neck Disability Index scores and pressure algometry in patients with neck pain. *Chiropractic* 1994;9:19–23.

40. Leach RA. An evaluation of the effect of chiropractic manipulative therapy on hypolordosis of the cervical spine. *J Manipulative Physiol Ther* 1983;6(1):17–23.

41. Fineman S, Borrelli FJ, Rubenstein BM, et al. The cervical spine: Transformation of the normal lordotic pattern into a linear pattern in the neutral posture: A roentgenographic demonstration. *J Bone Joint Surg* 1963;45-A:1179–1183.

42. Fountain FP, Minnear WL, Allison RD. Function of longus colli and longissimus cervicis muscles in man. *Arch Phys Med Rehabil* 1966;47:615–669.

43. Hogan N, Mussa-Ivaldi FA. Muscle behavior may solve motor control problems. In: Berthos A, Greaf W, eds. *The Head-Neck Sensory Motor System*. New York, NY: Oxford University Press; 1992:153–157.

44. Cavanagh PR. On "muscle action" vs. "muscle contraction." *J Biomechanics* 1988;1:69.

45. Lee SG, Ashton-Miller JA. Human cervical muscle recruitment and spine loading under 3-D quasistatic head loads: On synergies, agonism and antagonism. In: *Proceedings of the International Conference on Spinal Manipulation*. 1991:251–252.

46. Brink EE. Segmental organization of the upper cervical cord. In: Peterson BW, Richmond FJ, eds. *Control of Head Movement*. New York, NY: Oxford University Press; 1988:76–89.

47. Cholewicki J, Panjabi M, Khachatryan A. Stabilizing function of trunk flexor-extensor muscles around a neutral spine posture. *Spine* 1997;22(19):2207–2212.

48. Lewit K. *Manipulative Therapy in the Rehabilitation of the Locomotor System*. 2nd ed. Oxford: Butterworth-Heinemann; 1991.

49. Janda V. Muscles and motor control in cervicogenic disorders: Assessment and management. In: Grant R, ed. *Physical Therapy of the Cervical and Thoracic Spine*. New York, NY: Churchill Livingstone; 1994:195–216.

50. Conley MS, Meyer RA, Bloomberg JJ, et al. Noninvasive analysis of human neck muscle function. *Spine* 1995; 20:2505–2512.

51. Vitti M, Fujiwara M, Iida M, Basmajian JV. The integrated roles of the longus colli and sternocleidomastoid muscles: An electromyographic study. *Anat Rec* 1973;177:471–484.

52. Moroney SP, Schultz AB, Miller JAA. Analysis and measurement of neck loads. *J Orthop Res* 1988;6:713–720.

53. Harms-Ringdahl K, Ekholm J, Schuldt K, et al. Load moments and electromyographic activity when the cervical spine is held in full flexion and extension. *Ergonomics* 1986;29:1539–1552.

54. Carlsoo S. The static muscle load in different work positions: An electromyographic study. *Ergonomics* 1961;4:193–211.

55. Steen B. The function of certain neck muscles in different positions of the head with and without loading of the cervical spine. *Acta Morphol Neurol Scand* 1966;6:301–310.

56. Grice AS. Personal communication, 1989.

57. Parke WW, Sherk HH. Normal adult anatomy. In: The Cervical Spine Research Editorial Committee, eds. *The Cervical Spine*. 2nd ed. Philadelphia, Pa: Lippincott; 1989:11–32.

58. Nolan JP, Sherk HH. Biomechanical evaluation of the extensor musculature of the cervical spine. *Spine* 1988;13:9–11.

59. Mazzini L, Schieppati M. Preferential activation of the sternocleidomastoid muscles during voluntary rapid head rotations in humans. In: Berthoz A, Graf W, Vidall PP, eds. *The Head-Neck Sensory Motor System.* New York, NY: Oxford University Press; 1992:597–600.

60. Lehmkuhl LD, Smith LK. *Brunnstrom's Clinical Kinesiology.* 4th ed. Philadelphia, Pa: F.A. Davis; 1983.

61. Bagg SD, Forrest WJ. Electromyographic study of the scapula rotators during arm abduction in the scapular plane. *Am J Phys Med* 1986;65:111–124.

62. Paine RM, Voight M. The role of the scapula. *J Orthop Sports Phys Ther* 1993;18:386–391.

63. Michiels I, Grevenstein J. Kinematics of shoulder abduction in the scapular plane; On the influence of abduction velocity and external load. *Clin Biomech* 1995;10(3):137–143.

64. Poppen NK, Walker PS. Normal and abnormal motion of the shoulder. *J Bone Joint Surg* 1976; 58-A:195–201.

65. Basmajian JV, DeLuca CJ. *Muscles Alive: Their Functions Revealed Through Electromyography.* Baltimore, Md: Williams and Wilkins; 1985.

66. Behrsin JF, MaGuire K. Levator scapulae action during shoulder movement: A possible mechanism for shoulder pain of cervical origin. *Aust J Physiother* 1986;32:101–106.

67. Eliot DJ. Electromyography of levator scapulae: New findings allow tests of a head stabilization model. *J Manipulative Physiol Ther* 1996;19(1):19–25.

68. Engin AE. On the biomechanics of the shoulder complex. *J Biomech* 1980;13:575–590.

69. Wiedenbauer MM, Mortenson OA. An electromyographic study of the trapezius muscle. *Am J Phys Med* 1952;31:363–371.

70. Jones FP. The influence of postural set on pattern of movement in man. *Internat J Neurol* 1963;4(1):60–71.

71. Nashner LM, McCollum G. The organization of human postural movements: A formal basis and experimental synthesis. *Behav Brain Sci* 1985;8:135–172.

72. Kendall FP, McCreary EK. *Muscles: Testing and Function.* 3rd ed. Baltimore, Md: Williams and Wilkins; 1983.

73. Mannheimer JS, Rosenthal RM. Acute and chronic postural abnormalities as related to craniofacial pain and temperomandibular disorders. *Dent Clin North Am* 1991;35:185–208.

74. Black KM, McClure P, Polansky M. The influence of different sitting positions on cervical and lumbar posture. *Spine* 1996;21(1):65–70.

75. Mannheimer JS. Prevention and restoration of abnormal upper quarter posture. In: Gelb H, Gelb M, eds. *Postural Considerations in the Diagnosis and Treatment of Cranio-Cervical-Mandibular and Related Chronic Pain Disorders.* St. Louis, Mo: Ishiyaku EuroAmerica; 1991:93–161.

CHAPTER 3

Normal Function
of the Cervical Spine II
Neurophysiology and Stability

Donald R. Murphy

"Structure, therefore, is nothing else but the physical expression of function."

—Julius Wolff, MD, Lecture at the Second General Session of the 72nd
Assembly of German Natural Scientists and Physicians, 1900

INTRODUCTION

In the previous chapter, information was presented regarding the biomechanics of the cervical spine and normal posture. In this chapter, the discussion of the normal function of the cervical spine resumes with neurophysiology and stability mechanisms. These topics are of the utmost importance in understanding clinical syndromes that can develop in patients with cervical spine dysfunction.

For the purpose of presenting the various reflex and stability mechanisms involved in cervical function, these mechanisms will be taken out of the context of the entire body and examined in isolation. However, these mechanisms do not operate this way in life. It will be seen that the cervical spine is an area of great afferent activity, with large amounts of information being presented to the central nervous system (CNS) at any given moment. But this cervical input is part of a complex array of afferent information being presented to the CNS from the entire locomotor system as well as other afferent systems—such as sight, hearing, vestibular stimulation—and information from other sources, and should be looked upon as a part of this array, not as a completely separate entity.[1]

NEUROPHYSIOLOGY

Understanding neurophysiology as it relates to the cervical spine is at the heart of understanding cervical function. Whereas the lumbar spine is an area of the body that is called upon to bear great loads, the cervical spine is an area of the body that has great mobility and that influences neurological mechanisms throughout the entire locomotor system.

Much of the information presented here is derived from studies using animal models (most commonly the cat), not human models. The functional requirements of the quadruped differ greatly from those of the biped, due to the differences in the position of the head with respect to gravity. However, in areas of research in which both human and nonhuman vertebrates have been studied, the findings have generally been similar, particularly with regard to the somatosensory system related to the cervical spine.[1, 2]

We begin the discussion of cervical neurophysiology from the periphery, as normal control of movement is dependent on the quality of the information from peripheral structures.[3] In discussing joint and muscle receptors, it is important to be as specific as possible with regard to terminology. Those receptors that provide information regarding static position as well as the velocity and direction of movement in the locomotor system (i.e., those that are activated by mechanical stimuli) will be referred to as *mechanoreceptors*. They will not, in general, be termed *proprioceptors*, as proprioception specifically refers to the *perception* of movement and position of a body part[4] and this perception takes place in the cerebral cortex, not at the receptor level.[5] In addition, much of the sensory information used to control movement never reaches the level of conscious perception,[6] so a large part of the discussion of receptor function here revolves around the transmission of afferent information that remains subconscious.

JOINT MECHANORECEPTORS

Much has been made in some circles of the importance of joint mechanoreceptors in the spine, especially in the neck; in reality, however, their true function is unknown. McLain[7, 8] has demonstrated a relatively small population of mechanoreceptors in the cervical zygapophyseal joints. These were consistent in type to those arranged into the classification scheme proposed by Wyke.[9] In the cat, Richmond and Bakker[10] also showed a relative paucity of encapsulated receptors in the joints of the cervical spine. McLain[7] speculated that the small number of facet joint mechanoreceptors in the cervical spine may be related either to the relative functional insignificance of these receptors or to the fact that each receptor may have a large receptive field, thus innervating a large portion of the joint capsule. Recent work reported by Bolton[1, 2] supports the former notion. These experiments in the cat showed that when movement of the C1–C2 and C2–C3 motion segments was induced, recordings of afferent input from the joint capsules were rare, whereas those recorded from muscle afferents were abundant. This suggests that joint mechanoreceptors contribute little information with regard to cervical movements.

This situation has been demonstrated in extremity joints as well.[11–14] Clinically, it has been shown that abolition of joint afferent information, for example after joint replacement surgery, has no effect on joint position sense as long as muscle receptor afference is intact.[15–17] Unlike most extremity joints, the spinal joints have intrinsic muscles that directly cross the joint space and that contain an abundance of mechanoreceptors capable of detecting changes in position and movement, making it even less likely that mechanoreception from the joint capsules would be necessary for perception of movement in the spine.

If it is true that the mechanoreceptors in the cervical zygapophyseal joints play little, if any, role in signaling joint position and movement in the CNS, what is their role in normal cervical function? The answer to this question is not fully known. Proske et al[12] have suggested that, while they do not play a role in position sense, they may play a role in signaling joint movement and as end range detectors. This view, however, was based only on studies of extremity joints which, as previously stated, do not have spindle-rich intrinsic muscles that cross them. In the spine, Pickar and McLain[18] suggest that one possible role of facet capsule mechanoreceptors is the elicitation of somatoautonomic and somatosomatic reflexes. Investigations by Bolton[1, 2] have revealed involvement of the cervical spine afferents in these reflexes (see the discussion that follows), but have not demonstrated specific involvement of joint mechanoreceptors.

Perhaps the most telling research in this area is that of Johansson et al.[19–21] In these experiments, electrical stimulation of the articular nerves of the knee joint[19] as well as natural stimulation through movement of the knee[20] elicited dynamic responses of the gamma fusimotor neurons that supply the contractile portion of the muscle spindle (see later discussion). This reflex response was also shown to result from electrical stimulation of the posterior cruciate ligament.[21] These reflexes resulted in increased afferentation from the primary muscle spindle endings in the muscles around the joint. The responses were seen both ipsilaterally and contralaterally in both spinalized and intact cats. Interestingly, no force development was noted in the involved muscles, so it was not likely that activity in the alpha or beta motor neurons was elicited.

This finding suggests that joint mechanoreceptors may play a role in the polymodal regulation of muscle tone, as the reflex responses elicited appear to prime the stiffness in the involved muscle in order to preprogram its response to perturbation (Fig. 3–1). By increasing the afferentation arising from the muscle spindle, the reactivity of the muscle is increased, as well as its resistance to forces that would stretch it. It must be remembered, of course, that this work was done in the knee joint of the cat which, because of its easy access and the ability to work with spinalized models, is a more advantageous model with which to work, but may not necessarily translate completely to the human cervical spine. This work does, however, allow for the development of compelling theories as to the role that the cervical joint mechanoreceptors may play in normal function and, as will be explored in Chapter 4, dysfunction.

Additionally, it is believed that joint mechanoreceptors play a role in the modulation of nociceptive transmission from the joint, as part of the "gate control" of this transmission.[22] Transmission of afferent impulses along large-diameter fibers causes the activation of an inhibitory neuron, which then, through synapse with the projection neuron that relays the impulses to higher centers, causes

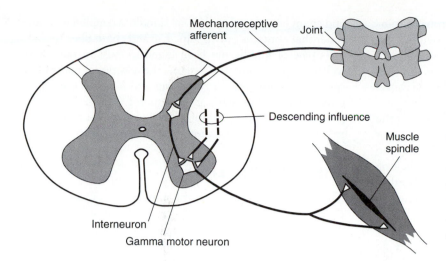

Figure 3–1. Model for the regulation of muscle tone by joint mechanoreceptors. Stimulation of joint mechanoreceptors causes excitation of the gamma motor neurons on both the ipsilateral and contralateral sides, causing increased afferentation from the muscle spindle, which, combined with influences from higher centers, increases muscle tone.

inhibition of this projection neuron. The mechanorecetive afferent also makes inhibitory synapse with the projection neuron. In order to maintain a pain-free state, there must be adequate balance between the afferentation from large-diameter fibers (e.g., those arising from joint mechanoreceptors) and small-diameter nociceptive fibers. A disruption of this balance can allow the nociceptive afferentation to "get through the gate" and reach higher levels in the CNS to produce the sensation of pain.

> **! CLINICAL PEARL**
>
> The role that the joint mechanoreceptors play in the regulation of muscle tone and nociceptive transmission is integral to normal joint function. When a joint develops joint dysfunction, this role is interfered with, leading to the development of both pain and muscle dysfunction. This interaction will be further explored in later chapters.

MUSCLE MECHANORECEPTORS—MUSCLE SPINDLE

Far more important than the joint mechanoreceptors in the transmission of mechanical information regarding the status of the neck are the mechanoreceptors in the cervical muscles. There are four types of mechanoreceptors in muscle, the most important of which are the muscle spindle and the Golgi tendon organ. Full details regarding the physiology of these receptors is beyond the scope of this book, but knowledge of their basic anatomy and physiology is necessary for a full understanding of the clinical concepts that will be presented later.

Muscle spindles are small, elongated structures that are found in a variety of locations in the muscles of the neck and that lie parallel to the extrafusal, contractile fibers of the muscle.[23] The spindle is made up of intrafusal fibers, the central portion of which is noncontractile and the outer portion of which is capable of generating contraction. Three types of intrafusal fibers are present in the muscle spindle: static nuclear bag fibers, dynamic nuclear bag fibers, and nuclear chain fibers. The innervation of each of these is somewhat different, and this difference has functional importance in muscle neurophysiology.

There are two afferent neurons that innervate the muscle spindle. A single group Ia fiber innervates all three types of intrinsic fibers, and its receptor is known as a primary ending. A group II afferent fiber innervates only the static nuclear bag fibers and the nuclear chain fibers. Its receptor is known as a secondary ending. Motor innervation to the muscle spindle is primarily provided by the gamma motor neurons, which innervate the outer, contractile portions of the muscle spindle.

The muscle spindle primary and secondary endings are responsive to stretch of the muscle or, more specifically, stretch of the intrafusal fibers of the muscle. The specific stimuli that elicit responses from each of the endings are different. The primary endings are sensitive to the rate of change in muscle length; that is, they communicate the velocity and acceleration of muscle stretch. During rapid stretch of the spindle, the velocity-sensitive primary endings increase their firing rate as the velocity of stretch increases. Likewise, when the muscle is shortened, the primary endings stop firing and return to their steady state firing rate when shortening ceases. So they are responsive to sudden, transient stimuli, such as quick taps and vibration, as well as to sudden perturbations. As muscle length becomes greater, the sensitivity of the primary endings decreases, unless velocity continues to increase. The secondary endings, on the other hand, are stimulated by the degree of change in muscle length; that is, they communicate the extent of muscle stretch. They are relatively unaffected by quick, sudden, transient stimuli. As the length of the muscle (thus the muscle spindle) increases, the firing of the secondary endings increases.

There are two types of gamma motor neurons that innervate the spindle. Dynamic gamma motor neurons innervate only the dynamic nuclear bag fibers while static gamma motor neurons innervate the static nuclear bag fibers as well as the nuclear chain fibers. Collectively, the gamma motor neurons are referred to as the fusimotor system (as opposed to the skeletomotor system made up of the alpha motor neurons). The purpose of the gamma motor neurons is to regulate the sensitivity of the spindle to change in velocity and length. They do this by eliciting shortening of the contractile portion of the spindle, thus causing stretch of the intrafusal fibers and increasing the firing of the primary and secondary endings.

! CLINICAL PEARL

It is these different functions of the intrinsic fibers and gamma motor neurons of the spindle that are involved in the development of increased or decreased muscle tone in the development of muscle dysfunction. This involvement will become clearer in later chapters.

In addition to the gamma motor neurons, the extrafusal fibers of the spindle are innervated by skeletofusimotor neurons called beta motor neurons.[23] These are collaterals of the alpha motor neurons and, like gamma motor neurons, have static and dynamic components. It is believed that their purpose is to ensure co-contraction of both the extrinsic and intrinsic muscle fibers so that significant unloading of the muscle spindle does not occur during muscle contraction.

There is an abundance of muscle spindles in the muscles of the cervical spine.[10, 24-28] While the large muscles of the neck contain a density of spindles that exceeds other large muscles of the body, the small intrinsic muscles contain an even greater proportion. Bakker and Richmond[29] found that the density of muscle spindles in the intrinsic muscles was two to five times that of the large dorsal muscles. The multifidi contained the greatest density of spindles.

The morphology of the spindles in the muscles of the neck is also different than that of other muscles in the body. There is a far greater number of what are called "conjunctive forms,"[30] groups of two or more spindles that are grouped together in a common capsule, in cervical muscles than in other muscles. These conjunctive forms of muscle spindles in the neck can be further grouped into what are called "spindle complexes"—groups of spindles lying close together and numbering up to 12 in a group. These complexes sometimes extend the entire length of the muscle and can then be intimately associated with the Golgi tendon organ at the myotendinous junction.[31] Probably the most common and best studied of the conjunctive form of spindles is the tandem spindle. This is a muscle spindle that contains the typical static bag fiber, dynamic bag fiber,

and chain fiber, but this classical spindle is coupled with another that contains only a static bag and chain fiber.[10, 26, 31] This type of spindle has been found to exist in human as well as cat neck muscles. Because the additional part of the spindle contains only a static bag and a chain fiber, it is only innervated by static gamma motor neurons. The purpose of these tandem spindles is believed to be to increase the static information coming from these muscles.

THE STRETCH REFLEX

The most basic function of the muscle spindle is the elicitation of the stretch reflex. This is a reflex in which a muscle contracts in response to stretch. There are two components of the stretch reflex—the dynamic component and the static component. The dynamic component is far more powerful than the static and arises from stimulation of group Ia afferents from the spindle that results from a rapid increase in length of the spindle. The Ia afferents have monosynaptic connection to the alpha motor neurons of both the homonymous muscle and its synergists, leading to contraction of these muscles. The static component is elicited by stimulation of the group II fibers, which have a weaker, polysynaptic connection to the alpha motor neurons. The static component is only elicited when the muscle is under a state of contraction, when even slow stretch will elicit the stretch reflex. So, when a muscle is at rest, rapid stretch of the muscle will cause elicitation of the dynamic stretch reflex, only.[23]

! CLINICAL PEARL

As will be seen in later chapters, the stretch reflex is only one component of the regulation of muscle activity during normal function. It does not generally function in isolation, but from a clinical standpoint, it becomes important in the neurological examination as well as in the examination and treatment of muscle dysfunction.

Understanding the function of the stretch reflex of the cervical spine is important to an understanding of the neurological examination. But in terms of cervical function, the monosynaptic stretch reflex plays little or no role. This is because the monosynaptic stretch reflex is weak or nonexistent in the cervical spine.[32] Abrahams et al[33] showed that only 1% of the motor neurons serving the cervical extensors could be excited to fire at monosynaptic latencies when the C2 or C3 nerves were stimulated in the cat.

This is not to say that when a cervical muscle is subjected to stretch the nervous system never responds by firing of the muscle's alpha motor neurons, leading to contraction. It is to say that the complexity of the neurophysiology of the cervical spine is such that the nervous system reserves the right to not produce reflex contraction of the muscle if it is not functionally advantageous. It does this by making this response polysynaptic rather than monosynaptic and, thus, subject to alteration at the interneuron level to suit the needs of the functional circumstances at any given moment in time.[34] This is another example of the principle that, as we have seen before and will see again, the neurophysiological mechanisms that govern the control of movement elsewhere in the body do not always apply to the cervical spine.

As will be seen, the elicitation of stretch reflexes is only one role that the muscle spindle plays—and this is a relatively minor role. The primary purpose of the muscle spindle is to apprise the central nervous system of the status with regard to the extent and velocity of length change in the muscle.

! CLINICAL PEARL

"Contrary to the earlier assumption of a joint receptor origin [of somatosensory information from the neck], recent studies provide strong evidence that the information essentially stems from muscle spindle receptors."[35]

MUSCLE MECHANORECEPTORS—GOLGI TENDON ORGAN

The Golgi tendon organ (GTO) is a small encapsulated receptor found most commonly at the myotendinous junction. It is innervated by a group Ib afferent fiber. The GTO is responsive to tension changes in the muscle; that is, when the muscles contracts, these receptors increase their firing rate. It is important to note that the GTO is only weakly and inconsistently responsive to stretch of the muscle.[15, 23, 36]. There are two reasons for this. The first is that the GTO is organized in *series* with the muscle fibers, as opposed to the spindle, which is arranged in *parallel*. Thus, stretch of the muscle is more likely to cause stretch of the spindle than the GTO. The second reason is that tendons have far greater resistance to stretch than do muscle fibers. Thus, when a muscle is subjected to stretch, the spindles will fire readily, but little or no response will be seen in the GTO.

It is commonly thought that the primary function of the GTO is to signal the nervous system when the muscle is subjected to a load that is so great that it threatens to cause damage to the muscle, and the nervous system responds to this by inhibiting the muscle to prevent damage. While this scenario does occur, it implies that the GTO plays little role in common, day-to-day function. This is hardly the case. In fact, the GTO is a highly sensitive receptor that is capable of responding to the contraction of a single motor unit.[37] Its purpose is to apprise the CNS with information regarding the level of active tension that is occurring in the muscle. This contributes to the overall picture that the locomotor system as a whole, through signals generated by the various receptors, presents to the CNS.

As with the muscle spindles, there is an abundance of GTOs in the cervical spine that far exceeds that in other parts of the body.[29] This contributes to the enormous amount of information that arises from the cervical muscles.

DISC MECHANORECEPTORS

Until relatively recently, the intervertebral disc was thought to be aneural. Recent studies, however, have revealed an abundance of neurological receptors in this structure. Mendel et al[38] showed that the cervical discs contain receptors that resemble Pacinian corpuscles in the superficial layers of the annulus and receptors resembling GTOs in the deeper layers. Interestingly, this was also shown in the lumbar spine by Roberts et al,[39] who found that the most common receptor was the GTO type, followed by the Pacinian type. They also found receptors that resemble Ruffini endings.

Bogduk et al[40] showed that the nerves to which these receptors are connected are the sinuvertebral nerve and the vertebral nerve. The vertebral nerve also carries sympathetic fibers. This finding was confirmed in the lumbar spine by Nakamura et al,[41] who showed an almost complete disappearance of the receptor networks following total bilateral resection of the sympathetic trunks. Mendel et al[38] showed that these nerves were all small in diameter (type III). Apparently, the intervertebral disc in the cervical spine plays a role in signaling position and movement, although under normal circumstances it is not known what role the receptors in the disc play in this process.

NOCICEPTORS

Nociceptors are those receptors that are best excited by noxious or potentially tissue-threatening stimuli and that signal the occurrence of this stimulation.[42, 43] They typically have a high threshold for activation.[43] As previously discussed, McLain[7, 8] found some mechanoreceptor endings in the cervical zygapophyseal joint capsules. Many of these were free nerve endings and were thought to be nociceptors. He also found this type of ending in the loose areolar tissue, dense connective tissue, and synovial lining around these joints. In addition, Giles and Harvey[44] have shown nociceptive innervation of the synovial folds in the lumbar spine. Nociceptors are also found in the muscles of the cervical spine.[45] These nociceptive endings in the cervical muscles, as is the case with the other receptor types, have great clinical importance that will be discussed in Chapter 4.

Bogduk et al[40] and Mendel et al[38] have demonstrated the presence of nociceptors throughout the cervical intervertebral discs. Their greatest concentration appears to be in the posterolateral portion of the disc, and they can be found as deep as the middle third of the annulus. These nociceptors have been shown to have direct reflex relation to the spinal muscles, particularly the multifidi,[46] and probably play an important role in producing spasm and antalgia.

Other tissues of the cervical spine that contain nociceptors and thus are capable of becoming painful include the ligaments that surround the vertebral bodies as well as the posterior arches, dura mater, periosteum of the vertebrae, and the nerve roots. Those tissues for which nociceptors have not been identified include the articular cartilage, the inner third of the annulus fibrosis (in normal discs), and the nucleus pulposus. Nociceptive mechanisms of the cervical spine will be explored in greater detail in Chapter 4.

OTHER RECEPTORS

Muscles contain a variety of receptors that signal various stimuli. The true function of many of these receptors is poorly understood. Low-threshold mechanoreceptors such as Pacinian corpuscles are excited by innocuous stretch or pressure. Thermoreceptors signal small and innocuous changes in temperature. Contraction-sensitive receptors are excited by moderate contraction or by stretch, although the threshold for this activation is much higher than that for the muscle spindle and GTO. They are thought to function as ergoreceptors, signaling the degree of work being performed by the muscle in order to trigger changes in cardiopulmonary function to adjust to this work.[42]

The nuchal ligament is well innervated and Fielding et al[47] have shown that stimulation of this ligament causes the generation of activity in the extensor muscles of the cervical spine. Receptors have been demonstrated in other tissues of the spine, as well. Most of this work has been done in the lumbar spine, and there is no reason to suspect that these findings would not also apply to the cervical spine. In fact, in most cases, receptors that have been identified in both the lumbar and cervical spines have been demonstrated to be more abundant in the cervical spine.[8]

The ligaments of the spine, such as the anterior and posterior longitudinal ligaments, also contain a number of mechanoreceptors, and these are believed to signal position and movement changes.[39] Jiang et al[48] have demonstrated Pacinian and Ruffini corpuscles in the interspinous and supraspinous ligaments of the lumbar spine.

MUSCLE TONE

Tone is a property of muscles that is often misunderstood. All normal muscles exhibit no electrical activity at rest. However, they have a "tonus" that relates to two factors:

1. The resistance of the muscle to passive stretch[49]
2. The readiness of the nervous system to activate the muscle in response to a stimulus or command[50]

Thus, when muscle tone is being assessed, these are the factors that need be considered. It is important to be aware that the first factor that relates to muscle tone, resistance to stretch, is determined by two things, the mechanical resistance created by the noncontractile elements in the muscle and the stretch reflex-induced contraction produced as a response to attempted lengthening.[49] According to Basmajian and DeLuca,[50] from a functional standpoint, the second of these factors, readiness of the nervous system to activate the muscle, is the more important. But as will be seen, resistance to stretch is of great clinical importance in the evaluation of muscle tone.

The neurological factors that contribute to muscle tone result in part from local phenomena and in part from cortical and brain stem phenomena. One important local phenomenon is the interaction between the joints and muscles, and the influence that the joint mechanoreceptors have on the activity of the gamma motor neurons. As discussed earlier, stimulation of the mechanoreceptors of the zygapophyseal joints can cause excitation of the gamma motor neurons and, thus, increase the sensitivity of the muscle spindle. This increased sensitivity decreases the threshold for the elicitation of the stretch reflex, thus increasing muscle tone. Regulation of stretch reflex sensitivity as well as readiness for activation are also influenced by afferent input from muscles and skin. In the cervical spine, this input influences the alpha motor neuron via polysynaptic pathways relayed through a circuit of interneurons.[49]

Input to the alpha motor neuron from higher centers can also both regulate the sensitivity of the stretch reflex and influence the readiness with which the nervous system activates the muscle. This can be in an excitatory or inhibitory direction. One important mechanism by which this occurs is via the descending bulbospinal pathway.[49] Bulbospinal fibers release serotonin and norepinephrine from their terminals in the vicinity of the alpha motor neurons. These chemicals greatly increase the excitability of the alpha motor neuron. The excitability of the alpha motor neuron is also influenced by descending reticulo-, vestibulo-, rubro-, and corticospinal fibers.[49]

FOCAL MOTOR PROGRAMS

Virtually all repetitive movements of the body are programmed in the CNS. Reflexes are usually programmed in the spinal cord,[51] although the more complex reflexes involving the cervical spine are more involved than this. Voluntary movements are programmed in the cerebral cortex as engrams.[52] It is not fully known where the memory for these programs is located in the CNS, but the programs are known to be highly plastic; that is, they are subject to change due to destruction of a portion of the CNS, injury, or dysfunction. The importance of motor programs in function and dysfunction in the cervical spine will be explored in other sections of the book.

These motor programs are dependent, in part, on afferent information that arises from the receptors in the locomotor system.[53] This afferent information provides the "data" that determine the precise neural activity patterns that are involved in each specific program. It is important to note that this afferent information is presented as a whole "picture" to the CNS, rather than as a group of individual messages from each receptor.[54, 55] The cervical spine, being the area of the locomotor system with the most abundant afferentation, has a particularly large impact on the CNS in this regard. This allows a holistic view of the activity in the locomotor system that the CNS can respond to in a variety of ways, according to a variety of different programs. The importance of motor programs will be further explored in other sections of the book.

CERVICAL–VESTIBULAR INTERACTION IN THE VESTIBULAR NUCLEUS

There is close and important interaction between vestibular and cervical afferent input to the vestibular nucleus. This interaction has clinical significance with regard to the diagnosis and treatment of disequilibrium and vertigo (see Chap. 10), but its functional implications are even more far reaching.

Neck mechanoreceptive and vestibular afferents converge in the vestibular nucleus.[34] The neck input appears to be from muscles only.[35, 56] The input from cervical receptors arises directly from connection of afferents from the cervical spine to the vestibular nucleus and from indirect connection via the central cervical nucleus, which receives afferents from the cervical spine and projects to the vermis of the cerebellum, which in turn sends projections to the fastigial nucleus of the cerebellum, which then projects to the vestibular nucleus[24, 57] (Fig. 3–2). In the simplest sense, the vestibular input provides information regarding the relationship between the head and space and the cervical input, information regarding the relationship between the head and the trunk, with the cervical input relating primarily to movement rather than static position.[58, 59] Important locomotor system input is also provided by the mechanoreceptors in the feet, providing information regarding the relationship between the trunk and the support surface.[60, 61] Significant input also arises from the retinae,[62, 63] with hearing playing a lesser but distinct role.[64] However, it is the interaction of all these inputs that allows the CNS to utilize this information. The closest interaction is between the vestibular apparatus and the cervical spine. The information is projected to the thalamus and then to the parieto-insular area of the cerebral cortex.[65, 66] (Fig. 3–3)

During slow movements of the head in space, the signal from the vestibular apparatus is very weak and the CNS cannot rely on it for perception of head movement.[60, 61, 67] So during slow movements of the head, the cervical spine is relied on to a greater extent to compensate for this. Cervical compensation also occurs in the presence of vestibular deficiency resulting from disease or injury.[68, 69] In addition, during many common movements the head moves both in space and in relation to the trunk. Because of this, the trunk must be used as a reference with regard to the position of the head in space. Therefore, for perception of head position in space to occur, perception of the position of the trunk is essential. This perception is provided by afferents from the cervical spine (head on trunk) and the feet (trunk on ground). Appropriate interaction of all these inputs, summated with that of the vestibular apparatus with regard to head position and acceleration, is necessary to establish the perception of the head in space by the CNS, and thus to elicit postural responses.[60, 61, 70, 71]

Thus, while input from the vestibular apparatus clearly plays the dominant role in equilibrium sense,[72] providing a sense of balance is only one aspect of the function of the vestibular nucleus and its related centers. Regulation of automatic locomotor movements, reflex activities, and postural stability requires a delicate interaction between the afferent input from the cervical spine and the labyrinths of the inner ear, as well as from the feet. In order for the CNS to efficiently provide this regulation, proper perception and

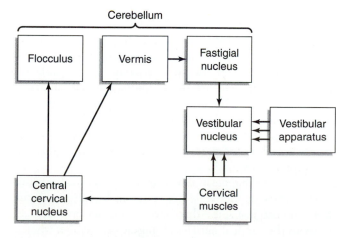

Figure 3–2. Cervical-vestibular interaction in the vestibular nucleus.

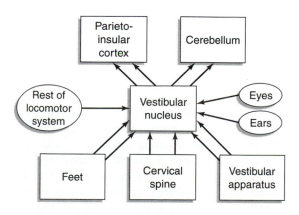

Figure 3–3. Pathways for equilibrium sense.

processing of afferent input from all the contributing systems is essential.

REFLEX ACTIVITIES INVOLVING THE CERVICAL SPINE

A reflex is "an involuntary and relatively stereotyped response to a specific sensory stimulus."[23] By definition, a reflex response requires a stimulus from the periphery. The cervical spine is an area of intense reflex activity. A variety of processes involved in cervical function are oriented around these reflexes.

The reflex is the simplest of the types of motor behaviors.[73] Reflexes form the basis of movement, and there is a hierarchy of control mechanisms that interact with these reflexes to produce various types of movements. Reflexes can be spinal or supraspinal (brain stem) with regard to their CNS pathways.[74] The spinal reflexes are the simplest (e.g., stretch reflex, withdrawal reflex) and are entirely contained in the spinal cord. The supraspinal reflexes are more generalized and produce semipurposeful–appearing movement patterns.[74] The reflexes related to the cervical spine discussed here are of the supraspinal type. Voluntary modulation of the activity of these reflex circuits is possible via descending cortical pathways.[73] These pathways, rather than providing detailed commands to the alpha motor neurons involved in the carrying out of the motor pattern, provide more general direction by acting on the brain stem pathways, the interneurons involved in the reflexes, as well as the alpha motor neurons themselves.[73] This modulation of the basic reflexes carried out by the cerebral cortical centers is largely driven by the nature of the engrams that are formed for a given movement pattern.[74]

It can therefore be seen that, while the reflex activities of the cervical spine can be overridden or modulated by the cortex, in most common activities, particularly automatic or semiautomatic activities, reflexes contribute a great deal to the determination of the specific combinations of muscle actions that carry out the desired movement pattern. Conscious control is involved only in the stimulation to initiate the action, the maintenance of the action for the duration desired, and the termination of the action.[74] If an error is detected, or the engram-driven process is not fully carrying out the desired movement, conscious substitution of individual components of the engram can be made.[74] This requires skill and, as will be seen, is subject to dysfunction.

Reflex activities in the cervical spine are unique in all the locomotor system. Several types of reflexes that occur in the cervical spine do not occur anywhere else and, conversely, many of the typical reflexes that occur in other parts of the locomotor system are absent in the cervical spine. This was discussed earlier with regard to the monosynaptic stretch reflex and reciprocal inhibition, both of which are virtually absent in the cervical spine. The crossed-extensor reflex is also absent in the cervical spine.[32]

The reflexes related to the cervical spine discussed thus far essentially fall under the category of postural reflexes. Postural reflexes are those that help maintain postural equilibrium and stability during the perturbations that are encountered in everyday activities, as well as in situations that have the potential to cause serious injury. Several different inputs contribute to the elicitation of these reflexes, and they are largely mediated through the vestibular nucleus in the brain stem. Efficient interaction between the input from the cervical spine and that from the rest of the locomotor system and with the vestibular and visual systems is essential for postural stability.

These postural "reflexes" are not true reflexes in the strictest sense.[34] While they, like reflexes, occur automatically and quite rapidly, they are subject to learning and refinement with practice. Also, although they are programmed in a relatively stereotyped spatiotemporal organization, this program can be altered.

An example of this program alteration in normal circumstances would be a situation in which one walks down a set of stairs in which each stair is of a height that is different from what one is used to. This may cause stumbling during the ascension of the first few steps, but then adjustments are made in the program to create the necessary alterations so that the remainder of the staircase becomes relatively easy.

! CLINICAL PEARL

The ability of the postural reflexes to become altered and to become more efficient with learning means that they can become altered in such a way as to place strain on the involved components of the reflex as well as on the locomotor system as a whole. It also means, however, that this dysfunction can be corrected with training. This aspect will be explored in future chapters.

The postural reflexes require input from the somatosensory, vestibular, and visual systems for their elicitation. The most important areas from which afferent input arises in the locomotor system are the cervical spine and the feet.[34, 60, 61] So essential information arises from the mechanoreceptors in the cervical spine (particularly the muscles) and the feet (from the joints, muscles, and skin) that apprises the CNS as to the state of affairs in the locomotor system. This information allows the CNS to formulate appropriate strategies for carrying out voluntary movements as well as moment-by-moment efferent responses to environmental stimuli.

Some of the reflexes that involve the cervical spine either directly or indirectly are initiated by afferent inputs from the cervical spine that have an impact on motor activity in the cervical muscles or muscles elsewhere, whereas others are initiated in receptors in other tissues such as the labyrinth or the retina that produce efferent activity projected to the cervical muscles. The purposes of the reflexes involved in the cervical spine are several:

1. Head movements occur almost constantly, and these movements must be compensated in order to maintain normal eye-head-neck-trunk relationships. These movements include the obvious, gross movements such as the boxer who must maintain head stability in space while bobbing and weaving to avoid punches and the jogger who must maintain a stable head-on-trunk relationship while preventing the head from flopping around during the body movements involved in this activity.[75] But more subtle head movements occur during blood pressure pulsations, respiration, and other physiological oscillations and these movements must also be compensated.[76]

2. The muscles of the trunk and limbs must be able to respond with alteration in activity to the needs of the performance of certain motor activities. This allows for optimum performance of the activity as well as proper maintenance of postural stability during activity.

3. Maintenance of visual fixation during head movements is required for proper maintenance of visual images on the retina.

4. Minor or major perturbations that have the capacity to cause injury must be responded to in order to protect the cervical tissues from damage.

Voluntary control of the compensatory movements required to maintain normal function during body movements would be impossible. Therefore, the muscle activity needed to allow for smooth movement and stability must be reflex in nature. These reflexes will be examined in isolation, but it is important to understand that it is their interaction with each other and with the function of the locomotor system as a whole that is essential in the normal carrying out of body processes with as little strain or injury as possible.

Tonic Neck Reflexes

Perhaps the best known of the cervical reflexes is the tonic neck reflex (TNR), which produces alteration of the tone of the muscles in the trunk and extremities in relation to cervical movements. The afferent arm of the reflex is initiated primarily in the spindles of the cervical muscles.[36, 77, 78] It was previously thought that the cervical joint receptors were the primary source of afferentation that produced the TNR. This supposition was based largely on the work of McCouch, Deering, and Ling,[79] who showed that cutting the large muscle nerves left the TNR unchanged while cutting the small nerves that carry joint receptor afferents abolished the reflexes. But, as Richmond and Bakker[10] pointed out, McCouch et al did not take into account the fact that the same small nerves that carry joint afferents also carry afferents from the small intrinsic muscles of the cervical spine, and these are probably the main source of

the elicitation of the reflexes. Suzuki et al[77] showed that removal of the skin overlying the cervical spine in cats has no effect on the TNR, so skin receptors do not play a role in its elicitation.

The alteration of muscle tone in the trunk and extremities that occurs as a result of cervical movements in the TNR is systematic and dependent on the direction of movement. When the cervical spine is rotated, there occurs an increase in the tone in the extensor muscles of the limbs on the side to which the chin is pointing and a decrease in the tone of the flexor muscles in these limbs. At the same time, the tone of the flexor muscles on the opposite side increases while the tone of the extensor muscles on this side decreases.[80–83] This is illustrated in Figure 3–4. Lateral flexion of the cervical spine produces the same changes, although more weakly than rotation.[81] In the upper extremities, on the side of limb extension there occurs abduction of the arm and forearm supination, with ad-

Figure 3–4. The tonic neck reflex related to rotation of the cervical spine.

(Reprinted with permission from Figure 39–6 of Ghez C. Posture. In: Kandel ER, Schwartz JH, Jessell TM, eds. Principles of Neural Science. 3rd ed. Norwalk, Conn: Appleton & Lange, 1991:596–607.)

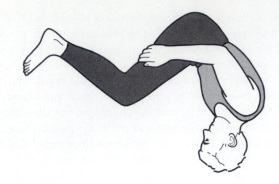

Figure 3–5. The tonic neck reflex related to flexion of the cervical spine.

(Adapted from Fukuda T. Statokinetic Reflexes in Equilibrium and Movement. Tokyo: University of Tokyo Press, 1984:19.)

duction and pronation occurring on the limb flexion side.[82, 83]

When the cervical spine is flexed, there occurs an increase in the tone of the flexor muscles of the spine and extremities and a decrease in the tone of the extensor muscles of the spine and extremities (Fig. 3–5). With extension of the cervical spine, the opposite response occurs; that is, increased tone of the extensor muscles of the spine and extremities and decreased tone in the flexor muscles (Fig. 3–6).

Fukuda[80] suggested that the functional significance of the TNR is such that it is put to use when there is a need to perform a certain action that requires a high degree of skill or power, and where the full concentration of the individual on accomplishment of the task is necessary. Again, using Figure 3–4, when a baseball player is attempting to catch a fly ball that is hit over his head and to his right, he must attempt, using his voluntary, cortical motor system, to move his gloved right hand to where he predicts the ball

will be. In order to maximize his ability to do this, involuntary (reflex) actions must take place. One of these is that the extensor muscles of the lower limb on that side must contract in order to leap into the air while the extensor muscles of the upper limb must contract to reach for the ball. At the same time, the flexor muscles of the limb on the opposite side must contract to allow for propulsion toward the ball, which was hit to his right.

The TNR is not manifest during usual activities under normal circumstances. This is partly because the reflex is overridden by voluntary action and partly because of the existence of the tonic labyrinthine reflex, which during flexion-extension and lateral flexion of the head and neck creates muscular reactions that are opposite those of the TNR. In normal circumstances these reflexes tend to cancel one another during these movements.[60, 77] However, during rotation of the head and neck, the tonic labyrinthine reflex is only weakly elicited, so that the TNR occurs without cancellation.[81]

In certain situations, the TNR and tonic labyrinthine reflexes are synergistic. An example of this is when a person performs a handstand (Fig. 3–7). Here, extension of the neck elicits the tonic neck reflex, which creates extension of the limbs and trunk. But because the head is held at

Figure 3–7. Interaction between the tonic neck reflex and the tonic labyrinthine reflex.

(Adapted from Fukuda T. Statokinetic Reflexes in Equilibrium and Movement. Tokyo: University of Tokyo Press, 1984.)

Figure 3–6. The tonic neck reflex related to extension of the cervical spine.

(Adapted from Fukuda T. Statokinetic Reflexes in Equilibrium and Movement. Tokyo: University of Tokyo Press, 1984:19.)

an angle of approximately −135 degrees (the angle at which the tonic labyrinthine reflex maximally activates the flexors of the trunk and extremities), balance is maintained, helping to prevent excessive TNR-induced extension.[80]

The elicitation of the TNR is brought about in two ways. One is via the connection of afferents from the cervical muscle spindles to the vestibular nucleus and the pontine and medullary reticular formation (Fig. 3–8). Vestibulospinal and reticulospinal neurons, via the medial and lateral vestibulospinal and reticulospinal tracts, respectively, then project to interneurons and propriospinal neurons throughout the spinal cord that are responsible for the distribution of patterns of excitation and inhibition to the alpha and gamma motor neurons of the extremity muscles involved in the reflex action. The neurons in these tracts make direct monosynaptic excitatory and inhibitory connections to the alpha and gamma motor neurons of the axial muscles of the cervical spine and trunk.[38] The other mechanism for the elicitation of the TNR is via signals from the upper cervical afferents that are sent to propriospinal neurons that project to the lower cord levels and make direct excitatory or inhibitory connections to motor neurons.[84]

Cervicocollic Reflex

The cervicocollic reflex (CCR) is elicited as a result of movement of the head on the trunk, and its purpose is to maintain alignment of the head with the trunk during perturbation.[34, 75] When the trunk moves relative to the head, the CCR causes the head to tend to turn in the same direction to maintain alignment. This primarily occurs during unexpected movements, such as being jostled in a crowd or bumping into an object while walking. During turning of the head, the CCR activates the muscles that move the head in the opposite direction in order to maintain stability and prevent overshooting. The CCR is opposed by the vestibulocollic reflex (VCR), which is present primarily in four-legged animals and is very weak in humans.[75] The purpose of the VCR is to keep the head in position during movements of the body that would tend to cause the head to move. It is active primarily in expected movements of the body and at relatively slow velocities, as in doing "The Twist," while the CCR is primarily active in unexpected perturbations.

It used to be thought that the CCR was a stretch reflex; however Richmond and Loeb[32] and Ghez[34] suggest that it is elicited via relay of afferents from the cervical muscles being stretched during a certain movement to the central cervical nucleus, which projects to both the flocculus of the cerebellum for modulation, and the vestibular nucleus, which then projects to the motor neurons of these same muscles[85] (Fig. 3–9).

Cervicorespiratory Reflex

This is a reflex that was recently discovered by Bolton and Yates.[2] It is believed to help regulate drive to the respiratory muscles during changes in posture.

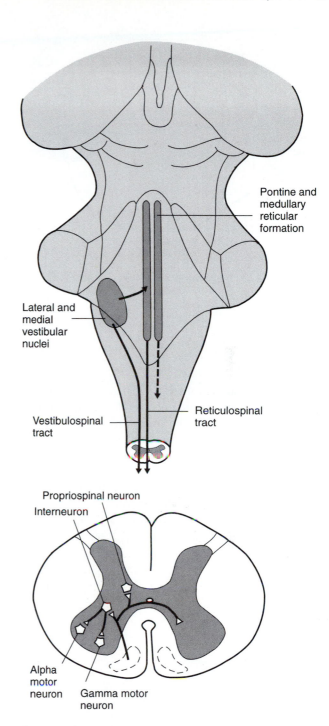

Figure 3–8. Central pathways of the tonic neck reflex.

Cervicosympathetic Reflex

This reflex was also recently discovered by Bolton and Yates[2] and is believed to help prevent orthostatic hypotension during changes in posture. Its efferent signals are carried by the greater splanchnic nerve.

Trigeminocervical Reflex

This is an aversion reflex that activates muscles in the cervical spine in response to tactile stimulus to the face.[86, 87] Its purpose is to withdraw from the stimulus. Several super-

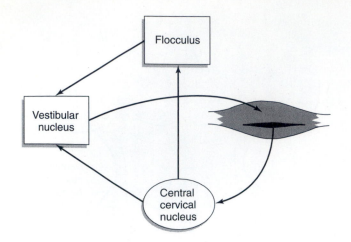

Figure 3–9. Pathway for the cervicocollic reflex.

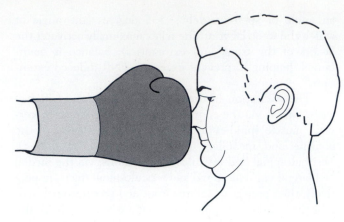

Figure 3–10. Manifestation of the trigeminocervical reflex. The upper cervical spine flexes while the lower cervical spine extends, creating a chin-tuck position. This allows withdrawal from the stimulus and increases the stability of the cervical spine.

ficial and deep muscles of the neck are activated by this reflex,[86] but the manifestation of the reflex is that of tucking in the chin and leaning the head back, so that the upper cervical spine moves into flexion while the lower cervical spine moves into extension (Fig. 3–10). This movement is created by simultaneous inhibition of the sternocleidomastoid and upper trapezius and excitation of the lower cervical extensors brought about by the stimulus.[88] This both allows for avoidance of a potentially injurious stimulus and

provides stability for the cervical spine against potential perturbation.

The pathway for the trigeminocervical nucleus is believed to be as follows: the afferent arm arises from the trigeminal nerve, with synapse in the caudal trigeminocervical nucleus. From here, impulses are sent to the accessory nucleus, where inhibitory postsynaptic potentials are produced, and to the lower cervical ventral horns, where excitatory postsynaptic potentials are produced[88] (Fig. 3–11).

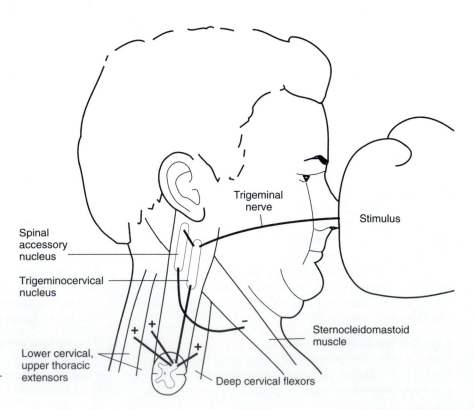

Figure 3–11. Pathway for the trigemino-cervical reflex.

REFLEX REGULATION OF EYE-HEAD-NECK COORDINATION

The cervical spine is unique in that it is responsible for maintaining stability of important sense organs, particularly those related to sight and sound. Unwanted displacement of the head in space must be counteracted in order to maintain normal positional relationships of these organs. With regard to sight, there are several reflexes that interact to provide stability of the eyes and head with movements of the body. These are quite complex and their coordination delicate. For this reason, efficient function is essential. The reflexes consist of the CCR, VCR, cervico-ocular reflex (COR), vestibulo-ocular reflex (VOR), smooth pursuit, saccades, and optokinetic reflex (OKR). All these reflexes have a direct or indirect relationship with the muscles of the cervical spine. Table 3–1 provides an overview of the reflex activities that involve the cervical spine.

Cervico-ocular and Vestibulo-ocular Reflexes

The COR is a reflex that has the purpose of maintaining fixation of the eyes on a target with movement of the neck.[89] When the head and neck move, the COR tends to keep the eyes in place to maintain ocular stability.

It was once thought that the joint receptors of the cervical spine played the primary role in providing the afferent input that produced elicitation of this reflex. This idea was mainly based on the work of Hikosaka and Maeda[90] and Maeda,[91] who showed that electrical stimulation of the "neck joints" after removal of the dorsal neck muscles evoked activity in the ipsilateral abducens nucleus. This effect was not seen with stimulation of the intact large dorsal neck muscles. But in these experiments, the intrinsic muscles that crossed the joints were left intact, and thus were not ruled out as the source of afferent input that brought about abducens activation. More recent evidence points to the mechanoreceptors in the cervical muscles, particularly the muscle spindles of the short-range rotators (i.e., the obliquus capitis posterior inferior, rectus capitis posterior major, splenius capitis, and sternocleidomastoid)[89, 92, 93] as the primary source of afferent input in the elicitation of the COR.

The COR interacts with the VOR and smooth pursuit, and is generally suppressed, playing more of a subordinate

Table 3–1: Reflex Activities That Involve the Cervical Spine

REFLEX	ELICITING STIMULUS	MOTOR RESPONSE	PURPOSE
Tonic neck reflex	Neck movement eliciting stretch to muscle spindles	Alteration of muscle tone in trunk and extremities	Assist postural stability, enhance coordination
Cervicocollic reflex	Neck movement eliciting stretch to muscle spindles	Eccentric contraction of the cervical muscles that oppose the eliciting movement	Maintain smooth, controlled cervical movement
Cervicorespiratory reflex	Neck movement eliciting stretch to muscle spindles	Alteration in respiratory rate	Assist adjustment in respiration with changes in posture
Cervicosympathetic reflex	Neck movement eliciting stretch to muscle spindles	Alteration in blood pressure	Assist prevention of orthostatic hypotension with changes in posture
Trigeminocervical reflex	Touch stimulus to the face	Head retraction	Protect against blows to the face
Cervico-ocular reflex	Neck movement eliciting stretch to muscle spindles	Movement of the eyes in the opposite direction of neck movement	Maintain gaze fixation during movements of the head
Vestibulo-ocular reflex	Head movement stimulating the semicircular canals	Movement of the eyes in the opposite direction of head movement	Maintain gaze fixation during movements of the head
Smooth pursuit	Visual target moving across the retinal field	Movement of the eyes in a direction in which a target is moving	Maintain gaze fixation on a moving target
Saccades	New visual target in retinal field	Movement of the eyes in the direction of a new target	Fixate eyes on a new target
Optokinetic reflex	Visual target moving across the retinal field causing perceived movement of the head	Movement of the eyes in the opposite direction of perceived head movement	Maintain gaze fixation on a moving target

role to the VOR.[89–91, 94, 95] However, in the presence of vestibular dysfunction[94–99] or increased muscle tone,[93, 94] the COR becomes prominent. The elicitation of the COR is such that when the head is turned in one direction, the eyes move in the opposite direction at an equal velocity and to an equivalent degree to maintain fixation of the eyes. It is stimulated by movement of the head on the trunk. The purpose of the VOR is the same as that of the COR (i.e., to maintain eye position with that of the head)[89, 100] however, it is stimulated by movement of the head in space and has a more powerful influence on eye movement, playing the dominant role in reflex maintenance of eye position.

The COR and VOR are elicited via afferentation from the muscle spindles of the intrinsic cervical muscles and the vestibular apparatus, respectively, to the rostral portion of the medial vestibular nucleus, followed by input to the flocculus of the cerebellum, where necessary modulation takes place and signals are sent back to the vestibular nucleus. The vestibular nucleus then projects to the abducens and oculomotor nuclei.[90, 100] This input is excitatory to the nuclei that move the eyes in the direction opposite head movement and inhibitory to the nuclei that move the head in the undesired direction[90, 100] (Fig. 3–12).

> ## ❗ CLINICAL PEARL
>
> Under normal circumstances these reflexes, particularly the VOR, are essential in maintaining fixation of the eyes during movements of the head. As a result, people with bilateral vestibular dysfunction are not be able to recognize faces or read signs while walking due to an inability to focus vision on these objects during the normal compensatory head movements that occur while walking.

Smooth Pursuit

The purpose of the smooth pursuit is to move the eyes in order to keep a moving target on the fovea,[100] so that when

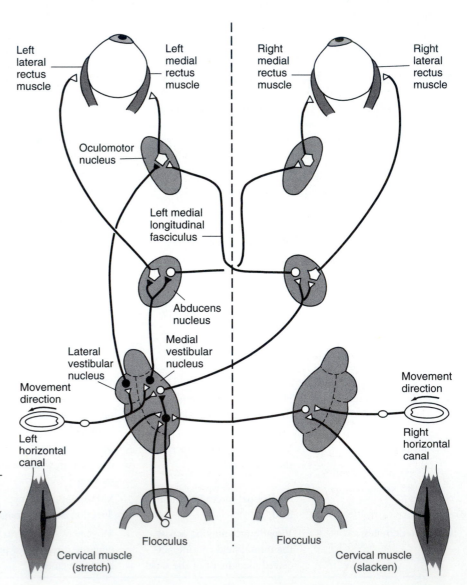

Figure 3–12. Pathway for the cervico-ocular and vestibulo-ocular reflexes.

(Adapted from Figure 43–11 of Goldberg ME, Eggers HM, Gouras P. The ocular motor system. In: Kandel ER, Schwartz JH, Jessell TM, eds. Principles of Neural Science. 3rd ed. Norwalk, Conn: Appleton & Lange, 1991:660–677.)

a target is moving across a visual field and the individual wants to follow it, the eyes, head, and neck can move in a coordinated fashion to maintain focus on the object. Smooth pursuit involves a greater degree of voluntary control than the COR and VOR. The stimulus for smooth pursuit arises from the retina, from which signals related to the target image are generated. Unlike the VOR and COR, these afferents bypass the vestibular nucleus and input directly to the cerebellum, where the input is modulated, and several cortical areas. Signals are then sent to the neural integrator and gaze center in the pons and are organized with those of the VOR and COR in the paramedian pontine reticular formation (PPRF), the area in the brain stem where integration of horizontal eye movements takes place,[94] before being sent to the oculomotor and abducens nuclei to elicit eye movements in the appropriate direction and to the appropriate velocity to follow the moving target[100] (Fig. 3–13). Signals are also sent to the cervical muscles, particularly the short-range rotators (i.e., obliquus inferior and rectus capitis posterior major, the splenius capitis, and—probably—the clavicular division of the sternocleidomastoid), to create movements of the neck.[90, 95, 101, 102] It is essential that this eye and neck movement is precisely coordinated. Without this, fixation on the target would be impossible.

This coordination requires adequate afferent input not only from the retinae, but also from the cervical mechanoreceptors, as in order for the cervical spine to perform this delicate movement, there must be constant feedback regarding its velocity and position.[103, 104] Interaction between afferents from the retinae, vestibular apparatus, cervical muscles, and extraocular muscles occurs in the frontal eye fields for this purpose.[102, 105, 106] Thus, there is close coordination between the VOR, COR, and smooth pursuit reflexes, and this coordination requires the PPRF.

Saccades

Saccades are quick, darting movements of the eyes that are designed to move the fovea toward an object of interest.[100] The typical example of this is reading. When words are being read across a page, the eyes quickly move from one word to the next. Unlike smooth pursuit, saccades do not require a visual stimulus for their elicitation but can be elicited by a sound, verbal commands, tactile stimuli, or memories of locations in space. Like smooth pursuit, saccades require delicate coordination with the cervical spine for their proper function.

Horizontal saccades are generated in the PPRF, although the command comes from the cerebral cortex.[100] Commands are generated from the frontal eye fields directly to the PPRF as well as to the superior colliculus, which then projects to the PPRF (Fig. 3–14). From there, excitatory and inhibitory signals are sent to the extraocular muscles to move the eyes in the desired direction. As with the other eye movements discussed, modulation is also made in the cerebellum.

> ## ! CLINICAL PEARL
>
> Only horizontal saccades are generated in the PPRF. Vertical saccades are generated in the rostral interstitial nucleus of Cajal.[107] This is why patients with progressive supranuclear palsy lose only vertical eye movements, while these movements are spared in those with "locked-in" syndrome (see Chap. 22). From a functional standpoint, horizontal saccades are the more important.

Concurrent activity in the cervical muscles is generated during saccadic movements, particularly in the short-range rotators (i.e., the splenius capitis and—probably—the obliquus capitis posterior minor, rectus capitis posterior major, and clavicular division of the sternocleidomastoid).[108] This allows appropriate eye-head-neck relationships while carrying out cervical movements. This muscle activity must be delicately balanced as it is designed to both initiate cervical rotational movement and brake it during the short saccadic eye movements.[108] As with the other oculomotor movements discussed, the proper elicitation of saccades requires adequate afferentation from the mechanoreceptors in the cervical spine.[109, 110] This allows the CNS to coordinate saccadic movements with head-neck movements while constantly being aware of head-neck position at each moment.

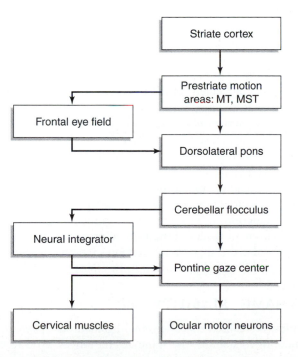

Figure 3–13. Pathway for smooth pursuit.

(Adapted from Figure 43–13 from Goldberg ME, Eggers HM, Gouras P. The ocular motor system. In: Kandel ER, Schwartz JH, Jessell TM, eds. Principles of Neural Science. *3rd ed. Norwalk, Conn: Appleton & Lange, 1991:660–677.)*

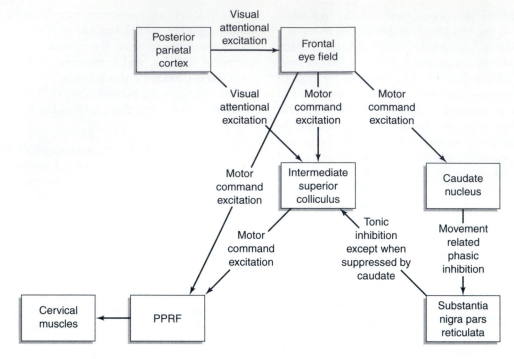

Figure 3–14. Pathway for saccades. (PPRF, paramedian pontine reticular formation.)

(Adapted from Figure 43–15 from Goldberg ME, Eggers HM, Gouras P. The ocular motor system. In: Kandel ER, Schwartz JH, Jessell TM, eds. Principles of Neural Science. 3rd ed. Norwalk, Conn: Appleton & Lange, 1991:660–677.)

Optokinetic Reflex

The optokinetic reflex is similar to the VOR in that its purpose is to maintain eye position with movements of the head.[100] However, the stimulus for this reflex is vision rather than vestibular signals. The visual system interprets movement of objects across the visual field as movement of the head, and the optokinetic reflex compensates for this by moving the eyes in the opposite direction of perceived head movement.

CERVICAL STABILITY

The stability of the cervical spine is determined by a number of factors. Traditionally, the greatest emphasis in considering stability of the cervical spine has been on the ligamentous structures and the role that they play in preventing excessive range of motion (ROM) at the intervertebral joint. However, more recently, there has been greater appreciation for the role of muscles, and, more important, the nervous system in the maintenance of stability of the spine. The muscular and nervous systems are essential for stabilization in the presence of microtrauma as occurs with common minor perturbations as well as macrotrauma such as that produced during motor vehicle accidents. This concept was introduced by Panjabi, in an influential paper published in the *Journal of Spinal Disorders*.[111] In it, he suggests that there are three subsystems

that interact in a delicate and intricate manner to maintain stability of the spine. These are:

1. The passive subsystem (ligaments, joint capsules, bones, facet joints, discs, passive mechanical properties of muscles), which functions to limit excessive movement of the intervertebral joints primarily at end ranges
2. The active subsystem (muscles), which functions to dampen sudden movements of the intervertebral joints that result from perturbations
3. The control subsystem (mechanoreceptors in the locomotor system that detect force, direction, and velocity of motion; neural control centers), which functions to read and interpret incoming signals from all tissues of the locomotor system and to order the appropriate responses required to provide stability and protection to the spine

DYNAMIC STABILITY

It must be realized that the spinal ligamentous system only functions to stabilize the spine at end ranges. And recent evidence suggests that the system may not even have the strength to serve this function to a great degree.[111] Regardless, most microtrauma and even some macrotrauma to the spine do not occur at end ranges but somewhere around the neutral zone.[112–114] The purpose of the stabilizing system of the spine is to, as Panjabi puts it, "provide sufficient stability to the spine to match the instantaneously varying stability demands due to changes in spinal posture and static and dynamic loads."[111] That is to say, the stabilizing system of the spine must be constantly active and easily adaptable to meet the ever-changing demands placed on it by the external and internal forces that are continually acting on the locomotor system.

To do this, there must be delicate, harmonious interaction between the three subsystems, particularly the active subsystem and the neural control subsystem. This interaction is illustrated in Figure 3–15. The CNS constantly monitors the signals from the receptors in the locomotor system, including those coming from the vestibular and visual systems, to assess the status of the body. It "listens" to these signals as a "symphony," not necessarily focused on any one signal, but rather on the combination of signals as an integrated whole, much as when one listens to a symphony orchestra, one hears the entire piece of music, rather than the individual instruments or notes.[115] When a perturbation is introduced to the system, such as being jostled in a crowd, or even in the simple act of taking a step, this "symphony" plays a certain "tune" that reflects what is occurring in the periphery. From this, the CNS determines the level of activity in the active subsystem that is required to maintain stability. This leads to a set of efferent signals that are sent to the specific muscles necessary to produce the force and direction of contraction required to create the appropriate postural reactions to meet the stability needs that have been established. These very muscles are not only tissues capable of generating force but, through afferentation from the GTOs, are also capable of monitoring the degree of force being produced. They report this to the CNS, which then makes the determination as to whether the force generated matches that previously determined to be required. If it does not, an adjustment is made (Fig. 3–16).

Several factors contribute to the efficiency and effectiveness of the spinal stability system. Cordo and Nashner[116] suggest that the postural reactions that occur in response to perturbation are determined by three things: postural set, somatosensory feedback, and focal motor program. That is to say, in order for the spinal stabilization system to optimally perform its task in producing the postural reactions that are required to maintain stability of the spine at any given moment, the following conditions must be satisfied:

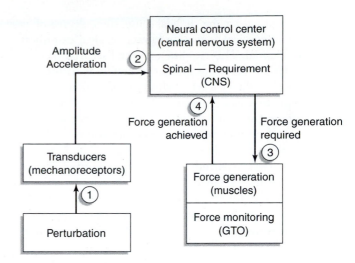

Figure 3–16. The stabilizing mechanism of the spine. When a perturbation is introduced to the spine (1), its amplitude and acceleration are communicated by the mechanoreceptors in the muscles, ligaments, and discs to the CNS (2), which determines the amplitude, speed, and direction of muscle contraction required to protect the tissues. This information is communicated to the appropriate muscles, which respond by generating force (3). The Golgi tendon organs (GTOs) of these muscles then communicate to the CNS the force that was generated in response to the command (4), and the CNS determines whether this matches that required.

(Adapted from Panjabi MM. The stabilizing system of the spine. Part I. Function, dysfunction, adaptation and enhancement. J Spinal Disord 1992;5(4):383–389.)

1. **Postural set.** As discussed earlier, proper posture is not only essential for preventing stress, strain, and injury to tissues during the maintenance of that posture, it is more important with regard to its impact on the quality of the movement that is derived from that set. This quality of movement also applies to the subcortical postural reactions that occur during the maintenance of spinal stability.

   Different head postures can create varying mechanical filtering characteristics because of the differences in the orientation of the joints and length-tension relationships of the muscles. This will alter the stabilization response to perturbation.[36] The position of maximum stability in the cervical spine is that of combined flexion of the upper cervical spine and extension of the lower cervical spine. Conversely, upper cervical extension combined with lower cervical flexion is the least stable position. When a stabilization response

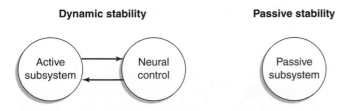

Figure 3–15. The stabilizing system of the spine.

(Adapted from Panjabi MM. The stabilizing system of the spine. Part I. Function, dysfunction, adaptation and enhancement. J Spinal Disord 1992;5(4):383–389.)

is required for the cervical spine, some degree of upper cervical flexion and lower cervical extension is adopted. This requires a postural set that provides the cervical stabilization system with the greatest ability to elicit this type of response.

2. **Somatosensory feedback.** Proper input from the afferent system is essential for the elicitation of efficient postural reactions to perturbations.[117] This enables the body to produce efficient stabilization responses to perturbations by allowing the CNS to detect the presence of the perturbation, to determine the direction and magnitude of the required correction, and to sense the postural set and support surface conditions under which the correction is to be made.[118]

! CLINICAL PEARL

The importance of the detection of the support surface conditions under which the stabilization response is to be made underscores the importance of foot function in the stability of the cervical spine. Disturbance of function in the foot can interfere with the normal transmission of information regarding the support surface. The clinical implications of this disturbance will be explored further in later chapters.

This information is actually provided by a combination of inputs from the visual, vestibular, and somatosensory systems. Of particular importance for the stability of the cervical spine is the somatosensory feedback from the entire locomotor system, particularly the cervical muscles, ligaments, and joint capsules, and from the muscle ligaments, joint, and skin receptors of the feet.[36, 67, 118–121] In the cervical spine, the muscles are responsible for signaling sudden stretch while the joint capsules and ligaments are responsible for priming the gamma system, and thus the muscle, for quick response.

These sensory systems function in the context of two different types of mechanisms: one that predicts the characteristics of stabilization responses based on past experience (focal motor program, see the discussion that follows) and one that monitors the progress of ongoing motor actions.[118] A particular pattern of afferentation from the cervical mechanoreceptors triggers the release of the necessary motor program that will provide the response required for the given perturbation. It can also update the motor program on a moment-by-moment basis as it is being executed, according to changes that may occur in the periphery.[122]

3. **Focal motor program.** The pattern by which the stabilization response to a particular perturbation

will occur is programmed in the nervous system.[123] Preprogramming of the stabilization response to perturbation is especially applicable to the anticipatory response to internal perturbation (see later discussion), as has recently been demonstrated in the lumbar spine by Hodges and Richardson.[124] However, even reactive responses are thought to represent preprogrammed motor patterns that are triggered by sensory cues.[125]

Thus, it is the interaction between these three factors that determines the precise response of the spinal stabilizing system to perturbation. This interaction must create effective responses in order for the cervical spine to withstand even the most minor of perturbations that it encounters during the course of everyday movements, let alone major trauma such as whiplash.

The spine is comprised of a series of individual segments that are separated by zygapophyseal joints and, at most segments, intervertebral discs. The discs have their own passive stabilization mechanism, but the zygapophyseal joints require a combination of passive and active elements to maintain stability. In particular, they require active stability to prevent excessive movements within the neutral zone. These movements, when allowed to occur to and beyond the limits of the neutral zone unchecked, can produce injury to the joint capsule.[111, 112, 114, 126] The most important subsystem in providing stability to the intervertebral joint is the active subsystem, under the direction of the neural subsystem (Fig. 3–17). The muscles best equipped to provide this dynamic stability are the small intrinsic muscles.[111, 127, 128]

In the cervical spine, the most important muscles are the multifidi, suboccipitals, including the rectus capitis anterior, and the deep cervical flexors. The enhanced ability of the small muscles to provide intersegmental stability is owing to the fact that they are positioned closer to the center of rotation and provide less deformation to the neural arch.[129] The reason these factors are essential is that because of them, these small muscles have a shorter reaction time than do the larger spinal muscles. This allows these muscles to behave as what Solomonow et al[111a] have referred to as "active ligaments," which can, unlike actual ligaments, increase or decrease tension to match the moment

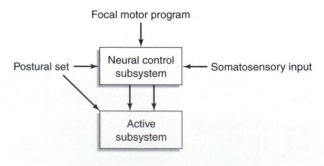

Figure 3–17. Dynamic stability.

to moment demands of the spinal stabilizing system. The stabilizing effect of the intrinsic muscles is especially important in the upper cervical spine where, as Winters and Peles[127] have shown through computer modeling, when only the larger muscles are used, focal areas of instability develop during normal movements. As Conley[130] has revealed, the large muscles of the cervical spine are active intermittently, primarily playing the role of torque production, while the deeper muscles show more continuous activity, consistent with a tonic, supporting role.

Winter[131, 132] has shown that there are two types of perturbation to which the spinal stabilization system must respond, each of which produces a distinct reaction by the neural control system:

1. External perturbations—forces acting on the body of which the individual is not aware; for example, standing on a bus or train, and having the vehicle accelerate unexpectedly, being jostled in a crowd, suddenly bumping into an object unexpectedly, or, as a more extreme example, cervical acceleration-deceleration forces as seen in whiplash. External perturbations produce reactive responses, based on the detection of the perturbation by the visual, vestibular, and somatosensory systems and the subsequent reaction by the CNS to stabilize the body.

2. Internal perturbations—forces acting on the body as a result of voluntary movements, such as raising the arms. Internal perturbations produce *proactive* responses in which the CNS produces an anticipatory response of certain key muscles to stabilize the body.[116, 133, 134] Cordo and Nashner[116] showed that the anticipatory responses in trunk muscles related to arm movements occur 60 msec earlier than the activation of the arm muscles. Gurfinkle et al[134] showed that with rapid movement of the arm in normal subjects, there is an initial movement of the head, neck, and upper thoracic spine in a rearward direction, much like tucking of the chin. This was most likely created by activation of the longus capitis and colli along with the extensors of the lower cervical and upper thoracic spine. Accompanying this movement was inhibition of the sternocleidomastoid and activation of the trapezius and splenius capitis. This was followed by activation of the ipsilateral hamstring and inhibition of the ipsilateral soleus. All this preceded the activation of the deltoid muscles that produced the arm movement. This response anticipates the need to stabilize the cervical spine in preparation for the perturbation produced by the movement on the arm.

With the internal and external responses to perturbation, the CNS prioritizes the area of the body to which the stabilization response occurs first. During gait, proactive stabilization responses occur with each step and occur in an above-down sequence; that is, the cervical spine is stabilized first, followed by a sequence of stabilization responses that end in the pelvis.[135] With external perturbations, such as bumping into an object while walking, the reactive stabilization response occur with greatest intensity at the site of the perturbation and then descends from above-down.[132]

! CLINICAL PEARL

Understanding external and internal perturbations and their respective responses will become important in Chapter 25, when we discuss sensorimotor training.

It is essential that these responses take place with great speed and efficiency; delay in any aspect of the stabilization response can lead to injury. Because of this, there must be limited involvement of the cerebral cortex in the process. A great degree of cortical involvement would lead to significant delays in the elicitation of responses, thus increasing the reaction time of the active subsystem.[136, 137] So the responses are generally too fast to be voluntary actions. But, as was previously discussed regarding the reflex activities related to the cervical spine, they are not subcortical reflexes in the truest sense, as they are too slow to be purely reflex in nature.[132] Rather, the nature of these responses is that of a "triggered response."[138]

The stabilization responses are evoked via a long-loop, transcortical pathway. They are brought about via afferent impulses from the receptors in the locomotor system that ascend in the dorsal column-medial lemniscal system. This input is then relayed through the thalamus and projected directly to the primary motor cortex and indirectly through the somatic sensory cortex[34] (Fig. 3–18). Based on this information, the force and direction of the response in the muscles required to achieve that stability necessary to avoid excessive movement outside the neutral zone, and the resultant injury, are encoded in the primary motor cortex, and efferent signals are sent along the corticospinal tracts to the necessary muscles.[139] Thus, the afferent impulses, while reaching the cerebral cortex, do not generally reach the level of conscious awareness.[124] However, the sensitivity of the muscular responses is largely regulated via subcortical bulbospinal pathways.

It is also essential that the response occur in a coordinated fashion, as the correct combination of muscles contracting in the required directions is necessary to adequately protect the tissues of the spine. This combined with the fact that the CNS is at the same time coordinating all of the movements that are simultaneously taking place to accomplish any desired tasks of the organism illustrates the enormous complexity of achieving stability at the same time as producing conscious and/or programmed

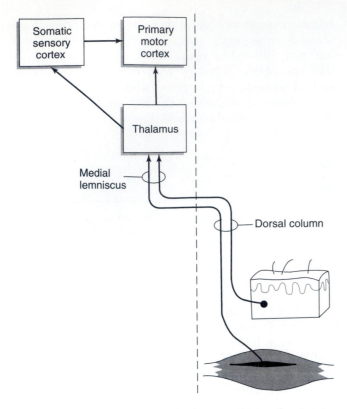

Figure 3–18. Afferent pathway for automatic spinal stabilization responses.

movements. Finally, but less significantly, there must be sufficient strength of the muscles that are called upon to act in stabilizing the spine to counteract the force of the perturbation that is acting upon the system.

PASSIVE STABILITY

As Panjabi et al state,[140] "the functions of a ligament are to provide stability to the joint, to act as a joint position transducer during physiologic motions, and to absorb energy during trauma." In terms of providing passive stability, their importance thus lies in providing stability in the presence of macrotrauma, where the integrity of end-range stability is threatened.

As is the case with the rest of the spine, the anterior and posterior longitudinal ligaments, zygapophyseal joint capsules, ligamentum flavum, and interspinous and supraspinous ligaments play a strong role in maintaining passive stability to the cervical spine.[141] The firm bond between the vertebral body and the intervertebral disc also provides essential stability.[142] A lesser role is played by the intertransverse ligaments, and the true importance of the interspinous and supraspinous ligaments is controversial.[141] The zygapophyseal joint capsules play a role in stability in lateral bending and rotation, but little role in flexion and extension.[143] But, as was stated earlier, the principal role that ligaments play in the spine is mechanoreception.

The cervical spine, unlike the other levels of the axial skeleton, features the presence of the nuchal ligament. This structure in humans is much smaller that those of quadrupeds, but appears to play a similar role[47] both as ligamentous support structure and as a source of mechanoreceptive afferent input which has particular interaction with the alpha motor neurons of the cervical extensors. Thus, when it is stretched, it causes activation of these muscles. This helps explain the absence of the flexion-relaxation phenomenon discussed in Chapter 2.

In the upper cervical spine, there are unique characteristics that require a different set of ligamentous support structures. The alar ligaments attach from the tip of the dens to the medial surfaces of the occipital condyles (see Chap. 1) and function to limit rotation and lateral bending of the upper cervical complex.[141, 144] It was previously thought that the left alar ligament limits rotation to the right (−y) and lateral flexion to the right (+z) and the right alar ligament limits rotation to the left (+y) and lateral flexion to the left (−z).[141] However, more recent evidence suggests that, at least with regard to rotational stability, both alar ligaments contribute to limit movement in each direction.[145, 146] The limitation of movement is greatest to the side opposite the location of the ligament; that is, the right apical ligament provides greater resistance to rotation to the left than to the right, and the left apical ligament provides greater resistance to the right than to the left. Rotational stability in the upper cervical spine is also provided by the tectorial membrane, which also helps to provide stability in flexion,[147] and the joint capsules.[148]

According to White and Panjabi,[141] the apical ligament contributes little to the stability of C0–C1 and nothing to C1–C2. The cruciate ligament, the major portion of which is the transverse ligament, is described by White and Panjabi[141] as the most important ligament in the upper cervical complex. Its purpose is to stabilize against anterior dislocation of C1 on C2. Swinkels and Oostendorp,[149] however, have stated that rupture of this ligament is compensated well by the alar ligaments.

CONCLUSION

It can be seen that the cervical spine is a neurologically complex area of the body. The neurophysiological information provided here is designed to provide the reader with an understanding of the basic mechanisms that govern cervical spine function and stability, and bring about the interaction that takes place between the cervical spine and the remainder of the locomotor system. This knowledge is essential in understanding cervical dysfunction and its impact on the development of clinical syndromes related to the cervical spine. The concepts introduced here will be revisited at various points in the book as they apply to the clinical evaluation and management.

REFERENCES

1. Bolton PS. The somatosensory system of the neck and its effects on the central nervous system. *J Manipulative Physiol Ther* 1998;21(8):553–563.

2. Bolton PS. The somatosensory system of the neck and its effects on the central nervous system. In: *Proceedings of the Scientific Symposium*. World Federation of Chiropractic, 1997:32–49.

3. Ghez C. The control of movement. In: Kandel ER, Schwartz JH, Jessel TM, eds. *Principles of Neural Science*. 3rd ed. Norwalk, Conn: Appleton & Lange; 1991:534–547.

4. *Dorland's Illustrated Medical Dictionary*. 26th ed. Philadelphia, Pa: Saunders; 1985.

5. Seaman DR. Proprioceptor: An obsolete, inaccurate word. *J Manipulative Physiol Ther* 1997; 20(4):279–284.

6. Martin JH. Coding and processing of sensory information. In: Kandel ER, Schwartz JH, Jessel TM, eds. *Principles of Neural Science*. 3rd ed. Norwalk, Conn: Appleton & Lange, 1991:329–352.

7. McLain RF. Mechanoreceptor endings in human facet joints. *Spine* 1994;19(5):495–501.

8. McLain RF, Raiszaden K. Mechanoreceptor endings of the cervical, thoracic and lumbar spine. *Iowa Othop J* 1995;15:147–155.

9. Wyke B. Neurology of the cervical spinal joints. *Physiother* 1979;65:73–76.

10. Richmond FJR, Bakker DA. Anatomical organization and sensory receptor content of soft tissues surrounding upper cervical vertebrae in the cat. *J Neurophysiol* 1982;48:49–61.

11. Tracey D. Joint receptors—changing ideas. *TINS* 1978;Sept:63–65.

12. Proske U, Schaible HG, Schmidt RF. Joint receptors and kinesthesia. *Exp Brain Res* 1988;72:219–224.

13. Goodwin GM, McCloskey DI, Matthews PBC. The contribution of muscle afferents to kinaesthesia shown by vibration induced illusions of movement and by the effects of paralysing joint afferents. *Brain* 1972;95:705–748.

14. Clark FJ, Horch KW, Burgess PR, Bach SM. Static awareness of knee joint angle is not affected by local anesthetic block of knee joint receptors. *Neurosci Absracts* 1975;1:132.

15. Brooks VB. *The Neural Basis of Motor Control*. New York, NY: Oxford University Press; 1986.

16. Grigg P, Finerman GA, Riley LH. Joint position sense after total hip replacement. *J Bone Joint Surg* 1973; 55A:1016–1025.

17. Cross MJ, McCloskey DI. Position sense following surgical removal of joints in man. *Brain Res* 1973;55:443–445.

18. Pickar JG, McLain RF. Responses of mechanosensitive afferents to manipulation of the lumbar facet in the cat. *Spine* 1995;20(22):2379–2385.

19. Johansson H, Sjolander P, Sojka P. Actions on gamma-motoneurones elicited by electrical stimulation of joint afferent fibers in the hind limb of the cat. *J Physiol* 1986;375:137–152.

20. Johansson H, Sjolander P, Sojka P. Fusimotor reflexes in triceps surae muscle elicited by natural and electrical stimulation of joint afferents. *Neuro-Orthop* 1988;6:67–80.

21. Johansson H, Sjolander P, Wadell I. Reflex actions of the gamma-muscles-spindle systems of muscles acting at the knee joint elicited by stretch of the posterior cruciate ligament. *Neuro-Orthop* 1989;8:9–21.

22. Seaman DR, Winterstein JF. Dysafferentation: A novel term to describe the neuropathophysiological effects of joint complex dysfunction. A look at likely mechanisms of symptom generation. *J Manipulative Physiol Ther* 1998;21(4):267–280.

23. Gordon J, Ghez C. Muscle receptors and spinal reflexes: The stretch reflex. In: Kandel ER, Schwartz JH, Jessel TM, eds. *Principles of Neural Science*. 3rd ed. Norwalk, Conn: Appleton & Lange; 1991:564–580.

24. Abrahams VC. Sensory and motor specialization in some muscles of the neck. *Trends Neurosci* 1981; 4:24–27.

25. Richmond FJR, Bakker GJ, Bakker DA, Stacey MJ. The innervation of tandem muscle spindles in the cat neck. *J Comparative Neurol* 1986;245:483–497.

26. Nitz AJ, Peck D. Comparison of muscle spindle concentrations in large and small human epaxial muscles acting in parallel combinations. *Amer Surg* 1986;52:273–277.

27. Cooper S, Daniel PM. Muscle spindles in man: Their morphology in the lumbricals and the deep muscles of the neck. *Brain* 1963;86:563–583.

28. Wilson VJ. Physiologic properties and central actions of neck muscle spindles. In: Berthoz A, Graf W, Vidall PP, eds. *The Head-Neck Sensory Motor System*. New York, NY: Oxford University Press; 1992:175–178.

29. Bakker DA, Richmond FJR. Muscle spindle complexes in muscles around upper cervical vertebrae in the cat. *J Neurophysiol* 1982;48:62–74.

30. Richmond FJR, Abrahams VC. Morphology and distribution of muscle spindles in dorsal muscles of the cat neck. *J Neurophysiol* 1975;38:1322–1339.

31. Richmond FJR, Abrahams VC. Morphology and distribution of muscle spindles in dorsal muscles of the cat neck. *J Neurophysiol* 1975;38:1322–1339.

32. Richmond FJR, Loeb GE. Electromyographic studies of neck muscles in the intact cat II. Reflexes evoked by muscle nerve stimulation. *Exp Brain Res* 1992;88:59–66.

33. Abrahams VC, Richmond FJR, Rose PK. Absence of monosynaptic reflex in dorsal muscles of the cat. *Brain Res* 1975;92:130–131.

34. Ghez C. Posture. In: Kandel ER, Schwartz JH, Jessell TM, eds. *Principles of Neural Science*. 3rd ed. Norwalk, Conn: Appleton & Lange; 1991:596–607.

35. Anastasopoulos D, Mergner TH, Becker W, Detytecke L. Sensitivity of external cuneate neurons to neck rotation in three-dimensional space. *Exp Brain Res* 1991;85:565–576.

36. Dutia MB. The muscles and joints of the neck: Their specialisation and role in head movement. *Prog Neurobiol* 1991;37:165–178.

37. Houk J, Henneman E. Responses of Golgi tendon organs to active contractions of the soleus muscle of the cat. *J Neurophysiol* 1967;30:466–481.

38. Mendel T, Wink CS, Zimny ML. Neural elements in human intervertebral discs. *Spine* 1992;17:132–135.

39. Roberts S, Eisenstein SM, Menage J, et al. Mechanoreceptors in intervertebral discs: Morphology, distribution and neuropeptides. *Spine* 1995;20(24):2645–2651.

40. Bogduk N, Windsor M, Inglis A. The innervation of the cervical intervertebral discs. *Spine* 1988;13:2–8.

41. Nakamura S, Takahashi K, Takahashi Y, et al. Origin of nerves supplying the posterior portion of the lumbar intervertebral discs. *Spine* 1996; 21(8):917–924.

42. Simone DA, Marchettini, Ochoa JL. Primary afferent nerve fibers that contribute to muscle pain sensation in humans. *Pain Forum* 1997;6(4):207–212.

43. Mense S. Peripheral mechanisms of muscle nociception and local muscle pain. *J Musculoskel Pain* 1993;1(1):133–169.

44. Giles LGF, Harvey AR. Immunohistochemical demonstration of nociceptors in the capsule and synovial folds of human zygapophyseal joints. *Br J Rheumatol* 1987;26:362–364.

45. Bogduk N. Innervation and pain patterns of the cervical spine. In: Grant R, ed. *Physical Therapy of the Cervical and Thoracic Spine*. 2nd ed. New York, NY: Churchill Livingstone; 1994:65–76.

46. Indahl A, Kaigle AM, Reikeras O, Holm SH. Interaction between the porcine lumbar intervertebral disc, zygaphysial joints and paraspinal muscles. *Spine* 1997;22(24):2834–2840.

47. Fielding JW, Burstein AH, Frankel VH. The nuchal ligament. *Spine* 1976;1:3–14.

48. Jiang H, Russell G, Raso VJ, Moreau MJ, Hill DL, Bagnall KM. The nature and distribution of the innervation of human supraspinal and interspinal ligaments. *Spine* 1995;20(8):869–876.

49. Davidoff RA. Skeletal muscle tone and the misunderstood stretch reflex. *Neurology* 1992;42:951–963.

50. Basmajian JV, DeLuca CJ. *Muscles Alive: Their Functions Revealed by Electromyography*. Baltimore, Md: Williams & Wilkins; 1985.

51. Guyton AC, Hall JE. *Textbook of Medical Physiology*. 9th ed. Philadelphia, Pa: Saunders; 1997.

52. Kupferman I. Learning and memory. In: Kandel ER, Schwartz JH, Jessel TM, eds. *Principles of Neural Science*. 3rd ed. Norwalk, Conn: Appleton & Lange; 1991:997–1008.

53. Gordon CR, Fletcher WA, Jones GM, Block EW. Adaptive plasticity in the control of locomotor trajectory. *Exp Brain Res* 1995;102:540–545.

54. Korr IM. The spinal cord as organizer of disease processes: Some preliminary perspectives. *J Am Osteopath Assoc* 1976;76:89–99.

55. Murphy DR. The locomotor system: Korr's primary machinery of life. *J Manipulative Physiol Ther* 1994;17(8):562–564.

56. Neuhuber WL, Zenker W. Central distribution of cervical primary afferents in the rat, with emphasis on proprioceptive projections to vestibular, perihypoglossal and upper thoracic spinal nuclei. *J Comp Neurol* 1989;280:231–253.

57. Hirai N. Cerebellar pathways contributing to head movement. In: Peterson BW, Richmond FJ, eds. *Control of Head Movement*. New York, NY: Oxford University Press; 1988:187–195.

58. Rubin AB, Young JH, Milne AC, et al. Vestibular-neck integration in the vestibular nuclei. *Brain Res* 1975;96:99–102.

59. Fredrickson JM, Schwarz D, Kornhuber HH. Convergence and interaction of vestibular and deep somatic afferents upon neurons in the vestibular nuclei of the cat. *Acta Otolaryngol* 1966;61:168–187.

60. Mergner T, Siebold C, Schweigart G, Becker W. Human perception of horizontal trunk and head rotation in space during vestibular and neck stimulation. *Exp Brain Res* 1991;85:389–404.

61. Mergner T, Hlavacka F, Schweigart G. Interaction of vestibular and proprioceptive inputs. *J Vestibular Res* 1993;3:41–57.

62. Gantchev GN, Draganova N, Dunev S. The role of visual information and ocular movements for the maintenance of body equilibrium. *Aggressologie* 1972;13B:55–61.

63. Black FO, Wall C, Nashner LM. Effects of visual and support surface orientation references upon postural control in vestibular deficient subjects. *Acta Otolaryngol* 1983;95:199–210.

64. Peterson H, Magnusson M, Johansson R, et al. Acoustic cues and postural control. *Scand J Rehabil Med* 1995;27:99–104.

65. Karnath HO. Subjective body orientation in neglect and the interactive contribution of neck muscle proprioception and vestibular stimulation. *Brain* 1994;117:1001–1012.

66. Grusser OJ, Pause M, Schreiter U. Vestibular neurones in the parieto-insular cortex of monkeys (*Macaca fascicularis*): Visual and neck receptor responses. *J Physiol* 1990;430:559–583.

67. Mergner T, Siebold C, Schweigert G, Becker W. Perception of horizontal head and trunk rotation in space: Role of vestibular and neck afferents. In: Berthoz A, Graf W, Vidall PP, eds. *The Head-Neck Sensory Motor System.* New York, NY: Oxford University Press; 1992:491–496.

68. Kobayashi Y, Yagi T, Kamio T. The role of cervical inputs in compensation of unilateral labyrinthectomized patients. *Adv Oto-Rhino-Lanryngol* 1988;42:185–189.

69. Shupert CL, Horak FB, Black LO. Effect of peripheral vestibular disorders on head-trunk coordination during postural sway in humans. In: Berthoz A, Graf W, Vidal PP, eds. *The Head-Neck Sensory Motor System.* New York, NY: Oxford University Press; 1992:607–610.

70. Mergner T, Huber W, Beckert W. Vestibular-neck interaction and transformation of sensory coordinates. *J Vest Res* 1997;7(4):347–367.

71. Zangemeister WH, Bulgheroni MV, Pedotti A. Differential influence of vertical head posture during walking. In: Berthoz A, Graf W, Vidal PP, eds. *The Head-Neck Sensory Motor System.* New York, NY: Oxford University Press; 1992:560–567.

72. Kelly JP. The sense of balance. In: Kandel ER, Schwartz JH, Jessell TM, eds. *Principles of Neural Science.* 3rd ed. Norwalk, Conn: Appleton & Lange; 1991:500–511.

73. Ghez C. The control of movement. In: Kandel ER, Schwartz JH, Jessel TM, eds. *Principles of Neural Science.* 3rd ed. Norwalk, Conn: Appleton & Lange, 1991:534–547.

74. Kottke FJ. From reflex to skill: The training of coordination. *Arch Phys Med Rehabil* 1980;61:551–561.

75. Gresty M. Stability of the head: Studies in normal subjects and in patients with labyrinthine disease, head tremor and dystonia. *Movement Disord* 1987;2:165–185.

76. Goldberg J. Nonlinear dynamics of involuntary head movements. In: Berthoz A, Graf W, Vidall PP, eds. *The Head-Neck Sensory Motor System.* New York, NY: Oxford University Press; 1992:400–403.

77. Suzuki I, Timerick JB, Wilson VJ. Body position with respect to the head and body position in space is coded by lumbar interneurons. *J Neurophysiol* 1985;54:123–132.

78. Wilson VJ. Physiologic properties and central actions of neck muscle spindles. In: Berthoz A, Graf W, Vidall PP, eds. *The Head-Neck Sensory Motor System.* New York, NY: Oxford University Press; 1992:175–178.

79. McCouch, GP, Deering, ID, Ling TH. Location of receptors for the tonic neck reflexes. *J Neurophysiol* 1951;14:191–195.

80. Fukuda T. *Statokinetic Reflexes in Equilibrium and Movement.* Tokyo: University of Tokyo Press; 1984.

81. Tokizane T, Murao M, Ogata T, Kondo T. Electromyographic studies on tonic neck, lumbar and labyrinthine reflexes in normal persons. *Jap J Physiol* 1951;2:130–146.

82. Hellebrandt FA, Houty SJ, Partridge MJ, Walters CE. Tonic neck reflexes in exercises of stress in man. *Am J Phys Med* 1956;35:144–159.

83. Hellebrandt FA, Schade M, Carns ML. Methods of evoking the tonic neck reflexes in normal human subjects. *Am J Phys Med* 1962;41:89–140.

84. Bolton PS, Tracey DJ. Spinothalamic and propriospinal neurones in the upper cervical cord of the rat: Terminations of primary afferent fibres on soma and primary dendrites. *Exp Brain Res* 1992;92:59–68.

85. Tjell C, Rosenhall U. Smooth pursuit neck torsion test: A specific test for cervical dizziness. *Am J Otol* 1998;19:76–81.

86. Abrahams VC, Kori AA, Loeb GE, et al. Facial input to neck motoneurons: Trigemino-cervical reflexes in the conscious and anaesthetised cat. *Exp Brain Res* 1993;97:32–30.

87. Di Lazzaro V, Restuccia D, Nardone R, et al. Preliminary clinical observations on a new trigeminal reflex: The trigeminocervical reflex. *Neurology* 1996;46:479–485.

88. Nishimura Y, Asahara T, Higuchi K, Tanaka T. Synaptic inhibition of accessory motoneurons evoked by stimulation of the trigeminal nerve in the cat. *Brain Res* 1992;585:291–294.

89. Barmack NH, Errico P, Ferraresi A, Pettorossi VE. Cervico-ocular reflexes with and without simultaneous vestibular stimulation in rabbits. In: Berthoz A, Graf W, Vidall PP, eds. *The Head-Neck Sensory Motor System*. New York, NY: Oxford University Press; 1992:202–207.

90. Hikosaka O, Maeda M. Cervical effects on abducens motoneurons and their interaction with vestibulo-ocular reflex. *Exp Brain Res* 1973;18:512–513.

91. Maeda M. Neck influences on the vestibulo-ocular reflex arc and the vestibulocerebellum. *Prog Brain Res* 1979;50:551–559.

92. Lennerstrand G, Han Y, Velay JL. Properties of eye movements induced by activation of neck proprioceptors. *Graefe Arch Clin Exp Opthalmol* 1996;234:703–709.

93. Botros G. The tonic oculomotor function of the cervical joint and muscle receptors. *Adv Oto-Rhino-Laryngol* 1979;25:214–220.

94. Gimse R, Tjell C, Bjorgen I, Saunte C. Disturbed eye movements after whiplash due to injuries to the postural control system. *J Clin Exp Neuropsychol* 1996;18:178–186.

95. Andre-Deshays C, Berthoz A, Revel M. Eye-head coupling in humans I. Simultaneous recording of isolated motor units in dorsal neck muscles and horizontal eye movements. *Exp Brain Res* 1988;69:399–406.

96. Huygen PLM, Verhagen WIM, Nicolasen MGM. Cervico-ocular reflex enhancement in labyrithine-defective and normal subjects. *Exp Brain Res* 1991; 87:457–464.

97. Dichgans J, Bizzi E, Morasso P, Tagliasco V. Mechanisms underlying recovery of eye-head coordination following bilateral labyrinthectomy in monkeys. *Exp Brain Res* 1973;18:548–562.

98. Kobayashi Y, Yagi T, Kamio T. Cervico-vestibular interaction in eye movements. *Auris Nasus Larynx* (Tokyo) 1986;13(suppl II):S87–S95.

99. Reker U. Quantitative measurements of the intensity of the cervico-ocular reflex. *HNO* 1985;33:426–429.

100. Goldberg ME, Eggers HM, Gouras P. The ocular motor system. In: Kandel ER, Schwartz JH, Jessell TM, eds. *Principles of Neural Science*. 3rd ed. Norwalk, Conn: Appleton & Lange; 1991:660–677.

101. Hinoki M, Terayama K. Physiological role of neck muscles in the occurrence of optic eye nystagmus. *Acta Otolaryngologica* 1966;62:157–170.

102. Roll R, Velay JL, Roll JP. Eye and neck proprioceptive messages contribute to the specification of gaze direction in visually oriented activities. In: Berthoz A, Graf W, Vidall PP, eds. *The Head-Neck Sensory Motor System*. New York, NY: Oxford University Press; 1992:193–196.

103. Pozzo T, Berthoz A, Lefort L. Head kinematics during complex movements. In: Berthoz A, Graf W, Vidall PP, eds. *The Head-Neck Sensory Motor System*. New York, NY: Oxford University Press; 1992:587–590.

104. Goldberg J. Nonlinear dynamics of involuntary head movements. In: Berthoz A, Graf W, Vidall PP, eds. *The Head-Neck Sensory Motor System*. New York, NY: Oxford University Press; 1992:400–403.

105. Dubrovsky BO, Barbas H. Frontal pojections of dorsal neck and extraocular muscles. *Exp Neurol* 1977;55:680–693.

106. Buisseret P. Suppression of cervical afferents impairs visual cortical cells development. In: Berthoz A, Graf W, Vidall PP, eds. *The Head-Neck Sensory Motor System*. New York, NY: Oxford University Press; 1992:188–192.

107. Fukushima K, Fukushima J. Involvement of the interstitial nucleus of Cajal in the mibbrain reticular formation in the position-related, tonic component of vertical eye movement and head posture. In: Berthoz A, Graf W, Vidall PP, eds. *The Head-Neck Sensory Motor System*. New York, NY: Oxford University Press; 1992:330–344.

108. Andre-Deshays C, Revel M, Berthoz A. Eye-head coupling in humans II. Phasic components. *Exp Brain Res* 1991;84:359–366.

109. Kowler E, Pizlo Z, Zhu GL, et al. Coordination of the head and eyes during the performance of natural (and unnatural) visual tasks. In: Berthoz A, Graf W, Vidall PP, eds. *The Head-Neck Sensory Motor System*. New York, NY: Oxford University Press; 1992:419–426.

110. Maeda M. Clinical and experimental investigations of visually guided eye and head movement: Role of neck afferents. In: Berthoz A, Graf W, Vidall PP, eds. *The Head-Neck Sensory Motor System*. New York, NY: Oxford University Press; 1992:648–653.

111. Panjabi MM. The stabilizing system of the spine. Part I. Function, dysfunction, adaptation and enhancement. *J Spinal Disord* 1992;5(4):383–389.

111a. Solomonow M, Zhou BH, Harris M, et al. The ligamento-muscular system of the spine. *Spine* 1998;(23):2552–2562.

112. Kaigle AM, Holm SH, Hansson TH. Experimental instability of the lumbar spine. *Spine* 1995; 20(4):421–430.

113. McConnell WE, Howard RP, Van Poppel J, et al. Human head and neck kinematics after low velocity rear-end impacts—understanding whiplash. 39th Stapp Car Crash Conference, 1995. SAE 952724.

114. Panjabi MM, Lyons C, Vasavada A, et al. On the understanding of clinical instability. *Spine* 1994;19(23):2642–2650.

115. Murphy DR. The locomotor system: Korr's primary machinery of life. *J Manipulative Physiol Ther* 1994;17(8):562–564.

116. Cordo PJ, Nashner LM. Properties of postural adjustments associated with rapid arm movements. *J Neurophysiol* 1982;47:287–302.

117. Gordon J. Spinal mechanisms of motor coordination. In: Kandel E, Schwartz J, Jessel T, eds. *Principles of Neural Science*. 3rd ed. Norwalk, Conn: Appleton & Lange, 1991:581–595.

118. Nashner LM, McCollum G. The organization of human postural movements: A formal basis and experimental synthesis. *Behav Brain Sci* 1985;8:135–172.

119. Wilson VJ. Physiologic properties and central actions of neck muscle spindles. In: Berthoz A, Graf W, Vidall PP, eds. *The Head-Neck Sensory Motor System*. New York, NY: Oxford University Press; 1992:175–178.

120. Karnath HO. Subjective body orientation in neglect and the interactive contribution of neck muscle proprioception and vestibular stimulation. *Brain* 1994; 117:1001–1012.

121. O'Connel, Dietz V, Gollhofer A, Kleiber M, Trippel M. Regulation of bipedal stance: Dependancy on "load" receptors. *Exp Brain Res* 1992;89:229–231.

122. Johannson RS, Westling G. Role of glabrous skin receptors and sensorimotor memory in automatic control of precision grip when lifting rougher or more slippery objects. *Exp Brain Res* 1984;56:550–564.

123. Jones GM, Watt DGD. Observations on the control of stepping and hopping movements in man. *J Physiol* 1971;219:709–727.

124. Hodges PW, Richardson CA. Inefficient muscular stabilization of the lumbar spine associated with low back pain: A motor control evaluation of transversus abdominis. *Spine* 1996;21(22):2640–2650.

125. Gielen CCAM, Ramaekers L, van Zuylen EJ. Long latency stretch responses as co-ordinated functional responses in man. *J Physiol (Lond)* 1988;407:275–292.

126. Panjabi MM. The stabilizing system of the spine. Part II. Neutral zone and instability hypothesis. *J Spinal Disord* 1992;5(4):390–397.

127. Winters JM, Peles JD. Neck muscle activity and 3-D head kinematics during quasi-static and dynamic tracking movements. In: Winters JM, Woo SLY, eds. *Multiple Muscle Systems: Biomechanics and Movement Organization*. New York, NY: Springer-Verlag; 1990:461–480.

128. Cholewicki J, McGill SM. Mechanical stability of the *in vivo* lumbar spine: Implications for injury and chronic low back pain. *Clin Biomech* 1996;11:1–15.

129. Panjabi M, Abumi K, Durenceau J, Oxland T. Spinal stability and intersegmental muscle forces: A biomechanical model. *Spine* 1989;14(2):194–200.

130. Conley MS, Meyer RA, Bloomberg JJ, et al. Noninvasive analysis of human neck muscle function. *Spine* 1995;20:2505–2512.

131. Winter DA. *ABC of Balance During Walking and Standing*. Waterloo, Ontario: Waterloo Biomechanics; 1995.

132. Winter DA. Human balance and posture control during standing and walking. *Gait Posture* 1995;3:193–214.

133. Lee WA. Anticipatory control of postural and task muscles during rapid arm flexion. *J Motor Behav* 1980;12:185–196.

134. Gurfinkle VS, Lipshits MI, Letienne FG. Anticipatory neck muscle activity associated with rapid arm movements. *Neurosci Lett* 1988;94:104–108.

135. Prince F, Winter DA, Stergiou P, Walt SE. Anticipatory control of upper body balance during human locomotion. *Gait Posture* 1994;2:19–25.

136. Janda V. Pain in the locomotor system: A broad approach. In: Glasgow EF, Twomey LT, Scull ER, et al, eds. *Aspects of Manipulative Therapy*. New York, NY: Churchill Livingstone; 1985:148–151.

137. Gahery Y, Massion J. Co-ordination between posture and movement. *Trends Neurosci* 1981;4:199–202.

138. Wilder DG, Aleksiev AR, Magnusson ML, et al. Muscular response to sudden load: A tool to evaluate fatigue and rehabilitation. *Spine* 1996;21(22):2628–2639.

139. Ghez C. Voluntary movement. In: Kandel ER, Schwartz JH, Jessel TM, eds. *Principles of Neural Science*. 3rd ed. Norwalk, Conn: Appleton & Lange, 1991:609–625.

140. Panjabi MM, Vasavada A, White AA. Cervical spine biomechanics. *Sem Spine Surg* 1993;5:10–16.

141. White AA, Panjabi MM. *Clinical Biomechanics of the Spine*. 2nd ed. Philadelphia, Pa: Lippincott; 1990.

142. Pal GP, Sherk HH. The vertical stability of the cervical spine. *Spine* 1988;13:447–449.

143. Onan OA, Heggeness MH, Hipp JA. A motion analysis of the cervical facet joint. *Spine* 1998;23(4):430–439.

144. Driscoll DR. Anatomical and biomechanical characteristics of upper cervical ligamentous structures: A review. *J Manipulative Physiol Ther* 1987;10(3):107–110.

145. Panjabi M, Dvorak, J, Crisco JJ, et al. Effects of alar ligament transection on upper cervical spine rotation. *J Orthopedic Res* 1991;9:584–593.

146. Crisco JJ, Panjabi MM, Dvorak J. A model of the alar ligaments of the upper cervical spine in axial rotation. *J Biomech* 1991;24(7):607–614.

147. Oda T, Panjabi MM, Crisco JJ, et al. Role of tectorial membrane in the stability of the upper cervical spine. *Clin Biomech* 1992;7:201–207.

148. Crisco JJ, Oda T, Panjabi MM, et al. Transections of the C1–2 joint capsular ligaments in the cadaveric spine. *Spine* 1991;16:S475–SS479.

149. Swinkels RAHM, Oostendorp RAB. Upper cervical instability: Fact or fiction? *J Manipulative Physiol Ther* 1996;19(3):185–194.

Dysfunction in the Cervical Spine

DONALD R. MURPHY

"When injured most tissues heal, but skeletal muscles learn."

—Janet Travell, MD

INTRODUCTION

As can be seen from the previous chapters, the normal function of the cervical spine is quite complex and requires a wide variety of activities to be coordinated so that individuals can engage in everyday activities with the least amount of strain and potential injury. Likewise, when dysfunction develops in the cervical spine, chain reactions can develop that affect the entire body.

In the area of cervical disorders, there has been a history of erroneous interpretation of pathoanatomy, such as "arthritis," "disc degeneration," and (worst of all) "pinched nerve," as being the most common cause of pain. High-tech testing has only reinforced this. In fact, many studies have demonstrated that structural abnormalities correlate poorly with the presence of spinal pain.[1-9] Simply put, the human body can, in many if not most cases, deal with most pathoanatomy quite adequately. However, disturbances of function can cause chain reactions to occur that present the body with a much greater challenge. This, of course, does not mean that pathoanatomical lesions do not produce pain in any patient; in fact, dysfunction and pathoanatomy often interact to produce clinical symptoms. But the presence of pathoanatomical lesions should never be assumed to be the primary factor in a cervical pain syndrome. Because the vast majority of patients with cervical spine syndromes will have some type of dysfunction as the most prominent factor in their clinical picture, dysfunction must be looked for before assigning any major role to pathoanatomy.

This chapter examines the types of dysfunction that can occur in the cervical spine. The discussion focuses on the ways in which they interact with each other and the ways in which they can disrupt function of the locomotor system as a whole and produce clinical syndromes.

JOINT DYSFUNCTION

Joint dysfunction is defined by Mennel[10] as "loss of joint-play movement that cannot be produced by voluntary muscles." While little is known about how joint dysfunction develops and what specifically happens when it occurs, it is theorized that when joint play becomes lost, the joint can become painful. In addition to this, reflex effects can occur wherein certain muscles become hypertonic and certain others become inhibited. This imbalance in the activity of muscles can lead to the development of chain reactions of dysfunction throughout the locomotor system, and faulty movement patterns.

Several processes or events can cause joint dysfunction in the cervical spine. They generally fall into three categories:[11]

1. *Trauma*. Trauma is probably the most common cause of joint dysfunction and can range from microtrauma, such as that created by an improper stabilization response to repetitive perturbation or asymmetrical loading from imbalance in the activity of the muscles that cross the joint, to macrotrauma, such as cervical injury in a motor vehicle accident.
2. *Immobilization*. Prolonged bed rest or use of a cervical collar are the most notable among the immobilization-related causes of joint dysfunction in the cervical spine.
3. *Resolution of some more serious pathological condition*. This category is particularly related to inflammatory conditions.

The precise mechanisms by which joint dysfunction develops are not known; however, there are several theories as to what can happen within a joint that can cause it to become dysfunctional. The primary theories were presented in a paper by Rahlmann.[12] These theories fall into four categories:

1. *Meniscoid entrapment*. Meniscoids, or joint inclusions,[13] are structures that are located within all segments of the cervical spine. Giles[13] has shown that, in the cervical spine, there are two types of meniscoid: a synovial fat-filled inclusion that projects into the superior aspect of the joint, and a fibro-adipose inclusion that projects into the inferior aspect. These structures have a tough, fibrous tip and their apparent function is to maintain congruence of the articular surfaces during movement.[14–16] Meniscoids have been shown to become entrapped between the articular surfaces[17] and when they do, they deform the articular cartilage and their tip becomes harder and more fibrotic. This deformation and fibrosis allows the meniscoid to become more firmly entrapped between the articular surfaces, thus creating mechanical restriction of the joint (Fig. 4–1). The immobilization itself can then cause the cartilage to become more deformable,[18] thus allowing further implantation of the meniscoid. In addition to the mechanical restriction, it has been suggested that traction applied to the meniscoid with attempted movement of the joint can stimulate nociceptive receptors in the joint capsule, producing reflex spasm of the small intrinsic muscles surrounding the joint, further restricting movement as well as causing pain.[18]
2. *Displaced disc fragments*. It is believed by some that joint dysfunction can be produced as a result of displacement of the nucleus pulposus within an intact

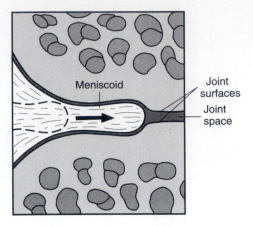

Figure 4–1. Entrapment of the intra-articular meniscoid as a possible cause of joint dysfunction. Position *a* is the normal position of the meniscoid. Position *b* represents entrapment of the hard edge of the meniscoid between the joint surfaces.

(Adapted from Lewit K. Manipulative Therapy in the Rehabilitation of the Locomotor System. 2nd ed. Oxford: Butterworth-Heinemann; 1991.)

but damaged annulus fibrosis. This is similar to what has been demonstrated as internal disc disruption,[19] which has been shown to occur in the cervical and lumbar spine. The displacement is believed to produce both mechanical restriction as well as muscle spasm through the stimulation of nociceptors in the disc.

3. *Muscle spasm*. As was discussed in Chapter 3, the intervertebral joints as well as the discs are well innervated by nociceptive receptors. These structures, therefore, are capable of generating noxious impulses following injury that project into the dorsal horn, with relay to various interneurons. Details of what occurs during this activity will be discussed later in the chapter, but certainly one of the things that can happen is reflex spasm of the muscles that cross the injured joint (multifidi, rotatores, etc.). These muscles, because they have direct influence on the movement of the individual joint, have the ability to restrict this movement when they are in spasm.[20] As will also be discussed later, this mechanism more likely involves muscle hypertonicity, not true spasm, as the latter is an acute situation and resolves spontaneously.
4. *Periarticular connective tissue adhesions*. The effects of immobilization on periarticular tissues are well known.[21] These effects include degeneration of articular cartilage; alteration of glycosaminoglycan, hyaluronic acid, and water content; contracture of the joint capsule; and ligamentous and intra-articular adhesions.[21, 22] In addition, resolution of the inflammatory process often results in fibrosis.[21] Fibro-

sis can cause passive restriction of the joint, which, in the case of the articular capsule, can be of a different magnitude on one side of the capsule compared to another, depending upon the position of immobilization.[21]

While none of these theories has universal acceptance, each of them has evidence to support it. It appears most likely that a combination of mechanisms is involved in the development of joint dysfunction. Which mechanisms are involved may be determined by a number of factors, including the specific segmental level that is involved. For example, internal disc disruption is a likely cause of an acute "locked joint" in the lower cervical spine, but, obviously, cannot be a factor in joint dysfunction in the upper two cervical segments, where there are no discs. Muscle hypertonicity is a likely candidate to be involved in dysfunction of most of the intersegmental joints of the spine but is an inadequate explanation for dysfunction of the sacroiliac, tibiofibular, and acromioclavicular joints,[23] which have no muscles that directly cross them.

Periarticular connective tissue adhesions are a likely cause of joint dysfunction, particularly in the chronic situation. All synovial joints have a capsule and surrounding ligaments and these tissues are susceptible to shortening, which has the potential to cause restriction in the movement of the joint. It does not, however, explain acute joint dysfunction, as adhesions require time to develop.

Meniscoid entrapment is likely to be a common cause of joint dysfunction, as this can occur in both the acute and chronic conditions and meniscoids have been demonstrated in joints of both the spine and extremities. In addition, an experiment reported by Lewit[23] demonstrated that when 10 patients were examined and found to have cervical joint dysfunction and then re-examined under general anesthesia with muscle relaxants, the restriction was still present and, in fact, was more easily detected due to the relaxation of the muscular system. However, as Lewit has pointed out,[23] when mechanical blockage occurs in a spinal joint, the muscular system inevitably becomes involved and increased tone in the intrinsic muscles surrounding a joint will further restrict movement of the joint.

MUSCLE DYSFUNCTION

Muscle is the only tissue in the body capable of generating forces on demand by the nervous system. As such, the muscular system plays an important role in the function of the locomotor system as a whole. Likewise, when disturbance in the function of a single muscle (or a combination of several muscles) occurs, this can have a wide-ranging impact on the function of the entire system.

Janda has delineated seven different types of muscle dysfunction.[24] The discussion that follows is closely based on Janda's classification system, with some modification.[25]

TYPES OF MUSCLE DYSFUNCTION

Janda has separated the types of dysfunction into two groups: structural and functional. The structural group contains disorders of muscle that are caused by structural lesions in the central nervous system (CNS) and are generally not of the type that are significant in functional pathology of the locomotor system. However, this group is included here for completeness.

The functional group contains disorders of muscle that arise as a result of some sort of functional disturbance in the locomotor system. The involved muscle may be the originator of this disturbance, or the origin may lie in another muscle, a joint, or practically any other tissue in the locomotor system. The mediator of the interaction of these functional disturbances is, of course, the nervous system. The functional disturbance may be hypertonicity—in which the involved muscle displays increased resistance or reactivity or both—or hypotonicity (also referred to as inhibition), in which there is a decreased readiness for the nervous system to activate the muscle.

Before discussing the types of dysfunction, terminology must be clarified to avoid confusion. In this classification system, the term *hypertonicity* is used throughout. Hypertonicity is, literally, an increase in muscle tone. As was discussed in Chapter 2, muscle tone is related to two qualities—the resistance of the muscle to passive lengthening (determined by both contractile and noncontractile factors), and the readiness of the CNS to activate the muscle in response to a stimulus or command. Note that nowhere in the preceding definition of muscle tone is the resting length or resting activity of the muscle included. The importance of this understanding will become evident as the discussion proceeds.

Structural Group

Spasticity
Spasticity occurs as a result of a lesion in the pyramidal (corticospinal) tracts or in the motor cortex. Spasticity features increased tone of certain predictable muscle groups, particularly flexors when it occurs in the extremities, and is seen after neurological injuries such as stroke, brain and spinal cord injuries, and CNS degenerative disorders.[26]

> ### ! CLINICAL PEARL
>
> It is important to note that the term *spastic muscle* applies to the condition described here and this term should *not* be used to describe "muscle spasm" (see later discussion). Improper use of the term *spastic* is a common mistake in the reporting of muscle injuries related to cervical trauma. Unless the trauma was severe enough to cause CNS injury, spasticity, or "spastic muscles," will not be part of the clinical picture.

Rigidity
Rigidity occurs as a result of a lesion in the extrapyramidal system and features increased tone in the muscles on both

sides of a given joint. It occurs in Parkinson's disease and other parkinsonian syndromes as well as focal dystonias, such as writer's cramp, spasmodic dysphonia, and spasmodic torticollis.[27, 28]

! CLINICAL PEARL

As was stated earlier with regard to "spastic muscles," *spasmodic* is a term that should be reserved for muscles that are affected by rigidity—a narrow definition. Therefore, *rigidity* or *spasmodic* are not terms that should be used to denote "muscle spasm," as may occur following soft tissue injury.

Functional Group

Limbic system dysfunction
The limbic system is the functional link between mental activity, particularly as related to emotions, and muscle activity.[29] There is also a direct connection between the thalamus and the limbic system that is involved in the memory of previous pain experiences.[30] When an individual experiences emotional stress, particularly as it relates to experiences that trigger previous pain memories, the physical manifestation of this is often increased tone in the muscular system that occurs in a certain distinct pattern.[24]

! CLINICAL PEARL

"Essentially there are no sharp demarcations between the physical, the mental, the emotional and the spiritual. Every thought, every emotion is attended by a vascular, myological, endocrine change, and also vice versa."

—Joseph Janse, DC

The muscles affected in limbic system dysfunction include those in the cervical spine, particularly the posterior cervical muscles, the sternocleidomastoid (SCM) and the upper trapezius, the lumbar muscles, particularly the erector spinae, and the muscles of the pelvic floor.[24] The affected muscles are not usually spontaneously painful (unless they contain myofascial trigger points; see later discussion) but are tender to palpation, and there is typically a gradual transition from the tender areas to the nontender areas.

The involved muscles are predisposed to developing myofascial trigger points (see later discussion) and are thus capable of creating referred pain syndromes, particularly headache, low back pain that involves a wide area of the lower back, and pelvic pain. Because of the involvement of the pelvic floor, female patients will also frequently report pelvic symptoms such as dysmenorrhea, dyspareunia, and urinary frequency.[24]

Interneuron dysfunction
Interneuron dysfunction is altered tone caused primarily by joint dysfunction although, as will be seen, muscle dys-

function itself can also cause altered tone. As was described in Chapter 3, there is a population of mechanoreceptors in the cervical zygapophyseal joints that is relatively small in number but is believed to have an influence on the activity of gamma motor neurons that innervate the muscle spindles. In addition, there are a great number of nociceptive afferents in the joint capsule,[31, 31a] far greater than the number of mechanoreceptors.[32] A large population of nociceptors located in the tissues surrounding the joints[33–35] also influence gamma motor neuron activity.

When a joint becomes dysfunctional (i.e., loses its normal joint play), a decrease in the activation of the mechanoreceptors as well as increased activation of the nociceptors in the joint capsule may develop. This alteration in the balance of activity between the two joint afferent systems has been termed *dysafferentation* by Seaman and Winterstein.[36] As Meyer et al[37] have pointed out, this alteration allows for the transmission of nociceptive impulses along the ascending nociceptive pathways relatively unchecked. Also, because of the influence of both afferent systems on the activity of the gamma motor neuron system, an alteration develops in the activity of the gamma motor neurons and, thus, an alteration in the sensitivity of the muscle spindle. The alpha motor neurons are unaffected at this level of dysafferentation.[38] Alteration in the activity in the gamma motor system, in turn, leads to disturbance of muscle tone. This disturbance can be that of increased[39, 40] or decreased[41–45] tone, depending on the muscle involved. It is believed that the specific disruption occurs in the interneuron network that is involved in the interaction between the mechano- and nociceptors and the fusimotor system[24, 46] (Fig. 4–2).

Certain muscles tend to easily become hypertonic in response to interneuron dysfunction, whereas others have a tendency to become inhibited. The reason for this is not fully understood. A list of these muscles, as they relate to the cervical spine, can be found in Tables 4–1 and 4–2.

A muscle that becomes hypertonic will demonstrate increased reactivity to stimuli. These stimuli can be peripheral, as in increased resistance to stretch or reflex contraction induced by stimulating another muscle,[28, 47, 48] or central, as in dominance of a centrally ordered movement pattern.[49, 50] In addition, a hypertonic muscle will tend to cause inhibition of its "antagonist."[51] An example of this would be a hypertonic upper trapezius causing reciprocal inhibition of the lower trapezius. Inhibited muscles tend to be left out of the movement patterns in which they are supposed to be involved.

If the affected muscle is one that tends to become inhibited, hypertonicity may develop in this muscle's synergists as the responsibility for carrying out certain movement patterns is placed on them as a result of the affected muscle's inhibition. An example of this would be an inhibited deep cervical flexor group (longus capitis, longus colli, and rectus capitis anterior) resulting in hypertonicity in the SCM.

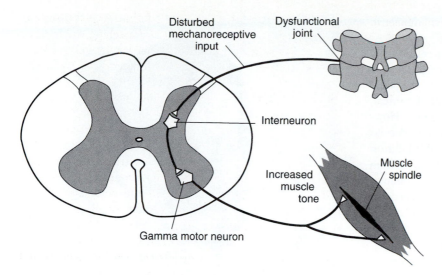

Figure 4–2. The mechanism by which joint dysfunction alters muscle tone.

It must be pointed out that as hypertonicity relates to increased muscle tone, it says nothing about increased resting electromyographic (EMG) activity. A hypertonic muscle, like a normal muscle, is silent at rest. What distinguishes a hypertonic muscle from a normal muscle is the degree of reaction to stimuli and degree of activation during centrally ordered movement patterns. Thus, the argument recently put forth by Lund and Donga[52] that pain cannot cause alteration of muscle activity, and that this activity cannot lead to the perpetuation of pain, does not hold up to scrutiny. This is because it is based on the many studies that have shown absence of *resting* EMG activity in muscles of chronic pain patients. Increased resting EMG activity, as will be seen later, occurs only in the acute stage of injury or dysfunction, and resolves soon after; thus, it cannot be expected in chronic pain patients. However, hypertonicity (and inhibition) is seen in chronic stages, although it cannot be detected by resting EMG. Studies that have assessed EMG during activity or during rest intervals between contractions have shown high correlation between patients with chronic complaints and those without.[40, 53–56] In addition, as was stated earlier, nociception arising from muscle, unless it is acute and quite intense, increases the activity of *gamma* motor neurons, not *alpha* motor neurons.[38] Thus, it creates hypertonicity and not

true spasm (see later discussion). Gamma motor neuron activity cannot be detected as resting EMG activity.

Distinction must also be made between "inhibited" and "weak." The term *weak* refers to the inability of a muscle to provide sufficient torque production. While this is an important function and requires assessment, especially during the neurological examination, it is not synonymous with "inhibited." The term *inhibited* refers to the inability of a muscle to *respond to stimuli*—be they external, in the form of perturbation, or internal in the form of central order—in the appropriate time or magnitude to adequately perform its function. A muscle that is inhibited may or may not be weak. And, a muscle that is hypertonic or has developed muscle tightness (see later discussion) may be weak. For example, it is not uncommon to encounter a patient whose deep cervical flexors do not activate sufficiently to maintain stability of the head when it is suspended in the supine position (see the Cervical Stability

Table 4–1: Muscles That Tend To Become Hypertonic

Temporalis	Sternocleido-mastoid	Upper trapezius	Rhomboids
Masseter	Suboccipitals	Levator scapulae	Pec major and minor
Scalenes			

Adapted from Janda V. Muscles and motor control in cervicogenic disorders: assessment and management. In: Grant R, ed. Physical Therapy of the Cervical and Thoracic Spine. New York, NY: Churchill Livingstone; 1994:195–216.

Table 4–2: Muscles That Tend To Become Inhibited

Suprahyoids	Rectus capitis anterior	Longissimus cervicis (lower cervical/upper thoracic extensor)	Serratus anterior
Longus capitis	Multifidis (lower cervical/upper thoracic extensor)	Middle trapezius	
Longus colli	Semispinalis cervicis (lower cervical/upper thoracic extensor)	Lower trapezius	

Adapted from Janda V. Muscles and motor control in cervicogenic disorders: assessment and management. In: Grant R, ed. Physical Therapy of the Cervical and Thoracic Spine. New York, NY: Churchill Livingstone; 1994:195–216.

test in Chap. 14), but with manual or dynamometric strength testing, they appear perfectly normal.

This is because strength activities are largely *cortical* processes; that is, when a patient is instructed to push against a certain object to determine the amount of torque production he or she can generate, a great deal of cortical, or conscious, activity is engaged to perform the task. However, inhibition arises from disturbance in *subconscious* processes. This can occur as a result of reciprocal inhibition by a hypertonic antagonist, from dysafferentation, or from an alteration of the CNS program for a certain common movement, in which the inhibited muscle does not become appropriately activated when that program is called into action. The reader is urged to understand this and not to confuse inhibition with weakness.

Both hypertonic and inhibited muscles will cause an alteration of the distribution of pressure over the joint(s) that they cross and, thus, may not only result from joint dysfunction, but produce joint dysfunction as well.[24] In addition, the resultant alteration of the movement patterns in which these muscles are involved will produce a distortion of the afferent "picture" that the CNS receives from the locomotor system,[57, 58] potentially leading to further disruption of centrally ordered motor programs. Both hypertonic and inhibited muscles are susceptible to the development of myofascial trigger points[51] and, thus, can themselves become sources of pain.

As will be discussed in more detail in Chapter 19, a hypertonic muscle exhibits features that can be detected on examination. The most prominent of these features is increased resistance to stretch; that is, when the examiner lengthens the involved muscle fully and then tries to stretch it beyond its resting length, the muscle offers greater resistance to the attempted lengthening than would a normal muscle. Another important feature of a hypertonic muscle that can be detected is the tendency for dominance on movement pattern examination. It is important to note that the muscle may or may not be of normal resting length. Some hypertonic muscles are shortened as compared to the muscle in its normal state, whereas others are of normal length. Therefore, resting length is not a reliable indicator of hypertonicity. Muscle tone must be determined by assessment of function.

Not only can dysafferentation from joint dysfunction lead to interneuron dysfunction, but nociception from muscle can as well. This will be discussed further in the section on faulty movement patterns that follows. In addition, direct impact to a muscle, even in the absence of actual structural injury, can produce interneuron dysfunction. An example of this is sudden "jolt" to the muscle in a low-speed, rear impact motor vehicle collision.[59]

Reflex spasm

Muscles often respond to nociception by "going into spasm;" that is, developing a sustained contraction. This is thought to be a protective mechanism to "splint" the in-

Figure 4–3. Reflex spasm due to cervical disc lesion.

jured tissue and protect it from further injury. Reflex spasm is the only type of muscle dysfunction in which there is continuous electrical activity throughout the entire muscle, as this is an actual muscle contraction. (As will be seen, electrical activity is found with myofascial trigger points, but this is limited to the area of the trigger point itself and does not involve the entire muscle.) Examples of reflex spasm are abdominal "rigidity" in the presence of acute appendicitis (though this is not true rigidity)[60] and antalgia related to lumbar or cervical disc lesions[61] (Fig. 4–3).

Reflex spasm is brought about by barrages of nociceptive impulses that, unlike the dysafferentation previously discussed, are of sufficient intensity to cause activation of alpha motor neurons in the muscle. Alpha motor neuron activation leads to contraction of the extrinsic fibers of the muscle (Fig. 4–4). This can occur as a result of intense nociception arising from virtually any tissue, but it is especially common when the pain-generating tissue is the intervertebral disc. Reflex spasm related to nociception from the intervertebral disc was demonstrated in an animal model by Indahl et al,[62] who stimulated the annular fibers of the disc in pigs and demonstrated a reactive increase in resting EMG activity in the multifidis and longissimus muscles at that segment.

 CLINICAL PEARL

When you see antalgia, think disc!

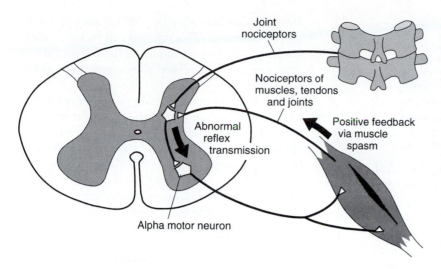

Figure 4–4. Neurological mechanisms of reflex spasm.

(Adapted from Zimmerman M. Basic neurophysiological mechanisms of pain and pain therapy. In: Jayson MIV, ed. The Lumbar Spine and Back Pain. *Edinburgh: Churchill Livingstone; 1992:43–59.)*

Reflex spasm itself can then become a source of pain, as the contraction can cause ischemia to develop within the muscle. Rather than resolving, as would occur after the relaxation of a normal muscle contraction, this ischemia is sustained. As muscle activity in the presence of ischemia stimulates the muscle's nociceptive afferents, use of the muscle can be painful.[63]

Reflex spasm is a self-limiting condition; that is, it resolves spontaneously as the intensity of the nociceptive impulses resolves (not necessarily as the *pain* resolves), though, as will be seen in Chapter 21, there are methods to hasten this resolution. As the intensity of nociception decreases, however, residual hypertonicity or, conversely, inhibition may remain in the muscle. This results from residual low-level nociception occurring, particularly in the presence of accompanying dysafferentation from joint dysfunction. For example, if a patient is injured in a motor vehicle accident that causes trauma to both the joints and muscles of the cervical spine, reflex spasm may develop due to intense nociception from these tissues. Regardless of what treatment is applied (or even no treatment), the intensity of the nociception will eventually decrease and the spasm will resolve. But if effective methods are not employed to restore function in the injured joints and muscles, thus normalizing the afferent input from these tissues, an underlying hypertonicity (in muscles that have a tendency to become hypertonic) or inhibition (in muscles that have a tendency to become inhibited) of the muscles involved may remain. This dysfunction can lead to the development of chronic pain. Residual dysfunction after the resolution of reflex spasm is common in patients who develop chronic pain after whiplash, as Fredin et al[40] have demonstrated. They found decreased ability to relax the upper trapezius, deltoid, and infraspinatus between repetitive shoulder flexion movements in 22 patients with chronic pain after whiplash compared to 27 controls. The patients also reported greater fatigue during these movements. Thus, appropriate management in the acute and subacute stages to restore normal function as quickly as possible is vital.

! CLINICAL PEARL

It is not uncommon, especially in the world of personal injury, to find inappropriate use of the word "spasm" to refer to virtually any condition that affects muscle. The term *spasm* should be reserved only for the clinical condition of reflex spasm as described here; thus, it is purely an acute phenomenon. The term does not apply to chronic conditions (except, in some cases, for acute exacerbation of a chronic problem), nor does it apply to any of the other types of muscle dysfunction.

Myofascial trigger points

Travel and Simons[64] define a myofascial trigger point (TrP) as "a hyperirritable spot, usually within a taut band of skeletal muscle, or in the muscle's fascia, that is painful on compression, and that can give rise to characteristic referred pain, tenderness and autonomic phenomena." Myofascial trigger points are common sources of pain in cervical syndromes, but they are usually the result of dysfunction elsewhere in the locomotor system.

A TrP develops when there occurs a localized shortening of a fascicle of muscle fibers in which a group of sarcomeres, rather than returning to their normal resting length, remain in a state of contracture (Fig. 4–5). This contracture can be palpated as a "taut band." TrPs occur as a result of the development of a focal area of metabolic distress within the fascicle[65] in which the shortening of sarcomeres causes disruption of vascular supply to the area, leading to a deficit in oxygen and ATP. The energy deficit does not allow the activation of the calcium pump that is required to release the overlapping of the actin and myosin filaments in the area. In the presence of injury, disruption

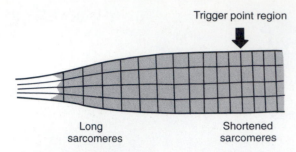

Figure 4–5. Focal shortening of sarcomeres in the development of a myofascial trigger point. Note that in the area of the trigger point, the sarcomere length is markedly reduced. This is palpable as a nodule at the nidus of the trigger point. Because the fascicle of muscle fibers maintains its normal resting length, the sarcomeres that are remote from the trigger point are abnormally lengthened. This is palpable as a taut band along the length of this fascicle.

(Adapted from Simons DG. Myofascial pain syndrome due to trigger points. In: Goodgold J, ed. Rehabilitation Medicine. *St. Louis: Mosby; 1988:686–723.)*

of the sarcoplasmic reticulum causes leakage of calcium ions into the intracellular environment, resulting in perpetuation of the contracture in the area of the TrP. Because this contracture is maintained by metabolic factors, the taut band is electrically silent although, as we will see, the TrP itself is not.

The disruption in vascular supply that is created by the localized contracture causes ischemia. Normal muscle contraction, in the presence of ischemia, can cause pain. In addition, the ischemic state allows the buildup of vasoneuroactive substances in the muscle.[63] These chemicals include bradykinin, 5-hydroxytryptamine, prostaglandins of the E type, leukotrienes, substance P, and high concentrations of potassium ions and are known to sensitize or activate type III (A delta) and IV (C) nociceptors in the muscle. Sensitization and activation of nociceptors can both produce and perpetuate nociceptive afferentation and pain perception.

It is believed that a TrP can develop in a muscle when that muscle is subjected to direct trauma, acute strain, sustained tension, overwork, hormonal or nutritional inadequacies, or joint dysfunction leading to dysafferentation and interneuron dysfunction.[66] Simons[65] has identified seven clinical features known to exist with TrPs:

1. *Local tenderness.* This results from the buildup of the vasoactive substances previously mentioned.
2. *Referred pain.* An active TrP will cause pain that will be perceived in remote areas. Each muscle has a characteristic distribution of referred pain that does not follow any known dermatome, sclerotome, or myotome.
3. *Palpable taut band.* This is caused by the local shortening of sarcomeres of the bundle of muscle

fibers that are harboring the TrP. It feels tense and ropy to palpation. This ropiness can be felt along the length of the taut band, and the nidus of the trigger point itself will feel more tense and nodular (see Chap. 19).
4. *Local twitch response.* Snapping the finger across the taut band will often create a twitch of the involved fibers. The twitch localized to the fascicle of muscle that contains the TrP and has been shown to be reflex in nature, mediated at the spinal cord level.[67]
5. *Metabolic distress.* This was discussed earlier.
6. *Relief by passive lengthening.* When done properly and within normal limits, passive lengthening of the fascicle of muscle fibers that contain one or more TrPs will restore the shortened sarcomeres to normal length and, thus, release the compressed blood vessels and restore normal metabolic processes (see Chap. 19).
7. *Weakness and fatigability.* Weakness of contraction without atrophy is frequently found in muscles that contain TrPs. This is caused by the CNS decreasing drive to the muscle as a result of the nociception. It is not to be confused with the inhibition discussed earlier. TrPs can occur in muscles that tend to become hypertonic or muscles that tend to become inhibited. In addition, a muscle may often tire easily because of the decreased circulation in the area of the TrP.

Recent research has demonstrated that there is spontaneous EMG activity in the nidus of the TrP that is not present in the rest of the taut band, or the other fascicles within the muscle.[68, 69] This finding caused Hubbard and Berkoff[68] to speculate that TrPs are generally located at the site of muscle spindles. If this is the case, it helps explain another mechanism by which TrPs can produce ongoing pain: As suggested by Kramis et al,[70] this mechanism involves afferentation from the muscle spindle that produces depolarization of sensitized wide-dynamic-range interneurons in the dorsal horn, causing transmission along central nociceptive tracts (see the explanation of this mechanism later in this discussion). But Simons et al[69] suggested that it is unlikely that evidence of spontaneous EMG activity in the nidus of a TrP indicates that the TrP is located at the site of a muscle spindle, as it is doubtful that a needle electrode would penetrate the fibrous capsule of the spindle. Much is still to be learned regarding the precise pathophysiology of the TrP phenomenon.

TrPs are classified as either active or latent. An active TrP is one that is spontaneously causing pain in the patient. A latent TrP is one in which the pathological features of the TrP phenomenon are present but there is no spontaneous pain being experienced by the patient. Latent TrPs can become activated in the presence of acute overload or strain to the muscle or, particularly in the case of TrPs in those muscles that cause referred head pain, emo-

Table 4–3: Muscles That Tend To Become Tight

| Masseter | Sternocleidomastoid | Levator scapulae |
| Suboccipitals | Upper trapezius | Pec major and minor |

Adapted from Janda V. Muscles and motor control in cervicogenic disorders: assessment and management. In: Grant R, ed. Physical Therapy of the Cervical and Thoracic Spine. New York, NY: Churchill Livingstone; 1994:195–216.)

tional stress (limbic system dysfunction) or hormonal or nutritional inadequacies.

Muscle tightness

Muscle tightness is a condition in which the connective tissue elements of a muscle are in a continuously shortened state and the muscle has increased reactivity to both central and peripheral stimuli.[24] As with hypertonicity related to interneuron dysfunction, this increased reactivity can be peripheral or central. So a muscle that is tight will have a tendency to dominate the movement patterns in which it is involved and provide greatly increased resistance to stretch. It will also tend to reciprocally inhibit its antagonists, causing those muscles to tend to be left out of the movement patterns in which they are supposed to be involved.

Because of the involvement of connective tissue contracture, muscle tightness is distinguished from hypertonicity related to interneuron dysfunction in that it is shortened in its resting state. A muscle affected by muscle tightness also tends to provide greater resistance to lengthening than does one with hypertonicity caused by interneuron dysfunction, because not only do the contractile elements provide increased resistance, the noncontractile elements do as well.

As discussed earlier in the section on interneuron dysfunction, there are certain muscles related to the cervical spine that tend to easily become hypertonic and certain muscles that tend to easily become inhibited. A similar pattern is seen with muscle tightness (Table 4–3). It can be seen that there is great overlap between those muscles that tend to become hypertonic (see Table 4–1) and those that tend to become tight (see Table 4–3).

> **! CLINICAL PEARL**
>
> Although TrPs can be found in muscles that tend to become inhibited, hypertonic, or tight, when a muscle actually has tightness, there generally will not be TrPs in it.

SKIN AND SUBCUTANEOUS SOFT TISSUE DYSFUNCTION

When joint or muscle dysfunction occurs, reflex changes can take place in the skin and subcutaneous tissue that can become their own locus of aberrant afferent input to the CNS, leading to pain and other reflex changes.[71] The most common of these is the hyperalgesic skin zone (HSZ).[71, 72]

The HSZ is an area of skin that develops increased sensitivity such that stimuli that are normally innocuous become painful. It occurs as a result of dysfunction in another part of the locomotor system and is frequently found in an area that is dermatomally or sclerotomally related to the area of dysfunction.[73, 74] HSZ can occur when the dysfunction from which it originated is actively producing pain or can become its own source of pain even when the original dysfunction is clinically quiescent.[72] The latter phenomenon was demonstrated by Lewis and Kellegren,[74] who, in their studies of referred pain resulting from injection of hypertonic saline into spinal tissues, showed that the zones of skin tenderness that developed in the areas of referred pain typically outlasted the pain by up to several hours. In clinical situations, where nociceptive stimulation lasts far longer than that induced by injection of hypertonic saline, plastic change can occur in the CNS (see later discussion) which can cause perpetuation of the HSZ.

The mechanism by which HSZ and other skin and subcutaneous dysfunction occurs is unknown, but Korr et al[75] found that myofascial insults induced either by injection of hypertonic saline or from specific postural stresses produced lowered electrical skin resistance in areas remote from the stimulation. They felt that these represented autonomic responses.

The area of skin affected by HSZ exhibits increased tension, manifested clinically as an increased resistance to stretch.[71] This increased resistance is also known to occur in skin overlying the spine, correlating to levels of joint dysfunction.[76, 77] The sensitivity of the HSZ can become significant enough to cause not only hyperalgesia (which is increased response to stimuli that are normally painful) but also allodynia (pain produced by stimuli that are normally not painful). So simply touching the skin lightly can produce pain that, at times, can be severe enough to be misdiagnosed as herpes zoster[72] or trigeminal neuralgia.[78]

FAULTY MOVEMENT PATTERNS

In many cases, particularly in the case of TrPs, muscle dysfunction can be a significant source of pain; that is, muscle can often be seen as a primary pain generator. But the phenomenon of muscle dysfunction also has wider ranging impacts that can lead to more widespread dysfunction and ultimately produce pain in areas remote from the origin. This wide-ranging impact was demonstrated by Wachter et al.[79] They showed that of 21 patients with chronic cervical pain after whiplash, half had increased tone in the thigh muscles compared to controls, as measured by the "modified pendulum" test in which the leg of the seated subject was extended at the knee and dropped, followed by measurement of the pendulum effect of the leg after dropping. They found in one subject that after injection of a TrP in the cervical spine that abolished his post-whiplash headache for 2 to 3 hours, there was a normalization of muscle tone in the legs. This spreading dysfunction can occur as a "chain reaction"[80] that can greatly complicate the clinical picture. One manifestation of this reaction is the development of faulty movement patterns.

As was discussed in Chapter 3, the muscular system supplies the most abundant somatosensory input of all locomotor structures. This abundance is a result of the density of mechanoreceptors that is present in this tissue. In addition, the muscles of the cervical spine have the greatest density of muscle mechanoreceptors, particularly muscle spindles, in the body. Thus, alteration of the function of muscles can have a great impact on the communication that occurs between the locomotor system and the nervous system. And alteration of the function of muscles in the cervical spine can have a particularly large impact on this communication. When a muscle develops dysfunction, the afferentation from that muscle can become disturbed due to change in the sensitivity of the muscle spindle.[39] Specifically, hypertonicity causes an increase in the sensitivity of the spindle, thus an increase in the afferent input from the spindle, and inhibition causes decreased sensitivity of the spindle and decreased afferentation. These effects can be enhanced by nociception arising from the muscle[81-86] and by direct injury to the muscle.[87]

Alteration in the afferentation from certain muscles can present a distorted "picture" to the CNS regarding the status of the locomotor system. The dysfunctional muscles will present a set of afferent signals that will be contradictory to those that are presented by the rest of the system. As a result, rather than being presented with a harmonious, coordinated picture of activity in the locomotor system, the CNS is presented with a jumbled, confused image.[57, 58] Because the focal motor programs of the CNS, including reflex and stability mechanisms as well as movement patterns, are dependent on a normal afferent system for their proper elicitation, muscle dysfunction, especially if it is widespread, can cause marked alteration in these programs. This alteration can be plastic; that is, the change in function that results can become semipermanent and remain until the pattern of afferent signals is again changed.

Motor program alteration was demonstrated by Gordon et al,[88, 89] who had subjects walk on a rotating treadmill for 2 hours while blindfolded. This activity caused an alteration in the manner in which the somatosensory system sent afferent signals to the CNS regarding this activity. The vestibular system was not stimulated by this activity, as there was no movement of the head in space. After 2 hours on the rotating treadmill, when the subjects performed the Stepping Test (see Chap. 14), in which they marched in place on solid ground, they tended to rotate in the same direction that the treadmill had been rotating. After just 2 hours of altered somatosensory afferentation, there was a change in the movement pattern for gait. In this experiment, normal gait was restored within 15 minutes (Fletcher WA, personal communication, 1998), but if the altered afferentation is sustained over a prolonged period of time, as

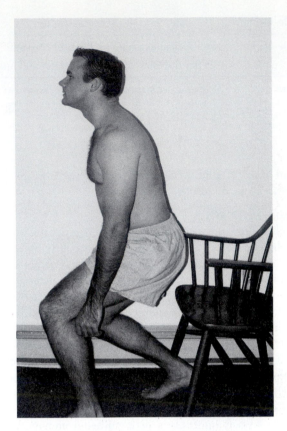

Figure 4–6. Faulty sit-to-stand pattern.

would be the case with joint and muscle dysfunction, a plastic change can occur in the CNS program by which the faulty pattern is perpetuated.

Faulty postural set also plays an important role in the development and perpetuation of faulty movement patterns. As was discussed in Chapter 2, all movements are derived from a certain postural set, that is, the specific posture in which the individual engages immediately prior to the onset of a certain movement pattern.[90, 91] The quality of the movement pattern is in part determined by the quality of the postural set from which it is derived. The relationship between postural set and subsequent movement pattern was demonstrated by Jones,[91] who found significant alteration in the sit-to-stand pattern derived from different postural sets. In those subjects whose postural set involved forward head placement, there was a greater degree of lumbar flexion and upper cervical extension associated with the subsequent movement pattern (Fig. 4–6). This movement represents an unstable and stressful pattern.

CERVICAL INSTABILITY

As Panjabi[92] has written, there are three subsystems that interact to provide the spine with the necessary stability to avoid injury. These are: (1) the active subsystem (muscles), (2) the passive subsystem (ligaments, joint capsules, bones, facet joints, discs, passive mechanical properties of muscles), and (3) the control subsystem (mechanoreceptors in the locomotor system that detect force, direction and velocity of motion, neural control centers). The active and neural control systems function to prevent movement that exceeds the normal neutral zones when internal or external perturbations are introduced to the spine (dynamic stability), while the passive subsystem functions to prevent excessive motion at end range (passive stability).

Stability in the cervical spine is provided by both these dynamic and static processes. Likewise, compromised stability of the cervical spine results from interference with either or both of these mechanisms. However, the size of the intervertebral neutral zone has been demonstrated to be a better indicator of spinal stability than gross range of motion.[93–97] As the job of the dynamic stabilizing system is to maintain the neutral zone within injury-free limits, this system is far more important than the passive system in protecting the intervertebral segments from injury on a daily basis.

DYNAMIC INSTABILITY

Panjabi defines that which is being referred to here as dynamic instability as ". . . a significant decrease in the capacity of the stabilizing system of the spine to maintain the intervertebral neutral zones within the physiological limits so that there is no neurological dysfunction, no major deformity and no incapacitating pain."[98] When dysfunction develops in either the active or neural control subsystems, a decrease in the reaction time of the active subsystem occurs, causing a delay in the stabilization response.[99] As a result, the response may be too slow to adequately keep the intervertebral neutral zones in check. This results in abrupt patterns of movement outside the normal neutral zones when perturbations are introduced (remember, these perturbations can even be in the form of normal activities such as movement of a limb) and can lead to pain and susceptibility to injury.

![CLINICAL PEARL]

The inability to stabilize the intersegmental joint in the presence of perturbations is one mechanism by which people with significant cervical dysfunction often have pain with common, everyday movements. Three other mechanisms by which this occurs will also be discussed here.

It should be remembered that there are three factors that determine the quality of a dynamic stabilization response: postural set, somatosensory input, and focal motor program.[100] There is great interaction between these three factors, and when dysfunction occurs that leads to the alteration of one, the others are generally affected as well.

FAULTY POSTURAL SET

As previously discussed, faulty posture not only affects specific tissues by placing increased strain on them during the maintenance of the posture, it also disturbs the postural set from which movement patterns will be derived. This includes the stabilization responses to internal and external perturbations. The postural set in which an individual engages at the moment of the introduction of the perturbation will, in part, determine the efficiency with which the stabilization response is carried out. In the case of the forward head posture, for example, there will be positional relationships that affect the afferentation from the tissues involved (influencing somatosensory input; see later discussion) as well as the moment arms of the muscles that are required to produce the response. As discussed in Chapter 3, those muscles that are shorter and whose muscle bellies are closer to the axis of rotation of the spinal segment(s) that they stabilize are the best equipped to produce fast, efficient stabilization responses. Forward head posture produces a destabilizing effect on the cervical spine in part because, as has been shown by Vasavada et al,[101] extension of the upper cervical spine increases the moment arm of the SCM for upper cervical extension, and flexion of the lower cervical spine increases the moment arm of the SCM for lower cervical flexion. This alteration in moment arms gives the SCM a greater mechanical advantage, at the expense of the deep cervical flexors and lower cervical/upper thoracic extensors. Because the SCM is a long muscle, it is not adequately suited for producing stabilizing responses, thus leading to a "destabilizing effect"[101] on the cervical spine.

![CLINICAL PEARL]

The effect of postural set on stability responses can easily be demonstrated. Have a person stand in a faulty postural set (see Chap. 14)—with the chin jutted forward, and hyperextension of the upper cervical spine, and hyperkyphosis of the thoracic spine—and gently but firmly apply a push to his or her upper thoracic area from behind. Note the magnitude of movement of the cervical spine in a mild "whiplash" fashion. Then place the individual in an optimum postural set (see Chap. 27)—with elevation of the posterosuperior portion of the head, elongated cervical spine, and chin slightly tucked—and introduce another push of the same magnitude to the same area. Note the marked difference in the resultant movement that occurs. This experiment illustrates why someone who is struck from behind in a motor vehicle accident will incur far greater injury if he or she is sitting in a faulty postural set as opposed to a correct postural set.

FAULTY SOMATOSENSORY INPUT

In order for appropriate stabilization responses to be elicited, there must be normal, harmonious communication between the locomotor system and the CNS[100, 102]

(Fig. 4–7). Joint, muscle, and skin dysfunction, as well as faulty movement patterns, can markedly disturb this delicate communication and thus compromise the quality of the stabilization mechanisms that are elicited in response to perturbations.

One of the functions of joint mechanoreceptors, in particular, is to prime the gamma motor neurons for quick response to external perturbation.[103–105] This priming readies the muscle spindle for sudden stretch and allows for an early, quick reflex response from the stabilizing muscles. With joint dysfunction, a decrease in the afferentation from these joint mechanoreceptors occurs, thus compromising on a segment-specific level the stability of the intervertebral joint. As a result, the presence of joint dysfunction can lead to dynamic instability of the segment involved. This phenomenon was suggested in the lumbar spine in a study by Hides et al,[106] who showed through scanning ultrasound decreased cross sectional area of the multifidis (a primary stabilizing muscle) at the level and side of acute or subacute low back pain. The segment at which the muscle wasting was found was identified in 24 of 26 subjects as exhibiting joint dysfunction, as determined by motion palpation examination.

> ### ❗ CLINICAL PEARL
>
> It may be difficult for some people to conceptualize the presence of instability in a segment that exhibits joint dysfunction, which, by definition, indicates hypomobility. However, remember that we are not referring to *passive* instability here, which would involve *excessive* mobility, but *dynamic* instability, which involves a decrease in the ability of the spinal stabilizing system to quickly activate the appropriate muscles to maintain the intersegmental neutral zones in response to perturbation. Dynamic instability is primarily a neurological phenomenon and occurs in the presence of *hypomobility;* that is, joint dysfunction.

Normal afferentation is important not only on a segmental level, but on a global level as well. One of the purposes of somatosensory input is to detect the support surface from which a stabilization response must be elicited. When stabilization responses are elicited in the standing position, the support surface is contacted by the feet. Thus, normal afferentation from the feet is essential in the efficiency of the response. Joint or muscle dysfunction in the feet can alter this afferentation.

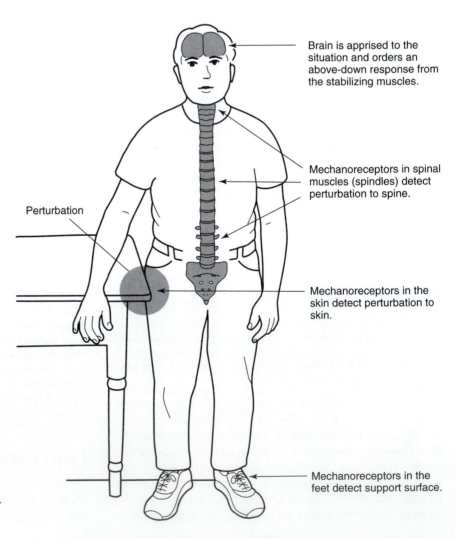

Brain is apprised to the situation and orders an above-down response from the stabilizing muscles.

Mechanoreceptors in spinal muscles (spindles) detect perturbation to spine.

Perturbation

Mechanoreceptors in the skin detect perturbation to skin.

Mechanoreceptors in the feet detect support surface.

Figure 4–7. Mechanisms of cervical stabilization.

FAULTY FOCAL MOTOR PROGRAM

Faulty somatosensory input resulting from chronic dysfunction in the locomotor system can produce alteration in the motor programs for a variety of locomotor activities, including those of stability mechanisms. The alteration is plastic[92] and tends to remain until a change is made in the program from the periphery. Plastic alteration in motor programs was demonstrated by Gurfinkle et al (as referenced by Gahery and Massion[107]), who showed that when individuals were confined to bed for "a few weeks" their stability responses to movement disappeared, but reappeared after movement was restored.

The faulty program may produce directions to the active subsystem such that excessive or insufficient muscle activity is generated, and the generation of this activity occurs too late to adequately stabilize the spinal segments. The instability that results leads to strain of the muscles involved in the response as well as the potential for overstretching of the joint capsule and abnormal loading of the disc that result when movements are allowed to exceed the intervertebral neutral zones.[92] Evidence of this program alteration was suggested in a study by Lauren et al,[108] in which tests of psychomotor speed were given to a group of 486 subjects. These tests consisted of quickly moving the hand from one pad to another on command. The authors found that those subjects who exhibited the greatest and least psychomotor speed had the greatest likelihood of developing neck pain over the next year. The authors suggested that the slow speed group were at risk due to inability to produce stabilization responses in time to reduce the effects of perturbations, while the high speed group were at risk due to overreaction of their responses. In either case, the motor program that determines these responses was dysfunctional.

Perturbations that have the potential to disturb the stability of the spine and produce microtrauma can be in the form of external events, such as being jostled in a crowd or riding on a train (external perturbations producing reactive responses). But it must be appreciated that even the simple movement of a limb serves as an internal perturbation to the cervical spine, to which the stabilizing system must respond effectively (with proactive responses) to maintain the intervertebral neutral zones within their normal limits.[109, 110]

MUSCLE FIBER TRANSFORMATION

With injury and dysfunction, an alteration can occur in the fibers of the cervical muscles that can impact the ability of these muscles to act as effective stabilizers. Uhlig et al[111] showed that in patients with chronic cervical pain resistant to treatment, a transformation of muscle fibers occurred in several cervical muscles from type I (slow, fatigue-resistant) to type IIB (fast, fatigable). Type I fibers have a slower reaction time but are very fatigue resistant,[112] and thus have a high endurance capacity. Their role in stabilization

comes from their ability to provide stability over a prolonged period of time. Type IIB fibers have a quick reaction time but fatigue easily;[112] thus, they are ideal for situations in which sudden, large perturbations are introduced to the system (e.g., being sharply pushed by another person or being struck in an automobile accident), but are not able to maintain their stabilization capacity with ongoing, low-grade perturbations (e.g., walking and extremity movements). As Sparto et al have shown,[113] fatigue is an important factor in the effectiveness of stability mechanisms—stability decreases as fatigue increases. Thus, the transformation of type I fibers to type IIB fibers compromises stability of the cervical spine by changing muscle fibers that are well equipped to contribute to ongoing stability into those that are ill-equipped for this function.

Hallgren et al[114] have shown that, in chronic head and neck pain patients, death of muscle fibers and infiltration of fatty tissues may occur in the rectus capitis posterior major and minor muscles. This change can lead to compromised stability in a number of ways. First, decreased afferentation from the mechanoreceptors in these muscles can lead to disturbance of the somatosensory input that is essential to stability responses, as well as perpetuating pain perception due to the decreased nociception-inhibiting function of mechanoreception. Second, the recti capiti, being small intrinsic muscles, are important segmental stabilizers. Degeneration decreases their ability to serve this function. Finally, because these tissue changes produce tightness in these muscles, the forward head posture that results can compromise the postural set of the head and neck.

PASSIVE INSTABILITY

Passive instability results from disruption of the passive subsystem of the spinal stability system,[92] which is primarily made up of the spinal ligaments. Thus, passive instability is also commonly referred to as ligamentous instability, although, as will be seen, there are varying degrees of stability loss that can occur with ligamentous injury. As discussed in Chapter 3, ligaments only provide stability to the intervertebral joints at end range. Thus, it is at end range, only, that disruption in the stabilizing function of ligaments is manifest. Passive instability is far less common than dynamic instability and usually occurs as a result of trauma in which there is marked injury to the ligaments.[115] Passive instability is considered a risk factor for chronicity in cases of whiplash.[116]

McGregor and Mior[117, 118] separate abnormally excessive motion of the cervical intervertebral joint into hypermobility and instability. They define segmental hypermobility as "the mobility of a given motion segment of the cervical spine which is excessive and is accompanied by local and/or peripheral symptoms, but not so extreme as to be life threatening or require surgery."[117] Instability is defined as: "The pathological state of motion at an intervertebral level in the cervical spine that results in clinically intolerable symptoms, as in cord or root damage, requiring prolonged bracing or surgery. Also involved are aberrations in neutral and/or flexion-extension x-rays, such as greater than 3.5 mm translation and/or greater than 11 degrees difference in vertebral angulation.[118] Both hypermobility and instability, as defined by McGregor and Mior, can be seen as different degrees of what we are discussing here under the heading of passive instability; that is, a decrease in the ability of the passive subsystem of the spinal stability system to adequately provide protection against injury to the spinal motion segment at end range.

Passive and dynamic instability interact in that the presence of passive instability exacerbates dynamic instability. This relationship was demonstrated experimentally by Ogon et al,[119] who found that in the normal spinal segment the velocity and acceleration of movements are fairly uniform regardless of direction of movement (i.e., flexion-extension, rotation, lateral flexion). But when a spinal motion segment is affected by passive instability, these parameters become unequal and vary depending on the direction of motion. Thus, in the presence of passive instability, the neural control subsystem has a variety of velocity and acceleration data to contend with and for which it must attempt to provide dynamic stability, and this places increased strain on this subsystem.

WHAT IS THE IMPACT OF CERVICAL DYSFUNCTION ON THE CNS?

As discussed in Chapter 3, the cervical spine is the most intense area in the locomotor system with regard to afferent input into the CNS, particularly from the muscle spindles of the intrinsic muscles. This afferent input provides important information to the CNS that is utilized in a variety of locomotor activities.

The most important connection between the cervical spine and the CNS in this regard is that to the vestibular nucleus. It is via this connection that the cervical spine can impact the activity of muscles throughout the locomotor system. This cervical-vestibular connection affects both the activity of individual muscles and the posture and stability mechanisms. Thus, with dysfunction in the cervical spine, individual muscle activity and postural and stability mechanisms can be disrupted.

Perhaps the most important reflex activity that can mediate alteration of function in the locomotor system as a result of cervical dysfunction is that of the tonic neck reflex (TNR). In normal circumstances, the TNR distributes muscle tone throughout the locomotor system as a result of cervical movements.[120–122] The TNR is usually quiescent but it becomes manifest in situations that require a high degree of skill or power. It also may become manifest in the presence of cervical dysfunction. This was suggested by Fukushima and Hinoki,[123] who showed that placing nor-

mal subjects in a cervical collar altered the EMG activity in the lower extremities during stepping activities. This alteration in muscle activity may cause the tendency to develop hypertonicity or inhibition of certain trunk or extremity muscles.

The connection of cervical afferents to the vestibular nucleus also allows the cervical spine to influence equilibrium sense. Disturbance of cervical input to the vestibular nucleus can manifest as vertigo or disequilibrium syndromes[124–127] in some patients, but it is usually well compensated. However, this compensation can place increased strain on the system as a whole, leading to breakdown and dysfunction. This was suggested by Abrahams and Falchetto[128] and Abrahams[129] in studying cats, wherein they showed that when the nerve to the biventer cervicis muscle (a muscle present in the cat, but not in the human) was cut, a variety of problems with gait and frequent falls occurred. But eventually, adaptation occurred and the cats were able to engage in normal activities without trouble, and only had problems when trying to jump and engage in rapid movements. This adaptation requires the remainder of the locomotor system to work harder to properly carry out simple movements, and thus lowers the margin of error in the system, predisposing to the susceptibility to injury and dysfunction.

With the cervicorespiratory reflex, afferentation from the cervical spine has influence on the drive to the respiratory muscles.[130] Although little is known about this recently discovered reflex, clinical manifestations of faulty breathing patterns are common in cervical patients.[131, 132] Faulty breathing is generally seen as an important source of overstrain to the cervical muscles, but it must be noted that the faulty breathing pattern may be initiated by cervical dysfunction and its effect on breathing via the cervicorespiratory reflex. Joint or muscle dysfunction, or both, in the cervical spine may alter the drive to the respiratory muscles such that there develops a tendency to overactivate the accessory muscles of respiration and inhibit the diaphragm. This association will be explored further in Chapter 14.

DISTURBANCE IN EYE-HEAD-NECK COORDINATION

Disturbance of eye-head-neck coordination and oculomotor reflexes resulting from cervical trauma is well documented.[133–139] It has been shown to be present in patients with "tension-type headaches" as well.[140, 141]

The most common oculomotor reflexes affected are saccades and smooth pursuit, although sympathetic-related eye functions have also been shown to be involved.[142–144] It is generally thought that this eye motility dysfunction, particularly smooth pursuit and saccades, relates to disruption in the normal afferentation from the mechanoreceptors in the cervical muscles as a result of trauma and muscle dysfunction. Hypertonicity of certain muscles in the

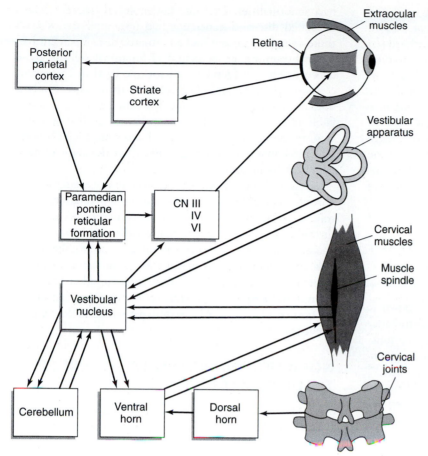

Figure 4–8. Control of eye-head-neck stability.

cervical spine, particularly the cervical rotators (SCM, upper trapezius, splenius capitis, obliquus capitis inferior) causes an increase in the afferent input from these muscles, whereas any muscles that may be inhibited produce decreased afferentation. This imbalanced input conflicts with afferent input from other sensory structures and creates alteration in the reflex processes that control these eye movements.[133, 137, 140, 141, 145] In addition, disturbance in the velocity of saccades is caused by the disruption of attentional processing that is common after cervical trauma.[146–148] Attentional processing is discussed in greater detail in Chapter 18. Control mechanisms for eye-head-neck stability are illustrated in Figure 4–8.

There is also evidence that oculomotor dysfunction may be a factor in the perpetuation of cervical pain. Hildingsson et al[134] assessed smooth pursuit and saccades in 39 subjects who had had cervical injury 6 months or more before the authors' assessment. Twenty still had disabling symptoms and the remainder were asymptomatic. They found disturbance of smooth pursuit in 18 of the 20 subjects that were still symptomatic and abnormal saccades in 9 of these 20. There was no difference in these functions between the asymptomatic group and a control group. In a second study,[135] the same group of researchers assessed 38 patients within 3 months of injury and again an average of 15 months after injury. They found that on initial exami-

nation, 8 subjects exhibited abnormal oculomotor function. Upon follow-up, these 8 subjects were still abnormal, but an additional 5 who were originally normal had developed oculomotor dysfunction. All of the 13 with oculomotor dysfunction at follow-up were still symptomatic, whereas only 5 of the 25 subjects with normal oculomotor function were symptomatic. These results do not demonstrate clearly that oculomotor dysfunction is the reason for chronicity in these cases, but suggest that it could possibly play a role.

⚠ CLINICAL PEARL

Karlburg et al[149] showed that restraining the cervical spine in a rigid cervical collar for 5 days produced a significant decrease in the velocity of voluntary saccades and alteration of smooth pursuit movements in 11 healthy subjects. This finding supports the argument against use of a rigid collar except in those extreme situations in which it may be necessary. And even then, use of a soft collar should be limited to the initial stages only (see Chap. 21).

Coordination of head and neck movements is closely related to that of eye movements and can also be disturbed by cervical spine dysfunction. The relationship between cervical spine dysfunction and coordination of head and neck movements was first shown by Revel et al,[150] who found a significantly decreased ability to reproduce head position in patients with chronic neck pain compared to controls. Head-neck incoordination has since been shown to occur after whiplash[151, 152] and in headache patients.[153] As with oculomotor dysfunction, it is believed that disturbance of normal afferentation from the muscles of the cervical spine is the cause of the incoordination. In this case, there is probably also involvement of joint dysfunction and the alteration of gamma motor neuron function that results from dysafferentation. The assessment and measurement of these functions will be discussed in Chapter 14.

CEPHALIC DYSFUNCTION RELATED TO CERVICAL DYSFUNCTION

Disturbance of certain brain functions has been shown to occur after cervical injury.[146–148, 154, 155] This disturbance includes attentional processing,[146, 147, 156] cognitive functions,[147, 156, 157] disturbed accommodation,[156] poor concentration,[146] and impaired adaptation to light intensity.[146] The common presence of these findings caused Radanov to coin the term "cervicoencephalic syndrome"[156] for cervical injury that also features a variety of symptoms and signs related to dysfunction in higher centers. These disturbances can be found in the absence of head injury[156] or evidence of morphological changes in the brain.[155] The symptoms related to this dysfunction can be virtually indistinguishable from those resulting from direct head injury.[158]

Although it has been suggested that this cerebral dysfunction is related to compromised blood flow to the brain resulting from cervical dysfunction,[159] this theory has been questioned.[160] Probably the most compelling theory is that originally proposed by Radanov,[156] who suggested that this dysfunction may be related to disturbed afferentation from the cervical spine to the brain stem, although, it may also relate to intense nociceptive bombardment alone. See Chapter 12 for greater detail regarding this phenomenon.

HOW DOES CERVICAL DYSFUNCTION CAUSE PAIN?

Pain is unique among sensory modalities; while, for example, hearing is directly related to the intensity of auditory signals, there is little relationship between intensity of nociceptive signals and pain experience.[161] To complicate matters further, research has demonstrated an inconsistent relationship between the presence of structural pathology and the presence of cervical-related pain.[162, 163] Boden et al[163] found that in 63 individuals with no history of neck pain, 19 percent had abnormalities that were demonstrable on magnetic resonance imaging scans. Fourteen percent of those under 40 years of age and 28 percent of those over 40

had abnormalities. Of those under 40, 10 percent had a herniated disc and 4 percent had foraminal stenosis. Of those over 40, 5 pecent had a herniated disc, 3 percent had bulging disc, and 20 percent had foraminal stenosis. Disc degeneration was found at at least one level in 25 percent of those under 40 and 60 percent in those over 40. This does not mean, of course, that structural pathology is incapable of creating pain in the cervical spine. It does mean that, in the majority of patients, doctors must look beyond structural abnormalities in the search for the cause of most pain and dysfunction.

The lack of evidence for a structural explanation for chronic neck pain has led to a greater appreciation of the role of dysfunction in the development of cervical syndromes. But the question remains: how does dysfunction cause pain? There are two general mechanisms by which this can occur. One is specific ongoing tissue irritation brought about by the dysfunction, and the other relates to central and peripheral nervous system changes that create an environment conducive to the perpetuation of the pain experience.

NOCICEPTION ARISING FROM DIRECT TISSUE DAMAGE

The simplest mechanism by which the experience of pain develops is that of activation of specific nociceptive receptors in a tissue by mechanical, chemical, or thermal (or a combination of these) means, which leads to transmission of impulses along small-diameter group III (A delta) and IV (C) fibers to the dorsal horn, where synapse occurs directly or indirectly with one of three classes of neurons.[164] Projection neurons relay the information to higher centers, excitatory interneurons relay the information to the projection neurons, and inhibitory interneurons modulate the amount of nociceptive transmission to higher centers. The most prominent tract in which this transmission is relayed is the lateral spinothalamic tract. Bolton and Tracey[165] have noted that in the rat, the majority of spinothalamic tract neurons are located in the first four cervical segments and that some of these cervical spinothalamic neurons have receptive field properties that include the entire body, unlike the majority of spinothalamic neurons in the other spinal cord levels. Projection neurons decussate before entering the spinothalamic tract. This tract then ascends in the anterolateral white matter to terminate in the thalamus.

Other spinal cord tracts that are responsible for transmission of nociceptive impulses from the cervical spine include:

The spinoreticular tract, which ascends both ipsilaterally and contralaterally in the anterolateral white matter. Some of the neurons in this tract synapse in both the reticular formation and the thalamus. Reticular formation neurons in turn project to the periaqueductal gray area, to influence descending pain modulation pathways (see later discussion).[166]

The spinomesencephalic tract, which also ascends in the anterolateral white matter and terminates in the mesencephalic reticular formation and the periaqueductal gray area.[164]

The spinocervical tract, which runs in the posterolateral white matter to the lateral cervical nucleus, which then sends projections across the midline to the medial lemniscus and then to various brain stem and thalamic nuclei.[164, 166]

The dorsal column tract, which ascends ipsilaterally and synapses in the nucleus gracilis and cuneatus, which in turn send projections across the midline to the thalamus.[164, 166]

The major tracts that carry nociceptive impulses from the cervical spine are depicted in Figure 4–9.

From the thalamus, transmission is made to a variety of cortical and subcortical centers, as depicted in Figure 4–10.[166] It is in these centers that localization as well as physical and emotional responses to the nociception are made.

PERIPHERAL SENSITIZATION AND ACTIVATION OF RECEPTORS

Acute pain that is experienced with direct tissue injury occurs as a result of mechanical or chemical sensitization and activation of nociceptors in the involved tissues. When a certain tissue in the cervical spine is damaged, be it muscle, ligament, joint capsule, disc, or other nociceptor-innervated tissue (Table 4–4), a variety of chemicals are released

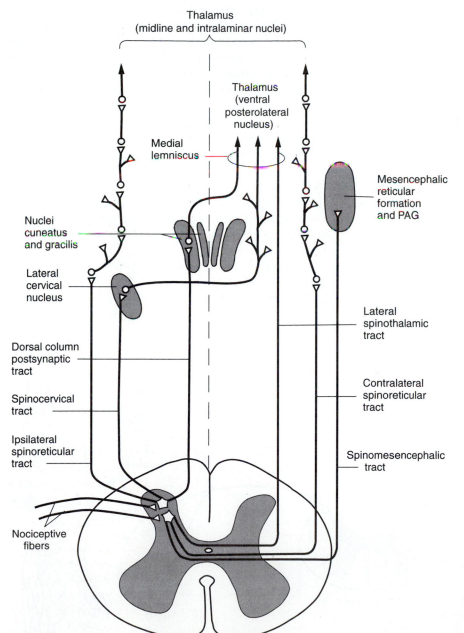

Figure 4–9. The major spinal cord tracts that carry nociceptive information from the cervical spine.

Figure 4–10. Pathways by which nociceptive impulses travel from the thalamus to the cerebral cortex.

(Reprinted with permission from Figure 13–10 of Haldeman S. The neurophysiology of spinal pain. In: Haldeman S, ed. Principles and Practice of Chiropractic. 2nd ed. Norwalk, Conn: Appleton & Lange; 1992:165–184.)

Table 4–4: Pain-sensitive Tissues in the Cervical Spine

Joint capsules	Ligaments
Muscles	Skin and subcutaneous tissue (including fascia)
Outer annulus of the disc	Blood vessels
Nerve root	Dura mater
Nerve root sleeve	Periosteum of the vertebrae

from the injured tissue and from the nociceptive receptors that have the ability to contribute to the development of this sensitization and activation. This chemical release results from cellular damage in the tissue as well as being part of the inflammatory process. The damage need not be gross and macroscopic; repetitive microtrauma can produce it as well.[167]

! CLINICAL PEARL

Peripheral sensitization of receptors is a second mechanism, this time applying to the acute stage, by which normal movement can become painful in patients with cervical dysfunction.

The course of events that occurs is illustrated in Figure 4–11. When damage occurs, various chemicals such as bradykinin, serotonin, prostaglandin E_2, and potassium ions are released from the tissue.[164] In addition, local mast cells release histamine. The peripheral terminals of nociceptive neurons also release chemicals that contribute to the process of nociceptive transmission. The most important and best known of these is substance P.[63, 164] Bradykinin, potassium ions, serotonin, and histamine serve to directly activate the nociceptive afferent neurons,[168] while prostaglandins, leukotrienes, and substance P serve to sensitize the receptor, reducing its threshold for activation by chemical or mechanical means, increasing spontaneous activity, and causing prolonged firing in response to stimuli that would normally be subthreshold, such as innocuous local pressure.[169, 170]

Peripheral sensitization leads to primary hyperalgesia, defined as an increased response of the afferent to a noxious stimulus.[170–172] Substance P also facilitates the release of histamine from mast cells, in addition to causing vasodi-

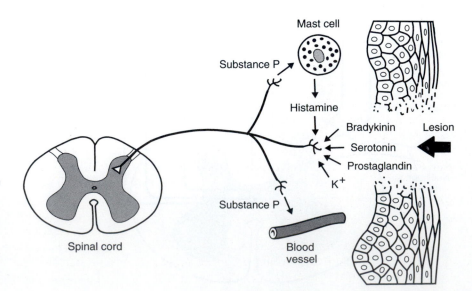

Figure 4–11. Nociception arising from acute tissue injury.

(Reprinted with permission from Figure 27–10 of Jessel TM, Kelly DD. Pain and analgesia. In: Kandel ER. Schwartz JH, Jessel TM, eds. Principles of Neural Science. 3rd ed. Norwalk, Conn: Appleton & Lange; 1991:385–399.)

latation of blood vessels, leading to edema and further release of bradykinin.[164] Recent evidence suggests that the chemical release by the peripheral terminals is carefully regulated at the level of the dorsal root ganglion and that modulation of nociceptive input, previously thought to only occur in the CNS (see later discussion), occurs in the periphery via this regulation.[173]

In joints, an additional phenomenon occurs that further leads to increased nociceptive transmission. A number of receptors, called "silent nociceptors," that lie within the joint capsule normally do not respond to mechanical stimulation, but in the presence of chemical sensitization resulting from tissue damage and inflammation, they "awaken" and become responsive, even to normal movement.[32, 63] By this mechanism, common movements can produce pain, as is commonly seen after injury such as whiplash trauma.

Dysfunction, in the form of joint dysfunction, muscle dysfunction, faulty movement patterns, or dynamic instability, can produce nociception directly or indirectly via the previously illustrated mechanisms. Directly, it can cause increased strain on the tissues involved in the dysfunction as they attempt to carry out normal movements. Indirectly, it can create increased strain on related tissues that may be affected by the dysfunction.

An example of dysfunction causing pain directly is hypertonicity of the upper trapezius and inhibition of the lower trapezius causing disruption of the normal pattern of shoulder abduction. This alteration can lead to increased strain on the upper trapezius due to overwork, leading to the development of myofascial TrPs in the muscle, which can cause sufficient chemical-mediated nociceptive transmission to create the experience of temporal headache. Or, depending on the specific types of activities in which the individual may engage on a regular basis, this same dysfunctional scenario may indirectly lead to the development of rotator cuff tendinitis as a result of increased strain on the rotator cuff with repetitive use of the upper extremity, as would occur with racquet or throwing sports. This repetitive action would lead to a combination of chemical and mechanical sensitization and depolarization of nociceptive afferents in the tendons of the rotator cuff.

Another example is microtrauma such as that produced as a result of functional instability at the intersegmental level. Continuous low-level injury to the zygapophyseal joint capsule as a result of repetitive compromise of the neutral zone of the intervertebral segment will produce the chemical response previously discussed which, due to sensitization, will set the stage for pain experience related to mechanical perturbation.

FACILITATION OF CENTRAL PAIN PATHWAYS

Perhaps the more powerful mechanism by which dysfunction can lead to pain, particularly chronic pain, results from alteration of CNS pain pathways. Recent research has contributed a great deal to our understanding of chronic pain in general, and of chronic neck pain in particular. One of the important concepts that has been discovered is that pain is not merely an acute phenomenon that signals actual or potential tissue damage, but that ongoing pain experience can involve, in addition to the peripheral stimulation of nociceptive afferents, several levels of the CNS.[174] As previously discussed, the chemical mediators produced as a result of tissue damage can cause either sensitization or activation of nociceptive receptors in the periphery, leading to the transmission of impulses along the group III (A delta) or group IV (C) fibers innervating the receptors. This process leads not only to transmission of impulses along the ascending nociceptive tracts, but also causes a variety of changes in the dorsal horn and other areas of the CNS, which have the potential to perpetuate nociceptive transmission and, thus, the experience of pain. The presence of dysfunction in the locomotor system greatly enhances these mechanisms.

These processes lead to sensitization of CNS pain pathways. Sensitization is a normal physiological phenomenon and under normal circumstances, when healing of the injured tissues takes place properly and without residual dysfunction, the sensitized state resolves. But if normal healing does not take place and, more importantly, residual dysfunction remains, the state of central sensitization may remain and chronic pain may result.[70] This pain experience can become independent of the degree of tissue nociception that is being generated.

CHANGES IN THE DORSAL HORN

Nociceptive input, particularly if it is intense, creates a central excitatory state that first involves the dorsal horn.[175, 176] In this state, the dorsal horn cells develop increased sensitivity to afferent stimuli. If this initial nociceptive input does not resolve, or resolves incompletely, a state of abnormal neural processing can develop that can lead to chronic changes.

As previously discussed, one of the classes of dorsal horn cells to which nociceptive afferent neurons synapse are projection cells that transmit signals to higher centers. There are two types of projection cells that perform this function. One type is nociceptive-specific and responds preferentially to noxious stimuli. The others are called "wide dynamic range" cells; they respond to a variety of stimuli, both noxious and non-noxious.[167] Both types of cells can become sensitized to nociceptive input, thus responding more intensely to subsequent stimuli. But the wide dynamic range neurons have been shown to become more intensely sensitized than nociceptive-specific neurons and, of course, these receive input from non-nociceptive sources as well as nociceptive.[70] In addition, once they are sensitized, wide dynamic range neurons often will respond as intensely to non-nociceptive input as they did to the original nociceptive input, due to strengthened synaptic links with these non-nociceptive afferents which are normally ineffectual.[37, 177] This causes the CNS to misinterpret the intense activity from non-nociceptive input, particularly from deep tissues such as joints, ligaments, and muscles, as being painful because of the intensity of the input. So by this mechanism, normal movement can continue to produce pain even in the absence of peripheral tissue damage, or in the presence of low-grade peripheral tissue damage.

! CLINICAL PEARL

Sensitization of wide dynamic range neurons is the third mechanism by which normal movement can become painful, this time in chronic cervical pain syndromes.

Wide dynamic range cells are also facilitated by attentional and behavioral processes.[178] Because these cells are capable of transmitting a variety of stimuli, both nociceptive and non-nociceptive, those stimuli to which the greatest conscious attention is paid are those most likely to be processed in higher centers. Also, when behavior of the locomotor system is consistent with a pain state (i.e., pain behavior), the afferent information coming from mechanoreceptors throughout the system reflects this state. This may increase the likelihood that wide dynamic range neurons will transmit mechanoreceptive signals along the central nociceptive pathways. Thus, when an individual pays greatest attention to the nociceptive impulses, and when the individual behaves as one would behave when in pain, the intensity of the pain experience will be greater.

In addition to primary hyperalgesia, which occurs as a result of peripheral sensitization, secondary hyperalgesia can occur, in which there is an increased response of the tissues around the original painful area to noxious stimulation.[37, 170, 171] The physiological purpose for this in the acute stage is probably to create pain in advance of the injured tissue being touched or otherwise stimulated in order to protect it.[179] Secondary hyperalgesia results from alteration of the receptivity of nociception-signaling interneurons in the dorsal horn, which, in addition to responding to noxious stimuli, develop the ability to fire in response to innocuous mechanical stimuli.[37, 180, 181] This secondary hyperalgesia can lead to the development of hyperalgesic skin zones; areas of skin that become painful to even innocuous stimuli that at times can be quite bothersome. Hyperalgesic skin zones will be further discussed in Chapter 14.

! CLINICAL PEARL

Secondary hyperalgesia is the fourth mechanism by which normal movements can cause the perception of pain in patients with cervical dysfunction.

Intense or persistent nociceptive input can also cause an increase in the receptive fields of dorsal horn cells,[37, 70, 169, 171, 175, 182–186] meaning they are capable of responding to input from a greater number of incoming afferent fibers, and a greater variety of types of stimuli. Interestingly, nociception arising from deep tissues causes expansion of the receptive fields of dorsal horn to both deep and cutaneous input.[183] "Windup" also occurs in which the normal stimulus-response relationship between primary afferent and dorsal horn neurons becomes altered. Windup causes the development of progressive increase in the firing of the dorsal horn neuron for the duration of the stimulus,[169, 171, 182, 184] and increased background activity in these cells,[171, 184] wherein spontaneous activity occurs independent of afferent input.

It is important to note that these alterations in the dorsal horn are not limited to the spinal cord segment(s) from which the injured tissue is innervated. Nociceptive afferents are capable of ascending or descending three to six cord levels and exerting their influence at these levels.[36] This, in addition to the widespread neurological effects of cervical dysfunction on other parts of the locomotor system discussed later, lead to the "chain reactions" that are common with cervical syndromes. It is also important to note that these alterations can be long-lasting even if the nociceptive input is short term.[183]

REFERRED PAIN

The cervical spine is notorious for creating pain that is perceived, not only in the cervical spine itself, but in other areas as well. This phenomenon is known as *referred pain*. As will be seen in Chapter 17, different cervical tissues and segmental levels can cause referred pain in various areas of the body and are important clues in the search for the primary pain generator in cervical spine syndromes. Several studies over the years have uncovered the patterns of referred pain that develop as a result of irritation to cervical tissues.[187–197] Each of these patterns has a characteristic distribution that can help identify the tissue from which it is arising.

The most likely mechanism by which referred pain occurs is the development of new receptive fields as a result of intense noxious stimulation of dorsal horn nocireceptive cells.[183, 198] A certain dorsal horn neuron may contain a receptive field for a certain area, but when subjected to intense nociceptive input, there occurs an awakening of previously dormant receptive fields of that cell for tissues that may be remote from that site. Thus, the patient can experience pain that appears to be arising from the remote tissue. The areas that are most likely to be included in new receptive fields of cervical cord segments are those of the upper limbs, head, chest, and thoracic area.[199] In general, referred pain from the upper cervical segments travels cephalad and that from the lower cervical spine travels caudad.

Several studies have shown that the size of the area of referred pain correlates with the intensity and duration of the primary nociceptive input.[197] These referred pain patterns do not follow a typical dermatomal distribution, as might be expected with pain arising from irritation to a nerve root. They are, however, segmentally organized, causing Inman and Saunders[200] to propose the concept of sclerotomes—that the areas to which pain is referred are areas that arise from the same embryological sclerotome during early development. The patterns can be useful for diagnostic purposes. These referred pain patterns and their clinical utility will be discussed further in Chapter 17.

One area in which understanding of the phenomenon of referred pain is particularly important is the role of the cervical spine in headache. There is a unique anatomical relationship between the dorsal horns of the upper three cervical spinal cord segments and the pars caudalis portion of the trigeminal nucleus, such that these areas are blended, with no anatomical distinction between the two.[201–206] This area has been termed by Bogduk the *trigeminocervical nucleus*,[207, 208] although it is not an actual anatomical nucleus in the typical sense (Fig. 4–12). The pars caudalis is that portion of the trigeminal nucleus in which pain and temperature change afferents synapse.

Thus, nociceptive information from tissues innervated by the first three cervical roots, because of the convergence of these pathways, can lead to pain being felt in any area innervated by the trigeminal nerve (Fig. 4–13). Conversely, nociception arising from the trigeminal system can be perceived as pain in areas innervated by the cervical system.[209]

Pain referral mediated through the trigeminocervical nucleus occurs as a result of the expansion of the receptive field of the neuron to which synapse is made to input from other afferents that synapse in the trigeminocervical nucleus.[210] This relationship will be discussed further in Chapter 8.

CHANGES IN HIGHER CNS CENTERS

Although far more is known about the mechanisms of central facilitation of nociceptive pathways capable of enhancing the perception of pain as they relate to the dorsal horn, there is substantial evidence that similar processes occur in higher levels of the CNS as well. Neuroplastic changes such as sensitization, expanded receptive field, and altered firing patterns have been demonstrated in the thalamus and other areas of the cortex that have a relationship with pain perception.[211] Melzack[212] proposed that there is a net-

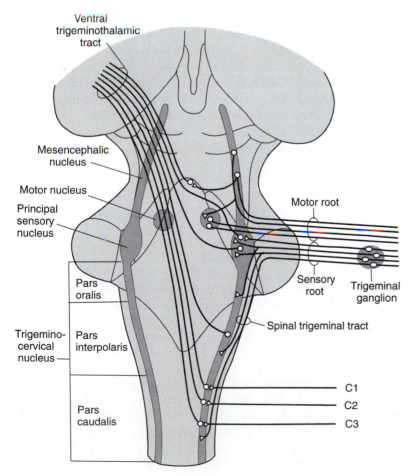

Figure 4–12. The trigeminocervical nucleus.

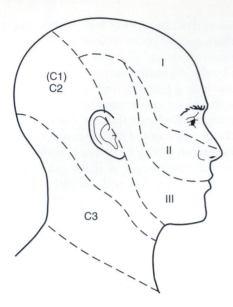

Figure 4–13. Areas from which nociception is mediated through the trigeminocervical nucleus. Sensory input is only occasionally seen in the C1 nerve root.

work of neurons scattered throughout the cortex, called a neuromatrix. This neuromatrix normally receives constant afferent input from receptors throughout the locomotor system and, in the relative absence of this input, leads to the psychological perception of pain. Melzack uses this to explain the phenomenon of phantom pain. Whether the alteration of afferent input that results from dysfunction in the locomotor system is sufficient to alter the activity of the neurons of this neuromatrix is unknown. Nonetheless, Canavero[213] disputes this theory, and suggests that a more local phenomenon that involves a reverberating circuit between the thalamus and the cortex is involved in the central facilitation of the perception of pain. He states that only a small portion of the thalamocortical system is devoted to direct sensory input from ascending pathways. A greater number of neurons in the thalamus receive input from the cortex. Thus, a large part of thalamic activity is devoted to re-entry, or reverberation of activity. Canavero feels that it is this reverberation of activity that leads to persistent pain perception. Coderre et al[184] have stated that stimulation of certain higher centers, including the thalamus, in patients undergoing surgery who have suffered chronic pain syndromes triggers the perception of this chronic pain. Pain memory rarely occurs in nonchronic pain sufferers. Therefore, there may be a central "pain memory" mechanism capable of being triggered even in the absence of peripheral stimulus.

Clearly, more work needs to be done to clarify the precise mechanisms by which cortical and subcortical processes increase pain perception. But one area for which much is known is that regarding function and dysfunction of the central inhibitory mechanisms of pain.

PAIN INHIBITORY MECHANISMS

Absence of pain is dependent upon a delicate balance between the anti- and pro-nociceptive systems.[213] The antinociceptive system acts primarily at the level of the dorsal horn and has components that arise both from the periphery and along descending tracts from the brain.

Peripheral Mechanisms

From the periphery, the mechanism is the well-known "gate control," first proposed by Melzack and Wall.[214] The original gate control theory has since been modified somewhat; however, it remains essentially the same from a conceptual standpoint. Afferentation from large-diameter, myelinated mechanoreceptive fibers have connection to the same nocireceptive projection neurons to which the nociceptive afferents synapse. In addition, each of the mechanoreceptive and nociceptive afferents have connection to an inhibitory interneuron in the dorsal horn, which serves to inhibit the transmission of impulses along the projection neuron. The mechanoreceptive afferent activates this inhibitory interneuron and effectively blocks nociceptive impulses from being transmitted along the ascending tracts.[164, 215] The nociceptive afferent inhibits the inhibitory neuron, thus preventing this interruption of nociceptive transmission, in addition to allowing the mechanoreceptive afferentation to facilitate transmission of impulses along the ascending nociceptive tracts (see Fig. 4–14).

As Kakigi and Shibasaki[216] have shown, the larger the diameter of the mechanoreceptive fiber, the more powerful the inhibitory effect. Thus, fibers such as those that transmit information related to movement (i.e., joint and muscle mechanoreceptors) have a greater impact than do smaller diameter fibers such as those that transmit tactile information. Injury or dysfunction decreases the responsiveness of these mechanoreceptors, thus interfering with their ability to inhibit nociceptive processing.[37]

As was discussed in Chapter 3, it is believed that one of the functions of joint mechanoreceptors is to contribute to the proper balance between these two afferent systems. This balance helps to modulate nociceptive transmission, and thus the experience of pain.

Central Mechanisms

In addition to this peripheral mechanism acting on the dorsal horn projection neurons, descending pathways from higher centers also serve to modulate nociceptive transmission and maintain a pain free state. This descending influence arises from a variety of centers, including the hypothalamus, locus ceruleus, nucleus raphe magnus (NRM), and ventrolateral medulla, but the central focus of this system is the periaqueductal gray area of the midbrain (PAG).

The PAG has two portions, the ventral portion and the dorsal portion. The ventral PAG projects via the NRM to the dorsal horn and primarily modulates nociception related to thermal stimuli.[171, 217, 218] It promotes immobility, recuperative behavior, and inhibition of the sympathetic system.

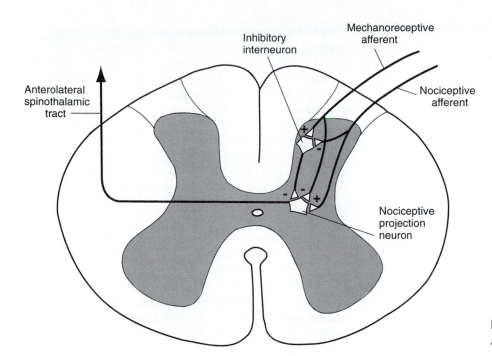

Figure 4–14. The gate control mechanism of nociceptive modulation.

The dorsal PAG projects via the nucleus paragigantocellularis to the dorsal horn and primarily modulates nociceptive input related to mechanical stimuli. It promotes fight-or-flight behavior, aversive actions, and stimulation of the sympathetic system.[164, 217, 218] Figure 4–15 illustrates the descending nociceptive modulating system.

> **! CLINICAL PEARL**
>
> As will be discussed in Appendix 19A, both the peripheral and central sources of nociceptive inhibition are activated during spinal manipulation.

Expectation, attention, arousal, and behavioral factors play a strong role in the function of this system.[178] Inputs to the PAG from higher brain centers, especially the frontal cortex, are essential for the initiation of descending nociceptive control.[219] As previously discussed with regard to wide dynamic range spinothalamic neurons, when attention is paid to pain, there occurs an inhibition of the descending modulating system. Also, pain behavior decreases the efficiency of this system. For these reasons, behavior and thought processes are extremely important in pain perception, particularly in chronic cervical pain situations. As will be seen in later chapters, this understanding is critical in the total assessment and management of the cervical patient.

In addition to the changes in the dorsal horn and cortical processing discussed thus far, nociceptive input, if intense and long lasting, can interfere with the function of the descending modulating system.[185] The mechanism by which this occurs in unknown.

> **! CLINICAL PEARL**
>
> Hoheisel and Mense[185] have pointed out that nociception arising from muscle is particularly powerful in inducing the plastic alterations in CNS processing of nociceptive information discussed in this section. This phenomenon of CNS alteration arising from muscle nociception is important because, while muscle may not always be the primary pain generator in a patient with a certain pain syndrome, muscle dysfunction that may be sufficient to cause facilitation of central pain processing will play an essential role in perpetuating the experience of pain, regardless of on what tissue the CNS focuses as the primary source. Thus, it is essential that clinicians look beyond the specific tissue that is generating pain, especially in chronic cases, and look for the key links in the chain of dysfunction that usually occurs with cervical pain syndromes. Particular attention must be paid to the muscular system in this regard.

FAULTY MOVEMENT PATTERNS AND CHRONIC CERVICAL PAIN

Faulty movement patterns represent an inappropriate manner in which the locomotor system behaves during everyday movements. This behavior presents a pattern of afferent activity to the CNS. The interpretation in higher cortical centers of the status of the locomotor system can be affected as a result. If the afferent "picture" that the locomotor system is presenting to the CNS is reflective of

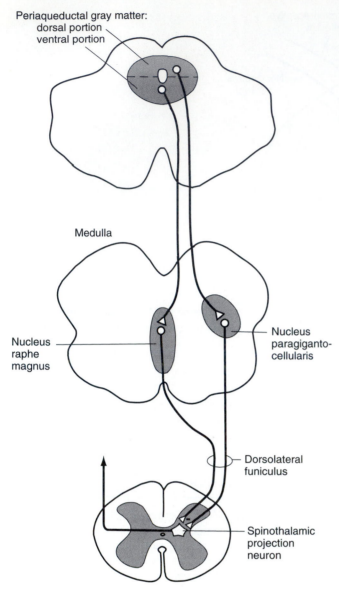

Periaqueductal gray matter:
dorsal portion
ventral portion

Medulla

Nucleus
raphe
magnus

Nucleus
paragiganto-
cellularis

Dorsolateral
funiculus

Spinothalamic
projection
neuron

Figure 4–15. The descending nociceptive modulating system.

behavior that suggests the presence of nociception, this may cause the actual perception of pain in the limbic system, independent of the degree of nociception that may be occurring.[220] Main and Watson[221] have noted that they have identified alterations in muscle recruitment patterns in low back pain patients by which they can identify patients from normal controls. As these patterns return to normal with treatment, there is a corresponding and associated decrease in fear avoidance behavior, suggesting that there may be a relationship between the aberrant movement pattern and the presence of the behavioral component of chronic pain.

Although locomotor system behavior, in the form of joint and muscle dysfunction and faulty movement pat-

terns, can produce and perpetuate changes in central processing of nociceptive input, it is important to note that this potentiation of central pain pathways still requires ongoing nociceptive input in order for the entire process to be "refreshed."[222] While nociceptive input must be intense in order to initiate the changes in the dorsal horn previously discussed, it need only be low grade for the purpose of perpetuation of these changes.[176] This is the reason why, even in chronic cervical pain patients, specific pain generators can often be identified. Thus far, with regard to the cervical spine, the most common site of pain generation has been demonstrated via anaesthetic injection techniques to be the zygapophyseal joints,[223–230] which have been shown to be the primary pain generator in about half of postcervical trauma patients whose pain has become chronic.

As the methods of detection of pain-generating tissues becomes more sophisticated, it can be expected that other tissues, particularly muscles, will be shown to be common generators of pain, as well. But in the patient with chronic pain, it is important to realize that the tissue identified by injection to be the primary pain generator may simply be the primary source of nociception that is contributing the *most* to the perpetuation and "refreshment" of central nociceptive transmission. Or, as Sheather-Reid and Cohen[176] have pointed out, injection of tissues that provides temporary relief of chronic pain may only be identifying these tissues as being most affected by the irritation produced by the overall locomotor system dysfunction or located in the area of greatest hyperalgesia. Nonetheless, these tissues should not be confused with the primary dysfunction that is underlying the entire process. The various mechanisms by which cervical dysfunction can cause pain have been presented here as separate entities; however, it is important to realize that they interact closely to produce the complex pain pictures that are seen with patients with cervical spine syndromes.

! CLINICAL PEARL

Noxious stimulation in one part of the body, if sufficiently intense, can inhibit nociceptive neurons in spinal segments innervating other tissues in the body.[217] The mechanisms and pathways by which this occurs are not clear, but it largely bypasses the PAG-NRM system. This helps explain the commonly seen phenomenon of a patient with severe cervical pain as a result of motor vehicle trauma developing low back pain several weeks after the initial traumatic event, at a time when the cervical pain is becoming less intense. In this situation, the injury to the lower back does not just somehow "appear," but, rather, the patient's perception of the nociceptive transmission from the injured lower back tissues becomes suprathreshold as a result of decreased inhibition of the CNS pathway for this transmission when the intensity of the cervical nociceptive transmission decreases.

CONCLUSION

To understand cervical spine syndromes, it is essential to look beyond pathoanatomy and towards dysfunction. There are several ways in which dysfunction can develop in the cervical spine, and several forms this dysfunction can take, ranging from joint dysfunction to muscle dysfunction, from faulty movement patterns to instability. In most cases, these different forms interact with each other to create a complex clinical picture.

Because of the exceptionally intense neurophysiological interaction between the cervical spine and the rest of the body, cervical spine dysfunction can have wide-ranging effects, leading to the development of "chains" of dysfunction. The purpose of this chapter was to present the current state of knowledge and theories regarding cervical spine dysfunction so that a foundation can be formed upon which strategies for diagnosis, treatment and rehabilitation can be understood. The remainder of this book will be devoted to exploring these strategies so that a systematic, rational approach can be taken to patients who are suffering from cervical-related syndromes.

REFERENCES

1. Friedenberg ZB, Miller WT. Degenerative disc disease of the cervical spine: A comparative study of asymptomatic and symptomatic patients. *J Bone Joint Surg* 1963;45A:1171–1178.
2. Boden SD, McCowin PR, Davis DO, et al. Abnormal magnetic resonance imaging scans of the cervical spine in asymptomatic subjects. *J Bone Joint Surg* 1990;72A:1178–1184.
3. Wood KB, Blair JM, Aepple DM, et al. The natural history of asymptomatic thoracic disc herniations. *Spine* 1997;22(5):525–530.
4. van Tulder MW, Assenfelft WJJ, Koes BW, Bouter LM. Spinal radiographic findings and nonspecific low back pain: A systematic review of observational studies. *Spine* 1997;22(4):427–434.
5. Wood KB, Garvey TA, Gundry C, Heitkoff KB. Magnetic resonance imaging of the thoracic spine: Evaluation in asymptomatic individuals. *J Bone Joint Surg* 1995;77A:1631–1638.
6. Boos N, Rieder R, Schade V, et al. The diagnostic accuracy of magnetic resonance imaging, work perception and psychosocial factors in identifying symptomatic disc herniations. *Spine* 1995;20(24):2613–2625.
7. Jensen MC, Brandt-Zawadzki MN, Obuchowski N, et al. Magnetic resonance imaging of the lumbar spine in people without back pain. *N Eng J Med* 1994;331:69–73.
8. Dabbs VM, Dabbs LG. Correlation between disc height narrowing and low back pain. *Spine* 1990;15(12):1366–1369.
9. Pettersson K, Hildingsson C, Toolanen G, et al. MRI and neurology in acute whiplash trauma: No correlation in prospective examination of 39 cases. *Acta Orthop Scand* 1994;65:525–528.
10. Mennel JM. *Joint Pain*. Boston, Mass: Little Brown; 1964.
11. Zohn DA, Mennel JM. *Musculoskeletal Pain: Diagnosis and Physical Treatment*. Boston, Mass: Little Brown; 1976.
12. Rahlmann JF. Mechanisms of intervertebral joint fixation: a literature review. *J Manipulative Physiol Ther* 1987;10:177–187.
13. Giles LGF. Lumbo-sacral and cervical zygapophyseal joint inclusions. *Man Med* 1986;2:89–92.
14. Saboe LA. Possible clinical significance of intra-articular synovial protrusions: A review of the literature. *Man Med* 1988;3:148–151.
15. Bland JH, Boushey DR. Anatomy and physiology of the cervical spine. *Sem Arthritis Rheum* 1990;20:1–20.
16. Bland JH, Boushey DR. The cervical spine, from anatomy and physiology to clinical care. In: Berthoz A, Graf W, Vidall PP, eds. *The Head-Neck Sensory Motor System*. New York, NY: Oxford University Press; 1992:136–140.
17. Giles LGF. Pressure related changes in joint articular cartilage. *J Rheumatol* 1986;13:1093–1095.
18. Lantz CA. Immobilization degeneration and the fixation hypothesis of chiropractic subluxation. *Chiropr Res J* 1988;1:21–46.
19. Schwarzer AC, Aprill CN, Derby R, Fortin J, Kine G, Bogduk N. The prevalence and clinical features of internal disc disruption in patients with chronic low back pain. *Spine* 1995;20(17):1878–1883.
20. Good AB. Spinal joint blocking. *J Manipulative Physiol Ther* 1985;8:1–8.

21. Wilson CJ, Dahners LE. An examination of the mechanism of ligament contracture. *Clin Orthop Rel Res* 1988;227:286–291.
22. Lederman E. *Fundamentals of Manual Therapy: Physiology, Neurology and Psychology*. New York, NY: Churchill Livingstone; 1997.
23. Lewit K. The muscular and articular factor in movement restriction. *Man Med* 1985;1:83–85.
24. Janda V. Muscle spasm—a proposed procedure for differential diagnosis. *Man Med* 1991;6(4):136–139.
25. Murphy DR. The seven types of hypertonicity of muscle. *J Myofasc Ther* 1995;1(4):33–36.
26. Young RR, Wiegner AW. Spasticity. *Clin Orthop* 1987;219:50–62.
27. Ludlow CL, Naunton RF, Sedory SE, Schultz GM, Hallet M. Effects of botulinum toxin injections on speech in adductor spasmodic dysphonia. *Neurology* 1988;38:1220–1225.
28. Simons DG, Mense S. Understanding and measurement of muscle tone as related to clinical muscle pain. *Pain* 1998;75(1):1–18.
29. Guyton AC. *Textbook of Medical Physiology*. 7th ed. Philadelphia, Pa: Lea and Febiger; 1989.
30. Lenz FA, Gracely RH, Zirh AT, et al. The sensory-limbic model of pain memory: Connections from the thalamus to the limbic system mediate the learned component of the affective dimension of pain. *Pain Forum* 1997;6(1):22–31.
31. McLain RF. Mechanoreceptor endings in human facet joints. *Spine* 1994;19(5):495–501.
31a. McLain RF, Raiszaden K. Mechanoreceptor endings of the cervical, thoracic and lumbar spine. *Iowa Orthop J* 1995;15:147–155.
32. Zoppi M, Chrubasik S. Neural control of joint pain. *Rheum Pain* 1997; Feb:2–8.
33. Mendel T, Wink CS, Zimny ML. Neural elements in human intervertebral discs. *Spine* 1992;17:132–135.
34. Bogduk N, Windsor M, Inglis A. The innervation of the cervical intervertebral discs. *Spine* 1988;13:2–8.
35. Giles LGF, Harvey AR. Immunohistochemical demonstration of nociceptors in the capsule and synovial folds of human zygapophyseal joints. *Br J Rheumatol* 1987;26:362–364.
36. Seaman DR, Winterstein JF. Dysafferentation: A novel term to describe the neuropathophysiological effects of joint complex dysfunction. A look at likely mechanisms of symptom generation. *J Manipulative Physiol Ther* 1998;21(4):267–280.
37. Meyer RA, Campbell JN, Raja SN. Peripheral neural mechanisms of nociception. In: Wall P, Melzack R, eds. *The Textbook of Pain*. 3rd ed. New York, NY: Churchill Livingstone; 1994:13–44.
38. Matre DA, Sinkaer T, Svensson P, Arendt-Nielsen L. Experimental muscle pain increases the human stretch reflex. *Pain* 1998;75(2,3):331–339.
39. Johansson H, Sojka P. Pathophysiological mechanisms involved in genesis and spread of muscular tension in occupational muscle pain and in chronic musculoskeletal pain syndromes: A hypothesis. *Med Hypotheses* 1990;35:196–203.
40. Fredin Y, Elert J, Britchgi N, et al. A decreased ability to relax between repetitive muscle contractions in patients with chronic symptoms after whiplash trauma to the neck. *J Musculoskel Pain* 1997;5:55–70.
41. Zoppi M, Chrubasik S. Neural control of joint pain. *Rheum Pain* 1997;Feb:2–8.
42. Young A, Stokes M, Iles JF. Effects of joint pathology on muscle. *Clin Orthop Rel Res* 1987;219:21–27.
43. Stokes M, Young A. The contribution of reflex inhibition to arthrogenous muscle weakness. *Clin Sci* 1989;67:7–14.
44. Hides JA, Stokes MJ, Saide M, Jull GA, Cooper DH. Evidence of lumbar multifidis muscle wasting ipsilateral to symptoms in patients with acute/subacute low back pain. *Spine* 1994;19(2):165–172.
45. Aniss AM, Gandevia SC, Milne RJ. Changes in perceived heaviness and motor commands produced by cutaneous reflexes in man. *J Physiol* 1988;397:113–126.
46. Van Buskirk RL. Nociceptive reflexes and the somatic dysfunction: A model. *J Amer Osteopath Assoc* 1990;90:792–809.
47. Davidoff RA. Skeletal muscle tone and the misunderstood stretch reflex. *Neurology* 1992;42:951–963.
48. Skoglund CR. Neurophysiological aspects on the pathological erector spinae reflex in cases of mechanical pelvic dysfunction. *Man Med* 1989;4(1):29–30.
49. Basmajian JV, DeLuca CJ. *Muscles Alive: Their Functions Revealed by Electromyography*. Baltimore, Md: Williams & Wilkins; 1985.
50. Janda V. Muscles and cervicogenic pain syndromes. In: Grant R, ed. *Physical Therapy of the Cervical and Thoracic Spine*. New York, NY: Churchill Livingstone; 1988:153–166.
51. Janda V. Muscles, central nervous motor regulation, and back problems. In: Korr IM, ed. *The Neurobiologic Mechanisms of Manipulative Therapy*. New York, NY: Plenum Press; 1978:27–42.

52. Lund JP, Donga R. The pain-adaptation model: A discussion of the relationship between chronic musculoskeletal pain and motor activtiy. *Can J Physiol Pharmacol* 1991;69:683–694.

53. Veiersted KB, Westgaard RH, Andersen P. Pattern of muscle activity during stereotyped work and its relation to muscle pain. *Int Arch Occup Environ Health* 1990;62:31–41.

54. Elert JE, Rantapaa-Dahlqvist SB, Henriksson-Larsen K, et al. Muscle performance, electromyography and fiber type composition in fibromyalgia and work-related myalgia. *Scand J Rheum* 1992;21:28–34.

55. Elert J, Brulin C, Gerdle B, Johansson H. Mechanical performance, level of continuous contraction, and muscle pain symptoms in home care personnel. *Scand J Rehab Med* 1992;24:141–150.

56. Elert J, Dahlqvist SR, Almay B, Eisemann M. Muscle endurance, muscle tension and personality traits in patients with muscle or joint pain—a pilot study. *J Rheumatol* 1993;20(9):1550–1556.

57. Korr IM. The spinal cord as organizer of disease processes: Some preliminary perspectives. *J Am Osteopath Assoc* 1976;76:89–99.

58. Murphy DR. The locomotor system: Korr's primary machinery of life. *J Manipulative Physiol Ther* 1994;17(8):562–564.

59. Elson LM. The jolt syndrome. Muscle dysfunction following low-velocity impact. *Pain Man* 1990;Nov/Dec:317–326.

60. Reilly BM. *Practical Strategies in Outpatient Medicine*. Philadelphia, PA: Saunders; 1984.

61. Roberts S, Eisenstein SM, Menage J, et al. Mechanoreceptors in intervertebral discs: Morphology, distribution and neuropeptides. *Spine* 1995;20(24):2645–2651.

62. Indahl A, Kaigle AM, Reikeras O, Holm SH. Interaction between the porcine lumbar intervertebral disc, zygapophysial joints and paraspinal muscles. *Spine* 1997;22(24):2834–2840.

63. Mense S. Peripheral mechanisms of muscle nociception and local muscle pain. *J Musculoskel Pain* 1993;1(1):133–169.

64. Travell JG, Simons DG. *Myofascial Pain and Dysfunction: The Trigger Point Manual*. vol. 1. Baltimore, Md: Williams & Wilkins, 1983.

65. Simons DG. Myofascial pain syndrome due to trigger points. In: Goodgold J, ed. *Rehabilitation Medicine*. St. Louis, Mo: Mosby; 1988:686–723.

66. Schneider MJ. *Principles of Manual Trigger Point Therapy*. Self-published; 1994.

67. Hong CZ, Torigoe Y, Yu J. The localized twitch responses in responsive taut bands of rabbit skeletal muscle fibers are related to the reflexes at spinal cord level. *J Muscluloskel Pain* 1995;3:15–32.

68. Hubbard DR, Berkoff GM. Myofascial trigger points show spontaneous needle EMG activity. *Spine* 1993;18:1803–1807.

69. Simons DG, Hong CZ, Simons LS. Prevalence of spontaneous electrical activity at trigger spots and at control sites in rabbit skeletal muscle. *J Musculoskel Pain* 1995;3:35–48.

70. Kramis RC, Roberts WJ, Gillette RG. Non-nociceptive aspects of persistent musculoskeletal pain. *J Orthop Sports Phys Ther* 1996;24:255–267.

71. Lewit K. *Manipulative Therapy in the Rehabilitation of the Locomotor System*. 2nd ed. Oxford: Butterworth-Heinemann; 1991.

72. Murphy DR. Hyperalgesic skin zone: A case report. *Chiro Tech* 1992;4:124–127.

73. Hochaday JM, Whitty WM. Patterns of referred pain in the normal subject. *Brain* 1967;90:481–496.

74. Lewis T, Kellegren JH. Observations related to referred pain, viscerosomatic reflexes and other associated phenomena. *Clin Sci* 1939;4:47–71.

75. Korr IM, Wright HM, Thomas PE. Effects of experimental myofascial insults on cutaneous patterns of sympathetic activity in man. *Neurol Transm* 1962;23:330–355.

76. Maigne R. *Orthopedic Medicine: A New Approach to Manipulation*. Springfield, Il: Charles C. Thomas; 1972.

77. Taylor T, Tole G, Vernon H. Skin rolling technique as an indicator of spinal joint dysfunction. *J Can Chiro Assoc* 1990;34:82–86.

78. Travell JG. Identification of myofascial trigger point syndromes: A case of atypical facial neuralgia. *Arch Phys Med Rehabil* 1981;62:100–106.

79. Wachter KC, Kaeser HE, Guhring H, et al. Muscle damping measured with a modified pendulum test in patients with fibromyalgia, lumbago and cervical syndrome. *Spine* 1996;21(18):2137–2142.

80. Lewit K. Chain reactions in disturbed function of the motor system. *Man Med* 1987;3:27–29.

81. Jovanovic K, Anastasijevic R, Vuco J. Reflex effects on gamma fusimotor neurones of chemically induced discharges in small-diameter muscle afferents in decerebrate cats. *Brain Res* 1990;521:89–94.

82. Johansson H, Djupsjobacka M, Sjolander P. Influences on the gamma muscle spindle system from muscle afferents stimulated by KCl and lactic acid. *Neurosci Res* 1993;16:49–57.

83. Djupsjobacka M, Johansson H, Bergenheim M, Wenngren BI. Influences in the gamma muscle spindle system from muscle afferents stimulated by increased intramuscular concentrations of bradykinin and 5-HT. *Neurosci Res* 1995;22:325–333.

84. Djupsjobacka M, Johansson H, Bergenheim M, Sjolander P. Influences on the gamma muscle spindle system from contralateral muscle afferents stimulated by KCl and lactic acid. *Neurosci Res* 1995;21:301–309.

85. Pederson J, Sjolander P, Wenngren BI, Johansson H. Increased intramuscular concentration of bradykinin increases the static fusimotor drive to muscle spindles in neck muscles of the cat. *Pain* 1997;70(1):83–91.

86. Matre DA, Sinkaer T, Svensson P, Arendt-Nielsen L. Experimental muscle pain increases the human stretch reflex. *Pain* 1998;75(2,3):331–339.

87. Edgerton VR, Wolf SL, Levendowski DJ, Roy RR. Theoretical basis for patterning EMG amplitudes to assess muscle dysfunction. *Med Sci Sports Exerc* 1996;28:744–751.

88. Gordon CR, Fletcher WA, Jones GM, Block EW. Adaptive plasticity in the control of locomotor trajectory. *Exp Brain Res* 1995;102:540–545.

89. Gordon CR, Fletcher WA, Jones GM, Block EW. Is the stepping test a specific indicator of vestibulospinal function? *Neurology* 1995;45:2035–2037.

90. Jones FP. The influence of postural set on patterns of movement in man. *Internat J Neurol* 1963;4:60–71.

91. Jones FP. Method for changing stereotyped response patterns by the inhibition of certain postural sets. *Psych Rev* 1965;72:196–214.

92. Panjabi MM. The stabilizing system of the spine. Part I. Function, dysfunction, adaptation and enhancement. *J Spinal Disord* 1992;5(4):383–389.

93. Panjabi M, Abumi K, Durenceau J, Oxland T. Spinal stability and intersegmental muscle forces: A biomechanical model. *Spine* 1989;14(2):194–200.

94. Panjabi MM, Lyons C, Vasavada A, et al. On the understanding of clinical instability. *Spine* 1994;19(23):2642–2650.

95. Mimura M, Panjabi MM, Oxland TR, et al. Disc degeneration affects the multidirectional flexibility of the lumbar spine. *Spine* 1994;19(12):1371–1380.

96. Wilke HJ, Wolf S, Claes LE, Arand M, Wiesend A. Stability increase in the lumbar spine with different muscle groups. *Spine* 1995;20(2):192–198.

97. Kaigle AM, Holm SH, Hansson TH. Experimental instability of the lumbar spine. *Spine* 1995;20(4):421–430.

98. Panjabi MM. The stabilizing system of the spine. Part II. Neutral zone and instability hypothesis. *J Spinal Disord* 1992;5(4):390–397.

99. Wilder DG, Aleksiev AR, Magnusson ML et al. Muscular response to sudden load: A tool to evaluate fatigue and rehabilitation. *Spine* 1996;21(22):2628–2639.

100. Cordo PJ, Nashner LM. Properties of postural adjustments associated with rapid arm movements. *J Neurophysiol* 1982;47:287–302.

101. Vasavada AN, Li S, Delp SL. Influence of muscle morphometry and moment arms on the moment-generating capacity of human neck muscles. *Spine* 1998;23(4):412–422.

102. Nashner LM, McCollum G. The organization of human postural movements: A formal basis and experimental synthesis. *Behav Brain Sci* 1985;8:135–172.

103. Johansson H, Sjolander P, Sojka P. Actions on gamma-motoneurones elicited by electrical stimulation of joint afferent fibers in the hind limb of the cat. *J Physiol* 1986;375:137–152.

104. Johansson H, Sjolander P, Wadell I. Reflex actions of the gamma-muscles-spindle systems of muscles acting at the knee joint elicited by stretch of the posterior cruciate ligament. *Neuro-Orthop* 1989;8:9–21.

105. Johansson H, Sjolander P, Sojka P. Fusimotor reflexes in triceps surae muscle elicited by natural and electrical stimulation of joint afferents. *Neuro-Orthop* 1988;6:67–80.

106. Hides JA, Stokes MJ, Saide M, Jull GA, Cooper DH. Evidence of lumbar multifidis muscle wasting ipsilateral to symptoms in patients with acute/subacute low back pain. *Spine* 1994;19(2):165–172.

107. Gahery Y, Massion J. Co-ordination between posture and movement. *Trends Neurosci* 1981;4:199–202.

108. Lauren H, Luoto S, Alaranta H, et al. Arm motion speed and risk of neck pain: A preliminary communication. *Spine* 1997;22(18):2094–2099.

109. Gahery Y, Massion J. Co-ordination between posture and movement. *Trends Neurosci* 1981;4:199–202.

110. Bouisset S, Zattara M. Segmental movement as a perturbation to balance? Facts and concepts. In: Winters JM, Woo SL-Y, eds. *Multiple Muscle Systems: Biomechanics and Movement Organization*. New York, NY: Springer-Verlag; 1990:498–506.

111. Uhlig Y, Weber BR, Grob D, Muntner M. Fiber composition and fiber transformation in neck muscles of patients with dysfunction of the cervical spine. *J Orthop Research* 1995;13:240–249.

112. Ghez C. Muscles: Effectors of the motor systems. In: Kandel ER. Schwartz JH, Jessel TM, eds. *Principles of Neural Science*. 3rd ed. Norwalk, Conn: Appleton & Lange; 1991:548–563.

113. Sparto PJ, Parniapour M, Reinsel TE, Simon S. The effect of fatigue on multijoint kinematics, coordination and postural stability during a repetitive lifting test. *J Orthop Sports Phys Ther* 1997;25:3–12.

114. Hallgren RC, Greenman PE, Rechtien JJ. Atrophy of suboccipital muscles in patients with chronic pain: A pilot study. *J Amer Osteopath Assoc* 1994;94:1032–1038.

115. Foreman SM, Stahl MJ. The domino theory of ligamentous failure in the lower cervical spine. In: Lawrence DJ, ed. *Advances in Chiropractic*. vol. 1. St. Louis, Mo: Mosby; 1994:175–192.

116. Croft AC. A proposed classification of cervical acceleration-deceleration (CAD) injuries with a review of prognostic research. *Palmer J Res* 1994;1(1):10–21.

117. McGregor M, Mior SA. Anatomical and functional perspectives of the cervical spine: Part II: The "hypermobile" cervical spine. *J Canad Chiro Assoc* 1989;33:177–183.

118. McGregor M, Mior S. Anatomical and functional perspectives of the cervical spine: Part III: The "unstable" cervical spine. *J Canad Chiro Assoc* 1990;34:145–152.

119. Ogon M, Bender BR, Hooper DM, et al. A dynamic approach to spinal instability: Part I: Sensitization of intersegmental motion profiles to motion direction and load condition by instability. *Spine* 1997;22(24):2841–2858.

120. Fukuda T. *Statokinetic Reflexes in Equilibrium and Movement*. Tokyo: University of Tokyo Press; 1984.

120a. Tokizane T, Murao M, Ogata T, Kondo T. Electromyographic studies on tonic neck, lumbar and labyrinthine reflexes in normal persons. *Jap J Physiol* 1951;2:130–146.

121. Hellebrandt FA Houty SJ, Partridge MJ, Walters CE. Tonic neck reflexes in exercises of stress in man. *Am J Phys Med* 1956;35:144–159.

122. Hellebrandt FA, Schade M, Carns ML. Methods of evoking the tonic neck reflexes in normal human subjects. *Am J Phys Med* 1962;41:89–140.

123. Fukushima H, Hinoki M. Role of cervical and lumbar proprioceptors during stepping: An electromyographic study of the muscular activities of the lower limbs. *Acta Otolaryngol (Stockh)* 1985;suppl 419:91–105.

124. Hulse M. Disequilibrium, caused by a functional disturbance of the upper cervical spine. Clinical aspects and differential diagnosis. *Man Med* 1983;1:18–23.

125. Lewit K. Disturbed balance due to lesions of the cranio-cervical junction. *J Orthop Med* 1988;3:58–61.

126. Fitz-Ritson D. Assessment of cervicogenic vertigo. *J Manipulative Physiol Ther* 1991;14(3):193–198.

127. Brown JJ. Cervical contribution to balance: Cervical vertigo. In: Berthoz A, Graf W, Vidal PP, eds. *The Head-Neck Sensory Motor System*. New York, NY: Oxford University Press; 1992:644–647.

128. Abrahams VC, Falchetto S. Hind leg ataxia of cervical origin and cervico-lumbar spinal interactions with a supratentorial pathway. *J Physiol* 1969;203:435–447.

129. Abrahams VC. Neck muscle proprioceptors and a role of the cerebral cortex in postural reflexes in sub-primates. *Rev Can Biol* 1972;31(suppl):115–130.

130. Bolton PS. The somatosensory system of the neck and its effects on the central nervous system. In: *Proceedings of the Scientific Symposium*. World Federation of Chiropractic; 1997:32–49.

131. Lewit K. Relation of faulty respiration to posture, with clinical implications. *J Amer Osteopath Assoc* 1980;79:525–529.

132. Chaitow L, Monro R, Hyman J, Witt P. Breathing dysfunction. *J Bodywork Mov Ther* 1997;1(5):252–261.

133. Fitz-Ritson D. Neural mechanisms involved in the control of the eye-head-neck coordinated movement: A review of the literature with emphasis on future directions for the chiropractic profession. *J Manipulative Physiol Ther* 1984;7:251–260.

134. Hildingsson C, Wenngren B, Bring G, Toolanen G. Oculomotor problems after cervical spine injury. *Acta Orthop Scand* 1989;60(5):513–516.

135. Hildingsson C, Wenngren B, Bring G, Toolanen G. Eye motility dysfunction after soft tissue injury of the cervical spine: A controlled, prospective study of 38 patients. *Acta Orthop Scand* 1993;64(2):129–132.

136. Barnsley L, Lord S, Bogduk N. Whiplash injury. *Pain* 1994;58:283–307.
136a. Brown S. Ocular dysfunction associated with whiplash injury. *Aust Physiother* 1995;41:59–60.
137. Gimse R, Tjell C, Bjorgen I, Saunte C. Disturbed eye movements after whiplash due to injuries to posture control system. *J Clin Exp Neuropsychol* 1996;18(2):178–186.
138. Tjell C, Rosenhall U. Smooth pursuit neck torsion test: a specific test for cervical dizziness. *Am J Otol* 1998;19:76–81.
139. Van Nechel C, Soeur M, Cordonnier M, Zanen A. Eye movement disorders after whiplash injury. In: Gunzburg R, Szpalski M, eds. *Whiplash Injuries: Current Concepts in Prevention, Diagnosis and Treatment of the Cervical Whiplash Syndrome.* Philadelphia, Pa: Lippincott-Raven; 1998:135–141.
140. Carlsson J, Rosenthal U. Oculomotor disturbances in patients with tension headache. *Acta Otolaryngol (Stockh)* 1988;106:354–360.
141. Rosenhall U, Tjell C, Carlsson J. The effect of neck torsion on smooth pursuit eye movements in tension-type headache patients. *J Audiol Med* 1996;5(3):130–140.
142. Horwich H, Kosner D. The effect of whiplash injuries on ocular functions. *South Med J* 1962;55:69–71.
143. Khurana RK. Oculocephalic sympathetic dysfunction in posttraumatic headaches. *Headache* 1995;35:614–620.
144. Brown S. Ocular dysfunction associated with whiplash injury. *Aust Physiother* 1995;41:59–60.
145. Botros G. The tonic oculomotor function of the cervical joint and muscle receptors. *Adv Oto Rhino Laryng* 1979;25:214–220.
146. Radanov BP, Hirlinger I, DiStefano G, Valach L. Attentional processing in cervical spine syndromes. *Acta Neurol Scand* 1992;85:358–362.
147. DiStefano G, Radanov BP. Course attention and memory after common whiplash: A two-year prospective study with age, education and gender pair-matched controls. *Acta Neurol Scand* 1995;91:346–352.
148. Radanov BP, Sturzenegger M, Di Stefano G. Long term outcome after whiplash injury: A 2-year follow up considering features of injury mechanism and somatic, radiologic and psychosocial factors. *Medicine* 1995;74:281–297.
149. Karlburg M, Magnusson M, Johansson R. Effects of restrained cervical mobility on voluntary eye movements and postural control. *Acta Otolaryngol (Stockh)* 1991;111:664–670.
150. Revel M, Andre-Deshays C, Minguet M. Cervicocephalic kinesthetic sensibility in patients with cervical pain. *Arch Phys Med Rehabil* 1991;72:288–291.
151. Heikkila H, Astrom PG. Cervicocephalic kinesthetic sensibility in patients with whiplash injury. *Scand J Rehabil* 1996;28:133–138.
152. Loudon JK, Ruhl M, Field E. Ability to reproduce head position after whiplash injury. *Spine* 1997;22:865–868.
153. Jull G. Management of cervical headache. *Man Ther* 1997;2:182–190.
154. Torrres F, Shapiro SK. Electroencephalograms in whiplash injury. *Arch Neurol* 1961;5:28–35.
155. King Liu Y, Chandran KB, Heath RG, Unterharnscheidt F. Subcortical EEG changes in Rhesus monkeys following experimental hyperextension-hyperflexion (whiplash). *Spine* 1984;9:329–338.
156. Radanov BP, Dvorak J, Valach L. Cognitive deficits in patients after soft tissue injury of the cervical spine. *Spine* 1992;17(2):127–131.
157. Radanov BP, Dvorak J. Impaired cognitive function after whiplash injury of the cervical spine. *Spine* 1996;21(3):392–397.
158. Barret K, Buxton N, Redmond AD, et al. A comparison of symptoms experienced following minor head injury and acute neck strain (whiplash injury). *J Acc Emerg Med* 1995;12:173–176.
159. Terrett AGJ. Cerebral dysfunction: A theory to explain some of the effects of chiropractic manipulation. *Chiropr Technique* 1993;5:168–173.
160. Budgell BS, Sato A. The cervical subluxation and regional blood flow. *J Manipulative Physiol Ther* 1997;20:103–107.
161. Fordyce WE, ed. *Back Pain in the Workplace. Management of Disability in Nonspecific Conditions.* Seattle, Wash: IASP Press; 1995.
162. Marchiori DM, Henderson CNR. A cross-sectional study correlating cervical radiographic degenerative findings to pain and disability. *Spine* 1996;21(23):2747–2752.
163. Boden SD, McCowin PR, Davis DO, et al. Abnormal magnetic resonance imaging scans of the cervical spine in asymptomatic subjects. *J Bone Joint Surg* 1990;72A:1178–1184.
164. Jessel TM, Kelly DD. Pain and analgesia. In: Kandel ER. Schwartz JH, Jessel TM, eds. *Principles of Neural Science.* 3rd ed. Norwalk, Conn: Appleton & Lange; 1991:385–399.

165. Bolton PS, Tracey DJ. Spinothalamic and propriospinal neurones in the upper cervical cord of the rat: Terminations of primary afferent fibres on soma and primary dendrites. *Exp Brain Res* 1992;92:59–68.

166. Haldeman S. The neurophysiology of spinal pain. In: Haldeman S, ed. *Principles and Practice of Chiropractic.* 2nd ed. Norwalk, Conn: Appleton & Lange; 1992:165–184.

167. Rosomoff HL, Fishbain D, Rosomoff RS. Chronic cervical pain: radiculopathy or brachialgia? *Spine* 1992;17:S362–S366.

168. Levine JD, Fields HL, Basbaum AI. Peptides and the primary afferent nociceptor. *J Neurosci* 1993;13:2273–2286.

169. Siddall PJ, Cousins MJ. Spinal pain mechanisms. *Spine* 1997;22(1):98–104.

170. Raja SN, Meyer RA, Campbell JN. Peripheral mechanisms of somatic pain. *Anesthesiology* 1988;68:571–590.

171. Sluka KA. Pain mechanisms involved in musculoskeletal disorders. *J Orthop Sports Phys Ther* 1996;24:240–254.

172. Chaplan SR, Sorkin LS. Agonizing over pain terminology. *Pain Forum* 1997;6(2):81–87.

173. Carlton SM, Coggeshall RE. Nociceptive integration: Does it have a peripheral component? *Pain Forum* 1998;7(2):71–78.

174. McMahon S, Koltzenburg M. The changing role of primary afferent neurones in pain. *Pain* 1990;43:269–272.

175. Woolf CJ. The dorsal horn: state-dependent sensory processing and the generation of pain. In: Wall P, Melzack R, eds. *The Textbook of Pain.* 3rd ed. New York, NY: Churchill Livingstone; 1994:101–112.

176. Sheather-Reid RB, Cohen ML. Psychophysical evidence for a neuropathic component of chronic neck pain. *Pain* 1998;75:341–347.

177. Mendel LM. Modifiability of spinal synapses. *Physiol Rev* 1984;64:260–324.

178. Dubner R. The effect of behavioral state on the sensory processing of nociceptive and non-nociceptive information. In: Fields HL, Besson JM, eds. *Progress in Brain Research.* Elsevier; 1988:213–223.

179. Campbell JN. The incongruent relationship between noxious and painful stimuli. *Pain Forum* 1996;5(3):165–166.

180. McMahon S, Koltenburg M. The changing role of primary afferent neurones in pain. *Pain* 1990;43:269–272.

181. Cervero F, Meyer RA, Campbell JN. A psychophysical study of secondary hyperalgesia: evidence for increased pain to input from nociceptors. *Pain* 1994;58:21–28.

182. Price DD. Characteristics of second pain and flexion reflexes indicative of prolonged central summation. *Exp Neurol* 1972;37:371–387.

183. Hoheisel U, Mense S, Simons DG, Yu XM. Appearance of new receptive fields in rat dorsal horn neurons following noxious stimulation of skeletal muscle: A model for referral of muscle pain? *Neurosci Lett* 1993;153:9–12.

184. Coderre TJ, Katz J, Vaccarino AL, Melzack R. Contribution of central neuroplasticity to pathological pain: Review of clinical and experimental evidence. *Pain* 1993;52:259–285.

185. Hoheisel U, Mense S. Long-term changes in discharge behavior of cat dorsal horn neurones following stimulation of deep tissues. *Pain* 1989;36:239–247.

186. Yu XM, Sessle BJ, Hu JW. Differential effects of cutaneous and deep application of inflammatory irritant of mechanoreceptive field properties of trigeminal brain stem nociceptive neurons. *J Neurophysiol* 1993;70:1704–1707.

187. Kellegren JH. Observations on referred pain arising from muscle. *Clin Sci* 1938;3:175–190.

188. Kellgren JH. On the distribution of pain arising from deep somatic structures with charts of segmental pain areas. *Clin Sci* 1939;4:35–46.

189. Campbell DG, Parsons CM. Referred head pain and its concomitants. *J Nerve Ment Dis* 1944;99:544–551.

190. Sinclair DC, Weddel G, Feindel WH. Referred pain and associated phenomena. *Brain* 1948;71:184–211.

191. Steinbrocker O, Isenberg SA, Silver M, et al. Observations on pain produced by injection of hypertonic saline into muscles and other supportive tissues. *J Clin Invest* 1953;32:1045–1051.

192. Feinstein B, Langdon JNK, Jameson RM, Schiller F. Experiments on pain referred from deep somatic tissues. *J Bone Joint Surg* 1954;36A:981–997.

193. Hochaday JM, Whitty CWM. Patterns of referred pain in the normal subject. *Brain* 1967;90:481–496.

194. Dwyer A, Aprill C, Bogduk N. Cervical zygapophyseal joint pain patterns I: A study in normal volunteers. *Spine* 1990;15(6):453–457.

195. Aprill C, Dwyer A, Bogduk N. Cervical zygapophyseal joint pain patterns II: A clinical evaluation. *Spine* 1990;15(6):458–461.

196. Dreyfuss P, Michaelson M, Fletcher D. Atlanto-occipital and lateral atlanto-axial joint pain patterns. *Spine* 1994;19(10):1125–1131.

197. Fukui S, Oheseto K, Shiotani K, et al. Referred pain distribution of the cervical zygapophyseal joints and cervical dorsal rami. *Pain* 1996;68:79–83.

198. Arendt-Nielsen L, Graven-Nielsen T, Drewes AM. Referred pain and hyperalgesia related to muscle and visceral pain. *IASP Newsletter* 1998;Jan-Feb:3–6.

199. Bogduk N. Innervation and pain patterns of the cervical spine. In: Grant R, ed. *Physical Therapy of the Cervical and Thoracic Spine*. 2nd ed. New York, NY: Churchill Livingstone; 1994:65–76.

200. Inman VT, Saunders JBCM. Referred pain from skeletal structures. *J Nerve Ment Dis* 1944;99:660–667.

201. Sessle BJ, Hu JW, Amano N, Zhong G. Convergence of cutaneous, tooth pulp, visceral, neck and muscle afferents onto nociceptive and non-nociceptive neurones in trigeminal subnucleus caudalis (medullary dorsal horn) and its implications for referred pain. *Pain* 1986;27:219–235.

202. Darby SA, Cramer GD. Pain generators and pain pathways of head and neck. In: Curl DD, ed. *Chiropractic Approach to Head Pain*. Baltimore, Md: Williams & Wilkins; 1994:55–73.

203. Nelson CF. The tension headache, migraine headache continuum: a hypothesis. *J Manipulative Physiol Ther* 1994;17(3):156–167.

204. Lord SM, Bogduk N. The cervical synovial joints as sources of post-traumatic headache. In: Allen ME, ed. *Musculoskeletal Pain Emanating from the Head and Neck: Current Concepts in Diagnosis, Management and Cost Containment*. New York, NY: Haworth Press; 1996:81–94.

205. Goadsby PJ, Knight PY, Hoskin KL. Stimulation of the greater occipital nerve increases metabolic activity in the trigeminal nucleus caudalis and cervical dorsal horn of the cat. *Pain* 1997;3(1):23–28.

206. Sessle BJ. Neurophysiological mechanisms related to craniofacial and cervical pain. *Top Clin Chiro* 1998;5:36–38.

207. Bogduk N. Cervical causes of headache and dizziness. In: Grieve GP, ed. *Modern Manual Therapy of the Vertebral Column*. Edinburgh: Churchill Livingstone; 1986:289–302.

208. Bogduk N. The anatomical basis for cervicogenic headache. *J Manipulative Physiol Ther* 1992;15(1):67–70.

209. Hu JW, Sessle BJ, Raboisson P, et al. Stimulation of craniofacial muscle afferents induces prolonged facilitatory effects in trigeminal nociceptive brainstem neurones. *Pain* 1992;48:53–60.

210. Yu XM, Sessle BJ, Hu JW. Differential effects of cutaneous and deep application of inflammatory irritant on mechanoreceptive field properties of trigeminal brainstem nociceptive neurons. *J Neurophysiol* 1993;70:1704–1707.

211. Backonja MM. Primary somatosensory cortex and pain perception. Part I. *Pain Forum* 1996;5(3):174–180.

212. Melzack R. Central pain syndromes and theories of pain. In: Casey KL, ed. *Pain and Central Nervous System Disease: The Central Pain Syndromes*. New York, NY: Raven Press; 1991:59–64.

213. Canavero S. Dynamic reverberation. A unified mechanism for central and phantom pain. *Med Hypotheses* 1994;42:203–207.

214. Melzack R, Wall PD. Pain mechanisms: A new theory. *Science* 1965;150:971–979.

215. Wyke BD. Neurologic aspects of pain therapy. In: Swerdlow M, ed. *The Therapy of Pain*. Philadelphia, Pa: Lippincott; 1980:1–30.

216. Kakigi R, Shibasaki H. Mechanisms of pain relief by vibration and movement. *J Neurol Neurosurg Psychiatr* 1992;55:282–286.

217. Wright A, Vicenzo B. Cervical mobilisation techniques, sympathetic nervous system effects and their relationship to analgesia. In: Shacklock M, ed. *Moving in on Pain*. Melbourne: Butterworth Heinneman; 1995:164–173.

218. Wright A. Hypoalgesia post-manipulative therapy: A review of a potential neurophysiological mechanism. *Man Ther* 1995;1:11–16.

219. Fields HL, Basbaum AI. Central nervous system mechanisms of pain modulation. In: Wall P, Melzack R, ed. *The Textbook of Pain*. 3rd ed. New York, NY: Churchill Livingstone; 1994:243–257.

220. Fields HL. Sources of variability in the sensation of pain. *Pain* 1988;33:195–200.

221. Main CJ, Watson PJ. Guarded movements: development of chronicity. In: Allen ME, ed. *Musculoskeletal Pain Emanating from the Head and Neck: Current Concepts in Diagnosis, Management and Cost Containment*. New York, NY: Haworth Press; 1996:163–170.

222. Bove GM, Light AR. The nervi nervorum: Missing link for neuropathic pain? *Pain Forum* 1997; 6(3):181–190.

223. Bogduk N, Marsland A. The cervical zygapophyseal joint as a source of neck pain. *Spine* 1988;13;610–617.

224. Bogduk N, Aprill C. On the nature of neck pain, discography and cervical zygapophyseal joint blocks. *Pain* 1993;54:213–217.

225. Lord S, Barnsley L, Bogduk N. Cervical zygapophyseal joint pain in whiplash. *Spine: State of the Art Reviews* 1993;7:355–372.

226. Barnsley L, Lord SM, Wallis BJ, Bogduk N. The prevalence of chronic cervical zygapophyseal joint pain after whiplash. *Spine* 1995;20(1):20–26.

227. Bogduk N. The anatomical basis for spinal pain syndromes. *J Manipulative Physiol Ther* 1995;18(9):603–605.

228. Lord SM, Barnsley L, Wallis BJ, Bogduk N. Chronic cervical zygapophyseal joint pain after whiplash: A placebo-controlled prevalence study. *Spine* 1996;21(15):1737–1745.

229. Lord SM, Barnsley L, Wallis BJ, Bogduk N. Third occipital nerve headache: A prevalence study. *J Neurol Neurosurg Psychiatr* 1994;57:1187–1190.

230. Lord SM, Bogduk N. The cervical synovial joints as sources of post-traumatic headache. In: Allen ME, ed. *Musculoskeletal Pain Emanating from the Head and Neck: Current Concepts in Diagnosis, Management and Cost Containment.* New York, NY: Haworth Press; 1996:81–94.

CHAPTER 5

Epidemiology of Cervical Spine Disorders

ERIC L. HURWITZ

"All truth passes through three stages: First it is ridiculed, second it is violently opposed, third it is accepted as being self-evident."

—Arthur Schopenhauer (1788–1860)

INTRODUCTION

Epidemiology is defined as "the study of the distribution and determinants of health-related states or events in specified populations and the application of this study to control of health problems."[1] Epidemiological methods are used primarily to estimate disease frequencies, to examine the effects of exposures on disease occurrence and disease prognosis, and to assess the effectiveness of health care on disease outcomes. This chapter focuses on the distribution and natural history of cervical spine disorders and factors associated with the prevalence and incidence of these disorders in the population.

EPIDEMIOLOGICAL CONCEPTS

MEASURES OF DISEASE FREQUENCY AND ASSOCIATION

Epidemiologists use a variety of measures to describe the frequency of disease and the relationships between exposures and outcomes. *Prevalence* is used to describe the proportion of the population having the disease or condition at a particular time. *Incidence* is used to describe the risk or rate of developing the condition in a population at risk. An incidence rate is the number of cases occurring in the population divided by the person-time at risk. Person-time is the total time (usually expressed in years) that members of the population spend at risk of developing the condition. Cumulative incidence, which is often called risk, is the proportion of the population at risk that develops the condition during a defined time period.

Risk factors are characteristics that influence the probability of disease onset, while prognostic factors influence the probability of recovery. Ratios and differences between risks and rates of disease in two or more exposure groups are used to describe associations between possible risk or prognostic factors for the condition and the condition itself. These effect measures are called rate and risk ratios and rate and risk differences. Ratio measures reflect the magnitude of the association between the exposure and disease, while difference measures reflect the impact of the exposure on the population. The null value, indicating equivalent risks or rates in each group, is 1.0 for ratio measures and zero for difference measures. Odds ratios, (ORs), which are ratios of the odds of exposure or disease in two populations, are used as measures of association in certain epidemiological study designs (e.g., case-control and cross-sectional studies) where exposure-specific risks are not known.

BASIC RESEARCH STRATEGIES

A variety of research strategies are employed to estimate disease frequencies and to assess the effects of possible risk or prognostic factors. Treatment and exposure effects are most appropriately estimated by conducting experiments, such as randomized clinical trials, where each subject in the study has an equal probability of receiving each treatment or exposure. The potential for confounding is minimized by ensuring comparability between exposure groups with respect to other risk or prognostic factors (assuming a large enough sample). Since experiments are generally not feasible for assessing the effects of typical exposures or purported risk factors, epidemiologists use observational designs to evaluate exposure effects.

Although the specific strategy depends on the nature of the research question, cross-sectional, cohort, and case-control designs are the three most common observational study designs used. Disease prevalence is most often estimated with cross-sectional studies by surveying a defined population and counting the number of members having the condition. Cohort studies are used to measure incidence of disease and to compare incidence between two or more exposure groups by following populations at risk over time and observing new cases of disease occurrence. Cohort studies may be prospective (in future time), retrospective (in past time), or they may involve both retrospective and prospective follow-up. Case-control studies, which compare the odds of exposure among those with the disease ("cases") with the odds of exposure among those without the disease ("controls"), are most often used to estimate the effects of exposures on rare diseases, where it would not be feasible to conduct cohort studies involving very large populations or very long follow-up periods, or both.

Case series are reported frequently in the literature and are useful for describing the distribution and character of existing disease and in the identification of new diseases, epidemics, and iatrogenic events. However, case series cannot be used to infer cause or to estimate treatment effects due to lack of comparison group(s). Additional information from appropriately selected noncase populations would provide clues as to the relative importance of specific exposures on disease occurrence. Case series are included in this chapter only if no other data are available. Although case reports cannot be used for causal inference, rigorously designed and executed single-subject (n-of-1) studies may be used to assess the effects of interventions on chronic or recurrent conditions at the individual level.[2, 3] Studies in which data from small studies of similar design are pooled, called meta-analyses, are conducted to obtain more precise estimates of overall effect or to identify differences in effects between studies.[4]

VALIDITY OF EPIDEMIOLOGIC DATA

Estimates of disease occurrence and exposure effect may be biased because of selection bias, measurement error or misclassification, and confounding. The potential for selection bias is greatest in nonpopulation-based case-control studies where study subjects may be different from members of the population at risk with respect to exposure and disease risk. Selection bias may also occur in cohort studies with large loss to follow-up and in nonpopulation-based occupational studies where persons with chronic pain, for example, may select out of certain jobs, which causes attenuation of the observed effect of the job (or related exposure) on pain occurrence.

Many studies examining the effects of occupational and psychosocial factors do not employ reliable and valid measures for assessing these factors, and investigators often fail to consider the frequency, intensity, duration, and timing of exposures, which may be important factors in describing the nature of many exposure–disease associations. Exposure and outcome assessments based on self reports or medical records may not be accurate because of recall and poor documentation, leading to potential misclassification and bias. Diagnostic criteria, especially for neck and upper extremity pain, headache, and temporomandibular disorders, are often not objective and consistent across studies, which makes validity questionable and interstudy comparisons difficult. The cross-sectional nature of many studies precludes the differentiation of risk factors and prognostic factors.

Since in observational studies the groups of persons with and without the purported risk factor may be different, on average, with respect to factors (potential confounders) affecting the risk of the disease or condition, the estimate of the exposure effect should be adjusted to control for these differences. Crude (unadjusted) effects, which are commonly reported in the literature reviewed later in this chapter, may be biased because of this lack of comparability between exposure groups. Furthermore, unlike randomization in experiments, adjustment cannot control for unknown factors that affect the risk of the outcome, nor under most circumstances can adjustment control for the selection of certain subjects versus others into the study.[4]

Finally, much of the data presented in this chapter originate from highly selected clinic or hospital populations, rather than from community-based populations. Even if the estimates of disease frequency or exposure effect are not biased (internally valid), the findings may not be generalizable (externally valid) to other settings and populations. While the heterogeneity of estimates observed between studies may be attributed to differences in methods, study populations, or bias, the relative importance of each in explaining the differences is difficult to determine.

NECK AND SHOULDER PAIN

Neck pain is one of the most prevalent and costly health problems facing the workplace and health-care communities.[5–7] Neck pain is one of the most common reasons for visiting an emergency department,[5] one of the principal reasons for visiting an ambulatory medical care provider,[6] and the second leading chief complaint reported by patients seeking chiropractic care.[8, 9] Thirty-three to sixty-six percent of whiplash victims have neck pain 6 months after the accident and 10 to 20 percent will have constant neck pain for 2 years or longer.[10–13] Investigators using insurance data from Sweden found that among injured motor-vehicle occupants, disability from injuries resulting in neck and shoulder pain increased from 19.2 percent in 1976–1978 to 46.9 percent in 1990–1992.[14]

PREVALENCE AND INCIDENCE

Table 5–1 shows the estimated frequencies of neck and shoulder pain. Fifty to seventy percent of the population will experience neck pain at least once in their lives,[15–17] and as much as one third of the population is affected each year.[18] About 10 percent of the population suffers from neck pain at any point in time.[18, 19] Women are more likely to report neck pain than men, and women are also more likely to report chronic neck pain[18, 20–22] and disability due to neck or shoulder pain.[21]

Bergenudd and Johnell[23] used pain drawings in a population-based study of 575 55 year olds in Sweden (323 males, 252 females) to estimate point prevalences of neck-shoulder pain of 1 percent among males and 2 percent among females, and point prevalences of thoracic or neck/shoulder pain, or both, of 1 percent among males and 5 percent among females. The investigators of a longitudinal study in Finland that repeated examinations of 154 13 year olds (82 males and 72 females) 25 years later found that females were more likely than males to report radicular neck pain (18 percent versus 8 percent), torticollis (25 percent versus 11 perent), other neck-shoulder pain (51 percent versus 28 percent), and any type of neck shoulder pain (56 percent versus 30 percent).[24]

RISK AND PROGNOSTIC FACTORS FOR NECK AND SHOULDER PAIN

Table 5–2 shows the possible demographic, physical, and psychosocial risk or prognostic factors for neck and shoulder pain. The greater population-based frequency of neck pain among females than males (previously reported) suggests that sex is a risk factor. The prevalence of neck pain has been found to increase with age,[18, 21, 22] indicating that age is a risk or prognostic factor. Makela et al[20] found the

Table 5–1: Frequencies of Neck and Shoulder Pain, Thoracic Outlet Syndrome, Whiplash, and Temporomandibular Joint Disorders, by Disorder and Frequency Measure

DISORDER	FREQUENCY MEASURE	POPULATION	FREQUENCY	REFERENCE(S)
Neck/Shoulder Pain	Lifetime prevalence (neck)	Total	50–70%	15–17
		Total	71%	20
	1-year prevalence (neck)	Female	40%	18
		Male	29%	18
		Total	34.4%	18
	1-month prevalence (shoulder)	Female 55 year olds	15%	23
		Male 55 year olds	13%	23
	1-month prevalence (neck/shoulder)	Total ≥30 years	41%	20
		Female ≥30 years	13.5%	20
		Male ≥30 years	9.5%	20
	1-week prevalence (neck/shoulder)	Female (any pain)	24.9%	21
		Female (disabling)	11%	21
		Male (any pain)	15.4%	21
		Male (disabling)	7%	21
	Point prevalence (neck)	Total	10%	19
		Female 55 year olds	2%	23
		Male 55 year olds	1%	23
	Point prevalence (neck >6 mos.)	Total 18–67 years	13.8%	18
		Female 18–67 years	17%	18
		Male 18–67 years	10%	18
Thoracic Outlet	1-year incidence	Total	<1/100–2/100	73, 74
Whiplash	1-year incidence	Total	<1/1000–4/1000	107, 108
Temporomandibular Joint Disorders	Point prevalence	Total	6–12%	126–128

Table 5–2: Putative Risk/Prognostic Factors for Neck/Shoulder Pain, Thoracic Outlet Syndrome, and Temporomandibular Joint Disorders, by Disorder and Type Of Factor

DISORDER	TYPE OF FACTOR	FACTOR	REFERENCE(S)
Neck/Shoulder Pain	Demographic	Female sex	18, 20–22, 35, 56
		Increasing age	18, 21, 22
	Physical	Obesity	20, 23
		History of neck/shoulder injury	20
		Parity	20
		Forward head posture	26
		Fast or slow arm motion speed	27
	Psychosocial	Psychological distress	25
		Weak sense of coherence	24
Thoracic Outlet Syndrome	Demographic	Female sex	75
	Physical	Obesity	75
		Poor posture	73
		Trauma	77
		Cervical ribs	76
		First rib abnormalities	76
		Large C7 transverse process	76
	Occupational—Job	Assembly line packer	72
		Assembly line worker	72
		Slaughterhouse worker	72
		Cash register operator	72
Temporomandibular Joint Disorders	Demographic	Female sex	129, 131, 135
	Physical	Neck/shoulder symptoms	138
		Whiplash injury	143
		Estrogen use	142
		Oral contraceptive use	142

prevalence of neck pain to be associated with history of injury to back, neck, or shoulder, being overweight, and parity, in addition to work-related mental and physical stress. Bergenudd and Johnell[23] found in their population-based study of 55 year olds in Sweden that women with shoulder pain or back pain, or both, tended to be heavier and reported their jobs as being more mentally demanding, compared to those without these symptoms. Although Viikari-Juntura et al[24] found in their longitudinal study in Finland that psychosocial factors in childhood had only minor, if any, predictive role of neck/shoulder pain in adulthood, they did find an association between having a weak sense of coherence and neck/shoulder pain in adults. High levels of psychological distress predicted disability from neck and shoulder disorders in a 10-year prospective study of 8655 farmers in Finland.[25]

In a study of healthy subjects, those with kyphosis and rounded shoulders were more likely to report interscapular pain, while those with a forward-head posture were more likely to report cervical and interscapular pain and headache.[26] Although those with generally more severe postural abnormalities were more likely to report pain, postural severity was not associated with pain severity. In a retrospective cohort study, family history of neck pain and expectation of disability were associated with persistent pain 1 to 3 years after a rear-end collision.[22] The investigators of a recent prospective study of 486 Helsinki city council workers found that very slow or very rapid arm motion speed predicted incident neck pain during a 1-year follow-up period.[27]

NECK PAIN IN THE WORKPLACE

Table 5–3 shows occupational-related physical and psychosocial factors that may affect the risk or prognosis for neck or shoulder pain.[14, 28–35] Occupational risk factors identified primarily from cross-sectional studies include repetition[32, 36–45] (ORs = 0.7 to 6.9); static posture[32, 39, 46] (ORs = 1.7 to 2.3); seated versus standing work[44] (OR = 3.9); awkward posture[47] (OR = 7.5); vibration[48] (OR = 4.2); physical load[49] (OR = 2.6); heavy workload[35, 50] (ORs = 4.1 to 8.0); "very stressful" work[51] (OR = 2.0);

and psychosocial factors[51-54] (ORs = 1.8 to 3.8). Psychosocial factors include factors such as high job demands, lack of social support from colleagues, competition, and low control over time.

The investigators of a recent 10-year prospective study of 902 metal-industry workers in Finland concluded that work-related psychosocial factors, such as poor satisfaction with social relationships at work and the psychological content of work, were associated with neck and shoulder pain at baseline and predicted change in occurrence of neck pain and other musculoskeletal disorders 10 years later.[55] These relationships were generally stronger among blue-collar compared to white collar workers, with the effects controlled for potential confounders including age, gender, social class, and physical workload. The investigators of a recent cross-sectional study of back and neck pain among 1449 public transit vehicle operators found that (1) ergonomic factors primarily related to seat and steering wheel position were the most important predictors of pain; (2) there was a dose–response relationship between years of driving and back and neck pain (OR = 3.43 for every 10 years of driving) after controlling for vehicle type, height, weight, age, and gender; and (3) the prevalence of pain among females was twice that of males.[56] Unfortunately, the authors' lumping together of back and neck pain complicates the interpretation of these findings.

Table 5–3: Occupational Risk/Prognostic Factors for Neck/Shoulder Pain, by Type of Factor

TYPE OF FACTOR	FACTOR	REFERENCE(S)
Physical	Arms raised above shoulder level	28
	Work with neck in bent position	28
	Work with twisted or bent posture	14, 29, 35, 47
	Work in static posture	32, 39, 46
	Work in seated position	44
	Monotonous work	14
	Work involving repetitive motion	32, 35–44
	Work with strenuous movements	14
	Work involving fast pace	28
	Physical stress	20
	Heavy physical loads	49
	Vibration	48
	Driving	56, 68
	Ergonomic factors	56
Psychosocial	Mentally stressful work	20, 51
	Low job satisfaction	29
	Poor psychosocial environment	30–33
	Psychologically demanding work	28, 34
	Lack of social support	51–55
	Competition	51–54
	Low control over time	51–54
	Heavy workload	35, 50
Occupation	Dentist	62–64
	Reindeer herder	65
	Medical secretary	32
	Forestry worker	66
	Construction worker	67
	Salesperson	54
	Driver	56, 68
	Video display terminal operator	51, 69
	Sewing machine operator	70, 71
	Lamp assembler	72
	Data entry operator	72
	Typist	72
	Scissor maker	72
	Assembly line packer	72

Waris[57] and Maeda et al[58] reviewed 20 and 15 primary studies, respectively, of occupational cervicobrachial syndromes. Waris[57] concluded that there is evidence for a relationship between occupational factors and cervical syndrome and acute "tension neck syndrome," and insufficient evidence for chronic "tension neck syndrome." Maeda et al[58] concluded that most of the studies were of poor quality; however, there is ample evidence from the well-designed studies to support causal associations between occupational factors and cervicobrachial disorders. Studies of neck and shoulder disorders in the workplace were also reviewed by Hagberg[59] and Anderson,[60] who concluded that comparing studies is fruitless because of lack of agreement on the definitions of cervical syndromes. Hagberg[59] reviewed 12 primary studies and concluded that occupational muscular stress may precede neck and shoulder disorders.

The vast majority of studies addressing occupational exposures and the risk of neck and shoulder pain (and related disorders) are plagued with limitations that preclude causal inference. Stock[61] considered 54 studies of occupational factors and musculoskeletal disorders of the neck and upper limbs for inclusion in a meta-analysis, of which only 3 met the inclusion criteria of having well-defined populations, explicit exposure criteria and definitions, measurement of outcomes using well-defined and explicit criteria, and employment of study designs that allowed for comparisons between groups.[61]

Table 5–3 lists occupations that may be associated with developing neck or shoulder pain, or associated with a poor prognosis.[32, 51, 56, 62–71] In a major review of neck and shoulder disorders, Hagberg and Wegman[72] calculated odds ratios as measures of association for a variety of occupations and tension neck syndrome (defined as pain, fatigue, and stiffness in the neck muscles). Occupations with a relatively higher prevalence of tension neck syndrome include film-rolling workers (OR = 118), industrial workers (OR = 5.9), lamp assemblers (OR = 5.1), data entry operators (OR = 2.3 and 4.9), typists (OR = 4.2), scissor makers (OR = 4.1), terminal operators (OR = 3.2), office workers (OR = 2.1), and assembly line packers (OR = 1.6).

THORACIC OUTLET SYNDROME

Thoracic outlet syndrome (TOS), which involves compression of one or more of the neurovascular components in the thoracic outlet, causes pain, numbness, weakness, and other symptoms.[73] Accurate estimates of the prevalence and incidence of TOS have not been reported. Some authors report the incidence as 0.3 to 0.7 percent per year,[74] whereas others believe the incidence is 1 to 2 percent.[73] Differences in diagnostic criteria and study populations probably explain much of this variation.

Table 5–2 lists possible risk or prognostic factors for TOS. Risk factors for TOS may include female sex and obesity.[75] Cervical ribs, which occur in 0.5 to 0.6 percent of the population and are twice as common in females, and other osseous abnormalities such as first rib abnormalities and large C7 transverse processes, are reported to be associated with about 30 percent of TOS cases.[76] The other 70 percent of cases are purportedly caused primarily by soft tissue structures in the thoracic outlet region. Empirical evidence from well-designed studies to support these statements is lacking. Although prior trauma was reported in 86 percent of TOS cases in one study[77] and poor posture has been reported as a predisposing factor,[73] the relative importance of these and other factors on TOS risk is unknown. Hagberg and Wegman's review[72] found assembly line packers (OR = 10), assembly line workers (OR = 3.9 and 9.6), slaughterhouse workers (OR = 2.5), and cash register operators (OR = 1.7) were relatively more likely than workers in other occupations to have thoracic outlet syndrome.

HEADACHE

Headache often accompanies neck pain.[10, 11, 21, 78, 79] An estimated 50 million headache sufferers lose 150 million workdays each year and cost businesses approximately $57 billion annually in lost productivity and medical expenses.[80] Headache accounts for 50 million visits yearly to U.S. health-care providers and constitutes 2.4 percent of all diagnostic clusters among primary care physicians.[81] Five to eight percent of all migraineurs in one study consulted nontraditional providers such as physiotherapists, herbalists, and chiropractors.[82] A survey of the U.S. population found that 6 percent of headache sufferers saw an alternative health-care provider (most commonly a chiropractor) within the past 12 months.[83]

The International Headache Society (IHS) has developed a classification system with standardized definitions for each type of primary headache.[84] The proper use of IHS diagnostic criteria in clinical and epidemiological research studies of headache should help to reduce misclassification and subsequent bias in the estimation of type-specific frequencies and exposure effects. Table 5–4 shows the estimated frequencies of any headache and specific types of headache in the population.

TENSION-TYPE AND MIGRAINE HEADACHE

The point prevalence of headache in the general population is estimated to be 16 percent.[85] The lifetime prevalence of tension-type headache in women and men is estimated to be 88 percent and 69 percent, respectively.[86] Rasmussen et al[86] conducted a population-based study of 760 25 to 64 year olds in Denmark and used IHS diagnostic criteria to estimate the 1-day point prevalence of any headache as 11 percent in men and 22 percent in women, and the 1-year period prevalence of migraine as 6 percent in men and 15 percent in women. These findings are consistent with a population-based study of 20,468 12 to 80

Table 5–4: Frequencies of Headache, by Type of Headache and Frequency Measure

TYPE OF HEADACHE	FREQUENCY MEASURE	POPULATION	FREQUENCY	REFERENCE(S)
Any Headache	Lifetime prevalence	Female	99%	86
		Male	93%	86
	Point prevalence	Total	16%	85
		Female	22%	86
		Male	11%	86
	Point prevalence (weekly aches)	Female	13.1%	21
		Male	6%	21
Tension-type Headache	Lifetime prevalence	Female	88%	86
		Male	69%	86
	1-year prevalence	Female	86%	86
		Male	63%	86
	1-week prevalence	Total	29%	85
Migraine Headache	Lifetime prevalence	Female	25%	86
		Male	8%	86
	1-year prevalence	Female	15–17.6%	86
		Male	6%	87
	1-week prevalence	Total	2%	85
	1-year incidence (with aura)	Female 12–29 years	14.1/1000	88
		Male 12–29 years	6.6/1000	88
	1-year incidence (without aura)	Female 12–29 years	18.9/1000	88
		Male 12–29 years	10/1000	88
Cervicogenic Headache	Point prevalence	Total 20–59 years	2.5%	85
		Headache sufferers 20–59	17.8%	85

year olds in the United States that employed modified IHS criteria, with male and female migraine prevalence estimates of 6 percent and 17.6 percent, respectively.[87] The prevalence of migraine peaks at about 40 years in both males and females; however, the sex-specific prevalence is higher in females than males at all ages over 12 years.[88] Evidence from National Health Interview Survey self-report data from 1981 through 1989 show the prevalence of migraine increasing 60 percent during this period.[89] The apparent increase in migraine prevalence may be real, or it may be explained by factors affecting self report, such as greater awareness, health-care use, and diagnosis of migraine.

The investigators of a population-based study of 12 to 29 year olds estimated the incidence of migraine with aura in males and females at 6.6 per 1000 person-years and 14.1 per 1000 person-years, respectively.[88] The estimates of incidence for migraine without aura in males and females were 10 per 1000 person-years and 18.9 per 1000 person-years, respectively. Although the overall incidence of tension-type headache is much greater than the incidence of migraine, the vast majority of sufferers do not seek care and there have been few population-based studies designed to

provide precise estimates of the incidence of tension-type headache.[82]

Table 5–5 lists possible risk or prognostic factors for each headache type. With the exceptions of age and sex, few other risk factors have been identified for tension-type and migraine headache. A recent cross-sectional study found a relationship between psychosocial variables and tension-type headache,[90] and past history of depression has been associated with tension-type headache in other studies.[91] Although many investigators have found appreciable cross-sectional associations between depression and anxiety disorders (e.g., panic, phobia, and generalized anxiety disorder), and migraine headache,[92] causal relationships cannot be inferred from these data. The results of one prospective study that addressed these relationships in young adults suggest the probable temporal sequence begins with anxiety, followed by migraine and, finally, depression.[93]

Population-based studies showing that about 70 percent of migraine sufferers have first-degree relatives with migraine[94] and twin studies finding greater concordance for migraine among monozygotic twins compared to dizygotic twins suggest a genetic etiology.[95] Other factors that were identified in a cross-sectional study of a general population

Table 5–5: Putative Risk/Prognostic Factors for Headache, by Type of Headache and Type of Factor

TYPE OF HEADACHE	TYPE OF FACTOR	FACTOR	REFERENCE(S)
Any Headache	Demographic	Female sex	21, 86
	Psychosocial	Stress	96
		Mental tension	96
	Other	Alcohol use	96
		Weather changes	96
		Menstruation	96
Tension-type Headache	Demographic	Female sex	86
	Physical	Sedentary activity	96
		Pericranial muscle tenderness	97
		Serotonin	99
	Psychosocial	Depression	91, 92
		Other psychosocial factors	90
Migraine Headache	Demographic	Female sex	86–88
		Family history of migraine	94, 95
		Age	86
		Low socioeconomic status	86
	Physical	Serotonin	99
Cervicogenic Headache	Demographic	Female sex	101
	Physical	Trapezius activity	103
	Occupational—Job	Managerial/professional	102

as possible risk or prognostic factors for tension-type and migraine headache were stress, mental tension, alcohol use, weather changes, and menstruation.[96] Sedentary activity in men was associated with tension-type headache only,[96] whereas a population-based study of 735 25 to 64 year olds found pericranial muscle tenderness to be associated with increased frequency of tension-type headaches but not migraine headaches,[97] suggesting an etiological or prognostic role for muscle factors in tension-type headache only. However, other investigators have found no correlation between electromyographic activity, muscle tenderness, and tension-type headache location.[98] Several investigators have suggested that an important factor in both migraine and tension-type headache etiology may be serotonin, which is increased in the plasma of migraine and tension-type headache sufferers during attacks.[99]

CERVICOGENIC HEADACHE

Population-based estimates of the prevalence and incidence of cervicogenic headache are almost nonexistent. The authors of a recent study of 826 randomly selected 20 to 59 year olds in Denmark estimated the prevalence of cervicogenic headache of about 2.5 percent.[85] Almost 18 percent of all headache sufferers were diagnosed with cer-

vicogenic headache according to a subset of the nonradiologic 1990 IHS classification criteria (e.g., pain localized to neck and occipital region, pain precipitated or aggravated by special neck movements or sustained neck posture, and resistance to or limitation of passive neck movements or abnormal tenderness of neck muscles). Nilsson[85] found that those with cervicogenic headache had a higher frequency of headache episodes compared to other headache sufferers (17 versus 9 headache days in the previous month). No differences were found between cervicogenic and noncervicogenic headache sufferers with respect to age, sex, or headache duration or severity.

Among a series of 127 headache patients who were all over the age of 50, 53 (41.7 percent) were classified as having cervicogenic pain.[100] Cervicogenic headaches have been found to be more common among females than males[101] and among females employed in managerial and professional occupations.[102] Recent evidence from a study comparing 17 cervicogenic headache patients with 17 healthy controls with respect to pain and electromyography levels suggests that the cervicogenic headache pain may be referred from the trapezius.[103] Other studies are needed to confirm this finding and to search for other risk factors for cervicogenic headache.

WHIPLASH

INCIDENCE

Estimates of the incidence of whiplash vary by more than tenfold. Mills and Horne[104] estimated the incidence of whiplash over a 12-month period in 1982 to 1983 in New Zealand and in Australia's State of Victoria to be 13 per 100,000 and 106 per 100,000, respectively. However, when only compensated whiplash injuries were considered, the rate in Victoria dropped to 39 per 100,000. Spitzer et al[105] used 1987 population-based data from Quebec to estimate annual incidence of compensated whiplash injury of 70 per 100,000. They found higher incidence rates among 20 to 24 year olds and among females compared to males (86 per 100,000 versus 54 per 100,000), which is consistent with Teasell.[106] Spitzer et al[105] also reported that the incidence of whiplash in Saskatchewan may be as high as 700 per 100,000. The annual rate of whiplash injury in the United States is estimated to be 4 per 1000, or about 1,000,000 injuries per year.[107] Barnsley et al[108] estimated the overall incidence of whiplash in Western societies to be about 1 per 1000, with a mean age in the thirties and no gender preponderance. Differences in estimates across sites may be due to differences in insurance, reporting, definitions, and other factors unrelated to risk of whiplash injury.

RISK AND PROGNOSTIC FACTORS

Table 5–6 lists potential risk and prognostic factors for whiplash injury. Otremski et al[109] identified all accident victims attending county hospitals in England over a certain period and concluded that females, persons aged 40 to 49, and persons wearing a seatbelt were more likely to suffer a whiplash injury compared to a nonwhiplash injury. Bourbeau et al[110] identified accident victims with whiplash injuries and compared them with those having other injuries, concluding that rear-end impact, collision with a heavier vehicle, and wearing a seatbelt were risk factors for whiplash. Galasko et al[111] identified post-road traffic accident patients attending selected hospitals in England during periods before and after seatbelt legislation (February 1982 to February 1983 versus February 1983 to February 1984). Their before- and after-legislation estimates of soft tissue injury of the cervical spine following traffic accidents were 7.7 percent (72 of 929) and 20.5 percent (193 of 940), indicating that seatbelts may be at least partially responsible for the increased proportion of traffic accidents resulting in soft tissue injury of the cervical spine. However, they also determined that the proportions increased from 30.9 percent in 1988 to 45.6 percent in 1991, suggesting that other factors, such as poor driving or a change in driving patterns, may also be responsible.[111] These findings should be viewed cautiously because of the non–population-based nature of the data: the study populations

Table 5–6: Putative Risk/Prognostic Factors for Whiplash Injury, by Type of Factor

RISK/PROGNOSTIC	TYPE OF FACTOR	FACTOR	REFERENCE(S)
Risk Factor	Demographic	Female sex	105, 106, 109, 112
		Age	105, 106, 109
	Physical	History of neck injury	112
		Collision with heavier vehicle	110
		Rear-end impact	110
		Seatbelt use	109–111
Prognostic Factor	Demographic	Female sex	105
		Increasing age	13, 105, 113
		Married/cohabiting	105
		Greater number of dependents	105
		Family history of neck pain	114
	Physical	Fatality/severe injury involved	105
		Stationary state of vehicle	115
		Lack of seatbelt use	105
		Unpreparedness at impact	115
		Rotated/inclined head position	13, 115
		Multiple injuries involved	105
		Initial head/neck pain intensity	13, 115
		Cervical spine degeneration	13
	Psychosocial	Expectation of disability	114

were comprised of only those persons who sought treatment and excluded persons in the populations at risk who suffered whiplash injuries but did not seek care. Dolinis[112] attempted to conduct a population-based study by identifying drivers who had a recent nonfatal, two-vehicle, rear-impact crash in South Australia, as reported to the South Australia police. Dolonis[112] concluded that having a history of neck injury (OR = 4.5) and being female (OR = 2.1) were independent risk factors for whiplash, while crash awareness, degree of forewarning, age, occupation, education, vehicle motion status prior to accident, and weight of either driver's car or striker's care were not predictive of whiplash injury. However, in light of a response rate of only 26 percent, these findings may not be valid.

Many studies have sought to identify factors that may predict delayed recovery or persistence of symptoms following whiplash injury (see Table 5–6). Spitzer et al[105] found that having multiple injuries, being female, being relatively older, having more dependents, being married or cohabiting, and being in a collision involving a fatality or a severe injury resulted in a longer time to return to usual activity, while seatbelt use resulted in returning to activity relatively sooner. Squires et al[113] interviewed 40 of 61 postwhiplash patients 15 years later. Of the 28 (70 percent) with neck pain or other symptoms referable to the accident, psychological disturbance was found in 52 percent versus 16 percent of those without symptoms. The 28 percent that deteriorated in the past 5 years were on average 5 years older than those who improved (18 percent) or were unchanged. Those with neck-related symptoms at 15 years were much more likely than those without symptoms to have had radiographic evidence of cervical spine degeneration at 11 years (21 of 26 or 80 percent versus 4 of 12 or 33 percent).[113]

Schrader et al[114] conducted a retrospective cohort study in Lithuania to identify factors associated with symptoms 1 to 3 years after a rear-end collision. Two-hundred-two persons exposed to collisions were compared to 202 persons not exposed and matched on age and sex. Similar proportions of both groups reported headache and chronic neck pain (10 percent in exposed versus 8 percent in unexposed), and no relation was found between severity of the impact and degree of pain. These authors found a family history of neck pain was the strongest predictor of having any neck pain (OR = 8.0), chronic neck pain (more than 7 days in the past month; OR = 3.2), and any headache (OR = 6.8), and that psychological symptoms were also predictive of any neck pain (OR = 1.6), chronic neck pain (OR = 2.1), any headache (OR = 1.9), and chronic headache (OR = 3.2). Use of seatbelts, headrest, and extent of car damage were not predictive of chronic neck pain and headache, and speed of the impact was not predictive of increased frequency of neck pain or headache.[114]

Sturzenegger et al[115] examined 117 postwhiplash injury primary care patients aged 19 to 51 years (mean age = 30.8; 58 percent female) 12 months after a baseline examination (mean 7.4 days postaccident), 28 of 117 or 24 per-

cent of whom were still symptomatic. They concluded that initial neck pain and headache intensity, head position (rotated or inclined), unpreparedness at impact, and stationary state of vehicle at impact were predictors of symptom persistence at 12 months, while baseline radiographic findings, baseline neurological loss, gender, vocational activity, and psychosocial factors were not predictive.[115, 116] The same patients were examined again 1 year later (2 years postaccident), 21 of 117 or 18 percent of whom continued to have accident-related symptoms.[13] Predictors of symptom persistence included being relatively older, rotated or inclined head position, having prior headache, greater initial neck pain and headache intensity, having more symptoms, radicular symptoms, and more radiographic evidence of cervical spine degeneration at baseline. Gender, vocational activity, and psychosocial factors were not found to be predictive of symptom persistence.

Borchgrevink et al[117] conducted a prospective study of 88 out of 353 patients admitted to an emergency department following car accidents. The 88 neck sprain patients, 18 to 70 years old (53 percent female) were examined within 4 days of being in the car accident and again 6 months later to determine predictors of symptom persistence (daily or constant neck pain, neck stiffness, or headache). Personality traits and psychiatric symptoms, as measured by the Millon Clinical Multiaxial Inventory, did not predict symptom persistence at 6 months, which is consistent with other studies.[118] Radanov et al[118] found psychological symptoms such as nervousness, irritability, and depression, as measured by the Freiburg Personality Inventory, are consequential to persistent injury-related symptoms rather than causal to them. Settlement of accident-related litigation has not been found to be predictive of symptom resolution in prospective[10, 119] or retrospective[120–124] studies.

TEMPOROMANDIBULAR JOINT DISORDERS

Temporomandibular joint disorders were recently defined by Dworkin and Massoth[125] as a heterogenous set of clinical conditions characterized by pain in the masticatory and related muscles of the head and neck, pain in the temporomandibular joint (TMJ) and associated hard and soft tissues, limitations in jaw function, and clicking and popping sounds in the TMJ. Persons who develop chronic TMJ-related pain may be similar to others with chronic pain syndromes with respect to the psychological and behavioral characteristics that precede or coexist with the chronic pain syndrome.

PREVALENCE AND INCIDENCE

There are very few reported estimates of the incidence or prevalence of TMD. Similarly, there is a dearth of research on the assessment of potential risk factors for TMD. Many of the estimates may be questionable and variable because of methodologic (e.g., clinic- versus population-based studies; examinations versus interviews) and definitional differences between studies. The prevalence of TMD in the general population has been estimated at 6 percent[126, 127] to 12 percent[128] in enrollees in health maintenance organizations (HMOs). The prevalence of TMD is two or more times greater in females than males, the prevalence is highest among females of reproductive age, and females are much more likely to seek TMD-related treatment.[129–131] Other investigators have noted that females have more problems with their masticatory systems than males, that TMD problems are more physically and psychologically severe in females,[132] and that females have a greater risk for disability.[133]

Schiffman et al[134] conducted a cross-sectional study of the prevalence of TMJ-related signs and symptoms among 269 female nursing students. Although 69 percent had clinically detectable TMD (19 percent had a joint disorder, 23 percent muscle, and 27 percent both), only 6.7 percent had ever sought TMD-related treatment. Dworkin et al[135] selected a probability sample of adults 18 to 75 years old enrolled in an HMO. They compared signs of TMD in clinic cases referred for treatment with community cases who reported pain but did not seek treatment in the past 6 months, and with persons in the community who did not report TMD symptoms. TMD-related pain was reported by 12.1 percent of the study population. A greater proportion of the clinic cases were female (84 percent) versus the community cases (75 percent), and the clinic cases had more pain on movement and palpation as well as more joint clicking. No differences were detected with respect to age, and TMD was found to be less prevalent among older persons, suggesting that TMD is a self-limiting condition.

Glass et al[136] conducted a telephone survey of 534 residents (217 males and 317 females) in Kansas City, Missouri, to estimate the prevalence of TMD-related symptoms. They found that 46 percent reported one or more of six symptoms, including nocturnal bruxism, diurnal clicking, jaw soreness, and joint sounds, with individual prevalences ranging from 10 to 19 percent; that there were no differences by sex; that the symptoms were more prevalent in those under age 45; and that the prevalence of reported pain increases as the number of reported symptoms increases. These findings are consistent with a prior survey conducted in St. Louis;[137] however, the results may not be valid because only 50 percent of those selected agreed to be interviewed and the validity of the interview instrument (i.e., how the symptoms relate to clinical findings) is unknown. Duckro et al[137] found symptom prevalences of 8 to 12 percent, with 149 of 500 respondents (30 percent) in their random telephone survey reporting at least one of the five symptoms.

RISK AND PROGNOSTIC FACTORS

The greater prevalence of TMD and TMD-related disability among females reported by these investigators suggests that sex may be a risk and prognostic factor for TMD. Signs and symptoms of TMD have been found to be more common in patients with neck and shoulder symptoms than in healthy controls,[138] and a higher prevalence of cervical signs and symptoms has been found in TMD patients than in healthy controls,[139, 140] although a recent study found no difference.[141] LeResche et al[142] conducted a case-control study of 1291 women with TMD and 5164 age-matched controls (age >40 years) and determined that those receiving estrogen were more likely to have TMD compared to those not receiving estrogen (OR = 1.32), and there was a dose-response relationship. The authors also conducted a case-control study of 1473 cases and 5892 controls 15 to 35 years old and determined that oral contraceptive use was associated with having TMD (OR = 1.16). Kolbinson et al[143] concluded after an exhaustive review of the literature that whiplash injury may be a risk factor for TMD, although much of the data were inconsistent, incomplete, and difficult to interpret due to methodological shortcomings of the primary studies and the lack of data on the natural history of TMD. The authors of a recent comprehensive literature review of the possible relationship between bruxism and TMD concluded that existing data could not be used to make a causal determination.[144]

Vimpari et al[145] found an association between depression, as measured by the Zung Depression Scale, and TMD symptoms in 780 55-year-old Finnish subjects. Subjective symptoms of TMD were found in 12.0 percent of the subjects, clinical symptoms in 4.9 percent, and depressive symptoms in 12.2 percent of the subjects. Depression and having symptoms in the shoulders or upper arms in the past 12 months increased the odds of having TMD (depression: OR = 2.40; shoulder/arm symptoms: OR = 2.06). Of the 10,549 TMD patients in a national study who completed the TMJ Scale (1579 males and 8970 females), females had higher severity levels for all physical and psychological symptoms (e.g., pain, palpation pain, perceived malocclusion, joint dysfunction, and limited range of motion) than males as well as greater severity of non-TMD symptoms, psychological factors, and stress.[132]

Schnurr et al[146] compared 202 TMJ patients with 79 non-TMJ pain patients and 71 healthy and pain-free students, finding no clinically important differences between groups with respect to personality type, hypochondriasis, anxiety, attitudes toward health care, or coping strategies. These findings are consistent with those of McKinney et al,[147] who found 78 TMD patients and 98 non-TMD patients to be similar with respect to levels of depression, anxiety, somatization, and illness behavior. Southwell et al[148] compared 32 TMJ patients with 32 sex- and age-matched dental clinic controls, finding that TMJ patients scored higher on the neuroticism and introversion scales of the Eysenck Personality Questionnaire, suggesting that TMJ patients have "stress-prone" personalities.

Kolbinson et al[143] indicate that nontrauma-related TMD is self-limiting in nature, while trauma-related TMD may or may not be self-limiting. De Boever and

Keersmaekers[149] reported similar treatment outcomes for trauma and nontrauma-related TMD. A 30-year prospective study on the natural progression of TMD revealed that TMD disorders follow a course irrespective of treatment.[150] Although Raphael and Marbach[151] found the course of TMD to be highly variable and independent of therapy, Marbach[152] found in his series of TMD cases that elevated levels of distress in 1 month were associated with higher levels of pain in the next month. Other studies have found that TMJ disc displacement has a prevalence of 33 percent in asymptomatic volunteers[153] and TMJ-related osteoarthritis and internal derangement is nonprogressive, and TMJ degenerative disease is self-limiting.[154] In a 5-year follow-up study of patients with masticatory myalgias, which comprise about 50 percent of all TMD cases,[155] 50 percent of patients reported freedom from pain after 1 year, 63.3 percent after 3 years, and 56.7 percent after 5 years.[156]

CONGENITAL MALFORMATIONS AND DEFORMITIES OF THE CERVICAL SPINE

Although congenital anomalies of the cervical spine are rare, the precise frequencies are unknown. The incidence of most anomalies is probably much higher than case reports would suggest since most are asymptomatic and do not present for clinical care. Many anomalies are discovered during post-traumatic radiographic examinations.[157]

UPPER CERVICAL SPINE ANOMALIES

Basilar Impression

Basilar impression is the most common congenital anomaly of the atlanto-occipital region.[157] Primary basilar impression is congenital, whereas secondary (acquired) basilar impression results from abnormal development or disease, such as Paget's disease, rickets, osteoporosis, renal osteodystrophy, rheumatoid arthritis, neurofibromatosis, or ankylosing spondylitis, which can cause softening around the base of the skull around the foramen magnum.[158] Although primary basilar impression initially develops in the embryo or fetus, symptoms do not usually occur until the teenage years or later. Symptoms are typically secondary to neurological or vascular impingement at the foramen magnum.[157]

Atlanto-occipital Fusion and Instability

Atlanto-occipital fusion involves partial or complete bony union of C1 to the base of the skull and is often associated with other cervical anomalies (e.g., basilar impression, Klippel-Feil syndrome).[157] Patients most often present with Klippel-Feil-type features, such as a short neck, low hairline, and limitation of neck mobility, and may present with torticollis or a high scapula.[158] The onset of neurological symptoms is usually delayed until the fifth decade and is often associated with trauma or an inflammatory process.[159]

Atlanto-axial instability may be congenital, or more commonly, secondary to trauma.[158] Persons with atlanto-axial instability usually become symptomatic in adulthood, with symptoms associated with cardiopulmonary arrest, motor weakness, vertigo, neck pain, and torticollis, or rarely, quadriplegia. Atlanto-axial instability is often associated with congenital scoliosis, osteogenesis imperfecta, neurofibromatosis, Morquio's syndrome, Larsen's syndrome, and Down syndrome, with a prevalence of 10 to 40 percent.[158]

Os Odontoideum

Os odontoideum is the most common odontoid process malformation.[158] Although one study of os odontoideum in identical twins[160] and the presence of os odontoideum with Klippel-Feil syndrome, Down syndrome, and other congenital conditions suggest a congenital etiology, longitudinal studies have shown development of post-traumatic os odontoideum in patients with radiographically normal spines prior to injury.[161] A recent study of identical twins demonstrating os odontoideum in only one twin posttraumatically[161] lends further support to an acquired etiology, which may be due to nonunion after fracture or secondary to vascular compromise. Whether congenital or acquired, trauma is frequently related to symptom onset, which includes neck pain, torticollis, headache, paresis, myelopathy, or ischemia from vertebral artery compromise.[158] Signs or symptoms of neurological compromise were observed in one third of os odontoideum patients in one study.[162]

Defects of the Atlas and Axis

Defects of the atlas and axis are caused by failure of fusion of the synchondroses of the developing cervical vertebrae.[157] Posterior arch defects are about four times more common than anterior arch defects; however, the incidence of both is probably less than 0.5 percent.[158] These defects may be asymptomatic or may be associated with neurological symptoms secondary to atlanto-axial instability.[158] A longitudinal study of 17 patients with congenital defects of the atlas ring demonstrated progression from flexible torticollis in early childhood to fixed torticollis in later years.[163]

LOWER CERVICAL SPINE ANOMALIES

Anomalous growth in the lower cervical spine is due to disruption during cervical spine differentiation.[157] The associated presence of multisystem involvement is due to the physical proximity of other developing structures at the time of disruption. The cause of lower cervical anomalies is probably multifactorial, including genetic, vascular, maternal substance abuse, and other factors.[158]

Klippel-Feil Syndrome

Klippel-Feil syndrome (KFS) is a congenital condition that involves fusion or segmental defects of the cervical vertebrae, or both, with associated low posterior hairline, restriction of neck motion, and a short neck in the majority of cases (53 percent of patients have the classic triad).[158] About 1 per 40,000 births is affected with KFS with two thirds of the cases being female.[164] A recent retrospective analysis of 57 KFS cases (17 males, 40 females) over a 25-year period revealed that KFS is associated with many anomalies, including scoliosis (70 percent), Sprengel's deficiency (26 percent), longitudinal arm deficiency (10.5 percent), and tetraparesis (5 percent). Cardiovascular anomalies were reported in 3.5 percent of the cases. Thirty-eight cases (67 percent) had nonscoliosis anomalies. Scoliosis was most severe in types I (cervical fusion with synostosis) and III (cervical and lower thoracic or lumbar fusion) compared to type II (isolated cervical fusion).[164] Scoliosis was recently reported in 78 percent of 111 KFS cases.[165] A 10-year follow-up of 32 KFS cases (10 male, 22 female) with congenital scoliosis found that 7 (22 percent) developed cervical or related symptoms.[166] Those with surgically fused cervicothoracic junctions were more likely to develop cervical symptoms, whereas those with congenital stenosis were more likely to develop upper extremity symptoms.

Cervical Ribs

Cervical ribs occur in 0.5 to 0.6 percent of the population.[76] Eighty percent of cases are bilateral and the frequency is twofold higher in females.[158] Cervical ribs occur when limb buds receive developmental contributions from cervical rather than thoracic vertebrae, which causes large ribs to form at C7.[158] Maternal exposure to alcohol may play an etiological role.[167] Cervical ribs are usually asymptomatic; however, the presence of cervical ribs may be a risk factor for thoracic outlet syndrome.[158]

INJURIES OF THE CERVICAL SPINE

CERVICAL SPINE FRACTURES

One population-based study describing the frequency of cervical spine fracture was found in the literature. The investigators used a cross-sectional design with administrative data from Manitoba to estimate the annual incidence of spinal fracture at 64 per 100,000.[168] Of the 944 patients identified over a 3-year period, 182 (19.3 percent) suffered cervical fractures and 286 (30 percent) suffered thoracic fractures. Of the cervical spine fractures, 82 (45 percent) were at C1–4 and 82 (45 percent) were at C5–7. One-hundred-forty (77 percent) were neurologically intact, while 42 (33 percent) experienced neurological injury.[168] Accidental falls and motor vehicle accidents were the most common mechanisms of injury, with the incidence of accidental falls relatively higher among females 70 years old and older, and the incidence of motor vehicle accidents higher among males 20 to 29 years old.

The annual incidence of spinal fracture rises dramatically with age, from less than 60 per 100,000 among females less than 60 years old to 438 per 100,000 among females 80 years old or older. The age-related increase among females may be due, at least in part, to osteopenia from primary osteoporosis, which is responsible for 1.5 million fractures per year.[169] The age-specific rates among males are higher than among females up to age 60, and are twice as high in the 15 to 29-year-old segment. These figures are consistent with other studies that have showed a young male predominance among trauma patients.[170–172] In a case series of 332 cervical spine injuries, 22 percent of those caused by accidents involved drugs or alcohol at the time of the accident.[170] A retrospective study of 5021 consecutive trauma patients admitted to a trauma center over a 1½-year period showed that the incidence of cervical spine injury is no higher among victims of trauma to the head, face, and clavicle than among nonhead-injured patients.[173]

CERVICAL SPINE INJURIES IN CHILDREN

The incidence of cervical spine injury in persons aged 15 years or younger is estimated to be 7.41 per 100,000 per year.[174] A retrospective analysis of 143 patients with cervical spine injuries from 1950 to 1991 found that children younger than 11 years old were most likely to be injured in falls and to suffer ligamentous injuries of the upper cervical spine, while those 11 to 15 years old were more likely to be injured during sports and recreational activities, to be male, and to suffer injuries to the lower cervical spine.[174] Another recent analysis of 34 patients with cervical spine injuries occurring over a 3-year period revealed that 68 percent were caused by motor vehicle accidents.[175] Of the 20 patients 8 years old or younger, 50 percent suffered injuries below C4, and of the 15 patients incurring injuries in motor vehicle accidents in this group, 12 (80 percent) were unrestrained or not restrained appropriately.

DEGENERATIVE DISORDERS OF THE CERVICAL SPINE

CERVICAL SPONDYLOSIS AND DISC DEGENERATION

Cervical spondylosis, which involves degenerative changes in the cervical spine, including spondyloarthrosis, apophyseal joint osteoarthritis, and disc degeneration, is extremely common. It is estimated that 90 percent of males over the age of 50 and 90 percent of females over the age of 60 have radiographic evidence of degeneration in the cervical spine[176] (Table 5–7). Gore et al[177] found 95 percent of males and 70 percent of females had at least one degenerative change by 60 to 65 years of age. The degenerative process has been seen in people as young as 30 years old and apparently begins in the intervertebral disc. C5–6 and C6–7 are the discs most commonly affected.[16, 177] The radiographic prevalence of advanced lateral atlanto-axial osteoarthritis (e.g., severe narrowing or obliteration of joint

Table 5–7: Frequencies of Fractures and Degenerative Disorders of the Cervical Spine, by Type of Disorder and Frequency Measure

TYPE OF DISORDER	FREQUENCY MEASURE	POPULATION	FREQUENCY	REFERENCE(S)
Cervical Spine Fracture	1-year incidence	Total	64/100,000	168
		Female <60 years	60/100,000	169
		Female 80+ years	438/100,000	169
Cervical Spondylosis	Point prevalence	Female 60+ years	70–90%	176, 177
		Male 50+ years	90%	176, 177
		Male 60–65 years	95%	177
Cervical Radiculopathy	1-year incidence	Total	83.2/100,000	184
		Female	63.5/100,000	184
		Male	107.3/100,000	184

space, subchondral sclerosis, and osteophytosis) was recently estimated to be 4.8 percent in a population of 355 patients aged 12 to 89 years old.[178] Not surprisingly, the prevalence increased with age, from zero among those less than 50 years old to 5.4 percent among 50 to 59 year olds, 8.3 percent among 60 to 69 year olds, 13.2 percent among 70 to 79 year olds, and 18.2 percent among 80 to 89 year olds.

Table 5–8 lists risk and prognostic factors for degenerative disorders of the cervical spine. Although age appears to be the major risk factor for degenerative changes, workers in certain occupations are more likely to have degenerative changes.[16, 72] Hult[17] reported that forest workers had a higher prevalence of radiographic evidence of degenerative changes than industrial workers. In an exhaustive review of the literature from 1966 to 1986, Hagberg and Wegman calculated ORs for the association between occupation and cervical spondylosis: meat carriers (OR = 8.4), dentists (ORs = 4.0 and 5.3), miners (ORs = 1.9 and 4.5), and heavy workers (ORs = 1.7). Cotton workers were less likely to have radiographic evidence of degenerative changes compared to the general population (ORs ranging from 0.57 to 0.75). Slaughterhouse workers, scissor makers, and civil servants were more likely to have cervical disc disease, with ORs of 8.5, 5.0, and 4.8, respectively.[72] Data entry operators, dockers, assembly line packers, and iron foundry workers were less likely to have cervical disc disease, with ORs of 0.54, 0.47, 0.27, and 0.07, respectively.

The effect of cervical spine injury on risk of degenerative changes in the cervical spine is not clear, although there is some evidence demonstrating a link. For example, Jonsson et al[179] found postmortem evidence of zygapophyseal joint injuries in 86 percent of motor vehicle accident victims examined. Among injured patients with no evidence of degenerative changes, Hohl[180] found radiographic evidence of cervical spondylosis in 39 percent of whiplash victims 7 years, on average, after the accident, rising to 60 percent among victims of the most severe acute whiplash injuries. These results should be interpreted cautiously be-

cause only 27 percent of the patients received follow-up examinations. More recent, albeit small, studies have found no relationship between whiplash injury and degenerative changes.[181, 182]

CERVICAL RADICULOPATHY

Disc herniation and cervical spondylosis are the most common causes of cervical radiculopathy.[183] Investigators employing a population-based survey in Rochester, Minnesota, from 1976 to 1990 identified 561 patients (332 males and 229 females, from 13 to 91 years old) with cervical radiculopathy.[184] They estimated the age-adjusted incidence of cervical radiculopathy to be 83.2 per 100,000 per year, with the highest age-specific rate of 202.9 per 100,000 per year for persons 50 to 54 years old.[184] The rate for males was almost twice that for females (107.3 versus 63.5 per 100,000 per year) (see Table 5–7). Cervical disc protrusion was present in 21.9 percent of the cases; 68.4 percent had radiographically confirmed spondylosis, disc protrusion, or both. The C7 nerve root was the most commonly affected. Although only 14.8 percent of the cases reported physical exertion or trauma preceding the symptoms, more than 40 percent of the cases reported a history of lumbar radiculopathy.[184] These data contrast to an earlier analysis from Rochester that used data from 1950 to 1974.[185] The authors of that analysis calculated an overall incidence of radicular symptoms caused by herniations or protrusions of 5.5 per 100,000 per year, with sex-specific rates of 6.5 per 100,000 per year for males and 4.6 per 100,000 for females.

A survey of 20 to 64 year olds with radiographically confirmed cervical prolapsed discs in New Haven and Hartford, Connecticut, between 1979 and 1981, found that males were 40 percent more likely to be affected than females, C5–6 and C6–7 were the most commonly affected discs (75 percent), and 23 percent of the cases were preceded by a motor vehicle accident.[186–188] Kelsey et al[186–188]

Table 5–8: Putative Risk/Prognostic Factors for Fractures and Degenerative Disorders of the Cervical Spine, by Disorder and Type of Factor

DISORDER	TYPE OF FACTOR	FACTOR	REFERENCE(S)
Cervical Spine Fracture	Demographic	Increasing age	169
		Female sex at age 60+	169
		Male sex before age 60	169–172
Spondylosis/Disc Degeneration	Demographic	Increasing age	176, 178
	Physical	Cervical spine injury	179, 180
	Occupational—Job	Forestry worker	72
		Meat carrier	72
		Dentist	72
		Miner	72
		Slaughterhouse worker	72
		Scissor maker	72
		Civil servant	72
Cervical Radiculopathy	Demographic	Male sex	184–188
		Increasing age	184–188
	Physical	Motor-vehicle accident	186–188
		Frequent lifting	186–188
		Cigarette smoking	186–188
		Frequent diving	186–188
Cervical Myelopathy	Demographic	Male sex	192
		Increasing age (50+)	192
	Physical	Cervical disc degeneration	176, 195
		Narrow spinal canals	189, 190
		Spinal cord injury	191
		Ossification of the PLL[a]	195

[a]PLL, posterior longitudinal ligament.

also reported that frequent lifting, cigarette smoking, and frequent diving were associated with prolapsed cervical discs (see Table 5–8). The recent study from Rochester found that about 75 percent of cervical radiculopathy patients reported symptom resolution with nonsurgical care.[184]

CERVICAL MYELOPATHY

Cervical myelopathy is the most serious condition resulting from cervical disc degeneration. Cervical myelopathy may also be caused by congenitally narrow spinal canals (10 to 13 mm)[189, 190] and by acute spinal cord injury.[191] Cervical myelopathy may involve upper and lower motor neuron abnormalities, reflex changes, and gait abnormalities.[176] The prevalence and incidence of cervical myelopathy are not known. Some authors believe cervical myelopathy is vastly underdiagnosed.[192, 193] More than twice as many males as females are affected, and the typical patient is more than 50 years old.[192] The intervertebral levels affected, in descending order of frequency, are C5–6, C4–5,

C6–7, and C3–4.[194] Some investigators have noted that the degree of cervical myelopathy depends on the magnitude of cord compression, the length of time that the cord has been compressed, and the nature of the compression (continuous or remittent)[195] (see Table 5–8). Although biologically plausible, there is no epidemiological literature to support these beliefs.

Pathophysiological etiologies for cervical myelopathy include disc herniation, spondylosis (e.g., due to repetitive or acute trauma or to aging), loss of vertebral height (e.g., from trauma or osteoporosis), degenerative changes interacting with prior acute trauma or a congenital anomaly (e.g., narrow spinal canal, Klippel-Feil syndrome), and ossification of the posterior longitudinal ligament.[195] The natural history of cervical myelopathy is variable, although it does parallel the normal aging process with some evidence that most untreated persons remain somewhat disabled with a gradual deterioration over time.[196] Other investigators have reported that 30 to 50 percent of patients with cervical myelopathy will show improvement with nonsurgical care.[197]

RHEUMATOID ARTHRITIS

The prevalence of rheumatoid arthritis (RA) in the United States is about 1 percent.[198] Females are twice as likely to be affected as males, and RA is most predominant in persons 30 to 60 years old. The cervical spine is one of the most common sites for RA involvement. Studies have shown that from 19 to 88 percent of RA patients have radiographic evidence of cervical spine involvement.[199, 200] This wide interstudy variability is probably due to differences in patient populations with respect to selection and diagnostic criteria, disease severity, time since onset, and other factors. The most frequent cervical spine abnormality among RA patients is anterior atlanto-axial subluxation (AAS), which is radiographically evident in 19 to 70 percent of RA cases.[199–201] Subluxations below C2 are seen in 7 to 29 percent of RA patients.[200, 202]

There is a dearth of information regarding the natural history of cervical spine involvement in RA.[202] In a 10-year follow-up of 41 RA patients with AAS, 27 percent became more subluxated, 12 percent became less subluxated, and 61 percent were unchanged.[203] Predictors of AAS progression include being male, a larger degree of baseline subluxation, cranial settling, and lateral subluxation.[204]

TUMORS OF THE CERVICAL SPINE

PRIMARY TUMORS

Primary cervical neoplasms account for about 1 percent of patients with primary bone tumors.[205] The investigators of a population-based study in Minnesota estimated the annual incidence of primary spinal tumors to be 2.5 per 100,000, while the prevalence was estimated to be 12.9 per 100,000.[206] Malignant neoplasms are more likely in older patients, whereas neoplasms found in children and adolescents are more likely to be benign.[207] Overall, benign primary cervical neoplasms are much more common and include hemangioma, osteochondroma, osteoid osteoma, osteoblastoma, and giant cell tumor of bone.[176] Malignant primary cervical neoplasms include chordoma, multiple myeloma, osteosarcoma, and chondrosarcoma. Intrinsic spinal tumors, which are classified as extradural (22 percent of primary spinal cord tumors), intradural-extramedullary (55 percent), and intramedullary (23 percent), are very rare.[176, 208] About 17.5 percent of intramedullary tumors occur in the cervical spinal cord, whereas intradural-extramedullary tumors, such as meningiomas and neurofibromas, are extremely rare in the cervical spinal cord.[209]

Of 58 cervical spine lesions observed over a 50-year period at Rizzoli Institute, 46 lesions (79 percent) were benign and 12 (21 percent) were malignant.[210] Of the 23 patients with primary tumors of the cervical spine, all of those under age 21 had benign tumors while 10 out of 14 (71 percent) of those over age 21 had malignant tumors.[211]

Of the benign tumors, osteochondroma (exostosis) is the most common. About 60 percent of all vertebral osteochondromas involve the cervical spine. Although aneurysmal bone cysts (ABC) and giant cell tumors are typically found in the thoracolumbar spine, 10 of 40 cases of ABC (25 percent) observed at Rizzoli Institute involved the cervical spine and 4 of 29 giant cell tumors (14 percent) involved the cervical spine.[210] Eosinophilic granuloma, which primarily affects children less than 10 years old and usually involves the skull, was found in the cervical spine in 6 of 52 cases (11 percent) observed at Rizzoli Institute.

A recent review of 41 patients diagnosed with benign cervical spine tumors at Rizzoli Institute from January 1952 through August 1988 described age at diagnosis, type of tumor, location, and presenting symptoms.[212] Thirty-nine patients (95 percent) presented with neck pain, 12 (29 percent) with accompanying torticollis, and the rest with accompanying neck stiffness; only eight (19.5 percent) had palpable masses. Fourteen patients (34 percent) were 10 years old or younger, 18 (44 percent) were 11 to 20 years old, and nine (22 percent) were 21 years old or older. The type of tumors, in descending order of frequency, were osteoid osteoma (44 percent), osteoblastoma (15 percent), ABC (15 percent), eosinophilic granuloma (12 percent), giant cell tumor (5 percent), osteochondroma (5 percent), hemangioma (2.4 percent), and Gorham's disease (2.4 percent). The vertebral locations represented, in descending order of frequency, were C4 (27 percent), C2 (24 percent), C7 (17 percent), C6 (15 percent), C5 (10 percent), and C3 (7 percent).[212] Beer and Menezes[213] reviewed the cases of 45 children 16 years old or younger diagnosed with a primary spinal tumor from 1951 through 1996. Of the 12 (27 percent) cases that involved the cervical spine, 7 (58 percent) were benign and 5 (42 percent) were malignant.

SECONDARY TUMORS

Metastatic tumors of the spine are much more common than primary spinal tumors, and in fact, account for 40 times as many patients as are affected by all other forms of bone cancer combined.[210] However, estimating the prevalence and incidence of spinal metastasis in general or by location is difficult because of the lack of population-based data. The primary sites that produced metastatic spinal tumors among 2748 cases reported in the literature, in descending order of frequency, were breast (21 percent), lung (14 percent), lymphoma (9 percent), prostate (7.5 percent), kidney (5.5 percent), gastrointestinal (5 percent), and thyroid (2.5 percent).[214]

The authors of a case series of 19 consecutive patients with cervical spine metastases noted that 40 percent of all spinal metastases identified during their 3-year review period were of the cervical spine, and of these, 57 percent were from the breast, prostate, or lung.[215] Although renal neoplasms were the most likely to metastasize to the spine (11 of 48 or 22.5 percent), only one of these metastasized to the cervical spine. The mean age at diagnosis was 61.1

(range = 30 to 85 years) and 18 of the patients (95 percent) were white. Sixteen cases (85 percent) involved the lower cervical spine only, with C5 and C6 predominating, and 17 cases (89 percent) involved multiple levels. They noted that of all neoplasms identified during their review period, 60 percent of breast neoplasms, 50 percent of lung neoplasms, 45 percent of prostate neoplasms, and 33 percent of bladder neoplasms localized to the cervical spine.[215]

CONCLUSION

Pain is the primary symptom associated with most of the disorders discussed in this chapter, including thoracic outlet syndrome, headache, whiplash, TMJ disorders, and degenerative conditions. Although sets of risk and prognostic factors have been identified for many cervical spine disorders, we have much less understanding of the epidemiology of pain and of pain-related disability and behavioral adaptations. Integrative research with the goals of increasing our understanding of the nature and mechanisms of the interactions between pain processing, neuroendocrine and immune factors, behavior, and their relationships to aberrant physiological responses and to the development of chronic pain, disability, and related disorders, promises to be a fruitful strategy to pursue in the coming years. A greater understanding of the etiology of pain and the interrelationships of pain and pain-related disability to psychosocial and behavioral factors should lead to the development of more effective therapeutic and preventive interventions for many cervical spine disorders.

REFERENCES

1. Last JM. *A Dictionary of Epidemiology.* 2nd ed. New York, NY: Oxford University Press; 1988.
2. Zucker DR, Schmid CH, McIntosh MW, D'Agostino RB, Selker HP, Lau J. Combining single patient (n-of-1) trials to estimate population treatment effects and to evaluate individual patient responses to treatment. *J Clin Epidemiol* 1997;50:401–410.
3. Backman CL, Harris SR, Chisholm JM, Monette AD. Single-subject research in rehabilitation: A review of studies using AB, withdrawal, multiple baseline, and alternating treatments designs. *Arch Phys Med Rehabil* 1997;78:1145–1153.
4. Rothman KJ, Greenland S. *Modern Epidemiology.* 2nd ed. Philadelphia, Pa: Lippincott-Raven; 1998.
5. Stussman BJ. *National Hospital Ambulatory Medical Care Survey: 1993 Emergency Department Summary. Advance Data from Vital and Health Statistics;* No. 271. Hyattsville, Md: National Center for Health Statistics; 1996.
6. Schappert SM. *National Ambulatory Medical Care Survey: 1994 Summary. Advance Data from Vital and Health Statistics;* No. 273. Hyattsville, Md: National Center for Health Statistics; 1996.
7. Clark W, Haldeman S. The development of guideline factors for the evaluation of disability in neck and back injuries. *Spine* 1993;18:1736–1745.
8. Hurwitz EL, Coulter ID, Adams AH, Genovese BJ, Shekelle PG. Use of chiropractic services from 1985–1991 in the United States and Canada. *Am J Public Health* 1998;88:771–776.
9. Shekelle PG, Brook RH. A community-based study of the use of chiropractic services. *Am J Public Health* 1991;81:439–442.
10. Norris SH, Watt I. The prevalence of neck injuries resulting from rear-end collisions. *J Bone Joint Surg (Br)* 1983;65:608–611.
11. Hildingsson C, Toolanen G. Outcome after soft-tissue injury of the cervical spine: A prospective study of 93 car-accident victims. *Acta Orthop Scand* 1990;61:357–359.
12. Barnsley L, Lord S, Bogduk N. Whiplash injury. *Pain* 1994;58:284–307.
13. Radanov BP, Sturzenegger M, Di Stefano G. Long-term outcome after whiplash injury. *Medicine* 1995;74:281–297.
14. Nygren A, Berglund A, von Koch M. Neck-and-shoulder pain, an increasing problem. Strategies for using insurance material to follow trends. *Scan J Rehab Med* 1995;32(suppl):107–112.
15. Horal J. The clinical appearance of low back disorders in the city of Gothenburg, Sweden. *Acta Orthop Scand* 1969;118(suppl):42–45.
16. Hult L. Cervical, dorsal and lumbar spinal syndromes. *Acta Orthop Scand* 1954;17(suppl):175–277.
17. Hult L. The Munkfors investigation: A study of the frequency and causes of stiff neck-brachialgia and lumbago-sciatic syndromes, as well as observations on certain signs and symptoms from the dorsal spine and the joints of the extremities in industrial and forest workers. *Acta Orthop Scand* 1954;16(suppl):12–29.
18. Bovim G, Schrader H, Sand T. Neck pain in the general population. *Spine* 1994;19:1307–1309.

19. van der Donk J, Schouten JASAG, Passchier J, Romunde LKJ, Valkenburg HA. The associations of neck pain with radiological abnormalities of the cervical spine and personality traits in a general population. *J Rheumatol* 1991;18:1884–1889.

20. Makela M, Heiliovara M, Sieveers K, Impivaara O, Knekt P, Aromaa A. Prevalence, determinants and consequences of chronic neck pain in Finland. *Am J Epidemiol* 1991;134:1356–1367.

21. Hasvold T, Johnson R. Headache and neck or shoulder pain—frequent and disabling complaints in the general population. *Scand J Prim Health Care* 1993;11:219–224.

22. Schrader H, Obelieniene D, Bovim G, et al. Natural evolution of late whiplash syndrome outside the medicolegal context. *Lancet* 1996;347:1207–1211.

23. Bergenudd H, Johnell O. Somatic versus nonsomatic shoulder and back pain experience in middle age in relation to body build, physical fitness, bone mineral content, gamma-glutamyltransferase, occupational workload, and psychosocial factors. *Spine* 1991;16:1051–1055.

24. Viikari-Juntura E, Vuori J, Silverstein BA, Kalimo R, Kuosma E, Videman T. A life-long prospective study on the role of psychosocial factors in neck-shoulder and low-back pain. *Spine* 1991;16:1056–1061.

25. Manninen P, Heliovaara M, Riihimaki H, Makela P. Does psychological distress predict disability? *Int J Epidemiol* 1997;26:1063–1070.

26. Griegel-Morris P, Larson K, Mueller-Klaus K, Oatis CA. Incidence of common postural abnormalities in the cervical, shoulder, and thoracic regions and their association with pain in two age groups of healthy subjects. *Phys Ther* 1992;72:425–431.

27. Lauren H, Luoto S, Alaranta H, Taimela S, Hurri H, Heliovaara M. Arm motion speed and risk of neck pain: A preliminary communication. *Spine* 1997;22:2094–2099.

28. Johansson JA, Rubenowitz S. Risk indicators in the psychosocial and physical work environment for work-related neck, shoulder and low back symptoms: A study among blue- and white-collar workers in eight companies. *Scand J Rehab Med* 1994;26:131–142.

29. Tola S, Riihimaki H, Videman T, et al. Neck and shoulder symptoms among men in machine operating, dynamic physical work and sedentary work. *Scand J Work Environ Health* 1988;14:299–305.

30. Linton SJ, Kamwendo K. Risk factors in the psychosocial work environment for neck and shoulder pain in secretaries. *J Occup Med* 1989;31:609–613.

31. Linton SJ. Risk factors for neck and back pain in a working population in Sweden. *Work Stress* 1990;4:41–49.

32. Kamwendo K, Linton S, Moritz U. Neck and shoulder disorders in medical secretaries. *Scan J Rehab Med* 1991;23:127–133.

33. Linton SJ. An overview of psychosocial and behavioral factors in neck-and-shoulder pain. *Scand J Rehab Med* 1995;32(suppl):67–78.

34. Theorell T, Hams-Ringdahlk, Ahlberg-Hulten G, et al. Psychosocial job factors and symptoms from the locomotor system: A multicausal analysis. *Scand J Rehabil Med* 1991;23:165–173.

35. Jacobsson L, Lindgarde F, Manthorpe R, Ohlsson K. Effect of education, occupation and some lifestyle factors on common rheumatic complaints in a Swedish group aged 50–70 years. *Ann Rheum Dis* 1992;51:835–843.

36. Onishi N, Namura H, Sakai K, et al. Shoulder tenderness and physical features of female industrial workers. *J Hum Ergol (Tokyo)* 1976;5:87–102.

37. Maeda K, Hirayama H, Takamatsu M. Occupational cervicobrachial disorders in workwomen in assembly lines of a cigarette factory. *Jpn J Indus Health* 1977;19:8–21.

38. Luopajarvi T, Kuorinka I, Virolainen M, et al. Prevalence of tenosynovitis and other injuries of the upper extremities in repetitive work. *Scand J Work Environ Health* 1979;5(suppl 3):48–55.

39. Kukkonen R, Luopajarvi T, Riihimaki V. Prevention of fatigue amongst data entry operators. In: Kvalseth TO, ed. *Ergonomics of Workstation Design.* London: Buttersworth; 1983;28–34.

40. Silverstein BA, Fine LJ, Armstrong TJ. Hand and wrist cumulative trauma disorders in industry. *Br J Indust Med* 1986;43:779–784.

41. Ohlsson K, Attewell R, Skerfving S. Self-reported symptoms in the neck and upper limbs of female assembly workers. *Scand J Work Environ Health* 1989;15:75–80.

42. Bergqvist-Ullman M, Wolgast E, Nilsson B, et al. The influence of VDT work on musculoskeletal disorders. *Ergonomics* 1995;38:754–762.

43. Ohlsson K, Attewell R, Paisson B, et al. Repetitive industrial work and neck and upper limb disorders in females. *Am J Indust Med* 1995;27:731–747.

44. Schierhout GH, Meyers JE, Bridger RS. Work related musculoskeletal disorders and ergonomic stressors in the South African workforce. *Occup Environ Med* 1995;52:46–50.

45. Hales TR, Bernard BP. Epidemiology of work-related musculoskeletal disorders. *Orthop Clin North Am* 1996;27:679–709.

46. Liss GM, Jesin E, Kusiak R, et al. Musculoskeletal problems among Ontario dental hygienists. *Am J Indust Med* 1995;28:521–540.

47. Welch LS, Hunting KL, Kellogg J. Work-related musculoskeletal symptoms among sheet metal workers. *Am J Indust Med* 1995;27:783–791.

48. Viikari-Juntura E, Riihimaki H, Tola S, et al. Neck trouble in machine operating, dynamic physical work and sedentary work: A prospective study on occupational and individual risk factors. *J Clin Epidemiol* 1994;47:1411–1422.

49. Berg M, Sanden A, Torell G, et al. Persistence of musculoskeletal symptoms: A longitudinal study. *Ergonomics* 1988;31:1281–1285.

50. Kuorinka I, Koskinen P. Occupational rheumatic diseases and upper limb strain in manual jobs in a light mechanical industry. *Scand J Work Environ Health* 1979;5:(suppl 3)39–47.

51. Marcus M, Gerr F. Upper extremity musculoskeletal symptoms among female office workers: Association with video display terminal use and occupational psychosocial stressors. *Am J Indust Med* 1996;29:161–170.

52. Hales TR, Sauter SL, Peterson MR, et al. Musculoskeletal disorders among visual display terminal users in a telecommunications company. *Ergonomics* 1994;37:1603–1621.

53. Bernard B, Sauter S, Peterson M, et al. Job task and psychosocial risk factors for work-related musculoskeletal disorders among newspaper employees. *Scand J Work Environ Health* 1994;20:417–426.

54. Skov T, Borg V, Orhede E. Psychosocial and physical risk factors for musculoskeletal disorders of the neck, shoulders, and lower back in salespeople. *Occup Environ Med* 1996;53:351–356.

55. Leino PI, Hanninen V. Psychosocial factors at work in relation to back and limb disorders. *Scand J Work Environ Health* 1995;21:134–142.

56. Krause N, Ragland DR, Greiner BA, Fisher JM, Holman BL, Selvin S. Physical workload and ergonomic factors associated with prevalence of back and neck pain in urban transit operators. *Spine* 1997;22:2117–2126.

57. Waris P. Occupational cervicobrachial syndromes. *Scand J Work Environ Health* 1979,6(suppl 3):3–13.

58. Maeda K, Horiguchi S, Hosokawa M. History of the studies on occupational cervicobrachial disorders in Japan and remaining problems. *J Hum Ergol* 1982;11:17–29.

59. Hagberg M. Occupational musculoskeletal stress and disorders of the neck and shoulder: A review of possible pathophysiology. *Int Arch Occup Environ Health* 1984;53:269–278.

60. Anderson JAD. Shoulder pain and tension neck and their relation to work. *Scand J Work Environ Health* 1984;10:435–442.

61. Stock SR. Workplace ergonomic factors and the development of musculoskeletal disorders of the neck and upper limbs: A meta-analysis. *Am J Indust Med* 1991;19:87–107.

62. Rundcrantz BL, Johnsson B, Moritz U. Cervical pain and discomfort among dentists: Epidemiological, clinical and therapeutic aspects. Part 1: A survey of pain and discomfort. *Swed Dent J* 1990;14:71–80.

63. Rundcrantz BL. Pain and discomfort in the musculoskeletal system among dentists. *Swed Dent J* 1991;76 (suppl):1–102.

64. Rundcrantz BL, Johnsson B, Moritz U. Pain and discomfort in the musculoskeletal system among dentists: A prospective study. *Swed Dent J* 1991;15:219–228.

65. Nayha S, Videman T, Laakso M, Hassi J. Prevalence of low back pain and other musculoskeletal symptoms and their association with work in Finnish reindeer herders. *Scand J Rheumatol* 1991;20:406–413.

66. Bovenzi M, Zadini A, Franzinelli A, Borgogni F. Occupational musculoskeletal disorders in the neck and upper limbs of forestry workers exposed to hand-arm vibration. *Ergonomics* 1991;34:547–562.

67. Holmstrom EB, Lindell J, Moritz U. Low back and neck/shoulder pain in construction workers: Occupational workload and psychosocial risk factors. Part 2: Relationship to neck and shoulder pain. *Spine* 1992;17:672–677.

68. Magnussen ML, Pope MH, Wilder DG, Areskoug B. Are occupational drivers at an increased risk for developing musculoskeletal disorders? *Spine* 1996;21:710–717.

69. Faucett J, Rempel D. VDT-related musculoskeletal symptoms: Interactions between work posture and psychosocial work factors. *Am J Indust Med* 1994;26:597–612.

70. Andersen JH, Gaardboe O. Prevalence of persistent neck and upper limb pain in a historical cohort of sewing machine operators. *Am J Indust Med* 1993;24:677–687.

71. Andersen JH, Gaardboe O. Musculoskeletal disorders of the neck and upper limb among sewing machine operators: A clinical investigation. *Am J Indust Med* 1993;24:689–700.

72. Hagberg M, Wegman DH. Prevalence rates and odds ratios of shoulder-neck diseases in different occupational groups. *Br J Indust Med* 1987;44:602–610.

73. Atasoy E. Thoracic outlet compression syndrome. *Orthop Clin North Am* 1996;27:265–303.

74. Lascelles RG, Schady W. The thoracic outlet syndrome. In: *Handbook of Clinical Neurology.* Vol. 7, *Neuropathies.* New York, NY: Elsevier Science; 1987.

75. Leffert RD. Thoracic outlet syndromes. *Hand Clin* 1992;8:285–297.

76. Urschel HC, Razzuk MA. Thoracic outlet syndrome. In: Sabiston DC, Spencer FC, eds. *Surgery of the Chest.* 5th ed. Philadelphia, Pa: WB Saunders; 1990.

77. Sanders RJ. *Thoracic Outlet Syndrome—A Common Sequela of Neck Injuries.* Philadelphia, Pa: JB Lippincott; 1991.

78. Radanov BP, Di Stefano G, Schnidrig A, Ballinari P. Role of psychosocial stress in recovery from common whiplash. *Lancet* 1991;338:712–715.

79. Radanov BP, Sturzenegger M, Schnidrig A, Di Stefano G, Aljinovic M. Factors influencing recovery from headache after common whiplash. *BMJ* 1993;307:652–655.

80. *Business and Health Special Report: Controlling Headache Costs.* Montvale, NJ: Medical Economics; 1992.

81. Cave DG. Analyzing the content of physicians' medical practices. *J Ambulatory Care Man* 1994;17:15–36.

82. Rasmussen BK, Jensen R, Olesen J. Impact of headache on sickness, absence, and utilization of medical services: A Danish population study. *J Epidemiol Comm Health* 1992;46:493–446.

83. Eisenberg DM, Kessler RC, Foster C, Norlock FE, Calkins DR, Delbanco TL. Unconventional medicine in the United States: Prevalence, costs, and patterns of use. *N Engl J Med* 1993;328:246–252.

84. Olesen J. *Classification and Diagnostic Criteria for Headache Disorders, Cranial Neuralgias and Facial Pain.* Copenhagen: The International Headache Society; 1990.

85. Nilsson N. The prevalence of cervicogenic headache in a random population sample of 20–59 year olds. *Spine* 1995;20:1884–1888.

86. Rasmussen BK, Jensen R, Schroll M, et al. Epidemiology of headache in a general population: A prevalence study. *J Clin Epidemiol* 1991;44:1147–1157.

87. Stewart WF, Lipton RB, Celentano DD, et al. Prevalence of migraine headache in the United States. *JAMA* 1992;267:64–69.

88. Stewart WF, Linet MS, Celentano DD, et al. Age and sex-specific incidence rates of migraine with and without visual aura. *Am J Epidemiol* 1993;34:1111–1120.

89. Lipton RB, Stewart WF. Prevalence and impact of migraine. *Neurol Clin* 1997;15:1–13.

90. Rasmussen BK. Epidemiology of headache. *Cephalalgia* 1995;15:45–68.

91. Marazziti D, Toni C, Pedri S, et al. Headache, panic disorder and depression: Comorbidity or a spectrum? *Neuropsychobiology* 1995;31:125–129.

92. Merikangas KR, Stevens DE. Comorbidity of migraine and psychiatric disorders. *Neurol Clin* 1997;15:115–123.

93. Merikangas KR, Angst J, et al. Migraine and psychopathology: Results of the Zurich cohort study of young adults. *Arch Gen Psych* 1990;47:849–853.

94. Stewart WF, Schechter A, Lipton RB. Migraine heterogeneity: Disability, pain intensity, and attack frequency and duration. *Neurology* 1994;44(suppl 6):24–39.

95. Larsson B, Bille B, Pedersen NL. Genetic influence in headaches: A Swedish twin study. *Headache* 1995;35:513–519.

96. Rasmussen BK. Migraine and tension-type headache in a general population: Precipitating factors, female hormones, sleep pattern and relation to lifestyle. *Pain* 1993;53:65–72.

97. Jensen R, Rasmussen BK, Pedersen B, Olesen J. Muscle tenderness and pressure pain thresholds in headache: A population study. *Pain* 1993;52:193–199.

98. Silberstein SD. Tension-type and chronic daily headache. *Neurology* 1993;43:1644–1649.

99. Lechin F, van der Dijs B, Lechin ME. Plasma neurotransmitters and functional illness. *Psychother Psychosom* 1996;65:293–318.

100. Pearce JM. Cervicogenic headache: A personal view. *Cephalalgia* 1995;15:463–469.

101. Sjaastad O. The headache of challenge in our time: Cervicogenic headache. *Funct Neurol* 1990;5:155–158.

102. Grimmer K. Relationship between occupation and episodes of headache that match cervical origin pain patterns. *J Occup Med* 1993;35:929–935.

103. Bansevicius D, Sjaastad O. Cervicogenic headache: The influence of mental load on pain level and EMG of shoulder-neck and facial muscles. *Headache* 1996;36:372–378.

104. Mills H, Horne G. Whiplash—Manmade disease? *NZ Med J* 1986;373:374.

105. Spitzer WO, Skovron ML, Salmi LR, et al. Scientific monograph of the Quebec Task Force on Whiplash-Associated Disorders: Redefining "whiplash" and its management. *Spine* 1995;20(suppl 8S):10S–73S.

106. Teasell RW, Shapiro AP. Cervical flexion-extension whiplash injuries. *Spine: State of the Art Reviews* 1993;7(3):373–390.

107. Evans RW. Some observations on whiplash injuries. *Neurol Clin* 1992;10:975–997.

108. Barnsley L, Lord S, Bogduk N. Whiplash injury. *Pain* 1994;58:283–307.

109. Otremski I, Marsh JL, Wilde BR, McLardy Smith PD, Newman RJ. Soft tissue cervical spinal injuries in motor vehicle events. *Injury* 1989;20:349–351.

110. Bourbeau R, Desjardins D, Maag U, Laberge-Nadeau C. Neck injuries among belted and unbelted occupants of the front seats of cars. *J Trauma* 1993;35:794–799.

111. Galasko CSB, Murray PM, Pitcher M, et al. Neck sprains after road traffic accidents: A modern epidemic. *Injury* 1993;24:155–157.

112. Dolinis J. Risk factors for "whiplash" in drivers: A cohort study of rear-end traffic crashes. *Injury* 1997;28:173–179.

113. Squires B, Gargan MF, Bannister GC. Soft-tissue injuries of the cervical spine: 15-year follow-up. *J Bone Joint Surg [Br]* 1996;78B:955–957.

114. Schrader H, Obelieniene D, Bovim G, et al. Natural evolution of late whiplash syndrome outside the medicolegal context. *Lancet* 1996;347:1207–1211.

115. Sturzenegger M, Radanov BP, Di Stefano G. The effect of accident mechanism and initial findings on the long-term course of whiplash injury. *J Neurol* 1995;242:443–449.

116. Radanov BP, Di Stefano G, Schnidrig A, Sturzenegger M. Common whiplash—psychosomatic or somatopsychic? *J Neurol Neurosurg Psychiatry* 1994;57:486–490.

117. Borchgrevink GE, Stiles TC, Borchgrevink PC, Lereim I. Personality profile among symptomatic and recovered patients with neck sprain injury, measured by MCMI-I acutely and 6 months after car accidents. *J Psychosom Res* 1997;42:357–367.

118. Radanov BP, Begre S, Sturzenegger M, Augustiny KF. Course of psychological variables in whiplash injury—a 2-year follow-up with age, gender and education pair-matched patients. *Pain* 1996;64:429–434.

119. Maimaris C, Barnes MR, Allen MJ. "Whiplash injuries" of the neck: A retrospective study. *Injury* 1988;13:393–396.

120. MacNab I. Acceleration extension injuries of the cervical spine. In: Rothman RH, Simeone FA, eds. *The Spine*. 2nd ed. Philadelphia, Pa: WB Saunders; 1982:647–660.

121. Gotten N. Survey of 100 cases of whiplash injury after settlement of litigation. *JAMA* 1956;162:865–867.

122. Gore DP, Sepic SB, Gardner GM, Murray MP. Neck pain: A long-term follow-up of 205 patients. *Spine* 1987;12:1–5.

123. Hohl M. Soft tissue injuries of the neck in automobile accidents. *J Bone Joint Surg* 1974;56:1675–1682.

124. Packard RC. Posttraumatic headache: Permanency and relationship to legal settlement. *Headache* 1992;32:496–500.

125. Dworkin SF, Massoth DL. Temporomandibular disorders and chronic pain: Disease or illness? *J Prosthet Dent* 1994;72:29–38.

126. Larach DC, Lipton JA. Responses to persistent jaw, face, and burning mouth pain in the United States. *J Dent Res* 1993;72:313.

127. Lipton JA, Ship JA, Larbach-Robinson D. Estimated prevalence and distribution of reported orofacial pain in the United States. *J Am Dent Assoc* 1993;124:115–121.

128. Von Korff M, Wagner EH, Dworkin SF, et al. Chronic pain and use of ambulatory health care. *Psychosom Med* 1991;53:61–79.

129. Von Korff M, Dworkin SF, LeResche L, Kruger A. An epidemiologic comparison of pain complaints. *Pain* 1988;32:173–183.

130. Stohler CS. Phenomenology, epidemiology, and natural progression of the muscular temporomandibular disorders. *Oral Surg Oral Med Oral Pathol Oral Radiol Endod* 1997;83:77–81.

131. Probert TC, Wiesenfeld D, Reade PC. Temporomandibular pain dysfunction disorder resulting from road traffic accidents—An Australian study. *Int J Oral Maxillofac Surg* 1994;23:338–341.

132. Levitt SR, McKinney MW. Validating the TMJ scale in a national sample of 10,000 patients: Demographic and epidemiologic characteristics. *J Orofac Pain* 1994;8:25–35.

133. Von Korff M, Dworkin SF, LeResche L. Graded chronic pain status: An epidemiologic evaluation. *Pain* 1990;40:279–291.

134. Schiffman EL, Fricton JR, Haley DP, Shapiro BL. The prevalence and treatment needs of subjects with temporomandibular disorders. *J Am Dent Assoc* 1990;120:295–303.

135. Dworkin SF, Huggins KH, LeResche L, et al. Epidemiology of signs and symptoms in temporomandibular disorders: Clinical signs in cases and controls. *J Am Dent Assoc* 1990;120:273–281.

136. Glass EG, McGlynn FD, Glaros AG, Melton K, Romans K. Prevalence of temporomandibular disorder symptoms in a major metropolitan area. *Cranio* 1993;11:217–220.

137. Duckro PN, Tait RC, Margolis RB, Deshields TL. Prevalence of temporomandibular symptoms in a large United States metropolitan area. *J Craniomandib Prac* 1990;8:131.

138. Kirveskari P, Alanen P, Karskela V, et al. Association of functional state of stomatognathic system with mobility of cervical spine and neck muscle tenderness. *Acta Odontologica Scand* 1988;46:281.

139. Clark GT, Green EM, Dornan MR, Flack VF. Craniocervical dysfunction levels in a patient sample from a temporomandibular joint clinic. *J Am Dent Assoc* 1987;115:251.

140. DeLaat A, Meuleman H, Stevens A. Relation between functional limitations of the cervical spine and temporomandibular disorders [Abstract]. *J Orofac Pain* 1993;1:109.

141. DeWijer A, DeLeeuw JR, Steenks MH, Bosman F. Temporomandibular and cervical spine disorders: Self-reported signs and symptoms. *Spine* 1996;21:1638–1646.

142. LeResche L, Saunders K, Von Korff MR, Barlow W, Dworkin SF. Use of exogenous hormones and risk of temporomandibular disorder pain. *Pain* 1997;69:153–160.

143. Kolbinson DA, Epstein JB, Burgess JA. Temporomandibular disorders, headaches, and neck pain following motor vehicle accidents and the effect of litigation: Review of the literature. *J Orofac Pain* 1996;10:101–125.

144. Lobbezoo F, Lavigne GJ. Do bruxism and temporomandibular disorders have a cause-and-effect relationship? *J Orofac Pain* 1997;11:15–23.

145. Vimpari SS, Knuuttila MLE, Sakki TK, Kivela S-L. Depressive symptoms associated with symptoms of the temporomandibular joint pain and dysfunction syndrome. *Psychosom Med* 1995;439–444.

146. Shnurr RF, Brooke RI, Rollman GB. Psychosocial correlates of temporomandibular joint pain and dysfunction. *Pain* 1990;42:153–165.

147. McKinney MW, Londeen TF, Turner SP, Levitt SR. Chronic TM disorder and non-TM disorder pain: A comparison of behavioral and psychological characteristics. *Cranio* 1990;8:40–46.

148. Southwell J, Deary IJ, Geissler P. Personality and anxiety in temporomandibular joint syndrome patients. *J Oral Rehabil* 1990;17:239–243.

149. DeBoever JA, Keersmaekers K. Trauma in patients with temporomandibular disorders: Frequency and treatment outcome. *J Oral Rehabil* 1996;23:91–96.

150. Boering G, Stegenga B, De Bont LGM. Clinical signs of TMJ osteoarthrosis and internal derangement 30-years after nonsurgical treatment. *J Orofac Pain* 1994;8:18–24.

151. Raphael KG, Marbach JJ. A year of chronic TMPDS: Evaluating patients' pain patterns. *J Am Dent Assoc* 1992;123:53.

152. Marbach JJ. Temporomandibular pain and dysfunction syndrome: History, physical examination, and treatment. *Rheum Dis Clin North Am* 1996;22:477–498.

153. Katzberg RW, Westesson P-L, Tallents RH, Drake CM. Anatomic disorders of the temporomandibular joint disc in asymptomatic subjects. *J Oral Maxillofac Surg* 1996;34:147–153.

154. DeLeeuw R, Boering G, Stegenga B, De Bont LGM. Symptoms of temporomandibular joint osteoarthrosis and internal derangement 30 years after nonsurgical treatment. *J Craniomandib Pract* 1995;13:81–88.

155. List T, Dworkin SF, Harrison R, Huggins K. Research diagnostic criteria/temporomandibular disorders: Comparing Swedish and U.S. clinics [Abstract]. *J Dent Res* 1996;75:352.

156. Huggins KH, Dworkin SF, LeResche L, Truelove E. Five-year course for temporomandibular disorders using RDC/TMD [Abstract]. *J Dent Res* 1996;75:352.

157. Bland JH. Congenital anomalies. In: Bland JH, ed. *Disorders of the Cervical Spine: Diagnosis and Medical Management.* 2nd ed. Philadelphia, Pa: WB Saunders; 1994;417–431.

158. Brinker MR, Weeden SH, Whitecloud TS. Congenital anomalies of the cervical spine. In: Frymoyer JW, ed. *The Adult Spine: Principles and Practice.* 2nd ed. Philadelphia, PA: Lippincott-Raven; 1997;1205–1222.

159. Hensinger RN. Congenital anomalies of the cervical spine. *Clin Orthop* 1991;264:16–38.

160. Kirlew KA, Hathout GM, Reiter SD, Gold RH. Os odontoideum in identical twins: Perspectives in etiology. *Skeletal Radiol* 1993;22:525–527.

161. Verska JM, Anderson PA. Os odontoideum: A case report of one identical twin. *Spine* 1997;22:706–709.

162. Fielding JW, Hensinger RN, Hawkins RJ. Os odontoideum. *J Bone Joint Surg* 1980;62A:376–383.

163. Doubousett J. Torticollis in children caused by congenital anomalies of the atlas. *J Bone Joint Surg* 1986;68A:178.

164. Thomsen MN, Schneider U, Weber M, Johannisson R, Niethard FU. Scoliosis and congenital anomalies associated with Klippel-Feil syndrome types I–III. *Spine* 1997;22:396–401.

165. Pizzutillo PD, Woods M, Nicholson L, MacEwen GD. Risk factors in Klippel-Feil syndrome. *Spine* 1994;19:2110–2116.

166. Theiss SM, Smith MD, Winter RB. The long-term follow-up of patients with Klippel-Feil syndrome and congenital scoliosis. *Spine* 1997;22:1219–1222.

167. Rogers JM, Mole ML, Chernoff N, et al. The developmental toxicity of inhaled methanol in the CD-1 mouse, with quantitative dose-response modeling for estimation of benchmark doses. *Tetrology* 1993;47:175–188.

168. Hu R, Mustard CA, Burns C. Epidemiology of incident spinal fracture in a complete population. *Spine* 1996;21:492–499.

169. Ryan TC, Taylor TKF. Odontoid fractures in the elderly. *J Spinal Disord* 1993;6:397–401.

170. Ersmark H, Dalen N, Kalen R. Cervical spine injuries: A follow-up of 332 patients. *Paraplegia* 1990;28:25–40.

171. Anderson P, Rivara FP, Maier RV, Drake C. The epidemiology of seatbelt-associated injuries. *J Trauma* 1991;31:60–67.

172. Johansson C, Mellstrom D, Rosengren K, Rundgren A. Prevalence of vertebral fractures in 85 year-olds. *Acta Orthop Scand* 1993;64:25–27.

173. Williams J, Jehle D, Cottington E, Shufflebarger C. Head, facial, and clavicular trauma as a predictor of cervical-spine injury. *Ann Emerg Med* 1992;21:719–722.

174. McGrory BJ, Klassen RA, Chao EY, Staeheli JW, Weaver AL. Acute fractures and dislocations of the cervical spine in children and adolescents. *J Bone Joint Surg* 1993;75:988–995.

175. Givens TG, Polley KA, Smith GF, Hardin WD. Pediatric cervical spine injury: A three-year experience. *J Trauma* 1996;41:310–314.

176. Clark CR. Differential diagnosis and nonoperative management. In: Frymoyer JW, ed. *The Adult Spine: Principles and Practice.* 2nd ed. Philadelphia, Pa: Lippincott-Raven; 1997;1323–1347.

177. Gore DR, Sepic SB, Gardner GM. Roentgenographic findings of the cervical spine in asymptomatic people. *Spine* 1986;11:521–524.

178. Zapletal J, de Valois JC. Radiologic prevalence of advanced lateral C1–C2 osteoarthritis. *Spine* 1997;22:2511–2513.

179. Jonsson H, Bring G, Rauschning W, Sahlstedt B. Hidden cervical spine injuries in traffic accident victims with skull fractures. *J Spinal Disord* 1991;4:251–263.

180. Hohl M. Soft-tissue injuries of the neck in automobile accidents. *J Bone Joint Surg [Am]* 1974;56A:1675–1682.

181. Parmar HV, Raymakers R. Neck injuries from rear impact road traffic accidents: Prognosis in persons seeking compensation. *Injury* 1993;24:75–78.

182. Robinson DD, Cassar-Pullicino VN. Acute neck sprain after road traffic accident: A long term clinical and radiological review. *Injury* 1993;24:79–82.

183. Ellenberg MR, Honet JC, Treanor WJ. Cervical radiculopathy. *Arch Phys Med Rehabil* 1994;75:342–352.

184. Radhakrishnan K, Litchy WJ, O'Fallon WM, Kurland LT. Epidemiology of cervical radiculopathy: A population-based study from Rochester, Minnesota, 1976–1990. *Brain* 1994;117:325–335.

185. Kondo K, Molgaard CA, Kurland LT, Onofric BM. Protruded intervertebral cervical disc. *Minn Med* 1981;64:751–753.

186. Kelsey JL, Githens PB, O'Connor T, et al. Acute prolapsed lumbar intervertebral disc: An epidemiologic study with special reference to driving automobiles and cigarette smoking. *Spine* 1984;9:608–613.

187. Kelsey JL, Githens PB, Walter SD, et al. An epidemiologic study of acute prolapsed cervical intervertebral disc. *J Bone Joint Surg* 1984;66A:907–914.

188. Kelsey JL, Githens PB, White AA, et al. An epidemiologic study of lifting and twisting on the job and risk for acute prolapsed lumbar intervertebral disc. *J Orthop Res* 1984;2:61–66.

189. Braakman R. Management of cervical spondylotic myelopathy and radiculopathy. *J Neurol Neurosurg Psychiatr* 1994;57:257–263.

190. Edwards WC, La Rocca SH. The developmental segmental sagittal diameter in combined cervical and lumbar spondylosis. *Spine* 1985;10:42–49.

191. Foo D. Spinal cord injury in 44 patients with cervical spondylosis. *Paraplegia* 1986;24:301–306.

192. Montgomery DM, Brower RS. Cervical spondylotic myelopathy: Clinical syndrome and natural history. *Orthop Clin North Am* 1992;23:487–493.

193. Dillin WH, Watkins RG. Cervical myelopathy and cervical radiculopathy. *Sem Spine Surg* 1989;1:200–208.

194. Crandall PH, Batzdorf U. Cervical spondylotic myelopathy. *J Neurosurg* 1966;25:57–66.

195. Batzdorf U. Complex cervical myelopathies. In: Frymoyer JW, ed. *The Adult Spine: Principles and Practice*. 2nd ed. Philadelphia, Pa: Lippincott-Raven; 1997:1401–1412.

196. Nurick S. The natural history and the results of surgical treatment of the spinal cord disorder associated with cervical spondylosis. *Brain* 1972;101–108.

197. La Rocca H. Cervical spondylotic myelopathy: Natural history. *Spine* 1988;13:854–855.

198. Bessette L, Katz JN, Liang MH. Differential diagnosis and conservative treatment of rheumatic disorders. In: Frymoyer JW, ed. *The Adult Spine: Principles and Practice*. 2nd ed. Philadelphia, Pa: Lippincott-Raven; 1997:803–826.

199. Kauppi M, Hakali M. Prevalence of cervical spine subluxations and dislocations in a community-based rheumatoid arthritis population. *Scand J Rheumatol* 1994;23:133–136.

200. Rajangam K, Thomas IM. Frequency of cervical spine involvement in rheumatoid arthritis. *J Indian Med Assoc* 1995;93:138–139.

201. Kauppi M, Sakaguchi M, Konttinen YT, Hamalainen M, Hakala M. Pathogenic mechanism and prevalence of the stable atlantoaxial subluxation in rheumatoid arthritis. *J Rheumatol* 1996;23:831–834.

202. Oda T, Fujiwara K, Yonenobu K, Azuma B, Ochi T. Natural course of cervical spine lesions in rheumatoid arthritis. *Spine* 1995;20:1128–1135.

203. Rana NA. Natural history of atlantoaxial subluxation in rheumatoid arthritis. *Spine* 1989;14:1054–1056.

204. Weissman BNW, Aliabadi P, Weinfield MS, et al. Prognostic features of atlantoaxial subluxation in rheumatoid arthritis patients. *Radiology* 1982;144:745–751.

205. Simeone FA, Rothman RH. *The Spine*. Philadelphia, Pa: WB Saunders; 1982.

206. Guidetti B, Mercuri S, Vagnozzi R. Long-term results of the surgical treatment of 129 intramedullary spinal gliomas. *J Neurosurg* 1981;54:323–330.

207. Weinstein JN, McLain RF. Primary tumors of the spine. *Spine* 1987;12:843–851.

208. Long DM. Cervical cord tumors. In: Baily RW, ed. *The Cervical Spine* (The Cervical Spine Research Society). Philadelphia, Pa: J.B. Lippincott; 1983:323–335.

209. Cassidy JR, Ducker TB, Dienes EA. Intradural tumors. In: Frymoyer JW, ed. *The Adult Spine: Principles and Practice*. 2nd ed. Philadelphia, Pa: Lippincott-Raven; 1997:1015–1029.

210. Boriani S, Weinstein JN. Differential diagnosis and surgical treatment of primary benign and malignant neoplasms. In: Frymoyer JW, ed. *The Adult Spine: Principles and Practice*. 2nd ed. Philadelphia, Pa: Lippincott-Raven; 1997:951–987.

211. Bohlman HH, Sachs BL, Carter JR, Riley L, Robinson RA. Primary neoplasms of the cervical spine: Diagnosis and treatment of twenty-three patients. *J Bone Joint Surg [Am]* 1986;68:483–494.

212. Levine AM, Boriani S, Donati D, Campanacci M. Benign tumors of the cervical spine. *Spine* 1992;17:S399–S406.

213. Beer SJ, Menezes AH. Primary tumors of the spine in children: Natural history, management, and long-term follow-up. *Spine* 1997;22:649–659.

214. Kostuik JP. Differential diagnosis and surgical treatment of metastatic spine tumors. In: Frymoyer JW, ed. *The Adult Spine: Principles and Practice*. 2nd ed. Philadelphia, Pa: Lippincott-Raven; 1997:951–987.

215. Rao S, Badani K, Schildhauer T, Borges M. Metastatic malignancy of the cervical spine: A nonoperative history. *Spine* 1992;17:S407–S412.

PART

2

Clinical Syndromes

CHAPTER 6

Cervical Trauma Following Motor Vehicle Collisions

Lawrence S. Nordhoff, Jr.

"As long as modern societies continue to be mobile with humans driving, there will be car crashes. Most crashes are not truly accidents, but instead involve human error. Many injuries could be prevented by simply making better cars and making our laws more severe for those who violate traffic laws. Our society needs to challenge itself by requiring that manufacturers make crashworthy vehicles. Doctors need to become more educated in diagnosis and management."

—L. S. N., Jr.

INTRODUCTION

When a physician in the emergency room or in private practice sees a patient with a cervical spine injury or is consulted for chronic neck pain, one of the more common considerations that enters into the possibility of causative events is the motor vehicle crash. The National Safety Council reports that annually there are about 2.3 million disabling injuries from motor vehicle crashes, about 730,000 nonfatal injuries in rear-end crashes, 640,000 nonfatal injuries in side crashes, and 60,000 nonfatal police reported injuries in frontal collisions. Rear-end crashes produce the greatest number of nonfatal injuries and injury accidents.[1]

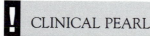
CLINICAL PEARL

There are about 4 to 5 million injury-producing car accidents annually in the United States.

The primary challenge to the physician is fundamentally found in the failure of the medical educational system, which has traditionally focused on pathological diseases and has put little emphasis on the common motor vehicle crash injury. In essence, the majority of physicians who exit medical and chiropractic colleges have little formal education in motor vehicle crash injury mechanisms, diagnosis, management, and prognosis. A second challenge concerns the amount of litigation that is involved; many physicians lack adequate history and treatment documentation forms and do not have the appropriate means to detail all of the factors that relate to these cases. Physicians often focus on the primary complaint and do not allow the patient to complete a questionnaire that provides secondary complaint information. Unlike most occupational, sports, or home injuries that usually involve one region of the body, the patient experiencing a motor vehicle crash case commonly presents with multiple symptoms. Typically two to four regions of the body incur injury. Injury patterns change in each collision vector and vary with the age of the occupant, size and physical condition, gender, seating position, pre-existing conditions, and other variables. These factors are discussed later in the chapter.

In this chapter, a *vector* is defined as the direction of impact between two vehicles. The term *minor injury*, as used in this chapter, indicates there is no risk of fatality. However, minor injuries can have varying severity of pain, treatment, and disability. Minor injuries include strains and sprains, disc herniations, and other soft tissue injuries. *Occupants* in this text refer primarily to the front seat driver and passenger unless specified otherwise. Two-vehicle crashes are considered in this text unless specified otherwise. The change in velocity, ΔV, is the measure of the velocity for a specific vehicle during a crash impulse.

VEHICLE DYNAMICS AND OCCUPANT KINEMATICS IN FRONTAL, SIDE, AND REAR-END CRASHES

To understand how neck injuries can occur, a brief analysis of how vehicles and occupants behave in crashes is necessary. The reader needs to consider vehicle crashworthiness, how vehicles crush, occupant interaction with various parts of the occupant compartment, and seatback interaction with occupants. As this chapter will show, each crash vector (impact direction) has unique properties that affect injury risk and types of injuries.

VEHICLE AND OCCUPANT DYNAMICS IN FRONTAL COLLISIONS

Frontal collisions are very fast events, lasting about 100 msec, which is about the time it takes for a person to blink his or her eyes once. In a frontal crash, there are three crush zones for the striking vehicle. The first zone is the bumper and area in front of the engine, which is relatively soft. The engine compartment is next and is very stiff. The structures behind the engine, which include the firewall and the front of the occupant cage, are the third area and are the second most rigid structure. In a frontal impact, the front bumper will first strike the front or side structures or the rear of another vehicle. When there is bumper-to-bumper impact, the front bumper of the striking and struck vehicle will absorb some of the energy, and if there is sufficient force, will crush. As these deceleration forces are transmitted into the frame of the entire vehicle, the occupant's body will continue to move forward at the same velocity as just prior to the impact.

> ## ! CLINICAL PEARL
>
> Newton's first law of motion says that a body in motion will continue to move until another force acts on it. The amount of space in front of the occupant and the path of motion of the occupant will determine the risk of striking the car's interior.

The occupant's body will move forward in a frontal crash until the seat belt system loads the person's body along the belt path. The driver will have loading from the shoulder harness in the left side of the neck and anterior chest wall. The lap portion will load the pelvis or lumbar region, depending upon the position of the belt at impact and whether the occupant slides below the belt. Seat positioning, occupant size, height, and posture, and vehicle interior design (window angle and steering wheel shape and size), and size of vehicle (less space for small cars) may leave the head or chest a distance of 4 to 18 inches from either the front windshield, header, or steering wheel. Figure 6–1 illustrates driver interaction with the steering system, knee bolster, and floor pan. Women are at higher risk, as they generally position their seats more forward than men, which places their bodies closer to the front car structures, thus increasing the likelihood of impacting the front interior.

Interior Occupant Interaction in Frontal Crashes
In frontal collisions, injuries occur primarily from contact with various structures within the occupant compartment. These contacts induce direct loading into soft tissues and bony structures. In addition, injuries can occur from rapid motion changes in various regions of the body with no direct loading. These inertial loading injuries are primarily strains and sprains or disc injuries.

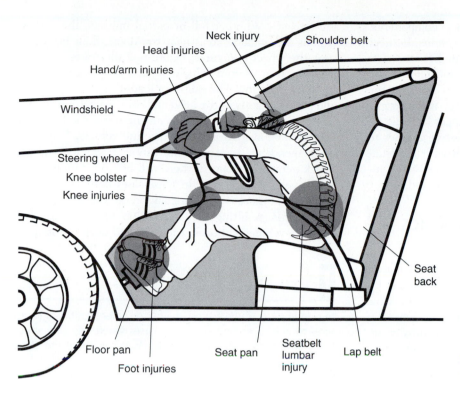

Neck injury
Head injuries
Hand/arm injuries
Shoulder belt
Windshield
Steering wheel
Knee bolster
Knee injuries
Seat back
Floor pan
Foot injuries
Seat pan
Seatbelt lumbar injury
Lap belt

Figure 6–1. Illustration of human interaction with interior of car in a frontal crash.

Seat Belt Interaction in Frontal Crashes

In a frontal crash, the seat belt system is typically the first contact source for the belted occupant. In fact, with all restrained occupants, regardless of seating position, the seat belt is responsible for generating more injuries than any other contact source within the vehicle. The majority of these injuries are minor and, therefore, are the product of the belt system operating in the manner in which it is designed. One study of 3276 front seat restrained occupants found 29.6 percent had minor injury directly from seat belt loading.[2] Morris and Thomas[3] found that 8 percent of unrestrained occupants reported neck injury compared to 20 percent having used seat belts. A study by Maag et al[4] of 3927 occupants in two-vehicle crashes shows that neck injuries occurred in 21 percent of the belted and 14 percent of the unbelted occupants.

There are several reasons why seat belts increase neck injury while reducing fatalities. First, the three-point belts are designed with asymmetrical geometry, with one shoulder being restrained. Second, the belts act as a fulcrum for energy to concentrate its loading on the occupant. With less of the human body to absorb energy, the neck takes the brunt of the forces. Third, submarining may occur in collisions in which the lap belt is loose; that is, the occupant slides down the seat under the shoulder harness or lap belt. There are several documented cases of hangman's noose types of neck injuries resulting from the occupant's interaction with the seat belt, typically involving children and small adults.

Airbag Interaction

As of 1997, federal law requires all passenger vehicles to have airbags. Most newer vehicles involved in frontal crashes have airbags. Recent studies that compare injury patterns in crashes involving airbag deployment to crashes not having airbags have made some interesting findings. Dischinger et al[5] found in their study that occupants having airbag deployment had fewer neck injuries and skull fractures. However, there were significantly more brain injuries and upper and lower extremity injuries in cases of deployment. As seen in studies that look at injury patterns associated with seat belt use, it is apparent that airbags also change the distribution of injuries.

Rebound Injuries in Frontal Crashes

If the occupants do not fully eject in a frontal crash, their bodies will usually rebound backward, typically moving into the seatback. If the impact is off center or if there is significant rotational force on the vehicle, then occupant motion becomes complex and both soft tissue and bony injuries can occur if the occupant hits the side structures of the vehicle.

Cervical Trauma in Frontal Crashes

The majority of neck injuries in frontal collisions are from deceleration inertial forces that occur over a short duration because the neck flexes and extends as the torso and shoulder are restrained by the seat belt system. Each body region of the occupant has its own deceleration rate during the crash impulse. When one shoulder is restrained, the head and neck rotate, adding rotational injury components. These injuries mainly include strains and sprains. Indirect loading to the cervical spine can occur in head impacts where the neck is compressed between the skull and the mass of the decelerating torso. If the neck is flexed at the time of impact, the majority of impact energy will be transmitted into the lower cervical spine and upper thoracic region. Cervical strains and sprains, compressive injuries to the disc, and fractures are commonly seen with head impacts. If bruising is noted along the neck from seat belt interaction, more serious injuries should be suspected.

VEHICLE AND OCCUPANT DYNAMICS IN SIDE IMPACTS

The National Safety Council estimates that approximately 30 percent to 40 percent of all two-vehicle crash types involve side collisions.[1] Most side collisions have the same crash time as frontal collisions, being around 100 msec in duration. In side crashes, the struck vehicle is usually impacted in its side structures by an incoming vehicle in an intersection. In most modern passenger cars, there are only 8 to 12 inches of distance between an intruding bumper and an occupant's body. The struck vehicle will usually have the loading increase on the suspension system opposite the impact side, resulting in the struck vehicle lifting on the same side as the striking vehicle. The bumper and front structures of the striking vehicle will either impact with its entire front end (full impact) or with a corner (par-

tial impact). Whether full or partial impacts, the contact regions can include areas near the doors, door beams, or near the wheel structures. Figure 6–2 illustrates an occupant's motion when a vehicle impacts on the same side as he or she is sitting. The side door loads the occupant's torso and pelvis laterally as the head and neck lag behind. As the torso moves laterally and pulls on the neck, the head will laterally flex away from the impacting vehicle. If impacts are perpendicular, are near the center of gravity, and the struck vehicle is stopped, there will be no rotation of the struck vehicle. However, in most cases both vehicles are moving and there is some angulation of both vehicles' impact points, resulting in postcollision vehicle spin. The spin of a vehicle will cause the head and neck to rotate.

> **! CLINICAL PEARL**
>
> In side impacts, there are no engines or other significant structures to absorb impact energy. In cases where the side structure contacts the occupant, the structure has about the same velocity as the striking vehicle.

Cervical Trauma in Side Crashes

Hobbs[6] found, in analyzing occupant kinematics in side crashes using crash dummies, that at 15 to 25 msec, the door will hit the dummy and at 30 to 35 msec, there will be maximum spine acceleration. The interior of the side door

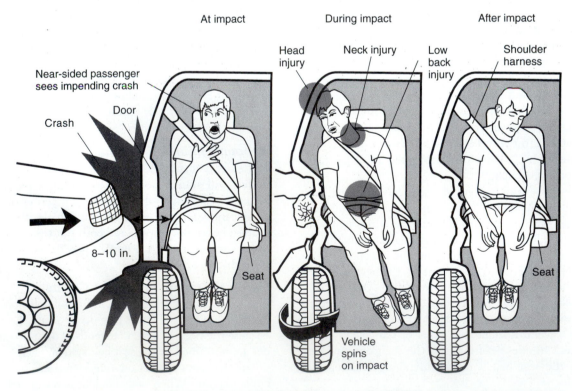

Figure 6–2. Occupant motion in a side crash.

will strike the occupant's body at the same velocity as the striking collision velocity. The occupant's torso and shoulder will rapidly move sideways as the vehicle moves in the direction of the postcollision. When the side of the vehicle slams into the occupant's body, the head and neck will lag behind, causing lateral flexion of the neck. The lag time of the head and neck while the torso and lower body move causes motion of these regions to be in the opposite direction. Cervical trauma in side crashes primarily involves disc injuries and strains and sprains from lateral flexion and rotation of the head and neck as the torso and shoulder are directly loaded by the side structures. In one side crash study, the C5–6 area was the primary region injured, with injuries to the disc being found to be first, joint injury second, and muscle injury third in frequency.[7] Occupants sitting nearest the impact (near sided) in lateral crashes will have significantly higher impact forces than occupants sitting on the opposite side of the crash (far sided). The near-sided occupant has one to three times more risk of injury than the far-sided occupant.

VEHICLE AND OCCUPANT DYNAMICS IN MODERATE TO HIGH VELOCITY REAR-END COLLISIONS

This part of the discussion looks at only rear-end crashes occurring at a velocity (ΔV) greater than 10 mph. Chapter 7 deals specifically with the low speed rear-end crash. Unlike frontal and side crashes, which historically have received funding for research, the high speed rear-end crash has been the focus of few studies. Most rear-end crash research has focused on low speed (2 to 5 mph) collisions. It is important for the reader to realize that in about 75 percent of rear-end crashes, the struck vehicle is stopped at the time of impact.[8]

> **! CLINICAL PEARL**
>
> To understand occupant kinematics, the reader must consider the role of the seatback and head restraint.

In the moderate to high speed rear-end collisions, the front bumper and front structures of the striking vehicle will impact the bumper, or if bumpers do not match, impact will occur to the trunk lid or to structures under the bumper. These impacts can be at a 12 o'clock position or can be off center, depending on avoidance maneuvering tactics of the striking vehicle's driver. In collisions where bumper-to-bumper contacts are made, the mostly elastic bumper will move forward, and depending on its type and shape, it will begin to deform. As the collision delta Vs increase, the struck vehicle's bumper, trunk, and eventually the frame and side structures will be damaged. The suspension and tire systems of the rear end of the struck vehicle will move downward as part of the forward motion. This downward motion is more dramatic in cases where the striking vehicle's center of gravity is higher. Regardless of the amount of damage, these impact forces from the striking vehicle will load the frame and then the occupant seat and seatback-head restraint structures.

> **! CLINICAL PEARL**
>
> Unlike the frontal and side crash, the primary element causing occupant kinematic motion in the rear-end crash is the elastic seatback and the lagging head and neck structures.

If the front seatback breaks, the inboard seat pin, which allows the seat to recline when the outboard lever is pushed, will usually break before the outboard side causing the seatback to twist and the occupant to move toward the center of the vehicle, which can complicate injury patterns. Overall, cervical injury risk decreases as impact speeds increase because of seat breakage. This is primarily due to the loading forces being axial and the amount of flexion and extension being dramatically reduced. Morris and Thomas[3] evaluated 243 rear-end impacts and correlated seatback breakage to neck injury outcome. They found neck injuries in 61 percent of cases where the seatback was not damaged and 39 percent where there was seatback damage.

Rebound Injury in Higher Speed Rear-End Crashes

A National Highway Traffic Safety Administration (NHTSA) study concludes that rebound injuries in rear-end crashes involving contact with front occupant cage structures such as the steering wheel, dashboard, and windshield, account for 28 percent of all the reported injuries. This is nearly as common as the percentage for injuries seen in frontal crashes.[9]

Cervical Trauma in Moderate to High Speed Rear-End Crashes

The risk of sustaining cervical injury can vary depending on the amount and type of motion of the head and neck, whether the seatback breaks, or if the occupant rebounds, hitting the front of the occupant space compartment. If the seatback does not break, the majority of injuries are caused by the differential motion between the seatback and occupant,[10] hyperextension of the neck over the head restraint, and rebound neck flexion as the head rebounds off the headrest. One study found that the headrest can move forward faster than seatback.[11] If the occupant has a typical seat which has poor head restraint positioning and the seatback does not break, the occupant's neck and head will extend beyond anatomical limits if the relative height of the occupant to the top of the head restraint allows for it to happen. In some vehicles with adjustable head restraints, such as in the Taurus, the head can hit the head restraint like a pile driver, forcing it rapidly into its most downward position. If the occupant is tall enough, if there is sufficient ramping up the seatback, if the head restraint is low enough and the head and neck can move over it, the head restraint acts as a fulcrum, which will significantly increase the likelihood of injury. In some cases, the neck can extend up to the point where occupants report being able to see the striking vehicle from behind and their eyeglasses or dentures are found in the rear seat. Occupants of pickup trucks can hit their heads on the cab's rear window.

Rebound injury may occur from the neck flexing over the shoulder harness, which will hold back the shoulder being restrained. If the occupant is seated close enough to the steering wheel, as is more common with women, or if the space is limited because the car is small or the occupant large, impacts to the dashboard, windshield, and steering system can occur.

Other types of injury mechanisms can occur in these higher speed crashes besides hyperextension and hyperflexion. These have been investigated in the low speed impacts but not in the high speed cases. However, I have concluded that most of the low speed injury mechanisms discussed in Chapter 7 would apply to the higher speed crashes and would simply be more extreme in magnitude. One volunteer study found that as the seatback loads the occupant's spine, the spine flattens and, as a result of this change in curves, the occupant becomes first taller and then shorter, or a lengthening-compression cycle occurs, causing microscopic damage to tissues.[12] One animal study found that in rear-end crashes, excessive venous pressure in the blood in the internal venous plexus within the intervertebral foramina would injure the cervical spinal ganglia due to an effect called a "blood hammer." Histopathological findings confirmed that there were signs of nerve cell membrane damage and dysfunction to the spinal ganglia. The authors found venous pressure gradients highest when the neck goes from extension to flexion motion.[13, 14]

In brief, several factors have been found to influence the risk of sustaining more severe neck injuries in rear-end crashes. These factors include the occupant having his or her head turned to the side at the time of impact or variations in seatback stiffness;[15] elastic rebound of the seatback, which can aggravate the violence of the whiplash-motion;[13] being a female occupant;[16] different car models;[13] being unaware of the impact;[17] being tall; and being out of position. Elderly occupants are more prone to injury as well. Fixed head restraints will lessen the risk for neck trauma. A real world German study of 520 rear-end crashes confirmed that the most important influences regarding neck injuries are (1) the car model (especially car mass, car structure, and car seat) and (2) the change of velocity (ΔV) of the struck car. This study in investigating neck injury frequency in several car models concluded that the neck injury factor was 5.5 times higher in the worst car than the best car. Smaller cars involved with larger vehicles did poorly also.[18]

IMPACT VELOCITY AND OTHER CRASH FACTORS IN FRONTAL, SIDE, AND REAR-END CRASHES

In vehicle-to-vehicle crashes, there are several other factors inherent to the vehicle and collision that can influence injury risk and severity. These are discussed next.

 CLINICAL PEARL

There is no typical crash.

VELOCITY THRESHOLD FOR NECK INJURY

When looking specifically at rear-end crashes, one emergency room study found that rear-end impacts of as little as 5 mph can give rise to significant symptoms.[19] Eichberger et al's[18] study of 520 real world rear-end crashes found about 20 percent of neck injury claims in real world rear-end crashes occurred at a ΔV of lower than 5 mph. Other studies have concluded that injuries often occur in low velocity rear-end impacts less than 12.4 mph[13] with no correlation being found between crash speed and duration of neck symptoms until side members collapse and permanent deformation is seen. Some neck injuries resulted from crashes at less than 6.2 mph.[20] One French study found that cervical injury frequency was higher in low speed rear-end crashes (36 percent of times by ΔV of less than 9.3 mph and 20 percent greater than 9.3 mph) than in the higher speed collisions (55 percent of the cases involving ΔV impacts of greater than 15.5 mph for car models newer than 1976) due to seatback breakage.[16] Foret-Bruno et al[21] concluded that rear impacts having a ΔV of less than 15.5 mph have about a 16.7 percent probability of causing a minor neck injury. Studies that look at neck injuries by speed limits have found significantly higher risks when the crashes occur in speed zones of less than 30 mph.[4] Other studies which look at velocity thresholds for low velocity rear-end crashes, are included in Chapter 7.

WHAT DELTA V IS NECESSARY TO CAUSE SERIOUS NECK INJURIES?

One of the questions facing the physician is what ΔV is necessary to cause cervical fractures or to put the occupant at risk for critical or fatal injury. Roberts and Compton's[22] study data within the National Accident Sampling Study (NASS) found that the 50th percentile for cervical fracture (all vectors) had a ΔV of 25 mph. One American and Canadian study of serious to fatal injuries to front occupants that focused primarily on the seat structures in rear-end impacts found about 50 percent of these cases would partially or totally eject through the rear structures of the vehicle with ΔVs as low as 18 mph.[23] One study evaluating crash data in the United States and England indicates that a frontal collision having a ΔV of 20 mph is the threshold for a critical to fatal neck injury.[24] When looking at fracture thresholds, the physician must consider head impacts, which will increase the risk of cervical fracture by three times.[21] The study also found that in side impacts involving ΔVs greater than 30 mph, there is risk for cervical fracture.[21]

SEAT BELTS AND NECK INJURY

A recent study of 3927 injured front seat occupants found that nonserious neck injuries were relatively more frequent in belted occupants, with 21 percent reporting neck sprains, compared to 14 percent of the unbelted occupants. However, seat belts were found to lessen the serious injuries as cervical fractures were found in 3 percent of the occupants using the belt system compared to 9 percent of unbelted occupants.[4] Morris and Thomas[3] found in their study of 11,866 occupants who sustained 42,876 injuries that 20 percent of seatbelt users and 8 percent of nonusers reported soft tissue injuries for all vectors. These authors felt that "what was certain is that soft tissue neck injuries can occur at comparatively low-speeds and are associated with seat-belt use."

CRASH VECTOR AND SEATING POSITION EFFECTS

Several authors have compared neck injuries by vector of crash. Table 6–1 summarizes six studies that look at the percentages of occupants reporting neck injury for each crash vector. The rear-end crash clearly puts the occupant at higher risk of sustaining neck trauma; almost twice as many injuries are reported as for frontal and side collisions. In rear-end crashes with similar masses, the occupants in the struck vehicle will have twice the relative risk of re-porting neck injury than those in the striking vehicle.[25] Maag et al[4] found that occupants involved in rear-end and near-sided side crashes were four times more likely to incur neck sprains than occupants involved in frontal or far-sided lateral crashes.

How crashworthy (aggressive) a vehicle is toward another vehicle can influence occupant injury risk. One study found that there are important differences in the relative risk of sustaining neck injuries even among cars of identical weight.[25] These authors found that variations in car construction between models can vary the magnitude of neck injury risk by 50 percent for poorly designed vehicles.[25] A vehicle can be aggressive, which means that the manufacturer makes the front end of the vehicle (often a sport utility vehicle or truck) very stiff. As a result of this design, when the aggressive vehicle impacts a softer passenger vehicle such as a standard-sized car, the car will crush more and put its occupants at higher risk of injury. Dissimilar heights of vehicles, which are common in the automotive industry, can cause the higher vehicle to hit the door panels of a lower riding vehicle in a side impact, thus striking the torso of the occupant. If all manufacturers designed vehicles of similar heights, the injury risk would be shared evenly. Furthermore, owners can make modifications after purchasing a vehicle, for instance, raising a truck height to the point that its bumper can actually contact the windows of passenger cars. There have been case reports of such "lifted" trucks rear-ending passenger cars at a closing velocity of less than 25 mph and literally decapitating the rear-seat occupants.

> ## ❗ CLINICAL PEARL
>
> Different models of vehicles (crashworthiness) can cause injury risk to vary by 50 percent.

Table 6–1: Comparison of Percentages of Occupants Reporting Neck Injuries by Crash Vector

AUTHOR	REAR CRASHES (%)	FRONTAL CRASHES (%)	SIDE CRASHES (%)
Spitzer et al[26]	39.5	11.8	18
Larder et al[27]	30.8	16.9	10.7–22.5
Morris and Thomas[3]	38	15	12–15
Foret-Bruno et al[21]	26.1	10.2	8.4
Galasko et al[28]	52	27	16
Sturzenegger et al[29]	38	36	16
Average	**37.6**	**20.4**	**14.2**

HUMAN FACTORS THAT INFLUENCE INJURY RISK AND SEVERITY

CHILDREN AND ELDERLY OCCUPANTS

Young and elderly occupants can be at increased risk of injury in motor vehicle crashes. Owing to differences in their size and shape, children will have different injury patterns which are more severe than those seen in adults. Children have a higher center of mass, larger head mass (about 25 percent of the entire body weight), and flatter pelvis, and are more likely to be improperly restrained than adults because of their size. One study of 2899 children involved in motor vehicle crashes found that 18.6 percent of children (ranging from infants to age 14) in the front seat and 12.3 percent of children in the rear seat reported neck injuries.[30] Another study of children in motor vehicle crashes found that seat belts caused fractures to the lumbar spine, with most children having seat belt bruising.[31] This study also found significant delays in physicians' diagnosis of these problems.[31] Another study, which looked at restrained 4- to 9-year-old occupants, reported spinal strains in 22 percent of restrained and 14 percent of nonrestrained children who sat in the front seat. Among rear-seated children, spinal strains were reported for 35 percent if restrained and 13% if not restrained. Three spinal fractures or cord injuries were found in unrestrained front-seated children and two were found in restrained rear-seated children. This study also found that 13 percent of 4- to 9-year old children placed the shoulder harness behind their backs. Rear-seated children sustained fewer serious injuries than children in the front seat.[32]

One study of 6000 traffic accident cases compared occupants over the age of 65 years to adults under age 65. The authors found that older occupants were more likely to sustain more serious injuries for any given accident and the fatality rate was almost 11 percent, which is much higher than that for younger occupants.[33] Older drivers are more prone to injury, because they have decreased soft tissue flexibility, less strength, less reserve capacity, and decreased bone strength. In addition, there is strong evidence that their capacity for repair is also decreased. One of the primary concerns for the physician is proneness to fracture and pathological ligamentous instability, particularly for higher speed crashes.

GENDER AND INJURY RISK

Women, when compared to men are significantly more prone to injury from motor vehicle accidents for any given vector. Morris and Thomas found 13 percent of men and 21 percent of women reported neck injury from all vectors.[3] A large French automotive study of 15,000 occupants involved in motor vehicle accidents found that in rear collisions, 42 percent of the women had cervical injuries, compared to 21 percent for the men.[16] In frontal collisions, this decreased to 17 percent for women and 7.5 percent for men, and in side collisions, women had a 13 percent and men a 6.5 percent frequency of neck injuries. The authors looked at frequency of cervical injury as a function of gender and the use of head restraints. They found that 15.3 percent of men and 30.3 percent of women in vehicles with head restraints reported neck injuries compared to 23.2 percent of men and 45.4 percent of females in vehicles without head restraints.[16] Insurance claim research in Sweden found that regardless of the size of the vehicle, women incur more neck injuries than men.[25]

> ! **CLINICAL PEARL**
>
> Women report more injuries than men by ratio of 2:1.

Generally, female occupants have smaller neck diameters, and thus weaker muscles, and have longer necks than their male counterparts. Women also have smaller body mass than men, which generally results in higher rebound velocities from the seat backs in rear-end crashes. Foust et al[34] found in their study of 180 adult volunteers that the range of motion for females was 1 to 12 degrees greater than their male counterparts. Both men and women were found to lose about 40 percent of their range of motion over their adult life span, with men losing about 25 percent by middle age as compared to women, who lost 13 percent in the same period. A comparison of neck flexor and neck extensor muscle strength revealed that men overall averaged about 8.3 ft/lbs more strength than women.

OCCUPANT SIZE, WEIGHT, AND HEIGHT

The size of the occupant is another injury risk parameter that needs to be considered. As Norin and Isaksson-Hellman note,[35] "[d]epending upon their size, occupants come into contact with different parts of the interior during a crash, and this will affect the risk of injury. The stiffness of the human frame is best observed in size or bulk. Generally speaking, the larger the occupant's mass the less injury will occur in a collision." Smaller unrestrained drivers in frontal crashes will usually have their heads propelled through the windshield first, whereas a large driver's head will usually hit the steering wheel first, then move to the windshield. Smaller occupants will usually have their seats closer to the windshield or steering wheel than larger counterparts, resulting in higher incidence of chest impacts onto the steering wheel and dashboard. The smaller occupant will have higher head injury levels as a result of having less body mass, incurring less belt stretch, and having higher head acceleration. Additionally if the shoulder harness for the small occupant is positioned close to the neck, the injury level will be greater. Taller occupants have been shown be at risk for higher neck injury.[35]

PRE-EXISTING COMPLICATING CONDITIONS

Patients who have significant pre-existing complicating conditions, either genetic or acquired, will have a lowered threshold for injury and will typically incur more severe injuries and require more treatment than the normal population. These pre-existing conditions can include: joint degeneration from trauma or aging, spinal stenosis, disc degeneration or protrusion, myofascial or fibrositis disorders, spinal surgery, thyroid disorders, healing disorders (diabetes), and severe nutritional disorders. One author concludes that adolescents, the elderly, and occupants having spinal degeneration are subject to neck trauma at lower impact forces than the healthier adult.[36]

! CLINICAL PEARL

Be cautious when indicating that a specific pre-existing condition is a complicating factor.

The physician needs to document factors that complicate recovery or worsen injury severity. At the same time, he or she must recognize that just because a patient is diabetic, it does not mean that the patient heals poorly. Physicians must correlate real life facts to the specific case. A physician can ask a diabetic patient how long it usually takes for skin wounds to heal, and compare the time frame to that for nondiabetic patients. Many diabetic patients maintain good control through diet and medication and have normal healing responses. If you feel that a condition has significantly complicated the case by either delaying or lessening a person's recovery, then adequately document your opinions in your notes, giving your reasoning. Just because someone has joint or disc degeneration does not mean that their prognosis is guaranteed to be poor. Pre-existing spinal degeneration clearly increases the risk of injury for the individual; however, in the real world some patients with degeneration have good recoveries.

GENETIC CONDITIONS

One of the more common genetic conditions seen in practice is spinal stenosis in the cervical spine. Pettersson et al[37] studied 48 whiplash patients, comparing initial and 12-month outcomes. They concluded that that the spinal canal was significantly smaller in patients who developed persistent symptoms than in those who had symptom resolution. Whether genetic or acquired, spinal stenosis reduces the ability of the spinal cord and nerve roots to move when the spine moves in various directions during a motor vehicle crash. Generally, patients with spinal stenosis are unable to tolerate extension postures for more than brief periods. If the patient's toes become numb or toe extensors become weak when the physician positions the patient

supine and holds the patient's neck in extension for 1 to 2 minutes, this indicates a long tract sign. If the patient develops chronic mid-scapular pain that does not resolve with treatment, the physician should consider cervical stenosis causing a long tract symptom as the problem.

Other genetic conditions, such as the Klippel-Feil syndrome, also warrant close analysis. Not only are bony tissues abnormal in size, shape, and function, but ligaments and muscles also vary immensely in their architecture, size, and attachment sites. Such conditions result in generalized weakness, and altered biomechanics, resulting in a loss of elasticity and strength that would be present in a normal spine.

CLINICAL PICTURE OF WHIPLASH INJURIES

Whiplash injuries occur as a result of occupant motions within a vehicle that is rapidly decelerating or accelerating. The vast majority of the claims that follow motor vehicle crashes involve soft tissue injuries. Many of these claimants or patients undertaking treatment for injuries will have symptoms that appear out of proportion to the objective findings found on physical and radiologic examination. Although the symptoms that follow in the acute to chronic cases are well defined, the actual anatomical lesions have been poorly defined. The discussion that follows will not focus on contact injuries or contusions that often occur.

Otremski et al's[38] study of 1197 crash occupants found that the typical neck injury occurred in a middle-aged female occupant wearing a seat belt in a low speed rear-end collision. Sturzenegger et al,[29] in their assessment of acute whiplash injuries, concluded that the following features of accident mechanisms were associated with more severe symptoms: an unprepared occupant (72.3 percent); rear-end collision, with or without subsequent frontal impact (62.1 percent); and rotated (27.7 percent) or inclined (12.4 percent) head position at the moment of impact.

! CLINICAL PEARL

The acute injury symptom complex is usually consistent in whiplash cases.

One study found that 87 percent of patients report multiple symptoms in the acute injury, with the mean patient reporting 3.1 symptoms after being injured.[29] The most common clinical symptoms include varying degrees of: neck pain (94.2 percent), headaches (71.5 percent), shoulder pain (48.9 percent), low back pain (37.2 percent), visual disturbances (21.1 percent), unsteadiness (16.1 percent), vertigo (4.4 percent), tinnitus (3.6 percent), and radicular irritation (10.2 percent).[29] Other common acute symptoms or injury complexes include fatigue, anxiety, sleep disruption, concussion, upper extremity symptoms, disc herniations, thoracic outlet syndrome, carpal tunnel syndrome, temporomandibular joint injuries, chest pain, middle back pain, and lower extremity symptoms. Less frequent reports are seen of shoulder and elbow injuries, menstrual irregularities, Bell's palsy, finger twitching, and finger flexor tendon injuries from the steering wheel being pulled out of an occupant's hands. The patterns of radiating symptoms may be of little value in locating the origin of the lesion. Radiating pain down the arm may be from thoracic outlet irritation, disc protrusion and disc fiber injury, nerve root irritation, myofascial trigger points, joint dysfunction, joint capsule inflammation, or double crush syndromes. Most of these acute symptoms lessen over time, with the exception of upper extremity symptoms, which usually are reported more frequently in chronic cases than in acute injuries.

Symptom onset delays are characteristic of whiplash injuries. Many patients experience little to no pain immediately following a motor vehicle crash. Others may note varying degrees of stiffness or pain. Gradually intensifying soreness and pain arising from normal inflammatory responses of the body to trauma typically begin from 12 hours to a few days later. In general, the more severe the symptoms and the more rapid their onset, the more severe the injury. The majority of clinical, automotive, and epidemiological studies report frequent delays in patients experiencing initial neck pain symptoms after being in a collision, anywhere up to 96 hours. These frequent delays in the onset of post-traumatic pain also account for many injuries not being reported to the police and being entered into national crash data. Radanov et al[39] found that the onset of neck pain occurred in 71 percent of the occupants within 24 hours and the remaining 29 percent had onset within a few days. Spitzer et al[26] found that 21 percent of occupants have delays in symptoms.

CLINICAL PEARL

Different body regions exhibit unique patterns of pain onset

Some degree of neck pain, soreness, or stiffness should be present within 1 to 2 weeks to be considered related to a collision. It is rare for an occupant to have absolutely no stiffness, ache, soreness, or pain and then develop the symptoms 1 month later. However, it is common for upper extremity symptoms and headaches to have delays of onset several weeks to months after the event. Radanov et al[39] found that on initial examination, 14 percent of patients reported trauma-related headaches; these figures increased to 21 percent at 3 months, and 30 percent at 6 months.

CLINICAL PEARL

If the patient initiates a first evaluation or care several weeks or months after the motor vehicle crash, it is imperative that the physician document why the delays occurred. In a lawsuit, the defense will most certainly look at your records. Consider transportation and monetary issues; maybe the patient was told the pain would go away and it persisted, or there were schedule conflicts. The physician will find it impossible to find referenced literature to support the hypothesis that a patient can have absolutely no degree of neck stiffness, soreness, or pain for several weeks and all of a sudden develop severe neck pain 1 to 9 months later. If the patient says he or she had no neck pain for the first few weeks, the physician needs to rephrase the question. The patient may interpret the term *pain* as meaning severe pain and not including soreness or aching, which are typical descriptors for lesser pain. If the patient states he or she had no initial pain, ask, "Did you have any stiffness, soreness, or aching type of feelings, discomfort or pain after the injury?"

HYPERFLEXION AND HYPEREXTENSION CERVICAL SPINE INJURIES

Hyperflexion injuries can be seen in a) frontal crashes due to inertia, and b) rear end crashes in which the occupant's head rebounds forward from an elastic seatback that does not break. Cervical flexion injuries primarily involve the trapezius muscles, semispinalis and splenius capitis muscles, levator scapulae muscles, rectus capitis muscles, suboccipital muscles, zygapophyseal joints and their capsules, nerve roots, damage to the posterior longitudinal ligament, and interspinous ligaments. Alar ligaments, longus and brevis cervicis muscles and other deep rotatory neck muscles, and disc fibers may be injured when head and neck rotation occur during the flexion motion.

Hyperextension cervical spine injuries can occur in rear-end and frontal crashes where there is sufficient velocity change and distance available to allow the neck to move backward beyond normal anatomical limits. This is more commonly seen when there is a low to absent head restraint or low seatback, particularly when combined with a taller person. As previously noted, I have seen several cases where the occupant reported seeing the front grill of the striking vehicle or the occupant's glasses and dentures were found in the rear seat after the crash. Hyperextension of the neck can cause injury to the sternocleidomastoid muscles, anterior and middle scalene muscles, longus colli, and other deep anterior neck muscles. In addition, the anterior longitudinal ligament, anterior spinal ligaments, disc fibers, and various fascia layers of the neck may incur injury. If the head is rotated at time of impact, the muscles involved will be more unilaterally involved with the anterior neck pain being worse on the opposite side to which the head was rotated. This means that if a driver and passenger are looking at each other with their heads turned, the driver should have more anterior neck pain on the left side and passenger more on the right side. Alar ligaments may be injured in rear-end crashes when the head is rotated at the time of impact.

I have found that patients will generally complain about anterior neck pain regardless of whether there was a flexion or extension injury. The only explanation I can offer for the consistent posterior pain is that there must be significantly fewer pain fibers in the anterior neck muscles or the nerves in the anterior neck muscles simply refer pain posteriorly. The easiest muscles that can be visualized by the clinician for swelling are the sternocleidomastoid and the scalene muscles. In some cases, the supraclavicular notch will be flat in appearance as a result of swelling. Taking a circumference measurement of the neck in the acute injury and comparing it to a measurement taken a few weeks after injury will objectively show swelling. Other objective findings of ligamentous instability include reversal of cervical curvature with sharp angulation, disruption of George's lines, and changes to the spaces between the odontoid process and the lateral masses of the atlas.

LATERAL FLEXION AND ROTATIONAL NECK INJURIES

The side crash is the most common cause of lateral neck injuries. All side crashes that have enough impact velocity to cause the struck vehicle to rotate after the collision will cause the head and neck to rotate due to the coupling nature of the cervical joints. Rotational injuries occur in frontal and rear-end crashes if the occupant is twisted at the time of impact or if the impact direction is not near the center of gravity, causing the vehicle or vehicles to rotate after the crash. Lateral flexion injuries will tend to focus on the longus capitis muscles, trapezius muscles, scalene muscles, and the sternocleidomastoid muscles, as well as deeper muscles and lateral ligaments of the spine. The disc and the fibers that hold the disc to the spine are particularly vulnerable to side crashes. Rotational spinal soft tissue injuries are primarily injuries to the ligaments and facet complex.[40]

PRIMARY CAUSES OF CHRONIC NECK PAIN AFTER WHIPLASH

There are several etiologies for chronic neck pain following whiplash injuries. The vast majority of studies have concluded that soft tissue pain is the primary cause and that there is, in fact, an organic basis for chronic pain. Less scientific sources, mostly editorials, feel that chronic pain is primarily based on financial motives of patients, attorneys, and physicians. The focus of this section is to give the best

estimate in ranking order for chronic neck pain following a motor vehicle crash. This is only an estimate as, to date, no large scale study has compared a population of people having no history of neck pain to the chronic whiplash patient. What is evident is that the vast majority of whiplash patients have multiple causes for chronic pain and the primary cause can vary for different individuals, depending upon the collision type, amount of motion, types of injuries, and aging effects.

The most likely source of chronic neck pain can be identified from injection studies of whiplash patients that sought to document the prevalence of zygapophyseal joint pain. In one study, the authors found that of 38 whiplash patients investigated with diagnostic blocks, 54 percent were confirmed as having pain from cervical zygapophyseal joint pain.[41] Lord et al[42] have confirmed the results of this study. Discoligamentous injury, which will cause scarring and ingrowth of new vasculature and sensory fibers, is a likely secondary cause of chronic pain. Research by Taylor and Twomey[43] confirms that disc injuries, particularly those near the vertebral rims, are common after neck sprains. A third likely cause, myofascial pain, is felt by some to account for the majority of persistent neck pain following whiplash injury.[44, 45]

Other sources of chronic neck pain also exist. Chronic pain may occur because the occupant is overly sensitive to noxious stimuli. It may also be the result of inactivity, which can make the occupant's neck and back biomechanically weak. In addition, there may be perpetuating factors such as poor ergonomic environments, poor posture, and psychosocial factors.

HEADACHE AND MIGRAINE

There is a wealth of literature on the topic of headache and migraine arising from whiplash injuries, and there is little debate that it is one of the most common syndromes that develop in these patients.[46, 47] Nordhoff looked at several studies showing the percentages of motor vehicle crash patients who have headaches. Averaging several studies revealed that about 52 percent of acute and 46 percent of chronic whiplash cases will report headaches.[48] When considering the pathogenesis of these postwhiplash headaches and migraines, the clinician must consider the type of injury. In whiplash injuries, most headaches arise from injury to the upper neck area. However, injuries to the lower cervical spine, sternocleidomastoid muscle, scalenes, temporomandibular joint muscles, and lower trapezius muscles can cause headaches. Head impacts can compress the neck, causing injury and inflammation to several types of pain-sensitive tissues capable of referring pain to the head. Yamaguchi's[49] study, which compared headache frequency to the severity of head injury, found that the mild head injury patients had more headaches, at 72 percent, compared to 33 percent for the severe head injury patients.

FIBROMYALGIA SYNDROMES

Fibromyalgia is a common post-traumatic diagnostic syndrome that may cause pain or paresthesias, or both. A recent study by Buskila et al[50] of 102 neck injury patients (67 whiplash cases) found that 21.6 percent of these patients were diagnosed as having fibromyalgia. Fibromyalgia syndrome (FMS) is a functional soft tissue disorder that usually effects several regions of the body. Post-traumatic FMS is usually unilateral in its presentation. The unilateral predominance is explained by the fact that most motor vehicle crashes load the human body with asymmetrical forces. FMS syndrome is often not diagnosed for 3 to 4 weeks and in some cases up to 4 to 9 months after an accident. According to the American College of Rheumatology, in order to make this diagnosis, the clinician needs to document (1) widespread pain in combination with (2) tenderness at 11 or more of the 18 points that have been established in the literature.[51] Several authors feel that FMS or myofascial pain is one of the most common causes of long-term persistent pain following whiplash injuries.[44, 52] Chester[53] found in his 7-month to 7-year study of 48 rear-end motor vehicle crash cases, that a diagnosis of fibromyalgia was present in more than 50 percent of the cases.

THORACIC OUTLET SYNDROME– CERVICOAXILLARY SYNDROME

Thoracic outlet syndrome (TOS) is one of the most common causes of upper extremity paresthesias following motor vehicle collisions and is usually suspected in crashes involving neck hyperextension motion. A recent report found 32 cases of TOS following motor vehicle crashes.[54] Another study found that 56 percent of TOS surgical cases were either from a rear-end crash (32 percent) or from frontal and side crashes (24 percent), with trauma from all causes accounting a total of 86 percent of all cases.[55] Common symptoms of TOS include shoulder, upper arm, lower arm, and hand paresthesias (primarily ulnar distribution) and pain that typically increases with arm abduction. Provocative arm maneuvers (abduction with external rotation or rapid hand grasping) should be performed on these patients to isolate scalene involvement. Observing for ischemia of the arm or hand during the abduction maneuvers can provide additional clues. An anatomical study of post-traumatic scalene muscles found that following neck injuries, the anterior and middle scalene muscles were fibrotic (having greater than 20 percent more connective tissue) and that these changes were consistent with trauma.[56]

VISUAL AND AUDITORY SYMPTOMS

Other common complaints following neck injury are reports of blurry vision, tinnitus, dizziness, or vertigo, either initially or in chronic stages. True vertigo is much more likely to develop than varying degrees of dizziness. Auditory and visual symptoms are most likely to occur if there is injury to the inner ear, temporomandibular joint, or the soft tissues of the neck that supply proprioceptive information. One study which used pigs in simulated rear-end crashes concluded that these types of symptoms had an anatomical site for injury, thus explaining the frequent occurrence. These authors hypothesized that injury to the lower cervical spinal ganglia as a result of a venous "blood hammer" effect as the neck moves in transition from flexion to extension in the lower cervical spine is a potential cause for these symptoms.[57] Sternocleidomastoid injuries, myofascial adhesions, muscle spasm in the paraspinal muscles, and joint irritation can result in visual and auditory symptoms.

> ## ❗ CLINICAL PEARL
>
> I have had several cases in which head rotation or digital pressure on the sternocleidomastoid or deep joint muscles would often reproduce or intensify the patient's tinnitus or dizziness.

Another author who has attempted to explain the symptom occurrence is Hinoki.[58] His hypothesis is that there is an overexcitation of the cervical proprioceptors, which is caused by an excitation of sympathetic beta-receptors in the muscle spindles. Some of the complaints of balance problems were explained by asymmetrical posture after whiplash injuries. Another study of 48 patients with chronic symptoms resulting from rear-end crashes found that 43 of these patients had specific difficulties in maintaining their balance in test conditions. This author also noted 12 patients having a diagnosis of perilymph fistula, 3 patients with stapes subluxation, and 16 with nystagmus.[53]

CERVICAL DISC INJURIES

Cervical disc herniations and the various symptoms that follow are common after cervical trauma in motor vehicle crashes. Hamer et al[59] compared 215 surgical patients having a whiplash history to 800 general orthopedic cases requiring cervical surgery; those patients having a whiplash injury had significantly higher risk of needing surgery than patients without the traumatic history. Another surgical study of 253 disc herniation patients found that the majority had a history of a flexion-extension injury or were involved in car crashes.[60] Pettersson et al[61] found, in a prospective magnetic resonance imaging (MRI) study of 39 patients 4 to 15 days after injury and at a 2-year follow-up, that 13 patients had disc herniations. Initially, ten patients were found to have disc herniations; seven with dural impingement, three with medullary impingement, and one with muscle edema and diffuse swelling. At 2 years, one patient's herniation had improved and two patients' disc herniation levels had deteriorated. These authors conclude that there is a poor correlation between the MRI findings and the clinical symptoms. Most MRI studies that focus on motor vehicle crashes will show old disc degenerative changes that are pre-existing. In my opinion, it is very unlikely that a single collision without head impact occurring at less than 30 mph can cause herniation of a healthy disc. Head impacts without skull fracture can lower the threshold. In most moderate to low speed crashes, there has to be pre-existing damage or weakening of the disc fibers to cause a symptomatic disc to enter into the clinical picture. It is important that the physician consider that "even when computed tomography shows cervical disc herniation it is unlikely to be the sole source of pain in these complicated patients."[45] The clinician may use frequency-selective fat-suppressed sequences or enhancement techniques to obtain a clearer understanding of what is causing the patient's clinical symptoms. Stäbler et al[62] used Gd-DTPA (Gadolinium)-enhanced MRI and found vascularized granulation tissue within the disc which indicates ingrowth of sensory fibers. The majority of authors do not recommend MRI studies of acute injuries unless pathological symptoms or signs are present. Even in chronic cases, the clinician does not need to order an MRI for most cases. If the patient has severe pain (level 8 to 10) for more than 3 weeks, then an MRI can be ordered. What makes a disc herniation suspicious? For the most part, the clinician needs to focus on symptom history, primarily during the first 2 weeks after the crash. I have found, in reviewing records of my cases and those of other physicians, that significant radiating pain, numbness, and tingling in the occupant's arm(s) within the first 2 weeks after a collision is almost always indicative of a herniated disc.

! CLINICAL PEARL

I have reconstructed several motor vehicle crashes where the closing (impact) velocity of the striking vehicle was in the range of 8 to 12 mph and the occupant in the struck vehicle, wearing a seatbelt, had a significant disc herniation in the neck or low back regions. Some of these cases required surgical intervention and resulted in permanent disability as a direct result of a low speed impact. In all cases that I have analyzed, there were reports of arm or leg pain or paresthesias following the crash. In addition, all of these cases had pre-existing disc degeneration and some degree of protrusion. Some of these cases were complicated by spinal stenosis. In all cases, the pre-existing disc was stable and the patient had no recent history of leg or arm symptoms.

CONCUSSION SYNDROMES

Mild brain injury or concussion can occur after whiplash injuries. More typically, the patient will feel "dazed" or "dizzy" after the collision. Loss of consciousness is not necessary for a concussion to occur. Rapid flexion and extension motion causes the brain to move within the skull, which leads to diffuse axonal injury. One large automotive study found that when an occupant hits his or her head in a motor vehicle crash, a ΔV of 10 mph was the threshold

Table 6–2: Common Concussion Symptoms

Loss of concentration	Fatigue
Memory loss or forgetful	Loss of coordination
Less mental stamina	Impaired judgment
Difficulties problem solving	Poor administrative function
Personality change	Reduced motivation
Language difficulty	Performance inconsistencies
Difficulty completing tasks	More shallow relationships
Difficulty anticipating	Loss of balance
Irritability	Dizziness or tinnitus

for mild head injuries.[63] There have not been any published studies that examined the velocity it takes to cause a concussion without head impact. However, I have found in my experience and reconstruction analysis that it takes a ΔV of at least 20 mph to cause concussion from inertial loading (no head impact) for most healthy adults. Elderly occupants have a lower threshold. Concussions are frequently misdiagnosed because most physicians are undereducated about this type of injury and do not allow the patient to indicate all of the secondary symptoms. I have frequently noted the absence of this diagnosis from physicians who take verbal histories. Table 6–2 outlines some of the more common symptoms that have been attributed to a concussion.

COMMON MISUSE OF SPASM, STRAIN, AND SPRAIN TERMINOLOGY

The terms *strain* or *sprain* and *spasm* are often misused in the medical and chiropractic community. A strain involves partial or complete tearing or injury to the muscles and fascia of the paraspinal muscles. A sprain to the neck and back involves a ligamentous injury with simultaneous trauma to muscles and fascia. It is impossible to injure spinal ligaments without involving paraspinal muscles. Another confusing term is *muscle spasm*. Many physicians erroneously believe that a muscle spasm is a tender muscle, a taunt muscle, a sore muscle, a trigger point, or just a tight muscle. However, true spasm is defined as "a sudden, violent, involuntary contraction of a muscle or a group of muscles, attended by pain and interference with function."[64] A leg cramp is a very brief muscle spasm. Anyone who has had a leg cramp can feel the muscle pull and deformity. A muscle spasm is simply a prolonged cramp. A muscle spasm can be an objective sign if used in its proper context. Muscle spasms are temporary conditions following spinal trauma and should be fully resolved within 2 to 3 weeks. If the patient continues to have significant muscle spasm beyond 2 to 3 weeks, a more detailed neurological examination is recommended. I have found that testing for vibration loss and subtle clonus can detect cord pressure. These cases usually involve patients who exhibit early significant radicular symptoms. A referral to a neurologist is recommended.

SOFT TISSUE INJURY HEALING

The recent Quebec Task Force has adopted a consensus that repair takes 4 to 6 weeks and remodeling takes up to 1 year following motor vehicle crashes.[26] There are four stages of wound repair:

Stage 1: The hemorrhagic or coagulation stage, in which cells are injured and die, muscles bleed, and coagulation begins.

Stage 2: The inflammatory stage, which is the result of the bleeding and other products that result from cell death and the normal response to cell death, injury, and bleeding. The inflammatory stage (macrophages and granulocytes) sets up an appropriate level of neovascular growth (angiogenesis) and collagen synthesis (fibroplasia).

Stage 3: The healing stage, in which active cell replacement or wound repair takes place. This is typically intensive from day 5 to 21 days after trauma, and decreases dramatically for the next 3 weeks.[65] Fibroblasts restore the normal continuity of the injured tissue. From a clinical viewpoint, fibroblasts replicate poorly in environments that lack oxygen, proper nutrition, and insulin. Wound repair is felt to conclude when the energy network that drives the repair process spanning the wound to both normal sides stops and the central area of the wound is no longer hypoxic.[66]

Stage 4: The remodeling stage is a slow, less intense reaction of soft tissue of reorientation of haphazard scar tissue. The fibers from the healed torn muscles remodel by aligning themselves along the lines of mechanical or motion stresses.

The intensity, quality, and time frame of healing response depend on the injury site, how the tissue was injured, the element of motion which affects the degree of vascular perfusion, and depth of injury.[66] Wound repair also depends on the extent of the injury, amount and type of motion (joint and soft tissue) in the healing tissue area, vascular supply inherent to the specific tissue, nutritional status, and genetics. Some patients simply heal faster and better than others. Tissues that are hypovascular, such as discs and ligaments, will usually take longer to heal. In my practice, I have found that cigarette smokers take longer to heal and have more residual myofasical pain.

> **! CLINICAL PEARL**
>
> Just because the active repair process is finished, the patient's progress will not stop, although it will slow down with time.

TIME OFF WORK AND TEMPORARY DISABILITY ISSUES

As noted earlier, according to the National Safety Council, there were about 2.3 million disabling injuries in 1995 from motor vehicle crashes in the United States.[1] It is well recognized that neck injuries cause a significant percentage of the disability associated with motor vehicle collisions.[67] The Insurance Research Council[68] reports in its review of over 62,000 claims throughout all 50 states that about 50 percent of all claimants will lose some time off work and of those who are off work, half will return to work within 7 days. This study also found that 20 percent of claimants have more than 30 days of disability. The Quebec Task Force found that 22.1 percent of occupants returned to work within 1 week, whereas 53 percent took more than 4 weeks to get back to work.[26] Several factors have been associated with longer temporary disability periods. Females and elderly occupants have significantly more disability.[26] Other factors that must be considered include: desire to return to work, self-employment versus being an employee, economic status, type of job demands, sedentary life style, family and social support system, and treatment delay. Noncompliance with treatment programs and home exercises can lead to delays in return to work. However, in my experience, it is the physician who is most likely to be able to get the patient back to work. Many patients are of the opinion that rest and sometimes prolonged time off work are beneficial to their recovery. It is essential for the physician to advise the patient that early return to either modified or normal home and work activity is very important to his or her recovery. As long as the activity is controlled, in the sense of attempting to avoid any new injuries or flare-ups, the patient will progress faster if he or she is physically active during the repair process.

PROGNOSIS FOR PATIENTS WITH NECK TRAUMA

One of the more challenging aspects of motor vehicle crash injuries is trying to determine long-term prognosis for patients who have undergone various types of treatment, and who continue to have persistent symptoms that influence their ability to function at work, home, or in other normal activities of living. An average of data from more than 30 published prognostic studies from 1980 to 1995 reveals that about 40 percent of occupants in all types of motor vehicle crashes who report neck injury initially will report some degree of chronic neck pain, soreness, stiffness, and a variety of other symptoms classic for the whiplash syndrome for anywhere from 6 months to 15 years.[48] Whether one looks at clinical studies or chronic intractable pain reports, the motor vehicle crash occupant is seen to have significantly more problems with long-term symptoms than patients with any other source of injury, including work-related, home, recreational, or sports injuries.

One of the few studies that compare the risk of occupants having sustained an impairment of more than 10 percent to the neck for more than 1 year was recently performed by Folksam Research in Sweden.[25] When percentages of occupants having permanent disability from minor neck injuries were compared by crash vector, it was found that 63.7 percent of occupants were involved in a rear-end impact, 23 percent in frontal crashes, and 8.8 percent in side crashes.[25] A Swedish insurance study of 12,000 claimants for 5 years found that the probability of sustaining a permanent impairment or disability was 10 percent for minor injuries of the neck, the back, skull and brain, and significantly less for other regions of the body. This study also found that occupants in more crashworthy vehicles (usually larger in size) had significant less chronic disability.[67]

The following is an overview of a few prognostic studies that have followed a group of patients over an interval of time. Norris and Watt[69] looked at long-term symptoms of 61 patients at about 2 years following the motor vehicle collision and evaluated their long-term status to initial injury severity. In group 1 (normal examination findings), 44 percent had residual neck pain, 37 percent had headaches, and 37 percent had upper extremity paraesthesias. In group 2 (normal examination with loss of range of motion), 81 percent had neck pain, 37 percent had headaches, and 29 percent had upper extremity paraesthesias. In group 3 injuries (abnormal range of motion and presence of objective neurological findings), 90 percent had residual neck pain, 70 percent had headaches, and 60 percent had upper extremity paraesthesias. The authors found that about 20 percent of each group had sufficient persisting neck pain severe enough to cause regular time off work. Radanov et al[39] found, in their study of 117 whiplash cases, that 27 percent still had post-traumatic headaches. Hildingsson and Toolanen[70] found, in their study of 93 car injury cases, that 29 percent had persistent neck pain, 25 percent had low back pain, and 15 percent had headaches. They also found that 43 percent had discomfort sufficient enough to interfere with their capacity to work an average of 2 years after injury. None of these cases were involved in litigation. Furthermore, none of these patients had neurological signs on initial examination. Four patients developed neurological signs, primarily sensory losses in the upper extremities. Squires et al[71] followed 40 whiplash patients for a mean of 15.5 years, finding that 70 percent continued to complain of symptoms referable to the original crash.

RISK FACTORS INFLUENCING PROGNOSIS

Several factors may have a significant role in treatment outcome and, therefore, are related to the prognosis for postcollision neck injuries (Table 6–3). The following list has been developed based on automotive research and clinical studies, as well as clinical experience. For all crashes,

Table 6–3: Risk Factors for Chronicity in Whiplash

FACTOR	SOURCE
Being involved in a rear-end crash	v Koch et al,[25] Sturzenegger et al[29]
Out-of-position occupant	Sturzenegger et al[29]
Unaware of impending impact	Ryan et al,[17] Sturzenegger et al[29]
Female occupant	Spitzer et al,[26] Squires et al[71]
Older occupants	Spitzer et al,[26] Squires et al[71]
Multiple injuries	Spitzer et al,[26] Radanov et al[39]
Greater than 10 cm distance between head and restraint	Olsson et al[20]
Prolonged discomfort for more than 3 months	Olsson et al[20]
Early onset of neck pain	Radanov et al[39]
Initial severity of neck pain	Ryan et al[17]
Early onset of numbness	Hohl[72]
Prolonged use of cervical collars	Hohl[72]
Sharp reversal or abnormal cervical curve	Norris and Watt,[69] Hohl,[72]
Need to resume physical therapy more than once	Hohl[72]
Construction of struck and striking vehicles	v Koch et al[25]
Mass ratios with smaller vehicles being worse	v Koch et al[25]
Seat belt use	Norris and Watt[69]
Pre-existing degeneration	Norris and Watt[69]

the following factors will influence risk: being involved in a rear-end crash, being in a less crashworthy vehicle, being in a small car, and being out of position. Human factors such as being female, elderly, having significant prior neck injury, prior cervical spinal surgery, and having significant degenerative joint changes will increase the risk of having long-term symptoms. When specifically addressing the rear-end crash, poor prognostic factors include: having the body twisted at the time of impact, a poor seatback design that is elastic and that has a head restraint more than 10 cm from the back of the occupant's head, being tall, being female, and being unaware of the impending crash. Post-collision factors include delays in initiating treatment, prolonged use of cervical collars,[72] having several flare-ups of pain during the course of treatment, having severe pain, being disabled in less than 12 hours, and having early radicular symptoms.

An English study compared whiplash patients to those who suffered neck injuries from other injury mechanisms. Between 10 and 15 years later, 62 percent of the whiplash group and 14 percent of the nonwhiplash group had residual problems.[73] One Australian study, in which a majority of cases were involved in rear-end crashes, found that unaware occupants had a 15 times higher risk of neck strain symptoms at 6 months.[17] In rear-end collisions, the duration of neck symptoms at 1 year after the crash was found to be significantly related to having a head restraint more than 10 cm behind the occupant's head.[20] Occupants whose heads were rotated at the time of impact were found to have significantly more long-term symptoms as well.[15] Norris and Watt[69] conclude from their study of 61 patients, that the presence of pre-existing spondyloarthrosis, postinjury neck pain or stiffness, C5–8 motor or sensory impairment, and muscle spasm adversely affect neck injury prognosis for rear-end collisions. They also conclude that any degenerative findings and abnormal cervical curves will appear to affect prognosis as well. A study of 78 patients in collisions in an initial and 6 month follow-up study found that psychosocial stress had little influence on the recovery outcome.[74]

HOW SOON CAN THE PHYSICIAN SAFELY PREDICT PROGNOSIS?

Prognosis is best predicted when the patient's pain intensity and functional capacity levels flatten out or plateau for a reasonable period without any significant flare-up of pain. I would suggest that when a patient's overall symptom intensity and frequency have stabilized for a period of 4 to 6 weeks without any significant flare-up, that the patient has reached MMI status. This plateau can occur as early as 2 to 3 months postcollision for patients with minor injuries or as late as 9 to 12 months later when injuries are more severe. Most authors feel that it is better to see how a patient responds to treatment and time before making a long-term prognosis. A rare author will feel that the initial presentation of the patient will adequately predict a long-term

prognosis.[69] However, making a prognosis at the initial visit may have some level of probability, which has not been yet defined in any large scale study; it does not allow for variations in the individual. If the type and patterns of symptoms and their onset are considered with severity of pain (i.e., early severe radicular pain), then some patients' outcomes can be predicted.

DOES LITIGATION, OR PENDING LITIGATION, HAVE ANY SIGNIFICANT INFLUENCE ON PROGNOSIS?

Substantial elements in our society embrace the theory that attorneys and the litigation process are responsible for the majority of long-term pain following motor vehicle crashes. Apparently, after litigation is concluded, a miracle happens and the pain goes away, sort of like a fairy tale. However, when one considers the prognostic literature that compares outcomes in tort states, states with no-fault insurance, and countries that do not have as many attorneys as the United States, there is an apparent theme. Litigation does not resolve chronic pain or its subsequent disability. There is no doubt that the process of taking depositions, arbitration hearings, and going through a trial will cause a patient to focus on his or her pain and activity level; however, this does not contribute a significant amount to the disability, in my experience. One excellent review of medical literature, evaluating 18 prognostic studies, concluded that only three studies favor the view that claimants improve after settlement.[75] Hodgson and Grundy[73] make a valid point; if litigation were a factor, why are occupants involved in rear-end crashes more commonly symptomatic, whereas those involved in frontal and side impacts had significantly fewer residual symptoms? Macnab and McCulloch's[76] viewpoint—that rear-enders incur most of the litigation—prompts the question of why litigation is not the same for various impact directions.

QUEBEC TASK FORCE WHIPLASH STUDY

This chapter would not be complete without a brief discussion of the Quebec Task Force guidelines.[26, 77] It is important for the reader to realize that this is the largest study of its kind in current print. There were two essential mandates of the Canadian insurance–funded study: (1) to review the base of medical literature and find the scientifically acceptable and clinically relevant studies, and (2) to make recommendations on diagnosis, treatment, and prognosis. The Task Force found 10,382 titles and abstracts for preliminary screening on the whiplash topic. Its independent reviewers concluded that only 62 studies were both "relevant and scientifically meritorious." It also reviewed insurance claim data of 3014 whiplash claims involved in various car accident vectors (front, side, rear), finding that 31 percent of crash events were documented as rear-end crashes and that these rear-end collisions resulted in higher rates of relapse or recurrences of symptoms. In addition, 59 percent of whiplash claims were reported among areas where speed limits were below 37 mph. Whiplash claims were notably higher for women and among seat belt users. About one fifth of occupants had delays in symptom onset. Occupants reporting prolonged disability include women, those with multiple injuries, elderly, those with a higher number of dependents, and those involved in a rear-end crash. The consensus of the Task Force was that repair takes 6 weeks and remodeling takes up to 1 year. The Task Force suggests that a 4 to 5 mph impact, which subjects the cervical spine to up to 4.5 g, is the threshold for cervical strain injury.

With regard to diagnosis and management, the Task Force developed a four-tier level of severity and recommended anterior-posterior open mouth, and lateral X-ray baseline views for levels 2 through 4. The Task Force recommends early interventions that promote mobilization, manipulation, and exercise in combination with limited use of medications. At 6 weeks, if the patient's case is not resolved (i.e., he or she is unable to return to work), a referral is recommended for specialized advice or a multidisciplinary team evaluation. The Task Force defined resolution of a case as the point when the patient was able to go back to work.

There were two major accomplishments of this study. First, the Task Force brought into perspective the poor scientific quality of these 10,000 studies. Second, it encouraged more collaboration between clinicians and research scientists. On the other hand, there were several inherent problems with this study, and physicians should be cautious about following its recommendations. A physician must be cautious when considering any study that admits that there was not one acceptable population-based study on the risk of whiplash disorder. In addition, the Task Force has not been able to add any scientifically valid treatment recommendations, as it only summarized the scant literature and based its opinion on the recommendations of a limited source of Task Force members, many whom were not clinicians. Cassidy[77] acknowledges that "although there is a vast literature on the subject of whiplash, it is obviously of poor scientific quality. The few randomized controlled studies of interventions in the literature were methodically weak, mixed treatment effects and were difficult to interpret." Another problem when relating the treatment standards of this Canadian study stems from the fact that by contract, patients in the United States have their conditions treated until the case is resolved; that is, when they reach maximal medical improvement and not when they are able to go to work.

CONCLUSION

Clearly, motor vehicle crashes are a major problem in modern mobile societies, and there are tremendous costs to the health care system from these injuries. I hope that the reader has a better understanding of frontal, side, and rear-end crash dynamics and occupant kinematics after reading this chapter. Each crash type has its own injury types, injury biomechanics, and injury threshold. Every occupant is unique and may vary in injury risk and prognosis. The physician needs to keep up to date on the literature that evaluates these injuries. I encourage my patients and friends to buy safe cars, preferably large cars, to drive safely, and to use safety devices in attempts to minimize injury risk.

! CLINICAL PEARL

The challenge for the physician is in preventing chronic pain and not in managing the acute injury.

Future legislative reform should focus on requiring manufacturers to make all motor vehicle safe. A 1997 report by the Insurance Institute for Highway Safety[78] that evaluated driver death rates for 140 models manufactured between 1991 and 1995—including sport utility vehicles, vans, and pick-up trucks—showed that 31 percent of the models sold in the United States have significantly more than average risk of causing fatality when compared to safer vehicles. Our society has the capability to manufacture safe vehicles. One must also wonder why Americans allow vehicles to be sold that can reach speeds of 140 mph. A solution to the problem of speeding on public roads would be to sell vehicles with governors that allow a top speed of 75 mph. Reform in the management arena should focus on isolating those who abuse the system, instead of punishing physicians.

REFERENCES

1. National Safety Council. *Accident Facts*. Chicago, Ill: National Safety Council; 1996.
2. Hill J, Mackay GM, Henderson S. *Seat Belt Limitations in Collisions that Involve no Compromise of the Passenger Compartment*. Society of Automotive Engineers, 1997; SAE paper 970118.
3. Morris AP, Thomas P. *Neck Injuries in the UK Co-operative Crash Injury Study*. Society of Automotive Engineers, 1996; SAE paper 962433.
4. Maag U, Desjardins D, Bourbeau R, Laberge-Nadeau C. Seat belts and neck injuries. International IRCOBI Conference on the Biomechanics of Impact, Lyon, France, September 12–14, 1990:1–13.

5. Dischinger PC, Ho SM, Kerns TJ, Brennan P. Patterns of injury in frontal collisions with and without airbags. International IRCOBI Conference of the Biomechanics of Impact, 1996:311–320.

6. Hobbs CA. *Dispelling the Misconceptions About Side Impact Protection.* Society of Automotive Engineers, 1995; SAE paper 950879.

7. Kallieris D, Schmidt G, Mattern R. Vertebral column injuries in 90 degree collisions: a study with post-mortem human subjects. International IRCOBI Conference on the Biomechanics of Impacts, Birmingham, UK, 1987:189–202.

8. Eberhard CD, Moffa PJ. Collision warning. Automotive Engineering, Society of Automotive Engineers, March, 1997:88–90.

9. Kahane CJ. *An Evaluation of Head Restraints—Federal Motor Vehicle Safety Standard 202.* NHTSA Technical Report, DOT HS–806–108. Springfield, Va: National Technical Information Service; 1982.

10. Romilly DP, Thomson RW, Navin RPD, et al. Low speed rear impacts and elastic properties of automobiles. 12th International Technical Conference on Experimental Safety Vehicles, NHTSA, 1989:1199–1205.

11. Geigl BC, Steffan H, Leinzinger P, Roll MM, Roll, Bauer G. The movement of head and cervical spine during rear-end impact. International IRCOBI Conference on the Biomechanics of Impact, Lyon, France, September 21–23, 1994:127–137.

12. McConnell WE, Howard RP, Guzman HM, et al. *Analysis of Human Test Subject Kinematic Responses to Low Velocity Rear End Impacts.* Society of Automotive Engineers, 1993; SAE paper 930889.

13. Svensson MY, Lövsund P, Håland Y, et al. *Rear-end Collisions—A Study of the Influence of Backrest Properties on Head-Neck Motion Using a New Dummy Neck.* Society of Automotive Engineers, 1993; SAE paper 930343.

14. Boström O, Svensson MY, Aldman B, et al. A new neck injury criterion candidate-based on injury findings in the cervical spinal ganglia after experimental neck extension trauma. International IRCOBI Conference on the Biomechanics of Impact, 1996.

15. Jakobsson L, Norin H, Jernström C, et al. Analysis of different head and neck responses in rear-end car collisions using a new humanlike mathematical model. International IRCOBI Conference on the Biomechanics of Impact, Lyon, France, September 21–23, 1994:109–125.

16. Foret-Bruno JY, Dauvilliers F, Tarriere C. Influence of the seat and head rest stiffness on the risk of cervical injuries in rear impact. Proceedings of the 13th ESV Conference in Paris, France; paper 91-S8-W-19, NHTSA; 1991.

17. Ryan GA, Moore VM, Dolinis J, et al. Crash severity and neck strain in car occupants. International IRCOBI Conference on the Biomechanics of Impacts, Lyon, France, September 21–23, 1994:97–107.

18. Eichberger A, Geigl BC, Moser A, Fachbach B, Steffan H. Comparison of different car seats regarding head-neck kinematics of volunteers during rear end impact. International IRCOBI Conference on the Biomechanics of Impact, 1996.

19. Morris F. Do head-restraints protect the neck from whiplash injuries? *Arch Emer Med* 1989;6:17–21.

20. Olsson I, Bunketorp O, Carlsson G, et al. An in-depth study of neck injuries in rear end collisions. International IRCOBI Conference on the Biomechanics of Impact, Bron, Lyon, France, 1990.

21. Foret-Bruno JY, Tarriere C, Le Coz JY, Got C, Guillon F. Risk of cervical lesions in real-world and simulated collisions. Proceedings of the 34th Association for the Advancement of Automotive Medicine, Scottsdale, Arizona, 1990.

22. Roberts VL, Compton CP. *The Relationship Between Delta V and Injury.* Society of Automotive Engineers, 1993; SAE paper 933111.

23. Saczalski KJ, Syson SR, Hille RA, Pozzi MC. *Field Accident Evaluations and Experimental Study of Seat Back Performance Relative to Rear-Impact Occupant Protection.* Society of Automobile Engineers, 1993; SAE paper 930346.

24. Langwieder K, Backaitis SH, Fan W, Partyka S, Ommaya A. *Comparative Studies of Neck Injuries of Car Occupants in Frontal Collisions in the United States and in the Federal Republic of Germany.* Society of Automotive Engineers, 1981; SAE paper 811030.

25. v Koch M, Kullgren A, Lie A, Nygren A, Tingvall C. Soft tissue injury of the cervical spine in rear-end and frontal car collisions. International IRCOBI Conference on the Biomechanics of Impact, Switzerland, September 13–15, 1995:273–283.

26. Spitzer WO, Skovron ML, Salmi LR, et al. Scientific monograph of the Quebec Task Force on whiplash-associated dsisorders: Redefining "whiplash" and its management. *Spine* 1995;20S(8S):1–73.

27. Larder DR, Twiss MK, Mackay GM. Neck injury to car occupants using seat belts. 29th Annual Proceedings, American Association for Automotive Medicine, Washington, DC, 1985:153–165.

28. Galasko CSB, Murray PM, Pitcher M, et al. Neck sprains after road traffic accidents: a modern epidemic. *Injury* 1993;24:155–157.

29. Struzenegger M, DeStefano G, Radanov BP, Schnidrig A. Presenting symptoms and signs after whiplash injury: The influence of accident mechanisms. *Neurology* 1994;44:688–693.

30. Lövsund P, Nygren Å, Salen B, Tingvall C. Neck injuries in rear end collisions among front and rear seat occupants. International IRCOBI Conference on the Biomechanics of Impact, Bergisch-Gladbach, Germany, 1988:319–325.

31. Rumball K, Jarvis J. Seat-belt injuries of the spine in young children. *J Bone Joint Surg (Br)* 1992;74-B:571–574.

32. Agran PF, Castillo DN, Winn DG. Comparison of motor vehicle occupant injuries in restrained and unrestrained 4 to 14 year-olds. *Accid Anal Prev* 1992;24:349–355.

33. McCoy GF, Johnstone RA, Duthie RB. Injury to the elderly in road traffic accidents. *J Trauma* 1989;29:494–497.

34. Foust DR, Chaffin DB, Snyder RG, Baum JK. *Cervical Range of Motion and Dynamic Response and Strength of Cervical Muscles.* Society of Automotive Engineers, 1973; SAE paper 730975.

35. Norin H, Isaksson-Hellman I. Injury potential prediction of a safety design feature. A theoretical method based on simulations and traffic accident data. International IRCOBI Conference on the Biomechanics of Impact, Verona, Italy, 1995:121–132.

36. Patrick LM. Neck injury incidence, mechanisms and protection. American Association for Automotive Medicine, 31st Annual Proceedings, New Orleans, Louisiana, 1987:409–433.

37. Pettersson K, Kärrholm J, Toolanen G, Hildingsson C. Decreased width of the spinal canal in patients with chronic symptoms after whiplash injury. *Spine* 1995;20:1664–1667.

38. Otremski I, Marsh JL, Wilde BR, et al. Soft tissue cervical spinal injuries in motor vehicle accidents. *Injury* 1989;20:349–351.

39. Radanov BP, Sturzenegger M, Di Stefano G, Schnidrig A, Aljinovic M. Factors influencing recovery from headache after common whiplash. *BMJ* 1993;307:652–655.

40. Yoganandan N, Haffner M, Maiman DJ, et al. *Epidemiology and Injury Biomechanics of Motor Vehicle Related Trauma to the Human Spine.* Society of Automotive Engineers, 1989; SAE paper 892438.

41. Barnsley L, Lord SM, Wallis BJ, Bogduk N. The prevalence of chronic cervical zygapophysial joint pain after whiplash. *Spine* 1995;20:20–26.

42. Lord SM, Barnsley L, Wallis BJ, Bogduk N. Chronic cervical zygapophyseal joint pain after whiplash. *Spine* 1996;21:1737–45.

43. Taylor JR, Twomey LT. Acute injuries to cervical joints: An autopsy study of neck sprain. *Spine* 1993;18:1115–1122.

44. Fricton JR. Myofascial pain and whiplash. *Spine* 1993;7:403–422.

45. Teasell RW, McCain GA. Clinical spectrum and management of whiplash injuries. In: Tollison CD, Satterthwaite JR, eds. *Painful Cervical Trauma: Diagnosis and Rehabilitative Treatment of Neuromusculoskeletal Injuries.* Philadelphia, Pa: Williams & Wilkins; 1992.

46. Kreeft JH. Headache following whiplash. *Spine* 1993;7:391–402.

47. Diamond S, Freitag FG. Headache following cervical trauma. In: Tollison CD, Satterthwaite JR, eds. *Painful Cervical Trauma: Diagnosis and Rehabilitative Treatment of Neuromusculoskeletal Injuries.* Baltimore, Md: Williams & Wilkins; 1992.

48. Nordhoff LS. *Motor Vehicle Collision Injuries: Mechanisms, Diagnosis, and Management.* Baltimore, Md: Aspen 1996.

49. Yamaguchi M. Incidence of headache and severity of head injury. *Headache* 1992;32:427–431.

50. Buskila D, Neumann L, Vaisberg G, Alkalay D, Wolfe F. Increased rates of fibromyalgia following cervical spine trauma: A controlled study of 161 cases of traumatic injury. *Arthritis Rheum* 1997;40:446–452.

51. Wolfe F, Smythe HA, Yunus MB, et al. The American College of Rheumatology 1990 criteria for the classification of fibromyalgia: Report of the multicenter criteria committee. *Arthritis Rheum* 1990;33:160–172.

52. Kraus H. Management of myofascial pain. In: Tollison CD, Satterthwaite JR, eds. *Painful Cervical Trauma: Diagnosis and Rehabilitative Treatment of Neuromusculoskeletal Injuries.* Baltimore, Md: Williams & Wilkins; 1992.

53. Chester JB. Whiplash, postural control, and the inner ear. *Spine* 1991;16:716–720.

54. Mailis A, Papagapiou M, Vanderlinden RG, Campbell V, Taylor A. Thoracic outlet syndrome after motor vehicle accidents in a Canadian pain clinic population. *Clin J Pain* 1995;11:316–324.

55. Sanders RJ, Pearce WH. The treatment of thoracic outlet syndrome: A comparison of different operations. *J Vasc Surg* 1989;10:626–634.

56. Sanders RJ, Jackson CGR, Banchero N, Pearce WH. Scalene muscle abnormalities in traumatic thoracic outlet syndrome. *Am J Surg* 1990;159:231–236.

57. Svensson MY, Lövsund P, Håland Y, Larsson S. The influence of seat-back and head-restraint properties on the head-neck motion during rear-impact. International IRCOBI Conference on the Biomechanics of Impacts, Netherlands, 1993:395–406.

58. Hinoki M. Vertigo due to whiplash injury: A neuro-otological approach. *Acta Otolaryngol (Stockh)* 1985; 419S:9–29.

59. Hamer AJ, Gargan MF, Bannister GC, Nelson RJ. Whiplash injury and surgically treated cervical disc disease. *Injury* 1993;18:549–550.

60. Lunsford LD, Bissonette DJ, Jannetta PJ, Sheptak PE, Zorub DS. Anterior surgery for cervical disc disease, Part I: Treatment of lateral cervical disc herniation in 253 cases. *J Neurosurg* 1980;53:1–11.

61. Pettersson K, Hildingsson C, Toolanen G, Fagerlund M, Björnebrink J. Disc pathology after whiplash: A prospective magnetic resonance imaging and clinical investigation. *Spine* 1997;22:283–288.

62. Stäbler A, Weiss M, Scheidler J, Krödel A, Seiderer M, Reiser M. Degenerative disk vascularization on MRI: Correlation with clinical and histopathologic findings. *Skeletal Radiol* 1996;25:119–126.

63. Malliaris AC, Hitchcock R, Hedlund J. *A Search for Priorities in Crash Protection.* Society of Automotive Engineers, 1982;SAE paper 820242.

64. *Dorland's Illustrated Medical Dictionary.* 28th ed. Philadelphia, Pa: WB Saunders; 1994.

65. Lehto M, Järvinen M, Nelimarkka O. Scar formation after skeletal muscle injury: A histological and autoradiographical study in rats. *Arch Orthop Trauma Surg* 1986;104:366–370.

66. Hunt TK. Basic principles of wound healing. *J Trauma* 1990;30S:122–128.

67. Krafft M, Kullgren A, Lie A, Nygren Å, Tingvall C. Car model safety rating based on real life accidents. International IRCOBI Conference on the Biomechanics of Impact, Berlin, Germany, September 11–13, 1991:25–39.

68. Insurance Research Council. *Auto Injuries: Claiming Behavior and Its Impact on Insurance Costs.* Oak Brook, Ill: Insurance Research Council; 1994.

69. Norris SH, Watt I, The prognosis of neck injuries resulting from rear-end vehicle collisions, *J Bone Joint Surg* 1983;65B:608–611.

70. Hildingsson C, Toolanen G. Outcome after soft-tissue injury of the cervical spine: A prospective study of 93 car-accident victims. *Acta Orthop Scand* 1990;61:357–359.

71. Squires B, Gargan MF, Bannister GC. Soft-tissue injuries of the cervical spine: 15-year follow-up. *J Bone Joint Surgery* 1996;78B:955–957.

72. Hohl M. Soft-tissue injuries of the neck in automobile accidents: Factors influencing prognosis. *J Bone Joint Surg* 1974;56A:1675–1682.

73. Hodgon SP, Grundy M. Whiplash injuries: Their long-term prognosis and its relationship to compensation. *Neuro-Orthopedics* 1989;7:88–91.

74. Radanov BP, Stefano G, Schnidrig A, Ballinari P. Role of psychosocial stress in recovery from common whiplash. *Lancet* 1991;338:712–715.

75. Mendelson G. Follow-up studies of personal injury litigants. *Int J Law Psychiatry* 1984;7:179–188.

76. Macnab I, McCulloch J. *Neck Ache and Shoulder Pain.* Baltimore, Md: Williams & Wilkins; 1994.

77. Cassidy JD. The Quebec Task Force on whiplash-associated disorders: Implications for clinical management and future directions for research. In: Allen ME, ed. *Musculoskeletal Pain Emanating from the Head and Neck: Current Concepts in Diagnosis, Management and Cost Containment.* New York, Ny: Haworth Medical Press; 1996.

78. Insurance Institute for Highway Safety. *Driver Death Rates: By Make and Model 1991–95 Models.* September 1997.

CHAPTER 7

The Mechanics of Low Speed Rear-End Motor Vehicle Collisions

Lawrence S. Nordhoff, Jr.

"It is interesting to note that not all things in life are clearly visible and objective. This is especially true in the low-speed rear-end crash. As humans we tend to depend on the dramatic events and opinions seen in the media. However, those committed to the well-being of mankind should not let societal bias and a few opinions lead us away from treating legitimate cases."

—L.S.N. Jr.

INTRODUCTION

Cervical injuries are frequently seen following low velocity rear-end crashes. These soft-tissue whiplash injuries are seen almost twice as frequently as those that are reported internationally in frontal and side crashes. There is general agreement among clinicians that significant injury or disability, or both, can occur in these low damage claims. In contrast, the insurance industry and the reconstruction community, whose primarily source of income are insurance companies, claim that these low damage crashes cannot cause injury. The objectives of this chapter are to review the literature, both automotive and clinical, and determine: (1) the crash dynamics for the vehicle and occupant, (2) the mechanisms of injury, (3) the speeds at which neck injuries occur, and (4) the challenges facing clinicians in this litigious environment. The chapter also addresses issues relating to reconstruction and physician perspectives. In addition, it evaluates whether there is any relationship between the damage to the vehicle and injury to the occupant in a low-speed rear-end crash.

ISSUES SURROUNDING LOW VELOCITY REAR-END IMPACTS

Low velocity rear-end impacts usually occur in one of the following situations: (1) the struck vehicle is stopped at a light or stop sign, (2) the struck vehicle is stopping rapidly due to changes in upcoming traffic speed, (3) a vehicle changes a lane in front of another vehicle and then slows down, or (4) a striking vehicle creates a chain collision in which an impacted vehicle is pushed into a third vehicle ahead. It has been estimated that in about 70 percent of the cases, the vehicle being struck in a rear-end crash is stopped.[1]

In many cases there can be varying extremes of damage to the rear and front ends of the two vehicles due to the differences in stiffness properties inherent in bumpers, varying distances from bumper to body, varying bumper heights, and different (i.e., isolator versus foam core) bumper systems. In some rear-end crashes the front end of the striking vehicle can have damage to the front hood, grill, and other areas that result in repair estimates totaling from $800 to $1,100, with little or no damage to the rear end of the struck vehicle. The structural damage from these low-speed crashes can vary from no visible external damage, to slight abrasions or scrapes of the bumper fascia, to minor indentations of the bumper, to more extensive damage that requires replacing the bumper or tail light fixtures, or repairing the trunk lid. In some cases, there is damage (wrinkling) to the rear side panels of the struck vehicle with little external damage to the bumper.

DEFINITIONS

A low velocity rear-end crash is defined in this chapter as a collision in which the struck vehicle's ΔV is less than 10 mph during the collision. A vehicle's ΔV is defined as a measure of the vehicle's change in velocity at its center of mass. It is the amount of acceleration that a vehicle's center of mass goes through from the initial impact to the end of the collision induced pulse. Mathematically, to calculate acceleration, you subtract the initial velocity from the ending velocity and divide that sum by the time it took. Most vehicles can start from a stopped position and accelerate within a distance of 4 feet to achieve a velocity of 5 mph. The coefficient of restitution (e) is the ratio of the rebound velocity to the impact velocity of two vehicles and measures the amount of bounce. In low speed crashes the amount of bounce (e) must be considered in any ΔV for the struck vehicle and closing velocity of the striking vehicle calculation. The g force for the low speed crash is the amount of acceleration for a vehicle during the crash impulse or for the occupant relative to the vehicle whose g forces primarily occur after the crash impulse has concluded. To calculate the g force, the amount of acceleration for the vehicle or occupant is divided by 32.2 ft/sec or gravity.

WHAT ARE THE CHALLENGES FACING THE PHYSICIAN?

The primary challenge facing the physician is understanding injury risk for this unique type of impact, the various mechanisms of injury, and how to correlate the few objective examination findings to support the degree of pain or disability with which the patient presents. When such a patient comes into the emergency department or private office for the initial office visit, and the physician becomes aware that his or her injuries were sustained in a low speed rear-end crash with minimal-to-no physical damage to the vehicle, a mental picture begins to form. The first thoughts that come to mind are, why does this patient have so much pain, and how do I manage this case? With the inherent litigation environment, many physicians are keeping their distance from these cases.

WHAT ARE THE CHALLENGES FACING THE ATTORNEY?

Recently, attorneys have been having significant difficulty settling many of their low speed rear-end collisions; in many instances, they are now refusing to accept these types of clients. Many insurance carriers have created an investment environment in which the plaintiff's attorney must invest heavily in the case.

 CLINICAL PEARL

In many cases, the plaintiff's attorney cannot win one of these low speed cases without investing around $12,000 for experts and depositions.

It is apparent that the tactics of forcing these issues to trial have worked for many insurance carriers, as the number of cases with legal representation has dropped in the past few years. Having little education in physics, traffic accident reconstruction, or studies that look at low speed injuries, many attorneys are unable to convince claim adjusters or juries that their clients sustained valid injuries. With most experts doing mostly defense work, it is also hard for the plaintiff's attorney to find an expert who will give credence to his or her side. These problems are compounded by inadequate paperwork by physician, incomplete documentation of examinations and history, delay in onset of pain, and large bills. All the above factors are complicated by television programs that try to dispute the validity of these injuries. The end result is that the general public (jurors) and many judges and physicians perceive these claims as being fraudulent or financially motivated.

WHY ARE THERE CHALLENGES FROM THE INSURANCE INDUSTRY?

Several American automobile insurance carriers have taken the stance that injuries cannot occur in a low speed rear-end crash when little vehicle damage exists. This industry is challenging its own clients in many cases.

! CLINICAL PEARL

The success of the insurance industry on this issue stems primarily from the inability of others to successfully challenge their position. The best experts in the field do primarily defense work.

Generally, most insurance carriers do much better in jury trials than they do in arbitration hearings, and with the recent success rates in obtaining favorable defense jury verdicts, the carriers have become very aggressive in taking these cases to trial. It appears that some carriers do not care if they lose a few cases. They simply want to win the majority of cases and send a clear message to plaintiff attorneys. The insurance industry has also successfully recruited a multibillion dollar traffic accident reconstruction and physician community to defend and endorse its "no possible injury" position. These engineers, physicists, mathematicians, kinesiologists, anatomists, physicians, and other specialities have jumped on the bandwagon to aid in the destruction of the occupant's and supporting physician's credibility. Although lacking scientifically valid large-scale studies that relate exact probabilities for injury risk for a rear-end crash for a specific individual, these so-called low speed crash experts will state, under oath, that there is no way that any injuries can occur in collisions that cause minimal damage, or occur at a ΔV of 5 mph or less. Often these medical experts—many of whom have never treated an actual patient—will also state under oath, with reasonable medical certainty, that an occupant's pre-existing disc bulging, or degenerative joint disease conditions were solely responsible for all of his or her current problems, even when the patient has no prior history of similar problems.

WHAT ARE THE CHALLENGES FACING THE OCCUPANT?

Typically, the occupant will see a physician or chiropractor within the first 2 weeks after the crash, or present to the emergency department the day after, reporting the injury and a variety of whiplash symptoms that have developed. In the fortunate cases, there is no difficulty with the insurance carrier regarding payment for the treatment and various diagnostic tests. However, in other cases the insurance carrier sends a letter to the occupant refusing to pay for any injury claims because of the limited extent of damage to the vehicle. The occupant then is forced to retain an attorney which is, by itself, a difficult process, with occupants often being told by several attorneys that they do not represent plaintiffs in low speed rear-end cases. To pay for treatment, the occupant will use his or her medical insurance, establish a lien with the physician or attorney, or pay for treatment out of pocket. As time moves forward, the attorney is frequently unable to obtain any reasonable settlement offer from the carrier. The case then moves into more serious maneuvering, involving depositions and nonbinding arbitration hearings, which often conclude with a plaintiff award from the arbitrator. These nonbinding plaintiff awards are usually refused by the carrier. The case finally ends up in court $1\frac{1}{2}$ to 2 years later. The occupant is frustrated because the insurance company (often his or her own company) has taken a position that there is no possible way that an injury could have been sustained and somehow any pain and any subsequent disability is solely motivated by attorneys and physicians. The occupant feels he or she is being treated like a criminal.

VEHICLE DAMAGE CORRELATION TO INJURY AND DELTA V

There is a common belief that occupant injury correlates to the amount of damage to the vehicle in all types of crashes. The crash literature does show an overall linear relationship between vehicle damage and injury production in most frontal and side crashes. However, in the low speed rear-end collision, this rule does not correlate well until the main body of the vehicle begins to crush. There is a conflict within the automobile industry between making bumpers inexpensive to replace and keeping customers safe if involved in a crash. The original concept of designing bumpers to primarily protect the occupant has become outdated. The federal government even compromised its early 1980 to 1982 5-mph bumper standard because of pressure from the automotive industry.

Current safety standards require a certain level of vehicle structural stiffness to protect the occupant in the striking vehicle at higher speed frontal crashes. However this stiffness creates more elasticity in the lower speed collision, and the vehicle structures being struck may have less aggressiveness. The crash dynamics of a vehicle become more favorable for the occupant as the amount of residual crush deformation increases.[2,3] This means that as the vehicle structures deform or crush permanently (plastic behavior), there is less injury risk. Hyde[4] concludes that the trivial rear-end crash, which causes little or almost no damage to the vehicles, can cause considerable neck injury and extensive disability to occupants. Collisions having little damage, because they cause the neck to move into hyperextension, are more likely to cause significant neck injuries than the high-damage crashes, which are more liable to cause the seatback to break or bend backward, allowing for mostly axial motion of the neck.

! CLINICAL PEARL

Vehicle damage does not correlate to injury risk in the low speed impacts.

There is a common misconception that the extent of occupant injury must correlate with the amount of damage to the vehicle that results from a crash. Robbins[4a] illustrated mathematically the error in this thinking by demonstrating that lower crush to the vehicle results in the occupant being subjected to greater kinetic energy.

When looking at reports by the National Highway Traffic Safety Administration (NHTSA), Romilly et al note that many of the personal injury claims that are being reported by the insurance and medical community have been associated with low speed rear-end crashes. Many of these crashes involve minimal structural damage resulting from impact speeds below 9.3 mph.[3] One study of 137 patients concluded that the amount of damage to the automobile and the speed of the cars involved in the crash bear little relationship to the injury sustained by the cervical spine.[5] These authors found that occupants who experienced rotation of the head, were involved in a rear-end crash, and were unprepared had a higher frequency of multiple symptoms.[5] Watts et al conclude that occupant injury can occur with either zero or very small amounts of vehicle damage.[6] Yet another crash study found that neck injuries often occur in rear-end crashes at less than 12.4 mph, showing no correlation between crash speed and duration of neck symptoms until side members collapse and permanent deformation is seen.[7] Parmar and Raymakers[8] found no relationship between long-term prognosis and the severity of damage the car sustained in rear impacts.

Even the reconstruction community has recognized that when using test subjects to develop injury and ΔV thresholds, many vehicles will be undamaged at severities that are above the range where human volunteers have reported neck and back symptoms in rear-end impacts. One reconstruction company found that although frontal and rear-end impacts are dynamically similar for both striking and struck vehicles, occupants will fare better in front-end impacts than in rear-end impacts.[9] These authors found that certain vehicles can sustain significant front or rear impacts without sustaining damage to either vehicle. Bailey et al[10] found in their extensive low speed tests (vehicle-to-vehicle) that the damage threshold for rear bumpers is in the range of 8 to 12 mph ΔV. Ford Escort vehicles were consistently found to have the highest threshold for bumper damage in their study. The authors concluded that the distance the vehicle moves forward after an impact usually does not provide a reliable way to estimate closing speed changes, because the distance a vehicle rolls forward after being hit depends on when and how hard the brakes were applied.

CLINICAL, AUTOMOTIVE, AND INSURANCE REPORTS VERIFYING INJURY AT LOW VELOCITY IMPACTS

Many automotive, clinical, and insurance studies have shown that neck injuries occur in low velocity rear-end collisions.[3, 11–13]

CLINICAL REPORTS

Clinical studies, usually from emergency departments, have concluded that rear-end impacts of as little as 5 mph

can give rise to significant symptoms.[14] Whiplash injuries may occur in low impact rear-end crashes.[15] These soft tissue injuries are nearly always caused by minor accidents with very little vehicle damage.[16] Otremski et al,[17] in a study of 1197 crash occupants, found that the typical neck injury occurred in a middle-aged female occupant wearing a seat belt in a low speed rear-end crash. This study found that soft tissue injuries of the cervical spine were frequent occurrences in motor vehicle crashes and were most commonly seen in low speed accidents. These authors found that the incidence of objective findings was low in these cases, which was consistent with other published studies.

AUTOMOTIVE REPORTS

Several reports, including those by the NHTSA show that the insurance industry is reporting a significant number of claims for the low speed, low-damage rear-end crash.[18] Other reports from the Society of Automotive Engineers and the International Conference of the Biokinetics of Impacts conclude that neck injuries often occur in low speed rear-end crashes.[7, 11] Several authors have found that significant neck injury can occur in rear-end collisions of 5 to 10 mph.[7, 14] Morris and Thomas conclude that soft tissue neck injuries certainly can occur at comparatively low velocities and are associated with seat belt use.[19] Svensson et al[20] conclude that neck injuries in rear-end crashes are usually caused by swift extension-flexion motion of the neck and mostly occur at low velocity impacts, typically less than 12.4 mph. A French crash study found that cervical injury risk was correlated to velocity and seatback breakage.[21] These authors found that injury risk decreases when impact speeds increase because of seat breakage. Thirty six percent of the cervical injuries were seen in impacts of less than 9.3 mph, whereas 20 percent occurred in impact velocities over 9.3 mph.[21]

McConnell et al[22] found that from a clinical standpoint, the threshold for mild cervical-dorsal-lumbar strain injuries was at 5 mph in their car crash test subjects. Another author concludes that one of the most common car collisions is the low velocity rear-end crash.[23] Although it usually involves a relative impact speed of 5 to 10 miles per hour or less and the vehicular damage is often minor, significant injury and pain may be claimed by the occupants of the struck vehicle. Only rarely do the occupants of the impacting vehicle report injury.[23] An Australian crash study found that neck strain was observed in crashes of low severity, with six cases having a ΔV of less than 6.2 mph and eight cases having a maximum residual deformation of less than 50 mm.[24] One reconstruction facility that has performed over 1000 crash tests has concluded that the crash severity, characterized as ΔV, tends to be associated with the onset of symptoms in rear-end crashes at about 4 to 5 mph ΔV, and in front-end collisions at around 7.5 to 12.4 mph ΔV.[9, 10]

STUDIES THAT COMPARE ACCIDENT RECONSTRUCTION DELTA V TO PHYSICIAN DIAGNOSIS

Three recent studies[24a–c] have analyzed the accident scene and damage to the target vehicle using traffic accident reconstructionists to determine ΔV and then compared these findings with the findings of the physician at a trauma unit to which the occupants were admitted. These three studies, which have totaled 1,154 real-world occupants who have been involved in rear-end crashes, have demonstrated a paradoxical relationship between ΔV and reported injuries. Hell et al[24a] reported that 53% of claims related to low ΔV collisions of up to 15 kmh. Otte et al[24b] concluded that about 37% of all neck injuries were seen in cases in which accident reconstructionists had determined ΔVs to be up to 10 kmh, and an additional 42% were seen in cases having ΔVs of 11–20 kmh. Eichberger et al[24c] found in their evaluation of 7,500 rear-end crashes that 27.2% of all neck injury claims were found in the 0–8 kmh range and 43.2% were of the 8–15 kmh range. They also found that injuries to the neck varied as much as 5.5 times from "good" to "bad" vehicle models and that car mass, vehicle crashworthiness, ΔV, and seatback factors had major influences on the risk of injury.

There are two primary reasons for this paradox.

- Acceleration forces to occupants are lower when kinetic energy is absorbed by a great deal of crush to the vehicle.
- In many high ΔV crashes, the seatback breaks. As the seatback breaks, the occupant undergoes greater axial motion and less "whipping", resulting in less injury to the cervical spine. This finding does not apply to the low back region, as injuries to this area will increase when the seatback breaks.

INSURANCE REPORTS

One insurance study found that about 20 percent of all injury claims were from crashes under 5 mph.[25] In Japan, the review of insurance claim patterns shows that approximately 50 percent of vehicle-to-vehicle accidents have resulted in neck injuries, particularly at low impact velocities.[13] In Sweden, claim researchers found that when considering the low amount of physical damage to vehicles in rear-end crashes, such a high incidence of neck injuries was not expected.[26] Another Swedish study found 5 of their 26 rear-end crash cases had an energy equivalent speed of less than 6.2 mph.[7] Other claim researchers have recognized the unique role of the rear-end crash, concluding that whiplash occurs frequently in rear-end crashes of low severity.[12] A Canadian review of more than 10,000 studies suggested that a 4 to 5 mph impact, which subjects the cervical spine to as much as 4.5 g's, constitutes the threshold for mild cervical strain injury.[27]

ELASTIC BEHAVIOR OF VEHICLES IN LOW-VELOCITY IMPACTS

The two-vehicle, bumper-to-bumper low velocity crash is mostly elastic in behavior. This elasticity is dominant until some permanent deformation is seen in either vehicle. The nonplastic behavior is primarily due to the elastic properties of the bumpers, the suspension system, and the cantilever-designed front seatback design. Romilly et al[3] summarized the elastic and plastic collision behavior well for low velocity impacts. They found that at low impact velocities, plastic behavior may be absent allowing most of the total impact energy to be recovered in elastic rebound. The preferred collision profile was found to occur when the vehicle behaved as a plastic body with large amounts of crush, which would reduce the overall acceleration to the occupant. They conclude that there is a major dilemma in our society as manufacturers and the insurance industry want to protect the consumer while keeping repair costs down. As vehicles are made to have less damage at low speed collisions, the occupant will have more violent motion, which increases the potential for injury. Vehicles that do not sustain permanent damage in low velocity crashes produce higher dynamic loading on their occupants than those that crush plastically under the same or possibly more severe impact conditions.

BUMPER DESIGN AND CRUSH THRESHOLD

Passenger vehicle bumper systems typically consist of an exterior plastic cover; a steel, aluminum, or reinforced plastic bumper beam, which spans the width of the car; and some type of impact absorber, which is attached to the frame of the vehicle. There are various types of impact absorbers, including isolators (piston and cylinder assembly), foam and honeycomb cores, deformable steel struts, rubber shear blocks, and leaf springs.[9] Today, most newer small and midsized passenger cars have foam core or honeycomb bumpers. The automotive industry has eliminated most isolator systems because cheaper systems are available, although some larger luxury cars still have them.

In crash tests, structural damage to the passenger car may precede bumper damage.[9] This is seen particularly in vehicles having foam core or honeycomb bumpers. Many of the newer smaller cars are getting away from isolators to the cheaper foam core systems. Szabo and Welcher[28] found, in their low speed crash tests, that there was no damage to the bumper systems for the struck and striking vehicles at the 5 and 10 mph tests, except for some bumper fascia scuffing and isolator striations. It is important for the reader to remember that many of these rear-end crash tests use Ford Escort vehicles because their bumpers have the highest threshold for damage (12 mph) and the investigators can do repeated tests without replacing the bumpers. In addition, many of the crash tests use barriers, sleds, and pendulums to reproduce real world crashes. Some testing facilities will modify the vehicles' seatbacks, or reinforce them to keep replacement costs down.

WHY DO SEATBACKS CAUSE INJURY?

The inherent design properties of passenger seats can create injury. In terms of safety design, some of the performance or protection properties needed for injury mitigation in high speed crashes result in different performance characteristics in the low speed crash. The seatback that is stiff enough to resist a high speed frontal, side, or rear-end collision may provide excessive elastic accelerations in the low speed crash.[29] There are significant differences between different models in front passenger seatback design and in how elastic seatbacks are during rear-end crashes. Although the research has clearly shown that safer seatbacks can be manufactured, the auto industry continues to produce seatbacks that fail to protect occupants to their best potential.

One study of 5 mph impacts found that significant occupant motion can be encountered in low velocity rear-end impacts because of the elastic rebound of the seatback.[29] The rear-end collision is unique in that it is the only type of crash in which the occupant has opposing loading from the elastic seatback, which rebounds forward at the same time the head and neck are maximally extending rearward. Seatback rebound increases the likelihood of injury.[30] The elastic (spring) rebound of the seatback can intensify the violence of the whiplash-motion and delay contact between the head and the head restraint.[20] Geigl et al[31] found, in their analysis of seatback and head restraints, that magnitude of head rotation was primarily dependent on the distance between the head and restraint. This study also found that in some cases the head restraint can be more elastic than the seatback, allowing for an increased gap to form. Romilly et al[3] found that in some cases, the passenger seats could have a rebound velocity 1.5 times higher than the initial impact velocity. This rebound spring effect, in conjunction with the ramping tendency, acts to increase the effective occupant change of velocity during the collision and thereby increases potential for injury.[7, 32] In addition, if the occupant is leaning forward in the seat at the time of rear impact (out-of-position), a longer time will elapse before the seat forces will build up, which increases the relative occupant velocity between the vehicle and the occupant.

HEAD RESTRAINT DESIGN

Most vehicles have head restraints that are designed poorly or, even if properly designed, are positioned too low, making them ineffective. One study found that 88 percent of all occupants had their head restraints positioned too low.[33] The literature consistently shows that abnormally positioned head restraints or their absence can significantly increase neck injury risk.[14, 34] The head restraint is the only passive safety measure for cars involved in rear collisions.

Short distances between the head rest and the occupant's head have been shown to reduce injury.[35] Kinematic analysis shows that small gaps in the head and torso position relative to seat and head restraint can markedly affect head rotational and shear velocities in relation to the thorax.[20, 21] Five mph crash tests with the head leaning forward at 20 degrees resulted in higher rearward velocities than did 11 mph tests with normally positioned occupants.[36] Ono and Kanno[13] found in their tests that about 50 percent higher bending moment for the neck occurred with low head restraints as compared to the properly positioned head restraints. One study concluded that occupants having 2.5 inches or more distance between head and head restraint sustained higher levels of neck injury and prolonged neck pain.[7]

If the occupant's neck extends over and contacts either the head restraint or the seat top, a fulcrum effect arises, thus significantly magnifying the acceleration levels to the neck and head structures.[12] This fulcrum effect may create 2 to 3 times higher acceleration levels for the occupant. In cases in which the head restraint is absent, video analysis shows that the head will sustain lower acceleration levels than if a head restraint is present; however, the head will have larger deflections.[3] Taller occupants have significantly higher risks of sustaining neck injury in the rear-end collision.[37] This increased frequency is because they are more often in a situation in which the head and neck exceeds the vertical support than their shorter counterparts.

LOW SPEED REAR-END CRASH DYNAMICS

Four stages of vehicle impact can be identified, as derived from the results of several low velocity impact studies that have used human volunteers.[10, 22, 29, 38, 39] They are: (1) vehicle impact, bumper and frame loading; (2) vehicle forward motion and peak seatback loading; (3) peak occupant loading; and (4) vehicle separation and restitution.

STAGE 1. VEHICLE IMPACT, BUMPER AND FRAME LOADING (0–60 MSEC)

Typically the front of the striking vehicle (usually braking) hits the rear bumper of another car. In the lower velocity crashes, the two colliding bumpers will flatten or sink inward and then the vehicles will separate and the bumper will resume its initial shape. In many cases, due to the type of bumper components involved or materials used (foam core or honeycomb), there may be no permanent external residual crush noted until impact velocities near 8 to 10 mph. Often there is only a scratch or scuff mark in the outer fascia. In either case, once impact occurs, the kinetic energy and motion forces move into the vehicle's frame, from which they are transmitted to the seat cushion and seatback. When the striking vehicle has a similar mass, the driver or occupants in the struck car can be visualized as having their torso and head struck by the seatback at about 70 to 150 percent of the striking vehicle's velocity. The seatback will rapidly accelerate forward and downward, as the striking vehicle's bumper pushes the rear of the struck car's downward. By 50 msec, in a 5 mph rear crash, the front occupants have not moved and the vehicle's front seats will move forward about 2 to 3 inches.[22] If the striking vehicle's front bumper or center of mass is lower than the struck vehicle, the downward motion will not occur.

> **! CLINICAL PEARL**
>
> Visualize the rear-end crash as causing the seatback to strike an occupant's torso and head at about 70 to 150 percent of the striking vehicle's velocity.

STAGE 2. VEHICLE FORWARD MOTION AND PEAK SEATBACK LOADING (60–80 MSEC)

Peak vehicle and seatback loading occur from 50 to 80 msec after impact. Thomson et al's[29] 5 mph rear-end crash study shows that at 50 msec, the struck vehicle has reached 60 percent of its maximum speed. A normally positioned occupant does not begin to move until about 50 msec. This delay is primarily due to occupant inertia. At about 60 msec after impact, the seatback cushion is compressed enough to move the subject's hips and low back forward and upward. At the same time, the seatback is flexing rearward with respect to the vehicle's motion.[22] At this stage, the struck vehicle's forward- and downward-moving seat base and seatback structures are being deflected downward and backward by the occupant. Most seatbacks are designed in a manner that results in the occupant's torso loading the seatback before the head strikes the head restraint.[29] This is due in part to different material properties (elasticity) in the seatback and head restraint and the occupant's initial seating position. As the rapidly accelerating forces of the seatback build up, the occupant's torso starts to slide up (seat drops under) and backward against the seat. The forward-moving chest and the lagging neck structures will cause the cervical spine to move in extension relative to the torso. As the occupant's torso is pushed forward with the accelerating seat motion, the head movement initially moves in mild flexion. McConnell et al[39] document 2 to 6 degrees of neck flexion. This is due in part to the frequent gap between the occupant's head and the head restraint. The cervical lordosis will flatten and possibly reverse if the head restraint design permits, in order to fill in the gap, thus causing the initial forward head motion. As the seatback loads the occupant, the spine flattens and elongates. The authors describe this as a rapid tension-compression effect. They also describe the torso moving forward as a result of seatback motion, which causes pulling of the sternocleidomastoid muscle because of subsequent cranial motion.

STAGE 3. PEAK OCCUPANT LOADING (80–120 MSEC)

The driver's and passenger's shoulders reach peak acceleration levels at about 100 msec, with the head reaching its first peak acceleration level at about 120 msec. The struck vehicle's acceleration levels are now lessening. Significant occupant motion has been demonstrated in the low speed rear-end collision resulting from the elastic rebound properties of the seatback and head restraints.[2, 20, 29] At about 100 msec, the seatback reaches its maximum rearward rotation of about 10 degrees.[40] High-speed film analysis shows that there is seatback-acceleration related straightening of the normal cervical, dorsal, and lumbar spinal curves against the forward moving seatback, causing an axial lengthening of the spine. The initial upward motion is immediately followed by a sudden and surprisingly vigorous descent of the torso, much like a rubberband, as the stretched and straightened spine structures are restrained and limited by the seat belt, and the spine forcefully returns to its normal state of curvature.[22] The seatback is now rebounding forward, pitching the occupant's torso forward. In addition, the head restraint, if present and if elastic, will provide some degree of recoil energy if the head strikes it. Volunteer tests indicate that head restraint contact will occur at about 120 msec.[22, 35] The head will have higher acceleration when rebounding due to the elastic spring effect. Szabo et al[38] found that the *head acceleration multiplication factor* (relation of vehicle acceleration to head acceleration) was 2 to 3 times higher for the head than for the vehicle in tests.

> **! CLINICAL PEARL**
>
> The head will accelerate 2 to 3 times faster than the impacted vehicle in human volunteer tests.

McConnell et al[22] found, in a 5 mph volunteer test, that there were 4.3 g's of acceleration in the forward direction at 120 msec and 4 g's backward at 220 msec to the cervical spine. This forward torso and shoulder motion is occurring at the same time the head and mobile neck structures are reaching peak rearward acceleration levels at about 108 msec. The shoulder was found to rebound forward of the head in all low speed tests. All photographic analysis tests show that the elastic properties of the seat allow the vehicle to almost reach its maximum forward velocity as the occupant's head reaches its maximum rearward velocity.[3]

Photographic analysis of low speed crashes shows upward motion of the torso and shoulders of about 3.5 inches. Cervical spine motion was shown upward to about one half inch in a forward-arcing movement.[22] Crash analysis also shows that the highest rebound velocity for the occupant will occur if the seatback starts to push forward when the crash pulse has concluded. Owing to the presence of the seat belt, the stopping distance for the rebounding occupant is extremely small. This study also found that the construction of the striking vehicle was important in the risk of sustaining injury.[40]

STAGE 4. VEHICLE SEPARATION–RESTITUTION (120–400 MSEC)

Both vehicles will separate at about 120 msec. The typical crash duration from beginning to end for the vehicle lasts about 200 msec.[29] Another study concludes that the occupant will continue to move relative to the vehicle from 200 to 400 msec from the time of impact.[22] The occupant's head will have its second peak acceleration level (about 6 g's) at about 220 msec. The occupant's seatback has moved forward and the head and neck are now rebounding forward due to elastic recoil of the head restraint and seatback. The seatback will continue to load the occupant even after the external crash forces have subsided.[29] At about 250 msec the seatback has returned to precrash angulation and the occupant's torso is rebounding forward and away from the seatback surface. The occupant's head may whip forward and backward or jiggle several times during this stage. At 250 msec, the seatback has returned to precrash configuration. One study found that the bumper isolators will return to normal at about 300 msec.[38]

LOW VELOCITY INJURY MECHANISMS

There are several neck injury mechanisms in low velocity rear-end crashes. These mechanisms have been theorized by authors who have performed volunteer testing that attempted to simulate the low speed crash. Most of these studies evaluated occupant motion and formulated theories based on the kinematic responses. There have been extremely few studies that attempted to correlate occupant dynamics to some anatomical lesion. Four mechanisms of neck injury are discussed next.

FIRST MECHANISM OF INJURY

For the rear-end collision, a first mechanism of neck injury involves the vertical (axial) lengthening of the spine during the crash sequence as the forward-moving seatback causes the normal spinal curves to straighten and elongate.[41] The study by McConnell et al[22] found an accordion effect of the spine as it is rapidly flattened and lengthened against the forward-moving seatback. Their study of human occupants concluded that injury could happen even when the head did not exceed its normal voluntary motion limits found prior to the crash. Figure 7–1 shows a summary of video analysis of a 5-mph ΔV rear-end impact as the occupant moves over a period of 400 msec. The arrows indicate the direction in which the g forces are being directed. It is apparent from this study that the motion that occurs to the occupant is complex and three-dimensional.

SECOND MECHANISM OF INJURY

A second mechanism of neck injury was found in a recent study that concludes, from detailed photographic analysis and instrumentation, that as the torso moves forward with the forward-moving seatback, the head lags behind. The sternocleidomastoid muscles, which attach to the clavicle and under the ears, are pulled forward. Figure 7–2 shows how the sternocleidomastoid muscles pull on the skull. The head is torqued with a clockwise motion, as illustrated by the ball-and-chain (Fig. 7–2) or tripod analogy (Fig. 7–3). This causes craniocervical motion. There is no global hyperextension in the low velocity crash. However, there can be segmental motion beyond normal anatomical limits, particularly if the occupant is unbraced or the head is turned at time of impact.

THIRD MECHANISM OF INJURY

Two studies have evaluated neck flexion-extension motion in pigs to see if the whiplash motion would increase cerebrospinal fluid (CSF) pressure gradients within the foramen magnum, spinal canal, and intervertebral foramina, possibly explaining the multitude of symptoms seen after a minor neck injury from a rear-end crash.[20, 42] These studies of anesthetized pigs exposed to swift extension-flexion motion of the neck found increases in CSF pressures of the magnitude of about 150 mm Hg, about 10 times greater than normal, primarily along the lower half of the cervical spine across the intervertebral foramina. The researchers later performed histopathological analysis of the pigs' cervical spinal ganglia. They found evidence of injury to the lower cervical and upper thoracic nerve roots and spinal ganglia. It was concluded that during a whiplash extension motion, blood in the internal venous plexus and transient CSF velocities can be expected to rise far above physiologically normal levels and then will reverse in a matter of milliseconds (a mechanism known as the "blood hammer") as the neck changes direction. The soft tissues around and within the lower cervical spine and upper thoracic spine sustain mechanical strain and stress due to these extension motions. The authors also found that the

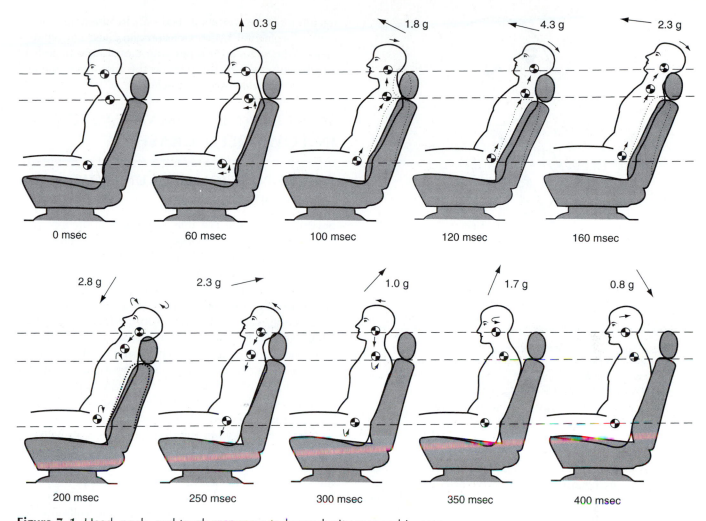

Figure 7–1. Head, neck, and trunk responses to low velocity rear-end impact.

(Adapted from McConnell WE, Howard RP, Guzman HM, et al. Analysis of human test subject kinematic responses to low velocity rear end impacts. Society of Automotive Engineers, 1993; SAE paper 930889.)

maximal pressure transients inside the spinal ganglia occur as the upper neck quickly changes from a flexion to extension shape.

> ### ❗ CLINICAL PEARL
>
> The "blood hammer" can injure spinal ganglia as the neck moves from extension to flexion.

FOURTH MECHANISM OF INJURY

Global hyperextension of the neck—that is motion beyond normal anatomical limits of ligaments, joint capsules, and muscles in the entire neck—can occur in some low velocity impacts. This is typically seen in crashes of greater than 5 mph ΔV, which still falls within the low velocity range as defined in this chapter. In crashes close to the 7 to 9 mph range, hyperextension is more likely to occur than at lower speeds even if the occupant is normally positioned. Hyperextension can occur in the lower range if the occupant is out of position (i.e., leaning forward prior to impact) or if, immediately before the rear-end crash, was involved in a frontal crash in which the occupant moved forward. Hyperextension can also occur when the head restraint is low, when the occupant is sufficiently tall enough for the head to extend over the head restraint, or when the seatback does not have a head restraint. If the occupant's head and neck are rotated at the time of impact, the ligaments and muscles are already under tension on the opposite side; thus, these joints can move beyond normal anatomical limits at dramatically lower amounts of extension. Occupants with pre-existing loss of anatomical range of motion, particularly elderly occupants with significant degenerative joint disease, or those with previous neck surgery or genetic fusion, may sustain extension injuries at lower velocities. According to Dunn and Blazer,[43] "the most injurious head

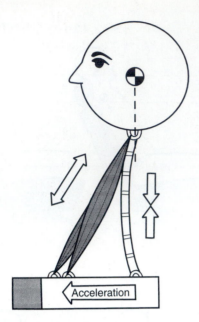

Figure 7–2. Head and neck "tripod."

(Adapted from McConnell WE, Howard RP, Poppel JV, et al. Human head and neck kinematics after low velocity rear-end impacts: Understanding "whiplash." Society of Automotive Engineers, 1995; SAE paper 952724.)

deflection in an acceleration injury is hyperextension, which is motion that goes beyond the normal physiologic range. Even though sustained in low-velocity rear-end collisions, this acceleration injury can produce forces significant enough to produce musculoligamentous tears with resultant hemorrhage and even disk disruption and avulsion

fractures of the vertebral bodies." In these low speed crashes, segmental hyperextension can cause an impingement of the rectus capitus posterior muscles and their dural attachment as the skull rotates on the atlas due to the pull of the sternocleidomastoid muscles.

VEHICLE AND HUMAN FACTORS IN LOW SPEED CRASHES

OUT-OF-POSITION AND UNAWARE OCCUPANTS

Several other factors can influence injury in the low speed crash, including the out-of-position occupant and the occupant who is unaware of the impending impact. Preimpact out-of-position occupants have been known to have increased injury potential.[30, 44] This can include an occupant who is bending forward in order to see oncoming traffic, a person reaching for papers on the floor, an occupant whose vehicle is involved in a frontal crash and then is rear-ended, and cases in which a car is braking hard to avoid an impact and the occupant is positioned forward at impact due to the rapid deceleration. In addition, occupants involved in multiple vehicle collisions, in which the struck car is pushed into another vehicle or object, thus effectively mispositioning the occupants, have an increased potential for injury. This malpositioning may be similar to a "karate chop" blow to the neck.[32] One Australian study found that unaware victims were 15 times more to likely to have persisting neck strain symptoms at 6 months than those who were aware of the impending collision.[24] A Swedish study of 163 rear-end crash occupants found that

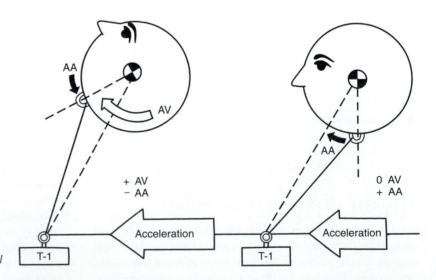

Figure 7–3. Ball-and-chain analogy.

(Adapted from McConnell WE, Howard RP, Poppel JV, et al. Human head and neck kinematics after low velocity rear-end impacts: Understanding "whiplash." Society of Automotive Engineers, 1995, SAE paper 952724.)

AV = Angular velocity
AA = Angular acceleration

the possibility of incurring long-term symptoms was significantly correlated with the occupant having the head rotated at the time of impact and having the seat inclined backward.[35]

OCCUPANT SEATING POSITION, SEATBACK, HEAD RESTRAINT, VEHICLE CRASHWORTHINESS, AND MASS RATIO FACTORS

The ability of the spine and soft tissues to tolerate these impact forces and motion depends on several variables, such as the occupant's size, age, health of the spine, and head and neck position at the time of the crash. Occupants in the rear seat have about half the frequency of injuries for front-seated occupants because the rear seat is directly attached to the vehicle's frame, significantly reducing the elastic properties. Carlsson et al[37] found 16 percent of rear seated occupants, 35 percent of drivers, and 25 percent of front seat passengers reported neck injuries in rear-end impacts. Data from the Folksam Insurance Company[26] found that 18.6 percent of front seat and 12.3 percent of rear seat occupants reported neck injury. Geigl et al[45] conclude that it is well known that seat construction has a large influence on the acceleration behavior of car passengers. The degree of head and spine motion also depends on the size and height of the occupant, rate of loading, presence or absence of head restraint, horizontal and vertical distance of head restraint from the back of the occupant's head, and the distance between torso and seatback. Also found to be influential are the plastic and elastic properties of the head restraint and seatback, presence of a seat belt, comparative size ratio of the impacting vehicles, and elastic-plastic characteristics of the bumper. Seat belts have also been shown to increase the incidence of neck injuries in rear-end crashes.[12, 19, 46]

Eichberger et al's[25] study of 520 rear-end crashes found, when comparing several car models for neck injury risk, that occupants in the less crashworthy car models were 5.5 times more likely to have neck injury than occupants in the best car models. Their study also found that occupants of smaller cars involved in rear-end crashes had significantly higher injury risk than those in larger models. In this study, the most important factors found to influence neck injuries in rear-end crashes include car model (especially car mass, car structure, and car seat stiffness and design), and the change of velocity of the struck car. A Swedish study of 8049 rear-end crashes found significant differences in neck injury risk for different models of cars (50 percent higher risk in less crashworthy vehicles) and in crashes involving smaller cars. They also found, in their analysis of different seatbacks, that the relative rebound velocity of the occupant could vary between 20 percent less than the car impact velocity or upward of 30 percent higher than the impact speed during a rear-end collision.[40]

HUMAN VOLUNTEER STUDIES THAT LOOK AT DELTA V THRESHOLDS

Several studies have attempted to estimate adult human thresholds for injury for specific vectors using human volunteer testing data or base estimates from mathematical models. When using human volunteers, primarily adult males, Bailey et al[10] concluded that ΔV associated with the onset of symptoms was 4 to 5 mph in rear-end crashes and 7.5 to 12.4 mph in frontal crashes. In looking for a general ΔV threshold for all impact vectors, one study, which based its information on data from the early 1970s, attempted to correlate injury threshold to impact velocities using mathematical models.[47] The author concluded that a 10-mph ΔV is the threshold for the 50th percentile male occupant. Further, a ΔV of 8.83 mph in extension injuries, 11.1 mph in flexion injuries, and 7.42 mph in lateral flexion injuries was the threshold using his mathematical constructs. However, this author also felt that there were considerable threshold variations due to factors such as occupant gender, age, size, and preexisting spinal disorders.[47] Because of other influences on injury risk, such as sitting posture and head restraint height, it is difficult to evaluate minor neck injury risk using impact speed, only.[13]

! CLINICAL PEARL

I find it difficult to justify adopting the limited findings of a handful of crash studies and then applying that very limited data to literally millions of people who have been injured in low speed crashes over the decades. In the past 4 decades, about 200 human test volunteers, only 40 being female, have participated in these simulated crashes. Most of these volunteers were employees of the firms publishing the data. None of the studies ever randomly selected subjects from the general population or used control groups. It is impossible to adopt these thresholds for practice guidelines when the vast majority of the organizations doing the low speed research assume that the human models used are typical occupants and that their calculations are mathematically solid. The authors of these studies have yet to publish any reliable probability figures for injury production based on vehicle damage, closing velocity, or ΔV.

There are several limitations to consider when attempting to validate human volunteer data in simulated crashes in order to apply the data to injury thresholds for the general population. Flaws in the majority of these volunteer studies include: (1) the absence of braking by volunteers; (2) the use of extremely small numbers in each study, usually ranging from four to ten volunteers; (3) the positioning of most volunteers in an upright and properly seated posture for the study; (4) the use of mostly male volunteers when most injuries occur to females in these ΔV ranges; (5) the use of mostly similarly designed (same size or model) vehicles and not accounting for more model variations; and (6) the failure to use randomly selected people from the general population as test subjects.

When attempting to develop valid injury-crash threshold concepts and answer the question of what ΔV is necessary for a specific individual in a specific vector and involving two specific vehicles to sustain injury, more studies are needed that look at variations of human occupants, vehicle crashworthiness, vector, and mechanisms of injury. There is a virtual lack of proof of a causal relationship between an injury mechanism and the designation of a specific medical syndrome. There is no valid model that defines a specific mechanism of injury for a specific individual in a type of crash. Although recent magnetic resonance imaging, electromyographic, and radiologic studies have strengthened the link between real world crashes and experimental studies, more sensitive, noninvasive techniques need to be developed so that independent large-scale studies can be carried out to validate these injuries. The medical system is plagued with lack of objective findings while at the same time significant pain and disability occur in many cases. I am not aware of any large-scale study that examines claim patterns and compares ΔV and damage profiles to injuries.

CHALLENGES FACING THE RECONSTRUCTIONIST

Clearly, reconstruction experts are unable to accurately estimate the ΔV and closing velocity for the struck and striking vehicle using motion, kinetic energy, or momentum equations in the vast majority of low velocity crashes. These formulas all require a certain amount of reliable data, such as the initial or ending velocities, the time it takes for a vehicle to stop, or the distance the vehicles moved prior to or following impact, skid marks before or after impact, pre-and postimpact positions of each vehicle, and the coefficient of friction/drag factor for braking or skidding. The only option currently available is to remove the damaged isolator from either vehicle and send it to a facility that can quantify the amount of force that went into its compression. The isolator can be compared to barrier tests if it has previously been tested on the specific vehicle model and year. In many instances where I have seen reconstruction ΔV estimates, there are no police reports, skid marks, or reliable speed estimates from any source at the scene of the collision. Often, the only evidence is a few poorly taken photographs.

When attempting to mathematically solve for the ΔV, the coefficient of restitution, or the difference between the closing and separating velocities, must be accounted for in the formulas. Vehicle-to-barrier restitution values are higher than vehicle-to-vehicle data and, if used, must be calculated for. As impact velocities increase, so too, does plastic behavior; thus, the restitution values will decrease as ΔV increases. In low velocity impact studies, King et al[9] concluded that the restitution values for vehicle-to-vehicle

collisions range from 0.25 to 0.75. However, when using the weights of the vehicles, the manufacturer figures do not include any cargo or occupants. Furthermore, the majority of computer software programs have difficulty accurately calculating the low velocity crash as most data were derived from high-speed collisions and there is very little reliable data for specific collisions in the programs. Some computer crash programs predict damage at every speed and do not account for a bumper damage threshold; therefore, they are of little use in evaluating low speed crashes.

When calculating g forces and closing velocity and ΔV of the striking vehicle, struck vehicle, and occupant and injury risk, the reconstructionist must account for the crashworthiness of the specific vehicles involved, types of bumper systems on each vehicle (isolator or foam core), impact points, and the amount of isolator motion. Other factors that need to be considered include the following: Were there any paint or grease scrape marks on the isolators? Did the isolator bottom out, fully rebound, or seize? Did the vehicle have a previous impact? Are there any leaks, damage or rust spots on the isolators indicating possible malfunction? Unfortunately, in many cases, the vehicles involved in the crash that is being investigated have been sold or are not available for personal inspection. Even if available, by the time the reconstructionist gets the case 1 to 2 years later, he or she cannot be certain of what might have occurred to the bumper system since the crash.

HOW CAN THE RECONSTRUCTIONIST ESTIMATE IMPACT VELOCITIES?

First of all, the reconstructionist must collect all of the available facts that relate to the case. Usually, the only information available includes the depositions of both parties, which describe the crash scene and the events before, during, and after the crash; some medical records; and occasionally a police report. In most cases, the struck car has a initial velocity of zero and the striking vehicle has an unknown speed at the time of impact, although the driver of the striking vehicle may state at deposition that he was traveling at 3 mph even though he or she was not looking at the speedometer just prior to impact. Typically, there is no police report or report of skid mark measurements, and the road surface type, (e.g., concrete or asphalt) is unknown, as is how worn the road surface was at the time of impact. Reconstructionists usually attempt to determine the ΔV by using motion formulas to predict velocity. Without knowing the amount of acceleration, the time, or the distance the vehicles moved before or after impact, the motion equations are impossible to solve reliably. When unable to solve mathematically, the reconstructionist will usually look at the damage profile next. The reconstructionist knows that under a certain impact velocity, there will be no damage to the bumper system and at a specified higher velocity, the bumper will be damaged along with the trunk and other structures of the vehicle. This range can vary dramatically, depending upon the type of vehicle (i.e., car or truck) and the specific model.

Once the reconstructionist determines the velocity range of when bumpers are initially damaged and at what ΔV the body of the vehicle is damaged, he or she can then look at the depositions and medical records to find notations about how the occupants moved in the crash. Then, the reconstructionist can use what is known about occupant motion in volunteer tests and correlate the occupant motion described in the crash to the motions seen in those tests. By taking this approach, the reconstructionist can narrow the range to a more realistic ΔV.

COMPARING ACTIVITIES OF DAILY LIVING TO ACCELERATION FORCES IN WHIPLASH

One of the more current strategies in the defense-oriented community is to compare g forces in normal activities of daily living and show that these forces are the same as those sustained in a typical whiplash case, thereby providing proof that these whiplash injuries are not organically based. This argument is frequently used by defense attornies in their opening statement to the jury. A defense attorney will make a statement to the effect that "we will prove beyond a reasonable doubt that the forces incurred in this crash were no more than those forces measured when a person sits in a chair or walks down a flight of stairs." The classic source for this argument was published in a recent study by Allen et al,[48] which compared head acceleration in volunteers who would bob their head, sit down, sneeze, cough, hop off a step, plop into a chair, and other motions. The authors found similar levels of head acceleration in their test volunteers as were seen in test subjects involved in low speed rear-end crashes. Their study found that plopping backward into a chair caused maximum peak head acceleration horizontally at 5.6 g's and vertically at 8.5 g's. The authors conclusion questions how people can be hurt in a whiplash injury when normal living motions cause similar forces on the head (less than 8 g's).

Allen et al's[48] study is not a study of whiplash but, in fact, of head acceleration. The eight volunteers in this study had accelerometers attached to helmets on their head. None of the volunteers was evaluated for neck or head motion. It is obvious that there are serious difficulties in accepting head injury potential and relating this to neck injuries in car crashes. Comparing this type of daily activity research, in which people are aware of what they are doing, to cases in which a seatback strikes an unaware occupant who is wearing a seat belt at similar g forces is unacceptable. The injury mechanisms are completely different. This type of research also fails to consider a person who falls down a step or whose chair slips out from underneath so that he or she hits the floor at similar g forces, resulting in surgery for herniated discs or torn ligaments. Another concern about these types of daily activity studies is that most volunteer test subjects are male, whereas most auto injuries occur to females. In addition, the seats are usually rigid and are not cantilevered, as are front seats in most automobiles, and the test subjects are aware that they are going to be tested. How can one compare g forces affecting a person going down a stair to the injury potential for someone who is unaware that a step exists and gets a jolt and pain from taking an unexpected step?

CAN THE PHYSICIAN CORRELATE HISTORY TO INJURY?

In biomechanical terms, injury production must be correlated to the human frame and its individual tolerance levels and crash factors, such as the size of the vehicle, seatback design, and crashworthiness. The physician must determine whether an injury occurred from the low speed rear-end crash and, if so, how severe it is. Utilizing history and examination forms, with enough detail specific to the rear-end crash, is important for an accurate diagnosis and treatment plan. The history intake form should ask questions regarding the occupant's awareness or lack of awareness of the impending impact, the seating position, and whether he or she was looking straight ahead or to the side, or bending forward to reach for something. Other important questions should include whether the vehicle's head restraints are adjustable or fixed, the position of the head restraint relative to the occupant's head, and the types of vehicles involved. In addition, the physician should request a copy of the police report for the file, if one is available.

What symptom profiles do these patients typically present with? When the physician asks the patient where he or she has pain, most patients will describe the primary complaints. This line of questioning can overlook many secondary or less intense symptoms, leaving them undocumented in the initial records. Instead, it is advised that the physician ask the patient to complete a questionnaire that lists all of the typical symptoms that might be present. Having the patient complete a pain drawing is an excellent approach, too. Table 7–1 compares occupants' reports of symptoms following rear-end crashes.

! CLINICAL PEARL

In reviewing my files and looking at other studies that have involved similar cases, I have noted that most patients will have initial complaints of neck stiffness or aching within 24 to 48 hours after the collision. By the time of the first office visit, most will have about two to four complaints, typically reporting some degree of neck pain or soreness, headaches, upper and lower back pain, and upper extremity symptoms.

Table 7–1: Comparison of Occupants Who Report Symptoms Following Rear-End Crashes

REPORT FEWER NECK INJURIES	REPORT MORE NECK INJURIES
Men (about 50% fewer reported claims)	Women (neck longer and has smaller diameter)
Aware of impending impact and has time to brace self (primarily muscle injury)	Unaware of impending impact with no time to brace self (involves ligaments and disc)
High or fixed head restraints	Low, absent, or adjustable head restraints
Seatback breaks (less neck-axial, more low back pain)	Seat does not break
Sitting with head positioned straight ahead	Head rotated at time of impact
Not wearing seat belt (i.e., 3-point restraint)	Wearing seat belt (neck and back injuries)
Young occupant	Elderly occupant
Shorter occupants	Taller occupants
Occupant in larger vehicle or collision in which there are similar mass ratios for vehicles	Occupant in smaller vehicle or collision in which mass ratios differ significantly
Properly positioned occupants to seat/restraint	Abnormally positioned occupants
Rear-seated occupants (seatback rigid)	Front-seated passengers (elastic seatback)
Spine joints and soft tissues in good health	Pre-existing degenerative joint disease or significant fibromyalgia

Less frequent complaints may include visual and auditory symptoms, lower extremity symptoms, glenohumeral, wrist and elbow joint pain, and rarely, finger joint pain from the steering wheel being pulled out of the driver's grasp. It is common for the patient to have delays in the onset of neck symptoms of some type (i.e., stiffness, soreness, or pain) for up to 1 to 2 weeks, but rare to have no degree of soreness and stiffness for the first couple of weeks and then develop severe neck pain. The onset of headaches and upper extremity symptoms will vary more dramatically than neck pain. Headaches or migraines and upper extremity symptoms can occur within the first few days. In about 35 to 40 percent of the cases, onset of severe symptoms may occur after 2 to 3 months.

The examination, which is correlated to the event history and subsequent subjective complaints, should be able to confirm a recent injury. If the patient indicates that his or her head was turned to one side at the time of impact, the examiner should pick up dominant bogginess, soreness, and some degree of spasm in the opposite sternocleidomastoid muscle. It is common for there to be no muscle spasm for the first 12 to 18 hours. If the occupant claims he or she was looking straight ahead, sternocleidomastoid muscle bogginess, soreness, and spasm should be symmetrical. In cases in which the head restraint was positioned low or was absent, additional anterior and posterior neck and upper dorsal pain and muscle spasm can be expected, as a result of more extension and flexion motion. Low back pain may be the result of the seat belt holding the pelvis down as the seatpan drops down and the seatback moves forward, and as lumbar flexion occurs. Most of the orthopedic and neurological tests will be negative. Typically, the foraminal compression test will increase neck soreness and, if the patient has lumbar pain, Kemp's test will elicit more pain as the patient is moved into extension. Only 2 to 3 percent of the cases I have examined have had any motor or sensory findings of objective significance. It is extremely rare to see any significant disruption of George's lines in the low velocity crash. If present, there is usually pre-existing history of a major ligamentous neck injury. Disc injuries can occur in the low velocity crash and will typically involve females more than their male counterparts. Early onset (less than 1 week) of severe arm or leg symptoms is classic for disc injury.

ADVICE FOR THE PLAINTIFF'S ATTORNEY

When accepting low velocity, low damage cases in today's defense environment, it is imperative that the physician's documentation be thorough and that the patient be discharged as soon as maximal medical improvement (MMI) status is achieved. The attorney will not do well by sitting back and waiting for the physician to notify him or her that the case is closed. If there are residual problems at MMI status, they should be outlined at the time of discharge and the patient referred to another provider if there are any options available that will further relieve the symptoms. Photographs of the vehicle are essential for all parties. If possible, get the repair shop to save the damaged bumper or isolators. Be certain to note any space narrowing between the bumper and the body on either side, any bumper contour changes, scrapes, abrasions, paint marks, trunk lid and body wrinkling, and bumper angulation changes. If the bumper is seen by a repair shop, be certain to get a copy of the repair report. Be sure to ask the patient if there was any difficulty in closing the trunk lid after the crash, as this indicates higher impact forces.

CONCLUSION

When treating patients involved in low velocity rear-end crashes, the clinician needs to recognize that these patients face a tough legal environment in confronting the insurance community. The treating physician needs to pay closer attention to details of the history and examination, making certain to document the onset of all symptoms. If the treating physician is faced with an upcoming trial in which a reconstruction report and a defense medical expert state that there is no possibility the occupant incurred any injuries at the velocity they have estimated, the physician should read the literature and become familiar with the references these experts cite. I would also suggest the treating physician conclude the treatment as soon as the patient has stabilized at a level of maximal medical improvement.

REFERENCES

1. Insurance Institute for Highway Safety. *Special Issue: Whiplash Injuries. Status Report.* 1995;30(8).
2. Matsushita K, Morita S. Relationship between vehicle front-end stiffness and dummy injury during collisions. 11th International Technical Conference on Experimental Safety Vehicles, NHTSA, 1989:529–537.
3. Romilly DP, Thomson RW, Navin RPD, Macnabb MJ. Low speed rear impacts and elastic properties of automobiles. 12th International Technical Conference on Experimental Safety Vehicles, NHTSA, 1989:1199–1205.
4. Hyde AS. *Crash Injuries: How and Why They Happen.* Key Biscayne, Fla, Hyde Association; 1992.
4a. Robbins MC. Lack of relationship between vehicle damage and occupant injury. Society of Automotive Engineers, 1997, SAE paper 970494.
5. Struzenegger M, DeStefano G, Radanov BP, Schnidrig A. Presenting symptoms and signs after whiplash injury: The influence of accident mechanisms. *Neurology* 1994;44:688–693.
6. Watts AJ, Atkinson DR, Hennessy CJ. *Low Speed Automobile Accidents: Accident Reconstruction, and Occupant Kinematics, Dynamics and Biomechanics.* Tucson, Ariz, Lawyers and Judges Publishing; 1996.
7. Olsson I, Bunketorp O, Carlsson G, et al. An indepth study of neck injuries in rear end collisions. International IRCOBI Conference on the Biomechanics of Impact, Bron, Lyon, France, 1990.
8. Parmar HV, Raymakers R. Neck injuries from rear impact road traffic accidents: Prognosis in persons seeking compensation. *Injury* 1993;24:75–78.
9. King DJ, Siegmund GP, Bailey MN. *Automobile Bumper Behavior in Low-speed Impacts.* Society of Automotive Engineers, 1993; SAE paper 930211.
10. Bailey MN, Wong BC, Lawrence JM. Data and methods for estimating the severity of minor impacts. In: *Accident Reconstruction: Technology and Animation V* (SP-1083), Society of Automotive Engineers, 1995; SAE paper 950352.
11. Langwieder K, Backaitis SH, Fan W, Partyka S, Ommaya A. *Comparative Studies of Neck Injuries of Car Occupants in Frontal Collisions in the United States and in the Federal Republic of Germany.* Society of Automotive Engineers, 1981; SAE paper 811030.
12. Nygren Å. Injuries to car occupants, some aspects of the interior safety of cars. A study of a five-year material from an insurance company. *Acta Otolaryngol* 1984;395:1–164.
13. Ono K, Kanno M. Influences of the physical parameters on the risk to neck injuries in low impact speed rear-end collisions. International IRCOBI Conference on the Biomechanics of Impacts, The Netherlands, 1993:201–212.
14. Morris F. Do head-restraints protect the neck from whiplash injuries? *Arch Emer Med* 1989;6:17–21.
15. Macnab I, McCulloch J. *Neck Ache and Shoulder Pain.* Baltimore, Md: Williams & Wilkins; 1994.
16. States JD, Balcerak JC, Williams JS, et al. *Injury Frequency and Head Restraint Effectiveness in Rear-end Accidents.* Society of Automotive Engineers, 1972; SAE paper 720967.
17. Otremski I, Marsh JL, Wilde BR, et al. Soft tissue cervical spinal injuries in motor vehicle accidents. *Injury* 1989;20:349–351.
18. Kahane CJ. *An Evaluation of Head Restraints—Federal Motor Vehicle Safety Standard 202.* NHTSA Technical Report, DOT HS–806–108. Springfield, Va: National Technical Information Service; 1982.
19. Morris AP, Thomas P. *Neck Injuries in the UK Co-operative Crash Injury Study.* Society of Automotive Engineers, 1996; SAE paper 962433.
20. Svensson MY, Lövsund P, Håland Y, et al. *Rear-end Collisions—A Study of the Influence of Backrest Properties on Head-Neck Motion Using a New Dummy Neck.* Society of Automotive Engineers, 1993; SAE paper 930343.

21. Foret-Bruno JY, Dauvilliers F, Tarriere C. Influence of the seat and head rest stiffness on the risk of cervical injuries in rear impact. Proceedings of the 13th ESV Conference in Paris, France, paper 91-S8-W-19, NHTSA, 1991.

22. McConnell WE, Howard RP, Guzman HM, et al. *Analysis of Human Test Subject Kinematic Responses to Low Velocity Rear End Impacts*. Society of Automotive Engineers, 1993; SAE paper 930889.

23. Orner PA. *A Physician-Engineer's View of Low Velocity Rearend Collisions*. Society of Automotive Engineers, 1992, SAE paper 921574.

24. Ryan GA, Moore VM, Dolinis J, Taylor GW. Crash severity and neck strain in car occupants. International IRCOBI Conference on the Biomechanics of Impacts, Lyon, France, September 21–23, 1994:97–107.

24a. Eichberger A, Geigl BC, Moser A, et al. Comparison of different car seats regarding head-neck kinematics of volunteers during rear end impact. International IRCOBI Conference on the Biomechanics of Impacts, 1996.

24b. Otte D, Pohlemann T, Blauth M. Significance of soft tissue neck injuries AIS 1 in the accident scene and deformation characteristics of cars with delta-V up to 10 km/h. International IRCOBI Conference on the Biomechanics of Impacts, 1997.

24c. Hell W, Langwieder K, Walz F. Reported soft tissue neck injuries after rear-end car collisions. International IRCOBI Conference on the Biomechanics of Impacts, 1998.

25. Eichberger A, Geigl BC, Moser A, Fachbach B, Steffan H. Comparison of different car seats regarding head-neck kinematics of volunteers during rear end impact. International IRCOBI Conference on the Biomechanics of Impact, 1996.

26. Lövsund P, Nygren Å, Salen B, Tingvall C. Neck injuries in rear end collisions among front and rear seat occupants. International IRCOBI Conference on the Biomechanics of Impact, Bergisch-Gladbach, Germany, 1988:319–325.

27. Spitzer WO, Skovron ML, Salmi LR, et al. Scientific monograph of the Quebec Task Force on whiplash-associated disorders: Redefining "whiplash" and its management. *Spine* 1995;20S(8S):1–73.

28. Szabo T, Welcher J. *Dynamics of Low Speed Crash Tests with Energy Absorbing Bumpers*. Society of Automotive Engineers, 1992; SAE paper 921573.

29. Thomson RW, Romilly DP, Navin FPD, et al. *Dynamic Requirements of Automobile Seatbacks*. Society of Automotive Engineers, 1993; SAE paper 930349.

30. Warner CY, Strother CE, James MB, et al. *Occupant Protection in Rear-End Collisions: II. The Role of Seat Back Deformation in Injury Reduction*. Society of Automotive Engineers, 1991; SAE paper 912914.

31. Geigl BC, Steffan H, Leinzinger P, Roll MM, Roll, Bauer G. The movement of head and cervical spine during rearend impact. International IRCOBI Conference on the Biomechanics of Impact, Lyon, France, September 21–23, 1994:127–137.

32. Blaisdell DM, Levitt AE, Varat MS. *Automotive Seat Design Concepts for Occupant Protection*. Society of Automotive Engineers, 1993; SAE paper 930340.

33. Stabler CE, Mackay KM, Parkin S. Head restraint positioning and occupant safety in rear impacts: The case for smart restraints. International IRCOBI Conference on the Biomechanics of Impact, 1996.

34. Nygren Å, Gustafsson H, Tingwall C. Effects of different types of headrests in rear-end collisions. 10th International Conference of Experimental Safety Vehicles, NHTSA, 1985.

35. Jakobsson L, Norin H, Jernström C, et al. Analysis of different head and neck responses in rear-end car collisions using a new humanlike mathematical model. International IRCOBI Conference on the Biomechanics of Impact, Lyon, France, September 21–23, 1994:109–125.

36. Strother CE, James MB. *Evaluation of Seat Back Strength and Seat Belt Effectiveness in Rear End Impacts*. Society of Automotive Engineers, 1987; SAE paper 872214.

37. Carlsson G, Nilsso S, Nilsson-Ehle A, Norin H, Ysander L, Örtengren R. Neck injuries in rear end car collisions. Biomechanical considerations to improve head restraints. Proceedings of the International IRCOBI/AAAM Conference Biomechanics of Impacts, Göteborg, Sweden, 1985:277–289.

38. Szabo TJ, Welcher JB, Anderson RD, et al. *Human Occupant Kinematic Response to Low Speed Rear-End Impacts*. Society of Automotive Engineers, 1994; SAE paper 940532.

39. McConnell WE, Howard RP, Poppel JV, et al. *Human Head and Neck Kinematics After Low Velocity Rear-End Impacts: Understanding "whiplash."* Society of Automotive Engineers, 1995; SAE Paper No. 952724.

40. v Koch M, Kullgren A, Lie A, Nygren A, Tingvall C. Soft tissue injury of the cervical spine in rear-end and frontal car collisions. International IRCOBI Conference on the Biomechanics of Impact, Switzerland, September 13–15, 1995:273–283.

41. Scott MW, McConnell WE, Guzman HM, et al. *Comparison of Human and ATD Head Kinematics During Low-Speed Rearend Impacts.* Society of Automotive Engineers, 1993; SAE paper 930094.

42. Boström O, Svensson MY, Aldman B, et al. A new neck injury criterion candidate—based on injury findings in the cervical spinal ganglia after experimental neck extension trauma. International IRCOBI Conference on the Biomechanics of Impact, 1996.

43. Dunn EJ, Blazar S. Soft-tissue injuries of the lower cervical spine. In: Griffin PP, ed. *Instructional Course Lectures.* American Academy of Orthopaedic Surgeons; 1987:36:499–512.

44. Benson BR, Smith GC, Kent RW, Monson CR. *Effect of Seat Stiffness in Out-of-Position Occupant Response in Rear-End Collisions.* Society of Automotive Engineers, 1996; SAE paper 962434.

45. Geigl BC, Steffan H, Dippel C, Muser MH, Walz F, Svensson MY. Comparison of head-neck kinematics during rear end impact between standard Hybrid III, RID Neck, volunteers and PMTO's. International IRCOBI Conference on the Biomechanics of Impact, Switzerland, September 13–15, 1995:261–270.

46. Orsay EM, Dunne M, Turnbull TL, Barrett JA, Langenberg P, Orsay CP. Prospective study on the effect of safety belts on motor vehicle crashes. *Ann Emerg Med* 1990;19:258–261.

47. Kornhauser M. *Delta-V Thresholds for Cervical Spine Injury.* Society of Automotive Engineers, 1996; SAE paper 960093.

48. Allen ME, Weir-Jones I, Motiuk DR, et al. Acceleration perturbations of daily living: A comparison to "whiplash." *Spine* 1994;19:1285–1290.

CHAPTER 8

Headache

CRAIG NELSON, DONALD R. MURPHY, JOANNE FOWLER, JANET WILTERDINK,
& ROWENA TABAMO

"The aim of life is to live, and to live means to be aware, joyously, drunkenly, serenely, divinely aware."

—Henry Miller

INTRODUCTION

The burden that chronic headaches imposes on society is substantial. Several comprehensive surveys have been published on headache prevalence and its socioeconomic impact.[1–7] While each of these studies views the problem from a slightly different perspective, they all conclude that the impact of headaches on the health and well being of individuals, and on the cost of headache disability, has been greatly underestimated.

In 1995, *Consumer Reports* conducted a survey of its readership[8] in which one of the questions asked regarded those conditions for which readers were most dissatisfied about their medical care. Some 70,000 people responded. Headache was the number one response. The top five responses are provided in Table 8–1.

A study in the *Journal of the American Medical Association* estimated that 27.3 percent of females and 13.9 percent of males suffer from severe headaches.[9] This survey found a 60 percent greater prevalence of headache in the lowest economic group than in the two highest groups. The authors believed that this relationship was at least partly the result of people with chronic severe headaches being unable to perform at work or school as well as others and thus earning lower incomes. This survey also found that over 10 million people suffer moderate to severe disability as a result of various forms of headache. This level of disability was defined as requiring bed rest or having severely impaired working ability.

A study in the *Canadian Journal of Neurologic Sciences* found that 36 percent of the Canadian population suffers from chronic tension headaches, of which 18 percent suffer some form of disability.[5] In addition, 14 percent suffer from migraine headaches and another 14 percent have both types of headaches. It was calculated that over 7 million work days per year were lost because of headaches.

A study published in the journal *Headache* calculated that in the United States, headache resulted in 74.2 million days of restricted work activity, costing an estimated $1.4 billion dollars in lost productivity.[7] In addition to the economic costs, the toll in human suffering caused by headaches is significant. In comparison to the general population with no chronic illnesses, chronic headache patients report significantly diminished health-related quality of life as measured by the standard SF-36 Health Survey.[10] The decrement in role functioning measured by this instrument was considerably greater for migraineurs than for persons with other chronic illnesses such as osteoarthritis, hypertension, and diabetes. So it can be seen that there is a great need for a continued push for the development and recognition of more effective approaches to this widespread problem.

Table 8–1: Top Five Conditions for Which People are Least Satisfied with Their Medical Care

CONDITION	PERCENT DISSATISFIED
1. Chronic headaches	24
2. Low back pain	19
3. Broken bones, torn ligaments	18
4. Anxiety, depression	15
5. Arthritis	14

DIAGNOSIS OF HEADACHE

For a patient presenting with the primary complaint of headaches, there is a fundamental diagnostic distinction that must be made between so-called primary or benign headaches and headaches caused by underlying organic disease. While this latter type of organic headaches represents only a small percentage of headache complaints, failure to quickly and accurately diagnose these conditions may have catastrophic consequences. It should also be noted that headache patients often harbor unexpressed fears and anxieties about the cause of their headaches, which compound their suffering. Even though these fears and anxieties are often clinically uninformed and exaggerated, they are nevertheless quite real and the reassurance provided by a competently rendered diagnosis can be therapeutically invaluable.

ADVANCED IMAGING AND HEADACHE DIAGNOSIS

The availability of advanced imaging techniques (computed tomography [CT] and magnetic resonance imaging [MRI]), which allow direct visualization of the contents of the cranial vault, provides physicians with a seemingly foolproof method of diagnosing organic headaches. The intuitive appeal of advanced imaging to both patients and physicians has resulted in high rates of utilization of advanced imaging for headache diagnosis. In two randomized clinical trials for tension and migraine headache conducted at Northwestern College of Chiropractic, 25 percent and 37 percent of patients, respectively, had previously undergone an advanced imaging examination for their headaches.

This enthusiasm for advanced imaging in the clinical context is, however, misplaced. Given the relative infrequency of intracranial masses or lesions presenting with the primary symptom of headache, and given the relatively clear clinical differences between benign and organic headache types, the use of imaging can easily be kept to a minimum even when erring on the side of caution. Several studies have shown that, in both adult and pediatric populations, imaging only very rarely contributes to an understanding of a patient's headache problem.

This discussion of headache diagnosis proceeds from the assumption that a thorough history and examination and a broad understanding of the clinical characteristics of headache will almost always result in a secure diagnostic conclusion. Only when uncertainty and concern remain after the history and examination should imaging be considered.

HEADACHE HISTORY

There are several clinical variables derived from the history that will dispel much of the uncertainty regarding possible organic causes of headache. The most important of these variables is the chronicity of the headache problem. The question is: How long has the patient had his or her headache problem in its present form? The probability of a headache being organically caused varies inversely with the chronicity of the problem. That is, the longer the problem has persisted, the less likely it is to be caused by an underlying organic process. When headaches are caused by organic disease, they will tend to progress in a manner that does not permit patients to ignore the problem for prolonged periods of time and patients will seek care relatively early. Conversely, when headaches are benign in nature, patients will frequently rely on self-care, or no-care until such time (often years after initial onset) as they feel the need for professional intervention. There is, of course, no well-defined threshold for what designates an onset as "recent," but when patients seek care within 6 months of the onset of their headache problem, a higher level of concern is appropriate. The clinical logic of this chronicity principle is not obvious to patients and, in fact, their intuition may tell them that *because* their headache problem has persisted for a long time it may indicate a serious organic disease. It is well worth the effort to explain this principle to patients and thereby provide an important reassurance.

A related question to be explored in the history is that of progression or change in headache symptoms. The clinical characteristics (frequency, severity, location, associated symptoms, etc.) of chronic, benign headaches tend to be stable, at least in the short run. When a patient reports that a long-standing headache problem, one that is presumably benign, has recently changed or progressed in some way, this should be regarded with the same concern as would a recent onset of headache.

The severity of headache pain can often mislead both patient and physician regarding possible organic causes of the headache. Our intuition tells us that the more severe the pain, the more likely it is to be caused by some malign process—the cause should resemble the effect. This intuition turns out to be false. The most severe headache pain, pain that can be completely disabling, is almost always the result of some variant of migraine headache. While headache pain this severe is in itself a serious health issue, it does not represent significant risk for a catastrophic event. Once again, reassuring the patient of this fact is essential in reducing the fear and anxiety associated with very severe headache pain. The severity of headache pain associated with organic causes is not uniform. Organic headaches can be severe, but they are as likely to be mild, or even incidental. The precise cause and location of the lesion will define the severity of these headaches.

The occurrence of any cognitive changes associated with a headache complaint will also differentiate between benign and organic causes of headaches. Even before any hard neurological signs (motor loss, sensory loss, reflex changes, etc.) are present, intracranial masses often produce subtle cognitive changes. These changes may include memory loss, confusion, and irritability. It is vital to explore this issue during the history, being aware that some prompting may be necessary to elicit relevant patient responses.

PHYSICAL AND NEUROLOGICAL EXAMINATION

Upon completion of a thorough headache history, the clinician should have formed a tentative impression regarding the possibility of an organic cause to the headache. This should be considered a diagnostic hypothesis and the examination following the history considered a test of that hypothesis.

All headache patients should receive a neurological screening examination. This examination should evaluate motor, sensory, visual, auditory, vestibular, and cerebellar functions. Also, signs of meningeal irritation should be evaluated. Any positive finding from this examination that cannot be accounted for by some benign cause or process should be viewed as evidence of an organic cause of the headache. In addition to vital signs, the physical examination should include auscultation and palpation of superficial vascular structures of the head and neck and palpation of the eye. The relevance of specific findings will be discussed later in this chapter.

DIFFERENTIAL DIAGNOSIS

The list of possible organic causes of headaches is, if not limitless, extensive. Of greatest concern are those causes that (1) present primarily as headaches and can be confused with benign headaches, (2) have a reasonable probability of being seen in an ambulatory care setting, and (3) represent a serious threat to the patient's well being if diagnosis is delayed. This list is much shorter and includes the following conditions: tumor headache, temporal arteritis, subdural hematoma, subarachnoid hemorrhage, meningitis, and acute glaucoma.

Tumor Headache

Even though it is not the most common cause of organic headaches, patients' anxieties about their headaches often are expressed as a fear of a brain tumor. When a brain tumor does occur, it is most likely to be seen in either children or in the elderly. The actual clinical presentation of a tumor headache is entirely dependent on its location, size, and rate of growth. As such, virtually any central nervous system sign may be present, or there may be a complete absence of hard neurological signs. If there is a typical tumor headache, it is one that is recent in onset (weeks to months), progressive in frequency and severity, and aggravated by any type of Valsalva maneuver. Cognitive changes are also common. Rarely, a tumor may impinge upon pain sensitive structures (e.g., the meninges) in such a manner as to produce headache pain in a point location.

> **❗ CLINICAL PEARL**
>
> Should a patient, in response to a request to identify the location of his or her headache pain, use an index finger to point at a spot on the skull, your level of concern should be raised.

Temporal Arteritis

Perhaps the most common of organic headaches and also the most commonly misdiagnosed, temporal arteritis is a granulomatous (i.e., aseptic) inflammation of cranial arteries, particularly the temporal artery. It occurs in the elderly population, and the patient will often have associated polymyalgia rheumatica. The location (temporal) and quality (throbbing) of the headache pain closely resemble that of migraine headache. Upon examination, the temporal artery will be palpably tender, thickened, and have a granular quality. An elevated sedimentation rate will confirm the diagnosis. The ophthalmic artery may be involved with the temporal artery or by itself. Arteries affected by this process have a high probability of becoming thrombosed and should this occur in the ophthalmic artery, blindness is a probable outcome. This result, and any other possible complications resulting from an occluded cranial artery, can be prevented with early diagnosis and treatment with corticosteroids.

Subdural Hematoma

Another organic type of headache affecting mainly the elderly is that caused by a subdural hematoma. Even in the healthy brain there is a degree of atrophy and shrinkage that takes place with age. This diminished volume of brain tissue creates a physical gap between the surface of the brain and the inner table of the skull. This gap is traversed by what are known as bridging veins. With relatively minor head trauma or with acceleration injuries, the atrophied brain may shift slightly within the skull, causing a tearing of these bridging veins, and thus create a subdural hematoma.

The low pressure of the venous system does not result in a catastrophic hemorrhage, but rather a slowly growing space-occupying lesion on the surface of the brain. Indeed, the patient will probably be unaware of this event having taken place at all. As the hematoma enlarges over weeks and months, it will cause increased intracranial pressure and neurological symptoms such as headache. Other symptoms are often vague cognitive and memory changes. Depending on the location of the hematoma, it may also produce focal neurological signs such as motor or sensory deficits. The increased intracranial pressure may also produce papilledema. The headache itself is not terribly revealing—it tends to be diffuse, of variable severity, and exacerbated by any Valsalva-type maneuver.

In any elderly patient with a recent onset of headache and a history of head or neck trauma, the possibility of subdural hematoma should be considered. Also bear in mind that the trauma, because it may have been trivial and several months in the past, may be poorly recalled by the patient. The suspicion of subdural hematoma is an indication for an imaging study. Assuming an otherwise healthy patient, surgical correction of the hematoma should result in a complete recovery.

Subarachnoid Hemorrhage

Unlike a subdural hematoma, a subarachnoid hemorrhage is arterial in nature and, therefore, is profoundly more threatening. These hemorrhages, which can occur at any age, result from the rupture of berry aneurysms of intracranial vessels. These aneurysms may exist asymptomatically for years, or even for a lifetime before rupturing spontaneously and unpredictably. Subarachnoid hemorrhages may be rapidly fatal or may produce such profoundly disturbing symptoms that emergency department treatment is the only reasonable action. But it is also possible that patients can remain ambulatory and conscious following the rupture of the aneurysm, and these patients do end up in ambulatory care settings. The headache associated with subarachnoid hemorrhage is notable for its virtually instantaneous onset and extreme pain. The onset has been described as feeling like being hit on the head with a baseball bat and the pain is described as the worst pain ever. The hemorrhage is also likely to produce signs of meningeal irritation such as nuchal rigidity and Kernig's sign. A subarachnoid hemorrhage is an extreme medical emergency and upon any suspicion of this condition, immediate evaluation in an emergency facility is the only acceptable course of action.

> **! CLINICAL PEARL**
>
> If a patient presents to an ambulatory care center complaining of the sudden onset of the worst headache he or she has ever had, subarachnoid hemorrhage should be suspected and it should be considered a medical emergency. Immediate referral to a hospital emergency room should be the course of action. Remember the rule that "patients are allowed to have two conditions at once" and subarachnoid hemorrhage can just as easily occur in a patient who is a chronic headache sufferer as in a patient who is not. Do not let the presence of a pre-existing headache condition deter you from taking the appropriate action, if subarachnoid hemorrhage is suspected.

Meningitis

Most febrile illnesses, including common self-limiting conditions such as influenza, have headache as a concomitant symptom and the combination of headache and fever is not particularly alarming. However, if a patient presents with fever, headache, *and* nuchal rigidity, the possibility of meningitis arises and alarm is appropriate. In such a patient, if hyperflexion of the cervical spine causes resistance, pain, muscular splinting, or any other defensive reaction, meningitis should be assumed. Only with immediate evaluation of the cerebrospinal fluid and antibiotic therapy can a positive outcome be hoped for.

Acute Glaucoma

Most cases of glaucoma are painless, but if increased intraocular pressure occurs acutely, it may produce pain in and around the eye that is interpreted by the patient as headache pain. It should not be difficult to differentiate between migraine pain in an ocular location and the pain of acute glaucoma. In acute glaucoma the eye itself is very tender to palpation. Vision will be blurred and not improved with refractory aids. The cornea will be cloudy and the conjunctiva injected with increased lacrimation. None of these characteristics are present with migrainous eye pain. Acute glaucoma must be referred immediately for medical or surgical intervention if vision is to be preserved in the affected eye.

As previously stated, this short list of conditions does not represent all possible circumstances where organic disease may present as headache. However, the clinical characteristics that differentiate these conditions from benign headaches are also likely to be present with any such headache-producing organic disease. Generalizing from the short list, we arrive at the principles of headache differential diagnosis outlined in Table 8–2.

CHRONIC HEADACHES

There are two competing points of view on the relationship between tension headaches and migraine headaches. The traditional view, which has been dominant until recently, held that tension and migraine headaches were dis-

Table 8–2: Principles of Headache Differential Diagnosis

If a patient has

(1) a history of a recent onset of headache, or;

(2) a history of a recent change or progression of headache symptoms, or;

(3) any hard neurological sign (motor, sensory, visual, cerebellar, etc.) associated with a headache, or;

(4) any cognitive changes (memory loss, confusion) associated with a headache, or;

(5) any physical findings (palpable tenderness of cranial structures, papilledema) associated with a headache;

then the possibility of organic disease is greatly elevated and individual findings will dictate whether and what further diagnostic procedures are necessary. If none of the preceding findings is present, and if the history is otherwise unremarkable, the possibility of a serious organic disease causing the headache is remote.

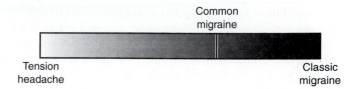

Figure 8–1. The tension headache–migraine headache continuum.

tinct and discrete diagnostic entities. The fact that many people seemed to have headache symptoms that were characteristic of both tension and migraine headaches was dealt with simply by regarding this as a case of co-morbidity; these persons simply had two different headache problems, just as one might simultaneously suffer from, say, gastritis and cholecystitis.

This view of tension and migraine headaches as discrete entities has been codified into rigid diagnostic guidelines by the International Headache Society (IHS). In its 1987 document "IHS Diagnostic Manual,"[11] tension and migraine headaches (and other headache types as well) were classified and categorized according to strict operational definitions. This diagnostic manual does eliminate most of the terminological confusion that had long plagued the headache literature, such as the archaic use of the term *muscle contraction headache* instead of the accepted term *tension-type headache*. However, in the process of eliminating this lexical chaos, these diagnostic guidelines have in the minds of many created a headache taxonomy that does not reflect pathophysiological or clinical realities. Implicit in the IHS diagnostic guidelines is the assumption that tension and migraine headaches are caused by different pathophysiological mechanisms—if they do not have different mechanisms, why bother to diagnose them as distinct entities? Also implicit in the guidelines is the assumption that the diagnosis of tension or migraine headaches should have a substantial and direct bearing on the management of the patient. There is reason to doubt both these assumptions.

An alternate view of tension and migraine headaches holds that these are not discrete entities, but simply different expressions of a common underlying problem or problems. This view is usually described as the continuum model of headaches (Fig. 8–1). There is a substantial body

of evidence, both basic scientific and clinical, that supports the continuum concept and it is our belief that this model best explains the phenomenon of chronic headaches.[12–20]

To understand the continuum model, it is first useful to review the traditional, discrete model of tension and migraine headaches. Tension headaches have traditionally been regarded as resulting from contraction and hypertonicity of cranial musculature (temporalis and frontalis), thus the use of the aforementioned term, muscle contraction headache. It was presumed that the contractions of these muscles were intrinsically painful, or might cause pain indirectly by producing a hypoxic condition in the scalp. Based upon this belief, muscle relaxants were once a common treatment for these types of headaches. This muscle contraction hypothesis was based, no doubt, on patients' subjective experience of this type of headache pain; a feeling of tightness was often experienced along with what was called a "hatband" distribution of the pain that roughly corresponded with the location of the temporalis and frontalis musculature. This hypothesis did not rest on any direct evidence of the hypertonicity of these muscles. When studies were undertaken to record and measure the activity of these muscles in headache patients, it was discovered that there was an insignificant relationship between headache pain (tension or muscle contraction headache) and the contractile state of these muscles. There was also little difference between headache patients and normal controls in terms of cranial muscular activity. These findings eventually led to the abandonment of the term muscle contraction headache.

The traditional view of migraine headaches viewed them as a purely vascular phenomenon. The pulsating quality of migraine headache pain clearly implicated blood vessels as the source of the headache pain; blood vessels are pain sensitive structures and dilation of cerebral vessels could easily produce headache pain. It was further assumed that in what was called classic migraine, (now called migraine with aura) the prodromal symptoms were caused by vasoconstriction. As with tension headaches, subsequent investigations revealed flaws and inconsistencies in the traditional view.[21] While there are definitely vasomotor irregularities in migraine patients, these irregularities do not correlate well with migraine symptoms. Vasodilatation sometimes occurs on the opposite side of the head from the headache pain, and in other cases the vasomotor activity may precede the onset of headache pain by several hours, or it may follow the onset of headache pain. And in some migraine patients, there appears to be minimal vasomotor disturbances. At most, vasodilatation and constriction can only explain a small part of the migraine phenomenon.

MECHANISMS OF HEADACHE PAIN

According to the continuum model, several physiological features conspire to produce the condition that manifests as chronic, recurrent headaches. These features interact in a way that not only produces headache, but also produces the unique characteristics of the condition in each patient. Understanding this interaction is essential to understanding each patient's clinical picture, and to devising a management strategy.

Dysfunction of the Descending Pain Inhibitory System

In addition to these problems with the traditional view, other investigations into chronic headaches began to suggest the existence of common tension and migraine headache mechanisms. A central feature of the headache continuum is the neurotransmitter serotonin. Serotonin, which is released by a wide range of neurons in the central nervous system, acts in several ways directly related to headache pain. First, it is a vasoactive substance. Depending on the receptor type, it can act both as vasoconstrictor or as a vasodilator. It may also mediate neurogenic inflammatory processes in blood vessels, further contributing to the evolution of pain.[22–27]

Serotonin also acts in ways that regulate the perception of pain. Several midbrain structures, particularly the periaqueductal gray (PAG) and the nucleus raphe magnus (NRM), send descending projections to dorsal horn and trigeminal nerve nuclei which inhibit the transmission of nociceptive stimuli to higher centers, and thus reduce the perception of pain (see Fig. 4–15). Artificial stimulation of these centers can produce complete analgesia in experimental animals. Dysfunction of this system is presumed to result in a lowered threshold to the perception of pain.

In both tension and migraine headache patients, serotonin metabolism is known to be aberrant. The precise nature of this aberration is not fully understood and it cannot be stated that serotonin activity in headache patients is either strictly hypoactive or hyperactive. It would be more accurate to characterize the aberration as a dysregulation of serotonin that results in oscillations of serotonin levels occurring over a much wider range than in normal subjects. These oscillations of serotonin may produce both a peripheral source of pain via vasodilatation and possibly inflammation, and an enhanced central nervous system sensitivity to peripheral sources of pain via the now dysfunctional descending pain inhibition system.

Autonomic Instability

Another physiological irregularity that is common to both tension and migraine headache patients is the occurrence of what is called autonomic instability.[28] When headache patients' basic vital functions (temperature, blood pressure, pulse, and respiration rate) are measured over prolonged periods of time, they are found to vary over a much wider range than in nonheadache subjects. This is true even when the headache subjects are asymptomatic; that is, during nonheadache periods. Other autonomic functions have not yet been studied in this way, but it is speculated that this same phenomenon might be observed in other physiological variables.

Autonomic centers such as the hypothalamus and locus ceruleus have a variety of functions, including the regulation of intracranial blood vessels,[29] interaction with the descending pain inhibitory system,[30] and regulation of the response to emotional stress.[31] Indeed, it may be that the serotonin dysregulation previously described is simply one other aspect of this autonomic instability.

Cervical Spine Dysfunction

Yet another pathophysiological process common to both tension and migraine headaches is dysfunction in the cervical spine. Spinal manipulation as a treatment for chronic headaches is predicated upon cervical spine dysfunction being a contributing factor in the etiology of these headaches. There is both a firm theoretical basis and empirical evidence for such a relationship.

First, when discussing headaches and the cervical spine, an important diagnostic distinction must be made between cervicogenic headaches and headaches caused or contributed to by cervical spine dysfunction. These two entities appear semantically identical, but they are not. This distinction is often not made and is the source of considerable confusion when discussing headache etiology.

The former, cervicogenic headache, is a discrete diagnostic category of headache, the principle etiology of which is presumed to be a specific disorder of the cervical spine. It is characterized by mild to moderate unilateral neck and head pain that does not side shift, and limited cervical range of motion. The headache pain is often precipitated, and can be provoked by the examiner, by movements of the neck. Symptoms of nausea, photo- or phonophobia, and other nonpain complaints, while sometimes present, occur much less frequently and less intensely than in common migraine headaches, a condition that is often confused with cervicogenic headache. Cervicogenic headache is caused by pain referring from tissues innervated by the C1, C2 and C3 segments (see Figs. 17–12 to 17–14). Cervicogenic headache, as it is defined by the IHS, is far less common than tension or migraine headaches.[32–34]

In contrast, the latter type of headache, those caused or contributed to by cervical spine dysfunction, may include all categories of tension and migraine headaches. In this case, when we use the term *cervicogenic*, we use it as a descriptor, not as a diagnosis. The role of the cervical spine may be one of several etiological or complicating factors. The actual clinical presentation of the headache pain will vary widely depending upon the primary diagnosis (tension or migraine) of the headache. The difference between cervicogenic headaches and headaches complicated by cervical spine dysfunction is probably not as distinct as the diagnostic categories suggest, and perhaps what is called "cervicogenic headache" is simply one point along the tension headache–migraine headache continuum.

The anatomical basis for the contribution of the cervical spine to chronic headaches has been well established. It is based upon the convergence of two peripheral systems of nociception: the trigeminal system and the cervical spinal nerve system, particularly from C1–3.[35–37] The primary cell body of each of the two systems is located in peripheral ganglia from whence they send projections centrally to synapse with the second order neuron. It is at this point that the convergence of these two systems occurs. The central projections from the trigeminal and cervical systems descend and ascend, respectively, several levels and terminate upon common second order neurons located in the trigeminal nucleus and in the dorsal horn of the cervical spinal cord. These second order neurons form a continuous column of cell bodies for which no anatomical, physiological, or functional distinctions can be drawn between the cervical and trigeminal systems. Because of the convergence of these two systems, this group of cells is more properly called the trigeminocervical nucleus (see Fig. 4–12). The functional effect of this convergence is that nociceptive input from these two systems is very poorly localized and pain stimuli arising from one can be interpreted subjectively as arising from the other. In other words, cervical spine dysfunction that produces pain can be felt as head pain or headache.

Bogduk[35] has demonstrated experimentally that disorders of the cervical spine can cause headaches. By administering anesthetic nerve blocks to the C2-3 zygapophyseal joints, he was successful in eliminating headaches in seven of ten patients with suboccipital headaches. These joints are innervated by branches of the dorsal ramus of the third cervical nerve (or third occipital, as it is called in his paper). Bogduk concludes that structures in addition to the zygapophyseal joints that are innervated by the first three cervical nerves may contribute to, or cause, headaches.

There is also a well-established clinical basis for the cervical spine–headache connection. Several studies have found functional abnormalities in the cervical spines of headache patients when compared to normal controls. The range of abnormalities include electromyographic (EMG) changes, reduced range of motion, palpable muscle spasm, and palpable tenderness.[38–64] Other studies have found differences between controls and headache patients on plain film radiography of the cervical spine.[65, 66]

Although these studies of the cervical spine and headaches do not present completely uniform results, their results do coalesce to suggest several conclusions:

The cervical spines of chronic headache patients, both tension and migraine, are functionally different from those of nonheadache subjects.

The cervical spines of tension and migraine headache sufferers are not markedly different from each other.

Pain stimuli arising from the cervical spine contributes to headache pain.

The cause-and-effect relationship between cervical spine dysfunction and headaches is probably reciprocal. In addition to cervical spine dysfunction being a source of headache pain, this pain may cause reflex changes in cervical spine musculature and produce mechanical dysfunction of the cervical spine.

In addition to these common pathophysiological mechanisms, there is other evidence that supports the continuum theory. The demographic distribution of tension and migraine headache patients is very similar. In both types of headaches, females outnumber males by about 3 or 4 to 1. The age distribution is very similar, with peak prevalence occurring between 35 and 45 years of age. Both headache types demonstrate similar psychological profiles that differ from nonheadache subjects: there is an increase in anxiety, depression, and hypochondriasis in chronic headache patients. It has long been known that there was a familial (presumably genetic) component to migraine headaches. Recent studies have shown that a very similar familial pattern exists for tension headache patients as well.

THE TENSION HEADACHE–MIGRAINE HEADACHE CONTINUUM

Putting together the aforementioned information allows the assemblage of a pathophysiological model for which a diagnostic and treatment strategy can be applied (Fig. 8–2). At the center of the model is the trigeminocervical nucleus, the central mediator of all pain perceived in the head, face, and upper cervical spine. There are essentially two primary sources of nociception that send afferents to the trigeminocervical nucleus in chronic headache patients. One is somatic and the other vascular. The somatic source may include cervical joint dysfunction, myofascial trigger points (TrPs), disc derangement, muscular and fascial adhesions, or other soft tissue abnormalities. The vascular source is the intracranial blood vessels that can become painful due to vasodilatation and inflammation that results from dysfunction in the central autonomic and serotonin regulatory systems.

The nociceptive afferentation from these sources is received by the trigeminocervical nucleus and has the potential to be transmitted to the thalamus and, ultimately, to higher centers to be experienced as pain. This transmission is under modulatory control of the descending pain inhibitory system, primarily arising from the PAG and NRM, and if this system is functioning properly, the likelihood of the experience of pain is greatly reduced. With dysfunction of the descending inhibitory system, however, the nociceptive input from the somatic and vascular sources is likely to reach the thalamus and cerebral cortex.

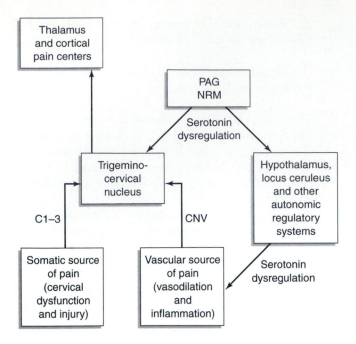

Figure 8–2. Pathophysiological model for chronic headache. NRM, nucleus raphe magnus; PAG, periaqueductal gray.

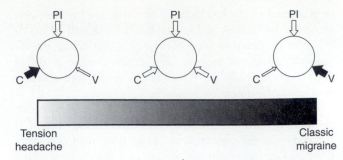

Figure 8–3. The relative involvement of the cervical (C), vascular (V), and pain inhibition (PI) components in headache pathophysiology.

So in the organization of the model, there are two potential sources of pain, but there must occur some type of dysfunction of three systems to cause these potential sources to generate nociceptive impulses and for these nociceptive impulses to reach a level in the cerebral cortex that allows for the experience of pain. Therefore, locomotor system dysfunction, primarily related to the cervical spine, dysfunction of the autonomic regulatory systems (involving, in part, dysregulation of serotonin), and dysfunction of the descending inhibitory system (also involving dysregulation of serotonin) all must occur to set the stage for the patient to experience chronic headache.

Patients with chronic headache have a widely varied presentation with regard to the quality of the headache pain, the nonpain symptoms they experience, and other related factors involved in chronic headache. This is easily understood in the continuum model. The particular clinical picture that will emerge from the combination of dysfunction involved in chronic headache will be determined by which pathophysiological features are most prominent in the individual patient. Looking once again at the continuum (see Fig. 8–1), the greater the involvement of the cervical dysfunction component, the more likely the clinical picture will resemble that typically described as tension headache. The greater the involvement of the autonomic regulatory systems (particularly related to serotonin regulation), the more likely the clinical picture will resemble migraine. Disruption of the descending pain inhibitory system is probably a common feature in all chronic headaches. This is illustrated in Figure 8–3. Most patients will fall

somewhere between these extremes, with features suggesting musculoskeletal and vascular (biochemical) involvement.

TREATMENT PRINCIPLES

The most compelling question regarding the continuum versus discrete diagnosis debate, is whether the specific treatment regimen for a particular patient will be defined by the diagnosis of tension or migraine headaches. The answer is that it largely will not. The treatment principles discussed here apply equally to patients who may be labeled as having tension headache and migraine headache and the variables in these principles will be influenced more by individual patient variation than by the particular diagnostic label.

The management strategy in each particular patient, therefore, will be determined by the most prominent pathophysiological features that are contributing to the individual patient's clinical picture. The further to the left on the continuum, the greater the likelihood that musculoskeletal treatment will play a prominent role in the management strategy. The further to the right on the continuum, the greater the likelihood that biochemical treatment will play a prominent role. Treatment directed to the descending pain inhibitory system should be a common feature in all patients. As the pathophysiological picture of most chronic headache patients falls somewhere between the two extremes of the continuum, in most cases a combined, multimodal approach will be required.

CERVICAL COMPONENT

The treatment approaches applied to address the cervical component will be determined by the specific dysfunctions that are found on examination. Identifying the primary pain-generating tissue(s) is of paramount importance, as this will, in most cases, allow for the application of treatment approaches that will decrease the level of nociception arising from these tissues. There will usually be several tissues contributing simultaneously, and the hallmark of their identification is the reproduction of the patient's headache pain upon examination. The most common cervical pain generators in the headache patient are the C0–1 (see Fig. 17–12), C1–2 (see Fig. 17–13), and C2–3 (see Fig. 17–14) intervertebral tissues and TrPs, particularly in the sternocleidomastoid (see Fig. 17–3), upper trapezius (see Fig. 17–4), suboccipitals (see Fig. 17–2), and splenius capitis (see Fig. 17–6) muscles.

! CLINICAL PEARL

It should be noted that while the diagnosis of occipital neuralgia is a common one, it is actually probably a quite rare cause of headache. Compression of the occipital nerve is an unlikely cause because, first, nerve compression does not generally cause pain but, rather, paresthesia, numbness and motor loss. Second, there are several structures that can cause pain that may be perceived in the area of the occipital nerve and rarely will there be signs of nerve entrapment. So if a patient comes to you saying that he or she has been diagnosed with occipital neuralgia, look for other potential sources of his or her pain!

It is important, however, that the pain generators not be assumed to be the primary problem. Dysfunction in the locomotor system as a whole that may be causing the pain generators to generate pain must be detected. This particularly involves looking at movement patterns and other tests presented in Chapter 14 that will identify key dysfunctions that may play a prominent role in the pathophysiology of the cervical component. The most important functional examination procedures are provided in Table 8–3.

Based on the findings from the history and examination, a treatment strategy is formulated that is designed to address both the nociception arising from the primary pain generators and those locomotor system dysfunctions that have been determined to be most significant. As joint dysfunction can be both a pain generator and a key dysfunction in the perpetuation of the condition, manipulation is often going to be an important component of treatment (see Chap. 18). Several studies have evaluated the role of manipulation in headache.[67–79] The most important of these are reviewed in Appendix B of Chapter 18. But it is important to realize that because of the multifaceted nature of the pathophysiology of headache, manipulation alone will be effective only in those patients in whom the cervical component is so prominent in the overall pathophysiological picture, and joint dysfunction is so prominent within the cervical component, that treating this alone will significantly alter the condition. This situation cannot be expected in all patients. The complexity of headache may be the reason for the mixed results in some of the studies that have evaluated singular treatment approaches, such as manipulation, in isolation of any others that may play a role in overall management. Despite this, however, most of the data regarding manipulation and headaches are favorable toward this form of treatment.

TrPs are often important pain generators in patients with headache, and ischemic compression (see Chapter 19) can be very helpful in rapidly reducing the pain. Postisometric relaxation (PIR) is also effective with TrPs, but its effect will not be as immediate. In those patients in whom TrPs are entrapped by significant adhesions within the muscle, Active Release Technique (see the appendix to Chap. 19) can be quite valuable, particularly with involvement of the suboccipital muscles. Application of these methods in combination is often necessary.

Table 8-3: The Most Important Functional Examination Procedures in the Headache Patient

PROCEDURE	SIGNIFICANCE IN THE HEADACHE PATIENT
Postural examination	Forward head posture suggests poor postural habits or imbalance between the upper cervical extensors and the deep cervical flexors, or both; shoulder unleveling suggests tightness in the upper trapezius
Cervical flexion movement pattern	Detects imbalance in the activity of the sternocleidomastoid and deep cervical flexors
Cervical stability test	Detects inhibition and poor stabilization function of the deep cervical flexors
Hip extension movement pattern	Detects hyperactivity of the cervical muscles and dysfunction of the motor program for gait
Shoulder abduction movement pattern	Detects hyperactivity in the upper trapezius and poor scapular stability
Stepping test	Detects faulty locomotor system kinesthetic awareness
Revel's test	Detects poor cervical kinesthetic awareness and suggests oculomotor dysfunction
Swallowing	Suggests underlying factor in cervical instability
Postural foot reaction	Detects foot instability, which can have an impact on cervical stability
S reflex	Suggests mechanical dysfunction of the pelvis, which can have an impact on the upper cervical spine

It has recently been discovered that the rectus capitis posterior minor muscle[79a] and the ligamentum nuchae[79b] are connected directly to the dura mater in the upper cervical spine by a connective tissue bridge. The development of tightness and/or adhesions in these structures may cause headache as a result of traction on the highly-innervated dura. If tightness and/or adhesions are found in these structures, carefully applied postfacilitation stretch (see Chapter 19) and/or Active Release Technique (see Chapter 19 appendix) should be used.

! CLINICAL PEARL

I have found a method that can be very helpful with an active headache episode and can often stop one it its tracks. While joint dysfunction often plays a primary role in the development of the condition, and factors such as heredity, diet, stress, and gender all play important roles, the actual pain itself most often arises from TrPs. When a patient consults me with a headache in progress (this is usually a patient who I am familiar with and have seen before), I find that, after ruling out red flags for serious disease, treating the involved TrPs with ischemic compression (see Chap. 19) often can completely eliminate, or at least markedly reduce the intensity of, the headache. The treatment must be done with extreme care as it is very easy to actually make the pain far worse.

When pressure is applied to a TrP, pain is produced. For a patient with a severe headache episode, I apply this pressure just enough so that the patient can feel the pain increase to the slightest degree. My command to the patient is "I am going to slowly apply pressure to this TrP and I want you to tell me the moment you begin to feel your headache get worse." This allows me to apply only the minimum amount of pressure required to stimulate the TrP without aggravation. I hold the slight amount of pressure steady and then say to the patient, "Now I want you to tell me when the pain that I have stimulated starts to die down." This allows me to have an idea of whether the TrP is going to let go. Usually within 30 seconds the patient tells me that the pain is starting to decrease. I then say to the patient, "Tell me when the pain that I have stimulated disappears completely." Usually another 30 seconds is required for this to occur. Once the pain from this particular stimulation is eliminated (the patient will still have the headache—there are invariably several more TrPs that are contributing to the pain and that need to be treated), I tell the patient, "I am now going to slowly increase the pressure on this TrP again and I want you to tell me the moment the pain that you felt before returns." When this happens I again stop and hold that pressure steady without increasing it until the patient once again tells me that it is starting to decrease and that it has gone away completely. I will usually do this a third time, gradually increasing the pressure applied to the TrP each time. This technique is then repeated with as many TrPs as I feel are contributing to the headache.

After this treatment, I apply a hot moist pack to the involved muscles and leave the patient in the darkened room for up to 20 to 30 minutes (or as long as is practical). Oftentimes by the time I take off the hot pack, the headache severity is only a fraction of what it was. Full recovery generally occurs shortly thereafter.

The specific therapeutic actions taken in response to findings on postural and movement pattern examination and functional testing will be determined by the findings on the individual examination procedures and the significance of these findings in the context of the overall clinical picture. They may include the use of sensorimotor training or cervical stabilization, or both. The key to the strategy for the management of the cervical component is to reduce the generation of pain by the primary pain generator(s) and to identify the key link in the chain of dysfunction that is leading to the perpetuation of the overall locomotor dysfunction and the production of pain by the primary pain generator(s). See Chapter 28 for specific protocols for management.

HEADACHE TRIGGERS

A second component of headache treatment is the identification of headache triggers. As described earlier, the autonomic regulatory systems of chronic headache sufferers appears to be unstable. Rather than responding with a smoothly graduated and measured physiological response to changes in the internal or external environment, the autonomically unstable subject responds with exaggerated oscillations. This instability may result in a cascade of physiological events that favor the formation of headaches. A headache trigger is any stimulus that initiates the cascade of events that leads to a headache.

The most common headache trigger is caffeine. It is a mild vasoconstrictor and has other central nervous system effects that may relate to headaches. The irony is that caffeine is often an effective headache remedy; precisely those effects that reduce headache pain (vasoconstriction), may act as a trigger under certain circumstances. Many chronic headache sufferers find themselves drawn to caffeine-containing beverages for their ameliorative effects. Whether, in an individual patient, the net effect of caffeine is to increase or decrease headache pain depends upon, as with the rebound phenomenon, frequency of use. Moderate, infrequent use is probably benign, but all headache patients should be encouraged to try a period of abstinence from caffeine to see if it produces any beneficial effects.

There is a large category of headache triggers comprised of vasoactive substances found in food. The two most conspicuous of these are the vasoactive amines tyrosine and phenylethylamine. These substances are nearly ubiquitous but are found in high concentrations in the following foodstuffs: aged cheeses, pickled or smoked fish, beans, chocolate, and aged, cured, or processed meats. Other common food triggers other than vasoactive amines include red wine, monosodium glutamate (MSG), artificial sweeteners, yeast breads and other yeast-containing products, and citrus fruits. Alcohol of any kind (even in moderation), because of its vasodilatory effects, may also be a headache trigger. Sugar, particularly in those who tend toward hypoglycemia, can also be a powerful headache trigger.

An important but often overlooked headache trigger is sleep, or more specifically, changes in sleep patterns. It is well established that there are regular diurnal fluctuations in physiological variables that are tied to sleep cycles. Any change in sleep patterns (over-sleeping, under-sleeping, changing times of retiring or arising) may upset the regular diurnal cycles and trigger a headache. Change in sleeping behavior is the primary cause of the weekend headache, a common complaint.

The identification and elimination of triggers can be a powerful tool in the management of headache, but there are several impediments to its implementation. First, the preceding list of triggers is not comprehensive. The comprehensive list of potential triggers would include, well, everything. Any compound that can be ingested and is biologically active in any way may, in certain individuals, act as a trigger. Second, a specific trigger may not invariably produce a headache. Only in certain concentrations or perhaps in combination with other compounds might a trigger be problematic. Third, the occurrence of headache following the ingestion of a trigger compound may be delayed long enough to mask the identity of the trigger or even to implicate the wrong compound. These limitations notwithstanding, the effort to identify triggers should always be a part of every headache consultation.

An important trigger of headache is emotional stress. Some studies have shown that up to 50 to 70 percent of headache sufferers cite this as the most important trigger to their headache.[21] It is thought that emotional stress can cause subtle increases in the tone of cervical muscles,[80] activating myofascial TrPs and producing headache pain. But perhaps more importantly, stress may decrease the effectiveness of an already dysfunctional descending pain inhibition system,[81] aggravating the serotonin dysregulation previously discussed. Thus, emotional and behavioral factors are of great importance in the dysfunction of the descending pain inhibitory system, and behavioral management is often invaluable in the management of the headache patient.

BEHAVIORAL MANAGEMENT

Headache experts have long recognized that behavioral as well as physical interventions are required to effectively treat chronic headache.[82–85] To ignore that cognitive, affective, and environmental factors can have physiological consequences severely limits the conceptualization of headache and can result in poor treatment outcomes, secondary to the repeated initiation of interventions that do not address the whole person. The behavioral model incorporates the roles of emotions, conditioning, stress, and inadequate coping into the development and maintenance of chronic headache and provides a framework for making treatment decisions.

By definition, pain involves an emotional component.[86] Pain is interpreted as a warning signal and leads to fear about the underlying cause. If headache persists, especially after treatment has been initiated, the anxiety associated with the pain is magnified, leading to a conviction that serious pathology is present. This preoccupation becomes resistant to reassurance on the part of the physician and leads to greater efforts on the part of the patient to seek a diagnosis and cure. Heightened irritability is likely to be present in reaction to persistent pain. The dysmodulation of the serotoninergic system in the brain associated with chronic headache can induce depression or exacerbate a pre-existing problem.[85] This fact can account for the degree of depression being proportional to the intensity and duration of the headache over time.

Fordyce[87] and Sternbach[88] have demonstrated how operant and classical conditioning can lead to the persistence of pain from several pathways. The basic tenet of operant conditioning is that any response that is reinforced (i.e., is met with positive consequences) will be repeated and become more durable. Furthermore, if the reinforcer is withdrawn, the response will be emitted with greater frequency in an attempt to reactivate the reinforcer. In headaches, for instance, pain and illness behavior can lead to increased attention and nurturing from family, the avoidance of responsibilities, and the prescription of analgesics and anxiolytics, all of which can reinforce the headache. Through operant conditioning, the response (headache) becomes more frequent. The removal of any of these reinforcers once the response (headache) is conditioned will result in an increase in the headache. With classical conditioning, the repeated pairing of a stimulus with a response results in the stimulus having the ability to consistently elicit the response. For instance, as headache persists, more frequent use of analgesic medication occurs, leading to tolerance or dependence on the analgesics and a regular pairing of medication and headache. The need for medication (tolerance or dependence) comes to elicit the response (headache) with which it has been paired. The patient is unlikely to realize or experience a craving for the medication, but rather the need for medication will elicit the headache. Parenthetically, such classical conditioning is not the etiology that underlies analgesic rebound headache, which is discussed later in this chapter. It is also important to remember that in the operant conditioning model, the reinforcers result from the misguided reactions of other, naturally occurring consequences of being ill, or from prescribed treatment. Similarly, in the classical conditioning paradigm, increased medication use is an effect of the headache, not the initial cause. In neither conditioning paradigm is the patient intentionally manipulating the situation.

Stress also provides a useful construct in conceptualizing the complex nature of chronic headache. Stress has been defined as the appraisal of circumstances as taxing or exceeding personal resources and endangering well being.[89] This definition captures the interaction of a person with his or her internal and external environment through the role of cognition (or attributions or expectations). Additionally, the perception of endangerment activates arousal levels that can lead to physiological symptoms or disease if the arousal level persists. Recurrent headache has come to be viewed as a stressor itself, capable of initiating this process.

From the behavioral model, it can be postulated that if a person with recurrent headache does not have self-management knowledge or skills (coping), dysregulation occurs resulting in chronic headache that can be resistant to intervention. Thus, treatment must be multidisciplinary and begin with a comprehensive assessment of the headache, including identification of the emotional, cognitive, and environmental factors involved. Thorough explanation of the headache and education of the patient regarding treatment is necessary to engage him or her in self-management (self-care). Great sensitivity is necessary when discussing the emotional, cognitive and conditioning aspects of the headache because it is easy for the patient to misperceive this aspect of headache as blaming him or her for the problem or dismissing the condition as "all in your head." Addressing medication issues, particularly analgesic overuse, must be a primary part of the treatment plan. Self-care interventions of relaxation, biofeedback, and cognitive behavioral therapies are implemented so patients can learn to intervene in the headache cycle to achieve amelioration. A single self-care intervention may be given or a combination chosen, depending on the response system that is the target of change.

The relaxation response has been described and researched over the years with good documentation of its effectiveness in treating headache.[84, 90] During the relaxation response, metabolism, blood pressure, heart rate, respiratory rate, and muscle tension all decrease.[90] Several techniques exist for teaching patients how to relax. Benson and Stark have found that the silent repetition of a word or phrase accompanied by the passive disregard of any intruding thoughts and a return to the repetition is effective in producing the relaxation response if practiced daily for 10 to 20 minutes.[90] Jacobson developed progressive muscle relaxation, a series of tension-release exercises with various muscle groups throughout the body.[91] If practiced daily for 15 to 20 minutes, it too can produce the relaxation response. Other techniques include autogenic training, guided imagery, self-hypnosis, and various forms of meditation.

Two types of biofeedback have been used for many years with headache with demonstrated effectiveness. EMG feedback measures muscle tension and helps the patient learn to decrease the tension. Thermal feedback measures skin temperature from a finger and, by teaching the patient to raise skin temperature, helps him or her to relax. Reduction of headache has been demonstrated with this method.[92] In biofeedback, electronic instruments measure physiological responses of interest and "feed back" information to the patient about these responses either visually or auditorily. With the feedback, the patient learns to change the response, such as muscle tension (EMG feedback) or temperature (thermal feedback), voluntarily. The typical session involves a baseline period to acclimate and stabilize the response, followed by the training or feedback part of the session. A voluntary control period, where the response is monitored while the patient attempts to change the response without the aid of the feedback is critical to demonstrate that the response has been learned and can be practiced at home.

Cognitive behavioral treatment is based on the fact that thinking or cognitive appraisal is instrumental in effecting mood and physiology. Cognitive restructuring teaches patients to systematically monitor maladaptive patterns of thoughts and how to revise them. It has been shown to effectively treat a variety of headache problems.[93] With cognitive therapy, patients are taught to monitor situations, their thoughts associated with these situations, and their responses emotionally and physically. Once associations or patterns are identified, patients can be taught to challenge maladaptive thoughts that lead to heightened arousal or other physiological responses connected to headache.

BIOCHEMICAL MANAGEMENT

Management of the biochemical component of headache pathophysiology can take on many forms, and often a combination of medical and nonmedical approaches is necessary.

Nonmedical Approaches

Dietary modification can be important and should be considered in all headache sufferers. This includes the elimination of those dietary factors that have been identified as being headache triggers (Fig. 8–4). Some investigators have suggested that food allergies may play a role in headache, and food allergens such as wheat, corn, citrus fruits, pineapple, grapes, soy, nuts, milk, eggs, beef, pork, shellfish, coffee, tea, colas, yeast and sugar should be identified and eliminated, as necessary.[94]

Regulation of blood glucose levels can also be important in dietary management. Altering the diet away from one that promotes rapid and wide fluctuations can help the patient to avoid hypoglycemic states that are often triggers of headaches. This involves eliminating cane sugar and other refined carbohydrates from the diet, limiting high carbohydrate foods such as breads, cereals, potatoes, and pasta, and never allowing more than 3 hours to pass without eating.[95]

In addition to recommendations for dietary changes, nutritional supplementation and use of herbal remedies can often be helpful. Perhaps the most common nutritional supplement used for headache sufferers is magnesium.[94, 96] It is believed that magnesium acts in a number of ways in affecting headache pathophysiology, including regulation of vascular tone and reactivity, calcium channel blockage, serotonin regulation, and regulation of inflammatory mechanisms.[94] Its distribution has been demonstrated to be abnormal in headache sufferers.[96] The evidence of effective-

NATIONAL HEADACHE FOUNDATION
428 W. St. James Pl., 2nd Floor, Chicago, IL 60614-2750
Toll Free (800) 843-2256 Fax (773) 525-7357
Web Site Address: www.headaches.org

DIET AND HEADACHE

Below is a list of foods that may trigger headaches. Dietary triggers do not necessarily contribute to headaches in all patients. Certain foods may trigger attacks in certain individuals, but not on every occasion. Be your own expert by trying to log the foods you have eaten before a migraine attack and see whether their removal reduces or eliminates your headaches.

AVOID:

Ripened cheeses (Cheddar, Emmentaler, Stilton, Brie, Camembert)
    (Permissible cheeses: American, cottage, cream, Velveeta)
Herring, pickled or dried
Chocolate
Anything fermented, pickled, or marinated
Sour cream (no more than 1/2 cup daily)
Nuts, peanut butter
Sourdough bread, breads and crackers containing cheese or chocolate
Broad beans, lima beans, fava beans, snow peas
Foods containing monosodium glutamate (MSG) - soy sauce, meat tenderizers, seasoned
    salt
Figs, raisins, papayas, avocados, red plums (no more than 1/2 cup daily)
Citrus fruits (no more than 1/2 cup daily)
Bananas (no more than 1/2 banana daily)
Pizza
Excessive amounts of tea, coffee, or cola beverages (no more than 2 cups daily)
Sausage, bologna, pepperoni, salami, summer sausage, hot dogs
Chicken livers, paté
Alcoholic beverages: (If you do drink, limit yourself to two normal size drinks selected
    from Haute Sauterne, Riesling, Seagram's VO, Cutty Sark)

A more complete diet listing is available to members of the foundation.

8/97

Your #1 Source for Headache Help

Figure 8–4. Dietary recommendations for headache.

(Used with permission, National Headache Foundation.)

ness of magnesium supplementation in patients with headache is only in the form of uncontrolled trials;[94, 96] however, it is suggested that this supplement may be helpful in certain patients. Gerber[94] suggests prescribing 600 mg per day in divided doses.

Schoenen et al[97, 98] recently demonstrated effectiveness of high-dose riboflavin for prophylaxis in patients diagnosed with migraine. A daily oral dose of 400 mg was found to significantly reduce attack frequency and headache days compared to placebo. There was a marginal superiority over placebo for headache severity and duration. It is believed that riboflavin positively influences mitochondrial energy metabolism.

Riboflavin has an excellent tolerability profile and no known risk of drug interactions[98a] and should be considered as a first-line biochemical approach.

Feverfew has been used for centuries as a headache remedy.[99] This herb is believed to affect serotonin regulation, inhibit platelet aggregation, and help in regulating blood vessel tone.[99, 100] One study[101] looked at 17 subjects who were already ingesting feverfew leaves for migraine prophylaxis and randomized them into two groups, one that continued taking feverfew and the other that was switched to placebo. They found that the placebo group experienced a threefold increase in headache frequency, while the feverfew group experienced no change. Another, larger trial[102] compared 72 patients randomized to either feverfew or placebo for 3 months, after which the placebo group began taking feverfew and the feverfew group began taking placebo. The authors found a 24 percent decrease in headache frequency and significant reduction in nausea and vomiting during feverfew treatment. Two other trials,[102a, 102b] however, have shown no benefit of feverfew. Gerber[94] recommends a dosage of 50 to 100 mg per day of a standardized extract or concentrate.

Although feverfew is considered relatively safe,[102c] one study reported a "post-feverfew syndrome"[101] in some patients, in which rebound of migraine symptoms, anxiety, insomnia, and muscle and joint stiffness was reported by long-time feverfew users after discontinuation. There are no changes in blood pressure, bodyweight, or hematological or biochemical profiles in this patient population.

Medical Approaches

Medical therapy in headache has two aspects—prophylactic and abortive. Prophylactic therapy aims to reduce the frequency and severity of headache attacks while abortive therapy aims to reduce the duration and severity of pain in individual attacks.[103]

Abortive Medications

When considering choices of abortive therapy, the practitioner should consider the intensity and severity of the pain and its associated symptoms. For acute attacks, analgesics are often the first line of therapy; aspirin, acetaminophen, and ibuprofen often provide relief for migraine and tension headache symptoms. These agents, when combined with caffeine, appear to have enhanced efficacy in

migraine attacks. Butalbital is a common adjunctive medication frequently used in combination preparations, which are believed to improve efficacy in both migraine and tension-type headaches. Indomethacin and naproxen may provide greater efficacy in patients with tension-type headaches that are resistant to aspirin or acetaminophen.[103]

Opioid analgesics are powerful pain relievers. However, tolerance potential for dependency and sedative side effects are serious drawbacks. Their use in the treatment of headaches of all kinds should be limited to very occasional severe attacks.

For acute headaches with migraine features, ergot alkaloids and the newer "triptans" (sumatriptan, rizatriptan) are attractive options, as they often provide early headache relief without disabling sedation and tolerance that may be produced by opioid analgesics. Because of their vasomotor effects, these medications are contraindicated in patients with coronary artery disease, peripheral vascular disease, cerebrovascular disease, Raynaud's disease, and hypertension. These agents vary in their onset and duration of effect, side effects, and available routes of administration. Ergotamine, for example, often causes intolerable gastrointestinal side effects, while sumatriptan is more frequently associated with headache recurrence.[104] Patients who do not respond to one agent may respond to others.

When nausea is a predominant feature of the headache syndrome, nonoral routes of administration of abortive agents are often used. Antiemetic agents such as promethazine, prochlorperazine, and metoclopramide often provide substantial relief of both the headache and nausea.[105]

Prophylactic Medications

Medications for prophylactic therapy should be considered when attacks occur more than 2 to 3 times per month. These agents have variable side effect profiles which should be considered when selecting a class of medication (Table 8–4). For example, in a depressed or dysthymic patient, tricyclic antidepressants would be a better choice than a beta blocker. Alternatively, in a patient with a weight problem, agents such as valproate and amitriptyline might be best avoided. Medications should be started at low doses and slowly increased. A period of 4 to 8 weeks of therapy is required before determining that any given agent or dose is ineffective; inadequate dose or duration of therapy is the most common cause of failure of drug therapy. After 6 to 12 months of good control of headaches, tapering and discontinuation of the prophylactic agent should be considered. The use of prophylactic agents for headache, in particular migraine, achieves significant improvement in frequency and severity of headaches in the majority of patients.[104, 106–108]

Rebound Headaches

A rebound headache is one that occurs when the physiological effects of an abortive medication wear off and the body attempts to reregulate itself. The body reacts to the

Table 8-4: Common Prophylactic Agents Used for Headache Prevention*

CLASS OF AGENT	PROTOTYPIC AGENT	STARTING DOSE	COMMON SIDE EFFECTS	CONTRAINDICATIONS
Tricyclic antidepressants	Amitriptyline	10 mg at bedtime	Sedation, dry mouth, tremor, weight gain, hair loss	Cardiac conduction defects, active coronary artery disease
Calcium channel blockers	Verapamil SR	120 mg daily	Hypotension, constipation, fluid retention	Hypotension, congestive heart failure, cardiac conduction defects, liver disease
Beta blockers	Propranolol SR	60 mg daily	Hypotension, bradycardia, depression, mental dulling	Hypotension, bradycardia, asthma, heart block, diabetes
Antihistamines	Cyproheptadine	4 mg at bedtime	Sedation, weight gain	
Anticonvulsants	Valproate	125 mg 3 times daily	Gastrointestinal upset, tremor, weight gain, hair loss	Liver disease, blood disorders
	Gabapentin	100 mg 3 times daily	Dizziness, somnolence, ataxia and fatigue	

* Second line agents for headache prophylaxis include lithium, methysergide, and corticosteroids. Use of these agents is limited to medically resistant patients because of potential for serious side effects.

presence of a vasoconstrictor or an anti-inflammatory agent by propelling itself in the direction of vasodilatation or inflammation and thereby producing a headache.

The phenomenon of rebound headaches was originally described in patients who used ergotamine on a daily or near daily basis. However, regular or frequent use of other abortive drugs including analgesics and high caffeine use are common in patients with chronic daily headache. During the history it should be established how often, and with what specific agents, a patient is using medication to relieve the symptoms of headache pain.

There is no absolute threshold regarding the rate of abortive medication use beyond which rebound headache is certain to occur. However, the likelihood of rebound headaches occurring does vary directly with the frequency of medication use. A good rule of thumb is that greater than once-per-week use of headache medication may produce rebound headache. The issue is not in doubt when, as is often the case, there is daily use of abortive medication to control headache symptoms.

The remedy for rebound headaches is discontinuation of the offending medication. Withdrawal of the agent results in significant improvement within 2 to 6 weeks. Prophylactic agents are often helpful in getting patients off of the drugs that caused the rebound headaches. Patients who take abortive therapy for any headache syndrome should be counseled to avoid use of these agents more frequently than 2 days out of any given week.[109–112]

Withdrawal of the offending agent will probably result in a short term worsening of symptoms. It is important to reassure patients that following this period of withdrawal their headaches will probably remit to a more manageable level. It should also be emphasized that by abstaining from frequent medication use, those same medications will be much more effective when used judiciously and infrequently.

! CLINICAL PEARL

The preceding discussion assumes that self-medication by the patient with over-the-counter (OTC) medications is responsible for rebound headaches. Of course prescription medications may also be responsible and, other factors being equal, may produce even more pernicious rebound headache because of the greater physiological effects of prescription compared to OTC medications. In the case of prescription medication, if the physician primarily responsible for the management of the patient is the one who prescribed the medication, discontinuation should be implemented. However, if the physician primarily responsible for the management of the patient is not the one who prescribed the medication, the prescribing physician should be consulted, particularly if the managing physician is not licensed to dispense the pharmaceuticals in question.

CONCLUSION

Chronic headache has a pathophysiology that is as widely varied as the patients that suffer from this complex disorder. A new model is emerging that recognizes that the underlying pathophysiological process that leads to the condition of chronic headache is similar regardless of whether the headache picture is one that would be labeled migraine or one that would be labeled tension-type headache.

Diagnosis and treatment should be predicated on recognition of the process that is headache, rather than on diagnostic labels. This often requires a multidisciplinary approach, in order to address those factors in the pathophysiological picture that are most prominent in each patient. Interprofessional cooperation can lead to optimum care for the patient.

REFERENCES

1. Linet MS, Stewart WF. Migraine headache: Epidemiologic perspectives. *Epidemiol Rev* 1984;6:107–135.
2. Lipton RB, Silberstein SD, Stewart WF. An update on the epidemiology of migraine. *Headache* 1994;34:319–328.
3. Lipton RB, Stewart WF. Migraine in the United States: A review of epidemiology and health care use. *Neurology* 1993;43(suppl 3):S6–S10.
4. O'Brien B, Goeree R, Streiner D. Prevalence of migraine headache in Canada: A population-based survey. *Int J Epidemiol* 1994;23(3):1020–1026.
5. Pryse-Phillips W, Findlay H, Tugwell P, Edmeads J, Murray TJ, Nelson RF. A Canadian population survey on the clinical, epidemiologic and societal impact of migraine and tension-type headache. *Can J Neurol Sci* 1992;19(3):333–339.
6. Rasmussen BK. Epidemiology of headache [Review]. *Cephalalgia* 1995;15(1):45–68.
7. Stang PE, Osterhaus JT. Impact of migraine in the United States: Data from the National Health Interview Survey. *Headache* 1993;33(1):29–35.
8. How is your doctor treating you? *Consumer Reports* 1995;Feb:81–88.
9. Stewart WF, Lipton RB, Celentano DD, Reed ML. Prevalence of migraine headache in the United States. Relation to age, income, race, and other sociodemographic factors. JAMA 1992;67(1):64–69.
10. Osterhous JT, Townsend RJ, Gandek B, Ware JE. Measuring the functional status and well being of patients with migraine headache. *Headache* 1994;34:337–343.
11. Headache Classification Committee of the International Headache Society. Classification and diagnostic criteria for headache disorders. *Cephalalgia* 188;8(suppl):1–96.
12. Anderson CD, Franks RD. Migraine and tension headache: Is there a physiological difference? *Headache* 1981;21(2):63–71.
13. Featherstone HJ. Migraine and muscle contraction headache: A continuum. *Headache* 1985;25(4):194–198.
14. Leston JA. Migraine and tension-type headache are not separate disorders. *Cephalagia*;1996:16:220–222.
15. Marcus DA. Migraine and tension-type headaches: The questionable validity of current classification systems. *Clin J Pain* 1992;8(1):28–36.
16. Mathew NT. Transformed migraine. *Cephalalgia* 1993;13(suppl 12):78–83.
17. Messinger HB, Spierings ELH, Vincent AJP. Overlap of migraine and tension-type headache in the International Headache Society classification. *Cephalalgia* 1991;11:233–237.
18. Nelson C. The tension headache, migraine headache continuum: A hypothesis. *J Manipulative Physiol Ther* 1994;17:156–167.
19. Rasmussen BK, Jensen R, Schroll M, Olesen J. Interrelations between migraine and tension-type headache in the general population. *Arch Neurol* 1992;49:914–918.
20. Scharff L, Turk DC, Marcus DA. Psychosocial and behavioral characteristics in chronic headache patients: Support for a continuum and dual-diagnostic approach. *Cephalalgia* 1995;15:216–223.
21. Olesen J. Clinical and pathophysiological observations in migraine and tension-type headache explained by integration of vascular, supraspinal and myofascial inputs. *Pain* 1991;46:125–132.
22. D'Andrea G, Welch KM, Riddle JM, Grunfeld S, Joseph R. Platelet serotonin metabolism and ultrastructure in migraine. *Arch Neurol* 1989;46(11):1187–1189.
23. Lance J, Lambert G, Goadsby P. 5-Hydroxytriptymine and its putative aetiological involvement in migraine. *Cephalagia* 1989;9:7–13.
24. Malmgren R. The central serotoninergic system. *Cephalalgia* 1990;10:199–204.
25. Marcus DA. Serotonin and its role in headache pathogenesis and treatment [Review]. *Clin J Pain* 1993;9(3):159–167.

26. Rajiv J, Welch K, D'Andrea G. Serotoninigeric hypofunction in migraine: A synthesis of evidence based on platelet dense body dysfunction. *Cephalalgia* 1989;9:293–299.

27. Takeshima T, Shimomura T, Takahashi K. Platelet activation in muscle contraction headache and migraine. *Cephalalgia* 1987;7(4):239–243.

28. Appel S, Kuritzky A, Zahavi I, Zigelman M, Akselrod S. Evidence for instability of the autonomic nervous system in patients with migraine headache. *Headache* 1992;32:10–17.

29. Bates D, Weinshilboum RM, Campbell RJ, Sundt TM. The effect of lesions in the locus coeruleus on the physiological responses of the cerebral blood vessels in cats. *Brain Res* 1977;136:431–443.

30. Jessel TM, Kelly DD. Pain and analgesia. In: Kandel ER, Schwartz JH, Jessel TM, eds. *Principles of Neural Science*. 3rd ed. Norwalk, Conn: Appleton & Lange; 1991:385–399.

31. Svensson TH. Peripheral, autonomic regulation of locus coeruleus noradrenergic neurons in brain: Putative implications for psychiatry and psychopharmacology. *Psychopharmacology* 1987;92:1–7.

32. Sjaastad O, Bovim G. Cervicogenic headache. The differentiation from common migraine. An overview. *Funct Neurol* 1991;6(2):93–100.

33. Sjaastad O. Cervicogenic headache: The controversial headache. *Clin Neurol Neurosurg* 1992;94(suppl):S147–S149.

34. Sjaastad O. The headache of challenge in our time: Cervicogenic headache. *Funct Neurol* 1990;5:155–158.

35. Bogduk N, Marsland A. On the concept of third occipital headache. *J Neurol Neurosurg Psychiatry* 1986;49(7):775–780.

36. Bogduk N. Cervical causes of headache and dizziness. In: Grieve GP, ed. *Modern Manual Therapy of the Vertebral Column*. Edinburgh: Churchill-Livingstone; 1986:289–302.

37. Bogduk N. The anatomical basis for cervicogenic headache. *J Manipulative Physiol Ther* 1992;15(1):67–70.

38. Blau JN, MacGregor EA. Migraine and the neck. *Headache* 1994;34(2):88–90.

39. Bodguk N, Corrigan B, Kelly P, Schneider G, Farr R. Cervical headache [Review]. *Med J Aust* 1985;143:202,206–207.

40. Boquet J, Boismare F, Payenneville G, Leclerc D, Monnier JC, Moore N. Lateralization of headache: Possible role of an upper cervical trigger point. *Cephalalgia* 1989;9:15–24.

41. Bovim G, Berg R, Dale LG. Cervicogenic headache: Anesthetic blockades of cervical nerves (C2/C5) and facet joint (C2/C3). *Pain* 1992;49:315–320.

42. Bovim G, Sand T. Cervicogenic headache, migraine without aura and tension-type headache. Diagnostic blockade of greater occipital and supra-orbital nerves. *Pain* 1992;51:43–48.

43. Dieterich M, Pöllmann W, Pfaffenrath V. Cervicogenic headache: Electronystagmography, perception of verticality and posturography in patients before and after C2-blockade. *Cephalalgia* 1993;13:285–288.

44. Farina S, Granella F, Malferrari G, Manzoni GC. Headache and cervical spine disorders: Classification and treatment with transcutaneous electrical nerve stimulation. *Headache* 1986;26:431–433.

45. Hack GD, Koritzer RT, Robinson WL, Hallgren RC, Greenman PE. Anatomic relation between the rectus capitis posterior minor muscle and the dura mater. *Spine* 1995;20(23):2484–2486.

46. Jaeger B. Are "cervicogenic" headaches due to myofascial pain and cervical spine dysfunction? *Cephalalgia* 1989;9:157–164.

47. Jensen OK, Justesen T, Neilsen FF, Brixen K. Functional radiographic examination of the cervical spine in patients with post-traumatic headache. *Cephalalgia* 1990;10(6):295–303.

48. Jensen R, Rasmussen BK, Pedersen B, Olesen J. Muscle tenderness and pressure pain thresholds in headache. A population study. *Pain* 1993;52(2):193–199.

49. Jensen R, Rasmussen BK. Muscular disorders in tension-type headache. *Cephalalgia* 1996;16:97–103.

50. Kidd RF, Nelson CM. Musculoskeletal dysfunction of the neck in migraine and tension headache. *Headache* 1993;33:566–569.

51. Lebbink J, Spierings ELH, Messinger HB. A questionnaire survey of muscular symptoms in chronic headache. An age- and sex-controlled study. *Clin J Pain* 1991;7(2):95–101.

52. Lenhart L. Post-traumatic cervical syndrome. *J Manipulative Physiol Ther* 1988;11(5):409–415.

53. Macpherson BCM, Campbell C. C2 rotation and spinous process deviation in migraine: cause or effect or coincidence? *Neuroradiology* 1991;33:475–477.

54. Mark BM. Cervicogenic headache differential diagnosis and clinical management: literature review. *J Craniomandib Pract* 1990;8:332–338.

55. Martelletti P, LaTour D, Giacovazzo M. Spectrum of pathophysiological disorders in cervicogenic headache and its therapeutic indications. *J Neuromusculoskel Syst* 1995;(3)4:82–87.

56. Michler RP, Bovim G, Sjaastad O. Disorders in the lower cervical spine. A cause of unilateral headache? A case report. *Headache* 1991;31:550–551.

57. Pearce JMS. Cervicogenic headache: A personal view. *Cephalalgia* 1995;15:463–469.

58. Pfaffenrath V, Dandekar R, Mayer ETH, Hermann G, Pöllmann W. Cervicogenic headache: Results of computer-based measurements of cervical spine mobility in 15 patients. *Cephalalgia* 1988;8:45–48.

59. Pikus HJ, Phillips JM. Characteristics of patients successfully treated for cervicogenic headache by surgical decompression of the second cervical root. *Headache* 1995;35:621–629.

60. Pozniak-Patewicz E. "Cephalgic" spasm of head and neck muscles. *Headache* 1976;15(4):261–266.

61. Vernon H, Steiman I, Hagino C. Cervicogenic dysfunction in muscle contraction headache and migraine: A descriptive study. *J Manipulative Physiol Ther* 1992;15(7):418–429.

62. Weiss HD, Stern BJ, Goldberg J. Post-traumatic migraine: Chronic migraine precipitated by minor head or neck trauma. *Headache* 1991;31:451–456.

63. Wilson PR. Chronic neck pain and cervicogenic headache [Review]. *Clin J Pain* 1991;7(1):5–11.

64. Winston KR. Whiplash and its relationship to migraine. *Headache* 1987;27:452–457.

65. Nagasawa A, Sakakibara T, Takahashi A. Roentgenographic findings of the cervical spine in tension-type headache. *Headache* 1993;33(2):90–95.

66. Wober-Bingol C, Wober C, Zeiler K, et al. Tension headache and the cervical spine—plain x-ray findings. *Cephalalgia* 1992;12(3):152–154.

67. Bitterli J, Graf R, Robert F, Adler R, Mumenthaler M. Zur Objektivierung der Manualtherapeutischen Beeinflussbarkeit des Spondylogenen Kopfschemerzes [Objective criteria for the evaluation of chiropractic treatment of spondylotic headache]. *Nervenarzt* 1977;48(5):159–162.

68. Boline PD, Kassak K, Bronfort G, Nelson C, Anderson AV. Spinal manipulation vs. amitriptyline for the treatment of chronic tension-type headache: a randomized clinical trial. *J Manipulative Physiol Ther* 1995;18(3):148–154.

69. Freitag FG. Osteopathic manipulative treatment of migraine. *Osteop Ann* 1983;11(6):3–7.

70. Hoyt WH, Shaffer F, Bard DA, et al. Osteopathic manipulation in the treatment of muscle-contraction headache. *J Am Osteopath Assoc* 1979;78(5):322–325.

71. Nelson C, Boline P, Evans R, Bronfort G, Anderson A. A randomized controlled trial of spinal manipulation, amitriptyline, and a combined therapy for the treatment of migraine headache. *J Manipulative Physiol Ther* 1998;21(8):511–519.

72. Nilsson N. A randomized controlled trial of the effect of spinal manipulation in the treatment of cervicogenic headache. *J Manipulative Physiol Ther* 1995;18(7):435–440.

73. Parker GB, Tupling H, Pryor DS. A controlled trial of cervical manipulation of migraine. *Aust N Z J Med* 1978;8(6):589–593.

74. Schoensee SK, Jensen G, Nicholson G, Gossman M, Katholi C. The effect of mobilization on cervical headaches. *J Orthop Sports Phys Ther* 1995;21(4):184–196.

75. Vernon H. Chiropractic manipulative therapy in the treatment of headaches: A retrospective and prospective study. *J Manipulative Physiol Ther* 1982;5(3):109–112.

76. Vernon HT. Spinal manipulation and headaches of cervical origin. *J Manipulative Physiol Ther* 1989;12(6):455–468.

77. Whittingham W, Ellis WB, Molyneux TP. The effect of manipulation (toggle recoil technique) for headaches with upper cervical joint dysfunction: a pilot study. *J Manipulative Physiol Ther* 1994;17(6):369–375.

78. Wight J. Migraine: A statistical analysis of chiropractic treatment. *ACA J Chiro* 1978;15:28–32.

79. Bove G, Nilsson N. Spinal manipulation in the treatment of episodic tension-type headache. A randomized, controlled trial. *JAMA* 1998;280:1576–1579.

79a. Hack GD, Koritzer RT, Robinson WL, et al. Anatomic relation between the rectus capitis posterior minor muscle and the dura mater. *Spine* 1995;20(23):2484–2486.

79b. Mitchell BS, Humphreys BK, O'Sullivan E. Attachments of the ligamentum nuchae to cervical posterior spinal dura and the lateral part of the occipital bone. *J Manipulative Physiol Ther* 1998;21(3):145–148.

80. Janda V. Muscle spasm—a proposed procedure for differential diagnosis. *Man Med* 1991;6(4):136–139.

81. Dubner R. The effect of behavioral state on the sensory processing of nociceptive and non-nociceptive information. In: Fields HL, Besson JM, eds. *Progress in Brain Research*. New York, NY: Elsevier; 1988:213–223.

82. Bakal DA. *The Psychobiology of Chronic Headache*. New York, NY: Springer; 1982.

83. Diamond, S, Dalessio, DJ. *The Practicing Physician's Approach to Headache*. 4th ed. Baltimore, Md: Williams & Wilkins; 1986.

84. Blanchard EB, Andrasik, F. *Management of Chronic Headaches: A Psychological Approach*. New York, NY: Pergamon Press; 1985.

85. Jay GW. *The Headache Handbook: Diagnosis and Treatment*. Boca Raton, Fla: CRC Press; 1998.

86. Fields HL, Basbaum AI. Central nervous system mechanisms of pain modulation. In: Wall P, Melzack R, eds. *The Textbook of Pain*. 3rd ed. New York, NY: Churchill Livingstone; 1994:243–257.

87. Fordyce, WE. Behavioral conditioning concepts in chronic pain. In: Bonica JJ, Lindblom U, Iggo A, eds. *Advances in Pain Research and Therapy*. vol 5. New York, NY: Raven; 1983.

88. Sternbach, RA. Psychological management of the headache patient. In: Diamond S, Dalessio DJ, eds. *The Practicing Physician's Approach to Headache*. 4th ed. Baltimore, Md: Williams & Wilkins; 1986.

89. Lazarus, RS, Folkman, S. *Stress, Appraisal and Coping*. NewYork, NY: Springer-Verlag; 1984.

90. Benson H, Stark M. *Timeless Healing: The Power and Biology of Belief*. New York, NY: Scribner; 1996.

91. Jacobson E. *Progressive Relaxation*. Chicago, Ill: University of Chicago Press; 1938.

92. Blanchard EB, Appelbaum KA, Rudnitz CL, et al. A controlled evaluation of thermal biofeedback and thermal biofeedback combined with cognitive therapy in the treatment of vascular headache. *J Consulting Clin Psychol* 1990;58:216–224.

93. Holroyd, KA, Penzien, DB. Pharmacological versus nonpharmacological prophylaxis of recurrent migraine headache: A meta-analytic review of clinical trials. *Pain* 1990;42:1–13.

94. Gerber JM. Nutrition and migraine: Review and recommended strategies. *J Neuromusculoskel Sys* 1997;5(3):87–94.

95. Theisler CW. *Migraine Headache Disease*. Gaithersburg, Md: Aspen; 1998.

96. Swensen RS. Is magnesium important in headache? *J Neuromusculoskel Sys* 1996;4(3):94–101.

97. Schoenen J, Lenaerts M, Bastings E. High dose riboflavin as a prophylactic treatment of migraine: Results of an open pilot study. *Cephalalgia* 1994;14:328–329.

98. Schoenen J, Jacquy J, Lenaerts M. Effectiveness of high-dose riboflavin in migraine prophylaxis. A randomized, controlled trial. *Neurology* 1998;50:466–470.

98a. Pryse-Phillips WEM, Dodick DW, Edmeads JG, et al. Guidelines for the nonpharmacologic management of migraine in clinical practice. *Can Med Assoc J* 1998;159(1):47–54.

99. Rose J. Feverfew in the treatment of migraine. *Clin Nutr Insights* 1998;6:1–2.

100. Diamond S. Herbal therapy for migraine. *Postgrad Med* 1987;82:197–198.

101. Johnson ES, Kadam NP, Hylands DM, et al. Efficacy of feverfew as prophylactic treatment of migraine. *Br Med J* 1985;91:569–573.

102. Murphy JJ, Heptinstall S, Mitchell JRA. Randomised, double-blind, placebo-controlled trial of feverfew in migraine prevention. *Lancet* 1988;2(8604):189–192.

102a. De Weerdt CJ, Bootsma HPR, Hendriks H. Herbal medicines in migraine prevention: randomized, double-blind placebo-controlled cross-over trial of a feverfew preparation. *Phytomed* 1996:3:225–230.

102b. Kuritzky A, Elhacham Y, Yerushalmi Y, et al. Feverfew in the treatment of migraine: Its effect on serotonin uptake and platelet activity. *Neurology* 1994: 44 Suppl2:293P.

102c. Vogler BK, Pittler MH, Ernst E. Feverfew as a preventive treatment for migraine: A systematic review. *Cephalagia* 1998;18:704–708.

103. Silberstein SD, Lipton RB. Overview of diagnosis and treatment of migraine. *Neurology* 1994;44:S6–16.

104. Moore KL. Management of chronic headache in the era of managed care. *The Neurologist* 1997;3:209–240.

105. Jones J, Sklar D, Dougherty J, White W. Randomized double-blind trial of intravenous prochlorperazine for the treatment of acute headache. *JAMA* 1989;261:1174–1176.

106. Raskin N, Schwartz RK. The prophylaxis of migraine: A long-term controlled study. *Neurology* 1980;30:25.

107. Ziegler DK, Hurwitz A, Preskorn S, et al. Propranolol and amitriptyline compared in the prophylaxis of migraine. *Arch Neurol* 1993;50:825–830.

108. Jensen R, Brinck T, Olesen J. Sodium valproate has a prophylactic effect in migraine without aura. A triple-blind placebo-controlled crossover study. *Neurology* 1994;44:647–651.

109. Mathew N. Chronic refractory headache. *Neurology* 1993;43:S26–33.

110. Mathew N, Stubits E, Nigam M. Transformation of episodic migraine into daily headache: Analysis of factors. *Headache* 1982;22:66–68.

111. Kudrow L. Paradoxical effects of frequent analgesic use. *Adv Neurol* 1982;33:335–341.

112. Saper JR. Drug overuse among patients with headache. *Neurol Clin* 1983;1.

CHAPTER 9

Cervical Radiculopathy and Pseudoradicular Syndromes

DONALD R. MURPHY, MARTIN I. GRUDER, & LAURA B. MURPHY

"It is only with the heart that one can see rightly; what is essential is invisible to the eye."

—The Fox

INTRODUCTION

The purpose of this chapter is to present those conditions that can produce neck pain and radiating or referred arm, chest pain, or thoracic pain, or a combination of all three. The clinical entities that can cause these symptoms are many and effective management depends on establishing the correct diagnosis. This includes both identifying the specific tissue(s) that are the primary pain generator(s) and any significant factors that serve to perpetuate the generation of pain by these tissues. Some of the conditions that can cause cervical radiculopathy are of a serious or surgical nature, and differential diagnosis is of the utmost importance, as these conditions can often cause rapidly progressive neurological deficit, and some can be life threatening.

CERVICAL RADICULOPATHY

Cervical radiculopathy includes any process that causes irritation, compression, or dysfunction of one or more of the cervical nerve roots. The clinical signs and symptoms are determined by the actual pathophysiological process involved. Although there is significant overlap, the signs and symptoms of radicular compression will differ from those of radicular irritation. Either of these processes can cause some degree of dysfunction of the nerve root.

PATHOPHYSIOLOGY

The pathophysiology of radiculopathy in the cervical spine is not fully understood but is thought to be similar to that in the lumbar spine.[1] Irritation to a nerve root may set up an inflammatory response that can be pain producing. Compression of a nerve root will not cause pain per se, but will cause neurological deficit. Biochemical mediators of inflammation and tissue degradation may cause reaction from the nerve root and have been implicated in discogenic radiculopathic pain. High levels of such mediators as phospholipase A2, matrix metalloproteinases, nitric oxide, prostaglandin E2 and interleukin-6 have been demonstrated in herniated lumbar and cervical discs[2-4] and are believed to cause nerve root pain, although the exact mechanism is not known. So the pain and neurological deficit are probably caused by a variety of factors, both mechanical and biochemical.

Several pathoanatomical processes can cause radiculopathy, and an important aspect of the differential diagnosis involves not only differentiating radiculopathy from other diagnoses that may involve a similar clinical picture, such as thoracic outlet syndrome or scalene trigger points, but also differentiating radiculopathy caused by herniated nucleus pulposus (HNP) from that caused by other space occupying lesions. This differentiation is discussed later in the chapter.

Studies vary somewhat regarding which single cervical nerve root is most commonly involved in cervical radiculopathy, but it is generally agreed that C6 and C7 are affected more often than the others.[5–9] Radiculopathy involving C4, C5, and C8 is less common, however, are by no means rare, so it is important to look for signs and symptoms that may reflect involvement of any cervical level.

In most cases, the clinical history and examination can establish the diagnosis of cervical radiculopathy. The most important signs and symptoms are those of pain, sensory changes such as paresthesia or numbness, decreased or absent muscle stretch reflex, and motor weakness. It is not always easy, however, to identify the involved root, as there is a great deal of variation in the distribution of both motor and sensory nerves from the cervical spine.[7, 10] (See Fig. 17–21 for a map of the dermatomes related to the cervical spine.) For this reason, signs and symptoms can vary from patient to patient. For example, some patients report pain, paresthesia, or numbness in all fingers of the involved hand, rather than localized to a single dermatome. However, knowledge of the "classic" signs and symptoms is helpful as a starting point from which to work in examining each individual patient.

 CLINICAL PEARL

Although it is commonly said that radiculopathic pain is limited to one specific dermatome and will be sharp, shooting and superficial, this is only uncommonly seen in clinical practice. Rather, the pain is usually diffuse, poorly localized, and deep. This may be because it is, in part, referred scleretogenous pain resulting from irritation to the dural sleeve which is densely innervated and, in the cervical spine, has direct projections to the dorsal root ganglion.[10a] Or, it may be because radicular pain is not referred along dermatomes but, rather, along what Slipman et al[10b] refer to as "dynatomes."

C5 Radiculopathy

With radiculopathy involving C5, there typically is no pain distal to the elbow and no numbness or paresthesia in the hand.[7, 11–13] The patient generally reports cervical pain along with pain in the shoulder, medial border of the scapula, and upper arm. Paresthesia or numbness or both may be seen over the deltoid area and radial aspect of the upper arm. The biceps reflex may be decreased or absent, although this is less likely than with C6 radiculopathy. Motor loss involves shoulder abduction. Table 9–1 summarizes these findings.

C6 Radiculopathy

Involvement of the C6 nerve root typically causes pain in the neck, shoulder, medial border of the scapula, radial upper arm and forearm, and thumb and index fingers. Paresthesia or numbness, or both, may be experienced in the thumb and index fingers and the radial aspect of the hand and forearm. The biceps or brachioradialis reflex, or both, may be decreased or absent and motor loss may been found in the biceps, brachioradialis, and wrist extensors.[7, 11–13] Refer to Table 9–2.

C7 Radiculopathy

Involvement of C7 causes more diffuse pain in the neck, on both the dorsal and palmar surfaces of the forearm, and along the medial border of the scapula. Numbness or paresthesia, or both, can be found in the middle finger. The triceps reflex may be decreased or absent and motor loss may be seen in the triceps, wrist flexors, and finger extensors.[7, 11–13] See Table 9–3 for a summary of findings.

C8 Radiculopathy

Involvement of C8 causes pain in the neck, scapula, ulnar aspect of the upper arm and forearm, and ring and little fingers. Numbness or paresthesia, or both, can be seen in the ring and little fingers as well as in the medial aspect of the forearm. Typically no decrease or absence of muscle stretch reflex can be assessed. Motor loss can be found in the finger flexors and abductor pollicis brevis.[7, 11–13] Refer to Table 9–4.

HERNIATED NUCLEUS PULPOSUS

HNP is the most common cause of cervical radiculopathy.[8] The concept of discogenic cervical radiculopathy only became widely recognized in 1943 with the publication of an

---

Table 9–1: Pain and Neurological Dysfunction Related to C5 Radiculopathy

	PAIN	SENSORY DISTURBANCE	REFLEX DISTURBANCE	MOTOR LOSS
Typically	Neck, shoulder, medial border of the scapula, upper arm	Deltoid area, radial aspect of the upper arm	Biceps	Deltoid, biceps, supra- and infraspinatus
Occasionally	Radial aspect of the forearm	Entire upper arm and radial aspect of the forearm	Brachioradialis	Brachioradialis

Adapted from Benini A. Clinical features of cervical root compression C5–C8 and their variations. Neuro Orthop 1987;4:74–88.

Table 9–2: Pain and Neurological Dysfunction Related to C6 Radiculopathy

	PAIN	SENSORY DISTURBANCE	REFLEX DISTURBANCE	MOTOR LOSS
Typically	Neck, shoulder, medial border of the scapula, radial upper arm and forearm, thumb and index fingers	Thumb and index fingers, radial aspect of hand and forearm	Biceps, brachioradialis	Biceps, brachioradialis, wrist extensors
Occasionally	Ring finger, all fingers at once		Triceps	Forearm pronators, triceps, deltoid

Adapted from Benini A. Clinical features of cervical root compression C5–C8 and their variations. Neuro Orthop 1987;4:74–88.

important paper by Semmes and Murphey.[14] A variety of clinical, pathological, and radiographic terms and categories have since been applied to disorders of the cervical disc that cause radiculopathy, and this can be a source of confusion. For imaging purposes, precise definitions are required to identify the specific characteristics of the abnormality on magnetic resonance imaging (MRI). For clinical purposes, the term HNP will be used, as this represents a focal displacement of nuclear material outside the peripheral disc margin. The clinical features of the various subcategories, such as protrusion, extrusion, subligamentous extrusion, transligamentous extrusion, and sequestration, while possibly important from an imaging standpoint, are not essential from the standpoint of clinical diagnosis and conservative management. Some clinicians will use the terms *soft disc* and *hard disc*—"soft" referring to herniation of disc material causing radiculopathy,[15, 16] and "hard" referring to the inclusion of cervical spondylosis and hypertrophic spur formation.[1, 15]

HNP is far less common in the cervical spine than in the lumbar spine. The ratio of symptomatic HNP in the cervical spine compared to the lumbar spine is 1:10.[1] Also, as will be seen, the management of cervical HNP is often vastly different from that of the lumbar spine, there being more rapid self-limitation in cervical HNP as compared to lumbar HNP.

HNP can occur as a result of sudden trauma that results in acute loading of the disc, as in the flexion phase of whiplash injury,[17] but it usually develops gradually, perhaps taking several years to progress. The process of HNP development in the cervical spine has not been as extensively studied as it has in the lumbar spine, but it is likely to be similar to the development of lumbar HNP.

As a result of recurrent flexion, loading, and rotational strains, circumferential tears develop in the anulus fibrosus (Fig. 9–1). Later, these circumferential tears coalesce to form radial tears, which gradually become larger and may extend from the periphery of the anulus to the nucleus (Fig. 9–2). The nucleus may migrate into the radial tear (Fig. 9–3). If this migration is sudden, it may be symptomatic, creating an acute disc derangement syndrome (see the discussion that follows and Chap. 26). However, if the migration occurs gradually, it may be well accommodated and occur asymptomatically. When the tear becomes nearly complete, it may require only a mild force to break though the remaining annular fibers and allow the nucleus to enter the lateral canal and cause radiculopathy (Fig. 9–4). It is for this reason that many patients with cervical radiculopathy related to HNP report that the pain began following a seemingly innocuous event such as turning to look around, or even that it began insidiously.

Table 9–3: Pain and Neurological Dysfunction Related to C7 Radiculopathy

	PAIN	SENSORY DISTURBANCE	REFLEX DISTURBANCE	MOTOR LOSS
Typically	Neck, dorsal, and palmar surfaces of the forearm, medial border of the scapula	Middle finger	Triceps	Triceps, wrist flexors, finger extensors
Occasionally	Lateral epicondyle area, index finger, ring finger, all fingers	Index finger; index and middle fingers; thumb, index, and middle fingers	Brachioradialis	Biceps, interossei, wrist extensors

Adapted from Benini A. Clinical features of cervical root compression C5–C8 and their variations. Neuro Orthop 1987;4:74–88.

Table 9–4: Pain and Neurological Dysfunction Related to C8 Radiculopathy

	PAIN	SENSORY DISTURBANCE	REFLEX DISTURBANCE	MOTOR LOSS
Typically	Neck, scapula, ulnar aspect of the upper arm and forearm, ring and little fingers	Ring and little fingers, medial forearm	None	Finger flexors, abductor pollicis brevis
Occasionally	All fingers, middle and ring fingers	Middle, ring and little fingers, ulnar side of the middle finger	Triceps	Triceps

Adapted from Benini A. Clinical features of cervical root compression C5–C8 and their variations. Neuro Orthop 1987;4:74–88.

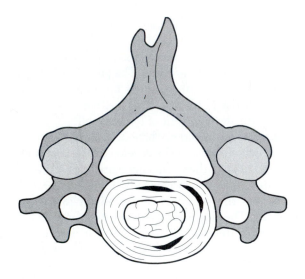

Figure 9–1. Circumferential tears in the anulus fibrosus.

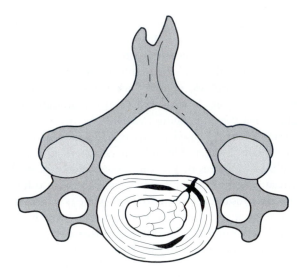

Figure 9–3. Disc derangement.

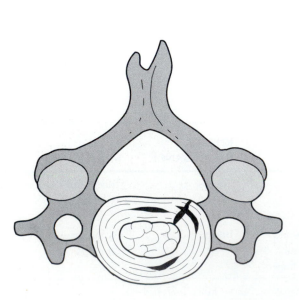

Figure 9–2. Radial tear in the anulus fibrosus.

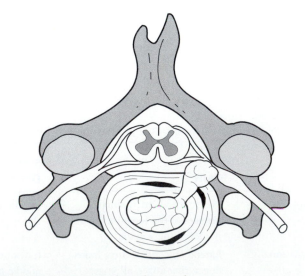

Figure 9–4. Herniated nucleus pulposus.

(Adapted from Connell MC, Wiesel SW. Natural history and pathogenesis of cervical disc disease. Orthop Clin North Am 1992;23:369–380.)

The nerve root affected will be determined by the disc level involved. Because the nerve roots exit at the level above the numbered vertebra to which they correspond (except C8, which exits between C7 and T1), HNP will affect the nerve root that is numbered according to the lower of the vertebrae between which the disc is located. Table 9–5 identifies the disc level that will affect each nerve root. The most commonly involved discs are C5–6 and C6–7.[13, 18]

As previously discussed, the precise mechanism by which HNP causes pain is not clear, although it is probably related to a combination of mechanical and biochemical factors. The presence of neurological deficit indicates a compressive lesion. It should be noted, however, that a significant number of asymptomatic people can be found to have HNP in the cervical spine.[19] So in a patient with neck and arm pain, the presence of HNP does not necessarily mean that radiculopathy related to HNP is the correct diagnosis. The nerve root must be specifically identified as the primary pain generator, and other possible pain generators ruled out, before this diagnosis can be given with confidence.

The nucleus pulposus is primarily composed of water and desiccates during the aging process. This desiccation is usually complete by age 40.[20] So, as a general rule, radiculopathy related to HNP is unlikely after age 40, although individual variations are not uncommon, and HNP in older patients is far from rare. Still, radiculopathy related to HNP is largely a syndrome of the young.

A recent anatomical study by Mercer and Bogduk[20a] suggests the possibility that the anatomy of the cervical disc may be different than was previously thought. They found the presence of only a thin layer of collagen in the posterior aspect of the disc, rather than a full posterior anulus. However, the cadaveric specimens that they dissected were mostly older; the youngest specimen was 39 years old, and only 3 specimens were under age 50. Further study will need to be done to determine if these are age-related changes, or if this disc morphology exists throughout life. If these findings are confirmed in younger specimens, it may necessitate a complete revision of the model of cervical HNP and disc derangement.

LATERAL CANAL STENOSIS

Lateral canal stenosis (LCS), which is frequently referred to as cervical spondylosis, is the second most common cause of cervical radiculopathy.[21] The term *lateral canal stenosis* is used preferentially here to cervical spondylosis, as the term *cervical spondylosis* refers to the degenerative changes themselves, which occur in almost all adults but are not necessarily a cause of symptoms. These symptoms occur as a result of the degenerative process, which, in part, involves the development of hypertrophic spurs along the margins of the disc, the joints of Luschka, and along the zygapophyseal joints. This spur development is often accompanied by hypertrophy of the ligamentum flavum. In most people, this is a painless process and occurs without consequence.[19, 22] However, if the spurs extend into the lateral canal where the nerve root exits and are positioned such that they cause compression or irritation to the root, radiculopathy can result (Fig. 9–5). If joint dysfunction is present at the same level, the resultant reduced motion of the segment will further render the nerve root susceptible to irritation or compression. As LCS results from degenerative changes, this type of radiculopathy generally occurs in people over the age of 40.

A recent experiment by Omarker and Myers[23] showed that the development of a decreased threshold for pain in a nerve root was more consistently seen with lesions that exposed the nerve root both to nuclear material and to mechanical deformation, as compared to either condition alone. This suggests that, although mechanical deformation alone (as would occur with LCS) or exposure to nuclear material alone (as would occur with HNP without deformation of the nerve root) is capable of producing pain, the combination of the two (as would occur with HNP with mechanical deformation) is more likely to produce pain. This helps explain why radiculopathy is more commonly associated with HNP than with LCS, even though

Table 9–5: Nerve Roots That Can Be Affected by HNP at Each Disc Level

DISC LEVEL	NERVE ROOT AFFECTED
C2–3	C3
C3–4	C4
C4–5	C5
C5–6	C6
C6–7	C7
C7–T1	C8

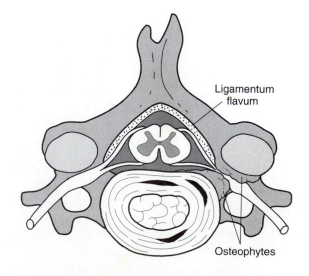

Figure 9–5. Lateral canal stenosis.

Ligamentum flavum

Osteophytes

cervical spondylosis is a virtually ubiquitous process. It also helps explain why many people with HNP do not experience pain, as in some cases there may not be sufficient mechanical deformation to produce pain.

OTHER SPACE-OCCUPYING LESIONS

Far less common, though extremely important, are infectious and neoplastic processes that can cause radiculopathy. The most common site of infection is the vertebral body and neural arch,[24] and abscess formation can lead to extension into the intervertebral foramen, causing nerve root compression or irritation. Because of the avascularity of the intervertebral disc, discitis will generally not be seen in adults, but may occur in children and should be considered seriously in a child presenting with radiculopathy.

Neoplastic processes that can cause radiculopathy include meningiomas, schwannomas, sarcomas, angiomas, chordomas, lipomas, epidermoids, melanomas, neuroblastomas, and metastatic tumors, most frequently from the breast, thyroid, and gastrointestinal tract.[25] These processes

frequently cause spinal cord compression as well as radiculopathy, but nerve root symptoms are often the initial manifestation. The clinical picture can greatly resemble that of HNP, lateral stenosis, or pseudoradiculopathy.

PSEUDORADICULOPATHY

> **! CLINICAL PEARL**
>
> Clinicians, *please* do not tell your patients that they "have a pinched nerve in their neck" unless they really do!

The presence of neck pain with pain radiating into the arm does not necessarily mean that the patient is experiencing cervical radiculopathy. There are other, more common, causes of pain in this distribution. Perhaps the most common is trigger points (TrPs) in the scalene muscles. TrPs in these muscles can cause pain in the shoulder and arm, frequently extending into the hand. Pain may also be experi-

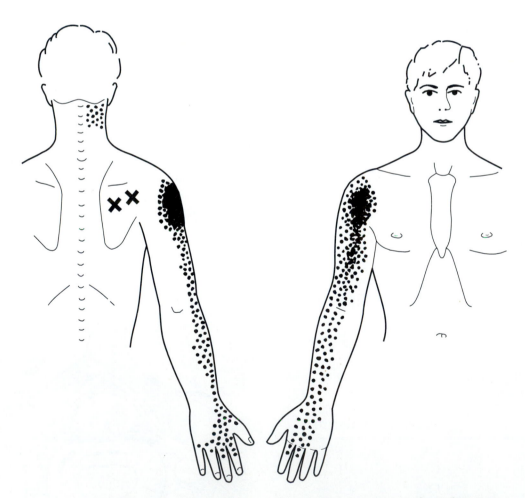

Figure 9–6. Referred pain pattern from myofascial trigger points in the infraspinatus muscle.

(Adapted from Travell JG, Simons DG. Myofascial Pain and Dysfunction: The Trigger Point Manual. Baltimore, Md: Williams & Wilkins; 1983:378.)

enced in the medial border of the scapula and in the chest (see Fig. 17–9). The chest referral can cause what has been referred to as "pseudo-angina."[26] Scalene TrPs are often accompanied by joint dysfunction in the lower cervical spine, which may produce local neck pain or contribute to the referral of pain into the arm. This combined pain pattern can be almost indistinguishable from that of radiculopathic pain.

Other muscles, when they develop TrPs, can cause referral of pain into the arm that can possibly be confused with radiculopathic pain. These include the infraspinatus (Fig. 9–6), supraspinatus (Fig. 9–7), and subclavius (Fig. 9–8). The pathophysiological mechanisms of TrPs were discussed in Chapter 4.

Joint dysfunction in the lower cervical spine can cause scleretogenous referral of pain into the upper extremity. This is most common at the levels of C5–6 through C7–T1 (see Figs. 17–16 to 17–19). Referral of pain into the arm can also be seen as a result of joint dysfunction at the first costotransverse joint. As previously stated, dysfunction in these joints is often accompanied by scalene TrPs, adding to the complexity of the neck-arm pain syndrome. Pathophysiological mechanisms, detection, and treatment of joint dysfunction are discussed in more detail in Chapters 4, 13, and 18.

Neck and arm pain may also be caused by disc derangement. The referral of pain into the arm is likely to be scleretogenous in nature from irritation of the annular fibers of the disc. It, like the other causes of radiculopathy and pseudoradiculopathy discussed, is often associated with joint dysfunction at the level of the derangement. Disc derangement is discussed in further detail in Chapter 26.

Other disorders that are capable of mimicking cervical radiculopathy include primary disease of the shoulder, such as rotator cuff tendinitis, and primary disease of the chest. Because the diaphragm receives innervation from C3, C4, and C5, lesions in the lung can refer pain into the C5 dermatome. A pancoast tumor, by impinging on the lower trunk of the brachial plexus, can simulate a C8 nerve root lesion.[10]

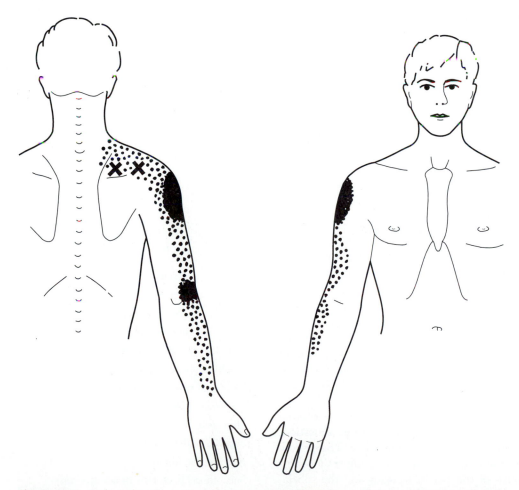

Figure 9–7. Referred pain pattern from myofascial trigger points in the supraspinatus muscle.

(Adapted from Travell JG, Simons DG. Myofascial Pain and Dysfunction: The Trigger Point Manual. Baltimore, Md: Williams & Wilkins; 1983:369.)

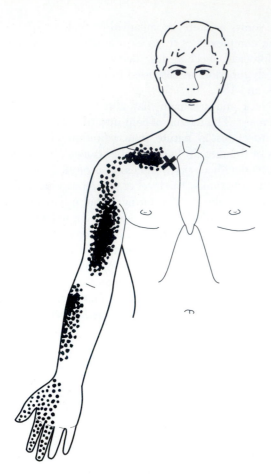

Figure 9–8. Referred pain pattern from myofascial trigger points in the subclavius muscle.

(Adapted from Travell JG, Simons DG. Myofascial Pain and Dysfunction: The Trigger Point Manual. *Baltimore, Md: Williams & Wilkins; 1983:580.)*

The clinical presentation can be neurogenic, vascular, or mixed, though in the majority of cases the dominant symptoms are neurogenic.[27–29] TOS is most commonly unilateral but bilateral involvement can often be found. Roos[30] has reported two types of patterns, one involving the upper roots of the brachial plexus (C5, C6, and C7) and the other involving the lower roots (C8 and T1). These patterns may occur separately or simultaneously. In the majority of cases, however, the lower trunk of the brachial plexus, which contains fibers from the C8 and T1 levels is involved.[27, 30] Although vascular involvement is less common, the potential consequences are more serious than with neurological involvement. Therefore, prompt and accurate diagnosis of the degree of vascular involvement is important, and appropriate actions must be taken.

The symptom complex may include pain in the shoulder, arm, or forearm, which may radiate into the hand and fingers. Pain may also be reported in the head, neck, face, and chest wall. The pain pattern with involvement of the lower nerves (C8, T1) could include pain in the supraclavicular and infraclavicular fossae, the back of the neck, the rhomboid area, the axilla and medial arm,[30] and may radiate into the hand and fourth and fifth fingers. Feeling of coldness and a "dead" feeling, hypesthesia, or "electric shock" sensations, in the C8 and T1 nerve root or ulnar nerve distributions, may be present.[27, 30] The pain pattern with involvement of the upper nerves of the brachial plexus (C5, C6, C7) can occur along the anterolateral aspect of the neck and may radiate up to the mandible, ear, into the upper chest anteriorly, posteriorly to the scapula, laterally over the top of the shoulder, and down the lateral aspect of the arm in the C5, C6, C7 dermatomes.[30] True numbness in the fingers, hand, or forearm may also be

THORACIC OUTLET SYNDROME

An important consideration in the patient who presents with symptoms such as pain in the cervical spine with pain or numbness and paresthesia in the upper extremity is that of thoracic outlet syndrome (TOS). TOS is being used here as an umbrella term that represents the various neurovascular entrapments that can occur as the brachial plexus passes from the cervical spine, between the anterior and middle scalene muscles and, along with the subclavian artery and vein, under the clavicle and pectoralis minor muscle and into the upper extremity.

These entrapments can produce a complex symptom picture involving upper extremity pain, altered sensation, motor dysfunction, and vascular insufficiency. The picture is thought to be due to compromise—by compression, irritation, or stretch—of the brachial plexus and the subclavian-axillary artery and vein as they exit the neck and traverse into the axilla. TOS has been referred to by a large number of diagnostic labels. Some of these labels are provided in Table 9–6.

Table 9–6: Diagnostic Labels That Have Been Used for Thoracic Outlet Syndrome

Cervical rib syndrome

Scalenus anticus syndrome

Costoclavicular syndrome

Hyperabduction syndrome

Pectoralis minor syndrome

Brachiocephalic syndrome

Nocturnal paresthetic brachialgia

Fractured clavicle-rib syndrome

Effort vein thrombosis (Paget–Schroetter syndrome)

Superior outlet syndrome

Naffziger syndrome

Subcoracoid pectoralis minor syndrome

First thoracic rib syndrome

Costoclavicular compression syndrome

Cervical rib and band syndrome

Table 9–7: Neurogenic, Arterial, and Venous Symptoms That May Be Seen in Patients with Thoracic Outlet Syndrome

NEUROGENIC	ARTERIAL	VENOUS
Pain—two patterns which may occur simultaneously	Ischemic pain—similar to that in neurogenic, although usually more diffuse and may be exercise-induced	Pain
Paresthesia—typically involving ulnar side or C8–T1 distributions of the hand; the entire hand may be involved	Numbness, coldness	Swelling of the entire limb
	Weakness	Nonpitting edema
	Pallor, skin color changes	Ecchymosis
Paresis—of the intrinsic muscles of the hand	Fatigue (exertional)	Increased limb girth
Early fatigability, progressive weakness, and dyscoordination	Episode may resemble Raynaud's symptoms	Venous collateralization with dilation or engorgement across the shoulder and superior chest wall
Atrophy and weakness of the intrinsic muscles of the hand	Muscle cramps with repetitive use	Stiffness of the fingers
Intermittent "cramping" of the hand	Gangrene or ulcerations of the digits in severe cases	Heaviness
		Cyanosis
		Fatigue

seen with involvement of either the upper or lower nerves.

Fatigue, loss of grip strength, incoordination (loss of dexterity), or clumsiness of the hand due to weakness of the intrinsic muscles are among the motor symptoms that may be reported. Sensory symptoms generally cover more than one dermatome and usually precede motor symptoms.[31] Symptoms may be aggravated with extreme positions of the neck and shoulder girdle and with heavy work, and the symptoms are often worse at the end of the day. Patients often report that they are awakened from sleep due to the symptoms.

With arterial involvement, coolness or intermittent ischemic episodes similar to those seen with Raynaud's phenomenon may also be reported.

The clinical picture varies depending on the components of the neurovascular bundle that are involved and, to a lesser extent, the site at which entrapment occurs. A summary of neurogenic, arterial, and venous signs and symptoms is presented in Table 9–7.

Various etiologies have been proposed for TOS. The feature they have in common is compression, irritation, or stretch on the neurovascular structures that pass from the neck to the axilla. The primary entrapment sites are discussed here, although there is some overlap. There is also a great deal of overlap in the clinical features related to each entrapment site. These features are both anatomical and functional in nature, and each contributes to the specific localized entrapment.

Probably the most important contributing factor in TOS is dysfunction of the first costotransverse joint.[27, 32–37] Also commonly involved are the joints of the cervical and upper thoracic spine.[27] Muscle dysfunction of the scalenes and pectoralis minor and faulty shoulder abduction pattern (see Chap. 14) are frequently seen.

TOS tends to be more common in certain occupations, such as electrician, painter, bricklayer, packer, assembly line worker, typist, cash register operator, and mason.[27, 38] Certain postures also tend to predispose an individual to TOS. These include "droopy" shoulders,[39] in which the individual has shoulders that tend to hang very low (Fig. 9–9), forward head posture (see Chap. 14), and round shoulders (see Chap. 14).

For the purpose of this chapter, classification is by the major sites of entrapments of the neurovascular bundle along its course from the intervertebral foramen of C5–T1 (though variations exist which may include C4 or T2, or both[40]) into the upper extremity. There are three main areas of entrapment: the interscalene triangle, the costoclavicular space and under the pectoralis minor muscle near its attachment to the coracoid process (see Fig. 9–10).

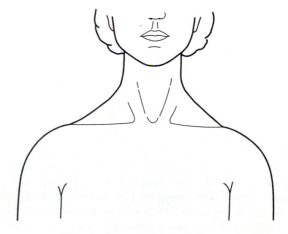

Figure 9–9. "Droopy" shoulders.

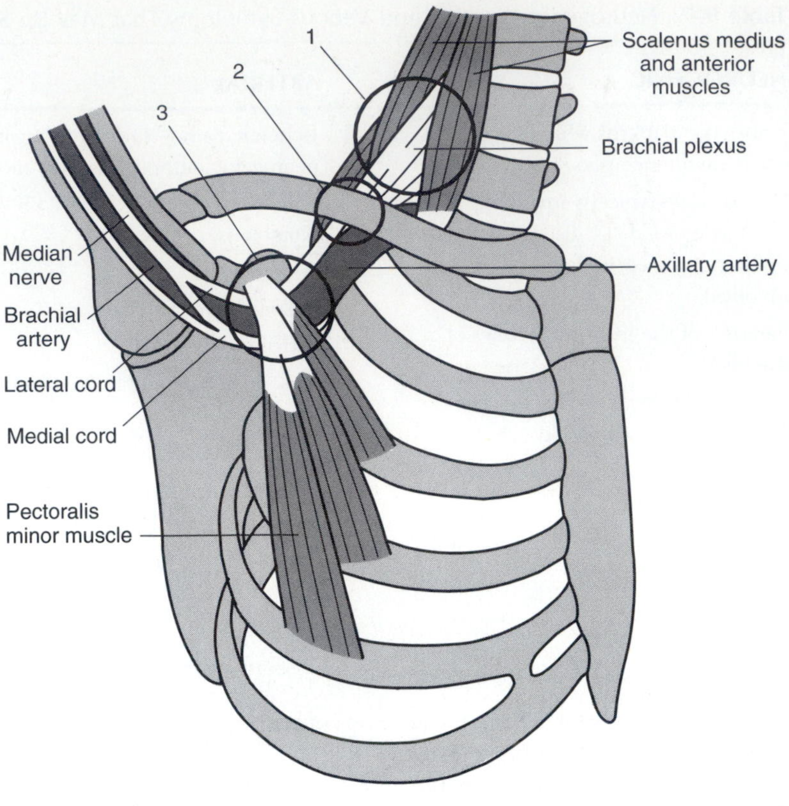

Figure 9–10. The three major entrapment sites in thoracic outlet syndrome: (1) interscalene triangle; (2) costoclavicular space; (3) space under the attachment of the pectoralis minor.

(Adapted from Travell JG, Simons DG. Myofascial Pain and Dysfunction: The Trigger Point Manual. Baltimore, Md: Williams & Wilkins; 1983:604.)

Scalenus Anticus Syndrome

The first site of entrapment is the interscalene triangle. The nerve roots of C5–T1 exit the neck from the intervertebral foramina and join to form the brachial plexus. The plexus then, along with the subclavian artery, passes through the interscalene triangle. The boundaries of this triangle are the middle scalene laterally, the anterior scalene medially, and the first rib inferiorly. The subclavian vein is not involved at this entrapment site as it usually passes anterior to the anterior scalene muscle. The brachial plexus or the subclavian artery can become entrapped here, although involvement of the artery is actually uncommon.[29]

Entrapment at this site can be accentuated by the presence of a cervical rib, although this anomaly is by no means necessary for symptom production.[29] If the cervical ribs are large, there is a greater likelihood of arterial involvement.[41]

> **!** CLINICAL PEARL

The presence of a cervical rib is not always associated with the presence of thoracic outlet syndrome. Only 5 to 10 percent of the people with cervical ribs are symptomatic.[27, 31] However, cervical ribs may be a contributing compressive factor in subclavian artery aneurysms. Nearly 50 percent of patients with subclavian artery aneurysm have a fully developed cervical rib. Most others generally have a different type of bony anomaly. Subclavian arterial damage under the age of 60 without a bony anomaly is unusual.[42] Some patients greater than 60 years of age may develop atherosclerotic subclavian aneurysms unrelated to bony abnormalities. Thus, if a cervical rib is noted on the radiograph, a thorough history should be taken to evaluate the suspicion of subclavian arterial involvement and aneurysm development.

In some cases, fibromuscular bands can develop between the anterior and middle scalene muscles or connecting from the first rib to a cervical rib or elongated C7 transverse process.[28] These may contribute to entrapment at this site; however, in the presence of normal function, these are unlikely to cause this form of TOS, as congenital bands are present in greater than 50 percent of the population and less then 1 percent of the population develops TOS.[28] Presence of scalenus minimus muscle may also contribute to entrapment.[28, 29]

The most important factors in the development of this syndrome are a combination of joint dysfunction of the first costotransverse joint and hypertonicity or adhesions in the scalene muscles. This can decrease the space available for the brachial plexus and restrict mobility of the area. Neurological symptoms predominate and most commonly relate to irritation, compression, or stretch of the lower trunk of the brachial plexus (C8 and T1).

Costoclavicular Syndrome

From the interscalene triangle, the brachial plexus and subclavian artery pass into the costoclavicular space where they are joined by the subclavian vein after it passes anterior to the anterior scalene muscle (Fig. 9–10). This is the second main area of entrapment. As the clavicle is depressed or the first rib elevated, the size of the costoclavicular space is reduced.[29] This may compress, irritate, or stretch the brachial plexus, the subclavian artery, or the subclavian vein as they pass between the first rib and the clavicle. The space can be narrowed by elevation of the first rib from scalene hypertonicity. The entrapment can be exacerbated by joint dysfunction of the sternoclavicular joint, as this joint serves as the fulcrum around which the clavicle elevates during activities involving the upper extremity. Restriction of this motion can lead to failure of the space to adequately expand during arm movements. Changes in the normal shape of either the first rib or clavicle resulting from postfracture callus formation may be a contributing factor to entrapment at this site.

Neurological symptoms are similar to those of the scalenus anticus syndrome. Arterial symptoms are as outlined in Table 9–7. Venous involvement is far more likely at this site, and this can be of serious concern. Venous signs and symptoms will include swelling of the entire limb, nonpitting edema, ecchymosis, stiffness of the fingers, cyanosis, and fatigue. This type of involvement is commonly seen in weight lifters, competitive swimmers, baggage handlers, and amateur wrestlers—individuals involved in vigorous physical activity with a dominance of the upper extremities.[43] If thrombosis occurs, it can lead to pulmonary embolus, so it is essential to recognize this syndrome and refer the patient for immediate anticoagulation therapy.

! CLINICAL PEARL

If venous symptoms are intermittent and disappear with rest and dependency of the arm, thrombosis has probably not yet occurred. However, if the symptoms are constant and do not change with rest and dependency, it is likely a thrombus has formed. Also, the thrombosed vein may be palpable in the axilla as a thickened cord. These findings strongly suggest venous thrombosis and the patient should be immediately referred.

Contributing factors particular to the costoclavicular syndrome include pseudoarthrosis of the clavicle; callus formation of the clavicle or first rib; malunion, nonunion, or comminuted fracture of the clavicle; bifid clavicle; and exostosis of either the first rib or clavicle. Also, carrying heavy loads or backpack usage may be aggravating.

Hyperabduction

After leaving the costoclavicular space, the three cords of the brachial plexus and the subclavian artery and vein pass into the axilla under the insertion of the pectoralis minor tendon on the coracoid process (see Fig. 9–10). At the point where they enter the axillary fossa, the subclavian artery and vein become the axillary artery and vein. At this third main site of entrapment, the neurovascular bundle may become compressed, irritated, or stretched, especially when the arm is elevated or abducted.

A fascial axillary sheath binds together the components of the brachial plexus and the axillary vessels as they pass the coracoid process under the insertion of the pectoralis minor muscle. Usually, in the upright anatomical position, little if any contact occurs between this axillary sheath and the pectoralis minor tendon or the coracoid process. When the arm is abducted and externally rotated, however, the neurovascular structures approach the coracoid process and this bone becomes a fulcrum around which the neurovascular structures stretch. The greater the abduction and external rotation, the more the neurovascular bundle will be stretched around the coracoid process. If the pectoralis minor muscle has muscle tightness (see Chaps. 4 and 19), contact between the neurovascular bundle and tendon and bone will occur sooner in the movement, and the stretch will be greater in degree. The stretch will be further accentuated if, in addition, tension is placed on the brachial plexus at one of the more proximal entrapment sites.

Neurological symptoms usually tend to be intermittent and only felt with hyperabduction of the arm.[38] Symptoms of pain and paresthesia may involve the lateral or medial cords.[44] Transient ischemia and edema may be present in some patients.[38] Symptoms may increase and the radial pulse may weaken or disappear with hyperabduction of the arm. Sleep postures involving the arm being held overhead may awaken the patient at night. Round shouldered posture (see Chap. 14) is particularly important as a predisposing factor in hyperabduction syndrome, as is tends to lead to tightness in the pectoralis minor.

CERVICAL SPONDYLOTIC MYELOPATHY

Cervical spondylotic myelopathy (CSM) is the most serious and disabling condition that results from the degenerative process in the cervical spine.[45] Its pathophysiology is identical to that of LCS, except that, in addition to (or instead of) osteophytes encroaching into the lateral canal, the encroachment occurs in the central canal, causing irritation or compression of the spinal cord. This is combined with hypertrophy or buckling of the ligamentum flavum (Fig. 9–11). CSM is more common in males and the onset of symptoms is usually insidious, although it can be precipitated by major or minor trauma.[21]

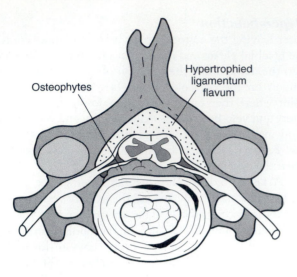

Figure 9–11. Cervical spondylotic myelopathy.

CSM is classified according to the anatomical location of the lesion.[46] This classification is as follows:

1. *Lateral.* This involves the nerve root only and is identical to what is referred to in this chapter as LCS.
2. *Medial.* This involves compression or irritation to the spinal cord without involvement of the nerve roots.
3. *Combined.* This involves a combination of compression or irritation to the spinal cord and the nerve root.
4. *Vascular.* This is the least common and involves compression of the anterior spinal artery, the posterior spinal arteries, or the radicular arteries, or all three.

The clinical picture of CSM is highly variable and depends on the site and level of the lesion.[47] The symptoms often begin as hypersensitivity and clumsiness in the hands and feet and a feeling of "tightness" in the legs, owing to spasticity. Many patients may also experience hyperalgesia in the arms or legs that is set off by the touch of the clothes on the skin. There may be sensory and motor loss at the level of compression with combined CSM, resulting from local radiculopathy, and there may be wasting in the hands. But upper motor neuron signs predominate below the level of the lesion. This manifests as weakness, difficulty with heel walk, hyperreflexia (although this may not be evident in the elderly patient), upgoing toes, positive Hoffman's sign (see Chap. 17), and pronator drift. There also may be signs of posterior column involvement, with loss of deep touch, vibration, and joint position sense. The patient may have difficulty maintaining Romberg's position (see Chap. 17) and may exhibit a wide-based gait. L'Hermitte's sign (see Chap. 17) may be present, with "electric shock" type pain extending into the extremities with cervical flexion.

It is not uncommon for the lower extremity findings to be asymmetrical, with hyperreflexia and upgoing toes on one side and normal findings on the other.[48] The patient may complain of pain in the lower back or legs, making the diagnosis more difficult.

The patient with CSM can develop signs of autonomic dysfunction, including abnormalities in function of the bowel, bladder or sexual organs.[49] This is an ominous sign that necessitates immediate surgical consult.

Plain film radiographs will demonstrate advanced degeneration, usually at multiple levels, and MRI will generally show the central stenosis. It is important to note, however, that there will often be several levels of stenosis evident on MRI and localization of the level of compression may need to be made based on examination findings. This will be discussed in more detail later in the chapter.

PATIENT ASSESSMENT AND DIFFERENTIAL DIAGNOSIS

HISTORY

The majority of patients with true cervical radiculopathy will have a herniated nucleus pulposus as the cause. HNP is followed in frequency by LCS. However, it is important that the physician not assume the presence of HNP in these patients, as the cause may be a serious medical or surgical condition that requires immediate attention.

In investigating the presence of possible cervical radiculopathy, differentiating it from other disorders that can cause similar symptoms, and identifying the involved root level, the history and examination are of paramount importance. In most cases, the diagnosis can be made without advanced testing. The principles guiding the workup of these patients are the same as those presented in Chapter 17 and revolve around three questions:

1. Are there any red flags for serious disease?
2. What is (are) the primary pain generator(s)?
3. What has gone wrong with this person as a whole that would cause the primary pain generator(s) to generate pain?

Rule Out Red Flags

There are several historical factors that help to increase the level of suspicion of the presence of serious disease, particularly tumor or infection. Younger or older patients who complain of neck and arm pain are more likely to have tumor or infection than middle-aged patients. Although the majority of patients in these age groups with true cervical radiculopathy will have HNP or LCS, with a patient who is under 20 years of age or over 50, suspicion should be raised of the possibility of tumor or infection.

As the most common extradural tumor that occurs in the cervical spine is metastatic disease,[25] a history of cancer should raise the level of suspicion that this may be the cause of the patient's radiculopathy. This particularly relates to the patient with a recent history of carcinoma of the breast, thyroid, or gastrointestinal tract.

It is important to ask the patient if he or she has had a recent infectious illness or fever, or constitutional symptoms, as this may suggest the presence of infection. Infection should also be suspected in a patient who is an intravenous drug user, has tested positive for human immunodeficiency virus (HIV), or whose immune system may be compromised by prolonged use of corticosteroids or recent transplant. Constitutional symptoms in the presence of recent unexplained weight loss suggest the possibility of tumor.

It is important to ask the patient what specific factors aggravate or relieve the pain. With HNP, LCS, or pseudoradiculopathy, the patient will usually have identified distinct movements or positions that increase or decrease the symptoms. If the patient reports that the pain remains unchanged despite alterations in position or movement, tumor or infection should be suspected.

Upper extremity vascular symptoms should be looked for, as their presence suggests thrombosis or embolization of the subclavian artery or blockage of the subclavian vein. Finally, if the patient reports lower extremity symptoms in addition to the neck and arm pain, it is important to consider the possibility of CSM or other spinal cord involvement. Table 9–8 lists the primary historical red flags in patients with neck and arm pain.

Identify the Pain Generator(s)

The history can also help localize the primary pain generator(s). Age is an important factor in differentiating radiculopathy related to HNP from that relating to LCS, although, as with virtually all the historical and examination findings presented here, age is not at all definitive in this differential. In general, however, patients with radiculopathy who are under 40 years of age are more likely to have HNP as the cause, whereas those over 50 are more likely to have LCS. Between 40 and 50, either condition could be present. Pseudoradiculopathy can occur at any age.

Table 9–8: Red Flags for Potentially Serious Disease in Patients with History of Neck and Arm Pain

FINDING	SUGGESTIVE OF
Age over 50 or under 20 years	Tumor or infection
History of cancer	Metastatic disease
Constitutional symptoms such as recent fever, chills, or unexplained weight loss	Infection or tumor
Recent bacterial infection, IV drug use, or immune suppression, such as from corticosteroids, transplant, or HIV	Infection
Pain that has no mechanical exacerbating or remitting factors	Infection or tumor
Symptoms in both the upper and lower extremities	Myelopathy
Venous symptoms	Subclavian venous thrombosis

It is often said that pain in patients with radiculopathy is well localized, sharp, shooting, and limited to a single dermatome, whereas pain referred from deep tissues is dull, diffuse, poorly localized, and follows a scleretogenous pattern. This, in the most technical sense, is true and, in the laboratory, if a nerve root is stimulated, the pain will be described as well localized, sharp, and shooting and will be limited to a single dermatome. And when deep tissues are injected, the pain is usually described as dull, diffuse, and poorly localized and will follow a scleretome.[50–53] Unfortunately, however, patients do not present in a laboratory, but, rather, in the "real world" and, more often than not, those with radiculopathy do not describe their pain with the classic "textbook" descriptors. While there are many patients whose pain follows a specific dermatome, in most cases the pain is described as deep, dull, diffuse, and poorly localized, probably because it represents scleretogenous referral of pain from irritation to the dural sleeve.[54] This makes the differential from pain related to pseudoradiculopathy more difficult. However, there are often subtle clues that can help in this differential.

Pain arising from radiculopathy is generally more disturbing to the patient than that from pseudoradiculopathy. The patient will often have a sense that something significantly wrong is occurring. He or she will tend to engage in more intense pain behaviors such as rubbing, grimacing, and moving gingerly. The patient may even strike the arm with the other hand for relief. The arm pain will frequently be more severe than the neck pain. Also, there is a much greater likelihood of antalgia. This probably arises from pain that is arising from the annular fibers of the disc rather than the nerve root, and must be differentiated from disc derangement (see Chap. 26 and the discussion that follows under examination). Patients whose pain is arising from joint dysfunction or TrPs, or both, will tend to have a less intense reaction to the pain, even though it can often be quite severe. They will also be less likely to exhibit antalgia. Of course, the absence of these findings does not rule out the possibility of radiculopathy, as if the pain is of lower severity, the patient's report and behavior will not be as distinct.

> ## ❗ CLINICAL PEARL
>
> As has been stated in other chapters, when you see antalgia, think disc! It is not uncommon for patients to present with marked antalgia without pain. Our experience is that this usually relates to acute disc derangement which, for some reason, causes nociceptive impulses that are of sufficient intensity to cause reflex spasm, but do not reach cortical levels. These patients typically respond well to a McKenzie approach (see Chap. 26).

The pain of cervical radiculopathy will usually improve with flexion of the neck and become worse with extension, although if chin retraction is performed prior to extension, this may relieve the arm pain. As Schultz[55] has noted, an important clue that strongly suggests the presence of radiculopathy is when the patient reports that certain arm positions dramatically relieve the pain. If the patient reports that the pain is relieved by pulling the arm into adduction, there is a good likelihood of C5 radiculopathy. If the patient reports that the pain is relieved by raising the arm overhead, there is a good likelihood that he or she has a C6 radiculopathy. If pressing the hand against the chest provides relief, there is a good likelihood of C7 radiculopathy. However, raising the arm overhead may be relieving with radiculopathy at any level, as well as with any of the thoracic outlet syndromes.[56] In addition, coughing, sneezing, or straining, because these maneuvers increase intrathecal pressure, may increase the pain of radiculopathy.

In a patient whose complaints include that of sensory changes, identification of the specific location of the changes is helpful. If the sensory loss covers only one specific dermatome, the diagnosis of radiculopathy and the level of involvement can be identified. If the sensory changes cover more than one dermatome, radiculopathy is less likely and TOS or peripheral neuropathy should be considered. If they involve both the upper extremity and the lower extremity or the trunk, myelopathy is suggested.

> ## ❗ CLINICAL PEARL
>
> It may be difficult at times to differentiate between sensory findings of the ulnar nerve and the C8 nerve root, as they both innervate the fifth digit and the medial aspect of the hand. However, always question the patient regarding extension of numbness or paresthesia above the wrist, and check this on examination, as the C8 dermatome includes the distal forearm above the wrist, while the ulnar nerve does not.

Historical factors that are useful for identifying the primary pain generator(s) are provided in Table 9–9.

EXAMINATION

Rule Out Red Flags

On examination, neurological status is of utmost importance. Significant weakness (weaker than 4/5) suggests the potential for permanent motor loss and may necessitate immediate surgical consult. Significant sensory findings or complete reflex absence are less ominous. Upgoing toes or Hoffman's reflex, or both, suggests upper motor neuron involvement possibly related to myelopathy. Horner's syndrome (ptosis, pupillary constriction, and loss of sweating over the forehead, all on the same side) suggests the possible presence of Pancoast tumor in the upper apices of the lung.

Fever strongly suggests the presence of infection, and, in these cases, infection should be assumed until ruled out.

Table 9–9: Historical Factors That Are Useful in Identifying the Primary Pain Generator(s)

FINDING	SUGGESTIVE OF	AS OPPOSED TO	BUT CONSIDER
Age below 40 years	HNP	LCS	Does not rule out pseudoradiculopathy, tumor, or infection
Age over 50 years	LCS	HNP	Does not rule out pseudoradiculopathy, CSM, tumor, or infection
Pain described as sharp, shooting, superficial, and localized to a specific dermatome	Radiculopathy	Pseudoradiculopathy	Does not rule out CSM; does not differentiate HNP from LCS
Pain described as severe and uncommonly disturbing	Radiculopathy	Pseudoradiculopathy	Does not completely rule out pseudoradiculopathy; does not rule out CSM; does not differentiate HNP from LCS
Pain increased with extension, decreased with flexion	Radiculopathy	Pseudoradiculopathy	Does not rule out CSM; does not differentiate HNP from LCS
Pain relieved by pulling arm into adduction	C5 radiculopathy	Radiculopathy at other levels	Does not rule out TOS; does not differentiate HNP from LCS
Pain relieved when elevating arm overhead	C6 radiculopathy	Radiculopathy at other levels	Does not completely rule out C5 or C7 radiculopathy, TOS, or pseudoradiculopathy
Pain relieved with hand pressed against the chest	C7 radiculopathy	Radiculopathy at other levels	Does not rule out TOS
Increased pain with coughing, sneezing, or straining	Radiculopathy	Pseudoradiculopathy, TOS	Does not rule out CSM; does not differentiate HNP from LCS
Sensory changes limited to single dermatome	Radiculopathy	Pseudoradiculopathy, TOS	Does not completely rule out TOS; does not differentiate between HNP and LCS
Sensory changes covering more than one dermatome	TOS or peripheral neuropathy	Radiculopathy	Does not differentiate between TOS and peripheral neuropathy
Presence of vascular symptoms	TOS	Radiculopathy or non-TOS pseudoradiculopathy	Vascular symptoms are uncommon in TOS, so cannot be relied upon for differential

CSM, cervical spondylotic myelography; HNP, herniated nucleus pulposus; LCS, lateral canal stenosis; TOS, thoracic outlet syndrome.

A palpable mass in the anterior cervical spine suggests infection or tumor. The presence of nonpitting edema in the upper extremity, especially accompanied by ecchymosis and a palpable cord in the axilla, strongly suggests venous effort thrombosis and should prompt immediate referral for anticoagulant therapy. Table 9–10 lists the primary red flags for serious disease that can be found on examination.

Identify the Pain Generator(s)

Two useful diagnostic tests in detecting cervical radiculopathy are the cervical compression and cervical distraction tests[57-58] (see Chap. 17). With these tests, reproduction of arm pain with compression and relief with distraction are highly suggestive of the presence of radiculopathy. The absence of positive findings on these tests, however, does not rule out the diagnosis. Another popular and useful test is the arm elevation test, or Bakody's sign[56, 58-62] (see Chap. 17). With this maneuver, the patient elevates the painful arm and places the palm of his or her hand on top of his or her head. This action is thought to cause relief of pain due to decreased traction on the brachial plexus; thus, relief of arm pain with this maneuver suggests the presence of radiculopathy. But the arm elevation test may also be positive with TOS.

In patients with TOS, there may be a positive Tinel's sign (tapping with a reflex hammer) in the supraclavicular fossa. With arterial involvement, a bruit may be heard on auscultation. Also, in a patient with hyperabduction syndrome, holding the arm elevated in hyperabduction may reproduce the symptoms within 1 to 2 minutes.

Table 9–10: Red Flags for Potentially Serious Disease in Patients With Neck and Arm Pain on Examination

FINDING	SUGGESTIVE OF
Weakness of 4/5 or less	Risk of permanent motor loss
Upgoing toes or other pathological reflexes	Myelopathy
Horner's syndrome	Pancoast tumor or other space-occupying lesion in the lower cervical or upper thoracic spine
Fever	Infection
Palpable mass	Fever or infection
Upper extremity edema	Subclavian venous thrombosis
Palpatory cord in the axilla	Subclavian venous thrombosis

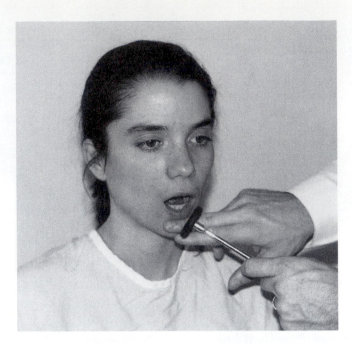

Figure 9–12. The jaw jerk reflex.

The Valsalva maneuver (see Chap. 17) is often positive in patients with radiculopathy. This test will create increased intrathecal pressure and may aggravate the pain of radiculopathy. The brachial plexus tension test (see Chap. 17) may help to differentiate radiculopathy or TOS from pseudoradiculopathy, as may the shoulder depression test (see Chap. 17).

Of obvious importance in the examination of the patient with neck and arm pain is the neurological examination (see Chap. 17). With true radiculopathy, there will often be detectable signs of neurological deficit, such as sensory loss to pinprick along a specific dermatome, decreased or absent muscle stretch reflex, or motor loss. These findings, however, are by no means necessary to make the diagnosis, as radiculopathy, particularly if it is related to irritation and not compression, may cause pain without neurological deficit.

Certain individual neurological tests are important with the neck and arm pain patient. These include Hoffman's sign, L'Hermitte's sign, and the examination for plantar response (see Chap. 17), all of which may suggest spinal cord involvement and raise the suspicion of the presence of CSM. In addition, for the patient with suspected CSM, it is important on examination to try to localize the level of the lesion, as radiographs and MRI will often reveal multiple levels of stenosis, only one of which may be symptomatic. Typically, the muscle stretch reflexes are hyperactive with spinal cord compression due to CSM. However, this does not differentiate spinal cord involvement from lesion of higher centers. The jaw jerk is a useful sign to rule out involvement of the central nervous system above the foramen magnum. With this reflex, the patient holds his or her mouth slightly open and the examiner's index finger is placed on the chin (Fig. 9–12). The finger is then tapped with a hammer. Normally, the jaw should open slightly, then return to position. With involvement of the corticobulbar tract or above, there is an abnormally brisk closing of the mouth in response to the tap.

The jaw jerk rules out involvement of the brain stem or above, but, as C5 is the highest cord level that is assessed in the routine reflex examination, the lesion can be located anywhere between C5 and the brain stem. The scapulohumeral reflex[63] is helpful for further localization. With this, the reflex hammer is used to tap either over the acromion or over the spine of the scapula (Fig. 9–13). Abduction of the arm or elevation of the scapula, respectively, is positive for localization of the lesion to the C1–3 cord segments.

In those patients with sensory deficit, the lesion can be localized by identifying the sensory level. This can be done by touching the patient lightly with a pin at a region in the thoracic spine at which he or she cannot feel the sharpness. The examiner then touches areas superior to this in a stepwise fashion until a level is reached at which the patient is able to feel the pinprick. The junction between the sensitive area and the area with hypesthesia is the sensory level, and generally corresponds to the level of cord compression.

Motion palpation is the primary method by which joint dysfunction is detected (see Chap. 13). This is important in assessing for the presence of pseudoradiculopathy although, as has been discussed, joint dysfunction is almost ubiquitous in patients with neck and arm pain. The most important levels to be examined are those from C4–5 to T3–4. Of particular importance, especially in those with TOS and scalene TrPs, are the first costotransverse joints. Palpation of the scalene muscles for TrPs is of paramount importance in the assessment for the presence of pseudoradiculopathy, as reproduction of the pain upon palpation of TrPs in these muscles is the hallmark of the diagnosis. Of course, patients with TOS related to the scalene muscles

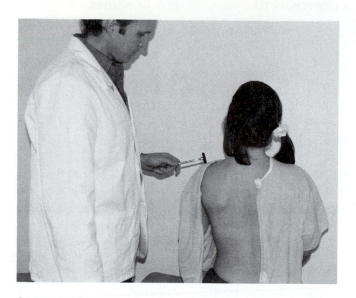
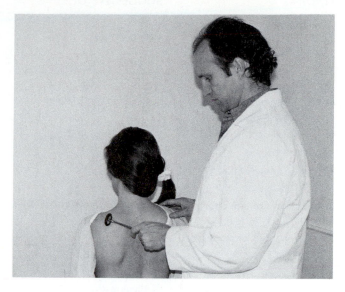

A   **B**

Figure 9–13. The scapulohumeral reflex. **A.** Elicited from the acromion process. **B.** Elicited from the superior angle of the scapula.

will often have scalene TrPs as well, so complete examination is necessary to determine the coexistence of scalene TrPs and TOS. Examination findings that help identify the pain generator(s) are listed in Table 9–11.

Identify the Dysfunctional Chain and the Key Link

This is where the commonalties of the syndromes of neck and arm pain become apparent. There often is a common component of locomotor dysfunction that can underlie and perpetuate any of these conditions. Probably the most common individual finding is that of joint dysfunction. Joint dysfunction can serve as both pain generator and key dysfunction. With true radiculopathy, joint dysfunction can most often be found at the level of involvement, but key joint dysfunction may be seen at other levels as well.

Faulty movement patterns (see Chap. 14) are common, particularly shoulder abduction, cervical stability, and breathing. Faulty breathing is particularly prevalent in patients with pseudoradiculopathy related to scalene TrPs and TOS. Faulty hip extension with hyperactivity of the cervical muscles, faulty swallowing, faulty postural foot reaction, and positive stepping test may be found, but less commonly. Postural analysis (see Chap. 14) is particularly important in patients with pseudoradiculopathy, especially those with TOS.

ADVANCED TESTS

In most patients, the physician should be able to arrive at the correct diagnosis without the use of advanced tests. Therefore, most of the time, no advanced imaging tests should be ordered except in specific clinical situations.

Pathoanatomical abnormalities such as HNP, spondylosis, and disc degeneration are frequently noted on imaging tests which have no relevance to symptom generation.[64–72] Unfortunately, these findings are frequently assumed to be the cause of the patient's symptoms. This assumption can lead to delay in appropriate treatment. Also, imaging studies are frequently an unnecessary expense; they frequently do not bear on management decisions. For example, in a middle-aged patient, particularly one between 40 and 50 years of age, with signs and symptoms of radiculopathy, it may seem reasonable to order an MRI for the purpose of differentiating between these diagnoses. But unless surgery is being considered, the management strategy will likely be identical regardless of whether the patient has HNP or LCS. The principles of decision making with regard to advanced tests can be found in Chapter 17.

IMAGING

When imaging is being considered, choosing the correct test is essential. Plain films, although their information is limited, are still often considered the recommended first line of investigation after the decision is made that imaging is necessary. Plain films, including oblique views, are often helpful in demonstrating the presence of LCS by osteophytes (Fig. 9–14). This may be a simple and inexpensive means by which LCS can be differentiated from HNP (although it does not rule out HNP). In patients with suspected CSM, the dimension of the cervical canal can be assessed with plain film radiographs. Sweeney[10] recommends measuring the anterior-to-posterior diameter of the cervical canal on the standard lateral view. For this, the level of the body of C5 is used. The minimum A-to-P

Table 9–11: Examination Findings Helpful in Identifying the Primary Pain Generator(s) in Patients with Neck and Arm Pain

FINDING	SUGGESTIVE OF	AS OPPOSED TO	BUT CONSIDER
Pain radiating into the arm with cervical compression test	Radiculopathy	Pseudoradiculopathy, TOS	Does not rule out CSM; does not differentiate HNP from LCS; negative finding does not rule out radiculopathy
Relief of arm pain with cervical distraction test	Radiculopathy	Pseudoradiculopathy, TOS	Does not rule out CSM; does not differentiate HNP from LCS
Relief of arm pain with the arm elevation test	Radiculopathy or TOS	Pseudoradiculopathy	Does not rule out CSM; does not differentiate HNP from LCS
Reproduction of arm pain with Valsalva maneuver	Radiculopathy	Pseudoradiculopathy, TOS	Does not rule out CSM; does not differentiate HNP from LCS
Reproduction of arm pain with the brachial plexus tension or shoulder depression tests, or both	Radiculopathy, TOS	Pseudoradiculopathy	Does not rule out CSM; does not differentiate HNP from LCS; may cause local pain with scalene TrPs, but will not usually cause radiating arm pain
Sensory changes limited to single dermatome	Radiculopathy	Pseudoradiculopathy, TOS	Does not completely rule out TOS, does not differentiate between HNP and LCS
Sensory changes covering more than one dermatome	TOS or peripheral neuropathy	Radiculopathy	Does not differentiate between TOS and peripheral neuropathy
Diminished or absent muscle stretch reflex	Radiculopathy	Pseudoradiculopathy	Does not rule out TOS or CSM; does not differentiate HNP from LCS
Motor loss	Radiculopathy	Pseudoradiculopathy	Does not rule out TOS or CSM; does not differentiate HNP from LCS
Hyperreflexia, upgoing toes	CSM	Radiculopathy, pseudoradiculopathy, TOS	Does not rule out other spinal cord syndromes or involvement of higher centers
Normal jaw jerk	CSM	Involvement of higher centers	Does not rule out other spinal cord syndromes
Positive scapulohumeral reflex	CSM at cord segments C1–3	Compression at other levels	Only implicates cord levels C1–3 in the presence of a normal jaw jerk
Lower cervical or first costo-transverse joint dysfunction, or both	Commonly found with HNP, LCS, CSM, TOS, and pseudoradiculopathy	Tumor or infection	Does not rule in or out any diagnosis
Scalene TrPs	Pseudoradiculopathy related to scalene TrPs	Radiculopathy	Does not rule out TOS
Relief of arm pain with neck retraction followed by neck extension	Pseudoradiculopathy related to posterior disc derangement	Radiculopathy	Does not completely rule out radiculopathy
Positive Tinel's sign in the supraclavicular fossa	TOS	Radiculopathy, other forms of pseudoradiculopathy	Does not completely rule out radiculopathy or scalene TrPs
Bruit on auscultation over the supraclavicular fossa	Arterial involvement on TOS	Radiculopathy, other forms of pseudoradiculopathy	Often present in normal subjects, so cannot be completely relied upon
Production of hand numbness upon hyperabduction of the arm	Hyperabduction syndrome	Radiculopathy, other forms of TOS	High false positive and false negative rate

CSM, cervical spondylotic myelography; HNP, herniated nucleus pulposus; LCS, lateral canal stenosis, TOS, thoracic outlet syndrome; TrPs, trigger points.

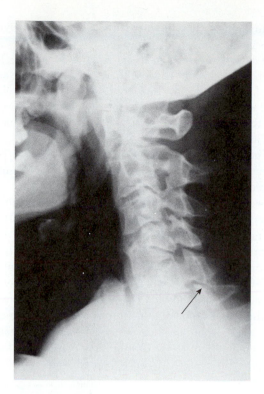

Figure 9–14. Oblique radiograph in a patient with lateral canal stenosis.

diameter of the canal should be no less than 11 to 12 mm (Fig. 9–15).

Given the limitations of plain films to image tissues other than bone, MRI is preferred for full evaluation of the cervical spine (Fig. 9–16). MRI allows for the assessment of bone as well as soft tissue and neural structures. Perhaps more importantly, especially to the surgeon, it allows for

the evaluation of the anatomical relationships between these structures. This is useful for determining surgical approach. MRI can often serve as a single test that helps differentiate HNP, LCS, and CSM, as well as identifying more serious disorders such as tumor, infection, or spinal cord pathology.

When it is suspected that disc derangement is the primary pain generator and this is not clarified on examination of response to loading (see Chap. 26), discography can be useful. This test is expensive and uncomfortable for the patient, but is more sensitive than MRI in detecting disc derangement.[73] With this method, contrast medium is injected into the disc and reproduction of the patients symptoms, along with demonstration of leakage of the contrast medium into the periphery of the disc, suggests the presence of internal disc disruption. Anesthetic can also then be introduced to abolish the symptoms to confirm the diagnosis.[74, 75]

The difficulty with discography is that it is inaccessible to many practitioners and can be quite painful to the patient. In addition, it can quite often be difficult for the patient to determine whether the injection reproduces his or her pain in its entirety. The procedure may also have a significant number of false positives.[76] Still, discography can be a useful tool when clinical examination does not produce a clear diagnosis.

There is little use for CT or myelography by the nonsurgeon in the evaluation of the cervical spine patient.

CLINICAL ELECTRODIAGNOSIS

As a disorder of the peripheral nervous system, cervical radiculopathy can be investigated by electrodiagnostic methods. The techniques that have been used the longest and have the greatest utility are nerve conduction studies and EMG.

Nerve Conduction Studies

Nerve conduction studies evaluate both motor and sensory nerve function. These functions are not evaluated at the

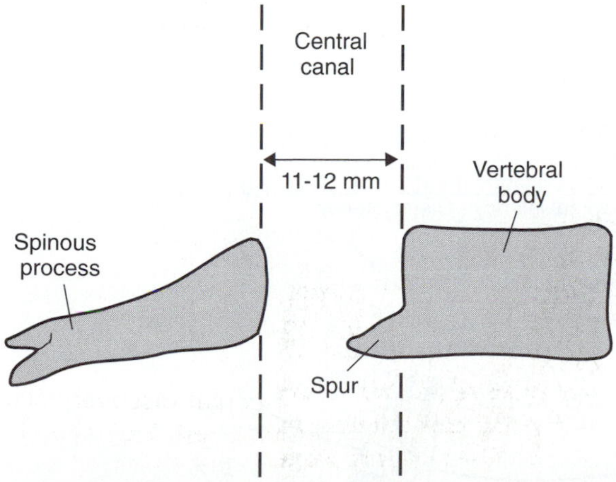

Figure 9–15. The normal central canal diameter in the cervical spine should be no less than 11 to 12 mm.

(Adapted from Cates JR, Soriano MM. Cervical spondylotic myelopathy. J Manipulative Physiol Ther 1995;18(7):471–475.)

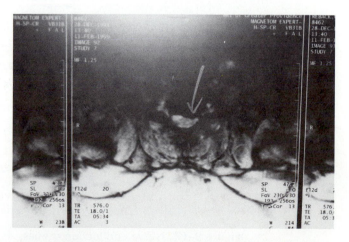

Figure 9–16. MRI of a patient with lateral canal stenosis.

same time as each demands a different technique. Variables that are assessed include amplitude, duration, latency, velocity, and "late reflexes."

Amplitudes represent the amount of electrical energy transmitted along the nerve upon external stimulation. They are measured as the height of the resultant wave form or action potential.

Duration refers to the width of the compound motor action potential (CMAP) or sensory nerve action potential (SNAP).

Latencies represent the time, measured in milliseconds, it takes from stimulation of the nerve until the formation of the sensory or motor action potential. Latencies are classified as *distal* and *proximal*, referring to the distance from the recording electrode to the point at which stimulation takes place. For example, motor latencies of the median nerve would be evaluated with a recording electrode placed over the lateral thenar muscles (abductor pollicis brevis). Stimulations would be performed over the nerve at the wrist, elbow, axilla, and possibly at Erb's point. The distal latency is measured from the wrist. The other stimulation sites would yield proximal latencies. Owing to technical limitations and factors specific to sensory nerve anatomy and physiology, sensory latencies are generally recorded at the distal stimulation site only.

Velocity, referred to as *conduction velocity* (CV) is a calculation of the speed at which an impulse travels along a motor nerve. It reflects the function of the fastest conducting axons of the nerve. CV is calculated using distal and proximal latencies from a nerve. The distal latency is subtracted from the proximal latency. The difference (msec) is divided by the distance between the proximal and distal stimulation sites (mm), measured using a tape measure on the skin surface. The product is the CV, which is given in meters per second (m/s) (Fig. 9–17).

"*Late reflexes*" refer to the *H-reflex* and *F-waves.* These tests are termed "late" because there is a delay in the arrival time of the stimulus to the recording site. The stimulation is performed distally and the impulse first travels proximally to the spinal cord. It then travels distally toward the recording site.

The *H-reflex* is performed in the lower extremity. It is an electrical version of the ankle jerk and is most useful in S1 radiculopathies.

F-waves are performed by supramaximal stimulation of motor nerves. The impulses generated by this stimulation travel both proximally and distally along the nerve. The proximally directed impulses eventually excite the anterior horn cells, which then initiate a distal impulse. The F-wave is formed when this distal impulse travels to the recording site muscle. The value of the F-wave is in its ability to examine conduction in proximal parts of the motor nerve that are not easily evaluated by standard nerve conduction tests. Owing to a variety of factors, however, this test is of only limited value in clinical practice.

Electromyography

EMG refers to the examination of electrical muscle activity. Although surface electrodes have been utilized in some clinical (as opposed to physiological) EMG applications, the standard for this type of examination is the needle electrode. This allows for the precise sampling of individual muscles, a necessity in performing the examination.

The electromyographer carries out the examination only after a thorough clinical evaluation has been com-

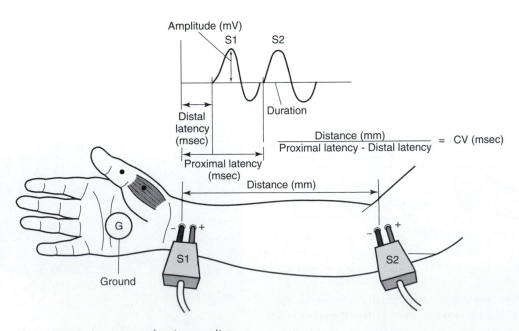

Figure 9–17. Nerve conduction studies.

(Adapted from Wilbourn A, Ferrante M. Clinical electromyography. In: Joynt R, Griggs R, eds. Clinical Neurology. Philadelphia, Pa: Lippincott-Raven; 1997:16.)

pleted. This allows for planning the general outline of the procedure, including the muscles to be sampled. The examination is dynamic in that the electromyographer can alter this plan after the examination has begun in response to the data that are being obtained.

The EMG examination consists of three parts. Electrical activity is first examined during needle insertion. Then spontaneous activity is looked for during rest. Finally, the examinee is asked to voluntarily contract the muscle being tested and the resulting activation of motor unit action potentials (MUAPs) is evaluated.

Patient preparation prior to an EMG examination is critical to obtaining good quality data. Postural comfort and modesty, room temperature, and skin surface cleanliness are all important factors. An often overlooked element is the patient's anxiety level as many patients have heard horror stories about the pain associated with this procedure from "well-meaning" friends and relatives. The electromyographer can attempt to reassure the patient but, in fact, patients' reactions to the pain of these examinations is quite variable. In the field today, the range of explanations is enormous, ranging from "This won't hurt a bit" to "This is a very painful test." While the former is an outright lie, destined to infuriate the patient, the latter may unnecessarily increase the patient's levels of anxiety and almost ensure higher levels of pain perception. An honest and simple statement such as, *"There will be some discomfort during this examination but it is probably not as bad as you are expecting. The needles we use are quite small and I'll do everything I can to complete your examination in the shortest time possible with the least amount of discomfort. Let me know how you are doing,"* is probably the best way to handle this situation.

! CLINICAL PEARL

Clinicians referring patients for EMG examinations may also need to deal with the patient's questions and concerns. Again, honesty is always the best policy and may prevent the return of an irate patient to your office seeking to inflict upon you the same level of pain you so callously visited upon him or her! It is also critical to impress upon the patient the clinical necessity for the proposed procedure and how this need outweighs concerns regarding any associated temporary discomfort.

During needle insertion the muscle should be relaxed. After the skin and underlying tissues are pierced, the needle is advanced in intervals. Insertional activity is the brief burst of electrical activity that occurs due to the resulting mechanical stimulation of muscle fibers. It is a normal finding and lasts no longer that 300 msec. At times, other electrical potentials immediately follow the insertional activity, making it appear longer in duration. This is called *increased insertional activity*. This is seen in a variety of disease processes, although it can be seen in normal subjects as well.[77]

Next, the muscle is examined while at rest. There should be no electrical activity seen in normal muscle. Occasionally, if the needle tip is in close proximity to the muscle end-plate, characteristic activity will be seen. The experienced examiner will be able to differentiate this benign "end-plate noise" from abnormal findings.

Other types of electrical activity seen at rest are considered abnormal. They include *fibrillation* and *fasciculation* potentials, *positive sharp waves*, *complex repetitive discharges*, and others. The reader is referred to an electrodiagnosis text (e.g. ref. 78) for a more complete discussion of these findings.

The final stage in the EMG examination involves patient participation. The examiner instructs the patient to voluntarily contract the muscle under study. As the patient performs the contraction, first lightly and then with greater force, it is possible to see and hear the pattern of recruitment of muscle fibers. At first a single MUAP is seen, and with increased force of contraction, it is joined by others, all firing asynchronously. Eventually the entire screen is filled with MUAPs. This is known as a "full interference pattern." In disease states affecting nerves and muscles, changes to this pattern will be seen. The changes can involve the shapes, size, or rate of firing of the MUAPs.

A recent study by Tsai et al[79] described a technique known as cervical root stimulation. In this technique, a monopolar needle electrode is inserted into the paraspinal muscles and compound MUAPs in distal muscles from the upper extremity are recorded. This technique was compared to conventional EMG studies, node conduction of velocity studies, and F waves. The authors found that while conventional EMG was abnormal in 56.2 percent of the cases, cervical root stimulation was abnormal in 78.1 percent. The authors concluded that this technique was a sensitive method for making a direct evaluation of proximal root conduction and felt it was a good method for presurgical evaluation of patients with cervical radiculopathy. As with many newer tests, only time will tell whether it is truly clinically useful and whether it will be widely adopted.

Clinical Utility of Electrodiagnosis

The usefulness of electrodiagnostics in clinical practice is a difficult subject to address. Although recent articles and books mention the limitations of these procedures, they all, nonetheless, continue to speak of their utility in glowing terms. To a certain extent, this may be due to the fact that the authors of this literature are almost universally clinical electrodiagnosticians who have obvious biases regarding what they do for a living.

It is important that clinicians not in electrodiagnostic practice, be they family practitioners, chiropractors, spine surgeons or others, have a realistic basis for determining the necessity of these procedures and for identifying those instances when truly *strategic* referrals should be made; that is, those for which there is a specific purpose for obtaining an electrodiagnostic study.

History and physical examination will, in the majority of cases, enable the clinician to arrive at a meaningful working diagnosis in patients with neck and arm pain. This being the case, when are electrodiagnostics called for? If the diagnosis is made with a high level of certainty, based on history and physical signs alone, in what situations would an EMG or nerve conduction studies be needed, warranted, or justified?

There are several purposes for which the use of electrodiagnosis can be unequivocally justified:

1. Exact localization of a problem, in order to direct the planning of treatment. This could apply to surgical procedures, injection therapy, and possibly in the application of more conservative modalities. In many cases the use of a diagnostic technique that yields anatomical information (such as MRI) may be more appropriate but, because imaging the peripheral nervous system is difficult, oftentimes physiological data is required.

2. Objective documentation of the existence of a lesion. This is especially helpful when only subjective findings are present in the clinical examination. Certain patients find themselves in the unenviable position of being thought a "hypochondriac" or "malingerer" by health care providers, third party payors, attorneys, and others involved in the health care system. Positive findings on an electrodiagnostic examination can make a serious difference to such a patient.

3. There are times when documentation is needed for reasons that are not strictly clinical. These would include issues of impairment assessment, employment suitability and risk, and other forensic applications. Although mentioned previously as a cautionary factor, it would require a rare naivete to not recognize that there are certain instances when medico-legal factors will prevail in the decision to order electrodiagnostic tests.

Many physicians would maintain that cases in which an exact diagnosis cannot be made after the history and physical or clinical examination absolutely require advanced diagnostic testing. However, while certain clinical situations may demand an exact anatomical and physiological diagnosis, there are many others in which a certain degree of relative uncertainty is well tolerated. In these cases, obtaining electrodiagnostic testing may be delayed for a reasonable period of time without any adverse effect to the patient. History and examination findings may provide sufficient data to allow the clinician to make certain decisions. Factors such as onset of the problem, subsequent course, level of symptomatology, and the patient's reaction to the problem may enable the nonsurgeon to adopt a diagnostic posture of "watchful waiting" while providing, if possible, either curative or palliative treatment directed toward a reasonable working diagnosis that is based on clinical findings. This is obviously determined much of the time by the type of treatment proposed. Many treatments such as manipulation, exercise, and anti-inflammatory drug therapies are relatively benign and may reasonably be instituted as a trial in testing the working diagnosis. A thorough understanding of the natural history of the condition is also required. This understanding allows the clinician to employ a trial of treatment and to know when this trial has been given sufficient time to have an effect on the patient's condition, and when additional diagnostic workup is needed.

Electrodiagnosis in Cervical Radiculopathy

Although patients with suspected radiculopathy are commonly referred for EMG and nerve conduction studies, the examination's usefulness is limited. Its major contribution is in ruling out other potential causes of the patient's complaints.

Nerve conduction studies are usually of little help in the diagnosis of cervical radiculopathy. Since fibers proximal to the dorsal root ganglion are affected with this condition, sensory nerve conduction studies, which assess postganglionic fibers, are normal. Motor nerve conductions are rarely affected, and if they are, only the amplitudes will be altered. But since muscles are innervated by multiple roots and compressive lesions rarely affect all fibers of a nerve root, it is extremely unlikely to find decreased amplitudes in a nerve root compression involving only one root.

The EMG portion of the examination may provide assistance in documenting a radicular lesion. The major finding is fibrillation potentials. These should be present in multiple muscles innervated by the nerve root in question. Muscles innervated by nerve roots just above and below the lesioned root should be unaffected. Additional confirmation is provided when the affected muscles within the same myotome are innervated by different peripheral nerves.

Examination of the paraspinal muscles is a necessity in suspected radiculopathy. Since these muscles receive innervation via the posterior primary ramus, any abnormalities found during examination effectively localize the lesion to a site proximal to the plexus and within the intraspinal canal.[78] Fibrillation potentials are, again, the most common abnormality found. This finding is not pathognomonic for radiculopathy, however, as it may also be seen in primary disorders of muscle. In addition, a radiculopathy does not always produce paraspinal muscle fibrillations.

The usefulness of EMG examination is affected by that point in the natural history of the disease the test is ordered. Fibrillation potentials rarely develop in less than 3 weeks of onset of cervical radiculopathy. To avoid equivocal test results, patients should not been sent for EMG examination and nerve conduction studies for at least 3 weeks. There is also a point after which reinervation of previously partially denervated muscles will occur. This occurs at approximately 6 months for muscles supplied by cervical roots. Test results after 6 months may therefore be un-

Table 9–12: Guidelines for Ordering Clinical Electrodiagnosis in Suspected Cervical Radiculopathy

1. When the exact location of the lesion must be known in order to plan treatment and the location cannot be determined by examination and imaging
2. When the exact diagnosis is uncertain based on history, examination and imaging and there is potential danger to the patient in not knowing the diagnosis (i.e., suspicion of infarction, metastatic disease, etc.)
3. When documentation of the presence of a lesion is required for medico-legal purposes
4. When it is impossible, based on history, examination, and imaging, to determine if the patient's symptoms are due to a local disease process (i.e., radiculopathy) or a more general one (i.e. polyneuropathy)

reliable. Table 9–12 summarizes guidelines for use of electrodiagnosis in cervical radiculopathy.

MANAGEMENT

As with all conditions involving the cervical spine, management should be founded on the principle of doing the least that is necessary to get the job done (see Chap. 28). This especially applies to the cervical radiculopathy patient, as oftentimes the pain is quite severe, the patient's distress quite dramatic, and the imaging findings quite alarming. Yet, this does not necessarily mean that invasive or long-term treatment is required. It is imperative that the physician avoid letting these factors drive his or her management decisions, as this can often lead to excessive care that is not only cost-inefficient, but often adds to the patient's distress and illness behavior.

Most patients with cervical radiculopathy will respond well to nonoperative management. The role of the nonsurgeon is to maximize recovery, help the patient avoid surgery, and recognize the need for surgical intervention if it arises.

CERVICAL RADICULOPATHY RELATED TO HNP

Cervical radiculopathy caused by HNP is, in most cases, a self-limiting condition with a favorable natural history. This does not necessarily mean, however, that patients with this condition will invariably become pain free in a short time. It does mean that in most cases the radiculopathy itself is destined to resolve by the very nature of the tissue that is creating the nerve root irritation or compression; the nucleus pulposus is primarily composed of water and, as such, will become absorbed with time when exposed to the environment outside its normal confines within the anulus.[80] Still, there are some patients who ex-

perience ongoing, long-term pain that is sometimes quite severe. In these patients, this pain does not generally relate to the radiculopathy itself but, rather, arises from related locomotor system dysfunction. Therefore, the management strategy for acute radiculopathy related to HNP revolves around five goals:

1. Monitoring neurological status
2. Reducing pain as quickly as possible
3. Hastening resolution faster than would occur by natural history
4. Correcting any residual joint dysfunction, muscle dysfunction, and faulty movement patterns
5. Improving cervical stability mechanisms to minimize microtrauma during healing and prevent reinjury

There is a great deal of variability in the clinical picture of patients with cervical radiculopathy related to HNP. Unlike in the lumbar spine, where the disc is subjected to great compression forces even in normal activities, cervical HNP usually resolves without the need for a great deal of treatment. There are certain notable exceptions to this, the most important being traumatically induced cervical HNP, as often occurs with whiplash injuries. But in the nontraumatic HNP, watchful waiting is usually the most important component of the management strategy. This often means that little or no treatment is necessary beyond self-care.

> **! CLINICAL PEARL**
>
> Ironically, sometimes even the most painful radiculopathy related to HNP requires far less treatment than a more moderate level of pain that is related to, for example, joint dysfunction. This shows that clinicians must not use the patient's level of pain or distress to determine the intensity of treatment.

Acute Stage

The patient should be seen at least weekly for the first 3 weeks to monitor neurological status, as progression of neurological deficit can, at times, be rapid. A greater frequency (3 to 5 times per week) may be required if significant concomitant joint and/or muscle dysfunction is being treated.

In the beginning stages, reducing nociception as quickly as possible is essential. A home regimen of ice is recommended. It is important, obviously, that the ice be placed over the area of the nerve root affected, not over the area of most intense pain. The ice should be applied for a full half-hour to allow for penetration of the cold to the area of the intervertebral foramen. A half-hour of application followed by 1 hour without ice is ideal, and the patient should be instructed to adhere as closely as possible to half-hour on, 1-hour off intervals. Sometimes electrical modalities such as interferential current, high volt galvanic, or microcurrent are effective for temporary pain relief, but these modalities should be limited to the acute phase, only, and used only as an adjunct to the more active forms of care discussed in the following paragraphs.[81]

Drug therapy can often be an important adjunction in acute management. Nonsteroidal anti-inflammatory drugs (NSAIDs) are perhaps the most commonly used agents for both their anti-inflammatory and analgesic properties.[82] NSAIDs can be obtained both by prescription and over the counter. Analgesics such as acetaminophen or opioids, while not providing an anti-inflammatory effect, may provide significant pain relief, and in some patients may be preferable to NSAIDs, especially in a patient who experiences gastrointestinal distress when taking NSAIDs. Muscle relaxants have been demonstrated to provide significant relief,[83] however their use is controversial because of questions regarding the appropriateness of inhibiting the central nervous system to reduce muscle spasm when this spasm has a protective purpose.[82] A single epidural steroid injection is often effective in rapidly reducing pain.[82a] This should be considered in the patient with severe pain while other treatments are being applied to facilitate resolution. This approach should not, however, be used in isolation of treatment approaches that are designed to improve function. Narcotics may be necessary in those patients whose acute pain does not respond adequately to initial acute care measures. Use of these agents should be strictly time limited, and they are inappropriate for chronic pain patients, as they frequently contribute to increased pain perception in these patients.[82]

An evaluation of symptomatic response to loading (McKenzie evaluation; see Chap. 26) should be undertaken at the initial examination, if at all possible. If a specific loading direction is determined to centralize the patient's pain, exercises in this direction should be instituted. This is an excellent way to decrease pain by reducing posterior disc derangement, but it also empowers the patient to be able to control his or her own pain with maneuvers that can be performed at home.

Manipulation is an important modality in the acute stage. In some patients, pain and muscle spasm precludes applying this procedure in the very early stages, in which case, oscillatory mobilization of grade III or IV or muscle energy manipulation should be instituted until manipulation with thrust can be tolerated. Manipulation likely improves the clinical picture via a number of mechanisms. One of these mechanisms is inhibiting nociceptive input[84–86] (see Appendix A in Chap. 18). Another is improving motion of the involved segment,[87, 88] which may help to both allow more freedom of movement of the nerve root and allow the mobilization of inflammatory fluid and exudates. Finally, correction of joint dysfunction will help reduce pain related to joint dysfunction and reflex spasm.[89, 90]

Manipulation should be directed toward any relevant joint that may be dysfunctional. Commonly, significant joint dysfunction can be found at the level of HNP. If this is the case, manipulation should be applied to this level, but care should be taken not to aggravate the condition. The maneuver should use the minimum of force (this should be the case with manipulation in any circumstance), and, during the set up before the thrust, constant monitoring of the patient's pain is essential. Any direction that causes peripheralization of the patient's pain should be avoided. There are those who feel that manipulation is contraindicated in the presence of HNP,[82a] however, practitioners who utilize manipulation on a daily basis generally consider it a relatively safe modality in these patients.[90a] Certainly, any clinician who does not feel confident in using manipulation in patients with HNP should not use this tool, and should recommend the patient to a clinician with experience in treating HNP patients. Manipulation should never be carried out in a patient with HNP unless the clinician applying the modality has a high degree of training, skill, and experience.

BenEliyahu[91] demonstrated the safety and effectiveness of including manipulation in the treatment of cervical radiculopathy caused by HNP. He studied 27 patients with radiculopathy related to HNP—of which 11 were cervical—who were treated with a combination of manipulation, traction, electrical modalities, ice, and home exercise. Twenty-two of the 27 had a "good" (visual analogue scale reduced to 2 or below) outcome. Nine out of the 11 cervical patients returned to their previous occupation. Importantly, no complications were noted in any patient, suggesting that manipulation by adequately trained practitioners in patients with cervical HNP can be carried out safely. Several other cases have been reported in the literature[92–94] of patients with cervical HNP treated with manipulation with positive clinical results and without complication.

Although its efficacy has not been clearly demonstrated,[95] cervical traction is often useful and can be performed in the office as well as at home by the patient. There are a variety of types of traction and methods of applying it, and it is our experience that a trial of both manual and home mechanical traction is frequently beneficial. A study by Zylbergold[96] compared three types of traction in patients with cervical spine disorders; static, intermittent, and manual traction were compared with a no traction group. While patients in all four groups experienced significant improvement, those receiving intermittent traction showed statistically significant improvements compared to patients in the no traction group in terms of decreased pain and increased range of motion. The ideal timing for intermittent traction is 10 seconds on, 10 seconds off intervals for up to 15 minutes.[96]

Over-the-door home traction is particularly useful, as it allows for the benefits of traction, but increases patient empowerment by putting the patient more in charge of his or her own recovery. Unfortunately, it is, by design, static as opposed to intermittent; however, it still can be beneficial to many patients. It is essential that the patient be instructed carefully about the proper use of the home traction unit and that the patient understand this proper use before being given the unit. The patient should sit facing the door (Fig. 9–18) with the head angulated 20 to 25 degrees.[97] The amount of weight will vary according to the patient. It is recommended that for female patients, 8 pounds should be initially tried. For males, the initial weight should be 10 pounds.[98] The weight can be gradually increased to 20 to 30 pounds,[99] depending on patient tolerance and therapeutic benefit. Care should be taken to monitor the patient when first performing the procedure, and it should be terminated immediately if there is any significant increase in pain or neurological symptoms. The traction should be applied for 15 to 20 minutes at a time, at least once to twice per day, depending on patient tolerance.[99] The patient should be instructed to terminate the procedure if he or she experiences peripheralization of the symptoms.

Manual traction can be applied intermittently or statically and has the benefit of allowing the clinician to control the amount of force, in addition to providing the ben-

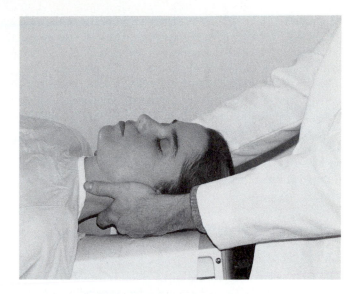

Figure 9–19. Manual traction.

efit of touch. The hands should be placed under the occiput of the supine patient (Fig. 9–19) with the headpiece of the table flexed to approximately 20 to 25 degrees. It is best to utilize a postisometric relaxation-type procedure of having the patient deeply inhale, followed by exhalation, at which time the traction should be applied by the clinician by moving the head cephalad. Repeating this several times is ideal.

> ## ❗ CLINICAL PEARL
>
> The treatment effects of manual traction can be improved by laterally angulating the cervical headpiece away from the side of pain.

Another treatment approach is advocated by Butler.[100] In treating patients with acute cervical radiculopathy, it is first determined whether treatment can be directed to some part of the nervous system other than the symptomatic area in order to change some of the tension on the affected nerve root. This could involve treatment either above or below the level of pain such as manipulation or mobilization to the thoracic spine or carpal tunnel. The second consideration is to direct mobilization to the injured nerve root. The stated rationale for this approach is to assist dispersal of either intra- or extraneural edema or blood. Various methods of placing tension on the affected limb or on adjacent structures are utilized.

Subacute Stage

Dynamic instability of both the cervical spine and the scapula is common in patients with HNP. This should be assessed for, using the Cervical Stability test and examining shoulder abduction movement pattern (see Chap. 14).

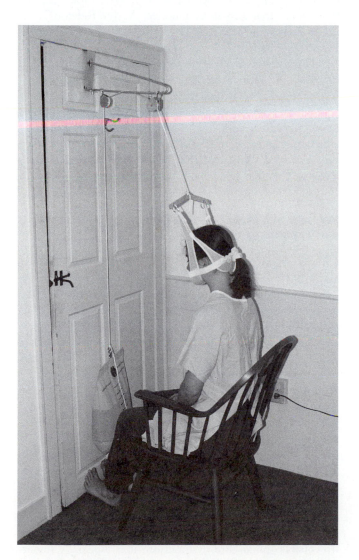

Figure 9–18. Over-the-door traction. The head should be angulated 20 to 25 degrees.

There may also be significant dysfunction of the tonic neck reflexes, as measured by the stepping test, or kinesthetic sensibility of the cervical spine, as measured by Revel's test (see Chap. 14). These functions should be assessed in the subacute stage, after initial pain relief is seen, and, if abnormal, may indicate the need for sensorimotor training or cervical stabilization (see Chap. 25). Saal et al[101] showed that 20 of 26 consecutive patients with cervical radiculopathy related to HNP had "good or excellent" results with a treatment regimen that included cervical stabilization, with only 2 patients needing surgery. No patients exhibited progressive neurological deficit.

CERVICAL RADICULOPATHY RELATED TO LCS

The management approach for LCS does not differ greatly from that for HNP, but there are a few specific features of LCS that require some alteration in management. Cervical radiculopathy related to LCS, because it results from a degenerative process, has a less favorable natural history than does HNP, but still usually responds well to nonsurgical methods.[45] However, the prognosis in LCS is commonly more guarded, and there is a greater likelihood that surgery may eventually become necessary. Also, patients with LCS are typically older than those with HNP. Because of this, there is generally less emphasis on stabilization exercise and more emphasis on improvement of mobility in these patients. Nonetheless, the management approaches discussed above apply to the LCS as well as the HNP patient.

CERVICAL SPONDYLOTIC MYELOPATHY

As do HNP and LCS, CSM generally has a favorable natural history. Many patients will improve without any treatment.[102, 103] So the management strategy for these patients should be quite similar to that for HNP and LCS: monitor neurological status, decrease symptoms as much as possible, improve function as much as possible, try to resolve the clinical manifestation of the condition more quickly than nature would by itself, and recognize the need for surgery.

There are some who believe that manipulation is contraindicated in patients with CSM.[46, 104] This belief is unfounded and not supported by any sound evidence. Although no large-scale studies have evaluated manipulation in patients with CSM, it is our experience, having treated many patients with this condition, that CSM is not, per se, a contraindication of this modality. Each individual case must be evaluated and a decision made based on the particular clinical features. For example, in a patient with significant stenosis of the central canal and advanced signs of spinal cord compression, it is best not to treat with high velocity, low amplitude manipulation. However, in a patient with early CSM, with more subtle signs of cord compression, a trial of skilled manipulation by a highly trained practitioner may not only be appropriate, but beneficial.

PSEUDORADICULOPATHY

Most cases of pseudoradiculopathy are related to joint dysfunction, muscle dysfunction, disc derangement, or any combination of the three. In these cases, the obvious treatment approach revolves around those methods that will correct this dysfunction. The reader is directed to Chapters 18, 19, 25, 26, and 28 for specific information regarding these methods.

In patients with TOS, it is best to try to identify which entrapment site is involved. This will allow treatment to be specific to the diagnosis. Manipulation of the first costotransverse joint is commonly required, as dysfunction of this joint is frequently a key link in the chain of dysfunction that leads to TOS.[34, 35] Manipulation to the cervical joint may also be necessary.[105] If scalenus anticus syndrome or costoclavicular syndrome are involved, postisometric relaxation (PIR) of the scalenes will usually be necessary (see Chap. 19). In the case of hyperabduction syndrome, PIR or postfacilitation stretch (PFS) to the pectoralis minor will probably be necessary (see Chap. 19). When localized adhesions are found in these muscles, Active Release Technique is excellent for releasing the entrapment (see the appendix to Chap. 19).

Normalization of cervical or scapular stability may be necessary if this is deemed to be a key link. If faulty breathing is present, this will require correction. See Chapters 25 and 27 for specific techniques. Postural correction is of utmost importance in patients with TOS.[27] This should be aimed at the specific postural faults (i.e., forward head posture, rounded shoulders) that are found on examination. Refer to Chapter 27 for more information.

WHEN SHOULD SURGERY BE RECOMMENDED?

Only a minority of patients with cervical radiculopathy and CSM require surgery. Even fewer patients with TOS require surgery. It is the responsibility of the nonsurgeon to determine whether surgery should be recommended. In general, severe or progressive neurological deficit, progressive myelopathy, or persistent, intractable pain, all of which fail to respond to nonsurgical methods, are considered the primary indications for surgical intervention.[106] However, as with the other aspects of the diagnosis and management of cervical radiculopathy and CSM, the determination must be made on an individual basis and there are situations in which deviation from the general rule must be made. There are cases, for example, in which motor weakness is so marked that a trial of nonsurgical care risks delaying surgery long enough for permanent motor loss to occur. Also, in a patient with CSM in whom bowel or bladder dysfunction is found, immediate surgical consult should be sought. Because of the potential consequences of irreversible spinal cord dysfunction, it is especially important to recognize the need for surgery in the patient with CSM.

Table 9–13: Indications for Surgery in Cervical Radiculopathy and Cervical Spondylotic Myelopathy

1. Progressive neurological deficit that does not improve with an adequate trial of nonsurgical care
2. Intractable pain that does not improve with an adequate trial of nonsurgical care
3. Progressive myelopathy that does not improve with an adequate trial of nonsurgical care
4. Severe motor loss, even if of recent onset
5. Bowel or bladder dysfunction

It is important to note that, in a patient with cervical radiculopathy related to HNP, the size of the herniation as demonstrated by MRI is not an indicator for the need for surgery. In fact, as Maigne and Deligne[107] showed, larger disc herniations actually regress to a greater degree with nonsurgical care than do smaller ones. Table 9–13 presents guidelines for surgical treatment of patients with cervical radiculopathy and CSM.

The nonsurgical practitioner plays an important role in the success of surgery. This is because it is the nonsurgeon who usually first speaks to the patient about the possible need for surgical intervention and, thus, has the earliest opportunity to prepare the patient for the operation. The attitude of the patient toward surgery and the patient's level of confidence that the surgery is necessary are essential in producing a positive outcome. Also, an important factor in the appropriateness of spine surgery in general is failure of an *adequate* trial of nonsurgical management.[108] Obviously, it is up to the nonsurgeon to be sure that the nonsurgical management that is applied is of the highest quality and has the best opportunity for resolving the condition.

 CLINICAL PEARL

As was stated earlier, in most cases of cervical radiculopathy, the diagnosis can be established and conservative treatment instituted without advanced testing. However, the orthopedist or neurosurgeon will require MRI to fully assess the patient in determining surgical technique and deciding on the direction of approach. So if, as a nonsurgical physician, you feel that surgical consult should be sought, and MRI has not yet been ordered, order an MRI before the patient sees the surgeon so that the surgeon can have the film in hand when he or she sees the patient.

CONCLUSION

Neck and arm pain, with or without neurological symptoms, is a common complaint. Many conditions can cause this complaint and accurate diagnosis is essential for effective treatment. The diagnosis must identify the actual process that is producing the symptoms (i.e., radiculopathy; peripheral entrapment; referred pain from muscles, joints, or ligaments) in addition to any key dysfunction that is occurring that may contribute to the perpetuation of the symptoms. In most cases, even in the presence of radiculopathy or myelopathy, nonsurgical methods are adequate to resolve the symptoms. When surgical intervention is necessary, however, proper patient selection helps to maximize success.

REFERENCES

1. Schutta HS. Intervertebral disc disorder and other spondyloarthropathies. In: Joynt RJ, Griggs RC, ed. *Clinical Neurology*. Philadelphia, Pa: Lippincott-Raven; 1996:3(41):1–152.
2. Saal JS, Franson RC, Dobrow R, et al. High levels of inflammatory phospholipase A-2 activity in lumbar disc herniations. *Spine* 1990;15:674.
3. Kang JC, Georgescu HI, McIntyre-Larkin L, Stefanovic-Racic M, Evans CH. Herniated cervical intervertebral discs spontaneously produce matrix metalloproteinases, nitric oxide, interleukin-6, and prostaglandin E2. *Spine* 1995;20(22):2373–2378.
4. Kawakami M. Possible mechanism of painful radiculopathy and lumbar disc herniation. *Clin Orthop Rel Res* 1998;351:241–251.
5. Henderson C, Hennessy R. Posterolateral foraminotomy as an exclusive operative technique for cervical radiculopathy: A review of 846 consecutively operated cases. *Neurosurg* 1983;13:504.
6. Dillin W, Booth R, Cuckler J, et al. Cervical radiculopathy: A review. *Spine* 1986;11:988–991.
7. Benini A. Clinical features of cervical root compression C5-C8 and their variations. *Neuro Orthop* 1987;4:74–88.
8. Ellenberg MR, Honet JC, Treanor WJ. Cervical radiculopathy. *Arch Phys Med Rehabil* 1994;75:342–352.
9. Radhakrishnan K, Litchy WJ, O'Fallon M, Kurland LT. Epidemiology of cervical radiculopathy: A population based study from Rochester, Minnesota, 1976 through 1990. *Brain* 1994:117:325–335.

10. Sweeney PJ. Clinical evaluation of cervical radiculopathy and myelopathy. *Neuroimaging Clin North Am* 1995:5(3):321–327.

10a. Yamada H, Honda T, Kikuchi S, Sugiura Y. Direct innervation of sensory fibers from the dorsal root ganglion of the cervical dura mater of rats. *Spine* 1998:23(14):1524–1528.

10b. Slipman CW, Plastaras CT, Palmitier RA, et al. Symptom provocation of fluoroscopically guided cervical nerve root stimulation: are dynatomal maps identical to dermatomal maps? *Spine* 1998;23(20):2235–2242.

11. Yoss RE, Corbin KB, MacCarty CS, et al. Significance of symptoms and signs in localization of involved root in cervical disk protrusion. *Neurology* 1960;60:673.

12. Hoppenfeld S. *Orthopedic Neurology. A Diagnostic Guide to Neurologic Levels*. Philadelphia, Pa: Lippincott; 1977.

13. Connell MC, Wiesel SW. Natural history and pathogenesis of cervical disc disease. *Orthop Clin North Am* 1992;23:369–380.

14. Semmes RE, Murphey F. The syndrome of unilateral rupture of the sixth cervical intervertebral disc. *JAMA* 1943;121:1209.

15. Ruggieri PM. Cervical radiculopathy. *Neuroimaging Clin N Am* 1995;5(3):349–366.

16. Yamano Y. Soft disc herniation of the cervical spine. *Internat Orthop* 1985;9:19–27.

17. Rizzolo SJ, Piazza MR, Cotler JM, et al. Intervertebral disc injury complicating cervical spine trauma. *Spine* 1991;16:S187–S189.

18. Ben Eliyahu DJ. Disc herniations of the cervical spine. *Am J Chiropractic Med* 1989;2(3):93–100.

19. Boden SD, McCowin PR, Davis DO, et al. Abnormal magnetic resonance imaging scans of the cervical spine in asymptomatic subjects. *J Bone Joint Surg* 1990;72-A:1178–1184.

20. Bland JH, Boushey DR. Anatomy and physiology of the cervical spine. *Sem Arthritis Rheum* 1990;20:1–20.

20a. Mercer S, Bogduk N. The ligaments and anulus fibrosus of human adult cervical intervertebral discs. *Spine* 1999;24(7):619–626.

21. Yu YL, Woo E, Huang CY. Cervical spondylitic myelopathy and radiculopathy. *Acta Neurol Scand* 1987;75:367–373.

22. Friedenberg ZB, Miller WT. Degenerative disc disease of the cervical spine: A comparative study of asymptomatic and symptomatic patients. *J Bone Joint Surg* 1963;45-A:1171–1178.

23. Omarker K, Myers RR. Pathogenesis of sciatic pain: Role of herniated nucleus pulposus and deformation of spinal nerve root and dorsal root ganglion. *Pain* 1998;78(2):99–106.

24. La Rocca SH, Eismont SJ. Other infectious diseases. In: Cervical Spine Research Society, eds. *The Cervical Spine*. 2nd ed. Philadelphia, Pa: Lippincott; 1989:552–563.

25. Long DM. Cervical cord tumors. In: Cervical Spine Research Society, eds. *The Cervical Spine*. 2nd ed. Philadelphia, Pa: Lippincott; 1989:526–543.

26. Nachlas IW. Pseudo-angina pectoris originating in the cervical spine. *JAMA* 1934;103:323–325.

27. Liebenson, CS. Thoracic outlet syndrome: Diagnosis and conservative management. *J Manipulative Physiol Ther* 1988;11:493–499.

28. Ault J, Suutala K. Thoracic outlet syndrome. *J Man Manipulative Ther* 1998:6:118–129.

29. Pratt, NE. Neurovascular entrapment in the regions of the shoulder and posterior triangle of the neck. *Phys Ther* 1988:66:1894–1900.

30. Roos DB. Thoracic outlet syndromes: Update 1987. *Am J Surg* 1987;154:568–573.

31. Krieg, L. Thoracic outlet syndrome: Pathology and treatment. *J Manipulative Physiol Ther* 1993;1:52–59.

32. Michael A. First rib function and the thoracic outlet syndrome. *J Orthop Med* 1995;17(2):56–61.

33. Lewit K. Impaired joint function and entrapment syndrome. *Manuelle Medizine* 1978;16:45–48.

34. Lindgren K-A, Leino E. Subluxation of the first rib: A possible thoracic outlet syndrome mechanism. *Arch Phys Med Rehabil* 1988;69:692–695.

35. Lindgren KA, Leino E, Manninen H. Cineradiography of the hypomobile first rib. *Arch Phys Med Rehabil* 1989;70:408–409.

36. Lindgren KA, Leino E, Hakola M, Hamberg J. Cervical spine rotation and lateral flexion combined motion in the examination of the thoracic outlet. *Arch Phys Med Rehabil* 1990;71:343–344.

37. Lindgren K-A, Leino E, Manninen H. Cervical rotation lateral flexion test in brachialgia. *Arch Phys Med Rehabil* 1992;73:735–737.

38. Pecina, MM, Krmpotic-Namanic J, Markiewitz, AD. *Tunnel Syndromes*. Boca Raton, Fla: CRC Press; 1991.

39. Swift TR, Nichols FT. The droopy shoulder syndrome. *Neurology* 1984;34:212–215.

40. Nichols HM. Anatomical structures of the thoracic outlet. *Clin Orthop* 1986;217:13–20.

41. Phillips H, Grieve GP. The thoracic outlet syndrome. In: Grieve GP, ed. *Modern Manual Therapy of the Vertebral Column*. Edinburgh: Churchill Livingstone; 1986:359–369.

42. Pailero PC, Walls JT, Payne WS, et al. Subclavian-axillary artery aneurysms. *Surgery* 1981;90:757–763.

43. Skerker RS, Flandry FC. Case presentation: Painless arm swelling in a high school football player. *Med Sci Sports Exerc* 1992;24:1185–1189.

44. Travell JG, Simons DG. *Myofascial Pain and Dysfunction: The Trigger Point Manual*. Baltimore, Md: Williams & Wilkins; 1983.

45. McCormick BM, Weinstein PR. Cervical spondylosis: An update. *West J Med* 1996;165:43–51.

46. Cates JR, Soriano MM. Cervical spondylotic myelopathy. *J Manipulative Physiol Ther* 1995;18(7):471–475.

47. Bland JH. *Disorders of the Cervical Spine: Diagnosis and Medical Management*. Philadelphia, Pa: WB Saunders; 1987.

48. Adams RD, Salam-Adams M. Chronic nontraumatic diseases of the spinal cord. *Neurol Clin* 1991;9:605–623.

49. Strubb RL. Spinal disease. In: Weisberg LA, Strubb RL, Garcia CA, eds. *Decision Making in Adult Neurology*. Toronto: BC Decker; 1987:14–15.

50. Feinstein B, Langton JNK, Jameson RM, et al. Experiments on pain referred from deep somatic tissues. *J Bone Joint Surg* 1954;36A(5):981–997.

51. Dwyer A, Aprill C, Bogduk N. Cervical zygapophyseal joint pain patterns I: A study in normal volunteers. *Spine* 1990;15(6):453–457.

52. Aprill C, Dwyer A, Bogduk N. Cervical zygapophyseal joint pain patterns II: A clinical evaluation. *Spine* 1990;15(6):458–461.

53. Dreyfuss P, Michaelson M, Fletcher D. Atlanto-occipital and lateral atlanto-axial joint pain patterns. *Spine* 1994;19(10):1125–1131.

54. Frykholm R. Cervical nerve root compression resulting from disc degeneration and root sleeve fibrosus. *Acta Chir Scand Suppl* 1951;160:1–148.

55. Schultz TS. Neck pain: A discussion of its pathogenesis and its evaluation. *J Disability* 1990;1(1):40–58.

56. Davidson RI, Dunn EJ, Metzmaker JN. The shoulder abduction test in the diagnosis of radicular pain in cervical extradural compressive monoradiculopathies. *Spine* 1981;6:441–445.

57. Bates B. *A Guide to Physical Examination and History Taking*. 4th ed. Philadelphia, Pa: JB Lippincott; 1987.

58. Farmer JC, Wisneski RJ. Cervical spine nerve root compression: An analysis of neuroforaminal pressures with varying head and arm positions. *Spine* 1994;19(16):1850–1855.

59. Beatty RM, Fowler FD, Hanson EJ. The abducted arm as a sign of ruptured cervical disc. *Neurosurgery* 1987;21:731–732.

60. Fast A, Parikh S, Marin EL. The shoulder abduction relief sign in cervical radiculopathy. *Arch Phys Med Rehabil* 1989;70:402–403.

61. Evans R. *Illustrated Essentials in Orthopaedic Physical Assessment*. St. Louis, Mo: Mosby; 1994.

62. Tandeter H, Spiegelmann R. Shoulder pain relieved by abduction: A sign of cervical radicular compression. *Can Fam Physician* 1997;43:511–512.

63. Shimizu T, Shimada H, Shirakura K. Scapulohumeral reflex (Shimizu): Its clinical significance and testing maneuver. *Spine* 1993;18:2182–2190.

64. Friedenberg ZB, Miller WT. Degenerative disc disease of the cervical spine: A comparative study of asymptomatic and symptomatic patients. *J Bone Joint Surg* 1963;45–A:1171–1178.

65. Gore DR, Sepic SB, Gardner GM, Murray MP. Neck pain: A long–term follow–up of 205 patients. *Spine* 1987;12:1–5.

66. Boden SD, McCowin PR, Davis DO, et al. Abnormal magnetic resonance imaging scans of the cervical spine in asymptomatic subjects. *J Bone Joint Surg* 1990;72–A:1178–1184.

67. Wood KB, Blair JM, Aepple DM, et al. The natural history of asymptomatic thoracic disc herniations. *Spine* 1997;22(5):525–530.

68. van Tulder MW, Assenfelft WJJ, Koes BW, Bouter LM. Spinal radiographic findings and nonspecific low back pain: A systematic review of observational studies. *Spine* 1997;22(4):427–434.

69. Wood KB, Garvey TA, Gundry C, Heitkoff KB. Magnetic resonance imaging of the thoracic spine: Evaluation in asymptomatic individuals. *J Bone Joint Surg (Am)* 1995;77A:1631–1638.

70. Boos N, Rieder R, Schade V, et al. The diagnostic accuracy of magnetic resonance imaging, work perception and psychosocial factors in identifying symptomatic disc herniations. *Spine* 1995; 20(24):2613–2625.

71. Jensen MC, Brandt–Zawadzki MN, Obuchowski N, et al. Magnetic resonance imaging of the lumbar spine in people without back pain. *N Eng J Med* 1994;331:69–73.

72. Dabbs VM, Dabbs LG. Correlation between disc height narrowing and low back pain. *Spine* 1990;15(12):1366–1369.

73. Schellhas KP, Smith MD, Gundry CR, Pollei SR. Cervical discogenic pain: Prospective correlation of magnetic resonance imaging and discography in asymptomatic subjects and pain sufferers. *Spine* 1996;21(3):300–311.

74. Roth DA. Cervical analgesic discography: A new test for definitive diagnosis of painful disk syndrome. *JAMA* 1976;235:1713–1714.

75. Simmons EH, Segil CM. An evaluation of discography in the localization of symptomatic levels of discogenic diseases of the spine. *Clin Orthop* 1975;108:57–69.

76. Bogduk N, Aprill C. On the nature of neck pain, discography and cervical zygapophyseal joint blocks. *Pain* 1993;54:213–217.

77. Wilbourn A, Ferrante M. Clinical electromyography. In: Joynt R, Griggs R, eds. *Clinical Neurology*. Philadelphia, Pa: Lippincott–Raven; 1997:1–76.

78. Thompson L. *The Electromyographer's Handbook*. Boston, Mass: Little, Brown; 1981.

79. Tsai CP, Huang CI, Wang V, et al. Evaluation of cervical radiculopathy by cervical root stimulation. *Electromyogr Clin Neurophysiol* 1994:34(6):363–366.

80. Ito T, Yamada M, Ikuta F, et al. Histologic evidence of resorption of sequestration-type herniated disc. *Spine* 1996;21(2):230–234.

81. Tan JC, Nordin, M. Role of physical therapy in the treatment of cervical disk disease. *Orthop Clin North Am:*1992;23(3):435–449.

82. Dillin W, Uppal GS. Analysis of medications used in the treatment of cervical disk degeneration. *Orthop Clin North Am* 1992;23:421–433.

82a. Rogers C, Joshi A, Dreyfuss P. Cervical intrinsic disc pain and radiculopathy. In: Malanga GA, ed. *Cervical Flexion-Extension/Whiplash Injuries. Spine: State of the Art Reviews* 1998;12(2):323–356.

83. Bercel NA. Cyclobenziprine in the treatment of skeletal muscle spasm in osteoarthritis of the cervical and lumbar spine. *Curr Ther Res* 1977;22:462.

84. Wright A, Vicenzo B. Cervical mobilisation techniques, sympathetic nervous system effects and their relationship to analgesia. In: Shacklock M, ed. *Moving in on Pain*. Melbourne, Australia: Butterworth Heinneman; 1995:164–173.

85. Wright A. Hypoalgesia post-manipulative therapy: A review of a potential neurophysiological mechanism. *Man Ther* 1995;1:11–16.

86. Vicenzino B, Collins D, Benson H, Wright A. An investigation of the interrelationship between manipulative therapy-induced hypoalgesia and sympathoexcitation. *J Manipulative Physiol Ther* 1998;21(70):448–453.

87. Yeomans SG. The assessment of cervical intersegmental mobility before and after spinal manipulative therapy. *J Manipulative Physiol Ther* 1992;15(2):106–114.

88. Cassidy JD, Lopes AA, Yonghing K. The immediate effect of manipulation versus mobilization on pain and range of motion in the cervical spine: A randomized, controlled trial. *J Manipulative Physiol Ther* 1992;15:570–575.

89. Shambaugh P. Changes in electrical activity in muscles resulting from chiropractic adjustment: A pilot study. *J Manipulative Physiol Ther* 1987;10(6):300–304.

90. Indahl A, Kaigle AM, Reikeras O, Holm SH. Interaction between the porcine lumbar intervertebral disc, zygapophysial joints and paraspinal muscles. *Spine* 1997;22(24):2834–2840.

90a. Croft AC. Appropriateness of cervical spine manipulation in disc herniation: a survey of practitioners. *Chiro Tech* 1994;8(4):178–179.

91. BenEliyahu DJ. Magnetic resonance imaging and clinical follow-up: Study of 27 patients receiving chiropractic care for cervical and lumbar disc herniation. *J Manipulative Physiol Ther* 1996;19(9):597–606.

92. BenEliyahu DJ. Chiropractic management and manipulative therapy for MRI documented cervical disk herniation. *J Manipulative Physiol Ther* 1994;17(3):177–185.

93. Brouillette DL, Gurske DT. Chiropractic treatment of cervical radiculopathy caused by a herniated cervical disc. *J Manipulative Physiol Ther* 1994:17(2):119–123.

94. Pollard H, Tuchin P. Cervical radiculopathy: A case for ancillary therapies? *J Manipulative Physiol Ther* 1995;18(4):244–249.

95. van der Heijden GJMG, Beurkens AJHM, Koes BW, et al. The efficacy of traction for back and neck pain: A systematic, blinded review of randomized clinical trial methods. *Phys Ther* 1995;75:93–104.

96. Zylbergold RS, Piper MC. Cervical spine disorders: A comparison of three types of traction. *Spine* 1985:10(10):867–871.

97. Kekosz VN, Hilbert L, Tepperman PS. Cervical and lumbopelvic traction. *Postgrad Med* 1986;80:187–194.

98. Fitz-Ritson D. Therapeutic traction: A review of neurological principles and clinical applications. *J Manipulative Physiol Ther* 1984;7:39–49.

99. Jackson R. *The Cervical Syndrome*. 4th ed. Springfield, Ill: Charles C. Thomas, 1978.

100. Butler DS. *Mobilisation of the Nervous System*. Melbourne, Australia: Churchill Livingstone; 1991:231–235.

101. Saal JS, Saal JA, Yurth E. Nonoperative management of cervical intervertebral disc with radiculopathy. *Spine* 1996;21(16):1877–1883.

102. Lees F, Turner JW. Natural history and prognosis of cervical spondylosis. *Brit Med J* 1963;2:1607–1610.

103. Nurick S. Natural history and results of surgical treatment of the spinal cord disorder associated with cervical spondylosis. *Brain* 1972;95:101–108.

104. Conley T, Schoenman K, Pudik T. Cervical spondylotic myelopathy. *Top Clin Chiro* 1995;2:48–53.

105. Mestagh B, Loomstein H, Lynn D. Thoracic outlet syndrome—an analysis of alternative treatments. Conference Proceedings of the Chiropractic Centennial Foundation, July 1995:342–343.

106. Ellenburg MR, Honet JC, Treanor WJ. Cervical radiculopathy. *Arch Phys Med Rehabil* 1994;75(3):342–352.

107. Maigne JY, Deligne L. Computed tomographic follow up study of 21 cases of nonoperatively treated cervical intervertebral soft disc herniation. *Spine* 1994;19(2):189–191.

108. Larequi-Lauber T, Vader JP, Burnand B, et al. Appropriateness of indications for surgery of lumbar disc hernia and spinal stenosis. *Spine* 1997;22(2):203–209.

CHAPTER 10

Cervicogenic Vertigo
and Disequilibrium

Don Fitz-Ritson

"It is almost impossible for all other systems of the Nervous System to function normally when there is a lack of stability, co-ordination and purposeful movement patterns, including normal feedback information, at the cervical level of the body. This area is the key point for controlling the head and the rest of the body in relation to the head."

—P. Bach-y-Rita, *Recovery of Function*[1]

INTRODUCTION

Cervicogenic vertigo is characterized by a feeling of unsteadiness when standing or walking[2] and can be induced by neck rotation while the head is stationary. Three disparate hypotheses have been proposed to explain the mechanism underlying this entity; they are identified as the vascular, neurovascular, and somatosenory input. This chapter begins with a brief review of these hypotheses as well as a fourth, proposed new sensory mismatch concept. The most common presenting signs and symptoms of cervicogenic vertigo, and a simple method for assessing aspects of this entity, are also presented, along with data from a comprehensive study of patients with this condition.

The effects of cervicogenic vertigo are body wide. This necessitates having in place a comprehensive program for effective management of the patient. The dynamic program outlined in this chapter involves a functional assessment, which identifies the effects of the disorder on the entire body; education to alleviate anxiety and empower the patient; and an outcome-based treatment program. Both the treatment and rehabilitation are time-targeted and specific to the patients' needs. An aspect of the treatment involves the use of a special laser for healing the injured tissues. This approach to management and rehabilitation is designed to decrease the duration and severity of the symptoms.

PROPOSED ETIOLOGIES OF CERVICOGENIC VERTIGO

Various hypotheses that have been proposed to cause cervicogenic vertigo are summarized next. However, the reader should keep in mind that vertigo and dizziness in neck disorders have also been suggested to arise from different combinations of these pathogenic factors.[3]

VASCULAR HYPOTHESIS

Vertebrobasilar ischemia—that is, episodic ischemia of the brain stem or the inner ear—resulting from vertebral artery compression[4] is considered to be a common cause of vertigo.[2] Although its importance as a cause of vertigo in neck disorders may have been overestimated,[5] the possibility of a vascular mechanism must be considered, particularly in elderly patients with known arteriosclerotic disease.

NEUROVASCULAR HYPOTHESIS

Barré, in 1926,[6] and others[7, 8] proposed that the sympathetic plexus surrounding the vertebral arteries could be mechanically irritated by degenerative changes in the cervical column. This hypothesis is contradicted by several reports indicating that sympathetic stimulation has little effect on the normal autoregulation of cerebral blood flow in intact animals.[9]

SOMATOSENSORY INPUT HYPOTHESIS

This hypothesis suggests that the symptoms of cervical vertigo result from a disturbed sensory input from the mechanoreceptors of the neck.[2, 10–12] There are no clear-cut methods for assessing cervical mechanoreceptive disturbances, but several animal and human studies support this hypothesis. In one study, Cohen[13] subjected monkeys to bilateral local anesthetic block or to bilateral sectioning of the dorsal roots C1–3. Both approaches resulted in severe defects in balance and motor coordination. The effects of the anesthetic block lasted for about 1 hour, while the root sectioning lasted for at least 3 weeks. In another study, Igarashi et al[14] found postural and dynamic ataxia after unilateral neck injection of local anesthetics or sectioning of the C1–2 dorsal roots in squirrel monkeys. The monkeys recovered about 1 hour after injection of local anesthetics, while recovery from unilateral sectioning of the dorsal roots took 8 days. Finally, De Jong et al[15] also found ataxia following injection of local anesthetics into one side of the neck in rabbits, cats, and monkeys.

SENSORY MISMATCH CONCEPT

According to this proposed ethiology, sensations of dizziness or vertigo arise because of a conflict between the converging input from the different sensory systems and the expected sensory patterns. A hypothesis put forward by Johansson and Sojka[16] to explain the genesis and spread of muscular tension in musculoskeletal pain syndromes may be extended to cover the proposed disturbed reflex mechanism in cervical pain syndromes. This proposed hypothesis is consistent with the findings of treatment-induced concomitant reduction of cervical pain, dizziness, and improved postural performance.[17–20]

Increased muscle spindle sensitivity may also be mediated via the sympathetic nervous system.[21] Thus, the somatosensory input hypothesis[12] and the neurovascular hypothesis[6] regarding the pathogenesis of cervical vertigo may be combined.

TYPES OF VERTIGO

MENIERE'S DISEASE

Meniere's disease is characterized by recurrent attacks of vertigo (paroxysmal vertigo) with fluctuating sensorineural hearing loss, tinnitus, and fullness in one ear.[22] Acute attacks can last up to several hours and residual symptoms can remain for days or even longer.[23] Meniere's disease has also been referred to as endolymphatic hydrops[24] and recurrent aural vetigo. The cause is unknown;[23] however, conditions ranging from polyarteritis nodosa to syphilis[24] and trauma to the cervical spine have been implicated.[25]

Davis[26] showed that vertigo resulted from cervical nerve root irritation, which he thought was caused by hypertrophic arthritis of the cervical spine and which responded to cervical traction. Jackson, as mentioned by Braaf and Rosner,[25] stated, "Meniere's syndrome maybe part of the cervical syndrome as much as the symptoms of equilibratory disturbances are very much the same in both instances and are due to reflex stimulation of the sympathetic nerve supply to the inner ear and to the eye."

BARRÉ-LIEOU SYNDROME

The Barré-Lieou syndrome was first described by M. Barré in 1926.[6] He described the syndrome as consisting primarily of suboccipital pain, vertigo that was usually precipitated by turning the head and not accompanied by any other vestibular dysfunction, and tinnitus along with visual symptoms. He noted that the patients were unable to read for long periods and usually had consulted a specialist in eye disease, although there were no objective findings.

Other secondary symptoms and signs include hoarseness that appears and disappears suddenly, severe fatigue, and radiographic findings localized to C4–5–6 levels. Patients also experience aching on one side of the face or the eye.[27] Similar symptoms have been observed in patients injured in traffic accidents, and attention has been focused on this relationship.[28]

One difficulty in assessing this syndrome is that the cranial symptoms are related to excessive movement of the neck. Research has suggested a variety of causes of Barré-Lieou syndrome. Some of the more prevalent theories focus on occlusion of the vertebral artery,[29, 30] involvement of the cervical sympathetic system,[27] and interference with neck reflexes.[31]

Stewart,[27] in his review of the neurological aspects of the cervical spine, outlined the following mechanism for the development of Barré-Lieou syndrome. He noted that the fifth cervical root contains sympathetic fibers that join the carotid plexus, furnishing sympathetic fibers to the neck and head. The sixth cervical root contains sympathetic fibers that proceed to the subclavian and brachial plexus. The seventh cervical root supplies sympathetic fibers to the cardioaortic and phrenic plexuses. There are also preganglionic sympathetic centers that arise from the medial lateral grey of the cervical cord at the C5 and C8 levels and produce fibers to form the white rami communicantes. The tangled web of sympathetic fibers follows the vertebral artery in its course in the transverse foramena of C4 to C6. This led Stewart to propose that changes in the position of the vertebra can precipitate a variety of symptoms.

CLINICAL PRESENTATION OF CERVICOGENIC VERTIGO

As previously noted, patients with cervicogenic vertigo experience feelings of unsteadiness when standing or walking.[2] These symptoms can also be induced by neck rotation while the head is stationary. This causes either a subjective or an objective sensation of movement. Both vertigo and dizziness appear to be on the same continuum, whereby dizziness is mild and vertigo is more severe.

Sandstrom[32] found vertigo and positional nystagmus in about 20 percent of patients with cervicobrachial pain and cervical spondylosis. In patients with whiplash injuries, the main symptoms are pain and stiffness in the neck and shoulder. Dizziness and vertigo are also reported by up to 80 to 90 percent of patients with chronic whiplash syndrome,[33, 34] and in one study, 48 percent of consecutive patients had neck rotationally induced cervicogenic vertigo.[35]

Brown[10] and Hulse[36] found that onset of neck pain precedes dizziness and vertigo. Attacks of more intense dizziness and vertigo, with a duration of seconds to minutes, may be triggered by head movements such as rotation or extension.

❗ CLINICAL PEARL

The feeling of imbalance may also be increased by peripheral visual stimulation such as that experienced when walking down the aisles of a supermarket or a narrow street, riding in a car, or walking and looking at box-patterned carpet.

Neck pain is a necessary symptom for the diagnosis of cervicogenic vertigo. Usually it is confined to the occipital region, but it may radiate into the temporal or temporomandibular areas, forehead, or orbital region. Headache is common. Generally, it is located to the occipital area, but it may also be described as a bandlike pressure around the head, thus resembling the description of tension headaches.[36]

Tinnitus occurs in about 30 percent of patients and may be accompanied by a sense of aural fullness. Some authors have also attributed low-frequency sensorineural hearing loss to cervical origins.[37]

Pain on palpation of the cervical muscles and findings of trigger points are considered important, especially when involving the short suboccipital muscles. Palpatory pain over the lateral mass of the atlas is considered to be of diagnostic importance. Many patients report a feeling of dizziness when the lateral mass of the atlas is palpated.[36]

Patients with cervical vertigo manifest no more than ordinary age-related degenerative changes on X-rays of the cervicogenic spine. The incidence of cervicogenic vertigo seems to be highest in the 30- to 50-year-old-age group, and a female preponderance is reported. Figures for the proportion of women with cervicogenic vertigo vary from 60 to 90 percent.[38]

REPORT OF A STUDY OF CERVICOGENIC VERTIGO

The next section summarizes results from a study of 235 patients with cervical trauma, ranging in age from 15 to 56 years, who were assessed and treated for cervicogenic ver-

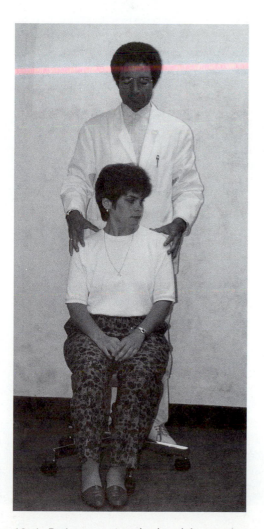

Figure 10–1. Patient rotating the head from side to side.

tigo.[38] One hundred twenty-three patients were female and 112 were male. Assessment and treatment were performed between 1986 and 1990. Consent was obtained from each patient. Subjects were included regardless of whether their complaint of vertigo was described as subjective (i.e., the patient feels that he or she is rotating) or objective (i.e., the patient feels that the room or environment is rotating).

METHOD

The method used to identify cervicogenic vertigo was the use of the "rotating stool test." This test is performed as follows:

1. Have the patient sit on a stool that rotates, with the thighs parallel to the floor. Ask the patient to close his or her eyes and shake the head from side to side as far and quickly as possible (Fig. 10–1). Some patients, because of pain, will have minimal side-to-side movements. If vertigo is present, it may originate either from the vestibular nuclei or from the muscles and joints in the cervical spine.

2. Next, have the patient sit upright, with the feet about 15 to 18 inches apart. Instruct the patient to use his or her feet to rotate the entire body on the stool from side to side. Have the patient do this a few times, to become comfortable with the procedure. When the patient is moving easily from side to side, stand behind the patient, cup the head to restrict its motion, and apply traction to the head via the mastoid processes. Instruct the patient to now close the eyes, while continuing to rotate the body from side to side (Fig. 10–2). If the patient now experiences vertigo, it originates from the tissues of the cervical spine. When the head is held stationary, there is no movement to affect the vestibular apparatus.

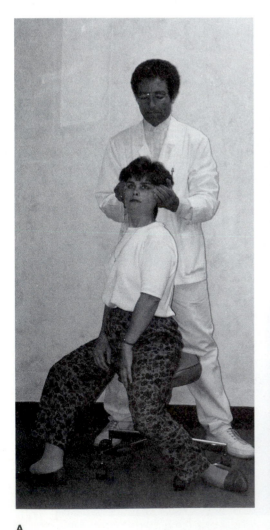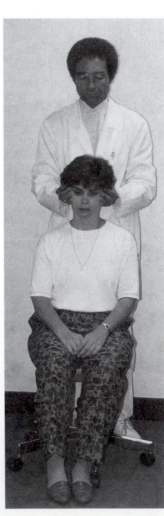

A   B   C

Figure 10–2. Patient rotating the body while the physician holds head steady.

In addition, the following activity, performed before the rotating stool test, was found to be helpful in accurately identifying patients with symptoms of cervicogenic vertigo:

1. Have the patient stand and rotate the body from side to side. This activates all the spinal, pelvic, and lower limb musculature.
2. Stand behind the patient and stabilize his or her head, while the patient continues to rotate the body. Note any unsteadiness with standing or walking (Fig. 10–3).

Cervicogenic vertigo was easily distinguished in patients who performed this activity and the rotating stool test. The working diagnosis of cervicogenic vertigo that was developed is founded upon the report of a feeling of unsteadiness when standing or walking,[39] which can be induced by neck-body rotation with the head held stationary.

 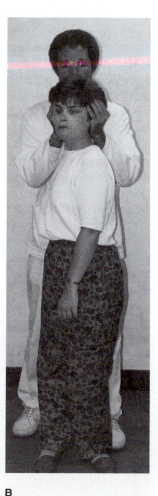

A   **B**

Figure 10–3. Patient standing and rotating the body while the physician holds the head steady

RESULTS

Of the 235 patients with cervical trauma, 112 (47.6 percent) were positive for the rotating stool test as previously defined; that is, they experienced true cervicogenic vertigo. An additional 41 patients (17.5 percent) had vertigo along with veering, and 27 (11.5 percent) had vertigo and nausea. Fifty (21.3 percent) of the patients had no vertigo while performing the test, and 5 patients were referred for further testing at the hospital's ear, nose, and throat department.

Seventy-three of the 112 patients (65.2 percent) had prominent upper cervical joint dysfunction at the occiput-atlas-axis, as revealed by motion palpation. The remaining 39 of 112 (34.8 percent) had either minor upper cervical joint dysfunction or no dysfunction. Sixty-nine of the 112 positive patients (61.6 percent) experienced acute symptoms, while 43 (38.4 percent) had chronic symptoms. After 18 treatments, 101 of the 112 patients (90.2 percent) were symptom free. Of the remaining 11 patients, 6 had decreased symptoms of vertigo and 5 experienced no change. Fifty-five of the 69 patients with acute symptoms had prominent upper cervical joint dysfunction. Forty-seven of the 55 patients (85.5 percent) with upper cervical joint dysfunction were symptom free and had no cervicogenic vertigo by their ninth treatment.

These findings suggest that dysfunction of the upper cervical muscles and joints may predispose to or be potent sources of cervicogenic vertigo.

MANAGEMENT AND REHABILITATION OF THE PATIENT WITH CERVICOGENIC VERTIGO

UNDERSTANDING COORDINATED MOVEMENT PATTERNS OF THE EYE, HEAD, AND NECK

As the results of the preceding study suggest, the etiology of cervicogenic vertigo can best be explained by the somatosensory hypothesis. To recap, this hypothesis states that cervicogenic vertigo is caused by abnormal sensory input from the cervical mechanoreceptors, which may be the result of trauma. To better understand the systems involved and their interactions, a brief review is necessary.

Complaints of impaired vision are frequent after whiplash injury, and their evaluation is often very difficult.[40, 41] One reason for this is the complexity of the systems that control sensory input. As Neububer and Bankoul[42] note, coordination of head, eye, and body movements requires processing of vestibular, visual, and somatosensory input.[43] Mechanoreceptive neck afferents, in particular those from the neck muscles, ascertain the position of the head relative to the trunk. They project inter alia directly to vestibular nuclei,[44] where mechanoreceptive signals converge with input from the labyrinth and oculomotor apparatus.[45, 46] Many of the efferent projections from that part of the vestibular nuclear complex are directed to the spinal cord.[40] The vestibular nuclear complex is not, however, the sole contributor to neck muscle control; the external cuneate nucleus,[47] the corticobulbar and the corticospinal higher centers,[48] and lower spinal centers[49] also provide input for neck muscle control.

The complexity of eye-head-neck interaction is illustrated when neck muscles are stimulated.[50, 51] Herman et al[52] found, when assessing subjects with idiopathic scoliosis, that a direct relationship exists between the visual system and a disordered axial motor system. That is, subjects with scoliosis and paraspinal muscular imbalances had inappropriate processing of afferent information in the brain stem nuclei as well as in higher centers.

In the human cervical intervertebral discs, nerve fibers enter in the posterolateral direction and are most numerous in the middle third of the disc. The presence of neural elements within the intervertebral discs indicates that the mechanical status of the disc is monitored by the central nervous system.[53]

PATIENT EDUCATION

Effective education helps to decrease patients' fears of more serious pathology. The education provided should detail the cause of the cervicogenic vertigo, why they are experiencing the signs and symptoms, and what they should expect in certain circumstances. Radanov[54] showed that patients with upper cervical injuries had what he termed "cervicoencephalic syndrome"; that is, these patients had difficulty with concentration and the processing of new information. With this in mind, it is important to have the patient restate his or her understanding of what has been discussed so the level of comprehension of the new information can be ascertained.

> ! CLINICAL PEARL
>
> Part of the education of patients involves empowering them to become active participants in their treatment and rehabilitation program. For this to occur, patients must understand what you are attempting to accomplish and the time frame in which you plan to work. They also have to become involved in setting goals and must understand the importance of their role in their own recovery.

One aspect of time-targeted goal setting involves using the Neck Disability Index of Vernon and Mior.[55] The tools are used to educate the patient about his or her level of disability and what the physician hopes to achieve in a specified time frame, such as 2, 4, 6, or 8 weeks. Ask questions such as the following: When would you like to be free of your cervicogenic vertigo? Your neck pain? When would you like to return to work? Carry out normal activities of daily living? Find out the patient's commitment level regarding punctuality and attendance.

OCCIPUT-ATLAS-AXIS FLEXION AND EXTENSION

The ability of the patient with cervical trauma to perform this maneuver is informative. Over the years, I have found that patients who are unable to perform occiput-atlas-axis flexion and extension on initial examination either have severe injury or pathomechanics of the upper cervical area, or a prognosis that should be considered guarded, or both. However, if these patients develop the ability to perform this maneuver, they accelerate their response to therapy. Figure 10–4 illustrates this maneuver.

RESTORING RANGE OF MOTION

One essential ingredient for quickly and elegantly returning function to the cervical spine is ensuring that shoulder joints and muscles have normal ranges of movement. The upper muscles of the girdle attach to the cervical spine, so if the shoulder girdles are balanced, stress is reduced to the cervical spine. I apply the reciprocal shoulder stretch to all patients from day 1 (Fig. 10–5). It stretches the majority of muscles in the girdles as it restores normal reciprocal motion. This prepares the cervical area for more detailed therapy.

After 1 week of therapy (i.e., three to four treatments), cervical traction with the Leander table can begin. With the patient prone and the Leander table in slow motion, have the patient place his or her hands on the table rests. Cup the patient's mastoid processes with your hands, apply cephalad traction, and allow the patient's body weight to traction the cervical and upper thoracic spines causally (Fig. 10–6). Begin with 15 seconds of four to six repetitions. Gauge the progress via the patient's response to therapy.

If, after a week, the patient's response to cervical traction is positive, begin prone active spinal extension (PASE). Have the patient, while prone, hold the head and neck suspended, tuck in the chin, and extend the cervical spine as a unit. Next, place one hand on the patient's sacrum and the other below the spinous process at the level of T6. Ask the patient to raise the head and neck with the chin tucked as a unit[56] (Fig. 10–7). When the patient lowers the head and neck, move your hand to below the T5 spinous process. Repeat to C7. This helps to restore extension at each level and also to return function to the muscles that control the cervical spine and originate as far down to the T6 level. There is often a noticeable increase in cervical motion after three to four treatments.

> ! CLINICAL PEARL
>
> If the patient exhibits flattening of the thoracic spine, PASE is contraindicated.

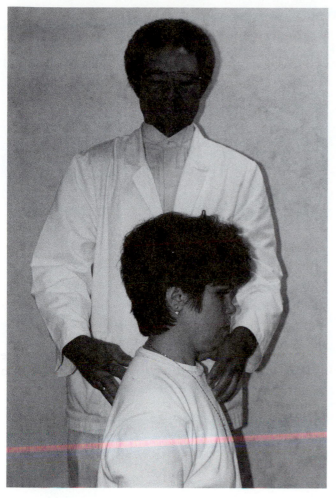

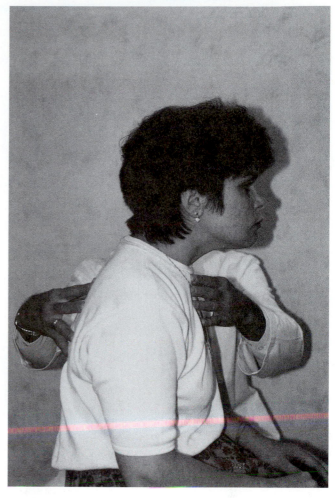

A   B

Figure 10–4. Occiput-atlas-axis flexion and extension. The physician stabilizes the upper body while the patient moves the head and neck forward.

LASER THERAPY

Utilizing a specially designed BioFlex laser (Dr. Don Fitz-Ritson, Toronto, Canada), which treats muscular pathology, I have been able to promote rapid and effective healing in the injured tissues. This is accomplished by using specific frequencies, power spectrums, and waveforms, which the manufacturer indicates cause relaxation of muscles, increased circulation, and promotion of collagen synthesis.

MANIPULATIVE THERAPY

Specific adjustments are administered to the area when indicated through accurate motion palpation. This therapy restores the normal integrity of the joints, as well as realigning the head and restoring its relationship to the cervical spine. This restoration of proper alignment is absolutely necessary for proper focusing of the eyes.

REHABILITATION AND EXERCISES

A program of phasic exercises is administered next.[57] The program consists of two levels, with each level performed for 2 weeks.

> **! CLINICAL PEARL**
>
> Before beginning rehabilitation exercises, be sure the patient has already conditioned the cervicothoracic area through appropriate range of motion, stretching, toning, and strengthening exercises.

Level 1

The exercises that comprise this level should be performed daily. Five to 10 repetitons of each exercise are recommended. The occiput-atlas-axis flexion and extension (see

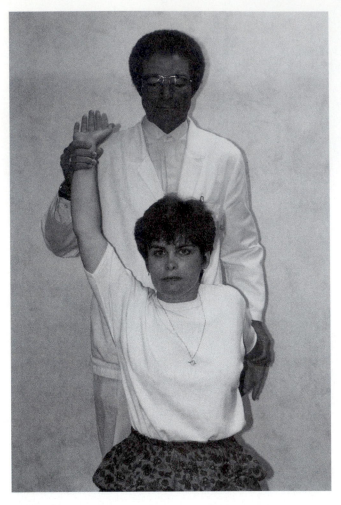

Figure 10–5. Reciprocal shoulder stretch.

Fig. 10–4), described earlier, is part of this series. Other exercises include the following:

Prone extension with chin in (Fig. 10–8)
Supine flexion with chin in (Fig. 10–9)

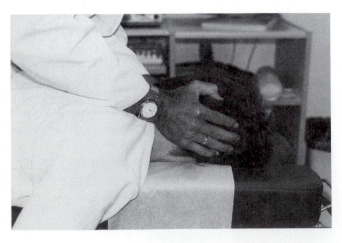

Figure 10–6. Cervical traction on the Leander table.

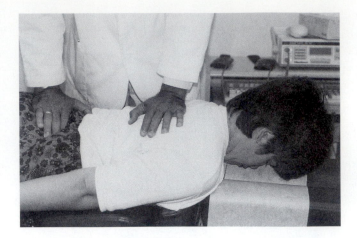

Figure 10–7. Prone active spinal extension.

Side posture, chin in, lateral flexion (Fig. 10–10)
Prone, extension, chin in, rotation with eyes leading head (Fig. 10–11)
Supine, flexion, chin in, rotation with eyes leading head (Fig. 10–12)
Side posture, lateral flexion, chin in, rotation with eyes leading (Fig. 10–13)
Eyes and head focused on hands, with slow left-to-right movements (Fig. 10–14)
Balancing on foam and slowly moving from side to side (Fig. 10–15)

Level 2
This level consists of the following exercises, which should be performed daily, with 5 to 10 repetitions of each exercise.

Balancing on Swiss ball, flexion with chin in (Fig. 10–16)
Balancing on Swiss ball, extension with chin in (Fig. 10–17)
Supine, chin in, flexion, rotation with eyes leading head (Fig. 10–18)
Prone, chin in, extension with eyes leading head (Fig. 10–19)
Full body rotation with eyes leading the head (Fig. 10–20)
Body rotation right, eyes leading head left (Fig. 10–21)
Eyes and head focused on hands, with faster left-to-right movements (Fig. 10–22)
Patient standing on foam, full body rotation with eyes leading the head (Fig. 10–23)
Patient standing on foam, body rotation left, eyes leading head right (Fig. 10–24)
Patient standing on foam, eyes and head focused on hand with fast left-to-right movement (Fig. 10–25)

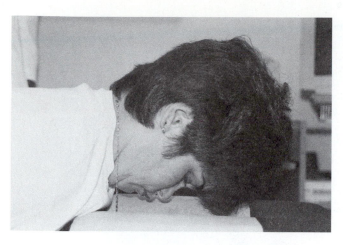

Figure 10–8. Prone extension with chin in.

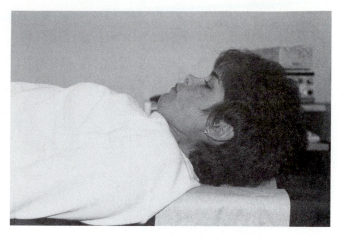

Figure 10–9. Supine flexion with chin in.

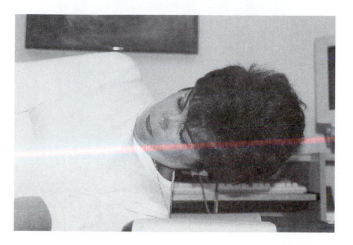

Figure 10–10. Side posture, chin in, lateral flexion.

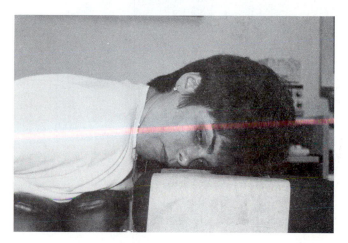

Figure 10–11. Prone, extension, chin in, rotation with eyes leading head.

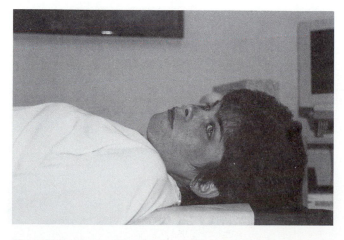

Figure 10–12. Supine, flexion, chin in, rotation with eyes leading head.

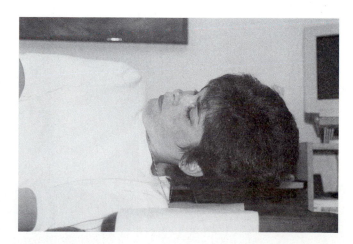

Figure 10–13. Side posture, lateral flexion, chin in, rotation with eyes leading.

Figure 10–14. Eyes and head focused on hands, with slow left-to-right movements.

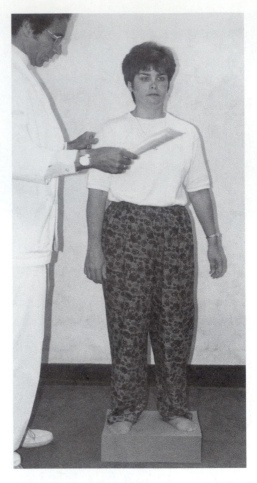

Figure 10–15. Patient balancing on foam and slowly moving from side to side.

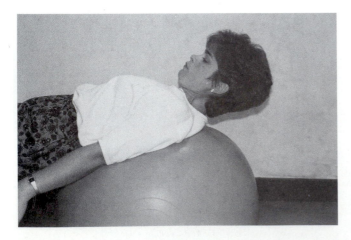

Figure 10–16. Patient balancing on Swiss ball, flexion with chin in.

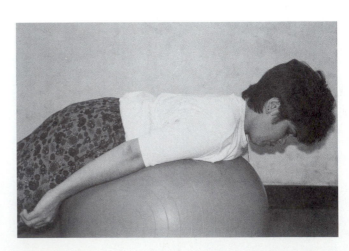

Figure 10–17. Patient balancing on Swiss ball, extension with chin in.

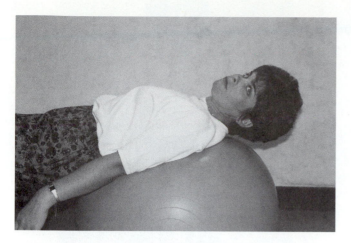

Figure 10–18. Supine, chin in, flexion, rotation with eyes leading head.

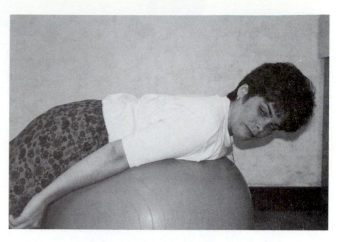

Figure 10–19. Prone, chin in, extension with eyes leading head.

Figure 10–20. Full body rotation with eyes leading the head.

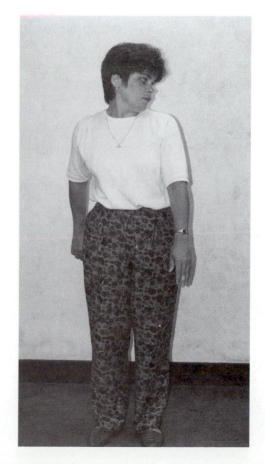

Figure 10–21. Body rotation right, eyes leading head left.

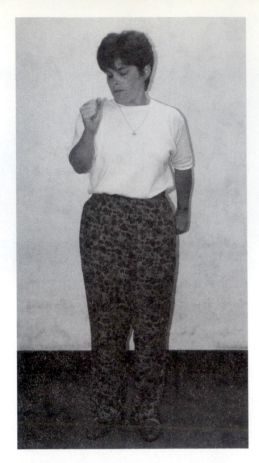

Figure 10–22. Eyes and head focused on hands, with faster left-to-right movements.

Figure 10–23. Patient standing on foam, full body rotation with eyes leading the head.

Figure 10–24. Patient standing on foam, body rotation left, eyes leading head right.

Figure 10–25. Patient standing on foam, eyes and head focused on hand with fast left-right movement.

The purpose of this rehabilitation program is to return the injured cervical spine and body efficiently and elegantly to preaccident levels.

Analysis of Preliminary Data Regarding Program Effectiveness

Data were obtained to evaluate whether patients with acute symptoms would respond favorably to the previously outlined exercise program. Over a 5-month period, 106 acutely injured patients were assessed in three clinics that deal exclusively with patients involved in motor vehicle crashes (D. Fitz-Ritson, unpublished data).

Forty-one patients were identified as having subjective or objective cervicogenic vertigo, along with unsteadiness upon either walking or standing. Twenty-six patients were females and 15 were males, ranging in ages from 23 to 57 years, with a mean of 34.5 years. Twenty-five patients had been injured in rear-end collisions, 7 in lateral crashes, 5 in frontal (head on) crashes, and 4 in crashes involving multiple mechanisms. On palpation, upper cervical joint dysfunction was noted in 30 (73 percent) of the cases.

After 2 weeks and an average of six treatments, which included soft-tissue therapy, laser therapy, and exercise, the following results were obtained:

Twenty-nine of 41 patients (71 percent) had no cervicogenic vertigo.
Twenty-four of 41 (83 percent) had upper joint manipulation.

After 4 weeks and an average of 12 treatments, during which manipulation was included for two of those weeks, the following results were documented:

Thirty-five of 41 patients (85 percent) had no cervicogenic vertigo.
Twenty-eight of 41 (68 percent) had upper joint manipulation.

After 6 weeks and average of 18 treatments, including manipulation, the following results were noted:

Three patients were discharged due to noncompliance.
One patient stopped attending.
Two patients, who were unconscious at the time of the injury, had approximately 50 percent resolution of their cervicogenic vertigo.

CONCLUSION

After 4 weeks of treatment, 85 percent of patients diagnosed with cervicogenic vertigo had responded favorably to these therapeutic interventions. In conjunction with the laser modality, which heals tissues, the rehabilitation program outlined in this chapter may be helpful for patients with cervical injuries.

REFERENCES

1. Bach-y-Rita P, ed. *Recovery of Function: Theoretical Considerations for Brain Injury Rehabilitation*. Baltimore, Md: Uni Oak Press; 1980:40.
2. Brandt T. *Vertigo: Its Multisensory Syndromes*. London: Springer-Verlag; 1991.
3. Pfaltz CP. Vertigo in disorders of the neck. In: Dix MR, Hood JD, eds. *Vertigo*. New York, NY: Wiley; 1984:179–197.
4. Sheehan S, Bauer RB, Meyer JS. Vertebral artery compression in cervical spondylosis. *Neurology* 1960;10:968–986.
5. Jongkees LB. Cervical vertigo. *Laryngoscope* 1969;79:1473–1484.
6. Barré M. Sur un syndrome sympathique cervical posterieur et sa cause frequente: l'arthrite cervicale. *Rev Neurol* 1926;33:1246–1248.
7. Bartschi-Rochaix W. *Migraine Cervicale*. Bern: H Huber Verlag; 1948.
8. Jackson R. *The Cervical Syndrome*. Springfield; Ill: Thomas; 1958.
9. Alm A. The effect of stimulation of the cervical sympathetic chain on regional cerebral blood flow in monkeys. A study with radioactively labelled microspheres. *Acta Physiol Scand* 1975;93:483–489.
10. Brown JJ. Cervical contribution to balance: Cervical vertigo. In: Berthoz A, Vidal P, Graf W, eds. *The Head-Neck Sensory Motor System*. New York, NY: Oxford University Press; 1992:644–647.
11. de Jong JM, Bles W. Cervical dizziness and ataxia. In: Bles W, Brandt T, eds. *Disorders of Posture and Gait*. New York: Elsevier, 1986:185–206.
12. Ryan G, Cope S. Cervical vertigo. *Lancet* 1955;31:1355–1358.
13. Cohen LA. Role of eye and neck proprioceptive mechanisms in body orientation and motor coordination. *J Neurophysiol* 1961;24:1–11.

14. Igasashi M, Alford BR, Watanabe T, Maxian PM. Role of neck proprioceptors for the maintenance of dynamic bodily equilibrium in the squirrel monkey. *Laryngoscope* 1969;79:1713–1727.

15. de Jong PT, de Jong JM, Cohen B, Jongkees LB. Ataxia and nystagmus induced by injection of local anesthetics in the neck. *Ann Neurol* 1977;1:240–246.

16. Johansson H, Sojka P. Pathophysiological mechanisms involved in genesis and spread of muscular tension in occupational muscle pain and in chronic musculoskeletal pain syndromes: A hypothesis. *Med Hypoth* 1991;35:196–203.

17. Carlsson J, Fahlcrantz A, Augustinsson L. Muscle tenderness in tension treated with acupuncture or physiotherapy. *Cephalalgia* 1990;10:131–141.

18. Carlsson J, Rosenhall U. Oculomotor disturbances in patients with tension headache treated with acupuncture or physiotherapy. *Cephalalgia* 1990;10:123–129.

19. Revel M, Minguet M, Gergoy P, Vaillant J, Manuel JL. Changes in cervicocephalic kinesthesia after a proprioceptive rehabilitation program in patients with neck pain: A randomized controlled study. *Arch Phys Med Rehabil* 1994;75:895–899.

20. Karlberg M. *The neck and human balance: A clinical and experimental approach to "Cervical Vertigo."* Doctoral dissertation, Lund University, Sweden 1995:6–7.

21. Hubbard DR, Berkoff G. Myofascial trigger points show spontaneous needle EMG activity. *Spine* 1993;18:1803–1807.

22. Hood NA. Diseases of the central nervous system. *BMJ* 1975;15:398–400.

23. Slater R. Vertigo. *Post Grad Med* 1984;5:58–67.

24. Sackett JF, Arenberg IK, Goldman G. The vestibular aqueduct: Tomographic evaluation in Meniere's disease: A preliminary report. *Head Neck Surg* 1980;2:282–286.

25. Braaf MM, Rosner S. Meniere-like syndrome following whiplash injury of the neck. *J Trauma* 1962;2:494–501.

26. Davis D. A common type of vertigo relieved by traction of the cervical spine. *Ann Intern Med* 1953;38:778–86.

27. Stewart DY. Current concepts of the "Barre syndrome" or the "posterior cervical sympathetic syndrome." *Clin Orthop* 1962;24:40–48.

28. Tamura T. Cranial symptoms after cervical injury: Aetiology and treatment of the Barre-Lieou Syndrome. *J Bone Joint Surg* 1989; 71B(2):283–287.

29. Limousin CA. Foramen arcuate and syndrome of Barre-Lieou: Its surgical treatment. *Int Orthop* 1980;4:19–23.

30. Buna M, Coghlan W, de Gruchy M, et al. Ponticles of the atlas. A review and clinical prospective. *J Manipulative Physiol Ther* 1984;7(4):261–266.

31. Ryan G, Cope S. Cervical vertigo. *Lancet.* 1955;11:1355–1358.

32. Sandstrom J. Cervical syndrome with vestibular symptoms. *Acta Otolaryngol (Stockh)* 1962;54:207–226.

33. Hinoki M, Hine S, Tada Y. Vertigo due to whiplash injury. In: Bustamante Gurria A, ed. *Oto-Rhino-Laryngology. Proceedings of the Ninth International Congress.* Amsterdam: Excerpta Medica; 1970:416–424.

34. Oosterveld WJ, Kortschot HW, Kingma GG, de Jong HA, Saatci MR. Electronystagmographic findings following cervical whiplash injuries. *Acta Otolaryngol (Stockh)* 1991;111:201–205.

35. Fitz-Ritson D. Assessment of cervicogenic vertigo. *J Manipulative Physiol Ther* 1991;14:193–198.

36. Hulse M. *Die zervikalen Gleichgewichtsstorungen.* Berlin: Springer-Verlag; 1983.

37. Blumenthal L. Tension headache. In: Vinken P, Bruyn G, eds. *Handbook of Clinical Neurology.* vol.5. Headaches and cranial neuralgias. Amsterdam: North-Holland Publ.; 1968:157–171.

38. Kuilman J. The importance of the cervical spine syndrome in otorhinolaryngology. *Pract Oto-Rhino-Laryngol* 1959;21:174–185.

39. Brandt T. Traumatic otolith vertigo. In: *Vertigo: Its Multisensory Syndromes.* London: Springer-Verlag; 1991:227–281.

40. Hulse M. Objective identification of vertebrogenic disorder of vision. *Man Med* 1990;28:23–27.

41. Hildingsson C, Wenngren B, Bing C, et al. Oculomotor problems after cervical spine injury. *Acta Orthop Scand* 1989;60:13–16.

42. Neububer W, Bankoul S. The "cervical portion" of the vestibular apparatus—Connections between cervical receptors and vestibular nuclei. *Man Med* 1992;30:53–57.

43. Fitz-Ritson D. Neural mechanisms involved in the control of the eye-head-neck coordinated movement: A review of literature with emphasis on future directions for the chiropractic profession. *J Manipulative Physiol Ther* 1984;7:251–260.

44. Fitz-Ritson D. The direct connections of the C2 dorsal root ganglia in the *Mecca irus* monkey: Relevance to chiropractic therapeutics. *J Manipulative Physiol Ther* 1985;8:147–156.

45. Roll R, Velay J, Roll J. Eye and proprioceptive messages contribute to the spatial coding of retinal input in visually oriented activities. *Exp Brain Res* 1991;85:423–431.

46. Huygens P, Verhagen W, Nicolasen M. Cervico-ocular reflex enhancement in labyrinthine-defective and normal subjects. *Exp Brain Res* 1991;87:457–464.

47. Anastasopoulos D, Merger T, Becker W, et al. Sensitivity of external cuneate neurons to neck rotation in three-dimensional space. *Exp Brain Res* 1991;85:565–576.

48. Berardelli A, Priori A, Inghilleri M, et al. Corticobulbar and corticospinal projections to neck muscle motoneurons in man. *Exp Brain Res* 1991;87:402–406.

49. Yamagata Y, Yates B, Wilson V. Participation of 1a reciprocal inhibitory neurons in the spinal circuitry of the tonic neck reflex. *Exp Brain Res* 1991;84:461–464.

50. Mergner T, Siebold C, Schweigart G, et al. Human perception of horizontal trunk and head rotation in space during vestibular and neck stimulation. *Exp Brain Res* 1991;85:389–404.

51. Taylor J, McClohey D. Illusions of head and visual target displacement induced by vibration of neck muscles. *Brain* 1991;114:755–759.

52. Herman N, Mixon J, Fisher P, et al. Idiopathic scoliosis and the central nervous system. A motor control problem. *Spine* 1985;10B:1–14.

53. Mendel T, Wink C, Zimny M, Neural elements in human cervical intervertebral disc. *Spine* 1992;17:132–135.

54. Radanov B, Dvorak J, Valach L. Cognitive deficits in patients after soft tissue injury of the cervical spine. *Spine* 1992;17(2):127–131.

55. Vernon H, Mior S. The Neck Disability Index: A study of its reliability and validity. *J Manipulative Physiol Ther* 1991;14:409.

56. Fitz-Ritson D. The chiropractic management and rehabilitation of cervical trauma. *J Manipulative Physiol Ther* 1990;13:17–25.

57. Fitz-Ritson D. Phasic exercises for cervical rehabilitation after "whiplash" trauma. *J Manipulative Physiol Ther* 1995;18:21–24.

CHAPTER 11

Orofacial Pain

DARRYL CURL

"Order and simplification are the first steps toward the mastery of a subject—the actual enemy is the unknown."

—Thomas Mann (*The Magic Mountain*, 1924)

INTRODUCTION

Patients with "TMJ" complaints often find themselves health care orphans. They are fortunate, indeed, if their jaw complaint is transient, for otherwise they may find themselves on an excursion to the dentist, osteopath, chiropractor, psychiatrist, ophthalmologist, otolaryngologist, and neurologist. Thereupon, they are X-rayed, massaged, medicated, manipulated, analyzed, fitted with splints, injected, stretched, relieved of their discs and condyles, and too often emerge with their temperomandibular joint complaint intact.

The clinician who is first encountering patients suffering from disorders of the orofacial area and the temporomandibular apparatus will immediately realize that there is an extraordinary amount written on the subject. He or she will also notice an unspoken, yet obvious, bias within the literature toward the differentiated type of jaw pain we now call temporomandibular joint disorders (TMDs). Admittedly, TMD, especially the classic form, leaves a distinctive footprint in the patient's history and in this respect its path is easier to track than other, albeit less glamorous, varieties of common aches and pains in the head and face.

The interactivity between the orofacial and temporomandibular apparatus with the cervical spine and the headache phenomena is one of the most fascinating (and frustrating) areas in health care (Fig. 11–1). Fortunately, clinicians and student alike can easily manage this complex interactivity by initially approaching the patient's presenting complaints in the realm of two basic differential diagnostic categories, namely:

1. Is the patient presenting with a disorder of the orofacial or temporomandibular apparatus manifesting as cervical pain or headache?
2. Is the patient presenting with a disorder of the cervical spine or headache manifesting as pain in the orofacial or temporomandibular apparatus areas?

This necessary first step in clinical decision making invariably guides the clinician to the correct pathway in diagnostic decision making. Essentially, when the clinician reaches a working diagnosis, he or she is actually developing a clinical theory that explains the patient's clinical predicament. This theory (i.e., the working diagnosis) is not set in stone once it is created. The working diagnosis is only the best estimate of the patient's condition based upon the avail-

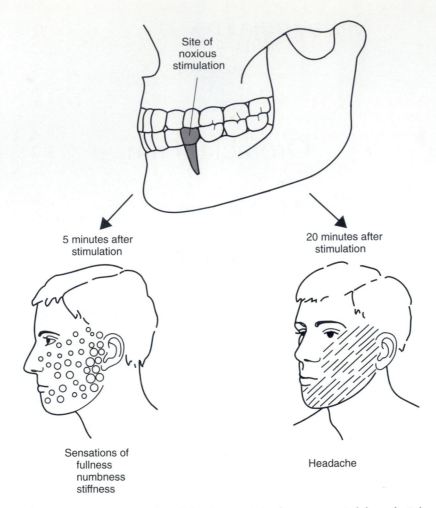

Figure 11–1. An example of the interactivity between painful orofacial and cervical structures is illustrated by these two common conditions.

(Adapted from: Wolff HG. Headache and Other Head Pain. *New York: Oxford, 1963.)*

able findings at the time of the encounter. Therefore, throughout each encounter with the patient clinicians should ask themselves the following queries.

What clinical theory am I trying to prove?
What facts do I have to back it up?
What facts are being ignored?

Patients suffering from orofacial pain or TMD are particularly vulnerable to inappropriate diagnoses for a variety of reasons, as outlined in Table 11–1. Because the typical adult displays one or more of the signs or symptoms of a temporomandibular disorder (Table 11–2), three basic clinical decision-making steps must be followed.

1. Is this an incidental discovery? The human temporomandibular joint functions in a widely normal physiological and structural range. The greatest challenge to clinicians is to resist the temptation to call these less-than-ideal but successful adaptations of the temporomandibular apparatus harbingers of disease, breakdown, or disaster.
2. Is this just a discovery of an old disorder? The jaw is the most active and powerful musculoskeletal structure of the human body. It is active for common functions when we are awake and while we are asleep (Table 11–3). We also use our jaw as a tool from

Table 11–1: Common Pitfalls in Diagnosis of TMDs

Errors in TMD diagnosis increase when the clinician fails to concern him- or herself with the following common pitfalls:

- Variation in the examiners' senses such as sight, hearing, touch (palpation), smell, or (uncommonly) taste. For example, the clinician cannot distinguish between small sore lymph nodes and a trigger point due to a diminished palpatory sense.
- The clinician's tendency to record inference rather than evidence. For example, the clinician may record joint locking rather than limited opening on the jaw range of motion study or muscle spasm rather than muscle hypertonicity on palpation of a patient with relatively normal jaw range of motion.
- The use of fuzzy or vague diagnostic classification schemes.
- Preconceived expectations. The clinician who sees a patient following a car accident *expects* the patient to suffer complaints attributable to whiplash. Preconceived expectation is also evident in the technology era. The introduction of surface electromyographic (EMG) devices provides a great opportunity to demonstrate the power of expectations. Every nonideal blip on the readout is deemed evidence of a muscle disorder—despite the fact that normative data and reliability studies are lacking.
- Clinical ignorance. The clinician may not know how to listen or inspect, where to touch or probe, or even how to properly interpret what he or she finds.
- Memory or recall. Delayed recording of examination data invariably leads to errors. Recall problems are also seen in patients, especially when they have given many histories to various clinicians or when large gaps in time transpire. Patients tend to exhibit substantial evolution of ideas or change their perceptions over the occurrence or timing of important health matters.
- Incorrect use of diagnostic tools. This problems is largely self-explanatory but is somewhat common in practice. For example, the mere act of palpating the temporomandibular joint often causes abnormal clicks or pops to appear. I cannot help but recall the behavior of one of my residents who would routinely insert the tip of the transilluminator in the mouth of a patient with pursed lips in a brightly lit room. Curiously, I asked the resident what test was being performed, whereupon came the reply, "Of course, Dr. Curl, you can see that I am transilluminating the maxillary sinuses!"

time to time (removing bottle caps, cutting packing tape or thread). Finally, the jaw is used in various ways for pleasure (kissing, sexual habits) as well as entertainment (singing, speeches, special sounds). Because of the jaw's never-ending workload and the considerable forces exerted by the jaw apparatus on a daily basis (it is commonly reported that the average female bites with an average of 250 pounds per square inch and the average male bites with an average of 350 pounds per square inch) it is subject to breakdown. Fortunately for the patient (and his or her physician), the temporomandibular joints are comprised of tissues that are highly adaptive and capable of remodeling and repair. Compounding the clinician's difficulties in discovery is the fact that the temporomandibular joint is a synovial joint. As such, it is subject to diseases and pathologies common to all synovial joints (Table 11–4).

Table 11–2: Common Indications of TMDs

Pain felt in the jaw joint or muscles, or both

Pain felt in the area of the ear, temples, or cheeks

Limited or deviated jaw mobility

Clicking, popping, or grinding of the jaw joints

Hypertrophy of the jaw muscles

Abnormal wear of the teeth

Table 11–3: Activities of the Jaw During Waking and Sleeping Hours

Speech	Eating
Nail biting	Ice chewing
Breathing	Lip moistening
Daytime clenching	Sexual intimacy habits
Tobacco chewing	Gum chewing
Nocturnal clenching	Smoking
Drinking	Humming
Facial gesturing	Lip biting
Dreaming	Tongue thrusting
Pen or pencil nibbling	Singing
Swallowing (we do this about 1500–2000 times per day)	Kissing
	Other oral habits
Whistling	

❗ CLINICAL PEARL

It is precisely the adaptive properties of the temporomandibular joint that serve as the foundation for rational TMD therapy. Consequently, I always devise my therapy to optimize the "natural" recovery properties of the temporomandibular joint apparatus.

3. Is this a discovery of a new disorder? Occasionally, clinicians will come across a brand new onset of TMD. Generally, these cases arise from acute overload secondary to any of the common jaw activities (chewing beef jerky, biting off a piece of hard bread or a steak sandwich). They also commonly occur from acute overuse (gum chewing or speaking for too many hours). From time to time, TMD arises from a traumatic event, particularly blunt trauma (fist fights), sports (elbow against chin contact), falls, and bodily contact with stationary or moving objects (steering wheel or air bag).

Table 11–4: Causes of Pain in the Region of the Temporomandibular Joint

In order to choose a correct and successful method of treatment, complaints of dysfunction and pain should be differentially diagnosed. Pain, when it occurs in the region of the temporomandibular joint, may arise from several causes:

Inflammation of the preauricular lymph node[1]

Otitis media or externa[2]

Referred pain from a trigger point[3]

Tenosynovitis of the temporalis tendon as it passes behind the zygomatic arch[4]

Trigeminal neuralgia[5]

Dental caries[6]

Bony tumors, both benign and malignant (primary and metastatic)[7, 8]

Inflammatory arthritides (i.e., ankylosing spondylitis, rheumatoid arthritis, juvenile arthritis, psoriatic arthritis, etc.)[9–14]

In the case of chronic pain, the practitioner must first differentiate whether the complaints are due to organic changes or psychosocial factors[15, 16]

No matter what the cause or etiology, the clinician must follow three basic time-honored principles. First, and foremost, is to begin with a clear diagnosis. Second, the clinician should select the treatment that is most logical (appropriate) for the diagnosis. Third, the cause, etiology, diagnosis, and treatment should be discussed with the patient to assure his or her informed cooperation in care.

Successful management of TMD depends on many factors. Early on, emphasis must be placed on prevention, which requires identifying habits and functions that place the patient at risk of injury. Once TMD has occurred, the emphasis is then placed on early diagnosis to include *all relevant aspects* of the condition. These aspects include biomechanical principles that have been introduced to explain the events of microtrauma and macrotrauma as mechanisms of injury. In this regard, stress-induced joint remodeling is viewed as a useful paradigm. Also included is the concept of environment (e.g., the workplace, the home, daily exercise routine, etc.), which should include—in addition to the physical domain—psychosocial factors with respect to musculoskeletal complaints and chronic pain.

IS THE PATIENT PRESENTING WITH A DISORDER OF THE OROFACIAL OR TEMPOROMANDIBULAR APPARATUS MANIFESTING AS CERVICAL PAIN OR HEADACHE?

The phenomena of heterotrophic pain (pain referral) and pain along an anatomical pathway typically account for the overlap in clinical symptomatology between localized orofacial or temporomandibular apparatus disorders and the complaint of headache or cervical pain. In some cases, the overlapping symptoms are quite persuasive to the point where the clinician is tempted to forego the studious clinical examination of the patient. In other words, the clinician commits the error of *preconceived expectations*. Occasionally, the clinician falls prey to the error of *clinical ignorance*, but this is easily overcome by following a good clinical examination strategy.

DISORDERS OF THE TEETH

Generally, dental disease does not confuse the patient or the clinician. Most often, toothache pain is localized and easily recognized. However, there are two important exceptions that are rather infamous for their tendency to be confused with headache or cervical pain (Fig. 11–2).

The condition most commonly known as *atypical odontalgia* is a dentoalveolar pain that persists without local cause.[17] The pain is nearly continuous and of many months' duration. Atypical odontalgia is a nonodontogenic form of toothache that is difficult to diagnose; therefore, it leads to a number of invasive dental procedures that normally worsen the pain condition. Often the diagnosis is discovered following a diagnostic block.

Generally, the patient is more than 40 years old and has a history of a dental infection or dental trauma. The condition is known to produce heterotrophic pain symptoms in other craniofacial areas; hence, the tendency to confuse this condition with sinus conditions, myofascial pain, TMD, or headache.

Not all dental infections are acutely painful. In fact, quite a few are relatively asymptomatic. The worst of this group is the *silent draining abscess* of a lower posterior tooth. These lesions tend to drain into the cervical lymph chain; hence, the tendency to produce neck pain. Worse yet is the tendency for physiotherapeutic measures to disperse

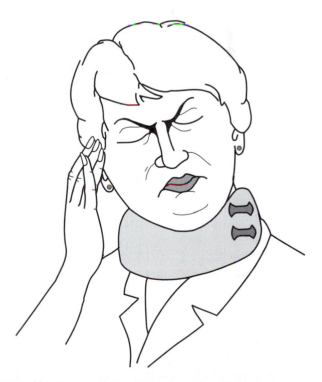

Figure 11–2. A typical odontalgia may mimic several conditions such as myofascial pain, TMD, or headache. Diagnostic blocks using a local anesthetic are very helpful to the diagnosis of this condition.

the infection, thus temporarily providing symptomatic relief. This condition is easily discovered by a studious look at the teeth followed up with a careful palpation of the regional lymph nodes.

! CLINICAL PEARL

One would think that no one could miss a draining abscess into the neck. However, I once evaluated a 17-year-old boy who had failed to respond to treatment for a presumed neck whiplash injury for 6 months. On examination, it was quite apparent that his neck pain was due to an abscessed lower left first molar.

ORAL LESIONS

Most oral lesions are easily recognized as the source of the patient's pain. Although these lesions may cause headache complaints or some degree of neck pain (via lymph node involvement), the clinician easily reaches the proper understanding of the patient's condition. However, *carcinomas of the oral cavity* can be formidable mimickers of neck or headache conditions. The clinician who elicits a careful history and pays close attention to the patient's overall poor response to therapy is most likely to uncover tumors within the cavities and chambers of the skull (Table 11–5).

! CLINICAL PEARL

I can recall a few cases referred to me in which the patient's headache or chronic neck pain was caused by a tumor of the sinus, oral cavity, mandible, or throat.

VASCULAR LESIONS

The clinician should always keep in mind two classic vascular disorders that mimic either headache or neck pain: temporal arteritis and facial migraine. *Temporal arteritis*

Table 11–5: Key Questions or Examination Findings Leading to Suspicion of Cranial or Oral Tumors

Does the patient complain of dysarthria, dysphagia, or dysphonia?

Is the neurological deficit progressing?

Is the pain persistent, constant, and progressive?

Does the condition persist despite rational intervention?

Has the lesion persisted for more than 30 days?

Does the lesion have irregular margins with patches of bleeding?

Does lymph node palpation reveal small, fixed, and shotty nodes?

Is the lesion on the posterolateral sulcus of the tongue?

(TA) is a condition in which certain arteries in the body become inflamed. TA gets its name because it often affects the arteries near the temples, although it can involve arteries in just about any part of the body (Fig. 11–3). The inflammation of the temporal artery leads to narrowing and sometimes to complete blockage of the blood vessel, resulting in ischemia and headache. When TA occludes the blood supply to the eye, vision impairment or blindness may develop suddenly.

Some of the more common symptoms in TA include pain in the jaw muscles when eating or talking (jaw claudication), headaches, and tenderness of the scalp over the temples (thus resembling tension headache). The TA headache is also brought on with considerable neck movement or exertion, thereby mimicking cervicogenic headache. The key clinical finding is palpatory ropiness and tenderness over the temporal artery pathway. Any time there is a complaint of visual disturbance, the patient should seek immediate specialty care.

The second condition to keep in mind is the variant of migraine known as *facial migraine*. It is estimated that as many as 25 percent of migraine sufferers have the facial variety.[18] This headache is brought on with midfacial pain, thus luring the clinician into believing the headache is due to a TMD, toothache, or sinus condition.

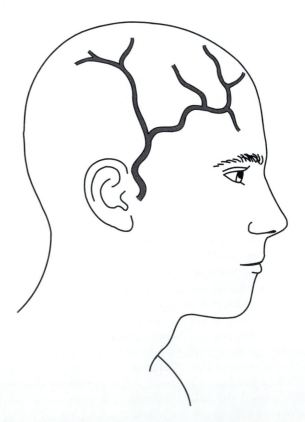

Figure 11–3. Pain in the territory supplied by the temporal artery and nodularity of the artery are key clinical findings in temporal arteritis.

NEUROLOGICAL LESIONS

Trigeminal neuralgia and atypical facial pain are common conditions of facial pain that mimic headache and, rarely, neck pain. Although these two pain conditions are classically well separated in textbooks, a straightforward diagnosis may not always be possible because of the overlapping clinical signs and symptoms.

Atypical facial pain (AFP) was first described by Temple Fay in 1927 as a vascular syndrome of dull, throbbing pain situated deep in the eye and malar region and often referred toward the ear, lateral neck, and shoulders.[19] However, AFP is now known to be a disorder that is mediated through the trigeminal nerve. AFP pain is lasting or occurs for long periods. Unfortunately, the symptoms are not clearly defined as they are in typical and atypical trigeminal neuralgia. AFP seems to affect people who are under high levels of stress or those with a history of psychiatric problems. In fact, Lehmann and Buchholz[21] believe that behind an "atypical face pain," a chronic depressive illness can be hidden. The symptoms of AFP, they believe, are part of an oligosymptomatic depressive disorder.

Trigeminal neuralgia is a disorder of the trigeminal nerve. This is one of the most painful problems that plagues human beings. In fact, its description first appeared in the scientific literature in 1672.[21] Far too often, when a person is suffering with severe facial pain with no apparent cause, the diagnosis given is trigeminal neuralgia. Because of this, the patient may be subjected to medications and even very serious surgical procedures that are unnecessary.

There are four forms of TN, as follows:

1. *Typical trigeminal neuralgia* is characterized as brief paroxysms of pain with pain-free intervals. The second division of the trigeminal nerve (the maxillary division), which supplies feeling to the midface, upper teeth and palate, seems to be involved most often. This pain can be triggered by touching a specific area of the skin while washing, shaving, applying makeup, brushing the teeth, kissing, or even by exposure to cold air. The pain is so severe that the sufferer will do virtually anything to avoid touching the trigger zone that produces the pain.
2. *Atypical trigeminal neuralgia* is characterized by somewhat constant intervals of painful paroxysms that last for minutes, with increasing and decreasing intensity. There are trigger zones with this type; however, there also is an area of dull aching that is intensified by touching the trigger zones. All three divisions of the trigeminal nerve seems to be affected equally. A history of trauma, especially after a surgical incision or blow to the face, raises the suspicion of this disorder.
3. Fromm et al[22] discovered that patients who subsequently developed typical trigeminal neuralgia experienced a prodromal pain that they termed *pretrigeminal neuralgia*. These patients described their prodromal pain as a toothache or sinusitislike or headachelike pain lasting up to several hours, sometimes triggered by jaw movements or by drinking hot or cold liquids.
4. The final variety is *tic douloureux*, which literally means unbearably painful twitch. The characteristic symptoms of tic douloureux are sharp electrical pain accompanied by a twitch.

! CLINICAL PEARL

An 82-year-old woman was sent to me in dire pain by emergency transport. She exhibited the classic signs of tic douloureux, which included a twitch just inferior to the zygomatic arch. This twitch erroneously led a neurologist to believe she suffered from some sort of TMD. As a result, she was injected with a corticosteriod and referred to a local temporomandibular joint clinic, where she was led to believe she suffered from spasm of the lateral pterygoid.

DISORDERS OF THE EYES

Eye strain looms as the greatest ocular cause of headache and neck pain. Generally, whenever eyestrain occurs, neck pain is also present (Fig. 11–4). This is because eyestrain and neck pain often share the same offending activities.

Of the eye strain factors studied by Vincent et al,[23] bright light, reading, working at the computer screen, and watching television were found to more commonly aggravate chronic headache than precititate acute headache. They concluded that eye strain factors are quite important in both the precipitation and aggravation of chronic headache.

Acute glaucoma commonly causes headache symptoms. Less than 5 percent of all glaucoma cases are in the acute category. Most cases of acute glaucoma are secondary to another pathology (e.g., iritis). The presentation of acute glaucoma is somewhat distinctive. Usually a limbic flush (red eye) develops first (depending upon the etiology), followed by a steamy or cloudy cornea. The cloudiness is due to corneal edema. The patient has significant eye pain because of the increased intraocular pressure. This pain can be confused with the retro-orbital eye pain of benign headaches, such as migraine or cervicogenic headaches. Acute glaucoma can be even more difficult to distinguish from headache when the patient also presents with nausea and vomiting.

DISORDERS OF THE EARS

Ear pain (*otalgia*) is one of the most frequently encountered pains in clinical practice. It is often associated with hearing loss, tinnitus, fullness in the ears, or disorders of balance. But ear pain does not always have an otogenic origin. In fact, it is commonly reported that a majority of otological

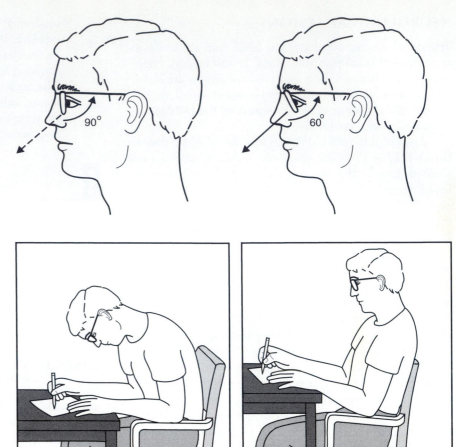

Figure 11–4. Eyestrain is often much more than just eye pain. Visual difficulties are often compensated with poor neck posture.

(Adapted from: Travell JG, Simons DG. Myofascial Pain and Dysfunction: The Trigger Point Manual. Baltimore, MD: Williams and Wilkins, 1983.)

complaints are nonotogenic. The clinician must keep in mind, however, that most ear pain has a pathological cause, even when the disorder does not arise from the ear. The etiology of ear pain can be so multifactorial (e.g., cervical arthritis, myofascitis, infections, Eustachian tube dysfunction, TMDs) that virtually all health care disciplines have been called on for proper diagnoses and treatment. Therefore, the clinician must be aware of the anatomical, muscular, and neuroanatomical relationships of the ear, head, and neck.

Ear infections that tend to drain into the cervical lymph chain may lead production of neck pain (Fig. 11–5). Ear disorders that produce vertigo may lead to neck pain or headache as a result of the disturbance of fine motor control of the neck musculature.[24]

Sudden hearing loss is common, but unexplained in many cases. Although usually attributed to a viral infection of the inner ear, the abrupt onset of the hearing loss in many patients argues against a viral etiology. Viirre and Baloh investigated cases of unexplained sudden hearing loss that meet the diagnostic criteria for migraine.[25] All of the patients had a sudden onset of hearing loss. Their study suggested that vasospasm of the cochlear vasculature during the migraine attack was the cause of the sudden hear-

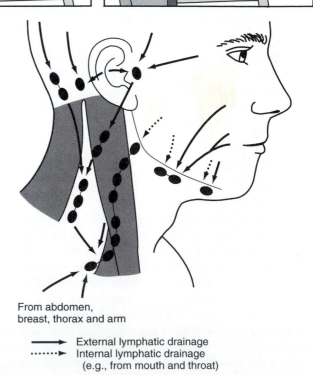

From abdomen, breast, thorax and arm

→ External lymphatic drainage
┄► Internal lymphatic drainage
(e.g., from mouth and throat)

Figure 11–5. Lymph drainage from the ear may inflame nodes in the neck or over the temporomandibular joint. These sore nodes may be confused with temporomandibular joint pain of myofascial trigger points.

ing loss in these patients. If the patient is unfortunate enough to have temporomandibular joint symptoms, the patient's hearing loss may erroneously be attributed to a TMD.

DISORDERS OF THE NOSE AND THROAT

Chronic nasal airway obstruction (CNAO) has profound effects on head, neck, and jaw posture. The developmental effects upon children are even more profound, if not sometimes devastating (Fig. 11–6).

CNAO is usually unilateral; however, it tends to be bilateral when caused by hypertrophic turbinates or adenoids. Hypertrophic turbinates are easily detected upon examination, and the history almost always reveals an

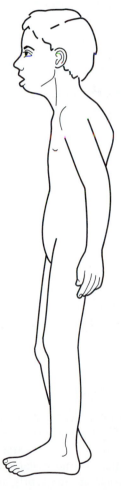

Figure 11–6. The posture of each child will vary to some degree. However, when the child exhibits the physical characteristics of chronic upper airway obstruction, careful consideration of the medical history must be taken. The child may have chronic upper respiratory allergies, repeated infections, enlarged tonsils or adenoids (or both), open-mouth posture (mouth breather), and forward head carriage.

association with nasal allergies. Trauma to the turbinates and vasomotor rhinitis also cause turbinate hypertrophy. Evidence of such factors is elicited in the history and during physical examination.

Adenoidal hypertrophy is the most common cause of nasal obstruction in young patients. Direct evaluation of the adenoids is difficult in the generalist's practice and is the domain of the otorhinolaryngologist. However, indirect evidence of adenoid hypertrophy are findings of persistent sore throat, a mouth-breathing habitus, difficulty with nasal breathing, a deeply arched palate, protrusive upper teeth, and a nasal quality to the voice.

Sinusitis is marked by an inflammatory condition of the lining of one or more of the nasal sinuses. The signs and symptoms of acute sinusitis are commonly known, with the most prominent complaint being headache. Examination of the face reveals focal tenderness upon palpation (Fig. 11–7). The patient might have a fever or an increased pulse rate. Clear or purulent nasal discharge is sometimes present. The mucous membrane of the nose can be reddened and boggy. The patient might even complain of a toothache-type pain. If fluid buildup occurs, a fluid line can appear on X-rays. Sinus conditions are known to mimic myofascial pain, cervicogenic headache, migraine, and TMDs.

Any condition that narrows the nasal passage, particularly in the region of the middle meatus (e.g., deviated septum, foreign bodies, polyps, vasomotor rhinitis, allergies), sets up an opportunity for sinusitis. Exuberant nose blowing or pressure changes during underwater activities can force secretions from the nose into the sinuses, thus contaminating them. Abscesses at the apices of the maxillary molars or bicuspids can develop into infectious sinusitis; an abscess first affects the maxillary sinuses.

Grisel's syndrome involves the subluxation of the atlanto-axial joint from inflammatory ligamentous laxity following an infection in the head and neck region. It is a rare condition, first described in 1830,[26] that usually affects children, but infrequent adult cases do occur. Patients generally seek treatment for progressive unrelenting headache or throat and neck pain. Neurological complications occur in approximately 15 percent of cases and can range from radiculopathy to myelopathy and even death.

TEMPOROMANDIBULAR DISORDERS

Temporal muscle tendinitis (TMT) is a common but frequently overlooked disorder (Fig. 11–8). TMT is another mimicker of headache because so many symptoms are similar to common migraine or tension headache pain. The TMT symptoms usually include pain near the temporomandibular joint and ear, ear fullness, temporal headaches, and facial pain. TMT is an overuse disorder and is classified as a tenosynovitis. Where gum or ice chewing is the cause, tooth sensitivity may be an associated complaint. If clenching is the cause, neck and shoulder pain may be seen in the stressed individual.

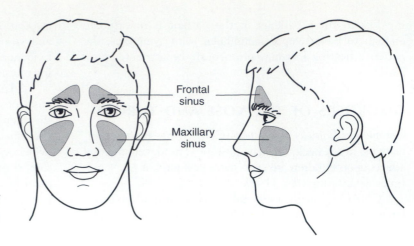

Figure 11–7. The maxillary and frontal sinuses of the face are illustrated. Only these sinuses are readily accessible to clinical examination.

> ## ! CLINICAL PEARL
>
> A patient with an unusual series of mysterious headaches was sent to me after exhaustive visits to numerous physicians. The problem turned out to be a simple case of TMT brought on by the coincidence of a preferred eating habit (peanuts) with new eyeglasses (the stem pressed too tightly against the temples).

Treatment primarily consists of cessation of the offending activity. Supportive care includes a soft diet, using moist heat, muscle relaxants, and anti-inflammatory medications, and sometimes physiotherapy. In extreme cases, injection of local anesthetics and other medications may be necessary.

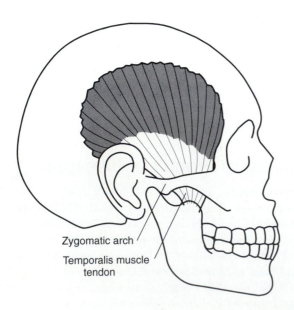

Figure 11–8. The temporal tendon is illustrated. Note that it is protected by the zygomatic arch, thus making extraoral palpation somewhat difficult.

The temporomandibular apparatus is also subject to *myofascial disorders*. For this reason, the clinician must keep in mind the pain referral patterns from the muscles of mastication.

IS THE PATIENT PRESENTING WITH A DISORDER OF THE CERVICAL SPINE OR HEADACHE MANIFESTING AS PAIN IN THE OROFACIAL OR TEMPOROMANDIBULAR APPARATUS AREAS?

The reader is reminded of the phenomena of heterotrophic pain, pain along an anatomical pathway, and the overlap in clinical symptomatology between localized orofacial or temporomandibular apparatus disorders and the complaint of headache or cervical pain. As always, the clinician must resist the temptation of *preconceived expectations* when examining the patient with disorders of the cervical spine or headache.

VASCULAR LESIONS

Carotidynia is a common neck pain syndrome that was first described in 1927.[27] The pain is typically dull, throbbing, continuous, and localized over the carotid bifurcation (Fig. 11–9) but may radiate to the ipsilateral mandible, cheek, eye, or ear. Symptoms are frequently aggravated by swallowing, chewing, and contralateral head movements. Hence, there is a tendency to mistake this condition for orofacial or temporomandibular joint disorders. The cardinal physical finding is tenderness on palpation of the carotid bulb, sometimes accompanied by prominence or throbbing of the carotid pulse. Although several serious conditions should be excluded, most cases follow a benign course.

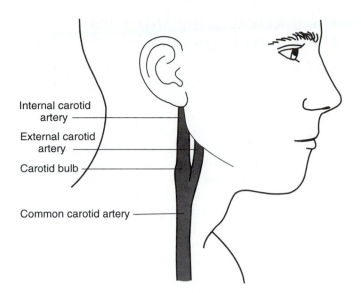

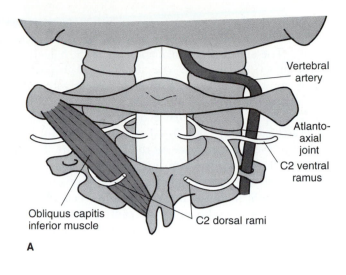

A

Figure 11–9. The carotid artery and bulb are easy to palpate once their anatomical layout is known. Be careful not to palpate both sides simultaneously so as not to restrict blood flow to the brain.

Thromboangiitis obliterans (Buerger's disease) is a nonatherosclerotic, inflammatory, occlusive vascular disease occurring almost exclusively in young male smokers. It involves principally medium-sized and small arteries and veins of the lower and upper extremities, and only rarely the visceral and cerebral blood vessels. Cases of Buerger's disease showing vascular lesions in the oral cavity (via the involvement of branches of the external carotid artery)[28] and of the temporal arteries[29] have been reported.

NEUROLOGICAL LESIONS

The cervicolingual syndrome also known as *neck-tongue syndrome* (NTS) is characterized by pain in the neck and altered sensation in the ipsilateral half of the tongue that is aggravated by neck movement. NTS has been attributed to damage to lingual afferent fibers traveling in the hypoglossal nerve to the C2 spinal roots. NTS is believed to be a result of the presence of a lateral atlanto-axial subluxation or of hypertonicity of the obliquus capitis inferior, either of which can cause compression of the C2 ventral ramus[30] (Fig. 11–10). Afferents fibers from the lingual nerve traveling via the hypoglossal nerve and ansa cervicalis to the second cervical root provide a plausible anatomical explanation for compression of that root, causing "numbness" of half the ipsilateral tongue.

The NTS patient usually presents with unilateral upper nuchal or occipital pain, with or without numbness in these areas, accompanied by simultaneous ipsilateral "numbness" of the tongue. These symptoms are reproducible by compression of the second cervical root in the atlanto-axial space on sharp rotation of the neck. There is no actual numbness of the tongue. Instead, there is hemi-

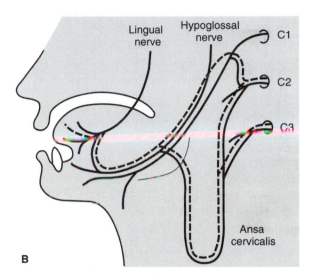

B

Figure 11–10A and B. Anatomy of neck-tongue syndrome.
(Adapted from: Terrett AGJ. Neck-tongue syndrome and spinal manipulation. In: Vernon H, ed. The Upper Cervical Syndrome: Chiropractic Diagnosis and Treatment. *Baltimore, MD: Williams and Wilkins, 1988:223–240.)*

paresis of the tongue, which is a proprioceptive disorder. In other words, the patient loses the position sense of the tongue and this highly abnormal sensation is usually conveyed by the patient as a weird type of numbness (dysesthesia).

The NTS patient may also present with occipital pressure; acute occipital pain of short duration radiating toward the ear with a burning, prickling sensation in this zone; and possible occipital-periorbital pain referral. Uncommonly there is sialorrhea (abnormal salivation), dysarthria, and less commonly symptoms in the arms and hands. Rarely, there is a lack of postural sensation in the cervical spine, resulting in instability of the head.[31]

NTS is also reported to occur with degenerative spondylosis and ankylosing spondylitis of the cervical spine.[32] The anatomical explanation for NTS, namely the interconnections between the lingual and hypoglossal nerves and the C2–3 nerve roots, is consistent with arthritis affecting the C1–2–3 articulation.

Facial pain can arise from *lesions affecting the nerve roots of the cervical plexus*. The C3–4 disc space is the most likely to be involved, but pressure on the C5 root can also produce facial, auricular, or retroauricular pain.[33] Findings on examination are sparse, although sensory impairment in areas of cervical plexus innervation has been observed. Paresthesia or episodic shocklike pain affecting the ear, para-auricular, lower occipital, and mandibular areas and prompted by head turning or extension are the most common complaints. Oftentimes, these symptoms mimic Eagle's syndrome as well as fracture of the styloid process.

❗ CLINICAL PEARL

A self-employed man in his late 40s was referred to me because of persistent neck, facial, auricular, and deep left-sided throat pain. These complaints arose as a result of a rear-end accident wherein the man's head was turned sharply to the left. After many "negative" examinations, he was referred to a neck surgeon who confirmed the presence of a left C5 facet fracture at the time of surgery.

ARTHRITIC DISEASE

The temporomandibular apparatus is not immune to the effects of *arthritic diseases* such as rheumatoid arthritis, systemic lupus erythematosis, ankylosing spondylitis, and psoriatic arthritis. On occasion, the temporomandibular joint is the initial site of onset.

Patients with rheumatoid arthritis and psoriatic arthritis show more frequent and severe signs and symptoms than subjects with ankylosing spondylitis. In general, the common signs and symptoms of TMD (pain during function, tenderness on palpation, and stiffness) are seen in rheumatoid arthritis, psoriatic arthritis, and ankylosing spondylitis. However, none of the signs and symptoms is pathognomonic for any of these arthritides.[34] Estimates are that about half of the patients with inflammatory rheumatic disease show a primary temporomandibular arthritis.[35]

The significant relationship between rheumatic disease and temporomandibular arthritis places a special burden on the clinicians who treat musculoskeletal disorders. As a rule, arthritic involvement of the temporomandibular joints should be suspected whenever the patient reports an abrupt change in jaw function, acute changes in the bite, crepitus or grinding sounds arising from the joint, joint swelling, or progressive increase in joint tenderness or stiffness. When arthritis is suspected, a prompt referral to an orofacial specialist or rheumatologist is in order.

THE CERVICAL SPINE AND TMDS—IS THERE A RELATIONSHIP?

In a few words, yes and no. The "no" side is supported by the empirical experience that common and somewhat dramatic cervical disorders (torticollis, neck fractures, cervical scoliosis) have not been shown to cause TMD. Further, the theory that neck sprain or strain leads to TMD has never been supported by credible scientific evidence.

In 1996, Wijer et al[36] specifically studied the relationship between TMDs and cervical spine disorders. The subjects included 111 consecutive patients with TMD and 103 consecutive patients with cervical spine disorders. They found that patients with cervical spine disorders reported *fewer* symptoms of TMDs than the subgroups of patients with TMDs. Hence, the authors conclude that the results of their study do not support the theoretical concept that cervical spine disorders may give rise to TMDs.

The "yes" side of the relationship question is supported by the deformities caused by forward head posture secondary to CNAO. In 1872, Tomes[37] coined the term "adenoid faces" to describe the craniofacial and head posture changes associated with CNAO. This condition is better termed the "long face syndrome" as it is characterized by an increased vertical height in the lower half of the face, a toothy smile, unusually deep palatal vault, and a steep jaw angle. Chronic nasal obstruction typically leads to disuse atrophy of the lateral cartilages of the nares, resulting in a slitlike opening with a narrow nasal vault (tension nose).

Then in 1962, Moss[38] further explained these changes in the "functional matrix theory" in an attempt to spell out the craniofacial distortions in nasally obstructed patients. He noted a significant relationship between nasal airway obstruction and certain craniofacial changes, including a "clockwise" rotation of the mandible in a more vertical and posterior direction, elongation of the lower face height, open bite, crossbite, retrognathia, and forward head carriage. The final result is best visualized when the child reaches puberty through early adulthood. At this stage, the individual variably exhibits the dento-craniofacial deformities previously noted, forward head carriage, abnormal cervical lordosis, rounded shoulders, a flattened chest wall, and a slouching posture.

The view that chronic nasal obstruction can effect musculoskeletal development is not without opposition. Clearly, there are cases of craniofacial problems in the absence of nasal obstruction and vice versa. Vig et al[39] assert that an obstacle to resolving the issue of musculoskeletal deformities following nasal airway obstruction has to do with the variable definition of mouth breathing. Mouth breathers may be patients who breathe with an open mouth but are partial nasal breathers, as well as those who fall in between the extremes of total nasal and total oral respiration. Vig's group also found that the nasal airflow in normal, "long-faced," and lip incompetent patients was not significantly different.

TEMPOROMANDIBULAR DISORDERS AS A GENERAL CLINICAL ENTITY

The general entity, now agreed-upon as TMD, has evolved from a host of confusing and conflicting terms (Table 11–6). Presently, TMD represents a set of related pathological changes that produce musculoskeletal symptoms in the jaw. However, the clinician is often reminded that the term TMD is purposely broad and is used only to convey a general concept that there is a population of patients suffering from abnormal function and pain of the muscles and joints of the jaw. The term TMD does not convey a mechanism of injury or disease, because TMD encompasses all of the specific conditions that afflict our patients.

! CLINICAL PEARL

Pain associated with jaw use, limited envelope of jaw movement, joint or muscle pain (or both) on examination, and abnormal joint sounds are all indications of TMD.

MAJOR CATEGORIES OF TMDS

Therapeutic strategies associated with these TMDs begin with a review of the major clinical categories embodying specific (target) disorders. The clinical classification of TMDs has evolved over the years to include:

> Muscle disorders
> Temporomandibular joint disorders
> Inflammatory disorders
> Disorders of mandibular mobility (hyper- or hypomobility)
> Growth disorders

Table 11–6: Terms That Have Been Used to Describe TMDs

Stomatognathic disorder

Craniomandibular disorder

Costen's syndrome

Myofascial pain dysfunction syndrome

Jaw whiplash

Temporomandibular joint syndrome

Cervicocraniomandibular disorder

Craniofacial disorder

Malocclusive disorder

Buzyness syndrome

Muscle Disorders

TMDs commonly manifest with functional disturbances. Within this group, the most common functional disturbance is muscle pain. Patients typically report pain associated with the use of the jaw, a pain that is aggravated by manual or functional palpation of the involved muscles. It is noteworthy that mandibular motion may be limited due to the inhibitory effects of pain via the muscle splinting effect.

Sometimes an acute malocclusion accompanies the muscle symptoms. When an acute malocclusion is present, the mechanism involves closing of the mandible from mandibular rest position, which is determined in large part by muscle tonus. When the mandible is brought from a muscularly altered mandibular rest position into intercuspal position the patient may perceive this as a "change in the bite."

Muscle disorders, as they apply to TMD, generally are subdivided into the following categories:

> Protective muscle splinting (trismus, bracing, guarding)
> Myospasms
> Myositis
> Myofascial pain (trigger point activity)
> Contracture
> Hypertrophy
> Dyskinesia (muscle incoordination)
> Dystonia
> Bruxism

Temporomandibular Joint Disorders

Temporomandibular joint disorders can manifest in a variety of specific disorders. Joint disorders resulting from interference with normal functioning of the articular disc (also known as disc displacement or internal derangement) occupy a position second only to muscle disorders. Bell[40] defines internal derangements of the temporomandibular joint as "morphofunctional disorders of the disc-condyle complex."

In recent years disc displacement disorders have been the focus of heated debate from researchers and clinicians. Nearly every conceivable treatment to the disc has been tried in vain attempts to "cure" the patient.

Inflammatory Disorders

Inflammatory disorders of the temporomandibular joint may be described as a continuous pain that is increased with function. Inflammatory joint pain is typically accompanied by hyperalgesia or allodynia in the area, with possible muscle splinting activity in those muscles that cross the joint.

Temporomandibular joint disorders generally are subdivided into the following categories:

> Arthralgia
> Capsulitis or synovitis
> Arthritic disease (systemic)
> Degenerative disease (osteoarthritis)
> Traumatic articular disease (sprain or strain, fracture)

Disc displacement without reduction (closed lock)
Disc displacement with reduction
Subluxation of the condyle
Dislocation of the condyle

Disorders of Mandibular Mobility

The abnormal jaw movement may be hypermobile or hypomobile. Hypermobile conditions are usually identified by maximal mandibular opening distances exceeding 55 to 60 mm. Hypomobile conditions are noted when mandibular movement is less than 40 mm of opening. Admittedly, there are exceptions to these numbers.

Hypermobility of jaw movement may be a normal variation in a person with generalized joint laxity. Or it may be a result of ligamentous tearing, stretching, or disruption from trauma. In any event, a hypermobile temporomandibular joint is more likely to suffer from disc dislocation or subluxation phenomena.

Hypermobile joints are known to dislocate beyond the crest of the articular eminence (condylar dislocation) (Fig. 11–11). Although simple manipulation procedures often reduce the joint to its original state, there have been reports of individuals who did not seek treatment and, years later, began forming a new articulation in this dislocated position.[41]

Hypomobility of jaw movement may be a normal variation in a small person or a person with a small mouth. Or, it may be a result of anterior disc dislocation (Fig. 11–12), intracapsular scar tissue formation, abnormal bone growth, or contracure of muscle. As a rule, patients with hypomobility are more likely to present to the clinic than their hypermobile counterparts because of the greater degree of impairment seen with limited mouth opening.

Disorders of mandibular mobility are generally subdivided into the following categories:

Hypermobility
Adhesion
Ankylosis
Coronoid process elongation
Fibrosis of muscle (contracture)

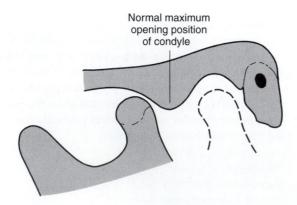

Figure 11–11. Hypermobility of the temporomandibular joint.

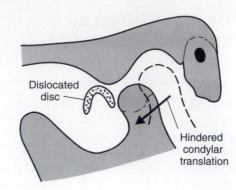

Figure 11–12. Hypomobility of the temporomandibular joint from anterior disc dislocation.

Growth Disorders

Growth disturbances may result from a variety of causes but can be grouped into hypoplasias, hyperplasias, and neoplasias. Genetic predisposition, birth or childhood trauma, and metabolic disorders are typical causes of hyper- or hypoplastic growth. Generally, these disorders are recognized early in the child's development and treated accordingly. Neoplasias, on the other hand, are rare in the temporomandibular joint system. In any event, these disorders are recognized by the tendency of the clinical symptoms to closely correlate with structural changes (e.g., bony deformity).

TREATMENT OF COMMON TEMPOROMANDIBULAR DISORDERS

A frequent criticism of temporomandibular therapists is that they are attempting to turn a simple jaw complaint into a regimen of extensive physical therapy and dental work or surgery, or both, to reposition the jaw. The controversy surrounding TMD therapy is fueled by the many myths and misunderstandings that persist regarding TMD. This is particularly true of theories of etiology, which are often spun from the creative minds of clinicians rather than developed through scientific research. Many of these etiological theories have been reinforced by the convictions of those who subscribe to a given theory as a result of empirical treatment successes they have obtained. I cannot help but recall a classic encounter with a clinician who claimed TMD arose because of an unleveling at the base of the spine. At the conclusion of his elaborate theoretical explanation, he announced that he had developed an intrarectal maneuver to level the sacral base and that his treatment has a 100% cure rate. When asked for the basis of his remarkable cure rate, he reported, "After one or two treatments, three at the most, my patients stopped complaining of jaw dysfunction." Obviously, his theoretical framework was reinforced by his empiric success.

CURRENT STATE OF UNDERSTANDING

As previously noted, TMD refers to a collection of medical and dental conditions affecting the temporomandibular apparatus. Depending on the practitioner and the diagnostic methodology, the term TMD has been cleverly used to characterize a wide range of conditions diversely presented as pain in the face or jaw joint area, headaches, earaches, dizziness, masticatory musculature hypertrophy, limited mouth opening, closed or open lock of the temporomandibular joint, abnormal occlusal wear, clicking or popping sounds in the jaw joint, and other complaints.

Although specific etiologies such as degenerative arthritis and trauma underlie some TMDs, as a group these conditions have no common etiology. Many still do not have an agreed upon biological explanation. The severity of these presenting conditions may range from clinically insignificant signs (e.g., painless popping) to seriously debilitating pain or dysfunction.

Broadly accepted, scientifically based guidelines for diagnosis and management of TMD are still unavailable. Nevertheless, practitioners have responded to their patients' needs by devising and employing a broad range of treatment approaches. Some of these include educational or behavioral counseling, pharmacological or mechanical approaches, occlusal therapies, and a variety of surgical procedures, or any combination of these. There is no doubt that in many cases, patients have improved no matter whose care they seek. Unfortunately there have also been some disasterous outcomes.

The absence of accepted guidelines for evaluation and diagnosis undermines the goal of consistent and conservative therapy. Unfortunately, the lack of standard treatment protocols means that patients may undergo therapy with inadequately tested approaches.

Apparently, this confusion has not gone unnoticed by the patient population. Patients suffering form pain and dysfunction in the temporomandibular region sometimes ignore appointments after the initial examination. This form of noncompliance is well known and is often studied in patients suffering from recurrent headaches, arthritis, and lower back pain.

De Boever et al[42] studied TMD patients who did not attend the next visit after their initial examination. The nonattenders had more pain and dysfunction at initial examination than did the treated patients while the treated patients reported a *shorter* duration of symptoms before seeking treatment than did the nonattenders. The nonattender's main reason for not returning was that symptoms improved enough or disappeared completely and spontaneously *without the proposed treatment*. At the time of the survey, 57 percent of the nonattenders reported to be symptom free or sufficiently improved. Most still had some symptoms such as clicking (59 percent) and reduced mouth opening (21 percent), but only 24 percent reported themselves to be in need of treatment.

SEQUELAE OF UNTREATED TMDS

Presently, TMD is classified based on signs and symptoms rather than by etiology. As this is the case, the signs and symptoms of TMD should be viewed in the larger context of other muscle and joint disorders. Several lessons can be learned from diagnostic and therapeutic approaches to other joint and muscle diseases.

An explanation for the nontreatment of TMD is at hand. Currently available epidemiological evidence suggests that TMD is frequently self-limiting.[43] The lower prevalence of TMD signs and symptoms at older ages reported in cross-sectional data is consistent with self-limiting signs and symptoms.[44] The few longitudinal clinical studies available at this time support this conclusion.[45]

At this time, well-designed, representative, cross-sectional and longitudinal studies of TMD are scarce. As a result, the natural history of TMD is not well defined. In addition, most studies are descriptive, with predictive or explanatory analyses virtually absent.[46] This means that the clinician and the patient must strive to develop a treatment plan that is evidence based and patient centered. Before agreeing upon any treatment plan, the clinician must weigh the patient's perception of pain and dysfunction and the impact of these on the patient's quality of life. In the absence of definite pathology, the clinician may work with the patient to devise a program of self-management supported by education and an understanding of the role of psychosocial factors. If the patient does not obtain adequate relief from these measures, the clinician may next consider a number of conservative, noninvasive, and reversible treatments.

SYMPTOMS, SIGNS, AND OTHER EXAMINATION DATA THAT PROVIDE A BASIS FOR INITIATING TREATMENT

Of course, initiation of therapy ought to be based on a thorough and sensitive study of the patient. Fortunately, signs and symptoms associated with certain TMDs are well established. However, the etiology of others remains ambiguous. Unfortunately for the clinician, too many assessment methods lack evidence of their diagnostic value (i.e., validity, reliability, specificity, sensitivity, and cost-effectiveness). Diagnosis and initial treatment, therefore, often depend on the clinician's experience and philosophy, rather than on sound clinical or scientific evidence.

Meanwhile, clinicians agree that diagnosis and initiation of treatment should be based on data derived from the physical examination and a well thought out medical and dental history. The history derives information from various quarters, including hearing, speech, swallowing or eating problems, pain and dysfunction, and consideration of psychosocial factors. The physical examination should encompass evaluation of oral and facial tissues, musculature of the head and neck, and neurological function. Attention should be paid to functional range of motion of the jaw, dental health, existence of parafunctional conditions (e.g., clenching, nail biting, pen chewing) and the presence of joint or muscle tenderness. Psychosocial assessments, by trained individuals, should determine the extent to which pain and dysfunction interfere with or diminish the patient's quality of life.

There is insufficient evidence at present to warrant "preventive" interventions to thwart the development of TMDs. For example, there is no clear evidence that orthodontic treatment or full mouth restorative procedures prevents, predisposes, or causes TMDs. Unfortunately for the patient, dentists may have made them undergo sessions of occlusal grinding, extensive (and expensive) fittings with crowns or bridges, and the "treatment" of displaced discs or noisy joints on the theory such care will prevent future onset of TMDs.

INITIAL MANAGEMENT AND TREATMENT OF PATIENTS WITH VARIOUS TMD CONDITIONS

Initial management is universally defined as the first treatment the patient receives after seeking care. The initial management of TMDs described in this chapter assumes that the clinician has identified the underlying systemic or overt joint disease. Patients with joint pain and painful muscle conditions associated with systemic disease obviously require specialty treatment for the underlying disease. On occasion, these patients may also need nonspecialty therapy directed specifically to the temporomandibular apparatus and related structures. Such treatment must be carefully coordinated with the specialist.

As was noted earlier, there is a lack of clinical studies concerning the use of therapeutic modalities offered for TMD patients. The clinician ought to keep in mind that most patients experiencing acute pain will have a self-limiting disorder and that a variety of different interventions will show improvements in the patient's pain and dysfunction. Hence, caution is urged with regard to use of invasive and other irreversible treatments, particularly in the initial management of TMDs.

Patient Education

Reassurance is invaluable. The patient should be educated regarding TMDs and the fact that most of these problems follow a benign course. Attention should be directed at eliminating certain behaviors that are perceived to be harmful, such as clenching and ice chewing, and recommendations for exercise and stress management should be given. Rest and dietary modifications are also useful.

The initial self-treatment program typically involves four tasks.

- First, an anti-inflammatory home care program is instituted. This can range in scope from over-the-counter medications to meditation, herbs, teas, dietary changes, or other anti-inflammatory measures.

- Second, the patient should be taught how to apply heat or ice as an aid to physiological relaxation and the eventual healing.
- Third, the patient should be advised to avoid mechanically stressful activities. A soft diet is typically recommended to prevent reaggravation during the acute phase of jaw pain and dysfunction.
- Fourth, the patient needs to practice the most important aspect of conservative therapy, namely, resting of the jaw. This is done by making the patient aware of unconscious poor habits such as posture, swallowing, clenching, or talking. The patient should also be instructed to practice the "lips apart and jaws relaxed" procedure.

Self-care programs are considered very important because a significant number of TMD patients undergo resolution of their symptoms without any other form of care. Approximately 10 to 30 days are usually required for home therapy to exert its maximum effect. As a rule, follow-up with aggressive treatment should be initiated only after it is shown that home care will not resolve the patient's complaints.

Pain Control

Pain control is always an important part of the initial symptom management. The pain control measures used for TMDs are similar to those that are useful for other painful musculoskeletal conditions. Meditation, herbs, over-the-counter nonsteroidal anti-inflammatory drugs (NSAIDs), and prescribed opiates are the mainstay of acute pain management. Muscle relaxant medications and low-dose antidepressants are also useful in the initial management of TMDs. Whatever the course of pain management, the clinician must weigh the risks against potential benefits, and do so within his or her professional competence in the administration and management of such strategies.

Physiotherapy

Physiotherapeutic applications to TMDs include a wide variety of manual techniques and treatment modalities. Most have been borrowed from treatment of other musculoskeletal disorders. As a rule, these therapies are conservative and noninvasive. Benefits to TMD patients have been described but are putative.

While the TMD patient is improving, an exercise regimen should be employed. Gentle, yet progressive, specific stretching exercises are usually helpful in remobilizing the jaw and in maintaining the patient's awareness of his or her habits, as well as improving muscular coordination.

Although physiotherapy can be performed by a dentist, chiropractor, or a physical therapist, only those trained in this area ought to apply the therapy. The management of acutely increased muscle tonicity generally includes the use of a vapocoolant spray or quick icing of the skin overlying the painful muscle while immediately stretching that muscle (stretch-and-spray). Those skilled in the use of physiotherapy are accustomed to the use of ice packs, heat packs, diathermy, and electrical or ultrasonic stimulation of the soft tissues. Additional therapeutic options include anesthetic injections and soft tissue mobilization and manipulation.

Intraoral Appliances

This form of therapy is unique to dentistry. Simple stabilization splints are used by many dentists for the early treatment of TMDs. Some argue this is because the general dentist is not comfortable with or trained in other forms of therapy. Nevertheless, if used, the dental splint should aid in maintaining the recovery achieved by physiotherapeutic intervention and a self-treatment program.

Splint therapy may be needed in some cases. The bruxing patient, for example, who shows accelerated dental wear may benefit from a protective splint. The purpose of the splint is not to reposition the jaw or directly stop the bruxing habit. The splint basically serves as a behavioral feedback device, making the patient aware of his or her destructive oral parafunctional habit.

Behavioral Medicine

In the event the patient continues to have a painful TMD, perpetuating causative psychosocial factors probably have not been clearly identified or are not being addressed. With the proper encouragement, the patient is usually receptive to a referral for behavioral medicine (stress control or relaxation training). For the patient with chronic pain, referral to a multidisciplinary pain clinic is indicated.

CONCLUSION

This chapter has attempted to guide the reader to a better understanding of the disorders of the orofacial area and the temporomandibular apparatus. Admittedly, this is a complex area, but the diligent clinician who pursues his or her good sense of clinical curiosity will eventually prevail where others have fallen short. Perhaps the best advice one can give to the patient with orofacial pain or TMD is the following: *"Philosophy, like medicine, has plenty of drugs, few good remedies, and hardly any specific cures."*[47]

REFERENCES

1. Bates B. *A Guide to Physical Examination.* 3rd ed. Philadelphia, Pa: JB Lippincott; 1983.
2. Myers LJ. Possible inflammatory pathways relating temporomandibular joint dysfunction to otic symptoms. *Cranio* 1988;6(1):64–70.
3. Travell J. Mechanical headache. *Headache* 1962;7:23–29.
4. Solberg WK. Temporomandibular disorders: Management of problems associated with inflammation, chronic hypomobility and deformity. *Br Dent J* 1986;160:421–428.
5. Friedman MH, Agus B, Weisberg J. Neglected conditions producing preauricular and referred pain. *J Neurol Neurosurg Psychiatry* 1983;46:1067–1072.
6. Shore N. *Temporomandibular Joint Dysfunction and Occlusal Equilibration.* 2nd ed. Philadelphia, Pa: JB Lippincott; 1976:160.
7. Tom BM, Rao VM, Farole A. Nondiscogenic causes of temporomandibular joint pain. *Cranio* 1991;9(3):220–227.
8. Nwoku ALN, Koch H. The temporomandibular joint: A rare localization for bony tumors. *J Maxillofac Surg* 1974;2:113–117.
9. Ronning O, Valiaho ML, Laaksonen AL. The involvement of the temporomandibular joint in juvenile rheumatoid arthritis. *Scand J Rheumatol* 1974;3:89–92.
10. Resnick D. Temporomandibular joint involvement in ankylosing spondylitis. Comparison with rheumatoid arthritis and psoriasis. *Radiology* 1974;112(3):587–91.
11. Ogus H. Rheumatoid arthritis of the temporomandibular joint. *Br J Oral Surg* 1975;12:275.
12. Morgan DH. The great imposter: Disease of the temporomandibular joint. *J Am Dent Assoc* 1976;235:2395.
13. Lowry JC. Psoriatic arthritis involving the temporomandibular joint. *J Oral Surg* 1975;33:206.
14. Vlain GS. Psoriatic arthritis and the temporomandibular joint. *J Dent* 1976;4:123.
15. Moulton R. Oral and dental manifestations of anxiety. *Psychiatry* 1955;4:261–273.
16. Curl DD, Shapiro CS. Head/neck pain: The need to identify the patient with acute versus chronic pain. *J Chiro Technique* 1989;1(3):101–105.
17. Graff-Radford SB, Solberg WK. Atypical ondontalgia. *J Craniomandib Disord Facial Oral Pain* 1966;6(4):260–266.
18. Merrill RL. Orofacial pain mechanisms and their clinical application. *Dental Clin North Am* 1997;41(2):167–188.

19. Brass LS, Amedee RG. Atypical facial pain. *J La State Med Soc* 1990;142(1):15–18.
20. Lehmann HJ, Buchholz G. Atypical facial neuralgia or depressive facial pain. Diagnostic aspects of a well-demarcated form of masked depression. *Fortschr Neurol Psychiatr* 1986;54(5):154–157.
21. Isler H. Independent historical development of the concepts of cluster headache and trigeminal neuralgia. *Funct Neurol* 1987;2(2):141–148.
22. Fromm GH, Graff-Radford SB, Terrence CF, Sweet WH. Pre-trigeminal neuralgia. *Neurology* 1990;40(10):1493–1495.
23. Vincent AJ, Spierings EL, Messinger HB. A controlled study of visual symptoms and eye strain factors in chronic headache. *Headache* 1989;29(8):523–527.
24. Chek P, Curl DD. Posture and headache. In: *Chiropractic Approach to Head Pain*. Baltimore, Md: Williams & Wilkins; 1996.
25. Viirre ES, Baloh RW. Migraine as a cause of sudden hearing loss. *Headache* 1996;36(1):24–28.
26. Mathern GW, Batzdorf U. Grisel's syndrome. Cervical spine clinical, pathologic, and neurologic manifestations. *Clin Orthop* 1989;244:131–146.
27. Hill LM, Hastings G. Carotidynia: A pain syndrome. *J Fam Pract* 1994;39(1):71–75.
28. Farish SE, el-Mofty SK, Colm SJ. Intraoral manifestation of thromboangiitis obliterans (Buerger's disease). *Oral Surg Oral Med Oral Pathol Oral Radiol Edontol* 1990;69(2):223–226.
29. Lie JT, Michet CJ Jr. Thromboangiitis obliterans with eosinophilia (Buerger's disease) of the temporal arteries. *Hum Pathol* 1988;19(5):598–602.
30. Bogduk N. An anatomical basis for the neck-tongue syndrome. *J Neurol Neurosurg Psychiatry* 1981;44(3):202–208.
31. Fortin CJ, Biller J. Neck tongue syndrome. *Headache* 1985;25(5):255–258.
32. Webb J, March L, Tyndall A. The neck-tongue syndrome: Occurrence with cervical arthritis as well as normals. *J Rheumatol* 1984;11(4):530–533.
33. Kessler LA, Abla A. Syndrome of the cervical plexus caused by high cervical nerve root compression. *Neurosurgery* 1991;28(4):506–509.
34. Kononen M, Wenneberg B, Kallenberg A. Craniomandibular disorders in rheumatoid arthritis, psoriatic arthritis, and ankylosing spondylitis. A clinical study. *Acta Odontol Scand* 1992;50(5):281–287.
35. Linke M, Horch HH, Herzog M, Albrecht HJ. TMJ examination in patients with underlying rheumatic diseases. *Dtsch Z Mund Kiefer Gesichtschir* 1989;13(6):407–414.
36. Wijer A, Leeuw JRJ, Steenks MH, Bosman F. Temporomandibular and cervical spine disorders: Self-reported signs and symptoms. *Spine* 1996;21(14):1638–1646.
37. Tomes CV. On the developmental origin of the v-shaped contracted maxilla. *Monthly Review of Dental Surgery* 1872;1:2–5.
38. Moss ML. The functional matrix: Functional cranial components. In: Krauss BS, Reidel, eds. *Vistas in Orthodontics*. Philadelphia, Pa: Lea and Febiger; 1962:85–90.
39. Vig PS, Sarver DM, Hall DJ, Warren DW. Quantitative evaluation of nasal airflow in relation to facial morphology. *Am J Orthod* 1981;79(3):263–272.
40. Bell W. *Temporomandibular Disorders: Classification, Diagnosis, Management*. Chicago, Ill: Year Book Medical; 1986.
41. Noach P. Dislocation/subluxation of TMJ—a case report. *J Dent Assoc S Afr* 1985;40(8):483.
42. De Boever JA, Van Wormhoudt K, De Boever EH. Reasons that patients do not return for appointments in the initial phase of treatment of temporomandibular disorders. *J Orofac Pain* 1996;10(1):66–72.
43. McNeill C. Management of temporomandibular disorders: Concepts and controversies. *J Prosthet Dent* 1997;77(5):510–522.
44. Ow RK, Loh T, Neo J, Khoo J. Symptoms of craniomandibular disorder among elderly people. *J Oral Rehabil* 1995;22(6):413–419.
45. LeResche L. Assessment of physical and behavioral outcomes of treatment. *Oral Surg Oral Med Oral Pathol Oral Radiol Endod* 1997;83(1):82–86.
46. Management of temporomandibular disorders. *NIH Technol Statement Online* 1996; April 29–May 1.
47. Sébastien-Roch Nicolas de Chamfort (1741–94), *Maxims and Considerations*, vol. 1, no. 17 (1796). The Columbia Dictionary of Quotations is licensed from Columbia University Press. Copyright © 1993, 1995 by Columbia University Press. All rights reserved.

CHAPTER 12

Neuropsychological Dysfunction Related to Cervical Trauma

GIUSEPPE DI STEFANO & BOGDAN P. RADANOV

"Natural science does not simply describe and explain nature; it is part of the interplay between nature and ourselves; it describes nature as exposed to our method of questioning."

—W. Heisenberg, *Physics and Philosophy*
(London: George Allen & Unwin, 1959)

INTRODUCTION

Whiplash-associated disorders are usually caused by a sudden acceleration followed by deceleration of the neck during car accidents when the patient's motor vehicle is hit from behind by another vehicle. Whereas most patients recover within some weeks, other patients develop chronic physical, psychological, and cognitive complaints. Objective tests often fail to find the underlying somatic reasons for the complaints, which causes whiplash to be one of the most controversial and least understood phenomena in the area of posttraumatic injuries. Despite a growing number of studies, the pathogenic mechanisms and the predictors for the course of recovery after whiplash are not yet clear. Etiological explanations range from lesions of various structures of the cervical spine[1] and the brain[2] to secondary gain and accident neurosis.[3, 4]

Similarly, there is a significant debate regarding the extent and the causes of neuropsychological dysfunctions relative to cervical trauma.[5] The older, mainly retrospective studies show a very heterogeneous clinical picture. Some of these studies revealed severe disorders of attention and memory,[6–10] whereas others failed to find any cognitive impairment after whiplash.[11–13] But due to severe methodological problems, such as unclear definition of injury, inclusion of cases with head injuries, retrospective research design, and highly selected samples, the validity of these studies is seriously compromised. Consequently, the retrospective studies are not supposed to reflect the real prevalence of neuropsychological dysfunctions after cervical trauma. In contrast to the retrospective research, most recent prospective studies using a clear definition of whiplash that excludes patients with possible traumatic brain lesions have shown homogenous results demonstrating mild to moderate attention deficits after whiplash.[2, 14–17] However, no significant dysfunctions of memory or other higher cognitive abilities were uncovered, and one particular prospective study did not reveal any neuropsychological impairment at all.[18]

The etiology of the neuropsychological impairment after whiplash remains an object of controversy. Some researchers have argued that a sudden hyperextension and hyperflexion of the neck can cause subtle brain lesions, which may explain the attention difficulties.[2] However, the empirical evidence for brain lesions after cervical trauma is not convincing. To our knowledge, no study using magnetic resonance imaging (MRI) in consecutive series of whiplash patients succeeded in finding brain lesions.[2, 19, 20] In this context, the recent development of new imaging techniques, such as single photon emission computed tomography (SPECT), seems of particular interest. The first studies performed with this method have shown a consistent pattern of parietal-occipital hypoperfusion in whiplash patients and in patients with nontraumatic cervical pain.[21–23] The authors believe that the hypoperfusion is most likely caused by a stimulation of pain-sensitive cervical afferents. The results do not show any signs of cerebral lesions after whiplash.

A recent study using positron emission tomography (PET) and SPECT in whiplash patients revealed most interesting correlations between the imaging results and the psychological distress.[24] In this study, a significant hypometabolism was found in the putamen and the fronto-polar and lateral temporal cortex of whiplash patients with persisting symptoms. In the absence of any structural cerebral lesions, as assessed by MRI, a significant correlation between the scores of the Beck Depression Inventory (BDI) and the hypometabolism in the fronto-polar region was found. This correlation raises the question of whether metabolic changes in the brain of whiplash patients could rather be explained through the presence of depression than by traumatic brain injury. However, the low sensitivity and the fact that neither PET nor SPECT can differentiate between functional alterations and microscopic brain damage raise doubts about the usefulness of these new imaging techniques. As long as these methodological and technical problems persist, we doubt whether PET and SPECT can provide objective findings about the origin of symptoms after cervical trauma.

An alternative hypothesis is provided by researchers who argue that secondary factors, such as the sensory input of chronic pain (i.e., nociception), sleep deprivation resulting from chronic pain, or side effects of centrally acting medication, might distract the cognitive processing of information and cause neuropsychological dysfunction.[17, 25] This assumption is confirmed by studies showing remission of cognitive impairment and of psychological distress after complete recovery from pain in whiplash patients.[26, 27] In our opinion, the hypothesis of nociception causing neuropsychological dysfunctions by absorbing the mental processing capacities and distracting the patient's attention seems very promising and deserves further research. Based on a better understanding of the nature of symptoms after cervical trauma, efforts have to be made to develop appropriate therapy and rehabilitation programs for both acute and chronic whiplash-associated disorders.

In this chapter, the prospective studies examining neuropsychological performance of whiplash patients are presented in detail and the possible causes for the cognitive impairment will be discussed. The proposed accident mechanism in whiplash and the evidence for brain lesions are reviewed first.

MECHANISM OF INJURY AND EVIDENCE FOR BRAIN LESIONS AFTER CERVICAL TRAUMA

One of the main features of whiplash is the lack of a direct force or impact to the head.[28] Usually, after a vehicle has been struck from behind, the trunk and the shoulders are accelerated by the back of the seat. Because of its mass, the head resists the forward movement, causing hyperextension of the neck. After a moment of inertia, the head is pulled forward and starts to accelerate too, resulting in hyperflexion of the neck when the car and the patient's trunk come to a stop. In their classical experiments, Severy et al[29] found that relatively small velocities of vehicles can result in enormous accelerations of the body. In a collision at 9.9 miles per hour, an acceleration of 11.3 g was measured on the neck. One g corresponds to the normal gravitational force on earth. This shows that the speed and the damage of cars involved in an accident may have little relationship to the forces transmitted to the patient's body.

Some authors argue that such an accident might cause brain lesions without direct impact to the head or loss of consciousness.[2] They hypothesize that, because of its inertia, the brain tends to maintain its position. This may cause an impact of the moving skull on the surface of the brain. Animal experiments provide empirical evidence for this hypothesis. Ommaya et al[30] have shown that cervical trauma without direct impact to the head can cause cerebral lesions in rhesus monkeys. Yet it remains unclear how far these findings can be generalized to real accidents in humans. However, brain lesions in humans after whiplash have been described by several authors. Ommaya and Yarnell[31] report two patients who had suffered subdural hematoma after whiplash without direct head impact or loss of consciousness. Other researchers report cases of transient global amnesia after cervical trauma without direct head injury or objective brain lesions.[32–34] But apart from these rare cases with striking neurological or neuropsychological sequelae, there is little evidence that brain lesions might be a common outcome after cervical trauma without direct head injury or loss of consciousness. In clinical practice, similar cases with such impressive neurological or neuropsychological findings are extremely rare.

Thus, there is no convincing evidence that whiplash might result in macroscopic or microscopic lesions of any part of the brain. According to the reviewed literature, this seems to be true for the majority of cases, where cervical trauma was not accompanied by loss of consciousness or retrograde and post-traumatic amnesia, and where no neurological symptoms or neuroanatomical lesions have been detected. Consequently, despite the similarity of cognitive complaints after mild head injury and after whiplash, a different underlying pathogenic mechanism has to be presumed. In the past, much confusion has been caused by the fact that patients with additional mild head injury were included in whiplash studies (e.g., ref. 35). As a consequence, in clinical routine as well as in research a clear definition of whiplash is required, including a distinction between whiplash and mild head injury. Because head injuries imply possible brain lesions, whereas the empirical evidence for such lesions in whiplash is lacking, the distinction between these two medical conditions is of crucial importance for understanding the sequelae of cervical trauma, in general, and the neuropsychological dysfunctions, in particular. Accordingly, we propose to define cervical trauma as sudden acceleration/deceleration of the neck resulting in soft-tissue injuries. In this diagnosis, we do not include fractures or dislocations of the cervical spine, herniation of the intervertebral discs, head contact injuries, loss of consciousness, or retrograde or post-traumatic amnesia.[36] According to the Quebec Task Force on Whiplash-Associated Disorders,[37] we make a distinction between the accident mechanism (whiplash or cervical trauma) and the clinical manifestations (whiplash-associated disorders) that may be the result of the impact. In this chapter, the terms *whiplash* and *cervical trauma* will be used synonymously.

DISORDERS OF ATTENTION

In the acute as well as in the chronic phase, patients who have sustained a cervical trauma often complain about attention impairment. Subjectively, this is mainly addressed as increased fatigue during mentally demanding work, loss of concentration (sometimes with sudden onset), difficulties in following conversations, higher rate of "unexplainable" mistakes during "easy" or automatic work routines, or reduced speed of information processing. Often, patients

report attention problems to be more disabling during activities of daily life and during work than pain itself. The importance of disorders of attention after whiplash is stressed by prospective studies, in which between 29 percent[2] and 38 percent[17] of symptomatic patients were found to complain about attention problems. In the neuropsychological literature, three main components of attention are distinguished:[38]

1. *General alertness*. This refers to an individual's ability to react to inner or outer stimuli and is reflected by the individual's reaction times. Impaired reaction times imply a slowed processing of information speed, which often underlies attention problems.
2. *Selective attention*. This concept refers to the individual's ability to selectively focus on relevant stimuli and to suppress the irrelevant ones.
3. *Vigilance*. This aspect of attention enables the individual to focus on a task over a longer period of time.

Despite these theoretical differentiations, the various aspects of attention are difficult to separate in practice. In clinical routine, attention deficits frequently appear as distractability, slowness of mental processes and impaired ability for focused behavior. The terms concentration and attention are often used synonymously.

Several prospective studies that have focused on attention deficits after cervical trauma are reviewed here in chronological order. Ettlin et al[2] examined 21 patients within the first 2 weeks after trauma. Follow-up examinations were performed with 15 patients after 3 months and with 4 patients after 2 years. Among others, their neuropsychological test battery included several attention and concentration tests. Compared to matched controls, whiplash patients displayed significantly lower performance in 5 out of 11 tests related to attention and concentration.

In another study by Keidel et al[16] 30 patients were tested within the first week after having sustained cervical trauma, and follow-up examinations were performed after 6 and 12 weeks. Again, several aspects of attention were tested with standardized neuropsychological tests. The longitudinal analysis of test performance reveals initial attention deficits. In this study, the initially impaired attention performance is found to recover within the first 12 weeks after the accident.

Radanov et al[17] examined a prospective sample of 117 whiplash patients within the first week after trauma. Follow-up examinations were performed after 3, 6, 12, and 24 months. Among other things, several attention tests were administered. At the 2-year examination, 21 patients were still symptomatic. This corresponds to a recovery rate of 82 percent of the initial sample. A comparison of the symptomatic patients to the recovered ones showed the symptomatic group to be significantly older, to have reported significantly more rotated or inclined head position at the time of impact, and to have higher pain ratings. Additionally, the symptomatic group reported more subjective complaints and showed more symptoms of radicular deficits during initial examination. This same group additionally was characterized by more signs of pre-existing cervical spine osteoarthrosis on initial X-rays and more reports of pretraumatic headache. With respect to attention functioning, the symptomatic group performed significantly worse on tests requiring a complex level of attention processing (i.e., focused and divided attention). The authors assume that the attention deficits were partially due to the adverse effects of analgesics that some patients were using. Sleep disturbances related to chronic pain, as reported by 67 percent of the symptomatic group, might additionally account for the attention problems.

In contrast to these reports of attention impairment after cervical trauma, the most recent study[18] did not reveal any attention deficits in a series of 29 consecutive whiplash patients.

To summarize, there is converging empirical evidence for a mild to moderate attention impairment in whiplash patients with chronic symptoms, especially a reduced speed of information processing and difficulties in divided attention tasks. These disturbances might well explain the subjective reports of distractibility, sudden loss of concentration, and a higher rate of mistakes at work. The origin of the attention impairment is not yet clear. We emphasize that all four reported studies used a strict definition of whiplash, excluding patients with possible cerebral lesions from the sample. Hence, cerebral lesions cannot be taken into consideration as a cause for the attention impairment. Some results in the reviewed studies suggest that secondary factors, such as medication, pain, or pain-related sleep disturbances, interact with attentional functioning. Although the detected cognitive impairment is not severe, there is no doubt that it might cause major difficulties in everyday situations and explain, at least in part, the disabling effect that cervical trauma can have in some cases.

DISORDERS OF LEARNING AND MEMORY

For a long time, neuropsychological studies of whiplash patients have focused on the assessment of various aspects of attention. Memory problems have either been neglected or were measured with methodologically inappropriate means. Considering that between 24 percent[2] and 33 percent[17] of chronic whiplash patients were found to complain about defective memory, the lack of studies on this subject is hard to understand. Most often, memory complaints of whiplash patients concern difficulties in recalling names or the contents of conversations, forgetting meetings and things to do, walking into a room without remembering what they were supposed to do there, or misplacing objects.

Recent prospective studies, in which memory performance after whiplash was assessed in a detailed way, have corrected this research deficit. These studies are presented here in chronological order. In the already mentioned study by Ettlin et al,[2] several neuropsychological tests were administered, covering, among other things, various memory aspects such as immediate and delayed recall of information and recall of verbal and visuo-spatial information. The statistical comparison between whiplash patients and matched controls showed only 1 significant difference out of 11 assessed memory variables. Thus, this study failed to find any disorders of learning and memory after whiplash. Similar results were obtained in the study by Keidel et al,[16] where neuropsychological testing revealed normal learning and memory functions in a group of patients with acute cervical trauma.

In two recent prospective follow-up studies, the course of learning and memory in the first 6 months[15] and the first 2 years[14] after having sustained cervical trauma has been assessed. Both studies are based on the same cohort of whiplash patients and analyzed various quantitative and qualitative aspects of learning and memory. To better understand the neuropsychological performance of whiplash patients, factors possibly interfering with learning and memory (e.g., medication, pain intensity, educational attainment, age, attention functioning) were assessed in conjunction. No systematic differences in learning and memory between whiplash patients and normal controls were found.[14] Additionally, a comparison of whiplash patients developing chronic symptoms and recovered whiplash patients revealed no significant group differences in learning and memory performance.[15] However, chronic patients were found to have poorer attention functioning when compared to the normal controls. Medication, pain intensity, educational attainment, and age could not explain the differences in attention functioning. These results are corroborated by Smed's study,[18] which did not reveal any learning and memory deficits at all.

Even if there is no empirical evidence for severe learning and memory deficits after cervical trauma, subjective memory complaints should be taken seriously during clinical examination or medico-legal evaluation. The results of the studies by Di Stefano and Radanov[14, 15] clearly show that subjective complaints of memory impairment or forgetfulness after whiplash may reflect attention deficits.

In summary, there is no prospective study showing learning and memory disorders after whiplash. Subjective memory complaints of whiplash patients are presumed to reflect a secondary phenomenon related to the aforementioned attention deficiencies and not a primary memory disorder such as is found after various types of brain lesions.

HIGHER COGNITIVE DYSFUNCTIONS

Usually, the term "higher cognitive functions" refers to cognitive abilities such as memory, language and attention, processing of emotional information, arithmetic, visuo-spatial, and executive functions.[38] In everyday situations, these functions interact with each other in a complex way. Actually, most human behavior and mental activity relies on a simultaneous combination of several cognitive functions. The purpose of neuropsychological assessment is to discriminate between the various cognitive functions and to measure them as accurately as possible. This goal is mainly achieved by means of various standardized neuropsychological tests, each focusing on selective cognitive aspects. Neuropsychological assessment can help to identify impaired cognitive functions and to distinguish them from preserved ones.

Surprisingly, only a few studies have examined cognitive functions other than attention and memory in a prospective way (Table 12–1). This may be because subjective cognitive complaints after cervical trauma are most often related to deficient attention and memory, whereas complaints regarding other mental functions (e.g., speech and language, visuo-perceptual, visuo-spatial and visuo-constructive disorders) are rare. In the two previous sections, findings related to the attention and memory performance of whiplash patients have been presented. In some of these studies other higher cognitive functions were additionally tested. These results are next reviewed briefly.

The previously mentioned neuropsychological test battery used by Ettlin et al[2] included arithmetic, visuo-spatial, and executive functioning tests. The comparison of whiplash patients and pair-matched normal controls did not reveal any performance differences in these tests measuring higher cognitive functions. Similar results were reported by Keidel et al,[16] who did not obtain any abnormal results in the LPS ("Leistungsprüfsystem"), a test battery assessing various higher cognitive functions, including language related skills, word fluency, visuo-spatial and percep-

tive abilities, concept formation, reasoning, and arithmetic abilities. These results were confirmed by Smed,[18] who administered several tests assessing visuo-spatial, perceptive, and executive functions and did not find any cognitive deficits whatsoever.

To our knowledge there are no other prospective studies examining higher cognitive functions after cervical trauma. This review makes clear that there is no empirical evidence for higher cognitive dysfunctions in whiplash patients. According to our definition of injury that excludes any trauma to the skull or brain, these types of neuropsychological disorders are not supposed to occur after whiplash injury. If neuropsychological assessment still reveals significant impairment of higher cognitive functions, doubts should be cast on the initial diagnosis of cervical trauma and the possibility of head injury should be considered. Careful analysis of all available information regarding the accident mechanism and the initial symptoms may, in some instances, reveal that the patient has suffered a significant head injury despite an initial diagnosis of cervical trauma. As mentioned previously, loss of consciousness, retrograde or posttraumatic amnesia, or bruises on the surface of the head might furnish evidence of a closed head injury with possible damage to the brain.

ROLE OF PSYCHOSOCIAL, LEGAL, AND CULTURAL FACTORS

A great deal of speculation and many misconceptions attend the role of psychosocial, legal, and cultural factors in the course of recovery after whiplash. Since the first published articles on this subject, psychological factors have been attributed an important role in recovery from cervical

Table 12–1: Summary of Prospective Studies Assessing Neuropsychological Capacities after Whiplash in Chronological Order

	ATTENTION	LEARNING AND MEMORY	VISUO-SPATIAL ABILITIES	EXECUTIVE FUNCTIONS	PROCESSING OF NUMBERS AND ARITHMETIC
Ettlin et al[2] (n = 21)	Impaired attention and concentration	Normal results	Normal results	Normal results	Normal results
Keidel et al[16] (n = 30)	Initial attention impairment	Initial impairment, then normal results in follow-ups	Normal results	Normal results	Normal results
Radanov et al[17] (n = 117)	Impairment of focused and divided attention	Normal results	Not tested	Not tested	Not tested
Di Stefano and Radanov[14, 15] (n = 117 and 86, respectively)	Impairment of focused and divided attention	Normal results	Not tested	Not tested	Not tested
Smed[18] (n = 29)	Normal results	Normal results	Normal results	Normal results	Not tested

trauma. Gay and Abbott[35] suspected that cervical trauma would not only traumatize the neck, but also the psyche. Compared to those with other injuries, they described the patients with cervical trauma to be more anxious, worried, and tense. From today's point of view, these changes of personality are not surprising, considering that a majority of the patients (62 percent) included in Gay and Abbott's study were suspected having suffered a brain injury.[35] By this serious methodological error, personality changes resulting from brain injury were confounded with abnormal emotional reactions or a predisposition for development of a psychoneurotic reaction. This mistake would influence the following several decades of research in whiplash patients.

For a long time, psychoneurotic aspects would be supposed to play a crucial role in patients development of chronic complaints after whiplash. In his description of 200 patients with brain injury, Miller[3] coined the term "accident neurosis," referring to the patient's conviction of unfitness for work, a conviction that seems not to be related to the medical condition. Other characteristics of an accident neurosis were the absolute denial of any degree of symptomatic improvement and, in some cases, a latency of several months between onset of symptoms and first appearance at the physician's office. In a follow-up study of 50 cases of accident neurosis, Miller noticed that nearly all patients were completely recovered after settlement. A similar opinion was published by Hodge,[4] who suspected that emotionally unstable whiplash patients find a new stability by seeking a financial compensation. He called this mechanism "whiplash neurosis." In his analysis, Farbman[39] concluded that emotional factors, overtreatment, previous diseases, and legal problems, would cause symptoms to last longer. After comparing whiplash patients in Australia with whiplash patients in Singapore, Balla[40] concluded that the physiological predisposition is irrelevant for the complaints. He writes that chronic disability after whiplash is socially determined by cultural values and sanctions and postulates chronic whiplash to be a social illness.

Together with a recent study from Lithuania,[41] these reports suggest that financial compensation may be the crucial factor in the development of chronic complaints after cervical trauma. However, all of these studies favoring a psychosocial etiology of symptoms are affected by serious methodological problems that call into question the reliability of the assessed variables and the validity of the findings. The samples are far from being representative, and the selection criteria often remain unclear. Additionally, all these studies are retrospective. The Lithuanian study is based exclusively on questionnaires filled out on average more than 21 months after the accident, which leads us to raise serious doubts about the quality of these data.

Considering that none of these studies used scientifically sound procedures for patient selection and injury definition, the hypothesis of whiplash being a psychiatric or culturally caused disease should be dismissed and regarded as a failed attempt to explain a still insufficiently explored medical condition. Recent methodologically appropriate research showed that litigation status did not predict employment status, suggesting that secondary gain does not figure prominently in explaining the level of functioning of these patients.[42] Additionally, a prospective study demonstrated that neither pretraumatic psychiatric symptoms nor personality traits such as neuroticism or depression could predict the course of recovery after whiplash.[43]

In an excellent analysis of pain and psychological symptoms in whiplash patients, Wallis et al[44] concluded that psychological disturbances exhibited by these patients are secondary to chronic pain. In their study, they found whiplash patients to manifest similar responses in a symptom checklist (SCL-90-R) as patients with chronic low back pain and those with rheumatoid arthritis. In contrast, the responses of whiplash patients differed markedly from a group of patients suffering from undifferentiated pain. This suggests that whiplash patients may have a psychological profile distinguishable from that of patients with more diffused chronic pain, but comparable to that of patients with similar medical conditions such as low back pain and rheumatoid arthritis.

It is possible that these patients may have a common underlying organic pathology that produces a similar profile of symptoms and psychological distress. To further validate this hypothesis, Wallis and Bogduk[45] asked pain-free persons to simulate chronic pain after a motor vehicle accident in order to ensure compensation. The naive subjects' scores were compared with those of whiplash patients, and striking differences between the two groups were obtained. They conclude that it is very difficult for an individual to fake a psychological profile typical of a whiplash patient. This study emphasizes that there is no legitimate reason to consider malingering to be common after cervical trauma. In view of these results, it seems to be more realistic and adequate to say that psychosocial, legal, and cultural factors can influence the subjective manifestation of symptoms, but do not determine the outcome after whiplash.

ROLE OF SECONDARY FACTORS SUCH AS NOCICEPTION, MEDICATION, AND SLEEP DISORDERS

Considering only prospective studies using a strict definition of whiplash that does not include patients with potential traumatic brain injury, we have shown in the previous paragraphs that the spectrum of possible neuropsychological impairment after such trauma can be limited to disorders of attention, with severity ranging from mild to moderate. The origin of this cognitive impairment is not yet clear. As outlined before, the attention impairment in whiplash patients cannot be explained by psychosocial factors nor by brain lesions. As far as we know, there are no prospective studies specifically focusing on the relationship between attention and factors possibly interfering with cognitive processes in whiplash patients. However, there is some evidence suggesting that pain, medication, and sleep disorders might be related to the attention problems.

Grigsby et al[46] have compared the neuropsychological performance of chronic pain patients with no known history of head trauma or neurological disorders on the one hand with patients who had sustained mild to moderate head trauma on the other. Some of the pain patients had suffered cervical trauma. Pain patients performed worse than head trauma patients on two of six information processing tests. These results suggest that pain may disturb cognitive performances that depend on attention, such as speed and capacity of information processing. The authors argue that pain represents a powerful sensory stimulus that activates several centers in the brain, such as reticular system, thalamus, limbic system, and cortex. As a sensory stimulus, nociception demands the patient's attention and represents a competitor for the finite attention resources, which may cause a disruption of the cognitive equilibrium that characterizes the brain's everyday functioning.

This hypothesis is supported by Jamison et al,[47] who found that the sensory input of nociception was a major contributor to concentration and memory problems in chronic pain patients. They argue that competing sensory stimuli have been shown to result in a decrease in the amount of information remembered by healthy volunteers. This mechanism may cause pain patients to be distracted by the continuous sensory input of nociception resulting in attention and memory problems. Further evidence is provided by Kewman et al,[48] who found cognitive problems in one third of patients with musculoskeletal pain. Direct empirical evidence for the pain hypothesis is provided by a study in which neuropsychological performance of whiplash patients was tested before and after immobilization of the cervical spine.[26] The whiplash-associated complaints—above all, pain—were completely cured by immobilization, and neuropsychological performance improved significantly after patients were symptom free.

In a recent study, a prospectively recruited sample of whiplash patients was compared to a group of patients with nontraumatic, rheumatic cervical disease.[25] Both medical conditions are characterized by similar physical and cognitive complaints. The fact that rheumatic symptoms—as opposed to whiplash-associated disorders—are not caused by a sudden trauma to the cervical spine, gives us the opportunity to study two similar clinical syndromes with two different medical histories. This may help us to better understand the etiology of cognitive complaints after whiplash. In this study, both pain groups showed a similar impairment of divided attention, whereas learning and memory were not affected. Medication, age, educational attainment, and psychosocial variables were not found to be systematically related to the neuropsychological findings. These results show that traumatic as well as rheumatic cervical conditions are characterized by a comparable level of cognitive impairment, emphasizing the role of nociception as an important factor in the etiology of neuropsychological impairment.

The reported studies suggest that pain has to be viewed as a complex response of the organism that incorporates subjective-psychological, motor-behavioral, and physiological-organic components,[49] which may interact with cognitive abilities. We assume that the emotional experience of pain is different from the noxious sensory input (i.e., nociception). Whereas the emotional experience of pain can be modulated by a variety of factors, such as personal history, previous experiences, culture, and emotional state, we refer to nociception as a sensory input exclusively. This makes it clear that nociception is different from the subjective perception of pain. Consequently, as demonstrated in a previous study,[36] we do not necessarily expect the subjective pain intensity reported by the patient to be significantly related to the deficit in attentional processing. In contrast, we expect the neuropsychological impairment to become greater as the noxious sensory input increases. However, reliable measures of nociception still have to be developed.

Nociception may interfere with cognitive information processing in several different ways. Since nociception has the function to register and to limit physical damage, it has a crucial biological role for the organism's survival. Therefore, we assume that the cerebral processing of noxious sensory inputs has a predetermined priority relative to the processing of other sensory information, such as visual inputs. In this proposed mechanism, the priority processing of noxious sensory inputs is a powerful competitor for the finite mental resources, particularly for attention. By absorbing the person's attention, nociception may diminish the available mental capacity and lead to the cognitive failures in everyday life that are typically reported by whiplash patients, such as increased fatigue during mentally demanding work and loss of concentration.

Other factors possibly related to cognitive impairment after whiplash may be medication with psychotropic side effects and pain-related sleep disturbances. According to Radanov et al,[17] 76 percent of patients with chronic complaints after whiplash suffer from pain-related sleep disturbances. However, the relationship between chronic pain-related sleep disturbances and cognitive performance has never been examined in whiplash patients. According to the distraction hypothesis for nociception, it can be speculated that chronic sleep disturbances may contribute to attention deficits by reducing the finite cognitive resources. Similarly, the role of psychotropic medication in cognitive impairment after whiplash remains unclear. In their prospective study, Radanov et al[36] found a partial interaction between medication with possible psychotropic side effects and neuropsychological test performance in the first 6 months after having sustained cervical trauma. This relationship was also confirmed later on in the 2-year follow-up examination.[17] Unfortunately, there are no other studies focusing on this aspect.

CONCLUSION

In the past, most research focusing on cervical trauma has been affected by methodological problems such as unclear definition of injury or biased sample selection, causing misconceptions and prejudices toward a still insufficiently understood medical condition. Major advances in the understanding of whiplash-associated disorders were made possible by recent research that adopted a clear definition of the accident mechanism and its sequelae.[37] In this context, the distinction between whiplash and head injuries plays a central role in understanding this medical condition. In this chapter, we have extensively reviewed the neuropsychological studies performed on whiplash patients. When considering only prospective studies with consecutive patient admission and exclusion of patients with possible traumatic brain lesions, the following conclusions can be drawn.

There is no evidence for significant learning and memory disorders or disorders of other higher cognitive functions—such as speech and language, arithmetic and executive functions, visuo-perceptual and visuo-constructive abilities—after whiplash. However, a mild to moderate impairment of attention—especially a reduced speed of information processing and difficulties in tasks involving divided attention—has consistently been reported by most researchers. Although the causes have not yet been uncovered, this cognitive impairment seems most probably to be related to nociception. According to the definition of injury used in this chapter, primary cognitive dysfunctions caused by brain lesions are not expected to occur after whiplash. Neither conventional techniques, such as MRI or electroencephalogram, nor the new functional imaging methods (PET and SPECT) have revealed any evidence of traumatic brain lesions after cervical trauma. If the neuropsychological examination still reveals severe cognitive deficits, the initial diagnosis of whiplash-associated disorders has to be questioned and a possible mild traumatic brain injury has to be taken into consideration. However, a traumatic brain injury after whiplash is very rare and can only be diagnosed if the usually adopted criteria for a head or brain injury (e.g., loss of consciousness, retrograde or post-traumatic amnesia, impaired responses according to Glasgow Coma Scale, detectable brain injury, neurological signs) are fulfilled.

Since a neuropsychological examination is a functional method, several aspects can contribute to the results. In the case of cervical trauma, we suggest a relationship between nociception and the impairment of attention. We suggest that nociception (i.e., the perception of a noxious sensory input) has an assigned biological function of damage registration and damage limitation. Because of its important role for an organism's survival, nociception is a very powerful competitor for the finite cognitive capacities. We propose that nociception demands the patient's attention and limits its available capacity for other mental tasks. This may cause a disruption of the cognitive equilibrium and a distraction of the cognitive processes, resulting in an impairment of attention. This hypothesis has found strong support in recent studies showing remission of cognitive impairment and of psychological distress after complete recovery from pain in whiplash patients.[26, 27] Earlier in this chapter, several additional experiments were presented that support this hypothesis.

This assumption has important implications for therapy. A coordinated treatment of pain and cognitive impairment seems indispensable. An early combination of medical pain therapy and neuropsychological training may prevent patients from developing chronic physical, neuropsychological, and psychological impairment after whiplash. To minimize neuropsychological complaints, special attention has to be paid to the type of prescribed medication. Whenever possible, medication with little or no psychotropic side effects should be chosen. It will be an important focus of future research to develop effective treatments for patients with whiplash-associated disorders.

REFERENCES

1. Barnsley L, Lord S, Bogduk N. Whiplash injury. *Pain* 1994;58:283–307.
2. Ettlin TM, Kischka U, Reichmann S, et al. Cerebral symptoms after whiplash injury of the neck: A prospective clinical and neuropsychological study of whiplash injury. *J Neurol Neurosurg Psychiatry* 1992;55:943–948.
3. Miller H. Accident neurosis. *BMJ* 1961;1:992–998.
4. Hodge JR The whiplash neurosis. *Psychosomatics* 1971;12:245–249.
5. Shapiro AP, Teasell, RW, Steenhuis R. Mild traumatic brain injury following whiplash. *Spine* 1993;7:455–470.
6. Berstad JR, Bærum B, Löchen EA, Mogstad TE, Sjaastad O. Whiplash: Chronic organic brain syndrome without hydrocephalus ex vacuo. *Acta Neurol Scand* 1975;51:268–284.
7. Bohnen N, Jolles J, Verhey FRJ. Persistent neuropsychological deficits in cervical whiplash patients without direct headstrike. *Acta Neurol Belg* 1993;93:23–31.

8. Kischka U, Ettlin TM, Heim S, Schmid G. Cerebral symptoms following whiplash injury. *Europ Neurol* 1991;31:136–140.

9. Radanov BP, Hirlinger I, Di Stefano G, Valach L. Attention processing in cervical spine syndromes. *Acta Neurol Scand* 1992;85:358–362.

10. Yarnell PR, Rossie GV. Minor whiplash head injury with major debilitation. *Brain Inj* 1988;2:255–258.

11. Olsnes BT. Neurobehavioral findings in whiplash patients with long-lasting symptoms. *Acta Neurol Scand* 1989;80:584–588.

12. Schwartz DP, Barth JT, Dane JR, Drenan SE, DeGood DE, Rowlingson JC. Cognitive deficits in chronic pain patients with and without history of head/neck injury: Development of a brief screening battery. *Clin J Pain* 1987;3:94–101.

13. Taylor AE, Cox CA, Mailis A. Persistent neuropsychological deficits following whiplash: Evidence for chronic mild traumatic brain injury? *Arch Phys Med Rehabil* 1996;77:529–535.

14. Di Stefano G, Radanov BP. Course of attention and memory after common whiplash: A two-years prospective study with age, education and gender pair-matched patients. *Acta Neurol Scand* 1995;91:346–352.

15. Di Stefano G, Radanov BP. Quantitative and qualitative aspects of learning and memory in common whiplash patients. *Arch Clin Neuropsychol* 1996;11:661–676.

16. Keidel M, Yagüez L, Wilhelm H, Diener HC. Prospektiver Verlauf neuropsychologischer Defizite nach zervikozephalem Akzelerationstrauma. *Nervenarzt* 1992;63:731–740.

17. Radanov BP, Sturzenegger M, Di Stefano G. Long-term outcome after whiplash injury—A two years follow-up considering features of accident mechanism, somatic, radiological and psychosocial findings. *Medicine* 1995;74:281–297.

18. Smed A. Cognitive function and distress after common whiplash injury. *Acta Neurol Scand* 1997;95:73–80.

19. Borchgrevink GE, Smevik O, Nordby A, Rinck PA, Stiles TC, Lereim I. MR imaging and radiography of patients with cervical hyperextension-flexion injuries after car accidents. *Acta Radiol* 1995;36:425–428.

20. Karlsborg M, Smed A, Jespersen H, et al. A prospective study of 39 patients with whiplash injury. *Acta Neurol Scand* 1997;95:65–72.

21. Otte A, Ettlin TH, Fierz L, Mueller-Brand J. Parieto-occipital hypoperfusion in late whiplash syndrome: First quantitative SPET study using technetium-99m bicisate (ECD). *Eur J Nucl Med* 1996;23:72–74.

22. Otte A, Mueller-Brand J, Fierz L. Brain SPECT findings in late whiplash syndrome. *Lancet* 1995;354:1513–1514.

23. Otte A, Ettlin TH, Nitzsche EU, et al. PET and SPECT in whiplash syndrome: A new approach to a forgotten brain? *J Neurol Neurosurg Psychiatry* 1997;63:368–372.

24. Bicik I, Radanov BP, Schäfer N, et al. PET with fluorodeoxyglucose and hexamethylpropyleneamine oxime SPECT in late whiplash syndrome. *Neurology* 1998;51:345–350.

25. Di Stefano G. *Neuropsychologische Defizite nach Beschleunigungsmechanismus der HWS*. Unpublished doctoral dissertation, University of Freiburg, Switzerland, 1997.

26. Radanov BP, Dvorak J, Di Stefano G. Attention processing in common whiplash before and with immobilization of the cervical spine. *Eur Spine J* 1993;2:72–75.

27. Wallis BJ, Lord SM, Bogduk N. Resolution of psychological distress of whiplash patients following treatment by radiofrequency neurotomy: A randomised, double-blind, placebo-controlled trial. *Pain* 1997;73:15–22.

28. Bogduk N. The anatomy and pathophysiology of whiplash. *Clin Biomechanics* 1986;1:82–101.

29. Severy DM, Mathewson JH, Bechtol CO. Controlled automobile rear-end collisions, an investigation of related engineering and medical phenomena. *Can Serv Med J* 1955;11:727–759.

30. Ommaya AK, Faas F, Yarnell P. Whiplash injury and brain damage. *JAMA* 1968;204:285–289.

31. Ommaya AK, Yarnell P. Subdural haematoma after whiplash injury. *Lancet* 1969;2:237–239.

32. Fisher CM. Whiplash amnesia. *Neurol*(Ny) 1982;32:667–668.

33. Hofstad H, Gjerde IO. Transient global amnesia after whiplash trauma. *J Neurol Neurosurg Psychiatry* 1985;48:956–957.

34. Matias-Guiu J, Buenaventura I, Cervera C, Codina A. Whiplash amnesia. *Neurology* 1985;35:1259.

35. Gay JR, Abbott KH. Common whiplash injury of the neck. *JAMA* 1953;152:1698–1704.

36. Radanov BP, Di Stefano G, Schnidrig A, Sturzenegger M, Augustiny KF. Cognitive functioning after common whiplash: A controlled follow-up study. *Arch Neurol* 1993;50:87–91.

37. Spitzer WO, Skovron ML, Salmi LR, et al. Scientific monograph of the Quebec Task Force on whiplash-associated disorders: Redefining "whiplash" and its management. *Spine* 1995;20:1S–73S.

38. Kolb B, Whishaw IQ. *Fundamentals of Human Neuropsychology*. New York, NY: WH Freeman; 1996.

39. Farbmann AA. Neck sprain: Associated factors. *JAMA* 1973;223:1010–1015.

40. Balla JI. The late whiplash syndrome: A study of an illness in Australia and Singapore. *Cult Med Psychiatry* 1982;6:191–210.
41. Schrader H, Obelieniene D, Bovim G, et al. Natural evolution of late whiplash syndrome outside the medicolegal context. *Lancet* 1996;347:1207–1211.
42. Swartzman LC, Teasell RW, Shapiro AP, McDermid AJ. The effect of litigation status on adjustment to whiplash injury. *Spine* 1996;21:53–58.
43. Radanov BP, Di Stefano G, Schnidrig A, Ballinari P. Role of psychosocial stress in recovery from common whiplash. *Lancet* 1991;338:712–715.
44. Wallis BJ, Lord SM, Barnsley L, Bogduk N. Pain and psychologic symptoms of Australian patients with whiplash. *Spine* 1996;21:804–810.
45. Wallis BJ, Bogduk N. Faking a profile: Can naive subjects simulate whiplash responses? *Pain* 1996;66:223–227.
46. Grigsby J, Rosenberg NL, Busenbark D. Chronic pain is associated with deficits in information processing. *Percept Mot Skills* 1995;81:403–410.
47. Jamison RN, Sbrocco T, Parri WCV. The influence of problems with concentration and memory on emotional distress and daily activities in chronic pain patients. *Int J Psychiatry Med* 1988;18:183–191.
48. Kewman DG, Vaishampayan N, Zald D, Han B. Cognitive impairment in muskuloskeletal pain patients. *Int J Psychiatry Med* 1991;21:253–262.
49. Flor H, Birbaumer N, Turk DC. The psychobiology of chronic pain. *Adv Behav Res Ther* 1990;12:47–84.

PART

3

Evaluation

CHAPTER 13

Evaluation of Joint Dysfunction of the Cervical Spine

George G. DeFranca

"Go gently, be pure, be brave. Be humble as the earth and as radiant as the sun."

—Sioux Indian saying

INTRODUCTION

In the realm of locomotor disturbances of the cervical spine, joint dysfunction of the posterior facet joints occupies a central role in pain generation. It can also perpetuate local or even distant joint and muscular dysfunctions and force biomechanical compensations via reflex arthrokinetic and neuromuscular processes. In addition, aberrant mechanoreceptor input from dysfunctional cervical facet joints can modulate motor output to the rest of the locomotor system. As a result, poor movement patterns occur that become "programmed" and learned if habituated. Unfortunately, the whole locomotor system suffers the consequences of cervical joint dysfunction as various kinetic chains are linked to the neck.

Thus, in assessing cervical pain syndromes, the importance of being able to detect and treat cervical joint dysfunction is central. This chapter concerns itself with the former while the latter is dealt with in Chapter 18. For the purposes of this chapter, serious disease has been ruled out and motor, sensory, and reflex abnormalities are not dealt with. What follows is a discussion of functional assessment of the cervical facet joints.

PRINCIPLES OF MOTION PALPATION

Life is movement and so it is with joint function in the locomotor system, especially that in the cervical spine, the most mobile aspect of the vertebral column. It stands to reason that proper assessment of a joint's function requires examination of its movement capabilities. Manual methods of treatment for vertebral joint problems, particularly those in the cervical spine, regularly depend on palpation findings regarding bony position, pain provocation, and joint motion. Bony position tends to be less reliable as an indicator of technique selection, but pain provocation and

joint motion offer more information. However, the issue of reliability and validity of these examination procedures raises a number of questions. There is now evidence in the form of clinical trials to support the use of manual techniques for the treatment of neck pain. Unfortunately, these same studies do not specify which clinical tests could be used to better identify who can benefit from this type of treatment.

Palpation forms a cornerstone in the conventional physical examination. It is standard medical practice to palpate for spasm, abdominal organs, lymph nodes, arterial pulses, and so on. However, these procedures can be subjective, and examiner error is commonplace. In the examination of the locomotor system, much emphasis is placed on the palpatory findings of joint motion, tissue textures, and muscle spasm. Examination of joint play motion is a specific type of palpatory assessment; however, it, too, tends to be subjective without universal standardization of technique protocol. Movement palpation has good face validity, meaning that it makes sense to assume that movement assessment palpatory procedures should be able to assess a joint's motion capabilities. However, it lacks predictive validity; that is, the ability to successfully predict a specific outcome. This is owing to its lack of inter-examiner reliability, or the ability of different examiners to successfully agree with one another on a specific outcome. Intra-examiner reliability, or the ability of an examiner to agree with him- or herself on his or her own findings, fares better and more closely represents clinical settings where individual practitioners solely care for their patients.

According to Maitland[1] "joint signs" fulfill a triad of physical findings that aid in selecting where and how to mobilize a joint. They consist of joint resistance, pain, and spasm. However, of these, pain provocation has been found to be the only test with good to excellent reliability.[2-4] Sandmark and Nisell[5] found cervical facet pain provocation via direct palpation to be the most appropriate of five examination tests that correlated well with self-reported questionnaires on neck pain.

Using joint resistance as a sole indicator for technique application can be fraught with error. Tests for mobility and resistance have consistently demonstrated fair to poor reliability between examiners.[2, 6] In addition, there is much variability in spinal segmental stiffness values between subjects and at different segmental levels within the same person. This makes it very difficult to judge which spinal segments have normal or abnormal stiffness.

The segmental movement examination of the cervical spine has been shown to be reliable in one notable study by Jull et al.[7] Even though one examiner was used, and the study sample was small, the excellent results achieved demand notice and further study. Jull et al[7] demonstrated 100 percent accuracy in finding symptomatic cervical facet joints when compared to radiologically controlled nerve

blocks and intra-articular injections. Additionally asymptomatic facet joints were also correctly identified. Criteria for a symptomatic facet joint were as follows: abnormal "end feel," abnormal quality of resistance, and reproduction of local or referred pain. In a later study, Jull et al[8] demonstrated excellent inter-examiner reliability between examiners when testing for the presence of painful upper cervical joint dysfunction.

Although further research needs to be done in this area, an approach using segmental examining techniques to search for both pain and restriction can be employed, especially when looking for both to occur concurrently. More importantly, if in doing so the patient's presenting symptoms are reproduced, treatment can be better directed. Oftentimes, the only findings one has to go on are derived from techniques of manual palpation. Reproduction of the patient's chief symptoms are of primary concern in the examination and, therefore, pain provocation is key. Even if this cannot be accomplished after careful examination, one should look for segmental changes that could be most responsible.[9]

An interesting study by Maher and Adams[10] demonstrated that the assessment was affected by visual input. The study showed that the examiners perceived a mechanical stiffness stimuli as slightly stiffer when vision was occluded. The suggestion is that visual input needs to be considered when making conclusions about palpating stiffness and that judgments made on stiffness magnitudes should be made either with visual input or visual occlusion but not with both. In other words, an examiner should be consistent with using occluded versus nonoccluded vision when making conclusions as to stiffness characteristics. Using visual and nonvisual inputs during the same assessment session may confuse the outcome.

To effectively examine a joint's motion capabilities, and therefore its functional capacity, its full range of motion must be assessed. A joint's total range of motion consists of three zones of movement and two barriers to movement (Fig. 13–1). The zones of movement are active, passive, and paraphysiological ranges. An elastic barrier of

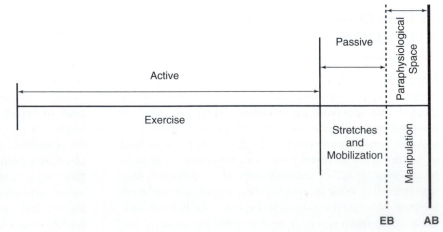

Figure 13–1. Range of motion. AB, anatomical barrier; EB, elastic barrier.

(From DeFranca GD, Levine LJ. Pelvic Locomotor Dysfunction: A Clinical Approach. Gaithersburg, Md.: Aspen Publishers; 1996, with permission.)

resistance separates the passive range of motion from the paraphysiological space. The anatomical barrier to movement consists of the ligaments and joint capsule and represents the ultimate restraint to joint motion.

Active range of motion entails having the patient move his or her joints through an active physiological motion using voluntary muscle contraction. Active range of motion conducted during an examination mainly demonstrates willingness of the patient to perform the movement. Voluntary movements and active exercises function within this range.

Passive range of motion consists of the soft tissue tension taken up to the paraphysiological barrier. Examination of passive movements assesses the integrity of the soft tissues and the joint's motion further into the range. Therapeutically, stretching and joint mobilization directly affect this part of a joint's range of motion.

The paraphysiological space entails joint play movements that are small and involuntary but necessary for normal painless active and passive ranges of motion to occur. It lies outside the passive range of motion. Joint manipulation allows entry into the paraphysiological space; mobilization and exercise do not.

Palpation examination of the cervical spine involves both static and dynamic procedures. Static palpation attempts to assess pain, muscle tension or spasm, soft tissue, and osseous changes. Dynamic or movement palpation is used to determine movement abnormalities such as joint restriction at end range, neutral, or through range. General or neutral scan techniques are used to quickly assess the overall mobility of the cervical spine and aid in localizing levels of gross motor disturbances (i.e., "resistance to neutral"). More specific movement palpation techniques attempt to further define movement abnormalities and provoke other joint signs such as pain and spasm. This is done using passive intersegmental motion palpation and is used to assess two types of movements: accessory or joint play and physiological movements. The scan examination aids in localizing a level of involvement, whereas specific palpation further defines the joint dysfunction.

Accessory movements are small involuntary joint play movements that cannot be performed actively by the patient. For instance, a long axis distraction of the first metacarpal-phalangeal joint is a joint play movement that cannot be performed actively by the patient, but needs to be done passively by an examiner. So, too, with individually directed pressures on the cervical vertebrae. Maitland discusses four types of accessory movements in the cervical spine.[11] Two are posterior-to-anterior (PA) pressures applied to the back of the motion segment, one being central over the spinous process, the other being placed unilaterally over each facet joint, lamina, or transverse process. A third entails directing a transverse pressure medially on the lateral aspect of the spinous process or articular pillar. A fourth accessory movement involves an anterior-to-posterior (AP) movement on the transverse process being ap-

plied from the front of the neck. The loss of joint play or accessory movements is significant because it is one of the earliest signs of aging in a joint and occurs earlier than changes seen with passive physiological movement.[12] Therefore, the loss of accessory movements is a subtle and sensitive indicator of joint pathomechanics.

Passive physiological movement testing involves moving a motion segment passively through a normal physiological movement that a patient can perform actively. For example, flexion, extension, rotation, and lateral bending are all movements that a patient can perform normally or physiologically. These motions can be taken to end range segmentally and tested for pain and joint play movement with over-pressure (i.e., "resistance to end range"). Additionally, accessory movements can be performed while a joint is held in its extreme physiological movement. For example, the neck can be laterally flexed while a central PA pressure is applied to a motion segment. This may elicit a patient's presenting symptoms more exactly.

Manual examination of the vertebral segments attempts to define the manipulable lesion, the main indication for joint manipulation. Mennell[13, 14] used the term joint dysfunction to denote the loss of normal joint play. This he called the manipulable lesion. The manipulable lesion is described by other terms, such as subluxation, somatic dysfunction, fixation, joint blockage, and segmental dyskinesia. Several factors characterize the manipulable lesion. Joint dysfunction is the main feature and is distinguished by a painful loss of involuntary joint play found on passive movement testing. Being involuntary it cannot be assessed via active range of motion testing but must be tested directly by passive segmental movement tests. It is caused by trauma, both intrinsic and extrinsic, but also by disuse, postural strain, immobilization, and pre-existing inflammations or disease. It can also be a manifestation of viscerosomatic disease.

Soft tissue changes in the nearby skin, subcutaneous tissue, muscles, and periarticular structures also characterize the manipulable lesion. The pain of joint dysfunction is sharp, occurs with movement, and alleviates with rest. It is not constant, as in inflammatory pain, nor is it nocturnal, as in more serious causes of pain. Movements and specific activities exacerbate the pain of joint play while rest alleviates it, and these clues should be searched for in the history.

Normal active joint motion and muscle function are dependent on the presence of normal joint play. Muscles that move a joint with joint dysfunction are adversely affected via arthrokinetic reflexes and become either hypertonic or inhibited. The muscles so affected cannot be restored to normal as long as the joint they serve is dysfunctional. Mennell[13, 14] states that exercising a dysfunctional joint can only delay recovery. Furthermore, impaired muscle function perpetuates abnormal joint function. Therefore, in the rehabilitation of the cervical spine, joint dysfunction must be treated so as to allow for normal active movements and exercise to take place.

EXAMINATION TECHNIQUE

The cervical spine is an area rich in anatomical variation. Being a small mobile stalk interposed between the rigid thoracic spine and heavy cranium, it affords great mobility yet is inherently unstable. The cervical spine can be arbitrarily divided into upper and lower regions for sake of simplicity and organization of examination. This should by no means imply simplicity of function, for it is the most complex region of the spine. In this chapter, the upper cervical spine includes the occipito-atlantal, atlanto-axial, and C2–3 articulations. The lower cervical spine entails the joints between C3 and C7.

The upper cervical spine frequently manifests symptoms above it, as headaches, whereas the lower cervical spine is associated with lower neck and upper extremity pain syndromes (Fig. 13–2A and B). The mid-cervical region (C3–5) commonly displays localized facet joint pain but can refer pain either above or below it.

> ### ! CLINICAL PEARL
>
> Upper cervical joint dysfunction often causes painful compensations to occur in lower cervical segments. In such cases, treatment should be directed at the dysfunctional upper cervical segments.

In addition to the craniocervical and cervicodorsal regions, the C2-3 segment can be considered a transitional level in its own right. It is the first cervical level to contain an intervertebral disc. In addition, the stout C2 vertebra is atypical with respect to the dens, its very large superior articular facets with the atlas, and its large bifid spinous process and lamina. Its spinous process is a focal attachment site for suboccipital and posterior spinal muscles, while anteriorly, it serves as the origin for the colli and scalene muscles.

Since joint dysfunction does not occur in isolation and has repercussions throughout the locomotor system, a discussion of muscle and soft tissue responses to dysfunction is necessary. As will be discussed later, locomotor disturbances tend to consistently occur in patterns; that is, grouped in a chainlike fashion, linking joint and muscle dysfunctions together.

The locomotor system "thinks" in terms of function, with its individual parts consequently integrated to work together as a system. No part functions in isolation but rather is intimately linked to the entire locomotor system via anatomical, neurophysiological, or biomechanical means. To understand how the locomotor system functions, we need to grasp two basic concepts, those of (1) tension and pain, and (2) chain reactions.

Pain in the locomotor system is usually associated with tension—be it in a muscle, joint, or "pain" point (peri-

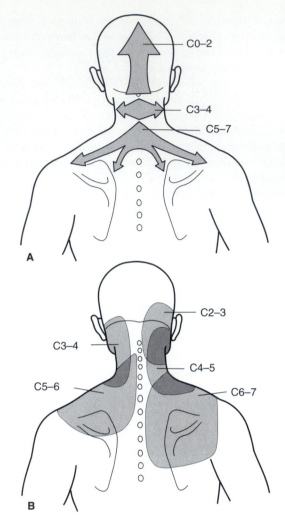

Figure 13–2. A. Common direction of cervical spine joint pain referral. **B.** Characteristic pain referral from cervical spine zygapophyseal joints.

(From Dwyer A, Aprill C, Bogduk N. Cervical zygapophyseal joint pain patterns I: A study in normal volunteers. Spine 1990;6:453–461, with permission.)

osteal insertion point). By identifying and releasing tension in the locomotor system, function can be restored and pain can be reduced. Assessing for tension in muscles, joints, and related periosteal pain points, therefore, should be an integral part of the examination for locomotor dysfunction (Table 13–1).

LOCOMOTOR CHAIN REACTIONS

Clinical experience shows that joint and muscle dysfunctions consistently occur in patterns. These patterns or groups emerge in chain-reaction fashion whereby one dysfunction can activate another. This occurs so often that the finding of one dysfunction should lead the examiner to search for other related dysfunctions. In addition, correc-

Table 13–1: Correlations Between Pain Points, Tight Muscles, and Dysfunctional Joints

PAIN POINT	TIGHT MUSCLE	JOINT DYSFUNCTION
Nuchal line	SCM, trapezius	C0–1
Posterior arch of C1	Short neck extensors	C0–1
Transverse process of atlas	SCM	C0–1
C2 spinous	Levator scapulae, SCM	C1–2, C2–3
Medial clavicle	SCM	—
First and second sternocostals	Scalenes, pectorals	Mid and low cervicals, ribs
Superior angle of the scapula	Levator scapulae	C2,3
Third rib angle	—	C0–1, C2–3
Erb's point	Scalenes	Mid and low cervicals

SCM, sternocleidomastoid.

tion of one "link" in the chain can often normalize the entire chain of dysfunction if it is the key link.

Key links often occur at spinal transitional areas, are usually chronically dysfunctional (often clinically "silent"), or commonly occur at the most distal link in kinematic chains. For example, an asymptomatic yet incredibly stiff cervicothoracic segment with chronic soft tissue changes and a boardlike lack of mobility can cause upper extremity pain syndromes. Pain often draws the attention away from the underlying problem, and a painful wrist or shoulder can be unsuccessfully treated for months until the cervicothoracic region is treated.

Besides being a dysfunctional joint, a key link can manifest as a tight and hypertonic muscle (e.g., a hypertonic sternocleidomastoid muscle). On the other hand, it may present as an inhibited lower trapezius muscle that allows the upper scapular fixators to painfully dominate function. There can also be more than one key link activating the chain of dysfunction.

Any dysfunction that maximally forces the locomotor system to compensate to it is a prime candidate to be a key link. Key links are, therefore, usually found in critical anatomical areas (spinal transitional areas), and areas of high innervation and control (e.g., craniocervical region, feet), and are chronically dysfunctional with evidence of related soft tissue changes, such as thickened and firm periarticular soft tissues, substantially shortened muscles, or very weak and inhibited muscles with atrophy.

Lewit[15] discusses several typical chain reactions that he has observed. In studying these patterns of dysfunction, their reason for existence seems to follow anatomical (i.e.,

scalene dysfunction and upper rib lesions), biomechanical (i.e., poor scapular stabilization and related dysfunctions), and neurophysiological (i.e., reciprocal inhibition, innervation patterns, and activation sequences) principles. These chain reactions or patterns of dysfunction consist of tension and dysfunction consistently observed in typical muscles and joints, respectively. In addition, associated painful periosteal points (pain points) are included. In assessing chain reaction dysfunction patterns, specific muscle tensions are searched for as signposts to related joint dysfunctions and vice versa. In addition, identifying a coexisting periosteal pain point can serve either as the corroborating sign to a specific muscle tension or the initial clue to the joint dysfunction associated with it.

The typical chain reactions found in the upper quarter, cervical spine, and upper thoracic spine can be organized into two main groups according to how they can be assessed clinically. The first group is termed "C0–1: SCM: Scalene," and the second, the "C2–3: Levator: Trapezius." Both chains can interrelate, making for a very confusing picture (Fig. 13–3A and B).

The *C0–1: SCM: Scalene* pattern involves the anterior aspect of the neck and trunk generally and is named after the major joint and muscle patterns of tightness that are commonly observed. The pectoral muscles are usually involved and, together with the scalene muscles, cause upper rib joint dysfunction and pain. The patient usually exhibits poor breathing patterns, headaches, neck pains, and a head forward posture.

The *C2–3: Levator: Trapezius* pattern generally affects the posterior aspect of the body and is also associated with a head forward posture, neck pain, and shoulder pain. In addition, poor scapular control is usually a dominant issue. This pattern also can intermingle with the chain pattern previously described.

The following discussion focuses on the static and dynamic or movement palpation examination of the cervical and upper thoracic spine. In addition, the upper three costotransverse, sternoclavicular, and scapulothoracic joints are considered, as they often relate to functional disorders of the cervical spine.

STATIC PALPATION

SOFT TISSUE PALPATION

Palpation of the soft tissues and osseous structures yields important clues as to areas of dysfunction. Unlike any other part of the human vertebral column, the cervical spine allows access to all of its sides via palpation. Examination should be performed in any position that is comfortable to both examiner and patient, and astute attention should be paid to the accurate identification of structures and their correct segmental level. With the patient prone and the neck in a neutral position, static palpation of many pertinent structures can easily be accomplished with the

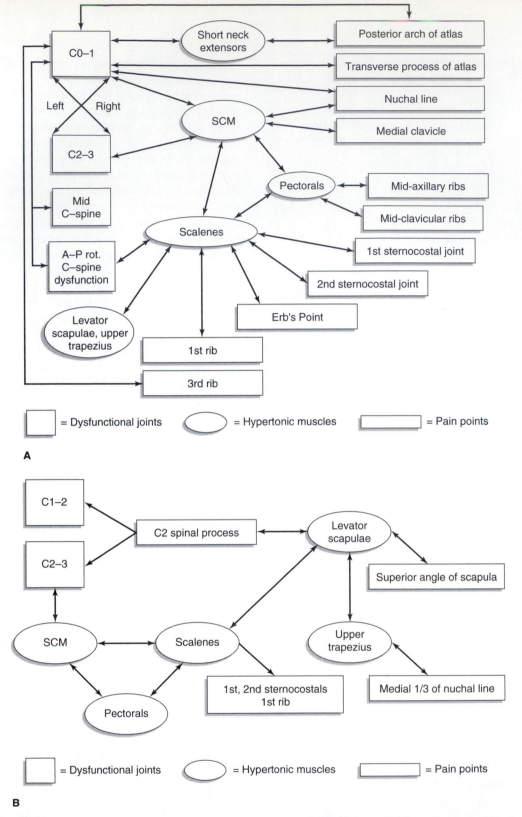

Figure 13–3. A. C0–1: SCM: Scalenes chain reaction. Diagram of interrelated joint and muscle dysfunctions and their associated pain points. The joint dysfunctions are on the left of the diagram represented by squares. Hypertonic muscles are situated near the middle represented by ovals. Periosteal pain points are on the right periphery and bottom of the diagram represented by rectangles. The crossed double arrows between C0–1 and C2–3 signify the occurrence of contralateral joint involvement between the different levels. For example, it is common to find a left-sided C0–1 joint dysfunction associated with a right-sided C2–3 joint dysfunction. **B.** C2: Levator: Trapezius chain reaction. Diagram of inter-related joint and muscle dysfunctions and their associated pain points named after the common C2 spinous pain point. Dysfunctional joints are represented by squares, hypertonic muscles by ovals, and pain points by rectangles.

patient fully relaxed. Osseous and ligamentous asymmetries in the craniovertebral region are the rule, as a perfectly symmetrical spine is a rarity. Additionally, the spinal transitional areas are "ontogenetically restless"[16] and congenital anomalies are, therefore, common in the upper cervical spine.

Initially, the general state of tension in the superficial posterior cervical musculature can be assessed with lightly probing fingertip pressures, working from the occiput to the upper thoracic spine and upper trapezius regions. Localized areas of spasm or hypertonus are searched for in the paraspinal muscles.

! CLINICAL PEARL

C0–1 dysfunction is commonly associated with hypertonic sternocleidomastoid and small neck extensor muscles. Tenderness is usually palpated at the origin of the sternocleidomastoid (SCM) on the lateral half of the superior nuchal line and its insertion on the medial clavicle, two important pain points. Tension in the short neck extensors is associated with a painful posterior arch of atlas.

Deeper palpation seeks to find segmental changes in muscle tone or soft tissue thickenings. Palpation using the thumb tips should be attempted from the lateral aspect of the spinous process out toward the lamina and facet joint region. The paraspinal muscles can be moved aside with the palpating fingers to feel these deeper structures. The superficial and deep paraspinal muscles often harbor local areas of thickening that can be painful. Just deep to these findings are commonly found thickened periarticular soft tissues. Some patients are more difficult to palpate than others, but it is surprising how much can actually be felt.

Changes found in the texture of the soft tissues are important to search for because they yield clues as to a condition's "age"; that is, whether it is acute or chronic. A common finding associated with joint and muscle dysfunction is thickening of the soft tissues, either the overlying skin and subcutaneous fascia or the periarticular tissues and capsular ligaments. Thickening of the soft tissues, by itself, is not as important as its textural quality. Therefore, the texture of the soft tissue thickening is very important to discern. A firm and stringy thickened texture signifies a chronic change. The feel can be compared to that of tough leather. This type of finding in the soft tissues overlying a very stiff facet joint usually correlates with a history of chronic stiffness and pain.

Soft tissue texture changes associated with conditions of more recent onset are softer and spongier. A sense of "bogginess" is imparted to the tissues, as is the patient's subjective feeling of inflammatory tenderness and pain. Soft and boggy soft tissue thickenings are key descriptors for conditions of recent onset, whereas firm and stringy thickenings denote chronic changes. In addition, recent soft tissue changes palpated on top of firmer, more chronic changes are often found in acute exacerbations of chronic dysfunctions.

The aforementioned chronic soft tissue changes may not be the pain generator causing the patient to present clinically. These textural changes could repesent the "silent tombstone" of a very chronic segmental dysfunction that insidiously forces the locomotor system to compensate to it in the form of painful secondary reactions. These painful compensatory reactions are commonly the pain generators that prompt the patient to seek attention. The secondary lesion may be adjacent to or at a distance from the primary chronic biomechanical fault.

Soft tissue thickenings are searched for in between adjacent spinous processes, the lateral aspect of the spinous processes, over the laminae and articular pillars, and over the cervical facet joint capsules. Tenderness and pain, both local and referred, are also searched for. Provocation of referred pain, especially that reproducing the patient's presenting chief symptom, is a very important finding. A common example is referred supraorbital or temporal headache pain elicited upon provocation palpation of the C2–3 or craniocervical facet joints (Fig. 13–4 and 13–5). Interestingly, manual techniques directed at normalizing joint function often yield normalization of these soft tissue changes to some extent over time.

Common soft tissue findings are painful deep thickenings over the C2–3 facet joint and craniocervical joint. Both sides can be involved, but one usually is more so. Joint play testing of these joints invariably reveals pain and stiffness. The upper fibers of the trapezius muscle just lateral to the C2–3 level are often thickened and usually harbor a painful trigger point. The suboccipital soft tissues are

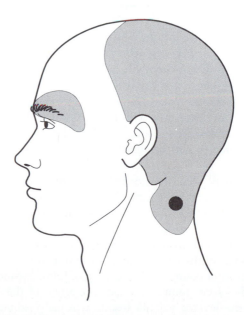

Figure 13–4. C2–3 facet joint pain referral. Note hemicranial distribution.

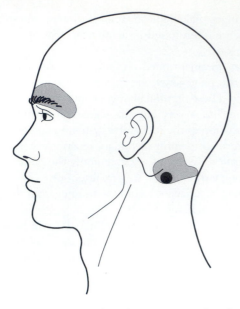

Figure 13–5. Occipito-atlantal joint pain referral.

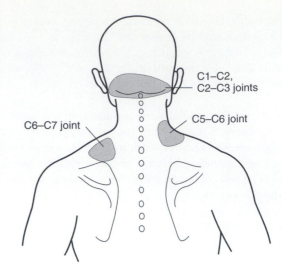

Figure 13–6. Painful tender points in relation to cervical spine joint dysfunction, according to Mennell.[13]

quite commonly thickened and feel firm, especially in patients with chronically stiff cervical spines and those with chronic headache. Localized painful thickenings are also common along the lateral aspects of the spinous processes.

! CLINICAL PEARL

The C2 spinous process represents an important diagnostic pain point because it indicates joint dysfunction at the C1–2 or C2–3 levels and tension in the levator scapulae muscle.

Soft tissue thickening is common over the upper thoracic region and is oftentimes exhibited as a dowager's hump. This is most notable in a head forward postural fault. Its significance is confirmed in the presence of painful skin rolling and excessive soft tissue thickening. The supraspinous ligaments will feel painfully thickened at the level of dysfunction and, often, the lateral aspect of the spinous process will be tender on the side of facet joint dysfunction.

Mennell[13] describes consistent palpatory pain spots relating to cervical facet joint dysfunction (Fig. 13–6). Tender pain points found at the nuchal line to either side of the midline are often found in pathology of the atlantodental joint and dysfunction of the C1–2 and C2–3 joints. The middle of the upper border of the trapezius muscle harbors a painful point in the presence of joint dysfunction of the C5–6 facet joint. The superior angle of the scapula where the levator scapula inserts is usually painful when the C6–7 joint is dysfunctional.

OSSEOUS PALPATION

Palpation of the osseous structures yields information as to painful and prominent spinous processes, alignment of structures, and exostotic thickenings. Older, more chronic exostotic changes feel hard yet have smooth and well-delineated borders. This is very common over the C2–3 joint region. More recent soft tissue changes over these exostotic thickenings give a spongier feel covering the underlying bone and signify more recent changes. Consequently, the osseous margins do not feel as defined.

Spinous process alignment is variable and, therefore, not a reliable indicator of abnormality. However, a prominent spinous process is regularly found that, when palpated, is stiff and painful.

! CLINICAL PEARL

A common finding is a painfully prominent C3 spinous, often found in headache patients. A centrally directed PA pressure usually reproduces the headaches or clues the examiner into palpating the C2–3 facet joint, which often reproduces similar results.

The C2 spinous process is the next largest palpable structure felt in the midline just below the external occipital protuberance. The posterior tubercle of the atlas can be palpated between the C2 spinous process and the occipital rim in patients who are slender and small, usually women and children. However, astute palpation on some patients can detect a slight midline firmness deep in the suboccipital tissues representing the posterior tubercle of the atlas. Palpating too firmly here, or anywhere in the suboccipital region, can elicit discomfort and painful reactions, including a latent onset of headaches and neck pain. Nausea and giddiness can also be evoked, signaling an irritable area or possible vertebral artery disease.

! CLINICAL PEARL

A tender posterior arch of the atlas indicates tension in the short neck extensors due to C0–1 joint dysfunction.

The lateral masses and craniovertebral joints can be palpated posterolaterally in patients who do not have thickened suboccipital tissues (Fig. 13–7). The transverse process of the atlas can be felt in most people just anterior and inferior to the mastoid tip. It is found between the mastoid process tip and the posterior aspect of the mandibular ramus. An important palpation landmark is a small sulcus felt just anterior to the transverse process tip and posterior to the mandibular ramus (Figure 13–8).

! CLINICAL PEARL

A painful atlas transverse process signifies C0–1 dysfunction and is associated with tension in the ipsilateral SCM muscle.

The craniovertebral joints are found midway between the atlas posterior tubercle in the midline and the transverse process tips laterally. Palpation pressure needs to be directed cranially and medially, toward the opposite eye. Capsular thickening and firm resistance that reproduce supraorbital or occipital headaches are common findings.

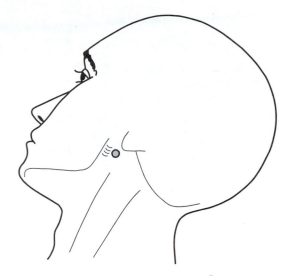

Figure 13–8. Small sulcus palpable anterior to transverse process of atlas.

The spinous processes should be aligned in the sagittal plane and scribe a lordotic arc. The two bifid processes on each spinous are usually asymmetrical. The large C2 spinous often overhangs the small, timid C3 spinous process. However, palpation of this little landmark is facilitated by flexing the upper cervical spine and palpating in a slightly cranial direction. The spaces between adjacent spinous processes should be assessed. A common palpable finding is the C6 spinous process palpating closer to that of C7. On the other hand, C4 often palpates as painfully prominent and is commonly associated with mid-cervical pain.

The inferior borders of the spinous processes of C2–6 lie on a level with the facet joints (Fig. 13–9). For example, the inferior tip of the C2 spinous process lies on a level with the joint between C2 and C3. The dorsal aspect of the facet joint is marked by a small bony protuberance that can be felt by moving the posterior muscle bellies medially and palpating deeply (Fig. 13–10). In many patients, a small groove can be palpated between the protuberances marking the joint line. Painful joint capsule thickening, either soft or hard, is commonly found over dysfunctional joints in this area.

The C7 and T1 spinous processes are equally large and long. To ascertain one from the other, the C7 and C6 spinous processes should be palpated simultaneously while extending the neck backward. Upon cervical extension, the C6 spinous process will disappear from palpation while C7 remains palpable. On the other hand, oscillating pressures directed caudally on the first rib can be palpated as small movements transmitted to the T1 spinous process.

The transverse processes can be palpated anterolaterally by moving the deep cervical musculature aside. The C2 transverse processes are the next largest anterolateral bony masses below the atlas transverse processes.

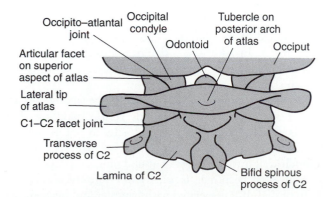

Figure 13–7. Cervicocranial osseous relations.

(From Grieve GP. Common Vertebral Joint Problems. New York, NY: Churchill Livingstone; 1988, with permission.)

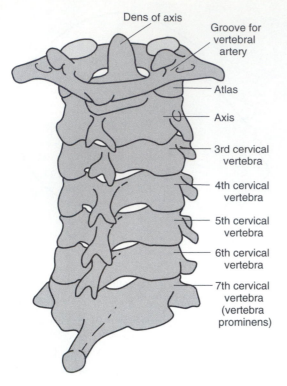

Figure 13–9. Anatomy of posterior aspect of cervical spine.

(From Clemente CD. Anatomy. A Regional Atlas of the Human Body. Philadelphia, Pa: Lea and Febiger; 1975, with permission.)

Facilitation of scalene palpation can be accomplished by feeling the anterior tubercles of the cervical transverse processes and having the patient take a deep breath. Contraction of the scalene muscles can be felt, and their muscle slips can then be palpated along their lengths.

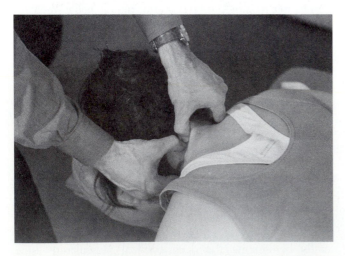

Figure 13–10. Palpation of cervical facet joint. Note tissue pushed medially.

! CLINICAL PEARL

Tension in the scalene muscle group indicates joint dysfunction of the mid- and lower cervical joints, particularly AP rotation and flexion dysfunctions. Tenderness at the sternocostal junctions of the first two ribs is also associated with scalene tension together with pectoral muscle tightness. Erb's point is located 2 cm above the clavicle at the posterior border of the SCM. It represents the area where the anterior and middle scalene muscles cross and where the cervical roots are located (where the superficial jugular vein crosses the SCM's posterior border). Tenderness here signifies cervical radicular involvement or scalene muscle tension.

The first rib can be palpated with the patient prone by directing both thumbs under the upper fibers of the trapezius and pressing towards the opposite hip (Fig. 13–11A). It palpates as a short, stout structure forming a wide blade with a small radius of curvature in the supraclavicular fossa. With the patient in the sitting position, the anterior curved aspect of the first rib is felt just posterior to the junction of the medial and middle thirds of the clavicle (Fig. 13–11B). Concurrently, it is found anterior to the mid-slope of the upper fibers of the trapezius muscle.

MOVEMENT PALPATION

Movement palpation can be divided into scan and joint-specific examinations. The scan examination is more general and identifies the level of the lesion. The joint-specific examination identifies particular parameters of joint motion that are abnormal and any elicited pain on provocation. The most important aspect of this examination is to assess each symptomatic motion segment specifically and fully in terms of movement restriction and pain response. Particular attention must be paid to the level of the lesion via astute landmark palpation. Joint resistance and pain should be assessed with respect to where they occur in the joint's range of motion (i.e., through range pain or end range pain). In addition, a determination as to whether pain or resistance or both simultaneously are limiting the motion should be made.

Joint pain occurring early in the range signifies an active or acute lesion that demands gentle handling. The pain is usually local, constant, and achy in nature and increases as one trespasses more into the range. Conversely, pain felt well into the range or at end range, especially after resistance has been met, is usually intermittent and can be sharp or dull. It is associated with capsular and ligamentous soft tissues that have adaptively shortened. Referred pain may be elicited in both types of situations, and its intensity is usually felt to a lesser extent distally.

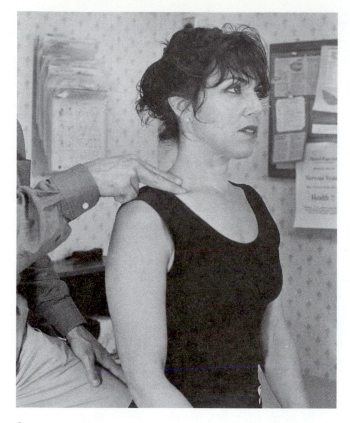

A

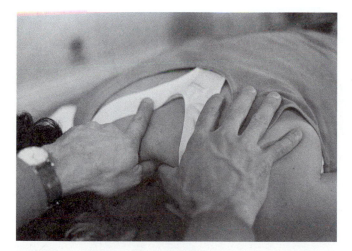

B

Figure 13–11. Palpation of first rib. **A.** Patient upright. **B.** Patient prone.

Normal joint motion is palpated as free and gliding. Resistance to motion in dysfunctional joints can be felt initially with a gradual increase in resistance the further in the range one moves, or it can be felt at the end range with an abrupt increase in resistance. Both responses, when coupled with their pain responses, help guide the way a joint is to be handled with mobilization techniques.

GENERAL SCANS

Gillet and Liekens[17] and Schafer and Faye[18] have developed scan and specific palpation procedures that adequately assess spinal motion to allow detection of joint dysfunction. A general sitting scan examination can be used that quickly localizes a level of resistance to neutral. The patient is seated upright making sure that slouching and head poking do not occur. The tips of the examiner's thumb and middle finger of one hand are used in a wide pincer grasp to palpate over the cervical facet joints while the head is stabilized with the other hand (Fig. 13–12). PA pressures are simultaneously employed through both fingers as they probe and slide quickly and smoothly up the cervical spine from the cervicodorsal region to the craniocervical joints. The spine is gently pushed out of its neutral resting posture into a few degrees of extension at each level and a "resistance to neutral" is observed for. Slight counterpressure is applied to the forehead to aid in extending the cervical spine facet joints over the probing fingers. The extension imparted is minimal. Once a level of motion resistance is identified, specific palpation in either the sitting or prone positions can be used to further elucidate the joint dysfunction.

Another form of scan examination can be used to differentiate upper from lower cervical joint problems. The pain response to gross cervical flexion and extension is noted. This is then compared to the pain response occurring during anterior and posterior glide of the head and

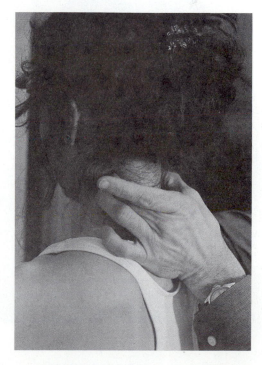

Figure 13–12. General motion scan examination.

neck (Fig. 13–13A and B). When the head translates forward in relation to the torso (i.e., chin poking), the upper cervical spine undergoes extension while the lower cervical spine flexes (Fig. 13–13A). With posterior gliding or chin retraction, the reverse occurs (Fig. 13–13B). If gross cervical spine flexion causes a painful response that is reproduced with chin poking and reduced with chin retraction, the lower cervical spine is incriminated as the painful site since it undergoes flexion in both maneuvers. If gross cervical spine extension is painful and the same response is reproduced with chin poking but not with chin retraction, the upper cervical spine is suspect because it undergoes extension during both maneuvers.

Combined movements can also be used to localize joint problems quickly. Quadrant testing the cervical spine places the facet joints into their close-packed positions, which stresses capsular ligaments. Painfully evoked quadrant tests can localize restricted dysfunctional joints. To quadrant test the cervical spine, it is placed into a position of extension, lateral flexion, and rotation where the rotation and lateral flexion are to the same side (Fig. 13–14). This maneuver close-packs the facets on the side to which the face is turned. Localized quadrant tests can be applied to each intersegmental level by using the palpating thumb

as the localizing fulcrum. A painfully restricted response is looked for.

SPECIFIC PROVOCATIVE PALPATION

The most important aspect of the cervical spine manual examination is specifically directed provocative palpation of individual motion segments. It is both specific and provocative in the sense that individual facet joints are assessed for painful joint restriction. After the scan examination identifies a level of lesion, the specific provocative palpation is performed to further characterize the joint dysfunction. An attempt is made to identify the plane of movement that is restricted to aid in the manipulative prescription.

Maitland[11] discusses various grades of movement describing both the examining and mobilizing procedures. These grades describe where they occur in the joint's range of motion and the amplitude of the movement used (Fig. 13–15). For instance, a grade I mobilization is a small amplitude movement occurring at the beginning of the range and can be almost imperceptible to an onlooker observing the examination. A grade II mobilization is a larger ampli-

A

B

Figure 13–13. A. Cervical spine anterior glide. **B.** Cervical spine posterior glide.

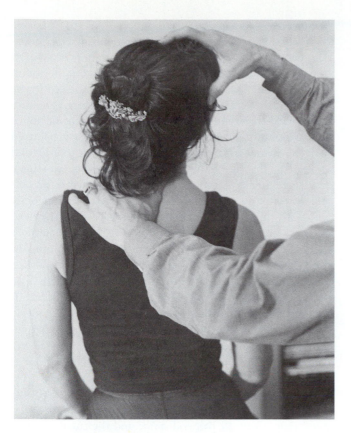

Figure 13–14. Cervical quadrant testing.

grade IV mobilization is like a grade I mobilization in amplitude; however, it starts and ends near the end range and applies more of a stretching force on the joint structures. Being able to relate the grade of movement used on the one hand, to the joint resistance and pain elicited on the other, aids in applying the appropriate therapeutic mobilization and manipulation techniques. A plus (+) or minus (−) sign can be used to denote a slightly more or less graded movement, respectively; that is, grade IV+ or grade II−.

A joint's "irritability" needs to be taken into consideration when examining a patient's painful condition. This pertains to the reactive nature of an articulation in terms of symptom production in response to provocation. The three parameters defining joint irritability are (1) the amount of movement needed to provoke symptoms, (2) the magnitude of the response, and (3) the time it takes for the joint to return to its undisturbed state. A very irritable joint is provoked into much painful rebellion with the least amount of movement and takes a long time to stabilize, anywhere from minutes to hours. These joint lesions need to be handled very carefully with examining techniques as well as therapeutic maneuvers. Irritable joints can only tolerate grade I examining movements and, therefore, demand grade I mobilization techniques in treatment. A person whose pain is moderately achy after several hours of exertion and returns to normal after several minutes of rest is not very reactive and can be examined more vigorously without fear of painful reprisal. Joints that evoke responses with only grade IV examining movements can be mobilized more vigorously with grade IV mobilizing techniques. It is therefore important to search for clues in the history to ascertain the reactive or nonreactive nature of the joint in question.

tude movement occurring within the range but not reaching either the beginning or end range regions. A grade III mobilization is similar to a grade II in amplitude; however, it starts within the range and ends at the end range of joint motion, therefore stretching the joint structures more. A

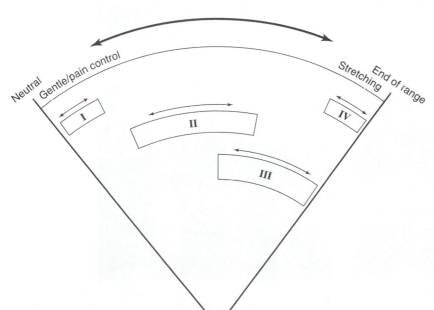

Figure 13–15. Grades of mobilization.

(From DeFranca GD, Levine LJ. Pelvic Locomotor Dysfunction: A Clinical Approach. Gaithersburg, Md.: Aspen Publishers; 1996, with permission.)

The two types of procedures for the cervical and upper thoracic spine that are discussed next are end range provocative testing using passive physiological movements and the testing of accessory movements from the neutral position.

CERVICAL SPINE

PASSIVE PHYSIOLOGICAL MOVEMENTS

The passive physiological movements of flexion, extension, rotation, and lateral bending can be assessed with the patient in the sitting or supine position. A unique factor of the cervical spine examination is that rotation can be examined in both PA and AP directions because of the accessibility of the anatomy.

Craniocervical Region

The upper cervical region demands astute attention to examination. The relationship between the transverse process of the atlas, mastoid process, and angle of the jaw during test movements forms the basis of assessment in this area. The small sulcus just anterior to the atlas transverse process is also used to assess changing relationships between the atlas and occiput. The test movements include rotation, lateral flexion, anterior glide, and flexion.

Rotation

As discussed in Chapter 2, a small amount of rotation occurs between the atlas and occiput. Rotation is assessed from both posterior to anterior and anterior to posterior on the same side. This motion is palpable and assessed for by observing the changing relationship between palpation landmarks. To examine PA rotation in the right occipitoatlantal joint, the right atlas transverse process is palpated with the examiner's right middle finger tip just inferior and anterior to the tip of the mastoid process (Fig. 13–16A). The small sulcus anterior to the atlas transverse process and posterior to the mandibular ramus is simultaneously felt. With the patient in a neutral sitting posture, the head and neck are passively rotated to the left by the examiner's indifferent hand contact on the cranial vertex. Normally, the palpating finger should sense the mastoid tip and bulge of the sternomastoid muscle covering the atlas transverse process to make it nonpalpable at the end of rotation. In addition, the small sulcus anterior to the transverse process should widen. In the presence of C0–1 joint dysfunction, the transverse process of the atlas will remain palpable and the sulcus will not widen.

To assess AP rotation of C0–1, the patient's head is rotated to the right while palpating the same landmarks (Fig. 13–16B). Normally, the mandibular ramus covers the atlas transverse process at the end range and the small sulcus is narrowed. In joint dysfunction of the C0–1 articulation,

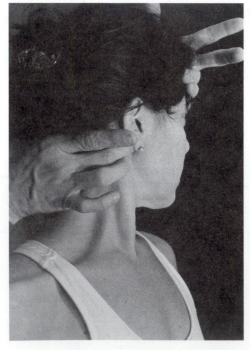

A

B

Figure 13–16. A. Posterior-to-anterior rotation palpation of right C0–1 joint. **B.** Anterior-to-posterior rotation palpation of right C0–1 joint.

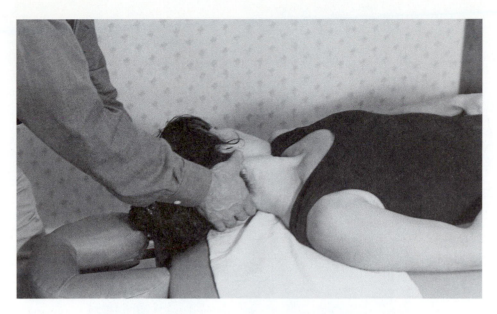

Figure 13–17. Posterior-to-anterior rotation palpation of right C0–1 joint supine.

the transverse process remains palpable and the sulcus width does not change. These movements are then repeated on the opposite side.

Rotation of the C0–1 joint can be assessed with the patient in the supine position by cradling the patient's head and upper cervical spine in one of the examiner's hands (Fig.13–17). The examiner's middle finger contacts the space between the left mastoid process and atlas transverse process while the thumb of the same hand palpates the same area on the right side. The occiput rests in the examiner's palm while the other hand supports and controls the head and neck movements. Rotation of the neck is performed as movement is palpated for and pain provocation is performed with slight over-pressure. The same movements as those previously mentioned should occur as the examiner monitors the changes occurring at each finger alternately. The advantage of this position is that the patient tends to be more relaxed.

Lateral Flexion

To assess for lateral flexion at the craniocervical joint, the space between the atlas transverse process and mastoid process is palpated (Fig. 13–18A). The examiner's middle finger feels for the space to open when the head is laterally flexed away from the contact and for it to close when the head is laterally flexed towards it. A springing action is induced at the end range while assessing for end play and pain provocation. In addition, a slight shifting of the atlas toward the side of lateral bending can often be perceived as the transverse process palpates more prominently. The same procedure is repeated on the opposite side and the findings are compared.

Lateral flexion can be assessed in the supine position by cradling the patient's head as previously mentioned for

rotation (Fig. 13–18B). Lateral flexion is localized to the upper cervical region as movement is palpated for and pain provocation is performed with slight over-pressure.

Anterior Glide

Anterior glide essentially consists of jutting the head forward on the cervical spine so that the occipital condyles glide anteriorly (Fig. 13–19). The upper cervical spine is actually extending. The space between the atlas transverse process and the mandibular ramus is palpated with one hand as the head is pressed forward with the other. The pad of the middle finger of the palpating hand is used while the palm of the other hand contacts the vertex. Normally the space opens and a sense of joint springing should be felt. Upon release of the forward gliding pressure the space should close. Joint dysfunction is evidenced by lack of motion and pain provocation. This is a difficult movement for some patients to perform. In such cases, the examiner can assist several repetitions of active chin poking and retraction so that patients can feel what is required of them. Sometimes palpation needs to be done as the patient actively performs a chin poking and retraction. The patient who exhibits great difficulty in performing this maneuver is usually the one who has very restricted craniocervical joints.

Flexion

Flexion is best examined with the patients supine. The examiner cradles both transverse processes of the atlas with the thumb pad and middle finger of one hand while the other hand flexes the occiput on atlas by pressing on the forehead (Fig. 13–20). The hand contacting the atlas both stabilizes and senses for movement while the hand pressing on the forehead senses for a springing sensation. Quite

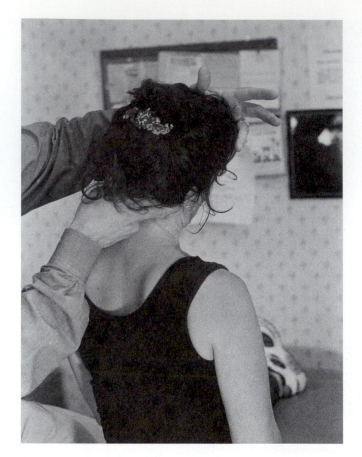

A

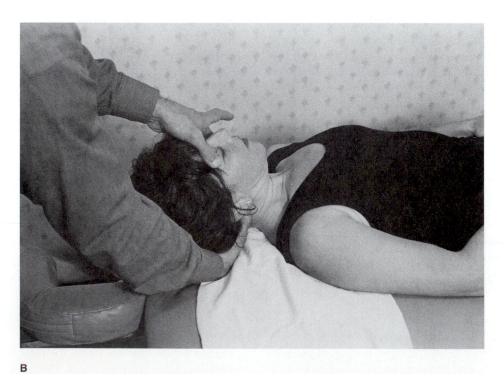

B

Figure 13–18. Lateral flexion palpation of C0–1. **A.** Patient sitting. **B.** Patient supine.

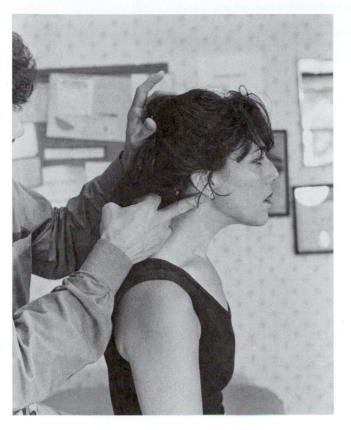

Figure 13-19. Anterior glide of C0–1.

commonly a block to motion is sensed as a result of hypertonic suboccipital muscles; this block is often found in patients exhibiting a head forward and chin-poking posture. In these cases, having the patient actively tuck in the chin may assist in feeling movement.

C2–7 Region

The rest of the cervical spine facet joints can be examined in extension, flexion, rotation, and lateral flexion. In addition, as in the craniocervical region, AP rotation can be palpated for. At the end range of motion, a joint play challenge is performed to assess joint restriction and pain provocation. Any resistance to movement resulting from segmental muscle spasm is also noted. Procedures are repeated bilaterally and the responses are compared. An organized sequence of examination entails the following: extension, PA rotation, lateral flexion, flexion, and AP rotation while in the seated position.

Extension

Unilateral facet extension is assessed with fingertip or thumb tip pressures of the palpating hand localizing an extension movement over the facet joint in question (Fig. 13–21). The indifferent hand controls the head and neck movements and imparts extension just to the level being examined and then slightly more as the palpating finger presses into full intersegmental extension unilaterally. It must be noted that this movement is not full gross cervical extension. Movement restriction and pain are present at a dysfunctional joint whereas painless free motion signifies normal function. Painful joint restriction in extension is often associated with a painfully stiff unilateral PA pressure at the same facet.

Posterior-to-Anterior Rotation

Because the palpating contact is posterior to the motion segment, and the movement imparted is rotation, although from a posterior to anterior direction, this motion assessment is termed PA rotation. While maintaining the same

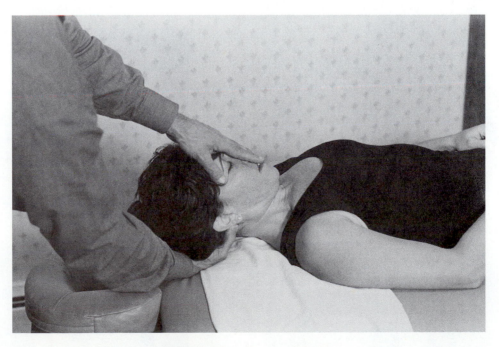

Figure 13-20. Flexion of C0–1.

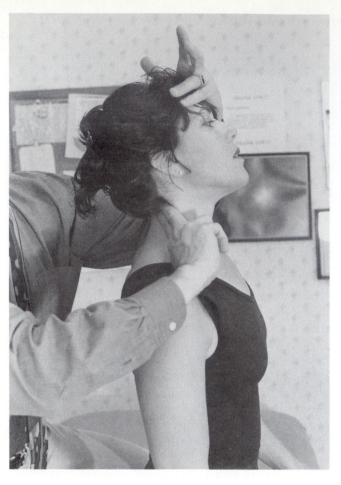

Figure 13–21. Extension palpation of C2–7.

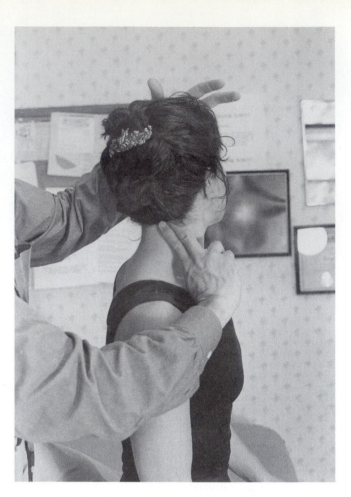

Figure 13–22. Posterior-to-anterior rotation palpation of C2–7.

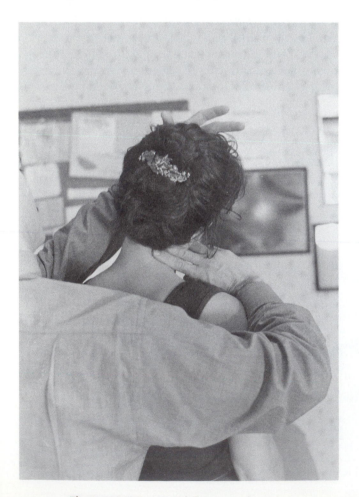

Figure 13–23. Lateral flexion palpation.

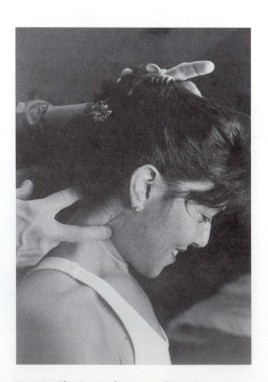

Figure 13–24. Flexion palpation of C2–7.

contact over the facet joint as previously described for extension, the head and neck are rotated away from the contact as the palpating finger follows the movement (Fig. 13–22). At the end range, a joint play challenge is applied and a springy, painless end feel should be palpated. Movement restriction and pain signify dysfunction.

Lateral Flexion

While still maintaining the same contact as for extension and rotation, the neck and head are laterally flexed over the palpating finger (Fig. 13–23). Because the articular pillars are posterolaterally placed, the examining movement is performed in slight posterolateral bending. A provocative springing motion at the end range aids in assessing for joint play and pain response. Lateral flexion dysfunctions are commonly coupled with extension joint restrictions.

Flexion

To assess intersegmental flexion, the pad of the examiner's index or middle finger palpates anteriorly as the spine is flexed over it (Fig. 13–24). The overlying muscle groups need to be pushed aside to acquire a deep contact over the anterior aspect of the transverse processes. The indifferent hand flexes the head and neck over the palpating finger just to the segmental level in question. More flexion is needed to assess the lower cervical motion segments. Provocative joint playing is performed to assess movement restriction and pain response.

Anterior-to-Posterior Rotation

This movement palpation assessment derives its name from the fact that a contact anterior to the motion segment is made, and rotation is imparted from an anterior to posterior direction. While maintaining the same contact as previously described for flexion, the neck and head are rotated to the side of contact as the palpating finger pulls posteriorly on the transverse process while following the gross movement of the cervical spine (Fig. 13–25). At the end range of motion, provocative joint springing is performed to assess joint play and pain response. These joint dysfunctions are very common and are often found in association with flexion fixations.

> ### ! CLINICAL PEARL
>
> AP rotation and lower cervical segmental flexion fixations are commonly found with cervicobrachial conditions, ipsilateral upper extremity disorders, and side of handedness. A common clinical finding is a firm, painful end feel during flexion or rotation (anterior to posterior) over the C5 and C6 levels, especially with cervicobrachial conditions and ipsilateral upper extremity disorders. Movement restriction is commonly found on the side of handedness. Firm pressure applied to the anterolateral aspect of the lower cervical motion segments often elicits referred pain onto the upper anterior chest wall, upper arm, or upper back medial to the scapula or a combination of all three—the so-called "door-bell sign." Maigne[19, 20] mentions that this upper back pain of cervical origin is quite consistent and is regularly found 2 cm lateral to the T5 and T6 spinous processes. Scalene and pectoral muscle tension is commonly associated with AP rotation and flexion dysfunctions.

ACCESSORY MOVEMENTS

As mentioned before, accessory movements are involuntary joint play movements. Essentially, various force vectors are applied to different aspects of the motion segment while the patient is prone to assess for motion restriction and pain provocation. They consist of central PA pressures over the spinous processes, unilateral PAs over the facet joints, and transverse pressures against the spinous processes or articular pillars. To further elicit the exact pain response from the patient, varying the pressures in different directions is helpful. For example, applying a medially directed pressure when performing a unilateral PA pressure at the C2–3 facet is a common and very important variation. This often elicits a response that reproduces the patient's symptoms by creating maximal joint gliding. In addition, unilateral AP pressure can be explored in the cervical region because of accessibility of the anterior regional anatomy. The elicited responses to these pressures help guide the application of therapeutic mobilization and manipulation techniques. The reader is referred to Maitland's work for a more complete discussion.[11]

Central Posterior-to-Anterior Pressures

The patient is prone with the head and neck in the neutral position while central posterior-to-anterior (CPA) pres-

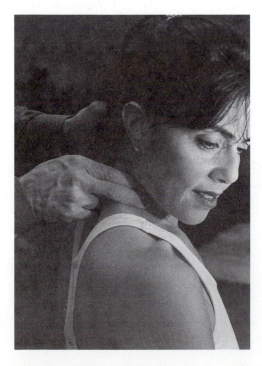

Figure 13–25. Anterior-to-posterior rotation palpation.

sures are directed through the spinous processes by using both thumb tips held together, thumbnail to thumbnail (Fig. 13–26A and B). The tips of the thumbs are used; however, the thumb pads can be used if discomfort is experienced by the patient from the contact. The hands and other fingers gently wrap around the cervical spine as the examiner is positioned at the head end of the table facing caudad (Fig. 13–26A). The arms are straight and the movement comes from the torso and arms, not the hands. Two to three oscillations are imparted to the motion segment to gain a sense of motion. A deeper, sustained pressure can be applied to elicit the patient's pain response.

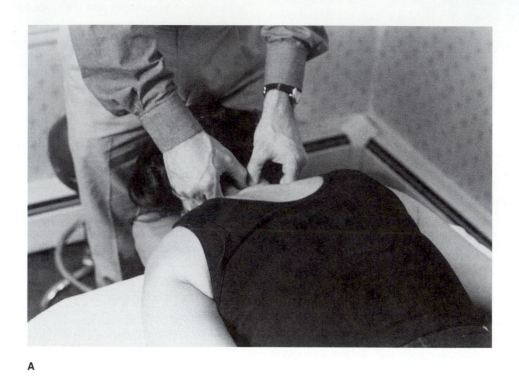

A

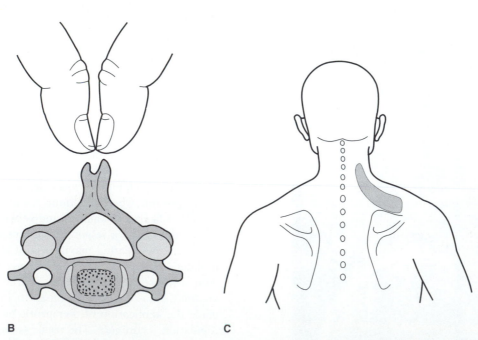

B

C

Figure 13–26. A. Examiner position for central posterior-to-anterior pressure. **B.** Anatomical view of central posterior-to-anterior pressure. **C.** Common pain referral from lower cervical spine facet joints.

The posterior tubercle of the atlas and each cervical spinous process are examined in this way, noting motion characteristics and pain responses. The atlas tubercle is difficult to palpate as is the small C3 spinous process. To facilitate examination, the patient can be asked to flex the upper cervical spine with a chin tuck. The fingers of both hands can gently lift the motion segments with anteriorly placed contacts on the transverse processes alternately with central PAs to gain a better feel for motion. A push-pull movement is used.

The C3 spinous process is commonly found to be prominent, stiff, and painful. Varying the CPA cephalad often reproduces a patient's headache along with the experience of a deep local pain. A prominent and stiff C4 spinous process often creates a local cervical pain when pressed upon, whereas the C5 spinous process, when stiff and painful, often refers pain into the top of the shoulder or suprascapular area (Fig. 13–26C). More commonly, the C6 spinous process causes this pain response with a CPA and palpates closer to the C7 spinous process, creating a gap between C5 and C6 and giving the C5 spinous process the appearance of being more prominent.[1]

Unilateral Posterior-to-Anterior Pressures

Unilateral PA pressures are applied over the articular pillars and facet regions of the cervical spine while the patient is prone with the head and neck in the neutral position (Fig. 13–27A). The double thumb contact previously described is used to palpate the posterior aspect of the facet region (Fig. 13–27B). The craniocervical joints are found lateral to the midline, about midway between the tip of the atlas transverse process and the mid-sagittal plane. The C1–2 facet is found more laterally than the rest of the cervical spine, and the lower facets need to be palpated from under the edge of the upper fibers of the trapezius muscle. The examiner must angle the pressures cephalad when examining the craniocervical and C1–2 joints. The middle three cervical facets are readily palpable.

A very important variation to unilateral PA pressures is to apply a slight medially directed angulation imparting maximal joint gliding[11] (Fig. 13–27C and D). This is especially so in the upper cervical spine, notably the C0–1 and C2–3 levels. It is also performed when assessing and treating for stiffness rather than pain. In a very painful segment, angling the pressure laterally is more tolerable. The C0–1 and C2–3 segments most commonly palpate as stiff and painful joints with soft tissue thickening layered over them.

! **CLINICAL PEARL**

A stiff and painful C0–1 joint dysfunction is commonly associated with a contralateral stiff and painful C2–3 joint dysfunction.

Maitland[11] discusses the differentiation of pain arising from the C1–2 versus the C2–3 facet joints by way of provocative palpation while varying neck rotation (Fig. 13–28). When a patient is prone with the head and neck in the neutral position, a unilateral PA pressure on C2 essentially assesses the C2–3 facet joint. If, however, the head is rotated approximately 30 degrees to the right, for instance, and a unilateral PA is performed on the right side of C2, then the C1–2 joint is being assessed. This is because, in this position, pressure on the right of C2 further increases its rotational movement against an already rotated atlas.

Transverse Pressures

A transverse pressure is applied to the lateral aspect of the spinous process to further assess the motion segment for motion and pain response (Fig. 13–29). Again, a double thumb contact is used, but this time one thumb is placed over the other's thumbnail for reinforcement. The paraspinal muscles need to be pushed aside with the palpating thumbs for the mid-cervical region. Gentle pressures are applied to the spinous process. An alternative method is to apply these same pressures to the articular processes. A transverse pressure can also be applied to the atlas transverse process with the head of the prone patient fully turned toward the examiner. Pressures are then applied with a bilateral tip-to-tip thumb contact. Again, signs of restriction and pain provocation are searched for.

Unilateral Anterior-to-Posterior Pressures

AP pressures should be assessed unilaterally on the transverse processes, especially in patients whose symptoms are anterior in origin or in those with any upper extremity related condition (Fig. 13–30). A double thumb contact can be used, and care in handling must be exercised because of the normal sensitivity in this area. The anteriorly placed muscles are gently pushed aside so that direct contact can be made on the transverse processes. The hands encircle the neck and movements are gently performed. If the person is prone, these same movements can be performed by lifting the transverse processes with the pads of the index or middle fingers. As with flexion and AP rotation joint fixations, pain elicited here often refers onto the upper anterior chest wall, arm, or upper back areas.

UPPER THORACIC SPINE

Pain and stiffness in the upper thoracic spine can also cause cervical symptoms. Likewise, lower cervical joint dysfunction and disc lesions often cause upper thoracic pain. As discussed earlier, the lower cervical spine commonly refers pain to the medial scapular region. Examination of upper thoracic joint function must be included in cervical pain syndromes. Upper thoracic joint dysfunction sometimes causes limited cervical range of motion or even referred pain to the head and upper extremities. Pain from the

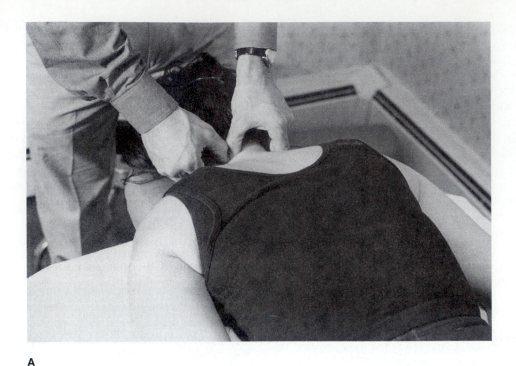

A

B

Figure 13–27. A. Examiner position for unilateral posterior-to-anterior pressure. **B.** Anatomical view of unilateral posterior-to-anterior pressure.

upper two thoracic segments is often felt horizontally across the upper back (Fig. 13–31). Examination of the upper thoracic spine for joint dysfunction is similar to that of the cervical region except for a few differences due to anatomical variation.

The first two thoracic segments are typically limited in their range of motion and movement is usually difficult to feel. Painful soft tissue thickenings in between the spinous processes and on their lateral aspect are very com-

mon and usually coincide with the level and side of joint dysfunction.

A stiff, boardlike upper thoracic spine is commonly seen in middle-aged and older individuals. Multiple segments and their corresponding costotransverse articulations typically are involved with joint dysfunction and local soft tissue thickening. Movement is very restricted with a firm and often rigid end feel. The skin and subcutaneous tissues can be surprisingly tough and thickened

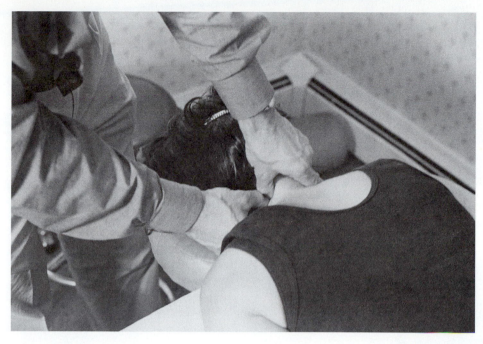

C

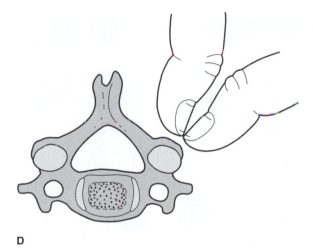

D

Figure 13–27 continued. C. Examiner position for unilateral posterior-to-anterior pressure directed slightly medially. **D.** Anatomical view of medially directed posterior-to-anterior pressure.

over the upper thoracic segments. A head forward posture, forward drawn shoulders, tight pectoral muscles, and poor scapular control frequently accompany this type of stiff upper thoracic spine. Poor upper thoracic joint function forces undue compensation by the cervical spine. Cervical motion tends to be focused into the mid and lower segments as the cervical-dorsal region is very restricted. Sometimes the line of the lower neck is almost horizontal in a severe head forward posture and most

! CLINICAL PEARL

Picking up a fold of skin between the fingers and rolling it first up the center of the spine, and then over either side, can be very informative, especially in the thoracic region. A positive finding occurs when the skin fold becomes quite painful and adherent to the underlying tissues over the level of dysfunction, making it difficult to continue rolling the skin fold. Rolling a fold of skin over each paravertebral trough area will be more painful and adherent on the side of joint dysfunction.

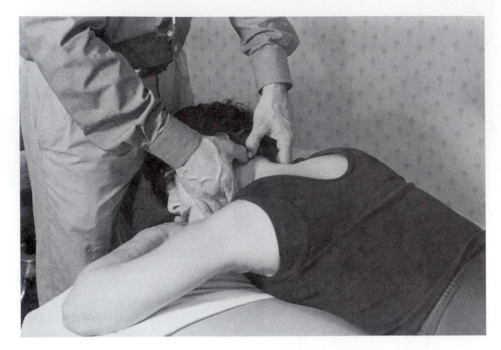

Figure 13–28. Unilateral posterior-to-anterior pressure with head rotation.

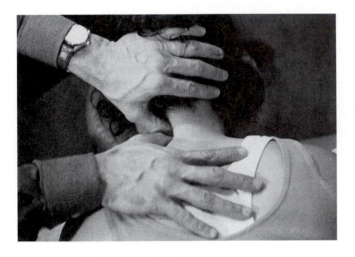

Figure 13–29. Transverse pressure.

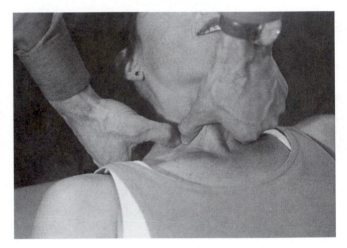

Figure 13–30. Unilateral anterior-to-posterior pressure.

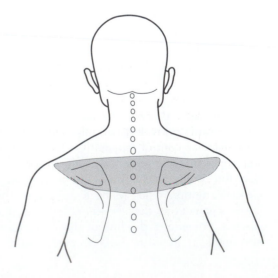

Figure 13–31. Pain referral from upper two thoracic joints.

neck extension appears to occur in the upper cervical spine.

One case presentation that may be seen is upper extremity paresthesias and headaches in women who are middle-aged and older. The symptoms occur during the nighttime hours or upon arising and are unilateral or bilateral, being glovelike in distribution. The headache is often occipital, frontal, or generalized and is not a consistent feature. Interestingly, stiff upper thoracic segments are a regular occurrence, especially at the T4 level; thus, the syndrome is named the T4 syndrome.[21] The T2–7 segments can be involved, but the T4 segment is by far the more common one affected. Joint dysfunction, soft tissue changes, and pain can be localized to the T4 segment and manipulative treatment directed at normalizing joint function is very helpful. Postural corrections usually need to be made with exercise instruction, and coexistent rib joint dysfunctions require treatment.

PASSIVE PHYSIOLOGICAL MOVEMENTS

In the upper thoracic spine, flexion, extension, rotation, and lateral flexion can all be assessed with the patient sitting or side-lying. The sitting variation is discussed here. The patient must sit upright without slouching. Some patients and examiners find it more comfortable to palpate the upper thoracic movements in the side-lying position. Essentially, the head and neck are cradled and moved by the examiner's cephalad hand and arm while the caudad hand palpates movement at the spinous processes (Fig. 13–32A–D). The supporting arm and hand move as one with the trunk to impart the various motions.

Flexion

The examiner's palpating thumb tip feels the interspinous space between two adjacent thoracic spinous processes while the other hand flexes the head and neck forward (Fig. 13–33A). The interspinous space should open and a springing sensation should be palpable at the end range with joint play provocation.

Extension

Extension appears to occur in two stages. The first stage is marked by spinous process approximation as the facet joints close in extension. Further extension causes the vertebral bodies to gap anteriorly, and this can be palpated at the spinous process as a subtle anterior translation (Fig. 13–33B). Shortened anterior longitudinal ligaments will cause lack of this movement. Joint play challenge can also be applied over each facet region to feel for joint restriction and to elicit pain as the head and neck are extended.

Rotation

For rotation, the examiner fully rotates the head and neck of the patient while the palpating thumb imparts additional rotational pressure on the thoracic spinous process (Fig. 13–34).

Lateral Flexion

To assess lateral flexion, the head and neck are laterally flexed as a unit by one hand while the palpating thumb of the other hand blocks motion at the spinous process being examined (Fig. 13–35). The thumb imparts a springing motion at the end range on the spinous process to assess mobility and any pain response.

ACCESSORY MOVEMENTS

The accessory movements of central PA pressures over the spinous process, unilateral PA pressures over the facet joint, and transverse pressures against the spinous process can be used to assess the upper thoracic spinal segments. Again, pain response, mobility, and elicited spasm are being assessed. The patient is positioned prone with the head and neck in the neutral position.

Central Posterior-to-Anterior Pressures

For this examination, the examiner is at the head end of the table and a double thumb contact is made on the spinous process (Fig. 13–36). In very large patients, a pisiform contact can be made instead of the thumbs. The spinous processes are often tender, but usually more in the mid-thoracic region. Pressure is applied perpendicular to the spinous process. The pads of the thumbs should be used and pressure is directed through them via the torso and arms.

Unilateral Posterior-to-Anterior Pressures

From the head end of the table unilateral PA pressures are applied over the transverse processes (Fig. 13–37). In addition, the costotransverse joints are examined at this time. This assessment is discussed in detail later in the chapter.

Transverse Pressures

When applying transverse pressures, an attempt is made to make a contact against the lateral aspect of the spinous process and not against its tip (Fig. 13–38). A slight anterior angulation facilitates this contact. One thumb pad contacts the lateral aspect of the spinous process while the other thumb reinforces it by pressing on the thumbnail. Pressure is exerted through the thumbs via the torso and arms.

RIB JOINTS

The upper costotransverse joints are commonly painful and stiff, being covered by ropy, knotted tender muscles. Two and even three levels are often involved.

 CLINICAL PEARL

Cervical and upper thoracic joint dysfunctions are often associated with coexisting costotransverse joint dysfunctions. A common example of this is the consistent finding of upper cervical joint fixations associated with joint dysfunction of the upper three costotransverse joints, most notably those of the first and third rib joints. The finding of one necessitates searching for the other.

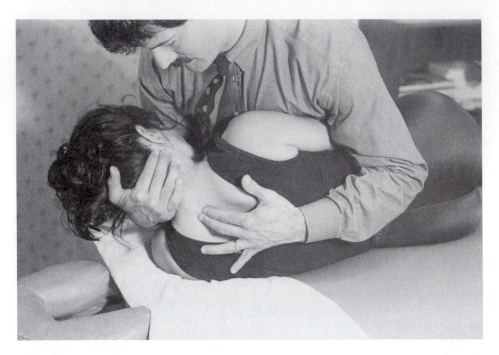

A

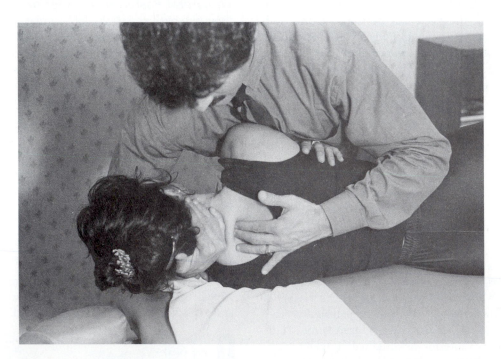

B

Figure 13–32. Palpation for upper thoracic movement with patient in side-lying position. **A.** Flexion. **B.** Extension.

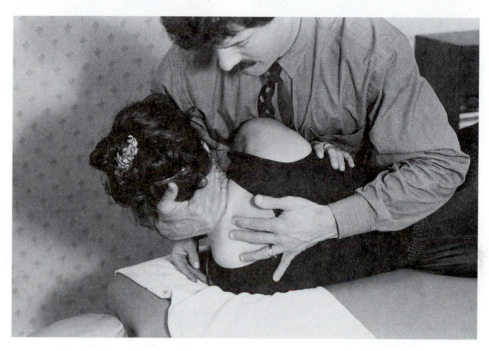

C

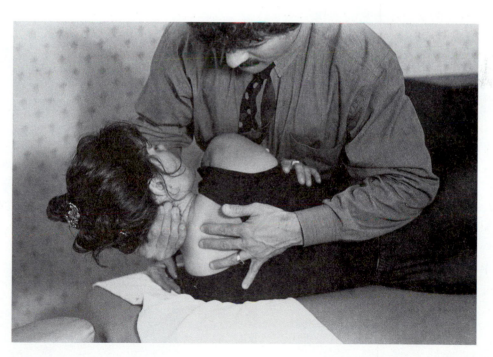

D

Figure 13–32 continued. Palpation for upper thoracic movement with patient in side-lying position. **C.** Lateral flexion. **D.** Rotation.

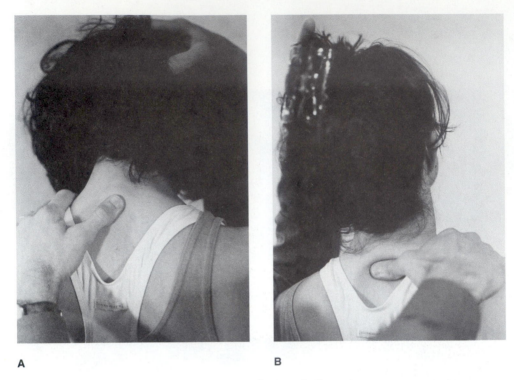

A   **B**

Figure 13–33. A. Flexion. **B.** Extension.

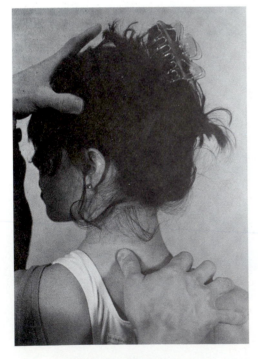

Figure 13–34. Rotation.

Figure 13–35. Lateral flexion.

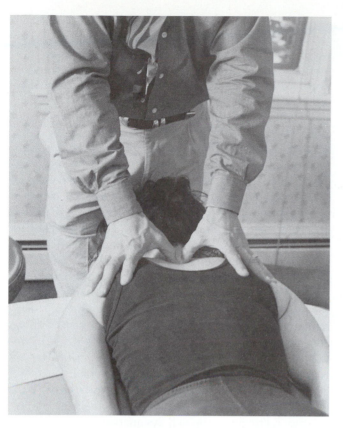

Figure 13–36. Central posterior-to-anterior pressure.

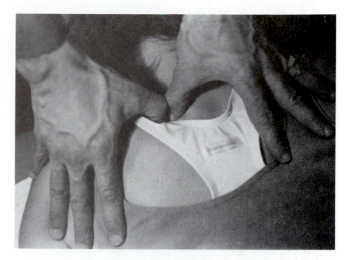

Figure 13–37. Unilateral posterior-to-anterior pressure.

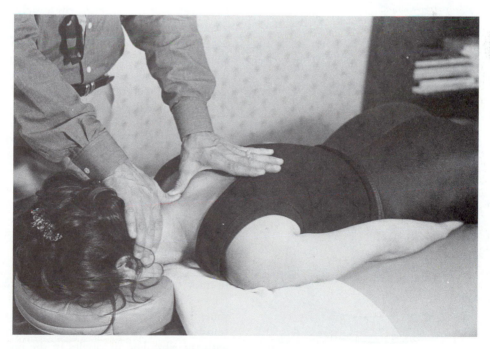

Figure 13–38. Transverse pressure.

The upper three rib joints are often involved with trauma to the neck, shoulder, or upper extremity and must be carefully assessed for pain and restriction in such cases. Additionally, the cause of neck ache and upper extremity heaviness that persists after cervical disc resolution can often be found in dysfunctional costotransverse joints of the upper three ribs.

Interesting anatomical relationships exist between the cervical spine and the upper ribs. The powerful anterior and middle scalene muscles link the cervical segments to the first and second ribs (Fig. 13–39). The anterior scalene muscle originates from as high up as the third cervical vertebra whereas the larger middle scalene has its origin at the second vertebral segment. Both the anterior and middle scalene muscles insert on the first rib while the posterior scalene inserts on the second rib. It is tempting to ponder the importance of this relationship for a consistent finding on examination in joint dysfunction of the first or second rib joints associated with a painfully stiff ipsilateral C2–3 facet joint and scalene muscle tension. Other muscles that attach to the first rib include the serratus anterior, subclavius, and intercostals. In addition, the costoclavicular ligament links the first rib to the shoulder girdle via the clavicle, and the suprapleural membrane attaches to its undersurface along the inner border. The serratus anterior, levator costae, and intercostals also insert onto the second rib. This area of anatomical diversity makes for a complex assessment of interrelated structures.

Painful dysfunction of the first costotransverse joint often presents as a deep ache in the root of the neck. Arm movements, especially pulling and lifting, are painful. Pain can sometimes be referred into the upper extremity and scalene muscle spasm and trigger points are commonly found. Lifting the head off the bed may irritate the pain as a result of scalene contraction. Pain can also be elicited on deep inspiration. The upper fibers of the trapezius muscle are often in spasm and cervical rotation toward the painful side is restricted. Cervical extension is painful and flexion feels tight and restricted. The angle of the first rib usually palpates as more elevated when compared to the nonpainful side. Grieve[22] mentions that patients with this condition present with an antalgic attitude of slight lateral flexion of the neck toward the painful side while reaching across with the opposite arm to rest the fingers on the painful "yoke" region. A subjective feeling of upper extremity heaviness is often reported.

Second rib joint pain and dysfunction typically present with painful prominences anteriorly at its sternal attachment and posteriorly at its angle. Patients are often only painfully aware of the rib's anterior attachment. A visible prominence of the anterior rib attachment just lateral to the sternal angle can be seen. Painful pectoralis fibers and trigger points are usually present. Cervical side bending, flexion, and extension provoke the upper pectoral pain.[22] As a differential point, careful palpation of the second rib angle is very painful, restricted, and elicits patients' presenting pain while examination of the first and third rib angles does not.

The third rib, when painful and dysfunctional, creates anterior chest pain that leaves patients with a sense that something is "stuck" there. As with second rib dysfunction, a painful prominence can be palpated and even seen, and deep chest pain is elicited on compression of the rib's anterior attachment. The posterior rib angle is also prominent and often exquisitely tender with palpably knotted and painful muscle tissue overlying it.

The following section outlines the manual examination of dysfunction of the upper three costotransverse joints. The palpable part of the rib is the rib angle or sometimes the tubercle just lateral to the transverse process. The transverse processes angle slightly cephalad to articulate with the ribs. The rib angles of the upper three segments are roughly on a level with the interspinous space above. The tip of the transverse process is about 2 inches lateral to the spinous process, and the rib angles are slightly more lateral than this. The first rib's tubercle and angle are one and the same.

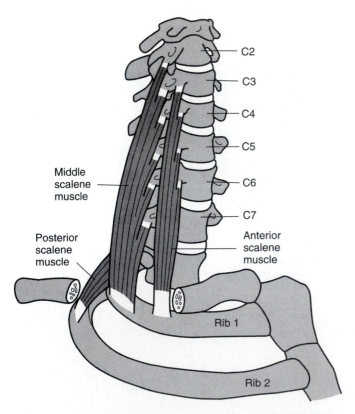

Middle scalene muscle

Posterior scalene muscle

Anterior scalene muscle

C2
C3
C4
C5
C6
C7

Rib 1

Rib 2

Figure 13–39. Oblique view of the three scalene muscles. A piece of the clavicle has been removed.

(From Travell JG, Simons DG. Myofascial Pain and Dysfunction. The Trigger Point Manual. Baltimore, Md: Williams and Wilkins; 1983, with permission.)

FIRST RIB

The first rib is commonly palpated as elevated and stiff when dysfunctional at its costotransverse articulation. Interestingly, this is often noticed on the side of hand dominance. The first rib is best examined with the patient in the seated position. The examiner palpates the anterior aspect of the first rib in the supraclavicular fossa with the index and middle fingers while the other hand fully rotates the head contralaterally (Fig. 13–40A). The examiner then flexes the neck onto the chest with it fully rotated. The palpating hand should feel the rib descend and a painless springing should be elicited upon provocative pressure. In the presence of rib joint restriction, the neck will not bend as far forward compared to when the other side is assessed.

An alternative technique is to extend the head and neck, rotate the head away, and laterally bend the neck over the palpating finger (Fig. 13–40B). Again, the rib should descend and provocative palpation should produce a painless springing sensation.

The first rib can also be examined prone with the patient's head and neck in the neutral position. The first rib can be found anterior and deep to the upper fibers of the trapezius muscle with a double thumb tip contact. The thumbs need to lift the anterior edge of the upper trapezius muscle and palpate deep to its border. The firm, wide first rib being easily located is pressed caudally toward the opposite hip joint. A dysfunctional first rib greets the palpating fingers with firm resistance and pain. The upper fibers of the trapezius muscle usually harbor a painful myofascial trigger point in association with this dysfunction. Levine (personal communication, 1997) states that a consistent finding with dysfunctional first rib joints is hypertonic upper trapezius muscle fibers that do not neccessarily harbor myofascial trigger points. Manipulative reduction of the joint restriction results in relaxation of the tense muscle.

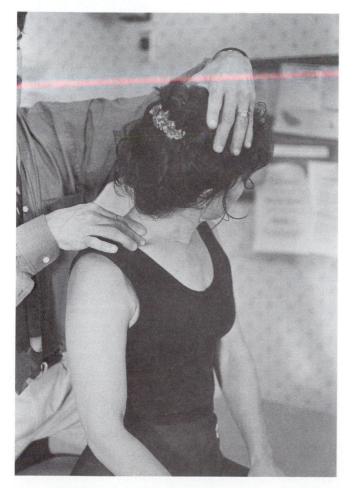

A

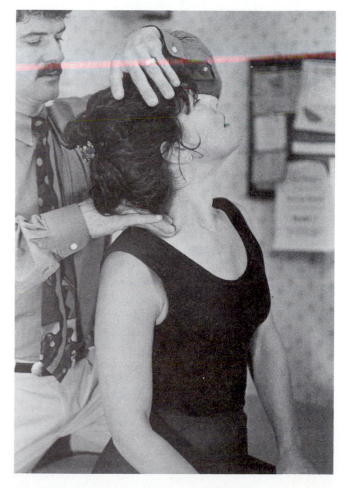

B

Figure 13–40. A and B. First rib palpation.

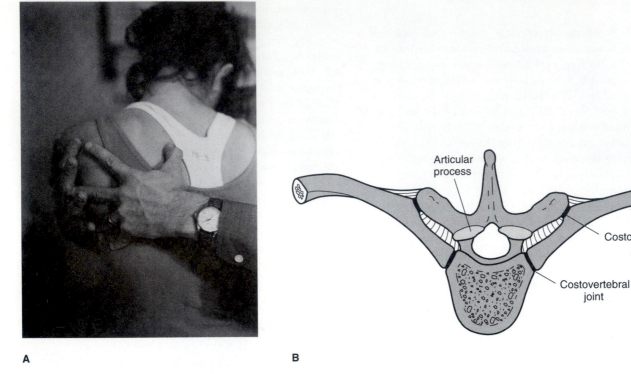

A   **B**

Figure 13–41. A. Rib angle palpation. **B.** Cross section at level of costotransverse and costovertebral joints.

SECOND AND THIRD RIBS

With the patient prone, the rib angles of the second and third ribs are palpated about 2½ inches lateral to their respective thoracic spinous process. Unilateral PA pressures applied to the rib angles elicit pain, and they feel restricted if dysfunctional. Care should be taken not to mistake painful soft tissue thickenings for rib angles. The rib angle palpates as a hard bony structure, whereas firm and painful soft tissue changes can be moved aside to palpate the deeper rib angle.

The rib angles can also be palpated with the examiner sitting behind the patient (Fig. 13–41A and B). The patient grasps the opposite shoulder with, for example, his or her right hand. The examiner reaches across the patient's chest with his left hand and grasps the patient's right upper arm. The examiner then pulls the upper torso around into left rotation, thus pulling the scapula away from the rib angles. The examiner's right thumb presses on each of the rib angles and springs them for motion and pain provocation. Often, the painful rib angle palpates as prominent and the local soft tissue and musculature are very tender.

COSTOSTERNAL JOINTS

The first seven ribs articulate anteriorly with the sternum at the costosternal joints (Fig. 13–42A). The first costosternal joint is a synchondrosis and is just deep and inferior to the clavicular insertion, being difficult to palpate. However, springing the first rib in the supraclavicular fossa,

as previously explained, while simultaneously palpating just inferior to the medial-most end of the clavicle often reveals movement at the anterior first rib insertion (Fig. 13–42B).

The second rib, more specifically its costal cartilage, inserts anteriorly at the sternal angle forming a true synovial joint. The third rib insertion is also a synovial joint and is the next palpable rib below this landmark. To assess pain and restriction at these joints, a double thumb contact can be used to apply unilateral AP pressures. The pressures can be angled in different directions to elicit symptoms more accurately.

> ## ! CLINICAL PEARL
>
> The second or third ribs, or both, are often painful and prominent anteriorly when dysfunctional posteriorly. Spasm and trigger points of the pectoral and scalene musculature are commonly associated with painful sternocostal joints.

STERNOCLAVICULAR JOINT

The sternoclavicular joint is linked to the cervical spine via the powerful sternocleidomastoid (SCM) muscle. Movements of the cervical spine are associated with coexistent sternoclavicular joint motion, especially cervical extension and rotation. Examination of the cervical spine

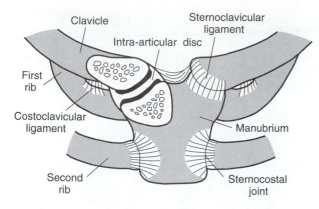

A

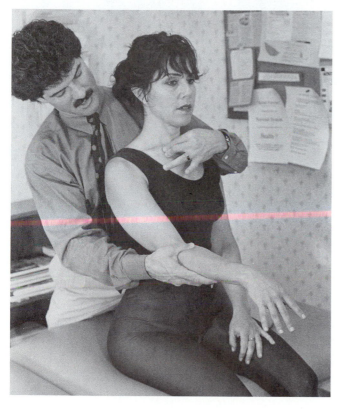

B

Figure 13–42. A. Sternum at junction of first rib, second rib, and clavicle. The right sternoclavicular joint is resected in the frontal plane to expose the intraarticular disc. Note palpable location of first rib just inferior to the medial clavicle. **B.** Sternoclavicular joint palpation with shoulder protraction.

should include assessment of the sternoclavicular joint, especially when pain occurs over the upper medial chest wall. In addition, clinical evidence suggests that joint dysfunction of the sternoclavicular joints can result in compensatory hypermobility of the lower cervical segments.[18]

> **⚠ CLINICAL PEARL**
>
> Care must be taken to assess the difference between a painful sternoclavicular joint and a painful medial clavicle pain point, which signifies tension in the SCM muscle and concomitant C0–1 joint dysfunction.

Accessory or joint play movements of the sternoclavicular joint can be palpated with the patient in the seated or supine positions. Sitting behind the seated patient, the examiner uses the right hand to cradle the patient's right elbow, for example. The examiner's left hand palpates the right sternoclavicular joint by reaching in front of and across the patient's chest. Holding the bent elbow, the examiner moves the shoulder girdle through various ranges of motion while the head of the clavicle at the sternoclavicular joint is palpated for movement and challenged for joint play. Shoulder girdle protraction is performed by pushing the patient's elbow forward and palpating for the clavicular head to depress into the joint. The elbow is then pulled rearward to impart retraction of the shoulder girdle while an anterior glide should be felt at the clavicular head (Fig. 13–43). It will palpate as being more prominent.

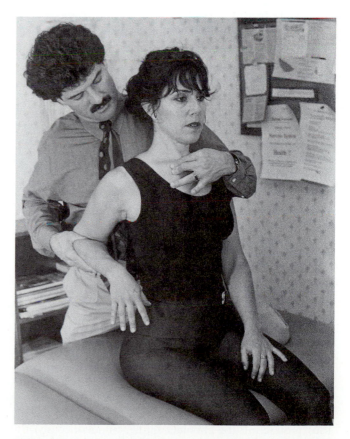

Figure 13–43. Sternoclavicular joint palpation with shoulder retraction.

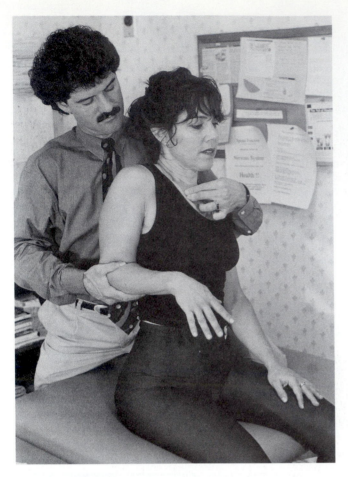

Figure 13–44. Sternoclavicular joint palpation with shoulder elevation.

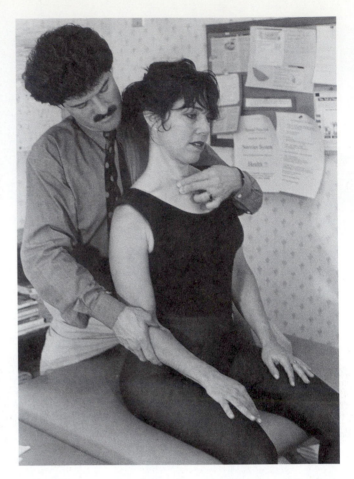

Figure 13–45. Sternoclavicular joint palpation with shoulder depression.

The elbow is kept by the patient's side while it and the humerus are raised vertically, thus shrugging the shoulder and inducing shoulder elevation (Fig. 13–44). Reciprocally, an inferior glide of the clavicular head should be palpated at the sternoclavicular joint. To elicit shoulder girdle depression, the elbow is pulled downward while a superior glide of the clavicular head should be palpated at the sternoclavicular joint (Fig. 13–45).

In the supine position, the clavicle is grasped between the forefinger and thumb of each hand just lateral to the sternoclavicular joint and a push- pull motion is used to assess superior-to-inferior glide (Fig. 13–46A). Joint mobility and pain provocation are assessed for and a comparison is made with the other side.

Another examining technique is performed with the patient supine while the examiner stands on the side of the patient to be examined facing cephalad. The examiner's right hand makes a hypothenar contact on the patient's right sternoclavicular joint, for example. The examiner's left hand pulls the patient's right arm toward the ceiling, thus protracting the shoulder girdle. Simultaneously, the sternoclavicular joint is depressed with the hypothenar

contact (Fig. 13–46B). Joint play challenge and pain provocation are performed.

ACROMIOCLAVICULAR JOINT

Because the acromioclavicular joint is integral in shoulder girdle and scapular movement which, if dysfunctional, can affect cervical spine function, its mobility needs to be assessed. Full overhead abduction and extreme horizontal adduction of the shoulder often cause pain in a dysfunctional acromioclavicular joint. A recent test for acromioclavicular joint pathology demonstrating good sensitivity and specificity was developed by O'Brien et al.[23] The patient's shoulder is flexed to 90 degrees with the elbow fully extended. It is then slightly adducted 10 to 15 degrees and fully rotated internally so that the thumb points downward. The examiner attempts to pull the arm down without overcoming the force of the patient's resisting contraction. The test is then repeated in the same position but with the arm fully rotated externally by placing the palm up. The test is considered positive if pain results during the first maneuver

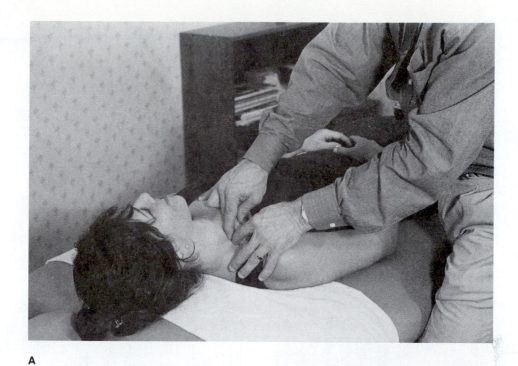

A

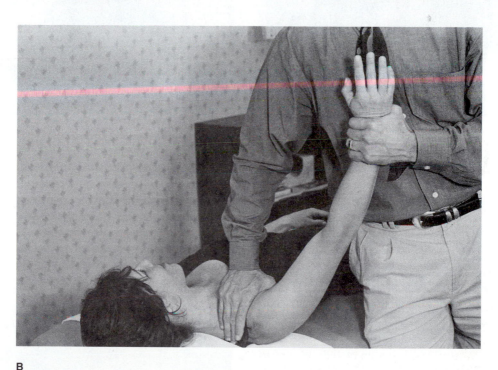

B

Figure 13–46. A. Superior-to-inferior glide palpation of sternoclavicular joint. **B.** Anterior-to-posterior pressure on sternoclavicular joint.

and is less or absent during the second maneuver. Pain localized to the acromioclavicular joint is diagnostic of pathology there, while pain or a painful clicking felt inside the shoulder joint is considered diagnostic of a glenoid labrum tear.

Three examining techniques of accessory movement can be used to assess acromioclavicular joint function. In the sitting position, inferior and superior glide movements can be assessed with the examiner sitting behind the seated patient. The right acromioclavicular joint, for ex-

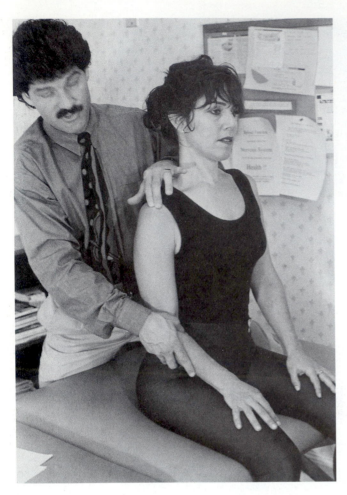

Figure 13–47. Acromioclavicular joint palpation with shoulder depression.

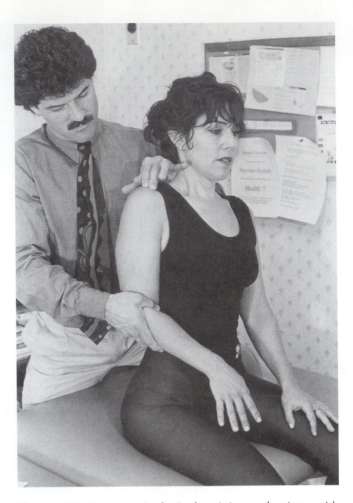

Figure 13–48. Acromioclavicular joint palpation with shoulder elevation.

ample, is palpated by the examiner's left hand. The patient's right hand rests on his or her lap while the elbow is maintained at a relaxed 90-degree angle. The examiner uses his or her right hand to push downward on the patient's bent arm (Fig. 13–47). This tractions the humerus and scapula away from the distal end of the clavicle, and a gapping of the joint should be palpated. The humerus, while being kept at the patient's side, is then raised upward to shrug the shoulder by lifting up under the bent elbow (Fig. 13–48). Palpation reveals the acromion to move above the level of the distal clavicle at the acromioclavicular joint. The patient can also be asked to actively shrug and depress the shoulder as the acromioclavicular joint is palpated. Dysfunction demonstrates a lack of movement, painful periarticular soft tissues, and pain provocation upon joint play challenge.

While sitting, the examiner can also face the seated patient from the side and place one thenar eminence posteriorly on the spine of the scapula and the other on the anterior aspect of the distal clavicle (Fig. 13–49). By pressing the hands together, an AP glide motion of the acromioclavicular joint can be palpated, and pain provocation is observed for.

In the supine position, the distal clavicle can simply be pinched between the thumb and forefingers of both the examiner's hands. A push-pull movement is then used to assess a shifting motion at the joint and pain provocation (Fig. 13–50).

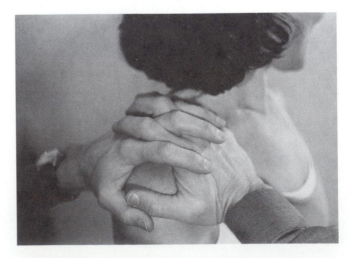

Figure 13–49. Acromioclavicular joint compression.

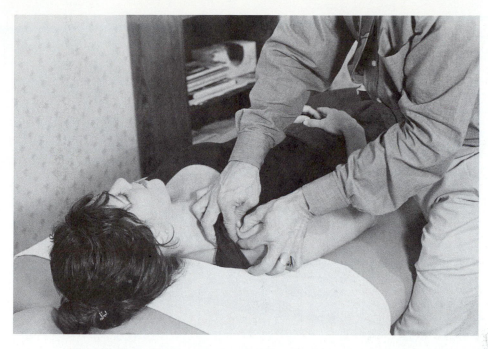

Figure 13–50. Superior-to-inferior glide of acromioclavicular joint.

SCAPULOTHORACIC JOINT

Although not a true anatomical joint per se, the scapulothoracic joint deserves consideration in cervical pain syndromes. Seventeen muscles insert on the scapula alone, three of which originate from the cervical and cranial regions (levator scapulae, trapezius, and omohyoid muscles). Cervical spine and scapular function and mobility have effects on each other, especially because of the attachments of the large and influential trapezius and levator scapulae muscles. As previously mentioned, important pain points found at the C2 spinous process and the superior angle of the scapula indicate tension in the levator scapulae and joint dysfunction at the C2–3 level. This dysfunction is commonly seen in patients manifesting a head forward posture.

Scapular mobility and control are often overlooked issues in the rehabilitation of cervical spine disorders. Uncoordinated movements and poor control of the muscles spanning the scapula and cervical spine can place undue tension on the locomotor system, causing persistence of pain and dysfunction. An example of this is seen in the forward head posture, where the levator scapulae act as tight check reins affecting cervical spine function.

Scapular mobility is assessed with the patient in the side-lying position and the side to be examined uppermost. The functional tracking of the scapula occurs in two basic patterns that need to be examined. One is from a superior and forward position (ie., a slight forward shrug) that leads diagonally downward to a slightly posterior and depressed position. The opposite to this is an upward and slightly posterior position (ie., a slight backward shrug) that leads diagonally downward to a forward and depressed position. Standing behind the patient, the examiner grasps the superior and inferior angles of the scapula simultaneously with both hands and passively moves it in these upward and downward glide movements (Fig. 13–51). In addition, straight forward and retracted positions are explored. The examiner tries to gain a sense of scapular mobility on the thoracic wall. Good muscle control is indicated by the patient who is able to relax the scapula for examination.

The examiner then faces the side-lying patient from the front and places both hands on the scapula so that the fingers wrap around and under its medial border (Fig. 13–52). An attempt is made to lift the medial border of the scapula off the thoracic wall and protract the scapula toward the examiner. It is easiest to start this subscapular exploration near the inferior angle and proceed cephalad. Restriction and pain are observed for. In the preceding two procedures, it is quite common for the patient to be unable to relax and fully "let go" of the scapula. This inability is in direct proportion to the lack of proper muscle control a patient has, and it is very common in postural and chronic cervical and shoulder pain syndromes.

In discussing scapular function, mention should be made of a condition often encountered, called the scapulocostal syndrome.[22] It consists of a painful medial scapular border independent of cervical and upper thoracic pain referral, crepitus upon scapular motion, poor scapular control, and oftentimes referred pain into the upper extremity upon pressure of painful nodular periscapular tissues. The scapula is usually found to be very adherent to the underlying thoracic wall and attempts to coax an examining finger

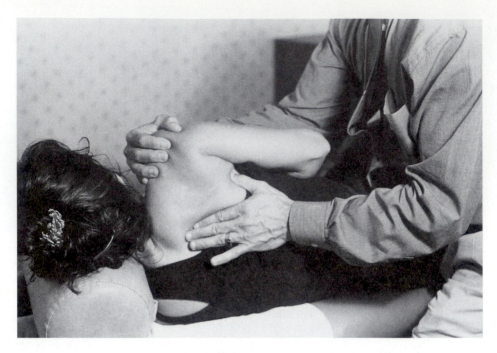

Figure 13–51. Superior-to-inferior glide of scapulothoracic joint.

under the scapula are met with resistance and pain. Painful costotransverse joints can be palpated and the medial aspect of the subscapularis muscle is tender. Passive movement of the scapula to its extreme ranges is met with pain and resistance. The cervical and upper thoracic spine movements are often unremarkable and do not contribute to the pain. Upper extremity use tends to exacerbate the pain as do poor sitting postures. Treatment of poor scapular mobility and muscle control in addition to postural advice need to be implemented.

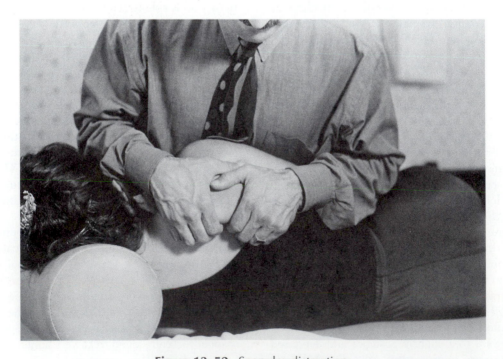

Figure 13–52. Scapular distraction.

CONCLUSION

Assessment of cervical facet joint dysfunction is an important and necessary part of any examination that concerns itself with cervical pain syndromes. Meticulous assessment of each motion segment's ability to move painlessly is key. Accurate palpation of anatomical structures aids in diagnosis. Pain provocation is an important finding in the examination of joint movement and should be coupled with joint resistance and soft tissue findings. Accessory or joint play movements and physiological movements are used to assess motion segment function. The upper thoracic spine and its adjoining rib articulations must be included in any assessment of cervical pain as should the sternoclavicular, acromioclavicular, and scapulothoracic joints.

REFERENCES

1. Maitland GD. *Peripheral Manipulation*. 2nd ed. Boston, Mass: Butterworths; 1977:15.
2. Matyas T, Bach T. The reliability of selected techniques in clinical arthrometrics. *Aust J Physiother* 1985;31:175–199.
3. Keating J, Bergman T, Jacobs G, Bradley D, Finer A, Larson K. Interexaminer reliability of eight evaluative dimensions of lumbar segmental abnormality. *J Manipulative Physiol Ther* 1990;13:463–470.
4. Potter N, Rothstein J. Intertester reliability for selected clinical tests for the sacroiliac joint. *Phys Ther* 1985;65:1671–1675.
5. Sandmark H, Nisell R. Validity of five common manual neck provoking tests. *Scand J Rehab Med* 1995;27;131–136.
6. Maher C, Latimer J. Pain or resistance—the manual therapists' dilemma. *Aust J Physiother* 1992;4:257–260.
7. Jull G, Bogduk N, Marsland A. The accuracy of manual diagnosis for cervical zygapophysial joint pain syndromes. *Med J Aust* 1988;148:233–236.
8. Jull G, Guy Z, Trott P, Potter H, Shirley D, Richardson C. Inter-examiner reliability to detect painful upper cervical joint dysfunction. *Aust J Physiother* 1997;43:125–129.
9. Grieve G. *Mobilisation of the spine*. 4th ed. New York, NY: Churchill Livingstone; 1984:111.
10. Maher CG, Adams RD. Stiffness judgements are affected by visual occlusion. *J Manipulative Physiol Ther* 1996;4:250–256.
11. Maitland GD. *Vertebral Manipulation*. 5th ed. Boston, Mass: Butterworths; 1986:171–232.
12. Magarey ME. Examination and assessment in spinal joint dysfunction. In: Grieve GP, ed. *Modern Manual Therapy of the Vertebral Column*. New York, NY: Churchill Livingstone; 1986:481–497.
13. Mennell JM. *Back Pain*. Boston, Mass: Little, Brown; 1960.
14. Mennell JM. *Joint Pain*. Boston, Mass: Little, Brown; 1964.
15. Lewit K. Chain reactions in disturbed function of the motor system. *J Man Med* 1987;3:27.
16. Schmorl G, Junghanns H. *The Human Spine in Health and Disease*. 2nd American ed. New York, NY: Grune and Stratton; 1971.
17. Gillet H, Liekens M. *Belgian Chiropractic Research Notes*. Huntington Beach, Calif: Motion Palpation Institute; 1984.
18. Schafer RC, Faye LJ. *Motion Palpation and Chiropractic Technic: Principles of Dynamic Chiropractic*. Huntington Beach, Calif.: Motion Palpation Institute; 1989.
19. Maigne R, Le Corre F. New ideas on the mechanism of common adult dorsalgias. *J Man Med* 1969;4:73.
20. Maigne R. La semeiologie clinique des derangements intervertebraux mineurs. *Ann Med Physique* 1972;15:275.
21. DeFranca GG, Levine LJ. The T4 syndrome. *J Manipulative Physiol Ther* 1995;18:34–37.
22. Grieve G. *Common Vertebral Joint Disorders*. New York, NY: Churchill Livingstone; 1981:233–236.
23. O'Brien SJ, Pagnani MJ, McGlynn S, et al. Abstracts. *J Shoulder Elbow Surg* 1997;6:175.

CHAPTER 14

Evaluation of Posture and Movement Patterns Related to the Cervical Spine

DONALD R. MURPHY

"Do not seek to follow in the footsteps of the wise, seek what they sought."

—Basho

INTRODUCTION

The examination of posture and movement patterns allows the clinician to assess the locomotor system in a global way in order to identify chains of disturbance that can have an impact on the system as a whole and can help identify localized dysfunction. This approach is based largely on the work of Vladimir Janda. As has been discussed in previous chapters, the locomotor system works as a functional whole and all movements occur as a result of a chain of muscle activity, with each muscle involved serving its own particular role in carrying out smooth, efficient, and stable movement patterns. When these patterns are altered in a way that makes them less efficient and stable, increased strain can occur on certain tissues that can lead to susceptibility to injury as well as chronic "overuse" (perhaps better described as "misuse") of the tissue. In addition, as was discussed in Chapter 4, behavior plays a strong role in the delicate balance between the nociceptive and the antinociceptive systems. Thus, if the behavior of the locomotor system—whether this behavior originates in conscious, cortical processes, or subconscious, programmed movement patterns—is reflective of a state in which a great amount of nociceptive impulses are arising from the system (regardless of whether this amount of nociceptive impulses actually is being generated), the central nociceptive pathways become facilitated and the cerebral cortex is likely to interpret this as pain. This can occur as a result of pain behavior or faulty movement patterns.

The examination of posture and movement patterns occurs in the subacute or chronic stages, only. In the acute stage, alteration of posture and movement is adaptive and expected. There is nothing to be gained by performing these examination procedures in the acute patient, and they will only lead the clinician away from the most important task that must be accomplished in the acute stage, that of rapid reduction of nociception and pain. The subacute or chronic stage, however, is the time to evaluate for the presence of significant dysfunctions that have the potential to perpetuate the patient's pain. This is also the time to look for chain reactions that may be present, the key links of which may require treatment or rehabilitation.

POSTURE

The role that "faulty" posture plays in the initiation and perpetuation of cervical spine syndromes is controversial. While many clinicians feel that deviations from what is considered "normal" posture predispose one to the development of symptoms, the evidence for this is not clear. Some studies have demonstrated a relationship between postural abnormalities and clinical syndromes,[1-4] while others have shown no relationship.[5-7] A high incidence of "abnormal" posture has been demonstrated in asymptomatic individuals.[5, 8, 9] However, it is not clear if this reflects the fact that posture plays little or no role in the development of pain, or if the quality of the research that is looking at this question has not yet risen to the level of providing definitive answers. Nevertheless, postural deviations must be looked at the same as any other history and examination factor—as potentially playing a role—but any role that they play must be determined in the context of the entire clinical picture.

Mannheimer[10] makes the point that determination of the impact that faulty posture has on the individual must take into consideration the individual's lifestyle activities. For example, habitual faulty posture may have little impact on an individual whose job involves a variety of movements that are carried out throughout the day, but in one who sits at a computer all day, faulty posture may have a huge impact.

In addition, as was discussed in Chapter 2, posture must be looked at not only in terms of a combination of static positional relationships, but also as a postural set from which movement patterns, including stability mechanisms, are derived. A certain postural deviation in a particular individual may not have any impact on the person's health unless it affects the quality of the movement patterns that are derived from that postural set.

The purpose of postural examination is twofold. First, it allows one to detect alterations in posture that may serve as important underlying factors for the perpetuation of pain, dynamic instability and dysfunction. An example of this would be someone who stands or sits in a habitual "slumped" posture (Fig. 14–1), which places strain on a variety of tissues in addition to having a great impact on the quality of the movement patterns and responses that are derived from that postural set. Second, it allows for the identification of subtle signs of underlying dysfunction that can increase the ease with which one detects this dysfunction. An example of this would be a high right shoulder that may be indicative of tightness in the upper trapezius or levator scapulae, or both.

The examination of posture should be systematic. It is best to begin with the head and gradually move downward. The patient's postural relationships should be examined from anterior, lateral, and posterior perspectives.

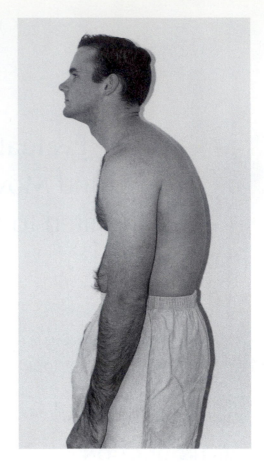

Figure 14–1. The habitual "slumped" posture.

ANTERIOR PERSPECTIVE

It is also best to start by looking at the patient from the anterior perspective (Fig. 14–2). The first positional relationship that should be noted is that of head alignment. It is not uncommon for patients suffering from chronic cervical spine syndromes to exhibit a head tilt or slight rotation of the head in normal stance (Figs. 14–3 and 14–4). This is often interpreted as indicating localized tightness of a specific muscle, but this is not likely to cause tilt or rotation. Many muscles act on the head, each capable of moving the head in a specific direction. Because of this, it is unlikely that any one muscle, on its own, would have a great impact on head position as tightness in a single muscle (or even in several) would be well compensated by the others. In addition, there are several postural reflexes, discussed in Chapter 3, that have the task of maintaining a stable head position. Thus, there is a strong neural drive to keep the head in normal alignment, and if these reflexes are operating normally, tightness in one or two muscles is not likely to be powerful enough to overcome them.

When deviation of the head in lateral flexion or rotation is seen in the patient with a chronic cervical-related

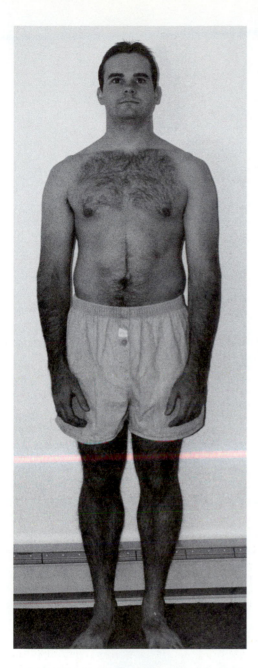

Figure 14–2. Assessment of posture from the anterior perspective.

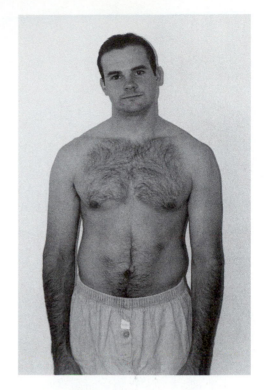

Figure 14–3. Head tilt.

occur in the cervical and ocular muscles, producing alteration of head posture. Further evidence is seen in the work of Bizzi and Polit,[12] who point out that the motor program utilized in turning the head involves ordering a given level of activity in the alpha motor neurons of the agonist and antagonist muscles. The activity of these muscles determines a particular length-tension relationship in each muscle. Thus, the final resting position of the head is determined by these length-tension properties and is dependent on the central nervous system (CNS) being aware of these properties. For this, the muscle receptors must accurately apprise the CNS as to these length-tension properties or else overshoot or undershoot will occur. With muscle dysfunction in the cervical spine, which can result in an alteration in the signal generation from the spindles, overshoot and undershoot is likely. In the static posture, this may manifest as head rotation or head tilt.

! CLINICAL PEARL

Almost invariably, the patient with head tilt or head rotation exhibits a positive Revel's test or stepping test, or both (see later discussion), suggesting, respectively, faulty detection of length-tension relationships or faulty tonic neck reflex and general kinesthetic awareness.

disorder (this does not refer to the acute cervical pain patient who may be antalgic), it is important to consider the possibility of dysfunction of postural reflexes as the cause. As Fukushima and Fukushima have shown,[11] the interstitial nucleus of Cajal, located in the midbrain reticular formation, has major outputs to the cervical (especially the sternocleidomastoid [SCM], splenius capitis, obliquus capitis inferior, and rectus capitis posterior major and minor) and extraocular muscles. This helps regulate head and eye posture. With unilateral dysfunction, abnormal activity can

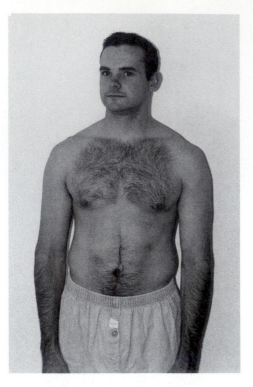

Figure 14–4. Head rotation.

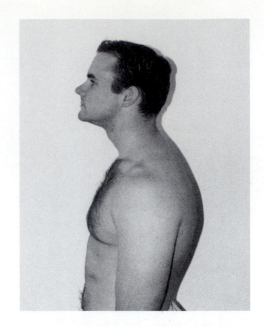

Figure 14–5. Forward head posture with posterior cranial rotation.

LATERAL PERSPECTIVE

Turning the patient to one side, the first relationship to look at is that of head placement, specifically to detect the presence of forward head placement (FHP). This finding is represented by positioning of the head anterior to the shoulders. FHP can be visually detected as placement of the external auditory meatus anterior to the clavicle.

Mannheimer[10, 13] discusses two different types of FHP; one in which posterior cranial rotation occurs, and one without posterior cranial rotation. In FHP with posterior cranial rotation (Fig. 14–5), the head is placed anterior to the shoulders and the upper cervical spine is positioned in slight extension. This posture can cause chronic shortening of the suboccipital muscles, which in turn predisposes these muscles to developing hypertonicity, tightness, and myofascial trigger points (TrPs). This, then, perpetuates the posture. It also places pressure on the C0–1 and C1–2 joints, which can lead to the development of joint dysfunction. Hypertonicity of both SCMs can be a cause or effect of FHP with posterior cranial rotation, and TrPs are often seen in these muscles.

This posture also has a destabilizing effect on the cervical spine, as described in Chapter 4, because it places the head in a postural set that interferes with normal movement patterns, particularly stabilization mechanisms, that are derived from that set. This usually involves overactivation of the SCM and inhibition of the deep cervical flexors and lower cervical and upper thoracic extensors. This postural set can also interfere with normal cervical flexion, swallowing, and sit-to-stand movement patterns (see later discussion). Watson and Trott[14] found a significantly increased incidence of FHP with cranial rotation in patients suffering from headache compared to controls.

In FHP without posterior cranial rotation (Fig. 14–6), the head is anteriorly placed but without extension of the

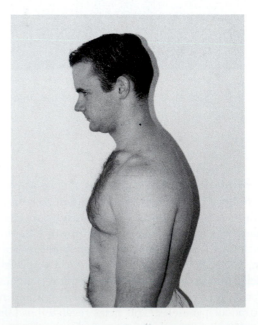

Figure 14–6. Forward head posture without posterior cranial rotation.

upper cervical spine. This posture generally occurs in the acute stage after cervical trauma. It is one possible manifestation of the general forward drawn posture (see later discussion and Chap. 20). It is often associated with hypertonicity of the posterior cervical muscles. Both the FHP with posterior cranial rotation and FHP without posterior cranial rotation are associated with loss or reversal of cervical lordosis,[9, 10, 13] but with posterior cranial rotation, there is lordosis in the upper cervical spine.

Moving downward in the examination of posture from the side, the relationship of the shoulders to the trunk, pelvis, and ankles is observed. Placement of the shoulders anterior to the midline of the trunk suggests the presence of anteriorly placed or "rounded" shoulders (Fig. 14–7). This can result from (or can cause) tightness or hypertonicity of the pectoralis major or minor, along with inhibition of the middle trapezius. Patients with this postural abnormality will often exhibit TrPs in any of these muscles. Anterior placement of the shoulder also serves as a postural set that can influence the pattern of shoulder abduction (see later discussion) in such a way that it causes overactivation of the upper trapezius, levator scapulae, or rhomboid, with inhibition of the middle and lower trapezius or serratus anterior.

Anterior placement of the shoulder in relation to the pelvis must also be assessed. This is part of the general forward drawn posture (see Chap. 20) and can be related to hypertonicity of the rectus abdominis muscles and also a cause of the development of TrPs in the erector spinae, posterior cervical, suboccipital, and gluteal muscles.

Moving further down the body, the position of the pelvis can be assessed. Specifically, this relates to the degree of anterior or posterior tilt that is present. Posterior tilt of the pelvis is associated with decrease in the lumbar lordosis, decreased thoracic kyphosis, and decreased cervical lordosis. It is typically a habitual posture and is not caused by any specific localized dysfunction, but rather is a result of poor postural habits. It contributes to the general "slumped" posture that is commonly seen, and it can lead to FHP (Fig. 14–1). Anterior pelvic tilt is less common and is associated with increased lumbar lordosis, which can then lead to increased thoracic kyphosis and increased cervical lordosis.

It is also important to look at the relationship between the pelvis and the ankles. Anterior placement of the pelvis causes the greater trochanter to be positioned well anterior to the lateral malleolus. This is also part of the general forward drawn posture (see Chap. 20).

! CLINICAL PEARL

One way to determine whether hypertonicity of the suboccipitals or posterior cervical muscles is a result of FHP or forward drawn posture that originates in the pelvis or lower extremities is to palpate these muscles while the patient is standing, to detect the degree of tension and tenderness. Then, have the patient sit and see whether the hypertonicity remains. Continuation of the hypertonicity suggests that it relates to FHP, whereas if it disappears, it likely relates to pelvic or lower extremity involvement.

POSTERIOR PERSPECTIVE

When observing the patient from behind, the clinician can look for head tilt or rotation; however, these are best seen from the anterior perspective. Shoulder level can also be detected, and it is best for the clinician to place his or her hands on the acromion processes of each shoulder to compare the relative heights. Unilateral elevation of a shoulder may be reflective of tightness in the upper trapezius (Fig. 14–8). Less commonly, it can relate to tightness in the levator scapulae. Moving downward, the position of the scapula should be assessed. Posterior placement of one scapula may be reflective of the presence of scoliosis. Displacement of the medial border of the scapula away from the body wall suggests inhibition of the middle trapezius (Fig. 14–9), while winging of the inferior angle away from the body wall suggests inhibition of the serratus anterior (Fig. 14–10).

Next, the height of the iliac crests should be evaluated. Differences in the relative heights of the iliac crests can be reflective of several processes, which must be differentiated from the others. The two deviations that are most commonly associated with unleveling of the iliac crests are pelvic obliquity and pelvic distortion. Pelvic obliquity oc-

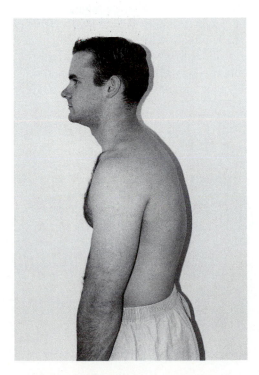

Figure 14–7. "Rounded" shoulders.

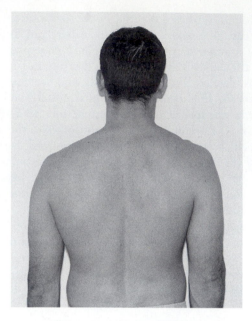

Figure 14–8. Unilateral shoulder elevation.

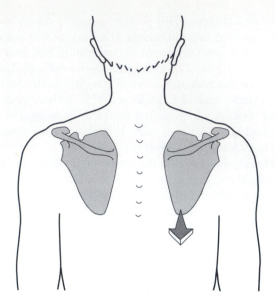

Figure 14–10. Winging of the scapula.

curs when the entire pelvis becomes tilted toward one side, but there is no alteration in the intrapelvic relationships (Fig. 14–11). With pelvic distortion, the pelvis remains level with respect to the floor, but there is internal deviation of the bones of the pelvis, such that one ilium rotates in a posterior-inferior direction and the other in an anterior-superior direction.[15] The sacrum also rotates, with the sacral base on the posterior-inferior side rotating in an anterior-inferior direction (Fig. 14–12).

Pelvic obliquity can be caused by anatomical short leg

or "functional" short leg (e.g., resulting from tightness of the quadratus lumborum). Pelvic distortion, however, is caused by joint or muscle dysfunction in the cervical spine, particularly the upper cervical spine.

There are several methods by which pelvic obliquity and pelvic distortion can be differentiated. One way is by placing the hands on the iliac crests and noting the relative heights. The hands can then be gradually moved medially along the crest until they reach the midline. If the hands meet in the midline, the ilia are aligned with each other, suggesting pelvic obliquity (Fig. 14–13). With pelvic distortion, the hands are offset, with the hand from the posterior-inferior ilium lower than the hand from the anterior-superior ilium (Fig. 14–14). Another method by which pelvic obliquity and pelvic distortion can be differentiated

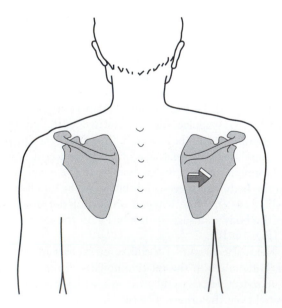

Figure 14–9. Displacement of the medial border of the scapula.

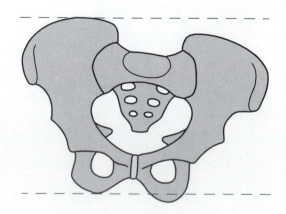

Figure 14–11. Pelvic obliquity.

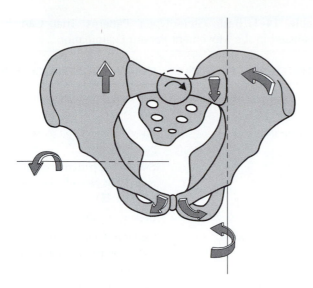

Figure 14–12. Pelvic distortion.

(Adapted from: Lewit K. Manipulation in the Rehabilitation of the Locomotor System. *2nd ed. Oxford: Butterworth-Heinemann; 1991.)*

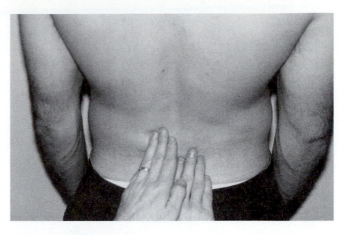

Figure 14–14. With pelvic distortion, as the hands move medially off the iliac crests, they will not meet.

is by palpating the posterior superior iliac spines (PSISs) and comparing their relative heights. With pelvic obliquity, the PSIS on the side that has the higher ilium should be equally elevated as compared to the other side. With pelvic distortion, the PSIS on the side on which the ilium appears higher is lower than the PSIS on the other side. Palpating the greater trochanter also reveals distinguishing findings. With pelvic obliquity, particularly related to anatomical short leg, the greater trochanter on the side of the high ilium should be equally elevated compared to the other side. With pelvic distortion, the greater trochanters should be similar in height.

Another important distinguishing feature is the presence of the overtake phenomenon. This phenomenon is unique to pelvic distortion and is seen when the patient flexes fully. The PSISs are first palpated in the upright position and their relative unequal heights noted. The patient is then asked to flex forward. The PSIS that appeared lower in the upright position appears higher in the fully flexed position (Fig. 14–15A and B). The overtake phenomenon strongly suggests the presence of pelvic distortion and implicates the cervical spine as the origin of the key dysfunction.

! CLINICAL PEARL

Patients with pelvic distortion will typically seek care for low back pain. The primary pain generator in most cases is the sacroiliac (SI) joint, most commonly on the posterior-inferior ilium side, but often in the anterior-superior ilium side. There may or may not be concomitant dysfunction of the involved SI joint, but the key link in the chain of dysfunction is almost invariably in the cervical spine. This is a relatively common cervical cause of low back pain.

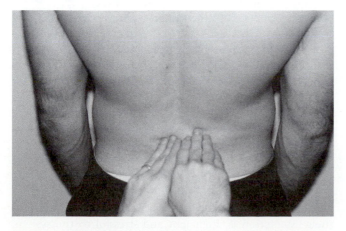

Figure 14–13. With pelvic obliquity, as the hands move medially off the iliac crests, they will meet.

The postural examination can include the lower extremities, and findings here can have great implications in patients with low back pain. However, they are of lesser importance in cervical patients, and thus will not be discussed. The interested reader is directed to the article by Tunnell[16] for further information.

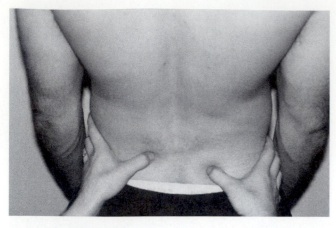

A

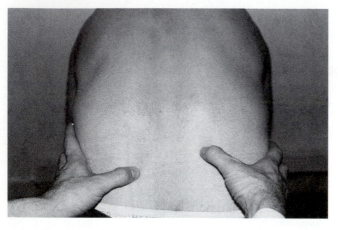

B

Figure 14–15. A and B. The overtake phenomenon in pelvic distortion. Finger positions are somewhat exaggerated for illustration purposes.

MOVEMENT PATTERNS

The examination of movement patterns is an essential part of the overall assessment of the patient with cervical spine syndromes. It allows the clinician to look globally at the patient with regard to the quality of movement related to certain basic stereotyped activities. It also allows the detection of important localized areas of dysfunction (key links) that may require treatment. In this way, it can provide for the clinician a "short cut" to the most significant areas of dysfunction, because by observing the quality of these movement patterns and detecting abnormalities, one can determine, or at least narrow down, the specific tissues that have become dysfunctional and where to direct specific treatment.

When examining movement patterns, it is important that movements that are representative of basic stereotyped patterns be included. These basic patterns include gait, prehension, eating, respiration, stability responses, and getting up from a recumbent or sitting position (Table 14–1).

Table 14–1: Basic Stereotyped Patterns That Can Be Assessed in the Movement Pattern Examination

STEREOTYPED PATTERN	EXAMINATION PROCEDURE
Gait	Hip extension pattern, stepping test
Prehension	Shoulder abduction pattern, push up pattern
Eating	Swallowing pattern, mandibular movement pattern (see Chapter 23)
Respiration	Breathing pattern
Stability responses	Cervical stability, shoulder abduction pattern, push up, postural foot reaction
Getting up from a recumbent or sitting position	Cervical flexion pattern, sit-to-stand pattern

These patterns are programmed in the CNS, and the programs call for specific muscles to become activated to specific magnitudes at specific points during the carrying out of each pattern.

Faulty movement patterns can result from alteration of the function of one or more of the muscles that are involved in the pattern. For example, if the upper trapezius becomes hypertonic as a result of trauma or dysafferentation related to dysfunction of a related joint, it may tend to dominate the movement patterns in which it is involved. For a muscle that tends to become inhibited, like the serratus anterior, trauma or dysafferentation, or both, may cause it to become activated to a lesser degree or even left out of the movement patterns in which it is supposed to be involved. In addition, faulty postural set alters the movement patterns that are derived from that set. For example, standing with a forward head posture negatively affects the stability responses that occur in response to perturbations that are introduced to the system while that postural set is taken.

There is another mechanism by which faulty movement patterns can develop. As was discussed in Chapters 3 and 4, CNS programs can become altered in a way that changes the timing and magnitude of activation of muscles in the program and even which muscles will be involved. This alteration can result from trauma, misuse, and peripheral dysfunction that can result in plastic alteration of the program, so that every time the program is ordered, the new pattern is carried out. The individual components (i.e., the muscles involved in the pattern) may or may not be normal, but the manner in which the CNS organizes their interaction is inefficient and stressful to the system. This programmatic alteration is common, and it is important to recognize it, as treatment may be markedly different than if the pattern is altered directly as a result of localized dysfunction of one or more of its components.

In other situations, a combination of factors may produce the faulty pattern. For example, trauma or dysafferentation, or both, may cause a particular muscle to become hypertonic, resulting in that muscle overactivating during the carrying out of a certain movement pattern. As this movement pattern is carried out repetitively over long period of time, the new, faulty pattern can become so well established in the CNS that a new program is created for that movement; this new program becomes accepted as "normal."

CERVICAL FLEXION

Evaluation of the cervical flexion movement pattern enables the clinician to assess the quality of coordinated muscle activity when the patient rises from a recumbent position. Normally, proper cervical flexion involves a balance between deep cervical flexors (longus capitis, longus colli, and rectus capitis anterior) and the SCM, which both flexes the lowers the cervical spine and extends the upper cervical spine.

Donaldson et al[17] demonstrated, using a dynamic surface electromyogram (EMG), that in headache patients who had myofascial TrPs in the SCM, there tended to be increased maximum amplitude of contraction of the SCM during cervical flexion compared to those patients without TrPs in these muscles. Barton and Hayes[18] showed that the SCMs of patients with unilateral neck pain and headache took longer to relax after contraction than those of pain-free controls after cervical flexion. Interestingly, this finding involved both muscles, even though the pain was unilateral. This suggests that the greater relaxation time was not related to pain, but to alteration in the program for cervical flexion.

Procedure
With the patient lying supine, the clinician places his or her finger at the midpoint of the patient's sternum and instructs the patient to raise his or her head off the table and touch the chin to the point at which the finger placed.

Normal Pattern
The chin tucks slightly first, then the patient's head smoothly rolls off the table while the cervical spine flexes (Fig. 14–16).

Faulty Pattern
The chin pokes out at the beginning of the movement and remains protruded throughout (Fig. 14–17). This finding is indicative of hypertonic SCMs and suboccipitals or inhibited deep cervical flexors, or both.

CERVICAL STABILITY

As was discussed in Chapters 3 and 4, the size of the intervertebral neutral zone has been demonstrated to be a bet-

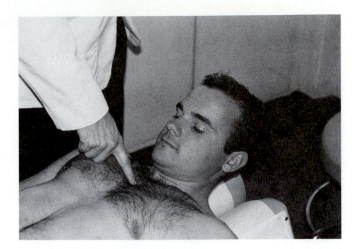

Figure 14–16. Normal cervical flexion movement pattern.

ter indicator of spinal stability than gross range of motion.[19–23] Unfortunately, there is no current method to measure the neutral zone in vivo. However, compromised stability of the cervical spine can be inferred by assessing those muscles that are the most important stabilizers of the cervical spine. Motion palpation (see Chap. 13) may help assess the state of the multifidis muscles.[24] The test presented here allows the assessment of the deep cervical flexors.

The deep cervical flexors, when acting as stabilizers, must have both a short reaction time (brought about by the type II fibers) and a long endurance capacity (brought about by the type I fibers). This procedure tests both functions as well as the balance between the deep cervical flexors and the SCM.

Watson and Trott[14] found that patients with headache performed significantly less well on this test than healthy controls. This was also found by Treleavan et al[25] in patients with postconcussion headache. Silverman et al[26]

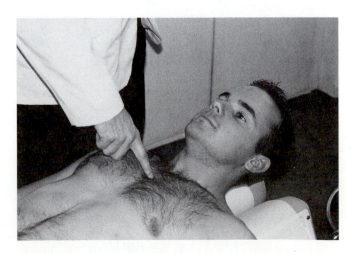

Figure 14–17. Faulty cervical flexion movement pattern.

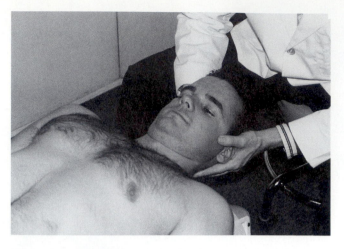

Figure 14–18. Initial position for the cervical stability test.

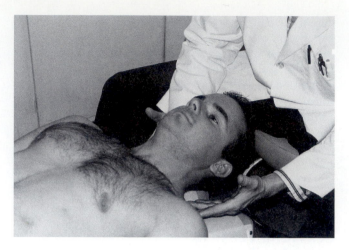

Figure 14–20. Chin poke on cervical stability test.

found true weakness (as opposed to inhibition, which they did not test for) in the deep cervical flexors in patients with chronic neck pain as compared to controls.

Procedure

With the patient supine, the clinician passively prepositions the head in the neutral position with the chin slightly tucked (Fig. 14–18). The clinician tells the patient that he or she is going to let go of the head and that the patient should continue to hold it in this exact position. The clinician then lets go of the head suddenly and observes how well the position is maintained for 10 seconds (Fig. 14–19).

Normal Pattern

The head position is maintained without excessive shaking.

Faulty Pattern

Any of the following responses is abnormal; they are listed from most to least common:

1. The chin pokes out (Fig. 14–20)
2. The head shakes excessively
3. The entire cervical spine flexes (Fig. 14–21)
4. The head drops into extension (Fig. 14–22)

These findings are indicative of inhibition of the deep cervical flexors or hypertonicity of the SCMs, or both. The presence of shaking suggests that transformation of type I to type II fibers has taken place in the deep cervical flexors.

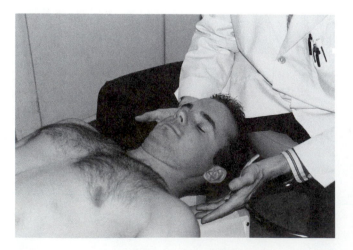

Figure 14–19. Cervical stability test.

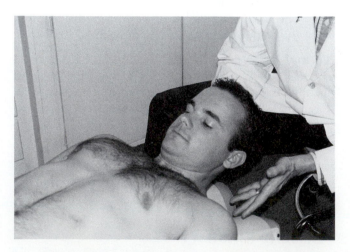

Figure 14–21. Flexion on cervical stability test.

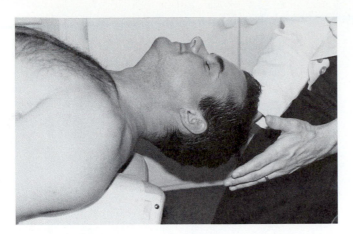

Figure 14–22. Extension on cervical stability test.

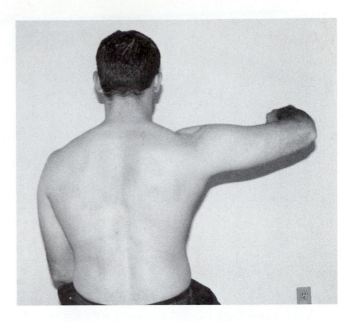

Figure 14–23. Shoulder abduction movement pattern.

SHOULDER ABDUCTION

The purpose of this test is to assess the efficiency of scapular stabilization during movements of the upper extremity. This is especially important for prehension, as part of the primitive movement of reaching out to grasp food and bringing it to the mouth. Abduction is used rather than flexion or any other movement because it most easily allows the visualization of all the components of scapular stabilization and has been demonstrated to be useful in assessing coordination of the muscles involved.[27]

The test assesses the balance between the upper, middle, and lower trapezii and the stabilization capacity of the serratus anterior. The upper trapezius and levator scapula have been demonstrated to be dominant in patients with cervical pain[28–32] and those with shoulder pain.[28, 33] This effect is especially noted after fatigue.[34] Imbalance of the muscles involved in this pattern has also been found in patients with brachial plexus irritation.[35] Alteration of this movement pattern can place increased strain on both the cervical spine and the rotator cuff.

Procedure
The patient is seated with his or her arm resting on the thigh. The clinician stands behind the patient. The patient is instructed to abduct the arm as far as possible (Fig. 14–23).

Normal Pattern
The first 30 to 60 degrees of motion should occur solely at the glenohumeral joint, with contraction of the upper trapezius to stabilize the scapula, but not to a degree that would create scapular movement. After this, the scapula rotates such that the acromion moves superiorward, the superior angle moves inferiorward, and the inferior angle, laterally. The scapula should remain firmly against the body wall.

Faulty Pattern
Anything that deviates from the normal pattern is described as faulty. The most common patterns are:

1. The superior angle of the scapula moves superiorward. This is indicative of levator scapulae hypertonicity.
2. The superior angle of the scapula moves superiorward and medially. This is indicative of rhomboid hypertonicity.
3. The scapula rises before the shoulder reaches 30 to 60 degrees of abduction. This is indicative of upper trapezius hypertonicity.
4. The scapula does not rotate at all, but rather elevates as the shoulder abducts. This is indicative of hypertonicity of the upper trapezius and levator scapulae or inhibition of the middle and lower trapezius, or both.
5. The inferior angle of the scapula moves away from the body wall during abduction or return to the starting position. This is indicative of inhibition of the serratus anterior.

Any of these faulty patterns can occur in combination, so a variety of possible patterns may be seen.

PUSH UP

The purpose of this test is to assess the functional ability of the scapular stabilizers. This is an especially important assessment in patients whose jobs involve pushing heavy objects. The push up test is particularly useful in evaluating

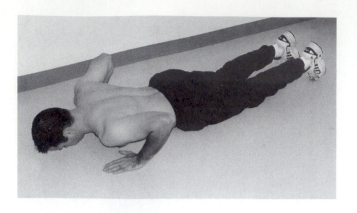

A

B

Figure 14–24. A and B. Push-up movement pattern.

the stabilization capacity of the serratus anterior, as subtle insufficiency of this muscle is not always revealed with the shoulder abduction test.

Procedure

The patient lies prone with his or her hands on the floor, preparing to do a push up maneuver (Fig. 14–24A). While keeping the knees on the floor, the patient pushes him- or herself up until the elbows are fully extended (Fig. 14–24B).

Normal Pattern

Movement is smooth, with the scapulae moving laterally as the pattern is carried out. The scapulae are maintained against the body wall.

Faulty Pattern

The following findings are abnormal:

1. Winging of the inferior angle of the scapula (Fig. 14–25); this is indicative of inhibition of the serratus anterior.
2. Elevation of the shoulders (Fig. 14–26); this is indicative of hypertonicity of the upper trapezius or

inhibition of the middle and lower trapezius, or both.
3. Medial rotation of the scapula; this is far less common than the previously listed findings, but would be indicative of hypertonicity of the upper trapezius or levator scapulae or inhibition of the middle and lower trapezius.

As noted earlier, any of these faulty patterns can occur in combination, so a variety of possible patterns may be seen.

An additional method that can be used in evaluating the activity of the serratus anterior was presented by Paine and Voight.[36] In this procedure, the patient stands facing a wall with his or her hands against the wall, below waist level, and the fingers pointing downward (Fig. 14–27). The patient then presses against the wall. Winging of the inferior angle of the scapula suggests inhibition of the muscle.

HIP EXTENSION

This test is commonly used in the evaluation of patients with low back pain, but it has implications for patients

Figure 14–25. Winging of the scapula on push-up movement pattern.

Figure 14–26. Shoulder elevation on push-up movement pattern.

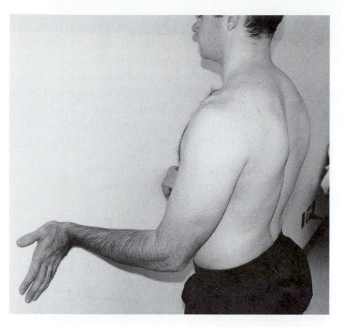

Figure 14–27. Winging of the scapula on wall push test.

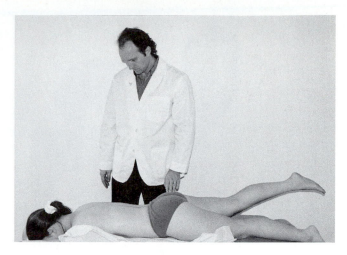

Figure 14–28. Hip extension movement pattern.

with primary cervical complaints as well. It assesses the pattern of contraction of muscles during a movement that mimics gait.

It was previously thought that there was a certain normal "firing order" of the muscles involved in this movement pattern, starting with the gluteus maximus or hamstrings and proceeding in a down-up direction to the thoracic muscles. This has recently shown to not be the case in normal circumstances.[37] In addition, it has been demonstrated that during normal gait, the muscular responses occur in an above-down sequence.[38–40] This test is still very helpful in assessing stability of the lumbar spine and pelvis as well as muscle imbalance in the cervical spine.

Procedure

The patient lies prone with the feet hanging off the end of the table. The clinician palpates the gluteus maximus on the tested side as lightly as possible and observes the lumbar and cervical spine. The patient is instructed to lift one leg into extension (Fig. 14–28).

Normal Pattern

The movement should occur smoothly with early and strong contraction of the gluteus maximus muscle. There should be virtually no movement of the lumbar spine and no contraction of the cervical muscles.

Faulty Pattern

Any of the following findings is considered abnormal:

1. Late or incomplete contraction of the gluteus maximus, or both; this is indicative of inhibition of the gluteus maximus.

2. Lateral or rotational movement of the lumbar spine; this is indicative of functional instability of the lumbar spine.
3. Hyperlordosis of the lumbar spine; this is indicative of tightness of the hip flexors.
4. Activation of the cervical erector spinae, upper trapezius, rhomboid, or levator scapulae muscles; this is indicative of hypertonicity of the involved muscle(s).

Again, any of these faulty patterns can occur in combination, so a variety of possible patterns may be seen.

SWALLOWING

Swallowing is a basic movement pattern that is performed countless times every day. The tongue should normally rest against the hard palate and be held there by negative pressure, with light contact of the tip of the tongue on the incisors.[10, 13] During swallowing, the tongue should increase pressure on the hard palate temporarily. Pressure of the tongue against the teeth is abnormal.

Procedure

The patient is first instructed to prepare to swallow. The clinician palpates the hyoid bone while at the same time placing one finger on the lower lip to prepare to part the lips at the very end of swallowing (Fig. 14–29). The patient then swallows and the clinician feels the hyoid. At the end, the clinician gently parts the lips.

Normal Pattern

The hyoid should move straight up and down, and the tongue should be placed on the hard palate just behind the upper incisors.

Faulty Pattern

A faulty pattern is seen when the hyoid moves anterior to posterior and, upon parting the lips, the tongue is pressed against the incisors (Fig. 14–30).

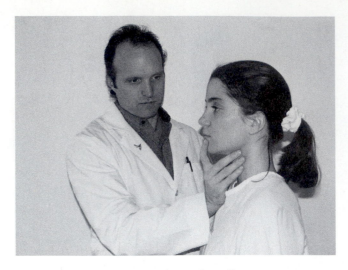

Figure 14–29. Examination of swallowing pattern.

Significance

Faulty swallowing can contribute to instability of the cervical spine as well as persistent forward head carriage.

Another clue that may identify a patient who engages in faulty swallowing is to examine the tongue. If the patient tends to maintain pressure against the incisors rather that on the hard palate, especially if this pressure increases during swallowing, the tongue may take on a scalloped appearance.[10, 13]

Other movement patterns have great relevance to cervical function and can be assessed; these, however, are not designed to uncover specific dysfunction but, rather, reveal inefficient use that has the potential to cause inordinate stress on some aspect of the cervical system.

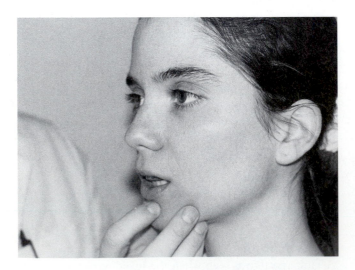

Figure 14–30. Faulty swallowing pattern.

SIT-TO-STAND

This movement pattern is very closely related to the cervical flexion pattern. Have the patient sit on a stool or chair (Fig. 14–31). Observe the patient from the side and ask him or her to stand up. The normal pattern would be for the patient to lead with the posterosuperior aspect of the head (Fig. 14–32). If the SCMs or suboccipitals, or both, are dominating, the patient will lead with the chin (Fig. 14–33). This is a faulty pattern.

BREATHING

Normal breathing is carried out primarily by the diaphragm, which contracts to depress the abdominal contents, thus increasing the volume of the thoracic cavity and creating a pressure gradient that forces air to rush into the lungs. During exercise or other high-intensity physical activity, the accessory breathing apparatus is utilized. This involves contraction of the scalene, upper trapezius, levator

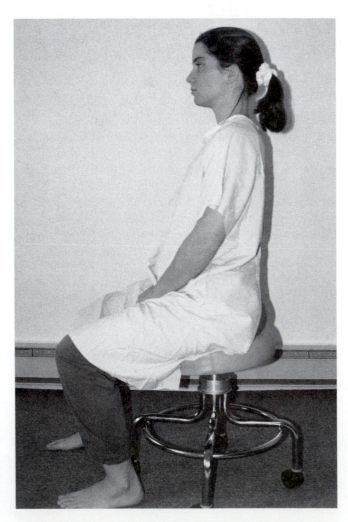

Figure 14–31. Start position for the examination of the sit-to-stand pattern.

Figure 14–32. Normal sit-to-stand movement pattern.

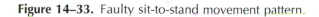

Figure 14–33. Faulty sit-to-stand movement pattern.

scapulae, SCMs, and pectoralis minor to elevate the shoulders and rib cage, allowing for further increase in the volume of the thoracic cavity so that more air can get in. With faulty breathing, the accessory breathing apparatus is utilized as the primary mechanism of breathing, a function it is not meant to perform.

While faulty breathing can place increased strain on the cervical spine due to excessive activity in the accessory breathing muscles, the faulty pattern itself can arise as a result of joint or muscle dysfunction in the cervical spine. It is especially important to look for this pattern in patients with cervicobrachial pain related to TrPs in the scalenes. Also, look for it in patients with scapular instability related to imbalance between the pectoralis minor and the serratus anterior.

Procedure

With the patient standing, the clinician stands behind the patient and watches his or her breathing, paying particular attention to the clavicles. The lateral rib cage can be palpated as well. It is important that the patient be unaware that his or her breathing is being evaluated, to avoid self-consciousness and possible alteration the natural breathing pattern.

Normal Pattern

Normally, the abdomen protrudes, followed by the lower rib cage flaring out laterally, and then the upper ribs rotating superiorward during inhalation. The shoulders and clavicles should remain relaxed and motionless.

Faulty Pattern

The clavicles rise and a furrow develops behind the clavicles. Contraction of the scalenes and SCMs may also be seen on inhalation, with little or no movement of the abdomen and lower ribs.

! CLINICAL PEARL

To evaluate the severity of the faulty breathing pattern, it should also be examined with the patient lying supine. It is easiest to breathe correctly in the supine position. If the patient displays a faulty pattern while supine, it suggests that the faulty pattern is well established in the CNS and will present a greater challenge to correction.

Significance

This faulty breathing pattern places inordinate strain on the muscles that make up the accessory breathing apparatus, particularly the scalenes, and predisposes them to developing myofascial TrPs.

OTHER FUNCTIONAL TESTS

STEPPING TEST

The purpose of this test is to assess the functional integrity of the tonic neck reflexes, as well as locomotor system afferent processing. It was originally deleveloped by Fukuda[41] as a test for dysfunction of the vestibular apparatus. But Fukushima and Hinoki[42] demonstrated that it detects alteration in the distribution of muscle tone to the lower extremities as a result of dysfunction of the tonic neck reflexes. Also, as Gordon and Fletcher[43, 44] found, the stepping test detects abnormality in general kinesthetic awareness in the locomotor system, rather than in the vestibular system.

Procedure

The patient stands with his or her eyes closed or wearing a blindfold with arms outstretched, horizontal to the floor, and parallel to each other. Ear muffs are placed over the ears to obliterate hearing. The clinician instructs the patient to step alternately as if marching, raising the knees to 45 degrees of hip flexion at a moderate pace (Fig. 14–34). This is carried on for 50 steps.

Normal Finding

After 50 steps, the patient should have rotated no more than 30 degrees to either side.

Abnormal Finding

Rotation in either direction to greater than 30 degrees within 50 steps is abnormal; this is indicative of a faulty tonic neck reflex mechanism or a deficit in general kinesthetic awareness, or both.

POSTURAL FOOT REACTION (VELE'S TEST)

The purpose of this test is to assess the automatic reaction of the intrinsic foot muscles to postural stress. This reaction is essential to maintaining stability of the locomotor system as a whole, and it has particular implications for the cervical spine. As Nashner and McCollum[45] and Mergner et al[46–48] have shown, for the nervous system to stabilize the head and neck, it must be aware of the position of head in space. This requires not only the vestibular system, but also knowledge of the head position in relation to the trunk, which, in turn, is dependent on knowledge of the position of the trunk relative to the ground. To determine the position of the trunk relative to the ground, normal afferentation from the foot is essential. In the presence of foot dysfunction, this afferentation is compromised, and additional responsibility may be placed on the cervical spine for this function.

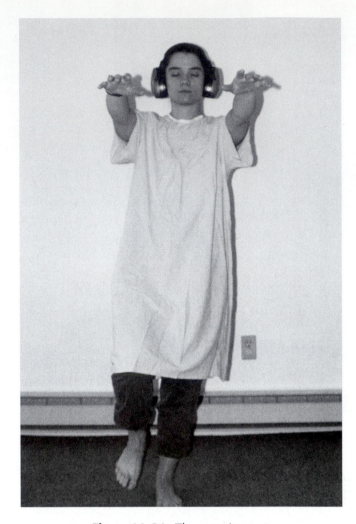

Figure 14–34. The stepping test.

Normal stability of the cervical spine is also dependent on a stable trunk in relation to the ground. The absence of a normal stability reaction in the foot may be reflective of a disordered postural stability system as a whole. This was illustrated in an experiment by O'Connel[49] in which healthy college students sat on a large swing and were asked, as the swing moved forward in its trajectory, to jump off and land on a mat. Postural responses were observed and time to achieve erect stance was measured. The students performed this action under three experimental conditions: (1) with no impedance of visual or foot afference, (2) blindfolded, and (3) blindfolded and after having their feet immersed in ice water for 20 minutes, effectively anesthetizing their feet.

O'Connel found that all subjects were able to achieve erect stance after the first series of jumps. The time from deepest knee flexion to erect stance varied from 0.21 to 0.53 seconds. In the blindfolded series, all subjects were again able to achieve erect stance, but knee flexion upon landing was found to be deeper in some subjects and the time to achieve erect stance varied from 0.22 to 0.77 seconds. In the third set of jumps, blindfolded and with the feet chilled, no subject was able to achieve erect stance without assistance. Two subjects ended up collapsing onto the floor.

Procedure

The patient is standing and looking straight ahead. The clinician asks the patient to lean his or her body weight forward so that body weight shifts to the forefoot (Fig. 14–35).

Normal Finding

An immediate reaction of the intrinsic foot muscles occurs such that the toes flex at the distal interphalangeal joints (Fig. 14–36).

Abnormal Finding

Anything that deviates from the normal is considered a faulty pattern. The common faulty patterns are:

1. Flexion of the proximal interphalangeal joints with extension of the distal interphalangeal joints, creating a "hammer toe"
2. No reaction, with falling forward

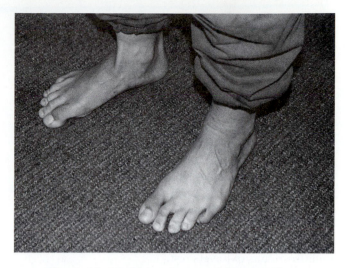

Figure 14–36. Normal postural foot reaction.

These findings are indicative of poor foot stabilization.

When this test is positive, it is important to assess the foot for local dysfunction. This includes the examination for joint dysfunction and improper positional relationships. The specific examination procedures for these dysfunctions are beyond the scope of this book, but can be found in other books (see refs. 50 and 51). Also important in the evaluation of foot function is assessment of the skin, for what Lewit calls "exteroceptive function."[52] For this evaluation, the patient should be supine and the examiner sitting facing the soles of the feet. The examiner then gently strokes the bottom of the patient's foot, feeling carefully for the degree of skin drag of the foot, and comparing this to the other side. Even more important than skin drag, however, is to ask the patient how sensitive the foot is to the stroking as compared to the other. Increased drag and decreased sensitivity is considered to be indicative of dysfunction.

REVEL'S TEST

The purpose of this test is to evaluate the kinesthetic sensibility of the cervical spine. It was developed by Michel Revel[53] who demonstrated that patients experiencing neck pain were significantly less accurate in repositioning the head to neutral from a rotated, flexed, or extended position than were normal controls.

Repositioning of the head requires, first, spatial awareness of the position of the head at rest. This is determined by integration of the signals arising from the spindles of the cervical muscles along with the vestibular apparatus and vision. This integration takes places in the partieto-insular vestibular cortex.[54] The most important of these inputs is that from the cervical muscles.[12] As was previously discussed, when the head is rotated, stretch signals arising from the cervical muscles (both agonists and antagonists) are altered accordingly. The length-tension levels are

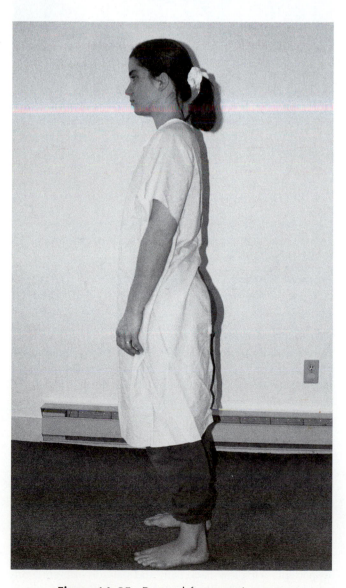

Figure 14–35. Postural foot reaction test.

recorded at each position, and memory of the length-tension relationship in the original position is stored.[12] In order for this to occur accurately, appropriate length-tension information must arise from the muscles. If this information is altered as a result of dysfunction, the ability to return the head from a fully rotated, flexed, or extended position to neutral may be impaired.

Significant dysfunction of repositioning as detected by Revel's test has been demonstrated in postwhiplash patients[55, 56] and has been shown to correlate well with the presence of oculomotor dysfunction, particularly smooth pursuit and saccades.[57] Thus, although there is currently no simple test that is convenient in the clinical setting for assessing oculomotor dysfunction in patients with cervical spine syndromes (see Chap. 4), its presence can be inferred from the results of Revel's test.

Procedure

The patient is seated 90 cm from a 40-cm diameter target that has concentric circles 1-cm apart (Fig. 14–37). The patient is blindfolded and is wearing a set of earmuffs with a laser pointer affixed to it. The head is aligned so that the laser pointer is positioned at zero on the target (Fig. 14–38). The patient is instructed to remember this position, then maximally rotate the head to the left and hold this position for 2 seconds. The patient is then instructed to return to the starting position. After this is done, a measurement is taken as to how far from the zero position the pointer rests (indicated as + or −, depending on whether

Figure 14–38. Starting position for Revel's test.

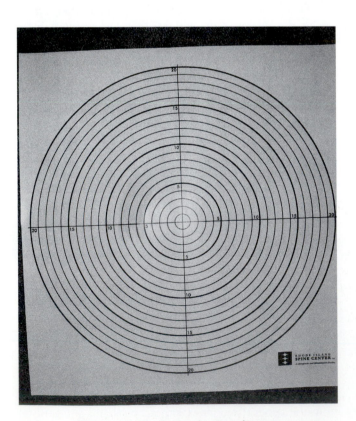

Figure 14–37. Target for Revel's test.

the patient over- or undershot the starting position). This procedure is then repeated with repositioning from rotation to the right, flexion, and extension.

Normal Finding

A repositioning error of 3 cm or less in all directions is normal.

Abnormal Finding

A repositioning error of 3 cm or more in any direction is abnormal; this is indicative of poor head repositioning related to faulty afferent input from the cervical muscles.

S REFLEX

In assessing patients with cervical spine syndromes, it is important to consider the role that dysfunction in the pelvis may play in the clinical picture. The S (Silverstolpe) reflex is a sign of mechanical pelvic dysfunction that can cause or perpetuate cervical problems. It was first discovered by Silverstolpe[58] and is a sign of dysfunction of the sacrotuberous ligament or pelvic diaphragm, or both. The S reflex may be present in patients with cervical spine syndromes as well as in patients with low back pain and pelvic symptoms. Silverstolpe has commonly found this sign to be significant in patients with headache and in performers with vocal problems (Lewit, personal communication, 1997).

Procedure

With the patient lying prone, the clinician places the tips of his or her fingers along the erector spinae muscles in the area between T5 and T11. The clinician then plucks the erector spinae muscles like a guitar string (Fig. 14–39) and observes for muscular reaction.

Normal Finding

There should be normal tension and lack of tenderness in the thoracic erector spinae muscles and no reflex activation with plucking of the fibers.

Abnormal Finding

Abnormal findings include tension and tenderness in the erector spinae muscles and reflex activation of the thoracic erector spinae and sometimes of the posterior cervical and ipsilateral hamstring muscles. These are indicative of dysfunction of the sacrotuberous ligament or the pelvic diaphragm, or both.

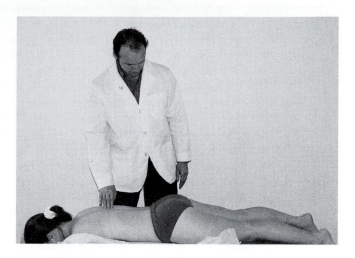

Figure 14–39. Examination for the S reflex.

CONCLUSION

In patients with cervical spine syndromes, it is essential that we look globally at the patient to assess the function of the locomotor system and detect dysfunction in this system that may have an impact on the complaints. Many clues to underlying dysfunction can be obtained by looking at posture and movement patterns, and by performing the other functional procedures that are presented in this chapter. These evaluations allow the clinician to determine the course of action in treatment that will most rapidly reduce the dysfunction and return the patient to as close to optimum health as possible. The decisions that will be made as a result of the findings of the examination of posture and movement patterns in the context of the entire patient examination, as well as those specific methods that can be used to correct the dysfunction, will be discussed in Chapters 17, 19, 25, and 28.

REFERENCES

1. Ayub E, Glasheen-Wray M, Kraus S. Head posture: A case study of the effects on the rest position of the mandible. *J Orthop Sports Phys Ther* 1984;5:179–183.
2. Treleavan J, Jull G, Atkinson L. Cervical musculoskeletal dysfunction in post-concussion headache. *Cephalalgia* 1994;14:273–279.
3. Greenfield B, Catlin PA, Coats PW, Green E, McDonald JJ, North C. Posture in patients with shoulder overuse injuries and healthy individuals. *J Orhtop Sports Phys Ther* 1995;21(5):287–295.
4. Troyanovich SJ, Harrison DE, Harrison DD. Structural rehabilitation of the spine and posture: Rationale for treatment beyond the resolution of symptoms. *J Manipulative Physiol Ther* 1998;21(1):37–50.
5. Dieck GS, Kelsey JL, Goel VK, et al. An epidemiologic study of the relationship between postural asymmetry in the teen years and subsequent back and neck pain. *Spine* 1985;10:872–877.
6. Braun BL. Postural differences between asymptomatic men and women and craniofacial pain patients. *Arch Phys Med Rehabil* 1991;72:653–656.
7. Harrison AL, Barry-Greb T, Wojtowicz G. Clinical measurement of head and shoulder posture variables. *J Orthop Sports Phys Ther* 1996;23:353–361.
8. Grimmer K. An investigation of poor cervical resting posture. *Aust Physiother* 1997;3:7–16.
9. Visscher CM, deBoer W, Naeije M. The relationship between posture and curvature of the cervical spine. *J Manipulative Physiol Ther* 1998;21(6):388–391.
10. Mannheimer JS. Prevention and restoration of abnormal upper quarter posture. In: Gelb H, Gelb M, eds. *Postural Considerations in the Diagnosis and Treatment of Cranio-Cervical-Mandibular and Related Chronic Pain Disorders.* St. Louis, Mo: Ishiyaku EuroAmerica; 1991:93–161.

11. Fukushima K, Fukushima J. Involvement of the interstitial nucleus of Cajal in the midbrain reticular formation in the position-related, tonic component of vertical eye movement and head posture. In: Berthoz A, Graf W, Vidall PP, eds. *The Head-Neck Sensory Motor System.* New York, NY: Oxford University Press; 1992:330–344.

12. Bizzi E, Polit A. Characteristics of the motor programs underlying visually evoked movements. In: Talbott RE, Humphrey DR eds. *Posture and Movement.* New York, NY: Raven Press; 1979:169–176.

13. Mannheimer JS, Rosenthal RM. Acute and chronic postural abnormalities as related to craniofacial pain and temporomandibular disorders. *Dent Clin North Am* 1991;35:185–208.

14. Watson DH, Trott PH. Cervical headache: An investigation of natural head posture and upper cervical flexor muscle performance. *Cephalalgia* 1993;13:272–284.

15. Lewit K. *Manipulative Therapy in the Rehabilitation of the Locomotor System.* 2nd ed. Oxford: Butterworth-Heinemann; 1991.

16. Tunnell P. Protocol for visual assessment: Postural evaluation of the muscular system through visual inspection. *J Bodywork Move Ther* 1997;1:21–27.

17. Donaldson CCS, Skubick DL, Clasby RG, Cram JR. The evaluation of trigger-point activity using dynamic EMG techniques. *Am J Pain Man* 1994;4(3):118–122.

18. Barton PM, Hayes KC. Neck flexor muscle strength, efficiency, and relaxation times in normal subjects and subjects with unilateral neck pain and headache. *Arch Phys Med Rehabil* 1996;77:680–687.

19. Panjabi M, Abumi K, Durenceau J, Oxland T. Spinal stability and intersegmental muscle forces: A biomechanical model. *Spine* 1989;14(2):194–200.

20. Panjabi MM, Lyons C, Vasavada A, et al. On the understanding of clinical instability. *Spine* 1994;19(23):2642–2650.

21. Mimura M, Panjabi MM, Oxland TR, et al. Disc degeneration affects the multidirectional flexibility of the lumbar spine. *Spine* 1994;19(12):1371–1380.

22. Wilke HJ, Wolf S, Claes LE, Arand M, Wiesend A. Stability increase in the lumbar spine with different muscle groups. *Spine* 1995;20(2):192–198.

23. Kaigle AM, Holm SH, Hansson TH. Experimental instability of the lumbar spine. *Spine* 1995;20(4):421–430.

24. Hides JA, Stokes MJ, Saide M, Jull GA, Cooper DH. Evidence of lumbar multifidis muscle wasting ipsilateral to symptoms in patients with acute/subacute low back pain. *Spine* 1994;19(2):165–172.

25. Treleavan J, Jull G, Atkinson L. Cervical musculoskeletal dysfunction in post-concussion headache. *Cephalalgia* 1994;14:273–279.

26. Silverman JL, Rodriquez AA, Agre JC. Quantitative cervical flexor strength in healthy subjects and in subjects with mechanical neck pain. *Arch Phys Med Rehabil* 1991;72:679–681.

27. Peat M, Grahame RE. Electromyographic analysis of soft tissue lesions affecting shoulder function. *Am J Phys Med* 1977;56:223–240.

28. Veiersted KB, Westgaard RH, Andersen P. Pattern of muscle activity during stereotyped work and its relation to muscle pain. *Int Arch Occup Environ Health* 1990;62:31–41.

29. Elert JE, Rantapaa-Dahlqvist SB, Henriksson-Larsen K, et al. Muscle performance, electromyography and fiber type composition in fibromyalgia and work-related myalgia. *Scand J Rheum* 1992;21:28–34.

30. Elert J, Brulin C, Gerdle B, Johansson H. Mechanical performance, level of continuous contraction, and muscle pain symptoms in home care personnel. *Scand J Rehab Med* 1992;24:141–150.

31. Elert J, Dahlqvist SR, Almay B, Eisemann M. Muscle endurance, muscle tension and personality traits in patients with muscle or joint pain—a pilot study. *J Rheumatol* 1993;20(9):1550–1556.

32. Fredin Y, Elert J, Britchgi N, et al. A decreased ability to relax between repetitive muscle contractions in patients with chronic symptoms after whiplash trauma to the neck. *J Musculoskel Pain* 1997;5:55–70.

33. Baybar SR. Excessive scapular motion in individuals recovering from painful and stiff shoulders: causes and treatment strategies. *Phys Ther* 1996;76:226–246.

33a. Eliot DJ. Electromyography of levator scapulae: New findings allow tests of a head stabilization model. *J Manipulative Physiol Ther* 1996;19(1):19–25.

34. McQuade KJ, Wei SH, Smidt GL. Effects of local muscle fatigue on three-dimensional scapulohumeral rhythm. *Clin Biomech* 1995;10(3):144–148.

35. Langley P. Scapular instability associated with brachial plexus irritation: a proposed causative relationship with treatment implications. *J Hand Ther* 1997;10:35–40.

36. Paine RM, Voight M. The role of the scapula. *J Orthop Sports Phys Ther* 1993;18:386–391.

37. Vogt L, Banzer W. Dynamic testing of the motor stereotype in prone hip extension from the neutral position. *Clin Biomech* 1997;12:122–127.

38. Prince F, Winter DA, Stergiou P, Walt SE. Anticipatory control of upper body balance during human locomotion. *Gait Posture* 1994;2:19–25.

39. Winter DA. Human balance and posture control during standing and walking. *Gait Posture* 1995;3:193–214.

40. Winter DA. *ABC of Balance During Walking and Standing.* Waterloo, Ontario: Waterloo Biomechanics; 1995.

41. Fukuda T. *Statokinetic Reflexes in Equilibrium and Movement.* Tokyo: University of Tokyo Press; 1984.

42. Fukushima H, Hinoki M. Role of cervical and lumbar proprioceptors during stepping: An electromyographic study of the muscular activities of the lower limbs. *Acta Otolaryngol (Stockh)* 1985;suppl 419:91–105.

43. Gordon CR, Fletcher WA, Jones GM, Block EW. Adaptive plasticity in the control of locomotor trajectory. *Exp Brain Res* 1995;102:540–545.

44. Gordon CR, Fletcher WA, Jones GM, Block EW. Is the stepping test a specific indicator of vestibulospinal function? *Neurology* 1995;45:2035–2037.

45. Nashner LM, McCollum G. The organization of human postural movements: A formal basis and experimental synthesis. *Behav Brain Sci* 1985;8:135–172.

46. Mergner T, Siebold C, Schweigart G, Becker W. Human perception of horizontal trunk and head rotation in space during vestibular and neck stimulation. *Exp Brain Res* 1991;85:389–404.

47. Mergner T, Hlavacka F, Schweigart G. Interaction of vestibular and proprioceptive inputs. *J Vestibular Res* 1993;3:41–57.

48. Mergner T, Huber W, Beckert W. Vestibular-neck interaction and transformation of sensory coordinates. *J Vest Res* 1997;7(4):347–367.

49. O'Connel A. Effect of sensory deprivation on postural reflexes. *Electromyography* 1971;11:519–527.

50. Mennel JM. *Joint Pain.* Boston, Mass: Little Brown; 1964.

51. Michaud TC. *Foot Orthoses and Other Forms of Conservative Foot Care.* Self-published; 1997.

52. Lewit K. Course on Manual Medicine and Locomotor System Rehabilitation, Prague, Czech Republic, 1997.

53. Revel M, Andre-Deshays C, Minguet M. Cervicocephalic kinesthetic sensibility in patients with cervical pain. *Arch Phys Med Rehabil* 1991;72;288–291.

54. Karnath HO. Subjective body orientation in neglect and the interactive contribution of neck muscle proprioception and vestibular stimulation. *Brain* 1994;117:1001–1012.

55. Heikkila H, Astrom PG. Cervicocephalic kinesthetic sensibility in patients with whiplash injury. *Scand J Rehabil* 1996;28:133–138.

56. Loudon JK, Ruhl M, Field E. Ability to reproduce head position after whiplash injury. *Spine* 1997;22(8):865–868.

57. Heikkila HV, Wenngren BI. Cervicocephalic kinesthetic sensibility, active cervical range of motion and oculomotor functions in patients with whiplash injury. *Arch Phys Med Rehabil* 1998;79:1089–1094.

58. Silverstolpe L. A pathological erector spinae reflex—a new sign of mechanical pelvis dysfunction. Proposal for treatment. *Man Med* 1989;4:28.

CHAPTER 15

Outcomes Management
of Cervical Spine Complaints

STEVEN G. YEOMANS

"In general, outcomes management is designed to establish baselines, document progress, assist in goal setting, and motivate patients. Hence, it has something to offer the patient, provider, and payor."

—S.G.Y.

INTRODUCTION

Today's insurance industry appears to be holding health care providers accountable for patient care based on proof of treatment benefit, demanding that "medical necessity" be present when care is delivered. Hence, providers are being requested to provide the "proof" that insurers are looking for. With this "paradigm shift" of accountability has come provider responsibility for collecting data and, because of this, outcomes management (OM) is becoming popular.

The reasons insurers give for reviewing so many claims is to assure quality and to contain costs, which may seem a like an oxymoron as it implies that quality comes cheaply. What insurers are really after is not the least expensive service at the expense of quality, but the "biggest bang for the buck." The use of OM may provide the insurer with the necessary information to be able to determine which providers are performing a quality service for a reasonable price, or offering a good value.

Prospective thinking providers are not waiting for insurers to gather data on a given patient population, such as members in a specific health maintenance organization (HMO) rather, they are opting to collect data or outcomes on their own patient population (not exclusive to only an HMO contract or only one insurer). Thus, prospective thinking providers are positioning themselves to be able to compete in a strong manner in an increasingly competitive market. The purpose of this chapter is to provide orientation for the reader to the methods of gathering outcomes that pertain to the cervical spine–injured patient.

CONCEPTS OF OUTCOMES MANAGEMENT

Before investigating the various outcomes assessment (OA) tools that are specific for cervical spine–related injuries, it is necessary to understand a few concepts regarding the OM process. OM can be defined as the measurement of the symptom(s) or function, or both, pertaining to a patient's clinical status. The process of assessing outcomes begins on the *initial visit*. This is essential in order to *establish baselines* and to help in goal setting. OA tools are simple to administer, time efficient (many OA tools are patient- rather than provider-driven), and low-tech (no expensive equipment is required). The critical issue is to establish functional goals, and then to follow those goals by documenting patient status and progress over time, utilizing OM. When clinical decision making is facilitated by the use of the outcome measures, an outcomes-based management approach is then established and the new paradigm has been adopted.

The promotion of quality without sacrificing cost is a critical component of OM.[1] The ratio of quality to cost defines value[2] and quality can be assessed by the demonstration of improved outcomes. Therefore, evidence-based treatment approaches can be assessed for both value and quality by the use of OM.[3]

CRITERIA FOR EVALUATING OUTCOMES INSTRUMENTS

Some of the criteria used to judge whether an OA tool is valuable or not are summarized in Table 15–1. These criteria will help you determine whether a specific tool is worth the financial expense or time spent in your clinic.[4]

The instruments utilized must be safe, which is not a problem with paper-and-pencil instruments but must be considered with functional testing. They must also be reliable, as they must be able to measure consistently over time and between observers. Instruments must also be valid, in that they must measure what they purport to; the inclusion of normative data is ideal, but unfortunately, these findings are not always available. Time and cost efficiency are also important criteria when selecting outcomes tools for clinical use. When an instrument succeeds in meeting all of these criteria, the tool can be confidently utilized in an OM system.

Table 15–1: Criteria for Evaluating Outcomes Assessment Tools

1. **Safety:** Given the known characteristics of the patient, the procedure should not be expected to lead to injury.
2. **Reliability:** The test score should be dependable across the evaluators, patients, and the date or time of administration.
3. **Validity:** The interpretation of the test score should be able to predict or reflect the patient's performance in a target work setting.
4. **Practicality:** The cost of the test procedure should be reasonable and customary. Cost is measured in terms of the direct expense of the test procedure plus the amount of time required of the patient, plus the delay in providing the information derived from the procedure to the referral source.
5. **Utility:** The usefulness of the procedure is the degree to which it meets the needs of the patient, referrer, and payer.

CLASSIFICATION OF OUTCOMES INSTRUMENTS

The cervical spine represents a specific region; hence, condition- or disease-specific questionnaires may best address the cervical injury or condition. However, because *patients* and not just *conditions* are being assessed, an orientation to the various categories of outcomes assessment is appropriate. More specifically, it does not take a great deal of clinical experience to realize that seemingly similar conditions in two different patients often yield significantly different treatment approaches and responses. Furthermore, practitioners often cannot predict the outcome of a case until some time passes and observation of the treatment response can be assessed. Use of a condition-specific questionnaire alone may be inadequate as it does not address how the condition is affecting the patient's general health and well-being. Therefore, utilization of a series of OA tools may be the best approach to a particular patient's needs, preventing the practitioner from developing tunnel vision by looking at only one facet of his or her condition.

OA tools can be classified into various categories, which helps the provider stay oriented to the goals that are

Table 15–2: Classification of Outcomes Instruments

ASSESSMENT GOALS	INSTRUMENT(S)
1. Pain Level	Visual Analogue Scale,[5] Numerical Pain Scale,[6] McGill Pain Questionnaire[7]
2. Disability LBP Neck	Oswestry Low Back Disability Questionnaire,[8] Roland-Morris,[9] Dallas Low Back Questionnaire,[10] Low Back TyPE,[11] NDI,[12] Headache Disability Index,[13] Dizziness Disability Index[14]
3. General Health	Dartmouth COOP charts,[15, 16] Health Status Questionnaire (HSQ 2.0),[17] SF-36[18–20]
4. Psychometrics	HSQ (questions 37–39)*,[17] SF-36*, Waddell's signs,[21] Modified Zung Depression Scale,[22] Modified Somatic Perception Questionnaire,[23] SCL 90-R,[24] Beck's Depression Inventory[25]
5. Patient Satisfaction	Chiropractic Satisfaction Questionnaire,[26] Visit-specific Questionnaire[27]

HSQ, Health Status Questionnaire; LBP, low back pain; NDI, Neck Disability Index; SCL 90-R, Symptom Checklist 90-Revised; SF-36, Short Form 36.
* Only parts of the questionnaire relate to the categories.

appropriate for a particular case. Some of the classification schemes that can be utilized are represented in Table 15–2. Although the use of many of the instruments listed in Table 15–2 may be appropriate in specific clinical cases, it is beyond the scope of this chapter and text to discuss each in great detail. This information is provided elsewhere (see ref. 28).

There are many different OM tools and determining what tool is most appropriate and when to use that tool is no easy task. To assist the provider in determining when goals of care are reached, OM includes valid and reliable, quantifiable measurements of patient symptoms, impairment/functional limitations, and disability/functional capacity. In other words, an OM tool can be subjective, tracking symptoms described by the patient through his or her responses to questions. An example of this is the measurement of pain. An OM instrument may also be objective; for example, a functional test that yields a quantitative result and, as with the subjective tools, can be repeated later for future comparison (i.e., for measuring outcomes). OM tools can also be specific to a condition and, hence, describe activity intolerance specific to that condition (i.e., disability). Therefore, outcomes categories that include subjective measures focus on the measurement of pain, general health, a specific condition or disease specific (disability), psychometric aspects, and patient satisfaction.

COLLECTING OUTCOME DATA: HOW TO START

OUTCOME DERIVED FROM SUBJECTIVE DATA

The process of collecting outcome information does not start or end with the use of OA instruments such as questionnaires and forms. Moreover, the use of OA tools does not diminish the importance of obtaining the standard history of the patient's presenting complaint(s). The patient history is the nucleus from which the outcomes tool selection is made. It is also the basis for determining which area must be examined by means of functional testing such as range of motion, muscle strength, palpatory tenderness, orthopedic and neurological testing, and so on. In addition, the history can effectively help follow outcomes if the *right* questions are asked and documented. Therefore, suffice it to say that an accurate history is the foundation upon which the entire case rests and from which outcomes data is collected.

The process of outcomes collection can be facilitated by taking an outcomes-oriented history. Often, when patients are asked to list pain-provoking factors, they respond with a short answer such as "bending, lifting, walking, and standing." This information, though "acceptable" by documentation standards, yields very little information for assessing improvement, a few weeks later when the same

question is posed and a similar response is gathered. In such cases, it may appear that no change has occurred with the current form of treatment; this in turn may prompt a third party, a patient, or even the treating clinician to question the benefit of the current treatment approach. However, if one were to ask outcomes-oriented questions at the initial visit—such as, "How far and how long can you bend before you feel pain or feel pain worsen?" "How much weight, from where to where, and for how long can you lift prior to pain worsening?" "How fast and how far can you walk prior to the onset of increased pain?" and, "How long can you stand prior to pain worsening?"—one would then be able to determine whether improvement had occurred, by asking the same questions at a follow-up visit. In other words, by *quantifying* the subjective complaints, which means using a method to measure the *amount* of change, the history can be useful in assessing outcomes. Similarly, if a patient, on the initial visit, reports that aspirin is "helpful," asking for the improved pain level obtained by the use of aspirin (ASA) can enable the provider to make a comparison 2 or 4 weeks later that may support his or her determination that improvement is being made—but only if the same question is asked. In this case, the patient's initial history might read, "3 ASA will reduce pain from 8/10 to 5/10 within a half hour and are taken 4 times a day." On follow-up, the same patient's history might read "2 ASA will reduce pain from 4/10 to 0/10 within 15 minutes and are taken only once a day now." In this example, the amount of medication required and its effect "tell a story" that the patient is improving.

When gathering information for a patient history, the provider should present the question in a manner that can allow for future reassessment or provide documented evidence of therapeutic benefit. The terms "hard" and "soft" describe the quality of the information collected from a patient; "hard" refers to quantitative information whereas "soft" refers to qualitative information only. Table 15–3 offers some common examples of hard versus soft history-gathering methods.

Although more information must be written or transcribed when gathering "hard" data, the improved quality of the office note speaks for itself. If the same "hard" questions are asked say every 2 to 4 weeks, with perhaps one sentence addressing one of the "hard" questions on each visit, the documentation will "tell a story." Progress (or the lack thereof) can then be followed and treatment modifications made promptly to optimize case management. By asking the patient for examples of activities of daily living (ADLs) that are no longer tolerated because of the presenting complaint, the provider can also track progress at a later date, for example, by commenting that the activity intolerance noted on day 1 is now tolerable. By asking additional questions about the intensity, frequency, and duration of pain or quantifying the ADL restriction, the note becomes outcomes oriented and subtler changes can be followed in future progress notes. One may, instead, rely on the use of

Table 15–3: Examples of Hard versus Soft History-gathering Methods

QUESTION	"SOFT" RESPONSE	"HARD" RESPONSE
Pain is provoked by:	Bending, Lifting, Walking, Standing	Bending for > 5 seconds, 30 degrees; Lifting 15 lbs; Walking more than ½ block or 5 minutes; Standing > 2 minutes, such as when washing dishes
Pain is improved by:	NSAIDs, Rest, Ice, Manipulation	Ibuprofen 600 mg reduces the pain from 8/10 to 5/10 in 20 minutes; Rest for 10 minutes supine with knees and hips at 90/90; 20 minutes of ice decreases pain 50%; Manipulation decreases pain 90% for 1 day
The quality of pain is:	Achy and sharp	Achy most of the time (2/10); sharp with quick movements (stand from sitting = 8/10); returns to a 2/10 within 5 minutes if the patient can rest
The severity of pain is:	Mild and at times, bad	3/10 right now, 2–3/10 on average, and 1 to 8/10 from least to most. It's 2–3/10 80% of the time
Timing of the pain is:	AM > PM	AM 6/10; after 1.5 hr 2–3/10; and 5/10 after work (8 hr).
The frequency of pain is:	Off and on	0/10 80% of the time and 8/10 with quick moves. Recovers back to a 0/10 in ½ hour with rest & ice.

condition-specific questionnaires to track ADL changes over time. But it is still important to gather information concerning the intolerance to specific activities from the patient's history, as a questionnaire may not include an ADL restriction that is unique for a particular patient. An example of an effective patient chart is one that includes both a history containing "hard" quantitative data and outcomes questionnaires tracking pain, quality of life or general health, and condition-specific information.

There are three essential steps in becoming outcomes based.

1. The provider must become aware of the various questionnaires or outcomes tools that can be utilized.
2. The tools must be administered, scored, and recorded in a convenient location—such as on an outcomes summary page—for recall and future comparison. Also, the same tools must be administered at the first visit to establish the baseline; at subsequent time intervals, such as every 2 weeks; and at the conclusion of care.
3. The scores must be compared and contrasted with the history and physical examination information and, most importantly, clinical decisions must be made based on the information reviewed.

Oftentimes, questionnaires are administered but not scored or are not readministered during follow-up visits. When this occurs, correlation with the other clinical information concerning the patient and critical decision making based on outcomes is not possible.

CERVICAL SPINE–SPECIFIC OUTCOMES ASSESSMENT TOOLS

PAIN QUESTIONNAIRES

A wide variety of tools exist for measuring a patient's perception of pain. It is beyond the scope of this chapter to discuss at length each of the many tools included in this category; therefore, only the "gold standard" tools are included for practical reasons. Commonly utilized tools for assessing pain intensity include the *Visual Analogue Scale (VAS)*,[5] the *Numerical Rating Scale (NRS)*,[6] and, for measuring the quality and location of pain, the *pain diagram (location and quality of pain)*.[29–37] The difference between the NRS and the VAS is that the NRS includes a numerical descriptive typically using a 10-point ordinal scale whereas in the VAS, the "number" being scored is blinded from the patient. The VAS usually utilizes a 10-cm horizontal line; the statement "no pain" is written on the left-hand side of the line, and on the right, "maximum" or "worst pain imaginable."

Von Korff et al[38] offered a triple VAS, in which pain is graded in three ways: right now, average, and at worst. For patients with chronic pain, referring to the last 3 months is appropriate for obtaining the average pain level. One final VAS score is calculated by averaging the three grades. If the score is less than 50 (the average times 10 to equal a score on a 100-point scale), the pain is considered "low intensity." If the score is greater than 50, the pain is considered "high intensity."

One important question that I also recommend asking is, "What is the level of your pain at its best?" This helps determine how close to zero (no pain) the pain intensity approaches. In addition, asking, "What percent of your waking hours is your pain intensity at its best?" (as well as at its worst) is also very practical, as it allows the provider to address the duration of pain intensity. The importance of this specific line of questioning becomes apparent if for example, a patient says his or her pain level is "6/10"; how is the provider to know if that represents pain right now, on average, or at worst? More importantly, if it is only 6/10 for a short time period at a frequency of once a week, and is 0/10 the remainder of the time, the patient may well be ready for discharge and certainly should be working, at least in some capacity. In other words, the information received from asking these additional questions regarding pain may lead to a completely different interpretation and,

hence, a different "clinical path" for patient case management may be taken. If one does not ask the appropriate question, one will not obtain the response needed to make good, rational clinical decisions. Thus, it is possible to be misguided by the use of OM results if the tools are not properly utilized or if the information is not correlated with the rest of the existing case information.

Many studies have found the blinding of the numbers on the VAS from the subject to be most valid and reliable; other studies have suggested that the VAS and the NRS are comparable.[39] In two studies, the NRS was reported to be more reliable than the VAS.[6,40] Table 15–4 offers a VAS/NRS scheme called the Quadruple Visual Analogue Scale (QVAS) that is useful in clinical practice.

Table 15–4: Quadruple Visual Analogue Scale

Name _____ Date _____ Date of Birth _____

INSTRUCTIONS: Please circle the number that best describes the question being asked.

     NOTE: If you have more than one complaint, please answer each question for each individual complaint and indicate which score is for which complaint.

EXAMPLE:

                  headache   neck   low back

No pain ——————————————————————————————— Extreme pain

    0   1   2   (3)   4   (5)   6   7   8   9   (10)

1. What is your pain RIGHT NOW?

No pain ——————————————————————————————— Extreme pain

    0   1   2   3   4   5   6   7   8   9   10

2. What is your TYPICAL or AVERAGE pain?

No pain ——————————————————————————————— Extreme pain

    0   1   2   3   4   5   6   7   8   9   10

3. What is your pain AT ITS BEST (How close to "0" does your pain get at its best)?

No pain ——————————————————————————————— Extreme pain

    0   1   2   3   4   5   6   7   8   9   10

     What percentage of your awake hours is your pain at its best? _____%

4. What is your pain AT ITS WORST (How close to "10" does your pain get at its worst)?

No pain ——————————————————————————————— Extreme pain

    0   1   2   3   4   5   6   7   8   9   10

     What percentage of your awake hours is your pain at its worst? _____%

GENERAL HEALTH QUESTIONNAIRES

The patient's general health and quality of life must be considered when collecting outcomes in any condition, including cervical spine complaints. Two commonly used methods of general health are the Dartmouth COOP Health Charts and the Health Status Questionnaire 2.0.

The Dartmouth COOP Health Charts, which were developed in 1987, utilize a combination of a verbal description and a pictorial representation of nine quality of life measures. These charts are: (1) physical function, (2) emotional functioning, (3) daily activities / role function, (4) social function / activities, (5) pain, (6) overall health, (7) health change, (8) quality of life, and (9) social support / resources. Figures 15–1 through 15–9 represent a conceptual outline of this instrument. Scoring is easy, as each chart represents one measure of health and is scored on a 1-to-5 ordinal scale where 1 represents no limitation and 5 represents the most significant limitation. This instrument can be used to monitor patient progress although its main strength lies in allowing the patient the opportunity to reveal, in a quantitative format, functional limitations that might otherwise go unrecognized.[41]

The strengths of the Dartmouth COOP Health Charts include the following:

Ease of administration (the instrument is typically self-reported)

Ease of understanding, as both verbal and pictorial methods are included

Ease of scoring, as each chart is individually scored between 1 and 5

Reading and language barriers are less of a problem because of the inclusion of a picture (this instrument is available in multiple languages as well)

Quick completion time (approximately 5 minutes).

The criteria previously mentioned for a "valuable test" have been met, and ease of use and understanding by both health care providers and patients has been demonstrated.[15, 16, 42] Permission must be obtained by both health care providers as well as researchers in order to use the Dartmouth COOP Health Charts. This can be accomplished by contacting Deborah Johnson, Dartmouth COOP Project; Dartmouth Medical School, Hanover, NH 03755-3862; 603-650-1974.

The Health Status Questionnaire 2.0 (HSQ 2.0) was developed by the Health Outcomes Institute (2001 Killebrew Drive, Suite 122, Bloomington, MN 55425; 612-858-9188). Other instruments that carry similar scales but slightly different scoring methods or verbal titles of some of the scales include the Short Form 36 (SF-36)[18–20] and the RAND 36-Item Health Survey 1.0.[19] There are eight scales derived from this instrument: (1) physical function, (2) social function, (3) role limitations due to physical problems, (4) role limitations due to emotional problems, (5) mental health, (6) energy / fatigue, (7) bodily pain, and (8) health

perception. Table 15–5 represents the first step in the scoring of this instrument—recoding of each question. Note that because of the slight variation in scoring and scale name, the tables represented in this text were taken from the HSQ 2.0 and should not be used for the RAND 36 or the SF-36. The second step in scoring involves averaging the recoded items relating to a specific scale. Table 15–6 represents each scale, the number of items (questions) that make up each scale, the specific scale items and questions and numbers, and the minimum number of items or questions needed to compute a score.

Figure 15–10 includes an example of computing the score of the Mental Health Scale, and Table 15–7 represents examples derived from a completed HSQ 2.0. Table 15–8 represents three additional questions related to (1) major depression, (2) dysthymia, and (3) risk of both major depression and dysthymia. Computer software is available for performing the recoding and scale scoring methods (CareTrak from Synergy Solutions, Inc., P.O. Box 5103, Grand Rapids, MN 55744-5103; 800-950-8133; e-mail: synergy@uslink.net). Although a simple manual calculator can be used, a computer scoring system typically results in a decreased likelihood of error.

! CLINICAL PEARL

Rules regarding missing responses are included in the scoring instructions as patients may leave one or more items blank on the survey. When this occurs, it is recommended that an estimate be made with regard to the missing item. This is done by averaging the completed items in the same scale and re-averaging the total number of items or questions. If a scale is missing more than half of the items or questions, do not estimate. *Example*: If a person leaves one item in the five-item mental health scale blank, use the average score across the four completed items and re-average using all five items (the four completed items and the one averaged item).

A "depression screener" is included in the HSQ in the final three items, question numbers 37, 38, and 39. When the answer to question 37 is answered "yes," the patient may be at risk for major depression. When questions 38 and 39 are answered positively, the patient may be at risk for dysthymia. When the answers to all three questions are positive, the patient is at risk for major depression superimposed on dysthymia. Caution must be exercised when positive answers to these questions are received, as major depression and dysthymia can only be diagnosed through a professional psychological evaluation. However, it is the intent of the HSQ to alert the provider by identifying individuals at risk who would benefit from an appropriate referral.

Instruments such as the HSQ 2.0, SF-36, and RAND 36 have formats in which more than one item or question is factored into the final score of the scale. This results in

Text continues on page 344.

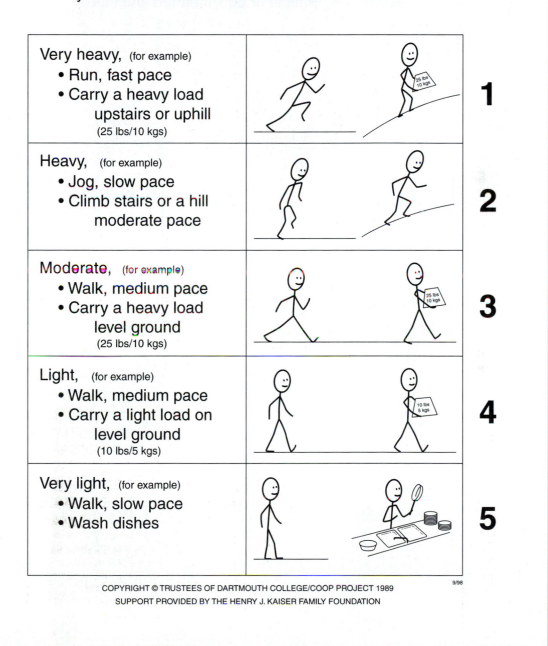

Figure 15–1. Physical Fitness component of the Dartmouth COOP Health Charts.

(Copyright © Trustees of Dartmouth College/COOP Project 1989. Support Provided by the Henry J. Kaiser Family Foundation.)

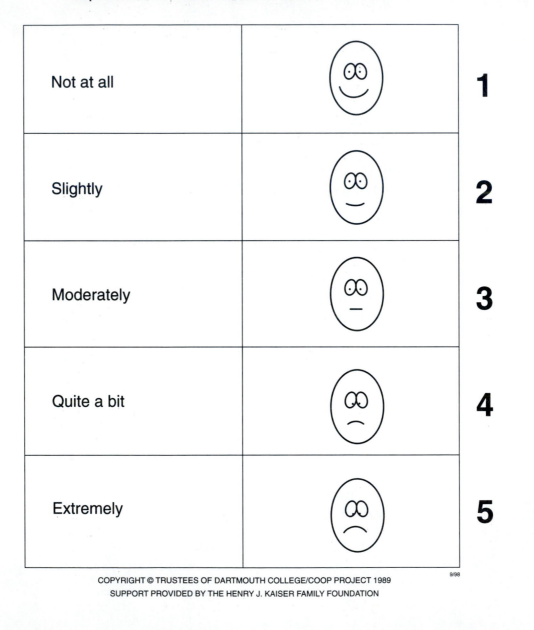

FEELINGS

During the past 4 weeks . . .
How much have you been bothered by
emotional problems such as feeling anxious,
depressed, irritable or downhearted and blue?

Not at all		**1**
Slightly		**2**
Moderately		**3**
Quite a bit		**4**
Extremely		**5**

9/98

Figure 15–2. Feelings component of the Dartmouth COOP Health Charts.

(Copyright © Trustees of Dartmouth College/COOP Project 1989. Support Provided by the Henry J. Kaiser Family Foundation.)

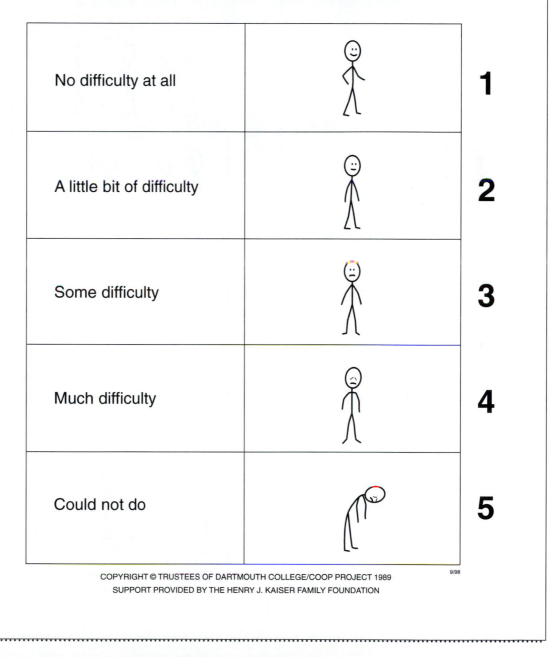

DAILY ACTIVITIES

During the past 4 weeks . . .
How much difficulty have you had doing your usual
activities or task, both inside and outside the house
because of your physical and emotional health?

No difficulty at all		1
A little bit of difficulty		2
Some difficulty		3
Much difficulty		4
Could not do		5

9/98

Figure 15–3. Daily Activities component of the Dartmouth COOP Health Charts.

(Copyright © Trustees of Dartmouth College/COOP Project 1989. Support Provided by the Henry J. Kaiser Family Foundation.)

SOCIAL ACTIVITIES

During the past 4 weeks . . .
Has your physical and emotional health limited
your social activities with family, friends,
neighbors or groups?

Not at all		**1**
Slightly		**2**
Moderately		**3**
Quite a bit		**4**
Extremely		**5**

9/98
COPYRIGHT © TRUSTEES OF DARTMOUTH COLLEGE/COOP PROJECT 1989
SUPPORT PROVIDED BY THE HENRY J. KAISER FAMILY FOUNDATION

Figure 15–4. Social Activities component of the Dartmouth COOP Health Charts.

(Copyright © Trustees of Dartmouth College/COOP Project 1989. Support Provided by the Henry J. Kaiser Family Foundation.)

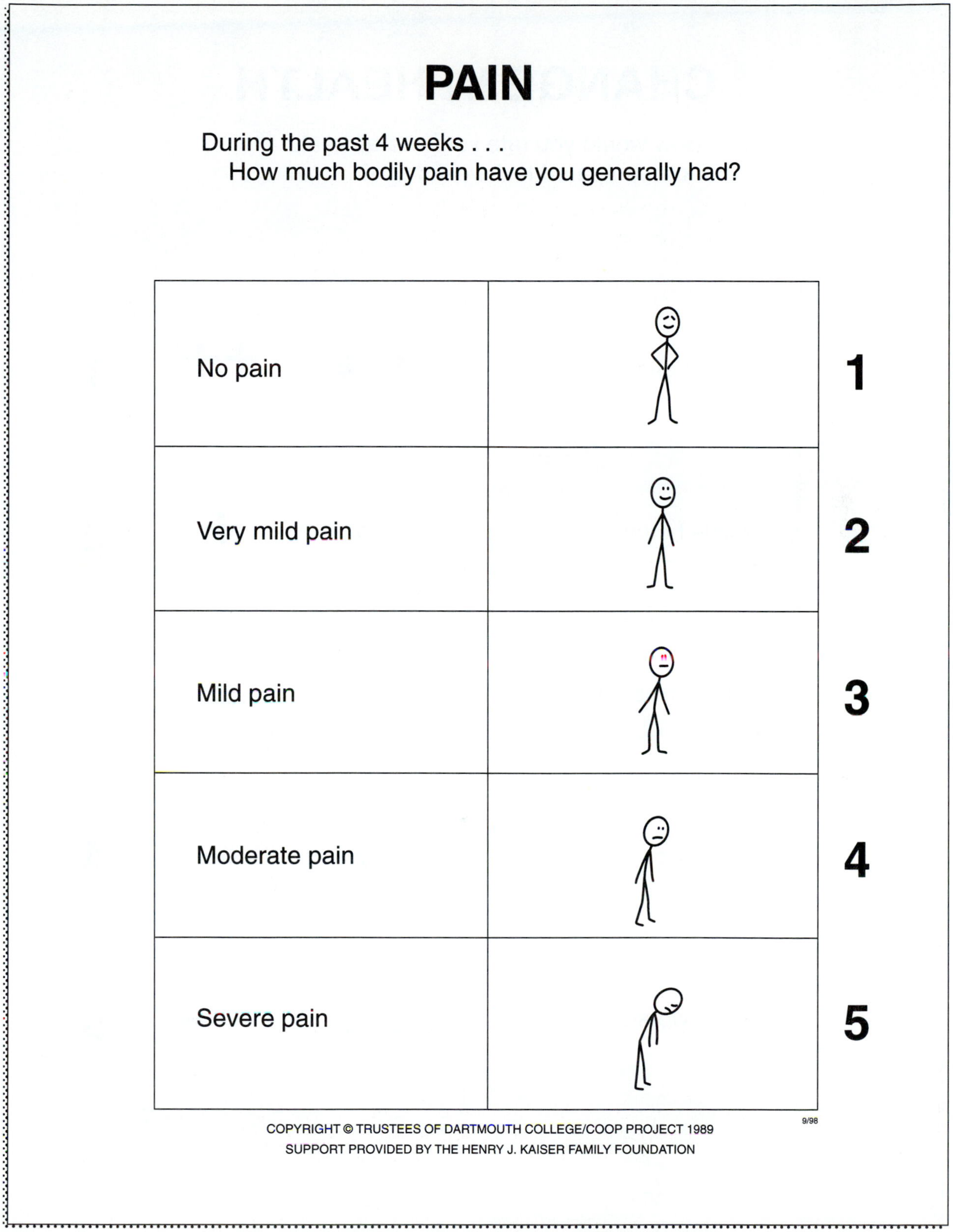

PAIN

During the past 4 weeks . . .
How much bodily pain have you generally had?

No pain		**1**
Very mild pain		**2**
Mild pain		**3**
Moderate pain		**4**
Severe pain		**5**

9/98

Figure 15–5. Pain component of the Dartmouth COOP Health Charts.

(Copyright © Trustees of Dartmouth College/COOP Project 1989. Support Provided by the Henry J. Kaiser Family Foundation.)

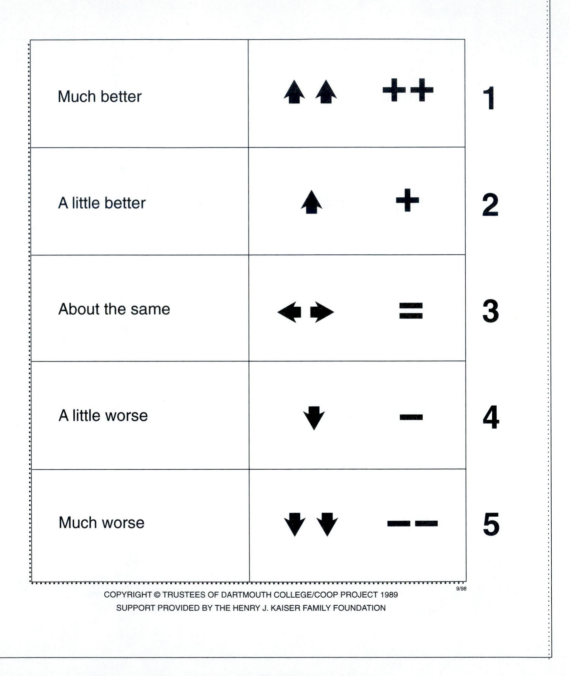

Figure 15–6. Change in Health component of the Dartmouth COOP Health Charts.

(Copyright © Trustees of Dartmouth College/COOP Project 1989. Support Provided by the Henry J. Kaiser Family Foundation.)

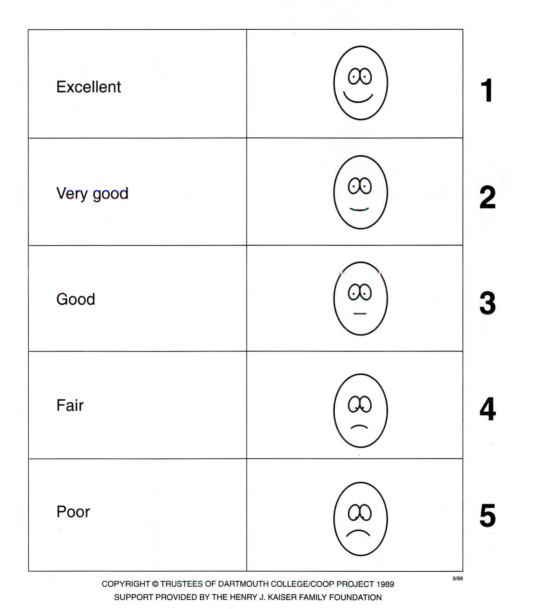

Figure 15–7. Overall Health component of the Dartmouth COOP Health Charts.

(Copyright © Trustees of Dartmouth College/COOP Project 1989. Support Provided by the Henry J. Kaiser Family Foundation.)

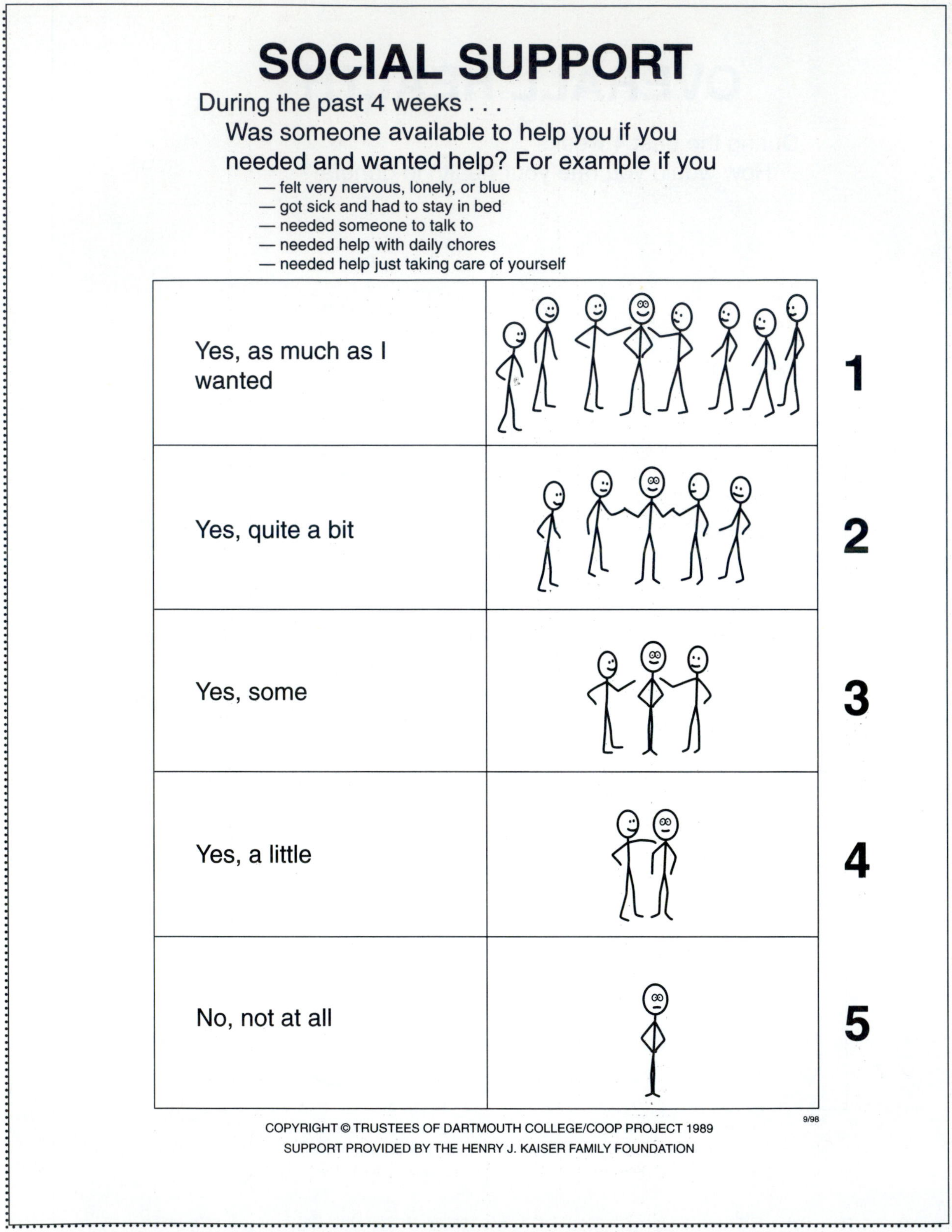
SOCIAL SUPPORT
During the past 4 weeks . . .
Was someone available to help you if you needed and wanted help? For example if you
— felt very nervous, lonely, or blue
— got sick and had to stay in bed
— needed someone to talk to
— needed help with daily chores
— needed help just taking care of yourself
Yes, as much as I wanted
1
Yes, quite a bit
2
Yes, some
3
Yes, a little
4
No, not at all
5
9/98
COPYRIGHT © TRUSTEES OF DARTMOUTH COLLEGE/COOP PROJECT 1989
SUPPORT PROVIDED BY THE HENRY J. KAISER FAMILY FOUNDATION

Figure 15–8. Social Support component of the Dartmouth COOP Health Charts.
(Copyright © Trustees of Dartmouth College/COOP Project 1989. Support Provided by the Henry J. Kaiser Family Foundation.)

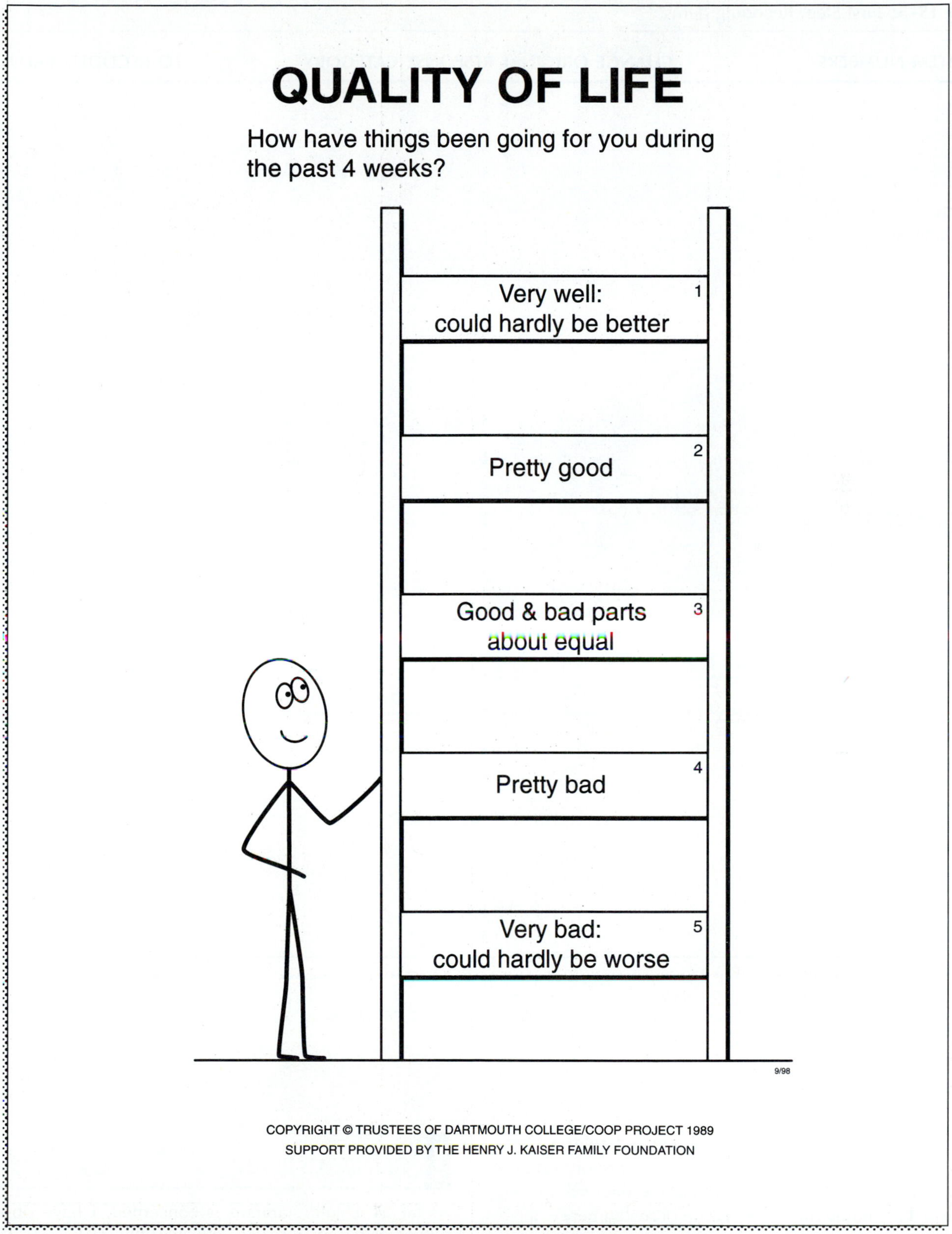

Figure 15–9. Quality of Life component of the Dartmouth COOP Health Charts.

(Copyright © Trustees of Dartmouth College/COOP Project 1989. Support Provided by the Henry J. Kaiser Family Foundation.)

Table 15–5: First Step: Recoding Items*

ITEM NUMBERS	CHANGE ORIGINAL RESPONSE CATEGORY[†]	TO RECODED VALUE OF
1	1	100
	2	85
	3	60
	4	25
	5	0
20, 22, 34, 36	1	100
	2	75
	3	50
	4	25
	5	0
3, 4, 5, 6, 7, 8, 9, 10, 11, 12	1	0
	2	50
	3	100
13, 14, 15, 16, 17, 18, 19	1	0
	2	100
21, 23, 26, 27, 30	1	100
	2	80
	3	60
	4	40
	5	20
	6	0
24, 25, 28, 29, 31	1	0
	2	20
	3	40
	4	60
	5	80
	6	100
32, 33, 35	1	0
	2	25
	3	50
	4	75
	5	100

*The first step in scoring this HSQ 2.0 is decoding the completed questionnaire by indicating the number of points per question answered by the patient.

[†]Precoded response choices as printed in the questionnaire. No recoding of items 2, 37, 38, 39 is necessary.

improved validity and reliability compared to the Dartmouth COOP charts, in which only one response determines the score. In addition, normative data have been published regarding the former group of scales; hence, a patient's results can be compared to the normative data in addition to his or her own follow-up score at a later date. However, issues of practicality and utility favor the Dartmouth COOP Health Charts, as they are quickly completed by the patient, easily scored by the health care provider, and meet the validity/reliability criteria previously discussed.[4]

 CLINICAL PEARL

As far as a gold standard is concerned, I have observed outcomes-based research utilizing the HSQ 2.0 (SF-36, RAND 36, etc.) more commonly than the Dartmouth COOP Health Charts.

Recently, the HSQ-12 and the SF-12 have been introduced. Reliability and validity criteria have been met but these instruments do not include all eight scales of the

Table 15–6: Second Step: Computing Scale Scores*

SCALE	NO. OF ITEMS	SCALE ITEMS	MINIMUM NO. OF ITEMS NEEDED TO COMPUTE A SCORE
Health Perception	5	1, 33, 34, 35, 36	3
Physical Functioning	10	3, 4, 5, 6, 7, 8, 9, 10, 11, 12	5
Role Limitations due to Physical Health	4	13, 14, 15, 16	2
Role Limitations due to Emotional Problems	3	17, 18, 19	2
Social Functioning	2	20, 32	1
Mental Health	5	24, 25, 26, 28, 30	3
Bodily Pain	2	21, 22	1
Energy/Fatigue	4	23, 27, 29, 31	2

*The scale, number of items, specific questions making up each scale, and minimum number of questions required to compute a score are listed.

36-item questionnaires.[43, 44] Regardless of the instrument utilized, the same tool must be used in follow-up in order to assess progress or change regarding quality of life issues. It has been my experience that an extra 5 to 10 minutes of time is needed for completion of the instrument. This, of course, varies and is dependent on patient compliance and educational level. In all cases, proper instruction by the staff person who provides the questionnaire to the patient is essential in helping the patient understand the importance of completing the instrument, thus minimizing both patient and support staff frustration.

CONDITION-SPECIFIC QUESTIONNAIRES

Unlike the many condition-specific outcome assessment questionnaires available for evaluating low back pain, few questionnaires are available for assessing patients who present with neck pain. In fact, the lack of an instrument specifically available to address the patient with activity intolerance due to a cervical spine complaint prompted Vernon and Mior to develop the *Neck Disability Index* (NDI).[17] More specifically, the authors, at the Canadian Memorial Chiropractic College, developed the NDI in a similar manner as the Oswestry Low Back Disability Questionnaire.[8, 45] In both of these instruments, there are ten categories of disabilities that are graded in terms of severity between 0 and 5. Totaling the points from each of the ten categories and doubling the number (so that the answer falls within a 0 to 100 scale) completes scoring. When less than ten categories are completed, the total number of categories completed *times* 5 is divided into the patient's total and multiplied by 100 (Table 15–9). The final score is then

Table 15–7: Third Step: Calculating Final Scores*

SCALE	NO. OF ITEMS	QUESTION NOS.	SCORES	AVERAGE
Health Perception	5	1, 33, 34, 35, 36	85 + 75 + 75 + 75 + 50 = 360/5	72
Physical Function	10	3–12	50 + 50 + 100 + 100 + 100 + 50 + 50 + 50 + 100 + 100 = 750/10	75
Role—Physical	4	13–16	100 + 100 + 0 + 100 = 300/4	75
Role—Emotional	3	17–19	100 + 100 + 0 = 200/3	7
Social Function	2	20, 32	75 + 100 = 175/2	88
Mental Health	5	24–26, 28, 30	80 + 100 + 80 + 100 + 80 = 440/5	88
Bodily Pain	2	21, 22	80 + 100 = 180/2	90
Energy/Fatigue	4	23, 27, 29, 31	80 + 80 + 100 + 80 = 340/4	85

*A final score for each of the eight scales is calculated by totaling the points for each question making up each scale and dividing by the number of questions (i.e., calculate the average).

FORMULA AND EXAMPLES

$$\frac{\text{Sum of Recoded Scale Items}}{\text{Number of Completed Scale Items}} = \text{Scale Score}$$

Example: Mental Health Scale calculation

Formula: $\dfrac{\text{HSQ24+HSQ25+HSQ26+HSQ28+HSQ30}}{5} = \text{Scale Score}$

Example: $\dfrac{80 + 100 + 80 + 80 + 80}{5} = 84$

Figure 15–10. The Mental Health Scale scoring is computed by adding the values for the recoded scale items and dividing by 5.

categorized into a chart to grade the level of disability. Reliability and validity have been established for the NDI.[12, 46] An interpretation or scale of the score is offered which can be used when initially assessing a patient as well as for future comparison at follow-up examinations.

! CLINICAL PEARL

It should be noted that, for consistency in scoring, when less than ten categories of the NDI are completed, the same categories that were omitted at the original examination should be omitted at future re-examinations.

Another condition-specific questionnaire that often helps to identify cervical spine dysfunction is the *Headache Disability Index* (see Table 15–10).[13] This instrument contains 25 questions, valued at a maximum of 4 points each (e.g., a maximum score of 100) for a "yes" response, an intermediate score of 2 for a "sometimes" response, or, lastly, 0 points for a "no" response. The response to each of the 25 questions determines the total score, but the total score

Table 15–8: Depression Risk Screener Interpretation*

	QUESTION NO.	RESPONSE (YES/NO)
At risk of major depression	37	YES
At risk of major dysthymia	38, 39	YES
At risk of both	37, 38, 39	YES

*These questions are not meant to result in a diagnosis but rather, are included to capture the risk factor of chronicity regarding depression.

can be broken down into "emotional" versus "functional" scores. Figure 15–11 describes the scoring methods.

! CLINICAL PEARL

The benefit of using a questionnaire such as the Headache Disability Index is that it provides *proof* to the third party payor, the patient, and the health care provider that the treatment being rendered is either of benefit to the patient or not. With this knowledge, the provider can then easily determine whether to follow the original clinical path if treatment benefit is supported by the questionnaire results, or to implement a change in the treatment protocol if no significant benefit is noted.

Another condition-specific questionnaire that may involve cervical spine dysfunction is the *Dizziness Handicap Inventory (DHI)* (Table 15–11).[14] This 25-item questionnaire was developed to evaluate the impact of vestibular system disease and dizziness on everyday life. The 25 questions are divided into three content domains that include functional, emotional, and physical aspects of dizziness and unsteadiness. Reliability and validity was demonstrated in a 106-subject study with good internal consistency and reliability. With the exception of the physical subscale, the mean values for the DHI scores increased significantly as dizziness episodes increased in frequency.[14] Test-retest reliability of the instrument was high. This questionnaire was modeled after the Hearing Handicap Inventory for the Elderly.[47] This questionnaire was also found to correlate with balance function tests, which included electronystagmography, rotational testing, and platform posturography.[48]

Recently, the Bournemouth Questionnaire (BQ), a short, multi-dimensional, self-report outcome measure has been validated for use in back pain patients.[48a] The BQ has been shown to be a valid, reliable and clinically responsive outcome measure for use in routine clinical practice. A neck pain version of the BQ is currently completing validation studies and the preliminary results appear promising (Humphreys BK, personal communication, 1999). The BQ contains 7 dimensions identified from the literature as being important in the investigation of patients with neck and back pain. Specifically, the BQ contains questions regarding patients' status for pain intensity, pain locus of control, physical disability, social and work interference, and anxiety and depression as registered on a 5-point numerical rating scale. It also documents patients' satisfaction with treatment and self-perceived global improvement. As the BQ is short and easy to fill out and score, it may be a useful outcome measure in the assessment, evaluation, and routine monitoring of neck and back pain patients in clinical practice.

Table 15–9: Scoring Technique for the Oswestry Low Back Disability Questionnaire and Neck Disability Index

1. Each of the ten sections is scored separately (0 to 5 points each) and then added up (max. total = 50).

Example:

Section 1. Pain Intensity	Point Value
A. _____ I have no pain at the moment	0
B. _____ The pain is very mild at the moment	1
C. _____ The pain is moderate at the moment	2
D. _____ The pain is fairly severe at the moment	3
E. _____ The pain is very severe at the moment	4
F. _____ The pain is the worst imaginable	5

2. If all ten sections are completed, simply double the patient's score.

3. If a section is omitted, divide the patient's total score by the number of sections completed times 5.

Formula: $\dfrac{\text{Patient's Score}}{\text{No. of Sections Completed} \times 5} \times 100 = \underline{\hspace{1cm}} \%$ Disability

Example:

If nine of ten sections are completed, divide the patient's score by $9 \times 5 = 45$; if

Patient's score:	22
Number of sections completed:	9(9 × 5 = 45)

$$22/45 \times 100 = 48\% \text{ disability}$$

4. Interpretation of disability scores (from original article):

SCORE	INTERPRETATION
0–20% Minimal Disability	Can cope with most ADLs. Usually no treatment needed, apart from advice on lifting, sitting, posture, physical fitness, and diet. In this group, some patients have particular difficulty with sitting and this may be important if their occupation is sedentary (typist, driver, etc.).
20–40% Moderate Disability	This group experiences more pain and problems with sitting, lifting, and standing. Travel and social life are more difficult and they may well be off work. Personal care, sexual activity and sleeping are not grossly affected, and the back condition can usually be managed by conservative means.
40–60% Severe Disability	Pain remains the main problem in this group of patients but travel, personal care, social life, sexual activity and sleep are also affected. These patients require detailed investigation.
60–80% Crippled	Back pain impinges on all aspects of these patients' lives, both at home and at work. *Positive intervention is required.*
80–100%	These patients are either bed-bound or exaggerating their symptoms. This can be evaluated by careful observation of the patient during the medical examination.

ADLs, activities of daily living.

From Fairbanks CT, Couper C, Davies JB, O'Brien JP. The Oswestry low back pain disability questionnaire. Physio Ther 1980;66:271–273.

Learning Resources
Centre

Scoring method for
Headache disability index

E = Emotionally based questions (#'s 1, 3, 5, 6, 8, 9, 10, 11, 12, 14, 20, 22, 23)
13 questions total

F = Functionally based questions (#'s 2, 4, 7, 13, 15, 16, 17, 18, 19, 21, 24, 25)
12 questions total

Score values

"YES" =   4 POINTS
"SOMETIMES" =   2 POINTS
"NO" =   0 POINTS

Final scores

Emotional = total sum of the scores for the "E" questions / total possible score (13 × 4 = 52) or,
Patients Score ("E" questions) / 52 ×100 = % total score (represented by emotionally based responses)

Functional = total sum of the scores for the "F" questions / total possible score (12 × 4 = 48) or,
Patients Score (F questions) / 48 ×100 = % total score (represented by functionally based responses)

Figure 15–11. Scoring method for the Headache Disability Index. Scoring can be reported on three scales—a 100-point total score, which is made up of 52 points from emotionally based questions, and 48 points from functionally based questions. Hence, since 100 points make up the total score, if the entire questionnaire is completed, the percent of emotional versus functional components can easily be compared.

OUTCOMES DERIVED
FROM OBJECTIVE MEASURES

Thus far, this discussion has been limited to the use of subjective instruments or questionnaires. The use of objective measures has traditionally been viewed as being more important than subjective data. However, reports have supported a higher sensitivity and specificity (reliability) regarding the use of pencil-and-paper questionnaire approaches when compared to many of the objective forms of evaluation.[49]

When applying OA principles utilizing objective data, the same rules apply as those discussed previously regarding the gathering of subjective outcomes data. Thus, when gathering data from an examination, it is important to document in a manner that will allow for future comparison in a quantitative manner. Failure to do so may result in premature claim closure due to lack of documented evidence of therapeutic benefit. "Hard" versus "soft" data is favored because it can serve as an OA item rather than simply a qualitative item. For example, when assessing nerve root impingement, an orthopedic test called the maximum cervical rotatory compression test is often utilized. Documentation of the results of this test are commonly reported as positive or negative, depending on the reproduction of pain with an emphasis on radiating pain into the upper extremity. However, if only a positive or negative result is documented, there is insufficient information to compare results to a follow-up examination performed at a later date. Hence, this level of documentation can be considered "soft" since the intensity, frequency, du-

Table 15–10: Headache Disability Index*

Name: _____ Date: _____ Age: _____ Scores Total: _____; E _____; F _____
                                                                                        (100)   (52)   (48)

Instructions: Please *circle* the correct response:

1. I have headache: [1] 1 per month [2] more than 1 but less than 4 per month [3] more than one per week
2. My headache is: [1] mild [2] moderate [3] severe

Instructions (Please read carefully): The purpose of the scale is to identify difficulties that you may be experiencing because of your headache. Please check off "Yes," "Sometimes," or "No" to each item. Answer each question as it pertains to your headache only.

	YES	SOMETIMES	NO
E1. Because of my headaches I feel handicapped.	☐	☐	☐
F2. Because of my headaches I feel restricted in performing my routine daily activities.	☐	☐	☐
E3. No one understands the effect my headaches have on my life.	☐	☐	☐
F4. I restrict my recreational activities (e.g., sports, hobbies) because of my headaches.	☐	☐	☐
E5. My headaches make me angry.	☐	☐	☐
E6. Sometimes I feel that I am going to lose control because of my headaches.	☐	☐	☐
F7. Because of my headaches I am less likely to socialize.	☐	☐	☐
E8. My spouse (significant other), or family and friends have no idea what I am going through because of my headaches.	☐	☐	☐
E9. My headaches are so bad that I feel I am going to go insane.	☐	☐	☐
E10. My outlook on the world is affected by my headaches.	☐	☐	☐
E11. I am afraid to go outside when I feel that a headache is starting.	☐	☐	☐
E12. I feel desperate because of my headaches.	☐	☐	☐
F13. I am concerned that I am paying penalties at work or at home because of my headaches.	☐	☐	☐
E14. My headaches place stress on my relationships with family or friends.	☐	☐	☐
F15. I avoid being around people when I have a headache.	☐	☐	☐
F16. I believe my headaches are making it difficult for me to achieve my goals in life.	☐	☐	☐
F17. I am unable to think clearly because of my headaches.	☐	☐	☐
F18. I get tense (e.g., muscle tension) because of my headaches.	☐	☐	☐
F19. I do not enjoy social gatherings because of my headaches.	☐	☐	☐
E20. I feel irritable because of my headaches.	☐	☐	☐
F21. I avoid traveling because of my headaches.	☐	☐	☐
E22. My headaches make me feel confused.	☐	☐	☐
E23. My headaches make me feel frustrated.	☐	☐	☐
F24. I find it difficult to read because of my headaches.	☐	☐	☐
F25. I find it difficult to focus my attention away from my headaches and on other things.	☐	☐	☐

*Tracking the headache patient can be difficult at best. This questionnaire allows for the assessment of the headache patient in a quantitative manner. The questionnaire should be administered at baseline or day 1 and at 4 weeks or discharge in order to track outcomes.

From Jacobson GP, Ramadan NM, et al. The Henry Ford Hospital headache disability inventory (HDI). Neurology 1994;44:837–842.

ration, and location of pain were not documented initially. More specifically, if the initial documentation included information such as "8/10 pain extended into the upper extremity to digits 4 and 5 within three seconds," future examination findings could be compared to this initial data if similar testing and documentation methods were utilized at the time of re-examination. The latter is an example of "hard" data; outcomes can be assessed at a later date because quantitative information was gathered rather than qualitative information only. Table 15–12 offers various examples of "hard" versus "soft" objective or physical examination data.

Several studies have been conducted to try to determine the reliability of various physical signs. One such

Table 15–11: Dizziness Handicap Inventory*

Name: _____ Date: _____ Age: _____ Score Totals: _____; E _____; F _____; P _____
(100)   (36)   (36)   (28)

Instructions: Please *circle* the correct response:

1. I have dizziness/unsteadiness: [1] 1 per month [2] >1 but < 4 per month [3] more than one per week
2. My dizziness/unsteadiness is: [1] mild   [2] moderate   [3] severe

Instructions (Please read carefully): The purpose of the scale is to identify difficulties that you may be experiencing because of your dizziness or unsteadiness. Please answer "Yes," "Sometimes," or "No" to each question. Answer each question as it pertains to your dizziness or unsteadiness problem only.

	YES	SOMETIMES	NO
P1. Does looking up increase your problem?	☐	☐	☐
E2. Because of your problem, do you feel frustrated?	☐	☐	☐
F3. Because of your problem, do you restrict your travel for business or recreation?	☐	☐	☐
P4. Does walking down the aisle of a supermarket increase your problem?	☐	☐	☐
F5. Because of your problem, do you have difficulty getting into or out of bed?	☐	☐	☐
F6. Does your problem significantly restrict your participation in social activities such as going out to dinner, going to movies, dancing, or to parties?	☐	☐	☐
F7. Because of your problem, do you have difficulty reading?	☐	☐	☐
P8. Does performing more ambitious activities like sports, dancing, household chores such as sweeping or putting dishes away increase your problem?	☐	☐	☐
E9. Because of your problem, are you afraid to leave your home without someone accompanying you?	☐	☐	☐
E10. Because of your problem, have you been embarrassed in front of others?	☐	☐	☐
P11. Do quick movements of your head increase your problem?	☐	☐	☐
F12. Because of your problem, do you avoid heights?	☐	☐	☐
P13. Does turning over in bed increase your problem?	☐	☐	☐
F14. Because of your problem, is it difficult for you to do strenuous house work or yard work?	☐	☐	☐
E15. Because of your problem, are you afraid people may think you are intoxicated?	☐	☐	☐
F16. Because of your problem, is it difficult for you to go for a walk by yourself?	☐	☐	☐
P17. Does walking down a sidewalk increase your problem?	☐	☐	☐
E18. Because of your problem, is it difficult for you to concentrate?	☐	☐	☐
F19. Because of your problem, is it difficult for you to walk around your house in the dark?	☐	☐	☐
E20. Because of your problem, are you afraid to stay home alone?	☐	☐	☐
E21. Because of your problem, do you feel handicapped?	☐	☐	☐
E22. Has your problem placed stress on your relationships with members of your family or friends?	☐	☐	☐
E23. Because of your problem, are you depressed?	☐	☐	☐
F24. Does your problem interfere with your job or household responsibilities?	☐	☐	☐
P25. Does bending over increase your problem?	☐	☐	☐

*This instrument captures three content domains, consisting of functional, emotional, and physical aspects of dizziness and unsteadiness. A total of 100 points (derived from 36% emotionally based, 36% functionally based, and 28% physically based questions) allows the provider to track progress over time, hence, assessing outcomes.

From Jacobson GP, Newman CW. The development of the dizziness handicap inventory. Arch Otolaryngol Head Neck Surg 1990;116:424–427.

Table 15–12: Examples of Hard versus Soft Physical Examination Data

TEST	"SOFT" RESPONSE	"HARD" RESPONSE
Maximum cervical rotatory compression test	Positive or "+" Negative or "−"	8/10 pain extending to left digits 4 and 5 after 3 seconds
Cervical distraction test	Positive or "+" Negative or "−"	Pain decreased from 8/10 to 2/10 and centralized within 2 seconds
Cervical palpation	Positive or "+" Negative or "−"	10/10 pain at C2 radiating to the vertex of the calvarium
Thoracic outlet test (Wright's test)	Positive or "+" Negative or "−"	Loss of the radial pulse with numbness to digits 4/5 occurred within 5 seconds
Vertebral-basilar insufficiency test	Positive or "+" Negative or "−"	Dizziness and nausea occurred within 7 seconds with maximum C-rotation / extension
Muscle testing of the upper extremities	"Weak"	A 4/5 or "good" muscle grade weakness of triceps and finger extensors
Sensory examination	Positive or "+" Negative or "−"	Partial sensory loss, hypothenar left hand (8 mm 2-point discrimination)
Cervical ROM	All decreased	Flexion 44° with decreased C and UE pain Extension 54° 3/4 pain to digits 4/5

C, cervical; ROM, range of motion; UE, upper extremity.

study, regarding low back pain, was conducted by McCombe et al.[50] The physical signs or tests studied were divided into three categories described as "most reliable," "potentially reliable," and "poor reliability." Eight tests were studied: pain pattern, posture, movement, tenderness, sacroiliac and piriformis tests, root tension signs, root compression signs, and inappropriate signs. Table 15–13 illustrates the results of this study. The authors drew the following conclusions:

Pain pattern—the more distal, the more agreement. Disagreement occurred when differentiating back

Table 15–13: Three Categories of Reliability When Comparing Various Physical Signs

TEST	MOST RELIABLE	POTENTIALLY RELIABLE	POOR RELIABILITY
Pain pattern	Thigh, leg	Buttock, foot pain	Back
Posture	Measure lordosis (cm)	NA	Spinal list measure (cm)
Movement	Flexion (Schoeber); pain on flexion; Lateral bend	Extension, rotation	Extension "catch"; lateral bend (cm)
Tenderness	NA	SI, iliac crest, midline	Paravertebral, buttock
SI and piriformis	Hip flexion (y/n)	Pain with ER	Maitland's test; SI compression; SI distraction
Root tension signs	SLR (onset and maximum)	Crossed SLR, SLR sciatic stretch test; SLR reproduces symptoms	NA
Root compression signs	Leg numbness (y/n)	Atrophy and weakness of the quadriceps femoris, calf, tibialis anterior, peroneus longus and brevis, knee extensor; Achilles DTR	Heel/toe strength, buttock atrophy, Patellar DTR
Inappropriate signs	NA	Distraction, simulation, over-reaction	Tenderness, regional motor/sensory disturbance

DTR, deep tendon reflex; ER, external rotation; n, no; NA, not available; SI, sacroiliac; SLR, straight leg raise; y, yes.
Based on data in McCombe PF et al. Reproducibility of physical signs in low back pain. Spine 1989;14:908–918.

from buttock pain and illustrates the importance for careful pain localization.

Tenderness—The most unreliable signs were paravertebral and buttock (soft tissue tenderness) while bony tenderness was "potentially reliable" or "reliable."

Root tension signs—Straight leg raise and femoral stretch were more reliable than bowstring in general. Specifically, the bowstring test for leg pain and the femoral stretch for low back pain were the most reliable for these two tests.

Root compression signs—There was good agreement between results when two surgeons performed the tests but not when a surgeon and a physical therapist performed the tests. This may reflect differences in training. Caution is therefore needed regarding reliability of test results when different types of providers perform these tests.

Inappropriate signs (Waddell's nonorganic signs[51])—No clear pattern emerged. The two unreliable signs (superficial tenderness and abnormal regional sensory or motor disturbance) appear to require more subjective judgment than pain with simulation or distraction. (Note that this finding conflicts with Korbon et al,[52] who found sensory, motor, tenderness, and straight leg raise distraction test or "flip sign" to be *most* reliable.)

Unfortunately, there is no similar study of physical signs relating to the cervical spine. However, several individual studies have reported validity and reliability in physical measures, including inclinometric mensurated cervical range of motion,[53] cervical spine strength,[54–58] forward head posture and weakness of the upper cervical flexor musculature in association with cervical headaches,[59] electromyogram-based instrumentation studies,[60–63] and cervicothoracic kyphosis and cervical inclination measurements in pain versus nonpainful subjects.[64] In addition, the validity of five common manual neck pain provocative tests were studied, as follows: (1) active rotation of the neck and upper thoracic spine with a passive manual stretch at the extreme position of ipsilateral rotation; (2) active flexion and extension of the neck and upper thoracic spine; (3) foraminal compression test; (4) the upper limb tension test (combination of a shoulder depression test and costoclavicular test); and (5) palpation of the cervical spine facet joints.[65] The results of this study revealed validity when comparing pain provocation in 75 randomly selected men out of a population of 3,144 electricians from Stockholm, Sweden (22 or 29%, with neck pain and dysfunction and 53 or 71%, without neck pain for at least 1 year) with tests 3, 4, and 5. The first test reproduced pain only in two of the neck pain subjects (sensitivity and specificity could not be measured) and the sensitivity was low in the second (27%) compared to tests 3 through 5 (77%, 77%, and 82%, respectively). Similarly, the specificity was 92%, 94%, and 79% for tests 3 through 5, respectively. The authors concluded that palpation over the facet joints was the most appropriate test of the five to use in epidemiological investigations because tests 3 and 4 were designed to provoke nerve root signs but only localized neck pain was provoked in this study. They did, however, admit that the small study population and absence of nerve root impingement were probably the reasons for the findings. They concluded that tests 3 and 4 (the nerve root tests) provoked localized pain due to the extreme positions of the neck and upper trunk by stretching the ligaments and muscles of the cervical spine and upper part of the back, neck, and shoulders. Since tests 3 and 4 did not provoke nerve tension signs in any of the subjects, they drew the conclusion that test 5 was the best as it did what it was designed to do (i.e., provoke localized pain).

This conclusion raises a very important issue when documentation (the patient's chart) lacks an explanation of the results of the provocative test. More specifically, a provocative pain response is important, although it may not be the defined response described in the literature, even when a test is "negative" according to its intended definition. Another example is that of a patient with localized pain in the cervical spine that increases during a cervical distraction (manual traction) test. A "positive" response is defined as reduction in neck or arm pain, or both. But if pain increases (not the intention of the test) it is *not* appropriate to describe the test as positive. This forces the health care provider to describe the test as negative. Many of these tests are "prescriptive," that is, a specific treatment approach is driven from the response to the test (e.g., cervical traction is indicated when neck or arm pain, or both, reduces during a cervical distraction test but is contraindicated when pain increases). It becomes obvious, then, as to why a description of the test response is preferred over a simple "soft" positive or negative form of reporting.

Soft tissue tenderness can be measured by *algometry* or a *rheumatology rating scale*[66] (grade 0 to IV) (Table 15–14). Severe pain intensity has been considered by some as pain greater than 6/10.[67] The measurement of physical capacity (isolated function of muscles or joints, or both) using inexpensive, low-tech approaches has also been reported.[68–70]

Table 15–14: Scheme for Grading a Patient's Response to Pain

GRADE	DEFINITION
I	Mild tenderness to moderate palpation
II	Moderate tenderness with grimace or flinch to moderate palpation, or both
III	Severe tenderness with withdrawal (+ "jump sign")
IV	Severe tenderness with withdrawal (+ jump sign) to non-noxious stimuli (i.e., superficial palpation, pinprick, gentle percussion)*

*In noninjured tissue, this is a sign of neuropathic pain.

These tests, in essence, evaluate impairment or dysfunction. For example, *range of motion, strength,* and *endurance* can all be tested. Alaranta et al[68] showed that low-tech tests are reliable and valid. Normative data has also been published on simple, inexpensive, squatting, trunk flexion, and trunk extension tests.[68]

Many other qualitative tests have prescriptive importance but have not been studied with reference to the criteria previously discussed, especially validity and reliability. Though these tests are important, as they help guide the health care provider in treatment, they are not quantitative and, hence, do not facilitate measuring outcomes. I recommend attempting to "quantify" any provocative or functional test, even though it may not be described in existing literature in that manner. More specifically, the use of a stopwatch to measure the loss of function or the onset of pain, or both, allows for future comparison (i.e., measures outcomes). For example, when performing the cervical flexion test, a stopwatch can be utilized to document the time at which the supine, head-flexed patient's chin protracts forward or the head drops downward.[71] Similarly, the shoulder abduction test, designed to offer the health care provider important information regarding the coordination of scapulo-humeral rhythm, can be measured using a standard goniometer. More specifically, as the elbow-flexed patient abducts the shoulder, the measurement is taken at the point where the shoulder shrugs upward (point of scapulo-humeral elevation). This is then compared to normative data that indicates that scapulo-humeral elevation should not occur prior to approximately 60 degrees.[72] These two examples illustrate how a previously qualitative test can be turned into a quantitative outcomes-oriented test. Techniques such as these allow for mensuration and, hence, quantification of otherwise qualitative tests. The provider should refer to other tests described elsewhere in this text and try to apply a quantitative approach whenever possible.

Of course, until validity and reliability issues are studied, the improvised methods of mensuration may be challenged. If, however, the measurement techniques appear to be useful clinically and "make sense," one can certainly argue that they have face or content validity.[73] Furthermore, if one finds the measuring method sensitive to detecting change over time (assessing outcomes), the responsiveness of the technique can be argued. Moreover, if we were to exclude all tests that have not been studied by randomized, double-blinded methods, we would not be able to provide ideas for future study with examination methods or concepts that may prove valid and reliable in future literature. Most importantly, not being able to improvise with techniques would remove the creativity or "art," which is the heart and soul of diagnosis and treatment.

CONCLUSION

With a little training, OM, especially when combining subjective and objective methods, can contribute greatly to the musculoskeletal practice. Improved goal setting, patient motivation, determination of the endpoints of care, data collection, medico-legal protection, and quality chart documentation are all clear benefits. The instruments mentioned in this chapter are included for ease of use. Software available to process the outcomes data generated from the various outcome assessment tools was also included in the chapter.

OM is here to stay. Instead of relying on unreliable, nonvalidated assessments of a patient's status and progress, which are of questionable value in an optimally managed practice, it is now feasible to modernize one's practice with little to no additional expense. As evidenced by managed care, OM will continue to become streamlined and will offer the health care provider the ability to compare patient data for epidemiological study, clinical research, and to determine the value of rendered health care. Instead of waiting and being forced to implement OM methods, providers can use the information included in this chapter to "jump start" the implementation of gathering outcome data in their practice today.

REFERENCES

1. Mayer TG, Polatin P, Smith B, et al. Contemporary concepts in spine care: Spine rehabilitation—secondary and tertiary nonoperative care. *Spine* 1995;20(18):2060–2066.
2. Frymoyer JW. Quality: An international challenge to the diagnosis and treatment of disorders of the lumbar spine. *Spine* 1993;18:2147–2152.
3. Hazard RG. Spine update functional restoration. *Spine* 1995;20(21):2345–2348.
4. Deyo R, Diehr P, et al. Reproducibility and responsiveness of health status measures, controlled clinical trials. *Spine* 1991;12:142S.
5. Huskisson EC. Measurement of pain. *Lancet* 1974;2:127.
6. Downie WW, Leatham PA, Rhind VA, et al. Studies with pain rating scales. *Anal Rheum Dis* 1978;37:378–381.
7. Melzak R. The McGill pain questionnaire: Major properties and scoring methods. *Pain* 1975;1:277–291.

8. Fairbank J, Davies J, et al. The Oswestry Low Back Pain Disability Questionnaire. *Physiotherapy* 1980;66(18):271–273.

9. Roland M, Morris R. A study of the natural history of low back pain, part II. *Spine* 1983;8(2):141–144.

10. Lawlis GF, Cuencas R, Selby D, McCoy CE. The development of the Dallas pain questionnaire: An assessment of the impact of spinal pain on behavior. *Spine* 1989;14:511–516.

11. Deyo RA, Cherkin DC, Franklin G, Nichols JC. Low back pain (forms 6.1 to 6.4), 10-12-92. Bloomington, MN: Health Outcomes Institute.

12. Vernon H, Mior S. The Neck Disability Index: A study of reliability and validity. *J Manipulative Physiol Ther* 1991;14(7):409.

13. Jacobson GP, Ramadan NM, et al. The Henry Ford Hospital headache disability inventory (HDI). *Neurology* 1994;44:837–842.

14. Jacobson GP, Newman CW. The development of the dizziness handicap inventory. *Arch Otolaryngol Head Neck Surg* 1990;116:424–427.

15. McHorney CA, Ware J, Rogers W, Raczek A, Lu JF. The validity and relative precision of MOS short- and long-form health status scales and Dartmouth COOP charts. *Med Care* 1992;30:MS253–MS265.

16. Kraus N. The Dartmouth Primary Care Cooperative ("COOP") Information Project. *Interstudy Qual Edge* 1991;1:33–39.

17. Health Outcomes Institute, Bloomington, MN (designed: 4-1-93).

18. Brazier J, Harper R, Jones SN. Validating the SF-36 Health survey questionnaire: New outcome measure for primary care. *Br Med J* 1992;305:160–164.

19. Goertz CMH. Measuring functional health status in the chiropractic office using self-report questionnaires. *Top Clin Chiro* 1994;1(1):51–59.

20. Albert TJ, Mesa JJ, Eng K, McIntosh TC, Balderston RA. Health outcome assessment before and after lumbar laminectomy for radiculopathy. *Spine* 1996;21:960–963.

21. Waddell G, McCulloch JA, Kummel E, Venner RM. Nonorganic physical signs in low-back pain. *Spine* 1980;5:117–125.

22. Zung WWK. A self-rating depression scale. *Arch Gen Psychiatry* 1965;32:63–70.

23. Main CJ. Modified Somatic Perception Questionnaire. *J Psychosom Res* 1983;27:503–514.

24. Bernstein IH, Jaremko ME, Hinkley BS. On the utility of the SCL-90-R with low-back pain patients. *Spine* 1994;19:42–48.

25. Beck A. *Depression: Clinical, Experimental and Theoretical Aspects.* New York, NY: Harper and Row; 1967.

26. Coulter ID, Hays RD, Danielson CD. The chiropractic satisfaction questionnaire. *Top Clin Chiro* 1994;1(4):40–43.

27. Cherkin D, MacCormack F. Patient evaluations of low-back pain care from family physicians and chiropractors. *Western J Med* 1989;150:351.

28. Yeomans S (ed). *The Clinical Application of Outcomes Assessment.* Stamford, Conn: Appleton and Lange; 1999, in press.

29. Keele KD. The pain chart. *Lancet* 1948;2:6.

30. Ransford HV, Cairns D, Mooney V. The pain drawing as an aid to psychological evaluation of patients with low back pain. *Spine* 1976;1:127.

31. Margolis RB, Tait RC, Krause SJ. Rating system for use with patient pain drawings. *Pain* 1986;24:57.

32. Margolis RB, Chibnall JT, Tait RC. Test-retest reliability of the pain drawing instrument. *Pain* 1988;33:49.

33. Tait RC, Chibnall JT, Margolis RB. Pain extent: Relations with psychological state, pain severity, pain history and disability. *Pain* 1990;41:295.

34. Uben A, Hstrom M, Bergenudd H. Pain drawings in chronic back pain. *Spine* 1988;13:389.

35. Vernon H. Pain and disability questionnaires in chiropractic rehabilitation. In: Liebenson C, ed. *Rehabilitation of the Spine: A Practitioner's Manual.* Philadelphia, Pa: Williams and Wilkins; 1996:61.

36. Ohlund C, Eek C, Palmblad S, Areskoug B, Nachemson A. Quantified pain drawing in subacute low back pain: Validation in a nonselected outpatient industrial sample. *Spine* 1996;21:1021–1031.

37. Bryner P. Pain drawing analysis: A review. *Chiro J Aust* 1993;23:86–91.

38. Von Korff M, Ormel J, Keefe F, Dworkin SF. Grading the severity of chronic pain. *Pain* 1992;50:133–149.

39. McDowell I, Newell C. *Measuring Health: A Guide to Rating Scales and Questionnaires.* New York, NY: Oxford University Press, 1987.

40. Bolton J, Wilkinson RC. Responsiveness of pain scales: A comparison of three pain intensity measures in chiropractic patients. *J Manipulative Physiol Ther* 1998;21:1–7.

41. Bass MJ. Assessing functional status in family practice. *Fam Med* 1992;24:134–135.

42. Nelson EC, Langraf J, Hays R, Wasson J, Kirk J. The functional status of patients: How can it be measured in physician offices? *Med Care* 1990;28:111–126.

43. Ware JE, Kosinski M, Keller SD. A 12-item short-form health survey (SF-12): construction of scales and preliminary tests of reliability and validity. *Med Care* 1996;32:220–223.

44. Ware JE, Kosinski M, Keller SD. *How to Score the SF-12 Physical and Mental Health Summary Scales.* 2nd ed. Boston, Mass: The Health Institute, New England Medical Center, December 1995.

45. Hudson-Cook N, Tomes-Nicholson K. *The Revised Oswestry Low Back Pain Disability Questionnaire.* Bournemouth, England: Anglo-European College of Chiropractic; 1988. Thesis.

46. Vernon H. Pain and disability questionnaires in chiropractic rehabilitation. In: Liebenson C, ed. *Rehabilitation of the Spine: A Practitioner's Manual.* Philadelphia, Pa: Williams and Wilkins; 1996:65.

47. Ventry I, Weinstein B. The hearing handicap inventory for the elderly: A new tool. *Ear Hear* 1982;3:128–134.

48. Jacobson GP, Newman CW, Hunter L, Balzer GK. Balance function test correlates of the dizziness handicap inventory. *J Am Acad Audiol* 1991;2:253–260.

48a. Bolton JE, Breen AC. Bournemouth questionnaire: A short form comprehensive outcome measure. I. psychometric properties in back pain patients. *J Manipulative Physiol Ther* 1999, accepted for publication.

49. Chapman-Smith D. Measuring results—the new importance of patient questionnaires. *Chiro Report* 1992;7(1):1–6.

50. McCombe PF, Fairbank CT, Cockersole BC, Pynsent PB. Reproducibility of physical signs in low-back pain. *Spine* 1989;14:908–918.

51. Waddell G, McCulloch JA, Kimmel E, Venner RM. Nonorganic physical signs in low back pain. *Spine* 1980;5:117–125.

52. Korbon GA, DeGood E, Schroeder ME, et al. The development of a somatic amplification rating scale for low-back pain. *Spine* 1987;12(8):787–791.

53. Mayer T, Gatchel RJ, Keeley J, Mayer H, Richling D. A male incumbent worker industrial database. *Spine* 1994;19:762–764.

54. Vernon HT, Aker P, Aramenko M, Battershill D, Alepin A, Penner T. Evaluation of neck strength with a modified sphygmomanometer dynamometer: Reliability and validity. *J Manipulative Physiol Ther* 1992;15:343–349.

55. Bohannon RW. Test-retest reliability of hand-held dynamometry during single session of strength assessment. *Phys Ther* 1986;66:206–209.

56. Hyde SA, Scott OM, Goddard CM. Myometer: Development of a clinical tool. *Physiotherapy* 1983;69:424–427.

57. Edwards RHT, McDonnell M. Hand-held dynamometer for evaluating voluntary muscle function. *Lancet* 1974;2:757–758.

58. Agre JC, Magness JL, Hull SZ, et al. Strength testing with a portable dynamometer: Reliability for upper and lower extremities. *Arch Phys Med Rehabil* 1987;68:454–458.

59. Watson DH, Trott PH. Cervical headache: an investigation of natural head posture and upper cervical flexor muscle performance. *Cephalgia* 1993;13:272–284.

60. Kenny WR III. Development and comparison of electrical strain dynamometer and cable tensiometer for objective muscle testing. *Arch Phys Med Rehabil* 1965;46:793–803.

61. Schuldt K, Harms-Ringdahl K. EMG/moment relationships in neck muscles during isometric cervical spine extension. *Clin Biomech* 1988;3:58–65.

62. Harms-Ringdahl K, Ekholm J, Schuldt K, Nemeth G, Arborelius UP. Load moments and myoelectric activity when the cervical spine is held in full flexion and extension. *Clin Biomech* 1988;3:129–136.

63. Schuldt K, Harms-Ringdahl K. Cervical spine position vs. e.m.g. activity in neck muscles during maximum isometric neck extension. *Clin Biomech* 1988;3:129–136.

64. Refshauge K, Goodsell M, Lee M. Consistency of cervical and cervicothoracic posture in standing. *Aust J Physiother* 1994;40:235–240.

65. Sandmark H, Nisell R. Validity of five common manual neck pain provoking tests. *Scand J Rehab Med* 1995;27:131–136.

66. Wolfe F, Smythe HA, Yunus MB, et al. The American College of Rheumatology 1990 criteria for the classification of fibromyalgia. *Arthritis Rheum* 1990;33:160–172.

67. Von Korff M, Ormel J, Keefe F, Dworkin SF. Grading the severity of chronic pain. *Pain* 1992;50:133–149.

68. Alaranta H, Hurri H, Heliovaara M, Soukka A, Harju R. Non-dynametric trunk performance tests: Reliability and normative database. *Scand J Rehab Med* 1994;26:211–215.

69. Yeomans SG, Liebenson C. Quantitative functional capacity evaluation: The missing link to outcomes assessment. *Top Clin Chiro* 1996;3(1):32–43.
70. Rissanen A, Alaranta H, Sainio P, Harkonen H. Isokinetic and non-dynametric tests in low back pain patients related to pain and disability index. *Spine* 1994;19:1963–1967.
71. Janda V. Evaluation of muscular imbalance. In: Liebenson C, ed. *Rehabilitation of the Spine: A Practitioner's Manual.* Philadelphia, Pa: Williams and Wilkins; 1996:102,106.
72. Janda V. Evaluation of muscular imbalance. In: Liebenson C, ed. *Rehabilitation of the Spine: A Practitioner's Manual.* Philadelphia, Pa: Williams and Wilkins; 1996:102,107.
73. Vernon H. Pain and disability questionnaires in chiropractic rehabilitation. In: Liebenson C, ed. *Rehabilitation of the Spine: A Practitioner's Manual.* Philadelphia, Pa: Williams and Wilkins; 1996:60.

CHAPTER 16

Diagnostic Imaging
of the Cervical Spine

Beverly L. Harger & Lisa E. Hoffman

"To affect the quality of the day, that is the highest of arts."

—Henry David Thoreau

INTRODUCTION

Several abnormalities affecting the cervical spine can cause pain and disability. In many of these disorders diagnostic imaging, by means of radiography and other advanced methods, is vital in establishing an accurate diagnosis and hence improving patient care. This chapter discusses some of the more common conditions affecting the cervical spine and its surrounding structures and describes the imaging appearance of each condition. The first part of this chapter is an overview of imaging techniques available and some basic principles of cervical spine imaging. The second part discusses and demonstrates examples of various conditions affecting the cervical region.

OVERVIEW OF DIAGNOSTIC IMAGING PROCEDURES

This section summarizes the various imaging procedures that are available for the evaluation of the cervical spine. Any practitioner that utilizes imaging tests must be cognizant of the necessity and appropriateness of each of these procedures.

PLAIN FILM RADIOGRAPHY

Examination of the Cervical Spine

Examination of the cervical spine varies depending on the specific clinical situation. The "basic" examination should consist of a three-view survey—an anteroposterior open mouth projection, anteroposterior lower cervical projection, and neutral lateral views. An anteroposterior open-mouth projection adequately demonstrates the atlas and axis. The anteroposterior lower cervical projection allows visualization of the remaining cervical vertebrae. This frontal radiograph is obtained with the patient either erect or recumbent in an anteroposterior projection with approximately 15 degrees of cephalad angulation of the tube. The lateral radiograph with the head in the neutral position should include the base of skull through T1. A swimmer's view may be added if C7 is not adequately demonstrated.

This basic examination may be supplemented with additional projections depending upon the clinical situation. Lateral radiographs obtained with cervical spine flexion and extension may be included. Forty-five-degree oblique projections are obtained with the patient sitting or standing. Although such projections are useful in the analysis of the intervertebral foramina, those in the lower cervical spine are better demonstrated on 55-degree oblique radiographs.[1] A pillar view for demonstration of the vertebral arches is obtained in an anteroposterior or posteroanterior position. For some portions of the cervical spine, additional radiographs are suggested. Specific projections are designated for the cervicobasilar and cervicothoracic regions. Numerous positioning texts are available and clinicians are strongly encouraged to refer to these publications for a more comprehensive review.

Role of Cervical Spine Radiographs for Biomechanical Assessment

The use of chiropractic radiography for biomechanical interpretation is not standardized and remains a source of controversy. The role of radiographs in evaluation of cervical spine biomechanics is controversial, though a number of chiropractic techniques incorporate such analysis into their treatment plans.[2, 3] Biological asymmetry, and positional and distortional factors, are the most commonly noted sources of error in radiographic evaluation of spinal biomechanics. To provide useful biomechanical information, which outweighs its inherent risks and costs, radiography should provide a relatively conclusive answer to the presence or absence of significantly abnormal biomechanics. Reproducible results with minimal variance on multiple measurements should be expected. Many studies suggest significant sources of error in radiographic evaluation of biomechanics.[3] Several studies have shown reasonable reliability when well trained interpreters and well-defined anatomical landmarks are used.[4-6] Still, evidence supporting reliability does not provide information about the clinical usefulness or construct validity of these measurements.

Role of Cervical Spine Radiographs for Monitoring Therapeutic Progress

In addition to the questions of reliability and usefulness of various measurements, the applications of these biomechanical assessments as indicators of therapeutic progress are a point of debate.[2] In our opinion, more research is needed before routinely using radiography to monitor therapeutic progress. This research should address whether the reliably measured changes are due to therapeutic intervention and whether changes are clinically meaningful.

Limitations of Plain Film Radiography

It is critical to understand the limitations of plain film radiography. It is well known that 30- to 50-percent destruction of bone is necessary before it becomes visible on plain film radiographs.[7] The plain film is also insensitive to many diagnoses requiring surgical intervention. For example, spinal stenosis, herniated nucleus pulposus, and intraspinal neoplasm cannot be diagnosed from plain films and require advanced imaging methods. In cases where plain radiography is insufficient, other specialized imaging techniques are available for evaluation of the cervical spine.

CONVENTIONAL TOMOGRAPHY

Conventional tomography is a useful adjunct to plain film radiography and should be used when standard and specialized views fail to provide needed information for correct diagnosis and adequate treatment. This modality can be applied to the cervical spine in cases of skeletal trauma to detect and delineate vertebral column fractures. For instance, fractures involving the odontoid process may be better demonstrated with conventional tomography.[8, 9] The superiority of computed tomography and magnetic resonance imaging in the evaluation of the cervical spine, however, has resulted in a significantly diminished role of conventional tomography.

COMPUTED TOMOGRAPHY

Computed tomography (CT) surpasses plain film radiography and conventional tomography in soft tissue contrast and osseous detail because of its enhanced spatial and contrast resolution. While the soft tissue contrast of CT is inferior to that of magnetic resonance imaging (MRI), the strength of CT lies in the ability to define osseous abnormalities. Fracture detection is 78 to 100 percent with CT.[9] Axial imaging alone produces results at the lower end of this range while use of thin (1.5-mm) sections with the addition of coronal and sagittal reformations is likely to result in sensitivity levels nearing 100 percent.[9] An in-depth explanation of the principle of computed tomography is beyond the scope of this chapter. What follows is an overview of some of the more important indications for CT of the cervical spine.

CT is frequently employed in the evaluation of complex fractures and dislocations of the cervical spine and has essentially replaced conventional tomography. CT is recommended as follow-up to abnormalities identified on plain film radiographs, providing the most useful information when directed through the area of known or suspected injury rather than as a screening tool for the full cervical spine.[9] Although most information is obtained from transaxial images, the benefits of coronal and sagittal reformations are significant in trauma settings, especially in cases of horizontally oriented fractures. CT is particularly suited to show bone fragments in the spinal canal, and these may be easily obscured on plain film. Jefferson or burst fractures of the atlas and atlanto-axial rotational fixation are also optimally imaged with CT. CT can be used to evaluate complex compression, hyperflexion, or hyperextension injuries; however, conventional tomography is often adequate and is commonly used. The role of CT in the evaluation of spinal neoplasm and infection has been largely relinquished to MRI. MRI is the modality of choice in the assessment of musculoskeletal tumors, and the early stages of infectious arthritis and metastasis are better defined by MRI or scintigraphy. In general, articular disorders do not warrant CT, though it may provide important information regarding the presence and extent of disease in joints that are difficult to image with plain radiography or conventional tomography (e.g., apophyseal, costovertebral, sternoclavicular and temporomandibular joints).[10]

COMPUTED TOMOGRAPHY-MYELOGRAPHY

In general, both CT-myelography and MRI define the spinal canal and associated soft tissue structures as well as detecting discogenic disease and quantifying thecal sac and cord compromise. CT-myelography does not have the capability of MRI to show internal cord architecture and identify subtle cord contusions. CT-myelography is most applicable to spinal canal pathology when MR imaging is not available or cannot be performed. It may be superior to MRI in the evaluation of nerve root avulsion and dural tears.[11]

MYELOGRAPHY

Myelography is an invasive procedure with a significant risk of complications, including hypersensitivity reactions, infection, and bleeding. CT and MRI leave limited use for myelography and it is now generally performed only when these modalities are not available.[11]

MAGNETIC RESONANCE IMAGING

Numerous studies support the assertion that MRI is superior to other modalities in the evaluation of soft tissues. This makes it particularly valuable in the evaluation of the spinal cord, intervertebral disc, and spinal ligaments. It is emerging as an essential tool following plain film radiography in the evaluation of these structures and in patients with neurological deficit. This modality has a significant value in imaging long segments of the spine at once and the tomographic ability to evaluate complicated regions such as the cervicothoracic junction. The advantages of MRI are essentially its soft tissue resolution and the ability to obtain direct sagittal images.

Spinal cord injury may result in mild edema to complete transection, or delayed sequelae such as atrophy and syringomyelia. MRI can identify and differentiate acute cord hemorrhage (intramedullary hematoma) and non-hemorrhagic cord contusion (intramedullary edema).[9] MRI is the only imaging tool capable of directly demonstrating many such intrinsic abnormalities.[9]

MRI plays an important role in the detection of traumatic disc herniation. Its role in the evaluation of isolated ligamentous injury is developing. Patients with injury to the anterior longitudinal ligament, posterior longitudinal ligament, ligamentum flavum, and interspinous ligaments may be at risk for delayed instability. These injuries may be evident on MRI, though they are usually found incidentally during investigation of other abnormalities.[9] Patients with signs of myelopathy, those with progressive or delayed neurological deficit, or those with neurological deficits not otherwise explained may benefit from MRI evaluation.

A prominent disadvantage of MRI is its inferior resolution of osseous structures. This particularly limits its ability to detect vertebral arch fractures, though most other fractures and dislocations are demonstrated.

Contraindications to MRI are usually associated with the effects of the magnetic field. Cochlear implants, metallic foreign bodies in the eye, ferromagnetic heart valves, intracranial aneurysm clips, intrauterine devices with metallic loops, permanent transcutaneous electrical nerve stimulation units, and some cardiac pacemakers may all result in significant patient morbidity or mortality if subjected to MRI.[11] High field scanners tend to have a relatively small bore size, which may make claustrophobic or obese patients poor candidates for examination.[11] Owing to limited information regarding potential effects on the fetus, it is recommended that pregnant women undergo MRI only when absolutely necessary.[11] Most orthopedic implants are not adversely affected, but image quality is degraded by these devices.[11]

RADIONUCLIDE SCAN

Radionuclide bone imaging is a sensitive indicator for any process that disturbs the normal balance of bone production and resorption. These processes may be manifested as regions of increased or decreased activity. Even though the bone scan is extremely sensitive, it is relatively nonspecific. Nonetheless, a major clinical application of radionuclide bone imaging is in the detection of osseous metastasis in patients with primary neoplasms that frequently spread to the bone (e.g., carcinoma of the prostate or breast).[12] Osseous metastatic lesions appear as focal areas of increased activity. Documenting the specific sites of involvement in patients with Paget's disease of bone and determining true activity of this disease process are other common clinical applications.[12]

VIDEOFLUOROSCOPY

Videofluoroscopy has limited use in evaluation of patients with cervical spine pain. The fluoroscopic evaluation of flexion, extension, and lateral flexion in patients who have undergone spinal arthrodesis (fusion) can be performed when there is a question of nonunion that cannot be demonstrated on routine flexion-extension radiographs.[13] Routine clinical use is discouraged since quantification of findings is difficult without sufficient data supporting normal findings and lack of clear definitions of abnormal findings. As new information emerges, however, the role of videofluoroscopy in the evaluation of the cervical spine may expand.

ULTRASONOGRAPHY

While the use of diagnostic ultrasound in evaluation of the abdomen and the appendicular musculoskeletal system is clear, much controversy surrounds the application of this modality to the adult spine. The American College of Radiology (ACR) and the American Chiropractic College of Radiology (ACCR) discourage general clinical use of this modality.[14] With the exception of the neonate spine,

Table 16–1: Common Segmental Abnormalities

SEGMENTAL ABNORMALITY	KEY FEATURES
Congenital block vertebra	Continuous cortical margin between vertebrae; narrowing of anteroposterior diameter; posterior element fusion (50%),[15] usually remnant disk (see Fig. 16–1)
Klippel-Feil syndrome	Two or more cervical block vertebrae; Sprengel's deformity (20–25%)[15] Clinical features—short, webbed neck; restricted cervical motion; low posterior hair-line[16]
Occipitalization	Posterior arch C1 fused to occiput; associated basilar impression; evaluate for subjacent instability

diagnostic ultrasound has not been established as a diagnostic tool in evaluation of the spine.[14] Despite the lack of methodologically sound data, overt commercialization of this technology exists and is a source of controversy. This is a noninvasive and easily acquired imaging modality, but it is extremely operator dependent and variability among different machines may be significant.[14] Lack of data supporting any cervical spine application and the proven abilities of other modalities result in no support for the use of this modality in evaluation of the cervical spine.[14] The existing guidelines on the use of diagnostic ultrasound are subject to change should new information regarding clinical applications be discovered.[14]

COMMON CONDITIONS AFFECTING THE CERVICAL SPINE

This section discusses the more common conditions affecting the cervical spine and its surrounding structures. Emphasis is placed on the imaging appearance of each condition.

CONGENITAL ANOMALIES

Congenital anomalies in the cervical spine are not uncommon. Clinically, they may represent incidental findings, complicating factors, indications for further evaluation, or

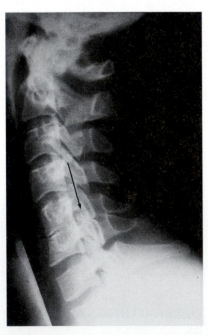

A

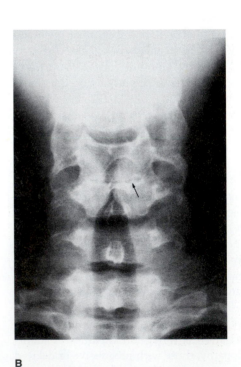

B

Figure 16–1. C5–6 Congenital synostosis. **A.** Lateral cervical view shows the classic narrowing of anteroposterior (AP) body diameter (wasp waist deformity) and remnant disc space of congenital synostosis. The posterior elements are not involved in this case. **B.** The synostosis is suggested by the narrowed disc space on the AP view.

Table 16–2: Differentiation Between Congenital and Acquired Fusion

	CONGENITAL FUSION	ACQUIRED FUSION
Anteroposterior diameter	Decreased anteroposterior diameter at fusion	No decrease in anteroposterior diameter
Disc space	Hypoplastic or rudimentary disc space; may show calcification	Disc space may be diminished in some acquired fusion processes
Apophyseal joints	Possible fusion (50% of cases)[15]	Almost never involved with acquired fusion processes
Spinous processes	Possible malformation or fusion of spinous processes	Almost never involved with acquired fusion processes

contraindications to certain treatments. When they occur alone, the more common anomalies have limited clinical significance. When multiple anomalies are identified, consideration should be given to the possibility of anomalies in other regions of the skeleton and in major organ systems, especially the renal system. Table 16–1 reviews the more common segmental abnormalities.

Congenital Block Vertebra

Segmentation anomalies may occur at any level. At C2 through C7, failure of segmentation or a congenital block vertebra is identified by the continuous cortical margin be-

tween vertebrae. This uninterrupted cortex is usually seen at both the anterior and posterior body margins. The intervening disc is usually remnant and often shows calcification. The classic appearance of a narrowing anteroposterior diameter of the block vertebrae at its mid-portion is secondary to fusion of the ring epiphyses (Fig. 16–1). The posterior elements are osseously fused in approximately 50 percent of cases.[15] Differentiation of congenital versus acquired fusion is based on radiographic appearance as well as clinical history (Table 16–2; Fig. 16–2).

Clinically, the block vertebra itself is insignificant. The associated intervertebral foramina may be narrowed, but

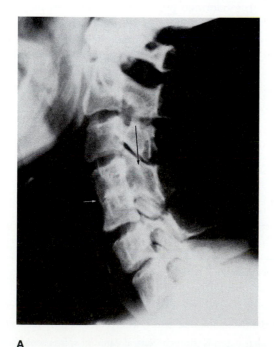

A

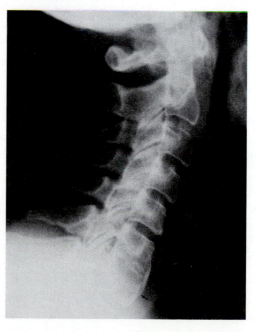

B

Figure 16–2. Differentiation between congenital and acquired fusion. **A.** Congenital synostosis. Note the classic findings of decreased anteroposterior diameter at fusion site, involvement of apophyseal joints, and malformation of spinous processes. **B.** Acquired synostosis. The normal sagittal body width and uninvolved posterior elements is consistent with acquired fusion. The bridging bone formation *(arrows)* and loss of disc space is often seen with surgical fusion.

Table 16–3: Methods for Determining Significant Basilar Impression on Neutral Lateral Cervical View

METHOD	LANDMARKS	COMMENTS
McGregor's line	Line drawn from posterosuperior margin of hard palate to inferior surface of occiput; odontoid apex to this line is measured (Fig. 16–4)	Odontoid apex should not lie more than 8 mm above this line in males and more than 10 mm above it in females[18]; abnormal superior position indicative of basilar impression
Chamberlain's line	Line drawn from posterior margin of hard palate to posterior aspect of foramen magnum; odontoid apex to this line is measured (Fig. 16–5)	Measurement of 7 mm or more is definitely abnormal[18]
MacRae's line	Line drawn between the anterior and posterior margins of the foramen margin; inferior margin of the occipital bone should lie at or below this line (Fig. 16–6)	Basilar impression present if inferior margin of the occipital bone is convex in the superior direction or lies above this line, or both[18]

the exiting nerve root is not compromised. These congenitally fused vertebrae may become clinically relevant due to changes at adjacent levels. The lack of intersegmental motion may translate into increased forces at other levels, especially the next movable caudal segment. This may result in hypermobility or instability as well as early degenerative changes.[15] The identification of multiple block vertebrae should alert the clinician to possible associated congenital syndromes, especially Klippel-Feil syndrome, which may have coexisting anomalies of the major organ systems.[15]

Klippel-Feil Syndrome

Radiographic findings minimally include two or more cervical block vertebrae. Sprengel's deformity is congenital elevation and medial rotation of the scapula and is seen in 20 to 25 percent of Klippel-Feil patients.[15] An anomalous osseous connection of the superior angle of the scapula to the transverse processes of the mid-cervical spine (omovertebral bone) may also be present.[15]

Klippel-Feil syndrome presents with clinical findings of a short, webbed neck, restricted cervical motion, and a low posterior hairline. Nearly one third of patients are deaf.[16] Approximately one half have an associated renal anomaly.[17]

Occipitalization

Occipitalization refers to failure of segmentation at the craniovertebral junctions. Usually the posterior arch of C1 is osseously fused to the occiput (Fig. 16–3). Less frequently, the anterior arch and lateral masses are also involved. Basilar impression is often associated with occipitalization.[15] In this case, the osseous margin of the foramen magnum is elevated relative to the base of the occiput. This may result in abnormal alignment of the tip of the odontoid process to the foramen magnum and associated compromise of the brain stem. Many methods exist for determining the presence of significant basilar impression (Table 16–3). Associated subjacent instability is of particular concern at this level. Without articulation at the craniovertebral junction, forces are increased at the C1–2 level.

Schisis Defects

Common schisis defects within the cervical spine are illustrated in Table 16–4.

Table 16–4: Common Schisis Defects of Cervical Spine

SCHISIS DEFECT	KEY FEATURES
Spina bifida occulta	Failure of osseous fusion of vertebral arches Lateral view—absent spinolaminar junction line
Spondylolisthesis	Most common C6[15]; associated with anterior subluxation and spina bifida occulta defect (Fig. 16–7)
"Butterfly" vertebra	Resultant of persistent notochordal tissue; midline defect; interpedicular distance widened
Diastematomyelia	Fibrous, cartilagenous, or osseous bar extends through central canal of spine; separates spinal cord into halves; surgical intervention usually required; magnetic resonance imaging or computed tomography required to fully evaluate
Hemivertebra	More common in thoracic spine; usually lateral which results in scoliosis; surgical intervention may be required when the resulting abnormal curvature is marked (Fig. 16–8)

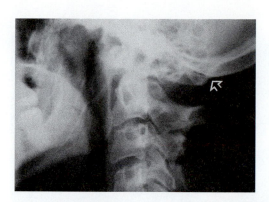

Figure 16–3. Occipitalization. Occipitalization is readily identified on this lateral radiograph. Note that the tip of the odontoid process extends well above McGregor's line. Basilar impression is often seen in conjunction with occipitalization and may make a diagnostic APOM radiograph difficult to obtain.

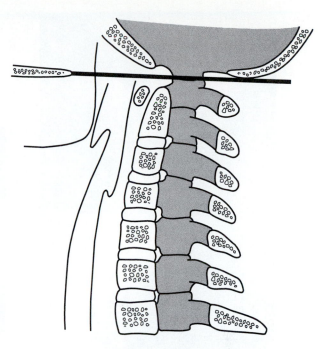

Figure 16–4. McGregor's line. Odontoid apex should not lie above a line drawn from the posterosuperior margins of hard palate to inferior surface of occiput.

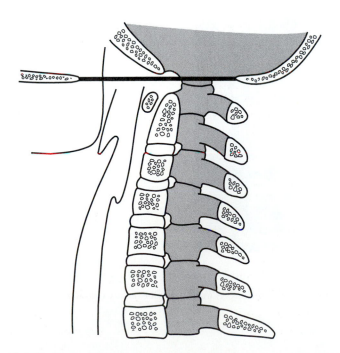

Figure 16–5. Chamberlain's line. Distance to odontoid apex is measured from a line drawn from posterior margin of hard palate to posterior aspect of foramen magnum.

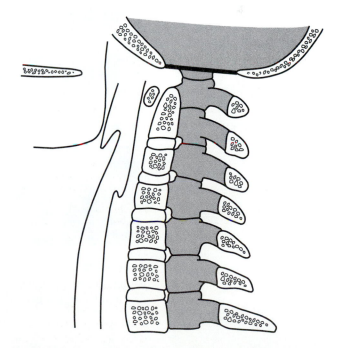

Figure 16–6. MacRae's line. Inferior margin of occiput should lie at or below line drawn between the anterior and posterior margins of foramen magnum.

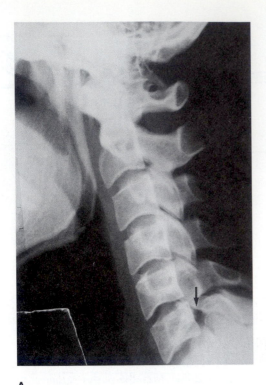

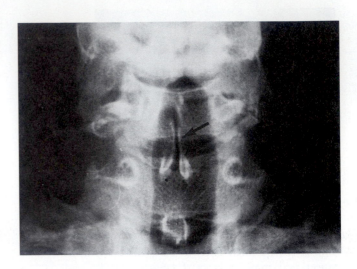

A

B

Figure 16–7. C6 spondylolisthesis. **A.** Lateral cervical spine. Bilateral congenital pars interarticularis defects and an accompanying anterior subluxation are seen at C6. **B.** The anteroposterior lower cervical radiograph shows a spina bifida occulta defect at C6. This defect frequently is found with congenital spondylolisthesis at this level.

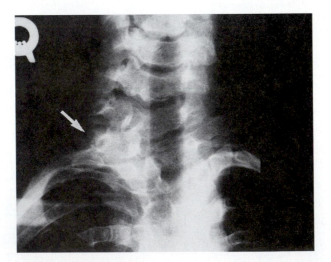

Figure 16–8. Hemivertebra. A hemivertebra with an articulating rib is seen between C7 and T1 on the right. This results in a short, congenital scoliosis.

Table 16–5: Odontoid Process Anomalies

ODONTOID PROCESS ANOMALIES	STABILITY	KEY CHARACTERISTICS
Agenesis or hypoplasia of dens	Unstable	Complete lack or small, osseous protuberance in place of normal dens; C1 anterior tubercle may be hyperplastic
Os odontoideum	Unstable	Round or oval ossicle present in place of dens; lucent cleft separates C2 body from ossicle; C1 anterior tubercle may develop angled posterior articulating surface and may be hyperplastic (Fig. 16–9)
Os terminale	Stable	Secondary ossification center at tip of dens does not osseously fuse

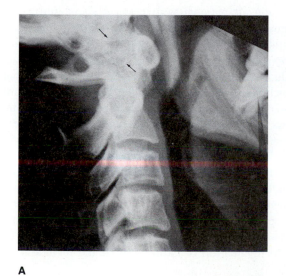

A

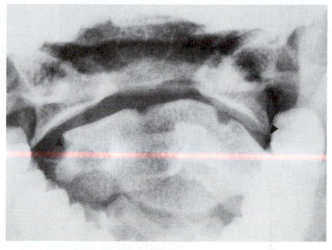

B

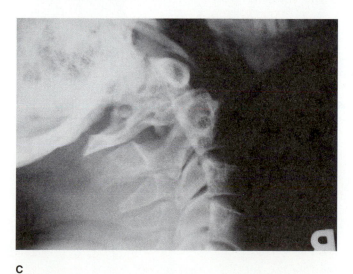

C

Figure 16–9. Os odontoideum. **A.** The os odontoideum is faintly visible on the lateral view. The corticated inferior margin of this os indicates its lack of attachment to the remainder of C2. **B** and **C.** Both the APOM and extension lateral radiographs show marked displacement of C1 relative to C2. Despite radiographic evidence of instability, surgical fusion was not recommended for this patient.

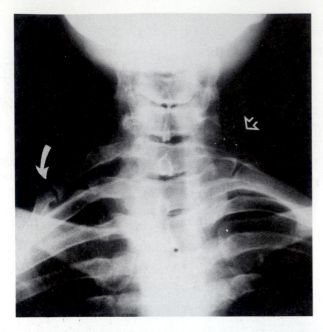

Figure 16–10. Cervical ribs. In this unusual case of cervical ribs, the cervical rib on the right has a pseudoarthrosis in its mid-portion. Changes on the left appear to be an elongated transverse process at C7 without an articulation.

Odontoid Process Anomalies

Abnormal development of the odontoid process of C2 is of particular concern because of the potential for instability. Three basic patterns of anomalous development are seen (Table 16–5).

Cervical Rib

Cervical ribs occur in about 0.5 to 1 percent of the population.[15] Anomalous rib development is most commonly seen at C7 and may be unilateral or bilateral (Fig. 16–10).[15] Cervical ribs range from small ossicles to fully formed ribs. Differentiation of cervical ribs from elongated C7 transverse processes may be difficult when articular spaces are not clearly visualized. Oblique radiographs may be helpful. In both entities, fibrous bands may extend from the end of the osseous structure to the sternum. Pressure from cervical ribs or associated fibrous bands may be responsible for thoracic outlet syndrome.

CERVICAL SPINE TRAUMA

Virtually all patients with cervical spine injuries and a normal level of consciousness have symptoms or signs referable to the cervical spine.[19] Initial radiographic evaluation of the cervical spine and contiguous structures includes assessment for the central canal or foraminal encroachment and instability. The neutral lateral, anteroposterior lower cervical and anteroposterior open-mouth views provide an appropriate initial evaluation for most cervical spine injuries.[20] Oblique, pillar (vertebral arch), and flexion-extension views may also be included in the initial examination or as follow-up. Vandemark developed a radiological algorithm for the traumatized patient that provides a reasonable approach to patient management.[19] The patient's risk of injury is assigned to one of four categories based on history and clinical presentation (Table 16–6). Evaluation of radiographs should include a careful

Table 16–6: Radiological Algorithm for Trauma Patients[19]

	CATEGORY 1	CATEGORY 2	CATEGORY 3	CATEGORY 4
History and/or physical findings	None	Indicates cervical spine involvement without likelihood that physiological range of motion exceeded	Force of injury suggests physiological range of motion exceeded	Force of injury suggests physiological range of motion exceeded; altered mental status; abnormal neurological findings; prominent cervical spine symptoms
Risk for spinal injury	None	Low	Moderate	High
Radiographic examination	Not initially indicated	Upright three view series	Supine lateral (cross-table), swimmer's view, anteroposterior lower cervical, and odontoid views	Lateral, anteroposterior lower cervical, odontoid, and shallow oblique radiographs performed with patient supine

Table 16–7: Abnormal Vertebral Alignment

ABNORMALITY	MEASUREMENT	COMMENTS
Loss of lordosis	Perpendicular lines to the horizontal line of C1 and a line to the inferior endplate of C7 are constructed. Normal values range from 23–44 degrees[21, 21a] (Fig. 16–11)	Not considered a strong indicator of underlying soft tissue injury; loss of lordosis may be secondary to muscle spasm
Acute kyphotic angulation	Single abrupt angular change in configuration of cervical curve	C5–6 segments most common levels of involvement; two adjacent spinous processes widely separated
Widened interspinous space	Interspinous space wider than 2 mm compared to other levels	May denote significant posterior ligamentous injury
Excessive sagittal vertebral body rotation	Lines drawn through anterior and posterior inferior vertebral body corners—extended anteriorly to point of intersection (Fig. 16–12)	Angles greater than 11 degrees between adjacent segments strong indicator for significant ligamentous injury[22]
Axial rotations (rotatory)	Displacement of spinous process from midline	May be due to torticollis, artifactual rotation of head, unilateral subluxation, or facet joint dislocation
Excessive sagittal translation	Cervical arc lines: anterior body margins, posterior body margins, spinolaminar junctions; and tips of spinous processes	Greater than a total of 3.5-mm translation strong indicator of segmental instability[22]; disruption of anterior and posterior body margins may also be associated with burst fragments or odontoid fracture, or both

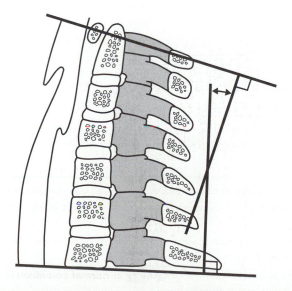

Figure 16–11. Angle of cervical curve. Perpendicular lines are constructed from a line drawn along the inferior endplate of C7 and a line drawn through the midpoints of the anterior and posterior tubercles of the atlas. The resultant angle is measured.

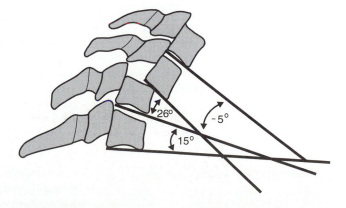

Figure 16–12. Sagittal body rotation. Angles greater than 11 degrees between adjacent segments are considered to be definitive radiographic evidence of segmental instability.

Table 16–8: Abnormal Joints

ABNORMALITY	MEASUREMENT	COMMENTS
Anterior atlanto-occipital dislocation	Distance between basion and posterior arch at spinolaminar junction < distance between opisthion and posterior margin of anterior arch[8]	Usually fatal
Widened atlantodental interspace (predental space)	Should not exceed 3 mm in adults and 5 mm in children less than 12 years of age[8, 23]	Isolated post-traumatic disruption of transverse ligament is infrequent
Widened intervertebral disc space	At the involvement, the disc space may be widened posteriorly and narrowed anteriorly[8, 24]	Strong indicator of serious ligamentous disruption
Vacuum phenomenon ("lucent cleft" sign)	Presence of small, smooth lucent cleft adjacent to the anterior vertebral endplate best demonstrated on extension lateral view	Associated with annular avulsion from the discovertebral junction
Widening of zygapophyseal joint	Joint space more than 2 mm may denote tearing of the facet joint capsule	Wide facet joint, wide interspinous space, compression fracture, and loss of cervical lordosis may denote significant tearing of the posterior ligamentous complex and instability

search for indirect indicators of trauma, such as alteration in vertebral alignment, abnormal joint spaces, and soft tissue abnormalities, as well as identification of direct indicators, such as fractures (Tables 16–7, 16–8, and 16–9).

Occipito-atlanto-axial Injuries

The cervicocranial junction is a transitional region and, as such, differs anatomically and functionally from the lower cervical spine. This is the most common site of cervical spine injury in children under 12 years of age.[13] Table 16–10 reviews the injuries most likely to occur at the cervicocranial region.

Lower Cervical Spine Injuries

Knowledge of the mechanism of injury and an understanding of normal anatomy guide radiological evaluation of this area. Osseous and articular anatomy and ligamentous at-

Table 16–9: Abnormal Soft Tissues

ABNORMALITY	COMMENTS
Widened retropharyngeal space	Tissue immediately anterior to the anteroinferior aspect of C2 body should not exceed 7 mm in children and adults; hematoma or edema will manifest as widening of the soft tissue space[8, 25]
Widened retrotracheal space	Tissue immediately anterior to the anteroinferior aspect of C6 body should not exceed 14 mm in children or 22 mm in adults[26]
Displacement of prevertebral fat stripe	A thin radiolucent vertical linear shadow corresponding to fatty areolar tissue is frequently observed adjacent to the anterior aspects of C6 and C7 vertebra[8, 27]; hematoma or edema will widen this soft tissue landmark
Tracheal deviation and laryngeal dislocation	Torticollis or hematoma may displace trachea
Soft tissue emphysema	Gas within neck's soft tissues indicative of tracheal laceration or transection, pneumothorax, or pneumomediastinum

Table 16–10: Occipito-atlanto-axial Injuries

TYPE	MECHANISM OF INJURY	STABILITY	RADIOGRAPHIC FINDINGS	COMMENTS
Atlanto-occipital dislocation	Controversial; possibly hyperextension and distraction	Unstable	Anterior displacement of basion; malalignment of spinolaminar line of C1 and posterior margin of foramen magnum; failure of clival line to intersect odontoid[13]	Rare, usually fatal[8]
Atlanto-axial subluxation	Not well understood	Unstable	Abnormal widening of atlanto-dental interval; >3 mm in adults; >5 mm in children[8, 23]	Rare, dens tightly bound to C1 by transverse ligament
Atlanto-axial rotary fixation (Fig. 16–13)	Occurs after minor trauma; may develop spontaneously after upper respiratory tract infection[28]	Stable	Dens is positioned eccentrically between lateral masses of C1; no change in relationship of C1 and C2 with contralateral rotation[28]	Patient presents with painful torticollis[28]
Posterior arch fracture	Compressive extension force	Stable	Vertical fracture lines extending through one or both sides of arch	Not associated with soft tissue swelling
Jefferson (burst) fracture (Fig. 16–14)	Compressive axial force	Unstable	Overhanging edges at the C1–2 facet articulation; atlantodental interval may be widened if rupture of transverse ligament is associated; posterior arch fracture	Usually associated with significant prevertebral soft tissue swelling; injury may be unilateral or bilateral
Anterior tubercle (avulsion)	Hyperextension	Stable	Fragment detached from inferior aspect of tubercle and displaces inferiorly	Usually associated with prevertebral soft tissue swelling
Odontoid fracture (Fig. 16–15)	Not well understood	Type 2—unstable; type 1 and 3—stable	Type 1—oblique fracture through tip of dens (rare); type 2—fracture at junction of dens with body of C2; type 3—horizontal fracture through C2 vertebral body	Type 2 fracture high rate of nonunion
Hangman's fracture (Fig. 16–16)	Vertical compression and hyperextension	Unstable	Fractures through neural arches; anterior subluxation C2 vertebral body	Usually little neurological damage due to decompression of spinal canal by separated fragments

tachments are essentially the same for the lower five cervical vertebrae. Table 16–11 discusses the mechanism of injury, stability, and roentgen findings seen with the most common lower cervical spine injuries.

CERVICAL SPINE DEGENERATIVE DISEASE

Primary and secondary degenerative joint disease of the cervical spine is prevalent in older populations, especially in those over 40 years old.[29] The intervertebral disc, uncovertebral or facet joints may be affected, though they are frequently involved concurrently. Most of the changes of degenerative disease are readily evident on plain film radiographs. The lack of significant correlation of the presence or severity of clinical symptoms to radiographic findings requires the clinical evaluation to be given careful consideration in relation to the radiographic findings.[30]

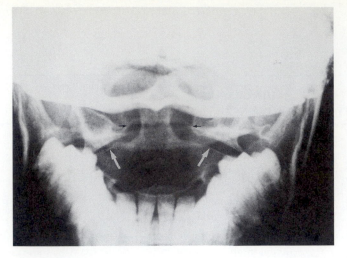

A

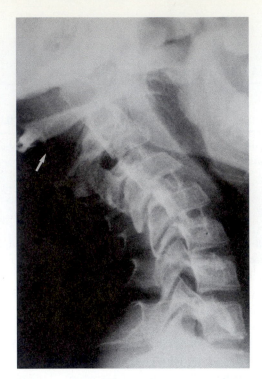

B

Figure 16–13. Atlanto-axial rotary fixation. **A.** APOM with rotary subluxation of C1. The rotational malposition is indicated by the asymmetry of the lateral masses, paraodontoid spaces, and C1–2 joint spaces. **B.** The lateral cervical view shows the lateral mass of C1 in profile posterior to the odontoid process. The atlantodental interval is not visualized. The cervical gravity line is markedly displaced posteriorly.

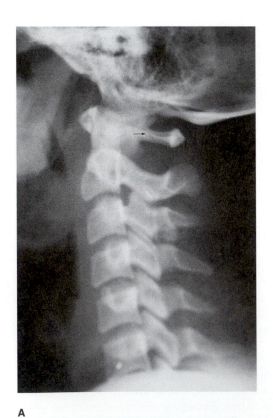

A

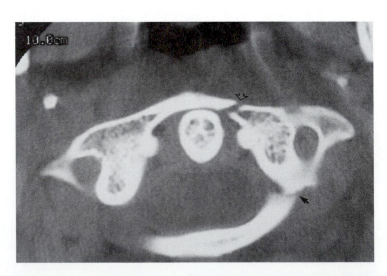

B

Figure 16–14. Jefferson fracture. **A.** Cross-table lateral cervical spine. A subtle fracture line is seen at the posterior arch of C1. This finding is often simulated by superimposition of the posterior margin of the lateral masses. Note the prevertebral soft tissue distention at the level of C1–2. **B.** Axial computed tomography clearly demonstrates the unilateral fractures through both the anterior and posterior arches adjacent to the left lateral mass in this Jefferson fracture. Offset of the lateral mass is minimal with the transverse ligament still intact.

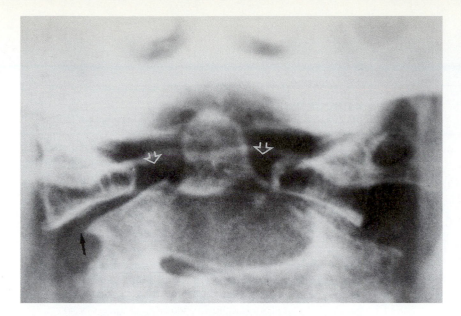

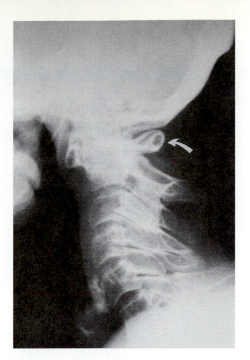

A

B

Figure 16–15. Odontoid fracture. **A.** Though a fracture line is not visible, the significant offset of the lateral masses of C1 and asymmetry of the paraodontoid spaces indicate significant trauma to the upper cervical spine. **B.** Marked offset of the posterior tubercle of C1 relative to the spinolaminar junction line (posterior cervical line) indicates the instability of this odontoid fracture.

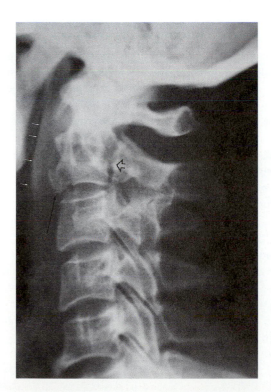

Figure 16–16. Hangman's fracture (traumatic spondylolisthesis). This lateral cervical spine radiograph clearly shows the bilateral pedicle fractures and the accompanying anteroinferior teardrop fracture. The retropharyngeal soft tissues exceed normal measurements in this recent fracture.

(Courtesy of Cynthia Peterson, DC, DACBR, Bournemouth, England.)

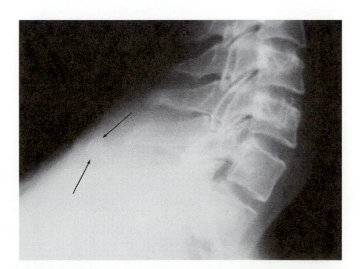

Figure 16–17. Clay shoveler fracture. Clay shoveler fracture or spinous process avulsion fracture is usually due to hyperflexion injury, but can be seen secondary to marked muscular contraction. The avulsed fragment can be differentiated from an unfused secondary ossification center by its lack of a complete cortical margin and the inferior displacement.

Table 16–11: Lower Cervical Spine Injuries

TYPE	MECHANISM OF INJURY	STABILITY	RADIOGRAPHIC FINDINGS	COMMENTS
Wedge compression fracture	Hyperflexion	Stable	Comminution of anterosuperior endplate of vertebra	Without concomitant injury to posterior vertebral body or posterior bony elements
Clay shoveler fracture (Fig. 16–17)	Hyperflexion	Stable	Oblique fracture of spinous process of C6 or C7	Avulsion of supraspinous ligament
Hyperflexion sprain (Fig. 16–18)	Hyperflexion	Unstable	Radiographs may be normal; may show widening of interspinous distance or apophyseal joint; with disruption of posterior annulus, widening of disc space or anterior displacement of superior vertebra[13]	Ligamentous injury with disruption of posterior ligamentous complex and facet joints
Bilateral articular facet lock (Fig. 16–19)	Severe flexion force	Unstable	Inferior articulating facets of superior vertebra locked anterior to superior articular of lower vertebra; anterior subluxation usually greater than half the width of vertebral body[13]	Complete ligamentous disruption of posterior and middle columns
Flexion teardrop fracture (Fig. 16–20)	Flexion and axial loading	Unstable	Small anteroinferior fragment; fragment typically remains aligned with body below[13]	Usually results in anterior cord syndrome; uncommon injury; associated with complete ligamentous and annular disruption
Unilateral lock facet	Combination of flexion and rotation	Stable	Abrupt rotation of facet joints at level of dislocation; loss of super-imposition of facets; anterior subluxation less than seen with bilateral facet lock[13]	Presence of neurological damage or associated facet fracture should suggest instability; oblique radiographs identify side of abnormality
Extension teardrop fracture	Hyperextension	Stable	Anteroinferior corner of vertebral body; fragment is smaller compared to flexion teardrop fracture[13]; negative for subluxation	Usually not associated with neurological deficit
Hyperextension sprain	Severe hyperextension force	Unstable	Difficult to detect radiographically; rupture of anterior longitudinal ligament and intervertebral disc may produce prevertebral hematoma and widening of anterior disc space	Severe neurological damage may occur; magnetic resonance imaging is optimal method for evaluation of spinal cord[13]
Pillar or facet fracture	Extension and rotation	Stable	Difficult to detect on plain film radiographs	Facet fractures may be associated with radiculopathy; most commonly occur at C6 or C7[13]

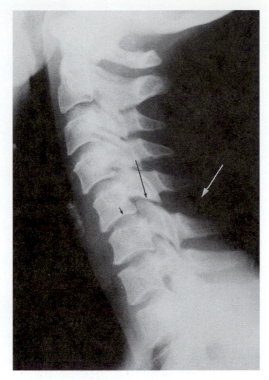

A

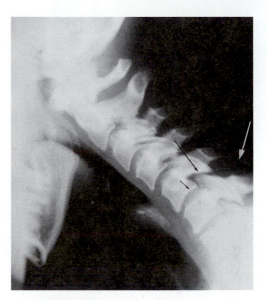

B

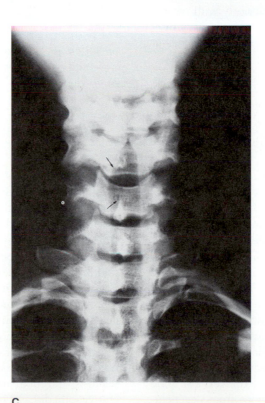

C

Figure 16–18. Hyperflexion sprain. **A.** Widening of the interspinous space, anterior wedging of the intervertebral disc space, and flexion subluxation of the facet joints are evident at C5–6. **B.** No remarkable increases in these findings are noted with flexion. **C.** The anteroposterior lower cervical radiograph reveals only the widening of the interspinous space.

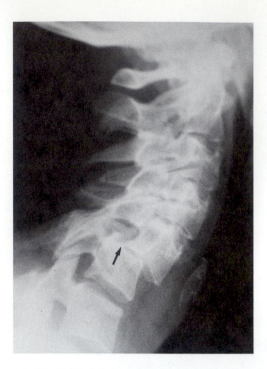

Figure 16–19. Bilateral articular facet lock. Neutral lateral cervical spine radiograph demonstrates greater than 11 degrees of sagittal rotation between adjacent vertebrae. The inferior facets of C5 are dislocated anteriorly with respect to the subjacent superior facets of C6. These findings indicate an unstable injury. Surgical fusion was performed.

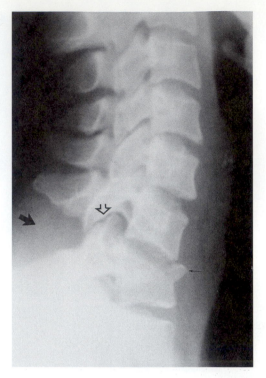

Figure 16–20. C7 teardrop fracture. Lateral cervical spine. The anterior body height of C7 is decreased by approximately 50 percent and a small fragment at the anterosuperior body margin is displaced. Note the slight bulge in the prevertebral soft tissues. Subluxation of the facets and widening of the interspinous space are present in this case of teardrop fracture.

Degenerative disc disease is seen most commonly at C5–6, C6–7, and C4–5 in order of frequency (Fig. 16–21).[30] It is least common at C2–3.[30] Some authorities have discussed the advantage of separating degenerative disc changes into findings reflecting dehydration and degeneration of the nucleus pulposus, termed *osteochondrosis*, and findings reflecting degenerative changes of the annular fibers, termed *spondylosis deformans*.[30] These changes are most often seen together, although one may be more pronounced, exist alone, or significantly predate other changes. Tables 16–12 and 16–13 discuss the radiographic features of osteochondrosis and spondylosis deformans. Additionally, Table 16–14 discusses the key radiographic features of other arthritides that may affect the cervical spine and how to differentiate these conditions from degenerative disc disease and degenerative joint disease.

Degenerative disease affecting the facet or uncovertebral joints, or both, may be secondary to degenerative disc disease or may arise separately. The C4–5 to C6–7 levels are most commonly involved in degenerative disease.[30] Involvement of the craniovertebral (C0–1) and atlanto-axial

(C1–2) articulations is uncommon.[30] If atlanto-axial subluxation is seen, it is most likely to be secondary to an inflammatory arthritide rather than degenerative disease (Table 16–15). Atlanto-axial subluxation is diagnosed when the distance between the posterior aspect of the anterior arch of the atlas and the anterior aspect of the odontoid process exceeds 3 mm in adults and older children or 5 mm in younger children (less than 12 years of age), or an interosseous distance that changes considerably between flexion and extension.[30]

Radiographic findings at the facet articulations include the basic findings of degenerative disease at any articulation: joint space loss, osteophyte formation, subchondral sclerosis, and subluxation. Uncovertebral arthrosis (degenerative joint disease) is often secondary to additional weight-bearing forces on the uncinates following intervertebral disc height loss. The primary radiographic findings are rounding of the uncinate processes and osteophyte formation.[30] The appearance of these hypertrophic changes and the resultant remodeling of the joint surface may simulate a transverse fracture of the vertebral body on the lateral view.[30]

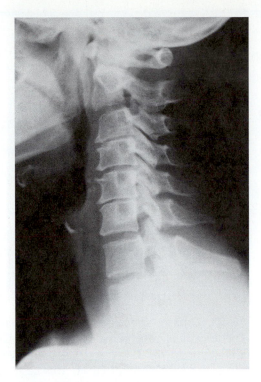

Figure 16–21. Degenerative disc disease. This lateral cervical spine radiograph demonstrates common findings of degenerative disc disease: disc height loss, spondylophyte (osteophyte) formation more prominent anteriorly, loss of lordosis, and mild retrolisthesis.

Many associated conditions should be considered when evaluating a patient with cervical spine degeneration. Table 16–16 reviews the most common complications of cervical spine degenerative disease and the imaging findings seen with each complication.

Table 16–12: Radiographic Features of Osteochondrosis

RADIOGRAPHIC FEATURES	COMMENTS
Decreased disc space height	Most consistent finding; may result in decrease of cervical lordosis; best identified on lateral view
Vacuum phenomenon	Result of nitrogen gas production in the degenerating nucleus pulposus; appearance of the gas density within the disc space is usually central and irregular; may be produced or accentuated with extension of the cervical spine
Endplate sclerosis	Best appreciated on the lateral view

Table 16–13: Radiographic Features of Spondylosis Deformans

RADIOGRAPHIC FEATURES	COMMENTS
Anterior spondylophytes (anterior vertebral body osteophytes)	Secondary to degeneration of the annular fibers; usually extend perpendicular to vertebral body, then extend inferiorly or superiorly; may grow very large, even causing dysphagia in a few cases[30]; should be differentiated from syndesmophytes of the inflammatory spondyloarthropathies
Posterior spondylophytes (posterior vertebral body osteophytes)	Are generally smaller, in comparison to anterior spondylophytes, but may be more significant due to their impact on neural structures[30]

CERVICAL SPINE LIGAMENTOUS INSTABLILITY

The term *instability* is often misunderstood because of historical misuse or overuse and, therefore, remains a controversial concept. Instability in this context is defined as ligamentous laxity to the degree that neurological structures may be compromised under conditions that would otherwise be considered normal physiological loading.[13, 32] Trauma to the cervical spine may result in segmental instability. Disruption of the posterior ligament complex (the ligamentum nuchae, the interspinous ligaments, the interfacetal capsules, the ligamentum flavum, and the posterior longitudinal ligament) results in the unstable segments.[33]

Table 16–14: Differential Diagnosis of Degenerative Disc Disease and Degenerative Joint Disease

DISEASE	KEY RADIOGRAPHIC FEATURES
Rheumatoid arthritis	Erosions; ankylosis
Ankylosing spondylitis (Fig. 16–22)	Ankylosis; marginal syndesmophytes
Psoriatic arthritis, Reiter's disease	Nonmarginal syndesmophytes, disc space not involved
Diffuse idiopathic skeletal hyperostosis (Fig. 16–23)	Flowing hyperostosis; disc space intact, facet joints not involved

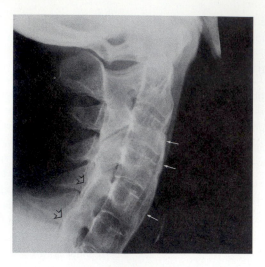

Figure 16–22. Ankylosing spondylitis. Smooth new bone anterior to the vertebral bodies (*arrows*) and bridging the intervertebral disc spaces is seen along with maintenance of intervertebral disc heights. In this case, involvement of the posterior elements helps differentiate this case of ankylosing spondylitis from diffuse idiopathic skeletal hyperostosis. The osteopenia seen here is also characteristic of ankylosing spondylitis. The integrity of the transverse ligament and stability at C1–2 should be of concern in this patient.

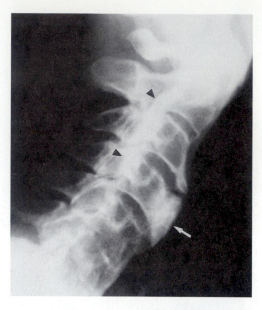

Figure 16–23. Diffuse idiopathic skeletal hyperostosis (DISH). The thick new bone formation anterior to C4 with lucencies anterior to the C3–4 and C4–5 intervertebral disc spaces are characteristic of DISH. This case is complicated by the associated ossification of the posterior longitudinal ligament (OPLL) seen posterior to the C2, C3, and C4 vertebral bodies. OPLL is often associated with DISH.

Plain film radiography is essential in the evaluation of the cervical spine if ligamentous instability is suspected. Since initial radiographs may be unrewarding because of protective muscle spasm, follow-up studies at 3 weeks posttrauma in symptomatic patients are required to evaluate for delayed instability.[22] The key radiographic features and alterations in alignment seen with cervical spine instability are reviewed in Tables 16–17 and 16–18. Advanced imaging may be helpful in the assessment of the extent of the injury. CT is required to detect subtle fracture that may not be appreciated on the plain film.[22] MRI can be utilized to evaluate for areas of edema and hemorrhage, as well as herniation of the nucleus pulposus.[22]

Table 16–15: Most Common Arthritides to Cause Atlantoaxial Subluxation

ARTHRITIDES	COMMENTS
Rheumatoid arthritis (Fig. 16–24)	Seen in 20–25% of patients with severe disease[31]; associated erosion of the odontoid may be severe
Psoriatic arthropathy	Seen in 45% of patients with spondylitis[31]
Juvenile chronic arthritis	Most commonly seen in seropositive juvenile onset adult rheumatoid arthritis[31]
Systemic lupus erythematosus	Unusual cause of atlanto-axial subluxation
Ankylosing spondylitis	Seen in 2% of cases[31]; usually a late feature

CERVICAL SPINE INFECTION

Approximately 2 to 5 percent of cases of osteomyelitis involve the spine, although the cervical region is the least commonly involved.[34] Infectious processes in the cervical spine may initially affect primarily bone (osteomyelitis), the intervertebral disc (infectious discitis), or the surrounding soft tissues (abscesses or cellulitis). Tuberculosis via hematogenous spread from pulmonary infection is the most common cause of spinal infection.[34] Pyogenic infections are most often of staphylococcal origin.[34] Other organisms that may infect the cervical spine and surrounding tissues include numerous other bacteria and a variety of fungi. A preceding infection of the genitourinary tract, respiratory tract, or skin is often noted with infectious processes affecting the musculoskeletal system.[34] Direct implantation of organism from penetrating wounds or surgery is another route of infection.

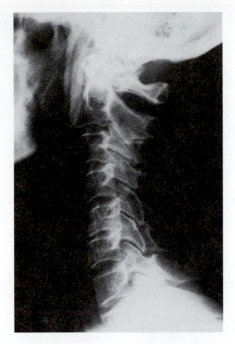
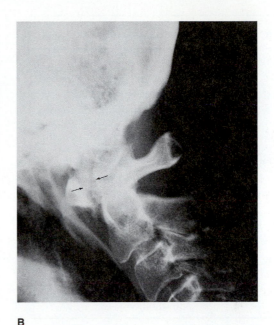

A   **B**

Figure 16–24. Rheumatoid arthritis/atlanto-axial subluxation. **A.** The neutral lateral radiograph of this patient with rheumatoid arthritis shows mild joint space loss and erosions at the C2–3 and C3–4 facet joints with mild anterolistheses at C3 and C4. Intervertebral disc height loss without osteophyte formation is seen at C5–6. **B.** The flexion lateral radiograph shows marked widening of the atlantodental interval. Rupture of the transverse ligament with subsequent instability at C1–2 is not uncommon in patients with rheumatoid arthritis.

Symptoms may or may not include the general signs of infection such as fever and malaise.[34] Spine pain, usually aggravated by motion, is another clinical feature.[34] Delayed diagnosis frequently occurs because the signs and symptoms can be vague and insidious.[34]

Most cases of osteomyelitis in the spine are associated with infectious discitis.[34] The earliest sign is loss of disc height.[34] Indistinct endplates differentiates this disc space loss from that of simple degenerative disease. Plain film radiographic diagnosis is usually delayed by 2 to 4 weeks

Table 16–16: Complications of Cervical Spine Degenerative Disease

COMPLICATION	IMAGING FINDINGS
Segmental instability	Excessive translation with dynamic study measuring 3.5 mm or greater is strong evidence of segmental instability[8, 24]; excessive vertebral body rotation with dynamic study assessed by lines drawn through anterior and posterior inferior vertebral body corners are extended anterior to point of intersection, angle greater than 11 degrees between adjacent segments is considered strong evidence of segmental instability[8, 24]
Degenerative anterior spondylolisthesis	Osteoarthritis of apophyseal joints; forward slippage of superior vertebra on inferior vertebra
Degenerative retrolisthesis	Posterior displacement of vertebra is characteristic
Synovial cyst	Rare before age 30 years; may be associated with disc degeneration and degenerative spondylolisthesis[30]; computed tomography or magnetic resonance imaging reveals mass adjacent to degenerative apophyseal joint
Spinal stenosis	Myelopathy or radiculopathy may be present
Ankylosis	Ankylosis of involved segments is uncommon and rarely affects more than two levels[30]

Table 16–17: Key Radiographic Features of Segmental Instability

RADIOGRAPHIC FEATURE	COMMENTS
Excessive translation with dynamic study	A break in a line drawn along the posterior vertebral body margins; 3.5 mm or greater translation is strong evidence of cervical spine instability
Excessive vertebral body rotation—sagittal plane with dynamic study	Lines drawn through the anterior and posterior inferior vertebral body corners are extended anterior to the point of intersection; angles greater than 11 degrees between adjacent segments are considered to be definitive radiographic evidence of segment instability

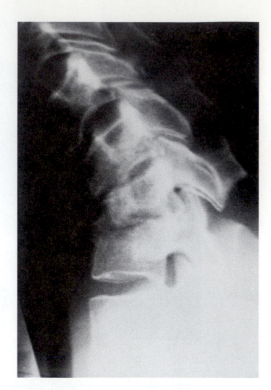

Figure 16–25. Infectious discitis. This patient developed neck pain and stiffness while hospitalized for endocarditis. Radiographic examination was performed weeks later when the pain persisted. In addition to the marked disc space loss, the sharp, angular kyphosis and loss of bony endplates indicates the destructive nature of infectious discitis.

Table 16–18: Alterations in Alignment

ALIGNMENT ALTERATION	COMMENTS
Anterior subluxation	A break in a line drawn along the posterior vertebral body margins
Acute kyphotic angulation	An abrupt angular change in configuration of the cervical curve at a single level
Widening of spinous-lamina space	A difference of 2 mm or greater, measured at the spinolaminar line, between adjacent cervical segments is considered interspinous separation (fanning).[8, 24]
Displacement of facets	The articular facets of the superior involved segment may be displaced anteriorly and superiorly; their relationship with the contiguous inferior segment may be altered[8, 23]
Widened intervertebral disc space	At the level of involvement the disc space may be wedged anteriorly (i.e., widened posteriorly and narrowed anteriorly)[8, 24]; these findings of anterior subluxation are exaggerated in flexion and reduced in extension
"Lucent cleft" sign	Significant injury of the intervertebral disc may be demonstrated on the lateral extension radiograph; when the annular fibers of the disc are partially avulsed from the anterior corner of the cartilaginous endplate, a "lucent cleft" may be seen[22]; this radiolucent cleft is not usually seen in the neutral lateral film; an extension view may be necessary to demonstrate this phenomenon; the "lucent cleft" sign is a small oval to round radiolucency near the anterior portion of the vertebral body endplate

following the onset of infection since detection often requires significant destruction of trabecular bone.[34] Destruction of the vertebral body endplates and pathological fracture are the usual presentation (Fig. 16–25).[34] Large soft tissue masses (abscess) may be present. Osseous fusion or abnormal curvatures, such as kyphosis in the cervical spine, may occur.

CERVICAL SPINE TUMORS AND TUMORLIKE LESIONS

The most common neoplasms, in order of frequency; key characteristics of malignant neoplasms; main features of benign tumors or tumorlike lesions; and tumor location as they relate to the cervical spine are reviewed in Tables 16–19 through 16–22.

RADICULOPATHY AND/OR MYELOPATHY OF INTERVERTEBRAL DISC HERNIATION OR SPINAL CORD LESION ORIGIN

Symptoms such as neck pain and radiculopathy may be caused by a cervical disc herniation. T1- and T2-weighted magnetic resonance images are usually sufficient to detect most disc herniations. Generally, on T1-weighted images, the disc lesions are seen as focal areas of intermediate signal intensity extending beyond the posterior vertebral body margin into the epidural space. On T2-weighted images and gradient-echo pulse sequences, the lower signal of the disc contrasts with the high signal of the cerebrospinal fluid.

Table 16–19: Common Neoplasms of the Cervical Spine in Order of Frequency[35]

Benign

Giant cell tumor (quasimalignant)

Aneursymal bone cyst

Osteoblastoma

Hemangioma

Osteochondroma

Osteoid osteoma

Eosinophilic granuloma

Malignant

Metastasis

Solitary plasmacytoma (myeloma)

Chordoma

Chondrosarcoma

Intramedullary processes commonly present as progressive myelopathies with increasing sensory and motor deficits. Acute exacerbations may be noted due to increases in tumor size, edema, hemorrhage, or rapidly expanding cysts.[37] The most common symptom in adults is axial pain at the level of the neoplasm rather than radiating pain.[37] The symptoms may be present from 2 months to 8 years with an average duration of 2 to 3 years.[37] The pain is often present for months or years before objective neurological findings are present.[37]

Table 16–20: Key Characteristics of Malignant Neoplasms of Cervical Spine

LESION	AGE/SEX	RADIOGRAPHIC FEATURES	COMMENTS
Metastatic bone tumors (Fig. 16–26)	>40 years	Most lesions are lytic; destruction of pedicle most common finding	Breast, prostate, and lung cancers most common primaries[35]
Multiple myeloma	>40 years	Discrete lytic lesions; generalized osteopenia; singular form—solitary plasmacytoma; involves vertebral body	Radionuclide study negative; clinical—bone pain, weight loss, lethargy, anemia[35]
Chordoma	>30 years	Lytic destruction of vertebral body without collapse; focal calcifications; anterior soft tissue mass	Most common cervical region locations—skull base and C2[35]
Chondrosarcoma	>40 years	Lobular radiopacities or purely lytic lesion; may affect vertebral body or neural arch; frequently involves more than one vertebra	Persistent, dull pain usual presenting symptom[35]

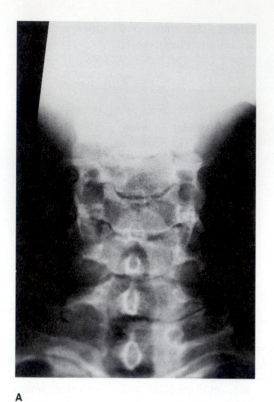

A

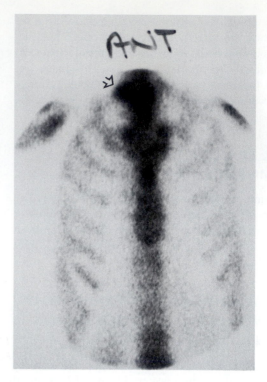

B

C

Figure 16–26. Missing pedicle, bronchogenic carcinoma. **A.** The right T1 pedicle is absent on this anteroposterior lower cervical radiograph. **B** and **C.** Radionuclide bone scans, performed in response to identification of this osteolytic lesion, show marked uptake at the same location (*arrows*). No other areas of increased uptake were identified. Further evaluation led to a diagnosis of metastasis from bronchogenic carcinoma.

Table 16–21: Key Characteristics of Benign Tumor or Tumorlike Lesions of Cervical Spine

LESION	AGE/SEX	RADIOGRAPHIC FEATURES	COMMENTS
Giant cell tumor (quasimalignant)	>20 years	Primarily lytic; somewhat expansile; vertebral body or neural arch, or both; soft tissue mass	May involve contiguous vertebrae
Aneursymal bone cyst	<20 years	Expansile lesions with thin cortex; primarily lytic; may involve contiguous vertebrae; CT may show fluid-fluid levels	Rapid onset of pain; pathological fracture and compression of spinal cord common complications
Osteoblastoma	<30 years	Lytic or bastic lesions; rapidly expansile; reactive sclerosis; stippled calcifications may be present	Rare; occur more frequently in posterior elements
Hemangioma	>20 years	Coarse, vertical striations; normal cortex; usually affects vertebral body	Generally asymptomatic
Osteochondroma	<30 years	Exostoses which may show calcifications	Uncommon in spine; local pain, neurological deficit, and palpable mass
Osteoid osteoma	<30 years	Dense, sclerotic lesion; frequently in the posterior arch	Clinical presentation—localized pain worse at night; salicylates relieve pain
Eosinophilic granuloma	<20 years	Lytic lesion of vertebral body; complete collapse of vertebral body; disc spaces preserved	Spontaneous resolution generally within 6 to 18 months
Paget's disease (Fig. 16–27)	>40 years	Lytic, mixed, and sclerotic phases; thickening of trabeculae and cortex; ivory vertebra	Mimics neoplasm; rarely undergoes malignant degeneration

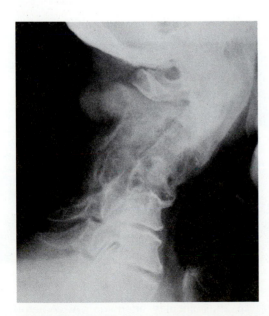

Figure 16–27. Paget's disease. This lytic process is affecting portions of C2, C3, and C4. The kyphosis could be due to the deformity of bone softening or pathological fracture. Radionuclide bone scan and follow-up radiographs of other involved areas revealed more characteristic findings in this case of Paget's disease.

The imaging modality of choice in cases of myelopathy and for evaluation of cord lesions is MRI (Fig. 16–28).[37] MRI is particularly superior in evaluating intramedullary lesions since it images not only changes in cord caliber but tissue changes as well.

Intramedullary tumors generally present on MRI as areas of multilevel cord expansion that are of heterogeneous signal intensity intermediate between the unaffected spinal cord and the cerebrospinal fluid on T1-weighted spin echo images and of increased signal on T2-weighted spin echo images.[37] Most low-grade tumors show some enhancement with contrast agents. Ependymomas, astrocytomas, and hemangioblastomas, the more common intramedullary tumors, tend to present with slightly decreased signal intensity on T1- and increased signal intensity on T2-weighted images.[37] Hemangioblastomas can be differentiated via MRI angiographic appearance.[37] Ependymomas and astrocytomas cannot be differentially diagnosed with MRI.[37] The administration of intravenous contrast agents with MRI improves the detection and definition of intramedullary tumors but does not improve the diagnostic specificity.[37]

MRI is also the choice for evaluating the associated cystic changes seen frequently with intramedullary neo-

Table 16–22: Tumor Location[35]

Body

Multiple myeloma

Eosinophilic granuloma

Chordoma

Hemangioma

Vertebral Arch

Osteoid osteoma

Osteoblastoma

Osteochondroma

Aneurysmal bone cyst

plasm, although histological confirmation of the nature of these cysts is still required. Syringomyelia and hydromyelia appear as sharply demarcated areas that are isointense with the cerebrospinal fluid.[37] Cysts filled with proteinaceous fluid are isointense with the cord and difficult to distin-guish. Most cysts expand the cord. Rostral and caudal cysts that show no wall enhancement with contrast agents are indicative of benign reactive cysts.[37] True tumor cysts are not isointense with the cerebrospinal fluid.[37]

PREVERTEBRAL SOFT TISSUE CALCIFICATIONS

Thyroid Lesions

The thyroid gland becomes more nodular with age. Solitary or multiple nodules occur in 90 percent of women after age 60 and in 60 percent of men after age 80.[38] Solitary thyroid

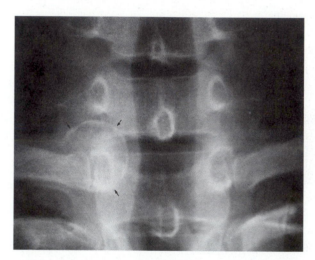

A

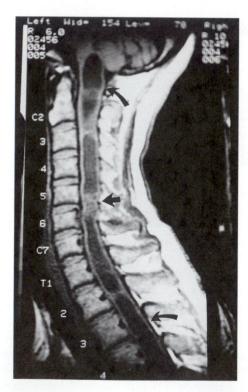

Figure 16–28. Ependymoma. This patient presented with progressive neurological symptoms affecting both upper and lower extremities. Plain film radiographs of the cervi-cal spine were negative. This T1-weighted magnetic reso-nance image reveals a well-defined, inhomogenous, in-tramedullary mass at the C5–6 level. Also present is extensive syrinx formation that extended well into the thoracic region. Magnetic resonance findings and histo-logical examination were consistent with a diagnosis of ependymoma.

B

Figure 16–29. Follicular adenoma. **A.** Anteroposterior spot projection shows a well-defined calcific density of a follicular adenoma, proven on fine-needle aspiration, overlying the right T1 pedicle. Observe the subtle smooth indentation on the tracheal air shadow. **B.** Lateral view demonstrates the location of the calcified nodule anterior to C7–T1 vertebral bodies overlying the tracheal air shadow.

nodules are four times more common in women than in men.[38] Thyroid lesions can be detected with careful neck palpation or can be seen incidentally on plain film radiographs when calcified. The clinical problem that must be addressed is whether a nodule is benign or malignant and euthyroid (normally functioning thyroid gland) or toxic.

After careful and thorough history taking and physical examination of a patient with a thyroid nodule or nodules, it is critical to ascertain whether the nodules are benign or malignant. The initial step and the best method to determine this is fine-needle aspiration.[38] The fine-needle aspiration biopsy should be performed by an experienced physician and interpreted by an experienced cytopathologist.[38] Ultrasound and radionuclide studies are not accurate in distinguishing benign from malignant nodules and, therefore, should not be used routinely in evaluating patients with thyroid nodules.[38] Both studies do, however, detect nonpalpable thyroid nodules. There are no pathognomonic diagnostic imaging findings that would indicate a certain thyroid lesion; however, in general, stippled calcification is suggestive of papillary carcinoma and peripheral rim calcification is more typical of benign lesions[38] (Fig. 16–29). Chest and neck plain film radiographs are sometimes utilized to evaluate large goiters, especially those with substernal extension. Enlargement of the thyroid gland from goiter is seen as a sharply defined, nonhomogeneous soft tissue mass in the lower neck causing displacement of midline structures such as the trachea or contrast-filled esophagus. The mass may be smooth or lobulated.[38] The enlarged thyroid gland can extend below the clavicles and behind the sternum known as the intrathoracic or plunging goiter. Calcification within the mass may be evident.

Hydroxyapatite Deposition Disease

Calcification within longus colli muscle may present as prevertebral soft tissue opacification (Fig. 16–30). Hydroxyapatite deposition generally occurs within the superolateral group of tendons at the insertion of the C2 and C3 anterior vertebral bodies.[39] This is a self-limiting condition with acute symptomatology. The patient usually presents with a painful stiff neck.[39] Other symptoms include muscle spasm, painful dysphagia, and a sense of globus hystericus, which slowly resolve within 1 to 2 weeks.[39]

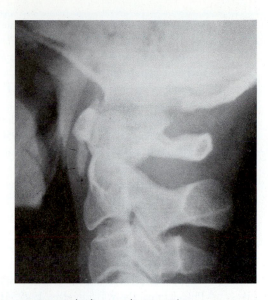

Figure 16–30. Calcific tendinitis. This patient presented with an acute onset of marked upper cervical spine pain and stiffness. Radiographs revealed a smooth bordered, oblong calcific density inferior to the anterior tubercle of C1 *(arrows)*. The symptoms of longus colli calcific tendinitis generally resolve in 1 to 2 weeks. Radiographic findings often take significantly longer to resolve.

CONCLUSION

Several abnormalities affecting the cervical spine can cause pain and disability. In many of these disorders, diagnostic imaging, by means of radiography and other advanced methods, is vital for accurate diagnosis. In establishing a correct diagnosis, it is essential that the physician understand the indications and limitations of each of the imaging modalities reviewed in this chapter. Furthermore, many common cervical spine disorders exhibit characteristic features. This chapter discussed the imaging appearance of numerous cervical spine disorders routinely seen in clinical practice.

REFERENCES

1. Marcelis S, Seragini FC, Taylor JAM, et al. Cervical spine: Comparison of 45 degrees and 55 degrees anteroposterior oblique radiographic projections. *Radiology* 1993;188(1):253–256.
2. Mootz RD, Hoffman LE, Hansen DT. Optimizing clinical use of radiography and minimizing radiation exposure in chiropractic practice. *Top Clin Chiro* 1997;4(1):34–44.
3. Sigler D, Howe J. Intra- and inter-examiner reliability of the upper cervical x-ray marking system. *J Manipulative Physiol Ther* 1985;9:75–80.
4. Owens EF. Line drawing analysis of static cervical X-ray used in chiropractic. *J Manipulative Physiol Ther* 1992;15:442–449.

5. Jackson BL, Barker W, Bentz J, et al. Inter- and intra-examiner reliability of the upper cervical marking system: A second look. *J Manipulative Physiol Ther* 1987;10:157–163.

6. Grostic J, DeBoer K. Roentgenographic measurement of atlas laterality and rotation: a retrospective pre- and post-manipulative study. *J Manipulative Physiol Ther* 1982;5:63–71.

7. Bachman AS, Sproul EE. Correlation of radiographic and autopsy findings in suspected metastases in the spine. *Bull NY Acad Med* 1940;44:169.

8. Montgomery JL, Montgomery ML. Radiographic evaluation of the cervical spine trauma: Procedures to avoid catastrophe. *Postgrad Med* 1994;95(4):173–196.

9. Cornelius RS, Leach JL. Imaging evaluation of cervical spine trauma. *Neuroimaging Clin North Am* 1995;5(3):451–463.

10. Andre M, Resnick D. Computed tomography. In: Resnick D, ed. *Diagnosis of Bone and Joint Disorders*. Philadelphia, Pa: WB Saunders; 1995:152.

11. Miller JS, Craw MM. Diagnostic imaging of the cervical spine following whiplash-induced injury. *Top Clin Chiro* 1997;4(1):26–33.

12. Alazraki N. Radionuclide techniques. In: Resnick D, ed. *Diagnosis of Bone and Joint Disorders*. Philadelphia, Pa: WB Saunders; 1995:434.

13. Pathria MN, Garfin SR. Imaging after spine surgery. In: Resnick D. *Diagnosis of Bone and Joint Disorders*. Philadelphia, Pa: WB Saunders; 1995:551.

14. Schultz GD. Diagnostic ultrasound of the adult spine: state of the technology. *Top Clin Chiro* 1997;4(1):45–49.

15. Guebert GM, Yochum TR, Rowe LJ. Congenital anomalies and normal skeletal variants. In: Yochum TR, Rowe LJ. *Essentials of Skeletal Radiology*. Baltimore, Md. Williams and Wilkins; 1996:197–306.

16. Hensinger RN, Lang JE, MacEwen GD. Klippel-Feil syndrome. A constellation of associated anomalies. *J Bone Joint Surg (Am)* 1974;56:1246.

17. Dahnert W. *Radiology Review Manual*. 2nd ed. Baltimore, Md: Williams and Wilkins; 1993:130.

18. Rowe LJ, Yochum TR. Measurements in skeletal radiology. In: Yochum TR, Rowe LJ. *Essentials of Skeletal Radiology*. Baltimore, Md: Williams and Wilkins; 1996:139–196.

19. Vandemark R. Radiology of the cervical spine in trauma patients: Practice pitfalls and recommendations for improving efficiency and communication. *Am J Roentgenol* 1990;155:465.

20. Pathria MN, Petersilge CA. Spinal trauma. *Radiol Clin North Am* 1991;29(4):847–865.

21. Harrison DD, Janik TJ, Troyanovich SJ, Holland B. Comparisons of lordotic cervical spine curvatures to a theoretical model of the static sagittal cervical spine. *Spine* 1996;21(6):667–675.

21a. Gore DR, Sepic SB, Gardner GM. Roetgenographic findings of the cervical spine in asymptomatic people. *Spine* 1986;11:521–524.

22. Smith GL, Harger BL, Keating JC. Cervical spine instability: Radiographic evaluation. *Top Diagnostic Radio Adv Imaging* 1993;1(3):19–23.

23. Wales LR, Knopp RK, Morishima MS. Recommendations for evaluation of the acutely injured cervical spine: A clinical radiologic algorithm. *Ann Emerg Med* 1980;9(8):422–428.

24. Berquist TH. Imaging of adult cervical spine trauma. *Radiographics* 1988;8(4):667–694.

25. Templeton PA, Young JW, Mirvis SE, et al. The value of retropharyngeal soft tissue measurements in trauma of the adult cervical spine: Cervical spine soft tissue measurements. *Skeletal Radiol* 1987;16(2):98–104.

26. Clark WM, Gehweiler JA, Laib R. Twelve significant signs of cervical spine trauma. *Skeletal Radiol* 1979;13:201.

27. Whalen JP, Woodruff CL. The cervical prevertebral fat stripe: A new aid in evaluating the cervical prevertebral soft tissue space. *Am J Roentgenol* 1970;109(3):445–451.

28. Fielding JW, Hawkins RJ. Atlantoaxial rotatory fixation: Fixed rotatory subluxation of the atlantoaxial joint. *J Bone Joint Surgery (Am)* 1977;59(1):37–44.

29. McRae DL. The significance of abnormalities of the cervical spine. *AJR* 1960;84:3.

30. Resnick D, Niwayama G. Degenerative disease of the spine. In: Resnick D, ed. *Diagnosis of Bone and Joint Disorders*. Philadelphia, Pa: WB Saunders; 1995:1236–1371.

31. Chapman S, Nakielny R. *Aids to Radiological Differential Diagnosis*. 2nd ed. Philadelphia, Pa: WB Saunders; 1990:62.

32. White AA, Southwick WO, Panjabi MM. Clinical instability in the lower cervical spine: A review of past and current concepts. *Spine* 1976;1:15–27.

33. Holdsworth FW. Fractures, dislocations and fracture dislocations of the spine. *J Bone Joint Surg Am* 1970;52A:1534–1551.

34. Smith GL, Taylor JAM. Infectious discitis in an immunocompromised patient. *Top Diagnostic Radiol Adv Imaging* 1995;3(1):5–7.

35. Yochum TR, Rowe LJ. Tumors and tumorlike processes. In: Yochum TR, Rowe LJ. *Essentials of Skeletal Radiology*. Baltimore, Md: Williams and Wilkins; 1996:975–1191.

36. Camins MB, Rosenblum BR. Osseous lesions of the cervical spine. *Clin Neurosurg* 1991;37;722–739.

37. Hoffman LE, Harger BL. Ependymomas: A case report. *Top Diagnostic Radiol Adv Imaging* 1996;4(2):18–20.

38. Ramos LS, Harger BL. Benign and malignant thyroid nodular diseases: four case reports. *Top Diagnostic Radiol Adv Imaging* 1996;4(2):5–12.

39. Rowe LJ, Yochum TR. Arthritic disorders. In: Yochum TR, Rowe LJ. *Essentials of Skeletal Radiology*. Baltimore, Md. Williams and Wilkins; 1996:948.

CHAPTER 17

History Taking
and Clinical Examination
of the Cervical Spine

DONALD R. MURPHY

"Listen, Doctor, the patient is telling you the diagnosis."

—Sir William Osler, MD

"History: The struggle between doctor and patient for information in which the doctor is frequently beaten."

—Karel Lewit, MD

INTRODUCTION

In assessing the patient with cervical-related complaints, certain principles must be followed that are not unlike those that apply to the assessment of patients with any neuromusculoskeletal disorder. There are three essential questions that one must ask oneself from the outset; these will direct the line of investigation in establishing a working diagnosis. The process of diagnosis, however, is ongoing and will continue as the management strategy is carried out and the patient's response to treatment is monitored.

During the patient workup, any condition that is capable of producing the symptoms that the patient is describing must be considered, and these conditions must be ruled out one by one until the most likely diagnosis is found. It is important to keep in mind that the majority of cervical spine syndromes are caused by some type of dysfunction, and usually a chain of dysfunction, but that pathoanatomy may in some cases occur in conjunction with this. Any suspicion of the presence of pathoanatomy must be considered in the context of the presence of functional pathology of the entire locomotor system. The modalities that are used to detect pathoanatomical changes should be used sparingly.

GENERAL PRINCIPLES

In evaluating a patient with a complaint related to the cervical spine, or one that may have a cervical component, it is important to have at the outset a clear view of the goals of the initial evaluation. Only by doing this can one be successful in establishing a working hypothesis upon which to base a rational management strategy. There are three essential questions of diagnosis that one must ask oneself in order to achieve this.

RULE OUT RED FLAGS

The foremost question is, *Is this a potentially serious or life-threatening condition?* Several conditions that may require immediate referral for further workup or emergency intervention can begin as neck, arm, or chest pain or headache. Often, these conditions, in their early stages, appear superficially identical to mechanical disorders of the cervical spine, but there are usually subtle (or not so subtle) clues that must be looked for in order to make an accurate diagnosis. This is true not only in the initial assessment, but also during subsequent encounters with the patient, as many times these clues do not reveal themselves until intervention is instituted.

The Agency for Health Care Policy and Research (AHCPR), in its guidelines on acute low back problems in adults,[1] provided an outline of those symptoms and signs that are most important to consider as red flags for serious conditions that can cause low back pain. There is a great deal of commonality between the red flags related to low back pain and those related to cervical pain. Tables 17–1 and 17–2 provide these red flags, adapted from the AHCPR low back pain guidelines. Tables 17–3 and 17–4 provide red flags for patients with headache.

IDENTIFY THE PRIMARY PAIN GENERATOR

The next question to ask oneself is, *What specific tissue(s) is (are) the primary source(s) of this patient's pain?* Several tissues in the cervical spine are capable of producing pain;[2, 3]

Table 17–2: Red Flags for Potentially Serious Conditions in Neck Pain Patients—Examination

FINDING	SUGGESTIVE OF
Pinpoint tenderness of the spinous process	Fracture or infection
Fever	Infection
Hyperreflexia with upgoing toes	Myelopathy
Palpable mass	Infection or neoplasm
Horner's syndrome	Tumor

they are listed in Table 17–5. Various conditions can cause these tissues to become painful. The most common conditions that serve as pain generators in cervical spine patients are myofascial trigger points (TrPs), joint dysfunction, internal disc derangement, and radiculopathy (Table 17–6). Of course, it is entirely possible, and quite common, to find more than one of these entities contributing at the same time to the overall pain picture. This complicates the clinical evaluation somewhat, but in most cases the painful tissues can be detected.

The importance of the identification of the primary pain generator(s) is so that strategies can be employed immediately to reduce its production of pain. The primary benefit of rapid pain relief is obvious—the reduction of the suffering of the patient—but it also, in the acute patient, helps reduce pain behavior. This aspect is essential in the

Table 17–1: Red Flags for Potentially Serious Conditions in Neck Pain Patients—History

FINDING	SUGGESTIVE OF
Major trauma such as motor vehicle accident or fall from a height	Fracture
Minor trauma in an older or potentially osteoporotic patient	Fracture
Age over 50 or under 20 years	Tumor or infection
History of cancer	Metastatic disease
Constitutional symptoms such as recent fever, chills, or unexplained weight loss	Infection or tumor
Recent bacterial infection, intravenous drug use, or immune suppression, such as from corticosteroids, transplant, or HIV	Infection
Pain that has no mechanical exacerbating or remitting factors	Infection or tumor
Symptoms in both the upper and lower extremities	Myelopathy

Table 17–3: Red Flags for Potentially Serious Disease in Headache Patients—History

FINDING	SUGGESTIVE OF
Sudden onset of severe headache in a patient who is not typically a headache sufferer	Intracranial hemorrhage
Changes in mood, personality, or mentation	Tumor or infection
Dysphagia, dysarthria, vertigo, or other bulbar symptoms	Tumor or vertebrobasilar dissection
Emesis	Tumor, infection, intracranial hemorrhage or vertebrobasilar dissection
Induced by coughing, sneezing, straining, or bending forward	Tumor or infection
History of cancer	Metastatic disease
Seizure	Early stage of tumor
Age over 50 years	Temporal arteritis, stroke
Visual loss	Glaucoma or other ocular disease

Table 17–4: Red Flags for Potentially Serious Disease in Headache Patients—Examination

FINDING	SUGGESTIVE OF
Fever	Infection
Papilledema	Tumor
Visual field abnormalities	Tumor
Exquisite scalp tenderness	Tumor
Hyperreflexia with upgoing toes	Tumor or infection
Nuchal rigidity or positive Kernig's sign, or both	Meningitis
Enlarged, tender temporal artery	Temporal arteritis
Leak of fluid from nose or ear with recent trauma	Skull fracture

Table 17–6: The Most Common Pain Generators in Cervical Spine Syndromes and Their Detection

PAIN GENERATOR	IDENTIFICATION
Myofascial trigger points (TrPs)	History and specific TrP palpation (see Chap. 19)
Joint dysfunction	History and motion palpation (see Chap. 13)
Internal disc derangement	History and response to spinal loading (see Chap. 26)
Radiculopathy	History, neurological examination, and nerve root tension signs

appropriate management of cervical spine syndromes and will be discussed further in later chapters.

It is also essential, however, to be clear on one point—do not confuse the *source* of the pain with the *cause* of the pain. That is to say, because a certain tissue is producing the actual nociceptive impulses that are leading to the experience of pain does not necessarily mean that this is the primary tissue to which the most attention must be directed during treatment. In fact, particularly in chronic conditions, it is far more common that the underlying *cause* of the generation of pain will be located somewhere remote from the actual *generator* of the pain.

IDENTIFY THE DYSFUNCTIONAL CHAIN AND THE KEY LINK IN THAT CHAIN

Finally, one must ask, *What has gone wrong with this person as a whole that would cause the primary pain generator(s) to generate pain?* The search for the answer to this question

Table 17–5: Tissues in the Cervical Spine That Are Capable of Generating Pain

Joint capsules

Muscles

Outer annulus of the disc

Nerve root

Nerve root sleeve

Ligaments

Skin and subcutaneous tissue (including fascia)

Blood vessels

Dura mater

Periosteum of the vertebrae

may involve assessment of the entire locomotor system to identify the key areas of dysfunction that may be involved. But consideration also must be given to the nonphysical (i.e., psychological, emotional, and spiritual) aspects of the patient in this search.

The relative importance of these three questions is different in different clinical situations. For example, in an acute, postwhiplash patient, ruling out red flags and identification of the primary pain generator(s) are of paramount importance, so that it can be determined if further investigation is necessary and the pain generator(s) can be identified and the pain quickly reduced. In this situation, the primary dysfunction and dysfunctional chain is of lesser importance. Once the subacute stage is reached, however, dysfunction becomes more important in the ongoing investigation. In the chronic patient, ruling out red flags is of lesser importance as, in most cases, if serious pathology was present, it would have fully manifested by the time the condition reaches chronic stages (though this is not always the case). Identification of the primary pain generator(s), while still important, takes a back seat to identification of the key dysfunction.

After these three essential questions have been answered, a strategy can be developed to address the significant factors as quickly and expeditiously as possible. This strategy development is discussed further in Chapter 28.

HISTORY

The importance of listening when interacting with a patient cannot be overstated. This perhaps is the single most important skill a health care provider can have, and one that is often neglected. This does not only apply to the history taking process, but to every interaction of any kind between provider and patient.

One of the essential aspects of listening that can dramatically enhance the recovery process is the quality of *em-*

pathy. Empathy is defined as, "understanding so intimate that the feelings, thoughts and motives of one are readily comprehended by another."[4] This is to be distinguished from *sympathy,* defined as, "a feeling or expression of pity or sorrow for the distress of another."[4] From the initial interaction with the patient through the final discharge, empathy should be provided in abundance and sympathy strictly avoided. This will be revisited in Chapter 28.

Effective history taking is an art form, a skill that is developed with practice. But there are important guidelines that one can follow that will dramatically improve one's ability in this process. Not all patients are good historians, so good history taking skills on the part of the provider are essential.

It is necessary for the provider to make the patient feel as much at ease as possible during the interview, as this will

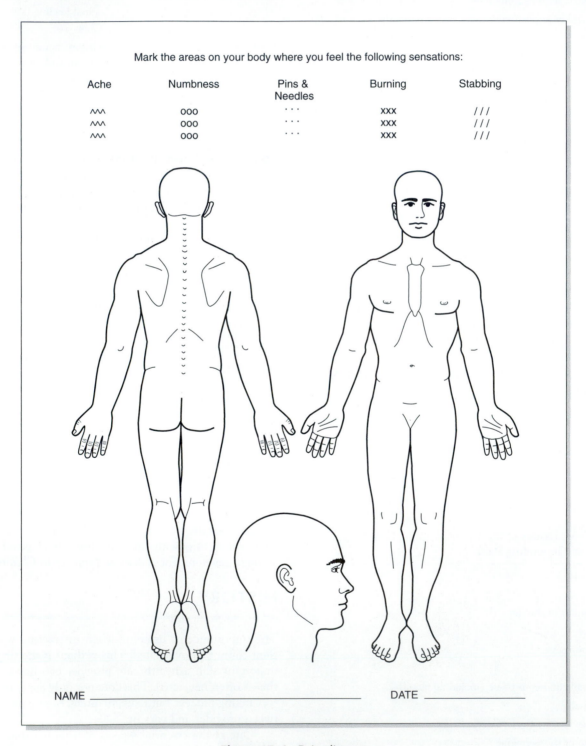

Figure 17–1. Pain diagram.

allow for easy exchange of information. The history taking process should not be an "interrogation," with rapid-fire questions being asked that demand quick answers.[5] Rather, it should be a comfortable process involving a give and take between provider and patient. Care needs to be taken to, on the one hand, avoid leaving out important information and, on the other hand, avoid allowing the patient to elaborate with so much irrelevant detail as to blur the important diagnostic information.

! CLINICAL PEARL

Some patients who have been in a motor vehicle accident (MVA) may be reluctant to provide certain information, such as whether they were wearing a seat belt or regarding previous injuries, for fear of negatively affecting their medicolegal case. This can backfire on them later when, in the course of litigation, these facts are revealed and it is discovered that they did not inform the provider of them. They need to be told to just present the facts as they are.

PAIN DIAGRAM

The pain diagram can be extremely valuable in initiating the investigation for the primary pain generator. The diagram is drawn in the patient's own hand and allows him or her to identify the precise symptoms experienced in precise location(s). An example of a pain diagram is provided in Fig. 17–1.

The patient can mark the areas of his or her body in which pain is experienced with whatever symbols corre-

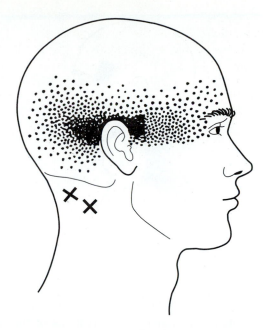

Figure 17–2. Trigger point referral patterns of the suboccipital muscles.

(Adapted from Travell JB, Simmons DG.[6] Myofascial Pain and Dysfunction: The Trigger Point Manual. Vol. 1. Baltimore, Md: Williams and Wilkins; 1983:322.)

spond most closely with what he or she is experiencing. The provider can then compare this drawing with the known pain referral patterns for the most common pain generating tissues in the cervical spine. Referred pain patterns for the most common TrPs involved in cervical spine syndromes are presented in Figures 17–2 through 17–11.[6]

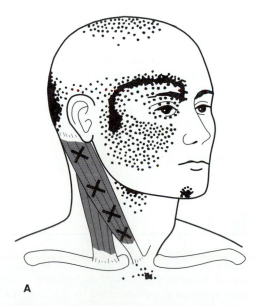
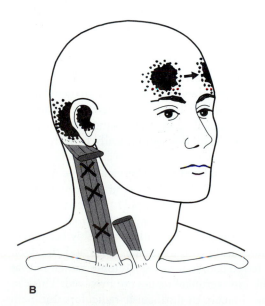

A   B

Figure 17–3. A and **B.** Trigger point referral patterns of the sternocleidomastoid muscle.

(Adapted from Travell JB, Simmons DG.[6] Myofascial Pain and Dysfunction: The Trigger Point Manual. Vol. 1. Baltimore, Md: Williams and Wilkins; 1983:203.)

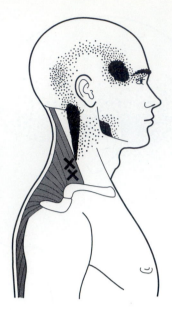

Figure 17–4. Trigger point referral patterns of the upper trapezius muscle.

(Adapted from Travell JB, Simmons DG.[6] Myofascial Pain and Dysfunction: The Trigger Point Manual. Vol. 1. Baltimore, Md: Williams and Wilkins; 1983:184.)

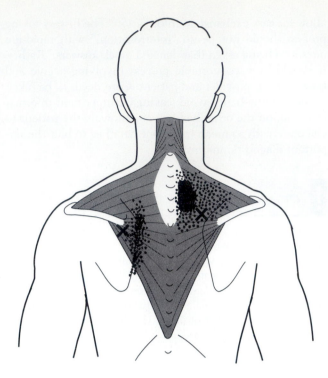

Figure 17–5. Trigger point referral patterns of the middle and lower trapezius muscles.

(Adapted from Travell JB, Simmons DG.[6] Myofascial Pain and Dysfunction: The Trigger Point Manual. Vol. 1. Baltimore, Md: Williams and Wilkins; 1983:185.)

This pain is frequently deep and aching in quality, although it can be quite sharp if severe. It may be associated with local burning pain in the affected muscle.

Referred pain patterns related to the intervertebral tissues are provided in Figures 17–12 through 17–20.[7–10] These referred pain patterns are scleretogenous in nature, and it should be noted that when the pain generator is the zygapophyseal joint capsule alone, the pattern is less extensive than when the intervertebral tissues in general are generating pain. As with TrP pain, the referred pain related to these tissues is typically deep and aching in quality and if it is described as sharp, this will typically be only in the local area of origin.

Patterns of pain related to the cervical nerve roots are provided in Figure 17–21.[11] These referred pain patterns are dermatomal in nature, but it should be noted that only uncommonly does referred pain related to radiculopathy follow these patterns precisely. Rather, probably because of concomitant irritation to the annular fibers and the dural sleeve, the referred pain follows a scleretome similar to that seen when the intervertebral tissues are involved. This can make it more difficult to distinguish radiculopathic pain from pain of intervertebral origin. However, when the pain is radiculopathic, it is likely to be more severe than that of intervertebral or zygapophyseal origin and is more likely to

be described as sharp in nature along the entire pattern. Radiculopathic pain is also more likely to extend fully into the distal aspects of the patterns, whereas this is relatively uncommon in nonradiculopathic pain.

Patterns of pain related to visceral disease can also encompass the cervical spine area, and mimic somatic disorders. Figure 17–22 provides the common sites of this referral.[12] It should also be noted that the referred pain elicited from scalene trigger points can be very similar in distribution to that of lower cervical dermatomal and scleretomal referral patterns.

! CLINICAL PEARL

In distinguishing pain of TrP origin from that of scleretogenous and/or dermatogenous origin, it is often noted that muscular pain is frequently described as "burning" in nature. This applies to the local pain over the muscle, and not to the referred pain pattern. So if the patient describes local burning pain with a dull ache referred into the extremity, suspect that the pain is arising from TrPs.

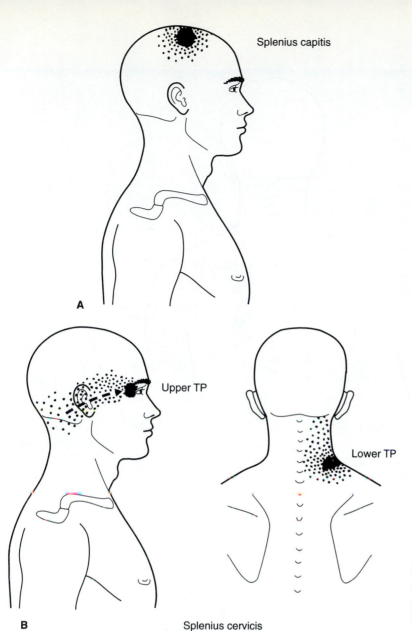

Splenius capitis

A

Upper TP

Lower TP

B

Splenius cervicis

Figure 17–6. Trigger point referral patterns of the splenius capitis **(A)** and cervicis **(B)** muscles.

(Adapted from Travell JB, Simmons DG.[6] Myofascial Pain and Dysfunction: The Trigger Point Manual. Vol. 1. Baltimore, Md: Williams and Wilkins; 1983:296.)

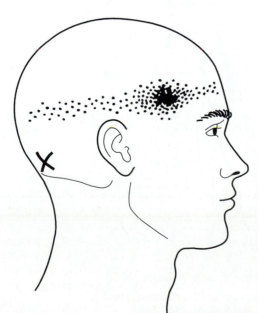

Figure 17–7. Trigger point referral patterns of the semispinalis capitis muscle.

(Adapted from Travell JB, Simmons DG.[6] Myofascial Pain and Dysfunction: The Trigger Point Manual. Vol. 1. Baltimore, Md: Williams and Wilkins; 1983:306.)

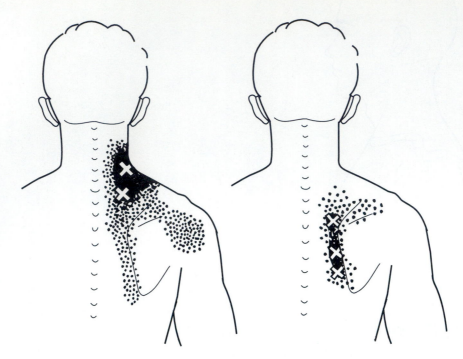

Figure 17–8. Trigger point referral patterns of the rhomboid and levator scapulae muscles.

(Adapted from Travell JB, Simmons DG.[6] Myofascial Pain and Dysfunction: The Trigger Point Manual. Vol. 1. Baltimore, Md: Williams and Wilkins; 1983:335, 426.)

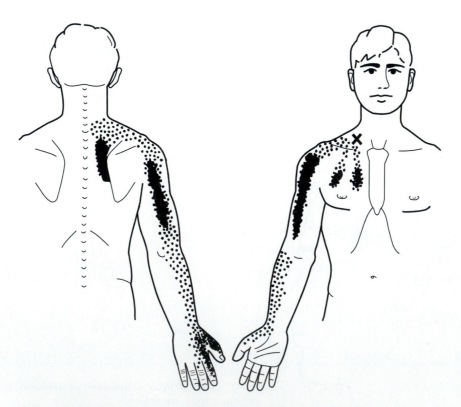

Figure 17–9. Trigger point referral patterns of the scalene muscles.

(Adapted from Travell JB, Simmons DG.[6] Myofascial Pain and Dysfunction: The Trigger Point Manual. Vol. 1. Baltimore, Md: Williams and Wilkins; 1983:345.)

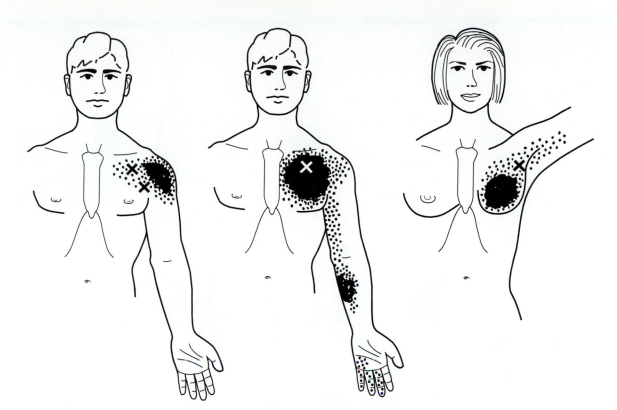

Figure 17–10. Trigger point referral patterns of the pectoralis major muscle.

(Adapted from Travell JB, Simmons DG.[6] Myofascial Pain and Dysfunction: The Trigger Point Manual. Vol. 1. Baltimore, Md: Williams and Wilkins; 1983:578.)

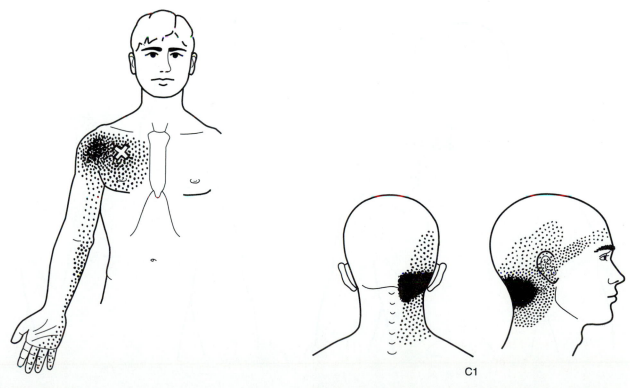

Figure 17–11. Trigger point referral patterns of the pectoralis minor muscle.

(Adapted from Travell JB, Simmons DG.[6] Myofascial Pain and Dysfunction: The Trigger Point Manual. Vol. 1. Baltimore, Md: Williams and Wilkins; 1983:599.)

Figure 17–12. Referred pain pattern of the intervertebral tissues at the C1 neurological level.

(Adapted from Feinstein B, Langton JNK, Jameson RM, et al.[7] Experiments on pain referred from deep somatic tissues. J Bone Joint Surg 1954;36A(5):155.)

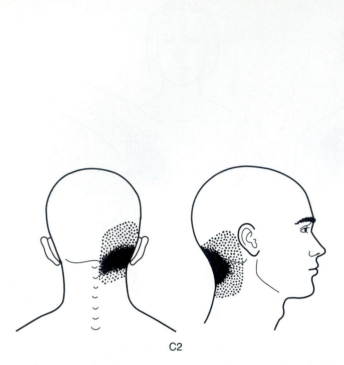

Figure 17–13. Referred pain pattern of the intervertebral tissues at the C2 neurological level.

(Adapted from Feinstein B, Langton JNK, Jameson RM, et al.[7] Experiments on pain referred from deep somatic tissues. J Bone Joint Surg *1954;36A(5):155.)*

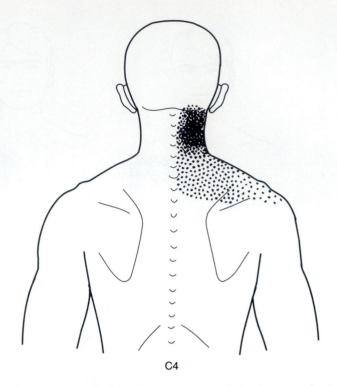

Figure 17–15. Referred pain pattern of the intervertebral tissues at the C4 neurological level.

(Adapted from Feinstein B, Langton JNK, Jameson RM, et al.[7] Experiments on pain referred from deep somatic tissues. J Bone Joint Surg *1954;36A(5):156.)*

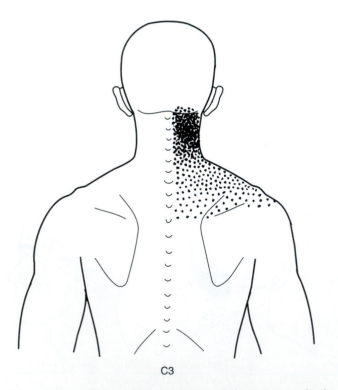

Figure 17–14. Referred pain pattern of the intervertebral tissues at the C3 neurological level.

(Adapted from Feinstein B, Langton JNK, Jameson RM, et al.[7] Experiments on pain referred from deep somatic tissues. J Bone Joint Surg *1954;36A(5):156.)*

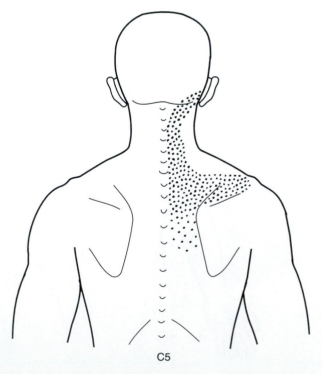

Figure 17–16. Referred pain pattern of the intervertebral tissues at the C5 neurological level.

(Adapted from Feinstein B, Langton JNK, Jameson RM, et al.[7] Experiments on pain referred from deep somatic tissues. J Bone Joint Surg *1954;36A(5):156.)*

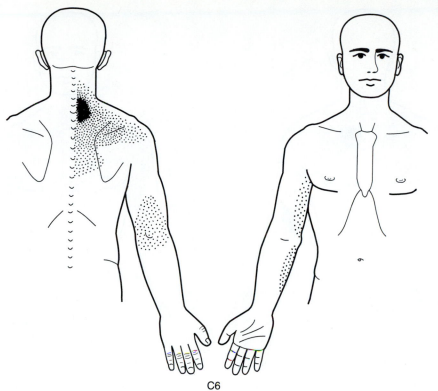

Figure 17–17. Referred pain pattern of the intervertebral tissues at the C6 neurological level.

(Adapted from Feinstein B, Langton JNK, Jameson RM, et al.[7] Experiments on pain referred from deep somatic tissues. J Bone Joint Surg 1954;36A(5):157.)

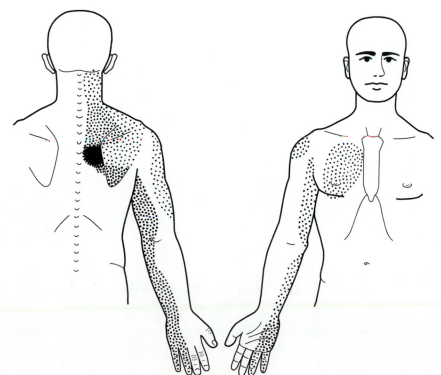

Figure 17–18. Referred pain pattern of the intervertebral tissues at the C7 neurological level.

(Adapted from Feinstein B, Langton JNK, Jameson RM, et al.[7] Experiments on pain referred from deep somatic tissues. J Bone Joint Surg 1954;36A(5):158.)

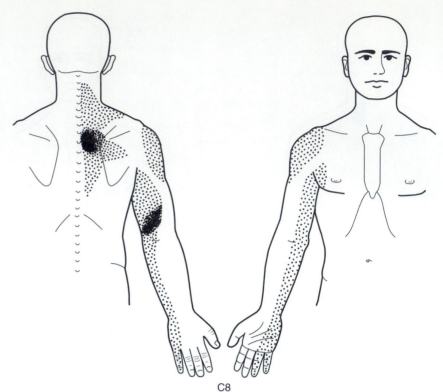

Figure 17–19. Referred pain pattern of the intervertebral tissues at the C8 neurological level.

(Adapted from Feinstein B, Langton JNK, Jameson RM, et al.[7] Experiments on pain referred from deep somatic tissues. J Bone Joint Surg 1954;36A(5):159.)

C8

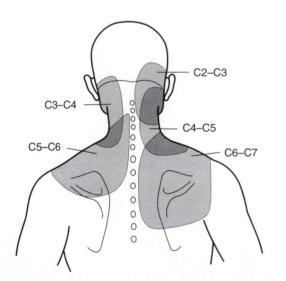

Figure 17–20. Referred pain patterns of the zygapophyseal joints of the cervical spine.

(Adapted from Dwyer A, Aprill C, Bogduk N. Cervical zygapophyseal joint pain patterns. I: A study in normal volunteers. Spine 1990;15(6):453–457.)

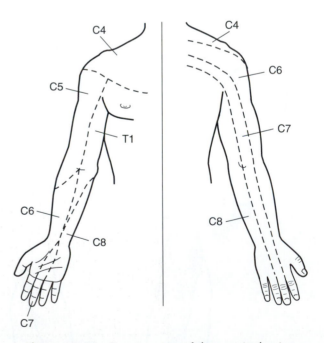

Figure 17–21. Dermatomes of the cervical spine.

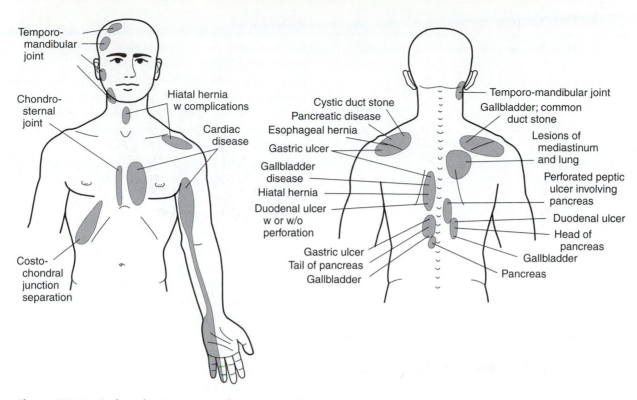

Figure 17–22. Referred pain patterns from viscera that can mimic cervical mechanical disorders.
(Adapted from Bland JH. Disorders of the Cervical Spine: Diagnosis and Medical Management. Philadelphia, Pa: WB Saunders; 1987:82.)

THE ORGANIZATION OF HISTORY TAKING

When taking the history, obtaining the information in an organized fashion is helpful in allowing the provider to make connections between the various factors in the case in a way that helps him or her establish a possible list of differential diagnoses. While every provider is unique and must adapt standard history taking principles to his or her own personal "style," one time-tested method is the use of the mnemonic OPQRST-AS. Each letter corresponds to a specific aspect of the history, and the mnemonic allows the provider to organize the interview in such a way as to maximize the quality of information gathering without wasting valuable time.

O—This stands for **onset.** That is, when did the symptoms first appear? This aspect establishes whether the complain is acute, subacute, chronic, or chronic-recurrent and whether there was a particular movement or activity that initiated the pain. A patient will not always volunteer that the problem is chronic-recurrent, so with acute patients, it is important to ask whether they have had the same or similar problems in the past and, if so, how many episodes they have had. This may be particularly important in the patient who has been involved in an MVA for purposes of apportionment of the degree of injuries to the MVA and the previous condition.

Also, in the post-MVA patient, it is essential to obtain specific information related to the accident, as provided in Table 17–7.[13–27] Perhaps the most important of these questions is whether the patient was aware of the impending impact. When a patient is not aware that he or she is going to be hit, the injuries are usually markedly more severe and are more likely to be longer lasting.[13, 14] The importance of risk factors for chronicity such as this will be discussed in Chapter 28.

Information regarding what movement or activity, if any, precipitated the pain can help in identifying the pain generator or key dysfunction. An example of this would be onset of neck and arm pain after starting an exercise program, which may suggest the scalenes as the primary pain generator and faulty breathing as a possible primary dysfunctional chain (though this must, of course, be distinguished from primary cardiac pain in the older individual). Information regarding onset can also alert the provider to the presence of a possible serious condition. An example of this is the sudden onset of severe headache in a patient with a negative headache history, which would be suggestive of acute cerebral hemorrhage. Included in the onset section should be previous providers that the patient has consulted regarding this condition and previous testing that has been performed, including the results. Also, included should be any previous treatment that the patient has received.

Table 17–7: Important Information To Be Obtained During History Taking in Patients Who Have Been Involved in Motor Vehicle Accidents

ACCIDENT-RELATED FACTOR	IMPORTANCE
Position in car (driver, front-seat passenger, rear-seat passenger)	Front-seat passengers are more likely to have long-term problems than drivers or rear-seat passengers[13, 14]
Year, make, and model of the vehicles involved	In rear-impact collisions, the greater the discrepancy in mass between the striking car and the struck car, the greater the ΔV (change in velocity of the struck car after the accident) and thus the greater likelihood for more significant injury of the occupant(s) of the struck car[15–18]
Estimated speed at the time of the accident	In rear-impact collisions, the passenger of a stationary car is more likely to have significant injury than one who is in a moving car[19]
Time of day (dawn, daylight, dusk, night)	This affects the ability of drivers to see
Road conditions (wet, dry, icy, snowing)	Icy or wet conditions allow for less friction upon braking, therefore increasing the impact velocity of the striking car as compared to dry conditions
Whether the patient's seat broke	In rear-impact collisions, the breaking of the seat back absorbs some of the energy of the collision, thereby imparting less to the occupant and reducing injury severity[20]
Whether the patient was wearing a seat belt and shoulder harness	The wearing of seat belts saves lives, but, especially with a shoulder harness, increases the severity of cervical injury[15, 21]
Whether the air bag deployed and, if so, whether the patient was struck by it	Air bags generally only deploy in frontal impacts, but when they do, they can strike the occupants and cause injury
The position of the patient, particularly head position (turned to talk to passenger, looking out the window, etc.) at the moment of impact	Having the head turned increases the severity of the injury[13, 19, 22]
Whether the patient had both or no hands on the steering wheel	This provides general information on the manner in which the patient braced him- or herself and can help explain upper extremity injuries
Whether the patient's brakes were applied	Not having the brakes applied increases the acceleration of the struck vehicle, and thus its occupant(s), increasing the severity of the injury
Whether the patient was aware of the impending impact	The occupant being unaware of the impending impact dramatically increases the severity of the injuries, because there is not enough time to prime the stabilizing system[19, 23]
Whether the patient struck anything in the inside of the vehicle	This increases the likelihood of further injuries, especially when there is head strike
Whether the patient's vehicle struck any other object after the initial impact	This increases the likelihood for further injuries, with different vectors than from the original impact[16, 24]
Whether the patient lost consciousness	This increases the likelihood of mild traumatic brain injury (MTBI), although its absence does not rule out MTBI[25]
Estimated property damage to the patient's vehicle	There is generally little relationship between damage to the vehicles and occupant injury;[26] however, this must be documented for possible future reference for medicolegal purposes
Estimated property damage to the other vehicle (if known)	See above
Whether the police came to the scene and a report made	It is important to obtain the police report to correlate it with the patient's description of the accident, which is often based on a fuzzy memory due to "shock"
When the symptoms first started (immediately, next day, several days later)	The earlier the onset of the symptoms, the greater the severity of the injury and the greater likelihood of long term problems[13, 19, 21, 22, 27]

Adapted from Croft AC. Whiplash: The Masters' Program Module 2 Notes. San Diego, Calif: Spine Research Institute of San Diego; 1996.

❗ CLINICAL PEARL

While it is important to ask the patient the investigations that have been done and the results, you must request the reports from these investigations; do not rely on the patient to accurately recall them. I can remember one patient that I saw complaining of neck and arm pain with numbness in the hand who told me that she "had an EEG" done by a neurologist. When I received the neurologist's records, I discovered that he had performed an EMG and that it had revealed median neuropathy!

P—This is actually separated into two sections, **Pr** and **Pa,** that is, **provoking factors** and **palliative factors.** In this section, the patient should be specifically questioned on those positions, movements or activities that increase his or her symptoms, and those that decrease them. These questions help obtain vital information that can be utilized both in identifying the pain generator and the dysfunctional chain that may be involved.

Provoking factors include movements of the cervical spine, coughing, sneezing, straining, sitting as opposed to standing, getting up from a seated position, and activities of daily living such as use of a computer. Palliative factors include movements, positions, and activities, but also whether previous treatments or attempts at self-care have been helpful. This aspect should include those medications and physical modalities that have been prescribed and home use of ice or heat.

❗ CLINICAL PEARL

Being precise in describing exacerbating and remitting factors is essential. I recall one patient who described numbness in his "hand" (he did not recall exactly what part of his hand) when sleeping with his arm elevated. This caused me to suspect the presence of a tight pectoralis minor causing compression to the brachial plexus. The patient later told a resident who was rotating with me, that this occurred only when his elbow was flexed, not when it was extended. When the resident told me this, it changed my suspicion to that of tardy ulnar palsy, which turned out to be the correct diagnosis.

Q—This stands for **quality,** or how the patient describes the pain. This aspect can be included in the pain diagram (see Figure 17–1), but it is best to repeat it during history taking to allow the patient to elaborate. The importance of inquiring about the quality of the pain is that, as stated earlier, the type of pain generated by the various pain-sensitive tissues in the cervical spine can be described differently. So this question can help to raise suspicion regarding the primary pain generator. For example, pain of muscular origin is often described as "burning" in quality, pain of joint capsule or ligamentous origin is often de-

scribed as a "deep ache," and pain of nerve root origin is often described as "sharp and superficial." As was stated earlier, however, true nerve root pain is uncommon and in a patient with radiculopathy, the pain generator is often the nerve root sleeve, which will produce pain that is described as a "deep ache." This pain, however, is usually more severe than ligamentous or capsular pain, and is generally much more disturbing to the patient. Any of the above tissues can produce pain that is described as "sharp," and this usually is reflective of increased severity of pain rather than implicating a particular tissue.

R—This stands for **radiation** or **referral.** It helps in identifying the primary pain generator and requires knowledge of the referred pain patterns that can result from nociceptive input from the various pain-sensitive tissues of the cervical spine (see Figures 17–2 through 17–22).

S—This stands for **site,** and allows the patient to indicate the primary area from which the pain appears to be arising. With both this aspect and referral or radiation, it is best to have the patient point with one finger to the exact area of pain. This helps to further localize the primary pain-generating tissue, in that if the patient is able to identify a specific location for the pain, it is more likely arising from nerve root irritation or from a superficial tissue such as the skin or subcutaneous tissue. On the other hand, deep tissues such as muscles or joint capsules tend to create pain that is more diffuse and poorly localized.

It is important, in patients with both local and referred pain, to ask which of the two is more severe. Typically, with referred pain related to joint dysfunction, myofascial trigger points or internal disc derangement, the local pain is more severe than the referred pain. But the opposite will often be the case in patients with radiculopathy.

T—This stands for **timing** and allows the patient to indicate whether the pain is worse at certain times of the day or during certain seasons or weather conditions. Burning pain that is worse at the end of the day often suggests poor muscular endurance, whereas pain that is worse in the morning suggests an articular origin. However, when patients describe persistent pain in the morning, especially when pain during the day has resolved with treatment, it is important to question them regarding the type and age of their mattress and pillow.

AS—This stands for **associated symptoms** and it is the point in the history at which the provider questions the patient with regard to other symptoms that may be accompanying the primary complaint. For example, in a patient experiencing neck pain with referral into the upper extremity, it is important to ask if the patient has been experiencing numbness, paresthesia, motor loss, gastrointestinal distress, or chest symptoms related to the pain. In a patient complaining of headache, questioning the patient with regard to blurred or double vision, dizziness, trouble with swallowing or speaking, numbness in the hands or face, or other bulbar symptoms is essential.

Particularly in the patient who has experienced cervical trauma, but in headache patients as well, it is important to inquire about visual disturbances such as difficulty reading, oscillopsia, impaired near-vision, difficulty with distance evaluation, and intolerance to moving objects in the visual field. This may be reflective of oculomotor dysfunction, which may need to be addressed in treatment.

REVIEW OF SYSTEMS

The history should also include a complete review of systems (Fig. 17–23). This is a general overview of the patient's health status and often reveals subtle clues that the patient may have overlooked, forgotten, or assumed were not relevant to his or her condition.

By the end of the patient history, the provider should have a list of potential answers to the three essential questions of diagnosis that were outlined earlier in the chapter; that is: (1) Are there any red flags for potential serious illness? (2) What is the primary pain generator(s)? (3) What has gone wrong with this person as a whole that would cause the primary pain generator(s) to generate pain? The examination will further narrow down the number of possible answers to these questions.

SAMPLE CASES—HISTORY

CASE 1

A 25-year-old female marketing assistant is seen with a complaint of headache. She actually has two different headache scenarios. One is described as a dull ache over the temporal areas bilaterally that she has had for over a year and that occurs several times per week. The other is of more recent onset (4 weeks) and is described as "sharp" and well localized to the right occipital area. This pain is much more severe than in the temporal headaches. She rates the temporal pain as follows:

- Currently, 5 out of 10.
- On average, 5 out of 10.
- At its worst, 5 out of 10.

She rates the right-sided occipital pain as follows:

- Currently, 8 out of 10.
- On average, 9 out of 10.
- At its worst, 10 out of 10.

Her Headache Disability Inventory score is 34. Her pain diagram is reproduced in Figure 17–24.

She states that there are no particular exacerbating or remitting factors related to the headaches and she regularly lifts weights without increasing pain. She denies the presence of neurological symptoms in the extremities as well as visual disturbances, dizziness, trouble swallowing or speaking, or other bulbar symptoms. She also denies recent fever or mental status changes.

She sits at a computer most of her workday and is nearsighted. Her eye prescription has recently changed, but this was before the onset of the more recent occipital headache.

Past medical history and review of systems are unremarkable. She is taking birth control pills but no other medications. Family history is unremarkable.

Questions
- Are there any red flags for serious disease?
- What do you suspect could be the primary pain generator(s)?
- What do you suspect could be the primary dysfunction(s)?
- What is the importance of the patient's age and gender?
- What will you look for on examination?

CASE 2

This 38-year-old female homemaker is seen complaining of left-sided neck, chest, and arm pain which began insidiously 5 days previously. She has no previous history of pain in this area. She describes the pain as "sharp and stabbing" and located in the lower cervical spine on the left, with referral into the left axilla, lateral arm and forearm, and into the dorsum of the hand. The arm and axillary pain is more severe than the neck pain. She is antalgic in forward head placement and left lateral flexion with her arm held adducted and across her chest as if it is in a sling. She is quite distressed over the intensity of the pain and breaks into tears several times during history taking.

She had been on hydrocodone bitartrate with acetaminophen, which did not reduce the pain, and a fentanyl patch, which made her sick.

The pain is aggravated by any movement outside of her antalgic position and she is not able to find any position, movement, or activity that provided substantial relief. She denies the presence of numbness or paresthesia in the upper extremities as well as motor weakness. She also denies the presence of precordial pain, shortness of breath, nausea, or gastrointestinal complaints. She rates her pain on a numerical rating scale as follows:

- Currently, 10 out of 10.
- On average, 10 out of 10.
- At its worst, 10 out of 10.

Her Neck Pain and Disability Index score is 68 percent. Her pain diagram is reproduced in Figure 17–25.

She has a history of two lumbar discectomies, the second of which included laminectomy, both of which failed to relieve chronic low back and leg pain that she had been experiencing. Otherwise, her past medical history is unremarkable. Review of systems is also unremarkable. Family history is remarkable for breast cancer in her older sister, who is undergoing chemotherapy.

Review of Systems

General:
___ Wt. change
___ Fever
___ Chills
___ Night sweats
___ Weakness
___ Fatigue

Eyes:
___ Vision
___ Pain
___ Discharge

Ears:
___ Hearing
___ Ringing
___ Pain
___ Discharge

Nose:
___ Pain
___ Bleeding
___ Taste

Mouth/Throat:
___ Sores
___ Bleeding
___ Taste

Skin:
___ Rash
___ Itching
___ Hair changes
___ Nail changes

Neurologic:
___ Headaches
___ Dizziness
___ Fainting
___ Convulsions

G-I:
___ Appetite
___ Abdominal pain
___ Vomiting
___ Diarrhea
___ Constipation

G-U:
___ Frequent urination
___ Painful urination
___ Incontinence
___ Impotence
___ Sterility

Cardio:
___ Murmur
___ Chest pain
___ Palpitations
___ Difficulty breathing
___ Cough
___ Wheezing
___ Blue extremities
___ Swollen extremities

Breasts:
___ Mass
___ Pain
___ Discharge
___ Self-exam

Psychologic:
___ Anxiety
___ Depression
___ Moods
___ Memory

**Musculoskeletal
Pain/Paresthesia:**
___ Neck
___ Upper extremities
___ Upper back
___ Lower extremities
___ Lower back

Additional Data: _____
_____

Figure 17–23. Review of systems form.

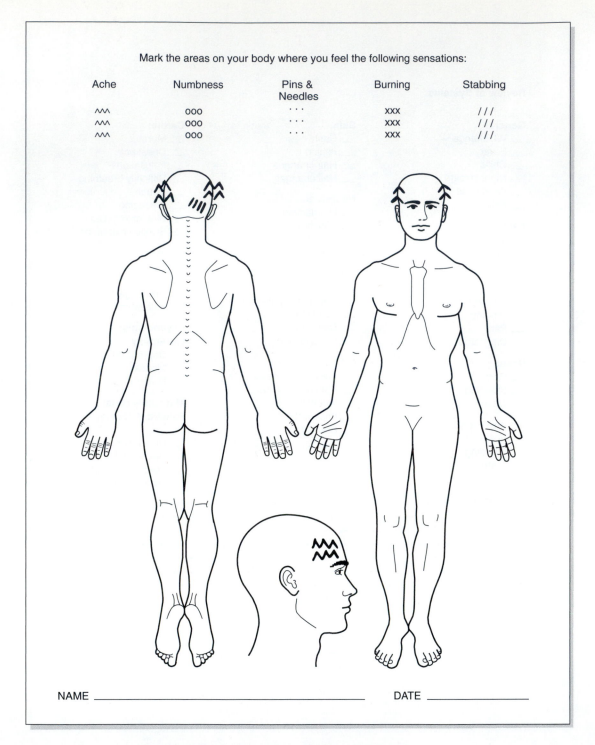

Figure 17–24. Pain diagram for Case 1.

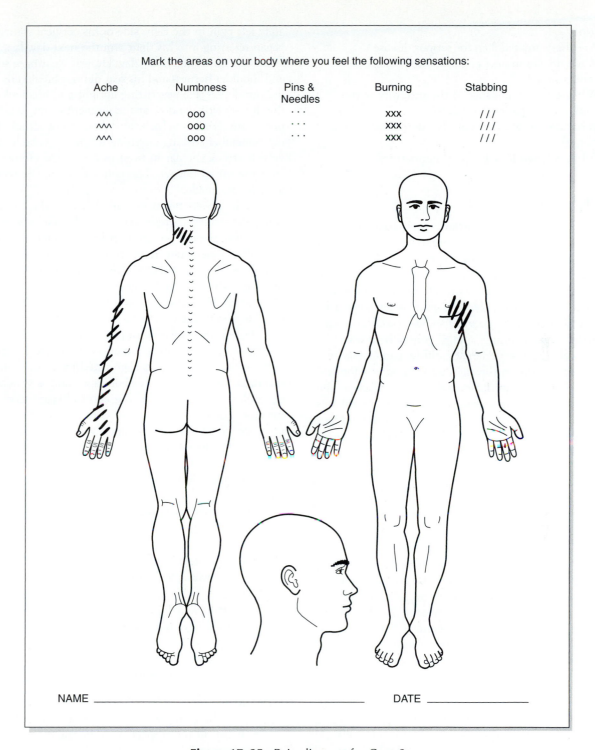

Figure 17–25. Pain diagram for Case 2.

Questions

- Are there any red flags for serious disease?
- What do you suspect could be the primary pain generator(s)?
- What is the significance of the intensity of the pain and the patient's distress?
- What do you suspect could be the primary dysfunction(s)?
- What will you look for on examination?

CASE 3

This 58-year-old male letter carrier is seen complaining of neck and bilateral arm pain. This began several years prior to his initial visit, but has gotten worse over the previous year. He describes the pain as being a dull ache over the lower posterior cervical spine with referral into the lateral arms and forearms bilaterally. The pain is aggravated by general movements of the cervical spine, as well as coughing, sneezing, and straining, and is generally relieved by rest. He has also been experiencing diffuse paresthesia over the lateral upper arm on the right and the lateral forearm on the left, but these do not disturb him as much as the pain. Further questioning reveals some feelings of weakness in the left lower leg and foot when walking, with mild foot drop. He rates his pain on a numerical rating scale as follows:

- Currently, 4 out of 10.
- On average, 5 out of 10.
- At its worst, 6 out of 10.

His Neck Pain and Disability index reveals a score of 48 percent. His pain diagram is reproduced in Figure 17–26.

Past medical history is remarkable for hypertension, for which he is taking a beta blocker and diuretic, and an ulcer, which had been successfully treated. Review of systems reveals occasional urinary frequency for which he has not seen his primary care practitioner. Family history is remarkable for stroke in his mother and heart disease in his father.

Questions

- Are there any red flags for serious disease?
- What do you suspect could be the primary pain generator(s)?
- What do you suspect could be the primary dysfunction(s)?
- What will you look for on examination?

CASE 4

This 39-year-old male attorney is seen complaining of pain in the right cervicothoracic junction. He had been in an MVA 8 months earlier in which the 1997 Toyota Camry in which he was sitting in the driver's seat at a traffic light was struck from behind by a 1988 Buick LeSabre. He immedi-

ately felt pain in the right side of his cervical spine, which began referring into his right arm the next day. It was mid-afternoon on a sunny, dry day. He was wearing a seat belt and shoulder harness and his seat did not break. His air bag did not deploy. He was sitting upright and was looking out the driver's side window at the moment of impact. He was not aware that his vehicle was about to be struck. He did not remember striking anything inside his vehicle, and his vehicle struck the car in front of it (a 1996 Honda Civic) after the initial impact. The police came to the scene and a report was made.

He had been taken by ambulance to the local emergency department, where cervical radiographs were taken and he was given a prescription for ibuprofen and a cervical collar. Emergency room records reveal that the radiographs were unremarkable. He was later seen by a chiropractor, who treated him with manipulation and ultrasound. The cervical and arm pain gradually resolved, but the pain in the cervicothoracic junction remained.

He describes the present pain as being a dull ache over the right cervicothoracic junction with referral into the right scapula. The pain is aggravated by all movements of the right arm, particularly abduction, and is generally relieved by rest. Rotation of the cervical spine to the right increases the pain as well, but more mildly. He denies the presence of neurological symptoms in the extremities as well as gastrointestinal or chest symptoms, but he states that he has noticed that his right eyelid has begun drooping somewhat. He is not sure when this started but is confident that it was not present before the MVA. He rates his pain on a numerical rating scale as follows:

- Currently, 6 out of 10.
- On average, 7 out of 10.
- At its worst, 9 out of 10.

His Neck Pain and Disability Index reveals a score of 54 percent. His pain diagram is reproduced in Figure 17–27.

Past medical history and review of systems are unremarkable. Family history is remarkable for prostate cancer for which his father recently had surgery.

Questions

- Are there any red flags for serious disease?
- What do you suspect could be the primary pain generator(s)?
- What do you suspect could be the primary dysfunction(s)?
- What will you look for on examination?
- Are there any significant risk factors for chronicity?

EXAMINATION

It has been said that 80 percent of the essential information needed to arrive at a working diagnosis comes from the history. In the case of cervical spine patients, the

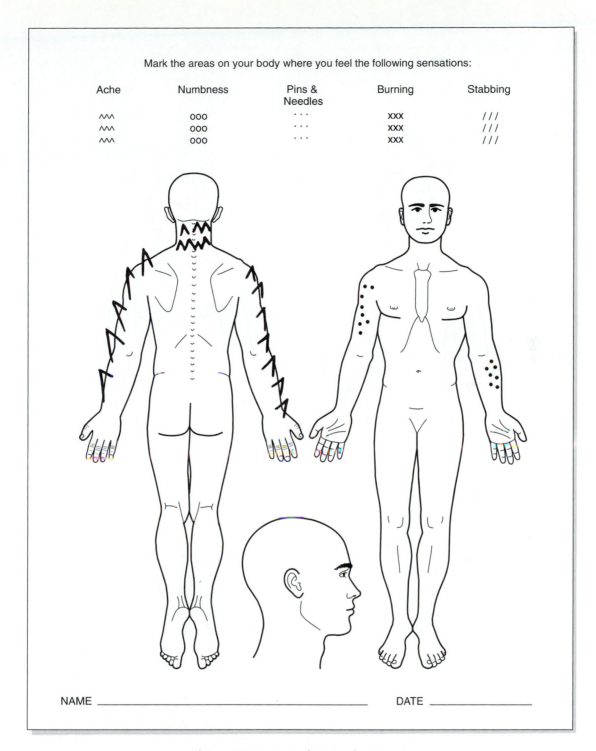

Figure 17–26. Pain diagram for Case 3.

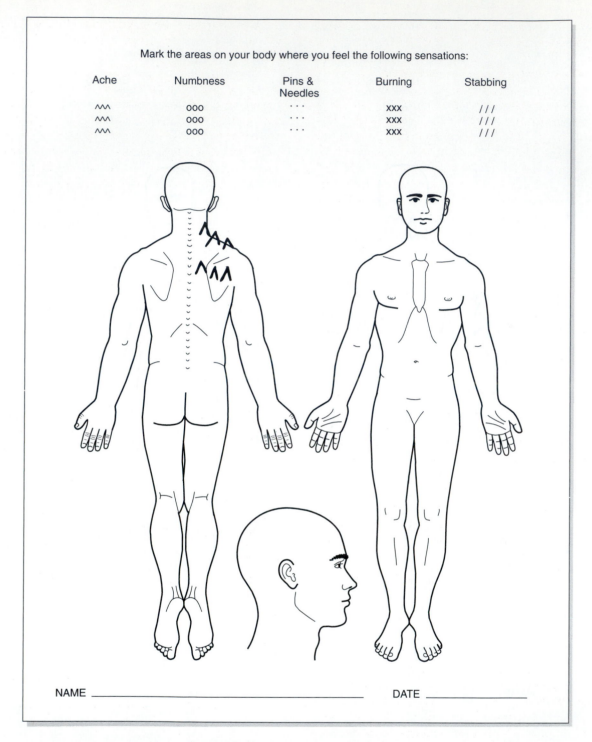

Figure 17–27. Pain diagram for Case 4.

percentage, while still greater than 50 percent, is somewhat less than 80 percent. While the history is of immense importance in the clinical evaluation of the patient, the physician's eyes and hands can uncover a great deal of vital information that the ears were not able to detect. The utilization of the information obtained during history taking can be affected by human factors such as bias, shyness, poor communication skills, and so forth, on the part of both the physician and the patient. But the information that the body provides to the eyes and hands of the physician is always accurate and the detection and utilization of this information is only at the mercy of the physician's human factors, over which he or she has some degree of control.

The clinical examination confirms or denies the impressions at which the physician arrived during the initial history taking and records review process. The two most important tools that are used in the process of examination are those of sight and touch (in addition to hearing). That is, the cornerstone of good examination is inspection, palpation, and auscultation. Palpation, in particular, is a skill that is invaluable in the assessment of locomotor system function, and there is no replacing well-developed palpation skills. Unfortunately, these modalities have been criticized in recent years for being "subjective." Poor interexaminer reliability is frequently found with many examination procedures that rely on inspection and palpation.[28–31] However, the experience of information sharing between physician and patient is a difficult one to objectify and to study scientifically, and is one in which a great variety of factors are involved other than merely whether a certain test is "positive" or "negative." Research into the effectiveness of examination procedures is still in its infancy[32] and conclusions should not be drawn from the preliminary work that has been done thus far. In addition, recent reliability studies that have improved on previous methodology[33–39] or that place palpation in the context of other clinical signs[40, 41] show better reliability of palpation procedures. Studies of examination procedures in which the procedure is taken out of the context of the history and examination process as a whole are bound to show poor reliability. Information regarding, for example, levels of significant joint dysfunction is obtained as much from the history as from palpation itself. Also, studies of palpation that do not include questioning the patient regarding pain, tenderness, or hyperalgesia during the procedure cannot adequately assess the situation that occurs in the "real world" clinical setting. Palpation alone is virtually worthless without the rest of the patient evaluation. The value comes from the entire package—history, examination, special tests, and response to treatment.

VITAL SIGNS

The examination is designed to finalize the answers to the three essential questions that have been discussed throughout this chapter: (1) Are there any red flags for potential serious illness? (2) What is the primary pain generator(s)?

(3) What has gone wrong with this person as a whole that would cause the primary pain generator(s) to generate pain?

With this in mind, the first procedure that must be performed is the taking of vital signs. Probably the most important of these actions in the cervical pain patient is taking the temperature. If vascular compromise is suspected, as may be the case with thoracic outlet syndrome (see Chap. 9), bilateral blood pressures may help clarify the diagnosis. Also, low or high blood pressure may have important implications in the headache patient.

 CLINICAL PEARL

In a patient experiencing cervical pain in the presence of fever, spinal infection should be assumed until it is proven otherwise.

INSPECTION

Inspection begins when the physician first lays eyes on the patient. Antalgia, gait, posture, stature, and mentation can be observed during the initial greeting, as well as throughout the history taking and examination process. These things should also be assessed systematically during the examination. The postural examination (see Chap. 14) consists of observing the patient standing at rest and can demonstrate not only potential underlying factors for the perpetuation of pain (i.e., "poor posture"), but also reveal clues as to the primary pain generator or the primary dysfunctional chain (see Chaps. 14 and 20). These findings must be considered in the context of the clinical situation. For example, the presence of head tilt in the acute patient may be reflective of antalgia, whereas in the chronic patient is may be reflective of poor neuromuscular communication and control (see Chap. 14).

! **CLINICAL PEARL**

When you see antalgia, think disc!

It is important during inspection to observe for skin lesions, scars, or visual masses, which can assist in identifying red flags or key dysfunctions. In addition, many of the important tests provided in the appendix to this chapter involve inspection and observation.

Inspection also allows the assessment of movement patterns and other neuromuscular functions related to the cervical spine. These include hip extension, shoulder abduction, cervical flexion, swallowing, and breathing, as well as the stepping test, postural foot reaction, and Revel's test (see Chap. 14). These tests are among the most important for identifying the primary dysfunctional chain.

PALPATION

Palpation encompasses static palpation, such as for skin temperature and texture, masses, myofascial trigger points, or soft tissue changes; motion palpation for assessing joint function; and muscle length tests for assessing muscle function. So it is utilized in the detection of red flags for serious disease, the primary pain generator(s), and the key dysfunctions and dysfunctional chains. There is no substitute for good palpation skills in examining patients with cervical spine syndromes.

An important aspect of palpation of the cervical spine is looking for lymphadenopathy and masses. Presence of lymphadenopathy suggests tumor, metastasis, or throat or ear infection.[12] When a mass is found in the cervical spine, it is important to ask the patient about any change in size over time. Rapid enlargement suggests malignancy or progressive inflammation. Stable size suggests chronic inflammation, slow-growing tumor, or congenital anomaly. Rapid fluctuation in size suggests a congenital cyst or recurrent inflammation.[42]

! CLINICAL PEARL

The general rule is that a palpable mass in the cervical spine that has been present for 7 days is probably inflammatory, for 7 months is probably neoplastic, and for 7 years is probably congenital.

One important purpose of palpation is to reproduce the patient's pain. If this can be done, one can be relatively confident that the primary pain generator has been found, although, this can sometimes be deceiving. As was discussed earlier, one of the most common pain generators in patients with cervical spine syndromes is the myofascial TrP. Palpation of TrPs can often exactly reproduce the pain that the patient is experiencing, but it must be noted that, because the provoking factors of the patient's pain discovered during history taking usually do not involve direct palpation of the pain generating tissue, the pain produced by palpation of the TrP may be more intense and somewhat different in character than that which the patient has been experiencing. For this reason, it is important to ask patients whether palpation reproduces the pain they are complaining of and, if not, whether the difference is one of intensity or character or one of location. If the intensity or character are different, but the location is the same, there is a good likelihood that this TrP is a primary pain generator.

If a good history was taken and the pain drawings were completed by the patient, it is not necessary to examine for TrPs every muscle that can cause pain in the neck or head. Knowledge of the referred pain patterns of the most important muscles (see Figs. 17–2 to 17–11) allows the physician to narrow down the examination to only those muscles that are likely to refer pain to the area of complaint.

Joint motion palpation not only helps identify potential primary pain generators but also key dysfunctions. This must be carried out in a way that maximizes reliability and validity of the findings. Therefore, it must include not only restriction of motion at neutral, but also loss of joint play at end range and production of pain[38, 43, 44] (see Chap. 13). Skin and subcutaneous tissue palpation can also detect the primary pain generator or the key dysfunction[45] (see Chap. 19).

Muscle length tests detect muscle hypertonicity or tightness that can be a significant dysfunction and contributor to the dysfunctional chain. It is not necessary to assess every muscle that can possibly be involved, as this would be exceedingly time consuming. Rather, the movement pattern and TrP examinations allow for the narrowing down of the most important muscles that must be evaluated. For example, if upon examining shoulder abduction movement pattern (see Chap. 14), one finds that the superior angle of the scapula is elevating instead of depressing, the levator scapulae should be evaluated for the presence of hypertonicity or tightness. There may be no need to evaluate other muscles. If, upon postural examination shoulder unleveling is detected, the upper trapezius on the side of the high shoulder will require specific assessment.

RANGE OF MOTION

The measurement of cervical range of motion (ROM) contributes virtually nothing to answering the three essential questions of diagnosis. However, pain and restriction on ROM does correlate well with the presence or absence of injury.[46–48] So for documentation and medicolegal purposes, there are those circumstances in which it has utility. But it should not be used for the purpose of obtaining information related to the establishment of a diagnosis. The normal ROM for the cervical spine is provided in Table 17–8 and the technique for measurement using dual inclinometers is provided in the appendix of this chapter.

Table 17–8: Normal Cervical Ranges of Motion

RANGE	NORMAL VALUE (DEGREES)
Flexion	50
Extension	60
Right lateral flexion	45
Left lateral flexion	45
Right rotation	80
Left rotation	80

Adapted from American Medical Association. Guides to the Evaluation of Permanent Impairment. 4th ed. Chicago, Ill: American Medical Association; 1993.

EXAMINATION FLOW

Effective examination requires that the information be obtained in an organized and systematic manner. This not only maximizes the assimilation of the information, it also makes the process easier on patients, as it is best to avoid making them repeatedly change from standing to lying to seated positions any more than is necessary.

An organized flow is provided here, to assist the physician in organizing his or her protocol. It must be remembered that the examination must be tailored to the clinical situation and the information that was obtained on history taking. Simply running through a group of examination procedures and hoping to come up with a diagnosis is not conducive to an effective examination. Rather, the examination should be specific to the individual patient in attempting to answer the three essential questions of diagnosis.

First, vital signs are taken in all patients (blood pressure, temperature, pulse, respirations). Height and weight can be measured if deemed necessary. A sample of the remainder of the examination flow is provided in Table 17–9.

IS "GEORGE'S TEST" NECESSARY?

It has previously been felt by many cervical spine specialists that what has come to be called "George's test" was a necessary part of the cervical spine examination in order to detect abnormalities in the vertebrobasilar system that may be reflective of increased risk to cervical manipulation. This test consists of four parts,[49, 50] including assessment of past medical history and family history for risk factors for stroke, taking bilateral blood pressures, auscultating the carotid and subclavian arteries for bruits, and performing the "vertebro-basilar artery functional maneuver," in which the cervical spine is placed in a position of maximum rotation and hyperextension and the patient is asked about symptoms that might be referable to vertebrobasilar ischemia. However, it has been demonstrated repeatedly[51–57] that there is little or no correlation between the findings of George's test and risk of vertebrobasilar dissection, and there is little agreement as to how the test should be performed and interpreted (see Chap. 22).

In spite of this, George's test has continued to be utilized, with the thought that for medicolegal purposes, it should be done to show that, if complications from cervical manipulation do occur, the practitioner at least performed the "screening procedure." This rationale is no longer credible. It makes no sense to subject the patient to a "screening procedure" that is completely invalid and only gives the practitioner a false sense of security regarding the degree of risk for the procedure. This, in light of the fact that complications from cervical manipulation are exceedingly rare,[58–63] can only lead to the conclusion that the four part George's test should be abandoned, for clinical and med-icolegal purposes. It should not be held as a yardstick for medicolegal cases.

One procedure that does make sense is what Ferezy has termed the "premanipulative position"[64] (originally suggested by Smith and Estridge[65]). This procedure can be performed, rather than at the initial examination only, during every visit in which cervical manipulation is applied. It consists of placing the patient into the position in which the manipulative maneuver is to be applied and, prior to the delivery of the thrust, oscillation, or muscle energy procedure (depending on the type of manipulation being used), asking the patient if he or she has any sensations that are unusual or disturbing, such as dizziness, numbness, headache, or visual changes. This may not only serve to identify the presence of vertebrobasilar compromise (though this may not always be reliable[54]), but it also affords the physician an opportunity to wait to be sure that the patient is fully relaxed and that conditions are such that the success and safety of the manipulation is maximized, and to obtain from the patient verbal consent to continue.

This, of course, is not to say that the other components of George's test (i.e., assessing risk factors, bilateral blood pressure, auscultation of the carotid and subclavian arteries) are never useful for other purposes. These elements can often be an important part of the overall workup of the cervical spine patient, depending on the clinical situation. It merely means that these tests should not be used routinely for the purpose of screening for the risk of vertebrobasilar dissection.

IMAGING AND OTHER ADVANCED TESTS

In recent years, good clinical evaluation tools have in many cases taken a back seat to modern, high-tech diagnostic tests, providing many physicians with a false sense of security that these tests can be relied upon in establishing a diagnosis. While tests such as magnetic resonance imaging (MRI) and electromyography (EMG) have made tremendous contributions to our ability to evaluate structural and functional abnormalities in our patients in a way that was only dreamed of just a few years ago, there have been problems with them that have limited their usefulness. The most important problem that has developed is that these tests, particularly imaging modalities such as radiography, computed tomography, and MRI, have placed unnecessary and deceptive emphasis on structural abnormalities as a cause of cervical spine syndromes.

In addition, in the modern era of concern for not only effectiveness in health care, but also efficiency (i.e., cost-effectiveness), there is little tolerance for ordering high-tech tests, even radiographs, without definitive evidence for their necessity. When patients complain of cervical-related pain, these tests are all too often ordered merely out of routine or because the examiner does not possess the

Table 17–9: Sample Examination Flow for Patients with Common Cervical Spine-Related Complaints*

EXAMINATION POSITION	PATIENT WITH NECK OR ARM PAIN	PATIENT WITH HEADACHE	PATIENT WITH DIZZINESS
Standing	Postural inspection (see Chap. 14) Heel, toe and tandem walking (see Appendix 17A) Postural foot reaction (see Chap. 14) Stepping test (see Chap. 14)	Postural inspection (see Chap. 14) Heel, toe and tandem walking (see Appendix 17A) Postural foot reaction (see Chap. 14) Stepping test (see Chap. 14)	Postural inspection (see Chap. 14) Heel, toe and tandem walking (see Appendix 17A) Postural foot reaction (see Chap. 14) Stepping test (see Chap. 14)
Seated	Spinal motion palpation (see Chap. 13) Shoulder abduction movement pattern (see Chap. 14) Cranial nerve examination (see Appendix 17A) Sensory, reflex and motor examination (see Appendix 17A) Rapid alternating movements, heel-to-shin, finger-to-nose, etc (see Appendix 17A) Plantar response (see Appendix 17A) Cervical compression (see Appendix 17A) Cervical distraction (see Appendix 17A) Valsalva maneuver (see Appendix 17A) Bakody's sign (see Appendix 17A) Brachial plexus tension test (see Appendix 17A) Shoulder depression (see Appendix 17A) Revel's test (see Chap. 14) Auscultation of subclavian arteries (see Appendix 17A)	Spinal motion palpation (see Chap. 13) Shoulder abduction movement pattern (see Chap. 14) Cranial nerve exam (see Appendix 17A) Sensory, reflex and motor examination (see Appendix 17A) Rapid alternating movements, heel-to-shin, finger-to-nose, etc (see Appendix 17A) Plantar response (see Appendix 17A) Auscultation of carotid arteries (see Appendix 17A) Revel's test (see Chap. 14)	Spinal motion palpation (see Chap. 13) Shoulder abduction movement pattern (see Chap. 14) Cranial nerve exam (see Appendix 17A) Sensory, reflex and motor examination (see Appendix 17A) Rapid alternating movements, heel-to-shin, finger-to-nose, etc (see Appendix 17A) Plantar response (see Appendix 17A) Hautant's test (see Appendix 17A) Rotating stool test (see Chap. 10) Auscultation of carotid arteries (see Appendix 17A) Revel's test (see Chap. 14) Hallpike maneuver (see Appendix 17A)
Supine	Foot motion palpation (if positive postural foot reaction) Assessment of foot skin drag (if positive postural foot reaction) (see Chap. 14) Abdominal examination Soto-Hall test (see Appendix 17A) Trigger point palpation Cervical flexion movement pattern (see Chap. 14) Cervical stability test	Foot motion palpation (if positive postural foot reaction) Assessment of foot skin drag (if positive postural foot reaction) (see Chap. 14) Kernig's test (see Appendix 17A) Trigger point palpation Cervical flexion movement pattern (see Chap. 14) Cervical stability test	Foot motion palpation (if positive postural foot reaction) Assessment of foot skin drag (if positive postural foot reaction) (see Chap. 14) Trigger point palpation Cervical flexion movement pattern (see Chap. 14) Cervical stability test
Prone	Hip extension movement pattern (see Chap. 14) Sacroiliac joint motion palpation	Hip extension movement pattern (see Chap. 14) Sacroiliac joint motion palpation	Hip extension movement pattern (see Chap. 14) Sacroiliac joint motion palpation

*There are a large number of other tests and examination procedures that may be required, depending on the findings on history and the other examination findings. Also, some of the procedures provided here will not be necessary in certain patients in certain clinical situations. The specifics of the examination should be decided upon by the physician in each circumstance.

Table 17–10: Imaging Modalities Most Commonly Used in Cervical Spine Patients

Plain film radiography

Conventional tomography

Computed tomography (CT)

CT myelography

Magnetic resonance imaging (MRI)

Bone scan

knowledge or skills to perform an appropriate diagnostic and functional evaluation of the patient. Nonetheless, there are clinical situations in which imaging and other special tests are extremely helpful in the assessment and management of the cervical spine patient, particularly in ruling out red flags and identifying the primary pain generator. See Table 17–10 for the most important imaging tests for the cervical spine patient and Chapter 16 for a detailed description of these tests.

DECISION MAKING IN ADVANCED TESTING

Several questions should be asked before ordering advanced testing. The first is, *Will this change my management approach?* If the findings of the test are likely to influence management decisions, it is likely the test is necessary. The most obvious example of this is the decision to recommend surgery in a patient with cervical radiculopathy. This decision cannot possibly be made until advanced testing (in this case, most commonly, MRI) has been performed to clarify the presence of a space occupying lesion like herniated nucleus pulposus (HNP). Another example, building on the previous one, is a case in which recommendation for surgery is being considered, MRI has been ordered and shows HNP, but it is not clear from the clinical findings that the HNP demonstrated on examination is producing the symptoms. EMG may be helpful in this case to clarify the presence and level of radiculopathy (see Chap. 9). With this second example, however, in most cases a good clinical examination should render the EMG unnecessary, particularly as usually substantial and progressive neurological deficit, easily detected on examination, should be present before surgical intervention is considered.

Another question to consider is, *Will this test assist in the current management strategy?* There are times when the patient's concerns are such that worrying about what is wrong creates so much distress as to interfere with the recovery process. In such cases, imaging to clarify the diagnosis may not be necessary for the physician, but it helps put the patient's mind at ease and can have a powerful effect on the patient. This indication for imaging may apply when a pathoanatomical lesion is the primary pain generator, in which case the modality demonstrates the presence of the lesion, or when some type of dysfunction is the primary pain generator, in which case the modality rules out pathoanatomy.

! CLINICAL PEARL

I can think of a recent case in which this principle applied. A patient was referred to me with neck and arm pain that was of a severity the likes of which I have rarely seen. She was doubled over and crying and had been in this state for several days. On examination, it was clear she had a radiculopathy, most likely C6. I saw no reason at the time to order imaging, as with little neurological deficit and such a recent onset, surgery was not a consideration. However, on speaking with her it appeared that, as distressed as she was about the intensity of the pain, a great deal of her distress revolved around not knowing what was causing it. My telling her that she "most likely" had C6 radiculopathy related to HNP was not very convincing, so an MRI was ordered. This demonstrated the presence of HNP at the level of C5–6. The clarification of the diagnosis calmed her mind to the extent that, while the acute pain was still considerable, the patient's distress and pain behavior decreased markedly and acute care measures could be instituted.

In addition to putting the patient's mind at ease, imaging to clarify the diagnosis can at times enhance the confidence of both the physician and patient in the treatment approach currently being employed, even if this treatment approach is unlikely to change as a result of the test. Confidence in the treatment approach is essential to its success and can greatly enhance the recovery process.[66]

Caution must, however, be exercised when this rationale is used as a reason for ordering imaging. First, it can at times be very dangerous to allow the patient's distress to dictate clinical procedures. Patients do not have the clinical perspective that physicians have, and every attempt must be made by the physician to confidently explain the working diagnosis to the patient. Before advanced testing is ordered the physician must be confident in the ability of the patient to understand the diagnosis in the context of the entire clinical picture and the patient's life in general. In addition, ordering imaging modalities must not serve as a substitute for the physician's confidence in his or her diagnostic ability. Advanced tests must not be used as a "crutch" by the physician to compensate for poor history taking and examination skills.

Another potential danger in ordering imaging for the purpose of easing the patient's distress or increasing his or her confidence is that, as was discussed earlier, the majority of cervical spine syndromes are caused by dysfunction, rather than pathoanatomy, but asymptomatic pathoanatomy is common. Thus, a patient with, for example, neck and arm pain caused by a combination of lower cervical joint dysfunction, scalene trigger points, and faulty breathing pattern may have unrelated and asymptomatic lower cervical disc herniation. Ordering an MRI in this patient to "rule out" cervical radiculopathy and put the patient's mind at ease may have the opposite effect of unnecessarily complicating the situation and creating confusion in the mind of the patient.

A third question to ask oneself when considering ordering imaging is, *Is there a reasonable likelihood that the test will uncover an abnormality (e.g., anomaly) that will substantially alter the treatment approach, and how potentially dangerous would treatment be if performed in the absence of awareness of this abnormality?* An example of this would be the consideration of using thrusting manipulation in the upper cervical spine. It is often advisable, though not routinely necessary, to obtain plain film radiographs prior to the institution of this treatment to rule out the presence of an anomaly that may render this treatment contraindicated (e.g., unstable os odontoideum or subluxation of the atlas related to absence of the transverse ligament). Although these anomalies are uncommon, the potential risk of the treatment being applied in their presence may dictate the need for radiographs to rule them out. Before the radiographs are obtained, however, one must ask, Can the treatment be altered in a way that increases safety without substantially reducing effectiveness (e.g., using a nonthrusting technique)?

Finally, the question must be asked, *Is there anyone else, besides the physician and the patient, who requires clarification that can be provided by an advanced test?* This particularly applies to patients who have been involved in an MVA in which medicolegal proceedings are taking place. Often, attorneys for both the plaintiff and defense benefit from the "objective" evidence that an advanced test may provide. The drawback to this is that in most cases of cervical injury resulting from MVA, these tests do not objectively demonstrate the cause of the patient's pain because the pain results from dysfunction, which the tests do not reveal. This can cause doubt as to the veracity of the patient's complaints.

For strictly clinical purposes, ordering imaging, in the absence of trauma, should be used only uncommonly and only when there is a sound rationale and a specific preconsidered purpose for the order. Minimalism should guide the process. Unfortunately, because of the litigious society in which we live, medicolegal considerations must also be involved in the decision. This reality dictates that imaging modalities sometimes be used in situations in which purely clinical considerations may not necessarily warrant the ordering of an advanced test. The decreased efficiency and increased cost that results from this are side effects of the legal environment in which most physicians work.

CERVICAL TRAUMA

Cervical trauma is a situation in which most patients will require at least plain film radiographs. This is because of the increased possibility of substantial injury to both bone and connective tissues that may be detected on plain films.

Table 17–11: American College of Radiology Criteria for Imaging After Cervical Trauma

PATIENT GROUP	RADIOLOGICAL EXAMINATION
Asymptomatic and normal examination	No radiographs appropriate
Symptoms of cervical injury and/or neurological signs	AP, lateral, and APOM views appropriate For oblique views, there was no consensus
Ligamentous injury suspected (this is based on the presence of continued pain) and plain films negative	Flexion and extension views For oblique views there was no consensus
Neurological signs and/or symptoms and normal plain films	MRI CT myelography For oblique views, there was no consensus
Screening films suggest injury to C0–2	Conventional tomography CT with reformatting For MRI and CT myelography, there was no consensus
Impaired consciousness	AP, lateral, and APOM views For oblique views, there was no consensus

AP, anteroposterior; APOM, anteroposterior open mouth; CT, computed tomography; MRI, magnetic resonance imaging.

Standard views should be obtained soon after the injury and, if it is deemed necessary, flexion and extension views should be taken as soon as the patient is able to move close to the full range in these directions to assess for passive instability. Sound guidelines have been provided by the American College of Radiology.[67] These are provided in Table 17–11.

OTHER SPECIAL TESTS

There are times when other tests are required to clarify the diagnosis in cervical patients. As with imaging modalities, these should only uncommonly be necessary. When they are necessary, however, they can be extremely valuable in determining the presence of more serious pathology (as would have been suggested by the presence of red flags on history and examination) and, in some cases, identifying the primary pain generator.

ELECTRODIAGNOSTIC TESTS

These modalities evaluate the function of the peripheral and central nervous system and detect interferences with this function.[68] In most cases, the tests that would be utilized in the cervical spine patient are EMG, nerve conduction studies, and somatosensory evoked potentials. Their purpose is to rule out radiculopathy, peripheral neuropathy, and central nervous system lesion.

In most cases, the differential diagnosis between radiculopathy, peripheral neuropathy, and pseudoradicular syndrome can be made on the basis of history and examination findings (see Chap. 9). However, in those uncommon circumstances in which the diagnosis may be in doubt, EMG/NCV is very reliable. Also, in medicolegal circumstances, these tests can help objectify clinical findings.

LABORATORY TESTS

Laboratory tests are often necessary in the presence of red flags for serious disease. Blood chemistry and complete blood count with differential are usually adequate for this purpose. These tests may include the following:[69]

- *Calcium, phosphorus, and alkaline phosphatase*—elevation suggests the presence of metabolic bone disease
- *Acid phosphatase*—in the male patient over 50, elevation suggests the presence of metastatic carcinoma from the prostate
- *Serum muscle enzymes* (CPK, SGOT, LDH, aldolase)—elevation suggests the presence of primary muscle disease
- *Blood glucose*—to assess for the presence of diabetes mellitus
- *Serum uric acid*—elevation suggests gout; however, only one in ten people with elevation have gout and it may be normal early in the disease process
- *Rheumatoid factors*—to assess for the presence of rheumatoid arthritis
- *Antinuclear antibodies*—these are seen in a variety of chronic diseases, including systemic lupus erythematosus (SLE), rheumatoid arthritis, scleroderma, dermatomyositis, and Sjogren's disease; it must be remembered, however, that they are present in 25 percent of healthy women over 60
- *LE cells*—to assess for the presence of SLE
- *HLA-B27*—primarily to assess for the presence of ankylosing spondylitis or Reiter's disease, as well as psoriatic arthritis and enteropathic arthritis
- *Erythrocyte sedimentation rate*—an excellent screening test that generally is elevated in the presence of some type of inflammatory process; it is nonspecific to type, although in ankylosing spondylitis, polymyalgia rheumatica, and discitis it may be the only positive lab finding; it can be elevated in infectious processes as well as noninfectious and carcinomatous processes
- *Erythrocytes*—anemia can be found in systemic illness such as SLE, collagen vascular diseases, as well as chronic infections

- *Leukocytes*—elevated leukocytes can be seen with infection (although its absence does not rule this out) as well as rheumatoid arthritis; leukopenia occurs with chronic collagen vascular disease and some viral infections; eosinophilia can be seen with polyarteritis and certain carcinomatous processes; monocytosis can be seen with collagen vascular diseases
- *Platelets*—thrombocytosis can occur in inflammatory and carcinomatous processes
- *C-reactive protein*—this can indicate the presence of rheumatic fever

DISCOGRAPHY

Discography, also referred to as provocation discography, is used less frequently in the cervical spine than the lumbar spine, and does not have the validity of lumbar discography, with a greater number of false positives.[70] Nonetheless, it can still can be a useful tool in identifying whether the disc is the primary pain generator in the case in which this tissue is suspected to be the primary source, but examination procedures, specifically involving assessment of response to loading (see Chap. 26) do not provide definitive findings.

The procedure involves injecting dye into the disc under fluoroscopic control.[71] A positive response is characterized by reproduction of the patient's pain upon injection, and leakage of the dye into the annulus of the disc, indicating internal disc disruption.

SAMPLE CASES—EXAMINATION

CASE 1 (SEE EARLIER HISTORY)

Examination reveals a well-nourished, pleasant woman who appears to be in no acute distress. Blood pressure is found to be 104/70 on the left. Temperature is 97.9° F, pulse is 84 per minute, and respirations are 16 per minute.

Heel, toe, and tandem walking are within normal limits. Romberg's position is held with eyes closed without difficulty. Examination of cranial nerves II through XII is within normal limits. Pupils are round, equal, and reactive to light and accommodation. Sensory response to pinprick in the upper and lower extremities is normal. Motor strength is 5/5 bilaterally throughout. Muscle stretch reflexes are 2+ and symmetrical throughout. Plantar responses are downgoing bilaterally. Rapid alternating movements, finger-to-nose and heel-to-shin movements are carried out without evidence of dysmetria or tremor.

Motion palpation reveals symptomatic pathomechanics at the level of C0–1 bilaterally. Palpation of the upper trapezius and sternocleidomastoid muscles reveals taut bands and twitch responses. Directly palpating the nodular portions of these taut bands reproduces the patient's temporal headaches. Taut bands are also noted in the right obliquus capitis inferior muscle. Directly palpating the nodular portions of these taut bands reproduces her right sided occipital pain.

Cervical flexion movement pattern is positive for inhibition of the deep neck flexors. Hip extension movement pattern is within normal limits. Plucking of the mid-thoracic erector spinae muscle on the left causes a twitch in both that muscle and the left hamstring. Tenderness is noted to palpation of the left sacrotuberous ligament.

Questions

- Are there any red flags for serious disease?
- What is the likely primary pain generator(s)?
- What is the primary dysfunction or dysfunctional chain?
- Is it necessary to order imaging or other tests? If so, which ones and why?

CASE 2 (SEE EARLIER HISTORY)

Examination reveals a well-nourished, pleasant woman who is crying and in obvious severe pain. Blood pressure is 136/86 on the left, temperature is 98.6° F, pulse is 96 per minute, and respirations are 20 per minute.

Examination of cranial nerves II through XII is within normal limits. Pupils are round, equal and reactive to light and accommodation. Sensory response to pinprick in the upper and lower extremities is normal. Motor strength is 5/5 bilaterally with the exception of the left triceps, which is 4+/5, although testing this muscle is painful and it is difficult to distinguish breakaway weakness related to pain and true motor loss. Finger extensors, however, are also 4+/5 and did not elicit pain upon testing. Muscle stretch reflexes are 2+ and symmetrical throughout. Plantar responses are downgoing bilaterally. Rapid alternating movements and finger-to-nose movements could not be performed due to pain, but heel-to-shin movements are carried out without dysmetria or tremor.

Auscultation of the heart is unremarkable.

All passive and active movements of the cervical spine are painful and loading in all directions peripheralizes the patient's pain. Attempting to move the patient's arm out of the adducted and internally rotated (hand against the chest) position also peripheralizes her pain. Motion palpation reveals symptomatic pathomechanics at the level of C6–7 on the left. Muscle palpation reveals diffuse tension and tenderness throughout the left scalene, posterior cervical, upper trapezius, and levator scapulae muscles.

Questions

- Are there any red flags for serious disease?
- What is the likely primary pain generator(s)?
- What is the primary dysfunction or dysfunctional chain?
- What is the significance of the arm position of relief?
- Is it necessary to order imaging or other tests? If so, which ones and why?
- What acute care strategy would be best for this patient?

CASE 3 (SEE EARLIER HISTORY)

Examination reveals a somewhat overweight, pleasant man who appears to be in no acute distress. Blood pressure is 146/94 on the left, temperature is 97.8° F, pulse is 80 per minute, and respirations are 16 per minute.

Examination of cranial nerves II through XII is within normal limits. Heel walking is difficult on the left. Toe and tandem walking are within normal limits. Sensory response to pinprick in the upper and lower extremities is normal. Motor strength is 5/5 bilaterally with the exception of left foot dorsiflexion, which is 4/5. Muscle stretch reflexes are 3+ and symmetrical throughout. Plantar responses are upgoing bilaterally. Hoffman's test is positive bilaterally. Rapid alternating movements, finger-to-nose and heel-to-shin movements are carried out without dysmetria or tremor.

Motion palpation reveals symptomatic pathomechanics at the level of C5–6 bilaterally and asymptomatic pathomechanics at the levels of T5–6, T12–L1, and L5–S1 bilaterally. Muscle palpation reveals tenderness and taut bands in the scalenes bilaterally. Directly palpating the nodular portions of these taut bands reproduces the patient's arm pain bilaterally.

Questions

- Are there any red flags for serious disease?
- What is the likely primary pain generator(s)?
- What is the primary dysfunction or dysfunctional chain?
- Is it necessary to order imaging or other tests? If so, which ones and why?
- Would nonsteroidal anti-inflammatory drugs be appropriate for this patient? Why or why not?

CASE 4 (SEE EARLIER HISTORY)

Examination reveals a well-nourished, pleasant man who appears to be in no acute distress. Blood pressure is 120/82 on the left and 122/82 on the right. Temperature is 98.6° F, pulse is 64 per minute, and respirations are 16 per minute.

Examination of cranial nerves II through XII is within normal limits with the exception of unequal pupil size, the right being smaller than the left. Pupils are reactive to light and accommodation. Heel, toe, and tandem walking are within normal limits. Sensory response to pinprick in the upper and lower extremities is normal. Motor strength is 5/5 bilaterally throughout. Muscle stretch reflexes are 2+ and symmetrical throughout. Plantar responses are downgoing bilaterally and Hoffman's test is negative. Rapid alternating movements, heel-to-chin and finger-to-nose movements are carried out without evidence of dysmetria or tremor.

Motion palpation reveals symptomatic pathomechanics at the right first costotransverse joints and C5–6 on the right. Muscle palpation reveals taut bands that exhibited twitch responses in the right rhomboid muscle. Directly palpating the nodular portions of these taut bands reproduces the patient's pain. Examination of movement patterns reveals elevation and medial deviation of the superior angle of the scapula on shoulder abduction. Cervical flexion, hip extension, swallowing, and breathing are within normal limits. The S reflex is absent and the stepping test is normal.

Questions:

- Are there any red flags for serious disease?
- What is the likely primary pain generator(s)?
- What is the primary dysfunction or dysfunctional chain?
- What is the significance of the shoulder abduction pattern being faulty while the hip extension pattern was normal?
- Is it necessary to order imaging or other tests? If so, which ones and why?

CONCLUSION

There is no substitute for a good patient workup, which revolves around the history and examination. It allows for interaction between physician and patient in which information regarding the patient's state of health is shared. This interaction involves both verbal and nonverbal communication, and it is important for the physician to be mindful of subtle signs that can be important clues to the correct diagnosis.

There are three essential questions of diagnosis that the physician must keep in mind at all times. These relate to the presence of symptoms or signs that may suggest potentially serious illness or injury, identification of the specific tissue that is the source of the patient's pain, and evaluation of the patient as a whole in the attempt to determine why this tissue would generate pain. The answers to these questions help the physician decide on the steps that need to be taken to further investigate the patient's complaint and to formulate a management strategy.

The initial encounter, however, is only the first step in the diagnostic process. Perhaps the most important tool that we have at our disposal is our treatment. A trial of treatment of what we think is the relevant key link in the suspected chain of dysfunction is the definitive tool in confirming or denying our initial working diagnosis. This aspect of management will be discussed further in Chapter 28.

REFERENCES

1. Bigos S, Bowyer O, Braen G, et al. *Acute Low Back Problems in Adults*. Clinical Practice Guideline, No. 14. AHCPR Pub. No. 95-0642. Rockville, Md: Agency for Health Care Policy and Research, Public Health Service, U.S. Department of Health and Human Services, U.S. Department of Health and Human Services; December 1994.
2. Massey AE. Movement of pain-sensitive structures in the neural canal. In: Grieve GP, ed. *Modern Manual Therapy of the Vertebral Column*. Edinburgh: Churchill Livingstone; 1986:182–193.
3. Seaman DR, Winterstein JF. Dysafferentation: A novel term to describe the neuropathophysiological effects of joint complex dysfunction. A look at likely mechanisms of symptom generation. *J Manipulative Physiol Ther* 1998;21(4):267–280.
4. Morris W, ed. *The American Heritage Dictionary of the English Language*. Boston, Mass: Houghton Mifflin Company; 1976.
5. Ferezy JS. *The Chiropractic Neurological Examination*. Gaithersburg, Md: Aspen; 1992.
6. Travell JG, Simons DG. *Myofascial Pain and Dysfunction: The Trigger Point Manual*. Vol. 1. Baltimore, Md: Williams and Wilkins; 1983.
7. Feinstein B, Langton JNK, Jameson RM, et al. Experiments on pain referred from deep somatic tissues. *J Bone Joint Surg* 1954;36A(5):981–997.
8. Dwyer A, Aprill C, Bogduk N. Cervical zygapophyseal joint pain patterns. I: A study in normal volunteers. *Spine* 1990;15(6):453–457.
9. Aprill C, Dwyer A, Bogduk N. Cervical zygapophyseal joint plan patterns. II: A clinical evaluation. *Spine* 1990;15(6):458–461.
10. Dreyfuss P, Michaelson M, Fletcher D. Atlanto-occipital and lateral atlanto-axial joint pain patterns. *Spine* 1994;19(10):1125–1131.
11. Rowland LP. Clinical syndromes of the spinal cord and brain. In: Kandel ER, Schwartz JH, Jessel TM, eds. *Principles of Neural Science*. 2nd ed. Norwalk, Conn: Appleton & Lange; 1991:711–730.
12. Bland JH. *Disorders of the Cervical Spine: Diagnosis and Medical Management*. Philadelphia, Pa: WB Saunders; 1987.
13. Parmar HV, Raymakers R. Neck injuries from rear impact road traffic accidents: Prognosis in persons seeking compensation. *Injury* 1993;24:74–78.

14. Harder S; Veilleux M; Suissa S. The effect of socio-demographic and crash-related factors on the prognosis of whiplash. *J Clin Epidemiol* 1998;51(5):377–384.

15. Croft AC. Advances in the clinical understanding of acceleration/deceleration injuries to the cervical spine. In: Lawrence DJ, ed. *Advances in Chiropractic*, Vol. 2. St. Louis, Mo: Mosby; 1995:1–37.

16. Nordhoff LS, Emori R. Collision dynamics of vehicles and occupants. In: Nordhoff LS, ed. *Motor Vehicle Collision Injuries. Mechanisms, Diagnosis and Management.* Gaithersburg, Md: Aspen; 1996:278–327.

17. Bailey M. Assessment of impact severity in minor motor vehicle collisions. In: Allen ME, ed. *Musculoskeletal Pain Emanating from the Head and Neck: Current Concepts in Diagnosis, Management and Cost Containment.* New York, NY: Haworth Press; 1996:21–38.

18. Gough JP. Human occupant dynamics in low-speed rear end collision: An engineering perspective. In: Allen ME, ed. *Musculoskeletal Pain Emanating from the Head and Neck: Current Concepts in Diagnosis, Management and Cost Containment.* New York, NY: Haworth Press; 1996:11–19.

19. Sturzenegger M, Radanov BP, Di Stefano G. The effect of accident mechanisms and initial findings on the long-term course of whiplash injury. *J Neurol* 1995;242:443–449.

20. Foret-Bruno JY, Dauvilliers F, Tarriere C. Influence of the seat and head rest stiffness on the risk of cervical injuries. 13th International Technical Conference on Experimental Safety Vehicles. S-8-W-19, 968–974; 1991.

21. Croft AC. Soft tissue injury: Long and short term effects. In: Foreman SF, Croft AC, eds. *Whiplash Injuries: The Cervical Acceleration/Deceleration Syndrome.* 2nd ed. Baltimore, Md: Williams and Wilkins; 1994:289–362.

22. Radanov BP, Sturzenegger M, Di Stefano G. Long term outcome after whiplash injury: A 2-year follow up considering features of injury mechanism and somatic, radiologic and psychosocial factors. *Medicine* 1995;74:281–297.

23. Croft AC. Low speed rear impact collisions: In search of an injury threshold. In: Allen ME, ed. *Musculoskeletal Pain Emanating from the Head and Neck: Current Concepts in Diagnosis, Management and Cost Containment.* New York, NY: Haworth Press; 1996:39–46.

24. Croft AC. Biomechanics. In: Foreman SM, Croft AC, eds. *Whiplash Injuries: The Cervical Acceleration/Deceleration Syndrome.* Baltimore, Md: Williams and Wilkins, 1988:1–72.

25. Swenson RS. Minor head injury. *J Neuromusculoskel Sys* 1997;5(4):133–143.

26. Robbins MC. Lack of relationship between vehicle damage and occupant injury. SAE 970494.

27. Croft AC. A proposed classification of cervical acceleration-deceleration (CAD) injuries with a review of prognostic research. *Palmer J Res* 1994;1(1):10–21.

28. Troyanovich SJ, Harrison DD. The reliability of chiropractic assessment procedures. *Chiro Tech* 1996;8(1):10–13.

29. Strender LE, Lundin M, Nell K. Interexaminer reliability in physical examination of the neck. *J Manipulative Physiol Ther* 1997;20(8):516–520.

30. Bogduk, N. Musculoskeletal pain: Toward precision diagnosis. *Proc 8th World Congress on Pain* 1997;8:507–525.

31. Rouwmaat PHM, Everaert D, Stappaerts KH, Aufdemkampe G. Reliability of manual skinfold tests in a healthy male population. *J Manipulative Physiol Ther* 1998;21(5):327–332.

32. Maher C. Pitfalls in reliability studies: Some suggestions for change. *Aust Physiother* 1993;39(1):5–7.

33. Lindgren KA, Leino E, Manninen H. Cervical rotation lateral flexion test in brachialgia. *Arch Phys Med Rehabil* 1992;72:735–737.

34. Maher C, Adams R. A psychophysical evaluation of manual stiffness discrimination. *Aust Physiother* 1995;41(3):161–167.

35. Sandmark H, Nisell R. Validity of five manual neck pain provocation tests. *Scand J Rehab Med* 1995;27:131–136.

36. Nilsson N, Christensen HW, Hartvigsen J. The intersegmental reliability of measuring passive cervical range of motion, revisited. *J Manipulative Physiol Ther* 1996;19(5):302–305.

37. Harrison AL, Barry-Greb T, Wojtowicz G. Clinical measurement of head and shoulder posture variables. *J Orthop Sports Phys Ther* 1996;23:353–361.

38. Jull G, Zito G, Trott P, et al. Inter-examiner reliability to detect painful upper cervical joint dysfunction. *Aust Physiother* 1997;43:125–129.

39. Gerwin RD, Shannon S, Hong CZ, et al. Interrater reliability in myofascial trigger point examination. *Pain* 1997;69(1,2):65–73.

40. Leboeuf C, Gardner V. Chronic low back pain: Orthopedic and chiropractic test results. *J Aust Chiro Assoc* 1989;19:1–6.

41. Leboeuf C, Gardner V, Carter AL, Scott TA. Chiropractic examination procedures: A reliability and consistency study. *J Aust Chiro Assoc* 1989;19:101–104.

42. Teaching rounds: Differential diagnosis of a neck mass. *Hospital Med* 1986;Dec:66–75.

43. Jull G. Manual diagnosis of C2-3 headache. *Cephalalgia* 1985;5(suppl):308–309.

44. Jull G, Bogduk N, Marsland A. The accuracy of manual diagnosis for cervical zygapophyseal joint pain syndromes. *Med J Aust* 1988;148:233–236.

45. Murphy DR. Hyperalgesic skin zone: A case report. *Chiro Tech* 1992;4:124–127.

46. Hagen KB, Harms-Ringdahl K, Enger NO, et al. Relationship between subjective neck disorders and cervical spine mobility and motion-related pain in male machine operators. *Spine* 1997;22(13):1501–1507.

47. Jordan A, Mehlsen J, Ostergaard K. A comparison of physical characteristics between patients seeking treatment for neck pain and age-matched healthy people. *J Manipulative Physiol Ther* 1997;20(7):468–475.

48. Vernon H. Correlations of self-ratings of pain and disability with impairment in chronic whiplash-associated disorder (WAD). Proceedings of the 1998 International Conference on Spinal Manipulation July 16–19, 1998 Foundation for Chiropractic Education and Research; 1998:51–52.

49. George PE, Silverstein HT, Wallace H, Marshall M. Identification of the high-risk pre-stoke patient. *J Chiro* 1981;15:S26–S28.

50. George PE. New techniques to identify the potential stroke victim. *Internat Rev Chiro* 1981; Jan–March:22–23.

51. Terrett AG. Vascular accidents from cervical spine manipulation: Report on 107 cases. *J Aust Chiro Assoc* 1987;17:15–24.

52. Terrett AG. Vascular accidents from cervical spine manipulation: The mechanisms. *J Aust Chiro Assoc* 1987;17:133–144.

53. Ferezy JS. Neural ischemia and cervical manipulation: an acceptable risk. *J Chiro* 1988;25:61–63.

54. Bolton PS, Stick PE, Lord RSA. Failure of clinical tests to predict cerebral ischemia before neck manipulation. *J Manipulative Physiol Ther* 1989;12:304–307.

55. Terrett AG. It is more important to know when not to adjust. *Chiro Tech* 1990;2:1–9.

56. Ferezy JS. Neurovascular assessment for risk management in chiropractic practice. In: Lawrence DJ, ed. *Advances in Chiropractic.* Vol 1. St. Louis, Mo: Mosby; 1994:455–477.

57. Terrett AG. *Vertebrobasilar Stroke Following Manipulation.* Des Moines, Iowa: National Chiropractic Mutual Insurance Company; 1996.

58. Carey PF. A report on the occurrence of cerebrovascular accidents in chiropractic practice. *J Canad Chiro Assoc* 1993;37(2):104–106.

59. Dabbs V, Lauretti WJ. A risk assessment of cervical manipulation vs. NSAIDs for the treatment of neck pain. *J Manipulative Physiol Ther* 1995;18(8):530–536.

60. Klougart N, Leboeuf-Yde C, Rasmussen LR. Safety in chiropractic practice. Part II: Treatment to the upper neck and the rate of cerebrovascular incidents. *J Manipulative Physiol Ther* 1996;19(9):563–569.

61. Klougart N, Leboeuf-Yde C, Rasmussen LR. Safety in chiropractic practice. Part II: Treatment to the upper neck and the rate of cerebrovascular incidents. *J Manipulative Physiol Ther* 1996;19(9):563–569.

62. Terrett AG. *Malpractice Avoidance for Chiropractors 1. Vertebrobasilar Stroke Following Manipulation.* Des Moines: National Chiropractic Mutual Insurance Company; 1996.

63. Coulter ID. Efficacy and risks of chiropractic manipulation: What does the evidence suggest? *Integrative Med* 1998;1(2):61–66.

64. Ferezy JS. Panel discussion at 1989 Cervical Spine Conference, New York Chiropractic College, New York, NY, 1989.

65. Smith RA, Estridge MN. Neurologic complications of head and neck manipulations. *JAMA* 1962;192:528–531.

66. Jamison JR. Nonspecific intervention in chiropractic care. *J Manipulative Physiol Ther* 1998;21(6):423–425.

67. Kathol MH. Cervical spine trauma: What is new? *Radiol Clin North Am* 1997;35:507–532.

68. Sachdeva K. Neurodiagnosis for neck injuries. In: Nordhoff LS, ed. *Motor Vehicle Collision Injuries. Mechanisms, Diagnosis and Management.* Gaithersburg, Md: Aspen; 1996:123–130.

69. Zohn DA, Mennel JMcM. *Musculoskeletal Pain: Diagnosis and Physical Treatment.* Boston, Mass: Little Brown; 1976.

70. Bogduk N, Aprill C. On the nature of neck pain, discography and cervical zygapophyseal joint blocks. *Pain* 1993;54:213–217.

71. Schellhas KP, Smith MD, Gundry CR, Pollei SR. Cervical discogenic pain: Prospective correlation of magnetic resonance imaging and discography in asymptomatic subjects and pain sufferers. *Spine* 1996;21(3):300–312.

Diagnostic Tests for the Cervical Spine Patient

Ronald Tyszkowski

1. CERVICAL COMPRESSION AND DISTRACTION[1]

Compression

With the patient seated, the examiner places downward pressure on the patient's head, while rotating the neck (Fig. 17A–1). The test is then repeated bilaterally. Localized pain indicates foraminal encroachment and radicular pain indicates pressure on the nerve root.

Distraction

With the patient seated, the examiner exerts upward pressure on the patient's head, thereby removing the weight from the patient's neck (Fig. 17A–2). Increased pain indicates muscle spasm and decreased pain indicates foraminal encroachment or facet capsulitis.

2. KERNIG'S SIGN[2]

The patient is placed in the supine position, and the examiner passively flexes the knee and hip of either leg to 90 degrees, respectively (Fig. 17A–3). The examiner then attempts to completely extend the leg (Fig. 17A–4). If pain prevents this, the sign is present. The sign is often accompanied by involuntary flexion of the opposite knee and hip and is present in meningitis.

3. VALSALVA MANEUVER

The examiner asks the patient to take a deep breath and hold the breath while bearing down, as if moving the bowel. A positive test is indicated by an increase in pain, which may be created by an increase in intrathecal pressure. This may be caused by a space-occupying lesion such as a herniated disc, a tumor, or osteophytes. Care should be taken in case dizziness or fainting occur, as the maneuver may constrict blood flow to the brain.

4. SOTO-HALL TEST[2]

The patient is placed in a supine position. The examiner places one hand on the sternum so that no flexion of the thoracic or lumbar spines can take place (Fig. 17A–5A). The examiner places the other hand under the occiput and flexes the head toward the chest. This produces a pull on the posterior ligaments of the spine and when the affected spinous process is reached, the patient will experience local pain (Fig. 17A–5B). Differential diagnosis includes subluxation, exostoses, sprain or strain, fracture, disc lesion, or meningial irritation.

5. HALL-PIKE MANEUVER[2]

The patient lies supine with the head off the examining table. The examiner provides support for the weight of the skull. The examiner tilts the patient's head to an angle of 45 degrees and turns it to one side. Reproduction of symptoms indicates benign positional vertigo (Fig. 17A–6). Symptoms should be reversed when the patient assumes an upright position.

6. L'HERMITTE'S SIGN[2]

The patient is seated. The examiner passively flexes the patient's head (Fig. 17A–7). A positive test is indicated by sharp pain down the spine and into the upper or lower limbs. This result indicates dural irritation in the spine.

7. RUST'S SIGN[2]

If the patient spontaneously grasps the head with both hands when lying down or when arising from a recumbent position, this is indicative of severe sprain, rheumatoid arthritis, fracture, or ligamentous instability (Fig. 17A–8).

8. SHOULDER DEPRESSION TEST[2]

With the patient seated, the examiner depresses the shoulder on the affected side and laterally flexes the cervical spine away from that side (Fig. 17A–9). This sign is positive if radicular pain is produced or aggravated. A positive sign indicates dural adhesions of the dural sleeves, spinal nerve roots, or adjacent structures of the joint capsules of the shoulder.

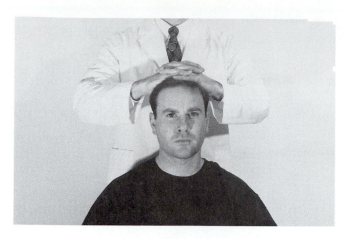

Figure 17A–1. Cervical compression.

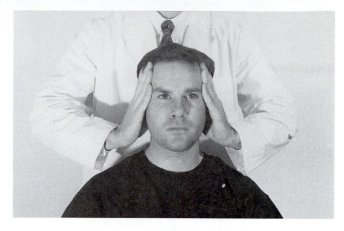

Figure 17A–2. Cervical distraction.

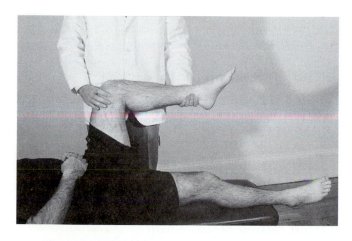

Figure 17A–3. Pre-test position for Kernig's sign.

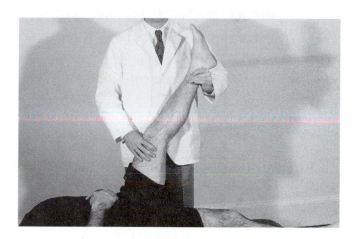

Figure 17A–4. Test for Kernig's sign.

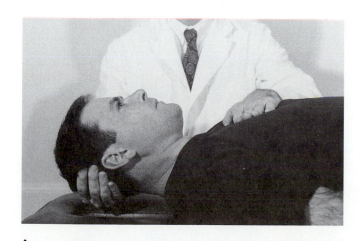

A

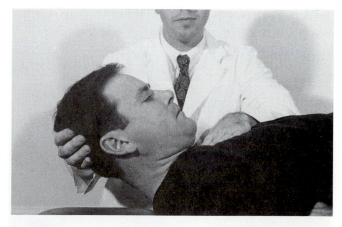

B

Figure 17A–5. A and **B.** Soto-Hall test.

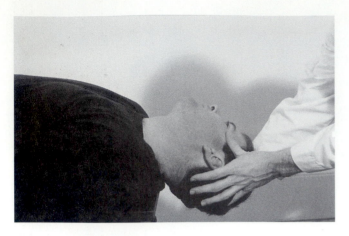

Figure 17A–6. Hall-Pike manuever.

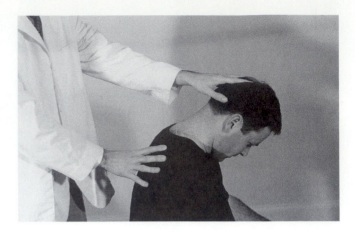

Figure 17A–7. L'Hermitte's sign.

9. CERVICAL RANGE OF MOTION: DUAL INCLINOMETER TECHNIQUE[3]

Flexion/Extension Measurement

Step 1

The examiner locates the T1 spinous process. With the patient seated, the first inclinometer is aligned in the sagittal plane and placed over the T1 spinous process while the second inclinometer is held over the occiput. The head should be in the neutral position while the inclinometers are set to 0 degrees (Fig. 17A–10A).

Step 2

The patient is asked to flex maximally and both angles are recorded (Fig. 17A–10B). The T1 angle is subtracted from the occipital angle to obtain the cervical flexion angle. The head is returned to the neutral position so that both inclinometers read 0 again.

Step 3

The patient is instructed to extend the neck as far as possible, with the examiner again recording both inclinometer angles (Fig. 17A–10C). The T1 angle is subtracted from the occipital angle to obtain the cervical extension angle. The patient is then asked to return the head to neutral position.

Step 4

The procedure is repeated three times. The cervical flexion angle and the cervical extension angle should be consistently measured within +/− 10 percent or 5 degrees, whichever is greater.

Lateral Flexion Measurement

Step 1

The examiner locates the T1 spinous process. With the patient seated, the first inclinometer is aligned in the coronal plane and placed over the T1 spinous process while the

Figure 17A–8. Rust's sign.

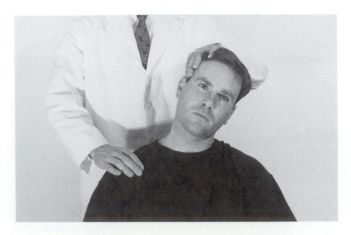

Figure 17A–9. Shoulder depression test.

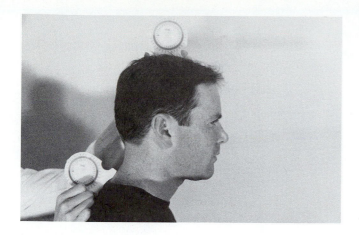

A

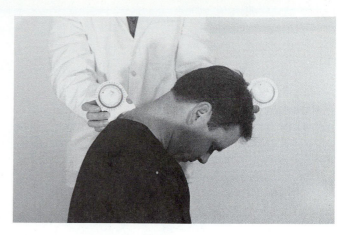

B

C

Figure 17A–10. A. Proper placement of inclinometers for flexion/extension measurement. **B.** Measurement of cervical flexion. **C.** Measurement of cervical extension.

second inclinometer is held over the occiput. The head should be in the neutral position while the inclinometers are set to 0 degrees (Fig. 17A–11A).

Step 2

The patient is asked to incline the head maximally to the right and both angles are recorded. The T1 angle is subtracted from the occipital angle to determine the degrees of right lateral flexion. The head is then returned to the neutral position.

Step 3

These steps are then repeated on the left side.

Rotation Measurement

Step 1

The patient is asked to lie supine on a flat examination table with shoulders exposed to permit observation of shoulder rotation. The examiner stands at the head of the table and places the inclinometer in the coronal plane with

the base applied to the forehead. The neutral 0 degree position is identified with the patient's nose pointing to the ceiling (Fig. 17A–12A).

Step 2

The patient is asked to rotate the head maximally to the right, and the cervical right rotation angle is recorded (Fig. 17A–12B).

Step 3

The patient is asked to rotate the head maximally to the left, and the cervical left rotation angle is recorded.

10. BRACHIAL PLEXUS TENSION TEST[4]

This test attempts to differentiate between local arm conditions and brachial plexus neural conditions with pain referral into the arm utilizing manuevers that stepwise

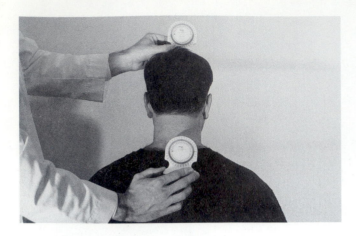

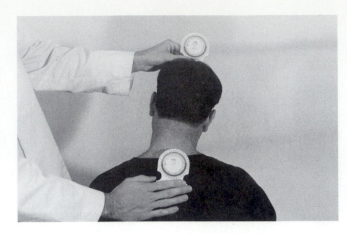

A

B

Figure 17A–11. A. Proper placement of inclinometers for lateral flexion measurement. **B.** Measurement of cervical lateral flexion.

increase tension in neural tissues. The position for the brachial plexus tension test is as follows: patient in supine position; glenohumeral joint abduction to 10 degrees, with maximal external rotation with the arm behind the coronal plane; elbow extension; wrist extension; supination of the forearm; shoulder girdle depression; and lateral flexion of the neck (Fig. 17A–13). The order of testing is as follows:

1. Patient is placed in supine position
2. Shoulder joint abduction
3. Shoulder joint external rotation
4. Shoulder gridle depression
5. Forearm supination
6. Wrist and finger extension
7. Elbow extension
8. Neck lateral flexion to the contralateral side

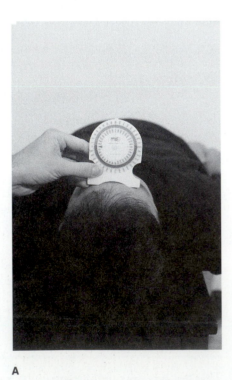

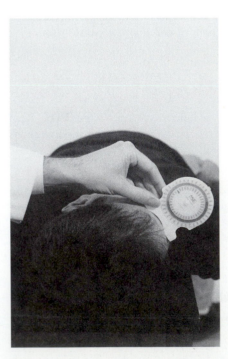

A

B

Figure 17A–12. A. Proper placement of inclinometers for rotation measurement. **B.** Measurement of cervical rotation.

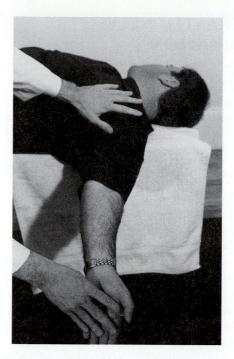

Figure 17A–13. Position for brachial plexus tension test.

Reproduction of symptoms and loss of normal extensibility indicate a positive test. (Note: Lateral neck flexion to the contralateral side is only used if the other testing was negative.)

11. ARM ELEVATION SIGN (BAKODY)[2]

While seated, the patient actively places the palm of the affected extremity on top of the head, raising the level of the elbow to the level of the head (Fig. 17A–14). The maneuver decreases stretching of the affected nerve root. This

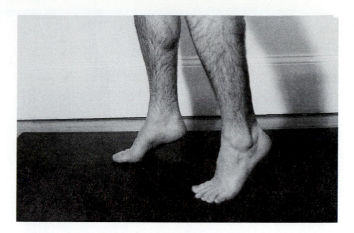

Figure 17A–15. Toe walking.

sign is present when radiating pain is lessened or disappears and suggests cervical radiculopathy or brachial plexus lesion.

12. TOE WALKING[1]

The patient is asked to take several steps while walking on his or her toes (Fig. 17A–15). This evaluates the strength of the plantar flexors of the foot and the integrity of the S1 nerve root.

13. HEEL WALKING[1]

The patient is asked to take several steps while walking on his or her heels (Fig. 17A–16). This evaluates the strength of the dorsiflexors of the foot and the integrity of the L4 and L5 nerve roots and is a subtle sign of upper motor neuron disease.

Figure 17A–14. Arm elevation sign.

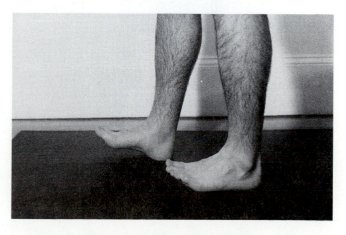

Figure 17A–16. Heel walking.

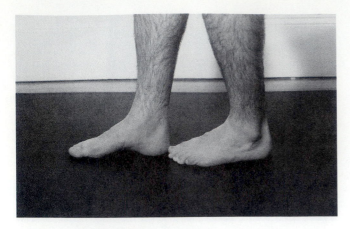

Figure 17A–17. Tandem walking.

14. TANDEM WALKING[1]

The patient is asked to walk heel to toe in a straight line—a pattern called tandem walking (Fig. 17A–17). Tandem walking may reveal ataxia not previously evident.

15. ROMBERG'S TEST[5]

The patient is asked to stand with the eyes closed (Fig. 17A–18). A small amount of swaying is normal. When cerebellar disease is present, the patient will swing wildly, but will not fall. With dorsal column disease, the patient will fall with the eyes closed.

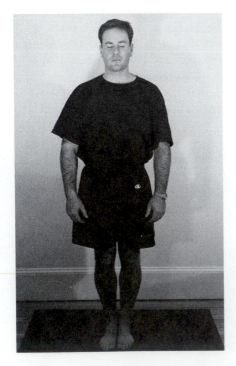

Figure 17A–18. Romberg's test.

16. CRANIAL NERVE EXAMINATION[1]

CN I—Olfactory

The sense of smell is accomplished by having the patient identify odors with each nostril. (Odors should be familiar ones such as coffee, orange, vanilla.)

CN II—Optic

This cranial nerve is tested in three ways; by examining visual acuity, visual fields, and optic fundi.

Visual Acuity

This is a test of central vision. If possible, the examiner should use a Snellen eye chart and light it well. The patient is positioned 20 feet from the chart. Patients who use glasses other than reading glasses should be instructed to use them. The patient is asked to cover one eye with a card and to read the smallest line possible. A patient who cannot read the largest letter should be positioned closer to the chart and the new distance noted. The examiner should determine the smallest line of print from which the patient can identify more than half the letters. The visual acuity designated at the side of this line, together with the use of glasses, if any, is recorded.

Visual acuity is expressed as a fraction (e.g., 20/30), in which the numerator indicates the distance of the patient from the chart, the denominator the distance at which a normal eye can read the letters.

! CLINICAL PEARL

For a routine examination of the cervical spine patient, it is adequate to test this aspect of cranial nerve II at the same time that visual fields and cranial nerves III, IV, and VI are being tested. If the patient can see the examiner's finger, then visual acuity is considered functional.

Visual fields by confrontation

This is a rough clinical test of peripheral vision. The patient is asked to cover one eye, without pressing on it, and to look at the examiner's eye directly opposite.

The examiner slowly brings a pencil or other small object from the periphery into the field of vision from eight separate locations (roughly 12, 1.5, 3, 4.5, 6, 7.5, 9, and 10.5 on the face of a clock) and asks the patient to say "now" as soon as it appears (Fig. 17A–19). During most of the examination, the examiner should keep the object equidistant between his or her own eye and the patient's so that the patient's visual field can be compared to the examiner's own.

Fundoscopic examination

If the examiner wears glasses for marked nearsightedness or astimagtism, he or she may choose to leave them on. If patients have refractive errors and the examiner cannot focus

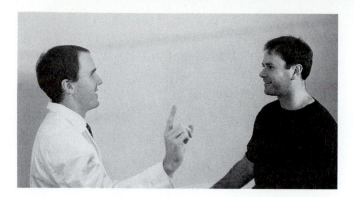

Figure 17A–19. Visual fields by confrontation.

clearly on their fundi, it may be easier to examine them with their glasses on. Patients with contact lenses should leave them in.

The room should be darkened. The examiner should switch on the ophthalmoscopic light, and adjust it to the large round beam of white light. The lens disc should be switched to 0 diopters (a lens that neither converges nor diverges the light rays). The examiner should keep his or her index finger on the lens disc, so that it can be focused during the examination (Fig. 17A–20).

The examiner should use his or her right hand and right eye for the patient's right eye and vice versa. The ophthalmoscope is held firmly braced up under the medial aspect of the examiner's bony orbit with the handle tilted laterally on a 20-degree slant from the vertical. The examiner should be able to see clearly through its aperture. The patient is asked to look slightly up and over the examiner's shoulder and gaze at a specific point on the wall.

From a position about 15 inches away from the patient and about 15 degrees lateral to the patient's vision, the light beam is shined on the pupil. The orange glow in the

pupil is called the red reflex. Any opacities interrupting the red reflex should be noted.

The light beam should be kept focused on the red reflex. The examiner should move in on a 15-degree line until the ophthalmoscope is very close to the eye, almost touching the patient's eyelashes. By placing the thumb of the opposite hand on the eyebrow, the examiner gains extra proprioceptive guidance as the patient gets closer, but this maneuver is not essential.

Both of the examiner's eyes should be kept open and relaxed, as if gazing into the distance. The fluctuating blurriness caused by the eye's automatic attempts to accommodate will then be minimized. Some patients may find the light to be too bright. By lowering the light's intensity somewhat the examiner can usually improve the patient's comfort and cooperation without impairing observations.

The examiner should now see the retina in the vicinity of the optic disc—a yellowish orange to creamy pink, oval or round structure. The disc will probably fill the field of gaze or exceed it. If it is not seen, the examiner should follow a blood vessel centrally until it is. The central direction can be determined by noting the angles at which vessels branch and the progressive enlargement of vessel size at each juncture as the disc approaches.

The optic disc can be brought into sharp focus by adjusting the lens disc. The examiner should note the following:

- The clarity of the disc outline. The nasal outline may normally be somewhat blurred.
- The color of the disc; normally this is yellowish orange to creamy pink.
- The possible presence of normal white or pigmented crescents around the disc.
- The size of the central physiological cup, if present. This cup is normally yellowish white. Its horizontal diameter is usually less than half the horizontal diameter of the disc.

Finally, the examiner should identify the arterioles and the veins, noting the relative sizes and the character of their crossings.

The patient is asked to look directly into the light and focus on the macula. This is an avascular area somewhat larger than the disc but has no distinct margins.

CN III—Oculomotor; CN IV—Trochlear; CN VI—Abducens

These three cranial nerves are tested together (Fig. 17A–21). The examiner:

1. Inspects the size and shape of each pupil
2. Tests the pupillary responses to light
3. Tests extraocular eye movements in the six cardinal fields of gaze
4. Looks for loss of conjugate movement in any of the six directions

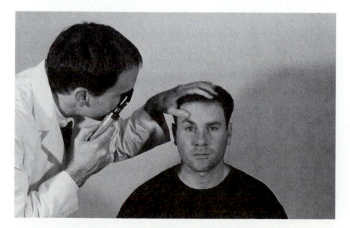

Figure 17A–20. Proper examiner position with respect to patient.

Figure 17A–21. Testing of cranial nerves III, IV, and VI.

5. Checks convergence of gaze and looks for nystagmus
6. Looks for ptosis of the upper eyelids

CN V—Trigeminal
The patient is asked to clench the teeth, and the examiner palpates the temporal and masseter muscles (Fig. 17A–22).

CN VII—Facial
The examiner inspects the face at rest and in conversation with the patient, and notes any asymmetry (Fig. 17A–23A–C). The patient is asked to:

1. Raise both eyebrows
2. Close both eyes tightly
3. Smile

Again, the examiner notes any weakness or asymmetry.

CN VIII—Acoustic
The examiner assesses hearing by gently rubbing two fingers next to the patient's ear (Fig. 17A–24). If hearing loss is present, then the examiner should test for lateralization and compare air and bone conduction.

CN IX—Glossopharyngeal and CN X—Vagus
The examiner listens to the patient's voice and notes any hoarseness and/or nasal quality. The patient is asked to open their mouth and say "aah." The examiner watches the movements of the soft palate and pharynx. The soft palate should rise symmetrically, the uvula should remain in the midline, and each side of the posterior pharynx should move medially (Fig. 17A–25).

Prior to testing the gag reflex, the patient should be warned. The examiner stimulates each side of the throat and notes the gag reflex. It may be diminished or absent even in normal people.

CN XI—Spinal Accessory
From behind the patient, the examiner notes any atrophy or fasciculations in the trapezius muscles and compares side to side. The patient is asked to shrug both shoulders upward against the examiner's hands. The strength of contraction should be noted (Fig. 17A–26A).

The patient is asked to attempt to turn his or her head to each side against the examiner's hand. The contraction of the opposite side sternocleidomastoid and the force of contraction should be noted (Fig. 17A–26B).

CN XII—Hypoglossal
The examiner inspects the tongue as it lies on the floor of the mouth looking for fasciculations. Some movements may be present in a normal tongue.

The patient is asked to stick out the tongue. The examiner looks for asymmetry, atrophy, or deviation from the midline. The patient is asked to move the tongue from side to side and the symmetry of movement should be noted (Fig. 17A–27).

17. SENSORY TESTING[1]

Full evaluation of the sensory system involves testing each kind of sensation: pain, temperature, light touch, vibration, position, and discriminative sensations. For patients with no neurological symptoms or signs, an abbreviated examination may be substituted, which should include assessment of pain in the hands and feet.

If a full examination is indicated, then assessment of vibration in the hands and feet, a brief comparison of light touch over the arms and legs, and assessment of stereognosis should be included. To make the examination as efficient as possible, the examiner should pay special attention to the following areas:

1. Assessment of stereognosis
2. Areas with symptoms of "numbness" or pain
3. Areas with motor or reflex abnormalities
4. Areas with trophic changes

Figure 17A–22. Testing of cranial nerve V; palpation of masseter muscles.

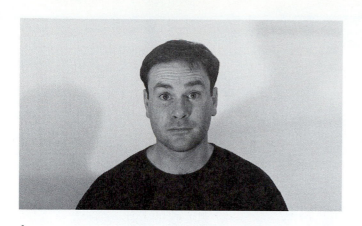

A

B

C

Figure 17A–23. A through **C.** Testing of cranial nerve VII.

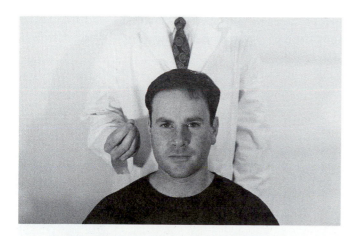

Figure 17A–24. Testing of cranial nerve VIII.

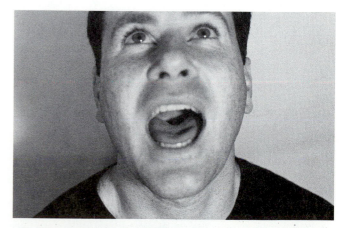

Figure 17A–25. Testing of cranial nerves IX and X.

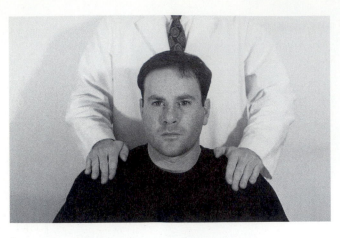

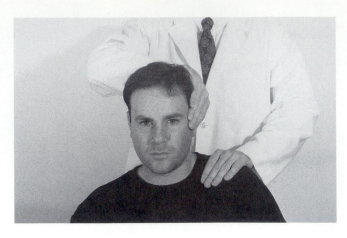

A

B

Figure 17A–26. **A** and **B.** Testing of cranial nerve XI.

Repeated testing at another time is often necessary to confirm abnormalities.

Patterns of Sensory Testing (see Fig. 17–21)

1. The examiner compares symmetrical areas on the two sides of the body, including arms, legs, and trunk.
2. When testing pain, temperature, and touch, the examiner should compare distal to proximal extremities.
3. When testing vibration and position, the examiner should first test fingers and toes.
4. The examiner should vary the pace of testing so that the patient does not merely respond to repetitive rhythm.
5. When an area of sensory loss or hypersensitivity is detected, the examiner should map out its boundaries in detail.

Sensory Tests

Pain

This test is performed using a sharp safety pin, occasionally substituting the blunt end for the point as a stimulus. The examiner stimulates in patterns outlined previously, and asks the patient "Is this sharp or dull?" or, when making comparisons using the sharp stimulus, "Does this feel the same as this?" (Fig. 17A–28). (Note: It is important that the examiner use as light a touch as the patient can perceive and not, under any circumstances, press hard enough to draw blood.)

Temperature

(This segment may be omitted if the pain testing is normal.) Using two test tubes, filled with hot and cold water, the examiner touches the skin and asks the patient to identify "hot" or "cold."

Figure 17A–27. Testing of cranial nerve XII.

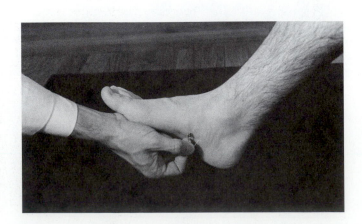

Figure 17A–28. Pain testing.

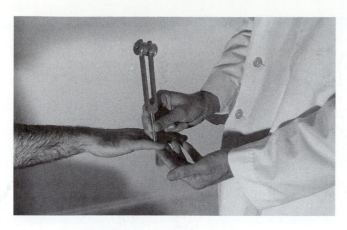

Figure 17A–29. Vibration testing.

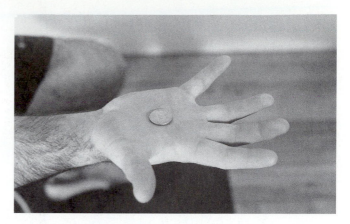

Figure 17A–31. Stereognosis testing.

Vibration

Using a relatively low-pitched tuning fork, preferably of 128 Hz, the examiner taps it on the heel of his or her hand and places it firmly over the distal interphalangeal joint of the patient's finger and big toe respectively. The patient is asked what he or she feels. To be certain, the patient is asked to inform the examiner when the vibration stops, and then the examiner touches the fork to stop the vibration. At this point, the patient should indicate that the vibration has stopped. If vibration sense is absent, then the examiner should move proximally along the extremity and re-test (Fig. 17A–29).

Position

The examiner grasps the patient's big toe, holding it by its sides between the thumb and index finger, and then pulling it away from the other toes to avoid friction. (This prevents extraneous tactile stimulation from indicating a change of position.) The patient is shown what is meant by "down" and "up" as the examiner moves the patient's toe clearly upward and downward. Then, with the patient's eyes closed, he or she is asked for an "up" or "down" response as the examiner moves the toe in a small arc. This

is repeated several times on each side, avoiding simple alternation of the stimuli. If position sense is impaired, then the examiner should move proximally along the extremity and re-test (Fig. 17A–30).

Discriminative sensations

Several additional maneuvers test the ability of the sensory cortex to correlate, analyze, and interpret sensations. Because discriminative sensations are dependent on touch and position sense, they are useful only when these sensations, when tested directly, are either normal or only slightly impaired.

STEREOGNOSIS. This refers to the ability to identify an object from its size and shape. The examiner places a familiar object in the patient's hand (such as a coin or a paperclip) and asks the patient to identify it (Fig. 17A–31).

NUMBER IDENTIFICATION (GRAPHESTHESIA). When motor impairment, arthritis, or other conditions prevent a patient from manipulating an object, the examiner should test the ability to identify numbers. With a blunt object the examiner draws a large number in the patient's palm, asking the patient to identify the number (Fig. 17A–32).

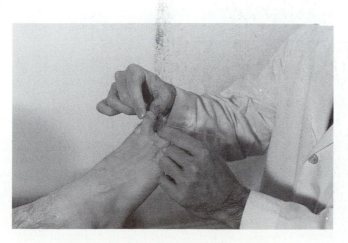

Figure 17A–30. Position sense testing.

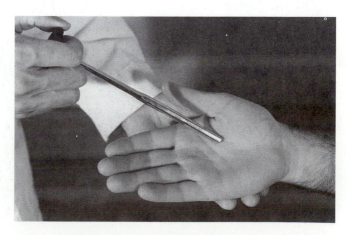

Figure 17A–32. Graphesthesia testing.

18. MOTOR STRENGTH TESTING[1, 6]

To test muscle strength, the patient is asked to move actively against the examiner's resistance or to resist movement. The examiner watches for muscular contraction and feels for strength exerted. He or she may be able to see or feel a weak muscular contraction even if it fails to move the body part.

Muscle strength may be graded on a 0 to 5 scale, as follows:

0	No muscular contraction detected
1	A barely detectable flicker or trace of contraction
2	Active movement of a body part with gravity eliminated
3	Active movement against gravity
4	Active movement against gravity and some resistance
5	Active movement against full resistance without evident fatigue; this is normal muscle strength

Spinal Cord Level	Movement Resisted
C5	Shoulder abduction (Fig. 17A–33)
C6	Wrist extension (Fig. 17A–34)
C7	Wrist flexion and finger extension (Fig. 17A–35)
C8	Finger flexion (Fig. 17A–36)
T1	Finger abduction and adduction (Fig. 17A–37)

19. MUSCLE STRETCH REFLEXES[1, 6]

To elicit a muscle stretch reflex, the examiner persuades the patient to relax, positions the limbs properly and symmetrically, and then strikes the tendon briskly, using a wrist movement. Reflexes are graded on a 0 to 4+ scale, as follows:

4+	Very brisk, hyperactive, indicative of upper motor neuron disease and associated with clonus
3+	Brisker than average; possibly indicative of disease
2+	Average; normal
1+	Somewhat diminished; low normal
0	No response

Biceps Reflex (C5, C6)

The patient's arms should be partially flexed at the elbows with the palms face down. The examiner places his or her thumb firmly on the biceps tendon. The examiner then strikes with the reflex hammer so that the blow is aimed directly through the digit toward the biceps tendon, observing flexion at the elbow, and watching for and feeling contraction of the biceps muscle (Fig. 17A–38).

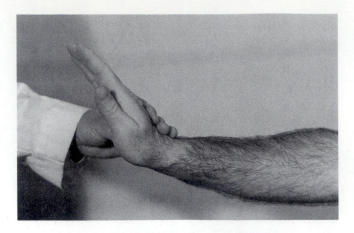

Figure 17A–34. C6: Testing wrist extension.

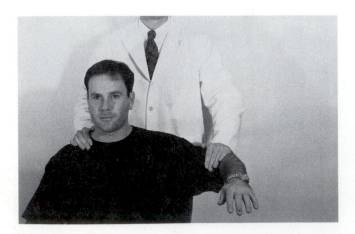

Figure 17A–33. C5: Testing shoulder abduction.

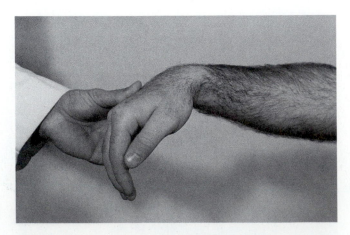

Figure 17A–35. C7: Testing wrist flexion and finger extension.

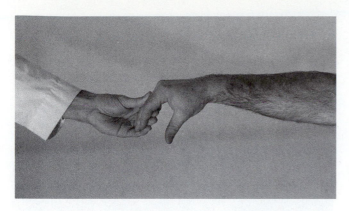

Figure 17A–36. C8: Testing finger flexion.

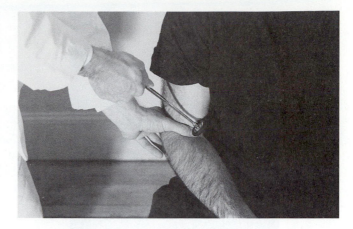

Figure 17A–38. Testing the biceps reflex (C5, C6).

Triceps Reflex (C6, C7, C8)

The patient's arm is flexed at the elbow with palm toward the body, and pulled slightly across the chest. The examiner strikes the triceps tendon above the elbow with a direct blow from directly behind, watching for contraction of the triceps tendon and contraction of the elbow (Fig. 17A–39).

Brachioradialis Reflex (C5, C6)

The patient's forearm should rest on his or her abdomen or in the lap. The examiner strikes the radius about 1 to 2 inches above the wrist, observing flexion and supination of the forearm (Fig. 17A–40).

Patellar Reflex (L2, L3, L4)

The patient may be either sitting or lying down as long as the knee is flexed. The examiner briskly taps the patellar tendon just below the patella, noting contraction of the quadriceps with extension at the knee (Fig. 17A–41).

Ankle Reflex (S1, S2)

With the leg flexed at the knee, the patient's foot is dorsiflexed at the ankle. The patient is persuaded to relax and

the examiner strikes the Achilles tendon, watching for plantar flexion at the ankle and noting the speed of relaxation after muscle contraction (Fig. 17A–42).

20. PLANTAR RESPONSE (ELICITATION OF BABINSKI RESPONSE)[3]

The examiner strokes the bottom of the foot along the lateral border of the foot and then across to the ball of the foot without touching the toes. A normal response is flexion of the big toe (Fig. 17A–43A). An abnormal response

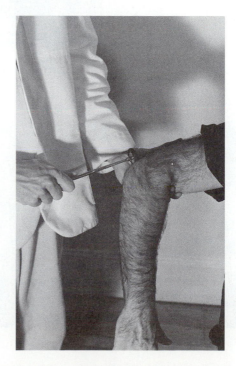

Figure 17A–39. Testing the triceps reflex (C6, C7, C8).

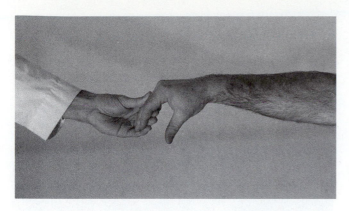

Figure 17A–37. T1: Testing finger adduction and abduction.

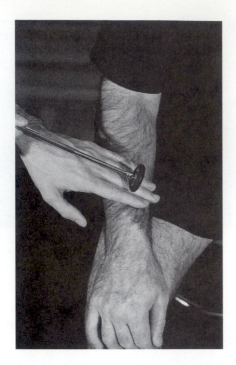

Figure 17A–40. Testing the brachioradialis reflex (C5, C6).

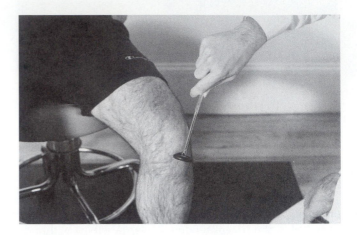

Figure 17A–41. Testing the patellar reflex (L2, L3, L4).

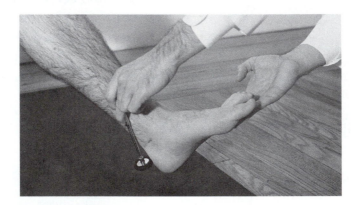

Figure 17A–42. Testing the ankle reflex (S1, S2).

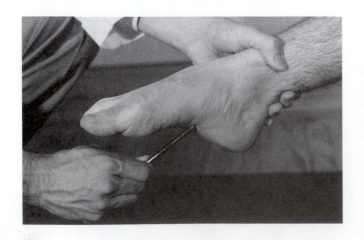

A

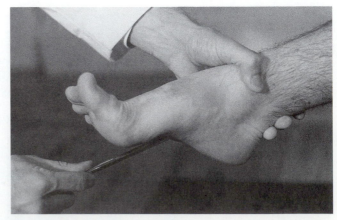

B

Figure 17A–43. A. Normal plantar response. **B.** Babinski response.

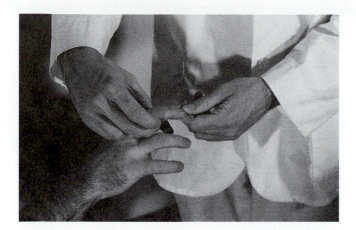

Figure 17A–44. Elicitation of the Hoffman response.

is extension of the big toe, also called a Babinski response. (Note: There is no "positive" or "negative" Babinski) (Fig. 17A–43B). An abnormal response is indicative of an upper motor neuron lesion and should be further investigated.

21. HOFFMAN RESPONSE[7]

The examiner flicks the distal phalanx of the index finger resulting in distal finger extension. A positive sign would be a "clawing" movement of the fingers, which is exaggerated contraction of the flexor muscles of the fingers (Fig. 17A–44). This is an upper extremity pathological reflex and would indicate a possible upper motor neuron lesion.

22. POINT-TO-POINT AND PAST POINTING[1]

Point-to-Point
The patient is asked to touch the examiner's index finger and then his or her own nose alternately several times (Fig.

17A–45). The examiner moves his or her index finger about so that the patient has to alter directions and extend the arm fully to reach it. The accuracy and smoothness of movements and the presence of any tremor should be noted. Clumsy and unsteady movements may indicate *cerebellar disease*. Such movements are called *dysmetria*.

Past Pointing
The examiner holds his or her finger in one place so that the patient can touch it with one arm and finger outstretched. The patient is asked to raise the arm overhead and lower it again to touch the examiner's finger. After several repeats, the patient is asked to close both eyes and try several more times (Fig. 17A–46). Normally a patient can touch the examiner's finger successfully with eyes open or closed. Repetitive and consistent deviation to one side (referred to as *past pointing*), worse with eyes closed, suggests *cerebellar or vestibular disease*.

23. HEEL-TO-SHIN TESTING[7]

The patient is asked to place the heel of one foot on the superior portion of the opposite shin, and run the heel down the length of the shin, over the foot, and off the big toe without breaking contact. Inability to maintain contact is indicative of leg dystaxia and cerebellar disease (Fig. 17A–47).

24. RAPID ALTERNATING MOVEMENTS[1]

The patient is shown how to strike one hand on the thigh with the palm, raise the hand, turn it over, and then strike the hand down on the same place with the dorsum of the hand (Fig. 17A–48). The patient is asked to perform this task as rapidly as possible. The examiner observes speed, rhythm and smoothness. This test is repeated on the opposite side.

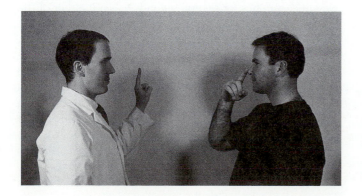

A

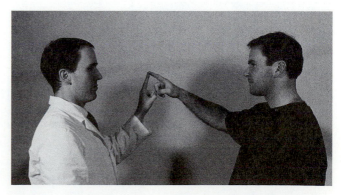

B

Figure 17A–45. A and **B.** Point-to-point testing.

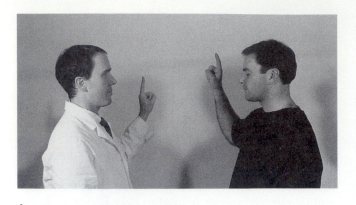

A

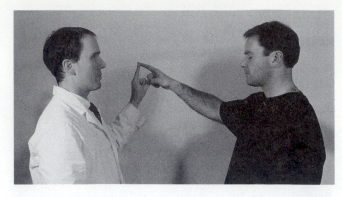

B

Figure 17A–46. A and **B.** Past pointing.

This is a test of dysdiadokinesia, in which one movement cannot be quickly followed by its opposite, and movements are slow and clumsy. Dysdiadokinesia is a sign of cerebellar disease.

25. AUSCULTATION[1]

The arteries that are most commonly auscultated in the cervical spine are the subclavian and carotid arteries bilaterally. The patient is placed in a seated position. The examiner stands behind the patient and ausculates with the stethoscope in the bell position.

Ausculation takes place in two positions on each side. First, the bell is placed over the supraclavicular fossa in order to auscultate the subclavian artery (Fig. 17A–49). The stethoscope is then moved to a position one third of the way up the lateral position of the neck, just anterior to the belly of the sternocleidomastoid muscle, to auscultate the carotid artery (Fig. 17A–50). The absence or presence of bruits is noted. If bruits are present, the examiner should retest with less pressure upon the bell of the stethoscope as increased pressure over the artery can simulate this phenomenon. If the bruit is still present, arterial stenosis should be ruled out.

26. VERTEBRAL ARTERY PROVOCATIVE MANEUVER

The examiner passively places the patient's head into extension and rotation. This position is held for 30 seconds on each side (Fig. 17A–51). The patient is asked to report any symptoms such as dizziness, nausea, or blurred vision. The examiner observes for nystagmus. A positive test may suggest vertebrobasilar arterial insufficiency.

27. HAUTENT'S TEST[8]

The patient is seated in a chair that supports the back, with both arms stretched forward. The examiner stands facing the patient, with the examiner's thumbs pointing at the patient's hands. The patient closes his or her eyes, while the examiner watches for several seconds to see if either of the patient's hands deviate to one side in relation to the examiner's thumbs (Fig. 17A–52A).

The test is then repeated with the head turned to the right, to the left, flexed, and extended (Fig. 17A–52B through 17–52E). While the patient moves the head to a new position, the examiner holds their hands to maintain positioning. A positive test is indicated by the presence of a "cervical pattern" in which the deviation of the hands to one side occurs with the head in neutral, and becomes greater with rotation to one side and less with rotation to the other. Deviation will also tend to become greater with extension and less with flexion. A positive test following movement of the head would implicate the cervical spine as a factor in disturbed equilibrium.

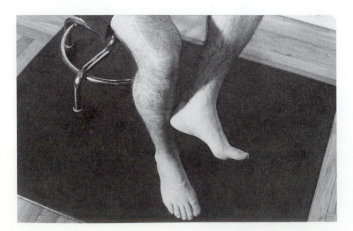

Figure 17A–47. Heel-to-shin testing.

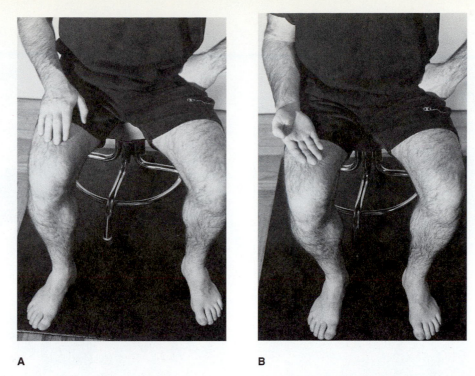

A   B

Figure 17A–48. A and **B.** Rapid alternating movements.

Figure 17A–49. Auscultation of the subclavian artery.

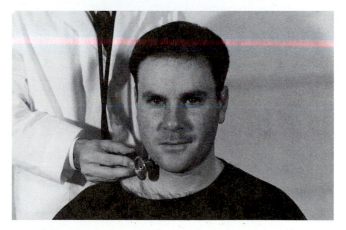

Figure 17A–50. Auscultation of the carotid artery.

Figure 17A–51. Vertebral artery provocative maneuver.

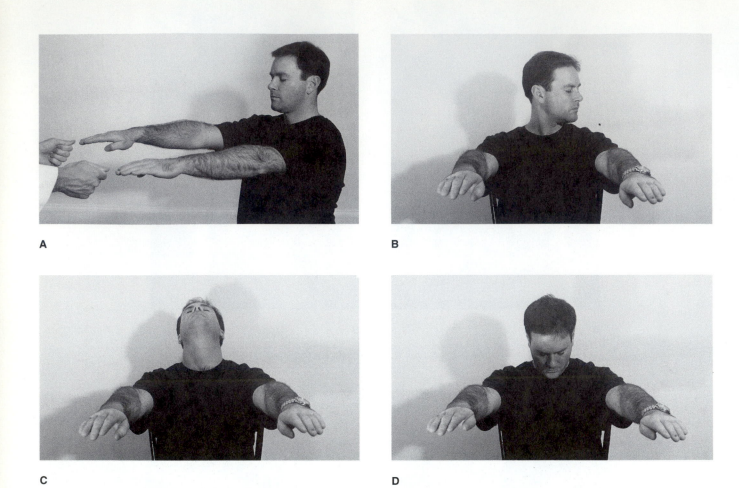

A

B

C

D

E

Figure 17A–52. A through **E.** Hautent's test.

REFERENCES

1. Bates B. *A Guide to Physical Examination and History Taking*. 4th ed. Philadelphia, Pa: JB Lippincott; 1987.
2. Evans R. *Illustrated Essentials in Orthopaedic Physical Assessment*. St. Louis, Mo: Mosby; 1994.
3. *American Medical Association Guides to the Evaluation of Permanent Impairment*. 4th ed. Chicago, Ill: AMA;1993.
4. Quintner, JL. A study of upper limb pain and paraesthesiae following neck injury in motor vehicle accidents: Assessment of the brachial plexus test of Elvey. *Br J Rheumatol* 1989;28:528–553.
5. Patten J. *Neurological Differential Diagnosis*. London: Harold Stark Ltd; 1980.
6. Hoppenfeld S. *Orthopaedic Neurology*. Philadelphia, Pa: JB Lippincott; 1977.
7. Ferezy J. *The Chiropractic Neurological Examination*. Gaithersburg, Md: Aspen; 1992.
8. Lewitt K. *Manipulative Therapy in the Rehabilitation of the Locomotor System*. 2nd ed. Oxford: Butterworth-Heinemann; 1991.

PART

4

Treatment

CHAPTER 18

Manipulative Techniques
for the Cervical Spine

GEORGE G. DeFRANCA

*"I slept and dreamed that life was happiness; I awoke and saw that life was service;
I served and found that in service happiness is found."*

—Unknown

INTRODUCTION

Cervical joint manipulation is a skillful art that demands much training, experience, and ability to become proficient in its use. When performed properly, while being cognizant of contraindications, cervical manipulation is a safe and effective form of manual treatment.

Joint manipulation and mobilization are specific yet different types of manual treatment. The distinction between the two depends upon parameters of amplitude and speed of movement, and the patient's ability to remain in control of the movement. This chapter focuses primarily on joint manipulation, following a limited discussion of joint mobilization.

MOBILIZATION

Mobilization is a form of manual therapy that uses oscillatory movements of various amplitudes to reduce pain, spasm, and restriction in articulations. These mobilizations are executed in certain parts of a joint's range of motion. Thrusting is not a feature of mobilization, and the movement imparted is still under the control of the patient should he or she decide to halt it. Mobilization also includes sustained stretches of variable vigor at the end range.

GRADES OF MOVEMENTS

The different amplitudes of mobilization are divided into four types or grades by Maitland[1] for ease of assessment and application (see Fig. 13–14). A fifth grade, grade V, is reserved to denote a manipulative thrust. Grade I is a small amplitude movement executed at the beginning of the joint's range. Grade II is a larger amplitude movement occurring within the joint's range of motion but not extending to the limit nor engaging any stiffness or spasm. Grade III is a large amplitude of movement that engages stiffness or spasm by extending to the limit of range. Grade IV is a small amplitude of movement, like a grade I movement; however, it occurs at the limit of range engaging stiffness or spasm.

Grades II, III, and IV can be applied either more or less vigorously and denoted with a plus (+) or minus (−) sign (II+, II−, III+, III−, etc.), respectively. The usual frequency of oscillations is two to three cycles per second for about 20 seconds; slower and gentler for painful joints, quicker and more abrupt for chronically stiff joints.

TECHNIQUE SELECTION

The choice of the mobilization grade used depends on the type of pain reaction and end-feel found during the examination of joint motion. Therefore, it is important to clinically determine whether the resistance to joint motion is from pain, spasm, or articular or periarticular tissues. For example, muscle spasm exhibits a "twanglike" end-feel and the muscle contraction may be visible. When encountering reflex spasm during mobilization movements, the treatment movement should be a sustained stretch just at the point of onset of pain or spasm. The pain and spasm should subside in about 20 seconds, at which time the joint can be challenged slightly more.

Similarly, pain is a predominant feature in acute conditions and painful joints, especially if irritable, demand respect. The speed and amplitudes of oscillations must be guided by the joint's pain response. Grade I and II oscillations are used mostly to reduce pain through mechanoreceptor stimulation. Gentle, slow oscillations can allow enough improvement to occur so movements of greater amplitude can be followed. A regular rhythm is used to "lull" the painful joint into quiescence and allow the patient to relax with the movements. Just as a painful myofascial trigger point can be "deactivated" by sustained pressure (ischemic compression), a painful joint motion can be rendered less so with continued gentle oscillating movements. It is amazing how a series of gentle grade I or grade II mobilizations can effectively tame a painful osteoarthritic cervical facet joint.

The beginning and ending pressures of the oscillations should be equal in rate, while the change from on-pressure to off-pressure should be almost imperceptible so they seemingly blend with each other. Usually, in joints that are not as painful, the beginning pressure is quicker than the off-pressure. However, if joint pain is provoked more with the off-pressure, then it should be the faster component. This causes a kind of recoil or rebound mobilization. Take, for instance, a posterior-to-anterior (PA) oscillation on the spinous process of C2 that elicits pain upon its release. To better mobilize in this case, the on-pressure is slower compared to a faster off-pressure in order to cause a rebounding mobilization from anterior to posterior (AP). Slow, gentle on-pressures followed by quick, almost abrupt, off-pressures will at first elicit a painful response. However, after 30 to 60 seconds of performing these "rebounding" oscillations, the pain usually subsides.

Shortened capsulo-ligamentous tissues are characteristic of chronic conditions where stiffness, rather than pain, is more of a feature. These joints can be handled more firmly without reprisal, especially near the end range of motion. Grade III and IV mobilizations are best used in this situation. This aids in stretching adaptively shortened or scarred capsulo-ligamentous structures. Maitland[1] describes a staccatolike oscillation combined with sustained stretching. Combining small grade IV amplitudes of oscillation near the end range with larger grade III amplitudes interposed works well. The larger amplitudes tend to abate any pain caused by the smaller end range oscillations.

Where in the range the pain or spasm occurs is also important. Grades I and II are used mostly to reduce pain if its onset occurs early in the range, whereas grades III and IV are used to stretch stiffened tissues felt further in the range.[1]

Mobilization techniques can often be used as preparatory maneuvers performed prior to a grade V manipulation, especially in chronic conditions. This creates greater relaxation of the periarticular soft tissues as well as of the patient. However, the very same techniques to next be described as manipulative procedures can be implemented as mobilizations by substituting a manipulative thrust with mobilizing oscillations or sustained stretching.

MANIPULATION

Joint manipulation is performed to restore joint play at dysfunctional joints. It is thought to work by: (1) releasing entrapped synovial folds or plica, (2) relaxing hypertonic muscles, and (3) disrupting articular or periarticular adhesions.[2] Fibrosis of the periarticular tissues can be a result of trauma and inflammation, immobilization, and degenerative joint disease.

A joint manipulation is defined as a high-velocity, low-amplitude thrust or impulse directed at restoring joint play. It is performed at the end of the usual passive range of motion, is usually associated with an audible "click," and because of its speed, is not under the voluntary control of the patient. Compared to the four grades of mobilization, it is given the designation grade V. It is similar to a grade IV mobilization in amplitude and position in the joint's range but differs in the velocity of delivery.[1]

The ultimate advantage of manipulation, as compared to mobilization, is that it provides rapid end range loading to dysfunctional joints. This has the effect of placing the articular capsule on a dynamic stretch, thus stimulating mechanoreceptor activity, causing a joint cavitation with an audible "crack" sound, and creating increased joint range of motion.

WHAT HAPPENS WHEN A JOINT IS MANIPULATED?

A joint's total range of motion is divided into three zones of movement: active, passive, and paraphysiological (see Fig. 13–1). An elastic barrier of resistance separates the joint's passive range of motion from the paraphysiological space. The limit of anatomical integrity represents the ultimate barrier—that of the restraining soft tissues in the form of a joint capsule and ligaments. Manipulation entails moving a joint with a high-velocity, low-amplitude thrust that is outside the patient's control to prevent it, yet accurate enough to enter the paraphysiological space after all the "slack" is removed. Slack is the motion in the active and passive ranges that needs to be taken up prior to engaging the elastic barrier. It is the sudden movement beyond the elastic barrier of resistance that is usually associated with the click sound common to manipulation. However, further movement would impose upon the integrity of the joint's soft tissue holding elements and risk injury. Although quick, the distance traversed during a manipulation is very small, usually on the order of 1/8 inch. It is usually associated with an audible click or pop due to a joint cavitation phenomenon.

Exercise works within the active range of motion and mobilization affects more the passive range of motion—neither affects the paraphysiological space. It is manipulation that affects the paraphysiological space. Mennell[3] states that exercise, being a voluntary activity, cannot restore joint play, an involuntary joint motion. The same can be said for passive stretching techniques. In fact, Mennell[3] states that exercise will delay the recovery of a dysfunctional joint if the joint play is not restored first. Exercising a dysfunctional joint too soon in treatment can cause painful exacerbations and reflex muscle reactions. Exercise therapy is most important, even mandatory, especially in locomotor disturbances. However, it should be used only when joint play has been restored. To neglect this notion would be akin to trying to loosen a rusty hinge by repetitively swinging the door back and forth, regardless of the squeaking and grinding. Although movement is attained, and noisily so, it occurs at the expense of the hinge's structural integrity. It would make much more sense to oil the hinge first and then work it in with movement; movement that would be easier, quieter, and more in harmony with the hinge's structure. So, too, with restoring joint play and exercise where in the above analogy the movement is exercise, the squeaking and grinding represent pain, and the lubricating oil depicts the restoration of joint play.

Therefore, in the overall treatment of joint injuries, the active, passive, and joint play (paraphysiological) ranges of motion must all be assessed. Oftentimes range of motion is seen to increase after a manipulation.[4] Joint mechanoreceptors are thought to be stimulated during manipulation which, in turn, create reflexogenic muscle tone changes in the muscles that serve the joint.

THE LOAD–SEPARATION CURVE

In 1947, two anatomists from Great Britain, Rolston and Haines,[5] researched joint dynamics occurring during a manipulative thrust. Using the metacarpal-phalangeal joint as their model, they observed under radiological examination the joint's reaction to axial traction. The results were plotted and a load–separation curve was graphically displayed. Tension was plotted on the horizontal x-axis and joint separation in millimeters was plotted on the vertical y-axis.

The load separation curve illustrated by Figure 18–1 demonstrates that as the joint slack is taken up, tension builds and, at the end of the joint's passive range of motion, a sudden gapping apart of the facet surfaces is seen to occur with a coexistent audible joint click.

Unsworth et al[6] evaluated the synovial fluid and concluded that the crack sound was due to a cavitation phenomenon involving a bubble of carbon dioxide being formed and breaking (cavitating). A radiolucent intra-articular space is also produced after the manipulation. It takes 20 minutes for the gases to be absorbed and the joint to stabilize. During this time, an audible click will not be heard if a second manipulation is attempted. In the meantime, the joint is considered physiologically unstable owing to its reduced coaptive force. Normally, the intra-articular pressure of synovial joints is subatmospheric and affords coaptive stability. For example, a synovial joint with concave–convex articular surfaces can be stripped of all its muscular and ligamentous attachments and the joint surfaces will still remain in coaptation. It is only upon drilling a hole through one of the joint surfaces that the articular surfaces will easily fall apart as the subatmospheric coaptive force is released. In this regard, Sandoz[7] states that it is good practice to rest the joint approximately 20 minutes

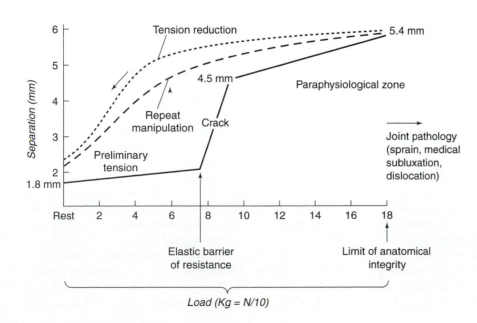

Figure 18–1. Load separation curve. An audible pop is heard at 8 kg of tension as the joint surfaces are separated. The small dashed lines signify the release of tension. Note that the separation of surfaces does not return to the original starting point. The middle curve indicates a second attempt at manipulation immediately after the first one. No crack sound is elicited.

(From Bergmann TF, Peterson DH, Lawrence DJ. Chiropractic Technique. New York, NY: Churchill Livingstone; 1993, with permission.)

postmanipulation before regular activities are resumed; that is, have patients lie down during the joint's refractory period or limit their activity for that time.

Sandoz[7] states that the following events occur at the moment of intrusion into the paraphysiological space:

- A sudden separation of the joint surfaces
- An audible cracking sound
- The appearance of a radiolucent space in the joint

Sandoz[7] also mentions that the active and passive ranges are increased temporarily after a manipulation as the paraphysiological space is added to them. He also comments that one must remain cautious when manipulating a joint during its refractory period because of the absence of the protective elastic barrier. The only barrier of resistance present in such a situation is the limit of anatomical integrity. Forceful manipulation can risk injury to the soft tissue holding elements of the joint.

Cervical manipulation can cause changes in the locomotor system at sites distant from the primary area treated; that is, thoracic or lumbar muscle spasm or improved range of motion after a cervical manipulation. These changes are mediated by the all-important nervous system. Manipulation should not be regarded as simply restoring motion in a restricted joint. Joint manipulation helps to reestablish the functional biomechanics of the locomotor system while simultaneously stimulating the nervous system via reflex phenomena (see Appendix 18A).

By stimulating joint mechanoreceptors, joint manipulation supplies a means of input to the nervous system on a reflex basis. Theoretically, dysfunctional joints and soft tissues supply the nervous system with abnormal afferent input that can engage reflex mechanisms, causing undesirable effects. Such consequences can be referred pain, muscle spasm, vasomotor changes, and even subtle visceral changes. Manipulating a dysfunctional joint can reduce its abnormal afferent input and subsequent reflexogenic effects and have far-reaching beneficial effects. Any afferent input into the system can potentially cause or influence motor responses, even if they are not observable on the exterior.

THE AUDIBLE "CRACK"

The significance of a joint's audible crack during a manipulation is debatable. Many manipulators feel that achieving an audible click is necessary for optimal results; others disagree. It is commonly observed that patients improve with manipulation even when an audible click does not occur. Certain patients have joints that just do not crack, regardless of the force used, how often they are manipulated, or the expertise of the manipulator. Nevertheless, the joint's range of motion and patient's symptoms seem to improve more rapidly when the joint is cavitated. Mierau et al[8] compared the effects of manipulation and mobilization on the range of motion of metacarpophalangeal joints. They found that manipulation associated with an audible

crack created a significantly larger range of motion than mobilization. This is not to say that every joint manipulation performed on every patient should result in a click, especially on the first attempt. Nor is it to say that an audible click should be the sole goal. However, somewhere along the patient's clinical course, if manipulation is indicated, the cavitation phenomenon is certainly welcomed.

As stated earlier, certain patients may not generate a crack sound upon joint manipulation. This occurs with two types of patients that are complete opposites clinically. The first type of patient exhibits very lax joints while the other has very tight joints. In the former situation, the lax joints have a larger joint volume and sufficient tension cannot be produced to generate an audible release.[9] In the tight-jointed individual, the limits of anatomical integrity are reached before enough capsular tension can be generated to create an audible crack.[9] Attempting to create an audible release by forcing a manipulation in these individuals is poor practice and is often met with equally poor results.

A joint should be "caressed" and coaxed to move, especially the joints in the cervical spine. If a joint clicks, so be it. If it does not, further coaxing can be attempted but the use of brute force should never be used, especially if only to fulfill the near neurotic whim of hearing an audible click.

In chronically stiff joints, manipulation should be used carefully. Years of poor joint function, adaptive shortening of periarticular tissues, and fibrosis do not readily reward the practitioner with an audible click, at least not in the beginning. This is a common occurrence with stiff osteoarthritic joints. Several visits over a few days using mobilization first, followed by manipulation on later visits, may produce a joint cavitation.

Interestingly, Meal and Scott[10] mention the effect of weather on the ability of a joint to produce an audible crack. When a low-pressure weather system was present, they observed the joints under study to crack more easily, with less tension and creating less noise.

SLACK REMOVAL

Most of the effort in joint manipulation involves taking all the slack out of the surrounding tissues while guarding neighboring joints that do not need to be manipulated. When a joint is taken to the end of its passive range of motion, right up to the elastic barrier, all slack is said to have been removed. This "preparation" of the joint is culminated by the grade V thrust itself, being directed at the joint restriction. The amount of force needed is minimal but the speed of execution is rapid in order to overcome the inertia of the restriction. It incorporates finesse and feel rather than force. The quick, short impulse allows safe entrance into the paraphysiological zone.

The importance of removing all tissue slack in order to meet the barrier of resistance can be illustrated by a simple experiment (Fig. 18–2). Suppose a bedroom door is slightly stuck in its door jamb and we want to open it, but we want

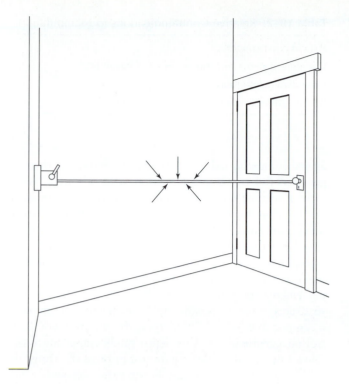

Figure 18–2. Door analogy and slack removal. Arrows indicate the various directions for applying finger flicks.

to do it in an unusual way. We tie one end of a strong industrial rubber band to the door knob and anchor the other end to a crank. Next, we crank up the tension in the rubber band just to the point where the door will fly open. The tension in the band is so much so that if we were to just flick it with our finger the door would immediately fling open. Do you think it would matter which direction we flicked the rubber band from? Not really. As long as the rubber band was "preloaded" to the threshold tension needed to open the door, and the direction of that tension was applied correctly, the door would fling open with minimal force in the direction we wanted. What the finger flick is actually doing is supplying just enough force to overcome the inertia holding the door closed.

The finger flick itself does not require tremendous effort, nor is the direction of its application to the rubber band important. The only thing that is important is that it occurs, but in conjunction with the correct preload tension. Most of the effort in opening the door is generated by the rubber band. So, too, is slack removal related to joint manipulation.

Most errors in manipulation arise from the inadequate removal of tissue slack. Unfortunately, many practitioners apply too much of the effort to the actual impulse thrust. The amount of tissue tension generated during slack removal is inversely related to the amount of impulse thrust required. If little slack is removed prior to a manipulation, one of two things will occur. Number one, the thrust will be dissipated in the extra tissue slack that is still present

and the joint's paraphysiological space will not be engaged. Number two, the extra slack needing to be taken up will most likely be incorporated with the impulse thrust. This creates a high-velocity, high-amplitude thrust—from the active and passive ranges of motion, right up to and through the elastic barrier—resulting in a potentially gross and painful manipulation. This result must be avoided at all costs. Problems with manipulation arise when the overzealous or impatient practitioner takes the joint through active, passive, and joint play ranges all in one quick movement. The joint mechanoreceptors react too briskly to be "fooled" and reflex muscle guarding is usually recruited, resulting in an unsatisfactory maneuver, to say the least.

Traction and slack removal should be performed slowly and gently with the practitioner being astute to any reaction from the joint, muscles, or patient in general. Needless to say, an uncomfortable position is not conducive to a relaxed patient. It is good practice to ask the patient if he or she feels comfortable just before the impulse thrust is delivered. Be mindful of the patient who is too embarrassed to volunteer this information.

The goal is to generate just enough tissue tension around the joint via slack removal so that a high-velocity, low-amplitude impulse is all that is necessary to "open the door." The vulnerability of the patient should be recognized and respected at all times, together with the realization that we manipulate living, feeling human beings, not just restricted painful joints.

CERVICAL ROTATION AND VERTEBROBASILAR INJURY

Cervical rotation is the motion that has the most impact on reducing vertebral artery perfusion, and it is the rotational manipulation that is most often incriminated in vertebrobasilar stroke.[11] Lateral flexion appears to have little effect on the vertebral arteries.[11] Unfortunately, there are no identifiable features that can reliably predict which patient is more likely to experience a vertebrobasilar injury following cervical manipulation. However, certain clues in the history can serve as risk factors that should alert the clinician to be cautious. These include dizziness, unsteadiness, giddiness, and vertigo. In addition, sudden severe unilateral head or neck pain that the patient states is different from anything he or she experienced before should raise a red flag in the clinician's mind. For a further discussion of vertebrobasilar injury, the reader is referred to Chapter 22.

Although extremely rare, on the order of 1 out of 1 million manipulations, vertebrobasilar injury from rotational manipulation is a serious potential sequela that must be kept in mind. A proper perspective regarding this risk must be maintained so that patients are not denied the benefits of cervical manipulation due to unrealistic fear of injury. On the other hand, care must be taken so as not to jeopardize the integrity of the upper cervical structures, including the vertebral arteries. Excessive rotation is to be avoided, especially in at-risk patients. Lateral flexion techniques can be substituted for rotational maneuvers.

Using the word "thrust" in regard to cervical spine manipulative techniques is a gross description of what should otherwise be described as a gentle, quick "nudge." Rotational cervical manipulations can be performed safely as long as thrusting is supplanted by gentle, low-amplitude, high-velocity impulses. Lateral flexion used in conjunction with rotation brings the joints to tension sooner, thus obviating the need for excessive rotation. Astute attention to technique setup and proper slack removal must be made so all that is needed is a slight quick movement to overcome the joint's movement restriction. Mennell (personal communication, September 1993) would often say that one must learn to "caress" the joints and try to move them "only 1/8 of an inch."

CONTRAINDICATIONS

Mobilization and manipulation are indicated when one determines that a joint's accessory or joint play movements need to be restored. According to Maitland,[1] hypermobile joints may need to be mobilized (not manipulated!) to reduce pain and increase their function, not to increase their range of motion. In this regard, grade I and II mobilizations are used to stimulate mechanoreceptor activity and reduce pain. Manipulation, on the other hand should not be used on hypermobile joints. Generally, mobilization and manipulation are used to increase joint motion. However, there are instances when mobilization and manipulation techniques are contraindicated.[12] These can be grouped into absolute and relative contraindications and are listed in Tables 18–1 and 18–2. Absolute contraindications are circumstances that place a patient at undue risk when a particular type of treatment is used. A relative contraindication is a circumstance that may place a patient at undue risk unless the treatment method is altered appropriately.[12]

Absolute contraindications are very straightforward; however, the relative contraindications carry some dis-

Table 18–1: Absolute Contraindications
to Manipulation[13]

Acute inflammatory arthritis

Fractures

Dislocations

Unstable os odontoideum

Malignancies

Bone infection

Clinical manifestation of vertebrobasilar injury

Acute myelopathy

Ankylosis

Table 18–2: Relative Contraindications to Manipulation[13]

Articular hypermobility

Postsurgical joints with no evidence of instability

Bone demineralization

Bleeding disorders and anticoagulant therapy

agreement among field practitioners depending on their experience. Relative contraindications demand careful assessment if manual techniques are to be considered for treatment. What might be a relative contraindication to an inexperienced clinician may not be one at all to an experienced practitioner. Conditions such as osteoarthritis and osteoporosis, although not contraindications, should be handled with care. Problems can be avoided so long as the movements are gentle and match the integrity of the joint structures treated. Small-amplitude thrusts or impulses mean just that—small 1/8-inch depths of movement. Control and gentleness at this depth rarely cause difficulties. Obviously, any increase in pain just prior to the thrust demands reassessment before following through with a manipulation.

Osteoarthritic cervical facet joints often respond well to gentle mobilizations and manipulations. Patients commonly present clinically with cervical spine osteoarthritis associated with headaches and neck pain. Radiographic evidence of facet arthrosis in these cases is a prevalent and often considerable finding. These patients have usually been told that they will have to learn to live with their arthritis and disability and are placed on anti-inflammatory medications. Yet despite their poor prognosis some, if not many, often respond very favorably to manual methods, attesting to the fact that a radiographic image is a poor indicator of a patient's subjective symptoms. In addition to joint mobilizations and gentle manipulations, soft tissue manipulations are very necessary and useful. Of course, in some cases, bony ankylosis needs to be ruled out if manual techniques are to be used, if for no other reason than the futility of trying to manipulate a fused joint.

Caution needs to be taken with the patient whose pain is too acute to allow effective application of manual techniques. Barring any pathology, this can be treated as a relative contraindication depending on the clinician's expertise; however, common sense should prevail and anti-inflammatory strategies can be used, such as electrotherapy, cryotherapy, and medication. Grade I and II mobilizations can be very effective in reducing pain and spasm over a 2- to 3-day period. Sustained traction often works wonders in painfully acute cervical joint dysfunctions. Just as much good can be accomplished by patiently coaxing rather than rushing the process. What may seem to be an attempt at a quick, miraculous maneuver to fix the acute pain more often results in an untimely, painful, and counterproductive treatment.

PREMANIPULATIVE PROVOCATIVE TESTING

Prior to any manipulative thrust, a premanipulative provocative test should be conducted to assess for pain and safety, and to acquaint the patient with the technique to be used. The manipulative technique is set up with complete slack removal, but a thrust is not delivered. During the technique's "dry run" an assessment is made as to patient comfort and ability to relax as the joint in question is preloaded. The clinician also assesses his or her own ability to properly set up the technique and to gain a sense of the amount of slack that needs to be taken up. If no problems are encountered with this premanipulative maneuver, an actual manipulation setup can then be made and a thrust safely attempted.

POSTMANIPULATION SIDE EFFECTS

Postmanipulative side effects are common but relatively minor when compared to the more serious yet rare complications that can arise from cervical manipulation. The most common side effects encountered entail local discomfort, radiating discomfort, headache, and fatigue. These can be predicted to some degree. Senstad et al[13] studied over 1000 patients undergoing more than 4700 treatments and observed some predictors to the more common side effects of spinal manipulation mentioned above (Table 18–3). Uncommon reactions such as dizziness and nausea were not associated with any specific predictors.

In their study, Senstad et al[13] found that when only the thoracic spine was manipulated, more patients complained of side effects than when the other spinal regions were solely treated. Headaches were the most common side effect from cervical and thoracic spine manipulations. The authors also observed that the number of reactions increased as the number of spinal regions treated was increased from one to three. Younger subjects (27 to 46 years of age) were more likely to expereince reactions when compared to older subjects (47 to 64 years). Women reacted adversely more often than men, and more reactions were observed after the first two treatment sessions, but especially the first.

Table 18–3: Predictors to Common Side Effects of Spinal Manipulation[14]

Female gender

Younger (27–46 years old) versus older (47–64 years old) patient

First treatment

Thoracic spine treatment (greatest number of reported reactions)

Cervical and thoracic spine, when only one area treated (more than lumbar)

Because of these observations, one should be careful to limit treatment to one area on the first treatment session, especially in younger women. Most importantly, force should not be substituted for skill nor should there be a quest to satisfy the neurotic need to hear an audible click by either clinician or patient. One should keep in mind that 85 percent of these reactions are only mild to moderate in nature and that 74 percent are transient, disappearing within 24 hours.[13]

MANIPULATION TECHNIQUES

Many fine techniques are used to manipulate joint dysfunction in the cervical and thoracic spines; only the more common ones are discussed in this section. The following section addresses techniques used to manipulate dysfunctions in the cervical and thoracic spine, costotransverse, sternoclavicular, acromioclavicular, and scapulothoracic joints. Assessment of joint dysfunction in these areas is discussed in Chapter 13. Unless otherwise stated, all joint manipulations presented in the following section describe manipulation of the right-sided articulation.

The setup of a manipulative technique entails the clinician's position, the patient's position, the manipulating hand's contact point, the stabilizing or "indifferent" hand's position (nonthrusting hand), and the direction of manipulation or line of drive. Additionally, the specific part of the patient's spine to be contacted needs to be considered (e.g., the spinous or articular process). The cervical spine can be easily manipulated in the sitting, supine, or prone positions depending on patient or clinician preference.

Cervical Spine

Manipulation of cervical spine joint dysfunction is predicated on palpation findings of painful joint restriction. In the evaluation of joint dysfunction discussed in Chapter 13, the manipulable lesion was primarily defined by movement restriction and pain, especially joint restriction that elicits pain on provocation. The plane or direction of joint restriction determines the type and direction of manipulative technique to be used. For example, consider assessing the right C2–3 facet joint for right lateral flexion joint play. If painful movement restriction is found, a manipulative technique that will increase right lateral flexion motion at that joint will be the indicated technique of choice. In general, the cervical spine manipulates easiest in rotation compared to the thoracic spine, which manipulates easiest in extension.

One of the most important regions to assess and manipulate in the entire spine when treating locomotor disturbances is the upper cervical area. It is rich in somatosensory input to the central nervous system and is associated with many reflexogenic affects on the entire locomotor system. Its biomechanical importance is reflected by the fact that an entire branch of clinical chiropractic practice pays attention solely to the upper cervical spine to the exclusion of other areas. Clinicians experienced in spinal joint manipulation frequently observe changes in subjective symptoms and objective signs occurring distant from the site of treatment. This is often profoundly observed when treating the upper cervical region.

Craniocervical Joints

Craniocervical joint dysfunction is characterized by pain and stiffness over the occipitoatlantal joint found midway between the midline and the tip of the atlas transverse process. Radiating pain as described in Chapter 13 can also be elicited. A firm block to movement palpation in the suboccipital region is felt during the scan examination discussed in Chapter 6. Restrictions are then sought for in both posterior-to-anterior and anterior-to-posterior rotations, lateral flexion, flexion, and anterior glide.

Occipital Lift

This technique can be used to manipulate any of the movement restrictions found at the craniocervical joints. Oftentimes these movement restrictions are found in combination and this technique usually addresses them all in one move. It can be performed in the supine, prone, or sitting positions (Fig. 18–3). The common contact point on the patient is the occipital rim located just behind and medial to the mastoid process. The lift technique attempts to manipulate the craniocervical joint by "lifting" the occipital condyles off the atlas articulations.

SUPINE OCCIPITAL LIFT. To manipulate the right craniocervical joint the patient lies supine while the clinician is positioned at the head of the table. The stabilizing hand (left) cradles the base of the occiput with the middle finger encircling the occipital rim just behind the mastoid process. The clinician faces the patient from the right side of the table at the level of the head and neck. The palm of the left hand cups the ear while the entire head and neck are rotated to the left so that the right articulation faces upward. The right hand makes a pisiform contact under the

Figure 18–4. Occipital lift using a thumb contact.

rim of the occiput with the fingers pointing cephalad along the side of the head (Fig. 18–4). An alternative method uses a thumb interphalangeal joint contact under the rim of the occiput while the palm of the hand contacts the zygomatic arch. Both hands exert firm traction cephalad to remove all slack while an important element of lateral flexion is added so that the head is lifted slightly off the table. Traction is assisted by the clinician using a cephalad body lean until the barrier of resistance is met. At the barrier, a high-velocity yet short amplitude impulse thrust is directed cephalad while a simultaneous movement of slight lateral flexion is added to impart a scooping type thrust.

PRONE OCCIPITAL LIFT. With the patient prone the head is fully rotated to the right so that the side of restriction is uppermost (Fig. 18–5). The clinician stands or kneels at the head of the table and supports the head and neck from underneath with the left (indifferent) hand contact. The head piece of the table is lowered slightly. The middle fin-

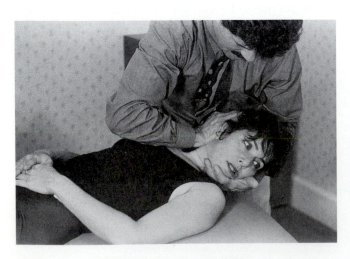

Figure 18–3. Occipital lift.

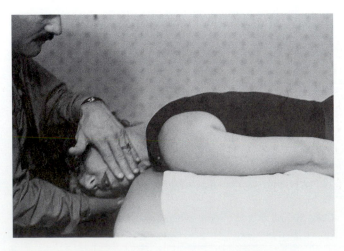

Figure 18–5. Prone occipital lift.

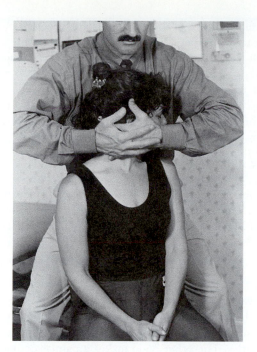

Figure 18–6. Sitting occipital lift.

SITTING OCCIPITAL LIFT. For the sitting technique, the clinician stands directly behind the sitting patient. The patient's head is turned fully to the left and the clinician's left hand reaches around to contact the right occipital rim just behind the mastoid process using the middle finger (Fig. 18–6). The thenar eminence of the left hand applies pressure above the zygoma and not on the temperomandibular joint. The clinician's right (indifferent) hand supports the contact hand by cupping over it. The clinician must squat down so that the patient's left parietal eminence is supported by his or her upper sternum. The shoulders of both clinician and patient should be parallel to each other and the patient's head is held firmly between the clinician's hands and sternum. Traction is exerted cephalad by the clinician straightening his or her knees and lifting the head with the arms and hands. A slight right lateral flexion is added to the upper cervical region by leaning forward over the patient while pulling the hands toward the sternal contact and rotating or supinating the palms upward. At the barrier of resistance, an impulse thrust is directed cephalad along with a slight scooping lateral flexion movement.

Occipital Rotation

This joint restriction is manipulated supine with the clinician at the head of the table. The patient's head and occiput is cradled in the left indifferent hand while it is rotated to the left and lifted or laterally flexed slightly off the table (Fig. 18–7). The thenar eminence of the contact hand (right) is placed on the zygomatic arch, the pisiform and hypothenar eminence is on the mandible, and the fingertips rest on the chin. End range is reached by flexing or "rocking" the chin onto the shoulder while simultaneously lifting or laterally flexing the head off the table slightly by action of the indifferent hand.[3] The contact hand simultaneously rotates the head further into the range and when the barrier of resistance is met, an impulse thrust is

ger of the indifferent hand is placed under the rim of the occiput while cupping the patient's ear in the palm. The contact hand tractions the patient's head down (floorward) and cephalad with a mid-forearm contact while the flexed wrist and hand gently contacts the upper occipital area. The fingers rest on the mandible for control, only, and are not used to pull or thrust. The whole cranium is tractioned cephalad (toward the clinician) and downward with the use of the indifferent hand and forearm of the contact hand. A manipulative thrust is delivered cephalad at the point the barrier of resistance is met.

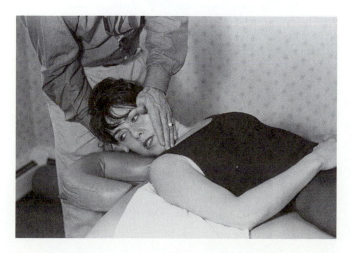

A

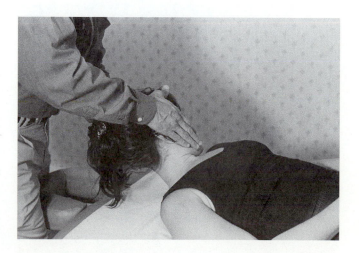

B

Figure 18–7. A. Occipital rotation. **B.** Note raised head and neck.

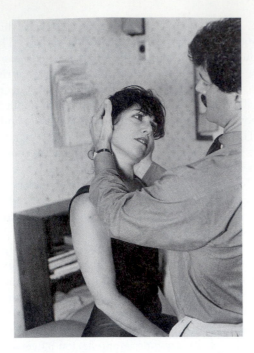

Figure 18–8. Anterior-to-posterior occipital rotation.

and inferior aspect of the right mastoid process. The clinician rotates the patient's head to the right while slightly laterally flexing it to the left (Fig. 18–8). Axial traction is applied using both hands while adding slight upper cervical flexion in order to stretch the right sternocleidomastoid muscle. Once the barrier is met, an impulse thrust is given with the right hand in a posterior and superior direction, creating an anterior-to-posterior lifting rotation.

Lateral Flexion

This technique is set up very similar to the supine occipital lift. The contact is on the lateral aspect of the mastoid process. The indifferent hand tractions cephalad while the contact hand supplies a lateral flexion movement localized to the craniocervical joint (Fig. 18–9). At the barrier an impulse thrust is delivered through the occipito-atlantal joints.

Flexion

With the patient supine, the clinician supports the base of the occiput with the indifferent hand while the tips of the thumb and middle fingers contact the transverse processes of the atlas. The other hand makes a palmar contact over the forehead while the fingers point down over the face (Fig. 18–10). The indifferent hand stabilizes the atlas vertebra as the occiput is flexed against it by the other hand. When the slack is taken up and barrier is met, a light impulse thrust is used to increase flexion at the craniocervical joints.

performed. In essence, the occiput is rocked or nodded forward while being rotated simultaneously on the atlas facet joints.

Another technique for rotation, this time from the anterior-to-posterior direction, can also be used. The clinician stands off to one side but facing the sitting patient. For a right-sided dysfunction, the clinician's indifferent hand (right hand) cups the left side of the patient's head and ear. The contact hand (left hand) cups the right side of the head and ear but makes a pisiform contact on the anterior

C1–7 Motion Segments

Rotation, Posterior-to-Anterior

With the patient supine, the clinician sits at the head of the table. The clinician's left hand cups the left side of the patient's head and ear while the right hand makes an index finger contact on the posterior arch of the atlas or articular pillar of the C2–7 segments (Fig. 18–11). The clinician moves slightly to the right side of the patient as

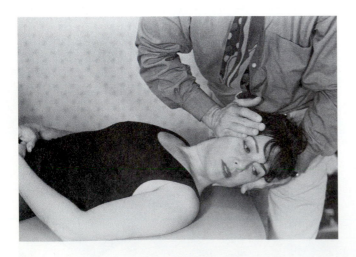

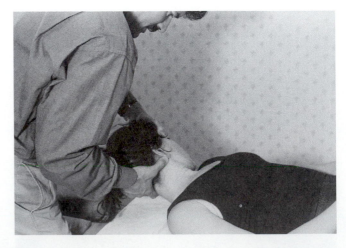

Figure 18–9. A. Lateral flexion at occipito-atlantal joint. **B.** Alternate technique for lateral flexion. After rotation to at least 45 degrees, lateral flexion is directed at the occipito-atlantal joint.

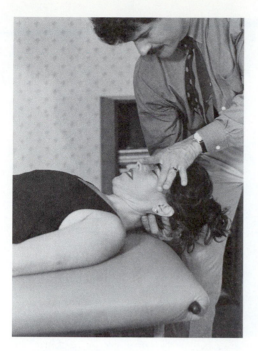

Figure 18–10. Flexion at occipito-atlantal joint.

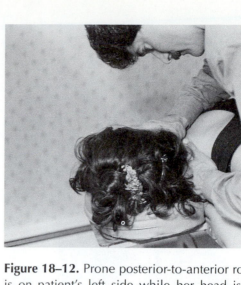

Figure 18–12. Prone posterior-to-anterior rotation. Contact is on patient's left side while her head is rotated to the right.

the head is rotated to the left until joint resistance is met. Lateral flexion is added to the level in question to further bring the joint to tension and an impulse thrust is then made. Care is taken to not overrotate the neck or thrust too vigorously.

The same technique can be performed in the prone or sitting positions. With the patient prone, the clinician stands on the left side (the side of joint dysfunction) facing cephalad. An indifferent hand contact is made with the right hand cupping the side of the patient's head and ear. An index finger contact is made on the posterior arch of

atlas or the articular pillar of segments C2–7 (Fig. 18–12). The head is pushed into right rotation by the indifferent hand while the contact hand moves along with the segment in question as it rotates around and underneath. Pressure is applied with the contact hand until the barrier is felt and an impulse thrust is made.

The clinician can also stand behind the sitting patient to manipulate this joint dysfunction. The patient should be sitting upright with the head and neck at a comfortable level for the clinician. The clinician supports the left side of the patient's head and neck with the left indifferent hand, cupping the ear with the palm. The right hand makes an index finger contact over the dysfunctional segment and rotates the head to the left while laterally flexing the neck slightly to the right using both hands (Fig. 18–13). The clinician must move slightly around the right side of the patient for optimal positioning, yet maintaining his center very close to the contact. A thrust is delivered when the barrier is met. By varying the angle of thrust and contact positions, this same technique can be adapted for lateral flexion and anterior-to-posterior rotation dysfunctions.

Rotation, Anterior-to-Posterior

Rotation from anterior to posterior can be manipulated with a similar supine setup to that previously described. To manipulate the C1–2 joint on the right side, the clinician reaches underneath the patient's head and neck with his or her left hand to make an index finger contact anterior to the right atlas transverse process. The right hand is the indifferent hand cupping the right side of the patient's head and ear. The head and neck are then rotated to the right, laterally flexed to the left, and flexed as a whole until joint resistance is met (Fig. 18–14). A pulling impulse manipulation is performed with the left hand while the right indifferent hand assists.

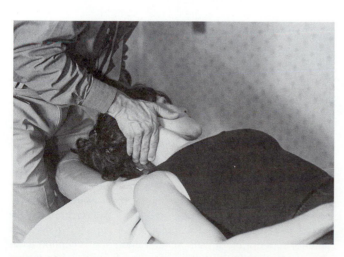

Figure 18–11. Posterior to anterior rotation technique for C1–7 motion segments.

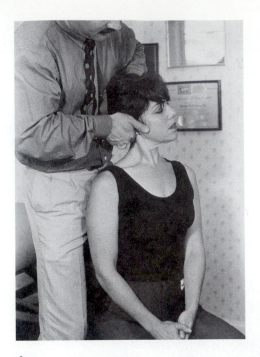
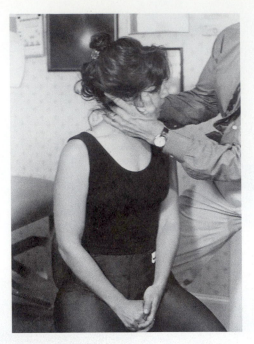

A **B**

Figure 18-13. A. Sitting posterior-to-anterior cervical rotation manipulation. **B.** Sitting rotational manipulation using a pull move. The middle finger contacts the dysfunctional cervical facet posteriorly while the indifferent hand cups the left side of the patient's head.

To manipulate the lower segments, an index finger contact is taken as previously described, but slightly lower than the level to be manipulated. The finger then initiates a soft tissue pull as it slides obliquely cephalad and medial in order to anchor on the right side of the respective spinous process of the level in question. By combining lateral flexion of the head to the left, rotation to the right, and cervical flexion, a line of tension can be localized to the

facet joint in question. A pulling type of impulse thrust is then given.

A sitting technique similar to the one discussed previously for posterior-to-anterior rotation dysfunctions can be used. However, the differences are that an index finger contact is taken anterolaterally on the transverse process and the patient's head is rotated and laterally flexed toward the contact hand (Fig. 18–15). Flexion is added to meet the barrier and an impulse thrust is made into the resistance by the contact hand.

![Figure 18-14 photograph]

Figure 18–14. Anterior-to-posterior rotation manipulation. Note the pull of the contact finger underneath the patient's neck.

! CLINICAL PEARL

Anterior-to-posterior rotational joint dysfunctions are common, yet clinical awareness of their existence is often lacking. As a consequence, their presence is very often overlooked. These joint dysfunctions in the upper cervical segments are often associated with sore throats, especially in children. These dysfunctions in the lower segments are often found in conjunction with chronic upper cervical joint dysfunctions, upper extremity pain syndromes, scalene muscle trigger points, and thoracic outlet conditions. Pain from these lower cervical anterior-to-posterior rotation dysfunctions often causes pain in the medial scapular region, upper extremity, or anterior superior chest wall. Schafer and Faye[14] mention a curious finding of the elicitation of a cough reflex when testing for this type of dysfunction at the atlas transverse process.

Figure 18–15. Sitting anterior-to-posterior rotation manipulation. Note anterior contact of clinician's right hand. Thrust is made into an anterior to posterior rotation.

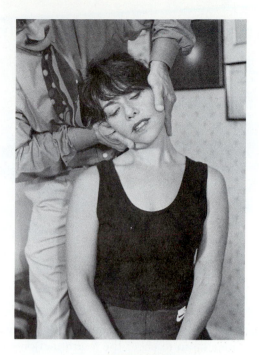

Figure 18–17. Sitting lateral flexion manipulation.

Lateral Flexion

A lateral flexion dysfunction is corrected with the patient supine and the clinician at the head of the table. The left hand cups the left side of the patient's head and ear and laterally bends the head and neck to the right. The right hand makes an index contact over the articulation in question after rotating the head slightly to the left (Fig. 18–16). Just enough lateral flexion is used to localize the manipulative thrust to the respective level. A thrust is given once the barrier is met.

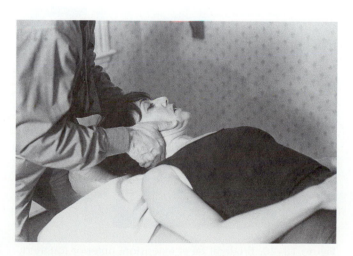

Figure 18–16. Lateral flexion manipulation.

A sitting variation of this technique can be performed as mentioned earlier in the posterior-to-anterior manipulation. The setup is exactly the same except the contact is made slightly more laterally than for the rotation technique. The head is rotated away from the side of contact only slightly and then laterally flexed to the level of joint dysfunction (Fig. 18–17). The clinician stands slightly to the side of contact and thrusts when the barrier is met.

Flexion

Flexion dysfunctions are commonly found in the lower cervical spine and can be manipulated. The clinician sits at the head of the supine patient. The left hand supports the left side of the patient's head cupping the ear. The right hand makes a contact over the right anterior aspect of the transverse process at the level in question using the proximal part of the index finger's proximal phalanx. The neck is flexed and laterally flexed slightly to the right to create tension at the level in question and an impulse thrust is made (Fig. 18–18). Flexion dysfunctions are often uncomfortable and regularly accompany the anterior-to-posterior rotation dysfunctions. They are sometimes corrected when manipulating the anterior-to-posterior rotation dysfunctions; however, if they are not, they need to be directly manipulated.

Thoracic Spine

Most thoracic spine manipulations are performed in either the supine or prone positions. This section focuses on the upper three thoracic motion segments followed by a discussion of costotransverse joint manipulations. Because of the muscle and fascial connections spanning the cervical and

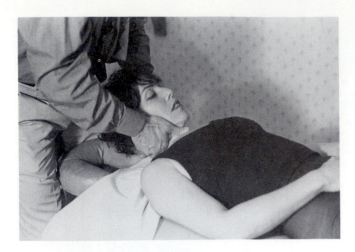

Figure 18–18. Flexion manipulation.

thoracic spines, movements of the neck can influence the thoracic spine down to about the fourth motion segment. As a consequence, head and neck positions can be used to bring upper thoracic segments to tension during manipulative techniques.

Thoracic spinal joint dysfunction is almost invariably linked with dysfunction of the related costotransverse joints. Therefore, by definition a thoracic motion segment must include the adjacent rib articulations as they all function together as one unit. Prone techniques are discussed first, followed by those in the supine position.

Prone Techniques

UNILATERAL FACET ROTATION. The clinician stands at the patient's shoulder level facing headward on the same side of the joint dysfunction; in this case, the left side. The indifferent hand (left hand) cups the base of the occiput and mastoid process with the palm while the thrusting hand (right hand) makes a pisiform contact over the left facet joint (Fig. 18–19). The pisiform should be placed just lateral to the spinous process. Too lateral of a contact from the spinous process will convert this technique into a costotransverse manipulation (see later discussion). The indifferent hand tractions cephalad and rotates the occiput away so that the face is turned towards the clinician. The contact hand presses firmly onto the facet joint and when the barrier is met, a thrust is made directed slightly lateral.

BILATERAL FACET EXTENSION/ANTERIOR LONGITUDINAL LIGAMENT. The clinician stands on either side, as previously described, but takes a bilateral pisiform contact over the facet joints of the same level such that the distal forearms are crossed and the clinician's shoulders are facing cephalad (Fig. 18–20). For example, if the clinician is on the left side of the patient, the right pisiform contacts the left facet joint while the left pisiform contacts the right facet joint. As the barrier of resistance is met by posterior-to-anterior pressure, a body drop impulse thrust is performed accentuating the side closer to the clinician or performed with equal pressure bilaterally if both facets are restricted.

To gap the anterior interbody space due to an adaptively shortened anterior longitudinal ligament, equal bilateral pressures are used and the motion segment is coaxed into further extension on each of three successive exhales performed by the patient. At the very limit of motion segment extension, a short quick body drop impulse is done.

EXTENSION, INTERSPINOUS CONTACT. The clinician stands as previously described, to the left of the patient. The left hand makes a "knife-edge" contact using the ulnar border of the fifth metacarpal placed between the spinous processes of the level in dysfunction. The right hand makes a thumb and index finger web contact under the base of

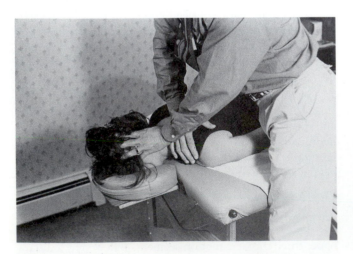

Figure 18–19. Unilateral facet rotation technique for left-sided joint dysfunction.

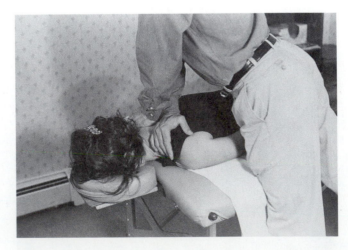

Figure 18–20. Bilateral facet extension, anterior longitudinal ligament manipulation.

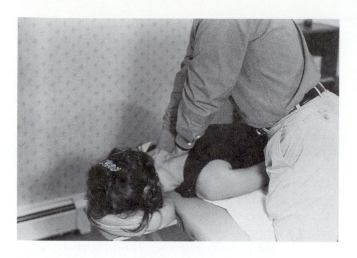

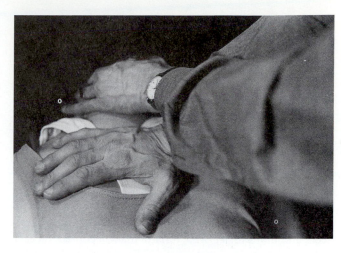

A   B

Figure 18–21. A. Interspinous contact. **B.** Close-up view with hands reversed.

the occiput. This hand is used to apply cephalad traction to the cervical spine and is placed over the left contact hand. As moderate cephalad traction is applied to the occiput, the contact hand presses down in between the spinous processes until the barrier is met and a thrust is delivered in a posterior-to-anterior direction (Fig. 18–21). The same procedure can be used to induce flexion into the motion segment by simply altering the arm of the interspinous contact so that it angles more cephalad during the thrust.

LATERAL FLEXION. For this technique the clinician stands on the side of the prone patient at shoulder level facing cephalad. The left hand makes a thumb contact against the left side of the spinous process at the level in dysfunction

while the hand and fingers rest over the upper fibers of the trapezius muscle. The clinician bends well over the patient and uses the right hand to cup the right side of the patient's head and neck as a unit. The right hand then laterally flexes the head and neck over the thumb contact, which acts as a fulcrum for the technique (Fig. 18–22A). Once the barrier is sensed by the thumb, an impulse thrust by the left hand from left to right is performed.

By switching hand positions and reversing the procedures of slack removal and thrusting, this technique can be repeated on the other side without the clinician switching sides (Fig. 18–22B). The only difference is that the clinician has to reach well over the patient to lower the elbow of the manipulating hand. The thrust is toward the clini-

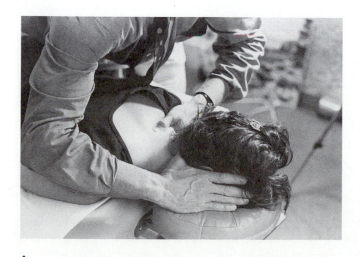

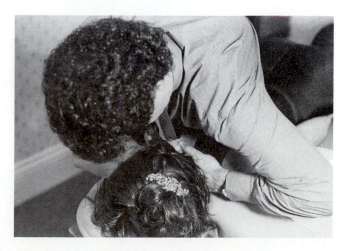

A   B

Figure 18–22. A. Lateral flexion; clinician is on the ipsilateral side. **B.** From the contralateral side.

cian with the right hand creating a more powerful technique as the strength of the clinician's pectoralis muscle is recruited. For both variations, as in any technique, success depends on maximal slack removal and meeting the barrier of resistance. In addition, the preceding technique can be performed from the head end of the table facing caudad. These same techniques can be used to reduce cervical lateral flexion dysfunctions by making the thumb contacts against the cervical motion segments.

CIRCUMDUCTION MOBILIZATION. This technique is quite effective in causing a general mobilization of the cervicodorsal region. The patient lies prone and the clinician stands to the side of the table facing cephalad. The thumb, web, and index finger of each hand make a contact on each side of the cervicodorsal region. The thumb pads simultaneously press against the lateral aspects of the spinous process to be mobilized. The web and index fingers of both hands grasp the upper trapezius and supraclavicular areas and help localize the mobilization to the cervicodorsal or upper thoracic regions (Fig. 18–23A). A circumduction motion in the transverse plane is performed in either direction. Small circular movements are progressed to ever widening ones.

Supine Techniques

CERVICOTHORACIC LOCALIZED TRACTION TECHNIQUE. This technique is an exceptionally specific and effective technique to mobilize the cervicothoracic region using a localized long axis distraction maneuver. The patient is supine with the cervicothoracic junction just at the edge of the table. The clinician cradles the occiput and upper cervical region with a cupped left hand and applies cephalad traction. Opposing this traction is a right-handed thumb contact blocking the superior aspect of the first thoracic spinous process. The web of the right hand encircles the supraclavicular region while the palm stabilizes the upper trapezius and superior aspect of the scapula. The fingers of the right hand stabilize the clavicle. The right hand essentially stabilizes the upper thoracic region while the thumb localizes specifically the segment against which a traction force can be applied via the left hand (Fig. 18–23B). The spinous processes of C6 through T4 can be used to create segmental traction. The traction hand can angle the cervical spine into extension, lateral flexion, and/or rotation to further localize tractional forces most effectively as determined by the patient's response. The traction hand can hold traction statically while the stabilizing thumb of the other hand firmly presses caudally using a steady pressure or oscillating mobilizations. Conversely, the thumb contacting the spinous process can statically hold the caudal vertebral segment of the motion unit while the other hand tractions the cervical spine using a steady pressure or oscillating mobilizations.

The hand contact for supine thoracic manipulations varies and deserves some explanation. In the first variation, the fingers are flexed so that the pads touch the volar aspect of the metacarpophalangeal joints (Fig. 18–24). The metacarpophalangeal joints are in a neutral position. Thumb is brought alongside the flexed index finger. The contact is made so that the spinous processes lie in the hollow formed by the palm. The thumb forms a bar that is placed between the spinous process in question and the flexed interphalangeal joints of the rest of the fingers are on

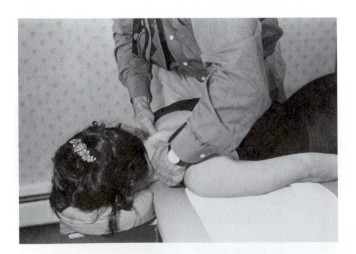

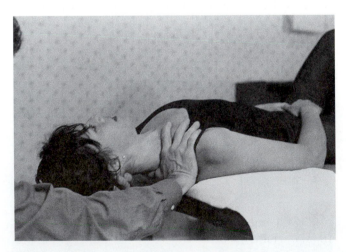

A

B

Figure 18–23. A. Circumduction mobilization. **B.** Localized traction of cervicothoracic junction. The caudal hand makes a palm and web of hand contact over the upper thorax and clavicle with a thumb pad contact over the spinous process of the first thoracic vertebra. The cephalad hand grasps the upper cervical spine and occiput and applies traction while the thumb on the caudal hand applies caudal pressure on the spinous process.

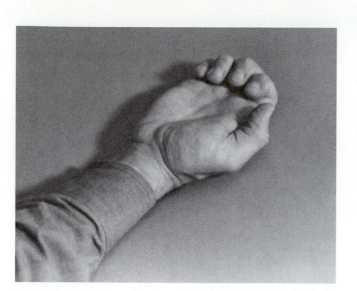

Figure 18–24. Contact hand position for supine thoracic techniques.

Figure 18–25. Second variation of hand position for supine thoracic techniques.

one side of the spine while the thenar and hypothenar eminences are on the other side.

The second variation is similar to the preceding one except that the fingers are flexed more, bringing their pads further into the palm of the hand (Fig. 18–25). The metacarpopahlangeal joints are flexed to about 45 degrees. This gives more depth to the hollow formed in the palm and creates more leverage.

A third variation entails holding the hand so that the third, fourth, and fifth fingers are flexed onto the palm while the index finger and thumb are held straight out as if using the hand to mimic a hand gun (Fig. 18–26). The flexed fingers and their knuckles are placed along one side of the spine over the facets while the thumb and thenar eminence are placed over the opposing facets. The index finger extends obliquely cephalad along the spine.

SUPINE EXTENSION. The patient lies supine with the arms crossed in front of the chest so that the left hand is on the right shoulder and the right arm crosses over top to grasp the left shoulder. The clinician stands to either side of the patient facing cephalad, in this case on the patient's left side. The clinician rolls the patient toward him or her with the right hand and places a left hand contact under the segment in question in the midline between the spinouses. The patient is then rolled onto the contact hand. The patient is told to tuck the chin in and flex the neck up (Fig. 18–27). The clinician's right hand controls the patient's upper body motion by contacting the patient's arms where they cross. The patient's upper body is rolled up into flexion by the clinician's right hand and is slowly lowered back over the contact hand that acts as a fulcrum. At the moment the segment in dysfunction is over the contact hand and the barrier is sensed, a thrust is exerted downward into

the table through the folded arms and thorax of the patient. Great leverage is on the side of the clinician so care must be exercised in being gentle.

SUPINE FLEXION. The same setup as previously described is adopted; however, the thrust is performed just before the upper body and segment to be manipulated is leveraged over the contact hand. In addition, the thrust is angled more cephalad along the long axis of the patient's upper arms (Fig. 18–28).

SUPINE LATERAL FLEXION. The setup is the same as previously described. This technique would be used to correct a left lateral flexion restriction. In making the contact with the left hand, the patient is rolled slightly more toward the clinician so that the contact can be made on the left side of the spine at the level of the dysfunction rather than in the midline (Fig. 18–29). The clinician's left hand crosses the midline and makes a thenar eminence contact against the left lateral aspect of the spinous process. Pressure is applied and the contact is pulled firmly against the spinous process in an attempt to laterally flex the segment to the left. The patient is then rolled only partially onto the contact and is not allowed to lie flat on his or her back, the right shoulder being almost 30 to 40 degrees off the table. This angled position allows the thrust to impart a left lateral bending force at the segment in question. By changing the contact this same technique can be used to manipulate the costotransverse joints (see later discussion).

SUPINE POSTERIOR GLIDE MOBILIZATION. This technique is similar to a supine thoracic technique; however, the edge of the table is used as a fulcrum for mobilizing the upper thoracic spine in the sagittal plane. The patient is supine with the segments to be mobilized placed over the edge of

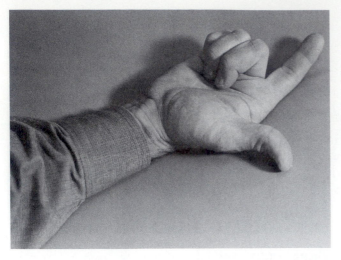

A

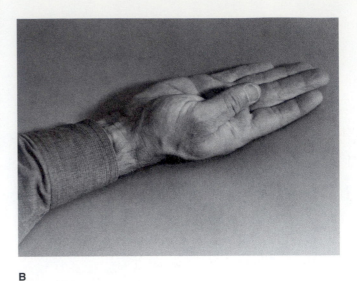

B

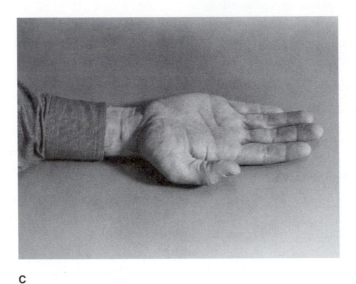

C

Figure 18–26. A. Third variation of hand contact for supine thoracic techniques. **B** and **C.** Additional contact hand positions not described in text: **(B)** flat hand; **(C)** raised thenar eminence.

the treatment table. The patients's hands are placed behind the neck with fingers interlaced and elbows together pointing upward. The clinician cradles the head and neck with one arm while the upper thoracic segments cephalad of the table's edge are contacted by the fingers. The fingers are held in a forked arrangement on either side of the segment to be mobilized, palpating the interspinous space for movement. The other hand is placed over the end of both elbows (Fig. 18–30). The neck and upper thoracic spine are held in a neutral position while the clinician imparts a posteriorly directed pressure through both elbows. This places a posterior glide mobilizing force at the segment stabilized by the table's edge. Using the elbows as levers, small amounts of upper thoracic flexion and extension can be performed while posterior glide movements are mobilized over the table's edge.

Rib Joints

First Rib

The spatulated blade of the first rib can be palpated in the supraclavicular fossa (see Chap. 13) and it can be manipulated in the seated, supine, or prone positions.

The seated manipulation mimics the seated examination maneuver with the addition of an impulse thrust. To manipulate the right side the clinician stands behind the seated patient and places his or her right foot on the table. The patient relaxes the upper extremity and trapezius region by resting the right arm on the clinician's knee. The clinician makes an index finger contact over the first rib in the supraclavicular fossa and angles his or her forearm so that the thrust is directed medially and caudad. The index finger contact employs the lateral aspect of the proximal

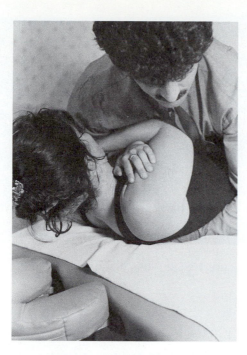

Figure 18–27. Supine extension technique. Note patient's thoracic spine is extended over the contact.

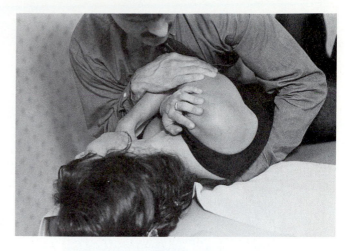

Figure 18–29. Supine lateral flexion technique. Note patient is rolled up onto contact to induce left lateral bending.

phalanx. The indifferent hand cups the side of the head and neck and laterally bends them as a unit over the contact hand (Fig. 18–31). The patient is asked to inhale and on the exhale, all slack is taken up, the barrier is met, and an impulse thrust is delivered.

In the prone position, the clinician stands on the left side of the patient facing cephalad and reaches well over to make an index finger contact on the right first rib (Fig. 18–32). The forearm is placed in position to thrust medially and caudad. To accomplish this, the elbow is held horizontal while pointing cephalad by internally rotating the shoulder. The indifferent hand cups the side of the head and neck and laterally flexes them as a unit over the contact. When the barrier is met an impulse thrust is delivered. If the clinician stays in this position but simply reverses the indifferent and contact hand positions, the left first rib can be manipulated by laterally flexing the head and neck over the left contact hand. Although it looks awkward, the former maneuver tends to be more stable and affords more leverage.

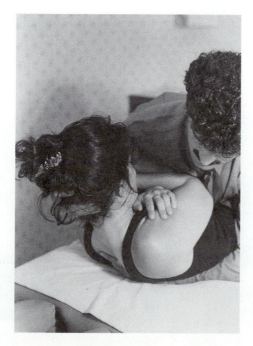

Figure 18–28. Supine flexion. Note patient's thoracic spine is still held in flexion, as compared to Figure 18–18.

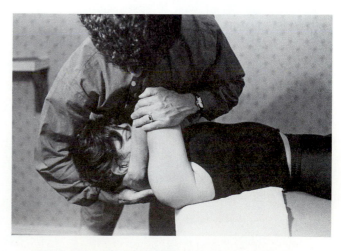

Figure 18–30. Supine posterior glide mobilization.

Figure 18–31. First rib manipulation.

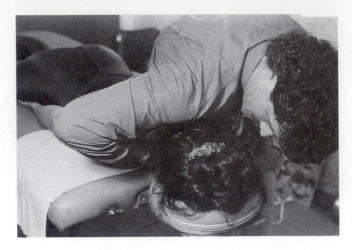

Figure 18–32. Prone first rib manipulation.

The same technique can be performed from the head end of the table. To manipulate the right first rib, the clinician approaches the prone patient from the head end of the table and makes a contact on the right first rib with the side of the left index finger (Fig. 18–33). The indifferent hand cups the left side to the patient's head and laterally flexes it over the contact hand. At the barrier resistance an impulse thrust is given.

Second and Third Costotransverse Joints

These joints can be manipulated in either the prone or supine positions. The contacts are taken approximately 2 inches lateral to the spinous processes on the rib angles. The rib angles are adjacent to the costotransverse joints in the upper thoracic segments. Oscillating pressures applied to the second or third costosternal rib insertion anteriorly, while simultaneously palpating for the movement at the posterior rib angle, facilitates accurate location of the correct rib level.

The same setup for the unilateral facet rotation technique mentioned earlier can be used for these rib levels (see Fig. 18–19). The only difference is a rib angle contact is taken and the thrust is directly slightly laterally.

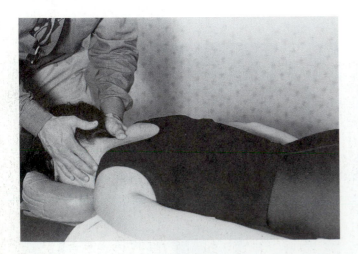

A   B

Figure 18–33. A and **B.** First rib manipulation.

A crossed bilateral pisiform contact can be taken on opposing rib heads. The side to be manipulated is closest to the clinician. The indifferent hand stabilizes the opposite side rib head to prevent undue motion segment rotation.

Supine rib techniques can be implemented and fashioned after the supine lateral flexion technique for the thoracic spine, previously discussed (see Fig. 18–29). As the supine patient is rolled toward the clinician, a thenar eminence contact is made under the "down-side" rib angle. The patient's thorax is rolled gently back onto the contact and a light thrust is made through the patient's arms and chest. Alternately, a thenar contact can be made on the "upper-side" rib angle by not having the contact hand cross the spine. The thorax is lowered onto the contact and a thrust is made. This latter variation is indicated in slender and smaller patients.

Sternoclavicular Joint

Schafer and Faye[14] and Gillet and Liekens[15] relate sternoclavicular joint dysfunctions to upper thoracic symptoms and, specifically, to cervicodorsal joint dysfunctions. Palpable soft tissue changes are often observed in the shoulder and upper back regions. The muscles and subcutaneous tissues that extend from the cervicodorsal region to the shoulder joint laterally often feel hard and contracted when the sternoclavicular joints are in chronic dysfunction. Cervical spine motion can elicit palpable movement changes in the sternoclavicular joint, most likely as a result of the sternocleidomastoid muscle linking the two. Clinically, joint dysfunction in the sternoclavicular joints is often found in association with lower cervical hypermobility and craniocervical joint dysfunction. Manipulation of dysfunctional sternoclavicular joints can aid in the restoration of normal cervical locomotor function.

The sternoclavicular joints can be manipulated with the clinician sitting behind the seated patient.[14] The clinician makes bilateral wrist contacts on the medial-most ends of both clavicles and presses his or her sternum against the mid- and upper thoracic spine of the patient. The clinician pulls the shoulders posteriorly with the forearms while the upper thorax is pushed anteriorly using the sternum (Fig. 18–34). At the barrier of resistance, an impulse pulling thrust is made with the arms while the sternum is thrust forward.

The joints can be manipulated in the supine position with the clinician standing at the level of the patient's shoulders facing cephalad. A bilateral thenar contact is taken on the medial-most aspect of both clavicles (Fig. 18–35). Pressure is applied anterior to posterior and laterally until the barrier of resistance is sensed and an impulse thrust is given.

Two other alternative supine techniques can also be used. In the first, the clinician stands at the side of the patient facing cephalad. The patient's right arm (to manipulate the right sternoclavicular joint) is held by the clinician's left arm and a right-handed thenar or pisiform contact is made on the medial-most end of the patient's

Figure 18–34. Sitting sternoclavicular joint manipulation.

right clavicle (Fig. 18–36). The clinician tractions the patient's right arm up toward the ceiling as pressure is applied onto the clavicle. A light impulse thrust is given when the barrier of resistance is met.

The other technique entails stabilizing the whole shoulder girdle and moving it as a unit in relation to the sternum. The clinician places his or her left hand under the patient's right scapula with his or her fingers grasping around its medial border. The patient's bent arm is cradled in the clinician's arm while a pisiform contact is made on the medial-most end of the clavicle, fingers pointing along it laterally (Fig. 18–37). Both the indifferent and contact hands traction laterally and thrust at the barrier.

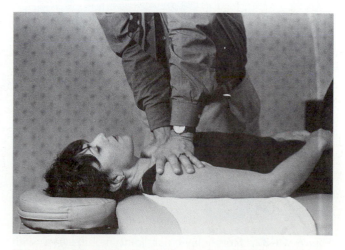

Figure 18–35. Supine sternoclavicular joint manipulation.

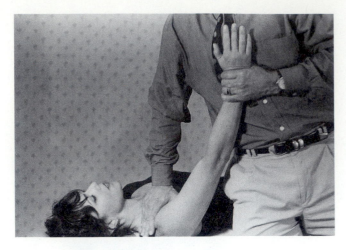

Figure 18–36. Sternoclavicular joint manipulation with arm traction.

Acromioclavicular Joint

The acromioclavicular joint is another extraspinal joint that, when in dysfunction, can contribute to continued cervical joint dysfunction, probably on a reflex basis. Assessment and treatment of acromioclavicular joint dysfunction should be considered in the management of cervical pain syndromes.

Acromioclavicular joint dysfunction can be manipulated with the patient in the seated or supine positions. The clinician sits behind the seated patient. The patient's arm is maximally flexed at the elbow and raised to 90 degrees of flexion at the shoulder joint (Fig. 18–38). The clinician cups and overlaps both hands over the olecranon process and pulls the arm directly backward. This exerts an anterior-to-posterior glide into the acromioclavicular joint via pressure imparted through the humerus and scapula rel-

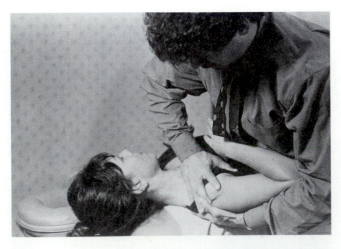

Figure 18–37. Sternoclavicular joint mobilization with scapular contact.

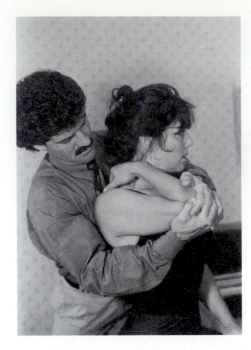

Figure 18–38. Acromioclavicular joint manipulation.

ative to the clavicle. An impulse thrust is directed posteriorly when the barrier is met.

A similar technique can be used in the supine position. The patient's bent elbow is placed pointing upward while the clinician presses posteriorly on the olecranon process. This imparts an anterior-to-posterior glide force into the acromioclavicular joint. A thrust is performed as the barrier is felt.

A very simple technique can be performed by pressing the acromion and distal end of the clavicle together in an anterior-to-posterior direction. The clinician cups the distal aspect of the acromion and clavicle with both hands in opposition and fingers interlaced (Fig. 18–39). An impulse manipulation or squeezing mobilization can then be performed by clasping the palms together.

Scapulothoracic Joint

Seventeen muscles attach to the scapula alone. It is directly linked to the cervical spine via the trapezius and levator scapulae muscles. The only osseous link the upper extremity has to the spine is via the scapula, clavicle, sternum, and upper rib attachments. The scapula functions to support upper extremity motion and provide attachments for muscles involved in that motion. Its movement on the thorax must be coordinated and stable to allow dynamic and mobile movements distally in the upper extremity. This necessitates proper neuromuscular control and range of motion. The scapulothoracic articulation, not a true joint but rather a physiological entity, is mobilized rather than manipulated. This is best performed with the patient in the side-lying position. Refer to Chapter 13 for scapulothoracic assessment.

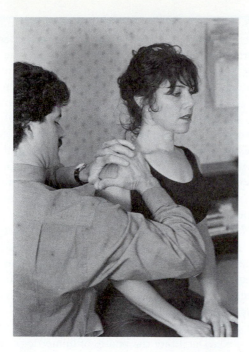

Figure 18–39. Acromioclavicular joint compression mobilization.

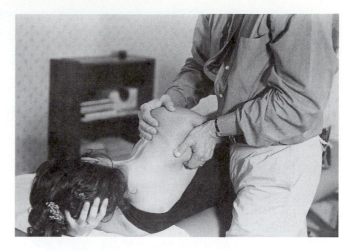

Figure 18–41. Lifting scapular mobilization.

To apply a general mobilization to the right scapulothoracic joint, the patient lies on the left side. The clinician stands behind the patient facing headward and grasps the top of the shoulder with a cupped cephalad hand (Fig. 18–40). The web of the caudad hand contacts the inferior angle of the scapula. The scapula is then glided along two diagonal tracks of motion. One track goes from a cephalad and slightly anterior position to a caudad and slightly posterior position. The other goes from a cephalad and slightly posterior position to a caudad and slightly anterior position. The scapula can then be passively circumducted on the thorax.

Another type of mobilization entails lifting the scapula off the thorax. The clinician stands behind the side-lying patient facing cephalad. The caudad hand grasps the inferomedial border of the scapula and works the fingers under its edge. The cephalad hand grasps the top of the shoulder (Fig. 18–41). The scapula is mobilized in various directions while the caudad hand attempts to lift the medial border off the thoracic wall.

A third type of mobilization is similar to the previous one. However, the clinician uses both hands to lift the medial border of the scapula off the thorax. The patient is placed in the side-lying position with the involved side up. The upper side arm is bent and placed along the lateral thorax with the scapula slightly retracted. The clinician faces the patient from the anterior and grasps the medial edge of the scapula with both hands (Fig. 18–42). The patient is stabilized in this position by the pressure of the clinician's sternum applied to the patient's upper shoulder and thorax. The fingers of both hands work their way

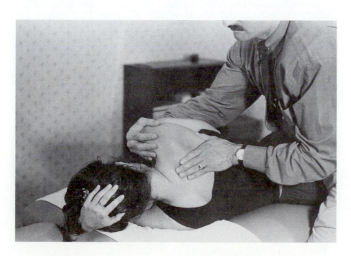

Figure 18–40. General mobilization of scapula.

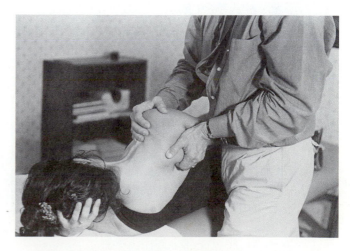

Figure 18–42. Scapular mobilization into protraction.

under the medial edge of the scapula. It is often easier to gain access to the underside of the scapula by starting at its inferior angle. Both hands then simultaneously protract the scapula as far as it will go as the clinician's hands, arms, and torso move as one unit pulling the scapula forward. The movement is reversed into retraction and another cycle of protraction is performed. Superior glide, inferior glide, and circumduction movements can also be conducted.

POSTISOMETRIC RELAXATION

Postisometric relaxation (PIR) is a gentle muscle energy technique that can be used to mobilize dysfunctional joints by relaxing the adjacent tight muscles.[16] PIR can be used instead of manipulative techniques in the case of relative contraindications or patient comfort or preference. Painfully acute joint conditions that demand gentle handling fare best with PIR. Children old enough to follow verbal commands welcome these gentle techniques. Any of the manipulations described in this chapter can be converted into gentle mobilization techniques by using PIR.

The joint to be mobilized is taken through its range of motion until a "barrier" is met. A light isometric contraction away from the barrier is initiated by the patient and resisted by the clinician for 8 to 10 seconds. After the contraction phase, the patient is instructed to inhale slowly and deeply and then to exhale, relax, and "let go." When the clinician senses full relaxation, the joint is moved into the direction of stretch to meet the next new barrier. The process is repeated 3 to 5 times.

For example, to mobilize left rotation of the right C2–3 facet joint, the clinician can use any of the rotational techniques described previously. The patient's head and neck are rotated to the left while maintaining contact on the right C2–3 facet joint. The rotation is stopped at the moment a barrier to movement is sensed. The patient is told to hold his or her head and neck still and not allow any motion to occur while the clinician gently tries to impart further left rotation. After 8 to 10 seconds, the patient inhales, holds his or her breath for a few seconds, and then exhales and is told to "let go." When the clinician senses full relaxation, the patient's head and neck are rotated further to the left until another barrier is met. The procedure is repeated three to five times.

Respiration can be used to facilitate or inhibit muscle contraction[16] and, therefore, the effects of PIR. Generally, with some exceptions, inspiration facilitates contraction while expiration inhibits it and fosters mobilization. An exception to this is during lateral flexion of the cervical spine.[16] The even segments (C0, C2, C4, etc.) respond as above; that is, tension is increased during inspiration and inhibited during expiration. The opposite is true for the odd segments. Therefore, to facilitate contraction in an odd segment expiration is used, and inhalation is used in the relaxation or mobilization phase.

In addition to phases of respiration, eye movements can be used to facilitate the phases of isometric contraction and relaxation in PIR.[16] Upward gaze facilitates contraction and downward gaze aids relaxation or mobilization. The patient is simply instructed to look either up or into the direction of the contraction and then look down or into the direction of the movement during the relaxation phase.

SKIN ROLLING

Rolling a fold of skin off the spine often elicits pain and resistance over dysfunctional segments (Fig. 18–43). The skin and fascia become very adherent, oftentimes painfully so, over dysfunctional upper thoracic segments. The skin in this area is commonly thickened, making it very hard to start a skin fold. It is necessary to release this skin and fas-

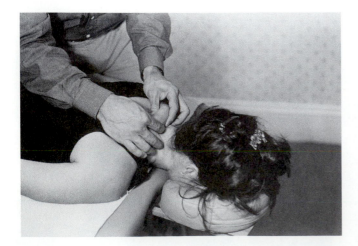

A

B

Figure 18–43. A and **B.** Skin rolling.

cial adherence when trying to restore function to the cervicodorsal region. Repeated skin rolling over the spine, both centrally and over each paraspinal region, can be very therapeutic. This is especially so in a chronically stiffened cervicodorsal region. Heat applications after skin rolling will help diminish post-treatment soreness.

CONCLUSION

Joint mobilization and manipulation are valuable tools used to restore mobility to joints restricted by joint dysfunction. The skill needed to adequately use these procedures comes with much training and experience. It is an art as much as it is a science. One needs to be aware of the appropriate indications and contraindications in using this form of treatment. The cervical and upper thoracic spine functionally interrelate very closely together with the associated rib joints, acromioclavicular joints, sternoclavicular joints, and scapulothoracic joints. Dysfunction of one may lead to dysfunction of other related structures in a chain-like fashion. Thrust and nonthrust techniques are commonly used in the successful treatment of painful cervical musculoskeletal disorders, and it is an advantage to the clinician to become proficient in their use.

ACKNOWLEDGMENTS

I would like to extend my gratitude and heartfelt thanks to Dr. Linda J. Levine for her clinical input, assistance in manuscript editing, and technical support. I would also like to thank Michael Bezoenik for the fine work and long hours spent during the photography sessions.

REFERENCES

1. Maitland GD. *Vertebral Manipulation*. 5th ed. Boston, Mass: Butterworths; 1986.
2. Shekelle PG. Spine update: Spinal manipulation. *Spine* 1994;19:858–861.
3. Mennell JM. *Back Pain*. Boston, Mass: Little, Brown; 1960.
4. Cassidy JD, Lopes AA, Yong-Hing K. The immediate effect of manipulation versus mobilization on pain and range of motion in the cervical spine: A randomized controlled trial. *J Manipulative Physiol Ther* 1992;15:570–575.
5. Roston JB, Haines RW. Cracking in the metacarpophalangeal joint. *J Anat* 1947;81:165.
6. Unsworth A, Dowson D, Wright V. Cracking joints. A bioengineering study of cavitation in the metacarpophalangeal joint. *Ann Rheum Dis* 1971;30:438.
7. Sandoz R. Some physical mechanisms and effects of spinal adjustments. *Ann Swiss Chiro Assoc* 1976;6:91.
8. Mierau D, Cassidy JD, Bowen V, Dupuis P, Noftall F. Manipulation and mobilization of the third metacarpophalangeal joint: A quantitative radiographic and range of motion study. *Manual Med* 1988;3:135–140.
9. Brodeur R. The audible release associated with joint manipulation. *J Manipulative Physiol Ther* 1995;18:155–164.
10. Meal GM, Scott RA. Analysis of the joint crack by simultaneous recording of sound and tension. *J Manipulative Physiol Ther* 1986;9:183.
11. Terrett AG. *Vertebrobasilar Stroke Following Manipulation*. West Des Moines, Iowa: National Chiropractic Mutual Insurance Co.; 1996.
12. Haldemann S, Chapman-Smith D, Petersen DM Jr. *Guidelines for Chiropractic Quality Assurance and Practice Parameters*. Gaithersburg, Md: Aspen; 1993.
13. Senstad O, Leboeuf-Yde C, Borchgrevink C. Predictors of side effects to spinal manipulative therapy. *J Manipulative Physiol Ther* 1996;19:441–445.
14. Schafer RC, Faye LJ. *Motion Palpation and Chiropractic Technic: Principles of Dynamic Chiropractic*. Huntington Beach, Calif: Motion Palpation Institute; 1989.
15. Gillet H, Liekens M. *Belgian Chiropractic Research Notes*. Huntington Beach, Calif: Motion Palpation Institute; 1984.
16. Lewit K. *Manipulative Therapy in Rehabilitation of the Motor System*. Boston, Mass: Butterworths; 1985.

Neurophysiological Effects of Cervical Manipulation

Donald R. Murphy

"If you knew Who walks beside you on the way that you have chosen, fear would be impossible."

—A Course in Miracles

INTRODUCTION

The primary purpose of manipulation is the correction of joint dysfunction. Joint dysfunction, as was discussed in Chapter 4, is a condition in which one of the joints of the spine or extremities has lost its normal joint play, that physiological motion that all joints possess and upon which the joint depends for normal function.

One of the effects of joint dysfunction is mechanical restriction of the movement of the joint. This can lead to increased strain on the tissues involved in the body's attempt to move that joint and in the tissues that must compensate for the inability of the involved joint to carry out its proper function. Manipulation helps to remove this mechanical restriction and eliminate the excessive strain, resulting in an increase in range of motion (ROM) of the joint.[1, 2] Although the increase in ROM is probably temporary,[3] it is thought that the improvement in joint play can be long term. However, several treatments may be required to achieve this. Improvement in joint play helps improve the function of the joint, leading to pain relief.

In addition to these mechanical effects of manipulation are neurophysiological effects that go far beyond the involved joint and its surrounding tissues. Because of the wide-ranging impact that cervical joint dysfunction can have on the locomotor system (see Chap. 4), cervical manipulation, and the improvement in function that it produces, can also have a wide-ranging impact. The purpose of this appendix is to summarize what is known about the neurophysiological effects of cervical manipulation.

LOCAL EFFECTS

The neurophysiological effects of manipulation primarily result from the changes that take place in the activity of the mechanoreceptors in the joint capsule. As was discussed in Chapter 3, the cervical capsular mechanoreceptors are thought to serve two primary functions. One is to influence the activity of the gamma motor neurons in the ventral horn.[4–6] This influence allows the cervical joint mechanoreceptors to affect muscle tone. When joint dysfunction develops, muscle tone may be altered, leading to hyper- or hypotonicity, depending on the muscle affected. This, in turn, can disrupt the afferentation arising from the mechanoreceptors in the cervical muscles, which have widespread connection throughout the central nervous system, and lead to dysfunction in other parts of the locomotor system.

The other primary function of joint mechanoreceptors is the "gate control" of pain. That is, stimulation of these receptors helps block impulses from nociceptive afferents from being transmitted along the spinothalamic tracts to the thalamus. With joint dysfunction, dysafferentation can occur[7] in which nociceptive input cannot be balanced by mechanoreceptive input.

Finally, nociception arising from the joint can cause pain, in addition to reflex spasm of related muscles via facilitation of alpha motor neurons in the ventral horn. This is exacerbated by the presence of dysafferentation, which

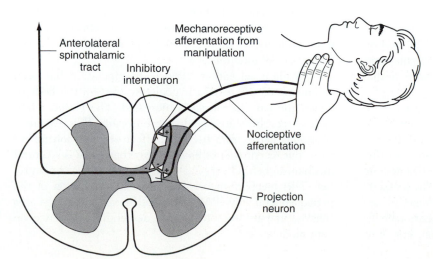

Figure 18A–1. The influence of cervical manipulation on muscle tone.

allows this nociceptive input to be transmitted relatively unchecked. Refer to Chapter 4 for further details of these effects of cervical joint dysfunction.

Understanding the theorized consequences of cervical joint dysfunction allows for the development of theories regarding the local effects of manipulation to correct this dysfunction. Manipulation is thought to produce a short-term, sudden burst of impulses from the mechanoreceptors in the joint capsule and the surrounding tissues.[8] In addition, the normalization of joint function is believed to cause normalization of the mechanoreception arising from the joint, correcting dysafferentation.

Cervical manipulation can have a regulating effect on muscle tone, as the normalization of joint function, and thus mechanoreceptor input, allows for appropriate afferent information influencing the activity of the gamma motor neurons (Fig. 18A–1). The resultant normalization of afferent input from muscle mechanoreceptors may then have

widespread effects throughout the central nervous system. This normalization of muscle tone may be one of increased tone[9] or decreased tone,[10–13] and this may be dependent on whether the involved muscle was rendered hypotonic or hypertonic, respectively, by the joint dysfunction that the manipulation was designed to correct.

In addition, by stimulating the large-diameter mechanoreceptive afferents, cervical manipulation is theorized to cause inhibition of spinothalamic projection neurons both via inhibitory synapse onto the projection neuron and by synapse onto an inhibitory interneuron which in turn synapses with the projection neuron (Fig. 18A–2). This is the well-known "gate control" theory of pain. Partly as a result of this effect, pain threshold is increased after manipulation[14, 15] and the patient experiences pain relief. If nociception is of sufficient intensity to cause reflex muscle spasm, the inhibition of spinothalamic projection of nociceptive impulses created by manipulation may lead to a

Figure 18A–2. The mechanism of local manipulation-induced antinociception.

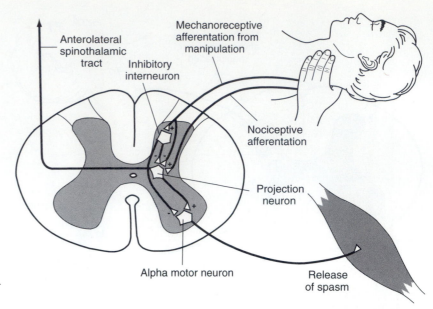

Figure 18A–3. The mechanism of relief of reflex muscle spasm by manipulation.

decrease in alpha motor neuron activity, leading to relief of muscle spasm (Fig. 18A–3).

An interesting group of studies was performed by Herzog et al[16–19] on the immediate effects of manipulation on muscle activity. While these experiments did not involve cervical manipulation specifically, they reveal some interesting findings that may be of importance to practitioners of manipulative therapy. These workers found that, when a high-velocity, low-amplitude thrust is applied to an intervertebral joint of the spine, there occurs a nearly immediate (50 to 200 msec) burst of activity in paraspinal muscles at both the level treated and other levels. They also showed activity response in a remote muscle (serratus posterior inferior with thoracic manipulation). Low-velocity manipulations produced a much smaller and relatively delayed response, or no response at all. Interestingly, some high-velocity manipulations produced audible joint cavitation, whereas others did not. Likewise, some low-velocity manipulations produced audible cavitation whereas others did not. But the presence of cavitation did not influence whether a burst of muscle activity was seen. That is, there was no greater likelihood of activity burst in the high- or low-velocity manipulations that produced cavitation as compared to those that did not produce cavitation.

It is difficult to tell whether the immediate burst of muscle activity demonstrated in these studies has any therapeutic import, or whether they merely represent epiphenomena, but it is possible that the essential feature in the elicitation of a response from the central nervous system with manipulation may be more dependent on the speed of the thrust than on whether audible cavitation takes place. It can certainly be said that low-velocity mobilizations may still be effective in correcting joint dysfunction, but they

may not create as great an immediate neurological effect as is seen with high-velocity manipulations.

Clinically, this was suggested by a recent study that compared high-velocity thrust manipulation and low-velocity muscle energy manipulation in patients with cervical pain.[20] Thirty patients with chronic cervical pain were randomized to receive either high-velocity thrust manipulation or muscle energy manipulation. Each group was treated twice per week for 3 weeks. It was found that the patients treated with high-velocity manipulation experienced a greater immediate relief of pain but that, at the end of the treatment period, there was no difference in pain levels, with pain decreasing in both groups to the same extent.

WIDESPREAD EFFECTS

In addition to the local effects previously discussed, more widespread neurological changes have been shown to occur following cervical manipulation. These effects may be more profound in their impact on pain relief and the improvement of function.

As discussed earlier, cervical manipulation has been demonstrated to create a hypoalgesic state in the body in which the pain threshold is increased. The patient often experiences this state as a decrease in pain. This hypoalgesia results partly from the local effect of "gate control" of pain. But recent studies have shown that there is a central mechanism behind cervical manipulation-induced pain relief. This mechanism revolves around stimulation of the periaqueductal gray (PAG) area in the midbrain—the area that is, in part, responsible for descending influence on pain modulation.[21, 22]

The PAG has two portions, the ventral portion and the dorsal portion. Each portion is capable of producing pain modulation, but there are differences in the modalities of nociception that each acts upon, the behavioral correlates that accompany this modulation, and the neurotransmitters that are used. The ventral PAG, in addition to creating analgesia, creates immobility, recuperative behavior, and sympathetic inhibition. The analgesic effect is blocked by the administration of noloxone, so it is considered an opioid form of analgesia. The dorsal PAG is associated with, in addition to analgesia, fight-or-flight behavior, aversive reactions, and stimulation of the sympathetic system. This effect is not blocked by noloxone, so it is considered a nonopioid form of analgesia.

The ventral PAG projects to the nucleus raphe magnus, which then projects to the spinal cord. It uses serotonin as a neurotransmitter and has been shown to create analgesia related to thermal nociceptive stimuli. The dorsal PAG projects to the nucleus paragigantocellularis, which then projects to the spinal cord. The dorsal PAG uses norepinephrine as a neurotransmitter and has been shown to play a key role in mediating analgesia related to mechanical nociceptive stimuli (Fig. 18A–4 and Table 18A–1).

Recent studies have shown that cervical manipulation, in addition to creating hyperalgesia to mechanical stimuli, also has a sympathoexcitative effect.[23, 24] This involves a variety of sympathetic functions, including sudomotor,[21, 23, 25–27] cutaneous vasomotor,[27] and cardiac and respiratory function.[24] These sympathetic functions do not arise from the same portion of the nervous system but, rather, have origins in different and distinct medullary centers. The finding that all these sympathetic functions have been shown to be stimulated by cervical manipulation argues against a local mechanism and suggests that the stimulation is arising from a common sympathoexcitation center higher in the nervous system. As cervical manipulation creates both sympathoexcitation along with hypoalgesia to mechanical, but not thermal, nociceptive input, the most likely source of these effects is the dorsal PAG. Further evidence for this was provided by Zusman et al,[28] who showed that there was no change in the hypoalgesic effect of passive motion by the administration of noloxone. In addition to nociceptive inhibition, noradrenergic projections also, either directly or via interneuron, connect to alpha motor neurons in the ventral horn, and may also synapse with gamma motor neurons. This causes a decrease in the activity of these motor neurons and, thus, reflex muscle spasm and muscle hypertonicity.[29]

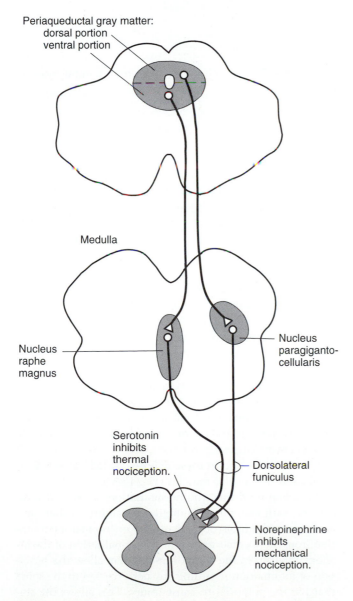

Figure 18A–4. The descending nociceptive modulating system.

Table 18A–1: The Differences Between the Ventral and Dorsal Periaqueductal Gray

VENTRAL PAG	DORSAL PAG
Creates analgesia to thermal nociception	Creates analgesia to mechanical nociception
Creates immobility, recuperative behavior, and sympathetic inhibition	Creates fight-or-flight behavior, aversive reactions, and sympathetic stimulation
Creates opioid analgesia	Creates nonopioid analgesia
Projects to the spinal cord via the nucleus raphe magnus	Projects to the spinal cord via the nucleus paragigantocellularis
Uses serotonin as neurotransmitter	Uses norepinephrine as neurotransmitter

The afferent pathway by which cervical manipulation stimulates the dorsal PAG is not understood but, as the known effects of joint mechanoreceptor afferentation are limited to local segmental processes, the stimulation may result from muscle spindle input as a result of stretch on the densely innervated intrinsic intersegmental muscles (i.e., suboccipitals, multifidi, intertransversarii, etc.). Afferentation from muscle spindles has a wide-ranging influence throughout the central nervous system.

Another more generalized neurophysiological effect of cervical manipulation includes influence on vision. A number of case series and case reports have been published demonstrating improvement or recovery of vision following cervical manipulation.[30–37] The prevailing theory as to the neurophysiological mechanism behind this effect was reviewed by Terrett[38] and revolves around the concept of cervical joint dysfunction resulting in impairment of vascular perfusion of the brain and cervical manipulation correcting this deficit. However, this theory has been questioned,[39] and Radanov et al[40, 41] have provided evidence that brain dysfunction is caused by intense nociceptive bombardment to the brain as a result of injury. The nociceptive bombardment that has been shown by Radanov et al to impair cortical function may not need to be of great intensity if the usual modulation by the segmental and descending inhibition systems (see earlier discussion) is impaired by joint dysfunction. In this case, manipulation may facilitate normal nociceptive modulation at both the segmental level as well as that descending from the dorsal PAG, decreasing the intensity of nociceptive input to the brain.

Carrick[42] showed that manipulation to the level of C2–3 on the side of an enlarged cortical map is associated with decreased cortical activity whereas manipulation on the side opposite an enlarged cortical map was associated with decreased cortical activity. He suggests that stimulation of joint and muscle receptors as a result of manipulation evokes changes in brain function that can be measured with physiological cortical maps. The methodology and findings of this study have been questioned,[43–46] and more work in this area will need to be done to assess its validity and clinical importance.

The effect of manipulation on kinesthetic sensibility was demonstrated by Rogers,[47] who evaluated 20 subjects with Revel's test (see Chap. 14). Ten of the subjects were treated six times with cervical manipulation over 3 to 4 weeks and the other ten subjects served as controls. It was found that nine of the ten treated subjects showed a mean improvement in Revel's test of 41 percent compared to a mean improvement of 12 percent in the control group. The difference was statistically significant.

The mechanism by which this improvement in cervical kinesthesia occurs probably relates to the normalization of muscle tone in the cervical spine that results from the correction of cervical joint dysfunction. As was discussed in Chapter 3, the mechanoreceptors from the cervical mus-

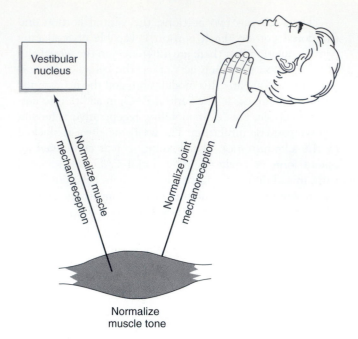

Figure 18A–5. The influence of cervical manipulation on the vestibular nucleus.

cles have direct connection to the vestibular nucleus in the brainstem. Joint dysfunction, by disrupting the tone of these muscles (causing either hyper- or hypotonicity), can cause an alteration in the coordination of the signals that are provided to the vestibular nucleus by the muscular mechanoreceptors. Correction of joint dysfunction restores normal tone to these muscles and, thus, normal afferentation from their mechanoreceptors, leading to improvement of the interpretation of position and movement of the cervical spine (Fig. 18A–5).

The influence of the cervical muscles on the vestibular nucleus is most likely the primary mediator of the neurophysiological effects of cervical manipulation on muscles throughout the locomotor system. Because the vestibular nucleus mediates most of the reflex activities related to the cervical spine (tonic neck reflex, cervico-ocular reflex, cervicocollic reflex), the normalization of cervical muscle tone via manipulation can have a positive influence on all the muscles involved in these reflexes, including extremity, trunk, and extraocular muscles (Fig. 18A–6).

Leading from this, the normalization of cervical muscle tone with manipulation improves stability mechanisms, as these mechanisms depend in part on normal afferentation from the locomotor system.[48] Normalization of the afferent input from the spinal muscles may allow the provision of information regarding any perturbation to the spine that has the potential to cause injury. This allows the stabilizing system of the spine (see Chap. 3) to engage in providing a quick response to prevent tissue damage.

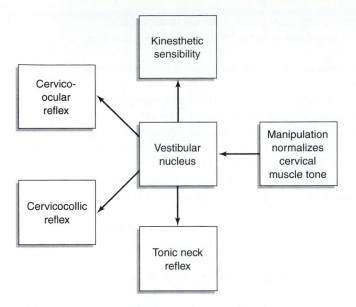

Figure 18A–6. The influence of cervical manipulation on reflex processes.

CONCLUSION

Research in the area of the neurophysiological effects of manipulation is in its infancy, and much work needs to be done to clarify what actually happens within the central nervous system as a result of manipulation to the cervical spine. In the area of nociceptive modulation, this research is well on its way; in other areas, it is lacking. The attempt in this appendix was to present the information that has been generated in the literature as well as propose some additional theories to be tested. This exciting area of research can help us further understand and improve the ways in which practitioners who utilize manipulation can help patients with this type of treatment.

REFERENCES

1. Yeomans SG. The assessment of cervical intersegmental mobility before and after spinal manipulative therapy. *J Manipulative Physiol Ther* 1992;15(2):106–114.
2. Cassidy JD, Lopes AA, Yonghing K. The immediate effect of manipulation versus mobilization on pain and range of motion in the cervical spine: A randomized, controlled trial. *J Manipulative Physiol Ther* 1992;15:570–575.
3. Nilsson N, Christensen HW, Harvigsen J. Lasting changes in passive range of motion after spinal manipulation: A randomized, blind, controlled trial. *J Manipulative Physiol Ther* 1996;19(3):165–168.
4. Johansson H, Sjolander P, Sojka P. Actions on gamma-motoneurones elicited by electrical stimulation of joint afferent fibers in the hind limb of the cat. *J Physiol* 1986;375:137–152.
5. Johansson H, Sjolander P, Sojka P. Fusimotor reflexes in triceps surae muscle elicited by natural and electrical stimulation of joint afferents. *Neuro-Orthop* 1988;6:67–80.
6. Johansson H, Sjolander P, Wadell I. Reflex actions of the gamma-muscles-spindle systems of muscles acting at the knee joint elicited by stretch of the posterior cruciate ligament. *Neuro-Orthop* 1989;8:9–21.
7. Seaman DR, Winterstein JF. Dysafferentation: A novel term to describe the neuropathophysiological effects of joint complex dysfunction. A look at likely mechanisms of symptom generation. *J Manipulative Physiol Ther* 1998;21(4):267–280.
8. Gillette RG. A speculative argument for the coactivation of diverse somatic receptor populations by forceful chiropractic adjustments: A review of the neurophysiological literature. *Man Med* 1987;3:1–14.
9. Rebechini-Zasadny H, Tasharski CC, Heinze WJ. Electromyographic analysis following chiropractic manipulation to the cervical spine: A model to study manipulation-induced peripheral muscle changes. *J Manipulative Physiol Ther* 1981;4(2):61–63.
10. Grice AS. Muscle tonus changes following manipulation. *J Can Chiro Assoc* 1974;18:29–31.
11. Shambaugh P. Changes in electrical activity on muscles resulting from chiropractic adjustment: A pilot study. *J Manipulative Physiol Ther* 1987;19:300–304.
12. Thabe H. Electromyography as a tool to document diagnostic findings and therapeutic results associated with somatic dysfunction in the upper cervical spinal joints and sacroiliac joints. *Man Med* 1986;2:53–58.
13. Nansel DD, Waldorf T, Cooperstein R. Effect of cervical spinal adjustments on paraspinal muscle tone: Evidence for fascilitation of intersegmental tonic neck reflexes. *J Manipulative Physiol Ther* 1993;16(2):91–95.
14. Terrett ACJ, Vernon H. Manipulation and pain tolerance: A controlled study of the effect of spinal manipulation on paraspinal cutaneous pain tolerance levels. *Am J Phys Med* 1984;63:217–225.

15. Vicenzino B, Collins D, Wright A. Cervical mobilisation: Immediate effects on neural tissue mobility, mechanical hyperalgesia and pain-free grip strength in lateral epicondylitis. *MPAA Conference Proceedings* 1995:155–156.

16. Suter E, Herzog W, Conway PJ, Zhang YT. Reflex response associated with manipulative treatment of the thoracic spine. *J Neuromusculoskel Sys* 1994;2(3):124–130.

17. Herzog W, Conway PJ, Zgang YZ, Gal J, Guimaraes ACS. Reflex responses associated with manipulative treatments on the thoracic spine: A pilot study. *J Manipulative Physiol Ther* 1995;18(4):233–236.

18. Herzog W. Mechanical and physiological responses to spinal manipulative treatments. *J Neuromusculoskel Sys* 1995;3(1):1–9.

19. Herzog W. On sounds and reflexes. *J Manipulative Physiol Ther* 1996;19(3):216–218.

20. Scott-Dawkins C. The comparative effectiveness of adjustments versus mobilisation in chronic mechanical neck pain. In: Proceedings of the Scientific Symposium, World Chiropractic Congress. June, 1997. World Federation of Chiropractic, Tokyo.

21. Wright A, Vicenzino B. Cervical mobilisation techniques, sympathetic nervous system effects and their relationship to analgesia. In: Shacklock M ed. *Moving in on Pain*. Melbourne: Butterworth Heinneman; 1995:164–173.

22. Wright A. Hypoalgesia post-manipulative therapy: A review of a potential neurophysiological mechanism. *Man Ther* 1995;1:11–16.

23. Vicenzino B, Gutschlag F, Collins D, Wright A. An investigation of the effects of spine manual therapy on forequarter pressure and thermal pain thresholds and sympathetic nervous system activity in asymptomatic subjects. In: Shacklock M ed. *Moving in on Pain*. Melbourne: Butterworth Heinemann; 1995:185–193.

24. Vicenzino B, Cartwright T, Collins D, Wright A. Cardiovascular and respiratory changes produced by lateral glide mobilization of the cervical spine. *Manual Ther* 1998;3:67–71.

25. Chiu T, Wright A. To compare the effects of different rates of application of a cervical mobilisation technique on sympathetic outflow to the upper limb in normal subjects. *Manual Ther* 1996;1:198–203.

26. Slater H, Vicenzino B, Wright A. The effects of a novel manual therapy technique on peripheral nervous system function. *J Man Manipulative Ther* 1994;2:156–162.

27. Vicenzino B, Collins D, Benson H, Wright A. An investigation of the interrelationship between manipulative therapy-induced hypoalgesia and sypathoexcitation. *J Manipulative Physiol Ther* 1998;21:448–453.

28. Zusman M, Edwards B, Donaghy A. Investigation of a proposed mechanism for the relief of spinal pain with passive joint movement. *Man Med* 1989;4:58–61.

29. Katavich L. Differential effects of spinal manipulative therapy on acute and chronic muscle spasm: A proposal for mechanisms and efficacy. *Manual Ther* 1998;3:132–139.

30. Gilman G, Bergstrand J. Visual recovery following chiropractic intervention. *J Behav Optometry* 1990;1(3):73–74.

31. Terrett AGJ, Gorman RF. The eye, the cervical spine and spinal manipulative therapy: A review of the literature. *Chiro Tech* 1995;7(2):43–54.

32. Gorman RF. Monocular visual loss after closed head trauma: Immediate resolution associated with spinal manipulation. *J Manipulative Physiol Ther* 1995;18(5):308–314.

33. Gorman F. The treatment of presumptive optic nerve ischemia by spinal manipulation. *J Manipulative Physiol Ther* 1995;3:172–177.

34. Stephens D, Gorman F. The association between visual incompetence and spinal derangement: An instructive case history. *J Manipulative Physiol Ther* 1997;20(5):343–350.

35. Stephens D, Bilton D, Pollard H, Gorman F. Wall perimetry in chiropractic. *J Manipulative Physiol Ther* 1998;21(1):32–36.

36. Stephens D, Gorman F, Bilton D. The step phenomenon in the recovery of vision with spinal manipulation: A report on two 13-year-olds treated together. *J Manipulative Physiol Ther* 1997;20(9):628–633.

37. Stephens D, Mealing, Pollard H, et al. Treatment of visual field loss by spinal manipulation: A report on 17 patients. *J Neuromusculoskel Sys* 1998;6(2):53–66.

38. Terrett AGJ. Cerebral dysfunction: A theory to explain some of the effects of chiropractic manipulation. *Chiro Technique* 1993;5:168–173.

39. Budgell BS, Sato A. The cervical subluxation and regional blood flow. *J Manipulative Physiol Ther* 1997;20:103–107.

40. Radanov BP, Dvorak J, Valach L. Cognitive deficits in patients after soft tissue injury of the cervical spine. *Spine* 1992;17(2):127–131.

41. Radanov BP, Dvorak J. Impaired cognitive function after whiplash injury of the cervical spine. *Spine* 1996;21(3):392–397.
42. Carrick FR. Changes in brain function after manipulation of the cervical spine. *J Manipulative Physiol Ther* 1997;20(8):529–550.
43. Seaman DR. Changes in brain function after manipulation of the cervical spine. Letter to the Editor. *J Manipulative Physiol Ther* 1998;21:295–296.
44. Troyanovich SJ, Roudebush M, Harrison D, Harrison D. Changes in brain function after manipulation of the cervical spine. Letter to the Editor. *J Manipulative Physiol Ther* 1998;21:297–299.
45. Lantz CA. Changes in brain function after manipulation of the cervical spine. Letter to the Editor. *J Manipulative Physiol Ther* 1998;21:426–427.
46. Meyer JJ, Anderson AV. Changes in brain function after manipulation of the cervical spine. Letter to the Editor. *J Manipulative Physiol Ther* 1998;21:498.
47. Rogers RG. The effects of spinal manipulation on cervical kinesthesia in patients with chronic neck pain: A pilot study. *J Manipulative Physiol Ther* 1997;20(2):80–85.
48. Panjabi MM. The stabilizing system of the spine. Part I. Function, dysfunction, adaptation and enhancement. *J Spinal Disord* 1992;5(4):383–389.

APPENDIX 18B

A Review of the Evidence of Efficacy of Cervical Manipulation

Kim Humphreys

INTRODUCTION

The cervical spine has increasingly become the focus of research interest, especially within the past few years. No doubt a major motivating factor for this trend has been our greater understanding of the magnitude of the problem associated with cervical spine disorders and its impact on society in terms of pain and suffering, cost of treatment, and time off work.[1, 2] Within the context of musculoskeletal conditions affecting the cervical spine, headache, whiplash injuries, and non-specific neck pain account for the vast majority of complaints seen by chiropractors and other practitioners of manual medicine.[1, 3–12]

The evidence of the effectiveness of any treatment method should be demonstrated in order for it to be considered as a valid treatment option in the management of these conditions and in order to help alleviate the burden of pain and suffering and its related cost of care.

The purpose of this Appendix is to review the current evidence for the effectiveness of manipulation for conditions affecting the cervical spine, such as headache and nonspecific neck pain, in light of current and previously reported research.

SPINAL MANIPULATIVE THERAPY

It is well known that spinal manipulative therapy (SMT) is a common method of treatment for low back and neck complaints, which is performed by several professional groups, including practitioners of chiropractic, osteopathy, manual medicine, and physiotherapy.[13] Of these professions world-wide, chiropractors are perhaps most commonly associated with the delivery of SMT for the treatment of mechanical low back and neck complaints.[3] Although spinal manipulation has been utilized as a treatment for various human conditions for centuries, relatively little research has been undertaken to evaluate its clinical effectiveness. Of the research that has investigated the effectiveness of SMT, the vast majority has been for low-back pain.[3, 14, 15] More recently, greater emphasis has been placed on investigating the effectiveness of manipulation for cervical spine complaints.[1] Although an excellent review of the literature on manipulation and mobilization of the cervical spine was published by Hurwitz et al in 1996,[16] a number of new studies have since been published. It would seem appropriate to reassess the established literature in light of the new studies. For the 1996 review, manipulation or SMT was defined as the "use of a short- or longlever high-velocity thrust directed to one or more of the joints of the cervical spine." It would seem appropriate to adopt the same definition of SMT for the current review.

HEADACHE

The traditional medical opinion in the diagnosis of headache is that the majority of headaches are either tension-type or migraine.[17] However, more recently both the International Headache Society (IHS)[18] as well as the North American Cervicogenic Headache Society (NACHS)[19] have produced definitions and criteria implicating the cervical spine as a common source of headache. According to the NACHS, cervicogenic headache may be defined as "referred pain perceived in any region of the head caused by primary nociceptive source in the musculoskeletal tissues innervated by cervical nerves." Results from three studies now suggest that the three most common headache groups include cervicogenic headache, tension-type, and migraine.[10, 20, 21]

It is a long held belief by practitioners of spinal manipulation that SMT is effective in the treatment of headache.[22] It is now suggested that the types of headaches most likely to respond to manipulation are the most common, namely tension-type, cervicogenic and migraine headaches.[9, 10, 22] However, clinically it is difficult to differentiate tension-type from cervicogenic headaches, and as a result it is not possible to separate the two forms of headache from the literature.[23] The most recent systematic review and best evidence synthesis of the literature evaluating the efficacy of spinal manipulation for headache and conditions other than spinal related pain was published in 1997 by Bronfort.[23] The following highlights the current state of evidence concerning SMT and its known effect on tension-type, cervicogenic headaches, and migraine headaches in light of this latest systematic review.

In the review by Bronfort,[23] a literature search of MEDLINE (from 1966 to first six months of 1996) and EMBASE (1974 to first six months of 1996) was conducted for all clinical studies (with or without control groups) and including retrospective and prospective clinical series. The methodological quality, magnitude of effect size, and statistical significance were considered for the identified studies in order to determine the level of evidence for the effectiveness of SMT in patients with tension-type and cervicogenic headache as well as migraine headache. The levels of evidence were graded according to an accepted hierarchy of 4 levels: A) strong evidence of efficacy or inefficacy; B) moderate evidence of efficacy or inefficacy; C) limited evidence of efficacy or inefficacy; and D) inconclusive evidence of efficacy or inefficacy.

Based on this methodology, 16 studies, which consisted of 6 randomised controlled trials and 10 other studies, were identified and evaluated. The 1995 study by Boline et al[24] comparing spinal manipulation to amitriptyline for the treatment of chronic tension-type headache was given the highest validity rating (77). This study was also given a quality score by Hurwitz et al of 77.[16] Overall 150 patients with headaches for over 3 months duration were randomly allocated to either 1) SMT, moist heat and light massage by a chiropractor, or 2) amitriptyline daily for 6 weeks. No differences were found between the groups at the end of 6 weeks in terms of headache pain intensity or frequency, general health status, or use of nonprescription drugs. The amitriptyline group did have marginally more effect on pain intensity at the end of the trial. However, 4 weeks post-treatment, the chiropractic group continued to maintain their improvement in headache duration, frequency, and general health status compared to the amitriptyline group.

The 1995 two-group randomized controlled trial by Nilsson[25] compared chiropractic SMT to deep friction massage and placebo laser for the treatment of cervicogenic headache over a period of 6 weeks. Thirty-nine patients were randomly allocated: 20 to the SMT group and 19 to the massage and laser group. Patients were evaluated in terms of NSAID use, headache hours per day, and pain reduction, analysed from patients' headache diaries. At the end of 6 weeks an overall trend in favour of SMT was observed with decreased NSAID use, fewer headaches per day, and pain reduction, although none of these were shown to have reached statistical significance ($p<0.05$). No follow-up studies were conducted to identify changes over time between these two groups. This study was given a validity score of 67 by Bronfort[23] but was not published in time to be evaluated by Hurwitz et al.[16]

Nilsson et al[9] have recently published a prospective randomized controlled trial with blinded observer to evaluate the effectiveness of SMT in the treatment of cervicogenic headache. As a result, no validity or quality scores are currently available.

A graphical analysis of the 1995 trial data[25] apparently identified that the two randomized groups were different from one another and that the study may have suffered from a type-2 error due to too few participants.[9] As a result, 53 subjects, who were suffering from cervicogenic headache and fulfilled the IHS criteria (with the exception of the radiological criteria), were recruited to the study from a group of 450 headache sufferers who responded to newspaper advertisements. Patients were asked to keep a headache diary for 1 week and then were randomly allocated to a treatment group based on the diary analysis of the blinded observer.

Twenty-eight patients were assigned to the chiropractic SMT group while 25 patients were assigned to the low-level laser and deep friction massage group. The SMT group received spinal manipulation twice a week for 3 weeks while the other group received soft tissue massage and laser for 3 weeks. During week 5, no treatment was given to either group but patients were required to fill out their headache diary. The blinded observer analysed the diary data at the end of week 5.

The results of the study showed that the main outcomes measures of analgesic use per day, headache intensity per episode, and number of headache hours per day, as registered in patients' diaries, were all shown to be significantly lower in the SMT group compared to the massage and laser group.

Jensen, Nielsen and Vosmar[26] published a study in 1990 comparing manual therapy including manipulation to the use of cold packs in patients who were experiencing posttraumatic headache of at least 1-year duration. This study received a quality score of 52 by Hurwitz et al[16] while Bronfort awarded it a validity score of 31. A total of 23 patients participated in this study and were randomly allocated to either two sessions of massage and cervical manipulation administered by a medical doctor (11 patients) or two sessions of cold packs (12 patients). The outcome measures used were: pain score, regional and segmental spinal ranges of motion, and the presence of any accompanying symptoms such as dizziness, visual disturbances, or ear pain. Patients were followed 2 weeks and 5 weeks post-treatment. At 2 weeks post-treatment, the SMT group demonstrated a 57% reduction of pain intensity and a 64% reduction in analgesic use. Both of these outcomes were statistically significant. However, by week 5 post-treatment, although the SMT still exhibited lower pain intensity and analgesic usage, the results were not significantly different from the control group.

An uncontrolled retrospective and prospective study of chiropractic treatment for tension-type headache was reported by Vernon in 1982.[27] Thirty-three patients were involved in this study: 18 in the prospective and 15 in the retrospective study. An average of nine SMT treatment sessions were given, with the outcome measures being frequency, duration, and intensity of headaches as demonstrated by patients' headache diary. This study represented the first time that a prospective cohort of headache sufferers was studied using standardized outcome variables (frequency, duration and intensity) as reported in a standardized outcome measure (headache diary).

Vernon reported that there was a significant reduction in headache activity with average frequency reduced from 13 to 3 headaches per month, average duration reduced from 12 to 2 hours, while average severity decreased from 3.5 to 1.5 on a scale of 5. Vernon also found that 90% of patients reported satisfaction with their treatment as measured by three Likert-scaled questions. Finally, patients were asked to report on any "autonomic" symptoms, such as dizziness, nausea, tinnitus, and aura. One-hundred percent relief was reported in the seven subjects who had previously suffered nausea; 97% relief was found in the nine subjects with prior dizziness. Both of these outcomes were statistically significant.[27]

Although appropriate statistical procedures and analysis were performed, this study suffered from its uncontrolled design. As a result, the author concludes that the results were unable to test the hypothesis of the efficacy of manipulation for tension-type headaches.

An osteopathic randomized controlled study of chronic muscle-contraction headache was published in 1979 by Hoyt et al.[28] Twenty-two patients were randomly allocated to one of three groups including either massage and SMT by an osteopath (10 patients), palpatory examination (6 patients), or supine rest for 10 minutes (6 patients). A statistically significant reduction in patient reported headache pain was found at 5 minutes post treatment in the massage and manipulation group compared to the other groups. However, no longer-term follow-up was conducted. This study was given a validity score of 50 by Bronfort[23] while Hurwitz et al[16] assigned it a quality score of 39.

In 1998, Bove and Nilsson[28a] published the results of a randomized controlled trial on the treatment of episodic tension-type headache by spinal manipulation. Consequently, this study has not been reviewed by Bronfort.[23] Seventy-five volunteer patients who met the International Headache Society criteria for episodic tension-type headache were recruited to the 19-week trial. Overall, 26 men and 49 women ranging from 20 to 59 years were included in the study and randomized either into a manipulation group (spinal manipulation and deep friction massage) or a control group (placebo laser and deep friction massage).

The authors were careful to point out that the addition of deep friction massage to both treatment and control group meant that spinal manipulation was the only factor not common to both and hence any differences observed should be more reliably attributed to spinal manipulation. Both groups received 8 treatments over a 4-week period performed by the same chiropractor. This was followed by an observation period.

The outcome measures included patient diary entries from weeks 7, 11, 15 and 18 compared to baseline levels recorded at weeks 1 and 2 for daily hours of headache, pain intensity per episode, and daily analgesic use. No statistical difference was found for the three outcome measures between the two groups. However, by week 7, a general trend of decreased daily headache hours and mean daily analgesic usage was observed for both groups. Neither group exhibited a change in headache pain intensity throughout the entire trial. The reduction in daily headache hours and analgesic use was maintained throughout the observation period.

The authors concluded that spinal manipulation did not appear to confer any additional positive effect on episodic tension-type treatment when compared to the control treatment. However, they conceded that due to small patient numbers, a Type II error could have occurred (true treatment effect not being detected). In addition, they did not mention the possibility that the application of two manual therapies in the treatment group could have been counterproductive or even irritating to some patients, resulting in a decreased overall effect for the spinal manipulation group. Finally, the inclusion of an active treatment form for both control and treatment groups meant that spinal manipulation would have to confer a significantly greater effect in addition to that of the deep friction massage effect to reach statistical significance.

The preceding has reviewed the current best evidence for the effectiveness of spinal manipulation in the treatment of tension-type/cervicogenic headache. Due to conflicting validity and quality scores for most of the randomized clinical headache trials discussed above, the author would agree with Bronfort[16] and strongly suggest that current best evidence still indicates that there is *moderate evidence for the efficacy of spinal manipulation* in the treatment of patients with chronic tension-type/cervicogenic headaches.

Migraine headache has been estimated to affect some 11 million adults in the United States with varying degrees of disability. It has also been estimated to cost the US economy up to 17 billion dollars annually due to health care costs and lost productivity from time off work.[29] Many practitioners of manual therapy hypothesize that there is a link between cervical spine dysfunction and migraine headaches[22] although as yet the etiology of migraine remains obscure.[30] Similarly, few studies regarding the efficacy of SMT for migraine headaches have been conducted.

A randomized clinical trial of cervical manipulation for migraine was reported on by Parker et al in 1978.[31] Eighty-five patients were randomly assigned to one of three groups, either SMT by a chiropractor (30 patients), SMT by a physiotherapist (27 patients), or cervical mobilization by a medical doctor (28 patients). Although 75% suffered from common migraine and 25% from classical migraine, subjects were not stratified when allocated to treatment groups. The outcome measures were pain intensity, disability score, and duration and frequency of attacks. The study included a 2-month baseline period, a 2-month treatment period, and a 2-month follow-up period. The average number of treatments given in the treatment stage was 7, for an average of less than 1 per week. This trial received a validity score of 65 by Bronfort[23] as opposed to a quality score of 55 by Hurwitz et al.[16]

The chiropractic SMT group showed a 15 to 17 point difference in pain intensity scores compared to the other groups. Overall there was a 40% reduction in migraine frequency in the chiropractic group, 34% in the physiotherapy mobilization group and 13% in the medical group, with an overall improvement of 28%. The chiropractic SMT group was also found to have significantly fewer severe headaches compared to the other groups. This was the only outcome measure for the study to achieve statistical significance (p=0.01). After 20 months there was found to be a small advantage for the chiropractic group in terms of headache frequency, although it was not statistically significant.

Vernon[22] reported on this study in his review of cervical manipulation in 1995. He suggests that there were a number of flaws with the study design including small number of patients, lack of stratification, too few treatments over too long a time frame, and lack of an effective control group as the study "control" group actually received a comparative form of treatment. However, taking these into account, Vernon suggests that the fact the chiropractic SMT group performed better than the other two groups should be encouraging for the use of spinal manipulation in the treatment and management of migraine.[22]

Recently, two studies on SMT and migraine have been reported.[29, 30] Nelson et al[29] conducted a prospective, randomized, parallel-group study comparing spinal manipulation, amitriptyline, and the combination of both therapies for the prophylaxis of migraine headache. The study consisted of a 4-week baseline period, an 8-week treatment period, and a 4-week follow-up period. Patients were followed up by a mail questionnaire at 6 months post-follow-up period to assess their current headache status. Nonrespondents were contacted by telephone and asked the questions in order to complete the follow-up. The outcome measures included self-report of current frequency and severity of headache pain. The headache frequency was measured by asking the question: "How often do you get a headache?" Subjects were to respond on a 5-point scale ranging from everyday (1) to less than once a month (5). Headache severity was measured on a 10 point numerical rating pain scale with 0 equal to "no pain" and 10 equal to "unbearable pain." Overall, 218 patients with migraine headaches were recruited for the study, with 155 subjects completing the follow-up questionnaire: 56 in the SMT group, 46 in the amitriptyline group, and 53 in the combined group.

For headache frequency, the amitriptyline group had the highest baseline level of frequency, followed by the combined group, and then the SMT group. At 6-months follow-up, all groups reported a decrease in headache frequency compared to baseline, with the SMT group showing the highest difference. As for headache pain, the SMT group had the highest mean score at baseline, followed by the amitriptyline group, and then the combined group. However, at 6-months follow-up, an increase in mean headache pain was observed with the greatest difference in mean scores being the amitriptyline group, followed by the SMT group, and then the combined group. It was not reported whether or not any of these differences for within and between treatment groups for headache frequency and pain reached statistical significance. The authors concluded that until the outcomes measures used in this study are validated against other outcomes measures used in short term studies, the meaning and significance of this study cannot be fully understood.[29]

A prospective clinical trial of 12-months duration utilizing cervical SMT for migraine patients was also recently reported by Tuchin.[30] The objective of the study was to assess the efficacy of chiropractic SMT in the treatment of migraine. The study design included three phases, namely a 2-month baseline period, followed by a 2-month treatment period, and then a further 2-month post-treatment period. The outcome measures included a patient headache diary to report frequency, intensity on a visual analogue scale, duration, disability, associated symptoms, and use of medication. The outcome measure used to assess disability was not reported.

Thirty-two patients were initially recruited through an advertising campaign. Of these, four patients withdrew during the study and a further four patients failed to complete the follow-up headache diaries, leaving 24 patients who completed the study.

At 6-months follow-up, means scores compared to baseline scores showed statistically significant improvement in migraine sufferers' frequency of headaches ($p<0.005$), visual analogue scale for pain ($p<0.01$), disability ($p<0.05$), and medication use ($p<0.01$). The mean number of migraine episodes also decreased from 7.6 to 4.1 compared to the baseline data. Five subjects reported being episode free at the 6-month follow-up.

This study shows some encouraging results for the use of SMT for migraine sufferers. However, as there was no control group or alternative therapy group, it would be difficult to judge the merits of SMT in comparison to commonly employed migraine treatments.

According to Bronfort,[23] the current evidence for the efficacy of SMT in the treatment of migraine suggests that although clinical studies have shown some promising results, there is insufficient data to draw any firm conclusions (Evidence Level D). It is hoped that the two new studies reported here will help to more firmly establish the role of SMT in the treatment of migraine headaches.

NON-SPECIFIC NECK PAIN

A substantially greater number of studies have evaluated the effectiveness of manipulation for neck pain than for headache. Of these, there is a paucity of reports on SMT and acute neck pain. Two studies have recently been published comparing chiropractic and physiotherapy treatment for low-back and neck pain.[32, 33] Skargren et al[32] published their report in 1997 on cost and effectiveness of physiotherapy versus chiropractic treatment, while Skargren and Oberg[33] reported on predictive factors for 1-year outcome of low-back and neck pain as a follow-on from the previous trial.

The 1997 report by Skargren et al,[32] was a randomized clinical trial where patients were allocated to either the physiotherapy or chiropractic group after attending a general practitioner for the complaint of low-back or neck pain. Patients' duration of complaint was categorized as

< 1 week, 1–4 weeks, 1–3 months or > 3 months. As a result, subjects in this study consisted of a mix of acute, subacute and chronic neck patients.

Overall, 323 patients were recruited for the study. Of the 70 neck-pain patients (approximately 22%), 41 patients were allocated to the chiropractic treatment group and 29 to the physiotherapy group. There was no report of the duration of neck pain for either group of subjects. The outcome measures included pain intensity on a visual analogue scale, pain frequency, function (Oswestry score, sick leave, duration of sick leave), use of pain medication, pain drawing, and general health. Neither group of practitioners was constrained as to the type of treatment offered.

The results indicated that 98% of patients in the chiropractic group received SMT, while the most common form of treatment for the physiotherapy group was McKenzie treatment, mobilization and soft tissue therapy. No difference was found between the chiropractic and physiotherapy groups in terms of pain, function, and general health immediately following the treatment and at the 6-month follow-up. However, there was a trend for fewer patients in the chiropractic group to be on sick leave after treatment (17% versus 18% for physiotherapy) which increased at six months (9% versus 15% for physiotherapy). This result was not statistically significant.

Skargen and Oberg[33] reported in 1998 a 1-year follow-up to the 1997 study.[32] No significant differences were found between the groups although a subgroup analysis indicated that patients with acute pain (<1 per week) benefited more from chiropractic manipulative care while patients with more chronic pain (>1 per month) benefited more from physiotherapy treatment. Although this study included neck pain patients ranging from acute to chronic, the lack of analysis of these patients does not allow one to comment on the effectiveness of chiropractic manipulation compared to physiotherapy treatment.

Also in 1998, Jordan et al[1] reported on a randomized, prospective clinical study comparing intensive training, physiotherapy, or manipulation for patients with chronic neck pain. Overall, 167 patients were screened for the study, with 119 patients being admitted (88 female and 33 male). Forty subjects (10 men and 30 women) were allocated to the intensive training group, 39 subjects (10 men and 29 women) to the physiotherapy group, and 40 subjects (11 men, 29 women) to the chiropractic treatment group. The outcome measures included self-reported pain (three 11-point box scales), disability (self-report disability index), medication use (yes or no), patient's perceived effect (six-point box scale) and physician's global assessment (five-point box scale). Patients were assessed at entry and completion of the study as well as by follow-up via a postal questionnaire at 4 and 12 months.

The results indicated that all three interventions produced a reduction in self-reported pain level and disability and medication use compared to baseline. This trend continued at 4-month and 6-month follow-ups. No significant differences were found between groups. Both the patient's perceived effect and physician's global assessment at the completion of the trial were similar for the three treatment groups. The patient's perceived effect was maintained at 4- and 12-month follow-up. The physician's global assessment was only completed at the end of treatment. The authors, however, conclude that because a control group was not used, it could not be determined whether the improvements were due to the treatment or simply due to the passage of time.

Koes et al in 1992 reported on a randomized clinical trial of manipulative therapy, physiotherapy, and treatment by the general practitioner for persistent back and neck complaints.[34] Also in 1992, Koes et al[35] reported on a 1-year follow-up to the previous trial.

One-hundred forty-four patients were randomly allocated to one of four groups. Group 1 (36 subjects) consisted of manipulation and/or mobilization by a physiotherapist. Group 2 (36 subjects) were given massage/heat/exercise modalities. Group 3 (32 patients) were given medication, advice on rest, exercise, and posture. Group 4 (40 subjects) were given detuned ultrasound. The outcome measures were severity of main complaint, physical functioning, and perceived global effect. Patients were followed-up at 6 weeks and 12 weeks, while the Koes et al study[35] reported on the 1-year follow-up. Bronfort allocated a validity score of 50 for this later study.[23]

The results indicated that the SMT and mobilization group fared better in terms of physical functioning, severity of main complaint, and perceived global effect at 6 and 12 weeks compared to the medical group (Group 3). However, the manipulation/mobilization group did not reach statistical significance when compared to Group 4 (detuned ultrasound). The 1-year follow-up showed that the manipulation/mobilization group maintained the statistically significant benefit compared to the medical treatment group (Group 3).

A 1992 randomized clinical study by Cassidy et al[36] looked at a combination of acute (16%), subacute (34%), and chronic (50%) neck pain patients with unilateral pain. One hundred patients were allocated to either a rotational manipulation group (52 patients) or a mobilization group (48 patients). Each group was given one treatment by a chiropractor. The outcome measures included self-reported pain improvement (numerical rating scale) and assessment of cervical range of motion. The manipulation group showed significantly less reported pain after treatment ($p=0.05$). However, after adjusting the groups for pretreatment differences, no statistical significance was observed ($p>0.05$). Range of motion showed a trend for greater increase in the manipulation group, but this was not statistically significant. Unfortunately, no longer-term follow-up was conducted.

In 1990, Vernon et al[37] reported on a randomized controlled trial of chronic mechanical neck pain patients allocated to either rotational manipulation or mobilization. One treatment was given by a chiropractor to each group. The outcome measure was change in pain pressure thresh-

old measured immediately following the treatment. A significant rise in pain pressure threshold immediately around the joint fixation was found in the manipulation group as compared to the mobilization group ($p<0.0001$). Again, this study suffers from the lack of a longer-term follow-up.

Howe et al[38] published a randomized clinical trial in 1983 comparing azapropazone plus rotational manipulation (Group 1) versus azapropazone only (Group 2). Patients were included in the trial if they had neck, arm, or hand pain originating from the cervical spine, as well as reduced range of motion. Eighty-seven percent of the patients had their complaint for less than 4 weeks duration while 81% had had previous attacks. Group 1 received between one to three treatments within a 1-week period. Sixty-eight percent of Group 1 and 6% of Group 2 reported immediate pain relief ($p<0.001$). However, no significant differences were found between the groups at 1- and 3-weeks follow-up. Group 1 also demonstrated immediate increase in cervical range of motion which was maintained at 1 and 3 weeks.

According to Bronfort,[23] there is inconclusive evidence for the short term efficacy of SMT for acute neck pain patients, while there is limited evidence of the short term efficacy of SMT for chronic neck pain patients. Although three recent studies have come to light,[1, 32, 33] their results suggest that the above statements currently represent a reasonable synopsis of the level of evidence in the literature for the efficacy of SMT for neck pain.

SUMMARY

Three excellent reports in the last few years have reviewed the literature for the effectiveness of manipulation of the cervical spine.[16, 22, 23] Vernon explored the literature to produce a report on the effectiveness of chiropractic manipulation in the treatment of headache in 1995. Hurwitz et al published their systematic review of the literature on manipulation and mobilization of the cervical spine in 1996. Finally in 1997, Bronfort reviewed the efficacy of manual therapies of the spine, which included manipulation for headaches and neck pain.

Although some recent research has been produced in the area of manipulation for tension-type/cervicogenic headaches, there is still only moderate evidence as to the efficacy of SMT for these types of disorders. However, this area does seem promising and it is hoped that more research will be forthcoming.

In the case of manipulation for the treatment of migraine headaches, there is more recent evidence to suggest an effect, but there is as yet insufficient evidence to draw conclusions about the efficacy of SMT for migraine. This area would also seem to be a promising one for future work by clinical researchers.

Similarly for nonspecific neck pain patients, there is inconclusive evidence of the effectiveness of SMT for acute neck pain and limited evidence for the effectiveness of manipulation for chronic neck pain.

Taken as a whole, the current body of research suggests that manipulation of the cervical spine for headache and neck pain is a valid form of treatment that does confer clinical benefit to the patient. Although the current level of evidence is weak, the body of research knowledge suffers from the lack of a sufficient number of sufficiently high quality studies. As Vernon[22] has pointed out, too many of the reported studies suffered from methodological flaws, especially in terms of sample size and the use of standardized and responsive outcome variables and outcome measures.

It is hoped that a trend towards the use of a wider range of research design will be seen in the future with clinical researchers utilizing more case series and cohort studies in addition to the randomized clinical trial to better study the spectrum of the human condition in the clinical setting.

REFERENCES

1. Jordan A, Bendix T, Nielsen H, Hansen FR, Host D, Winkel A. Intensive training, physiotherapy, or manipulation for patients with chronic neck pain. *Spine* 1998;23:311–319.
2. Bussieres A. A review of functional outcome measures for cervical spine disorders: Literature review. *JCCA* 1994;38(1):32–40.
3. Breen A. The chiropractic treatment of painful conditions: A review of scope and limitations. *Pain Reviews* 1996;3:293–305.
4. Borghouts JAJ, Koes BW, Bouter LM. The clinical course and prognostic factors of non-specific neck pain: A systematic review. *Pain* 1998;77:1–13.
5. Pedersen P. A survey of chiropractic practice in Europe. *Eur. J Chiropractic* 1994;42(suppl):3–28.
6. Makela M, Heliovaara M, Sievers K, Impivaara O, Knekt P, Aromaa A. Prevalence, determinants, and consequences of chronic neck pain in Finland. *Am J Epidemiol* 1991;134:1356–1367.
7. van der Donk J, Schouten JSAG, Passchier J, van Romunde LKJ, Valkenberg HA. The association of neck pain with radiological abnormalities of the cervical spine and personality traits in a general population. *J Rheumatol* 1991;18:1884–1889.
8. Cote P, Cassidy JD, Carroll L. The Saskatchewan health and back pain survey: The prevalence of neck pain and related disability in Saskatchewan adults. *Spine* 1998;23:1689–1698.
9. Nilsson N, Christensen HW, Hartvigsen J. The effect of spinal manipulation in the treatment of cervicogenic headache. *J Manipulative Physiol Ther* 1997;20:326–329.
10. Nilsson N. The prevalence of cervicogenic headache in a random population sample of 20–59 year olds. *Spine* 1995;20:1884–1888.
11. Smith BMT, Adams A. Whiplash: A selective annotated bibliography. *JCCA* 1997;41(2):91–104.
12. Watison A, Gargan MF, Bannister GC. Prognostic factors in soft tissue injuries of the cervical spine. *Injury* 1991;22:307–309.
13. Skargren EI, Oberg BE, Carlsson PG, Gade M. Cost and effectiveness analysis of chiropractic and physiotherapy treatment for low back and neck pain. *Spine* 1997;22:2167–2177.
14. Koes BW, Assendelft WJ, van der Heijden GJ, Bouter LM, Knipschild PG. Spinal manipulation and mobilisation for back and neck pain: a blinded review. *Br Med J* 1991;303:1298–1303.
15. Shekelle PG, Adams AH, Chassin MR, Hurwitz EL, Brook RH. Spinal manipulation for low-back pain. *Ann Intern Med* 1992;117:590–598.
16. Hurwitz EL, Aker PD, Adams AH, Meeker WC, Shekelle PG. Manipulation and mobilization of the cervical spine: A systematic review. *Spine* 1996;21:1746–1760.
17. Chapman-Smith D. Cervicogenic headache: New anatomical discovery provides the missing link. *The Chiropractic Report* 1998;12:1–8.
18. Olesen J. *Classification and diagnostic criteria for headache disorders, cranial neuralgias and facial pain.* Copenhagen: International Headache Society, 1990.
19. North American Cervicogenic Headache Society (NACHS) Formation Documents, 1995.
20. Pfaffenrath V, Kaube H. Diagnostics of cervicogenic headache. *Funct Neurol* 1990;5:159–164.
21. Sjaastad O, Fredriksen TA, Stolt NA. Cervicogenic headache, C2 rhizopathy, and occipital neuralgia: A connection. *Cephalgia* 1986;6:189–195.
22. Vernon, H. The effectiveness of chiropractic manipulation in the treatment of headache: an exploration in the literature. *J Manipulative Physiol Ther* 1995;18:611–617.
23. Bronfort G. Efficacy of spinal manipulation for headache and conditions other than spinal related pain: A systematic review and best evidence synthesis. In: Bronfort G, ed. Efficacy of manual therapies of the spine. Amsterdam, Vrije Universiteit, 1997.

24. Boline PD, Kassak K, Bronfort G. Nelson C, Anderson AV. Spinal manipulation vs. amitriptyline for the treatment of chronic tension-type headaches: A randomized clinical trial. *J Manipulative Physiol Ther* 1995;18:148–154.

25. Nilsson N. A randomized controlled trial of the effect of spinal manipulation in the treatment of cervicogenic headache. *J Manipulative Physiol Ther* 1995;18:435–440.

26. Jensen OK, Nielsen FF, Vosmar L. An open study comparing manual therapy with the use of cold packs in the treatment of post-traumatic headache. *Cephalgia* 1990;10:241–250.

27. Vernon HT. Manipulative therapy in the chiropractic treatment of headaches: A retrospective and prospective study. *J Manipulative Physiol Ther* 1982;5:109–112.

28. Hoyt W, Shaffer F, Bard D, et al. Osteopathic manipulation in the treatment of muscle-contraction headache. *J Am Osteopath Assoc* 1979;78:322–325.

28a. Bove G, Nilsson N. Spinal manipulation in the treatment of episodic tension-type headache: A randomized controlled trial. *JAMA* 1998;280(18):1576–1579.

29. Nelson CF, Bronfort G, Evans R, Boline P, Goldsmith C, Anderson AV. The efficacy of spinal manipulation, amitriptyline, and the combination of both therapies for the prophylaxis of migraine headache: results of a six-month follow-up. Proceedings of the 1998 International Conference on Spinal Manipulation. Vancouver, Foundation for Chiropractic Education and Research.

30. Tuchin P. Does chiropractic spinal manipulative therapy (SMT) for migraine produce results? Proceedings of the 1998 International Conference on Spinal Manipulation. Vancouver, Foundation for Chiropractic Education and Research.

31. Parker GB, Tupling H, Pryor DS. A controlled trial of cervical manipulation of migraine. *Aust NZ J Med* 1978;8:589–593.

32. Skargren EI, Oberg BE, Carlsson PG, Gade M. Cost and effectiveness analysis of chiropractic and physiotherapy treatment for low back and neck pain. *Spine* 1997;22:2167–2177.

33. Skargren EI, Oberg BE. Predictive factors for 1-year outcome of low-back and neck pain in patients treated in primary care: Comparison between the treatment strategies of chiropractic and physiotherapy. *Pain* 1998;77:201–207.

34. Koes, BW, Bouter LM, van Mameren H, et al. The effectiveness of manual therapy, physiotherapy, and treatment by the general practitioner for nonspecific back and neck complaints: A randomized clinical trial. *Spine* 1992;17:28–35.

35. Koes BW, Bouter LM, van Mameren H, et al. Randomized clinical trial of manipulative therapy and physiotherapy for persistent back and neck complaints: Results of a one year follow up. *BMJ* 1992;304:601–605.

36. Cassidy JD, Quon JA, LaFrance LJ, Yong-Hing K. The immediate effect of manipulation versus mobilization on pain and range of motion in the cervical spine: A randomized controlled trial. *J Manipulative Physiol Ther* 1992;15:495–500.

37. Vernon HT, Aker P, Burns S, Viljakaanen S, Short L. Pressure pain threshold evaluation of the effect of spinal manipulation in the treatment of chronic neck pain: A pilot study. *J Manipulative Physiol Ther* 1990;13:13–16.

38. Howe DH, Newcombe RG, Wade MT. Manipulation of the cervical spine: A pilot study. *J R Coll Gen Pract* 1983;33:564–579.

CHAPTER 19

Examination and Treatment of Muscle and Soft Tissue Dysfunction in the Cervical Spine

Donald R. Murphy

"We learn more by looking for the answer to a question and not finding it than we do from learning the answer itself."

—Lloyd Alexander

INTRODUCTION

In Chapter 4, the seven types of muscular dysfunction were discussed, and their characteristics were described in detail. This chapter discusses the methods by which to identify and distinguish each of the five functional types of muscular dysfunction and apply specific treatment approaches that are designed to address these unique characteristics for rapid improvement in function.

Each type of muscle dysfunction is manifested differently and has different neurophysiological characteristics. It is by these features that each type can be detected. Once the type of dysfunction involved has been identified, we can apply treatment in such a way as to reduce the pathophysiology that produces the alteration in function.

THE BARRIER

An essential concept in understanding the examination and treatment of muscle dysfunction (or joint dysfunction; see Chap. 13) is what Lewit describes as the "restrictive barrier."[1] All tissues have a barrier to stretch that, when reached, provides resistance to further stretch. This is a normal protective feature that prevents injury to the tissue from overstretching. When the tissue is lengthened, there is no resistance throughout most of the range of movement, followed by a gradual increase in resistance that becomes greatest at the end of the movement. The point at which resistance begins is the barrier. When this barrier is engaged, a certain amount of further elasticity can be felt, wherein slightly more stretch can be applied to the tissue, but with substantial resistance. This is known as "end feel." This end feel should be, according to Mennel (Mennel JMcM, personal communication, 1988), no more than $1/8$ inch. With most tissues, this barrier is purely passive, created by the inherent properties of the tissue (Figure 19–1A).

With dysfunction a "pathological restrictive barrier"[1] can develop (Figure 19–1B) in which the resistance develops more abruptly and a greater degree of resistance occurs. This can be detected only through skilled palpation

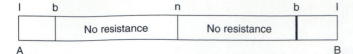

Figure 19–1. The restrictive barrier. As a tissue is lengthened from neutral (n), there at first is no resistance detected. The point at which resistance begins is the barrier (b). Beyond the barrier, resistance increases rapidly (end feel) until the anatomical limit of the tissue is reached (l). Normal tissue is depicted in **A.** In tissue with abnormally increased tension, as depicted in **B,** the barrier is reached sooner and is more abrupt than in the normal tissue. The barrier also provides greater resistance in this condition.

(Adapted from Lewit K. Manipulative Therapy in the Rehabilitation of the Locomotor System. *Oxford: Butterworth-Heinemann; 1991.)*

of the barrier. Correction of dysfunction is brought about by applying a procedure that creates release of the pathological barrier. As will be seen, the ability to engage the barrier, distinguish normal from abnormal, and sense its release is absolutely essential to the effective treatment of locomotor system dysfunction. Techniques to accomplish this are described in this chapter, but it requires a great deal of practice to develop the sensitivity to feel the barrier.

MUSCLE LENGTH TESTS

One of the most important methods by which individual muscle function is evaluated is through the use of muscle length tests. These tests allow the clinician to evaluate the tone of a muscle and to differentiate normal tone, hypertonicity, and tightness. This done is by lengthening the muscle to the point at which the barrier is engaged and assessing the degree of length that is attained, as well as the amount or resistance that the muscle provides when the clinician attempts to lengthen it beyond the barrier.

In the normal, relaxed patient, when stretch is applied slowly, there is no stretch reflex induced to passive stretch of the muscle.[2] Thus, any resistance at the barrier is related to passive elements in the muscle. With hypertonicity, the stretch reflex occurs more readily and provides additional resistance at the barrier that is palpable by the seasoned examiner. For this reason, it is essential that the lengthening be done slowly, so that normal and hypertonic conditions can be differentiated. It is also essential that the muscle is completely at rest, without acting against gravity, while the length test is being administered.

In the case of muscle tightness, a condition in which there is both hypertonicity and soft tissue contracture in the muscle, resistance occurs from both the stretch reflex and the passive elements. This provides a more abrupt resistance at the barrier. In addition, the muscle, when lengthened to the point of the barrier, appears abnormally shortened.

EXAMINATION AND TREATMENT OF THE FIVE FUNCTIONAL TYPES OF MUSCLE DYSFUNCTION

LIMBIC SYSTEM DYSFUNCTION

It will be recalled that limbic system dysfunction primarily arises from emotional stress. It is identified through the history and palpation. On history, there may not be any specific clues that lead to the diagnosis, but suspicion should be raised by carefully listening to the patient for subtle signs of great emotional stress.

 CLINICAL PEARL

Identification of excessive emotional stress in a patient must be done in a roundabout way. There are two reasons for this. One is that if you come right out and ask the patient, "Do you have a great deal of stress in your life?," hardly anyone in the Western world will not reply with something like, "Oh, yes, I am under so much stress. If only you knew!" The other reason is that many patients, especially if there is medicolegal involvement, are very sensitive to being told that the problem is "all in your head." Even if your intentions are good, asking pointed questions regarding emotional stress factors can cause the patient to withdraw from you.

With limbic system dysfunction, palpation will reveal a distinct area of tenderness over the involved muscles, particularly the upper trapezii and sternocleidomastoids, with nontender areas surrounding these areas. There is typically a gradual transition from the tender area to the nontender area.

 CLINICAL PEARL

This gradual transition is an important diagnostic clue. When you are palpating the patient, start palpating in the tender area, for example, the upper trapezius. Then gradually move your palpating fingers downward to the middle and lower trapezius; the patient will report that the tenderness gradually becomes less as you move downward.

Specific trigger points (TrPs) may be identified within the muscle; these should be palpated firmly to assess whether the referred pain they create reproduces all or part of the patient's symptoms. It is more common to find that there are no distinct TrPs, but rather, just generalized hypertonicity.

The treatment for limbic system dysfunction must involve some form of relaxation training if lasting relief of pain is to be expected.[3] This can take the form of meditation or biofeedback techniques that the nonpsychological practitioner can prescribe, or referral to a mental health professional for counseling. Meditation, in particular, can be a powerful tool in the treatment of patients with chronic cervical spine syndromes. It has been demonstrated that it is possible to reduce the sensitivity of the stretch reflex, and thus muscle tone, via conscious effort.[4-7] Kabat-Zinn et al[8] compared 90 chronic pain patients, including those with neck, head, and face pain, who were trained in mindfulness meditation, with 21 patients who were treated with nerve blocks, transcutaneous electrical nerve stimulation (TENS), physical therapy, analgesics, and antidepressants. The training period was 10 weeks. At follow-up after 2.5, 4.5, 7, and 12 months, they found a statistically significant improvement in present-moment pain, symptoms, mood disturbance, anxiety, and depression. No significant improvement was seen in the control group in any of these measures. All improvements except that of present-moment pain were maintained at 15 months follow-up.

Along with the relaxation training, the muscles can be treated with **postisometric relaxation** (see later discussion) to reduce tone, or **ischemic compression** (see later discussion) for any TrPs that may be present. However, the relief brought about by these techniques will be short lived if the limbic system dysfunction itself is not addressed.

INTERNEURON DYSFUNCTION

Interneuron dysfunction is alteration of muscle tone that results from joint or muscle dysfunction. Hypertonicity related to interneuron dysfunction can be detected by length tests. When the muscle is fully lengthened to the point of the barrier, further movement beyond this point is met with a distinct resistance that is greater than would be expected in a normal muscle. The muscle is also typically tender to palpation. It may or may not be shortened, and length changes should not be relied upon in the detection of hypertonicity.

The treatment of choice for joint dysfunction is **manipulation** (see Chap. 18). Changes in muscle activity have been demonstrated following manipulation.[9-14] See Appendix 18A for a detailed description of the neurophysiological effects of manipulation.

There are some clinical situations in which manipulation of the involved joint is not sufficient to resolve the hypertonicity of the muscle. This particularly occurs when the hypertonicity is well established as a result of a plastic change that has taken place in the neuromuscular system. In this case, treatment must be applied directly to the muscle to produce normalization of muscle tone. The best method for this is **postisometric relaxation (PIR).**

PIR is a method of gently reducing the tone of a muscle by utilizing isometric contraction.[15] When a muscle contracts isometrically, its alpha motor neurons are activated. When this isometric contraction is stopped, the muscle tends to relax more fully than it did before the onset of the contraction.[16, 17] Isometric contraction also decreases stretch perception in the muscle,[18] thus delaying the onset of the stretch reflex. This allows the clinician to reduce the tone of the muscle and, if necessary, to gently lengthen it.

Of utmost importance to the success of PIR is meeting the barrier. To do this the muscle is gently and fully lengthened while at complete rest. This requires that the patient and the involved muscle be placed in a position in which the muscle does not have to contract against gravity. As the full length of the muscle is reached, the clinician senses a point at which the muscle begins to provide resistance to further lengthening. This is the barrier. It is very subtle and requires great skill that can only come from many hours of practice.

After the barrier is met, the muscle is contracted isometrically. It is always best to provide for the patient a resistance against which to push in creating this contraction. The clinician can do this by placing his or her hand at a strategic location so that, if the patient were to push against this point, the muscle would naturally contract isometrically. It is important that this isometric contraction be very gentle, as a hard contraction runs the risk of over-facilitating the muscle, and worsening the hypertonicity.

Eye movements and breathing are often helpful in facilitating the gentle contraction of the muscle. When the eyes move in a certain direction, it causes certain muscles to become activated and certain others to become inhibited.[19] In general, for the cervical spine, the muscles that cause the head to move in the direction toward which the eyes are moving tend to become activated, while the muscles that tend to move the head in the opposite direction become inhibited. Inhalation causes most muscles to become activated and exhalation causes most muscles to become inhibited.[20] Thus, with PIR during the isometric contraction phase, the patient is told to move his or her eyes in the direction that facilitates the muscles and to breathe in. During the inhibition phase, the patient is told to look in the opposite direction and breathe out.

During the contraction phase, it is essential that the barrier remain engaged. Therefore, the muscle should not shorten during this phase. During the relaxation phase, the muscle is gently lengthened, but the clinician must wait to feel the release of the barrier before doing the lengthening. This can mean the difference between success and failure of the technique. Once the release of the barrier is sensed, the clinician gently *guides the muscle to lengthen* (do not stretch!) until a new barrier is met, at which point the lengthening stops and the process is repeated. Three to five repetitions is usually sufficient to achieve the desired result.

At times, the barrier does not release with the methodology described here. In these cases, the isometric contraction should be held longer—for 10 to 30 seconds—before the release is felt during the relaxation phase.

Table 19–1. Guidelines for Postisometric Relaxation

1. **Patient positioning**—The patient and the muscle being treated must be completely at rest.

2. **Lengthen the muscle fully**—Take the "slack" out of the muscle and extend it to its full resting length.

3. **Engage the barrier**—Feel the point at which resistance begins to increase.

4. **Isometric contraction**—Have the patient very gently and isometrically contract the muscle.

5. **Eye movements** (for some muscles)—Have the patient move his or her eyes in a direction that facilitates activity in the muscle.

6. **Breathing**—For most muscles, have the patient inhale deeply followed by exhalation (inhalation for the mandibular elevators).

7. **Wait!**—Do not lengthen the muscle until the release of the barrier is felt.

8. **Feel the release**—Sense the release of the barrier.

9. **Guide into lengthening**—Gently guide the muscle to lengthen until a new barrier is met, then stop. Remain at this new barrier for the next repetition.

10. **Repeat** 3–5 times.

However, most of the time, with cervical muscles, the isometric contraction need only last as long as it takes for the patient to inhale. Guidelines for PIR are provided in Table 19–1.

REFLEX SPASM

This is involuntary contraction of a muscle in response to intense nociception. It is a self-limiting condition, as it resolves upon reduction of the intensity of the nociception. Note that reduction of the intensity of the *nociception* does not necessarily mean reduction in the intensity of the *pain*. Therefore, reflex spasm may resolve in a patient in whom pain levels may remain relatively the same.

Reflex spasm can be detected by the visual assessment of antalgia. Also, the muscle will typically be painful to palpation. Electromyography (EMG) will reveal spontaneous activity, but use of this tool is usually not necessary for detection of reflex spasm. Length tests are not recommended.

The obvious treatment for reflex spasm is rapid reduction of nociception. See Chapter 21 for a description of the most effective methods. Reflex spasm related to spinal injury can be quickly relieved via manipulation. The mechanisms by which this occurs were demonstrated in an animal model by Indahl et al,[21] who stimulated the annular fibers of the disc in pigs and demonstrated a reactive increase in resting EMG activity in the multifidis and longissimus muscles at that segment. Injection of normal saline into the joint capsule of the segment, stretching the capsule in a way that is proposed to occur with manipulation, caused immediate or almost immediate reduction of the muscle activity.

MYOFASCIAL TRIGGER POINTS

This is a localized contracture of a fascicle of muscle fibers, which causes congestion to develop in a focal area, leading to ischemia and metabolite accumulation. TrPs are detected with palpation.

Several treatment approaches are effective in the treatment of TrPs. Possibly the most effective in rapidly reducing pain generation is **ischemic compression.** This is a method by which direct pressure is applied to the TrP for a certain amount of time, which varies depending on the technique used.

There are two methods that are popular in the application of ischemic compression. One was developed by Nimmo[22] and involves applying direct compression to the TrP, with enough pressure to elicit the referred pain pattern. It is important that the pressure applied not be so great that it causes significant pain for the patient, as it is important that the patient not tense the muscle, and thus obscure the TrP from compression. The pressure is held for 5 to 7 seconds, after which finger pressure is quickly withdrawn, another TrP is found, and compression is again applied for 5 to 7 seconds, followed by quick withdrawal and application of compression to a third TrP. After several TrPs are treated in this way, the practitioner returns to the first TrP and again treats it in the same manner, with repeated application to each of the treated TrPs. Each TrP is treated three times.

Another method, advocated by Travell and Simons,[23] involves, as with the Nimmo method, applying direct compression to the TrP, with enough pressure to elicit the referred pain pattern without causing significant pain. With this method, the pressure is held until the referred pain disappears, or up to approximately 1 minute (any more than this increases the risk of aggravating the TrP). Only one application is made to each TrP using this technique.

! CLINICAL PEARL

Choosing between the two techniques is a matter of personal preference on the part of the practitioner, but I have found that it is best to utilize the Travell and Simons method in most situations, as it allows the practitioner to eliminate the pain for the patient immediately. This has the psychological advantage of demonstrating to the patient not only that you know the source of his or her pain (by virtue of the fact that you reproduced it with compression of the TrP), but also that you are able to eliminate it, as the patient experiences this immediately. However, when several significant TrPs are to be treated, I like to use the Nimmo method, as it is more time-efficient.

The mechanism of action of ischemic compression is unknown, but several mechanisms, reviewed by Schneider,[24] have been proposed. The most compelling are direct mechanical lengthening of the shortened sarcomeres as a result of the pressure; reflex vasodilatation upon release of the compression, a response to the ischemia created by the compression that serves to flush out the chemical mediators from the area of the TrP; and "hyperstimulation" of nociceptive pathways that leads to the central release of pain-relieving opiates such as endorphin and enkephalin.

Two studies have assessed the efficacy of ischemic compression in the treatment of TrPs. Garvey et al[25] compared injection of 1 percent lidocaine, injection of 1 percent lidocaine with Aristopan, insertion of dry needle (acupuncture), and ischemic compression combined with topical vapocoolant spray. They found significant superiority of the ischemic compression treatment compared to the others. Hong et al[26] compared ischemic compression, spray and stretch using vapocoolant, ultrasound, and hydrocollator for the immediate effect on pressure pain threshold of TrPs (as measured by algometry) in the upper trapezius in 84 subjects. They found that ischemic compression provided the greatest increase in pain threshold of the four modalities.

Another method that is quite effective in relieving TrPs is **PIR** (see earlier discussion). PIR allows the practitioner to gently lengthen the shortened sarcomeres in the fascicle of muscle fibers that contain the TrP in a way that avoids overstretching, which can aggravate the TrP. When used for TrPs, it is especially important that the isometric contraction be as gentle as possible because too hard a contraction may cause the fascicle of muscle fibers that contain the TrP to become inhibited.

PIR has not been evaluated experimentally with regard to its effect on TrPs; however, Jaeger and Reeves[27] studied the effect of spray and stretch, a technique of lengthening of the shortened sarcomeres in which vapocoolant spray is used to induce reflex relaxation of the muscle rather than isometric contraction. In 20 subjects with myofascial pain in the head and neck, they found that spray and stretch resulted in decreased TrP sensitivity as measured by pressure algometry. Hong et al,[26] in the study mentioned earlier that compared ischemic compression, spray and stretch, ultrasound, and hydrocollator, found that spray and stretch was superior in increasing pain threshold to ultrasound or hydrocollator.

! CLINICAL PEARL

Years ago, I used spray and stretch technique almost exclusively as a method or normalizing length and tone to muscles. While I found it to be effective, there were several problems with it. The first, as has been discussed by Travell and Simons,[28] was that the chemical used, fluorimethane, is a chlorofluorocarbon, which may be harmful to the delicate ozone layer of the upper atmosphere. The second problem was the effect it had on my personal atmosphere—use of it in enclosed treatment rooms all day would cause me to be extremely light-headed by the end of the day. Finally, using fluorimethane necessitated that one hand be taken up with holding the bottle, whereas the use of PIR allowed me to have both hands free for the patient, maximizing the effectiveness of the treatment as well as providing additional therapeutic effects of touch. For these reasons, I abandoned fluorimethane in favor of PIR.

Although ischemic compression is more effective than PIR in producing immediate reduction of pain arising from a TrP, it is essential in most cases that restoration of normal length of the fascicle of muscle fibers that contain the TrP be accomplished at some point during the treatment program. This corrects function in the case in which the muscle is hypertonic as well as ensuring that the involved fascicle as a whole is normalized, rather than just the section containing the TrP.

! CLINICAL PEARL

There are exceptions to this approach. In general, ischemic compression should be used preferentially when treating muscles that tend to become inhibited, such as the middle and lower trapezius or infraspinatus, as inhibitory procedures can further aggravate, or promote the development of, muscle imbalance. Ischemic compression is also oftentimes more beneficial than PIR for muscles which are already quite short and difficult to lengthen, such as the suboccipitals.

MUSCLE TIGHTNESS

This is a state in which the muscle is hypertonic in addition to being shortened. Muscle tightness is detected with length tests. When performing a length test on a tight muscle, it will be noted that the muscle is shortened, that is, it cannot be lengthened to as great an extent as the same muscle in a normal circumstance. In addition to this, when the muscle is lengthened to the point at which the barrier is met, further movement beyond this point is met with an abrupt, hard resistance. This resistance is greater than that seen with hypertonicity, and differentiating between the two is essential if the correct treatment modality is to be chosen.

The treatment for muscle tightness is **postfacilitation stretch (PFS).** This is a method developed by Janda and is designed to both reduce the tone of the muscle and stretch the noncontractile elements that are maintaining the shortened state. PFS involves having the patient contract the muscle isometrically but, unlike PIR, this contraction is maximum or as close to maximum as possible. Also unlike PIR, the isometric contraction is performed with the muscle in the middle of its functional excursion, rather than at the barrier. Both these principles allow for the recruitment of the maximum number of motor units possible. The reason this is necessary is that muscle tightness involves hypertonicity and contracture of the *entire* muscle; thus, the entire muscle must be involved in treatment. No eye movements or breathing are used with PFS. The isometric contraction must be held for a full 10 seconds, after which the patient is told to completely let go of the muscle, so that it relaxes completely. This letting go is followed by a fast stretch of the muscle, to the point at which the barrier is reached. The stretch is then held for 10 to 15 seconds, followed by return to middle range. This process is performed three to five times. Table 19–2 provides guidelines for PFS.

The reason fast stretch is necessary when treating muscle tightness is that, first, fast stretch has been demonstrated to create a greater inhibition of the muscle than slow stretch.[29] Second, the stretch must be applied before the stretch reflex reaches its peak amplitude. Elicitation of the stretch reflex would interfere with the effectiveness of the technique. As Davidoff has discussed,[2] there is a latency between the onset of muscle stretch and the beginning of the stretch reflex. This latency is approximately 25 msec. For the first 25 msec, no contraction-related resistance is provided by the muscle, so the noncontractile elements are being stretched unopposed. It takes another 200 msec for the reflex contraction of the stretch reflex to reach peak amplitude, so the remainder of the stretch involves a rapidly increasing resistance, requiring speed in order to maximize the stretch with minimum contractile resistance.

It is important that the stretch position be held for 10 to 15 seconds to allow for stress relaxation (a gradual decrease in the tension provided by the noncontractile tissues of the muscle as the stretch is held) and creep (a gradual increase in length of the tissues as the stretch position is held) to occur.[30] Three to five repetitions of the maneuver are optimum; no benefit can be expected from a greater number.[30]

There are several contraindications to PFS; these consist of conditions and situations in which it should be fairly obvious that a vigorous stretch would not be appropriate. They include joint hypermobility, inflammatory disorders affecting muscle, and situations in which the stretch of the muscle would also stretch an inflamed nerve root, an example being use of PFS on the sternocleidomastoid muscle in the presence of cervical radiculopathy. In addition, great care must be taken in applying this technique in older patients or in children, although in the latter patient population, true muscle tightness in cervical muscles is rare anyway. Finally, PFS should not be applied unless it has been determined that true muscle tightness is present.

SKIN AND SUBCUTANEOUS SOFT TISSUE DYSFUNCTION

Often overlooked in cervical spine syndromes is the role that dysfunction in the skin and other soft tissues can play both in reflex changes that affect function as well as in causing localized pain. Several processes that can occur in these tissues can be important factors in the perpetuation of pain and dysfunction.

One factor is the hyperalgesic skin zone (HSZ).[20, 31] This is an area of skin that has developed increased sensitivity such that stimuli that are normally innocuous become painful. In addition, there develops increased tension in the tissue. This tension is palpable. There are several methods by which a HSZ can be detected. One simple method is assessing what Lewit[20] refers to as "skin drag." This involves lightly running a finger over the skin and assessing the friction in the involved area. An HSZ exhibits increased friction due to the excessive moisture. The patient also reports that the area is more sensitive than the same anatomical location on the other side of the body.

Table 19–2. Guidelines for Postfacilitation Stretch

1. **Patient positioning**—The patient and the muscle being treated must be completely at rest.
2. **Clinician positioning**—The clinician must be positioned such that he or she can provide resistance to a hard contraction from the patient.
3. **Start from mid-range**—The barrier is not engaged.
4. **Maximum or near-maximum contraction**—If the clinician is not able to resist the contraction, submaximal contraction should be used.
5. **Hold** the contraction for 10 seconds.
6. **Total relaxation**—The patient is told to completely let go of the muscle. The clinician should wait briefly to be sure that complete relaxation occurs before stretching.
7. **Fast stretch.**
8. **Hold** the stretch for 10–15 seconds.
9. **Return to mid-range.**
10. Repeat 3–5 times.

> **!** CLINICAL PEARL

As both Travell[32] and I[31] have reported, the pain experienced by a patient with HSZ can be so great as to be mistaken for trigeminal neuralgia or herpes zoster.

Skin stretching is another method of detecting HSZ. With this method, the skin is stretched either by placing the fingers on either side of the hyperalgesic area and gently moving them apart (Fig. 19–2) or by offsetting the fingers so that a fold of skin can be stretched between them (Fig. 19–3). In either case, the skin is gently lengthened until the restrictive barrier is engaged and the resistance at this barrier is assessed. Increased resistance at the barrier

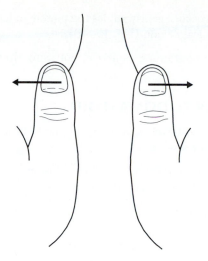

Figure 19–2. Skin stretching with the fingers parallel.

combined with the report of pain during springing palpation of the barrier are signs of HSZ.

Treatment of HSZ can be accomplished with a barrier release technique that is both effective and nonpainful. Using either of the above methods of stretching the skin, the barrier is engaged. It is important that movement beyond the barrier be avoided as this will cause pain and interfere with the effectiveness of the treatment. The skin is held at the barrier and the clinician waits to sense it release. As this occurs, the skin is gently lengthened until a new barrier is met, at which point the clinician again waits

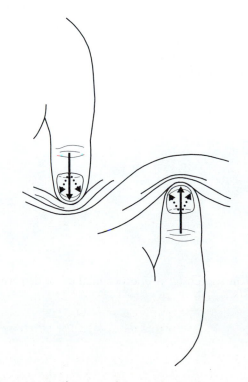

Figure 19–3. Skin stretching with the fingers offset.

for release. This should be done three to five times. As with PIR, subtlety is the key to the effectiveness of this technique, and sensing the release of the barrier is of paramount importance.

In addition to skin dysfunction, restriction of the movement between fascial layers and the development of adhesions in fascia and muscle can occur that can become significant sources of pain and dysfunction as well as of nerve entrapment. These adhesions require release. Perhaps the most effective method of accomplishing this is with what Leahy[33] has called "Active Release Techniques" (see Appendix 19A). With these techniques, the adhesion is identified by palpation and is contacted by the fingers or hand. The adhesion is then drawn under the contact, usually by lengthening the tissue and allowing the contact to pass longitudinally along the tissue and the lesion itself.

MUSCLE INHIBITION

There are several methods by which inhibition in the muscular system can be treated. An excellent hands-on method is rhythmic stabilization (RS). RS was developed as part of the Proprioceptive Neuromuscular Facilitation (PNF) system.[34] What is described next is actually a variant of the classical PNF method. For the purpose intended here, RS is designed to facilitate certain muscles that are inhibited. There are a wide variety of methods by which this is done, and certain principles are followed in applying the technique for facilitation.

When used to facilitate an inhibited muscle, the application of RS consists of first placing the muscle in a position that maximizes its ability to activate strongly, then applying pressure at a certain point and telling the patient to resist this pressure. The pressure is then applied rhythmically in a crescendo-decrescendo fashion, such that the clinician gradually increases it to a peak over 1 to 2 seconds, followed by a gradual decrease over 1 to 2 seconds. The peak pressure that is exerted by the clinician is determined by how much pressure the patient can resist without giving way or falling into a faulty recruitment pattern. In general, the goal should be to build up to the point at which RS can be applied to approximately 20 to 30 percent of the maximum voluntary contraction of the muscle.[35] The rhythmic contractions are repeated five to ten times, usually followed by a series of short, quick bursts. These are designed to improve reaction time in the neuromuscular circuit.

Several tricks can be used to maximize the effectiveness of the technique. These usually involve placing certain seemingly unrelated body parts in a position that causes reflex activation of the desired muscle or applying clinician pressure in a certain strategic spot to maximize recruitment of the desired muscle and minimize recruitment of muscles that the clinician does not want activated. An example is the middle and lower trapezius. Having the patient open the fingers as wide as possible during the RS procedure dramatically increases the activation of these muscles. Another example is facilitating the deep neck flexors. Applying pressure beneath the chin is optimal for recruitment of these muscles, whereas applying the pressure on the forehead would tend to activate the sternocleidomastoid.

SPECIFIC MUSCLES—INHIBITION AND LENGTHENING PROCEDURES

SUBOCCIPITALS

POSTURAL ANALYSIS SIGN. Forward-placed head.

MOVEMENT PATTERN SIGN. Chin poke on cervical flexion; activation of the posterior cervical muscles in general on hip extension test.

LENGTH TEST. None.

TRP REFERRAL PATTERN. The suboccipitals, sternocleidomastoid, splenius capitis, and upper trapezius are the muscles that most commonly harbor TrPs that are the primary pain generators in headache patients. Active TrPs in the suboccipitals may refer pain over the side of the head and behind the eye (see Fig. 17–2).

PIR. With the patient supine, the clinician blocks the C2 articular pillar with one hand and rotates and laterally flexes a few degrees away from the side being treated to place focus on that side. The clinician then flexes the upper cervical spine with the other hand to take up slack and meet the restrictive barrier (Fig. 19–4A). It is important to limit the movement to the upper cervical spine. This can be done by placing slight pressure caudally on the head while taking up slack. The patient will look up with his or her eyes and breathe in for the contraction phase and look down and breathe out for the relaxation phase. The clinician waits to feel for the release of the barrier and

when this occurs, gently guides the muscle to lengthen into upper cervical flexion (Fig. 19–4B).

PFS. Same positioning as above, but using the PFS procedure.

STERNOCLEIDOMASTOID

POSTURAL ANALYSIS SIGN. Forward-placed head and prominence of the muscle.

MOVEMENT PATTERN SIGN. Chin poke on cervical flexion test; chin poke on cervical stability test.

LENGTH TEST. None.

TRP REFERRAL PATTERN. As stated above, this muscle is among the most common sources of pain in patients with headache. Active TrPs in the sternocleidomastoid muscle may refer pain over the forehead and face, in and behind the ear, on top of the head, deep in the throat, and over the sternoclavicular joint (see Fig. 17–3).

PIR. The patient is supine, with his or her head off the end of the table. The clinician places his or her middle finger of the hand opposite the side of involvement under the occipital ridge (Fig. 19–5). The head is then moved into lateral flexion away from the side of involvement, rotation toward the side of involvement, extension of the lower cervical spine and flexion of the upper cervical spine to meet the restrictive barrier (Fig. 19–6A). The thumb of the hand on the involved side is then placed onto the forehead just over the patient's eye and the rest of that hand is rested on the side of the head (Fig. 19–6B). The patient pushes upward against the thumb, looks up, and takes a deep breath in for the contraction phase. The patient then stops pushing, looks down and breathes out for the relaxation phase. The clinician waits to feel the release of the barrier and then gently guides the muscle to lengthen toward the floor, while keeping the upper cervical spine flexed, until a new barrier is met (Fig. 19–6C).

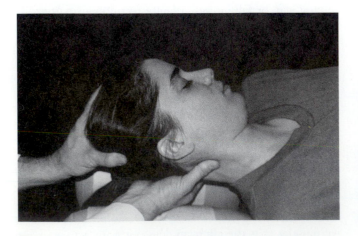

A

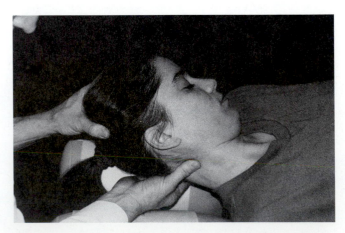

B

Figure 19–4. Suboccipital muscle PIR. **A.** Meeting the barrier. **B.** After release of the barrier.

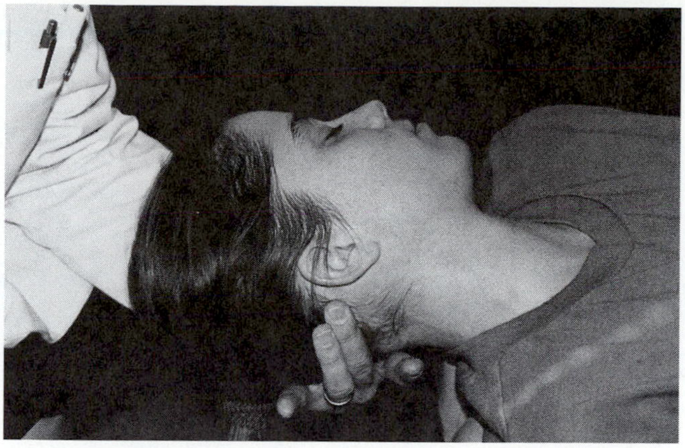

Figure 19–5. Finger placement for PIR of the sternocleido-mastoid.

PFS. The positioning described for the PIR technique is excellent for reducing hypertonicity in the sternocleidomastoid. However, it is insufficient for stretching the muscle in the presence of true muscle tightness (which, in the case of the sternocleidomastoid is relatively uncommon, but will be encountered). A modification of the traditional PFS technique is used for this muscle, one in which the fast stretch aspect is not utilized. Rather, a slow, controlled stretch is applied. As with PIR of this muscle, the patient is supine, with his or her head off the end of the table. The clinician's middle finger of the hand opposite the side of involvement is placed under the occipital ridge, as with PIR of this muscle (see Fig. 19–5). In order to fully stretch this muscle, however, the head must be placed differently than it was with PIR. For PFS, the head is rotated *away* from the side of involvement, laterally flexed away, and extended so that the head moves all the way down toward the floor. As with PIR of this muscle, the thumb of the hand on the involved side is then placed onto the forehead just over the patient's eye and the rest of that hand is rested on the side of the head (Fig. 19–7A). PFS is performed from this position in the traditional way, except that the fast stretch is replaced with a slow, careful stretch. The direction of stretch is in extension and lateral flexion away from the side of involvement (Fig. 19–7B).

Do not use the fast stretch aspect of the technique with this muscle. Common sense should dictate that we would not do this!

! CLINICAL PEARL

TrPs in the sternocleidomastoid muscle can be very temperamental, and care must always be taken when treating them with ischemic compression, as it is very easy to aggravate these TrPs and aggravate or provoke a headache.

SPLENIUS CAPITIS

POSTURAL ANALYSIS SIGN. None.

MOVEMENT PATTERN SIGN. None.

LENGTH TEST. This is a very long muscle and not very accessible to length testing. Its clinical importance is not as a muscle that develops hypertonicity and thus interferes with movement patterns, but rather as a common pain generator in patients with headache.

TRP REFERRAL PATTERN. To the top of the head (see Fig. 17–6). It should be noted that TrPs rarely occur in this muscle in isolation, but rather usually occur accompanying TrPs in the suboccipitals, sternocleidomastoid, or upper trapezius.

PIR. With the patient lying supine, the clinician places his or her hand on the posterosuperior portion of the patient's head as with the suboccipitals. The restrictive barrier is met by moving the head and neck into flexion, rotation approximately 45 degrees away from the side of involvement, and lateral flexion away from the side of involvement (Fig. 19–8A). It is important that the upper cervical spine be flexed as well as the lower cervical spine. The other hand is placed just behind the mastoid process to provide the patient with a tactile cue as to the direction in which to apply pressure during the contraction phase. The patient pushes against this hand, looks toward the side of involvement, and takes a deep breath in for the contraction phase, then stops pushing, looks to the opposite side, and breathes out for the relaxation phase. The clinician waits for the release of the barrier, then gently lengthens the muscle by moving further into flexion and lateral flexion (Fig. 19–8B).

PFS. This is not a muscle that tends to become tight, so PFS is not applicable.

UPPER TRAPEZIUS

POSTURAL ANALYSIS SIGN. Bilateral or unilateral elevated shoulders.

MOVEMENT PATTERN SIGN. Early elevation of the scapula on shoulder abduction test; scapular elevation on pushup test; activation on hip extension test.

LENGTH TEST. With the patient supine, the clinician places one hand on the point of the shoulder on the involved side. The other arm cradles the patient's head and the head is flexed, laterally flexed away, and rotated toward the side of involvement. The ipsilateral hand is used to push the shoulder inferiorward to lengthen the muscle until the restrictive barrier is met (Fig. 19–9). The clinician then feels for the amount of resistance to further stretching the muscle provides. Normally, the shoulder should move inferiorward several additional degrees and with little resistance.

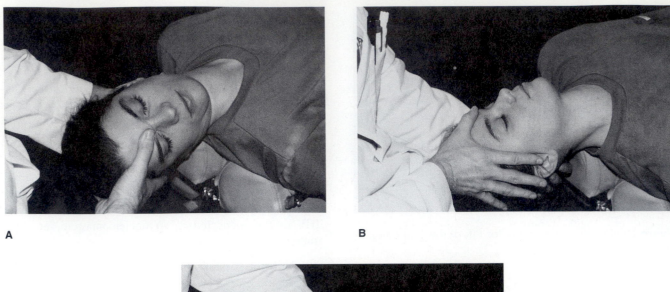

A

B

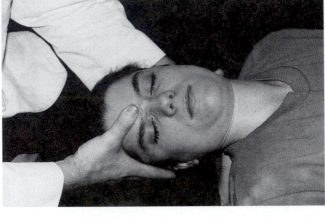

C

Figure 19–6. Sternocleidomastoid PIR. **A.** Meeting the barrier. **B.** Hand placement for resistance. **C.** After release of the barrier.

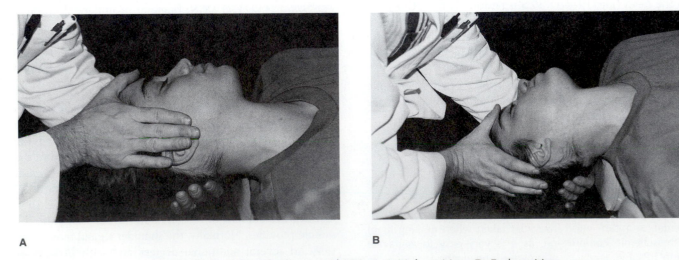

A

B

Figure 19–7. Sternocleidomastoid PFS. **A.** Initial position. **B.** End position.

A

B

Figure 19–8. Splenius capitis PIR. **A.** Meeting the barrier. **B.** After release of the barrier.

TRP REFERRAL PATTERN. As with the suboccipitals and sternocleidomastoid, TrPs in the upper trapezius are a very common pain generator in headache patients. Active TrPs may cause pain to refer up the side of the neck to the base of the skull and over into the temporal region and behind the eye. Uncommonly, pain may also be referred to the angle of the jaw (see Fig. 17–4).

PIR. Patient and clinician positioning are the same as that for the length test (see Fig. 19–9). The restrictive barrier is met in the same manner as previously described. The patient is instructed to gently press against the clinician's hand that is on the point of the shoulder, look up, and breathe in for the contraction phase, then stop pushing, look down, and breathe out for the relaxation phase. The clinician waits for the release of the barrier and then gently guides the muscle to lengthen by moving the shoulder inferiorward until a new barrier is met.

PFS. The clinician and patient positioning is the same as for PIR, but rather that taking up the slack in the muscle

and meeting the restrictive barrier, the muscle is maintained in a neutral position. The patient contracts the muscle strongly by pushing up against the clinician's hand as if trying to shrug. This contraction is held for 10 seconds, after which the patient lets go and a fast stretch is applied to the muscle by carefully moving the shoulder straight inferiorward.

LEVATOR SCAPULAE

POSTURAL ANALYSIS SIGN. Elevated superior angle of the scapula.

MOVEMENT PATTERN SIGN. Elevation of the superior angle of the scapula on shoulder abduction test; medial deviation of the inferior angle of the scapula on pushup test; activation on hip extension test.

LENGTH TEST. With the patient supine, the clinician places one hand on the superior angle of the scapula on the involved side. The other arm cradles the patient's head and the head is flexed, laterally flexed away, and rotated away from the side of involvement. The segments from C0 to C4 are then rotated as a unit, to ensure that the horizontally configured fibers that attach to C2, C3, and C4 are fully lengthened[36] (Fig. 19–10). With the hand on the superior angle of the scapula, the superior angle is pushed inferiorward to lengthen the muscle until the restrictive barrier is met. The clinician then feels for the amount of resistance the muscle provides to further stretching. Normally, the superior angle should move inferiorward several additional degrees and with little resistance.

TRP REFERRAL PATTERN. The levator scapulae should be examined for TrPs in the patient who is complaining of pain in the cervicothoracic junction. Active TrPs may also refer pain into the shoulder (see Fig. 17–8).

PIR. Patient and clinician positioning are the same as for the length test. The restrictive barrier is met in the same

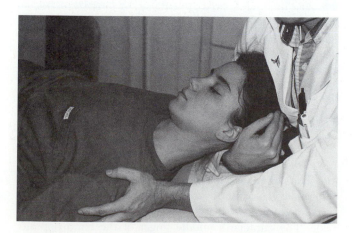

Figure 19–9. Length test for the upper trapezius.

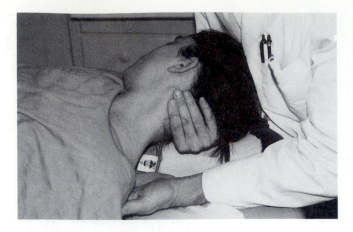

Figure 19–10. Length test for the levator scapulae.

manner as previously described. The patient is instructed to gently press against the clinician's hand that is on the superior angle of the scapula and breathe in for the contraction phase, then stop pushing and breathe out for the relaxation phase. The clinician waits for the release of the barrier and then gently guides the muscle to lengthen by moving the superior angle inferiorward until and new barrier is met.

An alternative method can be utilized which can be particularly useful when the upper part of the muscle contains TrPs. The patient is supine, with the hand on the involved side under his or her buttocks. The restrictive barrier is met by moving the head into flexion, lateral flexion away from the side of involvement, and rotation away from the side of involvement. The segments from C0 to C4 are then rotated as a unit, to ensure that the horizontally configured fibers that attach to C2, C3, and C4 are fully lengthened. The clinician then places his or her other hand just behind the C2–4 segments on the side of involvement (Fig. 19–11). The patient is instructed to press gently against the clinician's hand, look toward the side of

involvement, and breathe in for the contraction phase, then stop pushing, look away from the side of involvement, and breathe out for the relaxation phase. The clinician waits to feel the release of the barrier and then gently guides the muscle to lengthen into lateral flexion without losing the rotation and flexion until a new barrier is met.

PFS. Because the neck is a relatively unstable structure, when performing the vigorous PFS for the levator scapulae, the technique must be altered from that used for PIR. The clinician and patient are positioned the same as for the length test, but the muscle is maintained in a neutral position, rather than being taken to the restrictive barrier. The patient contracts the muscle strongly by pushing up against the clinician's hand as if trying to shrug. The patient holds this for 10 seconds, after which he or she lets go and a fast stretch is applied to the muscle by carefully moving the superior angle straight inferiorward.

SCALENES

POSTURAL ANALYSIS SIGN. Visual prominence of the muscles.

MOVEMENT PATTERN SIGN. Faulty breathing.

LENGTH TEST. None.

TRP REFERRAL PATTERN. TrPs in the scalenes are the most common primary pain generator in patients complaining of neck pain and radiating arm pain. They are also the most common pain generator in cases of "cervical angina" or "pseudocardiac disease." Active TrPs in this muscle can refer pain to the anterior chest, lateral and anterior aspect of the shoulder, down the front and back of the upper arm, and down the radial aspect of the forearm to the lateral hand and fingers. They also send pain to the medial border of the scapula (see Fig. 17–9). In addition to referred pain, the scalenes are a common source of neurovascular compression (see Chapter 9).

> ## ❗ CLINICAL PEARL
>
> This referral of pain into the medial border of the scapula is quite common, and I have seen a number of patients with this complaint who have had a variety of local treatments directed to the ribs, rhomboids, middle trapezius, and thoracic zygapophyseal joints. In many of these cases, simply palpating the scalenes, and locating and stimulating TrPs, exactly reproduced the pain, and treatment of the scalenes rapidly eliminated it.

PIR. The patient is supine, with the hand on the involved side under his or her buttocks. As with PIR of the sternocleidomastoid, the patient's head is off the end of the table. The clinician's middle finger of the hand opposite the side of involvement is placed under the occipital ridge

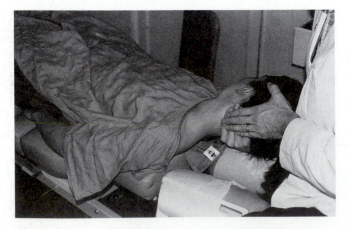

Figure 19–11. PIR for the levator scapulae. Alternative method.

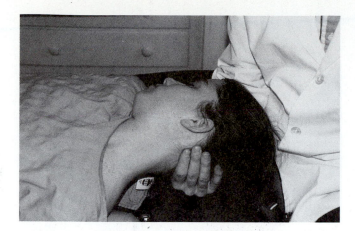

Figure 19–12. Hand placement for PIR for the scalenes.

(Fig. 19–12). The restrictive barrier is met by moving the head into lateral flexion away from the side of involvement, rotation slightly from that side, and extension of the *entire* cervical spine on the thoracic spine. It is essential to maintain a neutral lordosis so that the extension does not

occur at the upper cervical spine (Fig. 19–13A). The hand that is on the side of involvement is placed on the temporal bone. The patient presses against this hand and breathes in for the contraction phase and then stops pushing and breathes out for the relaxation phase (Fig. 19–13B). The clinician waits to feel the release of the barrier and then gently guides the muscle to lengthen into lateral flexion and extension.

If the clinician wants to put particular emphasis on releasing the anterior head of the scalene, the head should be laterally flexed and rotated to a lesser degree and the barrier should be met primarily in extension. The hand on the side of involvement should be placed more frontal (Fig. 19–13C). If the clinician wants to place particular emphasis on the posterior head of the scalene, there should a greater degree of lateral flexion of the head and less extension. The hand on the side of involvement should be placed on the parietal area (Fig. 19–13D). For the middle head, the standard technique is best.

PFS. None, as this is not a muscle that tends to easily become tight.

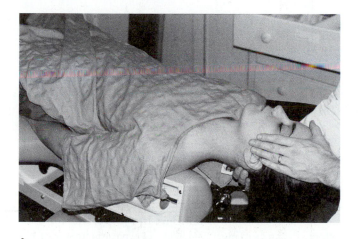

A

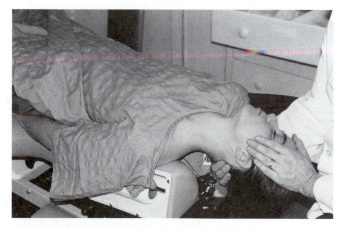

B

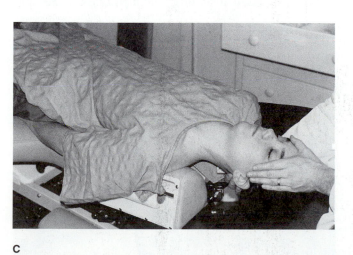

C

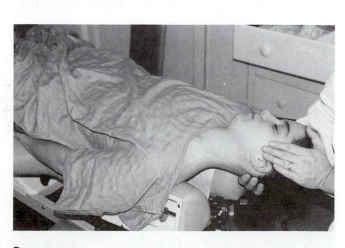

D

Figure 19–13. PIR for the scalenes. **A.** Meeting the barrier. **B.** After release of the barrier. **C.** Emphasis on the anterior head. **D.** Emphasis on the posterior head.

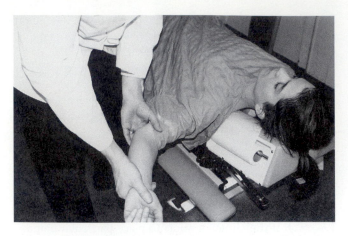

Figure 19–14. Arm placement for length test of the pectoralis major.

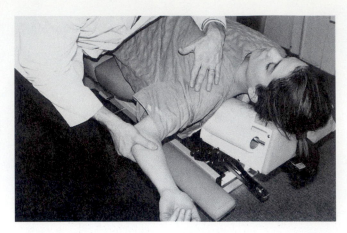

Figure 19–16. Length test of the sternal division of the pectoralis major.

PECTORALIS MAJOR

POSTURAL ANALYSIS SIGN. Rounded shoulder(s).

MOVEMENT PATTERN SIGN. None.

LENGTH TEST. There are actually three different portions of this muscle: the costal division, the sternal division, and the clavicular division. With the patient supine, the clinician supports the chest and prevents trunk rotation by placing his or her arm across the patient's chest (Fig. 19–14). The fingers of this hand can be used to palpate the tension in the fibers. The arm on the involved side is raised so that the shoulder is moved into abduction and external rotation. To test the costal division, the arm should be elevated to approximately 135 degrees of abduction (Fig. 19–15). While stabilizing the chest, the clinician checks for end feel. Normally, the arm should move a few degrees into extension without great resistance and there should be a soft end feel. For the sternal division, the same maneuver is performed but with the arm abducted to 90 degrees (Fig.

19–16). For the clavicular division, the arm should be resting at the side. Supporting the chest, the clinician pushes downward on the anterior aspect of the shoulder and tests for end feel (Fig. 19–17).

TRP REFERRAL PATTERN. Over the chest, into the shoulder, and down the arm to the hand (see Fig. 17–10). Travell and Simons[23] have reported that TrPs in the lower part of the pectoralis major can be a cause of cardiac arrhythmia.

PIR. PIR for this muscle is best done with the patient seated, as this allows for complete relaxation of the muscle by eliminating the tendency for it to contract under the force of gravity. For the costal division, the arm should be abducted to 135 degrees and externally rotated. It is important to be sure to maintain the support of the arm so that the muscle remains relaxed. Slack is taken up in the muscle and the restrictive barrier met by moving the arm into external rotation (Fig. 19–18A). The patient makes a fist and then presses it against the clinician's hand and

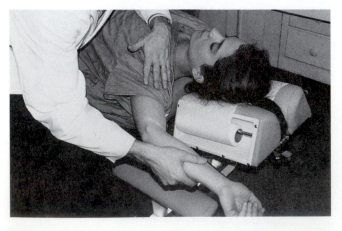

Figure 19–15. Length test for the costal division of the pectoralis major.

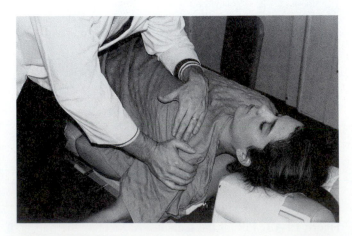

Figure 19–17. Length test for the clavicular division of the pectoralis major.

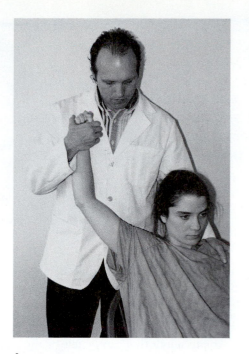
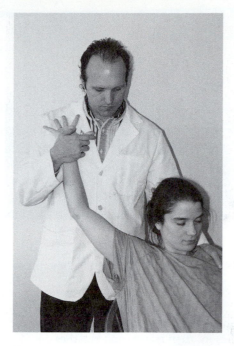

A   B

Figure 19–18. PIR for the costal division of the pectoralis major. **A.** Meeting the barrier. **B.** After release of the barrier.

breathes in for the contraction phase, then stops pushing, opens the hand, and breathes out for the relaxation phase. The clinician then waits for the release of the barrier and guides the muscle to lengthen into external rotation and horizontal abduction (Fig. 19–18B). For the sternal divi-sion, the PIR is the same except the arm is held at 90 de-grees of abduction (Fig. 19–19A and B). For the clavicular division, the patient is again seated and, with the arm at the side. The clinician moves the arm into extension and external rotation and takes up the slack to meet the barrier

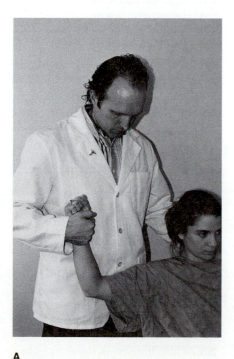
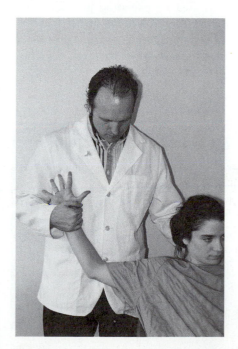

A   B

Figure 19–19. PIR of the sternal division of the pectoralis major. **A.** Meeting the barrier. **B.** After release of the barrier.

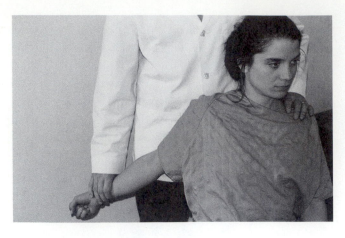

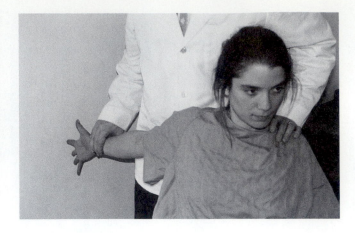

A   **B**

Figure 19–20. PIR of the clavicular division of the pectoralis major. **A.** Meeting the barrier. **B.** After release of the barrier.

(Fig. 19–20A). The patient pushes with a closed fist into flexion and breathes in, then relaxes and breathes out. The clinician waits to feel the release of the barrier and guides the muscle to lengthen into extension (Fig. 19–20B).

PFS. Same as for PIR, but with a hard contraction and fast stretch.

PECTORALIS MINOR

POSTURAL ANALYSIS SIGN. Rounded shoulder(s).

MOVEMENT PATTERN SIGN. Faulty breathing.

LENGTH TEST. None. Tightness is identified by palpation. The muscle can be located by palpating just below the clavicle and having the patient place his or her hand behind the back with the palm facing outward (Fig. 19–21). The clinican asks the patient to move the hand backward

away from the body. This causes contraction of the pectoralis minor that can be felt by the palpating hand.

TRP REFERRAL PATTERN. Over the chest, into the shoulder, and down the medial aspect of the arm to the hand (see Fig. 17–11). Like the scalenes, the pectoralis minor can be a source of irritation or compression of the brachial plexus (see Chap. 9).

PIR. The patient is seated. The clinician raises the arm on the involved side so that the shoulder is moved into abduction and external rotation. One hand is placed on the fisted hand on the involved side and the other is placed on the superior aspect of the scapula (Fig. 19–22A). It is important to be sure to maintain the support of the arm so that the muscle remains relaxed. Slack is taken up in the muscle and the barrier is met by moving the arm straight backward (Fig. 19–22B). The patient presses his or her fist against the clinician's hand and breathes in for the contraction phase, then stops pushing, opens the hand, and breathes out for the relaxation phase. The clinician waits for the release of the barrier and guides the muscle to lengthen into scapular retraction and depression (Fig. 19–22C).

PFS. Same as for PIR, but with a hard contraction and fast stretch.

DIAPHRAGM

POSTURAL ANALYSIS SIGN. None.

MOVEMENT PATTERN SIGN. Faulty breathing.

LENGTH TEST. None

TRP REFERRAL PATTERN. Deep in the anterolateral region of the lower border of the rib cage and in the upper border of the ipsilateral shoulder. The TrPs can be palpated by having the patient seated. The clinician stands behind the patient and, moving the patient into slight trunk flex-

Figure 19–21. Identification of the pectoralis minor can be made by having the patient place his or her hand behind the back and moving the hand straight posteriorward.

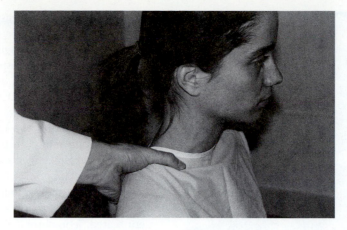

A

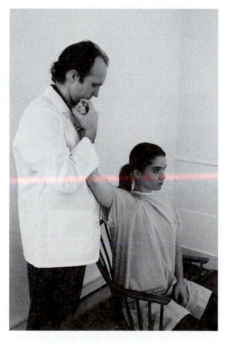

B

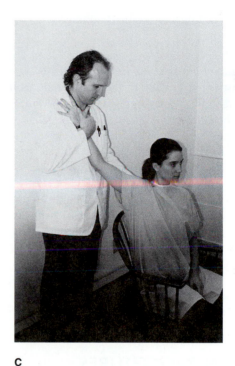

C

Figure 19–22. PIR of the pectoralis minor. **A.** Hand placement. **B.** Meeting the barrier. **C.** After release of the barrier.

ion, places the fingers just inferior to the costal margins and then moves them superiorward under the ribs (Fig. 19–23).

PIR. PIR of the diaphragm has been described by Lewit (personal communication, 1999) and can be performed by the patient. The patient is instructed to breathe in slightly, then hold his or her nose and breath in against a closed glottis. This is held for several seconds, after which the breath is *slowly* let out. The patient repeats this maneuver twice more and, on the third repetition, breathes out fully so that the breath is fully expelled.

PFS. None.

SACROTUBEROUS LIGAMENT/PELVIC DIAPHRAGM

POSTURAL ANALYSIS. None.

MOVEMENT PATTERN SIGN. Positive S reflex.

LENGTH TEST. None.

TRP REFERRAL PATTERN. None in cervical area.

PIR. PIR of the pelvic diaphragm has been described by Lewit[28a] and, as with the respiratory diaphragm, can be performed by the patient. The patient can be seated or lying on his or her side and is first instructed to co-activate the

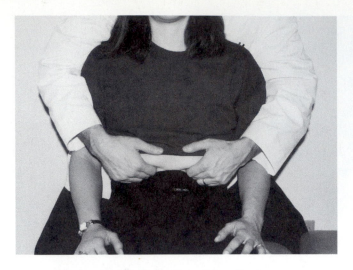

Figure 19–23. Palpation of the diaphragm.

deep abdominal muscles by drawing in the umbilicus. The patient is then instructed to draw in the anal region as if they are attempting to lift the anus straight superiorward. It is important that the patient avoid tensing the gluteal muscles during this maneuver. The patient is instructed to hold this contraction for several seconds, followed by slow relaxation. This is performed a total of three times.

A maneuver that may help the patient to sense the contraction of the pelvic diaphragm is to hold his or her nose and then attempt to breathe in against a closed glottis, then repeat the PIR procedure. This often enhances the contraction of the muscles and gives the patient a better sense of the movement created by the pelvic diaphragm, but should only be used for this purpose, and should not be a regular part of the PIR procedure.

Both the sacrotuberous ligament and pelvic diaphragm can also be treated with ischemic compression.

FACILITATION PROCEDURES

DEEP CERVICAL FLEXORS

POSTURAL ANALYSIS SIGN. Forward head posture.

MOVEMENT PATTERN SIGN. Chin poke on cervical flexion; chin poke, excessive shaking, flexion of the entire cervical spine or extension on cervical stability test.

TRP REFERRAL PATTERN. No referred pain pattern has been delineated for these muscles.

RS. The patient is lying supine. The clinician places one hand under the patient's chin and the other under the occiput. The patient is instructed to resist as the clinician rhythmically tries to pull the chin forward and upward, attempting to extend the upper cervical spine (Fig. 19–24A).

If the deep cervical flexors are so inhibited that they are not able to provide adequate resistance using the preceding technique (this would be evidenced by inability of the patient to resist extension the upper cervical spine), an alternate technique can be used. With this technique, the patient is sitting and a tongue depressor is placed in the patient's mouth and the patient is instructed to *gently* bite down on it while pressing his or her tongue against it. It is important that the patient sit in good postural alignment, with no forward head placement. The clinician performs RS by gently pulling the tongue depressor outward while the patient prevents chin poke (Fig. 19–24B). It is important that the clinician pressure be light so that the tongue depressor does not come out of the patient's mouth.

Ultimately, the optimal direction for RS of the deep cervical flexors is rotation.[29] This is performed with the patient seated. The clinician places one hand on the side of the head near the temporal bone and the other over the chin on the same side (Fig. 19–24C). The patient is instructed to tuck his or her chin, and RS is applied by the clinician attempting to push the head into rotation away from the side of contact. See Chapter 25 for additional facilitation methods using RS.

PATIENT EXERCISES. Chin tucks are performed in the sitting position in the beginning, with later transition to prone as the patient's deep cervical flexors become more active. The patient starts in the seated position and is instructed tuck his or her chin as far as possible (Fig. 19–25A). It is important that the head translate straight backward, with the upper cervical spine flexing and the lower cervical spine extending. When performing chin tucks in the prone position, the patient can lie on a bed or bench with his or her head hanging over the edge (Fig. 19–25B). The same chin-tuck movement is performed.

Supine cervical flexion is performed with the patient lying supine with his or her head supported. The patient is instructed to first tuck the chin, then raise the head off the support surface so the cervical spine moves into flexion (Fig. 19–26A and B). These exercises are designed primarily for cortical, isotonic strengthening. For subcortical stabilization exercises see Chapter 25.

MIDDLE AND LOWER TRAPEZIUS

POSTURAL ANALYSIS SIGN. Elevated shoulder, displaced medial border of the scapula.

MOVEMENT PATTERN SIGN. Decreased, absent, or reversed rotation of the scapula on shoulder abduction test; elevation or displacement of the scapula on push-up test.

TRP REFERRAL PATTERN. TrPs in these muscles can be an important cause of suboccipital headache. They can also cause pain in the shoulder and medial border of the scapula (see Fig. 17–5).

RS. There are several different methods by which activity in the middle and lower trapezius can be facilitated. The choice of methods is determined by clinician and patient preference, and also by the degree of inhibition that is present. It is usually best to start with the standard method and

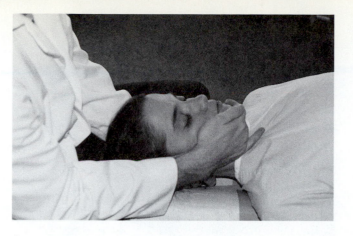

A

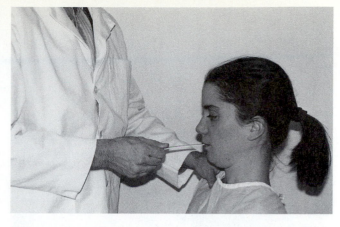

B

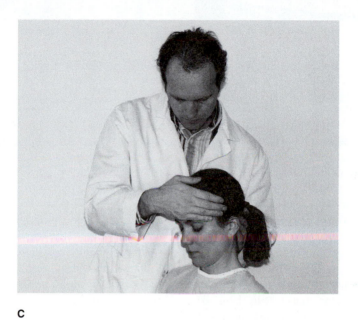

C

Figure 19–24. Rhythmic stabilization of the deep cervical flexors. **A.** In the supine position. **B.** Peel back level. **C.** In rotation.

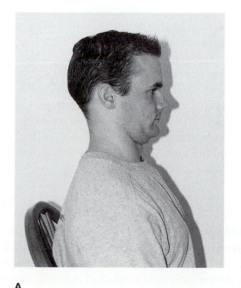

A

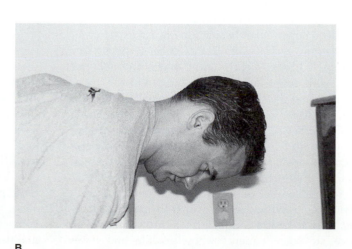

B

Figure 19–25. Chin tucks. **A.** In the seated position. **B.** In the prone position.

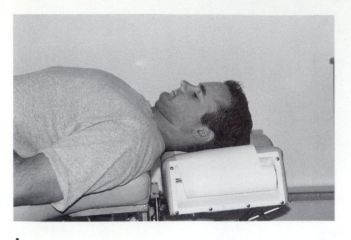

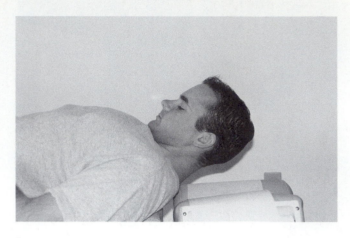

A

B

Figure 19–26 Cervical flexion. **A.** Initial upper cervical portion. **B.** Lower cervical portion.

monitor the response in the muscle. With the standard method, the patient is prone and the clinician stands at either side. The patient's arms are held at approximately a 45-degree angle at the sides, externally rotated and with the fingers opened as wide as possible (Fig. 19–27A). This position of external rotation with the fingers as wide as possible is important, as it primes the middle and lower trapezius for maximum activation. The clinician leans over the patient, being sure to rest his or her bodyweight on the table, and places his or her hands onto the posterior aspect of the thenar portion of the patient's hands (Fig. 19–27B). The clinician performs RS by pushing the patient's hands downward toward the floor while the patient resists.

If the patient can handle the technique at this level without excessive activation of the upper trapezii, which would be evidenced by elevation of the shoulders, the arms should gradually be raised to 90 degrees of abduction, and RS should be performed in this position (Fig. 19–27C). Up to this point, the primary focus has been on the middle trapezius. To place focus on the lower trapezius, RS should be performed with the arms raised to 110 degrees (Fig. 19–27D). It is important to watch closely for elevation of the shoulders at each point. If this occurs, the patient should be peeled back to the point at which this does not take place, with progression made on future visits.

If elevation of the shoulders occurs even with the arms held at a 45-degree angle, the patient should be peeled back to a lower level. The first peel-back level to attempt is with the patient lying prone. The clinician passively prepositions the scapula into depression and slight retraction (Fig. 19–28A). The clinician then instructs the patient to hold the scapula in this position while pressure is applied to the inferior angle of the scapula in the direction of elevation (Fig. 19–28B) and RS is performed in this manner.

There are some patients whose middle and lower trapezii are so inhibited that they are not able to maintain

scapular depression and retraction even in this position, in which case they must be peeled back further. In such cases, the patient can be placed in the side-lying position with the clinician standing at the anterior. The clinician passively prepositions the scapula into depression and slight retraction, in the same manner as the previous peel-back position (Fig. 19–29A). The clinician then instructs the patient to hold the scapula in this position while pressure is applied to the inferior angle of the scapula in the direction of elevation and protraction (Fig. 19–29B) and RS is performed in this manner.

PATIENT EXERCISES. One of the most important exercises to give a patient with inhibition of the middle and lower trapezii is the Brügger (see Chap. 25). This exercise not only activates the middle and lower trapezii, but also inhibits the upper trapezius pectoralis minor, and levator scapulae. Thus, it is especially important in the early stages when there may be significant inhibition of these muscles as well as hyperactivity in the upper trapezius or levator scapulae, or both.

Another important exercise is angels. These can be begun on the floor. The patient is supine with his or her shoulders and elbows abducted to 90 degrees, with hands supinated and fingers open as wide as possible. The knees and hips are flexed and the pelvis is anteriorly tilted so that the lumbar lordosis is accentuated (Fig. 19–30A). The patient is instructed to maintain pressure of the arms and hands against the floor and slowly slide his or her arms upward (Fig. 19–30B), then downward (Fig. 19–30C).

An advanced level of this exercise is to have the patient perform the angels while standing against a wall. Here, the head, thoracic spine, and buttocks should be in contact with the wall. The chin should be slightly tucked and the pelvis anteriorly rotated so that the lumbar lordosis is accentuated (Fig. 19–31). The arms are moved up-

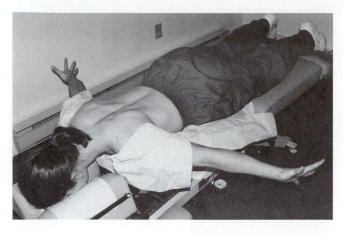

A

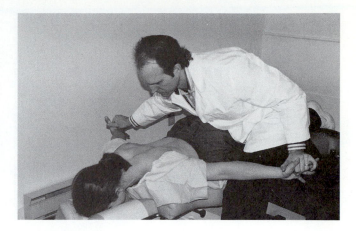

B

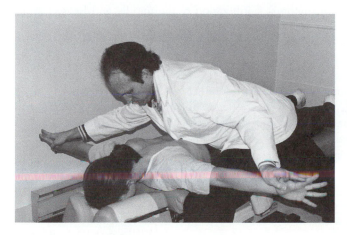

C

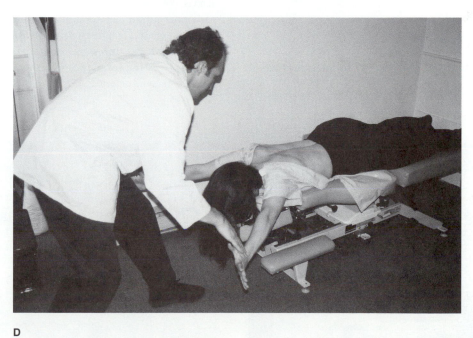

D

Figure 19–27. Rhythmic stabilization of the middle and lower trapezii. **A.** Initial position. **B.** Application of clinician pressure. **C.** Advanced level. **D.** Placing focus on lower trapezii.

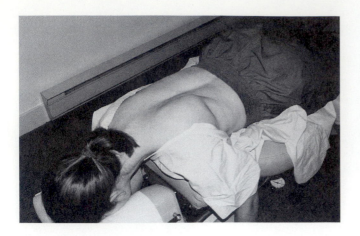

A

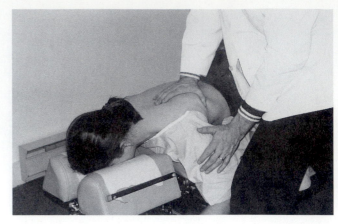

B

Figure 19–28. Peel-back level for rhythmic stabilization of the middle and lower trapezii. **A.** Initial position. **B.** Application of clinician pressure.

ward and downward in the same manner as was done on the floor. It is important to ask the patient where he or she feels the greatest muscle activity. The answer should normally be between the scapulae, in the area of the middle and lower trapezii. If the patient feels the exercise primarily in the area of the upper trapezii or levator scapulae, these muscles may be dominating the movement and the patient must be peeled back to the floor exercise. See Chapter 25 for other exercises that can be used to facilitate the middle and lower trapezii.

SERRATUS ANTERIOR

POSTURAL ANALYSIS SIGN. Winging of the inferior angle of the scapula.

MOVEMENT PATTERN SIGN. Winging of the inferior angle of the scapula upon lowering during the shoulder abduction or push-up tests.

TRP REFERRAL PATTERN. Over the axilla and lateral rib cage, occasionally along the lower medial border of the scapula and the medial arm and hand (Fig. 19–32).

RS. There are several methods by which RS can be applied in the activation of an inhibited serratus anterior. The challenge with facilitation of this muscle is minimizing the activity of the pectoralis minor during the procedure. The pectoralis minor can commonly be found to be tight or hypertonic, in the presence of an inhibited serratus anterior, and this can interfere with effective activation of the serratus. It is important to give these patients the Brügger exercise (see Chapter 25).

A

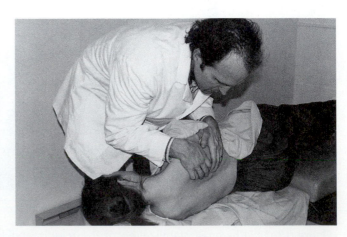

B

Figure 19–29. Further peel back for rhythmic stabilization of the middle and lower trapezii. **A.** Initial position. **B.** Application of clinician pressure.

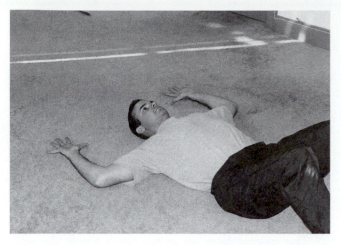

A

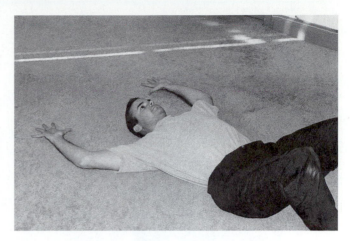

B

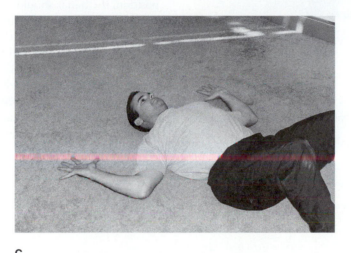

C

Figure 19–30. Floor angels. **A.** Starting position. **B.** Fully elevated position. **C.** Fully depressed position.

As with the middle and lower trapezius, having the hand open and the fingers spread as wide as possible is important in the facilitation of the serratus anterior, particularly as a closed fist tends to promote activation of the pectoralis minor, allowing this muscle to dominate the activity. A basic level method of RS is to have the patient supine, with the arm outstretched and the fingers spread (Fig. 19–33A). The clinician performs RS by stabilizing the scapula and pushing the arm in the direction of shoulder flexion (Fig. 19–33B).

Another method is to have the patient standing with his or her hands on the wall with the fingers spread as wide as possible and elbows extended (Fig. 19–34A). The hands should be slightly above shoulder level to place emphasis on the serratus anterior. The clinician pushes against the mid-thoracic area toward the wall and performs RS in this manner (Fig. 19–34B). The advantage of this method is that it activates the serratus anterior in a closed chain environment.

Another method of facilitation of the serratus anterior in a closed chain environment is to have the patient in the quadruped position with the hand on the involved side on the floor and the other hand in a handshake-like manner (Fig. 19–35). The clinician then performs RS in the direction of elbow flexion, extension, and movement left and right while the patient maintains stability of the scapula on the side that is in contact with the ground. It is important for the clinician to watch for winging of the scapula during this activity.

PATIENT EXERCISES. One effective exercise in strengthening the serratus anterior is the push-up with a plus. One must be very careful, however, to only use this exercise with a patient in whom no hypertonicity has been demonstrated in the pectoralis minor, as this exercise highly activates this muscle,[37] and hypertonicity in the pectoralis minor can significantly interfere with the function of the serratus anterior.[38] Also, patients with marked inhibition of the serratus

Figure 19–31. Wall angels.

may not be able to perform this exercise. In both these situations, peeling the patient back to the next exercise is necessary.

The patient is in the push-up position and performs a regular push-up but at the top adds a "plus" to the movement by pushing the shoulders into full protraction (Fig. 19–36). If the patient is not strong enough to perform this exercise in this manner, he or she can be peeled back to performing it with the knees on the floor. A further peel-back level would be to have the patient perform it against the wall.

The push-up with a plus exercise effectively activates the serratus anterior in an isotonic fashion. However, to train this muscle for stabilization, plyometric push-ups against the wall are far more effective. This exercise has the advantage of activating the serratus with far less involvement of the pectoralis minor than was seen with the push-up with a plus exercise, as well as facilitating quick, reactive stabilizing contractions of the serratus as opposed to cortically-driven isotonic contractions.

The patient places his or her hands against the wall with the elbows bent (Fig. 19–37A). As with RS in this position, the hands should be slightly above shoulder level. The patient then quickly pushes away from the wall so that the hands lose contact with the wall (Fig. 19–37B), followed by return to the wall (Fig. 19–37C). It is important that the landing on the wall be as "soft" as possible, so that the serratus is forced to work in its stabilizing function. An advanced level of this exercise is to have the patient maintain elbow extension throughout the exercise, causing the serratus to provide the impulse in both the concentric and eccentric portions of the maneuver. See Chapter 25 for other exercises that can be used to facilitate the serratus anterior.

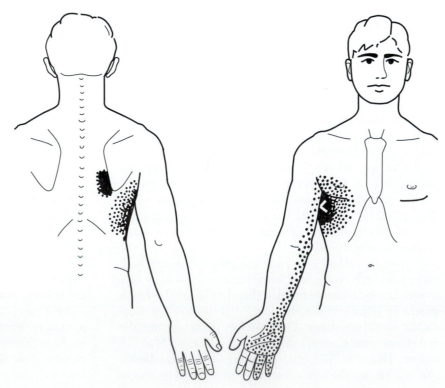

Figure 19–32. Referred pain pattern from TrPs in the serratus anterior muscle.

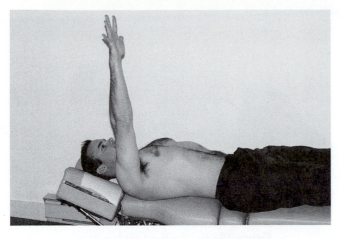

A

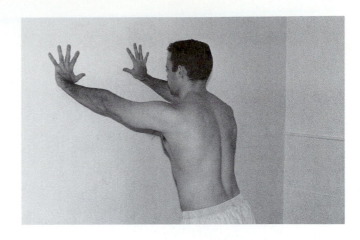

A

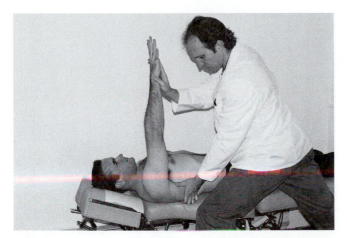

B

Figure 19–33. Rhythmic stabilization of the serratus anterior—basic level. **A.** Initial position. **B.** Application of clinician pressure.

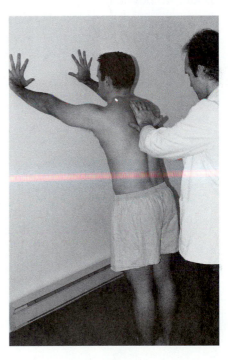

B

Figure 19–34. Rhythmic stabilization of the serratus anterior against the wall. **A.** Initial position. **B.** Application of clinician pressure.

CONCLUSION

As is the case in any area of the body, successful treatment of dysfunction in the locomotor system is dependent on accurate diagnosis. This means effectively identifying precisely the type of dysfunction that is present and understanding the physiological and clinical features of it so that the appropriate treatment approach can be taken. In this chapter, methods by which dysfunction in the muscular system and other soft tissues can be detected and treated were presented. This information, combined with that in Chapters 13 and 18, is designed to instruct in the primarily manual methods of diagnosis and treatment. Later, we will explore other methods, primarily exercise based, that can be used to further improve function in patients with cervical-related syndromes.

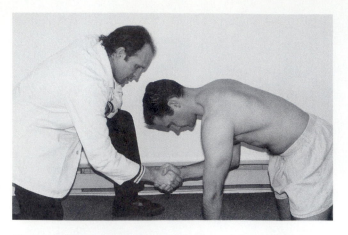

Figure 19–35. Rhythmic stabilization of the serratus anterior in the quadruped position.

Figure 19–36. Push-up with a plus.

A

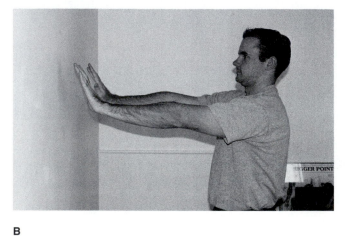

B

C

Figure 19–37. Plyometric push-ups against the wall. **A.** Initial position. **B.** The patient pushes away from the wall. **C.** Final position.

REFERENCES

1. Lewit K. Management of musclular pain associated with articular dysfunction. *Man Med* 1991;6(4):140–142.
2. Davidoff RA. Skeletal muscle tone and the misunderstood stretch reflex. *Neurology* 1992;42:951–963.
3. Integration of behavioral and relaxation approaches into the treatment of chronic pain and insomnia. NIH Technology Assessment Panel on Integration of Behavioral and Relaxation Approaches Into the Treatment of Chronic Pain and Insomnia. *JAMA* 1996;276(4):313–318.
4. Wolpaw JR. Reflexes capable of change: Models for the study of memory. *Fed Proc* 1982;42:2146.
5. Wolpaw JR, O'Keefe JA. Adaptive plasticity in the primate spinal stretch reflex: Evidence for a two-phase process. *J Neurosci* 1984;4:2718–2724.
6. Wolpaw JR. Adaptive plasticity in the primate spinal stretch reflex: Reversal and redevelopment. *Brain Res* 1983;278:299–304.
7. Evatt ML, Wolf SL, Segal RL. Modification of human spinal stretch reflexes: Preliminary studies. *Neurosci Lett* 1989;105:350–355.
8. Kabat-Zinn J, Lipworth L, Burney R. The clinical use of mindfulness meditation for the self-regulation of chronic pain. *J Behav Med* 1985;8(2):163–190.
9. Grice AS. Muscle tonus changes following manipulation. *J Can Chiro Assoc* 1974;18:29–31.
10. Shambaugh P. Changes in electrical activity on muscles resulting from chiropractic adjustment: A pilot study. *J Manipulative Physiol Ther* 1987;19:300–304.
11. Thabe H. Electromyography as a tool to document diagnostic findings and therapeutic results associated with somatic dysfunction in the upper cervical spinal joints and sacroiliac joints. *Man Med* 1986;2:53–58.
12. Herzog W, Conway PJ, Zgang YZ, et al. Reflex response associated with manipulative treatment of the thoracic spine. *J Neuromusculoskel Sys* 1994;2(3):124–130.
13. Guimaraes ACS. Reflex responses associated with manipulative treatments on the thoracic spine: A pilot study. *J Manipulative Physiol Ther* 1995;18(4):233–236.
14. Herzog W. Mechanical and physiological responses to spinal manipulative treatments. *J Neuromusculoskel Sys* 1995;3(1):1–9.
15. Lewit K. Postisometric relaxation in combination with other methods of muscular facilitation and inhibition. *Man Med* 1986;2:101–104.
16. Schieppati M, Crenna P. From activity to rest: The gating of excitatory autogenic afferences from the relaxing muscle in man. *Exp Brain Res* 1984;56:448–459.
17. Guissard N, Duchateau J, Hainaut K. Muscle stretching and motoneuron excitability. *Eur J Physiol* 1988;58:47–52.
18. Magnusson SP, Simonsen EB, Aagaard P, et al. Mechanical and physiological responses to stretching with and without preisometric contraction in human skeletal muscle. *Arch Phys Med Rehabil* 1996;77:373–378.
19. Sachse J, Berger M. Cervical mobilization induced by eye movement. *Man Med* 1989;4(4):154–156.
20. Lewit K. *Manipulative Therapy in the Rehabilitation of the Locomotor System*. Oxford: Butterworth-Heinemann; 1991.
21. Indahl A, Kaigle AM, Reikeras O, Holm SH. Interaction between the porcine lumbar intervertebral disc, zygapophyseal joints and paraspinal muscles. *Spine* 1997;22(24):2834–2840.
22. Cohen JH, Schneider MJ. Receptor-tonus technique: An overview. *Chiro Tech* 1990;2:13–16.
23. Travell JG, Simons DG. *Myofascial Pain and Dysfunction: The Trigger Point Manual*. Vol. 1. Baltimore, Md: Williams and Wilkins; 1983.
24. Schneider MJ. Chiropractic management of myofascial and muscular disorders. In: Lawrence D, ed. *Advances in Chiropractic*. Vol 3. St. Louis, Mo: Mosby-Yearbook; 1996:55–88.
25. Garvey TA, Marks MR, Wiesel SW. A prospective, randomized, double-blind evaluation of tripper-point injection therapy for low-back pain. *Spine* 1989;14:962–964.
26. Hong CZ, Chen YC, et al. Immediate effects of various physical medicine modalities on pain threshold of an active myofascial trigger point. *J Musculoskel Pain* 1993;1:37–53.
27. Jaeger B, Reeves JL. Quantification of changes in myofascial trigger point sensitivity with the pressure algometer following passive stretch. *Pain* 1986;27:203–210.
28. Travell JG, Simons DG. *Myofascial Pain and Dysfunction: The Trigger Point Manual*. Vol 2. Baltimore, Md: Williams and Wilkins; 1992.
28a. Lewit K. Chain reactions in the locomotor system in the light of coactivation patterns based on developmental neurology. *J Orthop Med* 1999;in press.

29. Vujnovich AL, Dawson NJ. The effect of therapeutic muscle stretch on neural processing. *J Orthop Sports Phys Ther* 1994;20:145–153.
30. Taylor DC, Dalton JD, Seaber AV, Garrett WE. Viscoelastic properties of muscle-tendon units. *Am J Sports Med* 1990;18(3):300–309.
31. Murphy DR. Hyperalgesic skin zone: A case report. *Chiro Tech* 1992;4(2):124–127.
32. Travell JG. Identification of myofascial trigger point syndromes: A case of atypical facial neuralgia. *Arch Phys Med Rehabil* 1981;62:100–106.
33. Leahy PM. Improved treatments for carpal tunnel syndrome. *Chiro Sports Med* 1995;9:6–9.
34. Adler SS, Beckers D, Buck M. *PNF in Practice: An Illustrated Guide.* Berlin: Springer-Verlag; 1993.
35. Jull G. Management of cervical headache. *Man Ther* 1997;2:182–190.
36. Diener I. The effect of levator scapula tightness on the cervical spine: Proposal of another length test. *J Man Manip Ther* 1998;6(2):78–86.
37. Mannion AF, Dumas GA, Stevenson JM, Cooper RG. The influence of muscle fiber size and type distribution on electromyographic measures of back muscle fatigability. *Spine* 1998;23(5):576–584.
38. Ludewig PM, Cook TM, Nawoczenski DA. Three-dimensional scapular orientation and muscle activity at selected positions of humeral elevation. *J Orthop Sports Phys Ther* 1996;24:57–65.

APPENDIX 19A

Active Release Techniques for the Cervical Spine

P. Michael Leahy & John M. Schneider

"The best answer is the simplest one. Finding it is complicated."

—P. M. L.

The answer we found is simple in principle, but it is not easy to perform effectively. Many providers, because of their extensive experience in soft tissue work or years of didactic study, make the mistake of assuming that Active Release Techniques (ART) are easy; however, there are no shortcuts. Only years of hard work will produce results.

Muscle and soft tissue dysfunction in the cervical spine are difficult problems for physicians to treat effectively. Many physicians are not properly trained in the evaluation and treatment of these conditions. Cervical dysfunction is often overlooked as an incidental finding that with time should heal without any intervention other than rest, anti-inflammatory medications, and muscle relaxants. Because of this mindset, too many patients are wrongfully being led down a road that leads to chronicity.

The changes in health care in the 1990s and into the new millennium are demanding more efficient and cost-effective ways of handling soft tissue injuries. Proper understanding of the anatomy and physiology of these tissues is essential. The pathophysiological process behind soft tissue dysfunction also needs to be understood if treatment of these conditions is to be successful. The ART soft tissue management system takes into account all of these factors, giving the physician the ability to treat these conditions effectively. Recent studies show that ART is a promising new treatment.[1]

ART treatment is a hands-on touch and case management system that allows a practitioner to diagnose and treat soft tissue injuries.[2] In this case, soft tissue refers primarily to muscle, nerve, fascia, and ligaments or tendons. Key entities include repetitive stress, adhesion, tissue hypoxia, and joint dysfuntion. While this definition seems overly simple, it serves as a starting point on which to build the rest of this discussion.

MECHANISM OF INJURY

To understand soft tissue injury, it is important to understand the mechanism of the injury. There are three types of injuries to the soft tissue that we are concerned with: acute injury, constant pressure or tension injury, and repetitive motion injury.

An acute injury is the result of a specific and direct trauma to the tissue. This immediately results in inflammation. The inflammatory cascade, once initiated, will lead to the cumulative injury cycle if not properly treated.[3]

The constant pressure or tension injury decreases circulation, leading to hypoxia. Cellular retention of calcium, poor repair, and altered function are but a few of the major results. Isometric contraction of a muscle and the muscle tension of poor posture are good examples of this mechanism.

Repetitive motion injury is related to specific physical factors. Like acute injury to tissue, a repetitive motion injury also leads to hypoxia and the cumulative injury cycle. The law of repetitive motion is used to help define the injury to the tissue. The formula used is presented in Figure 19A–1.

Vibration while using a jackhammer, for example, results in a number of repetitions **(N)** that is high, an amplitude of each repetition **(A)** that is low, and a relaxation time between repetitions **(R)** that is low. The result is an insult to the tissues that is very high. Posture that is poor and unchanging results in constant high forces in the musculature. In this situation, force or tension of each repetition of a percent of maximum muscle strength **(F)** is high, **A** is near zero, and **R** is essentially zero. The tissue insult is therefore high. A keyboard operator may experience 10,000 repetitions per day, a force of 2 percent of maximum, an amplitude of 10 percent of available, and a relaxation time of zero because the muscles never relax. This would also result in a high insult to the tissue. If the insult to the tissue is great enough it will lead to the cumulative injury cycle.

The cycle has three possible starting points depending on the injury. Each factor causes the next one in the cycle, which continually feeds the next part of the cycle (see Fig. 19A–2).

Acute injury enters the cumulative injury cycle (see Fig. 19A–2) with an original injury to the tissue that causes an inflammatory response by the tissue. This response causes fibroblasts to be attracted to the area, forming an adhesion in the tissue or between the tissue and its surrounding structures. If this is not treated properly and is allowed to persist for an extended period of time, the tissue becomes tight and weak. This leads to the tissue following the chronic portion of the cumulative injury cycle.

Repetitive injury to the tissue causes the muscles to tighten. The tissues that are adjacent may also become tight. As a result of weak and tight tissues, the internal forces acting on the tissues rise. These internal forces, friction, tension, and pressure, when high enough, can cause acute injury or inflammation without any external forces being applied to the tissues. Friction, tension, and pressure can also cause a decrease in the circulation to the tissue. This leads the tissue down the chronic portion of the cumulative injury cycle. The cellular hypoxia that is created chemotactically attracts fibroblasts to the area, which form an adhesion between two structures or within the muscle itself.[4] This adhesion causes the tissue to become weaker and tighter, further driving the cycle forward.

Many extrinsic factors affect the cycle, but they do so in predictable ways. Smoking, for example, tends to make circulation less efficient and helps perpetuate the cycle. Diabetes has a similar affect. Thyroid deficiencies tend to increase tension in the musculature and influence the total insult to the tissues as well as the "weak and tight" factor of the cumulative injury cycle. Hormonal changes with hysterectomy, excessive body weight, and pregnancy all lead to predictable changes in the factors involved.

DIAGNOSIS

Diagnosis of the correct soft tissue injury is important to maximize the likelihood of success in treatment. ART uses a three-part diagnosis; it is normal for the diagnosis to be made during the treatment phase. The first part is the identification of nature of the lesion, such as a tear, adhesion, or myofascitis. Next, the exact tissue that is involved in the injury must be known. Finally, the syndrome that is caused must be identified (e.g., rotator cuff syndrome, lateral epicondylitis, etc.).

When the physician is examining the area of the injury, it is important to evaluate four factors, as follows: (1) the texture of the tissue, (2) the tension of the injured and surrounding tissues, (3) the movement of the tissues, and (4) the function of the tissues.

The texture of the tissue tells the physician many things. Soft tissue undergoes many changes, all of which have their own unique feel. With an acute injury (24 to 72 hours postinjury), the tissue is inflamed and edematous. It is typically tender to palpation. After the inflammatory stage, the muscles become altered in tension and texture. The tissue now has hypertonic fibers and palpable bands that feel "stringy" to the touch. This change happens between 2 days and 2 weeks postinjury. As this cumulative process proceeds, the texture of the tissue develops into a lumpy, palpable adhesion. As this injury becomes more chronic, the tissue becomes more leathery in its texture. This takes a minimum of 3 months after the original injury.

The law of repetitive motion

$$I = \frac{NF}{AR}$$

In this model the factors are:

  I = insult to the tissue
  N = number of repetitions
  F = force or tension of each repetition as percent of
     maximum muscle strength
  A = amplitude of each repetition
  R = relaxation time between repetition (lack of pressure
     or tension on the tissue)

Figure 19A–1. The law of repetitive motion.

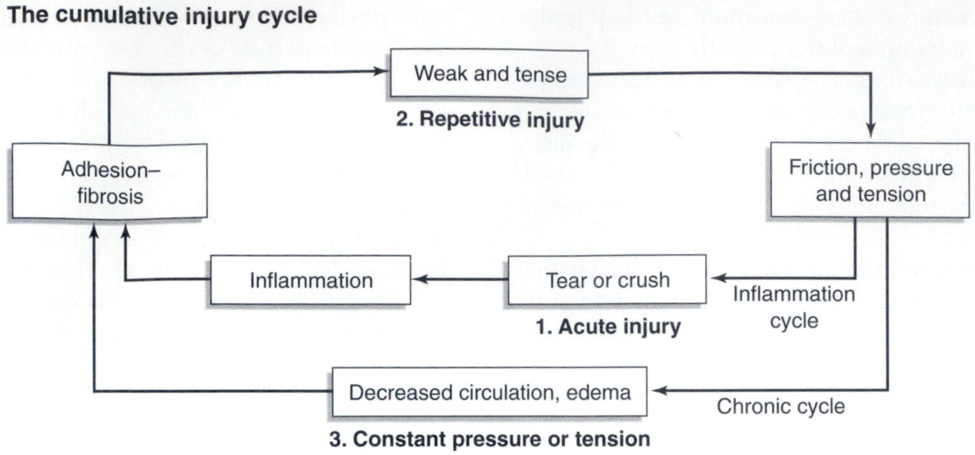

The cumulative injury cycle

Figure 19A–2. The cumulative injury cycle.

Tissue tension is difficult to quantify objectively. It takes the physician time to develop the touch necessary to distinguish tension between tissues. It is helpful to compare the tension in the injured tissue to the surrounding tissues and also to the tissue in the contralateral areas. Palpation of the injured tissue will reveal an increased tension during movements before surrounding tissues will draw tight. This tension may occur in any direction.

The movement of the tissues must also be identified to aid in the correct diagnosis. The joints and soft tissue must move together. Pain during active motion, passive motion, or both will determine what structures are involved. Pain with active motion, only, can be due to the contraction of the muscle. Pain with passive motion, only, will tend to suggest ligamentous, fascial, or capsular damage. Pain during both active and passive motion can implicate any of the tissues. The best way isolate the structures that are involved is to apply tension on a specific tissue during a specific movement and repeat with surrounding structures until the cause of the dysfunction is located.

Tissue function is the easiest of the four factors to assess. The standard examination techniques apply for soft tissue function. Sensory, motor, and reflex examinations are followed.

TREATMENT

After the lesion is found, it is treated by manipulation while drawing it under a specific contact. The most common method is to move the tissue from a shortened position to a fully lengthened position while the contact passes longitudinally along the soft tissue fibers and the lesion. As increased tension is palpated, the movement in the direction of tension is resisted.

Certain guidelines must be followed to ensure maximum benefit with minimum complication. If these rules are not understood and followed, patient welfare may be compromised. The rules are as follows:

1. *Use soft contact:* Use the specific contact described in the protocol. Hands-on instruction is most beneficial in learning a proper touch.
2. *Begin active, work longitudinally:* For many reasons, this method effectively breaks the adhesions in and between tissues. Although restrictions may be found in any direction, it is most important to establish longitudinal freedom of motion within a muscle. Then, if necessary, treat in other directions.
3. *Use active motion whenever possible:* This provides the patient with a sense of control and also inhibits pain. The methods of active motion are designed to maximize relative motion between tissues.
4. *Use slow motion:* If any motions are fast or quick, the tolerance of the patient is reduced and the muscle will tense.
5. *Evaluate patient tolerance:* The pressure and number of passes is always limited to patient tolerance. In general, three to five passes over a given area is the limit.
6. *Evaluate tissue tolerance:* It is sometimes necessary to delay a treatment due to tissue intolerance. This is indicated by physical as well as nonphysical indicators. When the tissue is sensitive from the previous treatment, it is better to delay the treatment and decrease the frequency of visits.
7. *For most long passes, work along the direction of venous and lymphatic flow:* Bruising and lymphatic edema are almost completely avoided by accurate methods. When motions are made against venous or lymphatic flow they are very short.
8. *Frequency = alternate days:* Treatment frequency is never more often than alternate days. Daily treat-

ment may lead to tissue intolerance and protracted treatment plans. In some cases, an even longer period between treatments is necessary.

PROTOCOLS

ART uses specific protocols for each muscle and peripheral nerve entrapment. Each protocol has specific hand contacts, patient motions, anatomical locations, and type of tension that must be learned in a "hands-on" environment. There are over 250 specific protocols for the human body. For example, treatment of the spine for symptom patterns of headache from the occipital to orbital regions would include soft-tissue consideration using the following specific protocols for various headache patterns (Table 19A–1).

The suboccipital muscles are best treated in the supine position. These muscles often entrap the occipital nerves or cause tension at the base of the skull which if left untreated will exert a tension on the aponeurosis over the top of the skull to the occular muscles. This causes the headache that seems to be "somewhere behind the eye."

The patient's head and neck are placed in the extended position with lateral flexion and rotation toward the lesion in order to shorten the muscles and fascia as much as possible. With 3 to 4 fingers, the traction of the tissue is accomplished ending at the lesion. As the head and neck are flexed, rotated, and laterally flexed away from the lesion, the contact is moved through the lesion with

Table 19A–1: ART® Treatment Protocols for Symptoms Related to Headache[2]

Greater occipital nerve at semispinalis capitis

Greater occipital nerve at superior nuchal line

Third occipital nerve at trapezius/semispinalis capitis

Lesser occipital nerve and great auricular nerve at sternocleidomastoid

Dorsal ramus of C-2 at inferior oblique

Suboccipital nerve at superior oblique

Upper trapezius

Semispinalis capitis

Splenius capitis

Superior oblique

Inferior oblique

Rectus capitis posterior

Longissimus capitis

Vertebral artery tension test

specific manipulation. Care must be taken to avoid excessive pressure, which may duplicate the headache pain to an inordinate degree. Manipulation of the atlanto-occipital joint after treatment is usually easier to accomplish and necessary as part of the treatment protocol.

REFERENCES

1. Mooney V. Overuse syndromes of the upper extremity: Rational and effective treatment. *J Musculoskel Med* 1998; Aug:11–18.
2. Leahy PM. Active Release Techniques Soft Tissue Management System/Spine, Active Release Techniques LLP, 1998.
3. Leahy PM. Improved treatments for carpal tunnel. *Chiro Sports Med* 1995;9:6–9.
4. Dawes KE, Peacock AJ. Characterization of fibroblast mitogens and chemoattractants produced by endothelial cells exposed to hypoxia. *Am J Resp Cell Mol Biol* 1994;10(5):552–559.

CHAPTER 20

Chain Reactions Related to the Cervical Spine

KAREL LEWIT & PAVEL KOLÁR

"Function is as real as Anatomy. It is, however, even more fundamental, for Structure develops to fulfill a Function and not the other way round."

"Every type of manipulation (including mobilization or thrust) whether applied to joints or to soft tissues is nothing but a form of passive motion, intended to restore impaired mobility."

—K.L., P.K.

INTRODUCTION

Interest in the spinal column is, as we know, the result of the steadily increasing numbers of patients suffering from pain of spinal (cervical) origin. One of the reasons why the health professions have so far been unable to deal effectively with this problem is that in the large majority of patients, there appears to be no adequate underlying cause for their pain—no well-defined pathological (structural) lesion explaining the condition. The experienced practitioner, however, whether medical physician, physiotherapist, chiropractor, osteopath, or even massage therapist, will find plenty of clinical signs such as faulty posture, movement restriction, soft tissue changes, muscular trigger points, hyperalgesic skin zones, and so on, related to the patient's pain. These patients are, therefore, classified or diagnosed as suffering from "nonspecific" or "idiopathic" pain.

In reality, these patients are suffering from quite specific and clinically diagnosable changes in function of the motor system, and it is not their fault that most of the health professions do not classify nor diagnose these changes as such. This is the more regrettable as changes in function are by definition reversible (i.e., treatable); however, treatment is by no means simple, it must be specific to be effective, and it requires a specific diagnostic approach. Indeed the importance and number of these patients is such that it should be our first diagnostic task to decide whether the patient is suffering (mainly) from a structural or a functional lesion, as the approach to treatment and management is basically different. We should, however, bear in mind that patients suffering from structural pathology usually have functional problems, too.

THE FUNCTIONAL APPROACH[1]

Of particularly importance for all of us who work with methods of physical medicine—whether we use massage, exercise, electrotherapy, manipulation, or treatment of trigger points by any method—is that each of these methods and techniques applies primarily to changes in function (dysfunction). Here again, it is worthwhile to point out that dysfunction, although (frequently immediately) reversible, is as real as structural pathology, just as physiology is as much of a science as anatomy. What, then, is the fundamental difference?

> ## ❗ CLINICAL PEARL
>
> Function is as fundamental as structure, like anatomy and physiology; both aspects, however, have to be distinguished, diagnosed, and treated.

First, the clinical picture is much more closely related to changes in function than to changes in structure. Indeed, as long as a structural change does not cause changes in function, the patient is usually symptom free. We are, on the other hand, increasingly familiar with structural changes entirely irrelevant to the patient's problem. This is not only true for the most frequent type, called "degenerative" changes, which are the rule above a certain age and frequently absent in the young, even in clinically serious cases. They remain the same whether the patient suffers from pain or happens to be pain free. The same can be even true for such sometimes important changes as disc prolapse, spondylolisthesis, or old compression fractures. On the other hand, it is exceptional if in a patient presenting symptoms there is no change in function relevant to his or her pain. For pain is a most important and powerful stimulus, which always causes reflex changes—motor and autonomic—with clinical manifestations (Fig. 20–1.)

The second fundamental difference lies in localization. Structural lesions of the motor system are localized, and we have to determine the nature of the pathology. Function, on the other hand, is never the result of one structure, but the result of correlation and interplay of many structures; as a rule it concerns the entire motor system. We, therefore, have to diagnose the most important chains[2] and the most important link in any chain.[3] This is borne out by treatment: In structural pathology, we apply a remedy to the le-

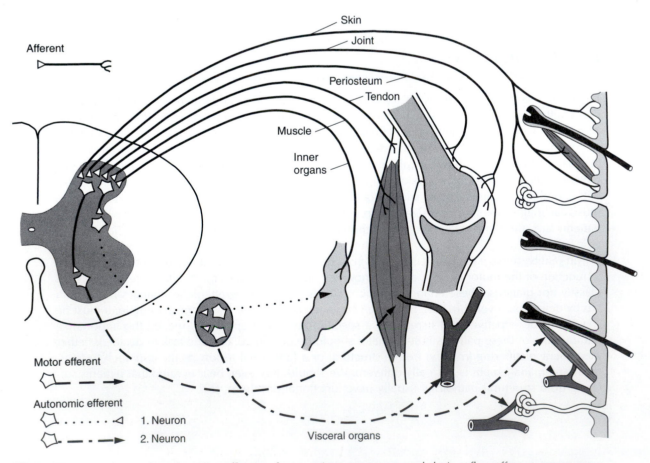

Figure 20–1. Diagram of nociceptive afferents from various structures and their reflex efferent responses.

sioned structure (e.g., surgery). If the remedy works, we go on applying it. In changes of function it is our aim to find the most relevant link of the chain and usually apply treatment there (a dysfunctional joint or trigger point); if treatment is successful (but symptoms still remain), this is usually because other links in the chain remain to be treated. If the lesion we first treated has not improved, we have to consider our first treatment as unsuccessful and should first consider the reason, before deciding whether to change or repeat the first treatment. For as changes in function are reversible, immediate improvement or even cessation of a lesion (link) should be expected, whereas in structural pathology the healing process is slower. In simple cases, therefore, something like a "miracle cure" can even be predicted in cases of functional changes.

! CLINICAL PEARL

Who treats where it hurts is lost—so, indeed, is his or her patient.

Hence the functional approach is, in its essence, holistic; the functional chains are widely considered to be the result of "reflex" mechanisms. In this connection it seems appropriate to quote Sherrington on the meaning of such "reflexes":

A simple reflex is probably a purely abstract conception, because all parts of the nervous system are connected together and no part of it probably ever capable of reaction without affecting and being affected by various other parts, and it is a system certainly never absolutely at rest.

When you or I sit down to write, or type, or play the piano, we have stored in our brains a considerably detailed representation of how the entire action is to be achieved.[4]

In reality motor function—and dysfunction—is concerned with motor programs, and a lesion of any link will affect the program as a whole. The tennis player with a lesioned arm or foot has to readjust his or her entire program of performance if one part of the motor system becomes dysfunctional. This, as we see, makes thinking in terms of function much more difficult, and holds for both diagnosis and treatment. The holistic approach is multifactorial, making statistical assessment much more difficult and at times impossible. Modern technology is also much less effective than in structural pathology, and we have to rely mainly on sophisticated clinical examination in which inspection and especially palpation play key roles. In short, we consider function to represent the software of the motor system.

The motor system functions according to programs that are partly innate and partly acquired, representing the software of the motor system.

We soon learned by experience that when we find a lesion localized at point A, we are likely to find one also at point B and if at B, very likely at point C. In this way the close connection between what may be called "key regions" became apparent; this was especially evident at the craniocervical junction, the cervicothoracic, the thoracolumbar, and between the pelvic regions and the feet. In other words, we noticed a number of regularly occurring chains of lesions that proved clinically helpful for quick orientation. Such traditional empirical concepts as the "meridians" of acupuncture came to mind. In modern, more scientific terms, however, we surmised a more rational explanation of such regularly occurring chain reactions.

Is there some underlying principle in the various chains and programs to be described in this chapter? The early ontogenesis of postural activity in infants (according to Kolár[5]) seems most relevant in this respect. The present view is that motor programming during the first few weeks of infancy is mainly of spinal or brain stem origin. The fundamental patterns of these programs can be explained by reciprocal activation and inhibition of agonists and antagonists. After a few weeks, however, the infant starts to use the eyes and to lift the head when prone. At the age of about 3 months, extension occurs in both the cervical and the lumbar region, if the infant supports the trunk on an elbow. This is not only the cardinal sign of normal development, but also is the decisive step in the development of human erect posture (unlike quadrupeds). The stages that follow enable straightening up to erect posture (Fig. 20–2A through D).

The role of the extensor muscles is obvious in this connection. There is a more subtle, but in no way less important, mechanism involved in the development of erect posture—balance. Erect posture that depended only on the extensors would be so labile as to be literally untenable. Therefore a mechanism of co-contraction of the flexors must develop.[5–8] The primitive (mainly spinal) mechanism of reciprocal stimulation-inhibition must be superseded by the cerebral (cortical) mechanism of co-contraction (i.e., balance and stabilization). Hence, the main function of the back muscles and the trunk flexors in humans is not forward or back-bending, but the antigravitational stability of human posture. This is no less true, of course, for the knee flexors and extensors. This basic pattern should have developed by the age of 3 months.[5]

! CLINICAL PEARL

Muscles called anatomical antagonists become synergists for the maintenance of postural function.

These mechanisms evidently apply to the cervical spine and head posture, and show new aspects of reflex mechanisms involved in programs and chains. It is important to know that erect neck posture is incompatible with

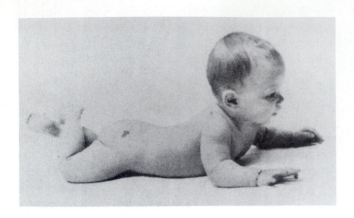

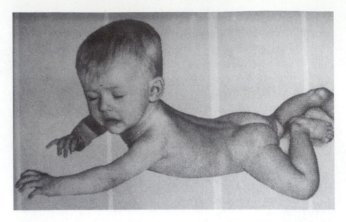

A

B

C

D

Figure 20–2. Infant prone: **(A)** supporting himself on the left elbow (end of third month); **(B)** supporting himself on the right elbow, reaching out with the left arm and hand (end of fifth month); **(C)** supporting himself on both arms (end of seventh month); other points of support are at the symphysis and the knees; **(D)** using the hands to achieve a vertical posture (end of ninth month). All show the same lordotic posture stabilized by co-contraction of the postural antagonists, with abduction of the thighs.

reclination of the head; in fact, if the neck is straight, there is some degree of flexion between occiput and atlas (see Fig. 20–6). Balanced posture as a result of physiological co-contraction of muscles places the most favorable load on all articular structures not only of the spinal column, but also of the peripheral joints—the correct "centration" of the joint (Fig. 20–3).

These mechanisms are evidence of the role of early development of posture. There is also something in the way of experimental evidence consisting in Vojta's[9] reflex stimulation techniques, which he applies mainly in infants suf-

fering from cerebral palsy, but which can also be demonstrated and applied in adults. By mechanical stimulation—digital pressure at certain points—he succeeded in establishing the physiological postural co-contraction patterns necessary for his patients to achieve erect posture. Some of these points may coincide with acupuncture points, but from the point of view of postural function, it is much more important that these points correspond to points of support, such as the elbows, other points on the trunk or head, or the knees, hands, or heels; that is, structures that we use if we (or, as previously illustrated, infants) want to get from

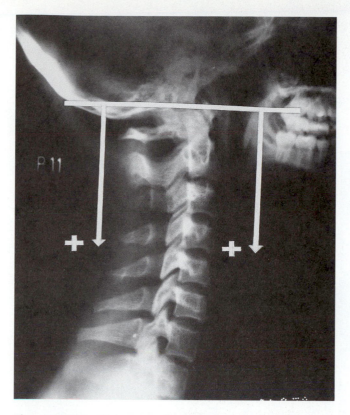

Figure 20–3. Diagram of physiological (symmetrical) forces acting on the cervical spine in the erect posture, producing the most favorable load at the joint structure ("centration").

recumbent to erect posture. It can easily be understood that these points are rich in receptors reacting to mechanical stimulation (Fig. 20–4).

If stimulation is carried out with the head, neck, and trunk in a neutral position, we also obtain a motor reaction

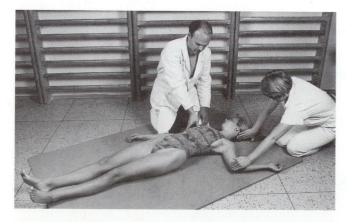

Figure 20–4. Stimulation producing reflex turning, according to Vojta. In this case reflex stimulation is carried out in a neutral head position at the left elbow, at the linea nuchae on the left, and at the fifth costosternal joint on the right.

during which a balanced co-contraction of the trunk and the extremities takes place. If the subject has his or her legs in abduction and external rotation, or in adduction and internal rotation, stimulation at the head (linea nuchae) and at the chest (fifth sternocostal joint) will bring the legs into the position of "centration"; that is, the position best suited for postural load (balance) (Fig. 20–5A through D). If, however, stimulation takes place with the head in reclination, the entire co-contraction pattern (i.e., the program or chain reaction) is altered. In other words, a changed function or dysfunction at one point alters the entire balance, program, or chain.

MUSCLE IMBALANCE

What Janda calls muscular imbalance may have its origin here.[10,11] If the same type of stimulation is carried out on a subject not in a balanced neutral position, but with the head in reclination, or even with the leg held in abduction and external rotation, the entire balanced co-contraction pattern is altered. There is increased tension in the upper part of the trapezius, levator scapulae, scaleni, pectorales, subscapularis, biceps, pronators, long head of the triceps, iliopsoas, quadratus lumborum, thigh adductors, rectus femoris, tensor fascia latae, hamstrings, triceps surae, and in particular, in the soleus and plantar flexors. There is, on the other hand, hypotonus in the deep neck flexors, lower trapezius, external shoulder rotators, supinators and extensors of the elbow and wrist, serratus anterior, midthoracic extensors, recti abdominis, gluteal muscles, vasti, and in the medial head of the gastrocnemius. The central origin of all these changes is obvious.

The simplest approach[2] seemed to be a rough analysis of such basic functions of the motor system as (1) gait, (2) body statics, (3) respiratory movements, (4) prehension, and (5) feeding. For each of these functions, we then examined the most important muscles, their attachment points, and possibly referred pain caused by trigger points (TrPs) and the joints involved in dysfunction. Tables 20–1 through 20–5 present the chains that resulted from this analysis; these chains have proved useful ever since. For this publication only those chains relevant to the cervical spine are discussed.

These chains are very useful both for diagnosis and for economical therapy. For example, if we find TrPs in the psoas, quadratus lumborum, and thoracolumbar erector spinae with restricted trunk rotation, we may either mobilize trunk rotation or relax any of these muscles; not only will the other two muscles relax, trunk rotation, too, will be restored. In epicondylar pain, we may either mobilize the elbow or relax the supinator, the finger extensors, or the bicep. We also know that this pain is linked with the cervical spine, which must be taken into account. The importance of balanced co-contraction patterns seems evident and easily explains joint lesions resulting from muscular dysfunction.

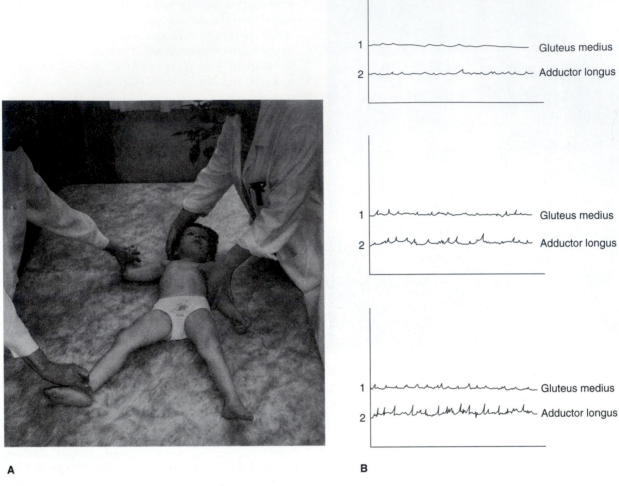

Figure 20–5. **A.** Stimulation (producing reflex turning) with the lower extremity in abduction. **B.** Electromyogram (EMG) registration of activity in the gluteus medius *(1)* and in the adductor longus *(2)* after 2, 4, and 6 minutes.

Table 20–1: Chain Reactions: Trunk—Body Statics

INCREASED MUSCLE TENSION	TENDER ATTACHMENT POINTS (REFERRED PAIN)	JOINT DYSFUNCTION (BLOCKAGE)
Sternocleidomastoid, short craniocervical extensors	Posterior arch of the atlas and transverse process	Craniocervical junction
Scaleni, deep neck flexors	Linea nuchae	Cervicothoracic junction
Digastrici	Spinous process of axis	Upper ribs
Upper trapezius, levator scapulae	Medial end of clavicle	Thoracolumbar junction (restricted rotation)
Iliopsoas, recti abdominus	Hyoid	Lumbosacral junction
Erector spinae, quadratus lumborum	Upper and vertebral margin	Sacroiliac joints
Hamstrings	Scapula	Feet
	Xiphoid	
	Pubic symphysis	
	Lowest ribs	
	Iliac crests	
	Fibular head	

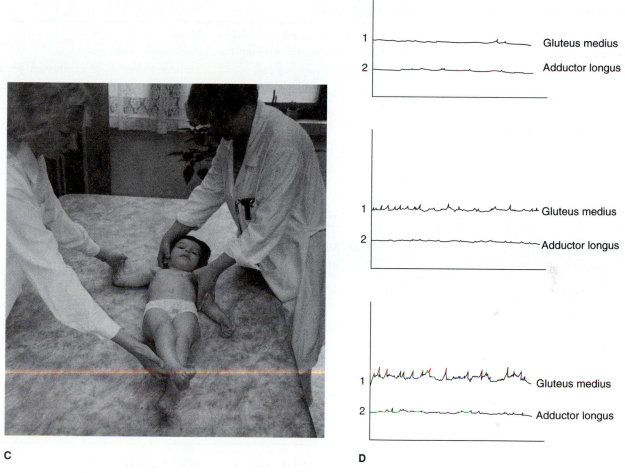

C

D

Figure 20–5 continued. C. Stimulation with the lower extremity in adduction. **D.** EMG activity in the gluteus medius *(1)* and in the adductor longus *(2)* after 2, 4, and 6 minutes.

Table 20–2: Chain Reactions: Lifting the Thorax at Respiration

INCREASED MUSCLE TENSION	TENDER ATTACHMENT POINTS (REFERRED PAIN)	JOINT DYSFUNCTION (BLOCKAGE)
Upper section of abdominal muscles	Atlas posterior arch and TvP	Craniocervical junction
Pectorals	Axis spinous process	Cervicothoracic junction
Scaleni with upper fixators of the shoulder girdle	Upper margin of scapula, sternocostal junctions	Upper ribs
Short extensors of the craniocervical junction	Upper ribs	

Table 20–3: Chain Reactions: Upper Extremity—Prehension; Impaired Flexion

INCREASED MUSCLE TENSION	TENDER ATTACHMENT POINTS (REFERRED PAIN)	JOINT DYSFUNCTION (BLOCKAGE)
Finger and wrist extensors	Styloid process and lateral epicondyle	Elbow
Thenar muscles	Attachment of supra- and infraspinatus	Acromioclavicular joint
Supinators	Attachment of levator scapulae	Mid-cervical spine, cervicothoracic junction
Biceps	Spinous process of axis	
Deltoids		
Supra- and infraspinatus		
Upper fixators of the shoulder girdle		
Interscapular muscles		

Table 20–4: Chain Reactions: Upper Extremity—Prehension; Impaired Extension

INCREASED MUSCLE TENSION	TENDER ATTACHMENT POINTS (REFERRED PAIN)	JOINT DYSFUNCTION (BLOCKAGE)
Finger and wrist flexors	Medial epicondyle	Carpal bones (carpal tunnel)
Pronators	Medial end of clavicle	Elbow
Subscapularis	Sternocostal junction	Glenohumeral joint
Pectorales	Erb's point	Craniocervical junction
Sternocleidomastoid	Atlas TvP	Cervicothoracic junction
Scaleni		Upper ribs

Table 20–5: Chain Reactions: Head and Neck—Feeding, Mastication, and Speech

INCREASED MUSCLE TENSION	TENDER ATTACHMENT POINTS (REFERRED PAIN)	JOINT DYSFUNCTION (BLOCKAGE)
Masticatory muscles	Hyoid	Temperomandibular joint
Digastricus	Atlas posterior arch and TvP	Craniocervical junction
Sternocleidomastoid	Axis spinous process	Cervicothoracic junction
Suboccipitals	Linea nuchae	Upper ribs
Upper trapezius	Upper margin of scapula	
Levator scapulae	Upper ribs	
Deep neck flexors		
Pectorales		

It is important to bear in mind that with all these changes, the soft tissue lesions—in particular hyperalgesic skin zones—and impaired mobility (resistance) of deep fascias are found mainly in the corresponding spinal segments.

THE CHAIN REACTION FROM SEVERE NOCICEPTION[5]

In the following chain, it must be borne in mind that the normal balance of the co-contraction pattern can be disturbed both by imbalance of agonist and activity, as is the case in Janda's muscular imbalance, or by both being hyperactive, as in painful disorders resulting from nociceptive stimulation, which causes co-contraction to immobilize the injured structures. This is particularly the case where TrPs are involved.

If, therefore, we find one TrP in a certain muscle, the entire pattern is bound to be affected. We expect a TrP in its antagonist; this is quite specific. If there is a TrP in the short thigh abductors, we expect a TrP in the caudal part of the gluteus maximus; with a TrP in the adductor longus, find one in the central part of the gluteus maximus and in the gluteus medius and minimus. With a TrP in the section of the pectoralis that attaches at the level of the fifth rib, we find a TrP in the longissimus thoracis. If there is a TrP in the pectoralis attaching itself more caudally, we also find a TrP more laterally in the iliocostalis thoracis.

In typical severe cases with chronic neck pain, we find increased tension with TrPs markedly on one side, usually the right. At inspection with the patient supine, the right shoulder protrudes ventrally and resists downward pressure. At examination, we usually find TrPs in a distribution, as listed in Table 20–6. This, indeed, corresponds to the co-contraction pattern of postural muscles subserving erect posture, according to developmental neurology.

On closer scrutiny we usually find much less noticeable TrPs on the left side in the pectoralis at the level of T6–7. Further TrPs correspond with this attachment point—in the subscapularis, at the upper section of the abdominal muscles; in the iliacus, long adductors, semi-membranosus, soleus, deep plantar flexors, and short toe extensors at the third and fourth metatarsal, gluteus medius, minimus, and the middle section of the gluteus maximus; in the iliocostalis, serratus anterior, and infraspinatus. On the side where changes are only slight, TrPs are less constant.

In addition there is restricted extension of the mid thoracic spine, movement restriction at the fibular head, and frequently at the metatarsophalangeal joints (II to IV) and at the cervical spine, in particular at the craniocervical and thoracolumbar junction and the upper ribs, and at the elbow and wrist. No less important than the relationship between agonists and antagonists is the close interrelation among the links of the entire chain to each other, so that, for example, dysfunction at the feet frequently causes relapses, including in the cervical spine.

This chain is, we believe, the result of nociceptive stimulation; its prevalent incidence on the right side is characteristic of the frequent incidence of asymmetrical signs of dysfunction, which remain unexplained.

BRÜGGER'S "STERNOSYMPHYSEAL" SYNDROME

According to Brügger,[12, 13] myofascial pain—in his terminology, "tendomyosis"—is mainly the result of faulty posture. This is owing to the fact that in many people, flexion is the predominating posture. Indeed, this is the position at work of most people in modern society; not only at office work, in front of the computer, but also when driving a car, on a tractor, or in front of a panel in the factory. This position is held to put an increased load on the spinal column, in particular on the disc.

At examination we regularly find increased tension with TrPs in the short extensors of the craniocervical junction, upper fixators of the shoulder girdle, pectorales, abdominal muscles, hip flexors, and adductors, and even in the flexors of the upper extremity. This chain is regularly found in the flexed working position; the moment the subject adopts a lordotic (relief) position, all or most of the tension vanishes, including the TrPs. There are few experiments that can more aptly demonstrate the reversibility of changes caused by dysfunction (Fig. 20–6).

Figure 20–6 shows the effect of forward tilt of the pelvis, lifting of the thorax, and elongating of the neck. It functions "like cogwheels," and we can also initiate the movement by elongating the neck. However, it is essential to have both legs in abduction and the feet in external rotation. If the legs are in adduction and the feet in internal rotation it is difficult to tilt the pelvis or even stretch the neck. Similarly, the upper extremities should not be in internal rotation and pronation.

Brügger therefore advocates seats (supports) that favor a lordotic position, and even advises his patients to stoop in a lordotic position—bending the knees at the same time. Indeed, he has worked out a system of gymnastics to combat kyphotic posture. It is significant that faulty respiration by lifting the thorax goes hand in hand with a faulty kyphotic posture, and Brügger's relief position has proved

---

Table 20–6: Chain Reactions from Severe Nociception

Neck: Sternocleidomastoid, scalenes, suboccipitals, splenius capitis and cervicis, upper trapezius, levator scapulae

Thorax: pectoralis major (upper part) and minor, subscapularis, rhomboids, serratus anterior, iliocostalis thoracis

Abdomen: obliques, rectus abdominis, longissimus thoracis, quadratus lumborum, psoas, iliacus, pelvic diaphragm (coccygeus)

Pelvis: short adductors, hamstrings, gluteus maximus and minimis, rectus femoris, tensor fascia lata

Foot: long toe extensors, tibialis anterior, soleus, short plantar extensors and flexors

Shoulder: subscapularis, infraspinatus, deltoid, teres major, triceps

Hand: pronators, supinators (biceps), finger extensors and flexors

Movement Restriction: mainly at key transitional areas of the spinal column (cervicocranial, cervicothoracic, thoracolumbar, and lumbosacral) and at T5–6, proximal tibiofibular joint and intertarsals, possibly the elbow

Trigger points are restricted to specific sites in each muscle, apparently producing immobilization of each section of the motor system; these sections always react simultaneously (under the control of the central nervous system)

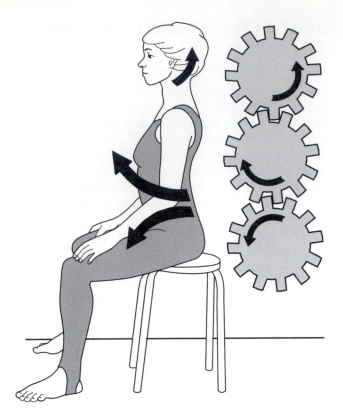

Figure 20–6. Brügger's "cogwheel diagram." Forward tilt of the pelvis causes lifting of the thorax and straightening of the neck (and vice versa); at the same time, the legs are abducted and in external rotation.

most useful for training correct breathing. There is a striking and obvious connection between the ontogenetic development of lordotic posture and Brügger's "sternosymphyseal" syndrome, even in such details as neck and head position: the neck should be straight, even lordotic, but the head should never be in reclination.

However important Brügger's contribution, there is the danger of one-sidedness in his attitude: he tends to avoid kyphosis even during stooping and unconditionally advocates a lordotic position. This can be exaggerated; many patients suffer most if they cannot change posture and suffer even when in a lordotic position for too long a time. It must also be kept in mind that the trunk and the spinal column are capable of movement in all planes, and neither flexion nor extension is abnormal in itself. There is yet another important point; in the extended standing position with legs apart and in external rotation, there is greatly reduced stability. With the legs parallel or in slight internal rotation and knees slightly bent, trunk extension is reduced, but there is much greater stability. (If we prepare to fight, we are not likely to adopt a lordotic position.) This, however, does not reduce the importance of correcting kyphotic posture in a population suffering from static overstrain. It is only necessary to point out

that this is not the only faulty program or the only important chain.

THE FORWARD DRAWN POSTURE

With a standing patient, observed from the side view, the forward drawn posture is a frequent phenomenon (Fig. 20–7).[14] Normally a plumb line from the outer acoustic meatus falls slightly in front of the ankle. In the forward drawn posture, the outer acoustic meatus, and thus the center of gravity, is shifted toward the metatarsals; this posture can result from a forward shift of the pelvis in relation to the feet, of the shoulders in relation to the pelvis, or of the head in relation to the shoulders, or a combination of all three.

Clinically, the most important feature is hypertonus with TrPs in the erector spinae throughout the back and neck. If the cause of this posture is not in the neck region, hypertonus disappears if the patient sits down. This difference is most noticeable at the neck, where hypertonus should then be compared standing and seated. With this difference, we find as a rule hypertonus with TrPs in the rectus abdominis at least on one side with tender attachment points at the symphysis and (less regularly) at the xiphoid. There is also hypertonus of the buttocks (usually on one side) with increased resistance against shifting of its underlying soft tissues in a cranial direction. As a rule we further find a TrP in the biceps femoris with restricted mobility of the fibular head (usually on the side of the TrPs in the rectus abdominis) and (less regularly) TrPs in the deep plantar flexors with restriction at the metatarsophalangeal joints, most frequently II through IV, possibly at the talocrural joint.

As the forward drawn posture affects all sections of the motor system, the patient may present symptoms in any of its regions. For treatment it is best to start at the most caudal point: if the feet are affected, at the feet (metatarsals); if only at the fibular head, at that joint; and if there is only hypertonus at the buttocks, then by soft tissue techniques applied there. The effect is always the same: hypertonus (TrPs) in the rectus abdominis and in the back and neck musculature disappears, the patient's posture is normalized; if there is restriction at the craniocervical junction, this disappears, too, as a rule. If, however, there is abnormal sensitivity at the soles of the feet (increased, decreased, asymmetrical) mere plantar stroking with an intensity pleasant to the patient will be just as effective.

A possible explanation for this chain could be the role of the hamstrings, which attach at the fibular head and harbor a TrP if there is restriction at the proximal tibiofibular joint. If this is the case, postural fixation of the pelvis is impaired and the rectus abdominis and the gluteals substitute for the hamstrings to keep it in the correct position. Again, as with Brügger's sternosymphyseal

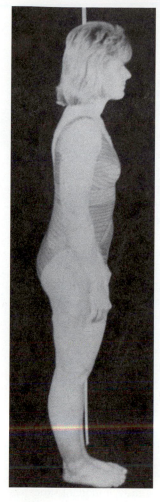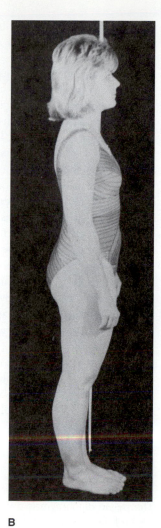

A　　　　　　　**B**

Figure 20–7. Forward drawn posture **(A)** before treatment; **(B)** after treatment; normalization.

syndrome, here, too, the underlying mechanism is a disturbed co-contraction pattern of the postural muscles—caused in this case most frequently by dysfunction of the lower extremities.

THE S-REFLEX

In 1989, Silverstolpe[15] described a reflex condition or chain: by snapping palpation of a TrP in the midthoracic region, they elicited dorsiflexion of the pelvis and demonstrated contraction of the lumbar erector spinae by electromyogram (EMG). At examination they further found a very tender point in the lateral gluteal region exactly at the level of the upper end of the intergluteal fold. Most important, they found a very tender point in the region of the sacrotuberous ligament. Massage of this point caused the entire syndrome to disappear. The authors called this phenomenon "pelvic dysfunction"; it is found more frequently on the left.

In a further paper,[16] they stressed the very frequent incidence of the reflex, noting that patients suffered not only from backache of various localization, but also neck pain and headache. The reflex can also be related to visceral pain and, most curiously, to dysphonia. For this reason, singers were very frequently the sufferers.

After observing Silverstolpe in 1991, we began to use his method to treat these patients. We, however, use only pressure at the pain point and wait for release. We are in full agreement with the response the authors describe. Indeed, one has only to touch the pain point for the TrP in the spinal erector spinae to disappear. Quite frequently the coccyx is also tender, not in the midline but on the side of the S-reflex. Where we differ from Silverstolpe is in the interpretation of the phenomenon. They ascribe the effect to the ligament to which the pressure is directed. The resistance we meet there and the release we obtain, however, is typical for a muscular TrP. Parallel with and just underneath the ligament lies the coccygeus muscle, part of the pelvic diaphragm. It seems more logical to attribute the effect of the maneuver to this structure. As in previous chain reactions, here, too, there is a postural reaction, affecting the motor system as a whole. This is easily explained by the function and importance of the pelvic diaphragm.

The pelvic diaphragm represents one of the walls of the abdominal cavity and plays a key role both in body statics and in respiration. The prominent TrPs in the thoracic region are related to pseudo-visceral symptoms, and the effect on respiration easily explains dysphonia in singers. This is of more than theoretical interest. As this syndrome frequently recurs, we think it most important to give specific exercise to the pelvic diaphragm. Indeed, it seems that the S-reflex is one of the few direct signs by which dysfunction of the pelvic diaphragm can be diagnosed.

It was not long before we found proof of this assumption; however effective the treatment by pressure or massage is for the moment, symptoms easily recur. Therefore, we considered how to contract and relax the pelvic diaphragm so as to obtain relaxation of the TrP at the coccygeus muscle. The following technique proved very successful:

1. We first seat the patient and show him or her how to draw in the navel, using the fingers to monitor (not to induce!) this movement (Fig. 20–8).
2. Once the patient does this correctly, and also relaxes, he or she lies on one side and puts the hand flat round the anus, trying to draw in that region (Fig. 20–9). It must be stressed that the buttocks must not be pulled together (!).
3. If the patient thinks he or she has achieved this, the patient is told to shut the nostrils with the other hand, and with the mouth shut, to perform a resisted inhalation. If the patient has really under-

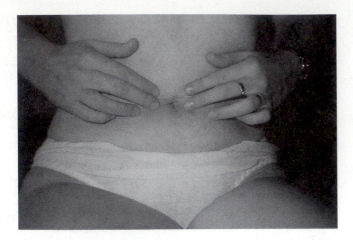

Figure 20–8. Drawing in the navel.

stood, he or she now feels the drawing in of the anal region much more and we know that the patient is now fully aware of it.

4. The maneuver then is repeated two to three times.

If properly carried out, this maneuver has the same effect as massage or pressure of the sacrotuberous ligament. Indeed, if we obtain the typical reaction of the spinal erector spinae and find the typical pain point at the buttocks, we now desist from the very painful palpation of the ligament and teach the patient to contract and relax both the deep abdominal muscles (drawing in the navel) and the pelvic diaphragm him- or herself—not only in the recumbent position, but also seated, standing, or even walking — and to do it several times a day, thus preventing recurrence. It must be stressed that the patient must perform the maneuver slowly, to obtain relaxation.

Some important implications must be pointed out. Panjabi[6, 17] has recently stressed the importance of the deep autochthonic spinal muscles for spinal stability. Several Australian authors[18, 19] demonstrated the importance

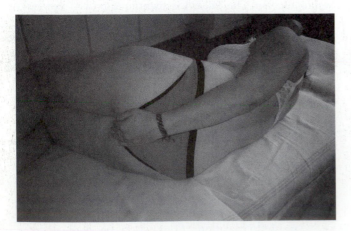

Figure 20–9. Drawing in the anal region.

of training the deep abdominal muscles together with the multifidus, to obtain spinal stability, by techniques which patients took several weeks to learn. These authors consider only individual muscles, but not what is in our opinion the crucial structure—the abdominal cavity (i.e., a fluid-filled cavity that can give support only if all its walls are functioning). This means not only the abdominal muscles and the back muscles, but also both diaphragms. We have, indeed, found that once there is a TrP at the diaphragm (on the side of the S-reflex palpated underneath the ribs, not unlike palpation of the gallbladder), this also disappears when the patient performs the exercise described. This, then, explains the efficacy of our technique: by restoring the stabilizing function of the abdominal cavity the (compensatory) spasm of the superficial spinal erectors becomes superfluous and the Silverstolpe phenomenon and its consequences clear up.

We thus treat the following chain: hamstrings (fibular head), adductors, pelvic diaphragm, deep abdominal muscles, erector spinae, diaphragm, shoulder girdle, and muscles of the orofacial system (i.e., both static and respiratory function). We do not limit ourselves now to patients with a fully developed Silverstolpe phenomenon, but examine the pelvic diaphragm if we suspect that static and respiratory function might be involved and there is no other more obvious explanation.

! CLINICAL PEARL

The pelvic diaphragm is one of the most important structures for both body statics and respiration; its dysfunction can best be detected by the Silverstolpe phenomenon and can be treated by the patient in the manner described herein.

VISCERAL PATTERNS

The chains of dysfunction dealt with thus far are the most typical and the most important; their expression can be modified by nociceptive stimuli arising from visceral organs.[20-22] In itself a visceral lesion, if painful, produces patterns or chains that are highly characteristic and therefore diagnostically very valuable. On the one hand, the belief of many practitioners that by treating the spinal column they could treat visceral organs cannot be upheld. On the other hand, the motor system and in particular the spinal column are a (diagnostic) mirror of what goes on in the organism—this point is underrated to this day. It holds true even during infancy, at the stage when upright human posture develops.

There are several visceral organs that can have a particularly potent impact on the motor system:

1. TrPs are found on the left side of the heart,[23, 24] in particular at the upper trapezius, sternocleidomastoid, scalenes, pectorales, subscapularis, erector

spinae, and their attachment points. There is movement restriction mainly at the cervicothoracic junction and the upper left ribs, in the thoracic spine between T3 and T5, and less regularly at the craniocervical junction. Faulty respiration by lifting the thorax is the rule.

2. The tonsils[25] are important, as they cause restriction at the craniocervical junction mainly between occiput and atlas, which is a most important key region, linked to the other key regions of the motor system. We also find spasm (TrPs) in the short extensors of the craniocervical junction, in the sternocleidomastoid, and in the muscles attached to the hyoid. This may interfere with head posture, causing head reclination and thus disturbing the entire postural co-contraction pattern.

3. The upper abdominal viscera seem to be of little relevance to the cervical spine; however, they frequently cause pain radiating into the upper extremity, possibly via afferent fibers of the phrenic nerve. In cases of recurrent cervicobrachial pain, it is therefore important also to look for (or exclude) lesions of the viscera of the upper abdomen.[26]

4. "Active" scars play an interfering role similar to that of visceral lesions.[27, 28] They, too, are a source of nociceptive stimulation, with reflex effects according to localization and intensity. There cannot, therefore, be a single characteristic pattern. Such scars can, however, and very frequently do modify or even produce a chain reaction in unpredictable ways. It is thus very important to diagnose and treat them. The characteristic features include increased skin drag in the area of the scar, increased resistance of the skin and the subcutaneous tissue to stretch and folding, and tenderness when exerting pressure on the tissue fold. Frequently, only part of the scar is "active." Treatment consists in stretching—not pressing!—the tissue fold with very little force; after engaging the barrier, we wait for release. A special approach is needed, however, for scars with a large surface adhering to the underlying bone. Here, treatment consists in gentle mobilization of the scar in the restricted direction (not unlike fascia).

To miss an active scar is a frequent cause of therapeutic failure; to give adequate treatment, on the other hand, is more than rewarding!

THE CRANIOCERVICAL JUNCTION AND THE OROFACIAL SYSTEM

This chain was summarized earlier in Table 20–5. However, it is of such practical importance that it warrants special emphasis. In our opinion, the orofacial system forms a functional unit with the craniocervical junction,[29] and it is no coincidence that clinical symptoms arising from either of these areas are almost identical. Indeed, the muscles of the orofacial system affect head posture via the diagastricus and the hyoid. What holds for the muscles is also true for the temperomandibular joint as a source of headache and disturbed equilibrium. Therefore, examination of the cervical spine must include the orofacial system and, if necessary, the expert opinion of the orthodontist. This is especially important after head injuries with or without concussion.

THE MID-CERVICAL SPINE, PAIN AT THE EPICONDYLES AND THE STYLOID PROCESS OF THE RADIUS, CARPAL TUNNEL SYNDROME, THE CERVICOTHORACIC JUNCTION, AND THE SYNDROME OF THE UPPER THORACIC OUTLET

It cannot be mere coincidence that a great many patients complain both of pain and dysesthesia in the upper extremity, including the wrists and elbows. They may suffer from the "repetitive strain syndrome" if their working conditions correspond to this diagnosis. What are the pathogenetic mechanisms underlying these chains? It seems unnecessary to insist upon the well-established relationship between the cervical spine and epicondylar pain[30] and between the cervicothoracic junction and the syndrome of the upper thoracic outlet. But it is necessary to explain the connection between epicondylar pain, pain at the styloid processes, the function of carpal bones, and carpal tunnel syndrome.[31] The key role is played by the radio-ulnar joint at the elbow.

At lateral (radial) or medial (ulnar) flexion at the wrist, there is concomitant pronation and supination of the forearm. If there is restriction at the radio-ulnar joint (at the elbow) lateral flexion at the wrist is affected and there is strain at the styloid processes, much more frequently on the radial side. This is a frequent complication after a fall on the hand with or without fracture of the radius, for obviously such an impact jams the radio-ulnar and radiohumeral joint via the radius.

! CLINICAL PEARL

Whether there is a Colles' fracture after a fall on the wrist or not, if there is pain at the wrist, examine and treat the elbow!

Because the carpal bones also take part in radial flexion, their function, too, suffers and the result is restriction of mobility there, which can be diagnosed clinically. Under normal conditions we meet next to no resistance at palpation if we try to move (shift) one carpal bone against the other. Even a slightly increased resistance is characteristic of carpal tunnel syndrome. Movement palpation, however, has to be carried out only with minimum force, which is not easy. The explanation is that the walls of the carpal tunnel must be fully mobile so as to adapt to the content during every movement and position of the hand. This is possible only if the mobility of the carpal bones is perfect. Impaired mobility can be regularly felt in the early reversible stages of the carpal tunnel syndrome, and treated by mobilization. Once adhesions at the transverse ligament develop, surgery becomes necessary.

! CLINICAL PEARL

Timely diagnosis and treatment of movement restriction of carpal bones can prevent surgery for carpal tunnel syndrome.

The relationship of thoracic outlet syndrome to the cervicothoracic junction is obvious, but it is important to understand that there are very many structures involved in this syndrome. Disturbance of any of them must be diagnosed for treatment to be successful; the low cervical and upper thoracic spine, the upper ribs, the scaleni with the upper fixators of the scapula, and also the pectoralis minor. Changes of function are frequent in all these structures, but each must be treated specifically. The underlying cause is frequently faulty respiration (lifting the thorax) combined with a kyphotic posture.

! CLINICAL PEARL

Indications for surgery in these patients result from the inability to diagnose and treat all of these changes in function.

It is interesting to note that dysesthesia resulting from carpal tunnel involvement occurs frequently in patients who also suffer from thoracic outlet syndrome, and vice versa, so that the same patient in whom we have treated carpal tunnel syndrome seeks our help again for dysesthesia in the upper extremity—this time, however, because he or she is suffering from thoracic outlet syndrome. The reason for this frequent coincidence is most probably the same type of faulty posture characteristic for both these conditions: a round-shouldered sitting posture, producing hypertonus of all the muscles of the shoulder girdle, and faulty respiration,[32] making relaxation almost impossible. The association with Brügger's sternosymphyseal syndrome is also obvious. Here, again, an abnormal co-contraction pattern of the postural muscles plays a prominent role and must be the object of the rehabilitation program. Correct breathing must be taught at the same time.

INTERFERENCE OF PROGRAMS OF DYSFUNCTION, STRATEGY, AND TACTICS—DECIDING ON THE MOST SUITABLE APPROACH

Clearly the chains and programs discussed in this chapter have more than one feature in common: faulty respiration and Brügger's sternosymphyseal syndrome; the crucial role trunk extension plays in Kolár's "chain reaction due to nociception," and again in the sternosymphyseal syndrome and in the forward-drawn posture; the close relationship between the preceding programs and body statics, and between respiration and the S-reflex. Every localized lesion has its repercussions throughout the motor system according to the co-contraction pattern acquired in infancy in the course of the first 3 months. As in most fields of medicine, it is the ontogenesis or the developmental aspect that best promotes theoretical understanding.

All these programs are frequently interfered with by visceral disease, trauma, or scars (nociception). In each case, we have to decide which program and which lesion constitutes the decisive element. In addition it is quite possible that other programs than those discussed here may exist.

It is no less important (and difficult) to determine at what point we should enter the programs and which is the most important and most accessible link of a chain. It is by no means true that if joints, muscles, fascia, and even surface sensitivity are involved, joints are necessarily the major element. There are certainly key regions, not all of them at the spinal column; one is that of the feet. We have already mentioned the crucial role of the hamstrings for fixation of the pelvis, and the role of fascias in the chronic stage of myofascial pain syndromes. Recent experience with exteroceptive stimulation[33] of the sole of the foot shows that a simple change in afferents can influence the entire motor system. This is also true when we treat scars. Here, too, we must carefully diagnose: whether the scar is active, whether sensitivity of the sole of the foot is normal (i.e., symmetrical, hyper- or hyposensitive). Since the wearing of shoes has deprived us of sensory inputs, such changes are frequent here.

To come to some important practical conclusions, if the case we are treating is not a straightforward or acute case, we should never treat individual lesions as we diagnose them, one after another. First, after taking a thorough history we should make a complete physical examination, and only then decide which type of dysfunctional program or even programs are involved. We must then decide which program is the more important, and at which point we should enter it (or them). There may even be links between them.

There is no easy solution to this question and there always remains an element of trial and error. As only gentle, physiological methods are used, no harm should be done.

There are, of course certain guidelines: a thorough case history should tell us where and in what circumstances symptoms first started. At examination, we note which change is very marked and which is only slight. No less important is whether we find change at a key region, a key joint, or a key muscle (e.g., the craniocervical area, the feet, the scaleni, the subscapularis, etc.). If we find a "stuck fascia" (with a pathological barrier when shifting), it is usually a sign of chronicity and should be treated first, as it causes recurrence of muscular TrPs and joint movement restriction. Whether to treat muscular spasm or joint movement restriction first is frequently a question of convenience, as the two lesions are very frequently interconnected. When using neuromuscular techniques, we treat both at the same time; if the fibula is restricted and there is the typical TrP in the biceps femoris, it is much more convenient to treat the joint; the reverse is true when the elbow presents epicondylar pain with TrPs in the supinator, or the finger extensors and biceps, or if there are more than one upper rib and TrPs in the subscapularis.

It is, therefore, mandatory after any treatment to immediately reexamine the patient in order to verify the working hypothesis; that is, whether the whole chain has been normalized or some part of it or, on the other hand, whether the hypothesis was incorrect, which is no less important. Sometimes we start with a lesion not because we are convinced that it is the most important in the chain, but because we want to find its relevance. This is particularly important with scars; if we begin elsewhere and the patient improves, we will never know whether the scar is relevant or not. If, however, we begin by treating the scar, and no effect is produced, we know that it is irrelevant and choose another link.

CONCLUSION

It is remarkable how few steps are required to normalize any number of lesions that constitute an entire chain. However, it is not only a question of effectivity; we can conclude that if our treatment is successful, then we have understood the pathomechanism or pathophysiology of the patient's problem. This is particularly important. It is no exaggeration to say that if the effectiveness of manipulative therapy has been proved by statistics—mainly in acute cases,[34] but much less so for long-term effects—this is because lesions have mainly been treated at the site of evident symptoms, while the underlying program or chain has not been recognized.

The diagnosis of chain reactions implies understanding of the dysfunctional program in disturbed function. This not only makes immediate treatment more effective, it also enables us to plan the most suitable rehabilitation.

REFERENCES

1. Lewit K. The functional approach. *J Orthop Med* 1994;16:74–74.
2. Lewit K. Chain reactions in disturbed function of the motor system. *J Manual Med* 1987;3:27.
3. Gutmann G. Die pathogenetische Aktualitätsdiagnostik. In: K Lewit, G Gutmann, eds. *Functional Pathology of the Motor System*. Rehabilitacia, Bratislava, Obzor Suppl 10–11;1975:15–24.
4. Pribram K. *Language of the Brain*. Englewood Cliffs, N.J.; Prentice Hall; 1971.
5. Kolár P. Diferenciace svalové funkce z hlediska posturální podstaty (Differentiation of muscle function with regard to its role in posture). *Medicina Sportiva Bohemica a Slovaca* 1996;5:4.
6. Panjabi MM. The stabilizing system of the spine. Part I. Function, dysfunction, adaptation, and enhancement. *J Spinal Disord* 1992;5:383–389.
7. Granata GL, Agarwal GC. The influence of trunk muscle coactivity on dynamic spinal loads. *Spine* 1995;20:913–919.
8. Crisco JJ, Panjabi MM. The intersegmental and multisegmental muscles of the lumbar spine. A biomechanical model comparing lateral stabilizing potential. *Spine* 1991;16:793–799.
9. Vojta V, Peters A. *Das Vojtaprinzip*. Heidelberg: Springer; 1992.
10. Janda V. *Muscle Function Testing*. London: Butterworth; 1983.
11. Janda V. Muscle and joint correlations. In: K Lewit, G Gutmann, eds. *Functional Pathology of the Motor System*. Rehabilitacia, Bratislava, Obzor, Suppl 10–11;1975:154–158.
12. Brügger A. *Das Sternale Syndrom*. Bern: Huber; 1971.
13. Brügger A. Die Funktionskrankheiten des Bewegungsapparates. *Funktionskrankheiten des Bewegungsapparates* 1986;1:69–129.
14. Lewit K. Verspannung der Bauch- und Beckenmuskulatur mit Auswirkungen auf die Körperstatik. *Manuelle Med* 1992;38:75–78.
15. Silverstolpe L. A pathological erector spinae reflex—a new sign of mechanical pelvis dysfunction. *J Manual Med* 1989;4:28

16. Silverstolpe L, Hellsing G. Cranial and visceral symptoms in mechanical pelvic dysfunction. In: JK Paterson, L Burn, eds. *Back Pain, an International Review*. Dordrecht: Kluwer; 1990:255.

17. Panjabi MM. Neutral zone and instability hypothesis. *J Spinal Disord* 1992;5:390–397.

18. O'Sullivan P, Twomey L, Allison G, Sinclair K, Knox J. Altered patterns of abdominal muscle activation in patients with chronic low back pain. *Aust J Physiother* 1997;43:91–97.

19. Wohlfahrt D, Jull G, Richardson C. The relationship between dynamic and static function of the abdominal muscles. *Aust J Physiother* 1993;39:9–13.

20. Kunert W. *Wirbelsäule und innere Medizin*. Stuttgart: Enke; 1975.

21. Schwarz E. Manuelle Therapie und innere Medizin. *Schweiz Rundsch Med (Praxis)* 1974;63:837–841.

22. Nansel D, Sslazak M. Somatic dysfunction and the phenomenon of visceral disease simulation: A probable explanation of somatic therapy in patients presumed to be suffering from true visceral disease. *J Manipulative Physiol Ther* 1995;18:379–397.

23. Schwarz E. Herz und Wirbelsäule. *Schweiz Rundsch Med (Praxis)* 1973;24:770–773.

24. Rychlíková E. Vertebragene funktionelle Störungen bei chronisher ischämischer Herzkrankheit. *Münch Med Wschr* 1975;117:127–130.

25. Lewit K, Abrahamoviç M. Kopfgelenkblockierungen und chronische Tonsillitis. *Manuelle Med* 1976;14:106–109.

26. Zbojan L. Vertebrogenní syndrom a viscerálne ochorenie (The vertebrogenic syndrome and visceral disease). *Çs Gastroent* 1985;19:277–278.

27. Huneke W. *Impletoltherapie*. Stuttgart: Thieme; 1952.

28. Gross D. *Therapeutische Lokalanästhesie*. Stuttgart: Hippokrates; 1972.

29. Gelb H, Bernstein I. Clinical evaluation of 2000 patients with temperomandibular joint syndromes. *J Prosthet Dent* 1983;49:234.

30. Maigne R. Le traitement des epicondylites. *Rheumatologie* 1957;6:293–295.

31. Lewit K. Impaired joint functions and entrapment syndromes. *Manuelle Med* 1978;16:45.

32. Parow J. *Funktionelle Atmungstherapie*. Stuttgart: Thieme; 1953.

33. Hermach H. Exteroceptive stimulation. In: K Lewit, ed. *Manipulative Therapy in Musculoskeletal Medicine*. 3rd ed. London: Butterworth-Heinemann (in press).

34. *Clinical Guidelines for the Management of Acute Low Back Pain*. Royal College of General Practitioners, Chartered Society of Physiotherapy, Osteopathic Association of Great Britain, British Chiropractic Association, National Back Pain Association, September 1996.

CHAPTER 21

Management of Acute Soft Tissue Injuries of the Cervical Spine

GARY F. IERNA & DONALD R. MURPHY

"If one advances confidently in the direction of his dreams, and endeavors to live the life which he has imagined, he will meet with a success unexpected in common hours."

—Henry David Thoreau

"There are two great puzzles in this world that foster debate among humans. One is the wonder of the universe, the other is whiplash."

—Murray Allen, MD

INTRODUCTION

Acute soft tissue injuries of the cervical spine plague society and present a challenge to those practitioners who manage patients with these injuries. Despite the fact that many whiplash injuries resolve within a short amount of time,[1] many others require effective treatment designed to reduce suffering and prevent chronicity. Difficulties in treating acute soft tissue injuries often result from a lack of complete understanding of the forces involved in the injury and the pathology involved. It can also be difficult to determine which structures are injured and are producing pain, and to determine the most appropriate management strategy.

Traditionally, there has been great uncertainty as to which management strategies have the greatest efficacy. This has lead to the development of various dogmatic approaches that lack a sound scientific foundation. Perhaps the most common ineffective approaches revolve around the long-term application of modalities such as cervical collars, anti-inflammatory medications, moist heat, massage, and manipulation. Each of these modalities can have great clinical utility when used judiciously, as part of a strategy designed to rapidly reduce pain and improve function. But when used singularly and without sound rationale, they may actually delay recovery. The job of the practitioner is to have a complete understanding of the injury and the various treatment options available and to administer the most efficacious treatment strategy possible, always keeping in mind the goals of treatment and avoiding any approach that would interfere with the attainment of those goals.

Essential to establishing an effective management strategy is making an accurate tissue-specific diagnosis. This can be difficult, due to both the paucity of information in the scientific literature regarding the pathology involved and the frequent failure of clinicians to fully appreciate the function of the locomotor system. This difficulty ultimately leads to failure in adequately designing a treatment and rehabilitation program. The purpose of this chapter is to provide the clinician with pertinent background information regarding the pathological processes involved in various acute soft tissue injuries and with the information required to make an appropriate working diagnosis. Once a working diagnosis is established, and the long-term goal of maximizing return of the patient to a pain-free functional state is understood, an appropriate management plan can be determined. It is only then that the clinician can take a pragmatic approach to determining those specific treatment and rehabilitation approaches that are to be applied.

No two injuries are the same; therefore, there is no "cookbook" recipe for the management of soft tissue injuries. The clinician must simply have a thorough understanding of the various factors involved and make appropriate decisions based on the current scientific understanding of the process. Indiscriminate use of any therapy without a logical rationale for how it will benefit the patient in achieving his or her long-term goals is inappropriate. Each clinical decision must be based on a sound understanding of the condition and must be adaptable to each patient's presentation and response to therapy.

UNDERSTANDING THE HEALING PROCESS

To maximize the healing potential and appropriately develop a management strategy, the clinician must have an understanding of the clinical phases of healing following acute cervical soft tissue injury. Van der Muellen[2] outlined the various physiological activities that take place following soft tissue injury, and this information can be integrated into the process of formulating an appropriate management strategy. It must be kept in mind, for example, that the duration and magnitude of each phase of healing will be related to the severity of the injury. Although the phases of healing discussed here provide a general framework of tissue healing, the actual clinical picture in each case is not always so well defined. For example, even though an injury may occur 2 weeks previous to the patient's initial presentation, the patient may still be experiencing an acute inflammatory response, related to repetitive trauma to the injured cervical structures, which results from failure of the muscular system to provide adequate support to the tissues. Therefore, the healing process must be seen as a continuum of events rather than consisting of well delineated phases. However, for the purposes of this discussion, the phases are presented as separate entities.

Acute Inflammatory Reaction Phase

This is the body's immediate response to injury. This phase can last up to 48 to 72 hours following the injury; the magnitude of the response is dependent upon the degree of tissue damage. Clinically, patients who experience an acute injury and are experiencing an inflammatory response often experience cervical pain even when they are at rest; for example, while lying in bed. Erect posture is not required for the patient to experience pain.

In the acute inflammatory response, the body attempts to remove the damaged tissues and prepare the environment for healing. Unfortunately, the response is often excessive and impedes optimal healing. The acute inflammatory response includes vasodilatation and increased permeability of capillaries, resulting in the exudation of white blood cells and various chemical by-products. Macrophages infiltrate the area and phagocytosis of the damaged tissues begins. As a result of capillary damage, a clot begins to form. In addition, fibroblastic infiltration occurs and early fibroblastic activity begins. The fibroblasts secrete collagen which is the foundation of scar formation. These physiological processes, as well as direct mechanical irritation of nociceptors, result in pain. Pain leads to reflex muscle spasm and pain behavior, which results in decreased movement of the injured area. This ultimately leads to fluid stasis and the establishment of a poor healing environment. The fluid stasis results in increased accumulation of tissue by-products, further sensitizing nociceptors. In addition, interstitial pressure increases, which slows the biochemical exchange of materials necessary for appropriate healing.

This process ultimately leads to the formation of what has been referred to as a "sensitizing soup."[3] This "soup" acts as a sensitizing agent to the nociceptors in the area and helps to perpetuate spasm of the surrounding musculature. It should be noted that although the spasm can be a source of pain, it serves a protective role, and any attempt to break the spasm, without addressing its underlying cause, should be avoided. It is, however, important to address this "soup" in the first few days following the injury, because the failure to appropriately control the inflammatory response will result in the "soup" becoming more organized and gel-like, which ultimately makes it very difficult to evacuate.

Intervention in the acute inflammatory reaction phase includes anti-inflammatory medications, nutritional supplementation, acupuncture, physiotherapy modalities, manual therapy, and promotion of activities that enhance fluid movement. Management strategy and goals during the acute phase should focus on the control of the inflammatory response and the education of the patient. This topic is discussed later in the chapter.

Repair and Regeneration Phase

This is the stage in which healing begins. The duration of this phase is highly variable and depends upon the severity of the injury. Van der Muellen[2] describes this phase as lasting from 48 hours to 6 weeks. Clinically, patients in this phase often state that they have minimal pain when they awaken; however, soon after assuming the erect posture, they develop neck pain.

It is during the repair and regeneration phase that granulation tissue is formed and there occurs an increase in collagen production. It is this collagen that ultimately provides the meshwork for the scar that attempts to provide stability to the spine. This new collagen is extremely fragile and can be easily disrupted. This collagen is deposited in a very unorganized fashion and lack of motion in the area can result in excessive disorganized scar formation. It, therefore, is important to control the forces being transmitted through the area to prevent collagen destruction, while still promoting the mobility required to prevent contracture. This approach will maximize the potential to restore stability while maintaining mobility. Although inflammation is resolving in this phase, repeated microtrauma to the area as a result of failure to control excessive forces can result in recurrence of the inflammatory response.

Appropriate management strategies for the patient become critical at this stage because ineffective approaches can contribute to the development of chronic pain, instability, and abnormal illness behavior. Clinicians must take an informed proactive approach to the injured patient to minimize the likelihood of chronic illness.

Remodeling and Maturation Phase

This phase can vary tremendously in duration. The duration can be based on several factors, including the severity of the injury, the healing capabilities of the patient, the manner in which the acute and subacute stages of healing were managed, and how the patient will be rehabilitated during this phase. It can vary from 3 weeks to 12 months, and the effectiveness of management strategies employed prior to and during this phase can have long-term implications for the patient. Patients in this phase quite often complain of minimal pain throughout their normal activities of daily living; however, they experience a greater degree of pain at the end of the day and following prolonged or excessive activity.

It is during the remodeling and maturation phase that maturation of the connective tissue occurs to form a stronger, more organized scar. Contracture of the scar tissue occurs and the healing response remodels the collagen based on the stresses to which it is subjected. It is unlikely that an active inflammatory response is present unless the patient has been poorly managed up to this point or the patient experiences exacerbation or reinjury.

IDENTIFICATION OF THE INJURED OR DYSFUNCTIONAL STRUCTURES

Just as the heart can refer pain to the neck, jaw, and left arm during a myocardial infarction, all structures of the musculoskeletal system can cause pain to refer to other areas. When treating musculoskeletal pain, the practitioner must first identify the site and quality of the pain and determine which structure(s) are the possible source(s) of the pain. In the acute stage, pain is the direct result of trauma to individual tissues and is often well localized. However, beyond the acute stage, when the function of the system is compromised, a chronic dysfunctional state may occur and pain referral distant from the source is common. It is important that the clinician become familiar with the various referred pain patterns and associated symptoms that can arise from cervical structures so that an appropriate tissue-specific "working" diagnosis can be made. This diagnosis is considered a "working" diagnosis because when dealing with pain, it is often difficult to ascertain the exact source of the pain without invasive procedures. A trial of treatment may be required to confirm or deny the "working diagnosis." In most cases, however, the pain pattern can be identified and provocative manual procedures and orthopedic tests can either provoke or alleviate the pain. From this, a reasonable determination of the pain generator(s) can be made. It is then up to the clinician to determine why those structures are producing pain

Several tissues are capable of producing pain following soft tissue injury to the cervical spine. Some of these soft tissue injuries result from serious injury; others are more benign, but potentially disabling.

SPINAL FRACTURES

Spinal fractures, though rare, can occur in hyperextension-hyperflexion injuries, and the practitioner must presume that one has occurred until proven otherwise. Failure to identify a fracture can be devastating for the practitioner who performs manual therapy. Fracture can occur at any cervical level and in a variety of locations in the vertebra. For those practitioners who perform manual therapy, a thorough diagnostic imaging evaluation should be performed prior to the institution of therapy.[4] Fractures of the upper cervical spine can often lead to serious neurological injury or even death. Many different fractures have been identified in whiplash injuries including odontoid process fractures,[5, 6] avulsion fractures, burst fractures, transverse process fractures, compression fractures, articular pillar fractures, fracture of the interarticular isthmus and lamina of one or more of the lower cervical vertebrae, fracture of the lateral process of C1 or C2, or both, clay shoveler's fracture, and fractures of the joints of Luschka.[7] Chapter 16 provides further details regarding cervical fractures.

LIGAMENTOUS INSTABILITY AND DISLOCATION

Most radiographs are performed within hours of cervical trauma and, as a result of muscle spasm splinting the injured area, subtle ligamentous injuries are not always visualized. The initial studies quite often focus on ruling out spinal fracture and dislocation. If the patient is still experiencing pain on examination 2 to 3 weeks after the injury, ligamentous instability should be suspected. In this case, follow-up radiographs, which should include a neutral lateral plus stress flexion and extension views, should be considered.[8]

Visualization of the biomechanical lines and the use of soft tissue measurements are essential to radiographic interpretation. In addition, specific radiographic signs of ligamentous instability should be observed (Table 21–1).

ESOPHAGEAL TRAUMA

Esophageal perforations have been reported in the literature following acute whiplash injuries and should be considered in those patients presenting with dysphagia.[9] Esophageal injuries are more likely to occur in those patients with pre-existing degenerative changes, particularly anterior osteophyte formation. In addition to esophageal perforation, prevertebral hematomas have been demonstrated, which can lead to airway obstruction and dysphagia.[10, 11]

Despite their low incidence, esophageal rupture and prevertebral hematoma must be detected when they occur and must be appropriately managed. Prevertebral air noted on lateral radiograph is the most important sign of esophageal rupture,[12] and presence of this sign should prompt immediate referral.

CLOSED HEAD INJURIES

Intracranial bleeding has been noted in whiplash injuries that do not involve direct head trauma.[13, 14] Minor brain injury has often gone undiagnosed because of a failure to investigate it or a limitation of the resolution of diagnostic imaging modalities. It has also been written off as "litigation neurosis." Fortunately, due to the advent of more advanced imaging software and single photon emission computed tomography (SPECT) scanning,[15] minor brain injuries are now being diagnosed.

Table 21–1: Radiographic Signs of Ligamentous Instability

Fanning of the spinous processes

Atlanto-dental interspace greater than 5 mm

Translation of one vertebra on the adjacent vertebra on flexion/extension views of greater than 3.5 mm

Gapping of the facet joint surfaces

VERTEBRAL ARTERY INJURY

The potential for vertebral artery injury following acute soft tissue injuries remains a real and potentially devastating complication that can result in severe neurological consequences, including death. Although vertebral artery injury following minor acute cervical spine trauma is rare, Freidman et al[16] demonstrated that in major acute cervical spine trauma, vertebral artery injury is common. They demonstrated, however, that in the majority of the cases, the vascular abnormalities identified by magnetic resonance angiography (MRA), remained clinically occult. This complication could potentially prove to be hazardous to practitioners who practice manual therapy. For this reason, a previous history of a motor vehicle accident may be a risk factor for vertebrobasilar artery insufficiency following manipulation.[17] Noninvasive assessment of the vertebral arteries by magnetic resonance imaging (MRI) or MRA, or both, should be considered in patients who have experienced severe injuries in high-speed crashes, particularly for those practitioners who are considering manual therapy.

> ### ⚠ CLINICAL PEARL
>
> One of the authors (GFI) recently had two patients who, following a severe motor vehicle accident (MVA), experienced a vertebrobasilar insufficiency. One patient was a 39-year-old, otherwise healthy man who was 6 months post-MVA and presented to my clinic for treatment of neck pain, occipital headache, and bilateral thoracic outlet syndrome. Vertebrobasilar provocative screening maneuvers were unremarkable; however, the patient did not respond favorably to his first gentle upper cervical thrust manipulation. The manipulation was performed at the level of the atlanto-occipital joint in lateral flexion and the patient stated it "did not feel right." Manipulation was subsequently discontinued. Eight weeks later, while on vacation, the patient suffered a Wallenberg's syndrome (see Chap. 22). The patient has since fully recovered. The second case was a 22-year-old woman who presented to my clinic 8 months post-MVA. On her third visit, an upper cervical thrust manipulation was performed, and the patient subsequently experienced a vertebrobasilar transient ischemic attack within 1 hour. The patient fully recovered within 24 hours; however, thrust manipulation was discontinued and the patient was informed of the mechanism of onset of her symptoms and advised against any further manipulations to the cervical spine. It should be noted that each of the cases involved rear-end collisions in which the patient's head was rotated at the time of impact.

VESTIBULAR DYSFUNCTION

Many patients who suffer traumatic soft tissue injuries to the cervical spine also suffer injury to the labyrinth.[18] This leads to a variety of symptoms that can be overlooked or dismissed by the clinician, particularly in patients for whom severe pain is their primary complaint. However, in addition to pain, many patients complain of a sense of disequilibrium and clumsiness following whiplash injuries and similar cervical trauma. The rapid oscillatory forces of cervical trauma can result in demonstrable inner ear dysfunction and loss of postural control.[18]

The clinician must be aware that labyrinthine damage, in addition to the sense of disequilibrium, can manifest itself in an increase in the resting tone of the antigravity muscles of the cervical spine, which can lead to the patient presentation of neck pain, stiffness, and headache, as well as temporomandibular dysfunction. A patient presenting with neck pain, stiffness, headache, and a sense of disequilibrium is often given the misdiagnosis of "cervicogenic vertigo" without proper workup. Inappropriate treatment is then provided, directed at the cervical spine or temporomandibular apparatus, based on the assumption that the source of the problem lies with the musculoskeletal structures.

Often helpful in the evaluation of these patients are vestibular function tests, which include electronystagmographic tests, moving platform posturography, vestibular autorotatory testing, and tympanometric fistula tests. Patients who demonstrate vestibular dysfunction must receive appropriate therapy, including possibly antivertigo medication, vestibular rehabilitation, and possibly acupuncture, if therapeutic success is to be achieved.

INTERVERTEBRAL DISCS AND RADICULOPATHY

Both anterior and posterior annular tears, avulsion tears of the anterior annulus from the vertebral end plate, and end plate fractures have been demonstrated in numerous case reports and scientific studies.[19] It has been suggested that forced compression of the anterior aspect of the disc during hyperflexion injury may cause the nuclear material to burst posteriorly. Conversely, during hyperextension injury, compression of the posterior annulus can result in the nuclear material bursting anteriorly. In addition, severe hyperextension can result in a tractioning force, resulting in avulsion of the annulus. It is presumed that as in the lumbar spine, compressive forces on the disc may result in end plate herniation.

It has been demonstrated that the outer one third of the annulus is innervated with both mechanoreceptive and nociceptive receptors[20] and, therefore, internal disruption of the disc can be a source of pain even if the spinal nerve roots are not involved. Pain can result from direct stimulation of the nociceptors as well through reflex spasm of segmentally related muscles due to the influence of intradiscal mechanoreceptors.[20] As previously noted, the C5–6 and C6–7 vertebral levels are most frequently injured in whiplash injuries, and pain from the discs at these levels can result in local neck pain as well as pain that refers to the interscapular region and upper extremity. This scleretogenous pain referral does not necessarily involve nerve root compromise.

The use of MRI and plain film x-rays can assist the clinician in identifying disc injuries.[21, 22] The presence of a vacuum phenomenon on plain films indicates avulsion of the annulus, and the presence of a tear-drop migration of nuclear material on MRI indicates internal disc derangement.[23] However, MRI has little utility in the acute whiplash patient unless there are signs of significant neurological injury.

Identification of the disc as a generator of pain in the acute patient may also be accomplished by examining the patient's response to loading (McKenzie evaluation; see Chap. 26). Centralization of pain with certain loading maneuvers suggests the presence of internal disc disruption (or, in McKenzie terms, derangement). Examination of response to loading has been demonstrated to compare well with discography in the lumbar spine,[24] however, its utility for cervical disc involvement has not been studied. Our clinical experience suggests that its utility in the cervical spine is somewhat less than in the lumbar spine, but it is still a useful, noninvasive tool for diagnosing internal disc derangement.

In contrast to internal disc derangement, herniated nucleus pulposus (HNP) can result in nerve root compromise, leading to radicular symptoms felt in the upper extremity. This can include dermatomal, myotomal, and scleretomal changes. A working diagnosis of cervical radiculopathy can usually be established by clinical history and examination. MRI and electrodiagnostic procedures should only be necessary if the diagnosis is not clear, and clarity is required to make treatment decisions, surgery is being considered, or objective confirmation is required for medico-legal purposes. Electrodiagnostic procedures, if they are necessary, should be delayed for at least 2 to 3 weeks[25] because neuromuscular changes will not be demonstrated in an acute radiculopathy unless total compression of the nerve root occurs.

The clinician must also watch closely for the development of cervical myelopathy. If HNP is significant enough to cause deformation and compression of the cervical spinal cord, signs and symptoms of cord compression may result. Symptoms may include sensory changes in the lower extremities, including paresthesia and loss of tactile and vibration sense. Lower extremity reflexes may appear hyperactive early in the process, with involvement of the upper extremities in more advanced disease. Loss of bowel and bladder control is a very serious finding. Plantar responses (Babinski sign) may be extensor. These patients require immediate surgical consult.

❗ CLINICAL PEARL

Patients who present with multiple level dermatomal changes usually are suffering from thoracic outlet syndrome and not multiple disc herniations. Patients are often given a diagnosis of multiple disc herniations because of arm symptoms and the presence of several cervical "disc bulges" on MRI. Quite often, the source of the problem is spasm of either the pectoralis minor muscle or the scalene muscles. This leads to compression of the entire neurovascular bundle and symptoms involving more than one dermatome (see Chap. 9). Electrodiagnostic studies can quite often be marginally positive, and the patient is then mistakenly given a diagnosis of multilevel disc herniations with radiculopathy without proper investigation and therapeutic intervention of the possible thoracic outlet syndrome as the cause.

ZYGAPOPHYSEAL JOINTS

Zygapophyseal joints are injured quite frequently in acute neck injuries. This results from the role they play in limiting end-range motion. While in most low speed, rear impact collisions the cervical spine as a whole does not reach the end range of flexion or extension,[26, 27] individual lower cervical segments, particularly C5–6 and C6–7, often greatly exceed the end range of extension.[28] Clinical and experimental studies have demonstrated that tears can occur in joint capsules following whiplash injuries.[29] This can result in segmental instability and lead to the development of chronic zygapophyseal joint pain. Barnsley et al[30] have demonstrated that in a population of patients with chronic neck after whiplash, the zygapophyseal joint was the most common pain generator. The difficult task for the clinician is to identify the symptomatic joint and determine the most efficient and efficacious form of treatment.

The most reliable way to diagnose the painful zygapophyseal joint is through anesthetic blocks of the joints themselves or the nerves that supply them.[30] This procedure, however, is invasive and is not always available to the clinician. In addition, it does not provide a long term solution to the problem.[31]

A more conservative approach to identifying the possibility that the zygapophyseal joints may be the source of acute neck pain is to first correlate the patient's pain pattern with those of each of the zygapophyseal joints. Dwyer et al[32] developed a pain map to determine which joint or joints should be initially investigated in a patient with suspected zygapophyseal joint pain (see Fig. 17–20). It should be noted that the zygapophyseal joints C2–3 and cephalad produce suboccipital pain and headache while joints below the level of C2–3 produce neck pain, interscapular pain, and shoulder pain.

Bogduk[33] proposes that the head pain produced by the upper cervical zygapophyseal joints is due to the convergence of the spinal and trigeminal afferents on the descending portion of the trigeminocervical nucleus. This referred pain phenomenon can often make it difficult to determine the exact source of neck pain and headache after whiplash. However, careful history taking can be extremely useful, in that once red flags for serious disease, including intracranial lesion, spinal fracture and dislocation, and radiculopathy have been ruled out, the location of the pain immediately following the injury (within minutes to

hours) should give an indication of the level and possible source of the pain. This is because, as was stated earlier, the pain that is experienced immediately after the trauma is generally well localized to the area from which it is arising. If the pain following the injury is primarily located in the neck, it is likely that the lower cervical segments were traumatized and are the present source of the pain. If neck pain and headache occur immediately following the injury, it is likely that upper cervical structures are the present source of pain. Barnsley et al[30] found that the most common levels for symptomatic zygapophyseal joints were C2–3 and C5–6. Also, in their study it was common to find patients with two levels of pain production, the most common double-level patterns being C2–3 with C5–6, and C5–6 with C6–7.

This situation leads to the difficult clinical task of confirming the initial suspicion as to the source of the patient's pain. The most appropriate conservative method is through motion palpation end-range provocative testing. Jull et al[34] found good reliability and validity of this type of motion palpation (see Chap. 13) in determining the symptomatic joint level. With a finding of abnormally resistant end-feel that, when springing palpation is applied, reproduces part or all of the patient's pain pattern, a sound clinical judgment can be made as to the probable level of pain generation. This determination will become very important when we discuss management of the injury.

MYOFASCIAL TRIGGER POINT PAIN SYNDROMES

Despite the lack of conclusive scientific evidence regarding the exact etiology of myofascial trigger points (TrPs) in the cervical musculature, clinicians must rely to a certain extent on empirical clinical evidence provided it is of sound scientific basis. The difficult and ironic situation that exists regarding TrPs, and other types of functional pathology of the locomotor system, is that, while they are a common cause of musculoskeletal pain, the objective diagnostic tests that are currently available are not capable of accurately identifying their presence. Travell and Simons[35] have, however, eloquently outlined the various myofascial TrP pain patterns and associated symptoms for each of the primary muscles of the cervical spine.

It is the job of the clinician to become familiar with the various pain syndromes that may develop as a result of cervical injury. By knowing the pain patterns that can be produced by TrPs in each cervical muscle, the practitioner can formulate a suspicion, based on the patient's description of his or her pain pattern, of what muscle is involved. Then, by palpating the muscle for a taut band and, if one is found, applying direct manual compression to the taut band, the patient's pain may be increased or reproduced. This strongly suggests that the TrP has been identified as the primary, or a contributing, pain generator. Then, if the appropriate treatment is applied (see Chap. 19) and resolution of the symptoms follows, the diagnosis is confirmed.

The following muscles are susceptible to developing myofascial TrP pain syndromes following acute injuries to the cervical spine: sternocleidomastoid, scalenes, posterior cervical muscles, suboccipital muscles, splenius capitis and cervicis, upper trapezius, levator scapulae, and pectoralis minor. They are discussed in detail in the next paragraphs.

Sternocleidomastoid

The sternocleidomastoid muscle is composed of two heads, the sternal division and the clavicular division. Quite often following an acute injury to the cervical spine, the sternocleidomastoid (SCM) develops multiple myofascial TrPs in either division or both. This muscle is often injured directly in a extension injury to the cervical spine. It will also tend to develop myofascial TrPs simply as a reaction to dysfunction of the upper cervical joints.

Referred pain and associated symptoms related to each division of the SCM are quite different. The sternal division tends to refer pain into the occiput, the vertex of the head, the temporomandibular joint, across the cheek, over the eye, to the throat, and the sternum (see Fig. 17–3). TrPs in the sternal division are often misdiagnosed as "atypical facial neuralgia," "sinus pain," or "temporomandibular joint syndrome." Associated autonomic phenomena may include twitching of the orbicularis oculi muscle as well as a full sensation within the sinuses without mucous production. TrPs in the clavicular division refer pain to the frontal region as well as to the ear. Patients quite often complain that the pain begins in the frontal region on one side and then migrates to the contrateral side, resulting in a severe frontal headache. Patients may also present with earache, with negative otoscopic examination. Nonpain symptoms involving the clavicular division include tinnitus, dizziness, and disturbed equilibrium.[36] This disequilibrium must be differentiated from true vestibular dysfunction. Of course, symptoms from both the clavicular division and the vestibular apparatus may occur simultaneously. Table 21–2 summarizes these symptoms.

Table 21–2: Associated Symptoms of Sternocleidomastoid Trigger Points

Postural disequilibrium

Temporomandibular joint pain

Tinnitus

Twitching of the orbicularis oculi

Coryza

Excessive lacrimation

Dry, nonproductive cough

Full sensation within sinuses

> ### ! CLINICAL PEARL

In patients with pain over the temporomandibular joint without primary dysfunction of the joint itself, investigate the sternal division of the SCM for TrPs, as this muscle often refers pain to the temporomandibular joint. Quite often these patients have had previous treatment of the temporomandibular joint which has failed, and the pain can be resolved by directing treatment to the sternal division of the SCM.

Scalenes

The scalene muscles are also frequently traumatized in extension injury. The damage to these muscles can be magnified when a lateral component is present, as when the patient's head is turned to one side at the moment of impact. When the scalene muscles become hypertonic as a result of either trauma or overuse, not only may TrPs develop, but thoracic outlet syndrome (specifically scalenus anticus syndrome) may occur as well. Patients with scalenus anticus syndrome will often complain of pain and paresthesia throughout the entire arm due to compression of the brachial plexus or subclavian artery, or both. The neurological signs and symptoms chiefly involve an ulnar distribution because of the elevation of the first rib and tractioning of the lower trunk of the brachial plexus. The median nerve can also become involved if the C5 and C6 nerve roots become compressed between the anterior and middle scalenes.

> ### ! CLINICAL PEARL

Patients with scalenus anticus syndrome often complain of pain and numbness throughout the entire arm, which is often exacerbated during sleep. Nighttime exacerbation is particularly likely when the patient sleeps in the lateral decubitus position, as this results in the cervical spine laterally flexing and causing further shortening of the scalenes on the down side and a stretching of the scalenes on the up side. This condition is often misdiagnosed as carpal tunnel syndrome because of the presence of hand pain and paresthesia that is worse at night. Although scalenus anticus syndrome occurring concurrently with carpal tunnel syndrome is possible, treatment of the scalenes should be considered. A useful diagnostic indicator of scalene involvement is the coexistence of ulnar and radial nerve involvement as well as a pain referral into the anterior chest or interscapular region.

Symptoms from scalene TrPs include pain on the radial side of the hand and forearm, the anterior chest and the interscapular region (see Fig. 17–9). Pain on the ulnar side of the hand with possible accompanying paresthesia, numbness, and dysesthesia can indicate compression of the neurovascular bundle.

Posterior Cervical Muscles (Semispinalis Capitis and Cervicis, Longissimus Capitis, and Multifidi)

The posterior cervical muscles may be directly traumatized during the flexion phase of injury. They may also develop spasm and hypertonicity as a protective reaction to vertebral motion segment trauma. In addition, hypertonicity of the posterior cervical muscles may result from vestibular injury, leading to the development of TrPs in these muscles. If this is the case, local treatment of the TrPs may be futile until the underlying vestibular dysfunction is addressed.

TrPs in the multifidis muscles generally produce local pain in the neck, whereas the semispinalis and longissimus muscles tend to refer pain cephalad to the occipital region and often to the apex of the skull (see Fig. 17–7). Patients often complain that their pain seems to "start as neck pain and then travel up the back of my neck to the top of my head."

Suboccipital Muscles (Rectus Capitis Posterior Major and Minor, Obliquus Capitis Superior, and Inferior)

With trauma to the upper cervical joints or ligaments, spasm can occur in the suboccipital muscles, which can lead to the development of TrPs in these muscles. Hypertonicity and subsequent TrPs can also develop whenever the structures within the skull are noxiously stimulated; therefore, caution must be exercised following a traumatic event when the suboccipital muscles develop myofascial TrP pain. These TrPs may be the painful expression of something more ominous, like upper cervical ligamentous damage or an intracranial lesion.

TrPs in these muscles tend to produce local suboccipital and occipital pain, as well as pain that can refer from the suboccipital region into the skull, the eye, and the forehead region (see Fig. 17–2). Patients often complain of stiff neck and headache and tend to rub their suboccipital region, often pointing to a tender spot. In addition to pain, TrPs in the suboccipital muscles can lead to disequilibrium. The clinician also must keep in mind that the suboccipital muscles are often the site of satellite TrPs from other muscles, particularly the SCM, upper trapezius, and lower trapezius. Therefore, careful evaluation of the other cervical muscles should be performed.

Splenius Capitis and Cervicis

The splenius capitis and cervicis are often traumatized during the flexion phase of an injury. TrPs in the splenius capitis often develop at the attachment site on the mastoid process and just inferior to it at the level of the upper cervical spine. These TrPs can refer pain to the vertex of the skull on the ipsilateral side (see Fig. 17–6). TrPs can develop in the upper and the lower portion of the splenius cervicis. Those in the upper portion of the muscle tend to refer pain diffusely into the skull and behind the eye (see Fig. 17–6). Patients often complain that "the pain feels like a stake is being driven through my head to the back of my

eye." In addition, it can result in blurring of the vision in the homolateral eye, which often results in what is described as "eye-strain headache" without identifiable visual abnormalities. Myofascial TrPs in the lower portion of the muscle can lead to an "achy" sensation at the angle of the cervical spine (see Fig. 17–6).

Upper Trapezius

The upper trapezius muscle is a common source of neck pain and temporal "tension-type" headache. The upper trapezius can be directly traumatized in lateral flexion injuries of the cervical spine. Trauma to the spinal joints and ligaments quite often leads to reflex spasm of the upper trapezius, leading to the development of TrPs. The upper trapezius muscle is often the site of musculoskeletal manifestation of limbic system dysfunction (see Chap. 4) and frequently the stress and emotional disturbance of being involved in trauma can lead to the development of myofascial pain related to this muscle.

When the superior border of the upper trapezius develops TrPs, pain is often referred cephalad along the muscle's edge to the posterolateral neck, mastoid region, angle of the jaw, above the eye, and most commonly to the temporal region (see Fig. 17–4). TrPs that develop in the belly of the muscle, just superior to the spine of the scapula, often cause suboccipital pain. This is frequently misdiagnosed as upper cervical joint dysfunction, and treatment directed to this area alone often fails. In addition to pain, TrPs in the upper trapezius can also result in a form of disequilibrium or vertigo as well as nausea.

Levator Scapulae

The levator scapulae muscle can be traumatized in flexion injuries; however, as with the upper trapezius, it can develop reflex spasm when the cervical joints or ligaments are injured. The levator scapulae quite often contributes to the "stiff neck" patients experience following cervical trauma. Cervical range of motion may be limited in contralateral rotation combined with flexion, and ipsilateral rotation combined with extension is often quite painful. The pain from TrPs in the levator scapula may remain local to the angle of the neck, or refer to the suboccipital region, the medial border of the scapula, and the posterior deltoid region (see Fig. 17–8).

Pectoralis Minor

Although not a muscle of the cervical spine, the pectoralis minor muscle is often involved in cervical spine trauma and is often overlooked as a source of symptoms radiating into the upper extremities. The brachial plexus and the axillary artery pass deep to the muscle and can be compressed when spasm or tightness develops in the muscle after whiplash injuries.

TrPs in the pectoralis minor muscle can lead to anterior chest wall and deltoid pain, as well as medial arm pain (see Fig. 17–11). Neurovascular compression can also occur and, in addition to the pain from the TrPs, numbness and pain in a radial distribution can be found.

THERAPEUTIC APPROACH

Acute soft tissue injuries of the cervical spine are essentially benign conditions, with the majority of patients recovering; however, a considerable percentage of patients become chronic pain sufferers.[37–41] Although certain factors have been determined to predispose patients to chronicity, the long-term efficacy and efficiency of the various management strategies have not been thoroughly examined. The practitioner who manages acute soft tissue trauma must understand the functions of the cervical spine, the mechanisms of the injury involved, and the dynamics of the healing process. He or she must also have the ability to accurately identify those structures that are injured or dysfunctional, conceptualize the short- and long-term goals, and appropriately design and apply a therapeutic regimen to accomplish those goals. The ultimate goals of clinicians who manage acute soft tissue injuries should be to (1) reduce the acute pain as quickly as possible and (2) prevent the development of chronic pain.

Prolonged immobilization of acute soft tissue injuries is generally considered to increase scar tissue, reduce cervical mobility, and promote pain behavior.[1] Normal function should be encouraged through return to normal activities of daily living as early as possible. Following the acute inflammatory and reaction phase, which usually lasts 48 to 72 hours after the injury, return to normal function should be encouraged.

The indiscriminate use of any therapy without an understanding of the pathology involved and the effects of the therapy is inappropriate. Rather, treatment should be directed toward specific physical findings and should be guided by predetermined goals. In general, these goals are to:

- Educate the patient
- Control the inflammatory response
- Reduce nociception from the primary pain generators
- Promote healing through controlled movements and reduced stresses
- Enhance neuromuscular and locomotor function
- Promote activity and independence from continued care

There are several treatment approaches to consider in the acute stage of cervical soft tissue injury. These are listed in Table 21–3 and will be examined separately, although several may be employed simultaneously.

PATIENT EDUCATION

Educating the patient regarding his or her condition is an important first step in recovery. There are several areas on which focus must be placed in patient education. These are listed in Table 21–4. It is essential to position the patient

Table 21–3: Therapeutic Considerations in Acute Soft Tissue Injuries of the Cervical Spine

Patient education

Pharmacological management

Nutritional management

Cervical collars

Surgical and invasive procedures

Passive modalities and electrotherapies

Acupuncture

Deep tissue massage

Muscle energy techniques

Joint mobilization and manipulation

Rehabilitative exercises

to become an active partner in his or her recovery and to be sure that the patient understands that his or her participation plays an integral role in recovery.

The patient should continue to perform as many activities of daily living as possible to minimize the effects the injury has on his or her lifestyle. Borchgrevink et al[42] demonstrated that patients who were advised to continue engaging in normal preinjury activities had a better 6 month outcome with regard to subjective symptoms, including pain localization, pain during daily activities, neck stiffness, memory and concentration, and neck pain and headache levels as measured with a visual analogue scale, as compared to those who were simply given time off from work and who were immobilized using a soft neck collar.

PHARMACOLOGICAL MANAGEMENT

Despite the paucity of data regarding the pharmacological management of acute soft tissue injuries involving the cervical spine,[1] a variety of medications are prescribed for patients including corticosteroids, nonsteroidal anti-inflammatory drugs (NSAIDs), analgesics, myorelaxants, and antidepressants. Oftentimes the possible benefit gained from prescribing certain medications is marred by inappro-

Table 21–4: Areas That May Be Covered During Patient Education

Basic anatomy and function of the cervical spine

The type of injury the patient sustained, including the soft tissues involved

The healing process

The type of treatment the patient will receive and the therapeutic goals of the program

Appropriate modification of activities of daily living

Emphasis on the patient's responsibility in the recovery process

priate advice given during the acute phase of the injury. For example, it is not uncommon for a patient to be prescribed a certain medication for acute pain or inflammation, but for this to be accompanied by recommendation for prolonged use of a cervical collar and inactivity. It has been demonstrated that early mobilization and an attempt to return to normal activities of daily living as soon as possible may have a significant long-term beneficial effect on acute neck injuries.[1, 42, 43] Therefore, it is most effective to prescribe medications that will help to reduce pain and inflammation in order to allow early activation along with the recommendation of return to normal activities. This takes full advantage of the beneficial effects of the medication.

Corticosteroids

Corticosteroids, in addition to having a powerful anti-inflammatory effect, have a neuroprotective effect. Petterssen[44] demonstrated that the administration of high-dose intravenous methylprednisolone in the very early phase of whiplash injuries (within 8 hours), significantly decreased the level of disabling symptoms and the duration of sick-leave periods on 6-month follow-up when compared to those who received placebo. Petterssen provided methylprednisolone bolus at a level of 30 mg/kg over the first hour followed by 5.4 mg/kg/hr for the next 24 hours. His study demonstrated that this very early intervention with corticosteroids may be beneficial in reducing long term disability and work incapacity.

Nonsteroidal Anti-inflammatory Drugs (NSAIDs)

The use of nonsteroidal anti-inflammatory drugs in the acute phase of the injury has proven beneficial and reduces long-term disability when the acute patient presents within 72 hours.[45, 46] Quite often, over-the-counter NSAIDs (i.e., ibuprofen, naproxen, aspirin, etc.) can be safely recommended to the patient, however, specific dosages must be taken to achieve an anti-inflammatory effect, otherwise these drugs will simply provide an analgesic effect and not obtain all desired results.[47] The Quebec Task Force[1] recommends the prescribed use of NSAIDs for no more than 1 week. The adverse effects from short-term and long-term use of NSAIDs should be considered and the patient should be advised of these. As with other forms of passive therapy, NSAIDs should not be viewed as a primary form of therapy; however, when NSAIDs are recommended for symptomatic relief with the goal of returning the patient to normal activities of daily living sooner, these drugs often provide significant benefit to the patient.

Analgesics

Although the use of narcotic and non-narcotic analgesic drugs enjoys widespread acceptance in the medical community and these drugs are frequently prescribed for whiplash patients, no studies to date have been conducted on the effects of analgesics on either the acute or chronic patient suffering from a whiplash-associated disorder. When non-narcotic analgesics are utilized in conjunction with other forms of treatment, limited efficacy has been demonstrated in the acute phase of whiplash.[45, 46, 48, 49] The use of narcotic analgesics in acute soft tissue injuries should be reserved for those severely injured patients whose pain levels produce significant disability. Patients whom the physician feels require narcotic analgesics to function, should be made aware of the long-term goals of activity and independence and how long-term narcotic use will impair their ability to fully recover. In addition, they should be advised of the adverse side effects of narcotics, including sedation and the potential for both physical and psychological dependency. Keeping this in mind, the prescription should be made for the minimal effective dose on a short-term basis of 1 week, eventually tapering the patient's use of the drug.[1]

Antidepressant Medications

No studies have been conducted on the efficacy of antidepressant medications in acute whiplash and, because of their temporal delay in therapeutic effect (often several days to several weeks), their usefulness in the acute pain setting is limited. Antidepressants or psychotherapeutic drugs may be considered for use in the chronic pain patient, both with and without psychosocial overlay, because of their analgesic effect.[50–52]

Muscle Relaxants

Despite the fact that there has not been a double blind controlled trial addressing the use of muscle relaxants for acute soft tissue injuries of the cervical spine, they are still widely used. It must be kept in mind that muscle spasm in acute injuries serves a protective role in limiting forces across injured structures. Pain that results in further muscle spasm is a sign to the patient to limit the painful activity. Considering that the principal action of muscle relaxants is to centrally reduce the activity of the muscles,[53] limiting the ability of muscles to contract during activities of daily living may diminish the locomotor system's inherent ability to protect itself; this may be detrimental to recovery. Therefore, from a theoretical standpoint, the daily use of muscle relaxants should be discouraged. In addition, the use of these medications in the early stages may contribute to long-term disability due to the sedative effects of muscle relaxants, which may decrease the patient's perceived functional levels. Where these medications may have benefit is for nighttime use. If pain prevents the patient from getting proper sleep, the use of muscle relaxants may prevent the detrimental effects of sleep deprivation.

NUTRITIONAL MANAGEMENT

Nutritional supplementation is a natural way to promote healing and should play an integral role in the management of acute musculoskeletal injuries. Nutrients may assist the healing process by reducing inflammation and the resulting adhesions, and by providing precursors for collagen matrix biosynthesis. The clinician should consider recommending a variety of supplements including a multivitamin/mineral, a series of antioxidants and a series of proteolytic enzymes which should hasten the healing process.

Nutritional recommendations differ for each phase of healing (Table 21–5). During the acute inflammatory phase, proteases, vitamin C, bioflavinoids, and curcumin may play a role in helping to control inflammation and reduce pain. It would also be prudent to include a multivitamin/mineral supplement as well as a series of antioxidants. During the repair and regeneration phase, vitamin C, bioflavinoids, thiamin (B1) and pantothenate can be recommended. In addition, a multivitamin/mineral and a series of antioxidants should be recommended. In recent years, glucosamine and chondroitin sulfate supplementation have come into favor in an attempt to provide the necessary precursors for collagen synthesis and thus proper repair of the injured soft tissues.[54] There are many commercially prepared supplements that can be recommended for patients.

CERVICAL COLLARS

The use of cervical collars has been a standard form of therapy prescribed by clinicians for many years to immobilize the neck following soft tissue injuries. The use of the collars, both soft and rigid, provides the patient with support in maintaining the cervical spine erect and may also function in reminding the patient of the injury, which prevents the patient from engaging in unexpected or excessive movement.

Several studies[1] have demonstrated that the use of cervical collars with other forms of passive therapy actually results in delayed recovery with regard to pain levels and restoration of range of motion. However, these studies illustrate the problem with addressing individual forms of therapy for a complex clinical condition such as whiplash and drawing sweeping conclusions based on the results. These studies simply looked at the use of collars and other passive therapies versus other more activating forms of therapy and determined that collars were less efficacious and therefore should not be recommended. There has yet to be published a study that looks at the judicious recommendation of using cervical collars as an adjunct to a management program which focuses on early patient activation, rehabilitation, and restoration of function.

The decision to recommend the time-limited use of cervical collars should be based on specific factors in each patient's condition and, in particular, on the individual's ability or inability to perform specific functional activities. If the time-limited use of cervical collars allows the patient to return to some of his or her activities of daily living sooner and is simply considered an adjunct form of management in the overall activation, rehabilitation, and restoration of function, the prudent use of collars is warranted. Where many clinicians and their patients experi-

Table 21–5: Nutritional Protocols for Acute Soft Tissue Trauma

KEY NUTRIENTS	DAILY DOSES
Acute Inflammatory Phase	
Pancreatin	1000–4000 mg
Trypsin/Chymotrypsin	500–1000 mg
Bromelain	500–2000 mg
Papain	500–1000 mg
+/− Fungal proteases	500–2000 mg
Vitamin C (ascorbate)	4000 mg (1000 mg q.i.d.)
Bioflavinoids (citrus)	2000 mg (500 mg q.i.d.)
Curcumin	2000 mg (500 mg q.i.d.)
Multivitamin/mineral supplement	
Beta-carotene	25,000–250,000 IU
Vitamin E (d-alpha-tocopherol or mixed tocopherol)	400–800 IU (400–800 mg)
Vitamin C (ascorbic acid, mineral ascorbate)	1000–5000 mg
Selenium (1:1 ratio from selenite, selenomethionine)	100–300 μg
Cysteine (N-acetyl-l-cysteine)	500–2000 mg
Repair and Regeneration Phase	
Vitamin C (ascorbate)	4000 mg (1000 mg q.i.d.)
Bioflavinoids	2000 mg (500 mg q.i.d.)
Thiamin (B1)	1000 mg (500 mg b.i.d.)
Pantothenate	2000 mg (500 mg q.i.d.)
Multivitamin/mineral	
Beta-carotene	25,000–250,000 IU
Vitamin E (d-alpha-tocopherol or mixed tocopherol)	400–800 IU (400–800 mg)
Vitamin C (ascorbic acid, mineral ascorbate)	1000–5000 mg
Selenium (1:1 ratio from selenite, selenomethionine)	100–300 μg
Cysteine (N-acetyl-l-cysteine)	500–2000 mg
Glucosamine salts	2000 mg (500 mg q.i.d.)
Chondroitin sulfates	2000 mg (500 mg q.i.d.)

Adapted from Bucci L. Nutrition applied to injury rehabilitation and sports medicine. In: Bucci L, ed. Nutrition in Exercise and Sports. Boca Raton, Fla: CRC Press; 1994:217–219.

ence difficulty, is when the use of collars becomes the mainstay of the overall treatment plan and inactivity and deconditioning result. Collar use may be recommended for sitting as a passenger in a motor vehicle, or in situations that require maintenance of an erect seated posture for extended periods of time (e.g., when sitting at a computer terminal). Use of a cervical collar should be limited to the

Table 21–6: Recommendations for the Use of Cervical Collars

1. Patients should be educated as to the long-term goals of therapy and, therefore, the detrimental effects of the long-term use of the cervical collars.
2. Collars should be recommended only for specific activities of daily living, and only if performing these activities without the collar becomes too difficult.
3. The recommendation of cervical collars should be predicated on the severity of the injury, and the collars should not be utilized beyond the repair and regeneration (subacute) phase of the healing process.
4. Patients should be weaned off the use of the collars as their recovery progresses.
5. The time-limited use of cervical collars should be an adjunct to the overall management process, focusing on early patient activation, rehabilitation, and restoration of function.

acute and subacute stages, and only if needed to allow the patient to perform activities of daily living that would otherwise be impeded by pain. Their use should never be recommended on a continued basis beyond the acute stage, and the patient should be encouraged to gradually decrease use of the collar as healing progresses.

The overall time frame for cervical collar use should be determined based on the severity of the injury. Table 21–6 outlines general recommendations for the use of cervical collars. A minor injury should not necessitate use of a cervical collar, a moderate injury may require the limited use of a collar for several days to a week, and a more severe injury may require recommendation of a collar for several days to several weeks. This is obviously a general guideline, and the specific recommendation for each patient must be determined individually. The greater the length of time the collars are utilized, the greater the likelihood of long-term disability.[55]

SURGICAL PROCEDURES

The need for surgery in acute soft tissue injuries is extremely rare. When the injury is severe enough to result in fracture or ligamentous instability leading to spinal cord injury, approximately 30 percent of the patients will not make it to surgery and will expire.[56–58] For those patients who do present to the emergency department with segmental instability or deformity, the goals of surgical intervention are to restore normal anatomy and stability, prevent neurological deficits, and, if neurological deficit is present, promote neurological recovery.[59] Surgical realignment, decompression, and fixation and fusion techniques are utilized to achieve these goals. The decision-making process on the particular surgical procedures and their exact timing are beyond the scope of this chapter; see Chapter 24 for further details.

PASSIVE PHYSIOTHERAPY MODALITIES

The use of passive physiotherapy modalities in the treatment of acute soft tissue injuries has been an integral part of patient management for many years. Recently, however, the paradigm has shifted to promote patient activation and rehabilitation and, as a result, many of the modalities have fallen out of favor. The clinician must remember that the passive modalities should only be used as an adjunct to help reduce inflammation, control pain, and, in particular, promote the activation of the patient. The use of passive modalities is often helpful during the acute and subacute phases of the injury and the decision to utilize a therapy should be based on sound therapeutic principles. Passive modalities should not be seen as a long-term form of treatment and their use should be time limited. Passive physiotherapy modalities can be grouped into three categories:

1. Ice/heat
2. Transcutaneous electrical neuromuscular stimulation (TENS)
3. Ultrasound

Ice/Heat

The use of ice and heat to help reduce inflammation and control pain has been advocated for years. Theoretically, ice should be applied in the acute phase to help reduce the inflammatory response and create an analgesic effect. However, ice can often increase pain that arises from a TrP. The application of moist heat, on the other hand, can relax the musculature and stimulate vasodilatation to help remove inflammatory exudates and by-products of muscle spasm. Heat, however, can increase the inflammatory response and thus should be avoided during the acute phase. The general recommendation should be to begin with the application of ice during the acute inflammatory reaction phase, as long as it is tolerated, and then progress to moist heat.

Transcutaneous Electrical Neuromuscular Stimulation

The use of electrotherapies in the management of acute soft tissue injuries has also been advocated for years. Various waveforms result in the stimulation of different receptors and axons, resulting in a variety of physiological responses. Some electromodalities are designed to stimulate large-diameter afferent fibers, resulting in pain inhibition; others are designed to stimulate muscle contraction in an attempt to reduce muscle spasm; and still others are designed to help reduce inflammation and promote healing (e.g., interferential therapy, electrical muscle stimulation, microcurrent stimulation, galvanic stimulation). In recent years, home TENS units have become available to help control pain on a continuous basis. The prudent use of various therapies is warranted during the acute and subacute phases, provided it is seen as an adjunct to the overall management strategy of rehabilitation and restoration of function and does not interfere with the body's protective mechanisms.

The application of TENS directly on the cervical spine can often be valuable in reducing pain and inflammation and can help facilitate tissue mobilization and activation. TENS may also be effective if applied on various acupuncture points to help control pain and reduce inflammation (see the later discussion of acupuncture). Microcurrent can also be very effective, when using probes, in rapidly reducing pain. One must be certain, however, to monitor the patient's response to the therapy. Patients occasionally complain of increased pain shortly after the application of pain-modulating TENS. This is quite possibly due to the fact that pain is a protective response of the body that involves muscular guarding, and the artificial removal of the painful stimulus may result in relaxation of this protection, resulting in exacerbation of the patient's symptoms. Electrical muscle stimulation techniques to reduce spasm should be used with caution during the acute and subacute phases. The goal of all treatment during these phases should be targeted toward the injured structure and not the protective spasm.

Ultrasound

Ultrasound can be very effective in controlling pain and reducing inflammation. Combining ultrasound and TENS can also be effective, particularly when addressing myofascial pain following acute soft tissue injury. Caution should be used when applying this therapy on the acute and subacute patient to avoid overheating the structures. Monitoring the patient's response following the therapy is advised.

ACUPUNCTURE

Acupuncture has been practiced in China for over 3000 years, and it was exposed to the Western world approximately 300 years ago. Traditional acupuncture is based on the belief that the world is regulated by two opposing cosmic forces, yin and yang, and the insertion of acupuncture needles restores balance to these forces in the body. Until recently, the practice of acupuncture was scorned as unscientific; however, in recent years, the use of acupuncture for pain control and many other purposes has received mainstream acceptance. Today, acupuncture is being practiced in the United States by thousands of practitioners both within and outside mainstream medicine.

The exact mechanism by which acupuncture assists in pain control is not completely understood. However, it is believed that dry needle stimulation of peripheral nerves leads to reflex changes and release of opioids at both the spinal cord level and in higher centers. Leon Chaitow[60] developed a series of points that are specific to the whiplash patient; these are provided in Table 21–7. The following auricular points can also be stimulated to obtain pain relief and edema reduction:

- Cervical vertebra point: Point is at the lower, medial aspect of the antihelix.

Table 21–7: Acupuncture Points Specific to the Whiplash Patient

POINT	LOCATION	NEEDLE INSERTION
Gallbladder 20 (GB 20)	Between the depression inferior to occipital protuberance and the mastoid bone	Insert needle 1 inch toward opposite orbit
Governor vessel 14 (GV 14)	In the mid-line between seventh cervical vertebra and first thoracic vertebra	Insert no deeper than 1 inch
Bladder 64 (Bl 64)	Point is on lateral surface of foot inferior to the tuberosity of the fifth metatarsal	Insert ½ inch

Adapted from Chaitow L. The Acupuncture Treatment of Pain. *Healing Arts Press; 1990.*

- Neck point: Point is at the junction of the antihelix and antitragus.

Additionally, acupuncture needles can be inserted directly into TrPs. Although the response is often short term, it provides the patient with significant relief and allows him or her to maintain a higher level of function with significantly less interference with activities of daily living.

Acupuncture has also been proven to be effective in treating the balance disorders caused by whiplash injuries. Fattori et al[61] inserted needles into acupuncture points Bladder 10 (Bl. 10) and Gallbladder 20 (GB 20) at a frequency of once per week for 3 weeks and found significant improvement in the patient's posturography results when compared to controls. The authors concluded that the use of acupuncture for balance disorders can be associated with or be a valid alternative to pharmacological treatment. Quite often the side effects associated with the medications for balance disorders can be quite disturbing, and therefore, the use of acupuncture should be considered for those patients who may be extremely sensitive to the medications.

DEEP TISSUE MASSAGE

Deep tissue massage helps to flush out fluids from the muscle,[62] reduce spasm,[63] and promote pain reduction.[64] It is one of the most effective tools for these purposes and is essential in rapidly reducing pain and spasm in the beginning stages, helping to prepare the patient for more active forms of care such as manipulation and exercise.

Deep tissue massage should be applied only by a trained practitioner, particularly in a patient with acute soft tissue injury, as there is a risk of further traumatizing the injured tissues. The patient's symptomatic response to the treatment should be closely monitored both immediately after treatment and the following day.

POSTISOMETRIC RELAXATION

In general, postisometric relaxation (PIR) is most useful in subacute and chronic stages, for the purpose of improving muscle function (see Chap. 19). However, there are times when it may be helpful in the acute stage to increase range of motion in order to allow the patient to begin range of motion exercises (see later discussion) as soon as possible. Great care must be taken never to vigorously stretch a recently traumatized muscle.

MOBILIZATION AND THRUST MANIPULATION

Mobilization

The introduction of controlled motion to injured structures assists in healing and should be considered as soon as patient tolerance allows. Caution must be taken, however, when the introduction of forces is considered in the traumatized spine as traumatic injury may sometimes compromise the passive stability of the spine. Gentle oscillatory mobilization techniques should be considered through the pain-free range of motion. This should assist in the healing process.

For intersegmental mobilization, the patient is placed in the supine position with the occiput resting in the palms of the clinician. The clinician's fingers are then placed on the lateral aspect of the articular pillars and the mobilization begins with gentle reciprocating lateral translatory movements of the fingers (Fig. 21–1). This generates intersegmental lateral flexion. The oscillations should begin slowly and be small in amplitude and can be progressed to more rapid movements with greater amplitudes. The spine is then mobilized in flexion and extension by placing the fingers beneath the articular pillars and gently oscillating each intervertebral joint into extension, allowing the spine to return to neutral between each oscillation (Fig. 21–2). Again, the oscillations begin slowly with small amplitudes and progress to more rapid movements of greater amplitude. The spine can then be mobilized in rotation by gently rotating the cervical spine to one side just short of the point of pain and gently oscillating the articular pillar into further rotation (Fig. 21–3). The opposite direction can then be mobilized. Finally, gentle intersegmental long axis traction can be performed by supporting the occiput and gently applying a long axis tractioning force and slowly releasing it. This can be repeated with increasing speed and amplitude as well. The goal of each movement is to main-

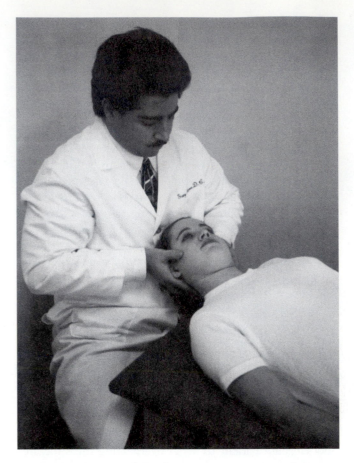

Figure 21–1. Intersegmental lateral flexion mobilization.

tain intersegmental mobility and prevent joint contracture. The patient's pain-free passive range of motion should increase following each mobilization, as well as following each session.

In addition to intersegmental mobility, it is important to maintain overall cervical spine mobility. Passive global range of motion mobilization should also be performed. This simply involves supporting the skull in the supine position and gently moving the entire cervical spine through flexion, extension, right and left lateral flexion, and right and left rotation. A gentle long axis tractioning force can also be applied during the movements. This also should be performed through a pain-free range of motion. This can be followed by active assisted range of motion exercises and then full active range of motion exercises.

Thrust Manipulation

If we consider the pathology involved in soft tissue injuries of the neck, the use of high-velocity thrust manipulation must be critically examined in the acute and subacute stages of healing. The body is attempting to stabilize the injured structures, and the introduction of a force that is designed to engage the restrictive barrier of the joint and increase the intersegmental motion may possibly interfere with this process. If thrust manipulation is being

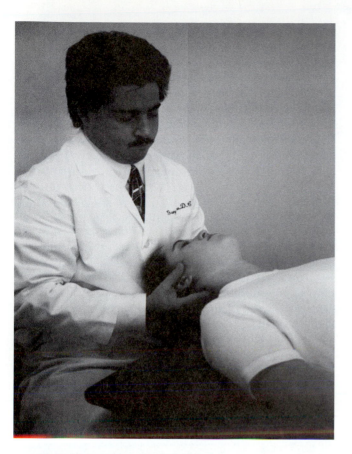

Figure 21–2. Intersegmental extension mobilization.

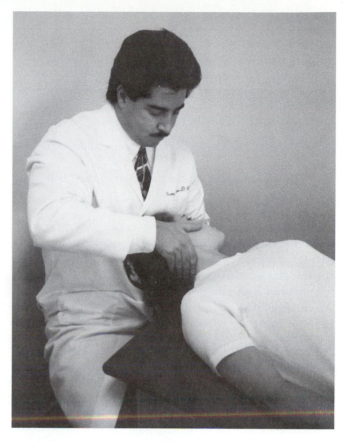

Figure 21–3. Intersegmental rotation mobilization.

considered, it should only be applied to those spinal segments that have been determined to be exhibiting joint capsular or ligamentous restriction of movement and a loss of joint play. It is important to minimize the use of thrust manipulation directly on those segments that have been traumatized or in adjacent segments. In addition, it may be prudent to wait until the repair and regeneration phase of healing has begun to utilize thrust manipulation. The time at which the repair and regeneration phase begins depends greatly on the severity of the injury and the quality of the healing process. It may be only several days in minor trauma or up to several weeks in more severe cases.

Despite the lack of a randomized double-blind controlled trial for the use of thrust manipulation in the treatment of whiplash (an uncontrolled trial recently suggested effectiveness[65]), this modality is considered by many clinicians to be a useful tool in the treatment of cervical trauma. Gentle thrust manipulation of the nontraumatized segments should be considered, particularly for the upper cervical and upper thoracic spine in an attempt to improve motion in distal segments. If, however, it has been determined that the upper cervical spine has been traumatized in the injury, thrust manipulation should not be applied to those segments in the acute stage.

! CLINICAL PEARL

The use of any technique designed to introduce motion into the spine (e.g., thrust manipulation, mobilization, and PIR) that consistently results in an increase in symptoms following its application should be reconsidered. If increase in symptoms occurs, it is quite possibly an indication that stability is required and not an increase in motion. It must be noted that some increase in pain after the first manipulation or mobilization session is normal. Repeated increase in pain after each session suggests, however, that increased mobility may not be indicated at that point in the process.

REHABILITATIVE EXERCISES

After the first 24 to 48 hours, a series of gentle exercises to further introduce motion to the cervical spine should be considered. The initial goals of incorporating rehabilitative exercise in acute soft tissue injuries are to:

- Prevent or minimize muscle wasting
- Prevent or minimize excessive scar formation
- Promote fluid movement in the injured area

Table 21–8: Hierarchy of Range of Motion Exercises

1. Passive range of motion
2. Active assisted range of motion
3. Active range of motion

- Promote activity to minimize fear avoidance behavior
- Restore proper pain-free function to the cervical spine

A series of range of motion and resistance exercises can be performed to patient tolerance as the patient progresses through the early phase of healing to minimize deconditioning and excessive dysfunction. There is a step-by-step hierarchy of both range of motion and resistance exercises which should be followed during the subacute phase of healing. These are provided in Tables 21–8 and 21–9.

Range of Motion Exercises

The goal of range of motion exercises is to maintain the mobility of the injured cervical spine and promote proper healing. In addition, movement of the cervical spine helps prevent the development of fear avoidance behavior, which can contribute to the development of a chronic pain syndrome.

Passive Range of Motion

Although passive range of motion (PROM) theoretically is a mobilization technique, it is an appropriate starting point for the rehabilitative exercise program. Gentle passive range of motion movements with the patient in the supine position, as described earlier, will help to maintain cervical range of motion. All planes of movement should be performed through a relatively pain-free range prior to the initiation of an active assisted range of motion.

Active Assisted Range of Motion

Once a relatively pain-free passive range of motion can be achieved, it is important to have the patient activate the musculature to maintain motion. Active assisted range of motion (AAROM) can be accomplished with the patient in the supine position with the clinician supporting the head and assisting the patient to move through all planes of movement. It can also be performed by simply allowing the patient to rest his or her head on the treatment table to

perform the movements. By providing support in the supine position, the cervical structures will not have to support the weight of the head against gravity. Another very effective and comfortable method to perform AAROM is with the use of the Occipital Float (OPTP; Winnetonka, Minnesota) (Fig. 21–4). This device is extremely effective in providing support in the supine position with minimal resistance to allow the patient to accomplish full range of motion through active muscular control. It is also a very effective tool to provide to patients for a home exercise program. When the patient can perform a relatively pain-free range of motion in all directions, weight bearing movements can then be added.

Active Range of Motion

Active range of motion exercises (AROM) are very simple to perform in the standing and seated position. These exercises add the resistance of gravity to the cervical musculature. All planes of movement should be performed and caution should be taken that the patient does not circumduct the cervical spine during these exercises. This movement quite often results in excessive pain due to the abnormal loading of the tissues.

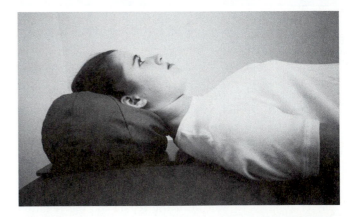

A

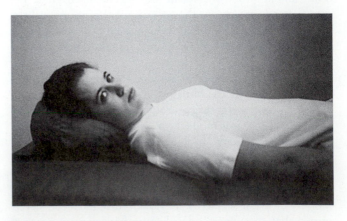

B

Figure 21–4. A and **B.** The use of the Occipital Float.

Table 21–9: Hierarchy of Resistance Training Exercises

1. Single angle, submaximal isometrics
2. Multiple angle, submaximal isometrics
3. Multiple angle, maximal isometrics
4. Small arc, submaximal isotonics
5. Full range of motion, submaximal isotonics

Resistance Training Exercises

Mild resistance exercises can be performed very early in the healing process to help maintain muscle strength and prevent significant atrophy of the cervical muscles. The resistance exercises should not cause sharp pain or excessive pain, but may produce mild delayed-onset muscle soreness. As rehabilitation progresses, the strength of the contraction and the holding time of the contraction can be increased to patient tolerance.

Single Angle, Submaximal Isometrics

It is best to begin these exercises in the neutral position due to the efficiency of the musculature in this position. The clinician must make certain the patient maintains a chin-tuck position to avoid chin poking, which places additional stress on the cervical spine. The options to the clinician include patient-controlled isometrics or clinician-controlled isometrics.

- *Clinician-controlled Isometrics.* The clinician can control the strength of the isometric contraction by simply placing the patient in the supine position and asking the patient to gently apply a force into the clinician's hand (Fig. 21–5). This should

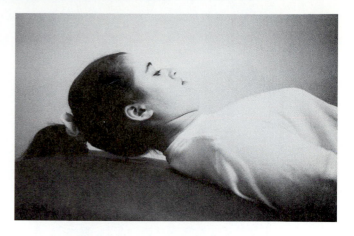

Figure 21–6. Hanging head isometrics.

be performed with resistance in all planes of movement.

- *Patient-controlled Isometrics.* Identical to the clinician-controlled isometrics, except that the patient places his or her hand on various points on the head and performs an isometric contraction. Again, all planes of movement should be performed.
- *Hanging Head Isometrics.* As many patients complain of inability to lift the head in the supine position, for example, when arising from bed, a simple exercise which can be performed on the treatment table and then continued at home, is to simply lift the head 1 inch off of the table, while maintaining the chin in a tucked position. This position is held for several seconds, followed by return of the head to the table. The patient can repeat this several times and increase the length of time the head remains elevated. This exercise can also be performed from the prone position and the lateral decubitus position (Fig. 21–6).
- *Neck Ball Isometrics.* Another effective way to perform isometric exercises is with the use of an 8-inch inflated neck ball (also known as a playground ball). Patients usually enjoy working with the neck balls and this appears to increase patient compliance. Simply have the patient place the ball against a wall and apply resistance with the cervical spine (Fig. 21–7). It is important that correct cervical spine posture be maintained, particularly in avoiding chin poking in the flexion movement. This can be prevented by avoiding forward translation during flexion. Posterior translation can be performed to help facilitate and strengthen the dorsal neck muscles and promote proper cervical postures. All planes of movement should be performed.

Multiple Angle, Submaximal Isometrics

After isometric exercises have been performed safely in the neutral position, the cervical spine can then be positioned

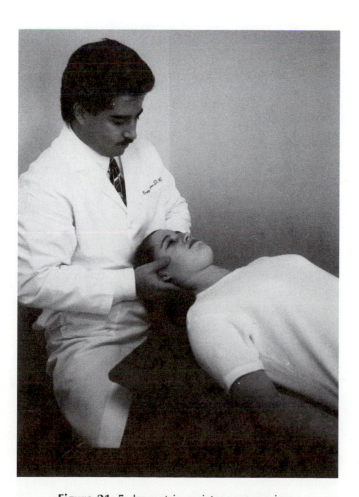

Figure 21–5. Isometric resistance exercises.

Figure 21–7. Neck ball isometrics.

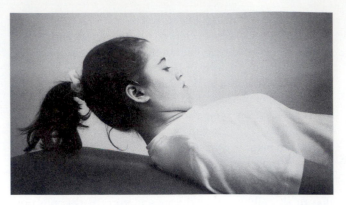

Figure 21–8. Hanging head isotonics.

in various angles to increase isometric strength throughout a wider range of motion. Positioning the cervical spine at 20-degree intervals in the range of motion and applying a submaximal resistance at each interval will result in strength gains throughout the full functional range of motion. The time each resistance is applied should also be increased as the patient progresses. All planes of movement should be performed.

Multiple Angle, Maximal Isometrics
Once submaximal isometric resistance can be performed throughout a full range of motion, the amount of force can be increased to achieve maximal multiple angle isometric resistance training throughout the full range of motion.

Small Arc, Submaximal Isotonics
When the patient is able to perform a series of isometric contractions through a full range of motion, small arc, submaximal isotonic exercises can then be instituted. The patient can quite simply use the weight of his or her own head to perform the isotonic exercises or use a neck ball (see earlier discussion) for this purpose. The patient can begin with small arcs (less than full range of motion) and progress to full range of motion exercises.

- *Hanging Head Isotonics.* Simply have the patient lie in the supine position and have him or her lift the head from the table. Make certain the patient begins the movement with tucking of the chin. This is accomplished through flexion of the head on the upper cervical spine. This will prevent the patient from poking the chin and thus promoting forward

head posture (Fig. 21–8). This exercise can then be performed in the prone position for extension and the lateral decubitus position for lateral flexion and rotation. All planes of movement should be performed.
- *Neck Ball Isotonics.* The use of an 8-inch neck ball is an inexpensive form of exercise and is quite easy for patients. In addition, it is more interesting than simple hanging head exercises and, therefore, patient compliance with a home exercise program is often greater. The ball should be placed against a wall (Fig. 21–9) and the patient should be placed in a correct posture. In the flexion exercises, the exercise should be initiated with a chin tuck, similar to hanging head isotonics, to prevent the development of forward head posture. To help facilitate and strengthen the deep cervical flexors, which quite often develop weakness and inhibition, repetitive chin tuck exercises against resistance can be performed to fatigue. Neck ball exercises can then be performed in extension as well, again attempting to maintain a chin-tucked position. This is done to prevent further tightening and hypertonicity of the suboccipital muscles. The exercises can also be performed in lateral flexion.

Full Range of Motion, Submaximal Isotonics
As the pain free range of motion increases, isotonic exercises can then be performed through a full range of motion. As a result of the physiological overflow which results from isotonic training, strength gains can be realized at 15 degrees on either side of the angle of applied resistance; therefore, resistance training can be performed initially through a limited range of motion and the actual strength gains will be appreciated through a greater range of motion. All planes of movement should again be performed.

For home exercise programs, a combination of isometric and isotonic exercises can be performed. It should be kept in mind that as the repair and regeneration phase of healing continues, cervical stabilization training may be necessary. This technique will be detailed in Chapter 25.

A

B

Figure 21–9. Neck ball isotonics. **A.** Starting position. **B.** Upper cervical flexion.

But early activation of the patient with range of motion, isometric, and isotonic exercises can assist in the long-term recovery of the patient.

Resistance exercises quite often result in the development of soreness in the cervical spine. Although this is inevitable in some cases, it should be minimized. If the patient complains of excessive soreness either during or following the application of the exercises, or even the next day, it may be prudent to advise the patient to reduce the amount of force he or she is applying.

Cardiovascular Conditioning

The use of cardiovascular conditioning in an acute soft tissue injury of the cervical spine is a very safe and effective way to activate the patient. Quite often, although an upper body ergometer should be avoided in these patients due to the excessive movement of the cervical spine, placing the patient on a recumbent bicycle or treadmill is quite effective and beneficial (Fig. 21–10). Cardiovascular conditioning increases cardiac output, releases endorphins, raises patient confidence, and prevents deconditioning. All of this assists in achieving the long-term goals of a pain-free functional cervical spine.

CERVICAL PILLOW

A cervical pillow is a special type of pillow that is shaped in such a way as to attempt to provide support for the cervical spine and maintain the normal cervical lordosis. There are a variety of types on the market, and these pillows have been prescribed for patients after acute cervical soft tissue injury for many years. Recently, these pillows have been subjected to scientific evaluation, and have been shown to reduce pain[66–68] and improve sleep.[66, 67, 69] Use of a cervical pillow is a good way to help reduce pain and dis-

comfort and, as with many of the other approaches discussed in this chapter, gives the patient another tool with which to reduce pain on his or her own. It is important to note that there is often an initial increase in discomfort when using a cervical pillow[68]; this should not necessarily be a sign that the pillow is contraindicated. In most cases, this discomfort subsides within one or two nights, and improved sleep follows.

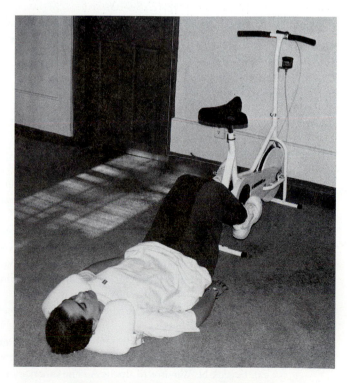

Figure 21–10. The recumbent bicycle.

CONCLUSION

Acute soft tissue injuries involving the cervical spine present a challenge to all clinicians. Although many will resolve without any long-term consequences, a large number of patients develop prolonged pain and disability. Clinicians must adopt an approach that attempts to minimize the risk of chronic disability. Although the current understanding of the pathology involved is limited, a pragmatic approach must be taken to patient management, particularly in the acute phase. The effectiveness of the management strategy during the early phases of recovery has been shown to significantly influence the long-term prognosis of the patient,[43, 44, 59] so there is a small window of opportunity in the acute stage to prevent chronicity. Keeping in mind the principles of effective management, including patient education; controlling the inflammatory response; treating the pain-producing structures; promoting healing through controlled movements and reduced stresses; enhancing neuromuscular and musculoskeletal performance; and ultimately promoting activity and independence from continued care, allows the clinician to determine those treatments that most closely follow these principles. The responsibility of the clinician is to continue to advance his or her understanding of the functions of the cervical spine, the healing process, the identification of the injured or dysfunctional structures, and the physiological responses and long-term effects of the therapeutic interventions. The clinician must always keep in mind the long-term functional goals of treatment when developing an appropriate management strategy for acute soft tissue injuries of the cervical spine.

REFERENCES

1. Spitzer WO, Skovron Ml, Salmi LR, et al. Scientific monograph of the Quebec Task Force on Whiplash-Associated Disorders: Redefining whiplash and its management. *Spine* 1995;20(suppl)8.
2. van der Muellen JCH. Present state of knowledge of processes of healing in collagen structures. *Int J Sports Med* 1982;3:4–8.
3. Wolf CJ. Generation of acute pain: Central mechanisms. *Brit Med Bull* 1991;47:523–533.
4. Crowther ER. Missed cervical spine fracture: The importance of reviewing radiographs in chiropractic practice. *J Manipulative Physiol Ther* 1995;18(1):29–33.
5. Signoret F, et al. Fractured odontoid with fractured superior articular process of the axis. *J Bone Joint Surg* 1986;68B:182–184.
6. Abel MS. Moderately severe whiplash injuries of the cervical spine and their roentgenological diagnosis. *Clin Orthop* 1958;12:189–208.
7. Barnsley L, Lord S, Bogduk N. Whiplash injury: Clinical review. *Pain* 1994;58:283–307.
8. Kathol MH. Cervical spine trauma: What is new? *Radiol Clin North Am* 1997;35:507–532.
9. Spengler CW, Benfield JR. Esophageal disruption from blunt and penetrating external trauma. *Arch Surg* 1976;111:663–667.
10. Howcroft AJ, Jenkins DH. Potentially fatal asphyxia following a minor injury to the cervical spine. *J Bone Joint Surg* 1977;59B:93–94.
11. Biby L, Santora AH. Prevertebral hematoma secondary to whiplash injury necessitating emergency intubation. *Anesth Analg* 1990;70:112–114.
12. Foreman SM, Croft AC. *Whiplash Injuries: The Cervical Acceleration/Deceleration Syndrome.* Baltimore, Md: Williams and Wilkins; 1988.
13. Ommaya AK, Yarnell P. Subdural hematoma after whiplash injury. *Lancet,* 1969;ii:237–239.
14. Ommaya AK, Faas F, Yarnell P. Whiplash injury and brain damage: An experimental study. *JAMA* 1968;204:285–289.
15. Bicik I, Radanov BP, Schafer N, et al. PET with fluorodeoxyglucose and hexamethylpropylene amine oxime SPECT in late whiplash syndrome. *Neurology* 1998;51:345–350.
16. Friedman D, Flanders A, Thomas C, Millar W. Vertebral artery injury after acute cervical spine trauma: Rate of occurrence as detected by MR angiography and assessment of clinical consequences. *Am J Roentgenol* 1995;164:443–449.
17. Terrett AGJ. Vascular accidents from cervical spine manipulation: the mechanisms. *J Austr Chiro Assoc* 1987;17(4):131–144.
18. Chester JB. Whiplash, postural control and the inner ear. *Spine* 1990;16:716–720.
19. Bogduk N. The anatomy and pathophysiology of whiplash. *Clin Biomech* 1986;1:92–101.
20. Bogduk N, Windsor M, Inglis A. The innervation of the cervical intervertebral discs. *Spine* 1988;13:2–8.

21. Davis SJ, Teresi LM, Bradley WGJ, et al. Cervical spine hyperextension injuries: MR findings. *Radiology* 1991;180:245–251.

22. Keller RH. Traumatic displacement of the cartilaginous vertebral rim: A sign of intervertebral disc prolapse. *Radiology* 1974;110:21–24.

23. Aprill C, Bogduk N. High-intensity zone: A diagnostic sign of painful lumbar disc on magnetic resonance imaging. *Br J Radiol* 1992;65:361–369.

24. Donelson R, Aprill C, Medcalf R, Grant W. A prospective study of centralization of lumbar and referred pain: A predictor of symptomatic discs and annular competence. *Spine* 1997;22(10):1115–1122.

25. Kimuro J. *Electrodiagnosis in Diseases of Nerve and Muscle: Principles and Practice*. 2nd ed. Philadelphia, Pa: FA Davis; 1989.

26. McConnell WE, Howard RP, Guzman HM, et al. Analysis of human test subject kinematic responses to low speed rear end impacts. SAE 930889; 1993.

27. McConnell WE, Howard RP, Van Poppel J, et al. Human head and neck kinematics after low velocity rear-end impacts—understanding whiplash. SAE 952724; 39th Stapp Car Crash Conference, 1995.

28. Grauer JN, Panjabi MM, Cholewicki J, et al. Whiplash produces an S-shaped curvature of the neck with hyperextension at lower levels. *Spine* 1997;22(21):2489–2494.

29. Taylor JR, Taylor MM. Cervical spine injuries: An autopsy study of 109 blunt injuries. In: Allen ME, ed. *Musculoskeletal Pain Emanating from the Head and Neck: Current Concepts in Diagnosis, Management and Cost Containment*. New York, NY: Haworth Press; 1996:61–79.

30. Barnsley L, Lord S, Wallis BJ, Bogduk N. The prevalence of chronic cervical zygapophyseal joint pain after whiplash. *Spine* 1995;20:20–26.

31. Barnsley L, Lord SM, Wallis BJ, Bogduk N. Lack of effect of intraarticular corticosteroids for chronic pain in the cervical zygapophyseal joints. *New Engl J Med* 1994;330(15):1047–1050.

32. Dwyer A, Aprill C, Bogduk N. Cervical zygapophyseal joint pain patterns I: A study of normal volunteers. *Spine* 1990;15:453–457.

33. Bogduk N. The anatomical basis for cervicogenic headache. *J Manipulative Physiol Ther* 1992;15(1):67–70.

34. Jull G, Bogduk N, Marsland A. The accuracy of manual diagnosis for cervical zygapophyseal joint pain syndromes. *Med J Aust* 1988;148:233–236.

35. Travell J, Simons D. *Myofascial Pain and Dysfunction: The Trigger Point Manual*. Baltimore, Md: Williams and Wilkins; 1983.

36. Weeks VD, Travell J. Postural vertigo due to trigger areas in the sternocleidomastoid muscle. *J Pediatr* 1955;47:315–327.

37. Norris SH, Watt I. The prognosis of neck injuries resulting from rear-end vehicle collisions. *J Bone Joint Surg* 1983;65-B:608–611.

38. Gargan MF, Bannister GC. Long-term prognosis of soft-tissue injuries of the neck. *J Bone Joint Surg* 1990;72-B:901–903.

39. Robinson DD, Cassar-Pullicino VN. Acute neck sprain after road traffic accident: A long-term clinical and radiological review. *Injury* 1993;24:79–82.

40. Parmar HV, Raymakers R. Neck injuries from rear impact road traffic accidents: Prognosis in persons seeking compensation. *Injury* 1993;24:74–78.

41. Radanov BP, Sturzenegger M, Di Stefano G. Long term outcome after whiplash injury: A 2-year follow up considering features of injury mechanism and somatic, radiologic and psychosocial factors. *Medicine* 1995;74:281–297.

42. Borchgrevink G, Kaasa A, McDonagh D, et al. Acute treatment of whiplash neck sprain injuries. *Spine* 1998;23(1):25–31.

43. Mealy, K, Brennan H, Fenelon GCC. Early mobilization of acute whiplash injuries. *Br Med J* 1986;292;8:656–657.

44. Pettersson K, Toolanen G. High-dose methylprednisolone prevents extensive sick leave after whiplash injury. A prospective, randomized, double-blind study. *Spine* 1998;23(9):984–989.

45. Foley-Nolan D, Barry C, Coughlan RJ, O'Connor P, Roden D. Pulsed high frequency electromagnetic therapy for persistent neck pain. A double blind, placebo controlled study of 20 patients. *Orthopedics* 1990;13:445–451.

46. Foley-Nolan D, Moore K, Codd M, Barry C, O'Connor P, Coughlan RJ. Low energy high frequency pulsed electromagnetic therapy for acute whiplash injuries. A double blind randomized controlled study. *Scand J Rehabil Med* 1992;24:51–59.

47. *Physician's Desk Reference*. 52nd ed. Montvale, NJ: Medical Economics; 1998.

48. McKinney LA. Early mobilization and outcome in acute sprains of the neck. *Br Med J* 1989;299:1006–1008.

49. McKinney LA, Dornan JO, Ryan M. The role of physiotherapy in the management of acute neck sprains following motor vehicle accidents. *Arch Emerg Med* 1989;6:27–33.

50. Siddal PJ, Cousins MJ. Pain mechanisms and management: An update. *Clin Exp Pharmacol Physiol* 1995;22:679–688.

51. Korzeniewski-Rybicka I, Paznick A. Analgesic effects of antidepressant drugs. *Pharmacol Biochem Behav* 1998;59:331–338.

52. Richmeimer SH, Bajwa ZH, Kahraman SS, Ransil BJ, Warfield CA. Utilization patterns of tricyclic antidepressants in a multidisciplinary pain clinic: A survey. *Pain* 1997;13:324–329.

53. Dillin W, Uppal GS. Analysis of medications used in the treatment of cervical disc degeneration. *Orthop Clin North Am* 1992;23:421–433.

54. Gottlieg MS. Conservative management of spinal osteoarthritis with glucosamine sulfate and chiropractic treatment. *J Manipulative Physiol Ther* 1997;20(6):400–414.

55. Hohl M. Soft tissue injuries of the neck in automobile accidents. *J Bone Joint Surg* 1974;56A:1675–1682.

56. Chestnut RM, Marchal LF. Early assessment, transport and management of patients with posttraumatic spinal instability. In: Cooper PR, ed. *Management of Post-traumatic Spinal Instability.* Park Ridge, Ill: American Association of Neurological Surgeons; 1990:1–17.

57. Cooper PR. Stabilization of fractures and subluxations of the lower cervical spine. In: Cooper PR, ed. *Management of Post-traumatic Spinal Instability.* Park Ridge, Ill: American Association of Neurological Surgeons; 1990:111–133.

58. Schlegel J, Bayley J, Yuan H, Fredricksen B. Timing of surgical decompression and fixation of acute spinal fractures. *J Orthop Trauma* 1996;10:323–330.

59. Mayer HM. Emergency care and surgery for whiplash injuries to the cervical spine. In: Gunzberg R, Szpalski M, eds. *Whiplash Injuries: Current Concepts in Prevention, Diagnosis, and Treatment of the Cervical Whiplash Syndrome.* Philadelphia, Pa: Lippincott-Raven; 1998:169–174.

60. Chaitow L. *The Acupuncture Treatment of Pain.* Healing Arts Press; 1990.

61. Fattori B, et al. Acupuncture treatment for balance disorders following whiplash injury. *Acupunct Electrother Res* 1996;21:207–217.

62. Cantu RI, Grodin AJ. *Myofascial Manipulation: Theory and Clinical Practice.* Gaithersburg, Md: Aspen; 1992.

63. Sullivan SJ, Williams LRT, Seaborne DE, Morelli M. Effects of massage on alpha motoneuron excitability. *Phys Ther* 1991;71:555–560.

64. Roy S, Irvin R. *Sports Medicine. Prevention, Evaluation, Management and Rehabilitation.* Englewood Cliffs, NJ: Prentice-Hall, 1983.

65. Woodward MN, Cook JCH, Gargan MF, Bannister GC. Chiropractic treatment of chronic "whiplash" injuries. *Injury* 1996;27:643–645.

66. Lavin RA, Pappagallo M, Kuhlemeier KV. Cervical pain: A comparison of three pillows. *Arch Phys Med Rehabil* 1997;78:193–198.

67. Persson L, Moritz U. Neck support pillows: A comparative study. *J Manipulative Physiol Ther* 1998;21(4):237–240.

68. Hagino C, Boscariol J, Dover, L et al:. Before/after study to determine the effectiveness of the align-right cylindrical cervical pillow in reducing chronic neck pain severity. *J Manipulative Physiol Ther* 1998;21(2):89–93.

69. Sanders GE, Mannello D, Dunphy F. Evaluation of Mediflow Waterbase Pillow: Satisfaction among asymptomatic subjects. Poster presentation at International Conference on Spinal Manipulation. Foundation for Chiropractic Education and Research, San Diego, Calif, June 1996.

CHAPTER 22

Vertebrobasilar Stroke Following Spinal Manipulation Therapy

ALLAN G. J. TERRETT

"All effective treatments have the potential to cause patient injury. Only an entirely inert therapy is totally without risk."

—A. G. J. T.

INTRODUCTION

Head and neck pain and dizziness are symptoms that chiropractors usually accept as indications of spinal joint or muscle lesions, or both, and therefore as indications for spinal manipulation therapy (SMT). While this is true in many cases, these same symptoms can indicate pathologies that contraindicate SMT. Vertebral artery dissection may cause symptoms such as head and neck pain or dizziness, which may prompt the patient to consult the practitioner.

The first mention of manipulative iatrogenesis appears to have been in 1871, when Wharton Hood wrote that "serious and often fatal results have occurred in the practice of all bone-setters."[1] The dangers of manipulation were apparently well known in 1871, and the first description of a case resulting in death was described the following year.[2] It has to be accepted that vertebrobasilar stroke (VBS) following SMT does occur. The temporal relationship between young healthy patients without osseous or vascular disease who attend an SMT practitioner and then suffer these rare strokes is so well documented as to be beyond reasonable doubt, indicating a possible causal relationship. Statements such as "chiropractic adjustments have always been safe"[3] and requoting statements such as "there is no conclusive proof that a chiropractic adjustment can or will cause a cerebrovascular accident (CVA),"[4] offer no help in accepting the problem, addressing the problem, or searching for solutions to the problem.

The issue has been confused by articles that talk about "neural ischemia."[5] This sounds harmless enough, a bit of dizziness. But often what we are dealing with and hopefully trying to prevent is trauma to blood vessel walls resulting in or aggravating intimal laceration, subintimal hemorrhages, vessel wall dissections, aneurysms, thrombus and embolus formation; producing central nervous system infarction; resulting in residual neurological deficit, tetraplegia, or death; not the occasional dizzy reaction.

Critics of SMT emphasize the possibility of serious injury, especially of the brain stem, due to arterial trauma after cervical SMT. It has required only the rare reporting of cases, many of which could have been prevented, to malign a therapeutic procedure that, in experienced hands, gives beneficial results with few adverse side effects.

Because VBS is responsible for the major criticism of SMT, it should be the primary objective of those involved in SMT to be on the lookout for the rare case, and take all available steps to minimize the occurrence of these accidents, for the benefit of the patient, the practitioner, the practice, and the profession. This chapter presents an analysis of VBS after SMT, based on 185 cases[6-119] collected from the English, French, German, Scandinavian, and Asian literature that were reported between 1934 and 1995.

INCIDENCE OF VBS FOLLOWING SMT

It is estimated that in the United States, approximately 125 million chiropractic visits occur annually (Haldeman S, personal communication, 1996). If it is assumed that one or more cervical adjustments occurs in half of these visits, then in the United States there would be 62.5 million visits each year where one or more cervical adjustments occurs.

In estimating incidence of VBS following SMT, it should be recognized that the actual incidence is not known, but can be expected to be higher than the reported incidence. Grieve[120] suggests an analogy to motor vehicle accidents, where the number of people injured according to reports in the press in no way gives any indication of the true incidence of people injured. Figures commonly quoted for serious injury following SMT have been: 1 in several tens of millions of manipulations;[121] 1 in 10 million;[122] 1 in 1 million;[123] and 2 to 3 per million.[65, 78] This indicates that

VBS is a rare iatrogenic complication when compared with complications of other therapeutic methods. It is to be noted that as the subject is being better investigated, the estimated incidence is increasing.

CASE ANALYSIS

Examination of the 185 cases described in the literature reveals the following age distribution, sex distribution, practitioner involved, and sequelae.

AGE DISTRIBUTION OF PATIENTS WHO SUFFERED VBS

It has been suggested that, "most risks of this nature are expected to be found in the elderly" because of spondylitic and arteriosclerotic changes.[124] Table 22–1 summarizes the age and gender of the cases reviewed. The age distribution graph of patients who suffered VBS following SMT (Fig. 22–1) easily dispels the idea that these injuries are more

Table 22–1: Age and Sex of People Suffering VBS after SMT

AGE (YEARS)	MALE Cases	MALE Deaths	FEMALE Cases	FEMALE Deaths	SEX UNKNOWN Cases	SEX UNKNOWN Deaths	TOTAL Cases	TOTAL Deaths
6–10	1						1	
11–15								
16–20	1		1				2	
21–25	4	2	3				7	2
26–30	6		18	2			24	2
31–35	18	3	28	6	1		47	9
36–40	15	3	18	4	2		35	7
41–45	12	1	9	2	3		24	3
46–50	2		6		1		9	
51–55	7	3	4	2			11	5
56–60	1		4	1			5	1
61–65	2						2	
66–70			2				2	
Age Unknown	5	1	6	2	5	2	16	5
Total	74	13	99	19	12	2	185	34

likely to affect the elderly. At first glance there does appear to be a predilection for SMT accidents in the 30- to 45-year-old group. Ladermann[60] noted this and mentioned that the average age is too young for gross anatomico-pathological alteration to be the cause. He proposed that the middle-age group was predisposed to post-SMT VBS because of a phase of joint instability occurring during middle life; and that this risk decreases with aging as arthrosis restores joint stability.

Closer analysis does not reveal any greater risk in any age range.[125, 126] The superimposed curve in Figure 22–1, is an age analysis of 6187 consecutive patient visits to an SMT practitioner's office (many patients are therefore recorded more than once); the solid line represents 10 percent. The increased number of accidents reported in the 30- to 45-year-old group appears simply to be a reflection of the age group most likely to seek the services of a practitioner of SMT. Therefore, factors such as a patient's age and the presence or absence of degenerative osseous or vascular changes do not appear to be important in assessing a patient's risk of manipulative iatrogenesis.[125–127]

AGE OF PATIENTS WHO SUFFERED POST-SMT VBS

Age and gender are known for 162 of the 185 patients. The age range for the patients was as follows:

- Males (n = 69): 7 to 63 years, with an average of 37.8 years
- Females (n = 93): 20 to 68 years, with an average of 37.1 years

The age distribution for mortality when age and gender were known was as follows:

- Males (n = 12): 23 to 51 years, with an average of age of 38.0 years
- Females (n = 17): 33 to 60 years, with an average of age of 38.7 years

The five cases of death where age was unknown were as follows: one male, two females, and two cases in which the gender was not stated.

SEX DISTRIBUTION OF PATIENTS WHO SUFFERED POST-SMT VBS

It has been stated that the group most at risk of VBS following SMT are young females. Of the 185 cases reviewed, the gender was known in 180 cases, which revealed:

- 77 males (42.8 percent); of whom 13 died (16.9 percent)
- 103 females (57.2 percent); of whom 17 died (16.5 percent)

At first glance there seems to be a greater risk for females. Closer examination reveals that this does not indicate a female sex predilection, but simply reflects the greater number of female patients seeking SMT. Studies have revealed the male–female patient percentages to be 40.7 to 59.3 percent, and 44.8 to 55.2 percent.[128, 129]

PRACTITIONER INVOLVED AND SEQUELAE

Table 22–2 lists the practitioner involved and the sequelae in the 185 cases of VBS. As is to be expected, the greater number of cases have involved chiropractors, because they perform most of this type of treatment. A simple analogy would be that complications following tooth extraction are much more common among members of the dental profession than among any other profession. In the United States, 94 percent of SMT is performed by chiropractors,

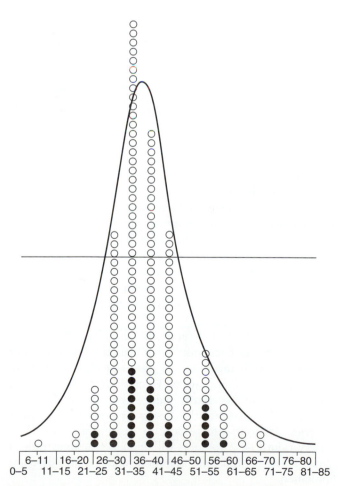

Figure 22–1. Age distribution of spinal manipulation therapy (SMT) vertebrobasilar stroke cases compared to distribution of patients attending SMT practitioner's office.

Table 22–2: Practitioner and Sequelae of 185 Cases of VBS (1934–1995)

PRACTITIONER	SEQUELAE							TOTAL
	CR	ACR	Unknown	RND	LIS-R	LIS	Death	
Chiropractor	6	8	9	36		5	13	77
Chiropractic	4	6	1	13	1		5	30
Medical Practitioner	5		5	7			8	25
Osteopath	2		1	5	1	1	3	13
Physiotherapist	2			5				7
Self-administered	1	1	1	2				5
Naturopath			1	1			1	3
Wife							1	1
Barber				1				1
Kung fu practitioner			1					1
Unknown	7		2	10			3	22
Total	27	15	21	80	2	6	34	185

ACR, almost complete recovery; CR, complete recovery; LIS, locked-in syndrome/tetraplegia; LIS-R, locked-in syndrome with recovery; RND, residual neurological defect.

*One case in the death column had been a case of tetraplegia.

4 percent by osteopaths, and 2 percent by medical practitioners.[130, 131]

MECHANISMS OF CEREBROVASCULAR INJURY

CLINICAL ANATOMY

The vertebral artery courses upward, encased within the transverse foramina of the cervical vertebrae, and on exiting the foramen in the axis vertebra, passes upward and laterally to reach the foramen of the atlas transverse process. The vertebral arteries are not freely movable at the C1 and C2 transverse foramina, but are relatively fixed by fibrous tissue. The vertebral artery then proceeds around the lateral mass of the atlas, enters the foramen magnum and, at the lower border of the pons, unites with the vertebral artery of the opposite side to form the basilar artery. The posterior inferior cerebellar arteries (PICAs), leave the vertebral arteries just before they join each other to form the basilar artery. The basilar artery passes up the anterior surface of the brain stem and divides to become the posterior cerebral arteries.

CLINICAL BIOMECHANICS

Rotation of the cervical spine to the extent of 45 to 50 degrees occurs chiefly at the atlanto-axial joint. This is about half of total cervical spine rotation.[132] Because the vertebral artery is fixed at the C1 and C2 transverse foramina during head rotation it is stretched, compressed, and torqued.

Research indicates that rotation is the single most effective movement producing decrease in blood flow; that is, it applies the greatest stress to the vertebral artery.[133–141] While cadaver studies[133–137] are important, the high percentages and early vertebral artery compromise are not reproducible in live subjects.[142–144] In one study of the vertebral arteries in 280 patients,[144] it was found that 5 percent lost the Doppler sounds during rotation to the end range, but none of these developed any signs or symptoms of brain stem ischemia. It is important to note that in no case of lateral flexion was there any loss of the Doppler signals;[144] and the cadaver study of Toole and Tucker[136] also indicated that lateral flexion placed less stress on the vertebral arteries. This should be considered when a rationale for the application of SMT to the upper cervical spine is developed.[125, 126]

During normal daily activities the blood flow in the vertebral arteries fluctuates,[145] but symptoms do not occur in healthy individuals due to adequate circulation from the opposite vertebral artery. Occlusion of one vertebral artery does not necessarily reduce the arterial supply to the posterior fossa via the basilar or posterior cerebellar arteries. Hence, compression or spasm of a vertebral artery from C–C2 rotation will induce symptoms only if flow in the contralateral vertebral artery is already compromised.

Normally during daily head movements, occlusion due to compression does not produce a decrease in flow suffi-

Table 22–3: Non-SMT Vascular Accidents Associated with Head Rotation or Extension

Childbirth[146]

By surgeon or anaesthetist during surgery[27, 147–149]

Callisthenics[36]

Yoga[36, 150]

Overhead work[151]

Neck extension during radiography[152]

Neck extension for a bleeding nose[152]

Turning the head while driving a vehicle[52, 61, 141]

Archery[153]

Wrestling[154]

Emergency resuscitation[155]

Star gazing[156]

Sleeping position[157]

Swimming[158]

Rap dancing[159]

Fitness exercise[160]

Beauty parlor stroke[161, 162]

Tai Chi[163]

Sexual intercourse[164]

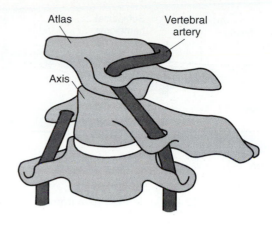

Figure 22–2. Stretch and compression applied to the vertebral artery between the atlas and axis vertebrae with contralateral rotation.

cient to produce ischemic signs and symptoms, or the development of infarction. In most cases the development of infarction indicates an underlying arteriopathic process other than brief occlusion.

There have been a number of cases where sustained or repetitive head position during normal activities has produced brainstem ischemic accidents in the absence of SMT (Table 22–3). Had these susceptible individuals presented to an SMT practitioner, the functional tests might have screened out some of those at risk, but could have precipitated VBS in others; and no doubt these patients would have been at high risk had they been treated by SMT. Even though the outcome may have been identical, the practitioner most likely would have been held responsible.

INJURY SITES

Injury to the vertebral arteries can occur anywhere along their path, by stretching, shearing, or crushing. Various authors postulate that there are seven potential sites in the cervical spine at which the vertebral artery can be compressed or injured by spinal movement.[125, 126] Rotation applies the greatest stress to the arterial structures in the upper cervical spine. The most reported site of post-SMT vertebral artery damage is between the C1–2 transverse processes, where the vertebral arteries are relatively fixed at the C1 and C2 transverse foramina (Fig. 22–2).

Injury to the internal carotid artery by the C1 transverse process has also been reported. Only five cases of internal carotid artery injury associated with SMT (2.7 percent) have been reported.[40, 51, 93, 105, 119]

ARTERIAL WALL TRAUMA

The mechanism of injury to the nervous system from a vertebrobasilar accident is brain stem ischemia, which may be due to (1) trauma to the arterial wall, producing transient vasospasm; or (2) trauma to the arterial wall, producing damage to the arterial wall; or both. There have been cases of VBS following SMT that were subsequently examined by angiograms and Doppler sonography, and in which no evidence of vascular injury could be found.[126] In these cases, it is believed that transient arterial spasm may be the mechanism for the neurological sequelae. Even in cases where arterial damage is found, the onset of symptoms is often immediate—too quick for clotting to have occurred—and this most likely indicates spasm.

Spasm would be particularly deleterious in the presence of hypoplasia or arteriopathy of the contralateral vertebral artery, or if the contralateral vertebral artery terminates in the PICA. Fortunately, in most cases, this spasm is transient and, if not accompanied by severe arterial damage or retraumatized, the patient soon recovers without any deficit. This appears to be a much more common happening than has been reported.

In most cases of VBS following SMT where angiography or autopsy findings are available, damage to the artery wall is found. One of the following mechanisms may occur:

- *Subintimal hematoma.* Compression or stretching of the vertebral artery wall may apply enough force to disrupt the vasovasorum, resulting in subintimal hematoma. This may decrease vertebral artery

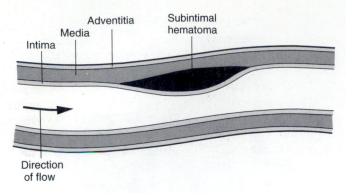

Figure 22–3. Subintimal hematoma.

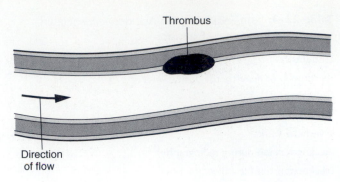

Figure 22–4. Intimal tear.

blood flow by occlusion of the lumen (Fig. 22–3). Intramural hematoma also may result in vasospasm.

- *Intimal tear.* The intima is the least elastic layer of the vessel wall, and the most likely to tear when the vessel is stretched or compressed. Exposure of the subendothelial tissue results in clot formation (thrombosis). The clot frequently remains adherent to the tear with propagation distally or proximally, or both, and may lead to vessel occlusion (Fig. 22–4). Following the intimal tear, the vessel (if not further traumatized) may undergo repair with no further symptoms, or it may go into spasm and progress through the changes described. Spasm may be induced following blood coagulation due to the release of thrombin, which is a potent constrictor of cerebral vessels.[165] Such spasm may then produce thrombosis.[166]
- *Intimal tear with embolic formation.* In this scenario, the propagating clot extends into the lumen. The blood flow may "break off" part and form an embolus (Fig. 22–5), which can then cause arterial occlusion distally, leading to infarction of the area supplied.
- *Vessel wall dissection with subintimal hematoma.* When the intima and the internal elastica are disrupted, allowing blood to dissect between them and the muscularis, a dissecting aneurysm is formed. The intramedial blood frequently compresses the true lumen, which accounts for the narrowed appearance angiographically. This also exposes the subendothelial tissue, which may result in thrombosis and occlusion of the vessel (Fig. 22–6). Dissecting hemorrhage can rupture through the intima, establishing communication with the true lumen (Fig. 22–7). Recanalization may occur, enlarging the true or false lumen.
- *Vessel wall dissection with pseudoaneurysm formation.* When the muscularis as well as the intima and internal elastica are disrupted, a pseudoaneurysm may

form as the remaining adventitia distends. As well as producing the changes previously described, this disruption may propagate distally to occlude the PICA (Fig. 22–8).
- *Perivascular bleeding (false saccular aneurysm).* Disruption in the continuity of the arterial wall allows blood to leak into the surrounding soft tissue and produce a periarterial hemorrhage, which is contained in the fascia. These changes may produce external compression of the vessel, resulting in either occlusion of the lumen or in turbulence, which may initiate thrombus and embolus formation (Fig. 22–9).

ONSET OF SIGNS AND SYMPTOMS

The onset of signs and symptoms of VBS following SMT can vary from immediately to many days afterward. The interval is probably related to the differing mechanisms of injury. When brain stem ischemia is due to vasoconstriction, symptoms would be expected immediately, whereas those (other than the pain of dissection) symptoms due to thrombus or embolus formation resulting from a vessel wall dissection would only become symptomatic after some time.

A review of the 185 cases reveals that the time between SMT and the onset of symptoms was specified in 138 cases, as follows:

- 69 percent during SMT
- 3 percent within moments or minutes of SMT
- 8.5 percent within 1 hour of SMT
- 8.5 percent 1 to 6 hours after SMT
- 5 percent 7 to 24 hours after SMT
- 6 percent 24 hours or more after SMT

Signs and symptoms of post-SMT vertebrobasilar ischemia usually occur in the practitioner's office (72 percent), and should be immediately recognized by the practitioner. The major signs and symptoms of vertebrobasilar

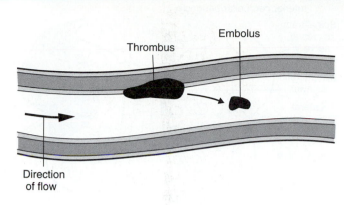

Figure 22–5. Intimal tear with embolic formation.

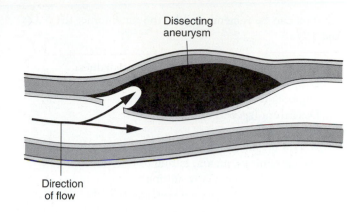

Figure 22–6. Subintimal hematoma with dissecting aneurysm.

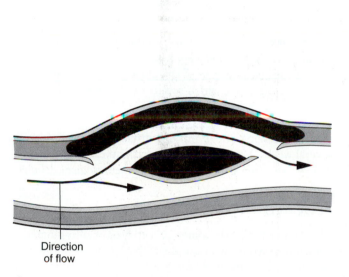

Figure 22–7. Rupture of a dissecting aneurysm through the intima.

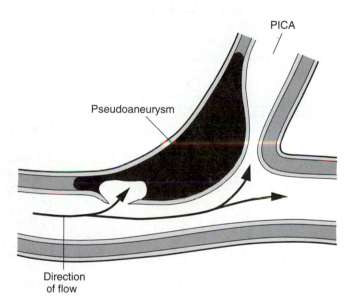

Figure 22–8. Occlusion of posterior inferior cerebellar artery (PICA) by distal propagation of dissecting aneurysm.

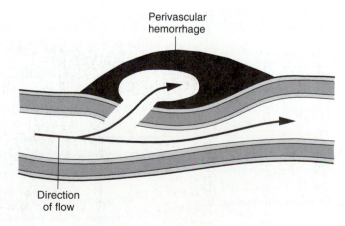

Figure 22–9. False saccular aneurysm.

ischemia can be remembered by the mnemonic, the 5 *D*'s
And 3 *N*'s:

Dizziness, vertigo, giddiness, lightheadedness
Drop attacks, loss of consciousness
Diplopia (or other visual symptoms)
Dysarthria (speech difficulties)
Dysphagia
Ataxia of gait (walking difficulties, incoordination of
the extremities, ataxia, falling to one side)
Nausea (with possible vomiting)
Numbness on one side of the face or body
Nystagmus

Dizziness is the most common symptom of vertebrobasilar
ischemia and may be unaccompanied by any other signs or
symptoms. Therefore, the absence of other brain stem signs
and symptoms does not always exclude the possibility of a
vascular cause. Also, the belief that dizziness is required before posterior brain circulation dysfunction can be diagnosed is incorrect, as isolated symptoms may occur without
dizziness.[167]

POST-SMT STROKE SYNDROMES

Post-SMT central nervous system injury (stroke) usually
conforms to one of the following syndromes: Wallenberg's
(dorsolateral medullary or retro-olivary) syndrome (occlusion of the PICA); "locked-in" (cerebromedullospinal dis-
connection) syndrome (occlusion of the basilar artery);
other brain stem syndromes; occipital lobe injury; cerebellar injury; or thalamus injury.

WALLENBERG'S SYNDROME

The dorsolateral medullary (retro-olivary) syndrome of
Wallenberg is usually produced by occlusion of the PICA,
but can also be produced by occlusion of the parent vertebral artery (syndrome of Babinski Nageotte). The signs and
symptoms are due to the destruction of the nuclei and
pathways located in the dorsolateral medulla oblongata
(Fig. 22–10). The following structures are involved:

- Inferior cerebellar peduncle, producing asynergia
  (ataxia) and hypotonia on the side of lesion
- Descending spinal tract and nucleus of cranial
  nerve V, producing loss of pain and temperature on
  the ipsilateral side of the face and loss of the
  corneal reflex
- Ascending lateral spinothalamic tract, producing a
  loss of pain and temperature on the contralateral
  trunk and limbs. Involvement of this tract and the
  trigeminal nerve tract results in an alternating
  analgesia.
- Descending sympathetic tract, which results in an
  ipsilateral Horner's syndrome

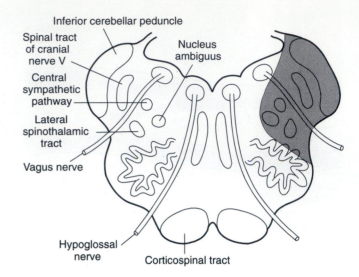

Figure 22–10. Cross section of the medulla oblongata.
Hatching indicates area involved in Wallenberg's syndrome.

- Lower vestibular nuclei, producing nystagmus, vertigo, nausea, and vomiting
- Nucleus ambiguus of the glossopharyngeal and
  vagus nerves, which results in hoarseness, dysphagia, or intractable hiccups

The acute signs and symptoms usually disappear within
several weeks. Most patients have a significant degree of recovery, but often experience residual neurological deficits.

"LOCKED-IN" SYNDROME

The "locked-in" syndrome, or cerebromedullospinal dis-
connection syndrome, is produced by occlusion of the mid-
basilar artery. This syndrome was first reported in the medical literature by Plum and Posner,[168] who described it as a
condition of total consciousness, with or without impaired
sensation, and no voluntary movement except vertical eye
movement and convergence (tetraplegic/quadriplegic). It is
interesting to read Alexander Dumas' description of this
syndrome—written in 1844,[169] 122 years before the first
description in the medical literature by Plum and Posner—
in the person of M. Noitier de Villafort in the novel, *The
Count of Monte Cristo.*

Interference to basilar artery blood flow in the region
of the midpons produces bilateral ventral pontine infarction, which effectively transects the brain stem at the midpons region (Fig. 22–11), resulting in patients who are conscious, paralyzed mutes—"a corpse with living eyes"
(tetraplegic/quadriplegic). The findings can be explained as
follows:

- Consciousness is retained because the reticular formation of the midbrain and rostral pons is unaffected, and the electroencephalogram is normal or
  near normal.

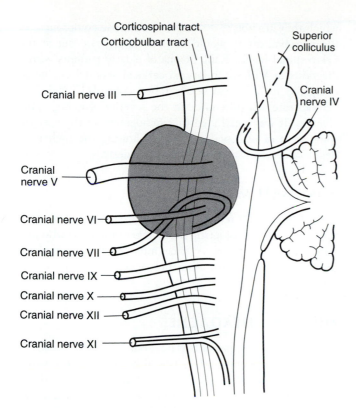

Figure 22–11. Area infarcted (ventral pons) in "locked-in" syndrome.

- Movement of the body is eliminated because the corticospinal tracts are destroyed, with resultant decerebrate rigidity.
- The nuclei of cranial nerves V to XII are destroyed, resulting in their paralysis. The oculomotor nucleus is above the infarcted area, but is paralyzed because its caudal connections to the para-abducens nucleus in the pons and the medial longitudinal fasciculus lie in the infarcted region.
- The sensations carried in the medial lemniscus are lost, but cutaneous sensation may be grossly intact because the lateral spinothalamic tract may be spared due to its lateral position in the brain stem.
- The patient can still hear because the auditory nerves ascend the brain stem lateral to the infarcted area.
- The cranial nerve IV nucleus and the superior colliculus of the quadrigeminal plate are spared, and therefore, the patient is still capable of convergence and upward gaze of the eyes. Using these eye movements, the patient is able to communicate using a code.

Most patients with locked-in syndrome die early in the course of the disease. The survivors usually remain in a chronic locked-in state, as the medullary vital centers automatically maintain respiratory and cardiovascular func-

tion. A few cases of substantial recovery have been reported.[88–90, 170, 171]

PATIENT HISTORY

Tables have been produced that attempt to identify pre-existing pathological or altered physiological risk factors of VBS if SMT is proceeded with.[172–175] It is now apparent that very few of the factors, either alone or in combination, specifically increases the susceptibility to post-SMT VBS. Different facets of the history are reviewed next.

PRESENTING COMPLAINT

The presenting complaint of patients who suffered VBS after SMT was given in 137 (74 percent) cases (Table 22–4). It can be seen that there is little that could alert the astute practitioner of an impending VBS, as most patients were young healthy individuals, suffering from musculoskeletal complaints such as head and neck or shoulder pain, without any predisposing VBS risk factors.

TRANSIENT ISCHEMIC ATTACKS

When a review of systems reveals transient ischemic symptoms, it strongly suggests the necessity for medical referral and for the exclusion of SMT. Patients with vertebrobasilar transient ischemic attacks may have many attacks before they suffer a VBS.[176] Symptoms due to vertebral artery compromise (5 Ds And 3 Ns), should alert the practitioner not to manipulate the neck, and indicate that the patient may require immediate medical referral.[176]

If the patient suffers from carotid transient ischemic attacks, medical referral is imperative as patients may suffer a complete stroke after only a few episodes; 10 percent in

Table 22–4: Major Presenting Complaint of Patients Who Subsequently Had an SMT-Induced VBS (n = 137)

COMPLAINT	PERCENT
Neck pain/stiffness	47.4
Neck pain/stiffness and headache	19.7
Headache	16.8
Torticollis	5.8
Low back pain	2.2
Abdominal complaint	2.2
Scoliosis/kyphoscoliosis	1.5
Head cold/cold in the head	1.5
Upper thoracic pain	1.5
Upper limb numbness	0.7
Hay fever	0.7

the first 6 months, then 6 percent a year.[176] Signs and symptoms of carotid artery ischemia include:

- Hemianesthesia
- Hemiparesis or monoparesis
- Headache
- Dysphasia
- Visual field disturbance
- Confusion
- Bruits

If, during the review of symptoms, a patient states that an audible bruit has recently developed (which may be associated with symptoms such as headache and neck pain), the patient should not be manipulated, as this may indicate signs of an impending spontaneous dissecting aneurysm.[91, 177]

CONTRACEPTIVES

Several authors have listed oral contraceptives as a potential risk factor. VBS following SMT in women taking oral contraceptives was only reported in four cases,[49, 60, 79, 119] indicating most likely no causal relationship. Also noted is that only one of these women was reported as smoker. Women taking oral contraceptives are at a greater risk of vertebrobasilar thrombosis than those not taking contraceptives.[178] However, as the source of the emboli in these cases is not from the vertebral arteries,[179] the taking of the contraceptive pill would not appear to predispose to any greater risk of post-SMT VBS.

CIGARETTE SMOKING AND ATHEROSCLEROSIS

In patients with other stroke risk factors, such as hypertension, hyperlipidemia, heart disease, or diabetes mellitus, chronic smoking enhances the decrease in cerebral blood flow.[180] A review of the 185 cases reveals that there were 11 patients who were recorded as smokers.

- Females: 7 cases (29 to 41 years), average age 37 years
- Males: 4 cases (33 to 55 years), average age 42 years

There was only one patient who smoked over the age of 45 years. Although chronic smoking appears to increase the risk of cerebral stroke, it does not appear to increase the risk of VBS after SMT; otherwise, such injuries would be expected to be more common in older age groups.

OSTEOARTHRITIS

Osteoarthritis does not appear to increase the risk of VBS after SMT. If it did, then it would be expected that the older age group would be at a significantly greater risk, which they are not,[125, 126] and osteoarthritic compromise of the vertebral artery would be most likely to occur at the C4–6 spinal levels. Radiographs of elderly patients with a diagnosis of VBI secondary to cervical spondylosis, when compared to age- and sex-matched controls,[181] failed to demonstrate any difference in the severity of radiographic changes. It was concluded that radiographs of the cervical spine were of little value, only confirming the high incidence of cervical spondylosis in the elderly.

POSTPARTUM

Only 4 of the 103 females were reported as being postpartum.[21, 56, 77, 91] Considering the number of women who present to SMT practitioners offices after childbirth complaining of neck pain, this does not appear to indicate any causal relationship.

MIGRAINE HEADACHES

Stroke in migraine patients is rare, but can occur, usually in the posterior cerebral artery (distal branches of the vertebral arteries).[182, 183] Several authors have mentioned that a history of migraine may be an important precipitating factor in some cases of post-SMT VBS.[57, 58, 89, 91,184–186] It has been shown that migraines are a stroke risk factor in young adults;[187, 188] and that vascular spasm in migraine patients may exacerbate injuries;[57] and migraineurs have been shown to be hypercoagulable.[189] While no definite predisposition can be demonstrated in migraineurs, it would appear to be unwise to stress or irritate the vertebral arteries during a migraine attack, when arteries are in an irritable state.

IMPORTANT RISK FACTORS

The most important VBS risk factors to identify in the history are (1) sudden severe pain in the side of the head or neck, which is different from any pain the patient has had before; and (2) dizziness, unsteadiness, giddiness, or vertigo.

SUDDEN SEVERE HEAD OR NECK PAIN

Many practitioners are not aware that the earliest symptom of vertebral artery dissection (VAD) (with or without SMT) usually manifests as severe head or neck pain, described as different from any previously experienced, which can occur minutes, hours, days, or even weeks before the onset of neurological dysfunction. One study[190] found the initial manifestation of VAD (not associated with SMT) was head pain in 60 percent of cases, vertigo and oscillopsia in 20 percent, and focal neurological deficits in 20 percent. Another study[191] found headache was the prominent symptom in 86 percent of patients. Research[192] indicates that irritation of the vertebral artery can produce pain from the forehead or cheek to the occiput or neck to the upper trapezius region. Report of this distinct type of pain, although nonspecific as an isolated symptom, should raise suspicion of the possibility of an underlying VAD. As long as symptoms of brain stem ischemia are absent, head or neck pain due to VAD will rarely be correctly diagnosed.

Although the majority of cases of head or neck pain are major indications for SMT, in some circumstances, the same symptom that prompts the patient to seek care may be due to VAD, which is a major contraindication to SMT. The problem for the practitioner is that often the head or neck pain due to VAD cannot be differentiated from a musculoskeletal lesion. This is a dilemma for the practitioner, as severe head or neck pain of a musculoskeletal origin (without signs of brain stem ischemia) that will respond to SMT is very common, whereas VAD is uncommon. The incidence of VAD has been reported to be only about one to six patients per year in a large hospital.[91, 190, 191, 193, 194]

To further complicate the problem, VAD may be totally asymptomatic. One study found three patients with asymptomatic VAD while investigating other suspected lesions.[190] These silent VADs appear to occur predominantly in cases of multiple dissections of cervical arteries.[91, 193, 195, 196] This finding raises the possibility of an underlying arteriopathy, which predisposes to vessel dissection.

A review of 27 cases of non-SMT VAD (where central nervous system dysfunction was not one of the earliest signs) revealed the delay in the onset of central nervous system dysfunction after the onset of headache or neck pain to be as follows:

- In 30 percent of cases, less than 1 day
- In 15 percent, 1 to 3 days later
- In 30 percent, 1 to 2 weeks later
- In 25 percent, 3 weeks or more

These findings suggest that many cases of VAD attributed to SMT practitioners may have existed prior to treatment, and may have been the cause of the symptoms that prompted the patient to seek care (or they may have been silent). Because these scenarios are possible, it is suggested that techniques that excessively stress the vertebral arteries not be used on any patient.

DIZZINESS, UNSTEADINESS, VERTIGO, OR GIDDINESS

The signs of vertebrobasilar ischemia (5 Ds And 3Ns), should be known to all SMT practitioners. Observant SMT practitioners would be aware that patients suffering from dizziness often respond dramatically following upper cervical SMT,[197–201] but other possible causes of dizziness have to be kept in mind. The problem for the practitioner is that: (1) dizziness is usually the prominent symptom of vertebrobasilar ischemia and is often unaccompanied by any of the other signs and symptoms; and (2) there is no simple method available to the SMT practitioner to determine whether the dizziness is due to vertebrobasilar ischemia (a contraindication to SMT), or to a disturbance of articular or muscle proprioceptive input (an indication for SMT).

Many cases have been reported in which SMT was proceeded with in a dizzy patient with disastrous results.[125, 126, 202] In these cases the practitioners may have had no effect, have aggravated already existing vertebral artery pathology, or have caused the vertebral artery damage; but they found themselves being blamed as having caused the VBS. Because the assessment methods available do not enable SMT practitioners to be absolutely sure whether or not a patient's symptoms of dizziness, giddiness, unsteadiness, or vertigo (or even head or neck pain) are caused by arterial wall pathology or not, in such patients it is recommended that treatment methods that excessively stress the vertebral artery walls not be used. SMT should be modified or other forms of therapy used (soft tissue therapy, accessory joint play movements, heat, ice, physiological therapeutics, etc). If after one or two treatment sessions the dizziness decreases, then this most likely indicates that vertebrobasilar ischemia was not the cause; normal SMT methods can then be used.

Two cases are presented next to illustrate a scenario in which dizziness in the history should alert the practitioner to modify or alter treatment. I have described similar cases in other articles and papers.[125, 126, 202]

Case A[67]

Following a rear-end motor vehicle injury, a 34-year-old male suffered persistent headache, dizziness, neck stiffness, and noted difficulty in walking and maintaining balance. He consulted a chiropractor, who decided to proceed with SMT. During the treatment he complained of dizziness, nausea, and faintness. He then suddenly became unresponsive with stiffening of all extremities and tongue biting. *Diagnosis:* Locked-in syndrome (tetraplegia).

Case B[74]

A 53-year-old male had a bout of vertigo and nausea which resolved over a few hours. Eight days later he had a sudden onset of vertigo, nausea, and vomiting. He then had cervical SMT from a chiropractor that afternoon and again the following morning without improvement. That evening he had persistent nausea and severe posterior headache. He was admitted to a hospital the following morning. Over the next 6 hours he became comatose and quadriplegic. On the fourth day of hospitalization, an angiogram revealed occlusion of the left vertebral artery at the C2–3 level, with a fresh thrombus. Despite aggressive neurological and pulmonary support, the patient died on the 27th day following hospitalization.

Note: This scenario, of there being definite brain stem signs and symptoms prior to treatment that should have warned the practitioner, may be much more common than the literature suggests, but because the reports were written by authors more interested in the neurological, postmortem, angiographic, computed tomographic (CT) or magnetic resonance imaging (MRI) scan findings, most likely this important point for SMT practitioners was not commented upon.

PATIENT EXAMINATION

Three major tests have been described as being able to detect patients at risk of VBS following SMT. They are blood pressure measurement, neck auscultation, and functional vascular tests.

BLOOD PRESSURE MEASUREMENT

A review of the cases reveals that the victims are usually young, and there is no consistently found hyper- or hypotension. Therefore, the taking of blood pressure does not appear to be particularly useful in determining any increased risk of VBS following SMT.

NECK AUSCULTATION

Review of the cases of post-SMT VBS reveals that the neck was auscultated for bruits in 18 cases.[126] In *none* of these was a vertebral artery bruit heard. Seventeen cases involved vertebral artery damage, of which 10 were confirmed by angiography and 1 was confirmed at postmortem. One case involved carotid artery damage[93] with positive arteriograph and surgical findings, and yet no carotid bruit was heard on neck auscultation.

As there were *no* arterial bruits detected after SMT, it would be highly unlikely that a bruit would have been detected prior to SMT. Therefore, it is my opinion that the taking of blood pressure and listening for bruits leads the practitioner into a false feeling that he or she is doing a relevant vertebrobasilar screening examination.

FUNCTIONAL VASCULAR TESTS

There are at least four variations of the vertebral artery patency tests.[172, 173, 175, 203-206] In all, the patient's head is held for a period in the premanipulative position (e.g., rotation, rotation with extension) before SMT, and the patient is observed for any signs and asked to report any symptoms of vertebrobasilar ischemia. Dizziness is the most common symptom of vertebrobasilar ischemia and may be unaccompanied by any other symptoms or signs; therefore, the absence of other brain stem signs and symptoms does not always exclude the possibility of a vascular cause.

These tests, when positive, indicate only that rotation has possibly produced brain stem ischemia, possibly due to compression of one vertebral artery, and inadequate patency of the opposite artery.

There are four major problems with these procedures as a predictor of VBS after SMT:

1. Even with a negative test result, VBS may still occur because these tests reproduce some of the

stresses of SMT on the osseous-articular-musculo-ligamentous-vascular structures, but cannot predict the effect of thrust, which may further stretch the vertebral artery and damage the vessel wall (see Fig. 22–2). Bolton et al[207] demonstrated the limited diagnostic value of these tests. In a patient in whom the pre-SMT tests failed to identify any vertebral artery problem, subsequent digital subtraction angiography revealed occlusion of one vertebral artery. Haynes,[144] in a study of the vertebral arteries in 280 patients, found that in 14 (5 percent), the Doppler sound stopped during neck rotation, but none of these patients developed any signs or symptoms of brain stem ischemia. A negative test result cannot be interpreted to mean that there is no arteriopathic process in the vertebral arteries. Therefore, these tests appear to be inadequate in all but the most grossly pathological or highly susceptible cases. There have been at least two cases in which patients suffered vertebral artery trauma after negative test results.[56, 72]

2. There is a problem of false-positive tests,[173] as vertigo and nystagmus of cervical origin (joint or muscle, or both) are well documented, with theories being related to the stimulation of cervical sympathetics or to cervical muscle and joint receptors.[143, 208-213] This type of dizziness can be expected to respond well to SMT. I have often experienced cases where testing prior to SMT produced dizziness, but the dizziness could not be reproduced after soft tissue therapy and gentle SMT, indicating vertebrogenic dizziness. Thiel et al[142] had an experimental group of 12 subjects who had positive functional vertebrobasilar tests and a history of dizziness or related symptoms during certain positions of the head and neck. Using duplex Doppler ultrasound, no decrease in vertebral artery blood flow was detected in these patients (or in the 30 subjects in the control group) during the functional vascular test position.

3. There is no evidence to suggest that these tests when positive indicate any underlying arteriopathy or altered anatomy that would predispose to arterial wall damage and VBS if SMT were proceeded with.

4. There have been cases in which merely placing the head into the rotated position has induced a stroke[24, 70, 214] (see Table 22–3).

Although we have to admit these inadequacies, when a test result is positive, caution is prudent.

RISK REDUCTION

Two major problems appear to occur in cases of SMT associated with VBS. They are (1) rotational SMT, and (2) continued treatment of a person with SMT after signs or symptoms of arterial damage have become evident. Once the practitioner is aware of these problems, changes in technique can easily be made so as to hopefully minimize these injuries.

ROTATIONAL SMT

Of the 185 cases reviewed, the method of SMT was described in 76 cases (41 percent). Rotation was used in 65.8 percent of cases; rotation with extension, flexion, or traction was used in 29 percent; toggle recoil repeated three times was used in 1.3 percent; and traction was used in 3.9 percent. In 94.8 percent of cases, rotation with or without other movements was used in the treatment. That rotation is the cervical movement most likely to damage the vertebral artery wall is supported by review of five sources:

1. Hemodynamic studies in cadavers
2. Hemodynamic studies in live subjects
3. The mechanism involved in non-SMT vertebral artery damage, which is usually neck rotation or rotation with extension
4. Post-SMT angiography, which consistently reveals the vertebral artery damage to be between C–C2 (rotation is the movement that compresses and stretches the vertebral artery most at this level)
5. Post-SMT VBS autopsy investigations, which consistently reveal the vertebral artery damage to be between C–C2

Some practitioners have considered that traction makes rotation SMT safer. This belief is not supported by one study of 41 cadavers (82 vertebral arteries), where extension and rotation occluded 5 (6 percent) vertebral arteries; when traction was then added, another 27 complete occlusions occurred (n = 32) or 39 percent; all occurred above the level of C2.[137]

CONTINUED TREATMENT OF A PATIENT AFTER SIGNS OF ARTERIAL DAMAGE HAVE BECOME EVIDENT

It has been documented[125–127, 202] that many cases of VBS after SMT could have been avoided had the practitioner understood that the symptoms post-SMT were due to arterial trauma, and that further trauma to an artery already undergoing pathological change can only be expected to aggravate rather than help the condition. The signs of vertebral artery damage can present in one of three ways:

1. Sudden onset of severe head or neck pain, or both
2. Vertebrobasilar ischemia (the 5 Ds And 3 Ns)
3. Both of these findings occurring together

As was already described, the earliest sign of damage to the vertebral artery wall is often head or neck pain. If head or neck pain occurs following upper cervical SMT, the practitioner should not remanipulate the neck in the mistaken belief that the first treatment was performed incorrectly and therefore must be done again. Patients whose head pain (usually occipital) or neck pain began during SMT usually describe the pain as:

- Immediate, suddenly, during SMT
- Distinctly different from pains previously suffered
- Sharp discomfort, excruciating, intense, violent, severe

If the pain occurs without the signs of ischemia, it is difficult for the practitioner to know whether it is a joint or muscle pain reaction to the SMT, but I would suggest that SMT not be repeated in the event that the pain is due to VAD.

Symptoms after cervical SMT, such as fainting and nausea, have been called by Maigne[121] "sympathetic storms." Several authors have postulated that irritation of the posterior cervical sympathetic nerves may cause spasm of the vertebrobasilar arteries and their branches.[121, 215–217] Although this is an attractive theory for various head, chest, and arm symptoms, it is not supported by research.[218, 219] A study of the neural control of vertebral artery blood flow found no evidence to support the contention that cervical lesions could affect hindbrain blood flow.[219] Vertebral artery blood flow was found to be profoundly unresponsive to stimulation of any component of the cervical sympathetic system, and it was concluded that the theory that irritation of cervical sympathetic nerves can alter vertebral artery blood flow is untenable.[219] Therefore, practitioners should be careful before ascribing post-SMT reactions to sympathetic storms, and be aware that they most likely indicate either alteration of upper cervical proprioceptive input or, more dangerously, brain stem ischemia induced by vertebral artery trauma.[125, 126, 202]

The problem for the practitioner is that dizziness is usually the prominent symptom in both cases and, in the absence of other signs of ischemia, it is not possible to determine the cause. These patients may subsequently respond well to SMT and suffer no ill effect, as dizziness usually responds well to SMT.[197–201] However, it is suggested that in such cases, because of the possibility of serious damage, it would be irresponsible to proceed with rotation thrust SMT techniques, which are the most likely to stress the vertebral artery wall. It seems to be courting possible disaster, as there are no diagnostic methods available to determine whether the symptoms such as post-SMT pain or dizziness are due to cervical joint and muscle dysfunction, sympathetic system stimulation, or to VAD. In these patients, other forms of therapy to the upper cervical spine should be used.

To illustrate the irresponsibility of continued manipulation of the neck after the onset of signs of brain stem ischemia, the following six cases are presented. I have described other similar cases elsewhere.[125, 126, 202]

Case 1[8]

Following manipulation, the patient said, "Oh, that was awful, something terrible has happened to me. That's awful. Let me up. I don't want any more; I can't stand any more." The chiropractor replied, "You will be alright. Let me get this other one." The patient then repeated, "I have had enough . . . don't . . . stop." The chiropractor continued to manipulate the patient. Immediately following the adjustment, she was unable to walk, her vision was impaired, she vomited, and she had a partial paralysis of the throat and vocal cords.

Note: When a patient tells you to stop treatment, you stop treatment.

Case 2[35]

A 52-year-old female was being treated biweekly by a chiropractor. Following each of these manipulations, she experienced transient dizziness and nausea, and sometimes 2-minute episodes during which she saw a zig-zag pattern of scintillating very bright lines across her visual field. On her last visit she became nauseated, vomited, felt numbness in her left cheek, and noted that when she tried to stand or walk, she veered and fell to the left. Examination disclosed numbness of the left side of her face and the right side of her body, diplopia, blurred vision, hoarseness, a left Horner's syndrome, and dysphagia. *Diagnosis:* Left Wallenberg's syndrome.

Note: Scintillating scotomas (zig-zag or flashing lights) across the visual field indicate occipital lobe ischemia. The occipital lobes are supplied by the terminal branches of the vertebral arteries. Often, SMT was continued after the onset of this symptom.

Case 3[44]

After chiropractic treatment, a 31-year-old female felt a sharp discomfort and seconds later experienced intense vertigo and flashes of light all over her visual fields. Within a minute, she noted the lower half of her visual fields had "blacked out." She communicated her distress to the practitioner, who, somewhat discomforted by all this, summoned his colleague. The colleague found it all most puzzling and promptly remanipulated the patient's neck. The patient then noted paresthesia in both arms and legs and found her face going numb, especially the right side. Her tongue was clumsy to the extent of rendering her inarticulate and dysphagic. She was dizzy, nauseated, and quite prostrated. She was taken to the hospital. Examination revealed bilateral ptosis, ataxia of the right arm and leg, rotatory nystagmus, and the right up-going plantar response. Angiography revealed a 3- to 4-cm attenuated segment of the right vertebral artery in the C1–2 region.

Case 4[57]

A 7-year-old boy suffered recurrent headaches for 4 months. A course of SMT was initiated. After one treatment session, the child became ill with severe occipital and bifrontal headaches, vomiting, and left facial weakness. A neurologist found no abnormalities the following day.

About 2 weeks later, the chiropractor resumed cervical manipulation, which produced severe headaches with intermittent vomiting and diplopia, difficulty with fine movements of left hand (writing), and ataxic gait. Examination revealed a right homonymous superior quadrantanopia, marked right dysmetria, dysdiadochokinesia, an intention tremor, and scanning speech. *Diagnosis:* Traumatic thrombosis of the left vertebral artery with emboli to the basilar, right superior cerebellar, and left posterior cerebral arteries.

Note: This case, and Hensell[48] indicate that a clear neurological report does not necessarily mean that the patient can be safely adjusted in the future. Many of the warnings are symptoms, and the signs when present are often transitory, not to be found on later examination. Their skill and training, as well as the emphasis on spinal manipulation, provide chiropractors with expert knowledge in the indications and contraindications of SMT. A neurologist is not an SMT expert.

Case 5[79]

A 45-year-old male with pain in the left shoulder and neck, was manipulated in an "unusually rough" manner by an osteopath. The following day he consulted a chiropractor, who briskly rotated his neck to the left and right. The patient had immediate onset of vertigo with nausea and vomiting, and his vision dimmed after an hour. These symptoms subsided sufficiently to allow him to drive home. That evening he went to a local emergency room where X-rays were taken. He was given a prescription for a muscle relaxant and sent home. The following day, because the symptoms were still troublesome, the chiropractor went to the patient's house and remanipulated his neck in the same manner. The patient then suffered persistent vertigo, disequilibrium, diplopia, tinnitus, and hearing loss. During approximately the next 10 days, he had cervical manipulations from other chiropractors without improvement. He then went to a hospital where examination revealed a sensorineural hearing loss, a right hypoplastic vertebral artery, and 20 to 30 percent stenosis of the dominant left vertebral artery between C1–2. The patient was treated with acetylsalicylic acid and dipyridamole for a month. Re-examination 6 months later revealed only a slight improvement in speech reception threshold.

Case 6[77]

A previously healthy 29-year-old woman who had been suffering neck stiffness for about 3 weeks was treated by a toggle recoil adjustment, which consisted of three thrusts to the upper cervical vertebrae. Immediately following the third thrust the patient experienced dizziness, tingling of the entire right side of her body, and severe headache. The chiropractor became frightened and told her it was not a normal reaction, then called another chiropractor (his uncle) who lived a few miles away. The patient had to be carried into the second chiropractor's office. Over the next 3 hours, both practitioners adjusted her upper neck region, at which time they decided they were dealing with a medical emergency and had the patient taken to hospital by ambulance. The patient came very close to death and was in an intensive care unit for about 7 weeks, after which she was transferred to a hospital for 2 weeks. Twenty-three weeks later, she still suffered neurological deficits which were expected to be permanent. She was having difficulty speaking, spastic weakness of the right extremities, slight incoordination of the left extremities (she needed a walking cane), and headaches. In this case, the plaintiff's counsel alleged the first chiropractor did not perform an adequate examination, that an ambulance should have been called when adverse signs and symptoms began, that the delay in receiving proper medical care may have endangered the patient, and that the additional chiropractic care could have increased irritation and possible trauma to the arteries and nerves in the neck.

Note: If any adverse signs or symptoms occur during treatment—*stop.* There is nothing to be gained from continuing to retraumatize an artery already undergoing pathological change. Left alone, the patient may recover. Continuing to treat the patient may result in death, tetraplegia, or permanent neurological deficit.

DID THE PRACTITIONER NECESSARILY CAUSE THE INJURY?

SCENARIO 1

When an apparently healthy young person with no known stroke risk factors suffers a post-SMT VBS, is there necessarily a cause-and-effect relationship, just because there is a temporal relationship? The usual interpretation has been that the SMT practitioner caused the stroke, most likely with rough or forceful SMT.[220]

SCENARIO 2

Many cases attributed to SMT practitioners may only have a coincidental relationship (not a cause-and-effect relationship). VAD can occur in the absence of trauma (spontaneous VAD), and produce musculoskeletal symptoms (head or neck pain) prior to brain stem neurological symptoms. Therefore, the pain due to arterial dissection may prompt the patient to seek care from an SMT practitioner. The patient with the stroke in evolution then attends the SMT practitioner, is treated, and subsequently suffers a stroke. The practitioner is then held responsible for having caused the arterial damage when, in fact, it was the pre-existing arterial pathology that caused the symptoms (head or neck pain) which caused the patient to seek the practitioner. In such a case, the practitioner either had no effect on the final outcome or may have only hastened the inevitable.

SCENARIO 3

Previous trauma may cause damage to the vertebral artery wall, producing a subclinical "precursor lesion," which may

increase the likelihood of VBS during SMT if techniques are used that stress the vertebral artery wall (or trauma, sports, etc). Three autopsy reports[87, 96, 221] found pathological changes in the involved artery, the ages of which could be accounted for by the times of previous SMT, before the SMT that caused the patient's death. This raises the possibility that arterial dissections after SMT are more common than practitioners or the literature suggest and that the injury heals, the symptoms resolve, and the patient has no further problems. Because it is possible that a patient may not have pain with the vertebral artery dissection, or that dissections may be produced by trauma to the artery walls during SMT, and that current diagnostic methods cannot alert practitioners to these possibilities, practitioners can minimize causing or aggravating existing abnormalities by using techniques that apply minimal stress to the arterial structures.

SCENARIO 4

Patients may present with an underlying arteriopathy. Fibromuscular dysplasia has been found in 23 percent and 33 percent of patients in two VAD studies.[91, 195] In the case of post-SMT VAD described by Peters et al,[119] examination of several arteries revealed a mediolytic arteriopathy with widespread mucoid degeneration and cystic transformation of the vessel wall caused by segmental degeneration of smooth muscle cells of the tunica media, which the authors believed were a predisposing factor to post-SMT VAD. Analysis of 11 patients with acute nontraumatic dissections of cervicocerebral arteries by Brandt et al[222] revealed ultrastructural abnormalities in 6 (55 percent). The major findings were collagen bundles containing composite fibrils and signs of elastic fiber degeneration with minicalcifications and fragmentations. The authors[222] stated, "preliminary data from our investigation indicate a correlation between spontaneous cerebral artery (carotid and vertebral) dissections and ultrastructural connective tissue abnormalities. This association could give new insight into the pathogenesis of arterial dissections and eventually lead to recognition of the protein and molecular defects." Mayer et al[223] and Rubin et al[224] describe a female patient who suffered multiple VAD (not associated with SMT); she had no stigmata of connective tissue disease apart from bluish sclera, and no family history of arterial dissection or congenital musculoskeletal disease. Analysis of the COL 1A1 gene that encodes the pro alpha 1 (I) chains of the type I procollagen revealed a point mutation in one allele, resulting in substitution of alanine for glycine (G13A) in about half of the alpha 1 (I) chains of type I collagen. The authors concluded that genetic disorders of collagen should be considered in the differential diagnosis of unexplained cervical arterial dissection.

These findings, therefore, suggest that:

- Many cases of arterial damage attributed to SMT practitioners may have already had a predisposing arteriopathy, or precursor lesion.

- The arteriopathy may have already been associated with arterial dissection prior to the patient seeing the SMT practitioner, and may have been the cause for the head or neck pain that prompted the patient to seek the practitioner.
- Since practitioners cannot readily examine for possible underlying genetic disorders of collagen, or protein and molecular deficits in arterial walls, then all cervical SMT should be performed using techniques that apply minimal stress to arterial structures.
- Even after taking all precautions VBS may still occur following SMT, but this does not necessarily implicate the practitioner as the cause, as it is possible that the patient already had a stroke in evolution, or an underlying pathology, or a precursor lesion when he or she presented to the practitioner.

EMERGENCY CARE

A practitioner may still be unfortunate enough to have a patient develop signs of brain stem ischemia, even, after all precautions have been taken (it may have been going to happen anyway). If post-SMT VBI signs occur, the following actions should be taken:[125, 126, 202, 220]

1. *Do not remanipulate the patient's neck.* There is nothing to be gained from retraumatizing an artery undergoing pathological change, and it may, in fact, result in further arterial damage and disaster.
2. *Observe the patient.* The symptoms may resolve within a short time, indicating either transient vertebrobasilar ischemia possibly due to spasm, or proprioceptive dizziness.
3. *Refer the patient.* If the symptoms do not subside, do not panic and remanipulate the patient's neck. The patient whose symptoms progress and do not abate needs to be hospitalized. The practitioner's assistance in describing what happened may be helpful in having the correct therapy instituted quickly.

CONCLUSION

Several authors have mentioned that patients with signs and symptoms of vertebrobasilar ischemia can respond beneficially following SMT. I agree that many cerebral and cranial nerve type signs or symptoms can respond to SMT,[225–232] but I hope readers can appreciate that a patient whose symptoms are due to vertebral artery trauma, with lumen constriction, thrombus, or embolus formation, is not likely to respond beneficially to SMT. This issue has been confused by some authors who have written about transient rotational occlusion that produced transient brain stem symptoms. What we are trying to prevent here is trauma to arterial structures resulting in intramural hemorrhages, lacerations, dissections, aneurysms, thrombus, and embolus formation with resultant central nervous system damage, not episodes of transient ischemia.

It is to be hoped that the incidence of these injuries will decrease as practitioners develop a better understanding of the pathology, warning signs in the review of systems and history, and warning signs during and after treatment that indicate that treatment should be altered or ceased; and the need in some cases for the patient to be hospitalized. It has been stated that all thrust techniques are ruled out as dangerous, and that "we should stay our hand until indications for thrust techniques are quite unequivocal."[120] It is my opinion that it is not thrust that is the most dangerous component of the manipulation, but extreme rotation. Techniques can be modified to abandon that component which appears to carry greatest risk for our patients.

Current knowledge is limited, and prediction of patients at risk of post-SMT VBS requires much further research, but the following conclusions are offerred:

- VBS following SMT is very rare (nobody knows what the true incidence is), but as has been described, many cases could have been avoided.
- As the subject of post-VBS is being better investigated, the estimated incidence is increasing.
- No age group or sex appears to be predisposed to post-SMT VBS.
- The fact that most reported cases involve chiropractors is to be expected, as chiropractors perform 94 percent of SMT in North America.
- Cadaver and in vivo studies on hemodynamic changes with neck movement indicate that rotation applies greater stress on the vertebral arteries than lateral flexion. While cadaver and in vivo studies both come to this conclusion, it is apparent that cadaver studies do not accurately reflect changes in the live human being.
- During normal daily activities in most people, vertebral artery blood flow fluctuates without detrimental effects.
- In many cases, the patient may have presented with an existing VAD, which may have caused the symptoms (head or neck pain) that prompted the patient to consult the practitioner. The practitioner, who is then held responsible for causing the patient's injury, may have had no effect on the final outcome, or merely hastened the inevitable. It is possible, though, that without trauma to the artery, the artery wall might have healed and the stroke might never have occurred.
- The most severe injuries following SMT are not cases of transient ischemia following transient compression or vasospasm, but of trauma to the vessel

wall (possibly already affected by an arteriopathy) resulting in disruption.

- SMT practitioners should know the signs and symptoms of vertebrobasilar ischemia (the 5 Ds And 3 Ns); should be aware that often dizziness or vertigo is the only symptom; and should determine whether any of the 5 Ds And 3 Ns are present prior to, during, or after SMT.
- Many of the reported cases of patient injury could have been prevented had the practitioner been aware of signs and symptoms of vertebrobasilar injury, which should have been elicited during the review of systems, or the case history, which should have indicated that SMT not be proceeded with. This situation may have occurred more commonly than the literature suggests.
- Many of the cases of patient injury may have been prevented had the practitioner performed a physical examination, including holding the head in the premanipulative position and observing for signs and symptoms of vertebrobasilar ischemia.
- The most severe injuries following SMT are not cases of transient ischemia due to compression or vasospasm, but of vessel wall laceration, dissection, and so on, possibly predisposed by an as yet unknown arteriopathy.
- Many of the previously supposed risk factors, as well as discrepancy of bilateral blood pressure and absence of neck auscultation findings, appear to be of no value in predicting risk.
- Functional vascular tests may result in false positive and false negative results, and there is no evidence to suggest that positive results have any correlation with future VBS if SMT is proceeded with. While

we have to admit these inadequacies, a positive result should indicate caution.

- Many cases of patient injury were caused, or made worse, because the practitioner did not stop treatment, which had the effect of further traumatizing an artery undergoing pathological change. This may have occurred more commonly than the literature suggests.
- It is not possible to predict all patients who may be presenting to our offices with pre-existing VADs (or other arteriopathic processes that may predispose to arterial dissection), as they may be silent or may, in fact, be causing the head or neck pain (without other warning signs) that prompted the patient to seek help. The absence of reported contraindications does not mean the patient will not suffer post-SMT VBS and, in fact, most of the reported cases did not document the supposed contraindications. Therefore, we cannot protect these patients by pre-treatment screening.
- Many of the cases that occurred in predisposed patients (pre-existing vertebral artery dissection, with or without examination findings) might not have occurred had the practitioners used a method of SMT that did not stress the vertebral artery walls (i.e., a technique that minimizes rotation in thrust techniques).
- Post-SMT dizziness may have many causes. The patient who does develop post-SMT dizziness should not be remanipulated, but instead observed. In most cases, the dizziness will resolve. If it does not, then transportation of the patient to the hospital is appropriate.

REFERENCES

1. Hood WP. *On Bone-setting (So Called), and Its Relation to the Treatment of Joints Crippled by Injury, Rheumatism, Inflammation*. London: Macmillan; 1871:10.
2. Anonymous. Bone setting extraordinary. *Lancet* 1872;2:900.
3. Durrett LC. Management of patients with vertebro-basilar ischemia. *Chiro Technique* 1994;6(3):95–97.
4. Savoie SM. The George's test: A review and update. *ICA Internat Rev Chiro* 1986;42(3):18–21.
5. Ferezy JS. Neural ischemia and cervical manipulation: An acceptable risk. *J Chiropr* 1988;25(8):61–63.
6. Foster v. Thornton. Medicolegal. Malpractice: Death resulting from chiropractic treatment for headache. *JAMA* 1934;103(16):1260. Malpractice: Cerebral hemorrhage attributed to chiropractic adjustment. *JAMA* 1935;105(21):1714. Malpractice: Death resulting from chiropractic treatment for headache. *JAMA* 1937;109(3):233–234.
7. Pratt-Thomas HR, Berger KE. Cerebellar and spinal injuries after chiropractic manipulation. *JAMA* 1947;133(9):600–603.
8. Bakewell v. Kahle. Medicolegal abstracts. Chiropractors: Rupture of brain tumor following adjustment. *JAMA* 1952;148(8):699. (See Krueger and Okazaki (1980) for discussion of this case 30 years later.)
9. Kunkle EC, Muller JC, Odom GL. Traumatic brain stem thrombosis: Report of a case and analysis of the mechanism of injury. *Ann Int Med* 1952;36:1329–1335.

10. Ford FR. Syncope, vertigo and disturbances of vision resulting from intermittent obstruction of the vertebral arteries due to defect in the odontoid process and excessive mobility of the second cervical vertebra. *Bull Johns Hopkins Hosp* 1952;91:168–173.

11. York v. Daniels. Medicolegal abstracts. Chiropractors: Injury to spinal meninges during adjustments. JAMA 1955;159(8):809.

12. Ford FR, Clark D. Thrombosis of the basilar artery with softenings in the cerebellum and brain stem due to manipulation of the neck. *Bull Johns Hopkins Hosp* 1956;98:37–42.

13. Schwarz GA, Geiger JK, Spano AV. Posterior inferior cerebellar artery syndrome of Wallenberg after chiropractic manipulation. *Arch Intern Med* 1956;97:352–354.

14. Attali P. Accidents graves apres une manipulation intempestive par un chiropractor. *Rev Rheum* 1957;24:652.

15. Boudin G, Barbizet J, Pepin B, Fouet P. Syndrome grave du tronc cerebral apres manipulations cervicales. *Bull Mem Soc Med Hop Paris* 1957;73:562–566.

16. Green D, Joynt RJ. Vascular accidents to the brain stem associated with neck manipulations. JAMA 1959;170(5):522–524.

17. Boshes LD. Vascular accidents associated with neck manipulation. JAMA 1959;171:1602.

18. Bouchet MM, Pailler P. Surdite brutale et chiropractie. *Ann Otolaryngol (Par)* 1960;77:951–953.

19. Hardin CA, Williamson P, Steegman A. Vertebral artery insufficiency produced by cervical osteoarthritic spurs. *Neurology* 1960;10:855–858.

20. Martin H, Guiral J. Surdite brusque au cours d'une manipulation vertebrale. *J Franc ORL* 1960;9:177–178.

21. Masson M, Cambier J. Insuffisance circulatoire vertebro-basilaire. *Presse Medicale* 1962;70(43):1990–1993.

22. Smith RA, Estridge MN. Neurologic complications of head and neck manipulations. JAMA 1962;182(5):528–531.

23. Pribek RA. Brainstem vascular accident following neck manipulation. *Wisc Med J* 1963;62(3):141–143.

24. Roche L, Colin M, DeRougemont J, et al. Lesions traumatiques de la colonne cervicale et attaintes de l'artere vertebrale. Responsabilite d'une examen medical. *Ann Med Leg* 1963;43:232–235.

25. Vedrine J, Spay G. Problemes medico legaux poses par les thromboses consecutives a un traumatisme fere des arteres vertebrales. *Lyon Medicale* 1968;27:5–21.

26. Jung A, Kehr P, Jung FM. Das posttraumatiche zervikal-syndrom. *Manuelle Medizin* 1976;14:101–106.

27. Brain L. Some unsolved problems of cervical spondylosis. *Brit Med J* 1963;1:771–777.

28. Godlewski S. Diagnostic des thromboses vertebro-basilaire. *Assises Med* 1965;23(2):81–92.

29. Janzen-Hamburg R. Schleudertrauma der Halswirbelsaule, neurologische Probleme. *Langenbecks Arch Klin Chir* 1966;316:461–469.

30. Nick J, Contamin F, Nicolle MH, et al. Incidents et accidents neurologiques dus aux manipulations cervicales: A propos de trois observations. *Bull Mem Soc Med Hop Paris* 1967;118(5):435–440.

31. Heyden S. Extra kranier thrombotischer Arterienverschlussals folge von Kopf und Halsverletzung. *Mat Med Nordm* 1971;23:24–32.

32. Wood MJ, Lang EK, Faludi HK, Woolhandler GJ. Traumatic vertebral artery thrombosis. *J La Med Soc* 1971;123(12):413–414.

33. Kanshepolsky J, Danielson H, Flynn RE. Vertebral artery insufficiency and cerebellar infarct due to manipulation of the neck. *Bull La Neurol Soc* 1972;37:62–66.

34. Lorenz R, Vogelsang HG. Thrombose der arteria basilaris nach chiropraktischen Manipulationen an der Halswirbelsaule. *Dtsch Med Wochenschr* 1972;97:36–43.

35. Kommerell G, Hoyt WF. Lateropulsion of saccadic eye movements. *Arch Neurol* 1973;28:313–318.

36. Nagler W. Vertebral artery obstruction by hyperextension of the neck; report of three cases. *Arch Phys Med Rehab* 1973;54:237–240.

37. Schmitt HP, Tamaska L. Disseziierende ruptur der arteria vertebralis mit todlichem vertebralis und basilaris—Verschluss. *Z Rechtsmedizin* 1973;73:301–308.

38. Schmitt HP. Manuelle Therapie der Halswirbelsaule. *Z Allgemeinmedizin* 1978;54:467–474.

39. Kramer KH. Wallenburg Syndrom nach manueller Behandlung. *Manuelle Medizin* 1974;12:88–89.

40. Lyness SS, Wagman AD. Neurological deficit following cervical manipulation. *Surg Neurol* 1974;2:121–124.

41. Mehalic T, Farhat SM. Vertebral artery injury from chiropractic manipulation of the neck. *Surg Neurol* 1974;2:125–129.

42. Kosoy J, Glassman AL. Audiovestibular findings with cervical spine trauma. *Tex Med* 1974;70:66–71.

43. Miller RG, Burton R. Stroke following chiropractic manipulation of the spine. *JAMA* 1974;229(2):189–190.

44. Bladin PF, Merory J. Mechanisms in cerebral lesions in trauma to high cervical portion of the vertebral artery rotation injury. *Proc Aust Assoc Neurol* 1975;12:35–41.

45. Davidson KC, Weiford EC, Dixon GD. Traumatic vertebral artery pseudoaneurysm following chiropractic manipulation. *Radiology* 1975;115:651–652.

46. Kipp W. *Todlicher Hirnstamminfarkt nach HWS-Manipulation* (dissertation). Tubingen: Eberhard Karls Universtitaet; 1975;39. (Cited by Ladermann).

47. Goodbody RA. Fatal post-traumatic vertebro basilar ischaemia. *J Clin Pathol* 1976;29(1):86–87.

48. Hensell V. Neurologische Schaden nach Repositions Massnahmen an der Wirbelsaule. *Med Welt* 1976;27(14):656–658.

49. Mueller S, Sahs AL. Brain stem dysfunction related to cervical manipulation. *Neurology (Minneap)* 1976;26:547–560.

50. Schmitt HP. Rupturen und thrombosen der arteria vertebralis nach gedecklen mechanischen Insulten. *Schweiz Arch Neurol Neurochirurg Psychiatr* 1976;119:363–369.

51. Beatty RA. Dissecting hematoma of the internal carotid artery following chiropractic cervical manipulation. *J Trauma* 1977;17(3):248–249.

52. Easton JD, Sherman DG. Cervical manipulation and stroke. *Stroke* 1977;8(5):594–597.

53. Zauel D, Carlow TJ. Internuclear ophthalmoplegia following cervical manipulation. *Ann Neurol* 1977;1(3):308.

54. Gorman RF. Cardiac arrest after cervical spine mobilization. *Med J Aust* 1978;2:169–170.

55. Nyberg-Hansen R, Loken AC, Tenstad O. Brainstem lesion with coma for five years following manipulation of the cervical spine. *J Neurol* 1978;218:97–105.

56. Parkin PJ, Wallis WE, Wilson JL. Vertebral artery occlusion following manipulation of the neck. *NZ Med J* 1978;88:441–443.

57. Zimmermann AW, Kumar AJ, Gadoth N, Hodges FJ. Traumatic vertebrobasilar occlusive disease in childhood. *Neurology* 1978;28:185–188.

58. Krueger BR, Okazaki H. Vertebral-basilar distribution infarction following chiropractic cervical manipulation. *Mayo Clin Proc* 1980;55(5):3220–3232.

59. Schellhas KP, Latchaw RE, Wendling LR, Gold LHA. Vertebrobasilar injuries following cervical manipulation. *JAMA* 1980;244(13):1450–1453.

60. Ladermann JP. Accidents of spinal manipulation. *Ann Swiss Chiro Assoc* 1981;7:161–208.

61. Sherman DG, Hart RG, Easton JD. Abrupt change in head position and cerebral infarction. *Stroke* 1981;12(1):2–6. (The first three cases were previously reported in Easton (1977).)

62. Dahl A, Bjark P, Anke I. Cerebrovaskulaere kompliskasjoner til manipulasjonsbehandling av nakken. *Tidsskr Nor Laegeforen* 1983;102(3):155–157.

63. Meyermann R. Möglichkeiten einer Schädigung der Arteria Vertebralis. *Manuelle Medizin* 1982;20:105–114.

64. Simmons KC, Soo YS, Walker G, Harvey P. Trauma to the vertebral artery related to neck manipulation. *Med J Aust* 1982;1:187–188.

65. Gutmann G. Verletzungen der Arteria Vertebralis durch manuelle Therapie. *Manuelle Medizin* 1983;21:2–14.

66. Braun IF, Pinto RS, DeFilipp GJ, et al. Brain stem infarction due to chiropractic manipulation of the cervical spine. *Southern Med J* 1983;76(9):1199–1201.

67. Horn SW. The "locked-In" syndrome following chiropractic manipulation of the cervical spine. *Ann Emerg Med* 1983;12(10):648–650.

68. Pamela F, Beaugerie L, Couturier M, et al. Syndrome de deefferentiation motrice par thrombose du tronc basilaire apres manipulation vertebrale. *Presse Medicale* 1983;12(24):1548.

69. Cellerier P, Georget AM. Dissection des arteres vertebrales apres manipulation du rachis cervical. A propos d'un cas. *J Radiol* 1984;65(3):191–196.

70. Daneshmend TK, Hewer RL, Bradshaw JR. Acute brain stem stroke during neck manipulation. *Br Med J* 1984;288:189.

71. Fritz VU, Maloon A, Tuch P. Neck manipulation causing stroke. *South African Med J* 1984;66:844–846.

72. Lindy DR. Patient collapse following cervical manipulation: A case report. *Br Osteopathic J* 1984;16(2):84–85.

73. Nielsen AA. Cerebrovaskulaere insulter forarsaget af manipulation af columna cervicalis. *Ugeskr Lager* 1984(22 Oct);3267–3270.

74. Zak SM, Carmody RF. Cerebellar infarction from chiropractic neck manipulation: Case report and review of the literature. *Ariz Med* 1984;41(5):333–337.

75. Bayerl JR, Buchmuller HR, Pohlmann B. Nebenwirkungen und Kontraindikationen der manuellen Therapie im bereich der Halswirbelsaule. *Nervenarzt* 1985;56(4):194–199.

76. Katirji MB, Reinmuth OM, Latchaw RE. Stroke due to vertebral artery injury. *Arch Neurol* 1985;42:242–248.

77. Modde PJ. *Chiropractic Malpractice.* Columbia, Md: Hanrow Press; 1985:269–270, 273–275, 311–318, 322–323, 329–331, 334–337.

78. Dvorak J, Orelli F. How dangerous is manipulation of the cervical spine? *Manual Med* 1985;2:1–4.

79. Brownson RJ, Zollinger WK, Madiera T, Fell D. Sudden sensorineural hearing loss following manipulation of the cervical spine. *Laryngoscope* 1986;96(2):166–170.

80. Miglets AS. Discussion. In: Brownson RJ, Zollinger WK, Madiera T, Fell D, eds. Sudden sensorineural hearing loss following manipulation of the cervical spine. *Laryngoscope* 1986;96(2):166–170.

81. Gittinger JW. Occipital infarction following chiropractic cervical manipulation. *J Clin Neuro Ophthalmol* 1986;6(1):11–13.

82. Terrett AGJ. Vascular accidents from cervical spine manipulation: report on 107 cases. *J Aust Chiro Assoc* 1987;17(1):15–24.

83. Dunne JW, Conacher GN, Khangure M, Harper CG. Dissecting aneurysms of the vertebral arteries following cervical manipulation: A case report. *J Neurol Neurosurg Psychiatry* 1987;50(3):349–353.

84. Bolton SP. Vascular accidents. *J Aust Chiro Assoc* 1987;17(2):75.

85. Fast A, Zinicola DF, Marin EL. Vertebral artery damage complicating cervical manipulation. *Spine* 1987;12(9):840–842.

86. Jentzen JM, Amatuzio J, Peterson GF. Complications of cervical manipulation: A case report of fatal brainstem infarct with review of the mechanisms and predisposing factors. *J Forensic Sci* 1987;32(4):1089–1094.

87. Sherman MR, Smialek JE, Zane WE. Pathogenesis of vertebral artery occlusion following cervical spine manipulation. *Arch Pathol Lab Med* 1987;111(9):851–853.

88. Povlsen UJ, Kjaer L, Arlien-Soborg P. Locked-in syndrome following cervical manipulation. *Acta Neurol Scand* 1987;76(6):486–488.

89. Carmody E, Buckley P, Hutchinson M. Basilar artery occlusion following chiropractic cervical manipulation. *Irish Med J* 1987;80(9):259–260.

90. Bell v. Griffiths. Hunter J (Judgement). Supreme Court, Common Law Division, Sydney; 14 Sep 1994.

91. Mas JL, Bousser MG, Hasboun D, Laplane D. Extracranial vertebral artery dissections: A review of 13 cases. *Stroke* 1987;18(6):1037–1047.

92. Chen TW, Chen ST. Brainstem stroke induced by chiropractic neck manipulation—a case report. *Chung Hua I Hsueh Tsa Chih* (Chinese Med) 1987;40(6):557–562.

93. Murthy JMK, Naidu KV. Aneurysm of the cervical internal carotid artery following chiropractic manipulation. *J Neurol Neurosurg Psychiatry* 1988;51(9):1237–1238.

94. Phillips SJ, Maloney WJ, Gray J. Pure motor stroke due to vertebral artery dissection. *Can J Neurol Sci* 1989;16(3):348–351.

95. Ponge T, Cottin S, Ponge A, et al. Accident vasculaire vertebro-basilaire apres manipulation du rachis cervical. *Rev Rhum* 1989;56(7):545–548.

96. Mas JL, Henin D, Bousser MG, et al. Dissecting aneurysm of the vertebral artery and cervical manipulation: A case report with autopsy. *Neurology* 1989;39(4):512–515.

97. Terrett AGJ. Osteopathic iatrogenics and the need for government regulation. *J New Zealand Register of Osteopaths* 1990;4:42–45.

98. Frumkin LR, Baloh RW. Wallenberg's syndrome following neck manipulation. *Neurology* 1990;40(4):611–615.

99. Raskind R, North CM. Vertebral artery injuries following chiropractic cervical spine manipulation—case reports. *Angiology* 1990;41(6):445–452.

100. Krieger D, Leibold M, Bruckmann H. Dissektionen der arteria vertebralis nach zervikalen chiropraktischen Manipulationen. *Dtsch Med Wochenschr* 1990;115 (15):580–583.

101. Malm J, Olsson T, Fagerlund M. Cervikal manipulation kan ge hjarninfarkt. *Lakartidningen* 1990;87(46):3877–3879.

102. Frisoni GB, Anzola GP. Vertebrobasilar ischaemia after neck motion. *Stroke* 1991;22(11):1452–1460.

103. Rothrock JF, Hesselink JR, Teacher TM. Vertebral artery occlusion and stroke from cervical self manipulation. *Neurology* 1991;41 (10):1696–1697.

104. Cook JW, Sanstead JK. Wallenberg syndrome following self-induced manipulation. *Neurology* 1991;41(10):1695–1696.

105. Braune HJ, Munk MH, Huffmann G. Hirninfarkt im Stromgebiet der arteria cerebri media nach Chirotherapie der Halswirbelsaule. *Dtsch Med Wochenschr* 1991;116(27):1047–1050.

106. Nakamura CT, Lau JM, Polk NO, Popper JS. Vertebral artery dissection caused by chiropractic manipulation. *J Vasc Surg* 1991;14(1):122–124.

107. Weinstein SM, Cantu RC. Cerebral stroke in a semi-pro football player: A case report. *Med Sci Sports Exerc* 1991;23(10):1119–1121.

108. *Saltzberg v Hawkins*. Los Angeles County Superior Court Case No. 697925. Kakita J and Jury. Judgement 13 Nov 1991. (Case also reported in: Chapman-Smith D. Who should manipulate—$1.3 million award against MD. *Chiro Report* 1992;6(6):6; and in Anonymous. MD's cervical manipulation causes woman's stroke. *MPI's Dynamic Chiro* 1991(Dec 20):33.)

109. Anonymous. A case of altered records. *Back Talk* (National Chiropractic Mutual Insurance Company) 1991;(Fall):5–6.

110. Sullivan EC. Brain stem stroke syndromes from cervical adjustments: Report on five cases. *J Chiro Res Clin Invest* 1992;8(1):12–16.

111. Johnson DW. Cervical self manipulation and stroke. *Med J Aust* 1993;158(4):290.

112. Hamaan G, Felber S, Haass A, et al. Cervicocephalic artery dissections due to chiropractic manipulations. *Lancet* 1993;341:764–765.

113. Sinel M, Smith D. Thalamic infarction secondary to cervical manipulation. *Arch Phys Med Rehabil* 1993;74:543–546.

114. Vibert D, Rohr Le Floch J, Gauthier G. Vertigo as manifestation of vertebral artery dissection after chiropractic neck manipulations. *J Oto-Rhino-Laryngology* 1993;55:140–142.

115. Carmichael JP. Transient global amnesia following rotational manipulation of the upper cervical spine. *Proceedings of the 1994 International Conference on Spinal Manipulation*. 1994;65.

116. Murase S, Ohe N, Nokura H, et al. Vertebral artery injury following mild neck trauma: Report of two cases. *No Shinkei Geka* 1994;22(7):671–676.

117. Bridges R. Trial or settlement: Circumstances that prompt the decision. *J Chiro* 1994;31(11):44–47.

118. Terrett AGJ. Misuse of the literature by medical authors in discussing spinal manipulative therapy injury. *J Manipulative Physiol Ther* 1995;18(4):203–210.

119. Peters M, Bohl J, Thomke F, et al. Dissection of the internal carotid artery after chiropractic manipulation of the neck. *Neurology* 1995;45:2284–2286.

120. Grieve GP. Incidents and accidents of manipulation. In: Grieve GP, ed. *Modern Manual Therapy of the Vertebral Column*. New York, NY: Churchill Livingstone; 1986;873–884.

121. Maigne R. *Orthopedic Medicine: A New Approach to Vertebral Manipulations*. Springfield, Ill: Thomas; 1972:155, 169.

122. Cyriax J. *Textbook of Orthopaedic Medicine. Vol 1. Diagnosis of Soft Tissue Lesions*. 7th ed. London: Bailliere Tindall; 1972;165.

123. Hosek RS, Schram SB, Silverman H, Meyers JB. Cervical manipulation. *JAMA* 1981;245:922.

124. Taylor HH. Letter to the editor. *J Chiro* 1981;18(6):11–12.

125. Terrett AGJ, Kleynhans AM. Cerebrovascular complications of manipulation. In: Haldeman S, ed. *Principles and Practice of Chiropractic*. 2nd ed. Norwalk, Conn: Appleton & Lange; 1992;579–598.

126. Terrett AGJ. Malpractice avoidance for chiropractors: Vertebrobasilar stroke following manipulation. West Des Moines, Iowa: National Chiropractic Mutual Insurance Company; 1996.

127. Terrett AGJ. Vascular accidents from cervical spine manipulation: the mechanisms. *J Aust Chiro Assoc* 1987;17(4):131–144.

128. Christiensen MG, ed. *Job Analysis of Chiropractic: A Project Report, Survey Analysis and Summary of the Practice of Chiropractic within the United States*. Greeley, Colo: National Board of Chiropractic Examiners; 1993;58.

129. Christiensen MG, ed. *Job Analysis of Chiropractic in Australia and New Zealand: A Project Report, Survey Analysis and Summary of the Practice of Chiropractic within Australia and New Zealand*. Greeley, Colo: National Board of Chiropractic Examiners; 1994;72.

130. Shekelle PG, Brook RH. A community based study of the use of chiropractic services. *Am J Public Health* 1991;81(4):439–442.

131. Shekelle PG, Adams AH, et al. The appropriateness of spinal manipulation for low back pain: Project overview and literature review. Santa Monica, Calif: RAND; 1991; Monograph No. R-4025/1–CCR/FCER.

132. Selecki BR. The effects of rotation of the atlas on the axis: Experimental work. *Med J Aust* 1969;56 (20):1012–1015.

133. deKleyn A, Nieuwenhuyse P. Schwindelanfaelle und nystagmus bei einer bestimmten Stellung des Kopfes. *Acta Otolaryng* 1927;11:155.

134. deKleyn A, Versteegh C. Ueber verschiedene Formen von Menieres Syndrom. *Dtsch Ztschr* 1933;132:157.

135. Tatlow WFT, Bammer HG. Syndrome of vertebral artery compression. *Neurology* 1957;7:331–340.

136. Toole JF, Tucker SH. Influence of head position upon cerebral circulation: Studies on blood flow in cadavers. *Arch Neurol* 1960;2:616–623.

137. Brown BSJ, Tatlow WFT. Radiographic studies of the vertebral arteries in cadavers. *Radiology* 1963;81:80–88.

138. Andersson R, Carleson R, Nylen O. Vertebral artery insufficiency and rotational obstruction. *Acta Med Scand* 1970;188:475–477.

139. Barton JW, Margolis MT. Rotational obstruction of the vertebral artery at the atlantoaxial joint. *Neuroradiology* 1975;9:117–120.

140. Grossman RI, Davies KR. Positional occlusion of the vertebral artery: A rare cause of embolic stroke. *Neuroradiology* 1982;23:227–230.

141. Yang PJ, Latack JT, Gabrielson TO, et al. Rotational vertebral artery occlusion at C1–2. *AJNR* 1985;6:98–100.

142. Thiel H, Wallace K, Donat J, Yong-Hing K. Effect of various head and neck positions on vertebral artery blood flow. *Clin Biomech* 1994;9:105–110.

143. Refshauge KM. Rotation: A valid premanipulative dizziness test? Does it predict safe manipulation? *J Manipulative Physiol Ther* 1994;17(1):15–19.

144. Haynes MJ. Doppler studies comparing the effects of cervical rotation and lateral flexion on vertebral artery blood flow. *J Manipulative Physiol Ther* 1996;19(6):378–384.

145. Bakay L, Sweet WH. Intra-arterial pressures in the neck and brain. *J Neurosurg* 1953;10:353–359.

146. Yates PO. Birth trauma to the vertebral arteries. *Arch Dis Child* 1959;34:436–441.

147. Fisher M. Basilar artery embolism after surgery under general anesthesia: A case report. *Neurology* 1993;43:1856.

148. Tettenborn B, Caplan LR, Sloan MA, et al. Postoperative brainstem and cerebellar infarcts. *Neurology* 1993;43:471–477.

149. Nosan DK, Gomez CR, Maves MD. Perioperative stroke in patients undergoing head and neck surgery. *Ann Otol Rhinol Laryngol* 1993;102:717–723.

150. Hanus SH, Homer TD, Harter DH. Vertebral artery occlusion complicating yoga exercises. *Arch Neurol* 1977;34:574–575.

151. Okawara S, Nibblelink D. Vertebral artery occlusion following hyperextension and rotation of the head. *Stroke* 1974;5:640–642.

152. Fogelholm R, Karli P. Iatrogenic brainstem infarction. *Eur Neurol* 1975;13:6–12.

153. Sorenson BF. Bow hunter's stroke. *Neurosurgery* 1978;2:259–261.

154. Rogers L, Sweeney PJ. Stroke: A neurologic complication of wrestling. *Amer J Sports Med* 1979;7(6):352–354.

155. Saternus KS, Fuchs V. Ist die arteria vertebralis bei der Reanimation gefahrdet? *Manuelle Medizin* 1982;20:101–104.

156. Barty GM. Expert testimony. *Klippel v Alchin*. Wagga Wagga, Australia; 1983(12 Aug):33.

157. Hope EE, Bodensteiner JB, Barnes P. Cerebral infarction related to neck position in an adolescent. *Pediatrics* 1983;72:335–357.

158. Tramo MJ, Hainline B, Petito F, et al. Vertebral artery injury and cerebellar stroke while swimming: A case report. *Stroke* 1985;16:1039–1042.

159. Dorey RSA, Mayne V. Break dancing injuries. *Med J Aust* 1986;144:610–611.

160. Pryse-Phillips W. Infarction of the medulla and cervical cord after fitness exercises. *Stroke* 1989;20:292–294.

161. Weintraub MI. Beauty parlor stroke syndrome: Report of 2 cases. *Neurology* 1992;42(Suppl 3):340.

162. Weintraub MI. Beauty parlor stroke syndrome: Report of five cases. *JAMA* 1993;269(16):2085–2086.

163. Oh VMS. Brain infarction and neck callisthenics. *Lancet* 1993;342:739.

164. Swords WJ. Postcoital vertebral artery dissection. 1996;54(7):2195–2196.

165. White RP, Chapleau CE, Dugdale M, Robertson JT. Cerebral arterial contractions induced by human and bovine thrombin. *Stroke* 1980;11(4):363–368.

166. Blaumanis OR, Gertz SD, Grady PA, Nelson ER. Thrombosis in acute experimental cerebral vasospasm. *Stroke* 1976;7(1):9–10.

167. Bogduk N. Cervical causes of headache and dizziness. In: Grieve GP, ed. *Modern Manual Therapy of the Vertebral Column.* New York, NY: Churchill Livingstone; 1986:289–302.

168. Plum F, Posner JB. *The Diagnosis of Stupor and Coma.* 3rd ed. Philadelphia, Pa: FA Davis; 1982:9.

169. Dumas A. *The Count of Monte Cristo.* Toronto: Bantam Books; 1956;203–210; originally published in 1844.

170. McCusker EA, Rudick RA, Honch GW, Griggs RC. Recovery from the "locked-in" syndrome. *Arch Neurol* 1982;39:145–147.

171. Khurana RK, Genut AA, Yannakakis GD. Locked-in syndrome with recovery. *Ann Neurol* 1980;8:439–441.

172. George PE, Silverstein HT, Wallace H, Marshall M. Identification of the high risk pre-stroke patient. *J Chiro* 1981;15:S26–S28.

173. Terrett AGJ. Importance and interpretation of tests designed to predict susceptibility to neurocirculatory accidents from manipulation. *J Aust Chiro Assoc* 1983;13(2):29–34.

174. Kleynhans AM, Terrett AGJ. The prevention of complications from spinal manipulative therapy. In: Glasgow EF, et al, eds. *Aspects of Manipulative Therapy.* 2nd ed. London: Churchill Livingstone; 1985;161–175.

175. Henderson DJ, Cassidy JD. Vertebral artery syndrome. In: Vernon H, ed. *Upper Cervical Syndrome: Chiropractic Diagnosis and Treatment.* Baltimore, Md: Williams and Wilkins. 1988;194–206.

176. Weiner HL. Transient ischemic attacks, when do they foreshadow a stroke? *Diagnosis* 1981;(Jul):51–57.

177. Mas JL, Goeau C, Bousser MG, et al. Spontaneous dissecting aneurysms of the internal carotid and vertebral arteries: Two case reports. *Stroke* 1985;16(1):125–129.

178. Bickerstaff ER. *Neurological Complications of Oral Contraceptives.* Oxford: Clarendon Press; 1975;57–58.

179. Ask-Upmark E, Bickerstaff ER. Vertebral artery occlusion and oral contraceptives. *Br Med J* 1976;1:487–488.

180. Rogers RL, Meyer JS, Shaw TG, et al. Cigarette smoking decreases cerebral blood flow suggesting increased risk for stroke. *JAMA* 1983;250:2796–2800.

181. Adams KHR, Yung MW, Lye M, Whitehouse GH. Are cervical spine radiographs of value in elderly patients with vertebrobasilar insufficiency? *Age Ageing* 1986;15:57–59.

182. Broderick JP, Swanson JW. Migraine related strokes: Clinical profile and prognosis in 20 patients. *Arch Neurol* 1987;44:868–871.

183. Gilroy J. *Basic Neurology.* 2nd ed. New York, NY: Pergamon Press; 1990;157.

184. Anonymous. Chiropractors urged to consider stroke risk. *Med World News* 1980(March 17);23.

185. Cashley MAP. Basilar artery migraine or cerebral vascular accident? *J Manipulative Physiol Ther* 1993;16(2):112–114.

186. Solomon GD, Spaccavento LJ. Lateral medullary syndrome after basilar migraine. *Headache* 1982;22:171–172.

187. Spaccavento LJ, Solomon GD, Mani S. An association between strokes and migraines in young adults. *Headache* 1981;21:121.

188. Solomon GD, Spaccavento LJ. Lateral medullary syndrome after basilar migraine. *Headache* 1982;22:171–172.

189. Dalessio D. Migraine, platelets, and headache prophylaxis. *JAMA* 1978;239(1):52–53.

190. Mokri B, Houser OW, Sandok BA, Piepgras DG. Spontaneous dissections of the vertebral arteries. *Neurology* 1988;38:880–885.

191. Sturzenegger M. Headache and neck pain: The warning symptoms of vertebral artery dissection. *Headache* 1994;34:187–193.

192. Nicholls FT, Mawad M, Mohr JP, et al. Focal headache during balloon inflation in the vertebral and basilar arteries. *Headache* 1993;33:87–89.

193. Hart RG, Easton JD. Dissections. *Stroke* 1985;16:925–927.

194. Biller J, Hingtgen WL, Adams HP, et al. Cervicocephalic arterial dissections. *Arch Neurol* 1986;43:1234–1238.

195. Hart RG, Easton JD. Dissection of the cervical and cerebral arteries. *Neurol Clin* 1983;1:155–182.

196. Chiras J, Marciano S, VegaMolina J, et al. Spontaneous dissecting aneurysm of the extracranial vertebral artery (20 cases). *Neuroradiology* 1985;27:327–333.

197. Fitz-Ritson D. Assessment of cervicogenic vertigo. *J Manipulative Physiol Ther* 1991;14(3):193–198.

198. Cote P, Mior SA, Fitz-Ritson D. Cervicogenic vertigo: A report of three cases. *J Canad Chiro Assoc* 1991;35(2):89–94.

199. Wing LW, Hargrave-Wilson W. Cervical vertigo. *Aust NZ J Surg* 1974;44(3):275–277.

200. Davis D. A common type of vertigo relieved by traction of the cervical spine. *Ann Int Med* 1953;38:778–786.

201. Jepson O. Dizziness originating in the columna cervicalis. *Nordisk Medicin* 1963;6(69):675–676. (Translated in: *J Canad Chiro Assoc* 1967;11:7–8,25).

202. Terrett AGJ. It is more important to know when not to adjust. *Chiro Technique* 1990;2(1):1–9.

203. Houle JOE. Assessing hemodynamics of the vertebrobasilar complex through angiothlipsis. *Digest Chiro Economics* 1972;15(2):14–15.

204. Kleynhans AM. The prevention of complications from spinal manipulative therapy. In: Idczak RM, ed. *Aspects of Manipulative Therapy*. Melbourne, Australia; Lincoln Institute of Health Sciences; 1980;133–141.

205. Terrett AGJ, Webb MN. Vertebrobasilar accidents following cervical spine adjustment/manipulation. *J Aust Chiro Assoc* 1982;12:24–27.

206. Grant R. Dizziness testing and manipulation of the cervical spine. In: Grant R, ed. *Physical Therapy of the Cervical and Thoracic Spine*. New York, NY: Churchill Livingstone; 1988;111–124.

207. Bolton PS, Stick PE, Lord RSA. Failure of clinical tests to predict ischemia before neck manipulation. *J Manipulative Physiol Ther* 1989;12(4):304–307.

208. Gayral L, France T, Nuewirth E. Oto-neuro-ophthalmologic manifestations of cervical origin. Posterior cervical sympathetic syndrome of Barre Lieou. *N Y State J Med* 1954;54:1920–1926.

209. Gray LP. Extralabyrinthine vertigo due to cervical muscle lesions. *J Laryngol* 1956;70:352–360.

210. de Jong PTVM. Ataxia and nystagmus induced by injection of local anaesthetic in the neck. *Ann Neurol* 1977;1:240–246.

211. Maeda M. Neck influences on the vestibulo-ocular reflex arc and the vestibulocerebellum. *Prog Brain Res* 1979;50:551–559.

212. Liedgren C, Odkvist L. The morphological and physiological basis for vertigo of cervical origin. In: Claussen C, ed. *Differential Diagnosis of Vertigo. Proceedings of the 6th Scientific Meetings of the NES, Finland 1979*. New York, NY: Walter de Gruyter; 1980;567–587.

213. Hulse M. Disequilibrium caused by a functional disturbance of the upper cervical spine. Clinical aspects and differential diagnosis. *Man Med* 1983;1:18–23.

214. Gatterman MI. Extreme caution advised. *J Chiro* 1982;19(9):14.

215. Neuwirth E. The vertebral nerve in the posterior cervical syndrome. *N Y State J Med* 1955;55:1380.

216. Stewart DY. Current concepts of "Barre syndrome" or the posterior cervical sympathetic syndrome. *Clin Ortho Rel Res* 1962;24:40–48.

217. Jackson R. *The Cervical Syndrome*. Springfield, Ill: Thomas; 1977;245–246.

218. Alm A. The effect of stimulation of the cervical sympathetic chain on regional cerebral blood flow in monkeys: A study with radioactively labelled microspheres. *Acta Physiol Scand* 1975;93:483–489.

219. Bogduk N, Lambert G, Duckworth JW. The anatomy and physiology of the vertebral nerve in relation to cervical migraine. *Cephalgia* 1981;1:1–14.

220. Terrett AGJ. A case of death following vertebrobasilar stroke (VBS) attributed to spinal manipulation therapy (SMT). *Aust Chiro* 1997(Oct);16–17.

221. Harper C. *Post Mortem Report*. Department of Neuropathology, Royal Perth Hospital, Perth, West Australia, 1985.

222. Brandt T, Orberk E, Hausser I, et al. Ultrastructural aberrations of connective tissue components in patients with spontaneous cervicocerebral artery dissections. *Neurology* 1996;46:A173, PO2.013.

223. Mayer SA, Rubin BS, Starman BJ, Byers PH. Spontaneous multivessel cervical artery dissection in a patient with a substitution of alanine for glycine (G13A) in the alpha 1 (I) chain of type I collagen. *Neurology* 1996 (Aug);47:552–556.

224. Rubin BS, Mayer SA, Starman BJ, Byers PH. Spontaneous multivessel cervical artery dissection in a patient with a substitution of alanine for glycine (GO13A) in the alpha 1 (I) chain of type I collagen. *Neurology* 1996;46:A173, PO2.013.

225. Terrett AGJ. The neck tongue syndrome. *J Aust Chiro Assoc* 1984;14(3):100–107.

226. Terrett AGJ. The neck tongue syndrome and spinal manipulative therapy. In: Vernon H, ed. *Upper Cervical Spine Syndrome: Chiropractic Diagnosis and Treatment*. Baltimore, Md: Williams and Wilkins. 1988;223–239.

227. Terrett AGJ. Tinnitus, the cervical spine, and spinal manipulative therapy. *Chiro Technique* 1989;1(2):41–45.

228. Terrett AGJ. Cerebral dysfunction: A theory to explain some of the effects of chiropractic manipulation. *Chiro Technique* 1993;5(4):168–173.

229. Terrett AGJ. Letter to the editor. *Chiro Technique* 1994;6(3):110–112.

230. Terrett AGJ. The cerebral dysfunction theory. In: Gatterman MI, ed. *Foundations of Chiropractic: Subluxation*. St. Louis, Mo: Mosby; 1995;340–352.

231. Terrett AGJ, Gorman RF. The eye, the cervical spine, and spinal manipulative therapy: A review of the literature. *Chiro Technique* 1995;7(2):43–54.

232. Terrett AGJ. Vertigo/Dizziness: A non-indication, indication and contraindication for chiropractic therapy, the dilemma. In: Robert J, ed. *The Puzzling Relationship of Vertigo and the Cervical Spine*. Proceedings of the 40th European Chiropractors Union Convention, Geneva, Switzerland, 16–18 May 1996: 59–62.

CHAPTER 23

Diagnosis and Treatment of Temporomandibular Disorders

CLAYTON D. SKAGGS

"There are more displaced diagnoses, than displaced discs."

—W. K. Solberg, DDS

INTRODUCTION

The temporomandibular joint (TMJ) system is often considered one of the most densely innervated regions in the body. Orofacial functions such as chewing, breathing, and swallowing are activities of daily living that precipitate frequent usage of this system. These factors, along with the synaptic connection of the TMJ system to afferents from the upper cervical spine via the trigeminocervical nucleus (see Fig. 4–12), make temporomandibular disorders (TMDs) a common area of nociception and dysfunction.

Owing to the frequent complexity of symptoms and the crossing of several disciplines, the diagnosis and treatment of TMD remains varied, with limited and immature guidelines. Although structural pathology does exist in the objective presentation of TMD, it is rarely the underlying cause of dysfunction. The majority of the literature and clinical evidence supports a conservative and functional approach to assessment and treatment.[1–9] As the depth of understanding of functional pathology linked to this disorder increases, its horrific and costly complexity will frequently be reduced to exciting simplicity. This chapter aims to bring the comprehension of TMD to a new level that will allow the clinician to approach it with certainty. The TMJ is an important part of the locomotor system and, therefore, should be treated as such.

FUNCTIONAL ANATOMY

The muscles of mastication are the key muscles when discussing TMD. The functions of this group include mastication, swallowing, and speech as primary functions, with respiration and emotional expression as secondary functions. The primary *actions* of the muscles of mastication involved in mandibular function include elevation (jaw closing) and depression (jaw opening). Protrusion (jaw jutting forward), lateral excursion, and retraction have secondary and synergistic action associated with the primary movements previously listed. For example, mandibular opening involves depression combined with chin retraction (Fig. 23–1). Normal chewing activity may involve opening with chin retraction, closing, and degrees of lateral excursion.

When considering the individual muscles of mastication and their treatment with relation to TMD the frequent approach is, unfortunately, often singular. The near unanimous attention goes to the lateral pterygoid muscle. The lateral pterygoid certainly warrants consideration. It plays a role in many aspects of mandibular movement, particularly if it is faulty. However, treatment approaches limited to the lateral pterygoid rarely end with permanent satisfaction for the patient or practitioner.

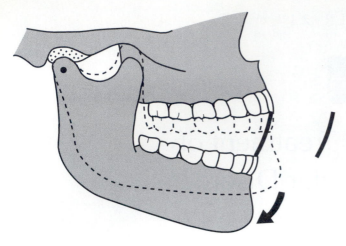

Figure 23–1. Normal opening of mandible. Rotational phase of depression combined with retraction.

The lateral pterygoid consists of two divisions, inferior and superior. The superior lateral pterygoid originates from the infratemporal surface of the greater wing of the sphenoid, and attaches to the disc (40 percent) and condyle (60 percent). Of clinical interest, several recent studies have shown no attachment to the disc in 30 percent of the population.[10, 11] The functions of the superior lateral pterygoid include stabilization during mandibular elevation and chewing and mandibular protrusion. The inferior lateral pterygoid originates at the outer surface of the lateral pterygoid plate and attaches to the neck of the condyle. Its primary role is protrusion. It assists in stabilization of rotary movement of the mandible provided there is proper activation of the depressors of the mandible.

The muscles involved in elevation of the mandible are the masseter, temporalis, and medial pterygoid. These are muscles involved in static, postural activity and are commonly overactive. Their tendency for tension and tightness corresponds with Janda's discussion of fundamental reflexes and the dominance of jaw closure with elements of fatigue, stress, or dysfunction.[12]

❗ CLINICAL PEARL

Four fundamental reflexes described by Janda include extension-adduction-rotation of the lower extremity (a part of the gait to escape impending danger), flexion-adduction-rotation of the upper extremity (to bring food to the mouth), *adduction of the jaw (closing of the mouth)*, and breathing.[12] He proposed that these reflexes and their subsequent actions would dominate during times of stress, fatigue and various structural lesions. *Clinically this correlates to the prevalence of parafunctional habits such as clenching and bruxism associated with TMD.*

Antagonists to the muscles of elevation are the muscles of mandibular depression. They often become inhibited and yet house trigger points as a result of effort to stabilize the mandible in the presence of dysfunction. The digastric muscle is considered the prime mover of mandibular depression, with the mylohyoid, platysma, and inferior lateral pterygoid muscles acting as synergists.

An important anatomical and functional link to the mandibular depressors is the hyoid bone. Reciprocal stabilization occurs between the hyoid and mandible during swallowing and chewing. To appreciate this phenomenon, simply swallow and notice your teeth come together to stabilize the mandible while the hyoid elevates. The hyoid, stabilized by surrounding muscular attachments, provides proximal stability for mobility of the mandible.

Three ligaments are involved in the condyle and disc complex of the TMJ. They are the capsular, collateral, and TMJ ligaments (Fig. 23–2). The capsular ligament is primarily responsible for maintaining the synovial fluid and is densely innervated. It is a common pain generator after abrupt trauma to the jaw. The medial and lateral collateral ligaments attach the disc to the condyle to allow a caplike mechanism for rotational articulation in the inferior joint of the condyle and disc complex. They aid in stabilization of the disc on the condyle and can also produce pain. The TMJ ligament has two components, an oblique and a horizontal division. The oblique TMJ ligament provides protection for the vital anterior structures of the neck as it limits rotation of the mandible to approximately two thirds of mandibular opening. Further mandibular rotation requires the condyle to move forward down the articular eminence of the temporal fossa, as with normal opening. This described function, powered by appropriate masticatory muscle activity, is the cornerstone for understanding functional pathology of TMD. It will be reviewed more extensively in the discussion of muscle imbalance that follows. The horizontal TMJ ligament serves primarily in a protective role, preventing direct posterior movement of the condyle.

The remaining component of the condyle and disc complex that has functional importance is the disc itself and the retrodiscal connective tissue. The disc is made up of fibrous connective tissue and is devoid of nerves or vessels. Its biconcave configuration, combined with intra-articular pressure, provide the main constructs for condyle and disc stability. The most functionally stable position for the condyle and disc complex is when it is in the most anterior and superior position of the temporal fossa (Fig. 23–3). This position is commonly referred to as "centric relation."[13, 14] This can also serve as a test position to determine if discal derangement is present (Fig. 23–4). A negative finding on centric relation testing signifies that disc derangement is not present or is not a causative factor in the patient's pain generation. Adequate skill is required to reduce the potential for false positive findings using this very valuable test.

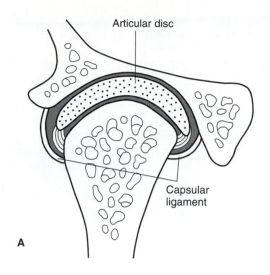

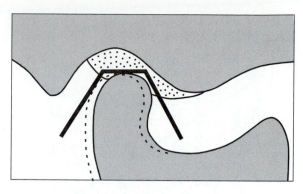

Figure 23–3. The most functionally stable position for the condyle and disc complex. This is commonly referred to as "centric relation."

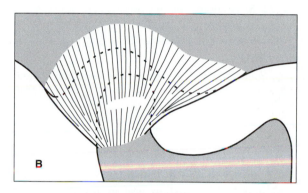

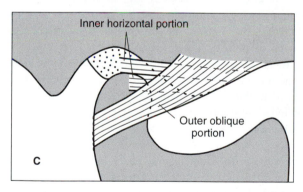

Figure 23–2. A. Temporomandibular joint (anterior view). The following are identified: AD, articular disc; CL, capsular ligament. **B.** Capsular ligament (lateral view). **C.** Temporomandibular ligament (lateral view). There are two distinct parts: the outer oblique portion (OOP), which limits rotational opening movement, and the inner horizontal portion (IHP), which limits posterior movement of the condyle and disc.

(Adapted from Okeson JP. Management of Temporomandibular Disorders and Occlusion. *3rd ed. St. Louis, Mo: Mosby Year Book; 1993.)*

! CLINICAL PEARL

If "centric relation" testing is negative for TMJ pain, it establishes a basis for a functional diagnosis and favorable prognosis. It confirms that the most functional, stable position for the TMJ is attainable without pain and is, therefore, suitable for rotational training of the mandible.

The retrodiscal tissue serves as one of the reasons why centric relation testing can be false positive if poorly performed. The retrodiscal tissue is highly vascularized and innervated and, thus, very pain sensitive. The retrodiscal tissue attaches to the posterior portion of the disc and acts as a guidewire along with the lateral pterygoid attaching anterior (Fig. 23–5). Poor technique in acquiring centric relation can compress the retrodiscal tissues and give a false indication of structural pathology

MUSCLE IMBALANCE

Muscle imbalance of the TMJ system has been linked to many postural and clinical presentations.[2, 5, 12, 15–25] They include, but are not limited to, forward head posture, malocclusion, respiratory obstruction, cervical segmental dysfunction, and sacroiliac dysfunction. The deduction and delineation for the etiology of muscle imbalance associated with TMD is beyond the scope of this chapter and, therefore, the imbalance itself is the focus here. Hyperactivity and tightness is primarily seen in the muscles of elevation and protrusion. These are the masseter, temporalis, medial pterygoid, and lateral pterygoid. These muscles will likely house trigger points and may also become shortened.

An astute student may have already concluded that the likely muscles of inhibition and weakness would be

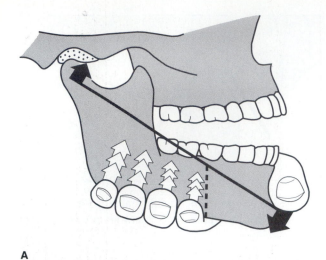

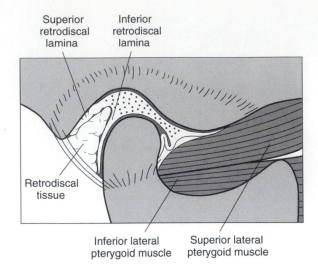

A

Figure 23–5. Anatomy of the retrodiscal tissue, showing the superior retrodiscal lamina (SRL), retrodiscal tissue (RT), inferior retrodiscal lamina (IRL), and superior lateral pterygoid (SLP).

(Adapted from Okeson JP. Management of Temporomandibular Disorders and Occlusion. 3rd ed. St. Louis, Mo: Mosby Year Book; 1993.)

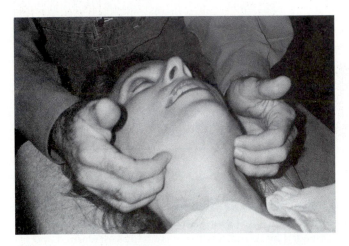

B

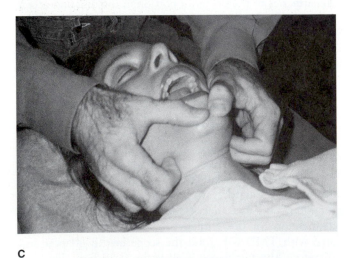

C

Figure 23–4. A–C. Centric relation provocation test.

those involved in mandibular depression. This is correct and most often involves the digastrics and mylohyoid. As Lewit describes,[26] these short and inhibited muscles also will house trigger points in their attempt at co-contraction to stabilize the TMJ in the presence of tightness or hyperactivity in the mandibular elevators.

In an effort to better understand the ramification of the aforementioned imbalance, let us now review the desired mandibular movement patterns. Many authors have concluded that opening of the mandible is the most revealing and diagnostic movement for mandibular dysfunction.[27, 28] Additionally, the rotational phase and initial phase of opening also appears to be the most crucial element with regard to stability and efficiency.[8, 13, 29, 30] During opening of the mandible, the condyle and disc complex should load in "centric relation" and allow for rotation of the mandible through approximately two thirds of mandibular opening. At the end of the rotational phase, the oblique TMJ ligament provides the anatomical stop and the condyle and disc complex must then move forward down the articular eminence of the temporal fossa to open further. This latter phase of opening is called translation (Fig. 23–6). Appropriate opening of the mandible would consist of near continuous retrusion of the chin through the full range of opening, including the phase that involves condylar translation. In a functional framework, proximal stability of the TMJ is provided by activation of the digastric muscle and its synergists for efficient distal mobility.

A mandibular movement pattern test (Fig. 23–7) has been suggested and is currently being validated.[31] The

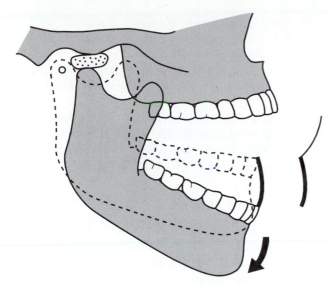

Figure 23–6. Translation phase of mandibular opening. The condyle and disc complex translates down the articular eminence of temporal fossa.

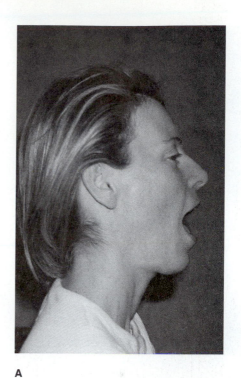

A

common movement failure associated with the previously stated imbalances is one of early protrusion. The early protrusive activity, largely due to lateral pterygoid hyperactivity and digastric weakness, often results in rotation occurring at the end of the movement rather than within the first two thirds of opening, as is desired. This causes rotation to occur in a very unstable condyle and disc position. There may be a loss of rotational movement altogether due to the vulnerability of the condyle and disc position. In my opinion, resolving abnormal mandibular opening is paramount to achieve permanent and satisfactory outcomes in treating TMD.

Lateral deviations and deflections when correlated with palpatory findings can offer important diagnostic information for treatment efficiency, although they are usually secondary to opening dysfunction. As is the case with other neuromuscular conditions, a comprehensive approach for TMD is essential. A treatment continuum that recognizes the entirety of the functional pathology is best suited for this type of imbalance.

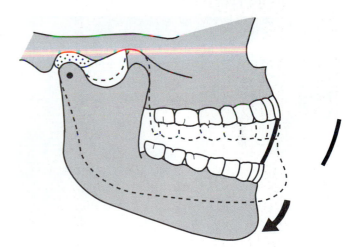

B

Figure 23–7. A and **B.** Mandibular movement test. The test can be performed with the patient seated or standing. The patient opens and closes the mandible. The test is marked pass/fail, with failure evidenced by protrusion on the initial phase of opening.

> **! CLINICAL PEARL**
>
> When dissected into functional chunks, TMD begins to resemble a low back syndrome, involving an inhibited and weak agonist (gluteus maximus/digastric) with overactive synergist (erector spinae/lateral pterygoid) and antagonist (psoas/masseter). Additional similarity exists in the historical pursuits of a structural etiology.

MANUAL TECHNIQUES FOR THE MUSCLES OF MASTICATION

MASSETER

The masseter is the agonist for mandible elevation and is a muscle that often requires treatment. It is frequently overactive and can become tight. It is sometimes associated

A

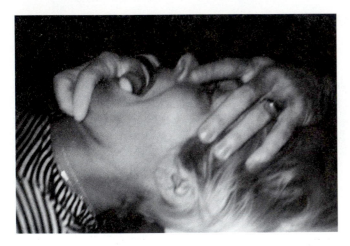

B

Figure 23–8. A and **B.** Postisometric relaxation of the masseter.

with prolonged usage of the mouth, as with a lengthy dental procedure, clenching, and bruxism. Clinical signs of dysfunction of the masseter include active trigger points and mandibular range of motion of 30 mm or less. This muscle responds very well to postisometric relaxation (PIR) (Fig. 23–8).

PIR for the masseter is performed as follows:

1. The practitioner is positioned at the head of the examination table facing caudally.
2. The practitioner places one hand on the patient's forehead as the stabilization hand and the other on the lower incisors of the mandible or on the chin.

3. Slack is then taken by opening the mandible through the proper *rotational* movement to the barrier of resistance.
4. From this point the patient applies pressure away from the barrier into the practitioner's thumb.

Unlike most PIR procedures, the contraction phase is performed with exhalation and the release phase is performed with inhalation. Having the patient simulate a yawn during the inhalation is very productive for the release.

LATERAL PTERYGOID

The lateral pterygoid is involved in most of the treatment plans for treating TMD. Its protrusive function is commonly dominant during mandibular opening, resulting in faulty movement. Often, chronic dysfunction is present and, therefore, connective tissue treatment in addition to relaxation techniques may be required (Figs. 23–9 and 23–10).

> ### ! CLINICAL PEARL
>
> During this procedure you may want to inform the patient that it will feel as if his or her jaw is going into the throat. As a practitioner, be aware of the small amount of retrusion that can actually take place. Be artful in your assessment of the barrier. Although the movement is small it can have a big effect for the patient, who often comments on tremendous relaxation and "looseness" felt in the jaws, and with minimal to no pain expense!

PIR for the lateral pterygoid is performed as follows:

1. The patient is supine and mouth slightly open.
2. The practitioner places a bilateral thumb contact on the distal portion of the mandible from above.

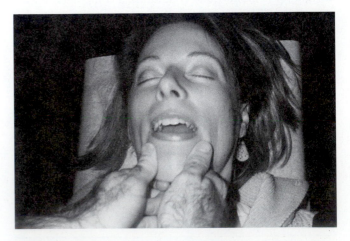

Figure 23–9. Lateral pterygoid postisometric relaxation.

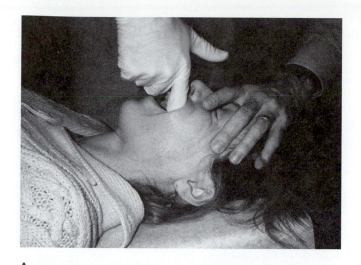
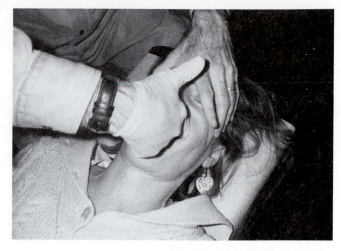

A

B

Figure 23–10. A and **B.** Lateral pterygoid myofascial release.

It is important that the line of drive or vector of force be directly posterior from the point of contact with the thumbs.

3. Slack is taken to the barrier of resistance.
4. The patient is then asked to gently press *directly* anterior and inhale; the patient then exhales and relaxes the jaw.
5. The practitioner, after waiting for relaxation, takes up the slack to meet a new barrier. This should only require three to four repetitions.

An alternative contact is to use the web of the hand on the mandible. This contact lacks the specificity of the thumbs for isolating the lateral pterygoid and therefore can sacrifice economy with the release.

Myofascial release for the lateral pterygoid is performed as follows:

1. The patient is supine. The practitioner sits at patient's head facing caudally.
2. The practitioner uses the opposite hand of the side receiving treatment to apply intra-oral contact. The same side hand contacts the frontal-temporal region. The intra-oral hand forms a gunlike configuration to allow deep penetration without impedance of the fingers into the face.
3. The arm is abducted to 90 degrees, with the elbow at 90 degrees, and the wrist adducts to approximately 40 degrees. The index finger enters along maxillary gingiva to the notchlike location inferior to the zygoma and is directed posteriorly towards the condyle.
4. No force is applied once initial contact is made. The weight of the arm with gravity allows for the release. Allowing the release to

occur is very important to avoid extreme discomfort.
5. The hand grasping the frontal-temporal region maneuvers the head in a rotation and decompressive movement, helping to relieve the tension.

Although this is a very sensitive area, a light contact and patience in waiting for the release can decrease the pain severity.

PROPRIOSENSORY STIMULATION AND MANDIBULAR STABILIZATION

TEMPOROMANDIBULAR JOINT MOBILIZATION

Recent quantitative studies have suggested a constantly moving, instantaneous axis of jaw rotation during opening that is different in every person.[32] Because of this variability, assessment of joint function should be focused primarily on symmetry of movement in relation to the opposing joint. Therefore, manual palpation would reveal the joint most requiring mobilization as the joint with the final translational position that is more posterior.

The purpose of mobilization is to reduce tension in the joint in an effort to normalize function. Thus, it may be applicable to mobilize both joints in the presence of asymmetrical motion. The success of the described mobilization in this chapter can limit the need for high-velocity thrusts to the TMJ. The benefit of thrusts in this region is easily equaled by combinations of softer muscle and joint techniques and, thus, the risk of sustaining hypermobility or injury can be avoided. Even in the presence of internal

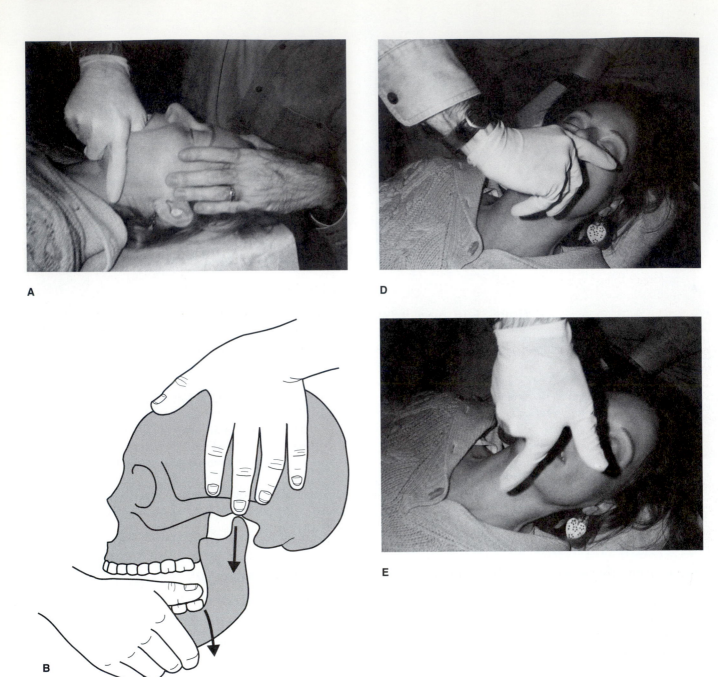

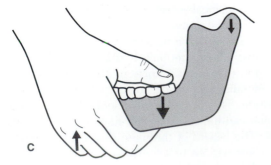

Figure 23–11. Temporomandibular joint mobilization: **(A)** caudal distraction, **(B)** caudal distraction, **(C)** caudal distraction, **(D)** medial distraction, **(E)** lateral distraction.

derangement, the described gentle procedure is extremely effective (Fig. 23–11).

TMJ mobilization is performed as follows:

1. Once the involved side is determined, the practitioner sits at the head facing caudally, on the side opposite the TMJ receiving treatment.
2. Palmar thumb contact is placed on lower molars with the inferior hand, while the superior hand palpates the joint (TMJ) anterior to tragus.
3. Slack is lightly removed and the barrier is engaged. The engagement of the barrier is first directed inferiorly, followed by medial and lateral directions. Asking the patient to accentuate respiration can assist the release. The barrier should not require longer than 25 seconds for release.
4. Medial and lateral mobilization for the condyle and disc complex is accomplished by holding a mandibular contact and performing supination and pronation of the hand. This movement is very similar to the screwing on and off of a lid.

HYOID MOBILIZATION

Owing to its anatomical relationship to the digastrics, the hyoid is often subject to abnormal tension and often requires treatment. Specific clinical indications for this can include difficulty swallowing, laryngitis, and hoarseness. The patient may also present with pain in the lower incisors, tongue, or mastoid.

Hyoid mobilization (Fig. 23–12) is performed as follows:

1. The practitioner sits at the head of the table facing caudally as the patient lies supine. Assessment is first conducted to determine the side of restriction.
2. An index or middle finger contact is placed bilaterally on lateral aspects of the hyoid. Side-

gliding motion is then applied to assess for restriction.

3. Once restriction is established, a light thumb contact is placed on the side of restriction; with the patient opening slightly (being sure to obtain pure condylar rotation), the patient gently tries to open the mouth, while the practitioner applies resistance.
4. The patient holds for 7 to 10 seconds and then relaxes the mandible. After waiting for relaxation, the hyoid will move away from the thumb.
5. The practitioner then takes up the slack to meet a new barrier. This procedure is repeated two to three times.

DIGASTRIC FACILITATION

Comparable to the middle and lower trapezius and the deep neck flexors, the digastric muscle is the key link to functional restoration in the management of TMD. It is active in co-contraction in an effort to stabilize the mandible. When it becomes inhibited, it can harbor abnormal tension and resultant trigger points. This sometimes warrants connective tissue techniques in addition to relaxation and retraining (Fig. 23–13).

Digastric proprioceptive neuromuscular facilitation is performed as follows:

1. Passive prepositioning is first used to make the patient aware of correct rotation (down and back) of the mandible during opening.
2. The patient is then taken through passive motion and asked to perform active motion with assistance.
3. Next, passive prepositioning is performed with isometric resistance to achieve rhythmic initiation.
4. Active motion without assistance is then observed for quality of movement.

For home training the patient is taught to palpate the submandibular muscles to assure proper activation and to develop kinesthetic awareness (see Fig. 23–13A and B). Rhythmic stabilization or a combination of isotonics maybe helpful in facilitating good or full contraction of the digastric (see Fig. 23–13C).

Once the patient is capable of performing mandibular depression properly, he or she is instructed to perform the rotational opening exercise to approximately one half to two thirds of total opening for 8 to 10 repetitions, 8 to 10 times a day. The patient may, at first, continue to facilitate the digastric with his or her fingers and eventually perform the movement unassisted through full mandibular opening. This final stage would be considered loaded mandibular depression. Here, the appropriate activation of the mandibular depressors loads the condyle and disc in centric relation and through preferred opening encourages normalization of function (see Fig. 23–13D).

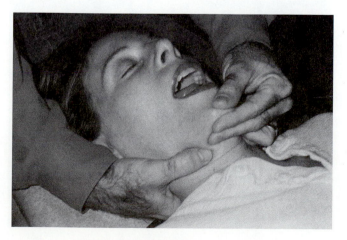

Figure 23–12. Hyoid mobilization.

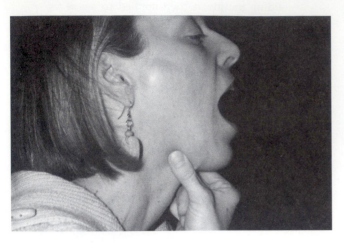

A

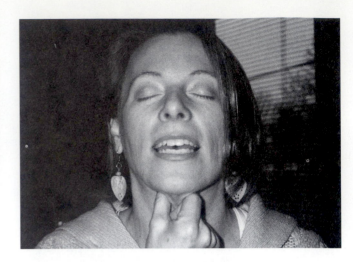

B

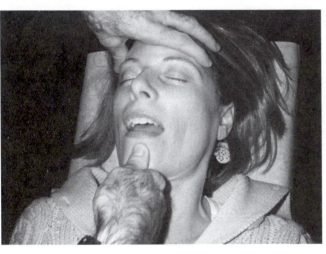

C

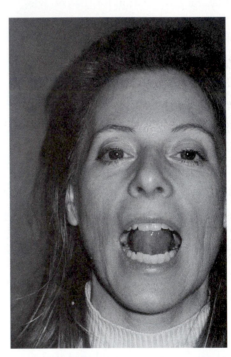

D

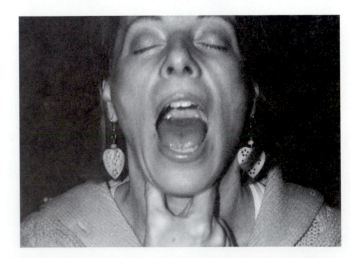

E

Figure 23–13. Digastric facilitation. **A** and **B.** Palpation of digastric activation. **C.** Rhythmic stabilization for the mandibular depressors. **D.** Loaded mandibular depression. **E.** Mandibular rotational exercises.

! CLINICAL PEARL

Teaching preferred mandibular depression is *essential* and requires skillful patience on the part of the practitioner. Utilization of auditory, visual, and kinesthetic cues is often necessary. Reassurance should be provided regarding nonpainful joint noise or muscle soreness associated with the retraining and pursuant normalization.

Patients who are unable to perform active motion and maintain quality of movement should not attempt it on their own. A peel-back exercise is to perform controlled mandibular rotations. This involves placing the tongue on the hard palate at a location below the nasal orifices. The patient is then instructed to gently open the mandible while maintaining tongue contact with the upper palate. This should only allow rotational opening to approximately one half to two thirds of total opening. This exercise can be performed for 8 to 10 repetitions, 8 to 10 times per day (see Fig. 23–13E).

ACTIVITY MODIFICATIONS

In the presentation of TMD there are a great number of parafunctional activities that can sabotage a well-meaning treatment plan. These include habits of lip biting, fingernail biting, pencil biting, teeth clenching, teeth tapping, and tongue thrusting. In a study by Conti et al,[33] 100 percent of the study population, who were considered to have severe TMD signs and symptoms, had three or more parafunctional habits. Ergonomic considerations include phone carriage, computer station, weight lifting, and other traditional preventative measures for maintenance of neutral or preferred spinal and postural position during activities. Fricton describes cognitive training as being very helpful for curbing these behaviors.[3] In addition to the aforementioned activities, rest position and swallowing should be understood and recognized for their importance. Optimum rest position for the jaw is reported as being a position where the tongue is in the roof of the mouth, the lips are together and the teeth apart.[1, 13, 34]

Education of this position, leading to kinesthetic awareness followed by habituation, can resolve many associated parafunctional activities. Swallowing function can also be a facilitator for normal function. During preferred swallowing the hyoid elevates. The efficiency of this action is provided by the tongue contacting the roof of the mouth and stabilization of the mandible through occlusion. Therefore, conscious effort to contact the roof of the mouth during swallowing activity by use of a mint or other object may be of benefit.

ILLNESS BEHAVIOR

TMD would make any list of top-ten conditions associated with abnormal illness behavior. In one study, total medical claim payments for patients with TMD were shown to be double those of patients without TMD.[35] In the same study, the utilization of professionals and institutional services was also twice as high for TMD populations. The chronicity and systemic associations are fascinating. Morrow and others[36] revealed the following: asymptomatic volunteers with anterior disc displacement (ADD) had twice the pain in other joints; symptomatic volunteers with or without ADD had four times the pain in other joints; and symptomatic volunteers with ADD had twice the likelihood of family affected by TMD. These findings suggest that with or without structural abnormality, the patient with TMD often has chronic neuromusculoskeletal pain presentations and illness behavior that may cross generations. Fricton and Olsen[37] showed that the only predictors for treatment outcome in a given TMD population were low self-esteem, low level of sleep, low energy, and having seen a large number of practitioners. Identification of risks of chronicity and appropriate patient activation must be utilized in this patient population.

! CLINICAL PEARL

In my lectures, I often describe my patients as wearing "TMJ" on their forehead. This label, with which they are often very attached, is a prescription for treatment failure and a life of chronic pain and dysfunction for the patient. It must be removed. Once structural pathology is ruled out, patients should be educated on "hurt versus harm." They should be moved toward pain confrontation and away from dramatization of joint noises and occlusal complications.

CONCLUSION

The treatment continuum for mandibular dysfunction or a given TMD often must be multifaceted (Table 23–1). Stabilization may require the assistance of dental medicine, most frequently in the form of splint therapy. It is encouraged that splints be applied after a conservative and active approach has been initiated to reduce the likelihood of illness behavior associated with passive correction. *It should be emphasized to the patient that the splint is merely to facilitate the process of returning normal function and does not replace nor can it accomplish the effect of his or her exercises and retraining.*[38–43]

The cervical spine undoubtedly plays a significant role in TMD and orofacial pain. Studies demonstrate high prevalence of cervical spine disorders associated with

Table 23–1: Treatment Approach for Altered Mandibular Function

Manipulate/mobilize the cervicocranial junction

Moblize and, if necessary, stabilize the temporomandibular joint

Relax and, if necessary, stretch the masseter, lateral pterygoid, suprahyoids, and suboccipitals

Train motor control of the mandibular depressors

Correct parafunctional habits, sitting, and standing posture

TMD.[1, 2, 44–46] In one study, cervical spine disorders were actually found with TMD (70 percent) more often than TMD was found alone (30 percent).[47]

! CLINICAL PEARL

"The jaw and cervical spine are of equal importance."
—K. Lewit, MD

Clearly, TMD and orofacial dysfunction should be a consideration when facing conditions and symptoms of the head, neck, and upper thorax. This includes findings of forward head posture, abnormal head or neck flexion, abnormal scapulohumeral rhythm, and their associated findings. Lewit[48] has said that the sternocleidomastoid is a common indicator for cervicocranial conditions. Therefore, the sternocleidomastoid should be closely monitored when there is suspicion of TMD and during the treatment process. Lewit

goes on to say that the sternocleidomastoid "is usually reactionary and is rarely in need of treatment. . . . it will resolve when the key link is satisfied."[48] Although this is often true, sternocleidomastoid relaxation can make the transition of correction more tolerable and pleasant during the pursuit of the key link in the chain of dysfunction that is usually present in these patients.

Early and late presentation following motor vehicle trauma is frequently theorized to include TMD.[49–51] Current evidence suggests motor vehicle trauma–induced TMD can increase the severity of symptoms and signs, increase morbidity, and produce poorer outcomes when compared to nontraumatic TMD.[52, 53] These studies were also clear of litigation bias. The approach recommended in this chapter is equally effective in treating trauma-induced TMD and nontrauma-induced TMD.

A holistic and educated view of TMD reveals the functional and neuromuscular complexity of this region. Okeson[2] verifies this in his guidelines for orofacial pain by stating, "although TMD was viewed as one syndrome, current research supports the view that TMD is a cluster of related disorders in the masticatory system that have many common symptoms." He goes on to say, "The clinical phenomenon of sensory, motor, and autonomic effects resulting from deep pain input are important because referral of pain from the cervical region is common and easily mistaken for masticatory pain."[2] By increasing the knowledge and skill of neuromuscular practitioners in the diagnosis and treatment of TMD and orofacial disorders, it is hoped the clinical pathways will be formalized to match the needs of the patient. Primary care of TMD belongs in the hands of a neuromusculoskeletal specialist.

REFERENCES

1. Fricton JR, Kroening RJ, Hathaway KM. *TMJ and Craniofacial Pain: Diagnosis and Management.* St. Louis—Tokyo: Ishiyaku EuroAmerica; 1988.

2. Okeson J. *Orofacial Pain: Guidelines for Assessment, Diagnosis, and Management.* Chicago: Quintessence Books; 1996.

3. Fricton J. Recent advances in orofacial pain and temporomandibular disorders. *J Back Musculoskel Rehabil* 1996;6:99–113.

4. Quinn JH. Mandibular exercises to control bruxism and deviation problems. *J Craniomandib Pract* 1995;13:30–35.

5. Skaggs CD. Multidisciplinary management of the cervicocranial/temporomandibular disorder. *Functional Orthodontist* 1993;10.

6. McNamara JA, Seligman DA, Okeson JP. Occlusion, orthodontic treatment, and temporomandibular disorders: A review. *J Orofacial Pain* 1995;9:73–90.

7. Stegenga B, de Bont LGM, Dijkstra PU, et al. Short-term outcome of arthroscopic surgery of the temporomandibular joint osteoarthrosis and internal derangement: A randomized controlled clinical trial. *Br J Oral Maxillofac Surg* 1993;31:3–14.

8. Mongini F. A modified extraoral technique of mandibular manipulation in disk displacement without reduction. *J Craniomandib Pract* 1996;13:22–26.

9. Sato S, Gato S, Kawamura H, Motegi K. The natural course of nonreducing disc displacement of the TMJ: Relationship of clinical findings at initial visit to outcome after 12 months without treatment. *J Orofacial Pain* 1997;11:315–320.

10. Naidoo LCD. Lateral pterygoid muscle and its relationship to the meniscus of the temporomandibular joint. *Oral Surg Oral Med Oral Pathol Oral Radio Endod* 1996;82:4–9.

11. Meyerberg M, Kubik S, Palla S. Relationships of the muscles of mastication to the articular disc of the temporomandibular joint. *Helv Odont Acta* 1986;30:1–20.

12. Janda V. Some aspects of extracranial causes of facial pain. *J Prosthet Dent* 1986;56:484–487.

13. Okeson JP. *Management of Temporomandibular Disorders and Occlusion*. 3rd ed. St. Louis, Mo: Mosby Year Book; 1993.

14. Dawson P. New definition for relating occlusion to varying conditions of the temporomandibular joint. *J Prosthet Dent* 1995;74:619–627.

15. Dijkstra PU, Lambert GM, et al. The relationship between temporomandibular joint mobility and peripheral joint mobility reconsidered. *J Craniomandib Pract* 1994;12:149–155.

16. Braun BL. Postural difference between asymptomatic men and women and craniofacial pain patients. *Arch Phys Med Rehabil* 1991;72:650–653.

17. Lynn JM, Mazzocco MW. Neuromuscular differentiation of craniocervical pain: Is it headache or TMD? *AJPM* 1993;3:181–190.

18. Wilson L, Dworkin SF, et al. Somatization and pain dispersion in chronic temporomandibular disorder pain. *Pain* 1994;57:55–61.

19. Gonzalez H, Manns A. Forward head posture: Its structural and functional influence on the stomatognathic system, a conceptual study. *J Craniomandib Pract* 1996;14:71–80.

20. Nobili A. The relationship between posture and occlusion: A clinical experimental investigation. *Cranio* 1996;14:274.

21. Pim Valk JW, Zonnenberg, JJ, et al. The biomechanical effects of a sagittal split ramus osteotomy on the relationship of the mandible, the hyoid bone, and the cervical spine. *Am J Orthod Dentofac Orthop* 1992;102(2):99–108.

22. Boyd CH. The effect of head position on electromyographic evaluations of representative mandibular positioning muscle groups. *J Craniomand Pract* 1987;5:50–53.

23. Hirayama K. The relationship between body posture and craniofacial morphology. *J Clin Pediatr Dent* 1993;17:133–137.

24. Schellhas KP, Pollei SR, Wilkes CH. Pediatric internal derangements of the temporomandibular joint: Effect on facial development. *Am J Orthod Dentofac Orthop* 1993;104:51–59.

25. Gregory TM. Temporomandibular disorder associated with sacroiliac sprain. *JMPT* 1993;16:256–266.

26. Lewit K. *Manipulative Therapy in Rehabilitation of the Locomotor System*. 2nd ed. London: Butterworth-Heinemann; 1991.

27. Kuwahara T, Bessette RW, Maruyama T. Chewing pattern analysis in TMD patients with and without internal derangement. *J Craniomandib Pract* 1995;13:2.

28. Rocobado M. Arthrokinematics of the temporomandibular joint. In: Gelb H, ed. *Clinical Management of Head, Neck and TMJ Pain and Dysfunction*. Philadelphia, Pa: WB Saunders; 1985.

29. Skaggs CD. Temporomandibular dysfunction. *J Bodywork Movement Ther* 1997;1(4):208–212.

30. Dawson PE. A classification system for occlusions that relates maximal intercuspation to the position and condition of the temporomandibular joints. *J Prosthetic Dent* 1996;75:60–66.

31. Skaggs CD. Validation of a functional test for mandibular opening. [Abstract]. 1999; in press.

32. Lindauer SJ, Sabol G, Isaacson RJ, Davidovitch M. Condylar movement and mandibular rotation during jaw opening. *Am J Orthod Dentofac Orthop* 1995;107:573–577.

33. Conti PC, Ferreira PM, Pegoraro LF, Conti JV, Salvador MCG. A cross-sectional study of prevalence and etiology of signs and symptoms of temporomandibular disorders in high school and university students. *J Orofacial Pain* 1996;10:254–262.

34. Carlson CR, Sherman JJ, Studts JL, Bertrand PM. The effects of tongue position on mandibular muscle activity. *J Orofacial Pain* 1997;11:291–297.

35. Shimshak D, Kent RL, DeFuria M. Medical claims profiles of subjects with temporomandibular joint disorders. *J Craniomandib Pract* 1997;15:150–159.

36. Morrow D. Relationship of other joint problems and anterior disc position in symptomatic TMD patients and in asymptomatic volunteers. *J Orofacial Pain* 1996;10:15–20.

37. Fricton JR, Olsen T. Predictors of outcome for treatment of temporomandibular disorders. *J Orofacial Pain* 1996;10:54–65.

38. Dao TTT, Lavigne FJ, Charbonneau A, Peine JS, Lund JP. The efficacy of oral splints in the treatment of myofascial pain of the jaw muscles: A controlled clinical trial. *Pain* 1994;56:85–94.

39. Kirk WS. Magnetic resonance imaging and tomographic evaluation of occlusal appliance treatment for advanced internal derangement of the temporomandibular joint. *J Oral Maxillofacial Surg* 1991;49:9–12.

40. Chung SC, Kim SH. The effect of the stabilization splint on the TMJ closed lock. *J Craniomandib Pract* 1993;11:95–107.

41. Helkimo E, Westling I. History, clinical findings, and outcome of treatment of patients with anterior disc displacement. *J Craniomandib Pract* 1987;5:270–276.

42. Moya H, Rocobado M, Miralles R, Zuniga C, Carvajal R, Santander H. Influence of stabilization occlusal splint on craniocervical relationships. Part I: Cephalometric analysis. *J Craniomandib Pract* 1994;12:47–52.

43. Just J, Ayer W, Greene C, et al. Treating TM disorders: A survey on diagnosis, etiology and management. *J Am Dent Assoc* 1991;122:56–60.

44. Steenks MH, Wifer A, Bosman F. Orthopedic diagnostic tests for temporomandibular and cervical spine disorders. *J Back Musculoskel Rehabil* 1996;6:135–155.

45. Rocobado M. Radiographic study of the craniocervical relation in patients under orthodontic treatment and the incidence with related symptoms. *J Craniomandib Pract* 1987;5:36–48.

46. Wijer A, Leeuw R, Steenks MH, Bosman F. Temporomandibular and cervical spine disorders. *J Back Musculoskel Rehabil* 1996;21:1638–1646.

47. Pandamsee M. Incidence of cervical disorders in a TMD population. *J Dent Res IADR* 1994; Abstract No. 680.

48. Lewit K. *Manual Medicine Teachers Course*. Tuscany, Italy; 1998,

49. Duckro PN, Chibnall JT, Greenberg MS, Schultz KT. Prevalence of temporomandibular dysfunction in chronic post-traumatic headache patients. 1997;8:228–233.

50. Garcia R, Arrington JA. The relationship between cervical whiplash and temporomandibular joint injuries: An MRI study. *J Craniomandib Pract* 1996;14:233–240.

51. Eversole JR, Machado J. Temporomandibular joint internal derangement and associated neuromuscular disorders. *J Am Dent Assoc* 1985;110:69–79.

52. Brooke RI, Lapointe HJ. Temporomandibular joint disorders following whiplash. *Spine* 1993;7:443–455.

53. Kolbinson DA, Epstein JB, et al. A comparison of TMD patients with or without prior motor vehicle accident involvement: Initial signs, symptoms, and diagnostic characteristics. *J Orofacial Pain* 1997;11:206–214.

CHAPTER 24

Operative Treatment of Cervical Spine Disorders

Mark Palumbo & Michael Barnum

"Criticism is something we can avoid easily —by saying nothing, doing nothing, and being nothing."

—Aristotle

INTRODUCTION

The vast majority of patients with cervical spine disorders can be managed successfully with nonoperative measures. However, there is a small but identifiable patient subgroup for which surgical management is warranted. To provide these select patients with an optimal clinical outcome, a multidisciplinary approach incorporating conservative care and consultation with a spinal surgeon is required.

In this chapter, operative indications and surgical techniques are be presented for common disorders affecting the cervicocranium (occiput through C2) and the lower cervical spine (C3 through C7). The primary focus is on the pathological conditions of degenerative disc disease and rheumatoid spondylitis. Neoplasm, infection, and major traumatic injuries are much less common and are beyond the scope of this discussion.

INDICATIONS FOR CERVICAL SPINE SURGERY

CERVICOCRANIUM

Degenerative Osteoarthrosis

Degenerative disease involving the atlanto-axial complex can cause occipitocervical pain. With advanced disease, the inflammatory process can progress to involve the ligamentous structures resulting in C1–C2 instability and potential spinal cord compression. Arthrosis of the lateral mass articulations can be identified by an open-mouth radiograph of the upper cervical spine and further delineated by plain tomography or computed tomography (CT) scan

(Fig. 24–1); flexion-extension views are useful to assess for subluxation.

Nonoperative treatment of this condition is adequate for the majority of patients with isolated occipitocervical pain. If conservative measures fail and pain becomes debilitating, consideration can be given to posterior atlanto-axial arthrodesis. Urgent posterior fusion is indicated for the patient with pain, instability, and myelopathy as a result of spinal cord compression. To prevent sensorimotor compromise in the neurologically intact patient with significant pain and associated instability, posterior fusion should be considered when radiological studies indicate that the space available for the cord within the spinal canal is less than 14 mm.[1]

through C6 vertebrae, our preference is to supplement cancellous bone grafting with posterior plate fixation. This fixation utilizes screws inserted into the lateral articular masses to achieve immediate stability and enhance fusion[27, 28] (Fig. 24–14). In the rheumatoid patient with suboptimal bone quality and for instability involving the cervicothoracic junction (C6–T1), interspinous wiring is the usual mode of fixation. We use a triple wire technique to secure the spinous processes of the unstable motion segment to each other and to two corticocancellous bone grafts[29] (Fig. 24–15).

CONCLUSION

Most disorders of the adult cervical spine can be managed effectively with nonoperative care. For those patients who fail to recover despite adequate conservative management, knowledge of the general indications and available methods for surgical treatment is important. By establishing a working relationship with an experienced cervical spine surgeon, the conservative practitioner can optimize the chance of a successful clinical outcome in this select group of patients.

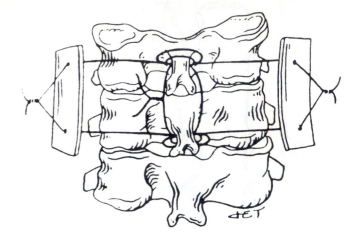

Figure 24–15. Posterior wire fixation. Three wires are used to affix the spinous processes of the unstable motion segment to each other and to two corticocancellous iliac bone grafts.

(Reprinted with permission from Abdu WA, Bohlman HH. Techniques of subaxial posterior cervical spine fusions. Orthopedics 1992;15:292.)

REFERENCES

1. Ghanayem AJ, Leventhal M, Bohlman HH. Osteoarthrosis of the atlanto-axial joints. Long-term follow-up after treatment with arthrodesis. *J Bone Joint Surg* 1996;78A:1300–1307.
2. Boden SD: Rheumatoid arthritis of the cervical spine: Surgical decision making based on predictors of paralysis and recovery. *Spine* 1994;19:2275–2280.
3. Boden SD, Dodge LD, Bohlman HH, Rechtine GR. Rheumatoid arthritis of the cervical spine: A long-term analysis with predictors of paralysis and recovery. *J Bone Joint Surg* 1993;75A:1282–1297.
4. Heller JG. The syndromes of degenerative cervical disease. *Orthop Clin North Am* 1992;23:381–394.
5. Dillin W, Booth R, Cuckler J, Balderston R, Simeone F, Rothman R. Cervical radiculopathy: A review. *Spine* 1986;11:989–991.
6. Gore DR, Sepic SB, Gardner GM, Murray MP. Neck pain: A long-term followup of 205 patients. *Spine* 1987;1–5.
7. Rothman RH, Rashbaum RF. Pathogenesis of signs and symptoms of cervical disc degeneration. *AAOS Instructional Course Lectures* 1978;27:203–215.
8. Blumberg KD, Simeone FA. Indications for surgery in cervical myelopathy: Anterior versus posterior approach. In: Rothman RH, Simeone FA, eds. *The Spine*. 3rd ed. Philadelphia, Pa: WB Saunders; 1992:613–625.
9. Montgomery DM, Brower RS. Cervical spondylotic myelopathy: Clinical syndrome and natural history. *Orthop Clin North Am* 1992;23:487–493.
10. Brooks AL, Jenkins EB. Atlanto-axial arthrodesis by the wedge compression method. *J Bone Joint Surg* 1978;60A:279.
11. Clark CR. Trauma and rheumatoid arthritis of the upper cervical spine. In: Sherk HH, ed. *The Cervical Spine: An Atlas of Surgical Procedures*. Philadelphia, Pa: JB Lippincott; 1994:127–144.
12. Grob D, Jeanneret B, Aeb M, Markwalder T. Atlantoaxial fusion with transarticular screw fixation. *J Bone Joint Surg* 1991;73B:972–976.
13. Wertheim SB, Bohlman HH. Occipitocervical fusion. *J Bone Joint Surg* 1987;69A:833.
14. Bohlman HH, Emery SE, Goodfellow DB, Jones PK. Robinson anterior cervical discectomy and arthrodesis for cervical radiculopathy: Long-term followup of 122 patients. *J Bone Joint Surg* 1993;75A:1298–1307.

15. Clements DH, O'Leary PF. Anterior cervical discectomy and fusion. *Spine* 1990;15:1023.

16. Gore DR, Sepic SB. Anterior cervical fusion for degenerated or protruded discs: A review of 146 patients. *Spine* 1984;9:667.

17. Smith GW, Robinson RA. Treatment of certain cervical spine disorders by the anterior removal of the intervertebral disc and interbody fusion. *J Bone Joint Surg* 1958;40A:607.

18. Henderson CM, Hennessy RG, Shuey HM, Shackleford KG. Posterior-lateral foraminotomy as an exclusive operative technique for cervical radiculopathy: A review of 846 consecutive operated cases. *Neurosurgery* 1983;13:504–511.

19. Murphey F, Simmons JC, Brunson B. Surgical treatment of laterally ruptured cervical disc: Review of 648 cases, 1939–1972. *J Neurosurg* 1973;38:679.

20. Scoville WB, Dohrmann GJ, Corkill G. Late results of cervical disc surgery. *J Neurosurg* 1976;45:203.

21. Silveri CP, Simpson JM, Simeone FA, Balderston RA. Cervical disc disease and the keyhole foraminotomy: Proven efficacy at extended long-term followup. *Orthopaedics* 1997;20:687–692.

22. Williams RW. Microcervical foraminotomy: A surgical alternative for intractable radicular pain. *Spine* 1983;8:708.

23. Bernard TN, Whitecloud TS. Cervical spondylotic myelopathy and myeloradiculopathy: Anterior decompression and stabilization with autogenous fibula strut graft. *Clin Orthop* 1987;221:149–160.

24. Bohlman HH. Cervical spondylosis and myelopathy. *AAOS Instructional Course Lectures* 1995;44:81–97.

25. Boni M, Cherubino P, Denaro V, et al. Multiple subtotal somatectomy: Technique and evaluation of a series of 39 cases. *Spine* 1984;9:358–362.

26. Hanai K, Fujiyoshi F, Kamei K. Subtotal vertebrectomy and spinal fusion for cervical spondylotic myelopathy. *Spine* 1986;11:310.

27. Anderson PA, Henley MB, Grady MS, et al. Posterior cervical arthrodesis with AO reconstruction plates and bone graft. *Spine* 1991;16(suppl):72.

28. Roy-Camille R, Saillant G, Mazel C. Internal fixation of the unstable cervical spine by a posterior arthrodesis with plates and screws. In: Sherk HH, ed. *The Cervical Spine*. 2nd ed. Philadelphia, Pa: JB Lippincott: 1989:390.

29. Bohlman HH. The triple-wire technique for posterior stabilization of fractures and dislocations of the lower cervical spine. In: Sherk HH, ed. *The Cervical Spine: An Atlas of Surgical Procedures*. Philadelphia, Pa: JB Lippincott; 1994:145–150.

PART

5

Rehabilitation

CHAPTER 25

Sensorimotor Training and Cervical Stabilization

Donald R. Murphy

"Any procedure, circumstance or induction that normalizes sensorial input and regulates motor response is good therapy."

—Joseph Janse, DC

INTRODUCTION

The purpose of sensorimotor training and cervical stabilization is threefold. The first purpose is to improve the efficiency and effectiveness of the common movement patterns in which the cervical spine and upper extremities engage on a regular basis. This includes the stabilizing system of the spine; that is, the neurological programs that govern the automatic stabilization responses that occur as a result of common perturbations to the cervical spine. The second purpose is to improve the efficiency of the reflexes that govern eye-head-neck-upper extremity coordination. Finally, and least significantly, is the improvement of strength in certain key muscles involved in the stability of the cervical spine.

Teaching a patient how to consciously carry out movement patterns correctly often leads to the patient performing them well in the office but not utilizing the proper pattern in his or her everyday movements. It thus becomes important to bypass cortical involvement by creating a new automatic motor program by which the patient carries out the movement correctly without having to "think" about it.[1]

As the stabilizing system of the cervical spine actually operates as a part of an integrated system that encompasses the entire body, it is important to begin by isolating certain aspects of the system and later to bring those parts into the whole in a training format that allows for integration of all the component parts of the universal stabilizing system of the body. That is to say that the mechanisms by which the cervical spine maintains its stability do not operate in isolation from the rest of the body but, rather, are simply localized manifestations of the whole-body stabilization system that is coordinated by the central nervous system (CNS). So when training the system, it is best to isolate certain parts of the system whose function may be impaired, followed by integrating these parts with the whole.

In the rehabilitation of patients with cervical spine syndromes, the primary focus must be on maximizing neurological integration and control. This starts with correcting peripheral joint, muscle, or skin and fascial dysfunction to normalize mechanoreceptive input to the CNS. Following this, techniques are applied that are designed to maximize the efficiency with which the CNS coordinates the body's movement patterns, including stability responses. Finally, training for endurance is essential.

This exercise approach can be carried out with a minimum of equipment. In fact, this is a big part of the effectiveness of the method, as it is very conducive to patients performing the exercises on their own at home, thus contributing to one of the most important aspects of good patient care—empowerment. It allows us to place the patient in charge of his or her own recovery and gradually transition greater responsibility to him or her as the patient is guided toward independence.

The minimal equipment necessary, along with the ease of home use of the exercises, also adds to the cost-effectiveness of the approach, an all-important factor that adds dramatically to the overall benefit of utilizing this method. In the modern era of health care, providing cost-effective care that is also effective clinically allows the clinician to offer the "best of both worlds."

SENSORIMOTOR TRAINING

Sensorimotor training is a method of stimulating the CNS through bombardment of afferent impulses. The CNS depends on afferent input from the periphery to appropriately order movement patterns that are harmonious and coordinated and that provide stability to the locomotor system.

As has been demonstrated in previous chapters, the locomotor system functions as an integrated unit. No activity of any particular muscle or muscle group occurs in isolation from the rest of the system. Because of this, it is important that in the rehabilitative process, the entire system be taken into consideration. In addition to this, it is essential to consider those locomotor system processes that are most important in promoting the stability and coordination of the system and to maximize their function to the fullest extent possible.

With sensorimotor training, an attempt is made to facilitate the automatic, reflexogenic reactions that the locomotor system creates in response to unexpected stimuli from the periphery. The purpose of this method is to change the program for a certain movement pattern from abnormal to normal. Thus, the indication for the need for sensorimotor training is detection of a faulty movement pattern in which it has been determined that the CNS program for that pattern has been pathophysiologically altered. The specific signs that may indicate the need for sensorimotor training in the cervical spine patient are:

- Faulty hip extension
- Faulty cervical flexion
- Faulty cervical stability
- Positive stepping test
- Faulty postural foot reaction (Vele's test)
- Positive Revel's test

These signs should not be seen as outright indications for sensorimotor training, as they often normalize with correction of joint, muscle, or skin and fascial dysfunction. But their presence increases the likelihood that this method will need to be instituted at some point in the rehabilitation process. This type of decision making is essential to the efficiency of rehabilitation and will be discussed further in Chapter 28.

THE SMALL FOOT

The foot is a very important, and often underappreciated, source of somatosensory input in to the CNS and appropriate afferentation from the foot is necessary for the proper elicitation of postural reflexes. The primary sources of this input are the cutaneous receptors in the skin on the bottom of the foot and the spindles in the intrinsic muscles. So, before any other sensorimotor exercise is given to the patient, it is essential that foot function be normalized. Joint play is first assessed and manipulation applied to any joint or joints of the foot that are found to be dysfunctional. Next, the patient is taught to, as Janda describes it, "make a small foot" (Fig. 25–1). This involves teaching the patient to tense the intrinsic muscles, particularly the quadratus plantae, adductor hallucis, interossei, and lumbricals of the foot by attempting to make the foot shorter and more narrow. It is important that the long muscles of the foot, the flexor digitorum and hallucis muscles, do not substitute. When this occurs, the foot takes a "hammer toe" posture (Fig. 25–2). Once the ability to make a small foot is established, the patient is instructed to maintain it during all exercises that he or she will be performing.

RESTING TONGUE POSITION

As with the small foot, it is important that the patient be taught to establish the normal resting tongue position against the hard palate. It is also essential to check the

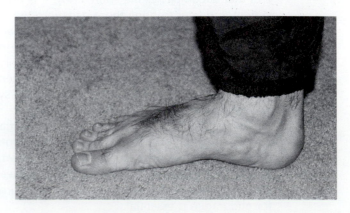

Figure 25–1. The small foot.

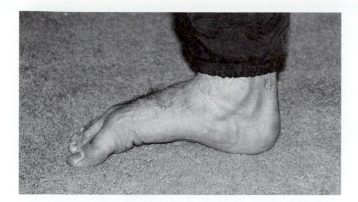

Figure 25–2. Improper technique in making a small foot.

swallowing pattern and to correct any dysfunction that is found (see Chaps. 14 and 27). The patient is then shown how to establish normal resting position by making a "cluck" sound. The position that the tongue takes against the hard palate just behind the upper incisors prior to making this sound is the normal resting position. The resting tongue position must be established before sensorimotor training can begin, and the position must be maintained during all exercises.

ROCKER BOARD

A beginning level of stimulation and challenge to the CNS can be introduced through the use of the rocker board (Fig. 25–3). The patient first stands on the board in a position such that the plane of instability of the board is front to back (Fig. 25–4). He or she is instructed to hold the small foot position. The patient is then placed in a balanced posture by instructing him or her to visualize a helium balloon attached to the posterosuperior portion of the head. This essentially causes the head to move superiorward and causes the neck to become longer.[2] The patient is then instructed to visualize his or her shoulders expanding outward and becoming wider. Finally, the patient is instructed to visualize his or her legs expanding away from the body toward the floor. This is a basic Alexandrian pos-

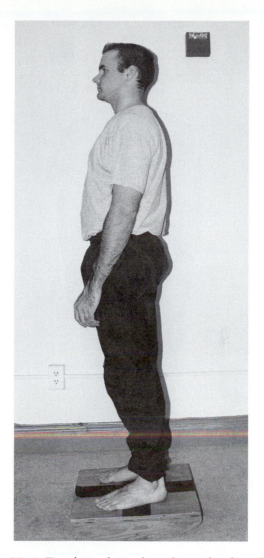

Figure 25–4. Two-legged stand on the rocker board with the board placed such that it is unstable from front to back.

ture.[2] The patient is told to maintain a quiet, balanced stance in this position.

Once the patient is able to maintain the quiet stance, the board is turned 90 degrees so that the plane of instability is left to right (Fig. 25–5). He or she is again instructed to hold the small foot position and go through the visualization processes to establish the Alexandrian posture. As the patient becomes able to maintain the quiet stance in this position, the board is rotated 45 degrees so he or she can stand on the board in an oblique position (Fig. 25–6). The small foot and postural set are again established. As soon as the patient becomes comfortable on two feet, he or she is progressed to standing on one foot on the board.

WOBBLE BOARD

Mastery of the rocker board allows the patient to progress to the wobble board. This is a board that is rounded on the

Figure 25–3. Rocker board.

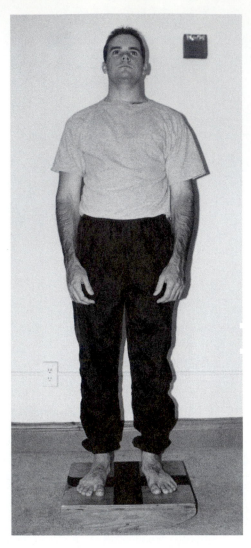

Figure 25–5. Two-legged stand on the rocker board with the board placed such that it is unstable from left to right.

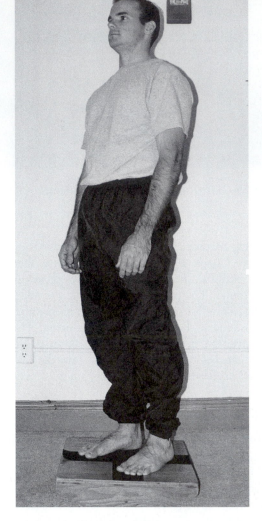

Figure 25–6. Two-legged stand on the rocker board with the board in the oblique position.

bottom and thus is unstable in all directions. This allows facilitation of postural reflexes in 360 degrees. As with quiet standing on the rocker board, the patient is instructed to maintain a small foot and an Alexandrian posture. Again, the patient should be progressed as quickly as possible to being able to stand on one foot on the wobble board (Fig. 25–7A and B).

! CLINICAL PEARL

To achieve the afferent bombardment required to create a plastic change in central motor programs, it is best to have the patient on one foot on the wobble board. Thus, it is essential to progress him or her to this point as quickly as possible. This is the point at which the greatest benefit is derived from sensorimotor training.

PERTURBATIONS

After the ability to maintain the quiet stance has been established, perturbations can be introduced. Perturbations are forces introduced to the CNS that upset equilibrium and facilitate automatic postural reactions.[3] Perturbations are important in the integration of long-loop reactions from the CNS as, in normal quiet stance on a rocker or wobble board, a condition in which destabilizing forces are small in amplitude, the monosynaptic stretch reflex of the ankle muscles is adequate to correct deviations, whereas larger amplitude disturbances, as can be created by introducing perturbations, are compensated by more neurologically complex reactions that involve higher centers, thus producing a greater response from the CNS.[4]

As was discussed in Chapter 3, Winter[5, 6] has shown that there are two types of perturbations, each of which cause a different response from the stabilizing system. External perturbations are forces acting on the body from the

A

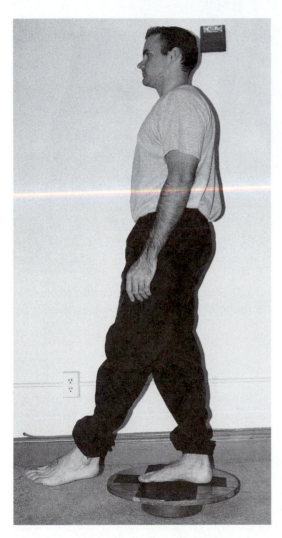

B

Figure 25–7. A. The wobble board. **B.** One-legged stand on the wobble board.

outside, which produce *reactive* responses, based on the detection of the perturbation by the visual, vestibular, and somatosensory systems and the subsequent reaction by the CNS to stabilize the body. Internal perturbations are forces acting on the body from within, as a result of voluntary movements, which produce *proactive* responses designed to maintain stability in anticipation of the disruption expected as a result of the movement.

Perturbations can be introduced to the body in a variety of ways, and specific stabilization responses can be elicited depending on the type, direction, and location of the imposed perturbation. External perturbations can be applied in two forms: a force directed to a certain body part or a force directed to the board itself. The former stimulates a reactive stabilization response that occurs in an above-down sequence;[5–7] that is, the cervical stabilizers react first, followed by the trunk and pelvic stabilizers. The latter stimulates a reactive response that occurs in a down-up sequence and primarily relies on an ankle strategy.[5–7] In sensorimotor training of spine pain patients, in which the improvement of spinal stability responses is the aim, the perturbations directed to the body should be emphasized, as those directed to the board are less effective in eliciting spinal stabilization responses and are more appropriate for rehabilitation of ankle instability.

Varying the placement and direction of the external perturbations allows the specific facilitation of certain muscles on which the clinician may desire to place emphasis. It had been shown that immediate response is seen in the muscles near the placement of the perturbation, in addition to the above-down stabilization response.[5] The perturbations can be provided by the clinician's hands, as this allows for control of the magnitude, frequency, and direction of the perturbation.

The deep cervical flexors are facilitated by applying the perturbation to the upper thoracic spine (Fig. 25–8). This causes a tendency for the chin to poke into protraction, thus causing the deep cervical flexors to counteract this in maintaining neutral head posture. The deep abdominal stabilizers are facilitated by applying the perturbation to the lumbosacral area (Fig. 25–9). This causes a tendency for increased lumbar lordosis and anterior tilt. The stabilizers of the trunk have to counteract this tendency by maintaining neutral posture. The gluteus maximus is facilitated by applying the perturbation to the anterior aspect of the hip joint (Fig. 25–10). This creates a tendency to cause hip flexion. Finally, the gluteus medius is facilitated by applying the perturbation in a lateral to medial direction to the opposite hip (Fig. 25–11). This must be done in the one-legged stand position, and it creates a tendency toward lateral pelvic shift.

Internal perturbations can be introduced via body movements. This is most easily carried out through the movement of the upper extremities. This movement can be begun by having the patient raise the arms overhead and back down again (Fig. 25–12A and B). As stated earlier, this action creates anticipatory reactions in the CNS that

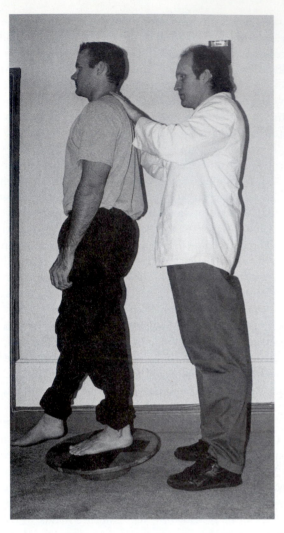

Figure 25–8. Applying perturbations to facilitate stabilization responses in the deep cervical flexors.

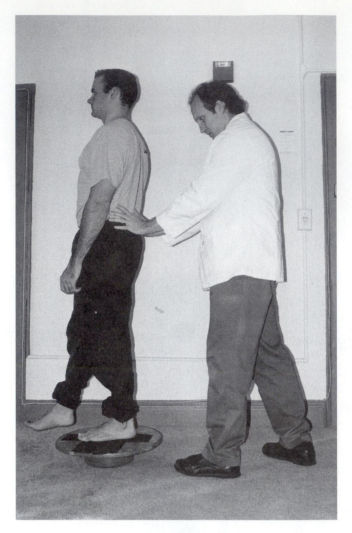

Figure 25–9. Applying perturbations to facilitate stabilization responses in the deep abdominal muscles.

facilitate stabilization responses that precede the actual movement. Both internal and external perturbations can be stimulated in sequence by throwing an object such as a basketball to and from the patient (Fig. 25–13). This can also be done with the use of a Body Blade, which the patient shakes while maintaining stability of the board. The Body Blade can be used to place facilitatory focus on the middle trapezius (Fig. 25–14), lower trapezius (Fig. 25–15), deep cervical flexors and abdominal stabilizers (Fig. 25–16), and serratus anterior (Fig. 25–17).

BALANCE SANDALS

Balance sandals have a hemisphere on the bottom of each (Fig. 25–18). They are particularly important in patients for whom the indication for sensorimotor training is a positive stepping test or faulty postural foot reaction, as they allow the patient to mimic gait in an environment of great

afferent stimulation and facilitate stabilization responses from the feet. The patient is first instructed to engage in a marching action and is carefully instructed in proper form (Fig. 25–19). It is important that the movement be isolated to the hips and that hiking of the iliac crests be avoided (Fig. 25–20). The feet, when contacting the floor, should be neutral with respect to dorsi- and plantar flexion.

Once the patient has mastered the marching form without shoes, he or she is instructed to do the same with shoes on (Fig. 25–21). The same form that was used without shoes must be utilized. The patient begins with marching in place and progresses to slowly moving forward, then backward. Lateral movements are then introduced.

Perturbations can be introduced while the patient is marching with the shoes via the use of pushes (external perturbations) (Fig. 25–22) and arm movements (internal perturbations) (Fig. 25–23). The Body Blade can also be used (Fig. 25–24).

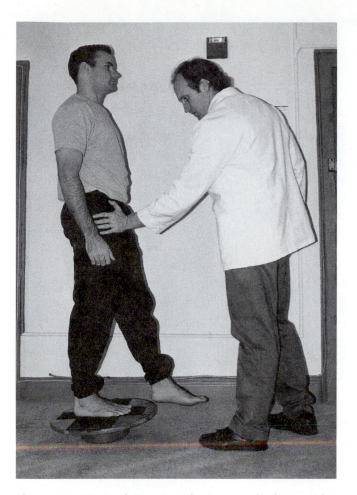

Figure 25–10. Applying perturbations to facilitate stabilization responses in the gluteus maximus.

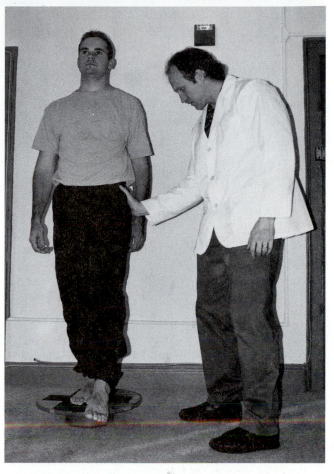

Figure 25–11. Applying perturbations to facilitate stabilization responses in the gluteus medius.

HIGHER LEVEL TRAINING

In some patients, particularly athletes who may require further fine-tuning of their neuromuscular systems, higher level activities can be performed. These include hopping from a wobble board to the floor, hopping from the floor to a wobble board, hopping from a wobble board to a rocker board, hopping from a rocker board to a wobble board, and hopping from a wobble board to another wobble board. These are very complex and potentially risky movements and should only be used in those who have a high degree of coordination and have been adequately prepared for this level of training.

EYE-HEAD-NECK COORDINATION

Particularly in patients who have experienced cervical trauma, eye-head-neck coordination must be trained.[8–11]

This involves stimulation of all the mechanisms involved in this coordination, which includes the visual, vestibular, and somatosensory systems. Sensorimotor training allows the clinician to perform this stimulation in an unstable environment that forces the CNS to adapt and thus maximizes the efficiency and the coordination of the involved systems.

As was discussed in Chapter 3, the cervical spine is involved in a number of reflex processes that help control and coordinate subconscious eye-head-neck movement patterns. The efficiency of these processes is essential to normal cervical (and thus, locomotor) function. It has been demonstrated that these processes can become disrupted in cervical injury[12–14] and tension headache[15] and that this disruption may be a factor in the development of chronic neck pain.[14] The disruption to these reflexes can be corrected through training.[10, 16, 17] This can be performed in an unstable environment through sensorimotor training.

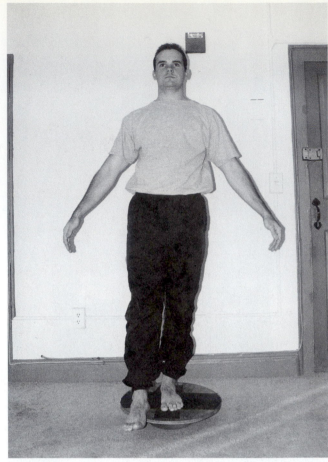

A

B

Figure 25–12. A and **B.** Facilitating proactive stabilization responses to internal perturbation.

Figure 25–13. Facilitating reactive and proactive responses.

Figure 25–14. Using the Body Blade to facilitate trunk stabilization responses as well as those in the middle trapezius.

Figure 25–15. Using the Body Blade to facilitate trunk stabilization responses as well as those in the lower trapezius.

In general, the patient should have progressed to the point of being able to maintain the quiet stance on one foot on the wobble board before beginning these exercises, as they are best done in this environment, although they can also be effectively utilized with two feet on the wobble board. First, a pen or similar object is held in front of the patient so that he or she can fix the gaze (Fig. 25–25A). The pen is then moved to the left while the patient follows it with his or her eyes, stimulating the smooth pursuit reflex (Fig. 25–25B). The pen should be moved as far to the left as the patient can follow while maintaining balance. The patient should freely turn the head and eyes as in normal pursuit of an object moving across the visual field. The pen is then moved back to neutral, followed by movement to the right in the same fashion (Fig. 25–25C). After again returning to neutral, the pen can be moved in a variety of directions, combining horizontal, vertical, and diagonal movements. After the patient learns to maintain stability while engaging in slow smooth pursuit movements, the speed can be increased by moving the pen faster.

! CLINICAL PEARL

With the smooth pursuit movements, it is important that the eyes and head move together, and not just the eyes alone. This is because, when the eyes move alone while fixating on an object, they move only in reference to a coordinate system that relates to visual space, but when eye movement occurs in conjunction with head movement, the movement occurs in reference to a coordinate system that includes the position of the head relative to the body and the position of the eyes in the orbits, therefore involving the cervical and extraocular muscle receptors.[18]

Figure 25–16. Using the Body Blade to facilitate trunk stabilization responses as well as those in the deep cervical flexors.

Figure 25–17. Using the Body Blade to facilitate trunk stabilization responses as well as those in the serratus anterior.

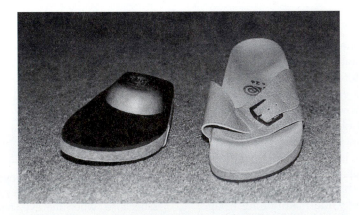

Figure 25–18. Balance sandals.

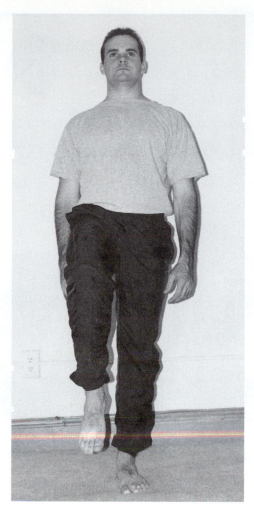

Figure 25–19. Proper form for marching in preparation for use of the balance sandals. Note that the hips remain level.

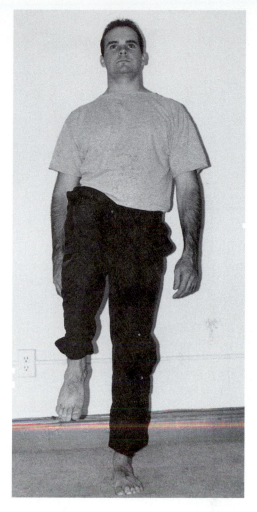

Figure 25–20. Improper form for marching.

Stimulation of smooth pursuit, with the inclusion of eye-head-neck-upper extremity coordination, can also be accomplished by having the patient throw a tennis ball into the air from one hand to the other, while following it with his or her eyes. As with the other smooth pursuit exercise, it is important that the head remain free to move along with the eyes.

Next, the patient is again asked to fix his or her gaze on the pen, but this time the head will move into rotation while maintaining gaze fixation, thus stimulating the vestibuloocular and cervico-ocular reflexes (Fig. 25–26A and B). This movement should also occur first in a horizontal plane, followed by combining horizontal, vertical, and diagonal planes. Following this, a magazine or book is held in front of the patient and he or she is asked to read aloud, stimulating saccadic movements of the eyes (Fig. 25–27).

SENSORIMOTOR TRAINING FOR SCAPULAR STABILITY

The patient is lying supine with his or her legs on a small Swiss gym ball. He or she is instructed to turn the hands outward with the fingers open as wide as possible and the thumbs pressed against the floor. The patient is then asked to raise the pelvis up into a bridge position (Fig. 25–28). Perturbations are introduced by the clinician via pushes on the ball (Fig. 25–29) or on the pelvis (Fig. 25–30).

TIMING

Maki and Whitelaw[19] showed that repeating any given perturbation results in a learning effect that leads to reduced response over time. This has also been shown to occur with the stimulation of eye-head-neck coordination,[20] where

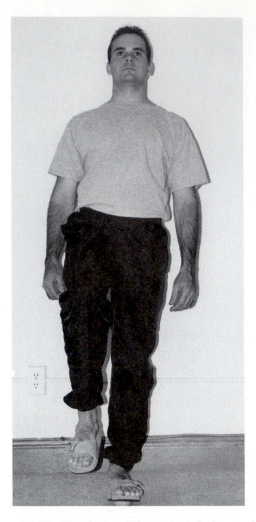

Figure 25–21. Marching while wearing balance shoes.

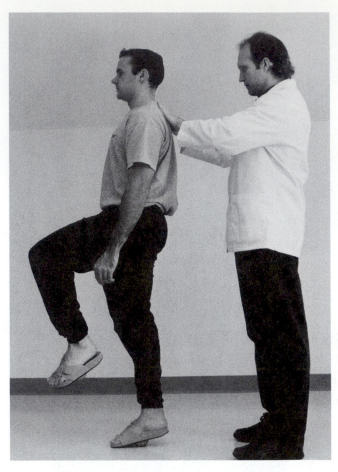

Figure 25–22. External perturbations with balance shoes.

the greater the repetition of the stimulus, the less likely a fully evoked response will be seen. It is therefore not productive to continue sensorimotor training for a prolonged period of time in each session. It has been my experience that the ideal training time for sensorimotor training is 2 to 5 minutes per session.

CERVICAL STABILIZATION

The purpose of cervical stabilization is to optimize the inherent automatic mechanisms that the cervical spine uses to maintain its stability. Whereas sensorimotor training is designed to specifically correct altered programs, which may include rompromised stability mechanisms but includes other patterns as well, cervical stabilization concerns itself primarily with stability. There is a degree of

overlap in the goals of the two methods, but cervical stabilization is more specific to this function.

The important components that need to be addressed with regard to the stability of the cervical spine are as follows:

- *Cervical stabilization:* Focus is on the multifidis, deep cervical flexors, and lower cervical extensors
- *Scapular stabilization:* Focus is on the middle and lower trapezius and serratus anterior
- *Lumbar stabilization:* Focus is on the transverse abdominis, internal oblique, and multifidis
- *Pelvic stabilization:* Focus is on the gluteus maximus and medius

To coordinate these mechanisms, some preliminary exercises must be given. First, the patient must be taught how

Figure 25–23. Internal perturbations with balance shoes.

Figure 25–24. Use of the Body Blade with balance shoes.

to establish the resting tongue position (see earlier discussion). Second, the patient must be taught the abdominal brace exercise, to facilitate the primary stabilizers of the lumbar spine.[21] This can be done in the supine position by having the patient draw the abdomen in such that the umbilicus moves posteriorward toward the spine. This maneuver selectively activates the transverse abdominis, internal oblique, and multifidis.[22] Finally, the patient is taught the cervical brace position, in which the chin is slightly tucked and cervical spine elongated. This action is very subtle and places the head in a neutral posture. It should not be an end-range chin retraction (Fig. 25–31).

The patient is then started on the quadruped track, done on the floor. The quadruped position allows for the facilitation of stabilization mechanisms in a relatively stress- and load-free environment that is still challenging to the stabilizing system.

It is absolutely essential that the exercises be performed with proper form and stability, as coordination and control are the most important aspects of an effective stabilization system that is capable of appropriately responding to potentially injurious perturbations. Training for endurance is important as well because, as Sparto et al[23] have shown, stabilization function degenerates as fatigue increases.

QUADRUPED TRACK

Exercise 1: Quadruped Static Hold
The patient is placed in the quadruped position and is instructed to maintain the resting tongue, cervical brace, and abdominal brace, positions. It is important that the patient maintain normal scapular stability with the scapulae held firmly against the thoracic cage (Fig. 25–31). He or she must be watched closely as this position is held for any loss of

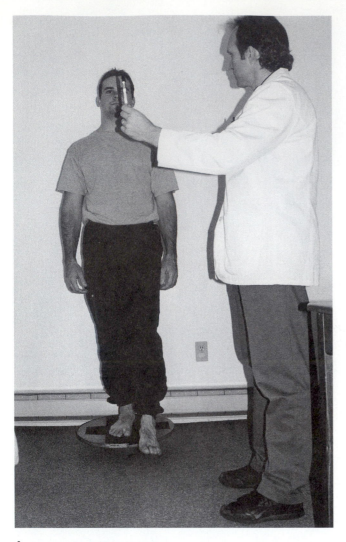

A

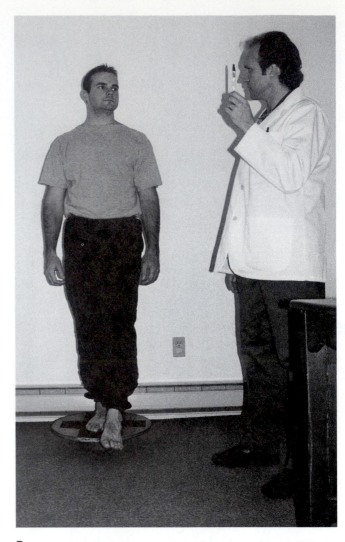

B

Figure 25–25. A–C. Stimulation of smooth pursuit.

stability, represented by chin poke, rising of the scapulae, movement of the lumbar spine, loss of abdominal brace, or shaking. Shaking indicates the substitution of phasic (type II) muscle fibers for tonic (type I) fibers and may be a sign that muscle fiber transformation has taken place (see Chap. 4). Static hold such as this should be performed primarily by tonic muscle fibers, and allowing the patient to fall into a pattern of using phasic fibers may reinforce the use of these fibers for static stability, a function for which they are poorly suited. The exercise ends at the point at which any of these changes occur. The exercise is progressed up to 30 seconds.

Exercise 2: Quadruped Book Balance

This is the same as Exercise 1, but a small hardcover book is placed on the back of the patient's head so that he or she

has to balance it (Fig. 25–32). Even more effective is a flexible ankle weight draped over the upper cervical spine and occiput. As with Exercise 1, the patient must maintain the quadruped position and proper cervical, scapular, and lumbar stability. The patient holds the position until he or she loses stability or begins to shake, or up to 30 seconds. At the point at which the patient is able to hold the position with good stability and without shaking for 30 seconds, a heavier book or ankle weight can be used.

Exercise 3: Quadruped Chin Retraction

The patient is placed in the quadruped position and is instructed to maintain the resting tongue, cervical, and abdominal brace and proper scapular positions. The patient is instructed to slowly retract the head as far as possible

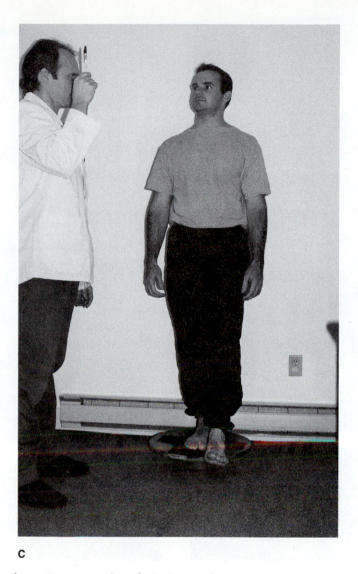

c

Figure 25–25 continued. A–C. Stimulation of smooth pursuit.

without losing stability (Fig. 25–33A). After a 2-second hold, the patient is instructed to slowly lower the head into protrusion (Fig. 25–33B). No static hold should be performed in the protruded position and the patient is instructed to return to the neutral position.

Exercise 4: Combining Cervical and Scapular Stabilization

The patient is in the quadruped position, holding the resting tongue position, the cervical and abdominal brace, and proper scapular position while balancing a book on his or her head as in Exercise 2. The hand on the involved side is on the floor and the other hand is held in a handshake-like manner (Fig. 25–34). The clinician then performs rhythmic stabilization in the direction of elbow flexion and ex-

tension while the patient maintains stability of the scapula on the side that is in contact with the ground. It is important for the clinician to watch for winging of the scapula during this activity

Exercise 5: Single Arm Raise

The patient is in the quadruped position, holding the resting tongue position, the cervical and abdominal brace, and proper scapular position. He or she is instructed to raise one arm overhead as high as possible without losing stability (Fig. 25–35). This arm is then lowered and the other raised in the same manner. For further facilitation of the middle and lower trapezius, the patient can be instructed to open the fingers as wide as possible while the arm is being raised.

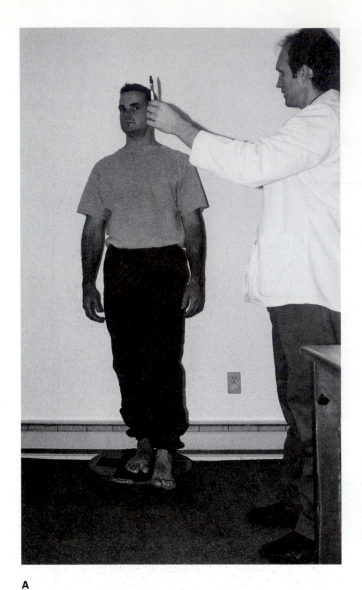

A

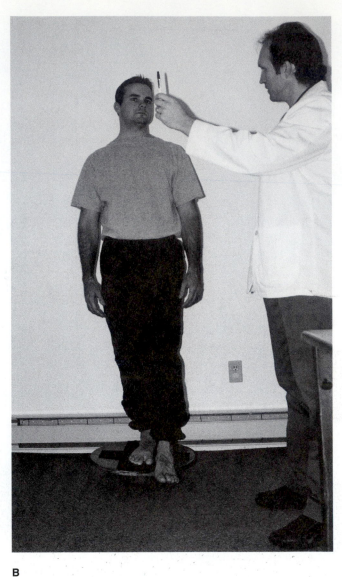

B

Figure 25–26. A and **B.** Stimulation of the vestibulo-ocular and cervico-ocular reflexes.

Exercise 6: Single Leg Raise

The patient is in the quadruped position, holding the resting tongue position, the cervical and abdominal brace, and proper scapular position. He or she is instructed to raise one leg behind as high as possible without losing stability (Fig. 25–36). This leg is then lowered and the other raised in the same manner.

Exercise 7: Cross-Crawl

The patient is in the quadruped position, holding the resting tongue position, the cervical and abdominal brace, and proper scapular position. He or she is instructed to raise one arm and the opposite leg as high as possible without losing stability (Fig. 25–37). This arm and leg is then lowered and the other arm and leg are raised in the same man-

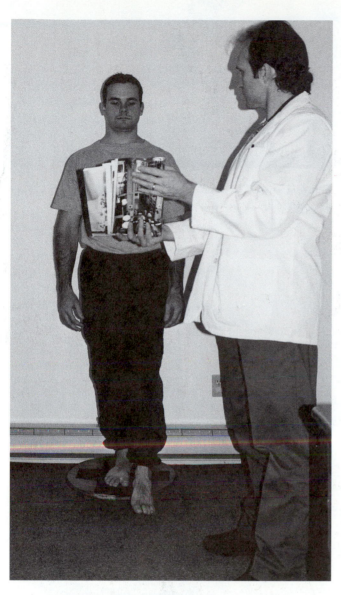

Figure 25–27. Stimulating saccadic reflexes.

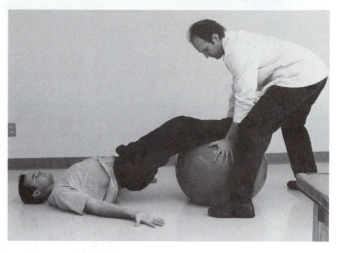

Figure 25–29. Perturbations to the ball in the floor bridge position.

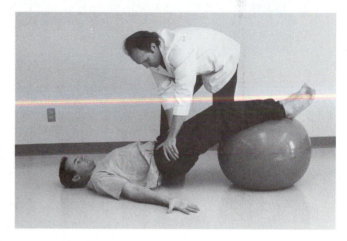

Figure 25–30. Perturbations to the pelvis in the floor bridge position.

Figure 25–28. The floor bridge position.

Figure 25–31. Quadruped static hold position.

Figure 25–32. Quadruped book balance.

A

B

Figure 25–33. A and **B.** Quadruped chin retraction.

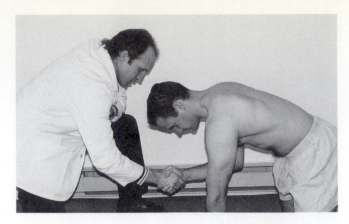

Figure 25–34. Rhythmic stabilization for the serratus anterior in the quadruped position.

Figure 25–35. Quadruped single arm raise.

Figure 25–36. Quadruped single leg raise.

Figure 25–37. Quadruped cross-crawl.

ner. For further facilitation of the middle and lower trapezius, the patient can be instructed to open the fingers as wide as possible while the arm is being raised.

Exercises 8 to 10

The patient performs exercises 5 through 7 progressively while balancing a book on his or her head (Figs. 25–38 through 25–40). To increase the stimulus for pelvic stability, a foam roll can be placed over the lumbosacral area and the patient instructed to maintain its balance while performing the exercise.

Figure 25–38. Quadruped single arm raise with book balance.

Figure 25–39. Quadruped single leg raise with book balance.

Figure 25–40. Quadruped cross-crawl with book balance.

Exercises 11 to 13

The patient performs Exercises 5 through 7 progressively while balanced on perpendicularly placed foam rolls (Figs. 25–41 through 25–43).

Figure 25–41. Quadruped single arm raise on foam rolls placed perpendicular.

Figure 25–42. Quadruped single leg raise on foam rolls placed perpendicular.

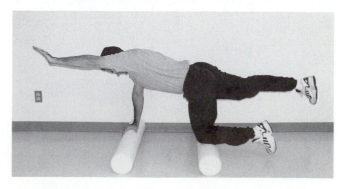

Figure 25–43. Quadruped cross-crawl on foam rolls placed perpendicular.

Exercises 14 to 16

The patient performs Exercises 5 through 7 while balanced on perpendicularly placed foam rolls and balancing a book on his or her head (Figs. 25–44 through 25–46).

Exercises 16 to 18

The patient performs Exercises 5 through 7 while balanced on parallel placed foam rolls (Figs. 25–47 through 25–49).

Figure 25–44. Quadruped single arm raise on foam rolls placed perpendicular and book balance.

Figure 25–47. Quadruped single arm raise on foam rolls placed parallel.

Figure 25–45. Quadruped single leg raise on foam rolls placed perpendicular and book balance.

Figure 25–48. Quadruped single leg raise on foam rolls placed parallel.

Figure 25–46. Quadruped cross-crawl on foam rolls placed perpendicular and book balance.

Figure 25–49. Quadrupled cross-crawl on foam rolls placed parallel.

Exercises 19 to 21

The patient performs Exercises 5 through 7 while balanced on parallel placed foam rolls and balancing a book on his or her head (Figs. 25–50 through 25–52). This exercise has a high degree of difficulty and most patients will not progress to this level.

Rhythmic stabilization can be applied in the quadruped track for facilitation of specific stabilization responses, such as for the deep cervical flexors and lower cervical/upper thoracic extensors (Fig. 25–53) and scapular stabilizers (Fig. 25–54) or for general trunk stabilization (Fig. 25–55).

Figure 25–53. Rhythmic stabilization for the deep cervical flexors in the quadruped position.

Figure 25–50. Quadruped single arm raise on foam rolls placed parallel and book balance.

Figure 25–51. Quadruped single leg raise on foam rolls placed parallel and book balance.

Figure 25–54. Rhythmic stabilization for the serratus anterior in the quadruped position.

Figure 25–52. Quadruped cross-crawl on foam rolls placed parallel and book balance.

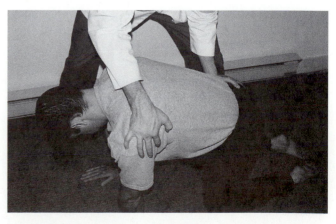

Figure 25–55. Rhythmic stabilization for the trunk stabilizers in the quadruped position.

PRONE GYM BALL WALKOUT TRACK

This track allows exercises to be performed in the unstable environment provided by the Swiss gym ball.

Exercise 1: Static Hold

The patient walks out on the gym ball in the prone position and is instructed to maintain the resting tongue and cervical and abdominal brace positions (Fig. 25–56). As with the quadruped static hold exercise, it is important that the patient maintain normal scapular stability with the scapulae held firmly against the thoracic cage. The patient must be watched closely as he or she holds this position for any loss of stability, represented by chin poke, rising of the scapulae, movement of the lumbar spine, loss of abdominal brace or shaking. The exercise ends at the point at which any of these changes occur. The exercise is progressed up to 30 seconds.

Figure 25–56. Prone gym ball walkout static hold.

Exercise 2: Book Balance

This is the same as Exercise 1, but a small hardcover book is placed on the back of the patient's head so that the patient has to balance it (Fig. 25–57). As with Exercise 1, the

Figure 25–57. Prone walkout static hold with book balance.

patient must maintain the quadruped position and proper cervical, scapular and lumbar stability. The patient holds the position until he or she loses stability or begins to shake, or up to 30 seconds. At the point at which the patient is able to hold the position with good stability and without shaking for 30 seconds, a heavier book can be used.

Exercise 3: Walkouts

The patient walks out onto the gym ball in the prone position while maintaining the resting tongue, cervical brace, and abdominal brace positions (see Fig. 25–56). The patient then walks back to the starting position, without losing stability (Fig. 25–58), then walks out again.

Figure 25–58. Walkouts.

Exercise 4: Chin Tucks

The patient walks out on the gym ball in the prone position and is instructed to maintain the resting tongue, cervical brace, and abdominal brace positions (see Fig. 25–56). The scapulae are held firmly against the thoracic cage. The patient is then instructed to tuck the chin as far back as possible (Fig. 25–59A) and hold it there for a second. The patient then slowly lowers the chin into a protruded position (Fig. 25–59B), followed again by chin tuck. It is important that the patient only hold the tucked position, not the protruded position.

Exercise 5: Double Arm Elevation

From the static hold position, the patient is instructed to slowly move backward on the ball by extending the arms overhead (Fig. 25–60). It is important that the clinician watch to be sure that the patient maintains the resting tongue, cervical brace, abdominal brace, and scapular position as he or she does this. The patient then returns to the static hold position.

For increased difficulty in the prone walkout track, the patient should move out farther on the ball so that the ball

A

B

Figure 25–59. A and **B.** Prone walkout chin retraction.

is lower on the legs (Fig. 25–61). To increase the stimulus for stabilization response, all of these exercises can be performed with the hands balancing on a duck walker (Fig. 25–62).

As with the quadruped track, rhythmic stabilization can be applied in the prone walkout track for facilitation of specific stabilization responses for the deep cervical flexors (Fig. 25–63) and scapular stabilizers (Fig. 25–64), or for general trunk stabilization (Fig. 25–65).

Figure 25–60. Prone walkout double arm elevation.

Figure 25–61. Increasing the difficulty of the prone walk-out track.

Figure 25–62. Use of the duck walker in the prone walk-out track. Fingers are spread as wide as possible.

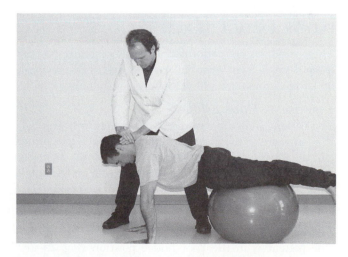

Figure 25–63. Rhythmic stabilization for the deep cervical flexors in the prone walkout position.

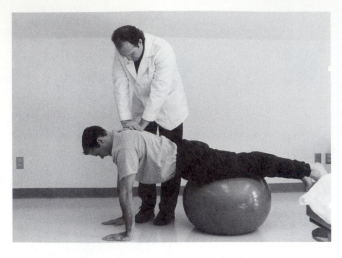

Figure 25–64. Rhythmic stabilization for the serratus anterior in the prone walkout position.

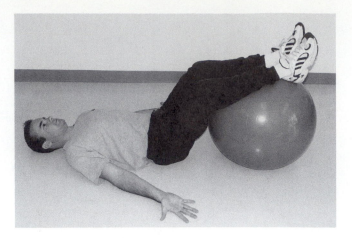

Figure 25–66. Preparation for the floor bridge track.

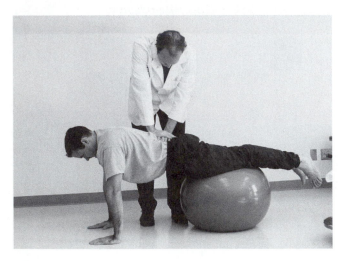

Figure 25–65. Rhythmic stabilization for the trunk stabilizers in the prone walkout position.

Figure 25–67. Floor bridge track single leg raise.

FLOOR BRIDGE TRACK

These exercises are performed in the floor bridge position using a small Swiss gym ball, as was described previously under sensorimotor training for scapular stability.

Exercise 1: Floor Bridges

The patient is supine with the legs on the Swiss gym ball. The arms are at the patient's sides, with the hands turned out, the fingers wide, and the thumbs against the floor (Fig. 25–66). The patient is instructed to perform an abdominal brace and slowly raise the pelvis into a bridge position (see Fig. 25–28). The patient then lowers back to the floor.

Exercise 2: Single Leg Raise

The patient is in the floor bridge position (Fig. 25–28). While maintaining the abdominal brace and using the arms to stabilize himself or herself on the floor, the patient raises

one leg into the air (Fig. 25–67). This leg is lowered back to the ball and the process is repeated with the other leg.

GENERAL EXERCISES

Brügger Exercise

The purpose of this exercise is to train the patient to facilitate the middle and lower trapezius and infraspinatus and inhibit the upper trapezius, levator scapulae, rhomboids, and pectoralis major and minor. It is also excellent for improving lumbar and cervical posture. The patient should do it as a regular exercise, in addition to using it as a "break" at work or home if he or she is sitting for a long time (see Chap. 27).

The patient sits with his or her ischial tuberosities at the edge of a chair, with the pelvis rocking forward into an anterior tilt, and the rest of the body upright (Fig. 25–68). The anterior tilt creates a natural lordosis in the lumbar spine and causes the chin to automatically assume a slightly "tucked" position. The patient is then instructed to open the fingers as wide as possible and externally rotate

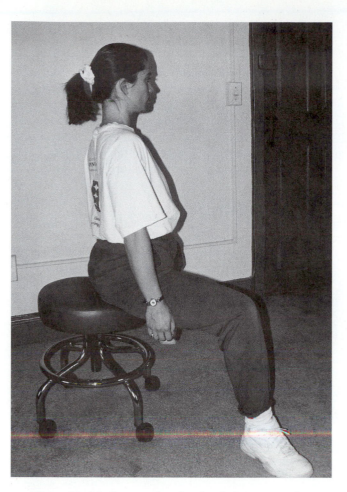

Figure 25–68. Preparation for the Brügger exercise.

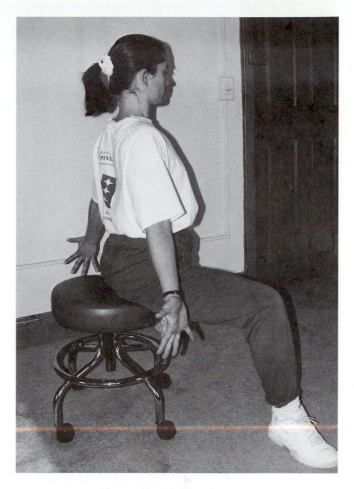

Figure 25–69. The Brügger.

the arms as far as he or she can (Fig. 25–69). The patient should feel the middle and lower trapezii contracting, although at first the feeling of stretch in the arms and pectorals may overpower this. The patient holds this position for 10 seconds.

> ## ❗ CLINICAL PEARL
>
> It is important that the patient not try to pull the scapulae together, as this will decrease the effectiveness of the exercise. There are two reasons for this. The first is that pulling the scapulae together will shorten the middle and lower trapezii and create active insufficiency,[24] in which the attachments of the muscles are so close together that full activation is compromised. The second is that the purpose of providing this exercise is to activate inhibited middle and lower trapezii. If these muscles are neurologically inhibited and the patient is instructed to try to consciously activate them, he or she is likely to recruit the upper trapezius or rhomboids, or both. By having the patient focus on opening the fingers and turning out the hands, rather than on the scapulae, the middle and lower trapezii will be indirectly, reflexively activated and much better recruitment of these muscles will occur.

This exercise can be modified to specifically target the lower trapezius by having the patient elevate the arms to 110 degrees and again opening the fingers as wide as possible and externally rotating the arms (Fig. 25–70).

TIMING

It is important to fit the duration of the stimulation during cervical stabilization training to the capacity of the CNS to produce stabilization responses. The CNS recruits motor neurons in a specific order to create smooth, coordinated and stable movement patterns. The order of recruitment is such that the smallest, most excitable alpha motor neurons, which innervate slow-twitch, fatigue resistant tonic muscle fibers, are recruited first.[4] As afferent input becomes greater, larger alpha motor neurons, innervating fast-twitch, easily fatigued phasic muscle fibers, such as those found in the deep cervical flexors and the gluteus maximus are recruited.[4] So, if the goal is to activate inhibited muscles, stimulation must be continued long enough to reach the point of recruitment of the larger motor neurons.

For this reason, it is best to use a combination of rhythmic stabilization maneuvers to create intense afferent input that will stimulate fast-twitch, phasic fibers, and

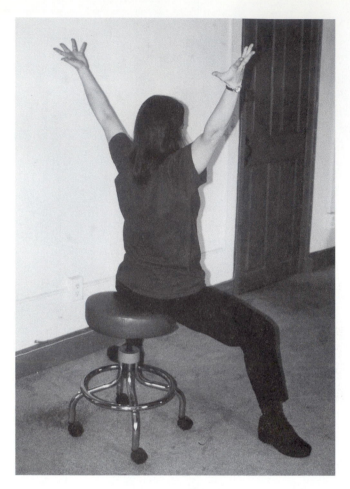

Figure 25–70. The Brügger, with emphasis on the lower trapezii.

endurance training (high repetitions or long static holds) to stimulate slow-twitch, tonic fibers. Sets and repetitions will vary, and the emphasis should be placed on maintaining stability throughout the entire exercise—this is far more important than performing the maximum number of repetitions. In general, the patient should perform the maximum number of repetitions that he or she is capable of while maintaining stability. At the point in the set at which stability is lost, the clinician should stop the set, and the patient should perform this number of repetitions in his or her home routine. The number of repetitions are gradually increased until 15 repetitions can be performed with good stability, after which time the patient is ready to progress to the next level of difficulty. The process is complete when the faulty pattern normalizes.

ISOTONIC AND AEROBIC TRAINING

In some patients and in some clinical circumstances, it may be desirable to include isotonic weight training and aerobic training in cervical stabilization. This approach allows for selective strengthening of important muscles involved in stabilization of the cervical spine and related areas. As stability is primarily a neural control process, rather than a strength process, this aspect of training is less important than that already presented. However, in those patients in whom weakness or deconditioning is a factor, or if it is seen that additional exercise training will contribute to patient empowerment, it is recommended that aerobic and strength training be instituted, and that it be targeted toward those areas that are most important for stability and coordination.

AEROBIC TRAINING

Properly instituted, aerobic training can be begun in the early stages of treatment. And in the presence of marked deconditioning, early institution can be of paramount importance. The use of the recumbent bicycle is invaluable here. As seen in Figure 25–71, the patient is supine with the cervical spine supported with a cervical pillow. This allows the patient to pedal in an environment in which the cervical spine is completely at rest.

It is best, especially if significant deconditioning is present, to start the patient at a low level of intensity and increase the intensity as the patient's aerobic condition improves. In patients who are over 40 years of age or who may be at risk of cardiovascular complication related to unfamiliar exercise, examination and clearance by a general internist or cardiologist is essential.

ISOTONIC STRENGTH TRAINING

Strength training can be performed with the simplest equipment—a Swiss gym ball and dumbbells are all that is really needed. The exercises are designed to strengthen those muscles that are most important in the stability of the cervical spine and scapulae.

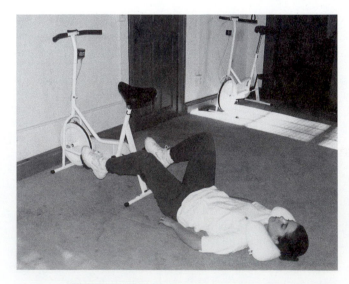

Figure 25–71. The recumbent bicycle.

Figure 25–72. Seated lateral raises.

Exercise 1: Seated Lateral Raises

The patient is sitting on the Swiss gym ball with a dumbbell in each hand, held at the sides. It is important that the patient maintain the cervical and abdominal brace and resting tongue position throughout the exercise. With the palms facing toward the patient, the dumbbells are raised to the sides, slightly anterior to the frontal plane, to greater than 90 degrees (Fig. 25–72).

Exercise 2: Seated Front Raises

The patient is sitting on the Swiss gym ball with a dumbbell in each hand, held at the sides. It is important that the patient maintain the cervical and abdominal brace and resting tongue position throughout the exercise. With the dumbbells facing to the posterior, they are raised alternately straight out in front to greater than 90 degrees (Fig. 25–73).

Exercise 3: Prone Lateral Raises at 90 Degrees

The patient is prone on the Swiss gym ball with a dumbbell in each hand, held at the sides. It is important that the patient maintain the cervical and abdominal brace and resting tongue position throughout the exercise. With the arms moving into external rotation as the movement is carried out, and the thumb pointing to the ceiling, the dumbbells are raised out to the sides (Fig. 25–74). The clinician should watch closely for chin poking during the performance of this exercise.

Exercise 4: Prone Lateral Raises with Elevation

The patient is prone on the Swiss gym ball with a dumbbell in each hand, held at the sides. It is important that the patient maintain the cervical and abdominal brace and resting tongue position throughout the exercise. With the arms moving into external rotation as the movement is carried

out, and the thumb pointing to the ceiling, the dumbbells are raised diagonally into elevation (Fig. 25–75). The clinician should watch closely for chin poking during the performance of this exercise.

Figure 25–73. Seated front raises.

Figure 25–74. Prone lateral raises.

Exercise 5: Upright Rows

The patient is standing holding a dumbbell in each hand in front, with the palms facing in. It is important that the patient maintain the cervical and abdominal brace and resting tongue position throughout the exercise. The patient raises the dumbbells upward, while keeping them close to his or her body (Fig. 25–76). The clinician should watch closely for chin poking during the performance of this exercise.

Exercise 6: Latissimus Pulldowns

The patient is sitting at a lateral pulldown apparatus or set up in a traction harness, with hands on the bar (Fig. 25–77). It is important that the patient maintain the cervical and abdominal brace and resting tongue position throughout the exercise. The bar is pulled downward as far as possible. A variety of positions and types of bars can be used for this exercise (Figs. 25–78A–C).

Exercise 7: Wall Chin Tucks

The patient is standing, facing the wall, with his or her face against a rubber ball that is placed just over the nose (Fig. 25–79A). It is important not to place the ball higher than this, up onto the forehead, as this will tend to facilitate the sternocleidomastoid and deemphasize the deep cervical flexors. The patient then nods his or her head for-

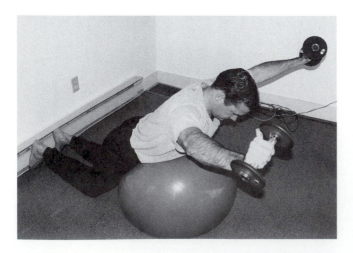

Figure 25–75. Prone lateral raises with elevation.

Figure 25–76. Upright rows.

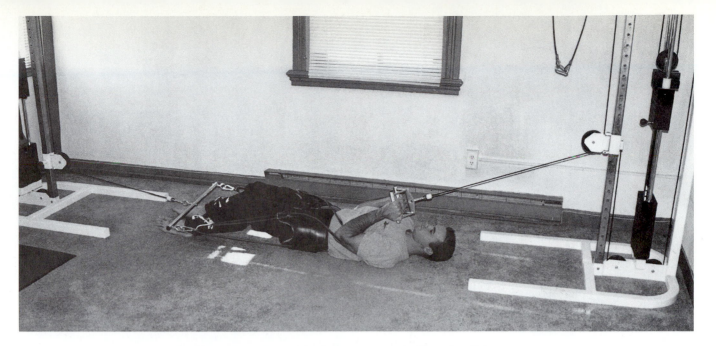

Figure 25–77. Traction harness setup for lateral pulldowns.

A

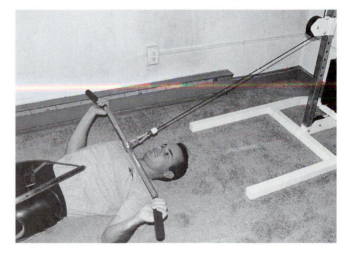

B

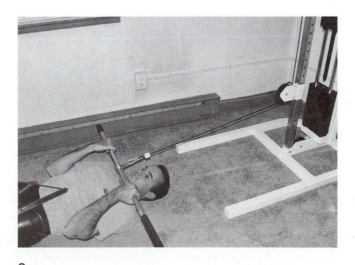

C

Figure 25–78. A–C. Variations in bars and grip for lateral pulldowns.

A

B

C

Figure 25–79. A–C. Wall chin tucks.

ward, limiting the movement to the upper cervical spine (Fig. 25–79B), followed by raising the head upward again into extension (Fig. 25–79C).

Exercise 8: Dynamic Cervical Range of Motion— Supine

The patient is lying supine on a bench or a Swiss gym ball with the head hanging freely. It is important that the patient maintain the abdominal brace and resting tongue position throughout the exercise. The patient is instructed to slowly lower the head into extension, after first retracting the head fully (Fig. 25–80A), followed by extension (Fig. 25–80B). The head is then returned to the original position by first moving the chin into the tucked position and then returning the head to neutral (Fig. 25–80C and D).

Exercise 9: Dynamic Cervical Range of Motion— Side Lying

The patient is lying on either side on a bench or a Swiss gym ball, with the head hanging freely. It is important that the patient maintain the cervical and abdominal brace and resting tongue position throughout the exercise. The patient is instructed to slowly lower the head into lateral flexion, then return to the neutral position, followed by raising the head into lateral flexion to the opposite side (Fig. 25–81A and B).

Exercise 10: Dynamic Cervical Range of Motion—Prone

The patient is lying prone on a bench or a Swiss gym ball, with the head hanging freely. It is important that the

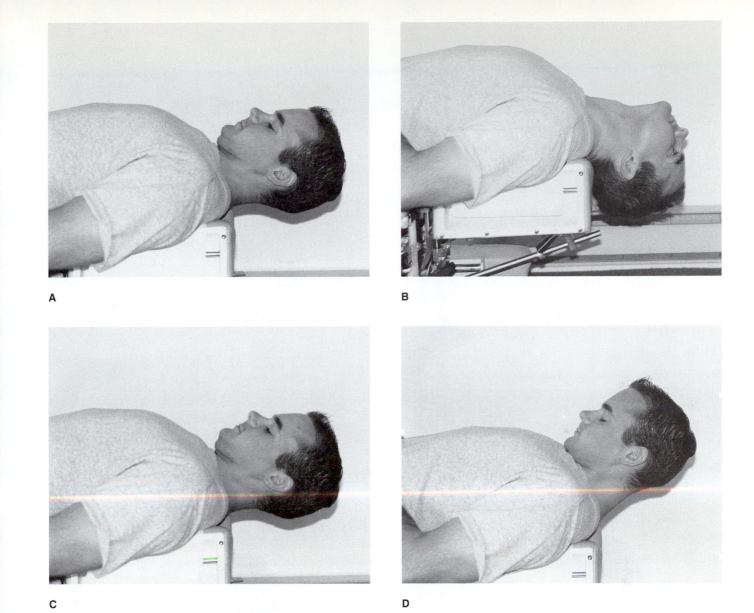

Figure 25–80. A–D. Dynamic range of motion—supine.

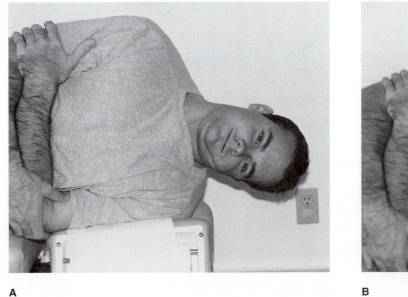

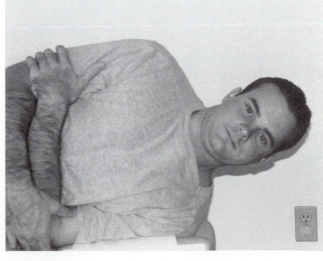

Figure 25–81. A and **B.** Dynamic range of motion—side lying.

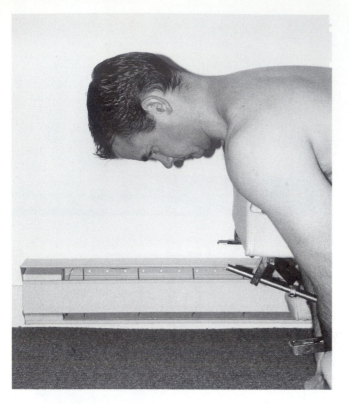

A

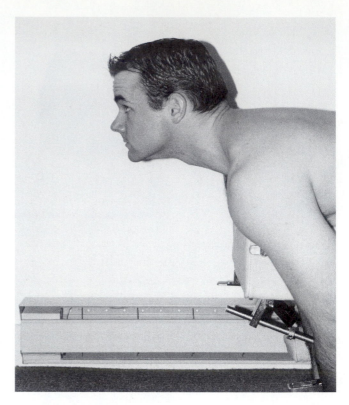

B

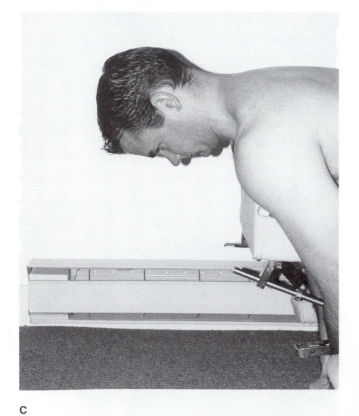

C

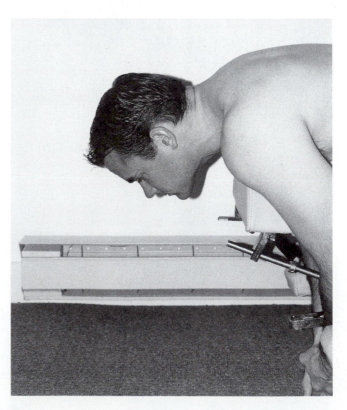

D

Figure 25–82. A–D. Dynamic range of motion—prone.

patient maintain the abdominal brace and resting tongue position throughout the exercise. The patient is instructed to slowly retract the head fully, then extend (Fig. 25–82A and B). The patient is then instructed to return to the neutral position (Fig. 25–82C), then lower the head into protraction (Fig. 25–82D), followed by return to the neutral position.

TIMING

Strength training should be initiated only after good stability mechanisms and movement patterns have been established, to avoid the risk of reinforcing improper neurological programs. In training for strength, a relatively low number of repetitions is best, ranging from eight to ten, over three sets. However, endurance is important in stability, so it is best to perform the exercises sequentially so that little or no rest between sets takes place. So if three sets of ten repetitions are desired, each exercise should be performed for one set, followed with as little rest as possible by the next exercise, and so on until all exercises have been performed for the first set. The patient then returns to the first exercise for the second set. This allows for training for strength, as each muscle does not become too exhausted to move the amount of weight needed to stimulate strength gains, while at the same time endurance is promoted because there is little or no rest between sets.

CONCLUSION

The inclusion of sensorimotor training and cervical stabilization can be instrumental in fully rehabilitating patients with cervical spine syndromes. While much work needs to be done in investigating efficacy, some preliminary studies have suggested that these methods have a role to play in the rehabilitation process. Saal et al[25] found, in an uncontrolled study, that 20 of 26 patients with cervical herniated nucleus pulposus documented on magnetic resonance imaging scans showed good to excellent results, based on measures of pain, function, and satisfaction, with a treatment approach that included cervical stabilization. Only 2 of the 26 patients required surgery. Karlburg et al[26] assessed 17 patients with dizziness suspected to be of cervical origin, one group of whom were treated with an approach that included cervical stabilization, and the other of whom were not treated in this fashion. They found that the treated group showed a significant decrease in intensity and frequency of dizziness episodes as well as a decrease in the velocity of body sway. There is also some empirical evidence of the effectiveness of cervical stabilization in patients with occupational neck or arm pain[27] and headache.[28]

By accurately identifying those specific patients that require sensorimotor training and cervical stabilization, we can move toward maximizing the effectiveness of the management of each patient's clinical condition.

REFERENCES

1. Janda V. Muscles and motor control in cervicogenic disorders: Assessment and management. In: Grant R, ed. *Physical Therapy of the Cervical and Thoracic Spine*. New York, NY: Churchill Livingstone; 1994:195–216.

2. Gelb M. *Body Learning*. New York, NY: Henry Holt; 1981.

3. Janda J, Va Vrova M. Sensorimotor training. In: Liebenson CS, ed. *Rehabilitation of the Spine: A Practitioner's Manual*. Baltimore, Md: Williams and Wilkins; 1996:319–328.

4. Davidoff RA. Skeletal muscle tone and the misunderstood stretch reflex. *Neurology* 1992;42:951–963.

5. Winter DA. *ABC of Balance During Walking and Standing*. Waterloo, Ontario: Waterloo Biomechanics; 1995.

6. Winter DA. Human balance and posture control during standing and walking. *Gait Posture* 1995;3:193–214.

7. Prince F, Winter DA, Stergiou P, Walt SE. Anticipatory control of upper body balance during human locomotion. *Gait Posture* 1994;2:19–25.

8. Fitz-Ritson D. Neural mechanisms involved in the control of the eye-head-neck coordinated movement: A review of the literature with emphasis on future directions for the chiropractic profession. *J Manipulative Physiol Ther* 1984;7:251–260.

9. Revel M, Andre-Deshays C, Minguet M. Cervicocephalic kinesthetic sensibility in patients with cervical pain. *Arch Phys Med Rehabil* 1991;72:288–291.

10. Revel M, Minguet M, Gergoy P, et al. Changes in cervicocephalic kinesthesia after a proprioceptive rehabilitation program in patients with neck pain: A randomized controlled trial. *Arch Phys Med Rehabil* 1994;75:895–899.

11. Loudon JK, Ruhl M, Field E. Ability to reproduce head position after whiplash injury. *Spine* 1997;22(8):865–868.

12. Hildingsson C, Wenngren B, Bring G, Toolanen G. Eye motility dysfunction after soft tissue injury of the cervical spine: A controlled, prospective study of 38 patients. *Acta Orthop Scand* 1993;64(2):129–132.
13. Hildingsson C, Wenngren B, Bring G, Toolanen G. Oculomotor problems after cervical spine injury. *Acta Orthop Scand* 1989;60(5):513–516.
14. Gimse R, Tjell C, Bjorgen I, Saunte C. Disturbed eye movements after whiplash due to injuries to posture control system. *J Clin Exp Neuropsychol* 1996;18(2):178–186.
15. Carlsson J, Rosenthal U. Oculomotor disturbances in patients with tension headache. *Acta Otolaryngol (Stockh)* 1988;106:354–360.
16. Fitz-Ritson D. Phasic exercises for cervical rehabilitation after "whiplash" trauma. *JMPT* 1995 18(1):21–24.
17. Heikkila H, Astrom PG. Cervicocephalic kinesthetic sensibility in patients with whiplash injury. *Scand J Rehabil* 1996;28:133–138.
18. Dubrovsky BO, Barbas H. Frontal projections of dorsal neck and extraocular muscles. *Exp Neurol* 1977;55:680–693.
19. Maki BE, Whitelaw RS. Influence of expectation and arousal on center-of-pressure responses to transient postural perturbations. *J Vestib Res* 1993;3:25–39.
20. Barmack NH, Errico P, Ferraresi A, Pettorossi VE. Cervico-ocular reflexes with and without simultaneous vestibular stimulation in rabbits. In: Berthoz A, Graf W, Vidall PP, eds. *The Head-Neck Sensory Motor System*. New York, NY: Oxford University Press; 1992:202–207.
21. Richardson C, Jull G, Toppenberg R, Comerford M. Techniques for active stabilisation for spinal protection: A pilot study. *Aust Physiother* 1992;38(2):105–112.
22. Richardson CA, Jull GA. Muscle control—pain control. What exercises would you prescribe? *Man Ther* 1995;1:2–10.
23. Sparto PJ, Parniapour M, Reinsel TE, Simon S. The effect of fatigue on multijoint kinematics, coordination and postural stability during a repetitive lifting test. *J Orthop Sports Phys Ther* 1997;25:3–12.
24. Lemkuhl LD, Smith LK. *Brunnstrom's Clinical Kinesiology*. 4th ed. Philadelphia, Pa: FA Davis; 1983.
25. Saal JS, Saal JA, Yurth E. Nonoperative management of cervical intervertebral disc with radiculopathy. *Spine* 1996;21(16):1877–1883.
26. Karlburg M, Magnusson M, Malmstrom EM, et al. Postural and symptomatic improvement after physiotherapy in patients with dizziness of suspected cervical origin. *Arch Phys Med Rehabil* 1996;77:874–882.
27. Grant R, Jull G, Spencer T. Active stabilisation training for screen based keyboard operators—a single case study. *Aust J Physiother* 1997;43:235–242.
28. Jull G. Management of cervical headache. *Man Ther* 1997;2:182–190.

CHAPTER 26

McKenzie Protocol in Cervical Spine Rehabilitation

Steven Heffner

"There may be psychological advantages in making patients responsible for their own treatment rather than victims of their own symptoms. If there is the slightest chance that patients can be educated in a method of treatment that enables them to reduce their own pain and disability using their own understanding and resources, they should receive that education. Every patient is entitled to this information, and every therapist should be obliged to provide it."

—Robin McKenzie, OBE, FCSP, FNZP (Hon), DIP MT

"The McKenzie System of neck and back care is a remarkable phenomenon among the various approaches. As a practitioner of two professions which strive to provide alternatives to orthodox medical practice, the McKenzie approach is quite appealing to me. Both chiropractic and acupuncture portray themselves as natural healing systems. What could be more natural than a method of self-treatment for the neck and back which explores the body's ability to heal itself without medication, heat, cold, electricity, ultrasound, needles, or a force introduced by the practitioner?

The McKenzie approach demonstrates the body has the mechanisms by which to correct itself, and the potential is great enough that the patient may develop skills to be self-reliant in achieving that goal."

—Gary Jacob, DC, LAc, CC RD, DipMDT, QME

INTRODUCTION

The two opening quotes serve as the best introduction to all that the McKenzie protocol embodies. The main purpose of this chapter is to explore the clinical reasoning resulting from McKenzie criterion regarding the nature and solution of common activity-related cervical complaints. This chapter attempts to give the reader a brief overview of the McKenzie system and treatment protocol as it pertains to evaluation and treatment of the cervical spine. Clinical competency in the McKenzie approach is greatly aided by study of McKenzie's original texts[1, 2] and by supervised clinical training. Supervised clinical training is particularly important, in order to develop the skills to best manage the fears faced by patients and clinician when the therapy involves promoting movement of the painful spine.

The definition commonly used for the McKenzie system is: *"Spinal therapeutics based on symptomatic and mechanical responses to spinal loading."* The logic of mechanical therapy is to:

1. Correct posture to relieve painful tension on normal tissues (postural syndrome)
2. Stretch to remodel shortened or contracted tissue (dysfunction syndrome)
3. Apply reductive pressures to relocate displaced tissue (derangement syndrome)

Its essence is summarized in the *3 R's*:

Re-education of posture
*Re*modeling of dysfunction
*Re*duction of derangement

CENTRALIZATION

Centralization is critical as a predictor of correct and incorrect movements or positions. It is often accompanied by improved mechanics.[3] The concept of centralization was taught to me by David Poulter, McKenzie Diploma Instructor and Head of the Faculty of the International McKenzie Institute. The following paragraphs describe centralization as it applies to the lumbar spine.

HYPOTHESIS

Centralization occurs as spinal structures that are able to refer symptoms into a limb distally are progressively and sequentially released from pressure. These structures include the extrathecal nerve root complex, the root dural sleeve, the posterior longitudinal ligament, and the outer annulus. Figure 26–1 is a pictorial representation of this hypothesis.

There is considerable support for this hypothesis in the literature. Pople and Griffith, in their paper on prediction of an extruded disc fragment,[4] showed that the pain pattern is highly predictable for an extruded disc. A sudden decrease in back pain, accompanied by an increase or production of leg pain (the leg pain becomes the predominate symptom), was found to be indicative of discal extrusion. A model to explain back pain is provided, linking it to the innervated annulus and posterior longitudinal ligament. As these two structures are breached, leg pain is produced by hitting the nerve root complex. Kuslich and Ulstrom have stated that back pain is commonly produced by the outer annulus and posterior longitudinal ligament, whereas buttock and thigh pain are produced by stimulating the dural sleeve, often in conjunction with the annulus. They further state that the nerve root complex is the only structure capable of producing leg pain.[5] Taking Pople and Griffith's description of the pain response to extrusion and reversing it, it is not difficult to imagine *centralization* taking place as the structures in the spine are sequentially released from pressure.

It is interesting to note that Smith and Wright demonstrated that as the nerve root complex was compressed, the extent of the radiation of the leg pain was directly proportional to the degree of pressure on the nerve root.[6] McKenzie quotes their work in his chapter on centralization: "Light pressure of the root will cause sciatica reaching down as far as the thigh whereas stronger compression will cause the sciatica to extend as far as the foot and toes. Thus it follows that centralization of pain would occur as pressure on the nerve root is reduced."[1]

In a prospective, blinded study, April and Medcalf used centralization of pain, during a standard McKenzie mechanical assessment, to predict discographic outcomes. They found that 74 percent of patients who centralized had positive discograms, and 91 percent of them had a competent outer annulus. Donelson reported that the outcome of this study would suggest that patients who centralize are discogenic with a competent annulus.[7]

DEFINITION

It is important to remember that *during* a loading strategy, a symptomatic response may occur. It is what happens when the loading strategy *ceases* that determines the use of the word "centralized." The centralization phenomenon is the result of the repetition of certain movements or the adoption of certain positions, in which peripheral pain originating from the spine and referred distally is made to move away from the periphery and toward the midline of the spine.

On cessation of the loading strategy, the change in the symptom presentation that occurred under loading is retained and the patient *remains better*. He or she has *centralized*. Once distinguished, movements that cause this occurrence can be used to abolish radiating and referred symptoms. In patients with pain of recent onset, this process can be extremely rapid and, in some cases, it may occur in a matter of minutes.

Centralization occurs only in the derangement syndrome during the reductive process. As reduction takes place, there may be a significant increase of localized central pain adjacent to or in the spine itself.

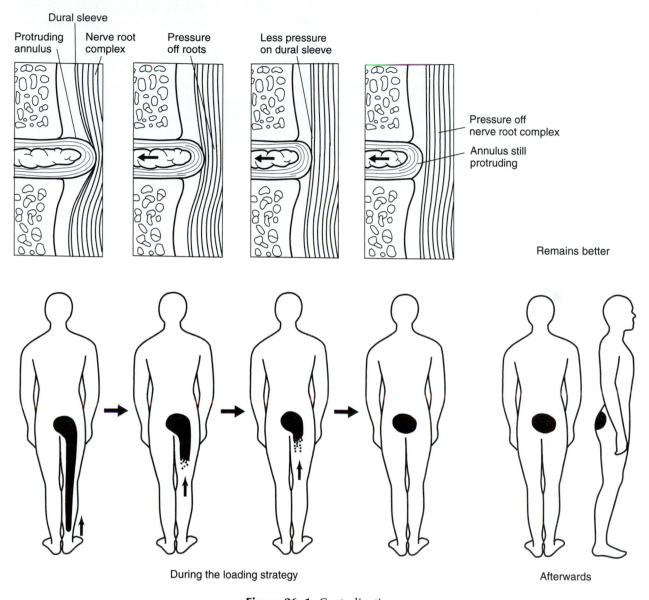

During the performance of a loading strategy
(repeated movements or static positioning)

Dural sleeve

Protruding annulus

Nerve root complex

Pressure off roots

Less pressure on dural sleeve

Pressure off nerve root complex

Annulus still protruding

Remains better

During the loading strategy

Afterwards

Figure 26–1. Centralization.

! CLINICAL PEARL

1. Once symptoms below the elbow have sequentially abolished, it is common for only the symptom of pain to remain above the elbow; hence, centralization refers to the perception of pain changing its distal location to a more proximal location toward the midline of the spine.
2. *During* the performance of a loading strategy, the symptomatic response should be noted, but it is only *after* the loading strategy that centralization can be said to have taken place. The symptomatic response obtained under loading must be retained; hence, centralize = better.
3. McKenzie hypothesizes that centralization occurs as a result of a progressive release of pressure from spinal structures that are able to refer symptoms distally into the limbs.

FOUR CERVICAL SYNDROMES OF McKENZIE THERAPY

Four syndromes are the foundation of the McKenzie treatment process. They are: (1) postural syndrome, (2) dysfunction syndrome, (3) derangement syndrome, and (4) cervical headache syndrome. Definitions, characteristics, effects of movements and positioning, and treatment protocols for each syndrome are described in the following pages.

POSTURAL SYNDROME

Patients with postural syndrome are usually younger than 30 years of age, have sedentary occupations, and frequently are deconditioned. They develop pain that appears locally, usually adjacent to the midline of the spinal column. The pain is provoked by mechanical deformation of soft tissues, which occurs only when spinal segments are subjected to *prolonged* static loading of the joints at end range. This occurs most frequently when poor sitting or standing postures are adopted. They frequently complain of pain either separately or simultaneously in the cervical, thoracic, or lumbar areas.

Pain from postural syndrome is *never* induced by *movement*, is *never* referred, and is *never* constant. There is no pathology, no loss of movement, and there are no signs in this syndrome. *There is nothing to see.*

Movements are normal, and patients with this syndrome are sometimes described as being hypermobile. The only objective information appears on examination of posture *at the time of onset of pain*, when the patient is seen to adopt poor postures and to "hang" at the end range of movement.[8]

Pain from postural syndrome could arise from any of the soft tissues adjacent to the vertebral segments. It is probably ligamentous in origin. Described simply, postural pain appears eventually from overstretching of normal tissue.

Postural syndrome is named according to the sustained spinal end range posture producing the pain. For example, sustained extension, sustained flexion, sustained lateral shift, or a combination of these or other postures.

! CLINICAL PEARL

1. Patients with postural syndrome will seldom present to your office for care because their pain is diffuse, not debilitating, intermittent, and they can abolish it by changing positions.
2. Postural syndrome patients will have no complaints in the better/worse section of the subjective history except with prolonged positioning. All movements are fine.
3. You can usually begin to suspect this syndrome from the subjective history alone. You can test then your suspicion during clinical examination by testing for any movement loss or production of symptoms from repeated test movements. If either of those is present, the patient does *not* have postural syndrome.

DYSFUNCTION SYNDROME

Patients with dysfunction syndrome are usually older than 30 years of age, except where trauma can be identified as the original cause of the problem. They commonly exhibit poor posture and also are frequently deconditioned.

They insidiously develop pain, which appears locally, adjacent to the midline of the spinal column. The pain is provoked on attempting *full* movement, by mechanically deforming shortened soft tissues in segments that have reduced elasticity and movement. The pain is *always* felt at *end range* and *never* felt *during* the movement. With the ex-

ception of a patient with an adherent nerve root, pain from dysfunction is *never* referred.

The loss of movement evident in this syndrome stems from two common sources. The first and most common cause is reduced spinal mobility resulting from poor postural habits maintained during the first few decades of life. This is especially so when the individual is under-exercised. Poor postural habits allow adaptive shortening of certain structures. The result is a gradual reduction of mobility with aging. The movements are generally those sagittal movements essential for the maintenance of the very erect posture.

The second cause of reduced spinal mobility is contracture of fibrous collangenous scar tissue developed during repair following trauma. An inextensible scar can form within, or adjacent to, otherwise healthy surrounding elastic structures, causing reduced mobility.[9] The pain resulting from stretching of this inextensible scar appears *only* on attempting *full end range movement*. It is not possible to identify the structure causing the pain of dysfunction, but any of the soft tissues next to the vertebral column may adaptively shorten or may be damaged. Thus, the pain may result from adaptive shortening or injury to any of the ligamentous structures in the segment, from the intervertebral disc, apophyseal joints, superficial or deep muscles and their attachments, or spinal ligaments. The pain may also result from adherence of the nerve root or dural sleeve following severe prolapsed or disc bulging but this is very easy to distinguish.

Described simply, the pain of dysfunction is produced immediately by overstretching of shortened tissues.

The nomenclature for the types of dysfunctions is derived from direction where the *motion* is restricted by the shortened structures, as follows:

- Extension dysfunction (extension limited by shortened structures)
- Flexion dysfunction (flexion limited by shortened structures)
- Retraction dysfunction (retraction limited)
- Rotation dysfunction (rotation limited)
- Lateral flexion dysfunction (lateral flexion limited)

And, in the case of major cervical trauma or surgery any combination or all of the preceding findings can be present.

! CLINICAL PEARL

1. Dysfunction syndrome is not frequently seen in the office, but it is more frequent than postural syndrome. When seen, it is often secondary to another complaint and incidentally found while treating the other condition. These patients are *avoiders;* if not, they probably would not have developed the condition in the first place. So they usually try not to perform the task that produces the pain and consequently do not seek medical care.

2. The condition must be of 6-week's duration or longer. One direction of movement will produce the pain. It will happen *every* time but will *not last*. You can confirm a suspicion of dysfunction syndrome, by noting the following: in the movement loss section of your assessment form (see Figure 26–3), there *must* be movement *loss*; repeated test movements in the restricted movement will produce end range pain but will not remain worse; and there will not be rapid changes in pain or mechanics. If any of these are not present, the patient does not have a dysfunction syndrome.

DERANGEMENT SYNDROME

Patients with this syndrome are usually between 20 and 55 years of age. As with postural and dysfunction syndrome patients, they generally have poor sitting posture. The pain is usually sudden in onset. That is, in a matter of a few hours or over a day or two, they change from feeling completely normal to being significantly disabled. Quite frequently this syndrome appears for no apparent reason. The symptoms may be felt locally, adjacent to the midline of the spine, or may radiate and be referred distally in the form of pain, paresthesia, or numbness. The symptoms are produced, abolished, increased, or reduced and made better or worse by the fulfillment of certain movements or the maintenance of certain positions. Pain from derangement syndrome may change, with regard to the area affected, which may increase or may move from the right side of the neck to the left.

Pathology must always be suspected when the patient describes pain that changes position and radiates when he or she changes position or performs different movements. When the referred pain changes its shape or position, displacement within the intervertebral disc is changing its shape or position. This occurs with movement or sustained positioning.

Pain from derangement syndrome is frequently constant in nature. There may be no position in which the patient can find relief. The pain, therefore, may be present whether movement is performed or not, and this pain is usually described as an ache.

The ache is then made worse by movement in certain directions and reduced by movement in other directions.[10] In the derangement syndrome, especially in severe cases, gross loss of movement may occur. Also, in severe cases, deformities such as kyphosis and scoliosis are frequently seen. Sudden loss of spinal mobility and the sudden appearance of deformity in acute low back and neck pain may be compared to the sudden locking that may occur in the knee joint, where internal derangement of the meniscus is common.

The mechanism of internal derangement of the intervertebral disc is not fully understood. The notion that tissue originating from the innermost aspect of the intervertebral disc can be displaced toward, and escape through the annular wall is well documented.[11] It is likely that there exists an early stage of displacement when migration of tissue is in its infancy; when small displacements are able to be replaced; when the displacement is, in fact, reversible.[12] The existence of the uncovertebral joints, described in earlier sections of this book, may produce horizontal fissures in early adolescence, providing an escape route for nuclear material even at an early age.[12, 13]

In lumbar spine patients under 50 years of age, internal derangement of the spinal segments may result from excessive displacement of the fluid nucleus/annulus complex. In patients over 50, derangement may result from displacement of the degenerated annulus or the now fibrosed nucleus, or both. In a recent study of the cervical spine intervertebral discs, it was revealed that by age 35, the nuclear material has fibrosed, making nuclear migration impossible.[14] Therefore, in cervical patients over 35 years of age, the derangement would be similar to that of a post-50-year-old lumbar patient. In fact, Mercer et al[15] have argued that because the nucleus pulposus becomes fibrotic at an early age, it is not possible that derangement syndrome could occur in the cervical spine. They opine that McKenzie practitioners have just treated the cervical spine as if it were a small lumbar spine. Such thinking is in error, because the McKenzie protocol does not state that a derangement must be that of displaced free-flowing nuclear material but rather can be of a fibrosed nuclear material common to the cervical spine.

Displacement of the fluid nucleus/annulus complex disturbs the normal resting position of adjacent vertebrae and, if excessive, will force deformity. Displacement also affects the ability of the joint surfaces to move in their normal paths, and deviation to the right or left of the sagittal plane will result when flexion or extension is attempted.

Described simply, the pain of derangement occurs as a result of anatomical disruption and displacement within the intervertebral disc. Specific derangements are presented in Table 26–1.

! CLINICAL PEARL

1. While obtaining the history and during the clinical examination, remember that this syndrome is the great impostor. It can resemble almost any spinal condition. In the history, possible signs of derangement may be present throughout. For this reason, it is very difficult to disprove. Therefore, try to rule out every other possible condition until only derangement is left, then test its possibility.
2. Remember that derangement is the only syndrome in which centralization takes place.
3. In derangement, look for rapid changes in symptoms and or movement loss that are dependent on the movement or position.
4. To be a derangement, both symptoms and mechanics (movement loss) *must* be present.

Table 26–1: Derangements

Posterior Derangements 1–6

Derangement 1   *One is central*
  Central or symmetrical symptoms
  Rarely, scapula or shoulder symptoms
  No deformity

Derangement 2   *Two is kyphotic*
  Central or symmetrical symptoms
  With or without scapula, shoulder, or arm symptoms
  Deformity of kyphosis

Derangement 3   *Three is unilateral*
  Unilateral or asymmetrical symptoms
  With or without scapula, shoulder, or arm symptoms
  No deformity

Derangement 4   *Four is torticollic*
  Unilateral or asymmetrical symptoms
  With or without scapula, shoulder, or arm symptoms
  With deformity of acute wry neck or torticollis

Derangement 5   *Five is in the arm*
  Unilateral or asymmetrical symptoms
  With or without scapula or shoulder symptoms
  Forearm symptoms distal to the elbow
  No deformity

Derangement 6   *Six is all the worst*
  Unilateral or asymmetrical symptoms
  With or without scapula or shoulder symptoms
  With forearm symptoms distal to the elbow
  With deformity of cervical kyphosis, acute wry neck, or torti-
  collis.

Anterior Derangement

Derangement 7   *Seven is the*
  Symmetrical or asymmetrical symptoms   *reverse of the*
  No deformity   *first**

---

*Jacob's Deranged Poem.[16]

CERVICAL HEADACHE SYNDROME

One of the several anatomical characteristics that is unique to the cervical spine, when comparing it with the lumbar spine, is the upper cervical complex, which has been described in detail in prior sections of this book. It is this occiput, atlas, and axis network that we are concerned with when evaluating and treating cervical headache syndrome.

It is widely understood that headache is one of the most widely reported complaints of patients who visit health care practitioners.[17, 18] The study by Frykholm[17] reported that of all the headaches reported in clinical practice, headache of cervical origin was the most frequent. Eisenberg et al's now famous study on alternative medicine, published in the *New England Journal of Medicine* in 1993,[19] found that of 27 percent of headache sufferers sought treat-

ment other than conventional medicine, and that the most frequent nonmedical health care professional consulted for headaches was a chiropractor.

There are many causes of headache, and excluding nonmechanical pathologies is imperative before applying any mechanical treatments. Only headache of mechanical origin is discussed here. And, of mechanically derived headaches, only those related to the upper cervical spine are discussed.

Once nonpathological headaches are have been ruled out, the next step is to assess whether the source of the mechanical headache is the lower or upper cervical area. If it is determined that the source of the headache is the lower cervical spine, treatment can be the same as for the other three syndromes.

It has been shown that the articulations of occiput-atlas, atlas-axis, and C2–3 are responsible for most but not all symptoms arising from this syndrome.[20–26] However, Fryholm states that headache can arise from any of the segments of the cervical spine.[17]

Once it has been determined that the headache arises from the upper cervical area, the treatment is singular to this syndrome. The exact origin of the mechanical cervical headache remains unknown. Postulations have included postural stress, contracture, or malpositioning, to name but a few.

It is arduous to conceptualize internal derangement in anatomical terms at the occiput-atlas-axis junctions as there are no intervertebral discs at these levels. As previously mentioned, headaches can originate from the C2–3 disc level or even from lower levels. Postural factors certainly play a role in many patients, for the correction of the faulty posture abolishes the pain. However, in some cases, even after the correction of posture some symptoms remain. Only with the application of rather dynamic flexion exercises do the headaches decrease or cease. Many have postulated that a neural component is responsible for these symptoms. As yet, the mechanical cause is a conundrum.

The occurrence of cervical headaches is not strongly correlated with age or sex, although a tendency toward women has been observed.[27] Cervical headaches can resemble migraine and be of such frequency and severity that complete disturbance of the normal lifestyle can result.

The ache from a cervical headache is usually noticed at the base of the occiput and adjacent areas, and it can radiate to the temporal and frontal regions. It is commonly unilateral and can switch sides. The headaches tend to be intermittent and episodic in nature. Cervical headache behaves characteristically. It is nearly always affected by *position* but not always by *movement*. It commonly arises as the result of static loading at end range positions, which cause postural distortion. Absence of limitation of motion is a frequent finding. A great majority of sufferers state that prolonged sitting (e.g., driving or office desk work) is the precipitating posture. Adoption of the protruded head posture on a routine basis is likely the cause in the production of the headache. But only rarely will patients be aware of the relationship between the postural factors and their chronic headaches.

When one is dealing with the upper cervical complex, especially with the possibility of increased forces needed in treatment of this fragile area, two major complications must be tested for and eliminated as a possibility before initiating mechanical treatment. These are unsuspected fracture or instability and vertebrobasilar insufficiency. These conditions have been described in previous sections of this book and therefore are not discussed in detail here.

EFFECTS OF REPEATED MOVEMENTS ON THE FOUR SYNDROMES

EFFECTS ON POSTURAL SYNDROME

Movement and repeated movements will not produce or affect the presenting symptoms in patients with postural syndrome.

EFFECTS ON DYSFUNCTION SYNDROME

Movement in the direction that stretches adaptively shortened structures will reproduce the patient's pain at the end of existing range, as follows:

- The pain disappears as soon as the end range stress is released.
- Repetition does not make the patient progressively worse.
- The condition does not remain worse as a result.

EFFECTS ON DERANGEMENT SYNDROME

The theory that Robin McKenzie has discussed in his books on the lumbar spine[1] and cervical and thoracic spine[2] is that movement influencing the location or displacement of the lumbar nucleus pulposus within the intervertebral disc is the cornerstone of the derangement syndrome. Kramer[12] describes experiments carried out in vitro on both lumbar and cervical discs by Vogel and Stahl.[28, 29] They studied intradiscal movements during symmetrical and asymmetrical loading.

These authors found that during symmetrical and axial loading, the nucleus expands and is retained only by the elastic annulus fibrosis. The nucleus returns to its initial form and central location on removal of the pressure. However, in asymmetrical loading the central part of the disk containing the nucleus migrates toward the area of least load. Thus, in forward bending there is a posterior migration; in hyperextension, an anterior migration; and in lateral flexion, migration is opposite the direction of bending. The greatest migration took place within 3 minutes of loading and, with continued asymmetrical compression, the nucleus pulposus was observed to migrate slowly to the area of least load in a matter of hours.[28, 29] *It is important to note that similar experiments on cervical discs yielded the same results.*

These findings are in agreement with the results of the in vitro experiments by Adams and Hutton,[30] who described gradual disc prolapse as a result of off-center loading. They state: "Postures involving unequal loading of the intervertebral disc cause the nucleus pulposus to become situated in an ever increasing eccentric position."[30] Kramer goes on to note that with the removal of asymmetrical loading, the nucleus pulposus remains in a displaced condition and only very slowly returns to its original central location. But he further states that the time for the relocation to a more central position can be *accelerated by compression in the opposite direction* or by traction, and that, with increasing age, the risk of migration diminishes. With age-related loss of elasticity, the annulus becomes weakened and susceptible to injury. Fissures and ruptures develop, which allow the degenerated nucleus to migrate.[12]

Movement in the direction that increases accumulation of nuclear/annular material produces, increases, or peripheralizes the patient's symptoms such that:

- Repetition results in a progressively increasing derangement and makes the patient progressively worse
- The condition remains worse as a result

Movement in the opposite direction decreases, centralizes, or abolishes the patient's symptoms such that:

- Repetition results in a progressively reducing derangement and makes the patient progressively better.
- The condition remains better as a result.

EFFECTS ON CERVICAL HEADACHE SYNDROME

This syndrome has the same movement effects as derangement syndrome. The main difference is that cervical headache syndrome usually responds to sustained positioning more so than repetitive movements.

TREATMENT OF THE FOUR SYNDROMES

ROLE OF POSTURAL CORRECTION IN THE FOUR SYNDROMES

Postural correction is the main treatment for patients with postural syndrome. It is an important component of treatment for patients with dysfunction syndrome because prolonged positioning can produce adaptive shortening. And it is essential in the treatment of patients with derangement syndrome and cervical headache syndrome.

TREATMENT OF CERVICAL POSTURAL SYNDROME

The patient is taught to perform the slouch–overcorrect procedure (Fig. 26–2) three times daily, 5 to 15 times at each session, for 3 to 4 days, minimum, or longer if needed. It takes approximately 1 week to teach the patient proper positioning, and approximately 3 weeks before the patient adopts the postures automatically.

After a day or two of correct sitting, the patient should be experiencing different pain symptoms or discomfort (e.g., mid-trapezius ache or general mid-back discomfort). If the patient does not complain of new pain, it is likely he or she has not maintained the corrected position often and long enough. New pain should not last longer than 5 to 6 days.

Prolonged standing does not generally exacerbate symptoms in the upper thoracic and cervical spine, as does prolonged sitting and lying. The most common relaxed and slouched standing position causes the chest and thoracic spine to move posteriorly as the pelvis moves anteriorly. The correction is best achieved by lifting the chest and thoracic spine and retracting the head and neck. At the same time, the pelvis is tilted slightly backward.

TREATMENT OF CERVICAL DYSFUNCTION SYNDROME

By applying the appropriate movement, one can have a significant influence on the remodeling of tissue and, ideally, this should occur during the process of repair. The longer the time lapse between repair and initiation of the recovery of full function, the more consolidated the repair will be. This in turn will make the task of remodeling more difficult and will extend the recovery time.

Correction is achieved in 6 to 10 weeks, provided all circumstances are favorable and the patient is well directed. In all dysfunction situations, exercises for the restoration of movement must be performed about 5 to 15 times per session. Sessions should be repeated at 2- to 3-hour intervals throughout the day.[31] The following directions should be given to the patient:

- Maintain correct posture at all times and, at the end of each session, perform retraction and extension.
- If exercise does not produce some minor pain, the movement has not been performed far enough and to end range.
- The pain characteristic should be similar in nature to that produced when you stretch your finger fully into extension.
- Pain should subside 10 to 20 minutes after completion of exercise.
- If the pain lasts continuously and is still evident the next day, overstretching (or derangement) has taken place and the number of exercises in each sequence or frequency of sequence must be reduced.
- If stretching results in a rapid increase or peripheralization of pain, the procedure should be discontinued immediately. If you are unable to adhere strictly to the recommended exercise program, recovery of full function is likely to take longer.

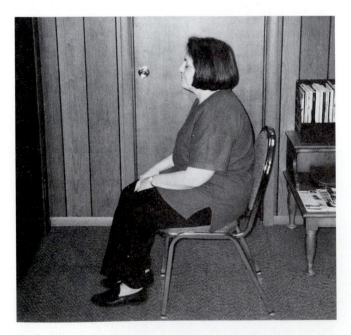

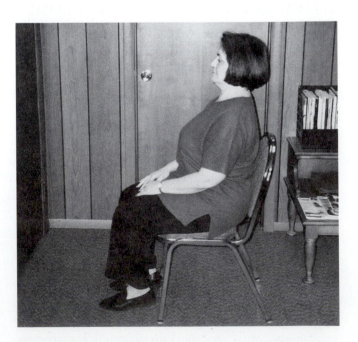

A   **B**

Figure 26–2. A. Slouch. **B.** Overcorrect.

TREATMENT OF CERVICAL DERANGEMENT SYNDROME

Movements or positions that reduce the displacement of the nuclear/annular material are referred to by Gary Jacob as the preferred loading strategy. The criteria for improvement (derangement reduction) are as follows:

- Symptoms abolish.
- Symptoms centralize.
- Symptoms decrease in intensity.
- Symptoms become intermittent.
- Symptoms decrease in frequency.
- Symptoms do not change but movement increases.

Treatment consists of the following four stages:

1. Reduction of the derangement, involving not more than one new procedure at any one session.
2. Maintenance of the reduction, through education regarding proper position in space when sitting, standing, and lying.
3. Recovery of function. Following successful and stable reduction of the derangement, it is important to introduce prohibited movements as soon as possible. Poor results occur if this is delayed.
4. Prevention of recurrence (prophylaxis) through education so patients fully understand their own potential to self-treat.

Test Movements for the Cervical Spine

The intensity and location of any symptom present is recorded prior to the performance of any movement. The assessment sheet shown in Figure 26–3 lists the test movements and positions to be performed. The production of pain during motion (PDM) or end range pain (ERP), or both, should be recorded. The patient then repeats the movement 10 or more times, always returning to the neutral or relaxed position. The maximum possible stretch is obtained during the last few movements. The test *movements* are as follows, with possible progression of forces included after the movement name in parentheses:

1. Protrusion—refer to Figure 26–4.
2. Retraction (no overpressure to patient overpressure to practitioner overpressure)—refer to Figure 26–5.
3. (a) Retraction, then extension (sitting)—refer to Figure 26–6A.
   (b) Retraction, then extension, then rotation (sitting)—refer to Figure 26–6B.
   (c) Retraction, then extension, supine lying (no overpressure to patient overpressure to practitioner pressure: traction/retraction)—refer to Figure 26–6C.

4. Lateral flexion (no overpressure to patient overpressure to practitioner overpressure)—refer to Figure 26–7.
5. Rotation (no overpressure to patient overpressure to practitioner over pressure)—refer to Figure 26–8.
6. Flexion (no overpressure to patient overpressure)—refer to Figure 26–9.

Cervical Static Mechanical Evaluation Test Postures

Some individuals will not experience provocation from the application of repeated movements and overpressure. In such patients, it is necessary to load the structure for a prolonged period of time before deformation is sufficient to reproduce the symptoms. Conversely, a prolonged period of time may be needed to reduce the deformation and for the symptoms to decrease or cease. Following are the sustained positioning tests performed, with the time frame for the position testing given in parentheses after:

1. Protrusion sitting (maximum of 3 minutes)
2. Retraction (maximum of 3 minutes)
3. Lying supine in retraction and extension (maximum of 3 minutes)
4. Lying prone in extension (maximum of 3 minutes), leaning on the elbows and resting the chin on the outstretched fingertips with the head facing forward and upward—refer to Figure 26–10.

Additional tests, if necessary, include similar tests for extremes of rotation and lateral flexion.

The test procedures for the cervical headache syndrome are as follows:

1. Sitting retraction (with progression of forces to overpressure and practitioner overpressure if needed)—as shown in Figure 26–5.
2. Flexion (with overpressure as needed)—as shown in Figure 26–9.
3. Rotation (with overpressure as needed)—as shown in Figure 26–8.

TREATMENT OF CERVICAL HEADACHE SYNDROME

Treatment is similar for patients with derangement syndrome in that postural correction is performed along with sustained or repetitive movements in the preferred loading strategy indicated by the objective testing procedures. If no lasting change in headache can be achieved after 2 weeks of mechanical loading strategies as described in the next section, the patient should be regarded as having a nonmechanical headache. In this case, the patient should be referred for further investigation and perhaps a trial of migraine medication, if this has not already been provided.

EXAMINATION

POSTURE

Sitting: *Good/Fair/Poor*   Standing: *Good/Fair/Poor*   Protruded head: *Yes/No*   Torticollis: *Right/Left/Nil*

Other Observations: ....

MOVEMENT LOSS	maj	mod	min	nil		maj	mod	min	nil
Protrusion					Sidebending (R)				
Flexion					Sidebending (L)				
Retraction					Rotation (R)				
Extension					Rotation (L)				

TEST MOVEMENTS: Describe effects on present pain - produces, abolishes, increases, decreases, centralises, peripheralises better, worse, no better, no worse, no effect

	PDM	ERP
Describe pretest pain sitting		
PRO		
Rep PRO		
RET		
Rep RET		
RET EXT		
Rep RET EXT		
Describe pretest pain lying		
RET		
Rep RET		
RET EXT		
Rep RET EXT		
(If required)		
SB (R)		
Rep SB (R)		
SB (L)		
Rep SB (L)		
ROT (R)		
Rep ROT (R)		
ROT (L)		
Rep ROT (L)		
FLEX		
Rep FLEX		

STATIC TESTS If required

Protrusion ....   Flexion ....

Retraction ....   Extension: sitting/prone/supine ....

NEUROLOGICAL

Motor Deficit: ....   Reflexes: ....

Sensory Deficit: ....   Dural signs: ....

OTHER

Shoulder girdle: ....

Special tests: ....

CONCLUSION

Posture   *Dysfunction*   *Derangement No.*   *Trauma*

Other ....

PRINCIPLE OF TREATMENT

Posture Correction ....

Flexion ....

Extension ....

Lateral ....

Other ....

BY PERMISSION OF THE McKENZIE INSTITUTE INTERNATIONAL
ORTHOPEDIC PHYSICAL THERAPY PRODUCTS, PO BOX 47009, MINNEAPOLIS, MN 555447 (612) 553-0452   ©1993, OPTP, Inc.

Figure 26–3. Cervical spine assessment sheet, side 2.

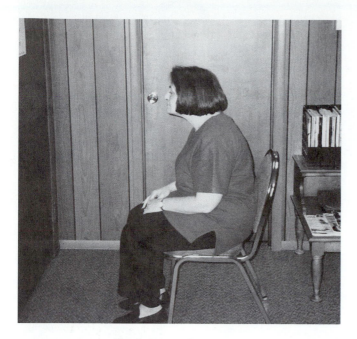

Figure 26–4. Protrusion.

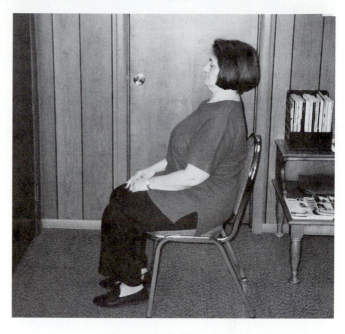

Figure 26–5. Retraction.

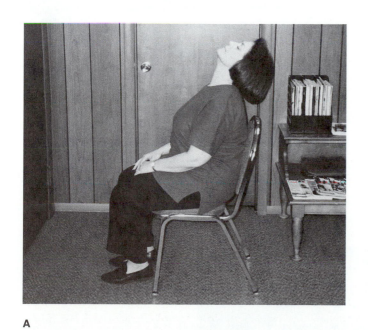

A

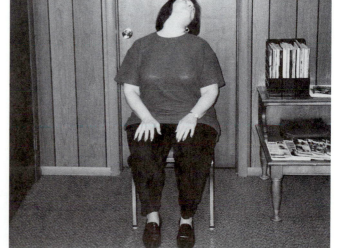

B

Figure 26–6. A. Retraction, then extension. **B.** Retraction, then extension, then rotation.

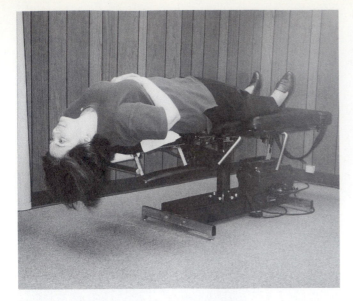

C

Figure 26–6 continued. C. Retraction, then extension in supine lying position.

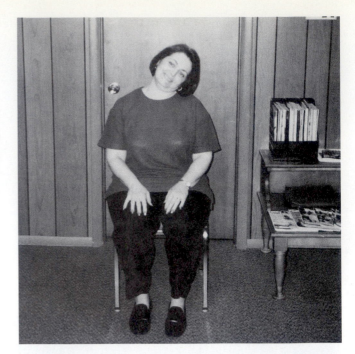

Figure 26–7. Lateral flexion.

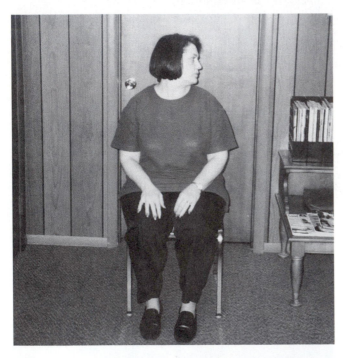

Figure 26–8. Rotation.

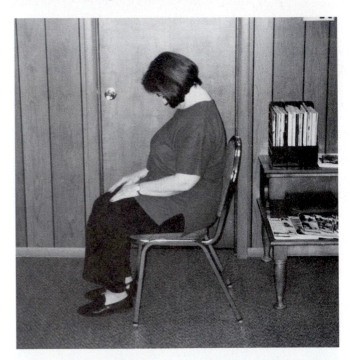

Figure 26–9. Flexion.

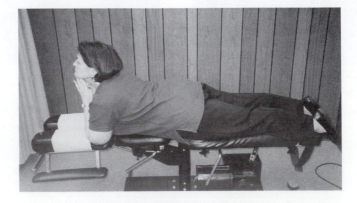

Figure 26–10. Prone in extension.

1. Try sustained positions initially, as most headaches of this type are produced by sustained positioning and they respond better to such.
2. Retraction with flexion overpressure is often the most effective technique.
3. If there is no response upon completion of the end range test procedures listed in the accompanying text, it is unlikely the headache is of mechanical origin.

PROGRESSION OF TREATMENT FORCES

The application of practitioner technique is a logical sequence based on making the correct mechanical diagnosis and then subjecting the patient to a series of mechanical pressures. These pressures are first self-generated, then externally applied as the need arises. As reduction fails to progress, more force is required. The sequence is as follows:

1. *Mechanical Diagnosis.* The correct mechanical diagnosis is essential for appropriate treatment. The effects of the proceedure or direction of applied forces depend on the mechanical diagnosis. In the case of derangement syndrome, use the movement that reduces the pain. In dysfunction syndrome, use the movement that produces the pain.
2. *Self-treatment procedures.* Explore the sagittal movements initally, then proceed to other movement planes as the results dictate.
3. *Overpressure.* Overpressure with an external force could include a towel, the edge of a chair, or practioner assistance.
4. *Mobilization Procedures/Practitioner Techniques.* Mobilization is more specific and more localized than overpressure. It entails a rhythmic, low-velocity, high-amplitude movement. Follow up with patient movement and posture control.
5. *Manipulation Procedures/Practitioner Techniques.* Manipulation is the last progression. It entails a high-velocity, low-amplitude movement. The force is applied at the end of the existing active end range. Follow up with self-treatment and posture control.

The progressions for application of force in modern mechanical therapy are as follows[2]:

Static Patient-generated Force
  1. Positioning in mid-range—refer to Figure 26–11A.
  2. Positioning at end range—refer to Figure 26–11B.
Dynamic Patient-generated Force
  1. Patient motion in mid-range—refer to Figure 26–12A.

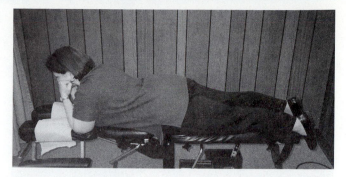

A

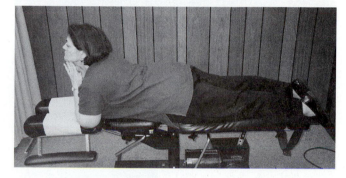

B

Figure 26–11. A. Positioning in mid-range—prone in extension. **B.** Positioning at end range—prone in extension.

  2. Patient motion to end range—refer to Figure 26–12B.
  3. Patient motion to end range with overpressure—refer to Figure 26–12C.
Practitioner-generated Forces
  1. Patient motion to end range with therapist overpressure—refer to Figure 26–13A.
  2. Practioner overpressure, mobilization—refer to Figure 26–13B.
  3. Practioner overpressure, manipulation—refer to Figure 26–13C.
  4. Traction: manual, intermittent, or sustained—refer to Figure 26–13D.

1. These techniques represent a progression of forces. Some benefit should be seen in the earlier portion of the progression before moving to more force.
2. Mobilization should be the premanipulative test before progressing to manipulation. Remember that mobilization can be discontinued, but once manipulation is begun it cannot be stopped.
3. Practioner techniques are frequently needed in mechanical therapy. But the ultimate goal is patient empowerment through self-treatment. Therefore, always return to self-treatment and posture control after a practioner technique.

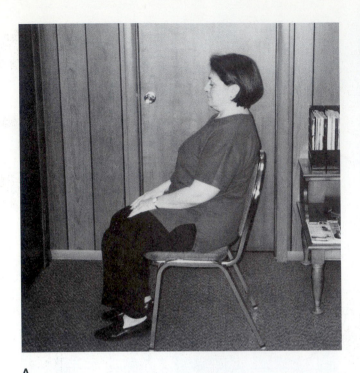

A

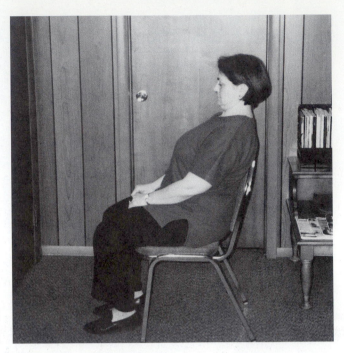

B

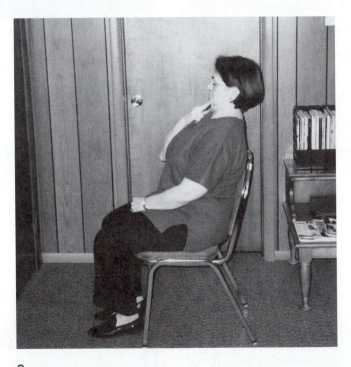

C

Figure 26–12. A. Patient motion in mid-range—retraction. **B.** Patient motion at end range—retraction. **C.** Patient motion to end range with overpressure—retraction with overpressure.

PREDISPOSING AND PRECIPITATING FACTORS FOR CERVICAL SPINE PAIN

The predisposing factors causing pain in the cervical spine have not been studied as extensively as those relating to the low back, but it is likely they are similar.[32] The three most common predisposing factors are (1) poor sitting postures, (2) frequent flexion of the neck, and (3) loss of extension of the lower cervical spine.

Poor sitting postures are the most common cause for failure of the articular supportive structures in the spinal column. They, therefore, become the number 1 predispos-

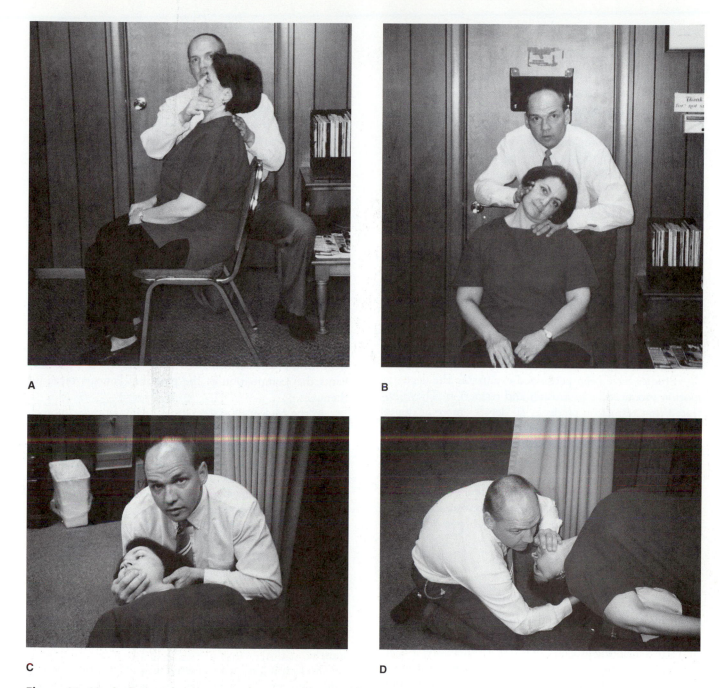

Figure 26–13. A. Patient motion to end range with practitioner overpressure—retraction with practitioner overpressure. **B.** Practitioner overpressure, mobilization—lateral flexion mobilization. **C.** Practitioner overpressure, manipulation—rotation manipulation. **D.** Traction—manual, intermittent, or sustained; traction, then retraction, then extension, supine.

ing factor in the development of mechanical disorders of the back and neck. Poor sitting postures lead to protruded head carriage and are commonly reported causes of neck pain. Static loading in faulty sitting or lying postures will lead eventually to problems within the cervical spine.

Frequency of flexion is the second most common predisposing factor in the production of cervical spine symptoms. This pertains to the frequency that the neck is flexed in daily living.

The first factor of prolonged sitting leads to postural static loading at end range of flexion in the lower and extension in the upper cervical segments. When this is added to the second factor, frequency of flexion, it is inevitable that creep, deformation, and eventually damage and displacement will follow.

Precipitating factors are such that lateral flexion or rotation movements of the head and neck that are performed while the head is in a protruded position, especially prolonged protrusion, can cause immediate symptoms. Trauma is also a common cause of cervical spine problems and is discussed at length elsewhere in this book. Adams and Hutton[30] have also demonstrated that the nocturnal imbibation of fluid causes the disc to become stiffer, placing the patient at risk until compressive forces reduce the fluid volume. This finding pertains especially to the first few hours after awakening, and patients should be educated to use caution during this time frame and avoid prolonged end range positions or extreme movements.

RETRACTION AND PROTRUSION

A unique feature of the upper cervical complex is the performance of translational movements, retraction and protrusion. Moffat, in his cinema-radiographic recordings of the motions of the cervical spine,[33] illustrated that in retraction of the head, the upper cervical segments flex and the lower segments extend. Protrusion is just the opposite, with the upper cervical segments extending and the lower segments flexing.

Studies have been performed evaluating the degree of motion produced by protrusion and retraction. They illustrated that retraction produces 10 degrees more flexion of the occiput than does flexion of the entire cervical spine. Protrusion produces 10 degrees more extension of the occiput than just extension of the cervical spine alone.[34]

The effect of motion on the upper cervical spine that these two translational movements produce is integral to the primary causation, treatment, and contraindications to treatment of both cervical trauma and cervical headache syndrome.

TRAUMA

Mechanical therapy applied to healing connective tissue and to remodeling scar tissue can influence the makeup and stress-adapting property of the scar. Therefore, it is imperative that after injury, some type of controlled movement be performed in a gentle, ordered fashion and on a regular basis.

THE ROLE OF THE McKENZIE PARADIGM IN REHABILITATION

The McKenzie system distinguishes itself among rehabilitation approaches by means of the criteria upon which it predicates evaluation and treatment methods. The McKenzie model accounts for spinal complaints by classifying the mechanical and symptomatic responses to spinal loading (forces applied by means of movement and positioning). It is important to watch and listen to the fluctuating manner in which patients report how movements and positionings of their spines affect them. The McKenzie approach explores activity-related solutions to activity-related complaints, employing the criteria of mechanical and symptomatic responses to loading to evaluate, treat, and provide prevention.

McKenzie protocols permit the employment of a *rehabilitation* approach during the acute phase of injury.[3] Rehabilitation utilizes active therapies to achieve restoration, self-sufficiency, and independent functioning skills. The clinician's responsibility is to introduce active therapy as soon as possible, and to identify cases in which active therapy is ineffective or inappropriate as soon as possible. The patient also has a responsibility to participate actively in exploring the potential benefits of self-generated movements.

Certain criteria of spinal evaluation and treatment are based on preconceived notions regarding the cause of common spinal complaints. The leading preconceived notions are that of inflammation and pain of muscular origin. Prescriptions for rest and use of medication are often the preferred strategies when treating inflammation and pain of muscular origin; exercise is frequently forbidden. However, treatment predicated on such preconceived notions prevents the examination of the potential benefits of active therapies.

In the McKenzie system, true inflammation is appreciated as a chemical event that would not be relieved greatly by mechanical factors. Contradictory to this, acute and chronic spinal complaints commonly included a history of certain activities, movements, or positioning that relieve the symptoms, suggesting the role of inflammation may not be valid. Prolonged rest, used to treat professed inflammation, promotes disability.[31]

Muscle spasm is the most commonly acknowledged pain of muscular origin. This notion leads to inactivity as the prescription to "relax" the spasm. Passive modalities and procedures are employed to this end as well. A diagnosis of "chronic spasm" sentences patients to prolonged inactivity (disability). True muscle spasm is uncommon since spasm is held to be a violent, involuntary contraction of a muscle.

McKenzie protocols determine, early in the course of care, who are the responders and nonresponders to mechanical therapies. Mechanical therapies include posture training, exercises, mobilization, manipulation, and advice pertaining to activities of daily living. If self-generated movements or clinician mobilization in all movement planes fails to provide relief, manipulation or other mechanical therapies are less likely to be of benefit. In fact, upon the application of progression of forces, if all movements or positions in all directions increase and worsen the patient's complaints, the clinician should suspect that a deleterious process is present that is not amenable to mechanical therapies. For patients who are identified as amenable to mechanical therapies, the clinician's task is to determine the preferred loading strategy, to begin active therapies immediately, and to avoid passive care and rest. This involves deciding which loading tactics to avoid, which to pursue, and when it is safe to reintroduce a previously avoided stratagem.

SPINAL MANIPULATION, REHABILITATION, AND McKENZIE PROTOCOLS

Current wisdom views manipulation as an efficacious approach worthy of consideration for acute, activity-related spinal complaints. The same cannot be said for passive nonmovement modalities that target inflammation or spasm, or both. The efficacy of spinal manipulation for acute conditions suggests that:

- Movement is of potential benefit for the acute spine.
- Aggressive movement is of potential benefit for the acute spine.
- Aggressive movement to end range is of potential benefit for the acute spine.

Manipulation, as in exercise, is a movement therapy. Both have been classified as forms of activation.

McKenzie employs a system of prescriptive exercise based on principles similar to that of spinal manipulation (i.e., end range loading). McKenzie protocols explore the mechanical and symptomatic responses to end range loading prior to introducing manipulative forces.

These protocols employ manipulation when patient self-generated movement to end range is illustrated to be of some, but incomplete, benefit. If self-generated end range loading results in complete recovery, manual therapies are not needed. And if only a parital response to self-generated loading is attained, the examiner has a good understanding of the directions in which to manipulate. In fact, the progression of forces would involve an interim technique before manipulation; that is, mobilization. Mobilization involves effectively taking the joint to physiological end range. If this resolves the complaints, there is no need to proceed to manipulation. The premanipulative end range mobilization testing illustrates the mechanical and symptomatic responses one can expect from end range loading.

Following is a list, from an article by Jacob, of eight effective interventions for physical complaints. These interventions apply to the application of the McKenzie protocol in acute as well as chronic patients.[32]

- Early activation with selected structured activities, including activities of daily living, that are appropriate to the individual's level of functioning
- Emphasis on the individual taking an active role in rehabilitation and sharing responsibility with practioners
- Emphasis on improvement in physical function and productivity, through graded mastery, and reduction

in disability, rather than only symptomatic relief or simply reducing illness behavior
- Strict reinforcement of safety practices and appropriate worker behavior
- Improvement of cognitive and behavioral skills, including activity control of symptoms and not vice versa (symptoms controlling the activity)
- Minimal time away from the workplace
- Education about prevention and management of work injury and chronic pain
- Analgesics and passive modalities used sparingly, if at all

! CLINICAL PEARL

1. McKenzie evaluation is an excellent "first strike" when it comes to rehabilitation of spinal complaints. The clinician can quickly and efficiently determine whether the patient will be amenable to movement or position therapy.
2. In the case of injured tissue, movement is to be initiated as soon as the inflammatory phase has been completed, usually within 5 days postinjury. The movements need to be performed safely, to end range, and regularly into the remodeling stage to minimize contraction of the scar and reorganize the collagen fibers in a lengthwise manner that produces optimum healing and strength.
3. Patients who can treat the condition themselves derive much greater benefit. Rehabilitation that can be performed at home is more convenient and thus may be performed more frequently. Also, it empowers patients by giving them control of their health, making the process more effacacious and prophylactic education/treatment much more proficient.

This brings us back full circle to the opening quotes from Robin McKenzie and Gary Jacob on the benefits of empowerment.

CLINICAL PRESENTATIONS

Three cases are presented next which illustrate the use of the McKenzie system in the evaluation and treatment of cervical spine pain.

CASE 1

Subjective History
The patient is a 20-year-old female clerical worker whose work duties involve remaining in one position for long periods of time, usually sitting. The patient describes central neck and headache pain that often travels down the entire spine to the lumbar region. She has not missed any work and has not discontinued any activities due to these symptoms.

The symptoms have been present for months and have gradually worsened to the point where they have become more frequent and are produced more rapidly. When asked how the symptoms began, the patient responds "for no apparent reason." The pain originated in the neck and is intermittent.

Guaranteed to produce the pain is prolonged sitting. The movement or position that helps the pain is to move out of the sitting position. She has no difficulty rising from sitting, and other movements and positions will not produce the symptoms. There are no mechanics (movement loss) present when she has the pain or when getting out of the painful position. She is better on the move and worse in one position (sitting only). Her diurnal cycle illustrates that she is fine when awakening and gradually gets worse as the day goes on. By the end of the cycle, she is better upon leaving work.

She has no disturbed sleep. Cough, sneeze, and swallow are negative. There is no dizziness, tinnitus, or nausea.

She has no prior incidences today, although she noticed some discomfort earlier in the day. It was short lived and resolved as soon as she changed positions. She has had no prior treatment. She takes no medicine and has had no diagnostic tests.

Clinical Examination

The patient had poor sitting posture during the subjective history, during which she illustrated a protuded head positioning. Standing posture was good.

Movement loss evaluation shows no movement loss in all arcs (all six normal arcs plus protusion and retraction).

Repeated movement testing is unremarkable in all tests, with no pain during motion or end range pain produced.

Static testing (with different head positions) was negative. Neurological testing was negative for all tests.

Conclusion

Postural syndrome—prolonged slouch sitting.

Treatment

The recommended treatment is postural correction through the use of a lumbar roll to maintain a retracted head position; instruction to change position regularly (approximately every 30 minutes or less if possible); and instruction in the slouch-overcorrect exercise so that the patient can learn her optimum sitting position without a roll.

The patient should be seen again in approximately 2 weeks to check postural changes. If necessary, the patient should be scheduled for a 1- to 2-month follow-up to check postural correction maintenance.

> ! **CLINICAL PEARL**
>
> 1. In Case 1, there is *no* movement loss present, repeated test movements and static positions *do not* produce the pain (except for the prolonged slouch sitting position), and the pain is intermittent.

2. Slouch sitting during the taking of the subjective history (25 to 40 minutes) may be negative. If so, ask the patient, "If sitting produces your pain, how long must you usually sit before producing your pain?" If this is a postural syndrome, the patient will usually respond that it is longer than they sat during the subjective history.

CASE 2

Subjective History

This 35-year-old male machinist was involved in a motor vehicle accident. His postures and stresses at work entail sitting, standing, and repetitively using his arms for fine manipulation. At home he usually watches television and does yard work. He has not discontinued any of his activities because of his condition.

His pain pattern encompasses the right posterior neck into the right medial border of the trapezius muscle. He has had the pain for 3 months since being a passenger in a car that was struck by another car on the passenger side. The pain is unchanging. The symptoms began in the neck and are intermittent.

Guaranteed to produce his pain is to turn his head to the right. Guaranteed to make the pain better is to avoid turning the head to the right. He denies any pain when bending the head, sitting, lying, and rising from lying. There is no difference in his symptoms during the diurnal cycle.

He denies any disturbed sleep. Cough, sneeze, and swallow are negative. His gait is normal. He disavows any history of dizziness, tinnitus, nausea, or motion sickness. He has had no previous episodes of neck pain.

Previous treatment for this condition included a visit to the emergency department immediately postaccident and three visits with his family physician in which prescription anti-inflammatory and analgesic medications were given. He took the medication for the first 3 to 4 weeks, then discontinued it. Plain film cervical spinal X-rays were taken in the emergency department and were read as normal.

The patient's general health is good. He denies any recent or major surgery. He has had no other accidents and has had no unexplained weight loss.

Clinical Examination

Sitting posture was poor during the subjective history, and a protruded head position was noted. Standing posture was good. No torticollis was present.

Movement loss evaluation revealed no movement loss present with the exception of right rotation, which the patient stated was moderate to severe.

Prior to any test movements or static positioning, the patient had no pain. Repeated test movements were unremarkable, except for right rotation (RR). This movement produced pain at end range only and was no worse afterward.

Static testing with the head in different positions was unremarkable. Neurological testing was negative.

Conclusion

Dysfunction syndrome—right rotation.

Treatment

The recommended treatment is postural correction (use of a lumbar roll to maintain a retracted head position) and repeated RR stretching of the adaptively shortened tissue to end range pain (optimally 10 to 15 times per 2 to 3 hours per day for 6 weeks or greater).

The patient should be evaluated 2 to 3 times for the first week before concluding that this is an inactive dysfunction. Once it is clear that this is an inactive dysfunction, the patient should be scheduled for treatment every 2 weeks for 6 to 8 weeks until there is no movement loss present and pain has been abolished.

! CLINICAL PEARL

1. This condition *must* be present for a minimum of 6 weeks.
2. Movement loss *must* be present.
3. End range pain *must* be produced in the direction of movement loss.
4. The pain must be no worse afterward.

CASE 3

Subjective History

The patient is a 40-year-old clerical worker whose postures and stresses at work involve prolonged sitting, walking, reaching, and typing. At home she runs 12 to 15 miles per week and lifts weights 3 times per week. She has not missed any work as yet but has had to stop her running and weight lifting over the past 3 weeks due to the worsening of her symptoms.

Her symptoms involve left neck and shoulder pain that radiates down her left upper extremity to produce numbness and tingling in her left hand and first three digits. The condition appeared for no apparent reason 6 months ago and originated in her neck. She has constant neck pain but intermittent upper extremity symptoms.

Guaranteed to produce or increase her symptoms are bending her head up or down and turning her head left. Afterward the pain lasts. She is also worse when sitting, rising from lying down, as the day progresses and in the afternoon, and when still. She is improved when lying down, in the morning, and while on the move, but the improvement does not last. She believes that her neck and upper extremity symptoms are related. Upon questioning, she states that she has movement loss associated with the symptoms and that when the symptoms are worse, her movement loss is also worse. When her symptoms are decreased, her movement loss is less.

She states that her sleep is disturbed because of the condition. She relates that she uses two pillows to sleep and sleeps in the prone and right and left side positions.

Cough, sneeze, and swallow are negative. She denies any dizziness, tinnitus, nausea, or motion sickness being present with this episode.

She reports that she has had between 1 and 5 previous episodes of neck pain over the past 10 years, but they were self-limiting within a few days. She denies any previous upper extremity complaints.

Treatment prior to this episode included visits to her family physician, who prescribed a muscle relaxant and anti-inflammatory medication. He referred her to a physical therapist, who performed passive modalities consisting of ultrasound and moist heat packs for 3 weeks. She was then referred to a chiropractor for spinal manipulations over a month's duration. The medication and manipulation gave temporary relief. The physical therapy had no effect.

She was then referred for a magnetic resonance imaging scan of the cervical spine, which revealed a bulging disc of moderate size. An electromyogram was performed, which disclosed a mild median nerve compromise at the wrist.

Her general health is excellent, and the only medication she is currently taking are the two previously described. She denies any recent or major surgery. She has had no accidents. She denies any unexplained weight loss.

Clinical Examination

Sitting posture was poor during the subjective history, and the patient presented a protruded head position. Standing posture was good, and no torticollis was present.

Movement loss evaluation revealed minimal flexion loss. The patient stated she had moderate retraction, left sidebending, and left rotation loss. She confirmed a major loss of extension to be present.

Slouch sitting during the subjective history increased her neck pain and produced her left upper extremity symptoms complete to the numbness of her three digits. Sitting erect with a retracted head posture abolished her upper extremity symptoms and decreased her neck pain.

Her pretest pain included left neck pain with numbness and tingling into the forearm of the left upper extremity.

Since sitting erect with a retracted head posture gave temporary relief, the repeated test movements were begun with retraction. Repeated retraction produced end range pain, but she was no worse afterward. Retraction with extension produced end range pain. Repeated retraction (to 10 repetitions) decreased the forearm and arm symptoms, but the improvement did not remain. Retraction with extension to 20 repetitions abolished the forearm symptoms, and the improvement remained while arm and neck symptoms increased. Retraction with extension to 30 repetitions abolished the arm symptoms, and they remained better while the neck pain increased and remained worse. The same movement to 40 repetitions resulted in no change in the present symptoms.

Re-examination of her movement loss revealed an increase in mobility of her retraction, extension, and left rotation.

Neurological examination was unremarkable.

Conclusion

Derangement 5, with a preferred loading strategy to retraction with extension.

Treatment

The recommended treatment is postural correction with a lumbar roll to maintain a retracted head position, and retraction with extension to be performed throughout the day.

❗ CLINICAL PEARL

1. Derangements can and do elicit variable answers on the subjective history (e.g., they can be constant or intermittent, be present for 1 day or 1 year, illustrate being worse on all the better/worse questions or on none of the questions).
2. Movement loss *must* be present in conjunction with symptoms.
3. This is the only syndrome in which centralization can take place.
4. As shown in Case 3, changes can be rapid.
5. Even though the patient in Case 3 had a unilateral condition and had movement loss in all planes, rotation or lateral flexion was not attempted because sagittal plane movements produced the desired results.

6. If, on the follow-up office visit, the patient's symptoms are no better, then the next step may be progression of forces in retraction with extension, or performing the movement unloaded (supine). The practitioner could also explore the other movement planes.

CONCLUSION

McKenzie therapy is an easily understandable, active care treatment program that, because it provides rapid results, is an excellent "first strike" for cervical spine rehabilitation. Patients are empowered through this therapy to take control of their health; they are not just active participants in care, they *are* the therapists. Therefore, the integral ingredient in this treatment program is *education*. In treatment of cervical spine patients, it is wise to remember the old Chinese proverb: "Give a person a fish and you feed them for a day. But teach them to fish and you feed them for life."

ACKNOWLEDGEMENTS

I wish to thank Robin McKenzie and the International McKenzie Institute for allowing me to use the cervical spine assessment sheet and the centralization figure; Gary Jacob for allowing me to use his poem and published material; and Ann Marsiglio for being my model in the photographs in the chapter.

REFERENCES

1. McKenzie RA. *The Lumbar Spine: Mechanical Diagnosis and Therapy.* Waikanae, New Zealand: Spinal Publications; 1981.
2. McKenzie RA. *The Cervical and Thoracic Spine: Mechanical Diagnosis and Therapy.* Waikanae, New Zealand: Spinal Publications; 1990.
3. Long AL. The centralization phenomenon: Its usefulness as a predictor of outcome in conservative treatment of chronic low back pain. (A pilot study.) *Spine* 1995;20(23):2513–2521.
4. Pople IK, Griffith HB. Prediction of extruded fragment in lumbar disc patients from clinical presentations. *Spine* 1994;19:156–158.
5. Kuslich SD, Ulstrom CL. The origin of low back pain and sciatica: A microsurgical investigation. In: *Microsurgery of the Lumbar Spine. Principles and techniques in Spine Surgery.* Rockville, Md: Aspen; 1990:1–7.
6. Smith MJ, Wright V. Sciatica and the intervertebral disc. *J Bone Joint Surg* 1958;40A:1401.
7. April C, Medcalf R, Donelson R, Grant W. Discographic outcomes predicted by the centralization of pain and directional preference: A prospective blinded study. Presented at the ISSLS, June 18–22, 1995.
8. Majeske C, Buchanan C. Quantitative description of two sitting postures, with and without a lumbar support pillow. *Phys Ther* 1984;64:1531–1535.
9. Morrison J. Tissue response to injury III—Pain. *Curr Orthop* 1987;1:284–289.
10. Donelson R, Grant W, Kamps C, Medcalf R. Pain response to sagittal end-range spinal motion: A prospective, randomized multicentered trial. *Spine* 1991;16:S206–212.
11. Adams MA, McNall DS. Prolapsed intervertebral disc, a hyperflexion injury. *Spine* 1992;7(3):184–191.
12. Kramer J. *Intervertebral Disc Diseases: Causes, Diagnosis, Treatment, Prophylaxis.* 2nd ed. New York, NY: Theime; 1990.

13. Tondury G. Entwidklungsgeschiehte und Fehlbildungen der Wirbelsaule. In: *Die Wirbelsaule in Forschurg und Praxis*, Bd 7 hrsg. von H Junghanns. Stuggart: Hippokrates; 1958.

14. Isu T, Iwasaki Y, Miyaska K, et al. A reappraisal of the diagnosis in cervical disc disease: The posterior longitudinal ligament perforated or not. *Neuroradiology* 1986;28:215–220.

15. Mercer SR, et al. Morphology of the cervical intervertebral disc: Implications for McKenzie's model of the disc derangement syndrome. *Man Ther* 1996;2:76–81.

16. Jacob G. The McKenzie Paradigm, Cervical and Thoracic Spine. Syllabus for Chiropractic Rehabilitation Courses.

17. Wyke B. The neurology of low back pain. In: MIV Jayson, ed. *The Lumbar Spine and Back Pain*. 2nd ed. Turnbridge Wells, England: Pitman Medical; 1980.

18. Fryholm R. The clinical picture. In: C Hirsch, Y Zotterman, eds. *Cervical Pain*. Oxford: Pergamon Press; 1971.

19. Eisenberg DM, Kessler RC, et al. Unconventional medicine in the United States—prevalence, costs, and patterns of use. *N Engl J Med* 1993;328:246–252.

20. Bogduk N. Innervation and pain patterns of the cervical spine. In: R Grant, ed. *Physical Therapy of the Cervical and Thoracic Spine*. New York, NY: Churchill Livingstone; 1988.

21. Edeling JS. The true cervical headache. *S Afr Med J* 1982;62:531.

22. Ehni G, Benner B. Occipital neuralgia and the C1–2 arthrosis syndrome. *J Neurosurg* 1984;61:961.

23. Jull G, Bogduk N, Marsland A. The accuracy of manual diagnosis for cervical zygapophysial joint pain syndromes. *Med J Australia* 1988;148;233–236.

24. Lewit K. Ligament pain and anteflexion headache. *Eur Neurol* 1971;5:365.

25. Sjaastad O, Saunte C, Hovdahl H, et al. "Cervicogenic headache." An hypothesis. *Cephalalgia* 1983;3:249.

26. Trevor-Jones R. Osteoarthiritis of the paravertebral joints of the second and third cervical vertebrae as a cause of occipital headache. *S Afr Med J* 1964;38:392.

27. McKenzie RA. Personal records, 1974.

28. Vogel G. Experimentelle Untersuchungen zur Mobeltat des Nucleus Pulposis in Lumbalen Bandscheiben. Dissertation. Düsseldorf, 1977.

29. Stahl C. Experimentelle Untersuchungen zur Biomechanik der Halswirbelsäule. Dissertation. Düsseldorf, 1977.

30. Adams MA, Hutton WC. Gradual disc prolapse. *Spine* 1985;10(6):524–531.

31. Allan DB, Waddell G. An historical perspective on low back pain and disability. *Acta Orthop Scand* 1989;60(suppl 234).

32. Jacob, G. The McKenzie protocol and the demands of rehabilitation. *Calif Chiro Assoc J* 1991;October:29,38.

33. Moffatt EA. The human neck: Anatomy, injury mechanisms and biomechanics. Society of Automotive Engineers, 1979;SP-438,31–36.

34. Penning L. Normal movements of the cervical spine. *AJR* 1978;30:137.

CHAPTER 27

Patient Education

RONALD J. TYSZKOWSKI

"The man who listens to Reason is lost: Reason enslaves all whose minds are not strong enough to master her."

—George Bernard Shaw

INTRODUCTION

Patient education can be frustrating to the clinician, as it is the area over which he or she has the least control. It is easy for the clinician to explain and demonstrate to the patient exercise and lifestyle activities. However, ultimately, it is up to the patient to understand what he or she is being told, to perform the home exercises, or to change his or her activities. Oftentimes, the only way of gauging to what extent this has been accomplished is the patient's self report.

Regardless of these problems, patient education is critical to the success of any treatment protocol. Proper education concerning home exercises, activities of daily living, and proper posture techniques often succeeds where the best clinician-applied treatment fails.

This chapter introduces several different categories of patient education, including posture training, ergonomics, and home exercise. All of these can significantly affect the prognosis and course of acute and chronic cervical syndromes.

POSTURE TRAINING

Proper posture dictates proper musculoskeletal function and actually can affect the entire person, including mood, blood pressure, pulse, and lung capacity. In fact, it can be argued that through these mechanisms, posture affects autonomic function and, ultimately, organism homeostasis.[1] Poor posture can develop as a result of obesity, weakened muscles, emotional tension, poor postural habits, and, sometimes, improper design of task elements (e.g., a computer workstation). Non-neutral postures are known to contribute significantly to cervical pain and trauma and should be avoided.[2]

It is clear that the clinician must have an effective method of managing the problem of poor posture, particularly in the care of cervical spine syndromes. The challenge he or she is faced with is how to do it correctly and easily.

Conscious or active change in posture (i.e., "straightening up") rarely lasts and often simply exchanges one form of muscle tension for another. The clinician as well as the patient must be aware that any permanent change in posture will occur gradually.

Training begins with helping the patient become aware of certain areas of his or her body, specifically, the base of the head and upper neck. Physiologically, the body responds to the position of the head above the shoulders. Observing movements of a blind individual demonstrates that he or she moves with the head balanced so that the ears are directly above the shoulders.[1] As Lennon et al. state, "The position of the head on the neck is vital because it governs all postural reflexes. If the head is misaligned, other parts of the body move in and out of line to maintain balance and thus energy is expended to counteract the effects of gravity."[1] For this reason, the proper positioning of the head is the cornerstone of postural training.

This concept should be emphasized to the individual. If the patient can release the head and neck to their natural anti-gravity positions, the entire body will follow.

As mentioned previously, proper position is not obtained or maintained through direct intervention or conscious activation of specific muscle groups. The patient must be encouraged to use mental imaging and his or her own breathing to cue the adoption of the proper head and neck positioning.

BASIC EXERCISE

In-office training begins with instruction of a basic relaxation exercise that cultivates awareness of breathing patterns and proper head and neck position. The patient is instructed to lie in a supine position on the floor or on a firm mattress (Fig. 27–1). The legs are placed in the hook-lying position, and the arms are placed outward at approximately 45 degrees. The head is placed on a firm 1- to 2-inch surface to promote upper cervical flexion. The eyes should always remain open, as this is not simply an exercise in relaxation (although this does occur) but an active, ongoing process.

The patient is instructed to relax and then to slow the rate of breathing, becoming aware of the cycle of inhalation and exhalation. Upon inhalation, the patient is instructed to expand the lower rib cage outward to both sides. Often it can be helpful to instruct the patient to place his or her hands on either side of the rib cage for feedback (Fig. 27–2). Then, during exhalation, the patient is asked to imagine his or her body lengthening, with the most posterior superior aspect of the skull as the apex or leading edge of the lengthening process. In effect, the patient is visualizing an expansion upward and outward with each inspiration and expiration cycle. This is called gravity-centered breathing.[1]

Freeing of the base of the skull from the neck should be emphasized. If the patient can focus his or her attention

Figure 27–2. The patient can get feedback in completing the proper breathing technique by placing his or her hands on the lower ribs.

to the base of the skull during the inhalation exhalation procedure, stress in any portion of the spine can be relieved (Fig. 27–3). The patient is instructed to continue this breathing cycle for several minutes in the office, until he or she understands it and can practice it without supervision.

! CLINICAL PEARL

It is amazing to feel relief of discomfort in the lumbar spine simply by consciously freeing one's own suboccipital portion of the neck and allowing the head to assume its proper position.

Figure 27–1. Patient lying supine in gravity centered breathing position.

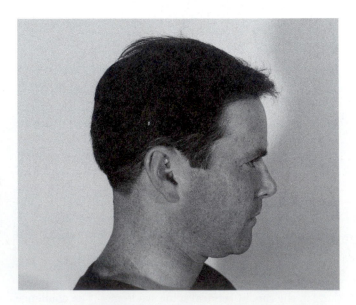

Figure 27–3. Proper positioning of the patient's head.

This task should be completed once daily for approximately 15 minutes. For patients who have considerable freedom within their work environment or their work schedule, this can be repeated several times throughout the day. Inevitably, while practicing, the mind will wander. It is important to emphasize that this is to be expected and is not an indication of failure on the part of the patient. It simply means that he or she needs to re-focus and begin the breathing cycle again.

The rest position is a position that can be taught to any patient, but should be strongly considered in those who undergo significant daily stress in the work environment. The position allows the patient to relax a variety of active and anti-gravity musculoskeletal structures.

STANDING AND SITTING

Once the basic technique has been satisfactorily understood, it can be applied to sitting and standing instruction. Again, it should be emphasized that there is no correct position per se.

Ideally, instruction in the standing position should begin in front of a full-length mirror so that the patient can see the lengthening process occurring. However, this is not crucial. Proper initial positioning is as follows. The feet are placed so that the heels are shoulder width apart with toes facing forward. Knees are slightly bent to remove excess tension. Pelvis and torso remain in a neutral position (Figs. 27–4 and 27–5). From this position, the patient is

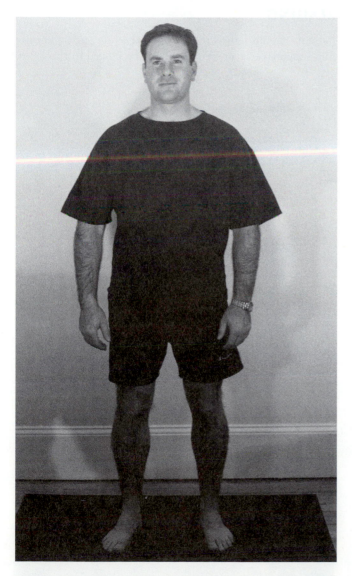

Figure 27–4. Proper standing position, front view: feet shoulder width apart facing forward, knees slightly bent, pelvis neutral, arms relaxed at sides, neutral head and neck posture.

Figure 27–5. Proper standing position, side view.

instructed to begin the breathing cycle, as was performed in the supine position, focusing on freeing or relaxing the base of the skull. This position can be adopted any time the patient has to stand for an extended period. It can also be incorporated into a daily routine.

Instruction in sitting should occur in a firm stool or chair with no arm support, and the arms relaxed (Fig. 27–6). Initially the patient should be instructed in the location of the ischial tuberosities. Then the difference between sitting on the sacrum (Fig. 27–7) and sitting on the ischial tuberosities (Fig. 27–8) should be explained and, preferably, demonstrated. Sitting on the superior aspect of the sacrum promotes slumping posture. Sitting on the ischial tuberosities promotes upright posture and forms the foundation for proper positioning. At this point, in order to maintain the correct posture, the patient is instructed to engage in the breathing cycle.

Sitting is probably the most difficult of the positions for patients to change. A slumping seated posture may initially be perceived by the subacute patient to be more comfortable. However, once the patient's level of awareness has been cultivated, he or she usually can no longer tolerate poor sitting posture.

Some additional considerations in the instruction of proper sitting posture include the following:

- The individual should maintain the knees at a level equal to, or slightly higher than, that of the hips. This enables the use of a backrest and allows alignment of spinal structures while sitting.
- Weight should be distributed uniformly under the thighs while sitting, to ensure proper balanced support of the spine, head, and shoulders.
- Reclined postures are acceptable, provided the chair gives adequate support to the individual's head, and the task is adjustable within the individual's viewing area.[2]

READING

Patients should be instructed to read while sitting upright in a supportive chair. A pillow may be placed in the lap to

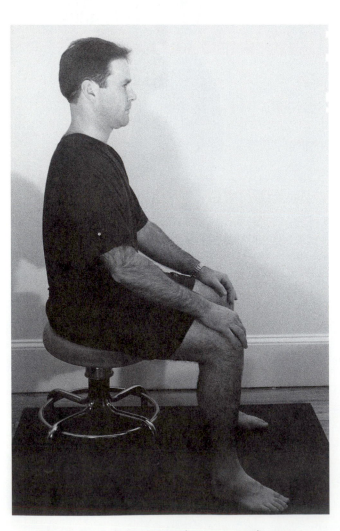

Figure 27–6. Proper seated position, side view.

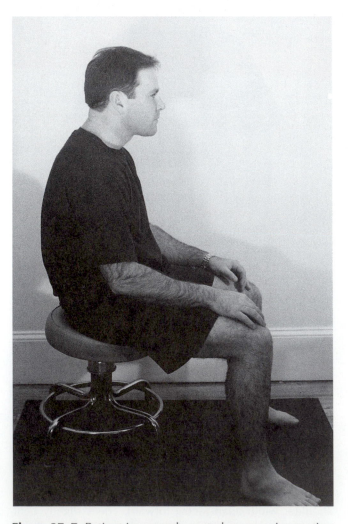

Figure 27–7. Patient improperly seated on superior portion of the sacrum.

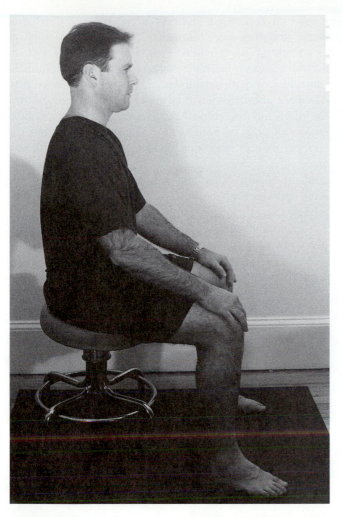

Figure 27–8. Patient properly seated on ischial tuberosities.

Figure 27–9. Proper reading position with arms supported and cervical spine neutral.

support the reading material. Adequate lighting is essential. The patient should be discouraged from reading in bed with pillows propping up the head as this often places the neck in extreme flexion and can be pain producing. Additionally, maintenance of this supported anterior head position may produce adaptive changes, possibly shortening of ligamentous structures, in the anterior and posterior cervical spine[3](Figs. 27–9 and 27–10).

SLEEPING

As most clinicians know, nothing will upset a patient more than being unable to sleep as a result of pain. Coaching the patient into a position that will facilitate sleep may help him or her to be more comfortable, accelerate the healing process and hasten recovery.

Sleeping instructions should begin with having the patient spend time trying to find the most comfortable position possible. Oftentimes, in an acute situation this is not possible. However, teaching the patient how to place the neck and shoulders in a neutral position can be beneficial.

The patient is instructed to lie on his or her side. The patient should begin by placing one or two pillows beneath the head so that the head and neck are parallel to the sleeping surface, with the symptomatic side up. The patient's knees can be bent and a pillow can be placed between them. Again, it should be emphasized that this position is a starting point. A large percentage of patients will not find relief in this position. The patient should be instructed to modify the position as necessary. If no position seems comfortable, and no red flags for serious disease are present, attempts should be made to reassure the patient as to the temporary nature of the situation, and the clinician's energy should be directed to pain relief (Fig. 27–11).

Cervical support pillows can bring relief to specific patients but are not a universal solution. Patients should be encouraged to try different pillows in their home and report results to the clinician.

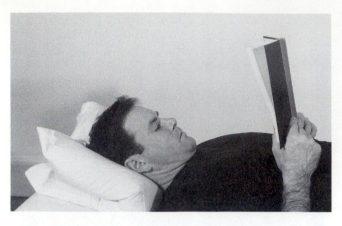

Figure 27–10. Improper reading position places excess stress on the cervical spine.

When giving patients advice concerning activities of daily living, the clinician should take care to not be overly strict. Patients are capable and perceptive, and usually have tried many alternatives on their own. It is sometimes necessary to provide several different options for them to try and have them report back to you as to which one works best.

ERGONOMICS

Ensuring safe and proper function within the work environment is an extremely important part of any patient education program. Significant dysfunction and injury can occur daily even in seemingly benign work environments. Ergonomics is the study of methods used for the "preservation of health and efficiency at work and in activities of daily living."[2] People working in ergonomically designed workplaces tire less quickly, are less stressed by poor envi-

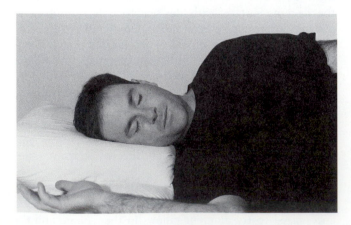

Figure 27–11. Proper lying down position.

ronmental conditions, are less likely to get injured, feel better, and work more effectively.[2]

Years ago, work-related musculoskeletal injuries in industrial settings were most commonly found in the lumbar spine. However, modern industrial design has changed this. The neck and shoulders now appear to be the critical area for injury and discomfort.[4] Additionally, a recent survey of ergonomic costs by Ford Motor Company showed that the cost per case of neck and head injuries was the highest among the injuries examined.[5] Now, more than ever, any clinician treating a patient with a cervical pain syndrome must consider ergonomic factors and address them appropriately.

Ergonomics of the workplace can be applied in three major areas[2]:

1. The design of equipment and furniture
2. The arrangement of the work environment
3. The design of job tasks that can be easily and effectively performed by the workplace user

This portion of the chapter addresses how the clinician can identify those at risk for injury and what can be done in each of these three categories to decrease that risk. This is by no means an exhaustive list of possible solutions, but merely a starting place for the clinician.

ERGONOMIC EVALUATION

For effective ergonomic solutions, there are no easy answers. "Which particular (ergonomic) measure is of major importance often has to be decided for each individual . . . after a careful analysis of the work tasks."[6] Each patient must be evaluated separately and decisions made based on specific work conditions and clinical findings. Implementation of ergonomic principles for the reduction of musculoskeletal stresses and accident prevention is the best approach to avoidance of injury and reduction of the individual's exposure to risk factors.[2]

Before dispensing ergonomic advice, the clinician must properly assess the risk involved in the patient's work tasks. Identification of basic risk factors for cervical injury in the workplace is a relatively straightforward task and can be adapted into the evaluation of the cervical spine patient.

GENERAL RISK FACTORS

The following are general risk factors for work injury[7]:

1. *Forcefulness.* Forcefulness is the amount of physical effort required by the person to perform a task or maintain control of tools and equipment. The greater the forcefulness, the greater the chance for certain types of work injury. A simple description of the job task usually gives an adequate idea of forcefulness.

2. *Poor design of equipment and furniture.* Large forces are not always necessary for injury to occur. Poor design of equipment and furniture can significantly affect risk of injury. Poor location or position of parts, equipment, or tools can result in awkward posture while performing a task, causing static loading or sustained exertion of vulnerable body structures. Similarly, mechanical contact stress as well as extreme temperatures and hand-arm vibration can increase risk of injury.

3. *Lack of task variation.* Lack of task variation can result in repetitive strain. The summation of forces over an 8-hour shift, whether it be assembly line work or key strokes, may result in a dangerous amount of stress to certain areas of the body. Factors such as the speed or frequency of the work or the duration of repetition can also be examined.

4. *Environmental factors.* Environmental factors, such as light, noise, temperature, and air quality are risk factors.

5. *Insufficient rest breaks.* Insufficient rest breaks over an 8-hour shift can magnify any of the preceding risk factors.

CERVICAL SPINE INJURY RISK FACTORS

All jobs or tasks that require the use of the upper extremity and upper back can constitute a source of stress and can produce cervical pain and discomfort.[2] Symptoms have been related to time spent in neck flexion, shoulder elevation, upper arm abduction, or total duration of activity.[8] The actual duration of contraction of muscles (i.e., the time between breaks) can also have an influence on the development of neck and shoulder pain.[8] Following are several questions that should be considered when workplace risk factors are suspected in a cervical spine patient.[6]

1. What Is the Thoraco-Lumbar Positioning?

The inclination of the thoraco-lumbar spine has an effect on activity of neck and shoulder muscles. A sitting posture in which the thoraco-lumbar spine is slightly inclined backward gives the lowest levels of muscular activity in the neck and shoulders (approximately 10 to 15 degrees).[9, 10] With slight inclination, however, it is important to position source documents to avoid extreme flexion while viewing, as this will increase the load on the cervical spine and activity of the cervical spine musculature,[9, 11] thereby increasing the likelihood of pain.[12]

By choosing a certain sitting posture for the patient, the clinician can significantly affect neck and shoulder activity. In order of most to least preferred, these are three recommended sitting postures: (1) seated with a slightly backward inclined posture, (2) seated with a vertical posture, (3) seated with a spine-neutral posture (Figs. 27–12 through 27–14).

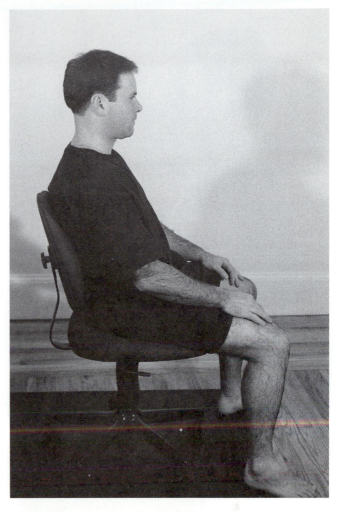

Figure 27–12. A sitting posture in which the thoraco-lumbar spine is slightly inclined backward gives the lowest levels of muscular activity in the neck and shoulders.

2. What Are the Upper and Lower Cervical Spine Positions?

Neck flexion increases the load on the cervical spine. Unnecessary forward flexion should be avoided.

3. What Are the Arm and Hand Positions?

Arm abduction increases upper trapezius, cervical erector spinae, and rhomboid activity. Arm elevation increases upper trapezius, thoracic erector spinae, rhomboid, and shoulder muscle activity. Some other arm and hand position factors that influence neck and shoulder activity include the following:

- A large horizontal distance between the work object and a plumbline through the shoulder
- High position of the work object
- High work table surface
- Weight and design of the tools used
- Other job-specific forces acting upon the arms and hands.

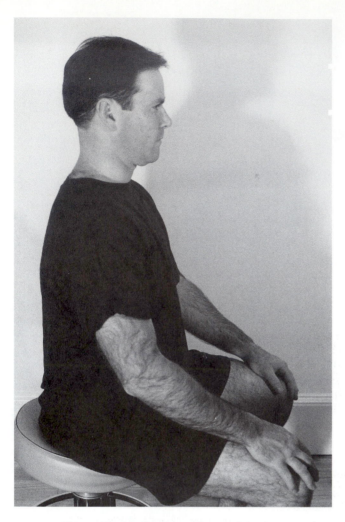

Figure 27–13. Straight spine positioning.

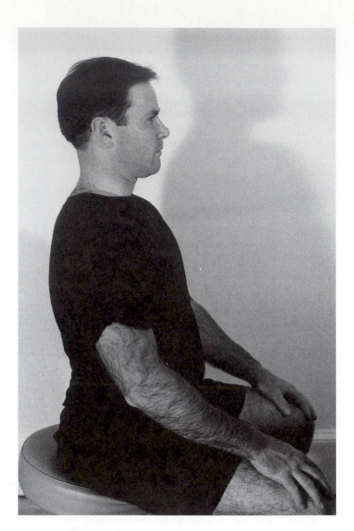

Figure 27–14. Neutral spine positioning.

4. For How Long Are These Positions Maintained?

Maintaining static positions for longer periods of time increase risk of injury. It has been shown that workers who were required to take more frequent breaks experienced less fatigue.[8] Decreasing the amount of fatigue decreases the risk of injury.

5. What Work Movements Are Being Performed?

The nature of the job task, whether it be repetitive lifting or exhaustive keyboard work, is important to assess when determining risk of injury.

6. How Repetitive Are the Movements?

Highly repetitive tasks negatively influence an individual's response to a particular load.

7. What Are the Weights of Objects Being Handled and What Are the Forces Required?

It seems logical to think that jobs requiring significantly more intense physical activity would produce a greater number of injuries than those that required less intense physical activity. However, many patients who present with musculoskeletal complaints are often employed in white-collar jobs, which do not necessarily require large forces to complete. So, although it is still important to assess the amount of physical activity necessary to complete a job when screening for ergonomic risk factors, the clinician should not be unduly influenced by how large or small the required forces are perceived to be.

8. What Other Factors That May Increase Muscle Activity, Such As Poor Lighting Conditions or Psychological Stress, Are Present?

Stress is endemic to our society. Most patients deal with a significant amount of stress in their lives. Simple questions about stress levels can give important information about significant risk factors. The clinician should also inquire about other irritating factors that might be present.

☒ CLINICAL PEARL

It must be remembered that the success of any ergonomic correction relies heavily on the cooperation of the employer. The clinician should be aware of this and be as diplomatic as possible in dealing with the employer, and should understand that a perfect ergonomic situation for the patient may not always be possible for many reasons beyond the clinician's control. For that reason, any ergonomic changes that are considered should be ranked, with high priority given to the ones with the most chance of having a positive outcome on the patient's condition. The clinician should endeavor to effect those changes first.

GENERAL WORKSPACE GUIDELINES WITH EMPHASIS ON THE COMPUTER WORKSTATION

The total number of ergonomic guidelines is limited only by the number of different jobs in existence. General workspace arrangements and layouts should allow for the following[13]:

- Adjustability to fit each worker's size
- Maintenance of neutral posture and avoidance of awkward or extended reaches and jerky movements while performing tasks
- A variety of working positions to avoid static posture
- A full range of motion and adequate leg room
- Adequate space for and access to all necessary tools and equipment
- Frequently used work items within easy arm's reach
- Unobscured line of sight

COMPUTER WORKSTATION GUIDELINES

The computer age is here, and it has brought with it an entirely new culprit in the generation of workplace injuries, the computer workstation. Keyboard workers have demonstrated a significantly greater risk of neck and upper extremity pain, ache, or discomfort.[14, 15] Fortunately, a significant amount of information is available on the prevention of these injuries. This, in turn, has spawned an entire industry devoted to the development of office equipment designed to lessen the chance of injury.

The next portion of this chapter presents some basic guidelines to reduce the risk of injury at the computer workstation. These recommendations are adapted from the publication, *Fitting the Job to the Worker*.[13]

1. The worker should maintain a neutral posture at the keyboard and mouse as much as possible. The worker's arms should hang comfortably at the sides, with the elbows bent to approximately 90 degrees, forearms parallel or at an angle of less than 90 degrees to the floor, knees slightly below hips, and wrists straight (Fig. 27–15).
2. The work surface should be large enough to support the keyboard, mouse, monitor, and documents. New developments in keyboard trays and mouse supports allow these two items to be stored below the desk, making better use of space. These trays also allow for optimal position of the wrists and hands when operating the computer.
3. The top line of the screen should be just below eye level to keep the worker's neck straight, approximately 5 to 10 degrees from the horizontal.

Figure 27–15. Proper workstation position.

(Courtesy of Bodybilt Inc., Navasota, Texas.)

This angle can be maintained for long periods of time with minimal discomfort and fatigue. The entire primary viewing area (top of screen to keyboard to source material) should be less than 60 degrees below the horizontal plane of the eyes.[2]

4. Monitors should be placed 18 to 30 inches away from the worker for viewing.

5. Keyboards and monitors should be detachable so that the worker, as necessary, can adjust the angle and position.

6. Keyboard and work surface edges should be rounded.

7. Documents should be at the same height and distance as the screen.

8. The screen and document should be easily viewed so that the worker's head is not turned to the side or tilted up or down regularly. Document positions for reading and typing significantly affect tension in the cervical extensor muscles.[16]

9. To prevent glare, the monitor and keyboard should be perpendicular to windows and between overhead lights. Glare reduction screens significantly reduce eyestrain and should be utilized whenever possible.

10. Screen contrast and brightness should be easily adjustable by the worker.

11. Screen characters should be clearly displayed, neither wavy nor flickering.

12. Forward head posture, when maintained over a long period of time, can have a detrimental effect on the cervical function of the patient (see Chaps. 4 and 14). Improper positioning at the computer workstation can easily result in this head posture (Fig. 27–16). Therefore, in any patient in whom forward head posture occurs as a result of the job, it is important to assess how this may be corrected.

13. Adequate seating is a necessity. The worker's chair should:
    a. Adequately support the back and legs
    b. Have padded seats
    c. Have separately adjustable back and seat cushions
    d. Permit the feet to be supported either on the floor or with a footrest
    e. Be adjustable while seated
    f. Swivel for most tasks
    g. Isolate the worker from whole body vibration
    h. Have adjustable arm supports when appropriate (Fig. 27–17).

14. The worker should not remain seated for more than one hour without a change in position.[17]

15. The worker should assume a position that minimizes elbow distance from the body with or without arm rests.[15]

Figure 27–16. Improper work position reinforcing forward head posture.

16. The worker should maintain no more than 30 degrees of forward flexion of the neck while reading or typing.[15]

17. Rotation of the head and neck should be avoided for any length of time.[15]

HOME EXERCISE

Specific home exercises are listed in Appendix 27A. Indications for each exercise are included within the discussions of specific cervical pain syndromes.

MEDITATION AND SPIRITUAL PRACTICE

Often, for patients the clinician perceives to be receptive, meditation can be introduced as a means to decrease stress and increase relaxation. There is a tremendous amount of information on this topic, and a suggested reading list is included at the end of the chapter. However, a basic meditation procedure can be quite easily taught to the patient.

The following technique is a combination of several different methods. The patient is instructed to sit comfort-

Figure 27–17. An example of a proper ergonomic chair. *(Courtesy of Bodybilt Inc., Navasota, Texas.)*

ably in a chair and relax. Then, he or she is instructed to become aware of the breath moving in and out of the lungs; specifically, the air as it moves in and out of the nostrils. Each time the thoughts wander, the patient should gently bring attention back to his or her breath. By placing attention on this one area, the patient can attempt to clear the mind of extraneous thoughts. This conscious effort to clear the mind is one of the key elements of meditation. By consistently and consciously freeing the mind, the patient can cultivate a more relaxed state. Relaxation in all its

forms can be an extremely useful adjunct to any care regimen, and clinicians are encouraged to discuss this option with their patients.

Spiritual practice is an extremely personal subject. However, it can have a profound effect on the attitude of the patient and, subsequently, on the healing and recovery process. If the patient already has a spiritual orientation, suggesting that he or she pursue this aspect of himself or herself in promoting health may be all that is needed. For those who do not have a spiritual orientation, a discreet way of prompting the patient to explore the spiritual side of life is to have several books on the subject available that the patient can look through while waiting for his or her appointment, or simply to suggest that the patient might find a particular one interesting. The clinician is advised to refrain from being overly "preachy," as this may frighten the patient away. Table 27–1 provides a list of suggested books and audiotape programs that may be introduced to the patient that may be helpful in getting him or her started on a spiritual path that may be of benefit in recovery.

CONCLUSION

The amount of time the clinician spends with the patient is limited, and the effects of any treatment may need to be amplified. Comprehensive patient education can accomplish this. Home exercise, advice on activities of daily living, and ergonomics are all significant tools for the practitioner to utilize in the care of patients with cervical spine syndromes. These methods can quite often be the difference between clinician–patient frustration, and problem resolution.

ACKNOWLEDGMENTS

The author would like to thank Bodybilt Inc. of Navasota, Texas, and Move Management of Providence, Rhode Island, for their assistance in the preparation of the photographs for this chapter. Thanks also to Susan and Michael Paquin, and Joanne Woerner for their assistance in the preparation of the figures.

674 Part 5 Rehabilitation

Table 27–1: Resources for Meditation and Spiritual Development

BOOKS

Title	Author	Publisher
A Course in Miracles®		Foundation for Inner Peace
The Holy Bible. New King James Version		
The Way and Its Power	Waley A	Grove-Atit
The Bhagavad Gita	Mascaro J	Penguin Group
Real Magic	Dyer W	Harper Collins
Your Sacred Self	Dyer W	Harper Collins
The Force	Wilde S	White Dove
Miracles	Wilde S	Hay House, Inc.
Affirmations	Wilde S	Hay House, Inc.
Ageless Body, Timeless Mind	Chopra D	Crown
The Seven Spiritual Laws of Success	Chopra D	Amber-Allen Success
For the Love of God	Shield B, Carlson R	New World Library
The Little Prince	Saint Exupery A	Harvest/HBJ
You Can Have It All	Patent A	Beyond Words
Gratitude, A Way of Life	Hay L	Hay House, Inc.
The Tao of Inner Peace	Dreher D	Harper Collins
A New Guide to Rational Living	Ellis A, Harper R	Prentice-Hall
The Prophet	Gibran K	Knopf
The Seven Habits of Highly Effective People	Covey S	Simon and Schuster
Be Here Now	Ram Dass	Crown

AUDIOTAPES

Title	Author	Publisher
Developing Your Sixth Sense	Wilde S	Nightingale-Conant
Infinite Self	Wilde S	Nightingale-Conant
The Art of Meditation	Wilde S	Hay House
The Secrets to Manifesting Your Destiny	Dyer W	Nightingale-Conant
Freedom Through Higher Awareness	Dyer W	Nightingale-Conant
The Higher Self	Chopra D	Nightingale-Conant
Magical Mind, Magical Body	Chopra D	Nightingale-Conant
Living Beyond Miracles	Chopra D, Dyer W	Amber-Allen
The Tao of Philosophy, Vol. 1	Watts A	Electronic University
The Tao of Philosophy, Vol. 2	Watts A	Electronic University

REFERENCES

1. Lennon J, Shealy C, Cady R, et al. Postural and respiratory modulation of autonomic function, pain and health. *Am J Pain Man* 1994;4:36–39.
2. Moty. *Ergonomic Considerations and Interventions*.
3. Mannheimer J. Prevention and restoration of abnormal upper quarter posture. In: Gelb H, Gelb M, eds. *Postural Considerations in the Diagnosis and Treatment of Craniocervical, Mandibular and Related Chronic Pain Disorders*. St. Louis, Mo: Ishiyaku Euroamerica; 1991.
4. Bullock M. Health education in the workplace. In: Isernhagen S, ed. *Work Injury Management and Prevention*. Rockville, Md: Aspen; 1988.
5. Pastula S, Reeve G. *The Economics of Ergonomic Disorders at Ford Motor Company*. Dearborn, Mich: Ford Motor Company.
6. Harms-Ringdahl K, Schuldt K. Neck and shoulder load and load elicited pain in sitting work postures. In: Bullock M, ed. *Ergonomics: The Physiotherapist in the Workplace*. New York, NY: Churchill Livingstone; 1990.
7. McPhee B. Musculoskeletal complaints in workers engaged in repetitive work in fixed postures. In: Bullock M, ed. *Ergonomics: The Physiotherapist in the Workplace*. New York, NY: Churchill Livingstone; 1990.
8. Pulket C, Kogi K. Fatigue of visual display unit operators in the freebreak system. *Abstracts of the XXI International Occupational Health Congress* 1984;364.
9. Schuldt K, Ekholm J, Harms-Ringdahl K, et al. Effects of changes in sitting work posture on static neck and shoulder muscle activity. *Ergonomics* 1986;12:1525–1537.
10. Schuldt K, Harms-Ringdahl K, Ekholm J, et al. Influence of sitting postures on neck and shoulder e.m.g. during arm-hand work movements. *Clin Biomechanics* 1987;2:126–139.
11. Harms-Ringdahl K, Ekholm J, Schuldt K, et al. Load moments and myoelectric activity when the cervical spine is held in full flexion and extension. *Ergonomics* 1986;12:1539–1552.
12. Eklund J, Corlett E. Evaluation of spinal loads and chair design in seated work tasks. *Clin Biomechanics* 1987;2:27–33.
13. *Fitting the Job to the Worker: An Ergonomics Program Guideline*. Olympia, Wash: State of Washington Department of Labor and Industries; 1994.
14. Mcphee B. Work related musculoskeletal disorders of the neck and upper extremities in workers engaged in light, highly repetitive work. In: Osterholz U, Karmaus W, Hullman B, Ritz B, eds. *Proceedings of an International Symposium: Work Related Musculoskeletal Disorders*. Bonn; 1987:244–258.
15. Welsh. *Physical Therapy, Ergonomics, and Rehabilitation*.
16. Hamilton N. Source document position as it affects head position and neck muscle tension. *Ergonomics* 1996;4:593–610.
17. Bendix T. Sitting postures—a review of biomechanic and ergonomic aspects. *Man Med* 1986;2:77–81.

RECOMMENDED READING

1. Caplan D. *Back Trouble*. Gainesville, Fla: Triad Publishing; 1987.
2. Gelb M. *Body Learning*. New York, NY: Henry Holt; 1981.

Patient Exercises
and Handouts

Ronald J. Tyszkowski

The following nine exercises and three patient handouts are set up on separate pages to facilitate copying and distributing them to patients.

CERVICAL SPINE HOME EXERCISE 1:
A. BREATHING

1. Stand facing a mirror that allows you to view your collarbones.
2. Place your hands on your lower ribs, with your fingers on your abdomen.
3. Slowly breathe in a normal breath, so that you feel your ribs expand outward underneath your hands and your abdomen expand forward. Repeat several times, breathing at a normal rate, until you are comfortable with this type of breath (Fig. 27A–1).
4. Now, watch your collarbones in the mirror, and try to breathe without raising them. This may take several tries to accomplish, but keep at it.
5. Remember, do not be frustrated if this is difficult at first. You are re-training your body to breathe correctly and this takes time. It is important to be consistent with your exercises.

Figure 27A–1. Breathing exercise.

B. SWALLOWING

1. Have a glass of water handy. Place a small mint or piece of candy on the roof of your mouth about 1 centimeter behind your front teeth. Hold it there with the tip of your tongue. This is the correct position of your tongue during swallowing.
2. Take a small sip of water, close your mouth and swallow while holding the candy in place with your tongue.

CERVICAL SPINE HOME EXERCISE 2: BRÜGGER EXERCISE

1. Sit with your "sit" bones on the edge of a chair with your arms hanging at your sides and your pelvis rocked forward so that your back arches. Spread your knees out wide and turn your feet outward (Fig. 27A–2A).
2. Place your tongue on the roof of your mouth, 1 centimeter behind your upper front teeth.
3. Open your fingers wide and place your hands so that your thumbs are pointing forward. Slowly turn your hands out so that your thumbs are pointing behind you and hold for 10 seconds (Fig. 27A–2B). Then, return to the starting position.

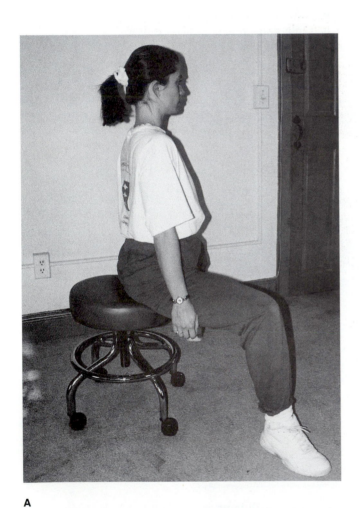

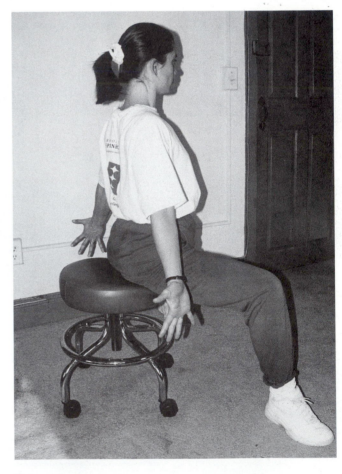

A

B

Figure 27A–2. A and **B.** Brügger exercise.

CERVICAL SPINE HOME EXERCISE 3: CHIN TUCKS

1. Start by sitting in an upright position (Fig. 27A–3A).
2. Retract your chin as far as it will go (Fig. 27A–3B). Be careful not to nod your head, or move your upper body. Hold this position for 2 seconds.
3. Release your chin back to neutral. Be careful not to overshoot your neutral position and poke out your chin.

Optional (Check with your doctor or therapist before performing this step): To increase the amount of movement, place one hand on your chin and gently press after completing step two (Fig. 27A–3C). After a 2-second hold, release your chin back to neutral. Again, be careful not to overshoot the neutral position and poke your chin.

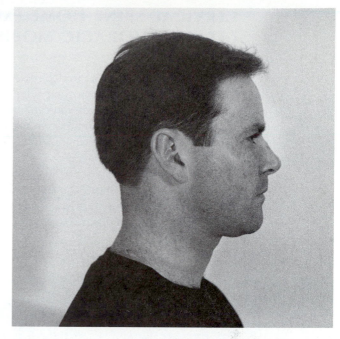

A

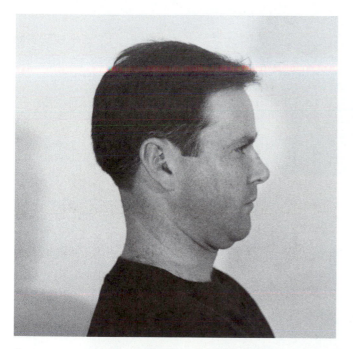

B

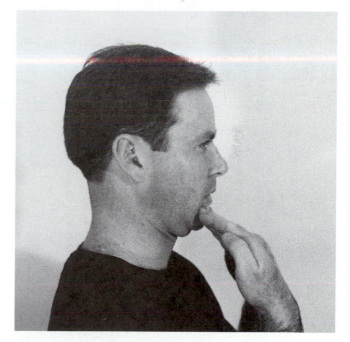

C

Figure 27A–3. A–C. Chin tuck exercise.

CERVICAL SPINE HOME EXERCISE 4: CERVICOTHORACIC MOBILIZATION

1. Start by sitting in an upright position.
2. Place both arms out to your sides at a 90-degree angle to the shoulder, spread your fingers as wide as you can, and point your right thumb up toward the ceiling and your left thumb down toward the floor.
3. Turn your head so you are facing the left thumb, which is pointing down toward the floor (Fig. 27A–4A).
4. Now, slowly turn your hands so that the thumbs switch places (the right thumb now pointing toward the floor and the left thumb pointing to the ceiling) and at the same time, turn your head to the right so that it is once again facing the thumb pointed down toward the floor (Fig. 27A–4B).
5. Repeat.

A

B

Figure 27A–4. A and **B.** Cervico-thoracic mobilization exercise.

CERVICAL SPINE HOME EXERCISE 5: ONE-LEGGED STANDING

1. Stand barefoot on a flat level space with a wall or a piece of furniture nearby to help with balance.
2. Slowly raise one leg so that you are standing on one foot.
3. Grip the toes of the foot on which you are standing. If you are able to hold this position for 30 seconds, do so and then switch legs. Otherwise, continue to try and balance, supporting yourself when necessary, for 30 seconds and then switch (Fig. 27A–5).
4. In the beginning, it is normal to lose your balance and have to grab something for support. Simply reposition yourself and start again. The more you do this exercise, the less frequently that will happen.

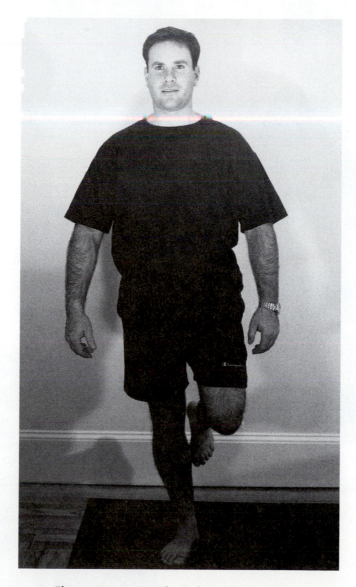

Figure 27A–5. One-legged standing exercise.

CERVICAL SPINE HOME EXERCISE 6: SIT-TO-STAND

1. Start by sitting in an upright position (Fig. 27A–6A).
2. Place your left foot slightly backward and lean forward at your waist until you begin to feel your body weight through your feet (Fig. 27A–6B).
3. With your arms relaxed at your sides, slowly stand up, leading with the top of your head (not your chin!) (Fig. 27A–6C).
4. Stand normally. Repeat.

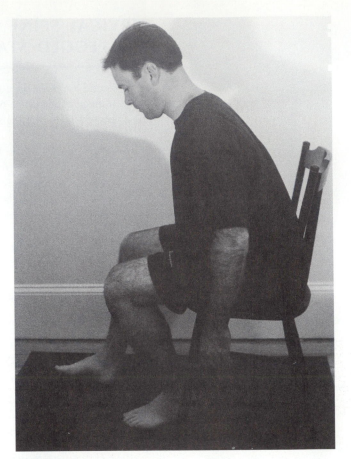

B

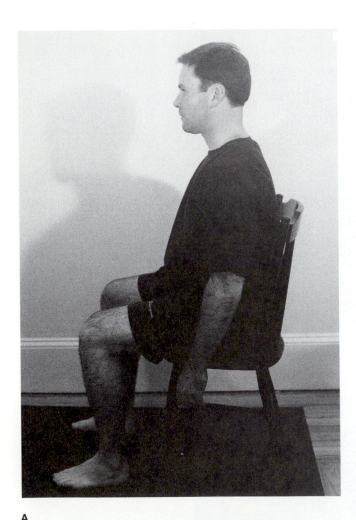

A

Figure 27A–6. A–C. Sit-to-stand exercise.

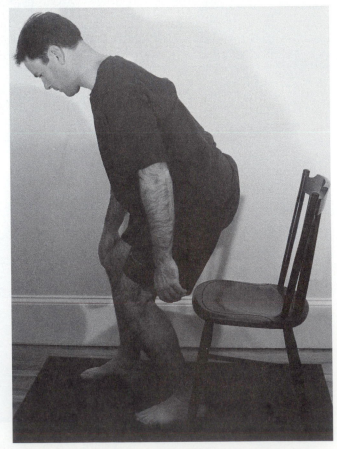

C

CERVICAL SPINE HOME EXERCISE 7: CERVICO-THORACIC STRETCH

1. Start by sitting in an upright position.
2. Inhale slowly.
3. As you exhale slowly, place your hands on your shoulder blades and point your elbows toward the ceiling. Then, slowly push your elbows as far as they can comfortably go toward the ceiling. (Do not drop your head forward. Do not raise your shoulders.)
4. Breathe in this position and hold for 6 seconds (Fig. 27A–7A and B).

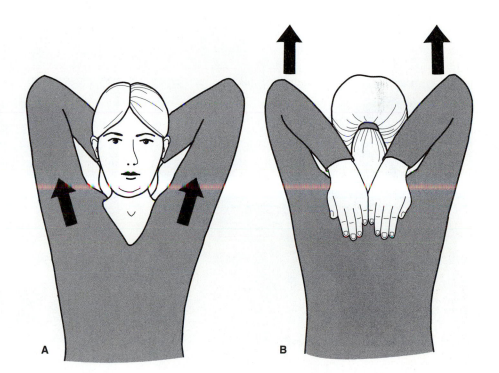

Figure 27A–7. A and **B.** Cervico-thoracic stretch exercise.

CERVICAL SPINE HOME EXERCISE 8: RHOMBOID DYNAMIC RANGE OF MOTION

1. Stand facing a wall. Place both arms directly out in front of you with your palms against the wall. Without bending your elbows, push away from the wall while leaving your palms against the wall (Fig. 27A–8A).
2. Then, relax your shoulders and allow them to come forward without bending your elbows (Fig. 27A–8B).

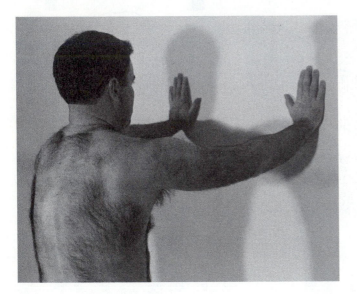

A

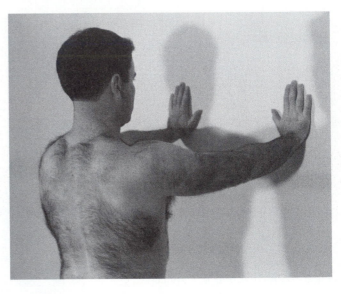

B

Figure 27A–8. A and **B.** Rhomboid dynamic range of motion exercise.

CERVICAL SPINE HOME EXERCISE 9: WALL ANGELS

1. Stand with your back to a wall. Place your arms up over your head against the wall with your palms facing outward (Fig. 27A–9A).
2. Keeping your arms tightly pressed against the wall, slowly bend your elbows and lower your arms until your arms touch your sides (Fig. 27A–9B).
3. Reverse this movement until your arms are overhead again. Repeat.

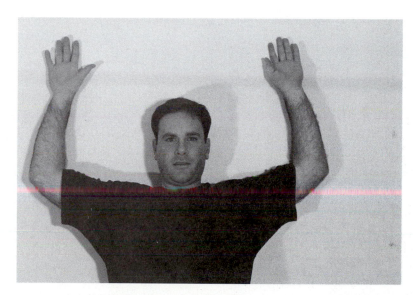

A

B

Figure 27A–9. A and **B.** Wall angels.

Intervertebral Disc: Basic Anatomy

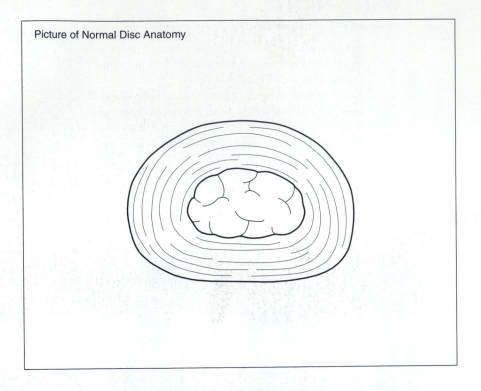

Picture of Normal Disc Anatomy

Notes:

_____

_____

_____

_____

Intervertebral Disc: Disc Derangement

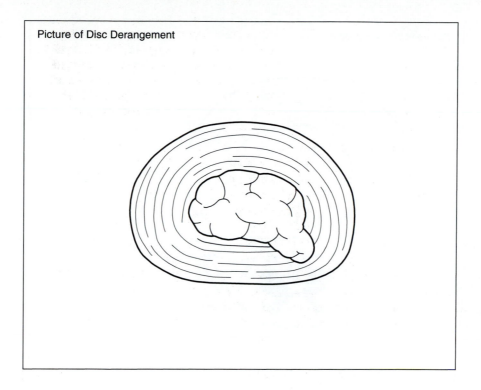

Picture of Disc Derangement

Notes:

_____

_____

_____

_____

Intervertebral Disc: Disc Herniation

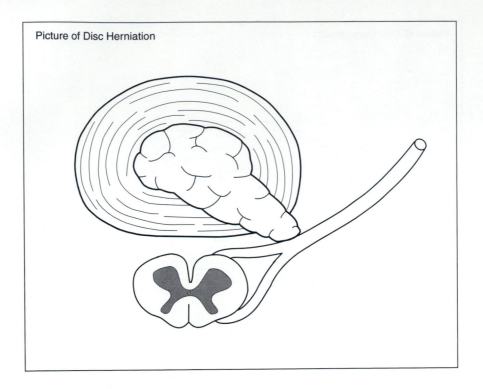

Picture of Disc Herniation

Notes:

_____

_____

_____

_____

PART

6

Management

Protocols for the Management of Patients with Cervical Spine Syndromes

Donald R. Murphy

"Think globally, act locally."

INTRODUCTION

The approach to protocols in this chapter is not based upon "cookbook" formulae; that is, first do A, then B, followed by C. Rather, it is *principle based,* meaning that a set of principles are presented that can be utilized in formulating a strategy for the resolution of the particular problem for which each individual patient seeks care.

The optimum approach to cervical spine disorders requires several key shifts in the paradigms, or frames of reference, from which physicians most typically have been oriented. The first paradigm shift has been discussed throughout this entire book; that is, from a focus on pathoanatomy to functional pathology as the explanation for most cervical spine syndromes. The second paradigm shift is that from *treatment* orientation to *management* orientation. *Treatment* refers to those specific techniques and approaches that a clinician applies to a patient. *Management* refers to the *entire clinical approach.* This includes the specific treatment that is being applied, but also includes the manner in which the clinician interacts with the patient, the decisions the clinician makes about the treatment approaches that should be applied in particular circumstances and at certain points in the recovery process (including those times in which *no* treatment is the best choice), and the decisions about referral of the patient for treatment approaches that another clinician may employ. Therefore, the most important aspect of management is the *strategy* the clinician employs for expeditious resolution of the problem.

The final paradigm shift, that from managing the *condition* or *injury* to managing the *patient,* parallels the second paradigm. This, of course, does not mean that injured tissues should be ignored, but rather that focus must be placed on what the patient requires to achieve maximum recovery. It is essential that the clinician avoids becoming so fixated in the injured tissue and the stages of healing, that he or she risks losing sight of the fact that it is a human being that is being cared for, not simply a collection of tissues.

It will be noted that most of the treatment procedures that are presented in this book, particularly those related to rehabilitation, are "low-tech" in nature. That is, they involve the use of as little equipment and technology as possible. This is by design. It is consistent with the concept of minimalism, which is discussed later in this chapter. This approach also enhances the empowerment of the patient, another important concept that is discussed, as it allows the patient to do more for himself or herself, with less reliance on the clinician. In addition, as has been discussed throughout the book, the most important factor in the etiology of most cervical spine syndromes is *dysfunction*. So, the most important component of treatment is the correction of this dysfunction. Correction of dysfunction is best done by means of hands-on approaches such as manipulation, PIR, PFS, and rhythmic stabilization techniques, along with exercise. Stabilization exercise requires the use of as little equipment as possible, as most exercise machines provide stability for the patient, defeating the primary purpose of stabilization. Finally, an important component of optimum management of patients with cervical spine syndromes is keeping the process cost-effective, so if the job can be done without expensive equipment, this is always best. The principles discussed here apply to any patient with a cervical spine syndrome, regardless of the diagnosis. As will be seen, however, there is some alteration in the case of the patient with whiplash.

It will also be noted that the protocols recommended in this chapter involve very little reference to published literature. There is a reason for this. As was identified specifically regarding whiplash by the Quebec Task Force on Whiplash Associated Disorders,[1] the current scientific literature offers the clinician very little in terms of guidance in the management of patients with cervical spine syndromes. And there does not appear to be a great deal on the horizon that the clinician will be able to turn to for this guidance. The research methods currently available are not able to reproduce the clinical environment and examine the dynamics of the clinician–patient interaction in such a way as to uncover meaningful information that can be used to optimize clinical care. For example, most randomized, controlled trials are designed to compare single, isolated treatments either with each other, to placebo, or to no care. But single treatments are rarely used in isolation in the clinical setting, nor should they be. More typically, a combination of treatments is utilized, and the components of that combination of treatments should be chosen on an individual basis. This approach is extremely difficult to study in the tightly controlled environment of a randomized trial.

Because of this paucity of useful data from randomized trials, empirical information derived from observation must be relied upon. These protocols are based on some of the scientific literature that is available, combined with empirical information derived from my interaction with various clinicians and observation of, and clinical care for, thousands of patients over a 12-year period.

THE PATIENT-CENTERED APPROACH

The most effective approach to care is one that is *patient centered*. This places the patient and his or her needs as the primary focus. The components of the patient-centered approach are[2]:

- Facilitation of the patient's inherent healing capacity
- Focus on the total person
- Respect for the patient's values, beliefs, health needs, and expectations
- Partnership between the practitioner and patient in decision making

Several aspects of the clinical interaction have effects, positive or negative, on the recovery process that go beyond the specific response to therapeutic interventions.[2] These nonspecific factors can be used to great advantage in enhancing the healing effect of the management strategy. The most powerful of these are[2]:

- The patient being provided with an acceptable explanation of the illness

- The clinician providing emotional support, including validation of the problem and empathy for the level of distress the patient is experiencing
- The intervention providing the patient with a sense of control over the condition
- The consultation providing the patient with a sense that "something can be done"

Another important aspect of the management approach relates to the expectation that the practitioner has with regard to the effectiveness of the management approach. Of course, it is essential that the practitioner be honest and realistic about what the patient can expect as a result of treatment. But, as Galer et al[3] have demonstrated, a positive expectation on the part of the practitioner regarding the response to treatment tends to be associated with greater pain relief reported by the patient. Thus, a positive attitude on the part of the practitioner can have a great impact on the results of treatment.

In Chapter 17, the concepts of *empathy* and *sympathy* were discussed, and it is necessary to approach these again here. The way in which the clinician and patient interact is critical to the process of the patient recovering from whatever ailment he or she is experiencing. This interaction is so powerful that it has a greater ability to "make or break" a case than any other single aspect of the management process.

Empathy helps provide for the patient the most important component of the process of restoration of health: personal empowerment. It communicates to the patient, "I understand and relate to what you are experiencing and acknowledge that your experience is relevant and very real." Sympathy, on the other hand, says, "You poor dear, things must be terrible for you." While there often is a strong tendency for patients to desire and actively seek sympathy, giving it to them only serves to further validate the sick role and cause them to identify more fully with their disability. And there is nothing more powerful than personal identity. If a clinician can help change a patient's identity from one that reflects a sick person to one that reflects someone who is well, he or she has done more for the patient's health than can any medication, manipulation, or exercise.

It is important to note, however, that as powerful as these nonspecific effects can be, they, as Jamison[2] has said, "will never be an adequate substitute for effective specific therapy." That is to say, quality care for cervical spine syndromes comes from a combination of patient empowerment *and* accurately diagnosing the problem and applying effective techniques for its correction.

CONCEPTUALIZING THE MANAGEMENT PLAN

In order to formulate a management strategy, some basic principles should be understood, and the plan should evolve from these principles. Following these principles allows the clinician to adopt a strategy that can be tailor-made for each individual patient.

WHAT IS "QUALITY CARE"?

The ingredients of quality care include:

1. Identifying the job that needs to be done.
2. Doing the job.
3. Monitoring the results.
4. Comparing the results with action 1.

Identifying the job that needs to be done includes identification of the goals of the patient, clinician, and payor; the important clinical factors contributing to the complaint; and the appropriate management strategy that will best contribute to resolution of the problem. Doing the job involves the application of the management strategy that was decided upon in the most effective and expeditious way possible. Monitoring the results involves measurement of outcomes, be it in a quantitative way (e.g., the Neck Pain and Disability Index or other outcome measurement instruments) or in a qualitative way (e.g., motion palpation

Table 28–1: The Components of the Formulation of a Management Strategy

COMPONENT	INCLUDES
1. Identifying the job that needs to be done	Ruling out red flags; identifying the primary pain generator(s); identifying the chain of dysfunction and the key link(s) in the chain; establishing a working diagnosis; establishing goals for resolution that includes those of the patient, clinician, and payor; assessing risk factors for chronicity; formulating a management strategy
2. Doing the job	Applying treatment and rehabilitation techniques; focusing on patient empowerment
3. Monitoring the results	Quantitative outcome measurement; assessing improvement in function
4. Comparing the results to action 1	Continually consulting the established goals to determine whether these goals are being achieved

to monitor improvement in joint function). Finally, the "job" that was originally identified as "needing to be done" must always be kept in mind and must serve as guide in directing the application of the management strategy (Table 28–1).

MINIMALISM

At all times, it is best to do as little as necessary to get the job done. This applies to both diagnostic approaches and treatment approaches.[4] There are many reasons for this, the most important of which relates to patient empowerment. The less that is "done to" the patient, the more he or she will be able to do on his or her own; and the less he or she feels like "a patient," the more the clinician can emphasize wellness behavior. In addition, decision making as to whether the current strategy is working according to expectation is made easier when fewer actual procedures are being applied to the patient. For example, in a patient with cervical radiculopathy who is being managed nonoperatively, one approach can be to treat the patient with nonsteroidal anti-inflammatory drugs (NSAIDs), home ice applications, manipulation, in-office traction, home traction, PIR to various muscles, interferential current therapy, hot packs, and McKenzie exercises. But suppose the patient is not responding. What should be stopped? What should be altered? What should be continued? This presents a confusing picture, indeed. Much more effective would be to identify the two or three things that are most important and treat only those, closely monitoring the results.

RED FLAGS, PAIN GENERATORS, KEY LINKS

In Chapter 17, the basic principles of diagnosis were described as being based on three questions: (1) Is this a potentially serious or life-threatening condition?, (2) What specific tissue(s) is (are) the primary source(s) of this patient's pain? and (3) What has gone wrong with this person as a whole that would cause the primary pain generator(s) to generate pain? Asking these questions, and seeking their answers, allows the clinician to then base the management strategy for each patient on what was discovered during the history and examination.

The discovery of red flags *may* cause the physician to further investigate through the use of imaging studies or other special tests or refer the patient to an appropriate specialist (although special testing or specialist referral in many cases will *not* be necessary and watchful waiting may be the best approach; this needs to be evaluated on an individual basis).

Identifying the primary pain generator(s) allows one to then choose the specific treatment modalities that can best reduce the generation of pain as quickly as possible, providing for rapid pain relief. It is important, however, that the primary pain generator not be assumed to be the primary problem. This is especially important in chronic conditions, in which the nervous system may have undergone plastic changes and significant locomotor system dysfunction may have developed. When these changes occur, the dysfunction can serve to both maintain central pain pathways and perpetuate the generation of pain by the primary pain generator(s), but may be quite remote from those pain generators. An example of this would be the patient who experiences cervical injury in a rear-end collision. Acute pain that arises from specific tissue injury predominates in the beginning, and the most appropriate treatment strategies should be directed toward the injured tissues (see Chap. 21). But in the patient who presents with a condition that is already chronic, more generalized dysfunction has likely developed, and this dysfunction is likely to perpetuate the central pain state as well as the generation of pain from the periphery. In this situation, focusing solely on the pain generating tissues without addressing the more generalized dysfunction will dramatically decrease the likelihood of success.

Hence, in the acute stage, after red flags have been ruled out, the choice of treatments should be based on rapid reduction of nociception. In the subacute and chronic stages, treatment approaches should be chosen on the basis of addressing pain generation as well as the identified key dysfunction(s) that is (are) occurring.

IDENTIFYING THE KEY LINK IN THE CHAIN OF DYSFUNCTION

As has been discussed throughout this book, most patients with cervical spine syndromes—regardless of whether their pain is recent in onset or more long-standing—have some type of underlying dysfunction that is chronic. And, as has been discussed, dysfunction in the locomotor system often occurs in chains, as a result of the alteration of neurological programs such as gait, prehension, breathing, and so forth. In addition to identifying the source of the nociception, it is essential that the clinician identify the dysfunctional chain that is most likely responsible for the perpetuation of the pain as well. Once this is accomplished, the clinician must identify the key link in that chain; that is, the joint, muscle, skin, fascial, or programmatic dysfunction that is most responsible for the perpetuation of the chain.

In this book, particularly in Chapters 13, 14, 19, and 20, a large number of methods have been presented to identify various types of dysfunctions that can potentially serve as key links in the chain of dysfunction in patients with cervical syndromes. The great variety of dysfunctions that can develop in the locomotor system, and the variety of procedures available for their detection, can be overwhelming and can lead to confusion on the part of the clinician in attempting to discover the primary dysfunctional chain that is occurring and to identify the key link in that chain. For this reason, the process is best kept as simple as possible. It should start general and become more localized as information is gathered. It is best to start with the most important programs for the cervical spine patient that can serve as chains of dysfunction. These are:

- Mastication, assessed primarily with the mandibular movement pattern and swallowing pattern tests
- Prehension, assessed primarily with the shoulder abduction movement pattern test
- Gait, as assessed primarily with the hip extension movement pattern test and the stepping test
- Breathing, as assessed primarily with breathing pattern test
- Arising from a supine or seated position, as assessed primarily with the cervical flexion movement pattern test
- Stability: cervical stability, as assessed primarily with the cervical stability and swallowing movement pattern tests; scapular stability, with the shoulder abduction and push-up tests; and postural stability, with the postural foot reaction test
- Eye-head-neck coordination, as assessed primarily with Revel's test

Pelvic function is also important in the cervical spine, as assessed primarily with the S-reflex. Posture (body statics) should also be assessed in all patients, as postural set can have an impact on all motor programs and postural assessment can provide clues to key dysfunctions.

It is not always necessary to assess all these programs in every patient. For example, breathing and prehension may be important in the neck or arm pain patient, but far less important in the headache patient, while pelvic function and eye-head-neck coordination may be far more important in the headache patient.

Once one or more dysfunctional chains are detected, a critically important question must be asked: What is the relevance of this faulty chain to the patient's complaint? This is an essential factor to consider, as the body is often perfectly capable of dealing with a certain program that may not be operating in a manner that would be considered normal; thus, it is wasteful to try to treat everything that is found. The determination of relevance will require a certain amount of clinical experience and trial and error, and there are no hard and fast rules in deciding the relevance of a certain faulty chain. An "educated guess" is often required in forming an impression, and a trial of treatment is almost always successful in confirming or denying this impression. As always, the principle of minimalism must be kept in mind.

! CLINICAL PEARL

Your most important diagnostic tool is a trial of treatment!

When a certain faulty chain is determined to be clinically relevant, specific localized joint, muscle, or skin and fascial dysfunction can be assessed as possible key links. The structures assessed should be those that are involved in the dysfunctional chain. Examples of the most important, but certainly not the only, areas to assess as possible key links are provided in Table 28–2.

For example, in a patient with faulty stepping test, the upper cervical joints, sternocleidomastoids, suboccipitals, splenii capitii, and feet should be examined. With faulty shoulder abduction, the sternoclavicular, glenohumeral, first costotransverse and cervicothoracic junction joints, along with the muscles found to be hyperactive in the movement pattern, should be examined. With faulty postural foot reaction, the joints, skin, and fascial tissues of the feet should be assessed.

Once localized dysfunctions involved in the faulty chain have been detected, another critical question must be asked: Are these dysfunctions the key link in the chain? As with the faulty chains, certain localized dysfunctions may be well tolerated by the body, and are not necessarily relevant to the patient's clinical complaint. Also, as with identifying the most important chain, the determination of the key link can only be made with certainty by a trial of treatment. Once again, minimalism should dictate. It is best to choose those two or three (or perhaps even one) dysfunctions that have the greatest likelihood of being the key link, treat them, and monitor the results.

The decision as to which dysfunctions to treat first as possible key links need not be complete guesswork. Certain factors may help increase the likelihood that a certain dysfunction is a key link, as follows:

- Because joint dysfunction is commonly the genesis of muscle dysfunction (and, thus, of faulty movement pattern), it is likely that at least one of the key links will be a joint.
- Areas that supply the most intense afferentation generally have a bigger impact on the nervous system when they develop dysfunction than do areas or less intense afferentation. Therefore, when found, they are more likely to be a key link. For example, in a patient with chronic headaches who has a positive stepping test and cervical stability test, joint dysfunction in the upper cervical spine will more likely be a key link than sternoclavicular joint dysfunction.
- As was discussed in Chapter 21, in a patient who has had trauma, as from a motor vehicle accident (MVA), the area of most intense pain in the acute stage often corresponds to the area of the key link. An example of this would be a patient with chronic pain near the medial border of the scapula with faulty scapular stability, in whom the most intense pain initially was in the area of C5. Commonly, joint dysfunction at C5 is a key link.
- Trigger points are common pain generators, but they are rarely key links.

It must be noted that not all patients will have a detectable dysfunctional chain. Frequently, a patient's cervical spine syndrome is explainable solely on the basis of local pain generators. This was alluded to in Chapter 9, when it was said that many patients with cervical radiculopathy related to herniated nucleus pulposus require little or no treatment. If there is no major dysfunctional chain, there will be little that needs to be done. This makes the clinician's job infinitely easier and, in most cases, makes for relatively quick resolution, even in chronic cases. So it is essential that the clinician avoid searching endlessly for a dysfunctional chain that does not exist. In these cases, the management consists only of treating the pain generators themselves, correcting local dysfunction, and educating the patient to avoid irritating the painful structures in the future. Again, it is always best to do the least that is necessary to get the job done.

MONITORING THE RESULTS

The results of treatment should be monitored using several strategies. First, the outcome measurement instruments that were used to determine pain intensity, disability level, and so forth (see Chap. 15) should be repeated to assess whether the treatment approach is creating a change in

Table 28–2: The Most Important Faulty Chains in Patients With Cervical Spine Syndromes, Their Detection, and the Most Important Dysfunctions to Assess as Possible Key Links

FAULTY PROGRAM	DETECTED BY	POSSIBLE KEY LINKS
Prehension	Shoulder abduction movement pattern test	First costotransverse joint dysfunction; upper cervical joint dysfunction; CT junction joint dysfunction; SC, AC, or glenohumeral joint dysfunction; upper trapezius, levator scapulae or rhomboid hypertonicity; pectoralis major hypertonicity; middle trapezius, lower trapezius, or serratus anterior inhibition
Gait	Hip extension movement pattern test; stepping test	SI joint dysfunction; upper cervical joint dysfunction; intertarsal, subtalar, or mortise joint dysfunction; hip joint dysfunction; upper trapezius, levator scapulae, or rhomboid hypertonicity; transverse abdominis, internal oblique and multifidis inhibition; gluteus maximus inhibition
Breathing	Breathing movement pattern test	First costotransverse joint dysfunction; lower cervical joint dysfunction; scalene hypertonicity; pectoralis minor hypertonicity; diaphragm inhibition
Arising from a supine or seated position	Cervical flexion movement pattern test	Upper cervical joint dysfunction; SCM hypertonicity; suboccipital tightness or adhesions; deep cervical flexor inhibition; fixed forward head posture
Cervical stability	Cervical stability test; swallowing movement pattern test	Upper cervical joint dysfunction; SC joint dysfunction; SCM hypertonicity; suboccipital tightness or adhesions; deep cervical flexor or lower cervical and upper thoracic extensor inhibition; fixed forward head posture
Postural stability	Postural foot reaction test	Intertarsal joint dysfunction; plantar skin and fascial dysfunction; mortise or subtalar joint dysfunction; upper cervical joint dysfunction
Scapular stability	Shoulder abduction movement pattern test; push-up test	First costotransverse joint dysfunction; upper trapezius, levator scapulae, rhomboid, or pectoralis major hypertonicity; middle trapezius, lower trapezius, or serratus anterior inhibition
Eye-head-neck coordination	Revel's test	Upper cervical joint dysfunction; SCM, suboccipital, or splenius capitis hypertonicity
Pelvic function	S-reflex	Sacrotuberous ligament dysfunction; pelvic diaphragm dysfunction

AC, acromioclavicular; CT, cervicothoracic; SC, sternoclavicular; SCM, sternocleidomastoid; SI, sacroiliac.

these parameters. The ultimate goal of treatment—the improvement in the functional ability of the patient and the maximization of his or her ability to engage in those activities of daily living that are meaningful to him or her—should always be paramount. Also, the movement pattern or other tests that were used to identify the dysfunctional chain should be used to determine if the treatment that is being applied to the suspected key link is working. Finally, the examination procedures that were used to determine the localized dysfunction (e.g., motion palpation, muscle length tests) should be used to assess whether the treatment is successfully improving local function.

HOW OFTEN SHOULD RESULTS BE MONITORED?

There are no definitive rules regarding the time frame for the determination of response to treatment. A variety of factors are involved in this, including whether an acute, subacute, or chronic condition is being treated; whether the onset of the condition was traumatic, as in a MVA; the age of the patient; and other clinical factors. However, outcome measurement instruments should be utilized every 2 to 3 weeks in nontraumatic conditions and every 2 to 4 weeks in acute traumatic conditions. This, of course, assumes that the patient requires care that lasts as long as 2 weeks. In many cases, less than 2 weeks of care are needed, in which case outcome measurements should be made on the first and last visit.

Pain generators, dysfunctional chains, and local dysfunction should be assessed at least as frequently and usually more frequently, than the outcome measurements. With these assessments, impatience is a virtue. In general, two or three visits should be enough to see a change in the condition—symptoms, pain generators, dysfunctional chain, local dysfunction, or any combination of these. The exception to this is the patient with soft tissue injury related to trauma, in which case longer periods of time should generally be expected before change occurs.

THE PASSIVE/ACTIVE CARE CONTINUUM

It is often noted that, in the management of spine-related disorders, an emphasis on what is called "active care" is desirable over an emphasis on what is called "passive care."[5] However, much confusion has arisen over this distinction. Certain treatment approaches have been dismissed as "passive," and others promoted as "active," often based on personal bias rather than on a definitive description of what constitutes "passive" and "active." It is suggested here that, rather than consider any particular treatment approach that may be applied to a patient with a cervical spine syndrome as necessarily "passive" or "active," it is most useful to consider the approach in the context of how "passive" or "active" it is compared to the other treatment approaches from which one has to choose.[6] In order to do this, the relative passivity or activity of a certain treatment approach must be determined by definitive criteria. The recommended criteria for this determination are provided in Table 28–3.

Using these criteria, the various common treatment approaches, rather than being placed into black-and-white categories of "passive care" or "active care," are placed on a

Table 28–3: Criteria for Determining the Relative Passivity or Activity of a Treatment Approach

1. The level of tissue mobilization that results
2. The level of stimulation of healing response that results
3. The degree to which the patient takes responsibility in the recovery process

Adapted from Murphy DR. The passive/active care continuum: A model for the treatment of spine related disorders. J Neuromuscukoskel Sys 1996;4(1):1–7.

continuum, with the relatively more passive forms toward the left and the relatively more active forms toward the right (Fig. 28–1.).

DECISION MAKING

Treatment approaches that are taken in each specific clinical situation must be based on a predetermined strategy for the management of the patient. Because of this, there is no "cookbook" formula that can be applied. The process of patient management must be unique to each individual patient's problem and must be designed to address the key components (or key links) that are contributing to the clinical syndrome.

From the passive-active care continuum (see Fig. 28–1), the initial treatment approach and the ongoing treatment plan can be conceptualized. Every attempt should be made to begin treatment as far to the right on the continuum as possible, and then to accelerate the process to the right as quickly as possible (over days, weeks, or months, depending on the situation). The ultimate goal of all management plans should be to help the patient get to the point at which he or she is independent from any clinician and either able to self-manage the condition, or be free of the condition and able to engage in normal ac-

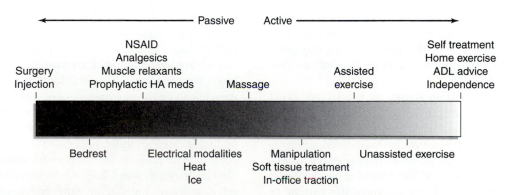

Figure 28–1. The passive-active care continuum. ADL, activities of daily living; NSAID, nonsteroidal anti-inflammatory drug.

(Adapted from Murphy DR. The passive/active care continuum: A model for the treatment of spine related disorders. J Neuromuscuoskel Sys 1996;4(1):1–7.)

tivities. There are, of course, those patients who will not completely reach this point, but approximating this as closely as possible must be foremost in the clinician's mind. Remaining too long at any one point along the continuum will compromise the process of functional restoration and patient empowerment and must be avoided.

THE EXCEPTIONAL CIRCUMSTANCE: WHIPLASH

Patients with cervical spine syndromes that result from injury related to MVAs often require a management strategy that is somewhat different from those whose pain has a nontraumatic etiology. Although the management follows the same principles (patient-centeredness, minimalism, identifying the job that needs to be done, doing the job, monitoring results, comparing results with goals, the passive-active care continuum), the process as a whole often takes longer and the treatment is often more intensive (this depends on a number of factors, including the severity of the injury and the presence of risk factors for chronicity).

The treatment in the acute stage is usually more intense than in patients with nontraumatic cervical syndromes (see Chap. 21) and progress is generally slower. Outcome measurements are generally made every 4 weeks, rather than every 2 weeks (however, if it is seen that the patient is making progress that is faster than expected, outcome measurement should be made sooner than planned). Once the acute, severe pain is decreased, the patient should be assessed for the need for exercise rehabilitation (see later discussion).

RISK FACTORS FOR CHRONICITY

It is important, in the subacute stage of whiplash injury, to assess the patient for risk factors for the development of ongoing chronic pain. The purpose of this assessment is to evaluate whether aggressive rehabilitation measures aimed at preventing the development of chronic pain are necessary or whether a relatively more "hands off" approach can be taken. It also allows the clinician to have a better perspective on when it is most appropriate to cease treatment and help the patient accept the reality of ongoing pain. The primary risk factors for chronicity in whiplash are provided in Table 6–3.

In a patient who exhibits significant risk factors, every attempt must be made to prevent chronicity. This means identifying the key dysfunctional chains that require exercise rehabilitation, and instituting this rehabilitation as quickly and aggressively as possible. It is essential to encourage active involvement on the part of the patient and make every attempt possible to empower the patient to take as full responsibility as possible in his or her own recovery, and to impart to the patient confidence in his or her ability to be successful.

Inevitably there will be some patients for whom aggressive rehabilitation is not be successful in completely eliminating their pain and disability. For these patients, early consideration of treatment cessation must be considered.

> ### ❗ CLINICAL PEARL
>
> Ceasing treatment of a patient who continues to experience pain is one of the most difficult things for a caring clinician to do. Naturally, we are all in this business to "help sick people get well" and our natural inclination is to continue seeking to end our patient's suffering, taking as much time and effort (and expense, as it turns out) as is necessary. However, there are times when the most compassionate thing that we can do is teach our patients how to best cope with chronic pain and allow them to detach from the treatment process. Treatment and rehabilitation, even when they have a functional orientation, naturally places a certain degree of focus on the patient's pain and, as a result, can reach a point at which the process merely reinforces the pain experience and pain behavior, leading to further dependency and despair. Knowing when to end treatment in this situation is a fine art, and one that requires a great deal of courage on the part of the clinician. Our job is to do what is best for our patients, and there are times when "cutting the umbilical cord" can empower the patient to move on with his or her life.

WHEN IS REHABILITATION NECESSARY?

First, it should be considered that virtually everything involved in the management process can be considered rehabilitation, as each procedure applied should be designed to in some way improve function. However, there are certain patients in certain clinical situations for whom exercise rehabilitative measures are required. Again, in the interest of minimalism, there are specific indicators for this approach. In the absence of these indicators, exercise rehabilitation is usually not necessary.

The most important indicator for the need for exercise rehabilitation is when the treatment of localized dysfunction fails to improve the identified faulty chain. When a certain faulty chain and the suspected key links in the chain have been identified, treatment is applied to the key links. It may happen that the localized dysfunctions that were felt to be the key links resolve with treatment but the faulty chain remains, or both the localized dysfunctions and the faulty chain fail to resolve with treatment. This finding is often an indication that the faulty chain has become a fixed program in the nervous system as a result of plastic alteration (see Chap. 4). In this case, correction of relevant joint, muscle, or skin and fascial dysfunction, while essential in establishing the afferent input necessary to carry out effective motor programs, is not enough to normalize the programmatic alteration, and rehabilitative methods are required. It is in this situation that sensorimotor training or cervical stabilization, or both, are necessary.

Again, the movement pattern and other functional tests are used to assess improvement in the relevant faulty chains in each patient. And the quantitative outcome measurements are used to monitor the effect of this improvement on pain and lifestyle activities. Where emphasis is placed in the exercise rehabilitation process is determined by the specific faulty program that is being treated. This, as always, must be decided on an individual basis, but there are certain general guidelines that can be followed. See Table 28–4 for these guidelines and Chapter 25 for the specific exercise methods. It must be noted that these are general guidelines, only, and should not be seen as rigid rules. As always, outcome should be closely monitored so that what is done is the least that is necessary to create a plastic alteration that restores the abnormal program to normal.

Other indications for exercise rehabilitation are sometimes found in the presence of a fixed program and other times not. These are: (1) significant deconditioning, in a patient in whom this deconditioning is deemed to be a significant factor in his or her condition, and (2) the presence of significant fear avoidance behavior (i.e., fear that movement will worsen symptoms).

Exercise is the obvious treatment of choice in deconditioning and should focus on cervical stabilization along with aerobic conditioning and weight training. With fear-avoidance behavior, stabilization is ideal, as the patient can be peeled back to the level at which he or she can work and intensity can be gradually increased. Gradually introducing increased intensity of exercise is often effective in illustrating to the patient that he or she is capable of engaging in activities that he or she previously thought were impossible. This approach is instrumental in empowering the patient to take control of the condition.

WHAT IF THE PATIENT IS NOT GETTING BETTER?

Once the management strategy is in place, treatment based on that strategy is instituted, and outcome monitored, what happens if the patient is not progressing as expected? In this instance, several possibilities need to be considered, as follows:

- The diagnosis is incorrect.
- The key link has not been identified.
- The key link has been identified, but the treatment being applied has not successfully resolved the dysfunction.
- There are other key dysfunctions in addition to, or instead of, what was thought to be the key link that require treatment.
- The faulty chain has become a fixed program in the nervous system and requires rehabilitation.
- There are factors in the lifestyle of the patient that are interfering with recovery.

Each of these possibilities must be investigated and acted upon.

Table 28–4: Guidelines for Deciding Which Exercise Rehabilitation Procedures to Use in Each Patient

FAULTY PROGRAM	EXERCISE REHABILITATIVE APPROACH	WHERE TO PLACE PARTICULAR FOCUS
Prehension	Cervical stabilization	Quadruped track; prone walkout track; floor bridge track
Gait	Sensorimotor training	One-legged stand on wobble board progression with perturbations
Arising from a supine or seated position	Cervical stabilization Sensorimotor training	Quadruped track, especially with book balancing; prone walkout track; one-legged stand on wobble board progression with perturbations for the deep cervical flexors
Cervical stability	Cervical stabilization Sensorimotor training	Quadruped track, especially with book balancing; prone walkout track; one-legged stand on wobble board progression with perturbations to the deep cervical flexors and use of body blade
Postural stability	Sensorimotor training	One-legged stand on wobble board progression and sandals
Scapular stability	Cervical stabilization	Quadruped track; prone walkout track; floor bridge track
Eye-head-neck coordination	Sensorimotor training	One-legged stand on the wobble board progression with eye-head-neck coordination exercises

CONCLUSION

The principles of diagnosis discussed in Chapter 17—ruling out red flags, identifying the pain generator, and identifying the key dysfunctions leading to and perpetuating pain generation—flow naturally into the principles of management. These principles are reducing generation of pain, correcting dysfunction, patient empowerment, transitioning from more passive to more active forms of care, monitoring outcomes, assessing risk factors for chronicity, knowing when to stop treatment, and minimalism.

Optimum care for patients with cervical spine syndromes necessitates following the principles of both diagnosis and management. The protocols provided in this chapter revolve around these principles. The application of effective techniques is only of benefit to a patient if they are applied for the correct diagnosis, at the correct time, and in an environment in which patient empowerment is at the forefront of the management strategy. Further research is needed to assess these protocols and to improve upon them.

REFERENCES

1. Spitzer WO, Skovron ML, Salmi LR, et al. Scientific monograph of the Quebec Task Force on Whiplash-Associated Disorders: Redefining "whiplash" and its management. *Spine* 1995;20(8S):2S–73S.
2. Jamison JR. Nonspecific intervention in chiropractic care. *J Manipulative Physiol Ther* 1998;21(6):423–425.
3. Galer BS, Schwartz L, Turner JA. Do patient and physician expectations predict response to pain-relieving procedures? *Clin J Pain* 1997;13:348–351.
4. Nelson C. Commentary: Where do we go from here? *J Manipulative Physiol Ther* 1995;18(3):178–182.
5. Haldeman S, Chapman-Smith D, Peterson DM, eds. *Guidelines for Chiropractic Quality Assurance and Practice Parameters*. Gaithersburg, Md: Aspen; 1993.
6. Murphy DR. The passive/active care continuum: A model for the treatment of spine related disorders. *J Neuromusculoskel Sys* 1996;4(1):1–7.

CHAPTER 29

Diagnostic and Management Techniques for the Difficult Cervical Spine Patient

Kim Garges, Arthur H. White, & Mary Koestler

"Men argue, nature acts."

—Voltaire

INTRODUCTION

A cost-conscious health care market is truly a formidable tergiversator of the difficult cervical spine patient. Managed care environments are making it increasingly difficult to care for patients who have had extensive but inadequate workups. Regional differences in acceptable testing protocols add to the confusion. The patient is often at odds with both the physician and the third-party payor. Time lapses between ordering and approving certain tests leave patients frustrated and angry. They may seek another physician who is less interested in patient welfare and more interested in capturing the managed care market, thereby offering treatment without adequate diagnostic information. Since they do not improve, these patients are later labeled as chronic pain sufferers and shunned by many physicians. A complete history of past imaging, medications, spinal injections, surgeries, and other treatments will help avoid the pitfalls of the patients' previous physician, as will obtaining copies of medical records and imaging before ordering any tests or therapy. Careful clinical examination and review of these medical records will avoid duplication and preserve the patients' health care budget.

The purpose of this chapter is to provide the nonsurgeon with an understanding of patients with difficult problems of the cervical spine. To this end, invasive tests and procedures have been described without superfluous detail. For the most part, descriptions of practical, applicable concepts from SpineCare* have been used in lieu of referenced data.

Difficult cervical spine patients can be divided into four categories. The first category includes those patients who have obvious pathology but in whom the disease is so extensive that conservative therapy† alone is ineffective, and a good surgical outcome is doubtful. Here, operative treatment may not appreciably alter lifestyle or improve pain scores. In the second group are those who demonstrate specific signs and symptoms of a lesion but in whom conventional

---

*SpineCare Medical Group/San Francisco Spine Institute, Arthur H. White, MD, Medical Director, Daly City, California.
†For the purpose of this chapter *conservative therapy* includes physical training, manual therapy, manipulation, acupuncture, and so on, but not medication. *Conservative treatment* includes medications.

testing (X-rays, scans, etc.) does not reveal the source of the pain. A third group includes those patients in whom the diagnosis is in question and, therefore, a treatment plan cannot be formulated based on a diagnosis. In this case there is no verifiable objective outcome. A fourth and special group of patients is those with neuropathic pain. This pain may occur secondary to nerve injury from disc herniations, foraminal encroachment, or postsurgery (Table 29–1).

REVIEW OF IMAGING AND OTHER TESTING

After a complete history and physical examination, imaging and minimally invasive procedures add greatly to confirming a diagnosis. Conventional studies include X-rays, MRI scans, CT scans, and electromyography (EMG/NCS).

X-rays should always include an AP, APOM, lateral, obliques, and lateral flexion/extension views. The occiput to the first thoracic vertebra should be clearly visible. A swimmer's view may help better visualize the lower cervical spine. Instability is indicated if a vertebra translates more than 3.5 mm or angulates greater than 11 degrees between segments on the lateral views.[1]

Table 29–1: Categories of Difficult Spine Patients

CATEGORY	CHARACTERISTICS	DIAGNOSIS	MANAGEMENT
I	**Obvious Pathology/Multilevel DDD** Extensive pathology Conservative therapy alone ineffective Doubtful good surgical outcome	X-rays, MRIs, CT scans EMG/NCS *(consider discograms if surgical consult indicated)*	Conservative treatment *(Exception: severe radiculopathy/ myelopathy—immediate surgical)* Stabilization/Strength training Stretching exercises Gentle manipulation Epidural injection SNRB/Periodic examination for myelopathic signs
II	**Specific Signs/Symptoms of Lesion** Conventional testing does not reveal pain source IDD and facet syndrome	X-rays, MRI, CT scans Discograms Facet blocks	Conservative treatment Pain management clinic Physical therapy Manipulation Stabilization training Surgery if all else fails
III	**Diagnosis in Question** Unable to formulate treatment plan based on diagnosis **Subgroups:**		
	a. Patient with or without organic disease Malingering, somatization, somatoform pain disorder, secondary gain	X-rays, MRI, CT scans Psychological evaluation	Conservative treatment Physical therapy Psychological support
	b. Fibromyalgia, fibromyositis, similar conditions	X-rays, MRI, CT scans	Conservative treatment Manual/physical therapy Rheumatology consult
	c. Pain generators not yet fully understood	X-rays, MRI, CT scans	Conservative treatment
IV	**Special Group: Neuropathic Pain** Sympathetically maintained pain—may occur secondary to nerve injury from disc herniations, foraminal encroachment, or postsurgery	X-rays, MRI, CT scans	Mainstay: conservative treatment Spinal cord stimulation Sympathetic blocks

CT, computed tomography; DDD, degenerative disk disease; EMG, electromyogram; IDD, internal disk disruption; MRI, magnetic resonance imaging; NCS, nerve conduction studies.

> **! CLINICAL PEARL**
>
> Check lateral flexion and extension views for instability. If present always evaluate for dynamic Hoffman's sign and other signs of myelopathy or spinal cord damage (Fig. 29–1).

MRI scans reveal changes in water and fat content. The MRI is of particular value in evaluating aging discs. The volume of the nucleus pulposus diminishes with decreasing hydration and increasing fibrosis.[2] Anhydrous material such as bone is not well visualized. Central canal and foraminal stenosis, if caused by bony impingement, may be underestimated on MRI. CT shows bone well but soft tissue is not as well visualized. Typically in the cervical spine, MRI scans are more useful than CT since lesions that affect the cervical cord and exiting roots are usually of the disc, and marginal osteophytes arising from the posterior aspect of the vertebral endplate. A MRI demonstrates focal effacement of the anterior cervical subarachnoid space and flattening or compression of the cervical cord. Postoperative patients with persistent or new symptoms should have a CT scan as well as an MRI with gadolinium. A nonunion at the graft site will be best seen on the CT, but scar tissue from previous surgery can be better differentiated from disc by gadolinium enhanced MRI scanning. Modes of failure other than nonunion, after anterior cervical arthrodesis, include collapse of the graft and the disc space with kyphosis, migration of the graft causing stenosis, and residual nerve-root or spinal-cord compression resulting in pain with or without paralysis[3] (Fig. 29–2).

Patients with neck pain and nerve symptoms in the upper extremities with or without recognizable pathology on scans, or in whom symptoms are not dermatomal and myotomal, may need electrodiagnostic studies as an extension of their clinical examination. These studies can be helpful in differentiating radiculopathy from peripheral nerve entrapment. Also, these studies can alert the physician to the possibility of a concomitant peripheral neuropathy with radiculopathy. In a small percentage of patients, the diagnosis of radiculopathy is established by EMG when the diagnosis on clinical grounds seems unlikely.[4]

> **! CLINICAL PEARL**
>
> Use electrodiagnostics to differentiate radiculopathy from peripheral nerve entrapment in difficult cases.

Other diagnostic and therapeutic procedures of particular value in difficult cervical spine cases include epidural injections, selective nerve root blocks, facet blocks, and discograms. The former three procedures can be therapeutic, whereas discograms are only diagnostic.

Epidural injections are performed by placing a needle in the interlaminar space between C7 and T1 under fluoroscopic control. Contrast media and steroid suspension are injected through a single syringe under image intensification. The purpose of the contrast material is to verify the flow of the mixture to the target level. Inflammation is a critical component of radicular pain and steroids work best when this inflammation is still acute, before progression to nerve-root fibrosis or axonal death occurs.[5] The steroid reduces swelling and inflammation surrounding the nerve roots and dura. Inflammation presumptively occurs with a herniated disc or other lesion that impinges on the dura and exiting nerve roots. By reducing the swelling, the space available for the nerve in the intervertebral foramina is increased, hence the pain due to the pressure on the nerve is reduced.

> **! CLINICAL PEARL**
>
> Steroids work best when inflammation is acute.

Selective nerve root blocks (SNRB) are performed through a transforaminal approach with the same mixture of steroid and contrast media, and under fluoroscopic image control. Selective blocks are more specific and far more accurate for a single nerve root than an epidural injection and, therefore, are more diagnostic, as well as being therapeutic. If symptoms decrease after an SNRB, a source of the pain has been identified and now a treatment plan specific for that area can be developed. The consequence of a misdirected injection into the vertebral artery makes this route of delivery much less favorable than the epidural approach in the cervical spine.

Facet injections are indicated for painful facet joints. Facet joint pain can usually be identified as axial pain that increases upon neck extension. If these joints are suspected to be problematic, a mixture of contrast media, corticosteroid, and lidocaine is injected via a posterior or lateral approach.

Discograms have no therapeutic value and are used only as a preoperative study. A needle is placed medial to the medial border of the sternocleidomastoid muscle and through the anulus, into the nucleus. Contrast media is injected into the cervical disc; the disc is pressurized through the syringe; and the patient's pain is noted as well as the dye pattern under fluoroscopy. If the disc is disrupted, the dye extends from the nucleus into anular fissures. This may cause significant pain if the fissures extend into the outer two thirds of the pain-sensitive anulus (Fig. 29–3).

A convincing, positive response to disc stimulation is one in which the patient reports exact or similar reproduction of pain on stimulation of a given disc but provided that stressing one or two

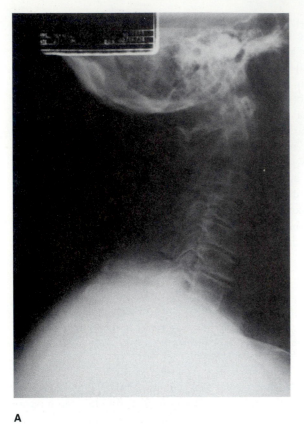

A

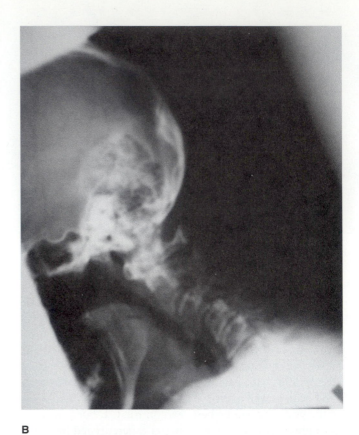

B

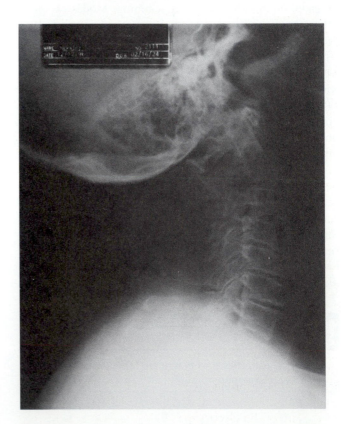

C

Figure 29–1. Lateral neutral **(A)**, flexion **(B)**, and extension **(C)** radiographs of a 60-year-old female with instability of C3–4. Patient complained of clumsiness of hands and gait, and exhibited positive Hoffman's sign and ankle clonus. Anterior cervical fusion resulted in resolution of complaints, Hoffman's sign, and ankle clonus.

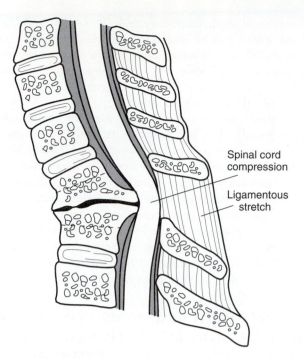

Figure 29–2. Anterior cervical fusion with collapse of graft.

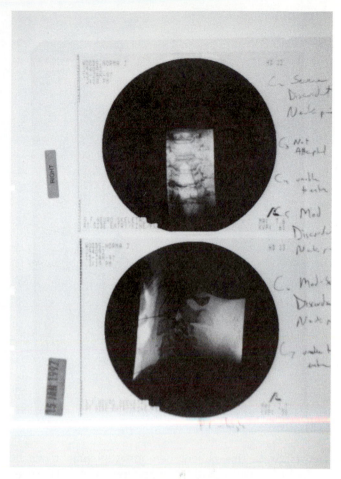

Figure 29–3. Discogram with needles in C2–3, C5–6, and C6–7 disk spaces. Demonstrated disrupted pattern of dye and discordant pain at all levels tested. C3–4 disk was not injected secondary to severe central stenosis and a herniated nucleus pulposus on MRI. C4–5 and C7–T1 could not be entered due to osteophytosis.

adjacent discs is painless or evokes pain totally foreign to the patient's previous experience. Any other pattern of response cannot be held to be reliably indicative that the disc stimulated is the source of the patient's pain. It may be possible for a patient to have two symptomatic discs, but under those circumstances, it is still mandatory to identify an adjacent disc that is asymptomatic. Without an asymptomatic "control" disc, there is no evidence that what they are reporting as disc pain is not simply the pain of needles felt in the back or neck.[6]

The morphology of the disc is not diagnostic; a convincing diagnosis is obtained only if the familiar (concordant) pain is reproduced and the disc appears disrupted. Discogenic pain may present as axial pain, headaches, interscapular pain, or upper extremity pain. It usually does not follow a dermatomal pattern.

Percutaneous radiofrequency techniques to coagulate the cervical dorsal rami near their origin have been used for pain suspected to originate from the zygapophysial joints.[7] This technique requires a skilled technician and careful attention to detail since the cervical cord is so near to the site of the electrode. Cervical medial branch nerve blocks anesthetize the small medial branches of the dorsal rami that supply the zygapophysial joints.[8] Radiofrequency techniques, medial branch blocks, and intra-articular facet injections have been successful conservative measures used for facet pain.

FOUR CATEGORIES OF DIFFICULT CERVICAL SPINE PATIENTS

PATIENTS WITH EXTENSIVE DISEASE

Patients who have painful degenerative disease at multiple levels (four or more) are usually better suited for conservative treatment than operative treatment (Fig. 29–4). Nonunions have been reported in as many as 50 percent of patients with multilevel fusions.[9] Those with severe radicular symptoms or myelopathy, or both, are exceptions and should be immediately referred for surgical consultation. In instances where urinary retention or incontinence, bowel incontinence, abnormal gait, upper extremity clumsiness, or severe intractable pain are caused by cervical cord or cervical nerve root impingement, surgical treatment is indicated before any conservative treatment care plan is

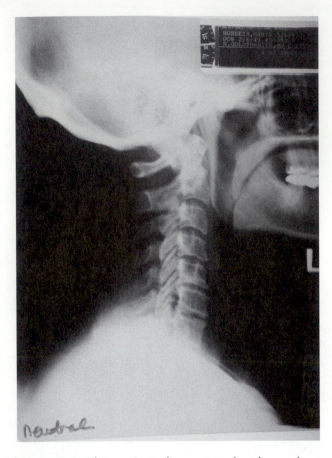

Neutral

Figure 29–4. This patient demonstrated only moderate multilevel degenerative changes on X-ray. However, discography demonstrated four levels (C2 through C6) of painful disks and disrupted patterns, along with a low pain threshold. She is not an operative candidate.

begun. The cervical spine levels responsible for the neurological changes should be decompressed and fused. Myelopathic symptoms correlate with at least 30 percent reduction of the cross-sectional area of the cervical cord to a value of about 60 mm by contrast CT.[10]

! CLINICAL PEARL

Patients with myelopathy should be referred for immediate surgical consultation.

Other cervical levels that appear degenerated on scan but are felt not to contribute to deficits are probably best left for conservative treatment. Multiple fused spinal segments create long lever arms, which increase the likelihood of accelerated degeneration above and below the fusion. Multilevel painful disease can be treated with a combination of conservative therapy and medications. Stabilization training, gentle manipulation, muscle stretching, and strengthening are a few of the more popular treatments.

Nonsteroidal antiinflammatory drugs (NSAIDs) and long-acting opiates may be used in combination. Epidural injections and SNRB are sometimes effective in the short term for degenerative disease but their effects usually dwindle with each successive block, and the cumulative cortisone dose limits their continued use.

Painful one- or two-level degenerative cervical disc disease usually does not present a treatment dilemma. If unresponsive to conservative therapy, NSAIDs are added to the regimen. Short-acting narcotic medication can be used occasionally for acute episodes, but their daily continued use is not indicated. Patients who require narcotics on a daily basis despite an adequate and aggressive conservative therapy plan may be candidates for cervical fusion. In that case an extensive workup, including MRI, diagnostic SNRB, and discograms, should be considered to evaluate possible pain generators prior to considering surgery.

PATIENTS WITH SYMPTOMS CONSISTENT WITH A LESION BUT WITH NEGATIVE CONVENTIONAL STUDIES: INTERNAL DISC DISRUPTION AND FACET SYNDROME

! CLINICAL PEARL

IDD and facet syndrome do not have neurological deficits associated with them.

Internal Disc Disruption

Patients who demonstrate symptoms consistent with a lesion but in whom conventional studies are unremarkable, present a diagnostic dilemma, especially in the managed care system:

- Physical examination is nonspecific.
- Limitation of forward flexion is common but muscle spasm is usually not present.
- There are no neurological changes.
- Palpation of the cervical discs anterior through the neck may produce concordant pain.
- MRI scanning may not reveal signs of disc involvement or appreciable foraminal or central canal stenosis.
- The facets may be free of obvious disease. Still the patient complains of headaches, shoulder pain, interscapular pain, arm pain, or neck pain.
- Nausea and vomiting are rare complaints but may occur.

In these cases the physician must be suspicious of internal disc disruption (IDD) as the cause. Discogram is the test of choice. As discussed earlier, this is a provocative test in

! CLINICAL PEARL

Discogram is the study of choice for patients with IDD.

which injection of the disc must cause the exact symptoms to be reproduced. IDD has been better described in the lumbar spine, but the concept is the same in the cervical spine. The condition usually results from traumatic axial loading such as a blow to the head or neck, or a flexion/extension injury. The symptoms can include local neck pain, headaches, interscapular pain, and nonspecific upper extremity referral from the dorsal ramus. The cartilage end plate separates from the vertebral body, and acute nutritional loss results in rapid disruption of the disc.[11] Radiography is unremarkable, and even MRI may be unrevealing.

Patients with disabling pain usually have seen many physicians without a diagnosis and become frustrated and depressed. Insurance providers in the managed care setting are reluctant to authorize further testing, including the controversial discograms. Pain clinics are sometimes recommended, where patients are given narcotics and become readily addicted. Physical therapy and manipulation may provide some relief, but results are variable and, in fact, increased pain may occur since already irritated nerve fibers in the outer two thirds of the anulus become stimulated with segmental motion.

Conservative therapy should be aggressive with goals of high levels of strength and impeccable dynamic body mechanic skills (cervical stabilization training). High levels of training may significantly improve function despite ongoing pain.[12] If an adequate course (3 to 4 months) of aggressive conservative therapy fails to provide relief and if lifestyle is totally unacceptable, surgical intervention should be considered. Surgical treatment should be discectomy and anterior interbody fusion. If painful IDD (by discography) includes more than three levels, surgical treatment should be considered cautiously since the outcome may not appreciably alter lifestyle and a fusion will render the discs above and below the fused segment vulnerable to accelerated degenerative disease.

Facet Syndrome

Facet syndrome is a controversial clinical entity. The small joints in the cervical spine may show no signs of degeneration on X-ray or scanning, yet the patient has pillar tenderness and increased pain upon extension that localizes to the facets. Neurological findings are absent. Diagnosis is confirmed by injection of the joint (facet block). Injection of contrast media should reproduce the pain (diagnostic injection). It has been demonstrated that distention of the joint with contrast media can induce not only neck pain but also referred pain characteristic of the segmental location of the stimulated facet.[13] Injecting a mixture of local anesthetic and cortisone (diagnostic and therapeutic injection) should render the joint less painful.

In theory, inflammatory adhesions of the facet joints and their capsules should cause a painful reduction in motion, as is the case for larger joints such as the knee and shoulder. Manipulation of peripheral joints, usually under anesthesia, followed by passive and active range of motion exercises, results in a more functional and less painful range of motion. Manipulation of the cervical spine should, therefore, have a parallel effect for cervical facet pain. The facets, we believe, are the target of all successful spinal manipulation, notwithstanding the popular belief that the placebo effect plays a role, which is the case with any form of treatment. The cervical facets are relatively small joints that become injured when subjected to increased violent loads as in flexion/extension injuries. Capsular inflammation then occurs, which leads to adhesions and persistent pain. Early manipulation followed by exercise programs can prevent long-term pain syndromes.

PATIENTS IN WHOM THE DIAGNOSIS IS IN QUESTION DESPITE AN EXTENSIVE WORKUP

The third group of patients is those in whom the diagnosis is in question despite an extensive workup. This group includes three subgroups of patients. The first subgroup consists of those patients with or without organic disease: malingering, somatization, somatoform pain disorder, secondary gain. Some patients use their physical symptoms as a way of dealing with their emotional lives (somatization).[14] They may blame their unhappiness and discontent on physical symptoms instead of admitting that a psychological problem is the cause. Moreover, they may be irritable, dependent, passive, or noncompliant. There may have been trauma that caused an initial physical injury but now, despite an adequate healing period, the disability persists. This is in contrast to malingering or "faking" disability. Malingering versus somatization is sometimes a difficult differentiation, and treatment personnel should include a psychiatrist or psychologist experienced in distinguishing between the two.

Psychological illness may predate the spine pain in some patients. "Somatoform pain disorder" is described in the *DSM-III-R* and includes somatization disorder, conversion disorder, somatoform pain disorder, and hypochondriasis. In all of these, the symptoms appear as a physical problem but evaluation cannot detect a condition of sufficient magnitude to account for the pain. To make the diagnosis of somatoform pain disorder there must be evidence of a psychological illness by criteria, not by exclusion.

Secondary gain is sometimes the engine that drives persistent pain and disability. This is a psychological problem that develops as a direct result of pain and injury where patients unconsciously use pain to avoid unpleasant things or to gain pleasant things (e.g., avoid the job they hate or gain attention they desire). Again, significant structural problems of the magnitude known to cause the presenting complaints are absent.[15] The treatment of this first subgroup requires a collective effort of mental health personnel, physical therapists, and the treating physician as a coordinator of the treatment plan.

Fibromyalgia, fibromyositis, and similar conditions comprise the second subgroup. The diagnosis is often in question and, although mechanical symptoms are present, the pain cannot be reliably provoked by specific maneuvers. Symptoms are not in a dermatomal distribution and neurological signs do not occur. Manual and physical therapy are effective over the long run for increasing function and decreasing pain but flare-ups are common. NSAIDs and corticosteroids help reduce symptoms, but patients using these long term must be monitored for side effects. Blocks and surgical intervention are not indicated. Medical management is best handled by a rheumatologist.

The third subgroup is an enigma. Patients who do not fit any other category may have pain associated with generators not yet fully understood. These may be biochemical in nature where traumatized areas are more sensitive. Nerves release chemicals in response to injury. Skin damage also releases chemicals that sensitize receptors. Ongoing disability in patients with vague complaints, and after exclusion of all other causes, may have biochemically supported pain. Conservative treatment is the mainstay in these patients.

PATIENTS WITH NEUROPATHIC PAIN

The fourth group of patients is those with neuropathic pain. This is pain arising from nerve injury or a functional abnormality of the nervous system. It may originate in nerve roots, peripheral nerves, or the central nervous system.[16] It is this group of patients that is most difficult to treat. The pain is present whether at rest or active. It is burning or aching and may be aggravated by activity, but only minimally relieved upon cessation of the activity.

Conservative treatment, including physical therapy, manipulation, exercise, and local injections, may aggravate the pain and cause days of increased symptoms. Inactivity causes deconditioning and depression, which adds to the patients' overall perception of disability and to the refractory nature of this pain to treatment. Surgery aggravates the symptoms if the nerve roots are manipulated. Medication side effects may prohibit the large doses necessary to relieve the pain.

Implantable spinal cord stimulators sometimes work well for this type of pain. They are first implanted by percutaneous insertion of an electrode that is attached to an external generator as a trial. If successful in alleviating the pain, the generator is implanted subcutaneously. Also, sympathetic blocks are useful both diagnostically and therapeutically. These are performed through an anterior cervical approach with the needle directed adjacent to the cervical sympathetic ganglia.

POSTOPERATIVE MANAGEMENT OF THE CERVICAL SPINE

Postoperative management is mainly directed toward rehabilitation after anterior cervical discectomy or after anterior cervical discectomy and fusion. The major factor determining when and how to proceed with rehabilitation is whether or not internal fixation has been used. Internal fixation involves the placement of hardware (plates and screws) attaching one vertebra to the next with an interposed bone graft in place of the disc (Fig. 29–5). Hardware confers immediate stability to the fixed spinal segments. A hard collar is usually unnecessary, and patients may begin physical therapy as soon as the wound is stable and their pain is controllable on non-narcotic medication. On the other hand, if internal fixation is not used, the patient is usually relegated to wearing a rigid collar for 6 to 12 weeks postoperation. In that case therapy is delayed until this collar is discontinued. Patients are graduated to a soft collar after a weaning period from the rigid collar. Therapy may begin after the weaning period.

Muscles are weaker and less responsive after rigid immobilization and, therefore, a longer period of strengthening and stabilization is necessary. Also, anterior cervical spine surgery is performed in the supine position and the shoulders are sometimes drawn caudad with tape on the shoulders and criss-crossed over the body and attached to the foot end of the operating table. This may cause a strain of the cervical musculature and especially the upper trapezius muscles. A common complaint is pain postoperatively in the strained muscles. The discomfort decreases as the therapy continues and the muscles are strengthened. Headaches sometimes also result from the strain and diminish with therapy.

A major concern after surgery is the increased risk to the discs adjacent to the fusion of accelerated degenerative changes, secondary to the longer lever arm. Therefore, patient education and cervicothoracic stabilization training with back school is extremely important. Ergonomically designed work environments are also important, especially for patients who perform repetitive movements with the cervical spine. Computer screens and television monitors should be positioned so that flexion, extension, and rotation are minimized. Repetitive tasks should not involve overhead reaching. Following the principles of stabilization training will avoid future trouble at adjacent levels.

! CLINICAL PEARL

Stabilization training reduces the risk of accelerated degenerative changes after cervical fusion.

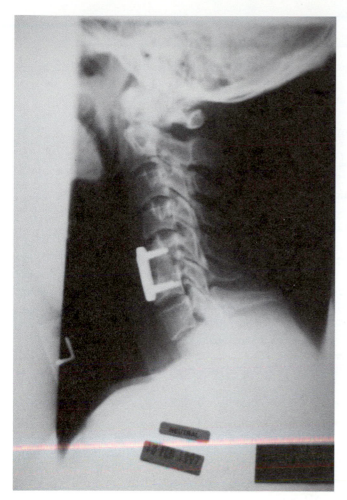

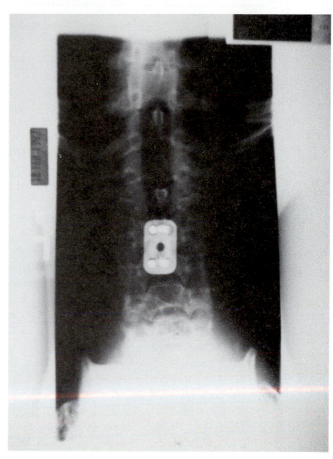

A

B

Figure 29–5. A and **B.** Anterior cervical fusion with plate fixation at C5–6. This patient is a professional athlete who had severe neck pain prior to surgery. He returned to athletics 3 weeks postoperatively with substantial reduction in pain and continued to improve as bony union developed.

Patients who have multilevel (greater than three) fusions and in whom internal fixation is not possible may need immobilization in a halo jacket. This obviously prohibits therapy until it is removed at 6 weeks to 3 months postoperation. The halo is usually followed by a rigid cervical collar for a weaning period, and then a soft collar is used as needed for comfort. Therapy begins when the patient is using the soft collar.

CONCLUSION

Difficult cervical spine patients are those who present either a diagnostic dilemma or a treatment dilemma for the physician. Patients with multilevel degenerative disease often present to the office, aware of the diagnosis, but unsatisfied with previously offered treatment options. They rarely need further diagnostic testing since they present with a file of imaging and physicians' office notes in hand, which displays the obvious pathology. Conservative treatment is the mainstay with careful periodic examinations for myelopathic signs. When the diagnosis is not clear on conventional studies, the physician must try provocative testing in order to identify a pain generator. Facet blocks and discograms are very helpful at this stage. If the diagnosis is still questionable, the final stage in the investigational protocol includes psychiatric cevaluation and referral to a rheumatolgist.

REFERENCES

1. White AA III, Panjabi MM, eds. *Clinical Biomechanics of the Spine*. 2nd ed. Philadelphia, Pa: JB Lippincott; 1990.

2. Pritzer KPH. Aging and degeneration in the lumbar intervertebral disc. *Orthop Clin North Am* 1977;8(1):65.

3. Zdeblick TA, Bohlman HH. Cervical kyphosis and myelopathy. Treatment by anterior corpectomy and strut-grafting. *J Bone Joint Surg* 1989;71-A:170–182.

4. Press JM, Young JL. *Electrodiagnostic evaluation of spine problems*. In: White AH, Schofferman JA, eds. *Spine Care*. St. Louis, Mo: Mosby; 1995:200.

5. Bogduk N, Aprill C, Derby R. Epidural steroid injections. In: White AH, Schofferman JA, eds. *Spine Care*. St. Louis, Mo: Mosby; 1995:326.

6. Bogduk N, Aprill C, Derby R. Epidural steroid injections. In: White AH, Schofferman JA, eds. *Spine Care*. St. Louis, Mo: Mosby; 1995:231–232.

7. Sluijter ME, Koetsveld-Baart CC. Interruption of pain pathways in the treatment of the cervical syndrome. *Anaesthesia* 1980;35:302.

8. Bogduk N, Marsland A. The cervical zygapophysial joints as a source of neck pain. *Spine* 1988;13:610.

9. White AA III, Southwick WO, DePonte RJ, Gainor JW, Hardy R. Relief of pain by anterior cervical-spine fusion for spondylosis. A report of sixty-five patients. *J Bone Joint Surg* 1973;55-A:525–534.

10. Penning L, Wilmink JT, Van Woerden HH, et al. CT myelographic findings in degenerative disorders of the cervical spine: Clinical significance. *Am J Roentgenol* 1986;146:793.

11. Selby DK. The structural degenerative cascade. In: White AH, Schofferman JA, eds. *Spine Care*. St. Louis, Mo: Mosby; 1995:16.

12. Schofferman JA. Diagnostic decision making. In: White AH, Schofferman JA, eds. *Spine Care*. St. Louis, Mo: Mosby; 1995:45.

13. Aprill C, Dwyer A, Bogduk N. Cervical zygapophyseal joint pain patterns. II: A clinical evaluation. *Spine* 1990;15:458.

14. Gatchel RJ. Psychosocial correlates of the deconditioning syndrome in patients with chronic low-back pain. In: White AH, Schofferman JA, eds. *Spine Care*. St. Louis, Mo: Mosby; 1995:543.

15. Schofferman JA. Diagnostic decision making. In: White AH, Schofferman JA, eds. *Spine Care*. St. Louis, Mo: Mosby; 1995:47.

16. Schofferman, JA. The structural degenerative cascade. In: White AH, Schofferman JA, eds. *Spine Care*. St. Louis, Mo: Mosby; 1995:24.

CHAPTER 30

Psychological Management of the Cervical Trauma Patient

ALLAN P. SHAPIRO & ROBERT W. TEASELL,

"Better an approximate answer to the right question than an exact answer to the wrong question."

—John Tukey

INTRODUCTION

Cervical trauma and particularly acceleration-deceleration ("whiplash") injuries are a common precipitant of chronic soft-tissue pain conditions. Although there are no definitive studies on incidence of chronic pain following whiplash, the best prospective study to date suggests that 24 percent of patients symptomatic at 1 week postinjury will continue to report symptoms after 1 year.[1] The majority of patients who recover will do so within the first 3 to 6 months.[1-4]

As with other chronic pain disorders, the pathophysiological basis of persistent pain following whiplash is not well understood.[5] Psychosocial problems frequently develop in response to chronic pain and disability. Because residual symptomatology is particularly common in patients who were occupants of stationary vehicles struck from behind,[1] there are often unresolved litigation and compensation issues. This combination of diagnostic uncertainty, psychological distress, and compensation/litigation has contributed to the widespread, albeit declining, belief that chronic whiplash pain is nonorganic or psychological in origin and tied in some way to the act of seeking compensation.

In this chapter we first review recent research that argues for an "organic" basis for chronic whiplash pain and convincingly demonstrates that emotional distress is a consequence of pain and associated limitations. Typical psychosocial consequences of chronic pain are discussed, particularly in reference to a constellation of personality characteristics postulated to place patients at greater risk for more severe pain, disability, and emotional distress. We also consider "psychological interventions," broadly defined, for these biopsychosocial consequences of chronic cervical pain. These include interventions that can be and often are implemented by various health professionals as well as those requiring more specialized psychological training and expertise.

EVIDENCE THAT PHYSICAL PATHOLOGY ACCOUNTS FOR CHRONIC WHIPLASH PAIN

The recent work of two research groups, Bogduk and colleagues in Australia and Radanov et al in Switzerland, provide convincing evidence that physical and not psychological factors account for nonresolution of symptoms in whiplash. In carefully controlled trials using diagnostic blocks of cervical zygapophyseal joints, the Australian group[6, 7] showed that chronic whiplash pain can be relieved. In these blinded studies, 50 and 68 consecutively referred patients with chronic pain following whiplash were injected with a short-acting (lignocaine) and a long-acting (bupivicaine) local anaesthetic. In the latter study[7] control saline blocks were also used. Well over half the patients obtained pain relief concordant with the expected duration of the anaesthetic. The same investigators[8] used radiofrequency neurotomy of the dorsal rami to achieve complete relief of chronic whiplash pain in patients with a median pain duration of 34 months. In this randomized, double-blind trial, 7 of 12 patients receiving the active treatment obtained complete pain relief for at least 6 months. Only 1 of 12 patients in the sham surgical placebo control condition reported similar relief. In a subsequent paper summarizing their work to date, these researchers[9] reported that a second neurotomy was successful in re-eliminating pain in 8 of 9 patients whose pain eventually returned (with nerve regeneration) after the first successful neurotomy. These demonstrations of facet joint involvement in chronic whiplash pain are consistent with previous experimental demonstrations of facet joint injuries in animals[10] and cadavers (e.g., ref. 11) subjected to acceleration-deceleration forces simulating "whiplash." Postmortem studies have also shown that facet joint injuries are common in motor vehicle accident (MVA) victims.[12]

The Australian researchers[13] also demonstrated that the psychological distress often evident in chronic whiplash patients is a consequence of the pain and has no etiological significance. As part of their experimental protocol, they administered the SCL-90, a widely used self-report measure of psychological symptomatology, both before and after radiofrequency neurotomy. The typical pretreatment SCL-90 profile revealed clinically significant elevations on scales reflecting somatic complaints, depression, and cognitive difficulties associated with excessive worry. Successful relief of pain following neurotomy resulted in significant reduction of all elevated scale scores to levels consistent with nonclinical (i.e., "normal") populations. Moreover, not only was eventual return of the pain followed by re-elevations of these SCL-90 scale scores, but successful repeat neurotomies again decreased these elevated scale scores to normal levels.

Further evidence for a physical basis for chronic whiplash pain comes from a prospective Swiss study, which suggested that biomechanical accident mechanisms associated with more severe injury predict nonresolution of whiplash.[1, 14] Patients recruited through family physicians underwent baseline physical examination, interview, and completed self-report questionnaires of mood, cognitive function, and personality within 10 days of injury. At 1-year postinjury, 24 percent of patients remained symptomatic. Baseline factors differentiating symptomatic from asymptomatic subjects were rotated or inclined head position at impact, unpreparedness at time of impact, their car being stationary when hit, and initial intensity of neck pain and headache. These researchers had previously demonstrated[15] in the same sample that a rotated or inclined head position and unpreparedness at time of impact was associated with more severe acute injury as evidenced by a higher frequency of multiple symptoms and radicular involvement, more signs on physical examination of cervical strain, and more severe headaches. Psychological factors assessed at baseline, including premorbid psychiatric history and neuroticism, were not predictive of failure of symptoms to resolve at either 6 months[1] or 1 year[14] postinjury.

PAIN "X" PERSONALITY INTERACTIONS: BIOPSYCHOSOCIAL VERSUS PSYCHIATRIC MODELS

Historically, a number of theorists have identified personality traits believed to be typical of chronic pain patients leading to the concept of a "pain prone" personality. Descriptions of these patients included extremely high activity levels premorbidly[16, 17]; high levels of perfectionism as part of an obsessive-compulsive personality[18]; and a reluctance or inability to verbalize emotional concerns.[16] These traits were hypothesized to be associated with specific psychological conflicts, which were expressed in the form of psychogenic pain. For instance, Blumer and Heilbronn[16] hypothesized that "pain prone" individuals had unconscious childhood needs to be dependent and cared for, which conflicted with their need to be viewed as "solid citizens (active, energetic, and independent)." This resulted in the "somatizing" of their psychic conflict into magnified medical complaints. That is, pain and associated disability was the only acceptable way of having their dependency needs met.

This erroneous view of chronic pain as nonorganic (psychogenic) and the failure of research to consistently identify a typical personality configuration among patients has led to a rejection of the concept of the pain prone personality.[19] Nevertheless, anecdotally we have observed similar traits in the chronic whiplash patients we treat. However, unlike traditional psychiatric models, we believe that these traits place patients at higher risk for developing more physical and emotional difficulties secondary to an organic pain condition. That is, premorbid personality factors interact with initial injury to produce more severe pain, disability, and emotional distress. The term "biopsychosocial" is used to emphasize that in addition to personality factors, there are a host of potential psychosocial variables (e.g., physical demands of job, culture, education, etc.) that affect patients' responses to any physical condition, including an organic pain disorder.

It should be noted that like other tertiary academic hospitals, we see a highly selected chronic pain population who are not representative of community samples. Relative to community samples, those seen in tertiary settings report more intense and constant pain, have more difficulties with activities of daily living, are more depressed and withdrawn socially, and show more long-term consequences as a result of unemployment, litigation, and substance abuse.[20] Accordingly, it is important to keep in mind that the "at-risk" population we describe represents a subset of patients, albeit those most severely affected by chronic cervical pain.

PROFILE OF THE "AT-RISK" PATIENT: THE "APS" PREMORBID PERSONALITY

The acronym "APS" describes a subset of chronic cervical pain patients who, prior to injury, could be characterized as being extremely *active* and *productive* as well as maintaining inordinately high *standards* for themselves. For instance, premorbidly, female patients would typically "do it all"—keep immaculate houses, do everything for and with their children, and work full time. They usually did not view their standards as high but rather as simply how things should be done—anything less was inadequate. The statement "if you are going to do something, you should do it right" typifies this belief. Similarly, while others often viewed them as "perfectionistic," typically they would disagree with this characterization. Their ability to be exceptionally well organized and get large amounts accomplished in a short period of time was a significant source of self-esteem. They often did things at a much faster pace than those around them.

As a consequence of their need to be extremely physically active and productive, these patients, once injured, try to maintain high levels of activity, resulting in higher pain levels as well as more frequent and severe exacerbations in pain. These pain "flare-ups" in turn, necessitate periods of relative inactivity because pain levels are so high there is little else patients can do. These down times are particularly difficult for APS patients because they feel "useless" when not active and productive and because of mounting anxiety, frustration, and irritability over everything that is not getting done. As well, because so much of their self-esteem is based upon their high levels of productivity, as the pain fails to remit and it is clear that a "cure" is not likely, they experience more pronounced depression.

High levels of pain, anxiety, frustration, irritability, and depression in the APS patient in turn places more stress on interpersonal and particularly family relationships. Premorbidly, APS patients relied on high levels of physical activity, distraction, and expending a lot of energy to "resolve" stressful situations. These coping strategies are no longer viable. High levels of activity exacerbate pain and the only real "fix" for them is to get rid of the pain. That is, not only do APS patients experience more pain and distress, but they are at a loss to know how to "turn off" the constant worry and concern that has now become a part of their lives.

It is important to emphasize that the psychosocial problems secondary to pain described in the following pages are not unique to APS patients. Similar difficulties are experienced in varying degrees by most, if not all, individuals with a significant, persistent pain problem. Later in the chapter, we describe in greater detail some of these "normal" biopsychosocial consequences of persistent pain and consider the ways in which APS personality characteristics render patients particularly vulnerable to these difficulties. However, we first consider a critical yet often overlooked variable—pain severity.

THE IMPORTANCE OF PAIN SEVERITY

Historically, pain severity has been either overlooked or viewed as inconsequential when considering the impact of pain on an individual's life. There are likely several reasons for this. When evaluating the effect of pain on a given individual, most laypeople and professionals alike naturally equate pain with their own past experience with a pain episode that typically was more mild, short lived, and nondisabling. Among professionals, failure to take into account differences in pain severity is also related to past research with chronic pain populations that failed to demonstrate a strong relationship between pain severity ratings and measures of function. However, more recent studies, primarily coming out of functional restoration programs (FRPs) for chronic musculoskeletal pain, have consistently found that higher levels of pain intensity are indeed associated with increased disability and predict poor outcome (e.g., refs. 21–23). Moreover, this research also demonstrates that pretreatment pain severity ratings are much stronger predictors of outcome than a range of psychological variables.[23]

Failure to find strong relationships between pain severity ratings and functional impairment in earlier pain research may have been due to the fact that this research was typically conducted in tertiary care settings where patients report much higher pain levels relative to community samples.[20] Research with cancer patients[24] indicates that to the extent that most patients rate their worst pain as between 7 and 10 (on a 10-point scale), one would find little relationship between different pain intensity ratings and functional status. In contrast, more recent research suggesting that pain and function are strongly related comes from treatment settings (FRPs) that serve a more diverse patient population with a much greater range of pain severity ratings.

Extrapolating from the work of Serlin et al[24] on cancer pain, average or worst pain ratings in the severe range (i.e., 7 or above on a 10-point scale) should alert the practitioner to a variety of potential psychological difficulties in the cervical trauma patient. The *Brief Pain Inventory (BPI)*[25] used by these researchers is well suited for assessing musculoskeletal pain, and its translations have proven sensitive across different cultures.[24]

HIGH PAIN INTENSITY IN THE APS PATIENT

As a consequence of their need to be extremely active and productive, APS patients continuously push themselves to and remain at the upper limits of their pain tolerance. Accordingly, it usually does not take much to bring them beyond this limit. For instance, either an extra half hour to finish some project or some emotional stressor often increases their pain to extremely high levels, the proverbial "pain flare-up." Indeed it is typical for these two factors, physical activity and stress, to occur simultaneously. For instance, as they are working at some task, APS patients will experience increasing pain levels—a signal that they need to stop, take a break, or switch to some activity not involving the same musculature. Instead, they become angry and frustrated with this imposed limitation, anxious and despondent because they cannot complete the task, and then push on in defiance of the limitations imposed by the pain. Even if they do stop and rest, any associated benefit is partially offset or completely negated by the psychophysiological concomitants of the emotional distress associated with not being able to finish the work. The ensuing pain flare-up is sufficiently severe to necessitate a more prolonged period of relative inactivity during which pain levels are so high there is *relatively* little the patient can do.

Forced inactivity secondary to a flare-up is also very stressful for APS patients as they worry about all the work piling up, become angry with others who are not sufficiently helpful, feel useless and inadequate because of their lack of productivity, and despair over the future implications of their condition. As pain levels begin to subside, they quickly resume their activity in an effort to catch up with everything that has been left undone, feel productive again, and decrease the anxiety associated with the period of nonactivity. The cycle then repeats itself, and it is not long until they are in their next flare-up. With each ensuing cycle, they push themselves a little harder, pain levels become a little higher, flare-ups occur a little sooner, periods of forced inactivity last a little longer, and emotional distress becomes greater. That is, ultimately these patients experience higher pain, more disability, and more distress as they go from one pain flare-up to the next.

There is a significant body of literature implicating the sympathetic nervous system in soft tissue pain.[26, 27] Possible mechanisms by which emotional distress increases underlying nociceptive input include reflex muscle spasm, ischemia, or release of pain-eliciting neurotransmitters. Not only are APS patients at increased risk for significant emotional distress secondary to chronic pain, but their usual coping strategies, activity and distraction, are no longer viable. Thus, as a consequence of pain, patients are not only forced into periods of inactivity, but during this inactivity must face a barrage of thoughts and emotions they are ill-equipped to deal with. In essence, APS patients find themselves without alternative skills with which to respond to what is now a very stressful existence. It is not surprising that periods of inactivity secondary to pain are extremely stressful and usually avoided unless pain becomes so severe that there is little choice. At that point, patients must not only endure high levels of pain but often find themselves dwelling on a host of seemingly insurmountable difficulties that reverberate in their minds and leave them feeling overwhelmed and out of control.

PSYCHOLOGICAL INTERVENTIONS FOR REDUCING PAIN SEVERITY: ACTIVITY PACING AND REDUCING EMOTIONAL DISTRESS

Education is the first step in the psychological management of the cervical trauma patient. From the outset, patients are told that two factors routinely and predictably exacerbate musculoskeletal pain—overactivity (i.e., repeatedly working well beyond one's pain tolerance) and emotional distress. Patients readily accept the former but may be resistant to the latter, especially if previously it was suggested, implicitly or explicitly, that their pain or disability is psychogenic. It is critical to emphasize that their pain is, indeed, physical but, as is the case for almost every medical condition, it is affected by stress, *whether they are aware of it or not.* The following quote can sometimes be helpful in making this point:

> Psychological and behavioral factors may affect the course of almost every major category of disease, including cardiovascular conditions, dermatological conditions, endocrinological conditions, gastrointestinal conditions, neoplastic conditions, neurological conditions, pulmonary conditions, renal conditions, and rheumatological conditions[28]

Patients are told that in order to manage pain (i.e., keep it at tolerable levels), it is necessary to pace their activities and keep stress levels down. They are warned that expectations and demands to fulfill their varied responsibilities—self and other driven—typically will undermine their ability to do so. Most self-help books on chronic pain (e.g., ref. 29) include chapters on activity pacing. Similarly, instruction in the use of various relaxation strategies (progressive muscle relaxation, breathing techniques, etc.) often available through books or cassette tapes can be helpful to reduce the physiological concomitants of stress, including stress associated with pain flare-ups. However, it would be naive to assume that after brief instruction in the use of these strategies, patients can and will successfully implement them. Patients are also not always forthcoming about their inability to do so. This is especially the case with APS patients who have particular difficulty with relaxation and pacing but often are reluctant to acknowledge it because this difficulty is seen as just another failure and increases feelings of inadequacy. Accordingly, it is particularly important to identify APS patients early in treatment. As discussed next, this is not as straightforward as it may seem.

IDENTIFYING THE APS PATIENT

APS patients are particularly difficult to identify, because they focus on their frustration and relative lack of activity during pain flare-ups and under-report the extent of their activity during nonflare-up periods. For instance, during relatively "good" days, they may insist that they are doing very little but, in reality, this is relative to premorbid activity levels which were exceedingly high. When they accurately report spending hours in the day "doing nothing" and insist that this constitutes "pacing," further questioning usually reveals that they are describing flare-up days when pain levels are so high they are unable to do anything else. Patients with APS characteristics seen in tertiary care settings after several years of increasing pain and disability may indeed be extremely disabled and relatively inactive. However, they too are usually pushing themselves to the upper limit of their pain tolerance and under-report activity on "good" days.

APS patients' tendency to focus on their frustrations with their limitations often leaves practitioners with the impression that these patients are "excessively" disabled and must be pushed to increase activity levels and "work through" their pain. Attempts to do so will only reinforce an already ineffective solution and go nowhere as pain levels and associated distress escalate further. Moreover, as patients complain of increased pain, practitioners may erroneously conclude that "emotional" or "motivational" factors must be inhibiting progress. Therapies aimed at reducing pain severity will also prove ineffective as patients continue to push themselves to the limits of their pain tolerance, experience repeated flare-ups, and remain highly distressed because they cannot maintain premorbid levels of activity.

We have not found traditional personality questionnaires helpful in identifying APS pain patients and are developing our own inventory to identify the constellation of personality characteristics described earlier. Our current

strategy involves asking patients to describe themselves and their activity patterns *before pain onset*. Patients who appear to fit the APS profile are instructed to "rest and do nothing" for 1 hour following every meal on a daily basis until the next appointment. We emphasize that resting only when pain levels are so high that nothing else is possible does not constitute proper pacing. APS patients, if questioned *very* closely (preferably with their spouse present), will report they were unable to carry out this assignment. This paves the way for the next intervention—*intensive* training in "pacing and stress management"; that is, mindfulness meditation.

MINDFULNESS MEDITATION FOR APS PATIENTS: LEARNING TO PACE AND REDUCE STRESS REACTIVITY

Our observation that APS patients are unable to sit and do nothing for an hour at a time and experience high levels of anxiety in trying has led us to adopt a very specific "stress management" technique—mindfulness meditation. Kabat-Zinn has reported both short-[30] and long-term[31, 32] benefits of mindfulness meditation in chronic pain. Although these studies do not involve appropriate controls and, therefore, are only suggestive at best, we are impressed by how well this technique and accompanying patient education materials[33] address the APS personality characteristics and associated difficulties in coping with pain. It should be noted that Kabat-Zinn[33] emphasizes that only those with advanced training in mindfulness meditation instruct patients in its use. Our own experience is that even with a combination of intensive group and individual instruction, APS patients struggle in their attempt to acquire these skills, and it is often necessary to address very difficult emotional issues that arise in the process. Accordingly, we would recommend against simply providing a patient with the commercially available materials and assuming that even if this does not prove useful, no harm is done. Not all patients are candidates for this intervention, and highly self-critical and often depressed APS patients not only struggle with this technique, but may well interpret their difficulty acquiring this skill as another personal failure.

When provided in the broader context of a pain management program, mindfulness meditation has the potential to help APS patients acquire skills to: (1) more optimally pace their activities, (2) reduce stress reactivity, and (3) reduce emotional distress in response to high pain intensity. In the next sections, we briefly discuss each in turn.

LEARNING HOW TO PACE: THE ART OF NONDOING

APS patients' inability to rest and "do nothing" unless pain is so intense that they have little choice renders them incapable of optimally pacing their activities. If they report that they can relax while doing nothing, it is usually because most everything is done. This is, of course, rarely the case because they cannot maintain premorbid levels of productivity and standards. In one of the two primary mindfulness meditation exercises, on a daily basis patients practice attending to their breathing for successively longer durations, working up to 45-minute periods over the course of 9 weeks. In our adaptation of this technique, individual counselling, group discussion, and supplementary reading materials are used extensively to facilitate acquisition of this skill, educate patients about the impact of APS personality characteristics on pain, and promote the importance of "nondoing."

Although the focus on breathing aids in relaxation, it is insufficient in itself to counter patients' overriding need to be active and productive and their accompanying intrusive thoughts about what they "should" be doing instead of meditating. The initial strategy for dealing with intrusive thoughts is to become aware that the mind is no longer on the breath and gently refocus on the breathing. Over time, patients also practice "stepping back" and observing, for an instant, the content of these thoughts, and then bringing the mind back to the breath.

! CLINICAL PEARL

This ability to assume the stance of an outside observer to one's thoughts without responding to them is a requisite skill in reducing stress reactivity.

REDUCING STRESS REACTIVITY: THE ART OF LETTING GO

APS patients' premorbid response to stressful circumstances was to remain active and distracted. In practicing mindfulness meditation, patients develop a new set of skills with which to respond to stressful circumstances and the intrusive thoughts that accompany them. Rather than using distraction, they are asked to: (1) become *more* aware or *mindful* of these thoughts; (2) step back and observe them as would an outside observer; (3) view them as simply thoughts, a creation of their minds, not necessarily reality; and (4) *let go* of these thoughts and return to the present moment by refocusing on their breathing. This process of detached self-observation is not only opposite APS patients' typical attempts at distraction but fundamentally different from other relaxation and meditatation techniques that promote distraction from intruding thoughts by focusing on some point or object to the exclusion of everything else.

This practice of detached self-observation, which eventually occurs for at least 45 minutes daily, teaches APS patients to sit quietly without becoming overwhelmed with mounting anxiety and the need to get up and be active and distracted. Once this skill is acquired, effective "pacing" can occur where not only do patients rest their bodies, but their minds remain relatively calm as well. This process of stepping back from a worry and concern does not, in itself, make the problem go away. Rather, it is a first step as the patient can now create some emotional distance, gain a new perspective, and perhaps see the problem more clearly and objectively, which then allows a more informed and measured response.

MAKING PEACE WITH PAIN: FOCUSING IN ON PAINFUL SENSATIONS

Acceptance or as we like to call it, *making peace* with pain, is a strong correlate of more optimal adjustment to chronic pain.[34] Rather than accepting their pain, APS patients wage an ongoing battle with it. As pain levels increase, they typically experience a cascade of distressing thoughts and associated emotions, depicted in Table 30–1, that become an integral component of their experience of pain. This "affective" or "suffering" component of pain perception[35] must also be addressed. High levels of emotional distress secondary to pain likely increase (via sympathetic nervous system activation) nociception and thereby exacerbate or prolong a pain flare-up.

The second mindfulness meditation exercise, the body scan, is a potentially powerful tool for decreasing emotional reactivity secondary to pain. Patients are instructed to direct their breath to different areas of their body, focus on any sensations associated with each area, then "let go" of that area and move on to the next body site. As they would in breathing meditation, during body scan they are to become aware of any intruding thoughts that take their focus away from these sensations, view them as "creations of the mind," let them go, and refocus on the sensation arising from the particular area of their body. Accordingly, in focusing in on areas that are painful, patients practice attending to the painful sensations themselves while becoming aware of and letting go of the thoughts and emotions (see Table 30–1) typically experienced in association with these painful sensations. To the extent that they learn to attend to the raw pain sensations themselves without becoming caught up in the cascade of distressing thoughts and emotions that typically accompany them, patients will decrease substantially the affective or suffering component of their pain experience.

THE BIOPSYCHOSOCIAL CONSEQUENCES OF PAIN

Pain, regardless of source, can affect every aspect of a patient's life. Persistent pain creates emotional distress, strains interpersonal relationships, and can result in work disability. In the remainder of this chapter we describe the most common biopsychosocial consequences of pain, ex-

Table 30–1: APS Patients' Cognitive–Affective Responses to Pain

THOUGHTS ABOUT	EMOTION
How pain interrupts ability to get things done	Frustration, anger, irritability
Driver responsible for accident and pain	Anger
Responses of societal agencies (insurance, health care professionals) patients look to for help:	Anger, depression
Pain is psychological or malingering	
Benefits are denied or inadequate	
Responses of friends, family:	Anger, hurt, depression
Pain is psychological	
Lack of emotional support	
Insufficient help with household	
Future impact of pain:	Anxiety (fear), anger, depression
Increased pain or disability with age	
Inability to work and financial hardship	
Negative effect on interpersonal relationships and children	
Enduring burden of pain over time:	Depression
"I'll always be like this."	
"I'll never be the same person."	
"I'm useless."	
"I'll never amount to anything."	

amine how APS characteristics render patients particularly vulnerable to these effects, and consider ways to address them. We begin with the impact of pain on mood and particularly depression, anger, and anxiety.

DEPRESSION

Depression is prevalent in patients with chronic cervical pain and chronic pain states generally with incidence ranging between 50 and 60 percent.[36] Depression in both pain and other chronic medical conditions may be conceptualized as a reaction to "loss" and an inevitable emotion associated with the process of grieving. This is well depicted in a popular self-help book on coping with chronic illness:

> . . . the process by which we acknowledge and come to terms with our losses is known as grieving. Although grieving is usually associated with death, it follows any kind of loss. . . . We grieve for ourselves. We are sad because of what we have lost, including our health, our normal routines, and the future opportunities that will never be. I grieved for the loss of control of my body, my sense of well being, and all those things that I might no longer be able to do.[37]

The process of grieving begins when it is clear to patients that their disabling symptoms will not resolve. Grieving may continue for many months and even years, depending on the extent of the losses and premorbid cop-

ing ability. APS patients are at particular risk for significant and long-lasting depression because they view their inability to maintain their premorbid standards as a sign of personal inadequacy and failure.

 CLINICAL PEARL

Recall that APS patients do not view their premorbid standards as high; rather, they simply did things "right." They are unable to adjust personal goals and standards because anything less is unacceptable

Interventions for Depression

Practitioners can facilitate the grieving process by explaining that unless there have been significant and progressive signs of improvement, symptoms present after 1 year usually do not resolve completely. Discussion and reading materials on coping with chronic illness can be particularly helpful in reassuring patients that the emotions they are experiencing are a "normal" reaction to loss. It is useful to encourage patients to begin considering the type of adjustments they may need to make long term (e.g., career change, different recreational pursuits, etc.), given that currently available treatments can at best help control but not eliminate the pain. The practitioner should not hesitate to broach this difficult topic as research clearly indicates that acceptance of the chronicity of pain[34] and the ability to flexibly adjust personal goals[38] is associated with better psychological adjustment.

The indications for psychiatric referral of depressed pain patients are symptoms of a major depressive episode, which may be responsive to anti-depressant medication. These include loss of appetite, anhedonia (loss of pleasure in all activities), early morning awakening, memory and concentration difficulties, and of course pronounced depressed mood. These signs are often difficult to assess. With the exception of anhedonia, all are common responses to pain or pain medication. Some neurovegetative signs of depression (appetite loss, sleep disruption) may be masked by low-dose antidepressants used primarily for sleep but at subtherapeutic doses for depression. Any indication of suicidal ideation warrants immediate referral as pain is rarely a reason for suicidal thoughts. Rather, suicidal intent is more often associated with significantly diminished self-esteem and pronounced depression. In making a referral, the practitioner should simply explain that although depression is a normal and understandable response to the losses associated with chronic pain, it decreases patients' ability to cope with illness but is often amenable to medication or counselling.

! CLINICAL PEARL

It should be noted that APS patients often do not like to use the term "depressed" because this is seen as a sign of "weakness."

ANGER

Fernandez and Turk[39] observed that anger is prevalent in many chronic diseases, and the same conditions that lead to frustration in these illnesses also hold true for chronic pain. These potential sources of frustration and anger include persistent somatic complaints, limited feedback on etiology, and repeated treatment failure. Anger over multiple losses is believed to be a common experience (along with depression) in the grieving process. From a biological perspective, anger may be an innate, "hard-wired" response to pain[39] because it had survival value in our animal ancestors. As previously discussed, APS patients have more intense pain, are more disabled, and experience a more profound loss of self-esteem. Accordingly, from either a grieving or biological perspective, they are at particular risk for struggling with the experience of anger.

Most of us have had the experience of feeling very time-pressured because of tasks that need to be done quickly and becoming very irritable or angry when our efforts to do so are blocked by a person or circumstance. One need only observe people caught in a traffic jam to test the veracity of this statement. Getting a lot done quickly is a core aspect of the APS personality. With the development

of pain, patients can no longer work at the same pace and perpetually feel things that must be done are piling up. Moreover, they are repeatedly blocked in their efforts to finish these tasks by increasing pain levels. Thus, frustration, anger, and irritability become frequent companions—especially at those times when relaxation is most critical—when pain is on the rise and patients need to calm their bodies and minds.

There are several other potential sources of anger in chronic pain, in general, and whiplash specifically. As noted by Shapiro and Roth,[40] the sense of victimization and associated anger present in most chronic whiplash patients is both normal and understandable when one considers the potential "losses" associated with chronic pain and the fact that these losses are the result of an accident in which the other driver can be held accountable. To the extent that the accident was caused by carelessness or, worse, criminal behavior (driving while intoxicated)—and therefore preventable—this anger would be even more intensified.[39] The advent of personal injury litigation will promote, intensify, and prolong this anger as patients are thrust into an adversarial medico-legal system in which they typically receive the message that their pain and disability are either nonexistent or exaggerated and reflect greed, laziness, or psychopathology. It is difficult to imagine a more anger-provoking circumstance than when one is profoundly suffering physically and emotionally because of another's carelessness but is then blamed for one's own suffering.

Moreover, another aspect of the APS personality that further intensifies the resulting sense of victimization are patients' high standards and strict adherence to the principles of honesty, integrity, and justice. Even if APS patients have learned that it is unrealistic to expect others to share their principles, they assume that their own adherence to these principals will be recognized and rewarded. They pride themselves on doing the right thing, which includes pushing themselves into high levels of pain to get things done. Accordingly, they feel particularly outraged and victimized when they are accused of just the opposite—exaggerating their pain and disability because of greed, avarice, laziness, wimpiness, or dislike of work.

Interventions for Anger

Therapeutic strategies for helping the cervical trauma patient optimally deal with anger require that one promote the expression of and normalize the experience of angry feelings. At the same time, it is necessary to convey the message that, as with any potential source of stress, there are significant physiological consequences of anger which, in turn, exacerbate pain. It is also critical to communicate the importance of "letting go" of the anger while at the same time acknowledging that it will be very difficult to do so because, on a regular basis, others will blame, criticize, or in some way question the legitimacy of patients' pain. It takes considerable psychotherapeutic skill to help patients "let go" of their anger. This is particularly the case for a

Table 30–2: Examples of Blaming and Nonblaming Statements

DON'T SAY	DO SAY
"You're not benefitting from treatment; maybe 'other things' are getting in the way."	"Some patients benefit, others don't. We don't understand this condition well enough to help everyone."
"I don't understand how you can be having that much pain" or "You have 'a low pain tolerance'/'more pain than you should'."	"Everybody is different; some patients have more pain than others."
"You need to improve your coping skills."	"Stress and overactivity always increase pain. You need to become an expert at pacing and reducing stress."

subset of APS patients whose all-consuming rage (at the other driver, lawyers, insurance company, etc.) appears to protect them from an extreme anger at themselves for being unable to maintain their premorbid standards, including being unable to overcome both pain and emotional distress in response to it. Ultimately, the task of enabling patients to express and let go of their anger is the purview of the skilled psychotherapist. However, as summarized in Table 30–2, there is much health and rehabilitation professionals can do so as not to blame the patient and, in so doing, add to his or her burden of pain and suffering.

ANXIETY

Anxiety is a normal part of life and a significant concomitant of any chronic illness and associated disability. Pain and disability may result in a host of stressors, including financial hardship, an uncertain future, concern about increased pain and disability in the long term, and interpersonal conflict. Pain itself is a stressor, as reflected by the use of relatively minor experimental pain stimuli in research examining psychophysiological responses to stress. Anxiety is often associated with the experience that things are piling up and ongoing worry about everything that is not being done because of pain. Anxiety is often a prominent aspect of depressive disorders. As previously discussed, APS patients continuously worry about tasks to be done and experience more severe pain and depression. Accordingly, they are particularly prone to anxiety-related symptoms. Wallis[41] found that 36 percent of patients with chronic whiplash scored above diagnostic levels on the SCL-90R anxiety subscale. It is likely that for some of these patients, high levels of anxiety reflected the co-occurence of panic disorder or post traumatic stress disorder (PTSD). These anxiety disorders are described next.

Post Traumatic Stress Disorder

Traumatic events may give rise to PTSD characterized by the following symptoms: persistent re-experiencing of the event as reflected by nightmares, intrusive memories, or flashbacks; symptoms of increased arousal, such as an exaggerated startle response or increased irritability; and avoidance of situations that remind the individual of the traumatic event. No studies have examined the incidence of PTSD among chronic whiplash patients. However, a recent review of the literature found that incidence of PTSD ranges between 10 and 45 percent among survivors of MVAs in which someone was sufficiently injured to require medical attention.[42]

Like chronic pain, PTSD is associated with high levels of emotional distress as well as disability and, therefore, failure to address it may contribute to poor outcomes in pain treatment programs.[43] To the extent that high levels of anxiety contribute to increased pain, the hyperarousal associated with PTSD will increase pain severity. Given the multitude of psychological problems that may occur in chronic pain, PTSD symptoms may either go unnoticed or be attributed to the pain itself. Accordingly, the health care practitioner should remain cognizant of the possibility of PTSD in cervical trauma and make an appropriate referral if there is some suspicion that it is present.

> ## ! CLINICAL PEARL
>
> If patients report having been afraid for their life at the time of the accident or acknowledge experiencing nightmares or significant anxiety driving since the accident, PTSD is a possibility.

Panic Disorder

Panic attacks can occur in the context of several different anxiety disorders, including PTSD, and are frequently reported by chronic cervical trauma patients. A panic attack is characterized by a period of intense fear and at least 4 of the 13 symptoms shown in Table 30–3.[28] Although there are no studies on the incidence of panic disorder in chronic cervical pain patients, Wallis[41] reported that 20 percent of a sample of chronic whiplash patients scored in the diagnostic range on a phobic anxiety subscale of the SCL-90R composed of items suggestive of panic. Using a structured interview, Katon et al[44] found that 11 percent of general pain center admissions met criteria for panic disorder. There is also a strong association between major depressive disorder and panic disorder, with the former preceding the latter in one third of patients presenting with both problems.[28] The heightened vulnerability of APS patients to depression may increase their risk of developing a panic disorder.

Although panic attacks may occur in reponse to identifiable situational triggers or stressors, this is not always the

Table 30–3: Symptoms of a Panic Attack

Palpations, pounding heart, accelerated heart rate

Sweating

Trembling or shaking

Shortness of breath or sensations of smothering

Feeling of choking

Chest pain or discomfort

Nausea or abdominal distress

Feeling dizzy, unsteady, lightheaded, or faint

Derealization (feeling of unreality) or depersonalization (being detached from oneself)

Fear of losing control or going crazy

Fear of dying

Paresthesias (numbness or tingling sensations)

Chills or hot flushes

From American Psychiatric Association Diagnostic and Statistical Manual of Mental Disorders. 4th ed. Washington, DC: APA; 1994:676.

case and patients often report they "come out of the blue." This spontaneous occurence, in combination with extremely intense physiological symptoms, contributes to patients' presenting with vague reports of "losing control," "going crazy," and fear of dying or having a heart attack. The practitioner should remain alert to such reports. Asking patients about the specific physical sensations associated with these episodes will often reveal symptoms suggestive of panic attacks. As with PTSD, the heightened anxiety, affective distress, and disability associated with panic disorder may exacerbate pain symptomatology and compromise treatment interventions for chronic pain. It is of note that panic disorder is emminently treatable with a short-term cognitive behavioural intervention developed by Barlow and colleagues.[45]

! CLINICAL PEARL

We have observed good response to this program despite the fact that multiple problems and worries secondary to chronic pain remain even after resolution of the panic attacks. That is, a panic disorder takes on a life of its own as the fear of having another panic episode increases anxiety levels and ultimately triggers subsequent attacks. Accordingly, panic disorder can be treated successfully without addressing the multitude of psychosocial stressors that may have contributed to its development. Antidepressant medication is also helpful in reducing panic attacks although relapse may occur once medication is discontinued.[46]

THE IMPACT OF PAIN ON INTERPERSONAL RELATIONSHIPS

Interpersonal difficulties are common among persistent pain patients, and this is no less true among patients with pain secondary to cervical trauma. As previously discussed, irritability is an ongoing problem and when expressed outwardly can put a strain on even the best relationships. Individuals with pain usually *look* fine and, as a consequence, others often maintain inaccurate expectations of patients' physical abilities or question the extent of or legitimacy of the pain problem. This is particularly the case with APS patients who feel weak and inadequate because of their disability and are reluctant to display outward manifestations of pain or verbalize the extent of their discomfort because they do not want to be viewed as "whiners" or treated like "invalids." Because of this reluctance to display or talk about pain, even well-meaning others often forget they have limitations and routinely ask patients to do things that are beyond their limits. In response, patients often feel angry that others "don't understand" or are "inconsiderate."

As discussed earlier, this credibility issue also arises because others naturally equate pain with their own experience of a pain episode that was often more mild and short-lived. Difficulty appreciating the extent of patients' pain and disability is compounded by the fact that pain levels vary and patients' activity levels and ability to do things also vary with pain levels. It is difficult for others to understand why on one day a patient can do a range of household chores while on the next almost nothing at all. This typically occurs when patients, frustrated with their limitations, go well beyond their limits to engage in activities that bring satisfaction only to "pay for it" with several days of more severe pain. This is particularly true of APS patients, who repeatedly push themselves to get things done and feel productive and then experience several days of disabling pain. Others often misinterpret these varying levels of disability as "motivational."

Invariably, significant others grieve the loss of the patients' "old self" and feel sad, angry, disappointed, and let down. This often is problematic in families of APS patients. These patients typically "did it all" before pain developed. Because of the credibility gap noted earlier, feelings of resentment, or simply force of habit, it may be particularly difficult for family to assume a greater share of household responsibilities. Their reluctance to help may also be related to their view that APS patients' need for order and cleanliness is excessive. Even when family members agree to help, they often discover that their efforts do not meet the standards or time urgency of the perfectionistic APS patient. Having always "done it all" for their families, APS patients feel especially hurt and resentful at this lack of support.

The end result is that APS patients end up pushing themselves even harder to complete the tasks that others have either refused to do, done "improperly," or have not completed soon enough. The physical effort involved, combined with concurrent anger and associated tension in response to this perceived lack of support, results in a quick escalation of pain levels. Patients then feel even more angry, and their underlying and lingering resentment invariably pervades other aspects of their relationships. Family and marital tension can become such a significant and pervasive source of chronic stress that it impedes both physical and psychological interventions.

Intervention for Interpersonal Difficulties

When the marriage is fundamentally sound and the main difficulty stems from miscommunication, misinterpretation, and difficulty changing well-established behavior patterns, a psycho-educational format can be quite helpful. Education focuses on the misinterpretation and miscommunication that occurs due to varying pain and disability levels and the development of more optimal communication skills. Emphasis is placed on the importance of pacing. Under guidance, couples negotiate a mutually acceptable redistribution of household and child care responsibilities that allows more optimal pacing. The couple must also agree to "let go" of excessively high standards regarding these tasks while acknowledging that this may not be easy for the other to do. Redistribution of household responsibilities must specifically define what is done, by whom (including other family members) and within what time frame while building in ways to flexibly alter or renegotiate the plan as dictated by changing circumstances.

In more dysfunctional marital relationships, there are usually fundamental problems that have predated the pain but kept in abeyance because (APS) patients were so busy they did not have to think about their underlying dissatisfaction. The APS patient's ability to "do it all" usually kept conflict at minimal or manageable levels. In either case, more intensive marital intervention must occur before one can proceed with the aforementioned psycho-educational intervention. In some cases resolution of these fundamental problems cannot be achieved and marital separation or divorce is the only solution to the chronic tension and anger that pervade the relationship.

COGNITIVE DIFFICULTIES

Patients with chronic whiplash pain often report difficulties with memory and concentration. A small minority report that these difficulties are so pronounced, they interfere with almost every activity and are as debilitating as pain itself. It has been argued that cognitive difficulties reported by whiplash patients are the result of mild traumatic brain injury (MTBI) sustained as a consequence of violent head movement during whiplash. However, a review of human research finds little or no evidence for enduring brain injury after whiplash.[47] Moreover, similar difficulties with cognitive functioning are well documented in other persistent pain conditions where there is no history of head or

neck trauma.[47] Recent research with "normal" subjects reveals that even a very brief experimental pain stimulus can interfere with cognitive processing.[48] As well, the disruptive effects of depression and anxiety or worry on cognitive functioning are well established.[47]

As previously discussed, APS patients are at greater risk for increased pain, anxiety or worry, and depression. These sequelae of pain will, in turn, render them more susceptible to difficulties with cognitive functioning. Moreover, problems with memory and concentration often leave APS patients feeling even more inadequate. Accordingly, they become particularly sensitive to difficulties with their memory, and often misinterpret normal forgetting as further evidence of their cognitive ineptitude. Their anxiety about forgetting can become so pronounced that it, in turn, interferes with ongoing cognitive processing. That is, every occasion to remember becomes a potential test of their adequacy, thus producing high "performance" anxiety, which, in turn, further disrupts their concentration and memory.

Patients presenting with cognitive difficulties should be reassured that these problems are quite normal effects of pain, medications, depression, worry, or sleep disruption. It is ill advised to raise the specter of MTBI as this will only sensitize patients to "normal" instances of forgetting and inattention, create further anxiety, and ultimately more cognitive difficulties.

WORK DISABILITY AND THE ROLE OF COMPENSATION OR LITIGATION

Much of the controversy surrounding the legitimacy of chronic pain disorders is related to physician and societal reactions to patients who claim disability and seek compensation.[19] For instance, although a pathoanatomic diagnosis cannot be made in up to 85 percent of patients with low back pain,[49] rarely is it suggested that the problem is psychological in acute or chronic patients who return to regular or near-regular function. That is, a diagnosis of psychogenic pain is reserved for those patients whose pain becomes both chronic and disabling and who understandably seek compensation through an existing insurance and medico-legal system.[19]

In their review of the literature on the effect of litigation on whiplash, Shapiro and Roth[40] concluded that there was no evidence that settlement of litigation leads to resolution of whiplash symptomatology. Although there are some reports of symptomatic recovery following settlement of claim, these retrospective studies invariably are based on nonrandom, unrepresentative, and poorly defined patient samples, do not include control groups, and fail to use standardized techniques of measurement or appropriate statistical analyses. Moreover, in the majority of these reports, a significant proportion of patients recover *prior* to settlement of litigation and resolution of a tort claim is not associated with symptomatic recovery for the majority.[40]

While patients do not recover with settlement of litigation, it would be naive to assume compensation has no effect. In our own research,[50] we found that compared to chronic whiplash patients who had completed litigation, active litigants reported higher pain severity, pain in more body sites, greater use of pain medication, and greater impact on day-to-day activities. However, there were no differences in employment. These results were interpreted as due, in part, to the stress associated with adversarial litigation which, in turn, increases pain severity. In Figure 30–1, we present a biopsychosocial model of the factors associated with failure to return to work after whiplash injury. According to this model, the impact of litigation or compensation on return to work is a function of patients' expectations regarding their ability to return to work and, once there, manage successfully despite residual pain. The lower this "self-efficacy" expectation, the greater the reliance on litigation and compensation. The factors influencing self-efficacy—pain, workplace and socioeconomic variables, and personality—are described next.

Pain

As described earlier, pain severity is central when considering the impact of pain on day-to-day functioning[24] and is the single best predictor of success (return to work) in functional restoration programs.[23] Stress, whether secondary to pain or the result of unrelated events, invariably increases pain by affecting the underlying pathophysiological mechanisms associated with soft tissue pain, increasing the affective component of pain perception, or both.

Personality

As depicted in Figure 30–1, personality can affect all aspects of this model. This is particularly true of APS patients who experience increased pain because they push themselves excessively in an attempt to maintain their premorbid levels of activity, productivity, and standards. They also experience more profound depression, anger, and anxiety because of their inability to moderate these excessively high standards. Moreover, APS patients will have little confidence in their ability to work with residual pain because of their perfectionistic tendencies. They do not view their standards as high but simply as adequate. From this perspective, if they are not "100 percent," they cannot do

their jobs as before. That is, work performance will be inadequate and failure guaranteed. The possibility of failing at a job not only produces anxiety about the financial repercussions, but the anticipation of failure is itself highly distressing and a significant threat to their now fragile self-esteem.

Workplace and Socioeconomic Factors

The ergonomic or physical demands of a job relative to patients' physical capacity is a critical variable influencing pain severity, self-efficacy, and disability. Whiplash patients not only experience neck pain and headaches but a significant proportion develop thoracic and low back pain. Involvement of multiple pain sites is associated with a particularly poor outcome in functional restoration programs.[51] Cervical pain and headaches are typically exacerbated by repetitive use of upper extremity musculature, sustained neck flexion, and sitting in one position for long periods of time. Increased low back discomfort is associated with repetitive lifting, bending or twisting, sitting or standing in one position for long periods, and extensive walking. Accordingly, not only do whiplash patients experience difficulty in traditional manual labour positions, but even so-called light duty (e.g., clerical) jobs involving mainly desk work can be problematic. Exacerbation of cervical pain typically leads to migrainous type headaches, which can last for days and are experienced as particularly debilitating. Given multiple pain sites and difficulty with both heavy and light duty work, whiplash patients are especially limited in vocational options.

Socioeconomic factors are closely related to ergonomic variables. Patients from lower socioeconomic backgrounds with less formal education and work in unskilled, semiskilled, or service positions have more physically demanding jobs and fewer alternative employment options if their current jobs are inconsistent with their physical limitations. Moreover, they are less financially secure and particularly fearful of returning to work and accepting a small settlement lest they eventually experience a deterioration in their condition, find themselves unable to work, and no longer have recourse through the courts. In contrast, professionals not only have much less physically demanding jobs but much more autonomy, which allows them to pace

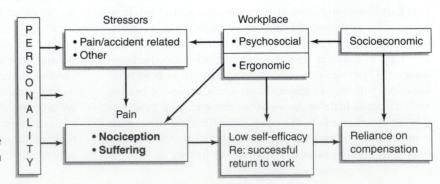

Figure 30–1. Biopsychosocial model of the effect of litigation or compensation on return to work.

their activities and maintain pain at tolerable levels. For instance, they usally have more opportunities to change positions frequently, alternate among various tasks requiring different postures and musculature, and take multiple breaks as long as their work eventually gets done.

Psychosocial workplace factors are also quite important. Patients often view management (or coworkers) as unsupportive of injured workers. Indeed, injured workers are often viewed as liabilities because of reduced productivity, burdensome work restrictions, higher absenteeism, and risk of reinjury. Patients may be quite reluctant to attempt a return to work fearing that, because of these issues, eventually they will be fired or laid off, will be unable to succeed at another job, and then find themselves without any recourse. Accordingly, they often look to the lawsuit to assure some semblance of financial security.

Interventions to Increase Self-Efficacy and Facilitate Work Re-entry

Returning to Figure 30–1, interventions to enhance self-efficacy must first address pain severity and the impact of stress. To the extent that high pain levels are secondary to failure to pace activities, stress, or both (as in the APS patient), instruction in pacing and stress reduction techniques is indicated. APS patients require particularly intensive intervention (mindfulness meditation) to enable them to pace and reduce stress reactivity. Individual, marital, or family therapy may prove necessary to address particularly significant and ongoing sources of stress, whether secondary to pain or not. If these interventions are successful, patients will report less pain, less frequent pain flareups, and less emotional reactivity. Decreased pain will translate into less irritability which, in turn, reduces marital or family tension. Intensive training in mindfulness meditation will enable APS patients to do things a little slower, not feel so time pressured, let go of some perfectionistic standards (at least with respect to upkeep of the home), and take breaks to relax without feeling so agitated when "nondoing." It is at this stage, once there is a new foundation to build upon, that traditional rehabilitation approaches will likely prove more successful.

Moving back to our biopsychosocial model (see Fig. 30–1), it is now necessary to address workplace factors. In some cases, very gradual physical and work conditioning (see the following paragraph) will be successful in eliminating discrepancies between job demands and a patient's physical capacity. However, certain jobs are simply too physically demanding or do not provide sufficient autonomy to allow patients to adequately pace their activities and keep pain within tolerable levels. Under these circumstances, vocational counselling or retraining is indicated. Similarly, when work environments are hostile toward injured workers, job change may be necessary.

Addressing ergonomic and psychosocial barriers to work reentry is necessary but often insufficient to alter low self-efficacy expectations. This is especially true for APS patients, who remain convinced that unless they can perform at their preinjury capacity, their work will be inadequate. Given their high anxiety about job performance and their tendency to push themselves excessively to do things "right," a very gradual return to work is often necessary. For instance, beginning at 1 hour per day and slowly increasing to 8 hours daily (over an 8-week period) will help keep pain under control, prevent patients from pushing themselves too hard, and allow for a gradual decrease in their performance anxiety. Similarly, arranging for the patient to be an "extra" worker during this conditioning period will help reduce anxiety about completing tasks and promote more support among coworkers. That is, coworkers will appreciate the *extra* assistance and patients will not see themselves or be viewed by others as liabilities because coworkers will not have to work harder to make up for their limitations. It should be noted that a gradual work reentry strategy is recommended even for APS patients who previously were "successful" in volunteer work placements or work simulation settings. That is, APS patients will not significantly alter their efficacy expectations until they have performed to their own satisfaction in a "real" job situation.

CONCLUSION

Historically, the absence of a clear pathophysiological basis for persistent pain following whiplash injuries, frequent occurence of psychological distress, and unresolved litigation issues contributed to the belief that chronic cervical pain following MVAs was psychological in origin. Recent research has convincingly demonstrated that in a large proportion of patients, persistent whiplash pain is associated with cervical zygapophyseal joint pathology and can be eliminated via neurotomy. Moreover, the psychological distress typically seen in association with this persistent pain also resolves after successful surgical intervention, demonstrating that psychosocial difficulties are secondary to pain and disability. Similar biopsychosocial consequences of pain are seen in other painful medical conditions and include depression, anxiety, anger, interpersonal conflict, cognitive difficulties, and work disability. Degree of pain severity is a critical, yet often overlooked variable in understanding these psychological sequelae of persistent pain. The acronym "APS" describes a subset of chronic cervical pain patients who, prior to injury, were extremely active, productive, and maintained inordinately high standards for themselves. These premorbid personality characteristics interact with initial injury to produce more severe pain, disability, and emotional distress.

Psychological intervention and specifically intensive training in pacing and stress management is indicated for APS patients. Symptoms of a major depressive episode, panic disorder, post traumatic stress disorder, or marital difficulties are other indications for psychological or psychiatric referral. A review of human research reveals no evidence for brain injury following uncomplicated whiplash and cognitive difficulties are best understood as normal effects of pain, medication, depression, worry, anxiety, or sleep disruption. A biopsychosocial model views the impact of litigation on return to work as a function of patients' expectation of their ability to succeed at work despite residual pain. This self-efficacy expectation is, in turn, influenced by a host of variables including severity of pain, ergonomic and psychosocial workplace factors, personality, socioeceonomic conditions, and environmental stressors, including the stress of adversarial litigation.

REFERENCES

1. Radanov BP, Sturzenegger M, DeStefano G, Schnidrig A. Relationship between early somatic, radiological, cognitive and psychosocial findings and outcome during a one year followup in 117 patients suffering from common whiplash. *Br J Rheumatol* 1994;33:442–448.
2. Gargan MF, Bannister GC. The rate of recovery following whiplash injury. *Eur Spin J* 1994;3:162–164.
3. Hildingsson C, Tollanen G. Outcome after soft tissue injury of the cervical spine. *Acta Orthop Scan* 1990;61:357–359.
4. Quebec Task Force on Whiplash Associated Disorders. *Spine* 1995;20:1S–73S.
5. Teasell RW, Shapiro AP. Whiplash injuries. In: Giles LGF, Singer KP, eds. *Clinical Anatomy and Management of Cervical Spine Pain*. Oxford: Butterworth Heinemann; 1998;71–86.
6. Barnsley L, Lord SM, Wallis BJ, Bogduk N. The prevalence of chronic cervical zygapophyseal joint pain after whiplash. *Spine* 1995;20:20–25.
7. Lord SM, Barnsley L, Wallis BJ, Bogduk N. Chronic cervical zygapophyseal joint pain after whiplash: A placebo-controlled prevalence study. *Spine* 1996;21:1737–1745.
8. Lord SM, Barnsley L, Wallis BJ, Bogduk N. A randomised, double-blind, controlled trial of percutaneous radio-frequency neurotomy for the treatment of chronic cervical zygapophyseal joint pain. *N Engl J Med* 1996;335:1721–1726.
9. McDonald G, Lord S, Bogduk N. Long-term audit of radiofrequency neurotomy for cervical zygapophyseal joint pain. Presented at Spine Society of Australia Scientific Meeting, 1997.
10. MacNab I. The whiplash syndrome. *Orthop Clin North Am* 1971;2:389–403.
11. Clemens HJ, Burrow K. Experimental investigation on injury mechanism of cervical spine at frontal and rear-front vehicle impacts. *Proc 16th Stapp Car Crash Conf* 1972;76–104.
12. Taylor JR, Twomey LT. Acute injuries to the cervical joints. *Spine* 1993;18:1113–1122.
13. Wallis BJ, Lord SM, Bogduk M. Resolution of psychological distress of whiplash patients following treatment by radiofrequency neurotomy: A randomised, double-blind, placebo-controlled trial. *Pain* 1997;73:15–22.
14. Radanov BP, Sturzenegger M. Predicting recovery from common whiplash. *Eur Neuro* 1996;36:48–51.
15. Sturzenegger M, DiStefano G, Radanov BP, Schnidrig A. Presenting symptoms and signs after whiplash injury: The influence of accident mechanisms. *Neurology* 1994;74:688–693.
16. Blumer D, Heilbronn M. The pain prone disorder: A clinical and psychological profile. *Psychosomatics* 1981;22:395–402.
17. Gamsa A, Vikis-Feibergs V. Psychological events are both risk factors in and consequences of chronic pain. *Pain* 1991;44:271–277.
18. Vanhoudenhove B. Prevalence and psychodynamic interpretation of premorbid hyperactivity in patients with chronic pain. *Psychother Psychosom* 1986;45:195–200.
19. Shapiro AP, Teasell RW. Misdiagnosis of chronic pain as hysterical. *NeuroRehabilitation* 1997;8:201–222.
20. Crook J, Tunks E. Defining the chronic pain syndrome: An epidemiological method. In: Fields, Dubner R, Cervero F, eds. *Advances in Pain Research and Therapy*. Vol. 9, New York, NY: Raven; 1985;871–877.
21. Carosella AM, Lackner JM, Feuerstein M. Factors associated with early discharge from a multidisciplinary work rehabilitation program for chronic low back pain. *Pain* 1994;57:69–76.
22. Dozois DJ, Dobson KS, Wong M, Hughes D, Long A. Predictive utility of the CSQ in low back pain. *Pain* 1996;66:171–180.
23. Feuerstein M. Functional restoration for spinal injuries: Successes, failures, and limitations. Paper presented at Whiplash Injury: New Developments, Current Controversies, Myths, and Realities. Toronto, Ontario, November 1994.
24. Serlin RC, Mendoza TR, Nakamura Y, Edwards KR, Cleeland CS. When is cancer pain mild, moderate or severe. Grading pain severity by its interference with function. *Pain* 1995;61:277–284.

25. Cleeland CS, Syrjala KL. How to assess cancer pain. In: Turk DC, Melzack R, eds. *Handbook of Pain Assessment.* New York, NY: Guilford Press; 1992:362–387.

26. Mense S. Neurophysiology of muscle in relation to pain. In: Vaeroy H, Merskey H, eds. *Progress in Fibromyalgia and Myofascial Pain.* Amsterdam: Elsevier Science Publishers; 1993:23–40.

27. Vaeroy H, Nyberg F. Endogenous opiate peptides, substance P, calcitonin gene related peptide and their relation to fibromyalgia. In: Vaeroy H, Merskey H, eds. *Progress in Fibromyalgia and Myofascial Pain.* Amsterdam: Elsevier Science Publishers; 1993:75–92.

28. *American Psychiatric Association Diagnostic and Statistical Manual of Mental Disorders.* 4th ed. Washington DC: APA; 1994:676.

29. Caudill MA. *Managing Pain Before it Manages You.* New York, NY: Guilford Press; 1995:61–65.

30. Kabat-Zinn J. An outpatient program in behavioral medicine for chronic pain patients based on the practice of mindfulness meditation. *Gen Hosp Psychiatry* 1982;4:33–47.

31. Kabat-Zinn J, Lipworth L, Burney R. The clinical use of mindfulness meditation for the self-regulation of chronic pain. *J Behav Med* 1985;8:163–80.

32. Kabat-Zinn J, Lipworth L, Burney R, Sellers W. Four year followup of a meditation based program for the self regulation of chronic pain. *Clin J Pain* 1986;2:159–173.

33. Kabat-Zinn J. *Full Catastrophe Living: Using the Wisdom of Your Body and Mind to Face Stress, Pain and Illness.* New York, NY: Delacorte; 1990.

34. McCracken LM. Learning to live with the pain: Acceptance of pain predicts adjustment in persons with chronic pain. *Pain* 1998;74:21–27.

35. Price DD, Harkins SW. Psychophysical approaches to pain measurement and assessment. In: Melzack R, Turk D, eds. *Handbook of Pain Assessment.* New York: Guilford Press; 1992:111–134.

36. Averill PM, Novy DM, Nelson DV, Berry LA. Correlates of depression in chronic pain patients: A comprehensive examination. *Pain* 1996;65:93–100.

37. Kobrin-Pitzele S. *Learning to Live With Chronic Illness.* Minneapolis, Minn: Thompson and Company; 1985:28.

38. Schmitz U, Saile H, Nilges P. Coping with chronic pain: Flexible goal adjustment as an interactive buffer against pain related distress. *Pain* 1996;67:41–51.

39. Fernandez E, Turk DC. The scope and significance of anger in the experience of chronic pain. *Pain* 1996;61:165–175.

40. Shapiro AP, Roth RS. The effect of litigation on recovery from whiplash. *Spine* 1993;7:531–556.

41. Wallis BJ. The psychological profile of patients with chronic neck pain following whiplash injury, before and after relief of pain. Dissertation. Newcastle, Australia, The University of Newcastle, 1997.

42. Blanchard EB, Hickling EJ. *After the Crash: Assessment and Treatment of Motor Vehicle Accident Survivors.* Washington, DC: American Psychological Association, 1997:21–34.

43. Geisser ME, Roth RS, Bachman JE, Eckert TA. The relationship between symptoms of post-traumatic stress disorder and pain, affective disturbance and disability among patients with accident and non-accident related pain. *Pain* 1996;66:207–214.

44. Katon W, Egan K, Miller D. Chronic pain: Lifetime psychiatric diagnoses and family history. *Am J Psychiatry* 1985;142:1156–1160.

45. Barlow DH, Craske MG, Cerny JA. Behavioral treatment of panic disorder. *Behav Ther* 1989;20:261–282.

46. Lydiard RB, Brawman-Mintzer O, Ballenger JC. Recent developments in the psychopharmacology of anxiety disorders. *J Consult Clin Psychol* 1996;64:660–668.

47. Shapiro AP, Teasell RW, Steenhuis R. Mild traumatic brain injury following whiplash. *Spine* 1993;7:455–470.

48. Crombez G, Eccleston C, Baeyens F, Eelen P. Habituation and the interference of pain with task performance. *Pain* 1997;70:149–154.

49. White AA, Gordon SL. Synopsis: Workshop on idiopathic low back pain. *Spine* 1982;7:141–149.

50. Swartzman LC, Teasell RW, Shapiro AP, McDermid AJ. The effect of litigation on adjustment to whiplash injury. *Spine* 1996;21:53–58.

51. Corey DT, Koepfler LE, Etlin D, Day IH. A limited functional restoration program for injured workers: A randomized trial. *J Occup Rehab* 1996;6:239–249.

Index

Learning Resources
Centre